Current Law

Legislation Citator

STATUTE CITATOR 2013

STATUTORY INSTRUMENT CITATOR 2013

Current Law

Legislation Citator

STATUTE CITATOR 2013

STATUTORY INSTRUMENT CITATOR 2013

SWEET & MAXWELL

Published in 2014 by Sweet & Maxwell, 100 Avenue Road, London, NW3 3PF, part of Thomson Reuters (Professional) UK Limited (Registered in England & Wales, Company No.1679046. Registered Office and address for service: Aldgate House, 33 Aldgate High Street, London, EC3N 1DL). For further information on our products and services, visit *http://www.sweetandmaxwell.co.uk*.

Computerset by Sweet & Maxwell. No natural forests were destroyed to make this product: only farmed timber was used and replanted.

A CIP catalogue record for this book is available from the British Library.

Crown copyright material is reproduced with the permission of the Controller of HMSO and the Queen's Printer for Scotland.

All rights reserved. No part of this publication may be reproduced, or transmitted in any form, or by any means, or stored in any retrieval system of any nature, without prior written permission, except for permitted fair dealing under the Copyright, Designs and Patents Act 1988, or in accordance with the terms of a licence issued by the Copyright Licensing Agency in respect of photocopying and/or reprographic reproduction. Application for permission for other use of copyright material, including permission to reproduce extracts in other published works, shall be made to the publishers. Full acknowledgement of the author, publisher and source must be given.

Thomson Reuters and the Thomson Reuters Logo are trademarks of Thomson Reuters.

Sweet & Maxwell® is a registered trademark of Thomson Reuters (Professional) UK Limited.

© 2014 Thomson Reuters (Professional) UK Limited

ISBN: 978-0-414-03173-9

PREFACE

The Sweet & Maxwell Current Law Service

The Current Law Service began in 1947and provides a comprehensive guide to developments in case law, primary legislation and secondary legislation in the United Kingdom and mainland Europe. The Current Law service presently consists of the Monthly Digest and the Yearbook, Current Law Statutes Annotated and the Bound Volumes, European Current Law, Current Law Week, the Case Citator and the Legislation Citator.

The Legislation Citator

The Legislation Citator comprises the Statute Citator and the Statutory Instrument Citator and has been published annually in this format since 2005.The Citators list all amendments, modifications, repeals, etc. to primary and secondary legislation made in the years indicated.

Updates to these Citators are available in Current Law Statutes Annotated. This Volume of Legislation Citator contains the Statute Citator 2013 and the Statutory Instrument Citator 2013.

The Statute Citator

The material within the Statute Citator is arranged in chronological order and the following information is provided:

(i) Statutes passed during the specified period;

(ii) Statutes affected during the specified period by Statute or Statutory Instrument;

(iii) Statutes judicially considered during the specified period;

(iv)Statutes repealed and amended during the specified period; and

(v) Statutes under which Statutory Instruments have been made during this period.

The Statutory Instrument Citator

The material within the Statutory Instrument Citator is arranged in chronological order and the following information is provided:

(i) Statutory Instruments amended, repealed, modified, etc. By Statute passed or Statutory Instrument issued during the specified period;
(ii) Statutory Instruments judicially considered during the specified period;
(iii) Statutory Instruments consolidated during the specified period; and
(iv) Statutory Instruments made under the powers of any Statutory Instrument issued during this period.

How To Use The Legislation Citator

The following example entries of the Statute and Statutory Instrument Citators indicate how to determine developments which have occurred to the piece of legislation in which you are interested. Entries to the Citators are arranged chronologically.

Statute Citator	
7. Business Rates Supplement Act 2009	— Chapter number, name of Act and year
Commencement Orders: SI 2009/2892 Art.2	— Commencement orders bringing provisions into force
Royal Assent July 02, 2009	— Date of Royal Assent
s.12, enabling SI 2009/2542	— Statutory Instruments made under the powers of s.1 of the Act
s.2. see *R. v Brown* [2009] Crim. L.R. 43	— Case judicially considering s.2
s.3, amended: 2010 c.3 s.2	— s.3 amended by Act (s.2 of Ch.3 of 2010) and two SIs
s.3, enabling: SI 2009/82; SI 2010/70	
s.4, repealed: 2010 c.3 Sch.4	— s.4 repealed by Sch.4 of Ch.3 of 2010
s.4A added: SI 2009/42	— s.4A added by SI number 42 of 2009

SI Citator	
3264 Agriculture (Cross compliance) Regulations 2009	— Number, name and year of SI
Reg.2, amended: SI 2010/65 Art.2	— reg.2 amended by art.2 of SI number 65 of 2010
Reg.3, revoked: 2010 c.23 Sch.15	— reg.3 revoked by Sch.15 of Ch.23 of 2010
Reg.4, see *R. v Smith* [2010] C.O.D. 54	— Case judicially considering reg.4

CONTENTS

CURRENT LAW

STATUTE CITATOR 2013

The Statute Citator covers the period 2013 and is up to date to February 24, 2014 (Orders and Acts received).

(i) Statutes passed between January 1, 2013 and February 24, 2014;
(ii) Amendments, modifications and repeals made to existing Statutes during this period;
(iii) Statutes judicially considered during this period;
(iv) Statutes under which Statutory Instruments have been made during this period.

Definitions of legislative effects:

''added'' : new provisions are inserted by subsequent legislation

''amended'' : text of legislation is modified by subsequent legislation

''applied'' : brought to bear, or exercised by subsequent legislation

''consolidated'' : used where previous Acts in the same subject area are brought together in subsequent legislation, with or without amendments

''disapplied'' : an exception made to the application of an earlier enactment

''enabling'' : giving power for the relevant SI to be made

''referred to'' : direction from other legislation without specific effect or application

''repealed'' : rescinded by subsequent legislation

''restored'' : reinstated by subsequent legislation (where previously repealed/ revoked)

''substituted'' : text of provision is completely replaced by subsequent legislation

''varied'' : provisions modified in relation to their application to specified areas or circumstances, however the text itself remains unchanged

ACTS OF THE SCOTTISH PARLIAMENT

2000

asp 1. Public Finance and Accountability (Scotland) Act 2000
s.4, applied: 2013 asp 4 s.4, s.6
s.21, amended: SSI 2013/177 Sch.1 para.4

asp 4. Adults with Incapacity (Scotland) Act 2000
applied: SI 2013/380 Reg.57, SI 2013/3029 Sch.13 para.1, Sch.13 para.9, SI 2013/3035 Sch.1, SSI 2013/50 Sch.1 para.21
Part 3, applied: SSI 2013/50 Sch.1 para.21
s.20, applied: SSI 2013/50 Sch.1 para.21
s.39, amended: SSI 2013/137 Reg.6
s.41, amended: SSI 2013/137 Reg.6

asp 5. Abolition of Feudal Tenure etc (Scotland) Act 2000
s.56, referred to: 2013 c.29 s.107

asp 7. Ethical Standards in Public Life etc (Scotland) Act 2000
applied: SSI 2013/197 Art.4, Sch.4 para.3
s.9, amended: SSI 2013/197 Sch.2 para.2
s.10, substituted: SSI 2013/197 Sch.2 para.3
s.11, substituted: SSI 2013/197 Sch.2 para.3
s.12, amended: SSI 2013/197 Sch.2 para.4
s.12, repealed (in part): SSI 2013/197 Sch.2 para.4
s.13, amended: SSI 2013/197 Sch.2 para.5
s.14, amended: SSI 2013/197 Sch.2 para.5
s.27, repealed: SSI 2013/197 Sch.2 para.6
s.28, amended: SSI 2013/197 Sch.2 para.7
Sch.1 para.5A, amended: SSI 2013/197 Sch.2 para.8
Sch.1 para.7, amended: SSI 2013/197 Sch.2 para.8
Sch.3, amended: 2013 asp 12 Sch.1 para.4

asp 8. Education and Training (Scotland) Act 2000
s.1, enabling: SSI 2013/75
s.2, enabling: SSI 2013/75
s.3, enabling: SSI 2013/75

2001

asp 8. Regulation of Care (Scotland) Act 2001
Part 3, applied: SSI 2013/50 Sch.1 para.15
s.44, applied: SSI 2013/141
s.44, enabling: SSI 2013/141
s.68, amended: SSI 2013/211 Sch.1 para.11
s.74, repealed: SSI 2013/211 Sch.2
s.76, repealed: SSI 2013/211 Sch.2
s.77, amended: SSI 2013/177 Sch.1 para.5

asp 10. Housing (Scotland) Act 2001
s.59, amended: SI 2013/496 Sch.11 para.6
s.60, amended: SI 2013/496 Sch.11 para.6
s.62, amended: SI 2013/496 Sch.11 para.6
s.91, applied: SI 2013/3029 Sch.5 para.21, SI 2013/3035 Sch.1
s.93, applied: SSI 2013/7
s.93, enabling: SSI 2013/7
s.109, enabling: SSI 2013/7
Sch.1 para.2, amended: SSI 2013/119 Sch.1 para.18

asp 14. Protection from Abuse (Scotland) Act 2001
s.1, applied: SSI 2013/357 Art.3

2002

asp 5. Community Care and Health (Scotland) Act 2002
applied: SI 2013/377 Reg.28
s.1, enabling: SSI 2013/108
s.2, enabling: SSI 2013/108
s.15, amended: 2013 asp 1 s.20
s.23, applied: SSI 2013/108
s.23, enabling: SSI 2013/108

asp 13. Freedom of Information (Scotland) Act 2002
applied: 2013 c.32 Sch.9 para.16, SI 2013/1119 Sch.2 para.2
s.4, enabling: SSI 2013/126
s.5, amended: 2013 asp 2 s.1
s.5, applied: SSI 2013/278
s.5, referred to: SSI 2013/278 Art.2
s.5, enabling: SSI 2013/278
s.7A, added: 2013 asp 2 s.1
s.18, amended: 2013 asp 2 s.2
s.25, amended: 2013 asp 2 s.3
s.26, applied: 2013 c.32 Sch.9 para.22
s.57, amended: SSI 2013/365 Art.2
s.59, amended: 2013 asp 2 s.4
s.59, enabling: SSI 2013/365
s.65, applied: SSI 2013/136 Art.3
s.65A, added: 2013 asp 2 s.5
s.72, amended: 2013 asp 2 s.4
s.72, applied: SSI 2013/278, SSI 2013/365
Sch.1 Part 5 para.49, amended: 2013 asp 12 Sch.1 para.6
Sch.1 Part 7 para.62, repealed: SSI 2013/126 Art.2
Sch.1 Part 7 para.62D, added: SSI 2013/126 Sch.1
Sch.1 Part 7 para.62ZZA, substituted: SSI 2013/197 Sch.2 para.10
Sch.1 Part 7 para.69, substituted: SSI 2013/126 Art.2
Sch.1 Part 7 para.72A, added: SSI 2013/126 Sch.1

Sch.1 Part 7 para.75ZA, repealed: SSI 2013/197 Sch.2 para.10
Sch.1 Part 7 para.79A, added: SI 2013/783 Art.8
Sch.1 Part 7 para.80AA, added: SSI 2013/126 Sch.1

asp 17. Debt Arrangement and Attachment (Scotland) Act 2002
s.2, enabling: SSI 2013/225
s.4, enabling: SSI 2013/225
s.5, enabling: SSI 2013/225
s.7, enabling: SSI 2013/225
s.7A, enabling: SSI 2013/225
s.10, referred to: SSI 2013/318 Reg.7
s.62, applied: SSI 2013/225
s.62, enabling: SSI 2013/225

2003

asp 1. Local Government in Scotland Act 2003
s.3, applied: SSI 2013/121 Art.7
s.4, applied: SSI 2013/121 Art.7
s.5, applied: SSI 2013/121 Art.7
s.12, applied: SSI 2013/121 Art.7
s.13, applied: SSI 2013/121 Art.7
s.20, applied: SSI 2013/200 Sch.1 para.6, Sch.2 para.8, SSI 2013/278 Sch.1
s.33, enabling: SSI 2013/45

asp 2. Land Reform (Scotland) Act 2003
s.7, amended: SSI 2013/356 Art.2
s.8, applied: SSI 2013/356
s.8, enabling: SSI 2013/356
s.98, applied: SSI 2013/356

asp 4. Public Appointments and Public Bodies etc (Scotland) Act 2003
applied: SSI 2013/197 Art.4, Sch.4 para.3
s.2, amended: SSI 2013/197 Sch.2 para.16
s.20, amended: SSI 2013/197 Sch.2 para.16
Sch.2, amended: 2013 asp 12 Sch.1 para.7

asp 7. Criminal Justice (Scotland) Act 2003
applied: SSI 2013/50 Sch.3 para.11
s.11, applied: SSI 2013/50 Sch.1 para.18
s.42, enabling: SSI 2013/302
s.53, amended: SSI 2013/211 Sch.1 para.12, Sch.2
s.56, applied: SSI 2013/43 Reg.9

asp 8. Building (Scotland) Act 2003
s.1, applied: SSI 2013/143
s.1, enabling: SSI 2013/143
s.24, enabling: SSI 2013/143
s.33, enabling: SSI 2013/143
s.36, enabling: SSI 2013/143
s.54, enabling: SSI 2013/143

asp 11. Agricultural Holdings (Scotland) Act 2003
s.9, applied: 2013 asp 11 Sch.19 para.13
s.10, applied: 2013 asp 11 Sch.19 para.13
s.11, applied: 2013 asp 11 Sch.19 para.13

asp 13. Mental Health (Care and Treatment) (Scotland) Act 2003
applied: SI 2013/377 Reg.28, SI 2013/3029 Reg.26, SI 2013/3035 Sch.1, SSI 2013/50 Sch.1 para.4
s.31, amended: SSI 2013/211 Sch.1 para.13
s.136, applied: SI 2013/376 Reg.19, SI 2013/377 Reg.31, SI 2013/379 Reg.63, Reg.96
s.136, referred to: SI 2013/381 Sch.1 para.5
s.259, applied: 2013 asp 1 s.9
Sch.2 Part 1 para.6, applied: 2013 c.25 Sch.5 para.12

2004

asp 4. Education (Additional Support for Learning) (Scotland) Act 2004
s.25, applied: SI 2013/377 Reg.28
Sch.1 para.9, applied: 2013 c.25 Sch.5 para.13

asp 8. Antisocial Behaviour etc (Scotland) Act 2004
s.12, applied: SSI 2013/150 Art.5, SSI 2013/194 r.31, r.32, r.34, r.35, r.84
s.82, applied: SSI 2013/50 Sch.1 para.16, Sch.3 para.9
s.83, applied: SSI 2013/50 Sch.3 para.9
s.88, applied: SSI 2013/50 Sch.3 para.9
s.102, applied: SSI 2013/194 r.83
s.112, amended: SSI 2013/211 Sch.1 para.14
s.116, repealed: SSI 2013/211 Sch.2
s.117, amended: SSI 2013/211 Sch.1 para.14
s.135, repealed: SSI 2013/211 Sch.2
s.136, repealed: SSI 2013/211 Sch.2
s.137, repealed: SSI 2013/211 Sch.2
Sch.4 para.4, repealed: SSI 2013/211 Sch.2

asp 9. Local Governance (Scotland) Act 2004
s.11, enabling: SI 2013/351, SSI 2013/351
s.16, enabling: SSI 2013/351

2005

asp 2. Emergency Workers (Scotland) Act 2005
s.1, applied: SI 2013/602 Art.24
s.1, referred to: SI 2013/602 Art.24
s.2, amended: SSI 2013/211 Sch.1 para.15
s.3, applied: SI 2013/602 Art.24
s.4, applied: SI 2013/602 Art.24

asp 5. Fire (Scotland) Act 2005
applied: SI 2013/602 Sch.3 para.12, SSI 2013/121 Sch.1
s.1, referred to: SI 2013/378 Reg.44, Sch.1 para.6

s.1A, applied: SI 2013/378 Reg.44, Sch.1 para.6
s.2, applied: SI 2013/378 Sch.1 para.6
s.6, referred to: 2013 c.25 Sch.1 para.9, SSI 2013/50 Sch.4 para.23
s.16A, amended: SI 2013/602 Sch.2 para.47
s.25, applied: SI 2013/602 Art.17, Art.18, Art.21, Art.22
s.27, applied: SI 2013/602 Art.17, Art.18, Art.21, Art.22
s.29, applied: SI 2013/602 Art.17, Art.18, Art.21, Art.22
s.40, applied: SSI 2013/97, SSI 2013/97 Art.2
s.40, referred to: SSI 2013/97
s.40, enabling: SSI 2013/97
s.41A, applied: SSI 2013/97 Art.3
s.41A, enabling: SSI 2013/97
s.61, amended: 2013 c.32 Sch.12 para.86
s.61, applied: 2013 c.32 s.89
s.61, repealed (in part): 2013 c.32 Sch.12 para.86

asp 6. Further and Higher Education (Scotland) Act 2005

applied: SI 2013/264 Sch.2 para.5, SI 2013/479 Sch.2 para.5, SSI 2013/84 Sch.2 para.5
s.3, amended: 2013 asp 12 Sch.1 para.8
s.4, amended: 2013 asp 12 Sch.1 para.8
s.4, disapplied: SI 2013/377 Reg.28
s.6, amended: 2013 asp 12 Sch.1 para.8
s.6, applied: SSI 2013/73 Sch.1
s.7, amended: 2013 asp 12 Sch.1 para.8
s.7, enabling: SSI 2013/319
s.7A, added: 2013 asp 12 s.5
s.7B, added: 2013 asp 12 s.8
s.7C, added: 2013 asp 12 s.8
s.7D, added: 2013 asp 12 Sch.1 para.8
s.9, amended: 2013 asp 12 Sch.1 para.8
s.9, repealed (in part): 2013 asp 12 Sch.1 para.8
s.9A, added: 2013 asp 12 s.2
s.9B, added: 2013 asp 12 s.14
s.9C, added: 2013 asp 12 s.3
s.9D, added: 2013 asp 12 s.4
s.10, amended: 2013 asp 12 Sch.1 para.8
s.11, amended: 2013 asp 12 Sch.1 para.8
s.11, disapplied: SI 2013/377 Reg.28
s.12, amended: 2013 asp 12 s.9
s.12A, added: 2013 asp 12 s.9
s.12B, added: 2013 asp 12 s.9
s.13, amended: 2013 asp 12 Sch.1 para.8
s.13A, added: 2013 asp 12 Sch.1 para.8
s.14, amended: 2013 asp 12 Sch.1 para.8
s.14A, added: 2013 asp 12 s.17
s.18, amended: 2013 asp 12 Sch.1 para.8
s.19A, added: 2013 asp 12 s.16
s.20, amended: 2013 asp 12 s.15, Sch.1 para.8
s.22, amended: 2013 asp 12 Sch.1 para.8
s.22, repealed (in part): 2013 asp 12 Sch.1 para.8
s.23A, added: 2013 asp 12 s.5
s.23B, added: 2013 asp 12 s.5
s.23C, added: 2013 asp 12 s.5
s.23D, added: 2013 asp 12 s.5
s.23E, added: 2013 asp 12 s.10
s.23F, added: 2013 asp 12 s.10
s.23G, added: 2013 asp 12 s.10
s.23H, added: 2013 asp 12 s.10
s.23I, added: 2013 asp 12 s.10
s.23J, added: 2013 asp 12 s.10
s.23K, added: 2013 asp 12 s.10
s.23L, added: 2013 asp 12 s.10
s.23M, added: 2013 asp 12 s.10
s.23N, added: 2013 asp 12 s.10
s.23O, added: 2013 asp 12 s.10
s.23P, added: 2013 asp 12 s.11
s.23Q, added: 2013 asp 12 s.12
s.23R, added: 2013 asp 12 s.13
s.24, amended: 2013 asp 12 Sch.1 para.8
s.25, amended: 2013 asp 12 Sch.1 para.8
s.25A, added: 2013 asp 12 Sch.1 para.8
s.26, amended: 2013 asp 12 Sch.1 para.8
s.26A, added: 2013 asp 12 s.19
s.28, amended: 2013 asp 12 Sch.1 para.8
s.31, amended: 2013 asp 12 Sch.1 para.8
s.34, amended: 2013 asp 12 Sch.1 para.8
s.35, amended: 2013 asp 12 Sch.1 para.8
Sch.1 para.4, substituted: 2013 asp 12 Sch.1 para.8
Sch.2, amended: SSI 2013/319 Art.2
Sch.2, applied: 2013 asp 11 Sch.2 para.17
Sch.2A Part 1, added: 2013 asp 12 s.8
Sch.2A Part 2, added: 2013 asp 12 s.8
Sch.2B para.1, added: 2013 asp 12 s.11
Sch.2B para.2, added: 2013 asp 12 s.11
Sch.2B para.3, added: 2013 asp 12 s.11
Sch.2B para.4, added: 2013 asp 12 s.11
Sch.2B para.5, added: 2013 asp 12 s.11
Sch.2B para.6, added: 2013 asp 12 s.11
Sch.2B para.7, added: 2013 asp 12 s.11
Sch.2B para.8, added: 2013 asp 12 s.11
Sch.2B para.9, added: 2013 asp 12 s.11
Sch.2B para.10, added: 2013 asp 12 s.11
Sch.2B para.11, added: 2013 asp 12 s.11
Sch.2B para.12, added: 2013 asp 12 s.11
Sch.2B para.13, added: 2013 asp 12 s.11
Sch.2B para.14, added: 2013 asp 12 s.11
Sch.2B para.15, added: 2013 asp 12 s.11
Sch.2B para.16, added: 2013 asp 12 s.11
Sch.2B para.17, added: 2013 asp 12 s.11
Sch.2B para.18, added: 2013 asp 12 s.11

asp 10. Charities and Trustee Investment (Scotland) Act 2005

s.12, applied: SSI 2013/362 Reg.1

s.34, applied: SI 2013/349 Reg.105, Sch.7 para.29
s.58, amended: SI 2013/496 Sch.11 para.7
s.64, enabling: SSI 2013/362
s.103, applied: SSI 2013/362
s.103, enabling: SSI 2013/362
Sch.2 para.2, applied: 2013 c.25 Sch.5 para.14

asp 16. Licensing (Scotland) Act 2005
s.87, applied: SSI 2013/261 Reg.2
s.87, enabling: SSI 2013/261
s.102, enabling: SSI 2013/199
s.108, enabling: SSI 2013/199
s.146, enabling: SSI 2013/199
s.147, enabling: SSI 2013/199, SSI 2013/261

2006

asp 1. Housing (Scotland) Act 2006
Part 1 c.4, applied: SSI 2013/20 Art.4
s.75, amended: SI 2013/1881 Sch.1 para.46
s.75, repealed (in part): SI 2013/1881 Sch.1 para.46
Sch.2 para.6, amended: SSI 2013/137 Reg.7

asp 6. Edinburgh Tram (Line Two) Act 2006
s.13, amended: SI 2013/2314 Art.6

asp 7. Edinburgh Tram (Line One) Act 2006
s.13, amended: SI 2013/2314 Art.6

asp 10. Police, Public Order and Criminal Justice (Scotland) Act 2006
applied: SI 2013/602 Sch.3 para.12, SSI 2013/121 Art.11
Part 1 c.2, applied: SSI 2013/121 Art.16
s.1, applied: SSI 2013/121 Art.11
s.7, applied: SSI 2013/121 Art.11
s.7, varied: SSI 2013/121 Art.11
s.8, applied: SSI 2013/121 Art.11
s.8, varied: SSI 2013/121 Art.11
s.15, applied: SSI 2013/121 Art.11
s.15, varied: SSI 2013/121 Art.11
s.32, applied: SSI 2013/121 Art.11
s.33, applied: SSI 2013/86 Reg.8
s.33A, applied: SI 2013/602 Art.3, Art.4, SSI 2013/118 Reg.5
s.34, applied: SSI 2013/121 Art.16
s.41B, applied: SSI 2013/118 Reg.6, Reg.7
s.41B, referred to: SI 2013/602 Art.3
s.41B, enabling: SSI 2013/118
s.41D, applied: SSI 2013/118
s.41D, referred to: SSI 2013/118
s.41D, enabling: SSI 2013/118
s.47, amended: SSI 2013/119 Sch.1 para.21
s.55, amended: SSI 2013/228 Art.2
s.55, enabling: SSI 2013/228
s.103, applied: SSI 2013/118
Sch.1 para.16, applied: SSI 2013/121 Art.11
Sch.1 para.16, varied: SSI 2013/121 Art.11
Sch.4 para.2, amended: 2013 c.22 Sch.8 para.172

asp 17. Planning etc (Scotland) Act 2006
s.58, applied: SSI 2013/26
s.58, enabling: SSI 2013/26

2007

asp 4. Adoption and Children (Scotland) Act 2007
applied: SI 2013/1465 Art.12
s.23, amended: SSI 2013/211 Sch.1 para.17
s.29, applied: SSI 2013/194 r.65
s.30, applied: SSI 2013/194 r.65
s.36, amended: SSI 2013/211 Sch.1 para.17
s.67, enabling: SSI 2013/310, SSI 2013/335
s.71, applied: SI 2013/3029 Sch.9 para.30, SI 2013/3035 Sch.1
s.72, amended: SSI 2013/211 Sch.1 para.17
s.79, amended: SSI 2013/211 Sch.1 para.17
s.89, amended: SSI 2013/211 Sch.1 para.17
s.90, amended: SSI 2013/211 Sch.1 para.17
s.95, amended: SSI 2013/211 Sch.1 para.17
s.95, applied: SSI 2013/194 r.77
s.96, amended: SSI 2013/211 Sch.1 para.17
s.96, applied: SSI 2013/194 r.77
s.96, repealed (in part): SSI 2013/211 Sch.2
s.97, amended: SSI 2013/211 Sch.1 para.17
s.106, amended: SSI 2013/211 Sch.1 para.17
s.106, repealed (in part): SSI 2013/211 Sch.2
s.110, amended: SSI 2013/211 Sch.1 para.17
s.117, enabling: SSI 2013/310, SSI 2013/335
s.119, amended: SSI 2013/211 Sch.1 para.17, Sch.2
Sch.1 para.6, applied: SSI 2013/310 Reg.4
Sch.2 para.9, repealed (in part): SSI 2013/211 Sch.2

asp 6. Criminal Proceedings etc (Reform) (Scotland) Act 2007
s.59, applied: SSI 2013/153
s.59, enabling: SSI 2013/153
s.76, applied: SSI 2013/50 Sch.4 para.3
s.81, enabling: SSI 2013/153

asp 12. Aquaculture and Fisheries (Scotland) Act 2007
Part 4, amended: 2013 asp 7 s.60
s.4A, added: 2013 asp 7 s.1
s.4B, added: 2013 asp 7 s.1
s.5, amended: 2013 asp 7 s.2
s.5A, added: 2013 asp 7 s.2
s.6, amended: 2013 asp 7 s.1
s.25, amended: 2013 asp 7 s.60
s.25, substituted: 2013 asp 7 s.60
s.26, substituted: 2013 asp 7 s.60

s.27, amended: 2013 asp 7 s.60
s.27, substituted: 2013 asp 7 s.60
s.28, substituted: 2013 asp 7 s.60
s.29, substituted: 2013 asp 7 s.60
s.30, substituted: 2013 asp 7 s.60
s.31, amended: 2013 asp 7 s.60
s.31, substituted: 2013 asp 7 s.60
s.32, substituted: 2013 asp 7 s.60
s.33, substituted: 2013 asp 7 s.60
s.43, amended: 2013 asp 7 s.1

asp 14. Protection of Vulnerable Groups (Scotland) Act 2007

applied: SSI 2013/194 r.90
Part 1, applied: SSI 2013/50 Sch.1 para.27
s.52, applied: SSI 2013/50 Sch.3 para.12
s.53, applied: SSI 2013/50 Sch.3 para.12
s.54, applied: SSI 2013/50 Sch.3 para.12
s.96, amended: SSI 2013/211 Sch.1 para.18, Sch.2
s.96, applied: SSI 2013/50 Sch.3 para.5
s.97, applied: SSI 2013/50 Sch.3 para.13
s.100, applied: SSI 2013/203
Sch.2 Part 2 para.11A, applied: SSI 2013/50 Sch.3 para.5
Sch.2 Part 3 para.15, amended: 2013 asp 12 Sch.1 para.9
Sch.2 Part 4 para.20, substituted: SSI 2013/203 Art.3
Sch.2 Part 4 para.20A, added: SSI 2013/203 Art.4
Sch.2 Part 4 para.20B, added: SSI 2013/203 Art.4
Sch.2 Part 5 para.28, enabling: SSI 2013/203

2008

asp 4. Glasgow Commonwealth Games Act 2008

Commencement Orders: SSI 2013/260 Art.2
s.1, referred to: SSI 2013/259 Art.2
s.1, enabling: SSI 2013/259
s.2, applied: SSI 2013/290 Reg.6
s.2, enabling: SSI 2013/290
s.3, enabling: SSI 2013/290
s.4, enabling: SSI 2013/290
s.5, enabling: SSI 2013/290
s.6, enabling: SSI 2013/290
s.10, applied: SSI 2013/290 Reg.12, Reg.14
s.10, enabling: SSI 2013/290
s.11, applied: SSI 2013/290 Reg.10
s.11, enabling: SSI 2013/290
s.12, enabling: SSI 2013/290
s.13, enabling: SSI 2013/290
s.14, enabling: SSI 2013/290
s.21, applied: SSI 2013/258 Reg.2
s.21, enabling: SSI 2013/258
s.30, applied: SSI 2013/160 Reg.3, Reg.4, Reg.5
s.30, enabling: SSI 2013/160
s.43, applied: SSI 2013/290
s.43, enabling: SSI 2013/160, SSI 2013/290
s.44, applied: SSI 2013/290
s.45, applied: SSI 2013/290
s.49, enabling: SSI 2013/260

asp 5. Public Health etc (Scotland) Act 2008

s.95, enabling: SSI 2013/201
s.96, enabling: SSI 2013/201
s.122, applied: SSI 2013/201

asp 6. Judiciary and Courts (Scotland) Act 2008

s.35, applied: SSI 2013/50 Sch.4 para.26
s.35, referred to: SSI 2013/50 Sch.4 para.26
s.62, amended: 2013 asp 3 s.15
s.62, repealed (in part): 2013 asp 3 s.15
Sch.1 para.2, applied: SSI 2013/50 Sch.4 para.28
Sch.1 para.9, applied: SI 2013/2192 Reg.17
Sch.3 para.2, referred to: SSI 2013/50 Sch.4 para.29

2009

asp 5. Health Boards (Membership and Elections) (Scotland) Act 2009

s.1, disapplied: SSI 2013/364 Art.3
s.4, applied: SSI 2013/364
s.4, enabling: SSI 2013/364
s.6, applied: SSI 2013/364 Art.3
s.10, enabling: SSI 2013/364

asp 6. Flood Risk Management (Scotland) Act 2009

s.5, applied: SSI 2013/314, SSI 2013/314 Art.2
s.5, enabling: SSI 2013/314

asp 12. Climate Change (Scotland) Act 2009

applied: 2013 asp 5 s.1

2010

asp 1. Arbitration (Scotland) Act 2010

applied: 2013 c.19 s.21, SSI 2013/288 Sch.3 para.6
varied: 2013 c.19 s.21

asp 5. Marine (Scotland) Act 2010

Commencement Orders: SSI 2013/276 Art.2
Part 4, applied: SSI 2013/288 Art.17
Part 7, applied: 2013 asp 7 s.7, s.35
s.22, enabling: SSI 2013/286
s.23, enabling: SSI 2013/286
s.24, applied: SSI 2013/286 Reg.8
s.24, enabling: SSI 2013/286
s.150, applied: 2013 asp 7 s.7
s.151, varied: 2013 asp 7 s.7, s.35
s.152, varied: 2013 asp 7 s.7, s.35
s.153, varied: 2013 asp 7 s.7, s.35

s.154, varied: 2013 asp 7 s.7, s.35
s.155, varied: 2013 asp 7 s.7, s.35
s.157, varied: 2013 asp 7 s.35
s.165, enabling: SSI 2013/276, SSI 2013/286
s.168, enabling: SSI 2013/276
Sch.2 para.1, substituted: 2013 asp 7 s.61
Sch.2 para.2, amended: 2013 asp 7 s.61
Sch.2 para.3, amended: 2013 asp 7 s.61
Sch.2 para.4A, added: 2013 asp 7 s.61

asp 8. Public Services Reform (Scotland) Act 2010
applied: SI 2013/3029 Sch.1 para.19, Sch.6 para.21, SI 2013/3035 Sch.1
Part 5, applied: SI 2013/376 Reg.35, SSI 2013/50 Sch.1 para.9
s.14, enabling: SSI 2013/197
s.15, enabling: SSI 2013/192
s.16, applied: SSI 2013/197
s.17, enabling: SSI 2013/24, SSI 2013/25, SSI 2013/220
s.18, applied: SSI 2013/24, SSI 2013/25, SSI 2013/220
s.19, applied: SSI 2013/197
s.25, applied: SSI 2013/24, SSI 2013/25, SSI 2013/192, SSI 2013/197, SSI 2013/220
s.26, applied: SSI 2013/24, SSI 2013/25, SSI 2013/197, SSI 2013/220
s.56, applied: SSI 2013/227 Reg.7
s.59, applied: SI 2013/3029 Sch.1 para.19, Sch.6 para.21, SI 2013/3035 Sch.1
s.78, applied: SSI 2013/227
s.78, enabling: SSI 2013/110, SSI 2013/205, SSI 2013/227
s.83, applied: SI 2013/3029 Sch.1 para.19, Sch.6 para.21, SI 2013/3035 Sch.1
s.104, applied: SSI 2013/110, SSI 2013/205, SSI 2013/227
s.104, enabling: SSI 2013/227
s.105, amended: SSI 2013/211 Sch.1 para.19
s.115, applied: SSI 2013/50 Sch.4 para.18
Sch.5, amended: SSI 2013/192 Art.2, SSI 2013/197 Sch.2 para.17
Sch.6, amended: SSI 2013/197 Sch.2 para.17
Sch.8, amended: SSI 2013/197 Sch.2 para.17, SSI 2013/211 Sch.1 para.19, Sch.2
Sch.12, applied: SI 2013/376 Reg.35
Sch.12 para.5, applied: SI 2013/376 Reg.35
Sch.12 para.6, applied: SSI 2013/205 Reg.3
Sch.12 para.12, amended: SSI 2013/211 Sch.1 para.19
Sch.12 para.12, applied: SSI 2013/50 Sch.3 para.4

asp 10. Interpretation and Legislative Reform (Scotland) Act 2010
Part 2, referred to: 2013 c.25 s.38

asp 13. Criminal Justice and Licensing (Scotland) Act 2010
Commencement Orders: SSI 2013/214 Art.2
s.102, referred to: SSI 2013/214 Art.3
s.132, amended: SI 2013/728 Art.3
s.201, enabling: SSI 2013/214
s.206, enabling: SSI 2013/214

asp 14. Crofting Reform (Scotland) Act 2010
s.4, amended: 2013 asp 10 Sch.1 para.2
s.5, amended: 2013 asp 10 Sch.1 para.2
s.10, amended: 2013 asp 10 Sch.1 para.2
s.15, amended: 2013 asp 10 Sch.1 para.2
Sch.2 Part TABLE, amended: 2013 asp 10 Sch.1 para.2
Sch.2 Part TABLEa, amended: 2013 asp 10 Sch.1 para.2

asp 16. Legal Services (Scotland) Act 2010
s.8, amended: 2013 c.24 Sch.6 para.193
s.15, amended: 2013 c.24 Sch.6 para.194
s.28, amended: 2013 c.24 Sch.6 para.195
s.49, amended: 2013 c.24 Sch.6 para.196
s.62, applied: SSI 2013/50 Sch.3 para.14
s.76, amended: 2013 c.24 Sch.6 para.197
s.92, amended: 2013 c.24 Sch.6 para.198
s.103, amended: 2013 c.24 Sch.6 para.199
s.113, amended: 2013 c.24 Sch.6 para.200
s.122, amended: 2013 c.24 Sch.6 para.201
s.125, amended: 2013 c.24 Sch.6 para.202
s.147, amended: 2013 c.24 Sch.6 para.203
s.149, amended: 2013 c.24 Sch.6 para.204
Sch.2 para.4, amended: 2013 c.24 Sch.6 para.205
Sch.5 para.4, amended: 2013 c.24 Sch.6 para.206
Sch.6 para.4, amended: 2013 c.24 Sch.6 para.207
Sch.7 para.3, amended: 2013 c.24 Sch.6 para.208
Sch.9, amended: 2013 c.24 Sch.6 para.209

asp 17. Housing (Scotland) Act 2010
s.18, amended: SI 2013/496 Sch.11 para.10
s.30, amended: SI 2013/496 Sch.11 para.10
s.80, amended: SI 2013/496 Sch.11 para.10
s.82, amended: SI 2013/496 Sch.11 para.10
s.87, amended: SI 2013/496 Sch.11 para.10
s.94, amended: SI 2013/496 Sch.11 para.10
s.96, amended: SI 2013/496 Sch.11 para.10
s.97, amended: SI 2013/496 Sch.11 para.10
s.98, amended: SI 2013/496 Sch.11 para.10
s.99, amended: SI 2013/496 Sch.11 para.10
s.165, applied: SSI 2013/45 Reg.5

2011

asp 1. Children's Hearings (Scotland) Act 2011
Commencement Orders: SSI 2013/98 Art.2, Sch.1; SSI 2013/190 Art.2; SSI 2013/195 Art.2, Art.3

applied: SI 2013/1465 Art.8, Art.9, Art.12, SSI 2013/50 Sch.1 para.29, SSI 2013/150 Art.20, SSI 2013/194 r.84, SSI 2013/200 Reg.6, Reg.27
referred to: SI 2013/3035 Sch.1, SSI 2013/212 Reg.12, Reg.13, Reg.14
Part 5, applied: SSI 2013/194 r.2
Part 9, applied: SSI 2013/194 r.22, r.26, r.55, r.81
Part 10, applied: SSI 2013/194 r.22, r.26, r.55, r.56, r.78, r.81
Part 11, applied: SSI 2013/194 r.22, r.26, r.55, r.81
Part 13, applied: SSI 2013/194 r.22, r.26, r.55, r.81
Part 15, applied: SSI 2013/194 r.2
s.1, applied: SSI 2013/150 Art.26
s.5, applied: SSI 2013/150 Art.4
s.6, amended: SSI 2013/211 Sch.1 para.20
s.6, applied: SSI 2013/150 Art.18
s.7, applied: SI 2013/1465 Art.4
s.8, applied: SSI 2013/194 r.79
s.23, applied: SSI 2013/150 Art.24
s.26, amended: SSI 2013/211 Sch.1 para.20
s.27, amended: SSI 2013/211 Sch.1 para.20
s.29A, added: SSI 2013/211 Sch.1 para.20
s.31, amended: SSI 2013/211 Sch.1 para.20
s.33, applied: SSI 2013/194 r.27, r.28, r.31, r.32, r.34, r.35, r.56, r.57
s.34, enabling: SSI 2013/212
s.37, applied: SSI 2013/194 r.29, r.39, r.40, r.71, r.72, r.91
s.37, referred to: SSI 2013/194 r.81
s.38, applied: SSI 2013/194 r.29, r.32
s.39, applied: SSI 2013/194 r.29, r.32
s.43, applied: SSI 2013/150 Art.16, SSI 2013/194 r.29, r.81
s.43, enabling: SSI 2013/172
s.45, applied: SI 2013/1465 Art.8, Art.9, SSI 2013/194 r.39, r.70, r.91
s.46, applied: SSI 2013/194 r.39, r.70, r.91
s.48, applied: SSI 2013/194 r.39, r.40, r.70, r.72, r.91, SSI 2013/200 Reg.6
s.49, applied: SSI 2013/194 r.39, r.40, r.71, r.91
s.50, applied: SSI 2013/194 r.40, r.71, r.72
s.55, applied: SI 2013/1465 Art.8, Art.9, Art.11
s.56, applied: SI 2013/1465 Art.8, Art.9, Art.11
s.56, referred to: SI 2013/1465 Art.8, Art.9
s.60, applied: SSI 2013/194 r.12
s.61, applied: SSI 2013/194 r.12, r.90
s.65, applied: SI 2013/1465 Art.8, Art.9
s.66, amended: SSI 2013/211 Sch.1 para.20
s.66, applied: SSI 2013/150 Art.15, SSI 2013/194 r.12, r.27, r.28, r.80, SSI 2013/205 Reg.10
s.67, amended: SSI 2013/211 Sch.1 para.20
s.67, applied: SSI 2013/146 Art.2, SSI 2013/205 Reg.10
s.67, referred to: SI 2013/1465 Art.13, Art.14
s.68, applied: SI 2013/1465 Art.8, Art.9, SSI 2013/194 r.12, SSI 2013/205 Reg.10
s.69, applied: SI 2013/1465 Art.8, Art.9, SSI 2013/150 Art.16, SSI 2013/194 r.2, r.12, r.22, r.26, r.27, r.28, r.29, r.37, r.38, r.55, r.80, r.81, SSI 2013/205 Reg.10
s.69, referred to: SSI 2013/150 Art.16
s.70, applied: SI 2013/1465 Art.13, Art.14
s.71, applied: SI 2013/1465 Art.13, Art.14
s.72, applied: SI 2013/1465 Art.8, Art.9, SSI 2013/194 r.12
s.73, applied: SSI 2013/194 r.23, r.44, r.61, r.62, r.63, r.64, r.65, r.66, r.70, r.73, r.76
s.74, applied: SSI 2013/194 r.23, r.44, r.61, r.62, r.63, r.64, r.65, r.66, r.70, r.73, r.76
s.75, applied: SSI 2013/194 r.61, r.62, r.63, r.64, r.65, r.66, r.70, r.73
s.76, referred to: SSI 2013/194 r.59
s.77, referred to: SSI 2013/194 r.59
s.78, amended: SSI 2013/211 Sch.1 para.20
s.78, repealed (in part): SI 2013/2042 Sch.1 para.42
s.79, applied: SSI 2013/194 r.3, r.19, r.45, r.46, r.48, r.49, r.52, r.53, r.54, r.55, r.61, r.62, r.63, r.64, r.65, r.66, r.73
s.79, referred to: SSI 2013/194 r.45
s.80, applied: SSI 2013/194 r.19, r.52, r.54
s.81, applied: SSI 2013/194 r.45, r.48, r.51, r.52
s.83, applied: SSI 2013/150 Art.8, SSI 2013/212 Reg.4, Reg.7
s.83, referred to: SI 2013/1465 Art.7, SSI 2013/205 Reg.6
s.83, repealed (in part): SSI 2013/211 Sch.2
s.87, applied: SSI 2013/212 Reg.4, Reg.7
s.88, applied: SSI 2013/212 Reg.4, Reg.7
s.89, applied: SSI 2013/194 r.14, r.27
s.90, applied: SSI 2013/194 r.59
s.91, applied: SSI 2013/194 r.37, r.60, r.61, r.62, r.90
s.91, varied: SSI 2013/194 r.68
s.92, applied: SSI 2013/194 r.61, SSI 2013/205 Reg.8
s.93, applied: SSI 2013/194 r.13, r.37, r.63, r.68, r.69, SSI 2013/205 Reg.8
s.93, varied: SSI 2013/194 r.68
s.94, applied: SSI 2013/194 r.13, r.37, r.63, r.68, r.69
s.95, applied: SSI 2013/194 r.64
s.96, applied: SSI 2013/194 r.41, r.73, SSI 2013/205 Reg.8
s.96, varied: SSI 2013/194 r.68
s.98, amended: SSI 2013/211 Sch.1 para.20
s.98, applied: SSI 2013/200 Reg.6, SSI 2013/205 Reg.8

s.99, applied: SSI 2013/200 Reg.6, SSI 2013/205 Reg.8
s.100, applied: SSI 2013/205 Reg.8
s.101, applied: SSI 2013/200 Reg.6
s.108, applied: SSI 2013/194 r.31, r.32, r.68
s.109, applied: SSI 2013/194 r.33, SSI 2013/205 Reg.8
s.110, applied: SSI 2013/200 Reg.6
s.115, amended: SSI 2013/211 Sch.1 para.20
s.115, applied: SSI 2013/194 r.31, r.32, r.33, SSI 2013/205 Reg.8
s.117, amended: SSI 2013/211 Sch.1 para.20
s.117, applied: SSI 2013/194 r.31, r.32, r.33, r.68, SSI 2013/205 Reg.8
s.119, applied: SSI 2013/194 r.31, r.37, r.57, r.60, r.61, r.62, r.68, r.90, SSI 2013/205 Reg.8
s.120, applied: SSI 2013/194 r.61, SSI 2013/205 Reg.8
s.121, applied: SSI 2013/194 r.58
s.123, applied: SSI 2013/194 r.17, r.61, r.63, r.78
s.126, applied: SSI 2013/193 Art.2, SSI 2013/194 r.42, r.74, r.81, r.92
s.126, referred to: SSI 2013/200 Reg.5
s.126, enabling: SSI 2013/193
s.127, applied: SSI 2013/194 r.82
s.128, applied: SSI 2013/194 r.83
s.131, applied: SI 2013/1465 Art.8, Art.9, SSI 2013/194 r.30, r.34, r.35, r.65, SSI 2013/205 Reg.7
s.131, varied: SSI 2013/99 Reg.7
s.132, applied: SSI 2013/194 r.88
s.134, applied: SI 2013/1465 Art.13, Art.14
s.136, applied: SSI 2013/194 r.36, SSI 2013/205 Reg.7
s.137, applied: SSI 2013/194 r.34, r.35, r.38, r.57, r.80, SSI 2013/205 Reg.15
s.137, varied: SSI 2013/99 Reg.7
s.138, applied: SI 2013/1465 Art.13, Art.14, SSI 2013/194 r.60, r.61, r.62, r.69
s.138, repealed (in part): SSI 2013/211 Sch.2
s.139, applied: SSI 2013/194 r.61
s.140, amended: SSI 2013/211 Sch.1 para.20
s.141, applied: SSI 2013/194 r.65
s.142, applied: SSI 2013/194 r.43, r.66
s.143, applied: SI 2013/1465 Art.8, Art.9, SSI 2013/149 Reg.9
s.145, applied: SI 2013/1465 Art.13, Art.14
s.145, disapplied: SI 2013/1465 Art.13
s.146, applied: SSI 2013/194 r.67
s.147, applied: SSI 2013/194 r.67
s.149, enabling: SSI 2013/149
s.150, applied: SSI 2013/210, SSI 2013/210 Reg.6, Reg.7, Reg.8
s.150, enabling: SSI 2013/210
s.151, applied: SI 2013/1465 Art.16, SSI 2013/212 Reg.4
s.151, referred to: SSI 2013/212 Reg.4, Reg.6
s.151, enabling: SSI 2013/212
s.152, enabling: SSI 2013/205
s.153, enabling: SSI 2013/205, SSI 2013/212
s.154, applied: SSI 2013/194 r.61, r.62, r.63, r.64, r.73, r.78, r.88, r.95, r.96, SSI 2013/200 Reg.6
s.155, amended: SSI 2013/211 Sch.1 para.20
s.156, amended: SSI 2013/211 Sch.1 para.20
s.156, applied: SSI 2013/194 r.27, r.28, r.31, r.32, r.34, r.35
s.158, applied: SSI 2013/194 r.62, r.76, r.88, r.93
s.159, amended: SSI 2013/211 Sch.1 para.20
s.159, applied: SSI 2013/194 r.88, r.92
s.160, applied: SSI 2013/194 r.48, r.50, r.66, r.88, SSI 2013/200 Reg.6
s.161, applied: SSI 2013/194 r.74, r.92, SSI 2013/200 Reg.6
s.162, applied: SSI 2013/200 Reg.6, SSI 2013/212 Reg.10
s.162, referred to: SSI 2013/212 Reg.5, Reg.11, Reg.12, Reg.13, Reg.14
s.162, enabling: SSI 2013/212
s.163, applied: SSI 2013/200 Reg.6
s.164, applied: SSI 2013/200 Reg.6
s.165, applied: SSI 2013/200 Reg.6
s.166, applied: SSI 2013/200 Reg.6
s.167, applied: SSI 2013/200 Reg.6
s.168, repealed (in part): SSI 2013/211 Sch.1 para.20
s.169, applied: SSI 2013/149 Reg.9
s.170, applied: SSI 2013/149 Reg.9
s.175, amended: SSI 2013/211 Sch.1 para.20
s.176, amended: SSI 2013/211 Sch.1 para.20
s.177, applied: SSI 2013/194
s.177, enabling: SSI 2013/194
s.178, applied: SSI 2013/194 r.6
s.182, amended: SSI 2013/211 Sch.1 para.20
s.190, enabling: SSI 2013/99
s.193, applied: SSI 2013/149 Reg.2, SSI 2013/194 r.99, SSI 2013/212 Reg.3
s.195, enabling: SSI 2013/194, SSI 2013/212
s.197, applied: SSI 2013/193, SSI 2013/194, SSI 2013/205, SSI 2013/210, SSI 2013/211, SSI 2013/212
s.199, applied: SSI 2013/194 r.90
s.200, applied: SSI 2013/193, SSI 2013/193 Art.3
s.200, enabling: SSI 2013/193
s.202, amended: SSI 2013/211 Sch.1 para.20
s.204, applied: SSI 2013/211
s.204, enabling: SSI 2013/147, SSI 2013/150, SSI 2013/211
s.205, enabling: SSI 2013/146, SSI 2013/150

s.206, enabling: SSI 2013/98, SSI 2013/190, SSI 2013/195
Sch.3 para.2, applied: SSI 2013/150 Art.23
Sch.3 para.7, applied: SSI 2013/150 Art.23
Sch.3 para.8, applied: SSI 2013/150 Art.20
Sch.3 para.10, applied: SSI 2013/150 Art.21
Sch.3 para.11, applied: SSI 2013/150 Art.21

asp 10. Local Electoral Administration (Scotland) Act 2011
s.2, applied: 2013 asp 14 s.5

asp 11. Certification of Death (Scotland) Act 2011
Commencement Orders: SSI 2013/159 Sch.1, Art.2
s.32, enabling: SSI 2013/159

asp 12. Public Records (Scotland) Act 2011
Sch.1, amended: SSI 2013/197 Sch.2 para.18

asp 13. Domestic Abuse (Scotland) Act 2011
s.3, applied: SSI 2013/357 Art.3

asp 14. Private Rented Housing (Scotland) Act 2011
Commencement Orders: SSI 2013/19 Art.2; SSI 2013/82 Art.3, Sch.1, Art.2
s.33, disapplied: SSI 2013/19 Art.3
s.41, enabling: SSI 2013/19, SSI 2013/82

asp 15. Forced Marriage etc (Protection and Jurisdiction) (Scotland) Act 2011
s.1, applied: SSI 2013/357 Art.3
s.5, applied: SSI 2013/357 Art.3

2012

asp 2. Budget (Scotland) Act 2012
s.4, amended: SSI 2013/117 Art.2
s.6, repealed: 2013 asp 4 s.8
s.7, applied: SSI 2013/117
s.7, enabling: SSI 2013/117
Sch.1, amended: SSI 2013/117 Art.3
Sch.2, amended: SSI 2013/117 Art.4

asp 3. National Library of Scotland Act 2012
Commencement Orders: SSI 2013/1 Art.2
s.10, enabling: SSI 2013/169
s.12, enabling: SSI 2013/1

asp 5. Land Registration etc (Scotland) Act 2012
s.117, enabling: SSI 2013/59
Sch.5 para.32, repealed: SI 2013/1575 Sch.1 para.16

asp 8. Police and Fire Reform (Scotland) Act 2012
Commencement Orders: SSI 2013/47 Art.2; SSI 2013/51 Art.2, Art.3
applied: SI 2013/602 Sch.3 para.5, SSI 2013/121 Art.3
Part 1 c.10, applied: SSI 2013/121 Art.16
s.6, applied: 2013 c.25 Sch.1 para.10
s.9, applied: SI 2013/602 Art.14, SSI 2013/35 Reg.2, SSI 2013/86 Reg.4
s.10, applied: SI 2013/602 Sch.3 para.6, Sch.3 para.7
s.15, applied: SSI 2013/35 Reg.2, Reg.31, Reg.32, SSI 2013/61 Reg.3, SSI 2013/76 Reg.2
s.15, enabling: SSI 2013/62, SSI 2013/76
s.16, applied: SSI 2013/35 Reg.2, SSI 2013/60 Reg.3, SSI 2013/61 Reg.3, SSI 2013/62 Reg.3
s.18, applied: SSI 2013/35 Sch.2 para.1
s.24, applied: SI 2013/602 Art.5, Art.7
s.25, applied: SI 2013/602 Art.14, SSI 2013/86 Reg.4
s.44, applied: SSI 2013/86 Reg.8
s.48, applied: 2013 c.25 Sch.5 para.23, Sch.6 para.10, SI 2013/602 Art.14, SSI 2013/42 Reg.2, SSI 2013/86 Reg.10
s.48, enabling: SSI 2013/35, SSI 2013/39, SSI 2013/40, SSI 2013/42, SSI 2013/43, SSI 2013/60, SSI 2013/61, SSI 2013/62, SSI 2013/122, SSI 2013/125
s.54, applied: SI 2013/602 Art.14, SSI 2013/35, SSI 2013/35 Reg.6, SSI 2013/39, SSI 2013/42, SSI 2013/43, SSI 2013/60, SSI 2013/61, SSI 2013/62, SSI 2013/122, SSI 2013/125
s.54, referred to: SSI 2013/35, SSI 2013/35 Reg.34, SSI 2013/39, SSI 2013/39 Reg.10, SSI 2013/42, SSI 2013/43, SSI 2013/43 Reg.5, Reg.24, SSI 2013/60, SSI 2013/61, SSI 2013/62, SSI 2013/122, SSI 2013/125
s.56, applied: SSI 2013/62 Reg.26, SSI 2013/63 r.3, r.4, r.5, Sch.1 para.4
s.56, enabling: SSI 2013/63
s.57, applied: SSI 2013/63 r.9
s.57, referred to: SSI 2013/63 r.9
s.59, applied: SSI 2013/63 r.10
s.61, applied: SSI 2013/86 Reg.8
s.72, applied: SSI 2013/76 Reg.2
s.73, applied: SSI 2013/76 Reg.2
s.78, applied: SSI 2013/121 Art.18
s.79, applied: SSI 2013/121 Art.18
s.80, applied: SSI 2013/121 Art.18
s.84, applied: SSI 2013/121 Art.4
s.87, applied: SI 2013/602 Art.13, SSI 2013/73 Art.2, Art.3, SSI 2013/76 Reg.2
s.87, enabling: SSI 2013/73
s.90, applied: SI 2013/602 Art.10
s.91, applied: SI 2013/602 Art.10
s.92, applied: SI 2013/602 Art.10
s.94, applied: SI 2013/602 Art.12
s.95, applied: SI 2013/602 Art.12
s.101, applied: 2013 c.25 Sch.1 para.9
s.125, applied: SSI 2013/119, SSI 2013/121

s.125, enabling: SSI 2013/35, SSI 2013/39, SSI 2013/40, SSI 2013/42, SSI 2013/43, SSI 2013/60, SSI 2013/61, SSI 2013/62, SSI 2013/63, SSI 2013/125
s.126, enabling: SSI 2013/119, SSI 2013/121
s.127, enabling: SSI 2013/119, SSI 2013/121
s.129, enabling: SSI 2013/47, SSI 2013/51
Sch.1 Part 1 para.7, applied: SSI 2013/76 Reg.2
Sch.1 Part 1 para.9, applied: SSI 2013/62 Reg.18
Sch.3 para.1, applied: SSI 2013/63 r.3
Sch.3 para.3, applied: SSI 2013/63 r.16
Sch.3 para.4, enabling: SSI 2013/63
Sch.5, applied: SSI 2013/35 Sch.3 para.8, Sch.3 para.9
Sch.5 para.3, applied: SSI 2013/35 Sch.3 para.4
Sch.5 para.5, applied: SSI 2013/35 Sch.3 para.4
Sch.5 para.8, applied: SSI 2013/60 Reg.3, Sch.2 para.6, Sch.2 para.7, SSI 2013/61 Reg.3, Sch.1 para.6, Sch.1 para.7, SSI 2013/62 Reg.3
Sch.7 Part 1 para.1, repealed: SI 2013/602 Sch.2 para.65
Sch.7 Part 1 para.33, amended: SSI 2013/47 Art.3
Sch.7 Part 2 para.54, amended: SSI 2013/51 Art.4
Sch.8, applied: SSI 2013/121 Art.11

asp 9. Long Leases (Scotland) Act 2012
Commencement Orders: SSI 2013/322 Art.2, Art.3, Art.4, Art.5, Sch.1
s.83, enabling: SSI 2013/322

2013

asp 2. Freedom of Information (Amendment) (Scotland) Act 2013
Commencement Orders: SSI 2013/136 Art.2, Art.3
Royal Assent, February 19, 2013
s.7, enabling: SSI 2013/136

asp 4. Budget (Scotland) Act 2013
Royal Assent, March 13, 2013
s.4, amended: SSI 2013/328 Art.2
s.7, applied: SSI 2013/328
s.7, enabling: SSI 2013/328
Sch.1, amended: SSI 2013/328 Art.3
Sch.2, amended: SSI 2013/328 Art.4

asp 6. High Hedges (Scotland) Act 2013
Royal Assent, May 02, 2013

asp 7. Aquaculture and Fisheries (Scotland) Act 2013
Commencement Orders: SSI 2013/249 Art.2
Royal Assent, June 18, 2013
s.66, enabling: SSI 2013/249

asp 8. Forth Road Bridge Act 2013
Royal Assent, June 28, 2013

asp 9. National Trust for Scotland (Governance etc.) Act 2013
Royal Assent, June 28, 2013

asp 10. Crofting (Amendment) (Scotland) Act 2013
Royal Assent, July 31, 2013

asp 11. Land and Buildings Transaction Tax (Scotland) Act 2013
Royal Assent, July 31, 2013

asp 12. Post-16 Education (Scotland) Act 2013
Commencement Orders: SSI 2013/281 Art.2, Sch.1, Art.2; SSI 2013/348 Art.2, Sch.1; SSI 2013/281 Sch.1
Royal Assent, August 07, 2013
s.23, enabling: SSI 2013/281, SSI 2013/348

ACTS OF THE PARLIAMENT OF ENGLAND, WALES & THE UNITED KINGDOM

1536

27. Church of Elsing Spytle, Parish Church of St Alphes Act 1536
repealed: 2013 c.2 Sch.1 Part 6

1 Will. & Mar. (1688)

2. Bill of Rights 1688
s.1, amended: 2013 c.20 Sch.1 para.2

1694

10. Orphans, London Act 1694
repealed: 2013 c.2 Sch.1 Part 6

8 & 9 Will. 3 (1696)

14. Rebuilding of St Paul#s and Westminster Abbey Act 1696
repealed: 2013 c.2 Sch.1 Part 6

15. Highways Surrey and Sussex Act 1696
repealed: 2013 c.2 Sch.1 Part 11

1697

18. Gloucestershire Roads Act 1697
repealed: 2013 c.2 Sch.1 Part 11

1700

2. Act of Settlement 1700
amended: 2013 c.20 Sch.1 para.3
s.2, amended: 2013 c.20 Sch.1 para.3

1710

17. New Churches in London and Westminster Act 1710
repealed: 2013 c.2 Sch.1 Part 6

1 Geo. 1 (1714)

23. Building of Churches, London and Westminster Act 1714
repealed: 2013 c.2 Sch.1 Part 6

8 Geo. 1 (1721)

29. Charterhouse Governors (Quorum) Act 1721
repealed: 2013 c.2 Sch.1 Part 1

1725

24. Gloucestershire Roads Act 1725
repealed: 2013 c.2 Sch.1 Part 11
37. Kensington, Chelsea and Fulham Roads (Tolls) Act 1725
repealed: 2013 c.2 Sch.1 Part 6

4 Geo. 2 (1730)

23. Oxford and Gloucester Roads Act 1730
repealed: 2013 c.2 Sch.1 Part 11
34. Fulham Roads Act 1730
repealed: 2013 c.2 Sch.1 Part 6

1731

4. Church at Woolwich Act 1731
repealed: 2013 c.2 Sch.1 Part 6

1732

8. Church of St George, Southwark Act 1732
repealed: 2013 c.2 Sch.1 Part 6

1736

18. Church of St Olave, Southwark Act 1736
repealed: 2013 c.2 Sch.1 Part 6

1738

7. Ealing Church Act 1738
repealed: 2013 c.2 Sch.1 Part 6

1742

6. Charterhouse Square Rates Act 1742
repealed: 2013 c.2 Sch.1 Part 6

1743

10. Oxford and Gloucester Roads Act 1743
repealed: 2013 c.2 Sch.1 Part 11

1745

15. Bethnal Green, Church Completion and Poor Relief Act 1745
repealed: 2013 c.2 Sch.1 Part 8
18. Gloucester Roads Act 1745
repealed: 2013 c.2 Sch.1 Part 11

1747

29. Orphans, London Act 1747
repealed: 2013 c.2 Sch.1 Part 6

1749

10. Fulham Roads Act 1749
repealed: 2013 c.2 Sch.1 Part 6

24 Geo. 2 (1750)

15. Islington Church Act 1750
repealed: 2013 c.2 Sch.1 Part 6
28. Gloucester and Oxford Roads Act 1750

repealed: 2013 c.2 Sch.1 Part 11

25 Geo. 2 (1751)

36. Disorderly Houses Act 1751
s.8, applied: SI 2013/435 Sch.1 Part 7

1753

70. Oxford and Gloucester Roads Act 1753
repealed: 2013 c.2 Sch.1 Part 11

1756

43. Bethnal Green Road Act 1756
repealed: 2013 c.2 Sch.1 Part 6
51. Gloucestershire Roads Act 1756
repealed: 2013 c.2 Sch.1 Part 11
58. Gloucester Roads Act 1756
repealed: 2013 c.2 Sch.1 Part 11
81. Berks Roads Act 1756
repealed: 2013 c.2 Sch.1 Part 11

1757

36. Passage from Charing Cross Act 1757
repealed: 2013 c.2 Sch.1 Part 6
64. Gloucestershire Roads Act 1757
repealed: 2013 c.2 Sch.1 Part 11
65. Gloucester Roads Act 1757
repealed: 2013 c.2 Sch.1 Part 11
77. Leatherhead and Guildford Road Act 1757
repealed: 2013 c.2 Sch.1 Part 11
78. Guildford and Farnham Road Act 1757
repealed: 2013 c.2 Sch.1 Part 11

1760

38. Croydon Parish Church Act 1760
repealed: 2013 c.2 Sch.1 Part 6

1764

90. Loddon and Clavering (Norfolk) Poor Relief Act 1764
repealed: 2013 c.2 Sch.1 Part 8

5 Geo. 3 (1765)

80. Oxford and Gloucester Roads Act 1765
repealed: 2013 c.2 Sch.1 Part 11

7 Geo. 3 (1767)

72. Queensborough Poor Relief Act 1767
repealed: 2013 c.2 Sch.1 Part 8
99. Addenbrooke's Hospital, Cambridge Act 1767
repealed: 2013 c.2 Sch.1 Part 1
105. Bethnal Green Road Act 1767
repealed: 2013 c.2 Sch.1 Part 6

1768

41. Gloucester and Oxford Roads Act 1768
repealed: 2013 c.2 Sch.1 Part 11
61. Abingdon to Swinford Roads Act 1768
repealed: 2013 c.2 Sch.1 Part 11

9 Geo. 3 (1769)

31. Magdalen Hospital, London Act 1769
repealed: 2013 c.2 Sch.1 Part 1

11 Geo. 3 (1771)

73. Oxford Roads Act 1771
repealed: 2013 c.2 Sch.1 Part 11

12 Geo. 3 (1772)

38. Christchurch, Middlesex Act 1772
repealed: 2013 c.2 Sch.1 Part 6

14 Geo. 3 (1774)

111. Gloucestershire Roads Act 1774
repealed: 2013 c.2 Sch.1 Part 11

1775

13. East and West Flegg Poor Relief Act 1775
repealed: 2013 c.2 Sch.1 Part 8
59. Mitford and Launditch (Norfolk) Poor Relief Act 1775

repealed: 2013 c.2 Sch.1 Part 8

73. Old Stratford to Dunchurch Road Act 1775
repealed: 2013 c.2 Sch.1 Part 11

16 Geo. 3 (1776)

9. Forehoe Poor Relief Act 1776
repealed: 2013 c.2 Sch.1 Part 8

23. London Streets Act 1776
repealed: 2013 c.2 Sch.1 Part 6

1778

49. Ratcliff Highway Act 1778
repealed: 2013 c.2 Sch.1 Part 6

50. Goodman#s Fields Act 1778
repealed: 2013 c.2 Sch.1 Part 6

73. London Streets Act 1778
repealed: 2013 c.2 Sch.1 Part 6

99. Berks Roads Act 1778
repealed: 2013 c.2 Sch.1 Part 11

102. Gloucester Roads Act 1778
repealed: 2013 c.2 Sch.1 Part 11

19 Geo. 3 (1779)

13. Hartsmere, etc (Suffolk) Poor Relief Act 1779
repealed: 2013 c.2 Sch.1 Part 8

93. Gloucester Roads Act 1779
repealed: 2013 c.2 Sch.1 Part 11

96. Guildford to Farnham Road Act 1779
repealed: 2013 c.2 Sch.1 Part 11

1780

70. Gloucester Roads Act 1780
repealed: 2013 c.2 Sch.1 Part 11

76. Burford to Preston Road Act 1780
repealed: 2013 c.2 Sch.1 Part 11

1781

87. Oxford Roads Act 1781
repealed: 2013 c.2 Sch.1 Part 11

1783

104. Gloucester Roads Act 1783
repealed: 2013 c.2 Sch.1 Part 11

106. Gloucestershire Roads Act 1783
repealed: 2013 c.2 Sch.1 Part 11

1788

60. Christchurch, Middlesex Improvement Act 1788
repealed: 2013 c.2 Sch.1 Part 6

1790

76. Hans Town, Chelsea Improvement Act 1790
repealed: 2013 c.2 Sch.1 Part 6

81. Manchester Poor Relief Act 1790
repealed: 2013 c.2 Sch.1 Part 8

106. Berks Roads Act 1790
repealed: 2013 c.2 Sch.1 Part 11

31 Geo. 3 (1791)

24. Oswestry Poor Relief Act 1791
repealed: 2013 c.2 Sch.1 Part 8

78. Ellesmere Poor Relief Act 1791
repealed: 2013 c.2 Sch.1 Part 8

103. Bicester to Aynho Road Act 1791
repealed: 2013 c.2 Sch.1 Part 11

111. Oxford and Gloucester Roads Act 1791
repealed: 2013 c.2 Sch.1 Part 11

32 Geo. 3 (1792)

159. Dunstable to Hockliffe Road Act 1792
repealed: 2013 c.2 Sch.1 Part 11

33 Geo. 3 (1793)

180. Bicester Roads Act 1793
repealed: 2013 c.2 Sch.1 Part 11

35 Geo. 3 (1795)

61. Bishopsgate Poor Relief Act 1795
repealed: 2013 c.2 Sch.1 Part 8

36 Geo. 3 (1796)

102. Lincoln Poor Relief Act 1796

repealed: 2013 c.2 Sch.1 Part 8

141. Old Stratford and Dunchurch Road Act 1796
repealed: 2013 c.2 Sch.1 Part 11

37 Geo. 3 (1797)

170. Adderbury and Oxford Road Act 1797
repealed: 2013 c.2 Sch.1 Part 11

39 & 40 Geo. 3 (1800)

38. Act of Union (Ireland) 1800
s.2, applied: 2013 c.20 s.4

1803

139. Forgery of Foreign Bills Act 1803
repealed: 2013 c.2 Sch.1 Part 2

48 Geo. 3 (1808)

48. Dublin General Post Office Act 1808
repealed: 2013 c.2 Sch.1 Part 4

1809

70. Dublin General Post Office Act 1809
repealed: 2013 c.2 Sch.1 Part 4

54 Geo. 3 (1814)

63. Dublin General Post Office Act 1814
repealed: 2013 c.2 Sch.1 Part 4

113. Dublin Site of Record Office Act 1814
repealed: 2013 c.2 Sch.1 Part 4

128. Dublin Foundling Hospital Act 1814
repealed: 2013 c.2 Sch.1 Part 4

55 Geo. 3 (1815)

152. Holyhead Roads Act 1815
repealed: 2013 c.2 Sch.1 Part 11

1820

29. Dublin Foundling Hospital Act 1820
repealed: 2013 c.2 Sch.1 Part 4

49. Dublin House of Industry Act 1820
repealed: 2013 c.2 Sch.1 Part 4

1 & 2 Geo. 4 (1821)

30. Holyhead Roads Act 1821
repealed: 2013 c.2 Sch.1 Part 11

3 Geo. 4 (1822)

26. Durham County Schools Amendment Act 1822
repealed: 2013 c.2 Sch.1 Part 1

35. Dublin Foundling Hospital Act 1822
repealed: 2013 c.2 Sch.1 Part 4

5 Geo. 4 (1824)

102. Dublin Justices Act 1824
repealed: 2013 c.2 Sch.1 Part 4

6 Geo. 4 (1825)

22. Jurors (Scotland) Act 1825
s.3, applied: SSI 2013/152 Art.15

100. Holyhead Road Act 1825
repealed: 2013 c.2 Sch.1 Part 11

7 Geo. 4 (1826)

76. Holyhead Bridges and Roads Act 1826
repealed: 2013 c.2 Sch.1 Part 11

7 & 8 Geo. 4 (1827)

35. London and Holyhead and Liverpool Roads Act 1827
repealed: 2013 c.2 Sch.1 Part 11

9 Geo. 4 (1828)

42. Church Building Society Act 1828
applied: SI 2013/641
repealed: SI 2013/641

75. Holyhead Roads Act 1828
repealed: 2013 c.2 Sch.1 Part 11

11 Geo. 4 & 1 Will 4 (1830)

37. Criminal Law (Scotland) Act 1830
s.2, repealed: 2013 c.2 Sch.1 Part 2
s.6, repealed: 2013 c.2 Sch.1 Part 2

2 & 3 Will. 4 (1832)

111. Lord Chancellor's Pension Act 1832
repealed: 2013 c.25 Sch.11 para.4

3 & 4 Will. 4 (1833)

41. Judicial Committee Act 1833
s.24, enabling: SI 2013/246

4 & 5 Will. 4 (1834)

44. Menai and Conway Bridges Act 1834
repealed: 2013 c.2 Sch.1 Part 11

6 & 7 Will. 4 (1836)

29. Dublin Police Act 1836
repealed: 2013 c.2 Sch.1 Part 4

35. London and Holyhead Road Act 1836
repealed: 2013 c.2 Sch.1 Part 11

1 & 2 Vict. (1837-38)

110. Judgments Act 1838
s.17, referred to: SI 2013/1046 r.40, r.57, SI 2013/1047 r.42, SI 2013/3208 r.41, r.58, r.117

2 & 3 Vict. (1839)

45. Highway (Railway Crossing) Act 1839
disapplied: SI 2013/2587 Art.3, SI 2013/3244 Art.3
s.1, applied: SI 2013/1030 Art.6

78. Dublin Police Act 1839
repealed: 2013 c.2 Sch.1 Part 4

3 & 4 Vict. (1840)

97. Railway Regulation Act 1840
disapplied: SI 2013/2587 Art.3, SI 2013/3244 Art.3

5 & 6 Vict. (1842)

24. Dublin Police Act 1842
repealed: 2013 c.2 Sch.1 Part 4

55. Railway Regulation Act 1842
disapplied: SI 2013/2587 Art.3, SI 2013/3244 Art.3
s.9, applied: SI 2013/1030 Art.6

7 & 8 Vict. (1844)

69. Judicial Committee Act 1844
s.1, enabling: SI 2013/246

8 & 9 Vict. (1845)

18. Lands Clauses Consolidation Act 1845
s.63, applied: SI 2013/3200 Art.19
s.68, applied: SI 2013/3200 Art.19

20. Railways Clauses Consolidation Act 1845
s.46, amended: SI 2013/2809 Art.3
s.46, applied: SI 2013/2809 Art.3
s.47, applied: SI 2013/1030 Art.6
s.58, applied: SI 2013/1967 Art.3, SI 2013/2809 Art.3
s.61, applied: SI 2013/2809 Art.3
s.68, applied: SI 2013/1967 Art.3, SI 2013/2809 Art.3
s.71, applied: SI 2013/1967 Art.3, SI 2013/2809 Art.3
s.72, applied: SI 2013/1967 Art.3, SI 2013/2809 Art.3
s.73, applied: SI 2013/1967 Art.3, SI 2013/2809 Art.3
s.77, applied: SI 2013/1967 Art.3, SI 2013/2809 Art.3
s.78, applied: SI 2013/1967 Art.3, SI 2013/2809 Art.3
s.78A, applied: SI 2013/1967 Art.3, SI 2013/2809 Art.3
s.79, applied: SI 2013/1967 Art.3, SI 2013/2809 Art.3
s.79A, applied: SI 2013/1967 Art.3, SI 2013/2809 Art.3
s.79B, applied: SI 2013/1967 Art.3, SI 2013/2809 Art.3
s.80, applied: SI 2013/1967 Art.3, SI 2013/2809 Art.3

s.81, applied: SI 2013/1967 Art.3, SI 2013/2809 Art.3
s.82, applied: SI 2013/1967 Art.3, SI 2013/2809 Art.3
s.83, applied: SI 2013/1967 Art.3, SI 2013/2809 Art.3
s.84, applied: SI 2013/1967 Art.3
s.85, applied: SI 2013/1967 Art.3, SI 2013/2809 Art.3
s.85A, applied: SI 2013/1967 Art.3, SI 2013/2809 Art.3
s.85B, applied: SI 2013/1967 Art.3, SI 2013/2809 Art.3
s.85C, applied: SI 2013/1967 Art.3, SI 2013/2809 Art.3
s.85D, applied: SI 2013/1967 Art.3, SI 2013/2809 Art.3
s.85E, applied: SI 2013/1967 Art.3, SI 2013/2809 Art.3
s.103, applied: SI 2013/1967 Art.3
s.105, applied: SI 2013/1967 Art.3, SI 2013/2809 Art.3
s.145, applied: SI 2013/1967 Art.3
Sch.1, applied: SI 2013/1967 Art.3, SI 2013/2809 Art.3
Sch.2, applied: SI 2013/1967 Art.3, SI 2013/2809 Art.3
Sch.3, applied: SI 2013/1967 Art.3, SI 2013/2809 Art.3

25. Maynooth College Act 1845
repealed: 2013 c.2 Sch.1 Part 1

10 & 11 Vict. (1847)

27. Harbours, Docks, and Piers Clauses Act 1847
applied: SI 2013/648 Art.53, SSI 2013/308 Art.3
varied: SSI 2013/46 Art.3
applied: SSI 2013/46 Art.3, SSI 2013/308 Art.3
varied: SSI 2013/308 Art.3
applied: SSI 2013/46 Art.3, SSI 2013/308 Art.3
varied: SSI 2013/308 Art.3
s.1, applied: SSI 2013/46 Art.3, SSI 2013/308 Art.3
s.1, varied: SSI 2013/308 Art.3
s.3, varied: SI 2013/648 Art.53, SSI 2013/46 Art.3, SSI 2013/308 Art.3
s.4, applied: SI 2013/648 Art.53
s.6, applied: SI 2013/648 Art.53
s.7, applied: SI 2013/648 Art.53
s.8, applied: SI 2013/648 Art.53
s.9, applied: SI 2013/648 Art.53
s.10, applied: SI 2013/648 Art.53
s.11, applied: SI 2013/648 Art.53
s.12, applied: SI 2013/648 Art.53
s.13, applied: SI 2013/648 Art.53
s.14, applied: SI 2013/648 Art.53
s.15, applied: SI 2013/648 Art.53
s.16, applied: SI 2013/648 Art.53
s.17, applied: SI 2013/648 Art.53
s.18, applied: SI 2013/648 Art.53
s.19, applied: SI 2013/648 Art.53
s.20, applied: SI 2013/648 Art.53
s.21, applied: SI 2013/648 Art.53
s.22, applied: SI 2013/648 Art.53
s.23, applied: SI 2013/648 Art.53
s.25, applied: SI 2013/648 Art.53
s.27, applied: SI 2013/648 Art.53
s.31, applied: SI 2013/648 Art.53
s.32, applied: SI 2013/648 Art.53
s.33, applied: SI 2013/648 Art.53, SSI 2013/46 Art.3
s.34, applied: SSI 2013/46 Art.3, SSI 2013/308 Art.3
s.34, varied: SI 2013/648 Art.53, SSI 2013/308 Art.3
s.35, applied: SSI 2013/46 Art.3, SSI 2013/308 Art.3
s.35, varied: SSI 2013/308 Art.3
s.36, applied: SI 2013/648 Art.53
s.37, applied: SSI 2013/46 Art.3, SSI 2013/308 Art.3
s.37, varied: SSI 2013/308 Art.3
s.38, applied: SSI 2013/46 Art.3, SSI 2013/308 Art.3
s.38, varied: SSI 2013/308 Art.3
s.39, applied: SSI 2013/46 Art.3, SSI 2013/308 Art.3
s.39, varied: SSI 2013/308 Art.3
s.40, applied: SI 2013/648 Art.53
s.41, applied: SI 2013/648 Art.53
s.42, applied: SI 2013/648 Art.53, SSI 2013/46 Art.3, SSI 2013/308 Art.3
s.42, varied: SSI 2013/308 Art.3
s.43, applied: SI 2013/648 Art.53
s.44, applied: SI 2013/648 Art.53
s.45, applied: SI 2013/648 Art.53
s.46, applied: SI 2013/648 Art.53
s.47, applied: SI 2013/648 Art.53
s.48, applied: SI 2013/648 Art.53
s.49, applied: SI 2013/648 Art.53
s.50, applied: SI 2013/648 Art.53
s.51, applied: SSI 2013/46 Art.3, SSI 2013/308 Art.3
s.51, varied: SSI 2013/308 Art.3
s.52, applied: SI 2013/648 Art.53
s.53, applied: SI 2013/648 Art.53

s.54, applied: SSI 2013/46 Art.3, SSI 2013/308 Art.3
s.54, varied: SSI 2013/308 Art.3
s.55, applied: SSI 2013/46 Art.3, SSI 2013/308 Art.3
s.55, varied: SSI 2013/308 Art.3
s.56, applied: SSI 2013/46 Art.3
s.57, applied: SSI 2013/288 Art.24
s.59, applied: SI 2013/648 Art.53
s.60, applied: SI 2013/648 Art.53
s.61, applied: SI 2013/648 Art.53
s.62, applied: SI 2013/648 Art.53
s.63, applied: SI 2013/648 Art.53, SSI 2013/46 Art.3, SSI 2013/308 Art.3
s.63, varied: SSI 2013/46 Art.3, SSI 2013/308 Art.3
s.64, applied: SSI 2013/46 Art.3, SSI 2013/308 Art.3
s.64, varied: SSI 2013/308 Art.3
s.65, applied: SSI 2013/46 Art.3, SSI 2013/288 Art.24, SSI 2013/308 Art.3
s.65, varied: SSI 2013/46 Art.3, SSI 2013/308 Art.3
s.66, applied: SI 2013/648 Art.53
s.67, applied: SI 2013/648 Art.53
s.68, applied: SI 2013/648 Art.53
s.69, applied: SI 2013/648 Art.53, SSI 2013/288 Art.24
s.70, applied: SI 2013/648 Art.53
s.71, applied: SI 2013/648 Art.53
s.79, applied: SI 2013/648 Art.53
s.80, applied: SI 2013/648 Art.53
s.81, applied: SI 2013/648 Art.53
s.82, applied: SI 2013/648 Art.53
s.83, applied: SI 2013/648 Art.53
s.84, applied: SI 2013/648 Art.53
s.85, applied: SI 2013/648 Art.53
s.86, applied: SI 2013/648 Art.53
s.87, applied: SI 2013/648 Art.53
s.88, applied: SI 2013/648 Art.53
s.89, applied: SI 2013/648 Art.53
s.90, applied: SI 2013/648 Art.53
s.92, applied: SI 2013/648 Art.53
s.97, applied: SI 2013/648 Art.53
s.98, applied: SI 2013/648 Art.53
s.99, applied: SI 2013/648 Art.53
s.100, applied: SI 2013/648 Art.53
s.101, applied: SI 2013/648 Art.53
s.102, applied: SI 2013/648 Art.53

11 & 12 Vict. (1848)

113. Dublin Police Act 1848
repealed: 2013 c.2 Sch.1 Part 4

12 & 13 Vict. (1849)

62. Advance of Money (Athlone to Galway Railway) Act 1849
repealed: 2013 c.2 Sch.1 Part 9

13 & 14 Vict. (1850)

81. Dublin Corporation Act 1850
repealed: 2013 c.2 Sch.1 Part 4

14 & 15 Vict. (1851)

99. Evidence Act 1851
s.7, applied: SI 2013/1554 r.35_2

16 & 17 Vict. (1853)

112. Dublin Carriage Act 1853
repealed: 2013 c.2 Sch.1 Part 4

17 & 18 Vict. (1854)

45. Dublin Amended Carriage Act 1854
repealed: 2013 c.2 Sch.1 Part 4

112. Literary and Scientific Institutions Act 1854
s.29, amended: 2013 c.22 Sch.9 para.12
s.30, amended: 2013 c.22 Sch.9 para.141

18 & 19 Vict. (1855)

65. Dublin Amended Carriage Act 1855
repealed: 2013 c.2 Sch.1 Part 4

19 & 20 Vict. (1856)

110. Dublin Hospitals Regulation Act 1856
repealed: 2013 c.2 Sch.1 Part 4

20 & 21 Vict. (1857)

31. Inclosure Act 1857
s.12, applied: SI 2013/3244 Art.61

67. Pimlico Improvement Act 1857

repealed: 2013 c.2 Sch.1 Part 6

81. Burial Act 1857

s.25, see *R. (on the application of Rudewicz) v Ministry of Justice* [2012] EWCA Civ 499, [2013] Q.B. 410 (CA (Civ Div)), Lord Neuberger (M.R.)
s.25, disapplied: SI 2013/586 Art.16

21 & 22 Vict. (1858)

84. Four Courts (Dublin) Extension Act 1858

repealed: 2013 c.2 Sch.1 Part 4

22 & 23 Vict. (1859)

52. Dublin Police Act 1859

repealed: 2013 c.2 Sch.1 Part 4

24 & 25 Vict. (1861)

28. Holyhead Road Relief Act 1861

repealed: 2013 c.2 Sch.1 Part 11

97. Malicious Damage Act 1861

s.36, applied: SI 2013/435 Sch.1 Part 7

98. Forgery Act 1861

s.34, applied: SI 2013/435 Sch.1 Part 7
s.36, applied: SI 2013/435 Sch.1 Part 7
s.37, applied: SI 2013/435 Sch.1 Part 7

100. Offences against the Person Act 1861

s.4, applied: SI 2013/435 Sch.1 Part 7, SI 2013/1852 Sch.1 para.3
s.16, see *R. v Smith (Joseph Alexander)* [2013] EWCA Crim 11, [2013] 2 Cr. App. R. 5 (CA (Crim Div)), Pitchford L.J.
s.16, applied: SI 2013/435 Sch.1 Part 7
s.17, applied: SI 2013/435 Sch.1 Part 7
s.18, see *R. v Anani (Khalid)* [2013] EWCA Crim 65, [2013] 2 Cr. App. R. (S.) 57 (CA (Crim Div)), Jackson, L.J.; see *R. v Clift (Leigh George)* [2012] EWCA Crim 2750, [2013] 1 W.L.R. 2093 (CA (Crim Div)), Lord Judge, L.C.J.; see *R. v Cripps (Russell)* [2012] EWCA Crim 806, [2013] 1 Cr. App. R. (S.) 7 (CA (Crim Div)), Rix, L.J.
s.18, applied: SI 2013/435 Sch.1 Part 7
s.20, see *R. (on the application of Jones) v First-tier Tribunal (Social Entitlement Chamber)* [2013] UKSC 19, [2013] 2 A.C. 48 (SC), Lord Hope, J.S.C. (Deputy President); see *R. v Cripps (Russell)* [2012] EWCA Crim 806, [2013] 1 Cr. App. R. (S.) 7 (CA (Crim Div)), Rix, L.J.; see *R. v Styler (Matt Donsson)* [2012] EWCA Crim 2169, [2013] 1 Cr. App. R. (S.) 120 (CA (Crim Div)), Richards, L.J.; see *R. v Topp (Bradley)* [2012] EWCA Crim 1861, [2013] 1 Cr. App. R. (S.) 82 (CA (Crim Div)), Aikens, L.J.; see *Sutton LBC v G* [2012] EWHC 2604 (Fam), [2013] 1 F.L.R. 833 (Fam Div), Hogg, J.
s.20, applied: SI 2013/435 Sch.1 Part 7
s.21, applied: SI 2013/435 Sch.1 Part 7
s.22, applied: SI 2013/435 Sch.1 Part 7
s.23, applied: SI 2013/435 Sch.1 Part 7
s.24, applied: SI 2013/435 Sch.1 Part 7
s.26, applied: SI 2013/435 Sch.1 Part 7
s.27, applied: SI 2013/435 Sch.1 Part 7
s.28, applied: SI 2013/435 Sch.1 Part 7
s.29, applied: SI 2013/435 Sch.1 Part 7
s.30, applied: SI 2013/435 Sch.1 Part 7
s.31, applied: SI 2013/435 Sch.1 Part 7
s.32, applied: SI 2013/435 Sch.1 Part 7
s.33, applied: SI 2013/435 Sch.1 Part 7
s.34, applied: SI 2013/435 Sch.1 Part 7
s.35, applied: SI 2013/435 Sch.1 Part 7
s.37, applied: SI 2013/435 Sch.1 Part 7
s.38, applied: SI 2013/435 Sch.1 Part 7
s.47, applied: SI 2013/435 Sch.1 Part 7
s.58, applied: SI 2013/435 Sch.1 Part 7
s.59, applied: SI 2013/435 Sch.1 Part 7
s.60, applied: SI 2013/435 Sch.1 Part 7
s.64, applied: SI 2013/435 Sch.1 Part 7

25 & 26 Vict. (1862)

37. Crown Private Estates Act 1862

s.1, applied: 2013 asp 5 Sch.3 para.3, 2013 asp 6 s.37

26 & 27 Vict. (1863)

92. Railways Clauses Act 1863

s.5, applied: SI 2013/2809 Art.3
s.6, applied: SI 2013/1030 Art.6
s.7, applied: SI 2013/2809 Art.3
s.12, applied: SI 2013/1967 Art.3, SI 2013/2809 Art.3

28 & 29 Vict. (1865)

18. Criminal Procedure Act 1865

s.5, applied: SI 2013/1554 r.50_8, r.62_15
s.6, applied: SI 2013/1554 r.50_8, r.62_15
s.7, applied: SI 2013/1554 r.50_8, r.62_15

73. Naval and Marine Pay and Pensions Act 1865

s.3, applied: 2013 c.25 Sch.5 para.25, Sch.6 para.12

30 & 31 Vict. (1867)

95. Dublin Police Act 1867
repealed: 2013 c.2 Sch.1 Part 4

133. Consecration of Churchyards Act 1867
applied: SI 2013/1918 Sch.2 para.1

31 & 32 Vict. (1868)

64. Land Registers (Scotland) Act 1868
s.25, enabling: SSI 2013/59

119. Regulation of Railways Act 1868
disapplied: SI 2013/2587 Art.3, SI 2013/3244 Art.3

32 & 33 Vict. (1869)

62. Debtors Act 1869
s.5, see *Bhura v Bhura* [2012] EWHC 3633 (Fam), [2013] 2 F.L.R. 44 (Fam Div), Mostyn, J.; see *Mohan v Mohan* [2013] EWCA Civ 586, [2013] C.P. Rep. 36 (CA (Civ Div)), Thorpe, L.J.; see *Zuk v Zuk* [2012] EWCA Civ 1871, [2013] 2 F.L.R. 1466 (CA (Civ Div)), Thorpe, L.J.
s.5, amended: 2013 c.22 Sch.9 para.78, Sch.10 para.2
s.5, repealed (in part): 2013 c.22 Sch.10 para.2

33 & 34 Vict. (1870)

35. Apportionment Act 1870
s.2, disapplied: 2013 c.1 s.1

36 & 37 Vict. (1873)

48. Regulation of Railways Act 1873
disapplied: SI 2013/2587 Art.3, SI 2013/3244 Art.3

60. Extradition Act 1873
repealed: 2013 c.2 Sch.1 Part 2

37 & 38 Vict. (1874)

81. Great Seal (Offices) Act 1874
s.9, enabling: SI 2013/986

38 & 39 Vict. (1875)

17. Explosives Act 1875
s.61, amended: 2013 c.32 Sch.12 para.51
s.74, amended: 2013 c.32 Sch.12 para.52
s.75, amended: 2013 c.22 Sch.8 para.14

39 & 40 Vict. (1876)

56. Commons Act 1876
s.30, amended: 2013 c.22 Sch.9 para.13

42 & 43 Vict. (1879)

11. Bankers Books Evidence Act 1879
s.6, applied: SI 2013/1554 Part 28
s.7, applied: SI 2013/1554 Part 28, r.28_1
s.8, applied: SI 2013/1554 r.76_1
s.10, amended: 2013 c.22 Sch.9 para.14

44 & 45 Vict. (1881)

41. Conveyancing Act 1881
s.9, varied: 2013 c.33 Sch.7 para.6

45 & 46 Vict. (1882)

43. Bills of Sale Act (1878) Amendment Act 1882
s.11, amended: 2013 c.22 Sch.9 para.15

61. Bills of Exchange Act 1882
s.81A, applied: 2013 c.10 s.12

75. Married Women's Property Act 1882
s.10, amended: 2013 c.22 Sch.11 para.2
s.17, amended: 2013 c.22 Sch.11 para.3

46 & 47 Vict. (1883)

3. Explosive Substances Act 1883
s.2, applied: SI 2013/435 Sch.1 Part 7, SI 2013/1852 Sch.1 para.23
s.3, applied: SI 2013/435 Sch.1 Part 7, SI 2013/1852 Sch.1 para.24
s.4, applied: SI 2013/435 Sch.1 Part 7

47 & 48 Vict. (1884)

31. Colonial Prisoners Removal Act 1884
applied: SI 2013/379 Reg.96

55. Pensions and Yeomanry Pay Act 1884
s.2, applied: 2013 c.25 Sch.5 para.26, Sch.6 para.13

72. Disused Burial Grounds Act 1884
applied: SI 2013/2587 Art.7

50 & 51 Vict. (1887)

54. British Settlements Act 1887
enabling: SI 2013/244, SI 2013/786, SI 2013/1443, SI 2013/1444, SI 2013/1446, SI 2013/1447, SI 2013/1718, SI 2013/1719, SI 2013/2598, SI 2013/2599, SI 2013/3160

51 & 52 Vict. (1888)

21. Law of Distress Amendment Act 1888
s.7, amended: 2013 c.22 Sch.9 para.16

52 & 53 Vict. (1889)

57. Regulation of Railways Act 1889
disapplied: SI 2013/2587 Art.3, SI 2013/3244 Art.3

69. Public Bodies Corrupt Practices Act 1889
s.1, applied: SI 2013/435 Sch.1 Part 7

53 & 54 Vict. (1890)

39. Partnership Act 1890
s.23, amended: 2013 c.22 Sch.9 para.118
s.38, amended: 2013 c.21 s.6

55 & 56 Vict. (1892)

23. Foreign Marriage Act 1892
repealed (in part): 2013 c.30 s.13
s.18, enabling: SI 2013/2875

58 & 59 Vict. (1895)

24. Law of Distress Amendment Act 1895
s.1, amended: 2013 c.22 Sch.9 para.17

59 & 60 Vict. (1896)

48. Light Railways Act 1896
s.26, amended: SI 2013/602 Sch.2 para.1

60 & 61 Vict. (1897)

30. Police (Property) Act 1897
s.2A, amended: 2013 c.22 Sch.8 para.15

62 & 63 Vict. (1899)

19. Electric Lighting (Clauses) Act 1899
Sch.1, applied: SSI 2013/264 Reg.4

2 Edw. 7 (1902)

8. Cremation Act 1902
s.8, applied: SI 2013/435 Sch.1 Part 7

37. Osborne Estate Act 1902
s.1, amended: 2013 c.24 s.62
s.1, repealed (in part): 2013 c.24 s.62

6 Edw. 7 (1906)

25. Open Spaces Act 1906
s.4, amended: 2013 c.22 Sch.9 para.115

32. Dogs Act 1906
s.3, amended: SSI 2013/119 Sch.1 para.1
s.8, amended: SSI 2013/119 Sch.1 para.1

34. Prevention of Corruption Act 1906
s.1, see *R. v Majeed (Mazhar)* [2012] EWCA Crim 1186, [2013] 1 W.L.R. 1041 (CA (Crim Div)), Lord Judge, L.C.J.
s.1, applied: SI 2013/435 Sch.1 Part 7

7 Edw. 7 (1907)

24. Limited Partnerships Act 1907
see *Certain Limited Partners in Henderson PFI Secondary Fund II LLP v Henderson PFI Secondary Fund II LP* [2012] EWHC 3259 (Comm), [2013] Q.B. 934 (QBD (Comm)), Cooke, J.
applied: SSI 2013/318 Reg.4
s.4, varied: SI 2013/1388 Reg.16
s.6, see *Certain Limited Partners in Henderson PFI Secondary Fund II LLP v Henderson PFI Secondary Fund II LP* [2012] EWHC 3259

(Comm), [2013] Q.B. 934 (QBD (Comm)), Cooke, J.
s.6, varied: SI 2013/1388 Reg.16
s.7, varied: SI 2013/1388 Reg.16
s.9, varied: SI 2013/1388 Reg.16
s.10, disapplied: SI 2013/1388 Reg.16

1 & 2 Geo. 5 (1911)

6. Perjury Act 1911
s.1, applied: SI 2013/435 Sch.1 Part 7
s.1A, applied: SI 2013/435 Sch.1 Part 7
s.2, applied: SI 2013/435 Sch.1 Part 7
s.3, applied: SI 2013/435 Sch.1 Part 7
s.4, applied: SI 2013/435 Sch.1 Part 7
s.5, applied: 2013 c.33 s.87, SI 2013/435 Sch.1 Part 7, SI 2013/971 Reg.26, SI 2013/1389 Reg.15, SI 2013/2605 Art.19
s.6, applied: SI 2013/435 Sch.1 Part 7
s.7, applied: SI 2013/435 Sch.1 Part 7
28. Official Secrets Act 1911
applied: SI 2013/1119 Art.66, SI 2013/2356 Reg.95, SSI 2013/174 Reg.8
34. Railway Companies (Accounts and Returns) Act 1911
repealed: 2013 c.2 Sch.1 Part 9

4 & 5 Geo. 5 (1914)

36. Osborne Estate Act 1914
repealed: 2013 c.24 s.62
47. Deeds of Arrangement Act 1914
s.10, amended: 2013 c.22 Sch.9 para.79
s.16, amended: 2013 c.22 Sch.9 para.79

5 & 6 Geo. 5 (1914-15)

90. Indictments Act 1915
s.5, applied: SI 2013/1554 r.14_1

6 & 7 Geo. 5 (1916)

24. Finance Act 1916
s.63, repealed: 2013 c.29 Sch.46 para.113

7 & 8 Geo. 5 (1917)

51. Air Force (Constitution) Act 1917
s.2, applied: 2013 c.25 Sch.5 para.27, Sch.6 para.14
55. Chequers Estate Act 1917
applied: SI 2013/537 Art.2
Sch.1, amended: SI 2013/537 Art.6

9 & 10 Geo. 5 (1919)

97. Land Settlement (Scotland) Act 1919
s.15, amended: SSI 2013/119 Sch.1 para.3

10 & 11 Geo. 5 (1920)

33. Maintenance Orders (Facilities for Enforcement) Act 1920
s.1, amended: 2013 c.22 Sch.11 para.5
s.3, amended: 2013 c.22 Sch.11 para.6
s.3, repealed (in part): 2013 c.22 Sch.11 para.6
s.4, amended: 2013 c.22 Sch.11 para.7
s.4, repealed (in part): 2013 c.22 Sch.11 para.7
s.4A, amended: 2013 c.22 Sch.11 para.8
s.6, amended: 2013 c.22 Sch.11 para.9
s.9, amended: 2013 c.22 Sch.11 para.10
s.11, amended: 2013 c.22 Sch.11 para.11
75. Official Secrets Act 1920
applied: SI 2013/2356 Reg.95, SSI 2013/174 Reg.8
s.8, applied: SI 2013/1554 r.16_1

12 & 13 Geo. 5 (1922)

35. Celluloid and Cinematograph Film Act 1922
repealed: SI 2013/448 Sch.1
51. Allotments Act 1922
s.6, substituted: 2013 c.22 Sch.9 para.59

13 & 14 Geo. 5 (1923)

20. Mines (Working Facilities and Support) Act 1923
s.15, applied: SI 2013/2809 Art.3

15 & 16 Geo. 5 (1925)

20. Law of Property Act 1925
s.53, see *Arif v Anwar* [2013] EWHC 624 (Fam), [2013] B.P.I.R. 389 (Fam Div), Norris, J.
s.53, disapplied: SI 2013/1388 Reg.21
s.64, applied: 2013 c.33 Sch.7 para.6, SI 2013/3110 Sch.5 para.16

21. Land Registration Act 1925
see *Groveholt Ltd v Hughes* [2012] EWHC 3351 (Ch), [2013] 1 P. & C.R. 20 (Ch D), David Richards, J.; see *Parshall v Bryans* [2013] EWCA Civ 240, [2013] Ch. 568 (CA (Civ Div)), Mummery, L.J.
applied: SI 2013/3110 Sch.5 para.16

61. Allotments Act 1925
s.8, see *Snelling v Burstow Parish Council* [2013] EWHC 46 (Ch), [2013] 1 W.L.R. 2271 (Ch D), Vivien Rose
s.8, disapplied: SI 2013/1967 Art.16

86. Criminal Justice Act 1925
s.33, applied: 2013 c.15 s.11, 2013 c.32 Sch.10 para.8, SI 2013/233 Reg.6, SI 2013/1389 Reg.50, SI 2013/1554 r.2_4, SI 2013/1635 Reg.23, SI 2013/1662 Reg.37
s.33, varied: SI 2013/2952 Reg.19
s.41, amended: 2013 c.22 s.32
s.41, applied: 2013 c.22 s.32, SI 2013/1554 r.16_1
s.41, disapplied: SI 2013/2786 Art.4

16 & 17 Geo. 5 (1926)

16. Execution of Diligence (Scotland) Act 1926
s.6, enabling: SSI 2013/345, SSI 2013/346

61. Judicial Proceedings (Regulation of Reports) Act 1926
s.1, applied: SI 2013/1554 r.16_1

18 & 19 Geo. 5 (1928)

32. Petroleum (Consolidation) Act 1928
s.25A, repealed (in part): SI 2013/448 Sch.1

19 & 20 Geo. 5 (1929)

29. Government Annuities Act 1929
s.48, amended: 2013 c.22 Sch.9 para.86
s.61, amended: 2013 c.22 Sch.9 para.86

34. Infant Life (Preservation) Act 1929
s.1, applied: SI 2013/435 Sch.1 Part 7

20 & 21 Geo. 5 (1930)

28. Finance Act 1930
s.42, amended: SI 2013/234 Art.5
s.42A, added: SI 2013/234 Art.4
s.42B, added: SI 2013/234 Art.4

51. Reservoirs (Safety Provisions) Act 1930
applied: SI 2013/1677 Sch.1 para.4, Sch.3 para.2

21 & 22 Geo. 5 (1931)

49. Finance (No.2) Act 1931
s.22, amended: 2013 c.29 Sch.46 para.114

22 & 23 Geo. 5 (1931-32)

20. Chancel Repairs Act 1932
s.3, amended: 2013 c.22 Sch.9 para.64
s.4, amended: 2013 c.22 Sch.9 para.64

23 & 24 Geo. 5 (1932-33)

4. Evidence (Foreign, Dominion and Colonial Documents) Act 1933
applied: SI 2013/1801 Art.3, SSI 2013/310 Reg.4

12. Children and Young Persons Act 1933
Part II, applied: SI 2013/3104 Sch.1 para.30
s.1, see *R. v Patel (Parulben)* [2013] EWCA Crim 965, [2013] Med. L.R. 507 (CA (Crim Div)), Jackson, L.J.; see *Sutton LBC v G* [2012] EWHC 2604 (Fam), [2013] 1 F.L.R. 833 (Fam Div), Hogg, J.
s.1, applied: SI 2013/435 Sch.1 Part 7
s.25, applied: SI 2013/435 Sch.1 Part 7, SSI 2013/50 Sch.1 para.6, Sch.3 para.3
s.26, applied: SI 2013/435 Sch.1 Part 7
s.34A, applied: SI 2013/1554 r.37_2, r.7_4
s.36, applied: SI 2013/1554 r.16_1
s.37, applied: SI 2013/1554 r.16_1
s.39, see *MXB v East Sussex Hospitals NHS Trust* [2012] EWHC 3279 (QB), (2013) 177 J.P. 31 (QBD), Tugendhat, J.; see *R. (on the application of A) v Lowestoft Magistrates' Court* [2013] EWHC 659 (Admin), (2013) 177 J.P. 377 (QBD (Admin)), Pitchford, L.J.
s.39, applied: SI 2013/1554 r.37_2, r.16_1, r.29_19
s.45, applied: SI 2013/1554 r.37_1
s.46, applied: SI 2013/1554 r.37_1
s.47, applied: SI 2013/1554 r.16_1
s.48, applied: SI 2013/1554 r.37_1
s.49, applied: SI 2013/1554 r.37_2, r.16_1
s.59, applied: SI 2013/1554 r.37_1
s.107, amended: SSI 2013/119 Sch.1 para.4
Sch.1, referred to: SI 2013/349 Reg.105, Sch.7 para.29

36. Administration of Justice (Miscellaneous Provisions) Act 1933
s.2, amended: 2013 c.22 Sch.17 para.32

s.2, applied: SI 2013/483 Reg.6, SI 2013/1554 r.12_4, r.14_1
s.2, referred to: 2013 c.22 Sch.17 para.2
s.7, amended: 2013 c.22 Sch.9 para.52

41. Administration of Justice (Scotland) Act 1933
s.18, applied: 2013 asp 3 s.14

24 & 25 Geo. 5 (1933-34)

40. Administration of Justice (Appeals) Act 1934
repealed: 2013 c.22 Sch.9 para.19

26 Geo. 5 & Edw. 8 (1935-36)

49. Public Health Act 1936
s.6, applied: SI 2013/2196 Reg.2, SI 2013/2210 Reg.2, SI 2013/2493 Reg.2, SI 2013/2591 Reg.2, SI 2013/2996 Reg.2
s.343, amended: SI 2013/755 Sch.2 para.1

1 Edw. 8 & 1 Geo. 6 (1936-37)

16. Regency Act 1937
s.3, amended: 2013 c.20 Sch.1 para.4

1 & 2 Geo. 6 (1937-38)

36. Infanticide Act 1938
s.1, applied: SI 2013/435 Sch.1 Part 7

2 & 3 Geo. 6 (1938-39)

72. Landlord and Tenant (War Damage) Act 1939
s.23, amended: 2013 c.22 Sch.9 para.52

82. Personal Injuries (Emergency Provisions) Act 1939
s.1, enabling: SI 2013/707
s.2, enabling: SI 2013/707

121. Official Secrets Act 1939
applied: SI 2013/2356 Reg.95, SSI 2013/174 Reg.8

5 & 6 Geo. 6 (1941-42)

13. Landlord and Tenant (Requisitioned Land) Act 1942
s.10, amended: 2013 c.22 Sch.9 para.98

7 & 8 Geo. 6 (1943-44)

5. Landlord and Tenant (Requisitioned Land) Act 1944
s.2, amended: 2013 c.22 Sch.9 para.98

10. Disabled Persons (Employment) Act 1944
applied: SI 2013/3029 Sch.9 para.51, Sch.10 para.46, SI 2013/3035 Sch.1

8 & 9 Geo. 6 (1944-45)

7. British Settlements Act 1945
enabling: SI 2013/244, SI 2013/786, SI 2013/1443, SI 2013/1444, SI 2013/1446, SI 2013/1447, SI 2013/1718, SI 2013/1719, SI 2013/2598, SI 2013/2599, SI 2013/3160

28. Law Reform (Contributory Negligence) Act 1945
applied: SI 2013/1637 Reg.15

43. Requisitioned Land and War Works Act 1945
applied: 2013 c.32 s.119
s.28, applied: 2013 c.32 s.119

9 & 10 Geo. 6 (1945-46)

73. Hill Farming Act 1946
s.21, amended: SI 2013/1036 Sch.1 para.188

80. Atomic Energy Act 1946
s.4, amended: 2013 c.32 Sch.12 para.35
s.5, amended: 2013 c.32 Sch.12 para.36
s.11, amended: 2013 c.32 Sch.12 para.37
s.18, amended: 2013 c.32 Sch.12 para.38

81. National Health Service Act 1946
Part IV, applied: SI 2013/335 Reg.42

10 & 11 Geo. 6 (1946-47)

41. Fire Services Act 1947
s.26, applied: 2013 c.25 Sch.5 para.20
s.26, enabling: SI 2013/703, SI 2013/736, SI 2013/1392, SI 2013/2125, SSI 2013/128, SSI 2013/185

44. Crown Proceedings Act 1947
see *O'Farrell v O'Farrell* [2012] EWHC 123 (QB), [2013] 1 F.L.R. 77 (QBD), Tugendhat, J.
applied: 2013 c.32 s.111, SI 2013/2605 Art.11
s.15, amended: 2013 c.22 Sch.9 para.20
s.17, applied: SI 2013/1554 r.65_12
s.20, amended: 2013 c.22 Sch.9 para.20
s.23, amended: 2013 c.22 Sch.9 para.20
s.24, amended: 2013 c.22 Sch.9 para.20

s.27, amended: 2013 c.22 Sch.9 para.20
s.28, amended: 2013 c.22 Sch.9 para.20
s.29, amended: 2013 c.22 Sch.9 para.20
s.38, applied: SI 2013/164 Reg.17, SI 2013/1877 Reg.21
s.38, varied: SI 2013/1389 Sch.1 para.3

48. Agriculture Act 1947

s.73, amended: SI 2013/1036 Sch.1 para.190
s.75, substituted: SI 2013/1036 Sch.1 para.191
s.75, enabling: SI 2013/1169
s.106, amended: SI 2013/1036 Sch.1 para.192
Sch.9, amended: SI 2013/1036 Sch.1 para.193
Sch.9 para.13, amended: SI 2013/1036 Sch.1 para.193
Sch.9 para.14, amended: SI 2013/1036 Sch.1 para.193
Sch.9 para.15, amended: SI 2013/1036 Sch.1 para.193
Sch.9 para.15A, added: SI 2013/1036 Sch.1 para.193
Sch.9 para.16, amended: SI 2013/1036 Sch.1 para.193
Sch.9 para.16A, amended: SI 2013/1036 Sch.1 para.193
Sch.9 para.17, amended: SI 2013/1036 Sch.1 para.193
Sch.9 para.19, amended: SI 2013/1036 Sch.1 para.193
Sch.9 para.22, amended: SI 2013/1036 Sch.1 para.193
Sch.9 para.23, amended: SI 2013/1036 Sch.1 para.193
Sch.9 para.23, applied: 2013 c.25 Sch.5 para.3

11 & 12 Geo. 6 (1947-48)

17. Requisitioned Land and War Works Act 1948

s.12, applied: 2013 c.32 s.119
s.12, repealed: 2013 c.32 s.128
s.13, repealed: 2013 c.32 s.128
s.14, repealed: 2013 c.32 s.128
s.15, repealed: 2013 c.32 s.128

26. Local Government Act 1948

s.62, amended: 2013 c.22 Sch.9 para.104
s.87, amended: 2013 c.22 Sch.9 para.104

29. National Assistance Act 1948

Part III, applied: SI 2013/377 Reg.28
s.22, applied: SI 2013/631 Reg.2, SSI 2013/40 Reg.2
s.22, enabling: SI 2013/518, SI 2013/631, SI 2013/633, SI 2013/634, SSI 2013/40, SSI 2013/41
s.26, see *R. (on the application of Chatting) v Viridian Housing* [2012] EWHC 3595 (Admin), [2013] H.R.L.R. 12 (QBD (Admin)), Nicholas Paines Q.C.; see *R. (on the application of Members of the Committee of Care North East Northumberland) v Northumberland CC* [2013] EWHC 234 (Admin), [2013] P.T.S.R. 1130 (QBD (Admin)), Supperstone, J.
s.26, applied: SI 2013/379 Reg.37, SI 2013/3029 Sch.9 para.32, SI 2013/3035 Sch.1
s.29, applied: SI 2013/3029 Sch.1 para.19, Sch.1 para.20, Sch.2 para.6, Sch.3 para.5, Sch.6 para.21, Sch.7 para.10, SI 2013/3035 Sch.1

47. Agricultural Wages Act 1948

s.1, repealed: 2013 c.24 Sch.20 para.2
s.2, amended: 2013 c.24 Sch.20 para.2
s.2, repealed (in part): 2013 c.24 Sch.20 para.2
s.3, repealed: 2013 c.24 Sch.20 para.2
s.3A, repealed (in part): 2013 c.24 Sch.20 para.2
s.4, repealed (in part): 2013 c.24 Sch.20 para.2
s.6, repealed (in part): 2013 c.24 Sch.20 para.2
s.7, repealed (in part): 2013 c.24 Sch.20 para.2
s.8, repealed (in part): 2013 c.24 Sch.20 para.2
s.9, repealed (in part): 2013 c.24 Sch.20 para.2
s.10, repealed (in part): 2013 c.24 Sch.20 para.2
s.11, repealed (in part): 2013 c.24 Sch.20 para.2
s.11A, repealed (in part): 2013 c.24 Sch.20 para.2
s.12, repealed (in part): 2013 c.24 Sch.20 para.2
s.13, repealed (in part): 2013 c.24 Sch.20 para.2
s.14, repealed (in part): 2013 c.24 Sch.20 para.2
s.15, repealed (in part): 2013 c.24 Sch.20 para.2
s.15A, repealed (in part): 2013 c.24 Sch.20 para.2
s.16, repealed: 2013 c.24 Sch.20 para.2
s.17, repealed (in part): 2013 c.24 Sch.20 para.2
s.17A, repealed (in part): 2013 c.24 Sch.20 para.2
s.18, repealed: 2013 c.24 Sch.20 para.2
s.19, repealed: 2013 c.24 Sch.20 para.2
Sch.1 para.1, repealed: 2013 c.24 Sch.20 para.2
Sch.1 para.2, repealed: 2013 c.24 Sch.20 para.2
Sch.1 para.3, repealed: 2013 c.24 Sch.20 para.2
Sch.1 para.4, repealed: 2013 c.24 Sch.20 para.2
Sch.1 para.5, repealed: 2013 c.24 Sch.20 para.2
Sch.1 para.6, repealed: 2013 c.24 Sch.20 para.2
Sch.1 para.7, repealed: 2013 c.24 Sch.20 para.2
Sch.1 para.8, repealed (in part): 2013 c.24 Sch.20 para.2
Sch.2, amended: 2013 c.24 Sch.20 para.2
Sch.2, repealed: 2013 c.24 Sch.20 para.2
Sch.4 para.1, repealed: 2013 c.24 Sch.20 para.2
Sch.4 para.2, repealed: 2013 c.24 Sch.20 para.2
Sch.4 para.3, repealed: 2013 c.24 Sch.20 para.2
Sch.4 para.4, repealed: 2013 c.24 Sch.20 para.2
Sch.4 para.5, repealed: 2013 c.24 Sch.20 para.2
Sch.4 para.6, repealed: 2013 c.24 Sch.20 para.2

56. British Nationality Act 1948

applied: SSI 2013/35 Reg.32

s.3, applied: SI 2013/2870 Art.188

12, 13 & 14 Geo. 6 (1948-49)

16. National Theatre Act 1949

s.1, repealed: 2013 c.2 Sch.1 Part 6

67. Civil Aviation Act 1949

s.8, enabling: SI 2013/2870
s.41, applied: SI 2013/2870 Art.160
s.41, enabling: SI 2013/2870
s.57, enabling: SI 2013/2870
s.58, enabling: SI 2013/2870
s.59, enabling: SI 2013/2870
s.61, enabling: SI 2013/2870

74. Coast Protection Act 1949

s.2A, amended: SI 2013/755 Sch.2 para.4
s.4, amended: SI 2013/755 Sch.2 para.5
s.4, repealed (in part): SI 2013/755 Sch.2 para.5
s.5, amended: SI 2013/755 Sch.2 para.6
s.8, amended: SI 2013/755 Sch.2 para.7
s.16, amended: SI 2013/755 Sch.2 para.8
s.17, amended: SI 2013/755 Sch.2 para.9
s.45, amended: SI 2013/755 Sch.2 para.10
s.47, amended: SI 2013/755 Sch.2 para.11
s.49, amended: SI 2013/755 Sch.2 para.12
Sch.1 Part I para.1, amended: SI 2013/755 Sch.2 para.13
Sch.2 Part I para.2, amended: SI 2013/755 Sch.2 para.14
Sch.2 Part II para.12, amended: SI 2013/755 Sch.2 para.14

76. Marriage Act 1949

see *A v A* [2012] EWHC 2219 (Fam), [2013] Fam. 51 (Fam Div), Moylan, J.; see *Shagroon v Sharbatly* [2012] EWCA Civ 1507, [2013] Fam. 267 (CA (Civ Div)), Thorpe, L.J.
applied: SI 2013/1918 Sch.2 para.1
Part III, applied: 2013 c.30 s.1
Part V, applied: 2013 c.30 s.1
s.3, amended: 2013 c.22 Sch.11 para.13, 2013 c.30 Sch.7 para.3
s.3, repealed (in part): 2013 c.22 Sch.11 para.13
s.25, amended: 2013 c.30 Sch.7 para.4
s.26, applied: 2013 c.30 Sch.7 para.1
s.26, substituted: 2013 c.30 s.3
s.26A, added: 2013 c.30 s.4
s.26B, added: 2013 c.30 s.5
s.27A, amended: 2013 c.30 Sch.7 para.5
s.27B, amended: 2013 c.22 Sch.11 para.14
s.27D, added: 2013 c.30 Sch.7 para.6
s.28A, amended: 2013 c.30 Sch.7 para.7
s.41, see *R. (on the application of Hodkin) v Registrar General of Births Deaths and Marriages* [2013] UKSC 77 (SC), Lord Neuberger, J.S.C.
s.41, amended: 2013 c.30 Sch.7 para.8
s.42, amended: 2013 c.30 Sch.7 para.9
s.42, substituted: 2013 c.30 Sch.7 para.9
s.43, amended: 2013 c.30 Sch.7 para.10
s.43, repealed (in part): 2013 c.30 Sch.7 para.10
s.43, substituted: 2013 c.30 Sch.7 para.10
s.43A, added: 2013 c.30 Sch.1 para.2
s.43B, added: 2013 c.30 Sch.1 para.2
s.43C, added: 2013 c.30 Sch.1 para.2
s.43D, added: 2013 c.30 Sch.1 para.2
s.44, amended: 2013 c.30 Sch.7 para.11
s.44A, added: 2013 c.30 Sch.1 para.3
s.44B, added: 2013 c.30 Sch.1 para.3
s.44C, added: 2013 c.30 Sch.1 para.3
s.44D, added: 2013 c.30 Sch.1 para.3
s.45A, amended: 2013 c.30 Sch.7 para.12
s.46, amended: 2013 c.30 Sch.7 para.13
s.46A, enabling: SI 2013/2294
s.48, amended: 2013 c.30 Sch.7 para.14
s.49A, added: 2013 c.30 Sch.7 para.15
s.53, amended: 2013 c.30 Sch.7 para.16
s.68, amended: 2013 c.30 s.6
s.69, amended: 2013 c.30 Sch.7 para.17
s.70, amended: 2013 c.30 s.6, Sch.7 para.18
s.70A, added: 2013 c.30 s.6
s.75, amended: 2013 c.30 Sch.7 para.19
s.78, amended: 2013 c.30 Sch.7 para.20
Sch.4 Part III, amended: 2013 c.30 Sch.7 para.21
Sch.4 Part IV, amended: 2013 c.30 Sch.7 para.21

88. Registered Designs Act 1949

applied: SI 2013/2533 Art.4
s.1, varied: SI 2013/2533 Sch.1 para.5
s.2, varied: SI 2013/2533 Sch.1 para.6
s.3, varied: SI 2013/2533 Sch.1 para.7
s.4, varied: SI 2013/2533 Sch.1 para.8
s.5, varied: SI 2013/2533 Sch.1 para.9
s.6, varied: SI 2013/2533 Sch.1 para.10
s.7, varied: SI 2013/2533 Sch.1 para.11
s.8, varied: SI 2013/2533 Sch.1 para.12
s.8A, varied: SI 2013/2533 Sch.1 para.13
s.8B, varied: SI 2013/2533 Sch.1 para.14
s.9, varied: SI 2013/2533 Sch.1 para.15
s.10, varied: SI 2013/2533 Sch.1 para.15
s.11, varied: SI 2013/2533 Sch.1 para.16
s.11A, varied: SI 2013/2533 Sch.1 para.17
s.11B, varied: SI 2013/2533 Sch.1 para.18
s.13, enabling: SI 2013/539
s.14, varied: SI 2013/2533 Sch.1 para.19
s.15, varied: SI 2013/2533 Sch.1 para.20
s.15A, varied: SI 2013/2533 Sch.1 para.21
s.15B, varied: SI 2013/2533 Sch.1 para.21

s.15C, varied: SI 2013/2533 Sch.1 para.21
s.16, varied: SI 2013/2533 Sch.1 para.22
s.17, varied: SI 2013/2533 Sch.1 para.23
s.19, varied: SI 2013/2533 Sch.1 para.24
s.20, varied: SI 2013/2533 Sch.1 para.25
s.22, varied: SI 2013/2533 Sch.1 para.26
s.23, varied: SI 2013/2533 Sch.1 para.27
s.24A, varied: SI 2013/2533 Sch.1 para.28
s.24B, varied: SI 2013/2533 Sch.1 para.28
s.24C, varied: SI 2013/2533 Sch.1 para.28
s.24D, varied: SI 2013/2533 Sch.1 para.28
s.24E, varied: SI 2013/2533 Sch.1 para.28
s.24F, varied: SI 2013/2533 Sch.1 para.28
s.24G, varied: SI 2013/2533 Sch.1 para.28
s.25, varied: SI 2013/2533 Sch.1 para.29
s.26, varied: SI 2013/2533 Sch.1 para.30
s.27, amended: 2013 c.22 Sch.9 para.21
s.27, varied: SI 2013/2533 Sch.1 para.31
s.27A, repealed (in part): 2013 c.22 Sch.9 para.21
s.28, varied: SI 2013/2533 Sch.1 para.32
s.30, varied: SI 2013/2533 Sch.1 para.33
s.33, varied: SI 2013/2533 Sch.1 para.34
s.34, varied: SI 2013/2533 Sch.1 para.34
s.35, varied: SI 2013/2533 Sch.1 para.35
s.36, varied: SI 2013/2533 Sch.1 para.36
s.36, enabling: SI 2013/444
s.37, varied: SI 2013/2533 Sch.1 para.37
s.37, enabling: SI 2013/539, SI 2013/2533
s.37A, varied: SI 2013/2533 Sch.1 para.38
s.43, varied: SI 2013/2533 Sch.1 para.39
s.44, varied: SI 2013/2533 Sch.1 para.40
s.47, disapplied: SI 2013/2533 Sch.1 para.4
s.47, enabling: SI 2013/2533
s.48, varied: SI 2013/2533 Sch.1 para.41
Sch.A1 para.1, varied: SI 2013/2533 Sch.1 para.42
Sch.A1 para.2, varied: SI 2013/2533 Sch.1 para.42
Sch.A1 para.3, varied: SI 2013/2533 Sch.1 para.42
Sch.A1 para.4, varied: SI 2013/2533 Sch.1 para.42
Sch.A1 para.5, varied: SI 2013/2533 Sch.1 para.42
Sch.1 para.1, varied: SI 2013/2533 Sch.1 para.43
Sch.1 para.2, varied: SI 2013/2533 Sch.1 para.43
Sch.1 para.2A, varied: SI 2013/2533 Sch.1 para.43
Sch.1 para.3, varied: SI 2013/2533 Sch.1 para.43

97. National Parks and Access to the Countryside Act 1949

s.1, repealed: SI 2013/755 Art.8
s.2, repealed: SI 2013/755 Art.8
s.3, applied: SI 2013/755 Sch.7 para.5
s.3, repealed: SI 2013/755 Art.8
s.4, repealed: SI 2013/755 Art.8
s.4A, amended: SI 2013/755 Sch.2 para.16
s.15A, amended: SI 2013/755 Sch.2 para.16
s.16, amended: SI 2013/755 Sch.2 para.17
s.21, amended: SI 2013/755 Sch.2 para.18
s.50A, amended: SI 2013/755 Sch.2 para.19
s.65, amended: SI 2013/755 Sch.2 para.20
s.85, amended: SI 2013/755 Sch.2 para.21
s.86A, amended: SI 2013/755 Sch.2 para.21
s.90, amended: SI 2013/755 Sch.2 para.22
s.91, amended: SI 2013/755 Sch.2 para.22
s.99, amended: SI 2013/755 Sch.2 para.23
s.114, amended: SI 2013/755 Sch.2 para.24
Sch.1 Part I para.2, amended: SI 2013/755 Sch.2 para.25

101. Justices of the Peace Act 1949

repealed: 2013 c.2 Sch.1 Part 5

14 Geo. 6 (1950)

12. Foreign Compensation Act 1950

s.7, enabling: SI 2013/236

29. Employment and Training (Northern Ireland) Act 1950

s.1, applied: SI 2013/628 Sch.1 para.2

37. Maintenance Orders Act 1950

s.4, amended: 2013 c.22 Sch.11 para.16, SI 2013/630 Reg.2
s.9, amended: SI 2013/630 Reg.2
s.15, amended: 2013 c.22 Sch.11 para.17
s.17, amended: 2013 c.22 Sch.11 para.18
s.17, repealed (in part): 2013 c.22 Sch.11 para.18
s.18, amended: 2013 c.22 Sch.11 para.19
s.18, repealed (in part): 2013 c.22 Sch.11 para.19
s.19, amended: 2013 c.22 Sch.11 para.20
s.19, repealed (in part): 2013 c.22 Sch.11 para.20
s.20, amended: 2013 c.22 Sch.11 para.21
s.22, amended: 2013 c.22 Sch.11 para.22
s.24, amended: 2013 c.22 Sch.11 para.23
s.25, amended: 2013 c.22 Sch.11 para.24
s.28, amended: 2013 c.22 Sch.11 para.25
Sch.2, amended: 2013 c.22 Sch.11 para.17

14 & 15 Geo. 6 (1950-51)

39. Common Informers Act 1951

Sch.1, amended: 2013 c.2 Sch.1 Part 2

65. Reserve and Auxiliary Forces (Protection of Civil Interests) Act 1951

Part V, applied: SI 2013/2356 Reg.85
s.2, amended: 2013 c.22 Sch.9 para.52
s.22, amended: SI 2013/1036 Sch.1 para.2
Sch.2 Part I, amended: SI 2013/602 Sch.2 para.2

15 & 16 Geo. 6 & 1 Eliz. 2 (1951-52)

10. Income Tax Act 1952
s.228, repealed: 2013 c.2 Sch.1 Part 10
s.400, repealed (in part): 2013 c.2 Sch.1 Part 10
s.406, repealed (in part): 2013 c.2 Sch.1 Part 10

39. Motor Vehicles (International Circulation) Act 1952
s.1, applied: SI 2013/3150
s.1, enabling: SI 2013/3150

52. Prison Act 1952
applied: SI 2013/378 Reg.13, SI 2013/3029 Reg.26, SI 2013/3035 Sch.1
s.37, enabling: SI 2013/485
s.38, applied: SI 2013/435 Sch.1 Part 7
s.42A, added: 2013 c.11 s.1
s.43, amended: 2013 c.11 s.1
s.47, enabling: SI 2013/2462

66. Defamation Act 1952
s.5, repealed (in part): 2013 c.26 s.2
s.6, repealed (in part): 2013 c.26 s.3

1 & 2 Eliz. 2 (1952-53)

14. Prevention of Crime Act 1953
s.1, applied: SI 2013/435 Sch.1 Part 7

20. Births and Deaths Registration Act 1953
applied: SI 2013/1616 Sch.1, SI 2013/1629 Reg.8
applied: 2013 c.13 Sch.1 para.5
s.34, applied: 2013 c.13 Sch.1 para.3

36. Post Office Act 1953
s.11, applied: SI 2013/435 Sch.1 Part 7

2 & 3 Eliz. 2 (1953-54)

39. Agriculture (Miscellaneous Provisions) Act 1954
s.5, amended: 2013 c.22 Sch.9 para.58, SI 2013/1036 Sch.1 para.195
s.5, repealed (in part): 2013 c.22 Sch.9 para.58
s.6, amended: SI 2013/1036 Sch.1 para.196
s.6, applied: SI 2013/1036 Sch.3 para.6
s.6, repealed (in part): SI 2013/1036 Sch.1 para.196
s.6A, added: SI 2013/1036 Sch.1 para.197

56. Landlord and Tenant Act 1954
Part II, applied: 2013 c.24 s.84
s.63, amended: 2013 c.22 Sch.9 para.52

70. Mines and Quarries Act 1954
applied: SI 2013/240 Art.7
s.79, applied: SI 2013/1471 Sch.2 para.29

3 & 4 Eliz. 2 (1954-55)

18. Army Act 1955
applied: SI 2013/1852 Art.3, Art.11

19. Air Force Act 1955
applied: SI 2013/1852 Art.3, Art.11

4 & 5 Eliz. 2 (1955-56)

44. Magistrates Courts (Appeals from Binding Over Orders) Act 1956
s.1, applied: SI 2013/1554 r.63_1

46. Administration of Justice Act 1956
s.40, amended: 2013 c.22 Sch.9 para.54

5 & 6 Eliz. 2 (1957)

52. Geneva Conventions Act 1957
s.1, applied: SI 2013/1852 Sch.1 para.26

53. Naval Discipline Act 1957
applied: SI 2013/1852 Art.3, Art.11

6 & 7 Eliz. 2 (1957-58)

30. Land Powers Defence Act 1958
applied: 2013 c.32 s.119
s.12, repealed: 2013 c.32 s.128
s.13, applied: 2013 c.32 s.119

33. Disabled Persons (Employment) Act 1958
s.3, applied: SI 2013/3029 Sch.10 para.47, SI 2013/3035 Sch.1

35. Matrimonial Causes (Property and Maintenance) Act 1958
s.7, amended: 2013 c.22 Sch.11 para.26

39. Maintenance Orders Act 1958
s.1, amended: 2013 c.22 Sch.10 para.4
s.1, repealed (in part): 2013 c.22 Sch.10 para.4
s.2, amended: 2013 c.22 Sch.10 para.5
s.2, repealed (in part): 2013 c.22 Sch.10 para.5
s.2A, amended: 2013 c.22 Sch.10 para.4, Sch.10 para.6
s.2A, repealed: 2013 c.22 Sch.10 para.6
s.3, repealed (in part): 2013 c.22 Sch.10 para.7
s.4, amended: 2013 c.22 Sch.10 para.8
s.4, repealed (in part): 2013 c.22 Sch.10 para.8
s.4A, amended: 2013 c.22 Sch.10 para.9
s.4A, repealed (in part): 2013 c.22 Sch.10 para.9
s.5, amended: 2013 c.22 Sch.10 para.10
s.5, repealed (in part): 2013 c.22 Sch.10 para.10
s.18, repealed: 2013 c.22 Sch.10 para.11
s.20, amended: 2013 c.22 Sch.10 para.12
s.20, repealed (in part): 2013 c.22 Sch.10 para.12
s.21, amended: 2013 c.22 Sch.10 para.13

47. Agricultural Marketing Act 1958
s.18, amended: 2013 c.22 Sch.9 para.57

51. Public Records Act 1958
s.2, enabling: SI 2013/3267
Sch.1 Part 1, amended: 2013 c.24 Sch.20 para.2
Sch.1 Part 2, amended: 2013 c.2 Sch.1 Part 10, 2013 c.22 Sch.8 para.16, 2013 c.24 Sch.4 para.21, SI 2013/2329 Sch.1 para.17
Sch.1 para.4, amended: 2013 c.22 Sch.10 para.14

69. Opencast Coal Act 1958
s.7, amended: SI 2013/755 Sch.2 para.26
s.14, amended: SI 2013/1036 Sch.1 para.198
Sch.8 para.7, amended: 2013 c.22 Sch.9 para.22

7 & 8 Eliz. 2 (1958-59)

49. Chevening Estate Act 1959
s.2, amended: SI 2013/2819 Reg.33
s.2, repealed (in part): SI 2013/2819 Reg.33

66. Obscene Publications Act 1959
s.2, applied: SI 2013/435 Sch.1 Part 7

72. Mental Health Act 1959
s.128, applied: SI 2013/435 Sch.1 Part 7

8 & 9 Eliz. 2 (1959-60)

16. Road Traffic Act 1960
s.223, applied: SI 2013/435 Sch.1 Part 7

33. Indecency with Children Act 1960
s.1, applied: SI 2013/435 Sch.1 Part 7

62. Caravan Sites and Control of Development Act 1960
s.1, see *White v South Derbyshire DC* [2012] EWHC 3495 (Admin), [2013] P.T.S.R. 536 (DC), Gross, L.J.
s.1, amended: 2013 c.14 s.13
s.3, amended: 2013 c.14 s.1, s.2
s.5A, added: 2013 c.14 s.1
s.7, amended: 2013 c.14 s.3
s.8, amended: 2013 c.14 s.1, s.3
s.9, amended: 2013 c.14 s.4
s.9A, added: 2013 c.14 s.4
s.9B, added: 2013 c.14 s.4
s.9C, added: 2013 c.14 s.4
s.9D, added: 2013 c.14 s.5
s.9E, added: 2013 c.14 s.5
s.9F, added: 2013 c.14 s.5
s.9G, added: 2013 c.14 s.6
s.9H, added: 2013 c.14 s.6
s.9I, added: 2013 c.14 s.6
s.10, amended: 2013 c.14 s.1, s.2
s.10A, added: 2013 c.14 s.1
s.12A, added: 2013 c.14 s.8
s.12B, added: 2013 c.14 s.8
s.12C, added: 2013 c.14 s.8
s.12D, added: 2013 c.14 s.8
s.12E, added: 2013 c.14 s.8
s.26, amended: 2013 c.14 s.13
s.26A, added: 2013 c.14 s.14
s.29, amended: 2013 c.14 s.1

65. Administration of Justice Act 1960
s.12, amended: 2013 c.22 Sch.9 para.52
s.13, see *B (Algeria) v Secretary of State for the Home Department* [2013] UKSC 4, [2013] 1 W.L.R. 435 (SC), Lord Neuberger (President); see *Thursfield v Thursfield* [2013] EWCA Civ 840, [2013] C.P. Rep. 44 (CA (Civ Div)), Lloyd, L.J.
s.13, amended: 2013 c.22 Sch.9 para.52, Sch.10 para.15
s.13, applied: SI 2013/1554 r.68_1, r.74_1

9 & 10 Eliz. 2 (1960-61)

33. Land Compensation Act 1961
see *Harringay Meat Traders Ltd v Secretary of State for Communities and Local Government* [2012] EWHC 1744 (Admin), [2013] P.T.S.R. 436 (QBD (Admin)), McCombe, J.
applied: SI 2013/533 Art.10, SI 2013/767 Art.11, SI 2013/1933 Art.30, SI 2013/2587 Art.35, SI 2013/3244 Art.31
varied: SI 2013/533 Art.10, SI 2013/1967 Art.26
Part I, applied: SI 2013/198 Art.6, Art.7, Art.8, Art.9, SI 2013/533 Art.3, Art.8, SI 2013/586 Art.11, Art.15, SI 2013/648 Art.15, Art.17, Art.22, Art.23, Art.32, Art.33, Art.34, Art.41, Art.42, SI 2013/675 Art.12, Art.13, Art.17, Art.18, Art.19, Art.23, Art.27, Art.28, Art.29, Art.34, Art.35, SI 2013/680 Art.12, Art.16, Art.17, Art.20, Art.21, Art.25, Art.26, Art.31, SI 2013/767 Art.8, Art.9, Art.13, SI 2013/1203 Art.15, Art.17, Art.22, Art.23, Art.24, SI 2013/1873 Art.12, Art.13, Art.16, Art.17, Art.21, SI 2013/1933 Art.8, Art.9, Art.14, Art.15, Art.16, Art.26, Art.27, Art.28, Art.32, Art.35, SI 2013/1967 Art.8, Art.9, Art.12, Art.14, Art.15, Art.22, Art.23, Art.24, Art.33, SI 2013/2587 Art.13, Art.19, Art.21, Art.23, Art.31, Art.32, Art.33, Art.37, SI 2013/2808 Art.13, Art.14, Art.17, Art.21, Art.25, Art.26, Art.30, Art.31, SI 2013/2809 Art.14, Art.18, Art.22, Art.23, Art.24, Art.28, SI 2013/3200 Art.16, Art.17, Art.18, Art.24, Art.25, Art.26, Art.30, SI 2013/3244 Art.10, Art.11, Art.16, Art.18, Art.20, Art.27, Art.28, Art.29, Art.33, Art.41
s.5A, applied: 2013 c.32 s.124

s.31, disapplied: SI 2013/2809 Art.9

34. Factories Act 1961

s.39, repealed (in part): SI 2013/448 Sch.1

s.176, amended: 2013 c.32 Sch.12 para.53

39. Criminal Justice Act 1961

s.22, applied: SI 2013/435 Sch.1 Part 7

55. Crown Estate Act 1961

applied: SI 2013/1978, SI 2013/1979

64. Public Health Act 1961

s.54, amended: SI 2013/755 Sch.2 para.27

10 & 11 Eliz. 2 (1961-62)

12. Education Act 1962

s.1, applied: SI 2013/3104 Sch.1 para.12, Sch.1 para.13

s.2, applied: SI 2013/3029 Sch.11 para.3, SI 2013/3035 Sch.1, SI 2013/3104 Sch.1 para.13

58. Pipe-lines Act 1962

s.10, applied: 2013 c.32 s.126

s.36, applied: 2013 c.32 s.126

s.40, applied: 2013 c.32 s.126

s.45, varied: 2013 c.32 s.126

s.66, amended: SI 2013/755 Sch.2 para.28

1963

27. Oaths and Evidence (Overseas Authorities and Countries) Act 1963

applied: SI 2013/1801 Art.3, SSI 2013/310 Reg.4

37. Children and Young Persons Act 1963

s.28, applied: SI 2013/1554 r.37_4

41. Offices, Shops and Railway Premises Act 1963

s.73, amended: 2013 c.22 Sch.9 para.114

s.90, amended: 2013 c.22 Sch.8 para.17

51. Land Compensation (Scotland) Act 1963

s.12, applied: 2013 c.32 s.124

1964

14. Plant Varieties and Seeds Act 1964

s.16, enabling: SI 2013/889, SSI 2013/326

s.29, amended: SI 2013/755 Sch.2 para.29

s.36, enabling: SI 2013/889, SSI 2013/326

16. Industrial Training Act 1964

applied: SI 2013/488 Sch.1

29. Continental Shelf Act 1964

applied: SI 2013/669 Art.1

s.1, enabling: SI 2013/3162

40. Harbours Act 1964

applied: SI 2013/1888, SSI 2013/288 Art.2

s.14, applied: SI 2013/1488 Art.8, SSI 2013/230, SSI 2013/288, SSI 2013/308

s.14, referred to: SSI 2013/308

s.14, enabling: SSI 2013/230, SSI 2013/288, SSI 2013/308

s.16, applied: SI 2013/1488 Art.8, SSI 2013/46

s.16, enabling: SSI 2013/46

s.17A, added: 2013 c.23 s.6

s.17B, added: 2013 c.23 s.6

s.17C, added: 2013 c.23 s.6

s.17D, added: 2013 c.23 s.6

s.17E, added: 2013 c.23 s.6

s.17F, added: 2013 c.23 s.6

s.30, applied: SSI 2013/288 Art.13

s.31, applied: SSI 2013/288 Art.13

s.40A, added: 2013 c.23 s.5

s.40B, added: 2013 c.23 s.5

s.40C, added: 2013 c.23 s.5

s.40D, added: 2013 c.23 s.5

s.44, amended: 2013 c.23 s.6, 2013 c.27 s.25

s.54, amended: 2013 c.23 s.5

s.54A, applied: SSI 2013/288

s.57, amended: 2013 c.23 s.5, s.6

s.57, referred to: SSI 2013/288 Art.13

s.58, amended: SI 2013/755 Sch.2 para.31

Sch.2, referred to: SSI 2013/230, SSI 2013/288, SSI 2013/308

Sch.2 para.9B, referred to: SI 2013/648 Art.68

Sch.3 Part I para.4, applied: SSI 2013/288

Sch.3 Part I para.5, applied: SSI 2013/46, SSI 2013/308

Sch.3 Part I para.6, applied: SSI 2013/288

Sch.3 Part I para.8, applied: SSI 2013/288

Sch.3 Part I para.9, applied: SSI 2013/288

Sch.3 Part I para.10, applied: SSI 2013/46, SSI 2013/46(c), SSI 2013/230, SSI 2013/288, SSI 2013/308

Sch.3 Part I para.10A, applied: SSI 2013/288

Sch.3 Part I para.15, applied: SSI 2013/46, SSI 2013/46(a), SSI 2013/288

Sch.3 Part I para.17, applied: SSI 2013/46, SSI 2013/230, SSI 2013/288, SSI 2013/308

Sch.3 Part I para.18, amended: SI 2013/755 Sch.2 para.32

Sch.3 Part I para.18, applied: SSI 2013/288

Sch.3 Part I para.19, applied: SSI 2013/46, SSI 2013/230, SSI 2013/288, SSI 2013/308

Sch.3 Part I para.21, applied: SSI 2013/46, SSI 2013/288

Sch.3 Part II para.26, applied: SI 2013/1488 Art.8

42. Administration of Justice Act 1964

s.26, amended: 2013 c.22 Sch.9 para.55

53. Hire-Purchase Act 1964

Part III, applied: SI 2013/3029 Sch.9 para.35, SI 2013/3035 Sch.1

74. Obscene Publications Act 1964

s.1, applied: SI 2013/435 Sch.1 Part 7

81. Diplomatic Privileges Act 1964

see *Al-Malki v Reyes* [2013] I.R.L.R. 929 (EAT), Langstaff, J. (President)

applied: SI 2013/1116 Art.3

84. Criminal Procedure (Insanity) Act 1964

applied: SI 2013/1554 r.76_4

s.4, applied: SI 2013/1554 r.33_1, r.42_8

s.4A, see *R. v B* [2012] EWCA Crim 770, [2013] 1 W.L.R. 499 (CA (Crim Div)), Aikens, L.J.

s.4A, applied: SI 2013/435 Sch.1 para.31, Sch.2 para.25

s.5, applied: SI 2013/1554 r.68_1, r.68_13

s.5A, applied: SI 2013/1554 r.68_1

1965

12. Industrial and Provident Societies Act 1965

s.1, amended: SI 2013/496 Sch.2 para.2

s.2, amended: SI 2013/496 Sch.2 para.2

s.5, amended: SI 2013/496 Sch.2 para.2

s.7A, amended: SI 2013/496 Sch.2 para.2

s.10, amended: SI 2013/496 Sch.2 para.2

s.16, amended: SI 2013/496 Sch.2 para.2, Sch.2 para.3

s.17, amended: SI 2013/496 Sch.2 para.2, Sch.2 para.4

s.18, amended: SI 2013/496 Sch.2 para.2

s.39, amended: SI 2013/496 Sch.2 para.2

s.39A, amended: SI 2013/496 Sch.2 para.2

s.39B, amended: SI 2013/496 Sch.2 para.2

s.42, amended: 2013 c.22 Sch.9 para.91

s.43, amended: SI 2013/496 Sch.2 para.2

s.43, substituted: SI 2013/496 Sch.2 para.5

s.44, amended: SI 2013/496 Sch.2 para.2

s.47, amended: SI 2013/496 Sch.2 para.2

s.48, amended: SI 2013/496 Sch.2 para.2

s.49, amended: SI 2013/496 Sch.2 para.2

s.50, amended: SI 2013/496 Sch.2 para.2, Sch.2 para.6

s.51, amended: SI 2013/496 Sch.2 para.7

s.52, amended: SI 2013/496 Sch.2 para.2, Sch.2 para.8

s.53, amended: SI 2013/496 Sch.2 para.2

s.55, amended: SI 2013/496 Sch.2 para.9

s.56, amended: SI 2013/496 Sch.2 para.10

s.56, substituted: SI 2013/496 Sch.2 para.10

s.58, amended: SI 2013/496 Sch.2 para.11

s.58, applied: SSI 2013/174 Reg.14, Reg.16

s.59, amended: SI 2013/496 Sch.2 para.2

s.60, amended: 2013 c.22 Sch.9 para.52, SI 2013/496 Sch.2 para.12

s.61, amended: SI 2013/496 Sch.2 para.13

s.66, amended: SI 2013/496 Sch.2 para.14

s.67, amended: SI 2013/496 Sch.2 para.15

s.70A, amended: SI 2013/496 Sch.2 para.16

s.72, amended: SI 2013/496 Sch.2 para.2, Sch.2 para.17

s.72A, amended: SI 2013/496 Sch.2 para.18

s.74, amended: SI 2013/496 Sch.2 para.2, Sch.2 para.19

s.76, amended: SI 2013/496 Sch.2 para.2

32. Administration of Estates (Small Payments) Act 1965

s.1, referred to: SSI 2013/174 Reg.22

s.6, applied: SI 2013/2356 Reg.82, SSI 2013/174 Reg.22

36. Gas Act 1965

s.8, amended: SI 2013/755 Sch.2 para.34

s.9, amended: SI 2013/755 Sch.2 para.34

s.15, amended: SI 2013/755 Sch.2 para.35

s.17, amended: SI 2013/755 Sch.2 para.36

Sch.2 Part II para.4, amended: SI 2013/755 Sch.2 para.37

Sch.2 Part II para.7, amended: SI 2013/755 Sch.2 para.37

Sch.2 Part II para.12, amended: SI 2013/755 Sch.2 para.37

Sch.2 Part III para.16, amended: SI 2013/755 Sch.2 para.37

Sch.3 para.4, amended: SI 2013/755 Sch.2 para.38

Sch.3 para.5, amended: SI 2013/755 Sch.2 para.38

Sch.3 para.6, amended: SI 2013/755 Sch.2 para.38

Sch.3 para.8A, added: SI 2013/755 Sch.2 para.38

Sch.4 Part II para.5, amended: SI 2013/755 Sch.2 para.39

Sch.6 para.2, amended: SI 2013/755 Sch.2 para.40

45. Backing of Warrants (Republic of Ireland) Act 1965

applied: SI 2013/1554 r.2_1

51. National Insurance Act 1965

applied: SI 2013/379 Sch.1 para.10

Part I, applied: SI 2013/377 Sch.2 para.2

s.36, amended: SI 2013/574 Art.11

s.36, applied: SI 2013/3029 Sch.1 para.16, SI 2013/3035 Sch.1

s.36, referred to: SI 2013/3029 Sch.1 para.16, SI 2013/3035 Sch.1

s.37, applied: SI 2013/3029 Sch.1 para.16, SI 2013/3035 Sch.1

s.37, varied: SI 2013/574 Art.11

56. Compulsory Purchase Act 1965

applied: SI 2013/533 Art.11, SI 2013/648 Art.31, SI 2013/675 Art.22, Art.24, Art.26, SI 2013/680

Art.18, Art.23, SI 2013/767 Art.12, SI 2013/1873 Art.20, SI 2013/1933 Art.24, Art.31, SI 2013/1967 Art.27, Sch.5 para.3, SI 2013/2587 Art.36, SI 2013/2808 Art.20, SI 2013/2809 Art.17, Art.21, Sch.7 para.3, SI 2013/3244 Art.32
referred to: SI 2013/533 Art.7, SI 2013/648 Art.27, Art.29, SI 2013/680 Art.21, SI 2013/1203 Art.20, SI 2013/1873 Art.18, SI 2013/1933 Art.23, Sch.8 para.3, SI 2013/1967 Art.18, Art.19, SI 2013/2587 Art.28, SI 2013/2808 Art.22, Sch.9 para.3, SI 2013/2809 Art.19, SI 2013/3244 Art.26
varied: SI 2013/767 Sch.1 para.3, SI 2013/2808 Sch.9 para.3, SI 2013/3200 Sch.3 para.3, SI 2013/3244 Sch.6 para.3
Part I, applied: SI 2013/533 Art.6, Art.13, SI 2013/648 Art.26, SI 2013/675 Art.21, SI 2013/680 Art.19, SI 2013/767 Art.8, Art.9, Art.14, Art.15, SI 2013/1873 Art.15, SI 2013/1933 Art.22, Art.33, Sch.8 para.3, SI 2013/1967 Art.17, Art.29, Sch.5 para.3, SI 2013/2587 Art.27, Art.38, Sch.5 para.3, SI 2013/2808 Art.19, Sch.9 para.3, SI 2013/2809 Art.16, Sch.7 para.3, SI 2013/3200 Art.20, Sch.3 para.3, SI 2013/3244 Art.24, Art.28, Art.29, Art.32, Art.35, Sch.6 para.3
s.1, applied: SI 2013/198 Art.11
s.1, varied: SI 2013/767 Art.4, SI 2013/1203 Art.2, SI 2013/3244 Art.24, Sch.6 para.3
s.2, varied: SI 2013/767 Art.4, SI 2013/1203 Art.2, SI 2013/3244 Art.24, Sch.6 para.3
s.3, applied: SI 2013/198 Art.11
s.3, varied: SI 2013/767 Art.4, SI 2013/1203 Art.2, SI 2013/3244 Art.24, Sch.6 para.3
s.4, varied: SI 2013/533 Art.6, SI 2013/767 Art.4, SI 2013/1203 Art.2, SI 2013/1933 Art.22, SI 2013/1967 Art.17, SI 2013/2587 Art.27, SI 2013/3244 Art.24, Sch.6 para.3
s.5, varied: SI 2013/767 Art.4, SI 2013/1203 Art.2, SI 2013/3244 Art.24, Sch.6 para.3
s.6, varied: SI 2013/767 Art.4, SI 2013/1203 Art.2, SI 2013/3244 Art.24, Sch.6 para.3
s.7, applied: SI 2013/680 Art.18, SI 2013/3200 Art.19
s.7, substituted: SI 2013/3244 Sch.6 para.4
s.7, varied: SI 2013/648 Sch.11 para.4, SI 2013/675 Sch.10 para.4, SI 2013/767 Art.4, Sch.1 para.4, SI 2013/1203 Art.2, SI 2013/1933 Sch.8 para.4, SI 2013/1967 Sch.5 para.4, SI 2013/2587 Sch.5 para.4, SI 2013/2808 Sch.9 para.4, SI 2013/2809 Sch.7 para.4, SI 2013/3200 Sch.3 para.4, SI 2013/3244 Art.24, Sch.6 para.3
s.8, applied: SI 2013/533 Art.11, SI 2013/675 Art.22, SI 2013/767 Art.6, Art.12, SI 2013/1873 Art.16, SI 2013/1933 Art.24, Art.31, SI 2013/2587 Art.29, Art.36, SI 2013/2808 Art.20, SI 2013/2809 Art.17, Art.21, SI 2013/3200 Art.18, SI 2013/3244 Art.32
s.8, disapplied: SI 2013/648 Art.31, SI 2013/675 Art.26, SI 2013/680 Art.23, SI 2013/1873 Art.20, SI 2013/1967 Art.27, SI 2013/3200 Art.22
s.8, referred to: SI 2013/648 Art.27, SI 2013/680 Art.20, SI 2013/1203 Art.18, SI 2013/1967 Art.19, SI 2013/3244 Art.26
s.8, substituted: SI 2013/3244 Sch.6 para.5
s.8, varied: SI 2013/648 Sch.11 para.5, SI 2013/675 Sch.10 para.5, SI 2013/767 Art.4, Sch.1 para.5, SI 2013/1203 Art.2, SI 2013/1933 Sch.8 para.5, SI 2013/1967 Sch.5 para.5, SI 2013/2587 Sch.5 para.5, SI 2013/2808 Sch.9 para.5, SI 2013/2809 Sch.7 para.5, SI 2013/3200 Sch.3 para.5, SI 2013/3244 Art.24, Sch.6 para.3
s.9, referred to: SI 2013/1967 Sch.5 para.6
s.9, varied: SI 2013/648 Sch.11 para.6, SI 2013/675 Sch.10 para.6, SI 2013/767 Art.4, Sch.1 para.6, SI 2013/1203 Art.2, SI 2013/1933 Sch.8 para.6, SI 2013/2587 Sch.5 para.6, SI 2013/2808 Sch.9 para.6, SI 2013/2809 Sch.7 para.6, SI 2013/3200 Sch.3 para.6, SI 2013/3244 Art.24, Sch.6 para.3, Sch.6 para.6
s.10, applied: SI 2013/198 Art.7, SI 2013/533 Art.8, SI 2013/648 Art.22, Art.25, Art.34, SI 2013/680 Art.18, Art.25, Art.26, SI 2013/767 Art.8, Art.9, SI 2013/1203 Art.23, Art.24, SI 2013/1933 Art.14, Art.27, Art.28, SI 2013/1967 Art.23, Art.24, SI 2013/2587 Art.21, Art.32, Art.33, SI 2013/3200 Art.16, Art.19, SI 2013/3244 Art.18, Art.28, Art.29
s.10, varied: SI 2013/767 Art.4, SI 2013/1203 Art.2, SI 2013/1933 Sch.8 para.6, SI 2013/2809 Sch.7 para.6, SI 2013/3244 Art.24, Sch.6 para.3
s.11, amended: SI 2013/2809 Sch.7 para.7
s.11, applied: SI 2013/533 Art.12, SI 2013/648 Art.28, SI 2013/675 Art.23, Art.28, Sch.13 para.2, SI 2013/680 Sch.7 para.4, SI 2013/767 Art.8, Art.14, SI 2013/1203 Art.19, SI 2013/1873 Art.17, SI 2013/1933 Art.27, Art.32, Sch.15 para.3, SI 2013/1967 Art.23, Art.28, Sch.9 para.18, Sch.9 para.55, SI 2013/2587 Art.32, Art.37, SI 2013/2808 Art.21, Art.25, SI 2013/2809 Art.9, Art.18, Art.23, Sch.10 para.17, SI 2013/3200 Art.25, SI 2013/3244 Art.28, Art.33, Sch.10 para.42, Sch.11 para.4
s.11, disapplied: SI 2013/1873 Sch.5 para.4
s.11, referred to: SI 2013/1967 Sch.5 para.7
s.11, varied: SI 2013/648 Sch.11 para.7, SI 2013/675 Sch.10 para.7, SI 2013/767 Art.4, Sch.1 para.7, SI 2013/1203 Art.2, SI 2013/1933 Sch.8 para.7, SI 2013/2587 Sch.5 para.7, SI 2013/2808

Sch.9 para.7, SI 2013/3200 Sch.3 para.7, SI 2013/3244 Art.24, Sch.6 para.3, Sch.6 para.7
s.12, amended: SI 2013/2809 Sch.7 para.7
s.12, referred to: SI 2013/1967 Sch.5 para.7
s.12, varied: SI 2013/648 Sch.11 para.7, SI 2013/675 Sch.10 para.7, SI 2013/767 Art.4, Sch.1 para.7, SI 2013/1203 Art.2, SI 2013/2587 Sch.5 para.7, SI 2013/2808 Sch.9 para.7, SI 2013/3244 Art.24, Sch.6 para.3, Sch.6 para.7
s.13, amended: SI 2013/2809 Sch.7 para.7
s.13, applied: SI 2013/198 Art.11, SI 2013/533 Art.8, SI 2013/648 Art.33, Art.34, SI 2013/675 Art.28, Art.29, SI 2013/680 Art.25, Art.26, SI 2013/767 Art.8, Art.9, SI 2013/1203 Art.23, Art.24, SI 2013/1933 Art.27, Art.28, SI 2013/1967 Art.23, Art.24, SI 2013/2587 Art.32, Art.33, SI 2013/2808 Art.25, Art.26, SI 2013/2809 Art.23, Art.24, SI 2013/3200 Art.25, Art.26, SI 2013/3244 Art.28, Art.29
s.13, disapplied: SI 2013/198 Art.11
s.13, referred to: SI 2013/1967 Sch.5 para.7
s.13, varied: SI 2013/648 Sch.11 para.7, SI 2013/675 Sch.10 para.7, SI 2013/767 Art.4, Sch.1 para.7, SI 2013/1203 Art.2, SI 2013/2587 Sch.5 para.7, SI 2013/2808 Sch.9 para.7, SI 2013/3244 Art.24, Sch.6 para.3, Sch.6 para.7
s.14, varied: SI 2013/767 Art.4, SI 2013/1203 Art.2, SI 2013/3244 Art.24, Sch.6 para.3
s.15, varied: SI 2013/767 Art.4, SI 2013/1203 Art.2, SI 2013/3244 Art.24, Sch.6 para.3
s.16, varied: SI 2013/767 Art.4, SI 2013/1203 Art.2, SI 2013/3244 Art.24, Sch.6 para.3
s.17, varied: SI 2013/767 Art.4, SI 2013/1203 Art.2, SI 2013/3244 Art.24, Sch.6 para.3
s.18, varied: SI 2013/767 Art.4, SI 2013/1203 Art.2, SI 2013/3244 Art.24, Sch.6 para.3
s.19, varied: SI 2013/767 Art.4, SI 2013/1203 Art.2, SI 2013/3244 Art.24, Sch.6 para.3
s.20, applied: SI 2013/1967 Sch.5 para.8
s.20, varied: SI 2013/648 Sch.11 para.8, SI 2013/675 Sch.10 para.8, SI 2013/767 Art.4, Sch.1 para.8, SI 2013/1203 Art.2, SI 2013/1933 Sch.8 para.8, SI 2013/2587 Sch.5 para.8, SI 2013/2808 Sch.9 para.8, SI 2013/2809 Sch.7 para.8, SI 2013/3200 Sch.3 para.8, SI 2013/3244 Art.24, Sch.6 para.3, Sch.6 para.8
s.21, varied: SI 2013/767 Art.4, SI 2013/1203 Art.2, SI 2013/3244 Art.24, Sch.6 para.3
s.22, amended: SI 2013/3244 Sch.6 para.9
s.22, referred to: SI 2013/1967 Sch.5 para.9
s.22, varied: SI 2013/648 Sch.11 para.9, SI 2013/675 Sch.10 para.9, SI 2013/767 Art.4, Sch.1 para.9, SI 2013/1203 Art.2, SI 2013/1933 Sch.8 para.9, SI 2013/2587 Sch.5 para.9, SI 2013/2808 Sch.9 para.9, SI 2013/2809 Sch.7 para.9, SI 2013/3200 Sch.3 para.9, SI 2013/3244 Art.24, Sch.6 para.3
s.23, varied: SI 2013/767 Art.4, SI 2013/1203 Art.2, SI 2013/3244 Art.24, Sch.6 para.3
s.24, varied: SI 2013/767 Art.4, SI 2013/1203 Art.2, SI 2013/3244 Art.24, Sch.6 para.3
s.25, varied: SI 2013/767 Art.4, SI 2013/1203 Art.2, SI 2013/3244 Art.24, Sch.6 para.3
s.26, varied: SI 2013/767 Art.4, SI 2013/1203 Art.2, SI 2013/3244 Art.24, Sch.6 para.3
s.27, varied: SI 2013/767 Art.4, SI 2013/1203 Art.2, SI 2013/3244 Art.24, Sch.6 para.3
s.28, varied: SI 2013/767 Art.4, SI 2013/1203 Art.2, SI 2013/3244 Art.24, Sch.6 para.3
s.29, varied: SI 2013/767 Art.4, SI 2013/1203 Art.2, SI 2013/3244 Art.24, Sch.6 para.3
s.30, varied: SI 2013/767 Art.4, SI 2013/1203 Art.2, SI 2013/3244 Art.24, Sch.6 para.3
s.31, varied: SI 2013/767 Art.4, SI 2013/1203 Art.2, SI 2013/3244 Art.24, Sch.6 para.3
s.32, varied: SI 2013/767 Art.4, SI 2013/1203 Art.2, SI 2013/3244 Art.24, Sch.6 para.3
s.33, applied: SI 2013/648 Art.38
Sch.1 para.10, referred to: SI 2013/1967 Sch.5 para.6
Sch.1 para.10, varied: SI 2013/648 Sch.11 para.6, SI 2013/675 Sch.10 para.6, SI 2013/767 Sch.1 para.6, SI 2013/2587 Sch.5 para.6, SI 2013/2808 Sch.9 para.6, SI 2013/3200 Sch.3 para.6, SI 2013/3244 Sch.6 para.6
Sch.2 para.2, referred to: SI 2013/1967 Sch.5 para.6
Sch.2 para.2, varied: SI 2013/648 Sch.11 para.6, SI 2013/675 Sch.10 para.6, SI 2013/767 Sch.1 para.6, SI 2013/1933 Sch.8 para.6, SI 2013/2587 Sch.5 para.6, SI 2013/2808 Sch.9 para.6, SI 2013/2809 Sch.7 para.6, SI 2013/3200 Sch.3 para.6, SI 2013/3244 Sch.6 para.6
Sch.3 para.3, varied: SI 2013/533 Art.6, SI 2013/1967 Art.17
Sch.4 para.2, referred to: SI 2013/1967 Sch.5 para.6
Sch.4 para.2, varied: SI 2013/648 Sch.11 para.6, SI 2013/675 Sch.10 para.6, SI 2013/767 Sch.1 para.6, SI 2013/1933 Sch.8 para.6, SI 2013/2587 Sch.5 para.6, SI 2013/2808 Sch.9 para.6, SI 2013/2809 Sch.7 para.6, SI 2013/3200 Sch.3 para.6, SI 2013/3244 Sch.6 para.6
Sch.4 para.7, referred to: SI 2013/1967 Sch.5 para.6
Sch.4 para.7, varied: SI 2013/648 Sch.11 para.6, SI 2013/675 Sch.10 para.6, SI 2013/767 Sch.1 para.6, SI 2013/1933 Sch.8 para.6, SI 2013/2587 Sch.5

para.6, SI 2013/2808 Sch.9 para.6, SI 2013/2809 Sch.7 para.6, SI 2013/3200 Sch.3 para.6, SI 2013/3244 Sch.6 para.6

57. Nuclear Installations Act 1965

applied: SI 2013/1471 Reg.14
referred to: 2013 c.32 s.74, s.113, s.116
s.1, applied: 2013 c.32 s.82
s.1, substituted: 2013 c.32 Sch.12 para.17
s.3, applied: 2013 c.32 s.82
s.3, substituted: 2013 c.32 Sch.12 para.18
s.4, applied: 2013 c.32 s.82
s.4, substituted: 2013 c.32 Sch.12 para.19
s.5, applied: 2013 c.32 s.82
s.5, substituted: 2013 c.32 Sch.12 para.20
s.6, applied: 2013 c.32 s.82
s.6, substituted: 2013 c.32 Sch.12 para.21
s.12, disapplied: 2013 c.32 s.107
s.19, amended: 2013 c.32 Sch.12 para.22
s.22, applied: 2013 c.32 s.82
s.22, substituted: 2013 c.32 Sch.12 para.23
s.24, amended: 2013 c.32 Sch.12 para.24
s.24A, amended: 2013 c.32 Sch.12 para.25
s.24A, applied: 2013 c.32 s.82
s.26, amended: 2013 c.32 Sch.12 para.26, SI 2013/755 Sch.2 para.41
s.27, repealed (in part): 2013 c.32 Sch.12 para.27
Sch.1 para.3, amended: 2013 c.32 Sch.12 para.28
Sch.2 para.1, amended: 2013 c.32 Sch.12 para.29
Sch.2 para.1, substituted: 2013 c.32 Sch.12 para.29
Sch.2 para.2, amended: 2013 c.32 Sch.12 para.29
Sch.2 para.2, substituted: 2013 c.32 Sch.12 para.29
Sch.2 para.5, amended: 2013 c.32 Sch.12 para.29
Sch.2 para.5, substituted: 2013 c.32 Sch.12 para.29
Sch.2 para.6, amended: 2013 c.32 Sch.12 para.29
Sch.2 para.6, substituted: 2013 c.32 Sch.12 para.29
Sch.2 para.7, amended: 2013 c.32 Sch.12 para.29
Sch.2 para.7, substituted: 2013 c.32 Sch.12 para.29
Sch.2 para.8, repealed: 2013 c.32 Sch.12 para.29
Sch.2 para.8, substituted: 2013 c.32 Sch.12 para.29

69. Criminal Procedure (Attendance of Witnesses) Act 1965

s.2, amended: 2013 c.22 Sch.17 para.33
s.2, applied: SI 2013/435 Sch.1 para.13, SI 2013/1554 Part 28, r.61_7, r.28_1
s.2A, applied: SI 2013/1554 r.28_5
s.2C, applied: SI 2013/1554 r.76_1
s.2D, applied: SI 2013/1554 Part 28
s.3, applied: SI 2013/1554 Part 28, r.62_5
s.4, applied: SI 2013/1554 Part 28, r.18_2

1966

4. Mines (Working Facilities and Support) Act 1966

s.7A, amended: SI 2013/755 Sch.2 para.42

51. Local Government (Scotland) Act 1966

s.24, enabling: SSI 2013/37
s.24A, enabling: SSI 2013/37
s.24B, enabling: SSI 2013/37

1967

8. Plant Health Act 1967

s.1, amended: SI 2013/755 Sch.2 para.43
s.2, enabling: SI 2013/23, SI 2013/888, SI 2013/1477, SI 2013/2687, SI 2013/2691, SI 2013/2939, SSI 2013/5, SSI 2013/187, SSI 2013/366
s.3, enabling: SI 2013/23, SI 2013/572, SI 2013/888, SI 2013/1477, SI 2013/1658, SI 2013/2687, SI 2013/2691, SI 2013/2939, SSI 2013/5, SSI 2013/187, SSI 2013/366
s.4, enabling: SSI 2013/5, SSI 2013/187, SSI 2013/366
s.4A, enabling: SI 2013/572, SI 2013/1658

10. Forestry Act 1967

applied: SI 2013/1821 Art.4
s.1, amended: SI 2013/755 Sch.2 para.45
s.1, applied: SI 2013/755 Sch.7 para.5
s.1, repealed (in part): SI 2013/755 Sch.2 para.45
s.2, amended: SI 2013/1821 Art.12
s.3, amended: SI 2013/755 Sch.2 para.46
s.5, amended: SI 2013/755 Sch.2 para.47
s.6, amended: SI 2013/755 Sch.2 para.47
s.7, amended: SI 2013/755 Sch.2 para.48
s.7A, amended: SI 2013/755 Sch.2 para.49
s.8, amended: SI 2013/755 Sch.2 para.50
s.8A, amended: SI 2013/755 Sch.2 para.51
s.9, amended: SI 2013/755 Sch.2 para.52, Sch.2 para.53
s.10, amended: SI 2013/755 Sch.2 para.52, Sch.2 para.54
s.11, amended: SI 2013/755 Sch.2 para.52, Sch.2 para.55
s.12, amended: SI 2013/755 Sch.2 para.52, Sch.2 para.55
s.13, amended: SI 2013/755 Sch.2 para.52, Sch.2 para.55
s.14, amended: SI 2013/755 Sch.2 para.52, Sch.2 para.56
s.15, amended: SI 2013/755 Sch.2 para.52, Sch.2 para.57
s.16, amended: SI 2013/755 Sch.2 para.52, Sch.2 para.58
s.17, amended: SI 2013/755 Sch.2 para.52
s.17A, amended: SI 2013/755 Sch.2 para.52, Sch.2 para.58

s.17B, amended: SI 2013/755 Sch.2 para.52, Sch.2 para.58
s.17C, amended: SI 2013/755 Sch.2 para.52
s.18, amended: SI 2013/755 Sch.2 para.52, Sch.2 para.59
s.19, amended: SI 2013/755 Sch.2 para.52, Sch.2 para.60
s.20, amended: SI 2013/755 Sch.2 para.52, Sch.2 para.61
s.21, amended: SI 2013/755 Sch.2 para.52, Sch.2 para.61
s.22, amended: SI 2013/755 Sch.2 para.52, Sch.2 para.62
s.23, amended: SI 2013/755 Sch.2 para.52, Sch.2 para.63
s.24, amended: SI 2013/755 Sch.2 para.52, Sch.2 para.64
s.25, amended: SI 2013/755 Sch.2 para.52, Sch.2 para.65
s.26, amended: SI 2013/755 Sch.2 para.52, Sch.2 para.66
s.27, amended: SI 2013/755 Sch.2 para.52, Sch.2 para.67
s.28, amended: SI 2013/755 Sch.2 para.52, Sch.2 para.68
s.29, amended: SI 2013/755 Sch.2 para.52
s.30, amended: SI 2013/755 Sch.2 para.52, Sch.2 para.69
s.31, amended: SI 2013/755 Sch.2 para.52
s.32, amended: SI 2013/755 Sch.2 para.52, Sch.2 para.70
s.33, amended: SI 2013/755 Sch.2 para.52
s.34, amended: SI 2013/755 Sch.2 para.52, SI 2013/1036 Sch.1 para.199
s.35, amended: SI 2013/755 Sch.2 para.52, Sch.2 para.71
s.36, amended: SI 2013/755 Sch.2 para.52
s.37, amended: SI 2013/755 Sch.2 para.72
s.37, substituted: SI 2013/755 Sch.2 para.72
s.38, amended: SI 2013/755 Sch.2 para.73
s.39, amended: SI 2013/755 Sch.2 para.74
s.40, amended: SI 2013/755 Sch.2 para.75
s.41, amended: SI 2013/1821 Art.13
s.41, applied: SI 2013/1821 Art.13
s.46, amended: SI 2013/755 Sch.2 para.76
s.48, amended: SI 2013/755 Sch.2 para.77
s.49, amended: SI 2013/755 Sch.2 para.78
Sch.1, applied: SI 2013/1821 Art.14
Sch.1 Part I para.6, applied: SI 2013/1821 Art.14
Sch.1 Part I para.7, amended: SI 2013/1821 Art.12
Sch.6 para.4, amended: SI 2013/755 Sch.2 para.79

13. Parliamentary Commissioner Act 1967
applied: SI 2013/160 Sch.1 para.2
s.4, enabling: SI 2013/238
s.5, enabling: SI 2013/238
Sch.2, amended: 2013 c.19 s.21, 2013 c.24 Sch.4 para.22, 2013 c.2 Sch.1 Part 10, 2013 c.22 Sch.8 para.18, 2013 c.24 Sch.20 para.2, 2013 c.32 Sch.12 para.54, SI 2013/64 Art.3, SI 2013/238 Art.2, SI 2013/252 Sch.1 Part 1, SI 2013/755 Sch.2 para.80, SI 2013/2329 Sch.1 para.18, SI 2013/2352 Sch.1 para.1, SI 2013/2853 Art.2
Sch.3 para.10, amended: SI 2013/238 Art.3

22. Agriculture Act 1967
s.46, amended: SI 2013/755 Sch.2 para.82
s.49, amended: SI 2013/755 Sch.2 para.83
s.50, amended: SI 2013/755 Sch.2 para.84
s.52, amended: SI 2013/755 Sch.2 para.85
s.57, amended: SI 2013/755 Sch.2 para.86
s.67, repealed (in part): 2013 c.24 Sch.20 para.2

48. Industrial and Provident Societies Act 1967
s.1, amended: SI 2013/496 Sch.3 para.2, Sch.3 para.3
s.3, amended: SI 2013/496 Sch.3 para.2
s.4, amended: SI 2013/496 Sch.3 para.2, Sch.3 para.4
s.5, amended: SI 2013/496 Sch.3 para.2
s.7, amended: SI 2013/496 Sch.3 para.5

58. Criminal Law Act 1967
s.4, applied: SI 2013/435 Sch.1 Part 7
s.5, applied: SI 2013/435 Sch.1 Part 7

77. Police (Scotland) Act 1967
applied: 2013 c.25 Sch.1 para.10, SI 2013/602 Sch.3 para.3, Sch.3 para.9, Sch.3 para.10, Sch.3 para.12, SSI 2013/39 Sch.2 para.4, SSI 2013/43 Sch.3 para.7, SSI 2013/121 Art.14, Sch.1
s.9, applied: SSI 2013/121 Art.16
s.11, applied: SI 2013/602 Sch.3 para.14
s.12, applied: SI 2013/602 Sch.3 para.16, Sch.3 para.17
s.12A, applied: SI 2013/602 Sch.3 para.10
s.13, applied: SI 2013/602 Sch.3 para.19
s.19, applied: SSI 2013/119 Art.3
s.26, applied: SI 2013/602 Sch.3 para.10, SSI 2013/63 Sch.1 para.4
s.26, repealed (in part): SI 2013/602 Sch.2 para.4
s.26A, applied: SSI 2013/121 Art.18
s.27, applied: SI 2013/602 Sch.3 para.10
s.27, repealed: SI 2013/602 Sch.2 para.4
s.30, applied: SSI 2013/63 Sch.1 para.2, Sch.1 para.4, SSI 2013/119 Art.2, SSI 2013/121 Art.12
s.32A, applied: SI 2013/602 Sch.3 para.11
s.32A, repealed: SI 2013/602 Sch.2 para.4
s.33, applied: SSI 2013/121 Art.18
s.38, applied: SI 2013/602 Sch.3 para.10
s.38A, applied: SI 2013/602 Sch.3 para.10
s.38A, referred to: 2013 c.22 Sch.8 para.10
s.42, repealed: SI 2013/602 Sch.2 para.4

s.46, applied: SSI 2013/121 Art.17
Sch.3, applied: SSI 2013/121 Art.12
Sch.3 para.1, varied: SSI 2013/121 Art.12
Sch.3 para.2, varied: SSI 2013/121 Art.12
Sch.3 para.6, varied: SSI 2013/121 Art.12
Sch.3 para.7, varied: SSI 2013/121 Art.12
Sch.3 para.9, varied: SSI 2013/121 Art.12
Sch.3 para.10, varied: SSI 2013/121 Art.12

80. Criminal Justice Act 1967
s.9, see *R. (on the application of ET) v Islington LBC* [2012] EWHC 3228 (Admin), [2013] 2 F.L.R. 347 (QBD (Admin)), Cranston, J.
s.9, applied: SI 2013/1554 r.27_1, r.33_3, r.28_4
s.10, applied: 2013 c.22 Sch.17 para.13, SI 2013/1554 r.33_3, r.12_4, r.35_2
s.89, applied: SI 2013/435 Sch.1 Part 7

87. Abortion Act 1967
s.1, see *Doogan v Greater Glasgow and Clyde Health Board* [2013] CSIH 36, 2013 S.C. 496 (IH (Ex Div)), Lord Mackay of Drumadoon; see *SB (A Patient) (Capacity to Consent to Termination), Re* [2013] EWHC 1417 (COP), [2013] 3 F.C.R. 384 (CP), Holman, J.
s.1, applied: SSI 2013/50 Sch.1 para.8, Sch.4 para.3

88. Leasehold Reform Act 1967
s.9, amended: SI 2013/1036 Sch.1 para.4
s.14, amended: SI 2013/1036 Sch.1 para.5
s.21, amended: SI 2013/1036 Sch.1 para.6
s.27, amended: SI 2013/1036 Sch.1 para.7
s.31, amended: SI 2013/1036 Sch.1 para.8
s.37, amended: SI 2013/1036 Sch.1 para.9
Sch.1 para.5, amended: SI 2013/1036 Sch.1 para.10
Sch.2 para.2, amended: SI 2013/1036 Sch.1 para.11
Sch.2 para.4, amended: 2013 c.22 Sch.9 para.99

1968

2. Provisional Collection of Taxes Act 1968
s.1, amended: 2013 c.29 Sch.35 para.1
s.1, repealed (in part): 2013 c.2 Sch.1 Part 10

18. Consular Relations Act 1968
Sch.1, referred to: SI 2013/749 Reg.8

19. Criminal Appeal Act 1968
Part I, applied: SI 2013/1554 r.68_1, r.71_2, r.71_3, r.71_4, r.68_2, r.71_9, r.74_1
s.1, applied: SI 2013/1554 r.68_1, r.68_3, r.68_4
s.7, see *R. v Lawrence (Nyira)* [2013] EWCA Crim 1054, [2013] 2 Cr. App. R. 24 (CA (Crim Div)), Hallett, L.J.
s.7, applied: SI 2013/1554 r.68_14
s.8, applied: SI 2013/1554 r.14_1, r.68_14
s.9, applied: SI 2013/1554 r.68_1
s.10, applied: SI 2013/1554 r.68_1
s.11, see *R. (on the application of Modhej) v Secretary of State for Justice* [2012] EWCA Civ 957, [2013] 1 W.L.R. 801 (CA (Civ Div)), Lord Judge, L.C.J.
s.11, applied: SI 2013/1554 r.68_3, r.68_4
s.12, applied: SI 2013/1554 r.68_1, r.68_3, r.68_4, SI 2013/2786 Art.5
s.13, applied: SI 2013/1554 r.68_1
s.15, applied: SI 2013/1554 r.68_1, r.68_3, r.68_4, SI 2013/2786 Art.5
s.16A, applied: SI 2013/1554 r.76_4, r.68_1, r.68_3, r.68_4, SI 2013/2786 Art.5
s.18, applied: SI 2013/1554 r.68_2, r.65_3
s.18A, applied: SI 2013/1554 r.68_2, r.65_3
s.22, applied: SI 2013/1554 r.68_11, r.65_5, r.68_12
s.23, see *R. v SV* [2013] EWCA Crim 159, [2013] 1 Cr. App. R. 35 (CA (Crim Div)), Davis, L.J.
s.23, applied: SI 2013/1554 r.68_7
s.31, applied: SI 2013/1554 r.68_3, r.69_3
s.31, referred to: SI 2013/1554 r.71_6, r.71_7, r.71_10
s.31C, applied: SI 2013/1554 r.65_5
s.33, applied: SI 2013/1554 r.74_1, r.74_2
s.34, applied: SI 2013/1554 r.74_2

20. Court Martial Appeals Act 1968
s.12, referred to: SI 2013/1852 Art.3
s.39, amended: SI 2013/1852 Art.15
s.40, amended: SI 2013/1852 Art.15
s.49, applied: SI 2013/1852 Art.26
s.49, enabling: SI 2013/2524

27. Firearms Act 1968
see *R. v Davies (Joseph)* [2012] EWCA Crim 2201, [2013] 1 Cr. App. R. (S.) 121 (CA (Crim Div)), Roderick Evans, J.
applied: SI 2013/449 Reg.3, SI 2013/602 Sch.3 para.1, SSI 2013/50 Sch.1 para.5, Sch.3 para.3
s.1, see *Smart v Forensic Science Service Ltd* [2013] EWCA Civ 783, [2013] P.N.L.R. 32 (CA (Civ Div)), Moses, L.J.
s.1, applied: SI 2013/435 Sch.1 Part 7
s.2, applied: SI 2013/435 Sch.1 Part 7
s.3, applied: SI 2013/435 Sch.1 Part 7
s.4, applied: SI 2013/435 Sch.1 Part 7
s.5, see *R. v Bewley (William)* [2012] EWCA Crim 1457, [2013] 1 W.L.R. 137 (CA (Crim Div)), Moses, L.J.; see *R. v Nightingale (Danny Harold)* [2013] EWCA Crim 405, [2013] 2 Cr. App. R. 7 (CA (Crim Div)), Lord Chief Justice; see *R. v Ramzan (Rauf Mohammed)* [2012] EWCA Crim 2891, [2013] 2 Cr. App. R. (S.) 33 (CA (Crim

Div)), Rafferty, L.J. DBE; see *R. v Williams (Orette)* [2012] EWCA Crim 2162, [2013] 1 W.L.R. 1200 (CA (Crim Div)), Davis, L.J.
s.5, applied: SI 2013/435 Sch.1 Part 7
s.7, applied: SSI 2013/50 Sch.1 para.5, Sch.3 para.3
s.9, applied: SSI 2013/50 Sch.1 para.5, Sch.3 para.3
s.9, enabling: SI 2013/2970
s.13, applied: SSI 2013/50 Sch.1 para.5, Sch.3 para.3
s.16, applied: SI 2013/435 Sch.1 Part 7
s.17, applied: SI 2013/435 Sch.1 Part 7
s.18, applied: SI 2013/435 Sch.1 Part 7
s.19, applied: SI 2013/435 Sch.1 Part 7
s.20, applied: SI 2013/435 Sch.1 Part 7
s.21, applied: SI 2013/435 Sch.1 Part 7
s.26A, enabling: SI 2013/1945
s.26B, enabling: SI 2013/1945
s.27, enabling: SI 2013/2970
s.28, enabling: SI 2013/2970
s.30D, applied: SI 2013/602 Sch.3 para.1
s.42, applied: SI 2013/435 Sch.1 Part 7
s.42B, amended: SI 2013/602 Sch.2 para.5
s.52, applied: SI 2013/602 Sch.3 para.1
s.53, enabling: SI 2013/1945, SI 2013/2970
s.54, repealed (in part): 2013 c.22 Sch.8 para.19, SI 2013/602 Sch.2 para.5
s.57, see *R. v Bewley (William)* [2012] EWCA Crim 1457, [2013] 1 W.L.R. 137 (CA (Crim Div)), Moses, L.J.
s.57, amended: SI 2013/602 Sch.2 para.5
Sch.1 para.5, amended: SI 2013/602 Sch.2 para.5
Sch.2 para.18, amended: SI 2013/602 Sch.2 para.5

34. Agriculture (Miscellaneous Provisions) Act 1968
s.46, repealed (in part): 2013 c.24 Sch.20 para.2

41. Countryside Act 1968
substituted: SI 2013/755 Sch.2 para.89
s.1, repealed: SI 2013/755 Sch.2 para.90
s.2, amended: SI 2013/755 Sch.2 para.91
s.2, repealed (in part): SI 2013/755 Sch.2 para.91
s.2, substituted: SI 2013/755 Sch.2 para.91
s.4, amended: SI 2013/755 Sch.2 para.92
s.8, amended: SI 2013/755 Sch.2 para.93
s.12, amended: SI 2013/755 Sch.2 para.94
s.13, amended: SI 2013/755 Sch.2 para.95
s.15, amended: SI 2013/755 Sch.2 para.95
s.15A, amended: SI 2013/755 Sch.2 para.95
s.16, amended: SI 2013/755 Sch.2 para.96
s.23, repealed (in part): SI 2013/755 Sch.2 para.97
s.24, amended: SI 2013/755 Sch.2 para.98
s.24A, amended: SI 2013/755 Sch.2 para.99
s.37, amended: SI 2013/755 Sch.2 para.100
s.38, amended: SI 2013/755 Sch.2 para.101
s.41, amended: SI 2013/755 Sch.2 para.102
s.45, amended: SI 2013/755 Sch.2 para.103
s.46, repealed (in part): SI 2013/755 Sch.2 para.104
s.49, amended: SI 2013/755 Sch.2 para.105

46. Health Services and Public Health Act 1968
s.63, applied: SI 2013/3029 Sch.11 para.4, SI 2013/3035 Sch.1

48. International Organisations Act 1968
s.1, enabling: SI 2013/785
s.6, applied: SI 2013/1116 Art.3
s.6, enabling: SI 2013/1116
s.10, applied: SI 2013/785
Sch.1, applied: SI 2013/1119 Art.2
Sch.1 Part IV, applied: SI 2013/1116 Art.3

52. Caravan Sites Act 1968
s.3, amended: 2013 c.14 s.12
s.5, amended: 2013 c.22 Sch.9 para.63

55. Friendly and Industrial and Provident Societies Act 1968
s.3A, amended: SI 2013/496 Sch.4 para.2
s.4, amended: SI 2013/496 Sch.4 para.2
s.4A, amended: SI 2013/496 Sch.4 para.2
s.9C, amended: SI 2013/496 Sch.4 para.2, Sch.4 para.3
s.11, amended: SI 2013/496 Sch.4 para.2, Sch.4 para.4
s.12, amended: SI 2013/496 Sch.4 para.2
s.13, amended: SI 2013/496 Sch.4 para.2
s.14, amended: SI 2013/496 Sch.4 para.2, Sch.4 para.5
s.14A, amended: SI 2013/496 Sch.4 para.6
s.18, amended: SI 2013/496 Sch.4 para.7
s.21, amended: SI 2013/496 Sch.4 para.8

59. Hovercraft Act 1968
s.2, amended: 2013 c.22 Sch.9 para.141

63. Domestic and Appellate Proceedings (Restriction of Publicity) Act 1968
s.1, amended: 2013 c.22 Sch.9 para.23, Sch.10 para.16, SI 2013/294 Sch.1
s.4, amended: SI 2013/294 Sch.1
s.4, repealed (in part): SI 2013/294 Sch.1

64. Civil Evidence Act 1968
s.11, applied: SI 2013/486 Reg.27
s.12, amended: 2013 c.22 Sch.10 para.17

67. Medicines Act 1968
Part II, applied: SI 2013/532 Sch.4 para.6
s.58, enabling: SI 2013/1855
s.69, applied: SI 2013/349 Sch.2 para.2, SI 2013/898 Sch.1 para.22
s.72, applied: SI 2013/349 Reg.74, SI 2013/898 Reg.35
s.72, referred to: SI 2013/349 Reg.74
s.74A, applied: SI 2013/1506 Reg.18

s.74B, applied: SI 2013/1506 Reg.18
s.74C, applied: SI 2013/1506 Reg.18
s.74D, applied: SI 2013/1506 Reg.18
s.74E, applied: SI 2013/1506 Reg.18
s.74F, applied: SI 2013/1506 Reg.18
s.74G, applied: SI 2013/1506 Reg.18
s.74H, applied: SI 2013/1506 Reg.18
s.74I, applied: SI 2013/1506 Reg.18
s.74J, applied: SI 2013/1506 Reg.18
s.74K, applied: SI 2013/1506 Reg.18
s.74L, applied: SI 2013/1506 Reg.18
s.75, applied: SI 2013/349 Sch.2 para.4
s.129, applied: SI 2013/532
Sch.3 para.28, amended: 2013 c.22 Sch.9 para.111

70. Law Reform (Miscellaneous Provisions) (Scotland) Act 1968
s.10, applied: SI 2013/486 Reg.27

1969

10. Mines and Quarries (Tips) Act 1969
Part I, applied: SI 2013/1471 Sch.2 para.43, SI 2013/1896 Reg.3
Part II, applied: SI 2013/1896 Reg.3
s.28, amended: 2013 c.22 Sch.9 para.52

32. Finance Act 1969
s.11, repealed (in part): 2013 c.2 Sch.1 Part 10
s.60, repealed: 2013 c.2 Sch.1 Part 10
Sch.20 para.11, repealed: 2013 c.2 Sch.1 Part 10

46. Family Law Reform Act 1969
s.2, repealed (in part): 2013 c.22 Sch.11 para.210

48. Post Office Act 1969
s.3, referred to: 2013 c.24 Sch.21 para.3
s.3, repealed: 2013 c.24 Sch.21 para.2

57. Employers Liability (Compulsory Insurance) Act 1969
s.3, amended: SI 2013/602 Sch.2 para.6

63. Police Act 1969
repealed: 2013 c.2 Sch.1 Part 2

1970

30. Conservation of Seals Act 1970
s.10, amended: SI 2013/755 Sch.2 para.107
s.10, repealed (in part): SI 2013/755 Sch.2 para.107
s.13, amended: SI 2013/755 Sch.2 para.108

31. Administration of Justice Act 1970
s.11, see *Mohan v Mohan* [2013] EWCA Civ 586, [2013] C.P. Rep. 36 (CA (Civ Div)), Thorpe, L.J.
s.11, amended: 2013 c.22 Sch.9 para.52, Sch.10 para.18
s.11, repealed (in part): 2013 c.22 Sch.10 para.18
s.28, amended: 2013 c.22 Sch.10 para.18
s.41, amended: 2013 c.3 Sch.1 para.2
s.41, applied: SI 2013/1554 r.76_1
s.43, amended: 2013 c.22 Sch.9 para.52
Sch.9 Part I para.13A, added: 2013 c.3 Sch.1 para.3

33. Law Reform (Miscellaneous Provisions) Act 1970
s.2, amended: 2013 c.22 Sch.11 para.27

34. Marriage (Registrar General's Licence) Act 1970
applied: 2013 c.30 s.1
s.1, amended: 2013 c.30 s.7, Sch.7 para.23
s.2, amended: 2013 c.30 Sch.7 para.24
s.13A, added: 2013 c.30 Sch.7 para.25

36. Merchant Shipping Act 1970
s.27, applied: SI 2013/435 Sch.1 Part 7

44. Chronically Sick and Disabled Persons Act 1970
s.21, amended: 2013 c.4 s.1, s.2, s.3, s.4, s.5, s.6, SI 2013/2042 Sch.1 para.1, SSI 2013/119 Sch.1 para.6
s.21, applied: SI 2013/362 Reg.13
s.21, varied: 2013 c.4 s.1
s.21, enabling: SI 2013/438, SI 2013/2203
s.21A, applied: SI 2013/362 Reg.13

45. Matrimonial Proceedings and Property Act 1970
s.30, amended: 2013 c.22 Sch.11 para.28
s.39, amended: 2013 c.22 Sch.11 para.28

1971

23. Courts Act 1971
s.16, repealed (in part): 2013 c.22 Sch.13 para.31
s.21, amended: 2013 c.22 Sch.13 para.32
s.24, amended: 2013 c.22 Sch.13 para.34, Sch.13 para.89
s.24, repealed (in part): 2013 c.22 Sch.13 para.89
s.30, amended: 2013 c.22 Sch.9 para.74
s.42, repealed (in part): 2013 c.22 Sch.9 para.24
s.52, repealed (in part): 2013 c.22 Sch.10 para.19
Sch.2 Part IA, amended: 2013 c.22 Sch.14 para.13

27. Powers of Attorney Act 1971
applied: SI 2013/380 Reg.57, SI 2013/3029 Sch.13 para.1, Sch.13 para.9, SI 2013/3035 Sch.1

29. National Savings Bank Act 1971
s.2, enabling: SI 2013/8
s.3, enabling: SI 2013/8
s.4, enabling: SI 2013/8
s.7, enabling: SI 2013/8
s.8, enabling: SI 2013/8

32. Attachment of Earnings Act 1971
s.1, amended: 2013 c.22 Sch.9 para.25, Sch.10 para.21
s.1, repealed (in part): 2013 c.22 Sch.10 para.21

s.2, amended: 2013 c.22 Sch.9 para.25, Sch.10 para.22
s.3, amended: 2013 c.22 Sch.9 para.25, Sch.10 para.23
s.3, repealed (in part): 2013 c.22 Sch.10 para.23
s.4, amended: 2013 c.22 Sch.9 para.25
s.5, amended: 2013 c.22 Sch.9 para.25
s.6, amended: 2013 c.22 Sch.9 para.25, Sch.10 para.24
s.8, amended: 2013 c.22 Sch.9 para.25, Sch.10 para.25
s.10, amended: 2013 c.22 Sch.9 para.25, Sch.10 para.26
s.10, repealed (in part): 2013 c.22 Sch.10 para.26
s.11, amended: 2013 c.22 Sch.10 para.27
s.13, amended: 2013 c.22 Sch.9 para.25
s.15D, amended: 2013 c.22 Sch.10 para.28
s.16, amended: 2013 c.22 Sch.10 para.29
s.17, amended: 2013 c.22 Sch.9 para.25
s.18, amended: 2013 c.22 Sch.10 para.30
s.18, repealed (in part): 2013 c.22 Sch.10 para.30
s.20, amended: 2013 c.22 Sch.10 para.31
s.21, amended: 2013 c.22 Sch.10 para.32
s.23, amended: 2013 c.22 Sch.9 para.25, Sch.10 para.33
s.23, repealed (in part): 2013 c.22 Sch.9 para.25
s.25, amended: 2013 c.22 Sch.9 para.25
Sch.1 para.15, amended: 2013 c.22 Sch.9 para.25

38. Misuse of Drugs Act 1971

applied: SI 2013/349 Sch.4 para.5, Sch.4 para.6, Sch.4 para.8, Sch.6 para.2, Sch.7 para.3, Sch.7 para.4, Sch.7 para.6, SI 2013/373 Reg.11, SI 2013/898 Sch.4 para.5, Sch.4 para.6, Sch.4 para.8, Sch.6 para.4
s.2, applied: SI 2013/239
s.2, enabling: SI 2013/239
s.2A, applied: SI 2013/1294 Art.2
s.2A, enabling: SI 2013/1294
s.2B, applied: SI 2013/1294
s.4, see *Brodie (George) v HM Advocate* 2013 J.C. 142 (HCJ), The Lord Justice General (Gill); see *Coalter (Adrian Robert) v HM Advocate* [2013] HCJAC 115, 2013 S.C.L. 1024 (HCJ), Lord Eassie; see *HM Advocate v B* [2013] HCJ 71, 2013 S.L.T. 810 (HCJ), Lord Jones; see *R. v Bamford (Martin Craig)* [2012] EWCA Crim 820, [2013] 1 Cr. App. R. (S.) 4 (CA (Crim Div)), Rafferty, L.J.; see *South Lanarkshire Council v George* 2013 Hous. L.R. 49 (Sh Ct (South Strathclyde) (Hamilton)), Sheriff Principal B A Lockhart; see *Stewart (Chrisopher Ian) v HM Advocate* [2013] HCJAC 64, 2013 S.C.L. 719 (HCJ), Lord Clarke
s.4, applied: SI 2013/435 Sch.1 Part 7, SI 2013/1852 Sch.1 para.21
s.5, applied: SI 2013/435 Sch.1 Part 7, SI 2013/1542 Art.14
s.6, see *R. v Bamford (Martin Craig)* [2012] EWCA Crim 820, [2013] 1 Cr. App. R. (S.) 4 (CA (Crim Div)), Rafferty, L.J.
s.6, applied: SI 2013/435 Sch.1 Part 7
s.7, applied: SI 2013/177, SI 2013/177 Art.2, SI 2013/624
s.7, enabling: SI 2013/176, SI 2013/177, SI 2013/624, SI 2013/625
s.7A, enabling: SI 2013/1294
s.8, applied: SI 2013/435 Sch.1 Part 7
s.9, applied: SI 2013/435 Sch.1 Part 7
s.10, enabling: SI 2013/176, SI 2013/625
s.11, applied: SI 2013/435 Sch.1 Part 7
s.12, applied: SI 2013/435 Sch.1 Part 7
s.13, applied: SI 2013/435 Sch.1 Part 7
s.22, enabling: SI 2013/176, SI 2013/625
s.31, applied. SI 2013/176, SI 2013/625
s.31, enabling: SI 2013/176, SI 2013/625, SI 2013/1294
Sch.2 Part II para.1, amended: SI 2013/239 Art.3, Art.4
Sch.2 Part II para.2A, amended: SI 2013/239 Art.5

48. Criminal Damage Act 1971

s.1, applied: SI 2013/435 Sch.1 Part 7, SI 2013/1852 Sch.1 para.22
s.2, applied: SI 2013/435 Sch.1 Part 7
s.3, applied: SI 2013/435 Sch.1 Part 7

56. Pensions (Increase) Act 1971

see *Royal Mail Group Ltd v Evans* [2013] EWHC 1572 (Ch), [2013] Pens. L.R. 239 (Ch D), Asplin, J.
applied: SI 2013/602 Sch.3 para.10, SI 2013/2356 Reg.16, Reg.24, Reg.25, Reg 26, Reg.27, Reg.28, Reg.29, Reg.31, Reg.41, Reg.42, Reg.44, Reg.45, Reg.47, Reg.48, SI 2013/2588 Reg.3, SSI 2013/174 Reg.1, Reg.2, Reg.3, Reg.4, Reg.5, Reg.10, Reg.11, Reg.12, Reg.14, Reg.15, Reg.17, Reg.20, Reg.21
Part III, applied: SSI 2013/174 Reg.2
s.1, applied: SI 2013/604 Art.3, Art.4
s.5, applied: SSI 2013/174 Reg.11, Reg.12
s.5, enabling: SI 2013/2588
s.8, applied: SI 2013/604 Art.2
s.8A, added: 2013 c.25 Sch.8 para.4
Sch.2 Part I, referred to: SI 2013/2588 Reg.3
Sch.2 Part I para.1, repealed: 2013 c.25 Sch.11 para.7
Sch.2 Part I para.2, repealed: 2013 c.25 Sch.11 para.7

Sch.2 Part I para.3, repealed: 2013 c.25 Sch.11 para.7
Sch.2 Part I para.4B, added: 2013 c.25 Sch.8 para.5
Sch.2 Part I para.4ZA, added: 2013 c.25 Sch.8 para.5
Sch.2 Part I para.15, amended: SI 2013/602 Sch.2 para.7
Sch.2 Part I para.15, repealed (in part): SI 2013/602 Sch.2 para.7
Sch.2 Part I para.15B, added: 2013 c.25 Sch.8 para.5
Sch.2 Part I para.16B, added: 2013 c.25 Sch.8 para.5
Sch.2 Part I para.20B, added: 2013 c.25 Sch.8 para.5
Sch.2 Part I para.20C, added: 2013 c.25 Sch.8 para.5
Sch.2 Part I para.22A, added: 2013 c.25 Sch.8 para.5
Sch.2 Part I para.22B, added: 2013 c.25 Sch.8 para.5
Sch.2 Part I para.29A, added: 2013 c.25 Sch.8 para.5
Sch.2 Part II para.39A, added: 2013 c.25 Sch.8 para.5
Sch.2 Part II para.43, amended: SI 2013/602 Sch.2 para.7
Sch.2 Part II para.43A, added: 2013 c.25 Sch.8 para.5
Sch.2 Part II para.44, amended: SI 2013/602 Sch.1 para.1
Sch.2 Part II para.44A, added: 2013 c.25 Sch.8 para.5

57. Pool Competitions Act 1971
repealed: 2013 c.2 Sch.1 Part 7

60. Prevention of Oil Pollution Act 1971
s.1, enabling: SI 2013/2944

61. Mineral Workings (Offshore Installations) Act 1971
s.1, applied: SI 2013/2605 Art.36

69. Medicines Act 1971
s.1, enabling: SI 2013/532, SI 2013/1855

77. Immigration Act 1971
see *Pembele (Paragraph 399(b)(i): Valid Leave: Meaning), Re* [2013] UKUT 310 (IAC), [2013] Imm. A.R. 845 (UT (IAC)), Judge Kebede; see *Syed (Curtailment of Leave: Notice), Re* [2013] UKUT 144 (IAC), [2013] Imm. A.R. 685 (UT (IAC)), Judge Spencer
applied: SI 2013/379 Reg.12, SI 2013/1460 Reg.2, Reg.8
disapplied: SI 2013/1460 Reg.2
Part III, applied: SI 2013/1460 Reg.15, Reg.18
s.3, see *Ahmad (Removal of Children over 18: Pakistan), Re* [2013] Imm. A.R. 1 (UT (IAC)), Collins, J.; see *Pembele (Paragraph 399(b)(i): Valid Leave: Meaning), Re* [2013] UKUT 310 (IAC), [2013] Imm. A.R. 845 (UT (IAC)), Judge Kebede; see *R. (on the application of Essa) v Upper Tribunal (Immigration and Asylum Chamber)* [2012] EWCA Civ 1718, [2013] Imm. A.R. 644 (CA (Civ Div)), Maurice Kay, L.J.; see *R. (on the application of New London College Ltd) v Secretary of State for the Home Department* [2013] UKSC 51, [2013] 1 W.L.R. 2358 (SC), Lord Hope, J.S.C. (Deputy President); see *Syed (Curtailment of Leave: Notice), Re* [2013] UKUT 144 (IAC), [2013] Imm. A.R. 685 (UT (IAC)), Judge Spencer
s.3, applied: SI 2013/376 Reg.9, SI 2013/3029 Reg.28, SI 2013/3035 Sch.1
s.3, referred to: SI 2013/617 Sch.1 para.1, Sch.7 para.1
s.3A, applied: SI 2013/1749
s.3A, enabling: SI 2013/1749
s.3B, applied: SI 2013/1749
s.3B, enabling: SI 2013/1749
s.5, see *Ahmad (Removal of Children over 18: Pakistan), Re* [2013] Imm. A.R. 1 (UT (IAC)), Collins, J.; see *R. (on the application of George) v Secretary of State for the Home Department* [2012] EWCA Civ 1362, [2013] 1 W.L.R. 1319 (CA (Civ Div)), Maurice Kay, L.J.
s.5, varied: SI 2013/1460 Reg.6
s.8, applied: SI 2013/1460 Reg.2
s.8, referred to: SI 2013/1460 Reg.2
s.8B, enabling: SI 2013/678, SI 2013/1745
s.24, applied: SI 2013/1460 Reg.18
s.25, applied: SI 2013/435 Sch.1 Part 7
s.25C, referred to: SI 2013/470 Art.4
s.26, applied: 2013 c.22 s.55
s.28A, applied: SI 2013/1460 Reg.18
s.28A, referred to: 2013 c.5 s.4
s.28AA, referred to: 2013 c.5 s.4
s.28B, applied: SI 2013/1460 Reg.15, Reg.18
s.28B, referred to: 2013 c.5 s.4
s.28C, referred to: 2013 c.5 s.4
s.28CA, applied: SI 2013/1460 Reg.18
s.28CA, referred to: 2013 c.5 s.4
s.28D, applied: SI 2013/1460 Reg.15, Reg.18
s.28D, referred to: 2013 c.5 s.4, SI 2013/1554 r.6_30
s.28E, applied: SI 2013/1460 Reg.15, Reg.18
s.28E, referred to: 2013 c.5 s.4
s.28F, referred to: 2013 c.5 s.4
s.28FA, applied: SI 2013/1460 Reg.18
s.28FA, referred to: 2013 c.5 s.4

s.28FB, referred to: 2013 c.5 s.4
s.28G, applied: SI 2013/1460 Reg.15, Reg.18
s.28G, referred to: 2013 c.5 s.4
s.28H, applied: SI 2013/1460 Reg.15, Reg.18
s.28H, referred to: 2013 c.5 s.4
s.33, applied: SI 2013/617 Sch.4 para.2, SI 2013/1460 Reg.2, SI 2013/2276 Reg.2
Sch.2 Part I para.1, applied: SSI 2013/76 Reg.2
Sch.2 Part I para.8, disapplied: SI 2013/1460 Reg.6
Sch.2 Part I para.9, disapplied: SI 2013/1460 Reg.6
Sch.2 Part I para.10, disapplied: SI 2013/1460 Reg.6
Sch.2 Part I para.10A, disapplied: SI 2013/1460 Reg.6

80. Banking and Financial Dealings Act 1971
applied: 2013 asp 14 s.17, Sch.2 para.8, Sch.2 para.17, Sch.2 para.19, Sch.2 para.29, Sch.3 para.1, Sch.3 para.14, Sch.4 para.42, Sch.4 para.60, SI 2013/362 Reg.3, SI 2013/486 Reg.10, SI 2013/1852 Art.20, Art.21, Art.23, SI 2013/2996 Reg.2, SI 2013/3028 Reg.1, SI 2013/3197 Art.4, SSI 2013/288 Sch.2 para.4

1972

18. Maintenance Orders (Reciprocal Enforcement) Act 1972
s.3, amended: 2013 c.22 Sch.11 para.30
s.3, repealed (in part): 2013 c.22 Sch.11 para.30
s.4, amended: 2013 c.22 Sch.11 para.31
s.5, repealed (in part): 2013 c.22 Sch.11 para.32
s.7, amended: 2013 c.22 Sch.11 para.33
s.8, amended: 2013 c.22 Sch.11 para.34
s.8, repealed (in part): 2013 c.22 Sch.11 para.34
s.9, repealed (in part): 2013 c.22 Sch.11 para.35
s.10, amended: 2013 c.22 Sch.11 para.36
s.14, amended: 2013 c.22 Sch.11 para.37
s.14, repealed (in part): 2013 c.22 Sch.11 para.37
s.17, amended: 2013 c.22 Sch.11 para.38
s.18, amended: 2013 c.22 Sch.11 para.39
s.18, enabling: SI 2013/3204
s.21, amended: 2013 c.22 Sch.11 para.40
s.23, amended: 2013 c.22 Sch.11 para.41
s.23, repealed (in part): 2013 c.22 Sch.11 para.41, Sch.11 para.43
s.26, amended: 2013 c.22 Sch.11 para.42
s.27B, amended: 2013 c.22 Sch.11 para.43
s.27C, amended: 2013 c.22 Sch.11 para.44
s.27C, repealed (in part): 2013 c.22 Sch.11 para.44
s.28, amended: 2013 c.22 Sch.11 para.45
s.28, repealed (in part): 2013 c.22 Sch.11 para.45
s.28A, amended: 2013 c.22 Sch.11 para.46
s.28A, repealed (in part): 2013 c.22 Sch.11 para.46
s.28B, repealed: 2013 c.22 Sch.11 para.47
s.32, amended: 2013 c.22 Sch.11 para.48
s.32, repealed (in part): 2013 c.22 Sch.11 para.48
s.33, amended: 2013 c.22 Sch.11 para.49
s.33, repealed (in part): 2013 c.22 Sch.11 para.49
s.34, amended: 2013 c.22 Sch.11 para.50
s.34, repealed (in part): 2013 c.22 Sch.11 para.50
s.34A, amended: 2013 c.22 Sch.11 para.51
s.34A, repealed (in part): 2013 c.22 Sch.11 para.51
s.35, amended: 2013 c.22 Sch.11 para.52
s.36, amended: 2013 c.22 Sch.11 para.53
s.38, amended: 2013 c.22 Sch.11 para.54
s.38, repealed (in part): 2013 c.22 Sch.11 para.54
s.38A, amended: 2013 c.22 Sch.11 para.55
s.42, amended: 2013 c.22 Sch.11 para.56
s.47, amended: 2013 c.22 Sch.11 para.57

48. Parliamentary and other Pensions Act 1972
s.26, repealed: 2013 c.25 Sch.11 para.5
s.27, repealed: 2013 c.25 Sch.11 para.5
s.28, repealed: 2013 c.25 Sch.11 para.5
s.31, repealed: 2013 c.25 Sch.11 para.7
s.36, repealed: 2013 c.25 Sch.11 para.7
s.37, repealed: 2013 c.25 Sch.11 para.7

54. British Library Act 1972
s.4, amended: SI 2013/2352 Sch.1 para.3

61. Land Charges Act 1972
applied: SI 2013/503 Reg.22
s.1, amended: 2013 c.22 Sch.9 para.97

62. Agriculture (Miscellaneous Provisions) Act 1972
s.20, enabling: SSI 2013/5, SSI 2013/187, SSI 2013/366

65. National Debt Act 1972
s.1, applied: SI 2013/501 Reg.4, SI 2013/588 Reg.4
s.3, enabling: SI 2013/416

68. European Communities Act 1972
see *R. (on the application of GI (Sudan)) v Secretary of State for the Home Department* [2012] EWCA Civ 867, [2013] Q.B. 1008 (CA (Civ Div)), Laws, L.J.
applied: SI 2013/2217
referred to: SI 2013/271
s.1, amended: 2013 c.5 s.3
s.2, see *Pryce v Southwark LBC* [2012] EWCA Civ 1572, [2013] 1 W.L.R. 996 (CA (Civ Div)), Pill, L.J.; see *Robertson v Swift* [2012] EWCA Civ 1794, [2013] Bus. L.R. 479 (CA (Civ Div)), Mummery, L.J.
s.2, applied: 2013 c.24 s.75, s.78, 2013 c.32 s.114, Sch.5 para.4, SI 2013/440 Art.1, SI 2013/441 Art.1, SI 2013/532 Reg.1, SI 2013/768, SI 2013/889, SI 2013/1001, SI 2013/1240, SI

2013/2591, SI 2013/2750, SI 2013/2775, SI 2013/2949, SI 2013/3032, SI 2013/3235, SSI 2013/366
s.2, referred to: SI 2013/768, SI 2013/1477, SI 2013/2139, SI 2013/2196, SI 2013/2210, SI 2013/2493, SI 2013/2687, SI 2013/2691, SI 2013/2750, SI 2013/2775, SI 2013/3235, SSI 2013/83, SSI 2013/217, SSI 2013/256, SSI 2013/266, SSI 2013/305
s.2, enabling: SI 2013/65, SI 2013/109, SI 2013/141, SI 2013/163, SI 2013/164, SI 2013/174, SI 2013/181, SI 2013/228, SI 2013/233, SI 2013/261, SI 2013/264, SI 2013/271, SI 2013/283, SI 2013/336, SI 2013/340, SI 2013/395, SI 2013/407, SI 2013/414, SI 2013/425, SI 2013/429, SI 2013/479, SI 2013/486, SI 2013/504, SI 2013/516, SI 2013/517, SI 2013/525, SI 2013/532, SI 2013/536, SI 2013/554, SI 2013/603, SI 2013/732, SI 2013/761, SI 2013/768, SI 2013/795, SI 2013/804, SI 2013/816, SI 2013/817, SI 2013/821, SI 2013/822, SI 2013/829, SI 2013/877, SI 2013/908, SI 2013/950, SI 2013/1037, SI 2013/1096, SI 2013/1105, SI 2013/1125, SI 2013/1162, SI 2013/1232, SI 2013/1241, SI 2013/1244, SI 2013/1329, SI 2013/1387, SI 2013/1388, SI 2013/1389, SI 2013/1391, SI 2013/1431, SI 2013/1445, SI 2013/1473, SI 2013/1478, SI 2013/1506, SI 2013/1507, SI 2013/1575, SI 2013/1605, SI 2013/1637, SI 2013/1652, SI 2013/1653, SI 2013/1655, SI 2013/1656, SI 2013/1662, SI 2013/1667, SI 2013/1672, SI 2013/1675, SI 2013/1683, SI 2013/1687, SI 2013/1753, SI 2013/1768, SI 2013/1773, SI 2013/1785, SI 2013/1797, SI 2013/1821, SI 2013/1855, SI 2013/1857, SI 2013/1865, SI 2013/1876, SI 2013/1877, SI 2013/1881, SI 2013/1908, SI 2013/1950, SI 2013/1964, SI 2013/2012, SI 2013/2013, SI 2013/2014, SI 2013/2033, SI 2013/2071, SI 2013/2181, SI 2013/2212, SI 2013/2217, SI 2013/2228, SI 2013/2269, SI 2013/2272, SI 2013/2327, SI 2013/2506, SI 2013/2593, SI 2013/2619, SI 2013/2620, SI 2013/2667, SI 2013/2696, SI 2013/2701, SI 2013/2720, SI 2013/2728, SI 2013/2815, SI 2013/2854, SI 2013/2874, SI 2013/2876, SI 2013/2893, SI 2013/2919, SI 2013/2945, SI 2013/2949, SI 2013/2952, SI 2013/2971, SI 2013/2985, SI 2013/2987, SI 2013/2996, SI 2013/3007, SI 2013/3008, SI 2013/3032, SI 2013/3036, SI 2013/3043, SI 2013/3049, SI 2013/3074, SI 2013/3075, SI 2013/3076, SI 2013/3077, SI 2013/3078, SI 2013/3079, SI 2013/3080, SI 2013/3081, SI 2013/3113, SI 2013/3115, SI 2013/3118, SI 2013/3133, SI 2013/3134, SI 2013/3135, SI 2013/3150, SI 2013/3169, SI 2013/3171, SI 2013/3180, SI 2013/3182, SI 2013/3184, SI 2013/3185, SI 2013/3207, SI 2013/3210, SI 2013/3220, SI 2013/3231, SI 2013/3235, SI 2013/3243, SI 2013/3270, SSI 2013/2, SSI 2013/9, SSI 2013/12, SSI 2013/77, SSI 2013/84, SSI 2013/116, SSI 2013/123, SSI 2013/127, SSI 2013/131, SSI 2013/151, SSI 2013/173, SSI 2013/177, SSI 2013/189, SSI 2013/221, SSI 2013/222, SSI 2013/265, SSI 2013/282, SSI 2013/292, SSI 2013/307, SSI 2013/309, SSI 2013/323, SSI 2013/326, SSI 2013/333, SSI 2013/336, SSI 2013/340
s.11, applied: SI 2013/435 Sch.1 Part 7
Sch.2 para.1, disapplied: 2013 c.24 s.75, s.78
Sch.2 para.1A, applied: SI 2013/950, SI 2013/1329, SI 2013/1478, SI 2013/2196, SI 2013/2210, SI 2013/2493, SI 2013/2591, SI 2013/2952, SI 2013/3133, SI 2013/3135
Sch.2 para.1A, enabling: SI 2013/164, SI 2013/233, SI 2013/336, SI 2013/795, SI 2013/804, SI 2013/889, SI 2013/1241, SI 2013/1477, SI 2013/1506, SI 2013/1768, SI 2013/1877, SI 2013/2012, SI 2013/2139, SI 2013/2687, SI 2013/2691, SI 2013/2750, SI 2013/2775, SI 2013/2919, SI 2013/2949, SI 2013/2996, SI 2013/3007, SI 2013/3182, SI 2013/3207, SI 2013/3235, SSI 2013/83, SSI 2013/116, SSI 2013/151, SSI 2013/189, SSI 2013/217, SSI 2013/256, SSI 2013/266, SSI 2013/305, SSI 2013/307, SSI 2013/340, SSI 2013/366
Sch.2 para.2, applied: SI 2013/283, SI 2013/761, SI 2013/768, SI 2013/816, SI 2013/817, SI 2013/1821, SI 2013/1857, SI 2013/2005, SI 2013/2876, SI 2013/2893, SI 2013/3008, SI 2013/3150

70. Local Government Act 1972

referred to: SI 2013/680 Art.7
Part VA, applied: SI 2013/1050 Reg.8
s.14, varied: SI 2013/2277 Art.5
s.54, applied: SI 2013/2156
s.58, applied: SI 2013/2156
s.58, enabling: SI 2013/2156
s.80, applied: SI 2013/218 Reg.5
s.89, varied: SI 2013/2277 Art.4
s.101, applied: SI 2013/218 Reg.22, SI 2013/362 Reg.15
s.101, disapplied: SI 2013/218 Reg.29, SI 2013/3029 Reg.12
s.101, varied: SI 2013/218 Reg.3
s.102, applied: SI 2013/362 Reg.15
s.102, varied: SI 2013/218 Reg.4
s.104, disapplied: SI 2013/218 Reg.5

s.123, see *R. (on the application of London Jewish Girls High Ltd) v Barnet LBC* [2013] EWHC 523 (admin), [2013] P.T.S.R. 1357 (QBD (Admin)), Mitting, J.
s.123, applied: SI 2013/3110 Sch.5 para.10
s.123, disapplied: SI 2013/1967 Art.43, SI 2013/3110 Sch.5 para.10
s.146, amended: 2013 c.22 Sch.9 para.52
s.151, applied: SI 2013/3104 Sch.1 para.20
s.225, applied: SI 2013/1798 Reg.4, SI 2013/2959 Art.7
s.228, applied: SI 2013/1798 Reg.4, SI 2013/2959 Art.7
s.265, enabling: SI 2013/643
s.266, enabling: SI 2013/643
Sch.12 Part IA para.6A, varied: SI 2013/2277 Art.5

71. Criminal Justice Act 1972
s.36, see *R. v B* [2012] EWCA Crim 414, [2013] 1 W.L.R. 320 (CA (Crim Div)), Lord Judge, L.C.J.
s.36, applied: SI 2013/1554 r.70_1, r.74_1, r.74_2, r.76_1

1265. Health and Personal Social Services (Northern Ireland) Order 1972
Art.30, applied: SI 2013/3029 Sch.1 para.20, Sch.6 para.21

1973

18. Matrimonial Causes Act 1973
see *Hudson v Leigh* [2009] EWHC 1306 (Fam), [2013] Fam. 77 (Fam Div), Bodey, J.; see *Independent Trustee Services Ltd v GP Noble Trustees Ltd* [2012] EWCA Civ 195, [2013] Ch. 91 (CA (Civ Div)), Lloyd, L.J.; see *P v P (Financial Remedies: Disclosure)* [2012] EWHC 1733 (Fam), [2013] 1 F.L.R. 1003 (Fam Div), Moylan, J.; see *Vince v Wyatt* [2013] EWCA Civ 495, [2013] 1 W.L.R. 3525 (CA (Civ Div)), Thorpe, L.J.; see *W v W (Financial Remedies: Confiscation Order)* [2012] EWHC 2469 (Fam), [2013] 2 F.L.R. 359 (Fam Div), Ryder, J.
applied: SI 2013/3174 Art.3, Art.4
s.1, amended: 2013 c.30 Sch.4 para.3
s.1, applied: SI 2013/104 Reg.25
s.4, amended: 2013 c.22 Sch.11 para.59
s.11, repealed (in part): 2013 c.30 Sch.7 para.27
s.12, see *Hudson v Leigh* [2009] EWHC 1306 (Fam), [2013] Fam. 77 (Fam Div), Bodey, J.
s.12, substituted: 2013 c.30 Sch.4 para.4
s.19, repealed: 2013 c.13 Sch.2 para.1
s.22A, applied: 2013 asp 11 Sch.1 para.4, Sch.1 para.5
s.23, see *Hamilton v Hamilton* [2013] EWCA Civ 13, [2013] Fam. 292 (CA (Civ Div)), Thorpe, L.J.
s.23, applied: SI 2013/3177 Sch.5 para.1, Sch.6 para.1
s.23A, applied: 2013 asp 11 Sch.1 para.4, Sch.1 para.5
s.24A, applied: 2013 asp 11 Sch.1 para.4, Sch.1 para.5
s.25B, applied: SI 2013/503 Reg.5, SI 2013/3177 Sch.5 para.1, Sch.6 para.1
s.25C, applied: SI 2013/503 Reg.5
s.25E, applied: SI 2013/3177 Sch.5 para.1, Sch.6 para.1
s.32, see *O'Farrell v O'Farrell* [2012] EWHC 123 (QB), [2013] 1 F.L.R. 77 (QBD), Tugendhat, J.
s.32, amended: 2013 c.22 Sch.11 para.60
s.33, amended: 2013 c.22 Sch.11 para.61
s.33, repealed (in part): 2013 c.22 Sch.11 para.61
s.35, amended: 2013 c.22 Sch.11 para.62
s.35, repealed (in part): 2013 c.22 Sch.11 para.62
s.36, amended: 2013 c.22 Sch.11 para.63
s.36, repealed (in part): 2013 c.22 Sch.11 para.63
s.38, amended: 2013 c.22 Sch.11 para.64
s.38, repealed (in part): 2013 c.22 Sch.11 para.64
s.48, amended: 2013 c.22 Sch.10 para.34
s.52, amended: 2013 c.22 Sch.11 para.65

21. Overseas Pensions Act 1973
applied: SI 2013/602 Sch.3 para.10
s.2, amended: SI 2013/602 Sch.2 para.9

26. Land Compensation Act 1973
s.20, applied: SI 2013/2809 Art.32
s.20A, applied: SI 2013/2809 Art.32
s.28, varied: SI 2013/2809 Art.32
s.44, varied: SI 2013/648 Sch.11 para.2, SI 2013/675 Sch.10 para.2, SI 2013/767 Sch.1 para.2, SI 2013/1933 Sch.8 para.2, SI 2013/1967 Sch.5 para.2, SI 2013/2587 Sch.5 para.2, SI 2013/2808 Sch.9 para.2, SI 2013/2809 Sch.7 para.2, SI 2013/3200 Sch.3 para.2, SI 2013/3244 Sch.6 para.2
s.58, varied: SI 2013/648 Sch.11 para.2, SI 2013/675 Sch.10 para.2, SI 2013/767 Sch.1 para.2, SI 2013/1933 Sch.8 para.2, SI 2013/1967 Sch.5 para.2, SI 2013/2587 Sch.5 para.2, SI 2013/2808 Sch.9 para.2, SI 2013/2809 Sch.7 para.2
s.59, amended: SI 2013/1036 Sch.1 para.201
s.61, amended: SI 2013/1036 Sch.1 para.202

33. Protection of Wrecks Act 1973
s.1, applied: SI 2013/1636
s.1, enabling: SI 2013/1636

35. Employment Agencies Act 1973
applied: SI 2013/1893 Sch.2

41. Fair Trading Act 1973
s.118, amended: SI 2013/1773 Sch.1 para.38

Sch.11 para.11, amended: SI 2013/294 Sch.1

43. Hallmarking Act 1973

s.2, amended: SI 2013/251 Art.3
s.3, amended: SI 2013/251 Art.4
s.4A, added: SI 2013/251 Art.5
s.5, amended: SI 2013/251 Art.6
s.6, applied: SI 2013/435 Sch.1 Part 7
s.13, amended: SI 2013/251 Art.7

45. Domicile and Matrimonial Proceedings Act 1973

s.5, amended: 2013 c.22 Sch.11 para.66, 2013 c.30 Sch.4 para.6
s.5, repealed (in part): 2013 c.13 Sch.2 para.2
s.6, amended: 2013 c.30 Sch.4 para.7
Sch.A1 para.1, added: 2013 c.30 Sch.4 para.8
Sch.A1 para.1, amended: 2013 c.30 Sch.4 para.10
Sch.A1 para.2, added: 2013 c.30 Sch.4 para.8
Sch.A1 para.3, added: 2013 c.30 Sch.4 para.8
Sch.A1 para.3, substituted: 2013 c.30 Sch.4 para.10
Sch.A1 para.4, added: 2013 c.30 Sch.4 para.8
Sch.A1 para.5, added: 2013 c.30 Sch.4 para.8
Sch.A1 para.6, added: 2013 c.30 Sch.4 para.8
Sch.1 para.2, amended: 2013 c.30 Sch.4 para.9

50. Employment and Training Act 1973

applied: 2013 c.32 s.101
s.2, applied: SI 2013/376 Reg.66, SI 2013/379 Reg.27, Reg.39, SI 2013/628 Sch.1 para.2, SI 2013/2540 Reg.2, SI 2013/3029 Sch.1 para.3, Sch.2 para.5, Sch.6 para.5, Sch.6 para.18, Sch.6 para.19, Sch.6 para.30, Sch.7 para.8, Sch.7 para.10, Sch.9 para.18, Sch.10 para.39, SI 2013/3035 Sch.1
s.2, referred to: SI 2013/3029 Sch.9 para.18, SI 2013/3035 Sch.1
s.11, applied: SI 2013/2540 Reg.4, Reg.5

51. Finance Act 1973

s.56, enabling: SI 2013/494, SI 2013/525, SI 2013/532, SI 2013/1240, SI 2013/1241, SI 2013/1700, SI 2013/2033, SI 2013/2327, SI 2013/2949, SI 2013/3050, SSI 2013/151
Sch.16A para.1, repealed: 2013 c.2 Sch.1 Part 10
Sch.16A para.2, repealed: 2013 c.2 Sch.1 Part 10
Sch.16A para.2A, repealed: 2013 c.2 Sch.1 Part 10
Sch.16A para.3, repealed: 2013 c.2 Sch.1 Part 10
Sch.16A para.4, repealed: 2013 c.2 Sch.1 Part 10
Sch.16A para.9, repealed: 2013 c.2 Sch.1 Part 10

52. Prescription and Limitation (Scotland) Act 1973

s.6, see *David T Morrison & Co Ltd (t/a Gael Home Interiors) v ICL Plastics Ltd* [2013] CSIH 19, 2013 S.C. 391 (IH), Lady Paton
s.6, applied: 2013 c.15 s.2, s.3
s.19BA, added: SI 2013/2604 Art.6
s.19C, amended: SI 2013/2604 Art.6

63. Government Trading Funds Act 1973

s.1, enabling: SI 2013/490
s.6, enabling: SI 2013/490

65. Local Government (Scotland) Act 1973

s.26, applied: SSI 2013/115
s.26, enabling: SSI 2013/115
s.56, repealed (in part): SSI 2013/211 Sch.2
s.90, applied: SSI 2013/278 Sch.1
s.96, applied: SSI 2013/121 Art.7
s.97, amended: SSI 2013/177 Sch.1 para.1
s.97, applied: SSI 2013/121 Art.7
s.97A, applied: SSI 2013/121 Art.7
s.97B, applied: SSI 2013/121 Art.7
s.98, applied: SSI 2013/121 Art.7
s.99, applied: SSI 2013/121 Art.7
s.100, applied: SSI 2013/121 Art.7
s.101, applied: SSI 2013/121 Art.7
s.101, referred to: SSI 2013/121 Art.7
s.101A, applied: SSI 2013/121 Art.7
s.102, applied: SSI 2013/121 Art.7, Art.10
s.103A, applied: SSI 2013/121 Art.7
s.103B, applied: SSI 2013/121 Art.7
s.103C, applied: SSI 2013/121 Art.7
s.103D, applied: SSI 2013/121 Art.7
s.103E, applied: SSI 2013/121 Art.7
s.103F, applied: SSI 2013/121 Art.7
s.103G, applied: SSI 2013/121 Art.7
s.103H, applied: SSI 2013/121 Art.7
s.103J, applied: SSI 2013/121 Art.7
s.118, applied: SSI 2013/121 Art.7
s.163, applied: SSI 2013/278 Sch.1
s.233, enabling: SSI 2013/115
Sch.7A Part I para.5, amended: SSI 2013/211 Sch.1 para.2

1974

7. Local Government Act 1974

applied: SI 2013/235 Sch.3 para.21
Part III, applied: SI 2013/2356 Sch.2 Part 4
s.9, repealed: SI 2013/755 Sch.2 para.110

23. Juries Act 1974

applied: SI 2013/1554 r.39_2
s.1, amended: 2013 c.8 s.2, 2013 c.22 Sch.9 para.96
s.1, repealed (in part): 2013 c.8 s.2
s.2, amended: 2013 c.22 Sch.9 para.96
s.7, amended: 2013 c.22 Sch.9 para.96
s.9, applied: SI 2013/1554 r.39_2
s.9A, applied: SI 2013/1554 r.39_2
s.12, amended: 2013 c.22 Sch.9 para.96
s.17, amended: 2013 c.22 Sch.9 para.96
s.20, applied: SI 2013/1554 r.62_5
s.23, amended: 2013 c.22 Sch.9 para.96

Sch.1 Part I, amended: 2013 c.8 s.2
Sch.1 Part I, referred to: SI 2013/1616 Sch.1
Sch.1 Part I para.1, amended: 2013 c.8 s.2
Sch.1 Part I para.1, substituted: 2013 c.8 s.2
Sch.1 Part I para.1A, amended: 2013 c.8 s.2
Sch.1 Part I para.2, amended: 2013 c.8 s.2
Sch.1 Part I para.3, amended: 2013 c.8 s.2
Sch.1 Part I para.4, amended: 2013 c.8 s.2
Sch.1 Part II, amended: 2013 c.8 s.2
Sch.1 Part II, referred to: SI 2013/1616 Sch.1
Sch.1 Part II para.5, amended: 2013 c.8 s.2
Sch.1 Part II para.6, amended: 2013 c.8 s.2
Sch.1 Part II para.7, amended: 2013 c.8 s.2
Sch.1 Part II para.8, amended: 2013 c.8 s.2
Sch.1 Part III, amended: 2013 c.8 s.2

37. Health and Safety at Work etc Act 1974

applied: SI 2013/240 Art.3, Art.4, Art.5, Art.6, Art.7, Art.8, Art.9, Art.10, Art.11, Art.13, SI 2013/349 Sch.4 para.28, Sch.5 para.18, SI 2013/898 Sch.4 para.27, Sch.5 para.16, SI 2013/1506 Reg.3, Reg.8, Reg.10, Reg.17, Reg.19, SI 2013/1893 Sch.2, SI 2013/3104 Sch.1 para.20, Sch.5 para.21
Part I, applied: 2013 c.32 s.69, s.74, s.112, Sch.9 para.15
s.1, applied: 2013 c.32 s.69, SI 2013/645 Reg.9, SI 2013/1506 Reg.3, SI 2013/1507 Reg.1
s.2, applied: SI 2013/645 Reg.9, SI 2013/1506 Reg.3, SI 2013/1507 Reg.1
s.3, applied: SI 2013/645 Reg.9, SI 2013/1506 Reg.3, SI 2013/1507 Reg.1
s.4, applied: SI 2013/645 Reg.9, SI 2013/1506 Reg.3, SI 2013/1507 Reg.1
s.5, applied: SI 2013/645 Reg.9, SI 2013/1506 Reg.3, SI 2013/1507 Reg.1
s.6, applied: SI 2013/645 Reg.9, SI 2013/1506 Reg.3, SI 2013/1507 Reg.1
s.7, applied: SI 2013/645 Reg.9, SI 2013/1506 Reg.3, SI 2013/1507 Reg.1
s.8, applied: SI 2013/645 Reg.9, SI 2013/1506 Reg.3, SI 2013/1507 Reg.1
s.9, applied: SI 2013/645 Reg.9, SI 2013/1506 Reg.3, SI 2013/1507 Reg.1
s.10, applied: SI 2013/645 Reg.9, SI 2013/1506 Reg.3, SI 2013/1507 Reg.1
s.11, amended: 2013 c.32 Sch.12 para.2
s.11, applied: SI 2013/449(b), SI 2013/1507(b), SI 2013/1667(b), SI 2013/448, SI 2013/645, SI 2013/645 Reg.9, SI 2013/1471, SI 2013/1506, SI 2013/1506 Reg.3, SI 2013/1507 Reg.1, SI 2013/1512
s.12, applied: SI 2013/645 Reg.9, SI 2013/1506 Reg.3, SI 2013/1507 Reg.1
s.13, amended: 2013 c.32 Sch.12 para.3
s.13, applied: SI 2013/645 Reg.9, SI 2013/1506 Reg.3, SI 2013/1507 Reg.1
s.14, amended: 2013 c.32 Sch.12 para.4
s.14, applied: 2013 c.32 s.90, s.114, Sch.9 para.17, SI 2013/645 Reg.9, SI 2013/1506 Reg.3, SI 2013/1507 Reg.1
s.15, amended: 2013 c.32 Sch.12 para.5
s.15, applied: 2013 c.32 s.81, s.114, SI 2013/645 Reg.9, SI 2013/1506 Reg.3, SI 2013/1507 Reg.1
s.15, enabling: SI 2013/448, SI 2013/449, SI 2013/645, SI 2013/950, SI 2013/1471, SI 2013/1506, SI 2013/1512, SI 2013/1667, SI 2013/2987
s.16, applied: SI 2013/645 Reg.9, SI 2013/1506 Reg.3, SI 2013/1507 Reg.1
s.17, applied: SI 2013/645 Reg.9, SI 2013/1506 Reg.3, SI 2013/1507 Reg.1
s.18, amended: 2013 c.32 Sch.12 para.6
s.18, applied: SI 2013/645 Reg.9, SI 2013/1506 Reg.3, Reg.17, SI 2013/1507 Reg.1
s.18, disapplied: SI 2013/1506 Reg.8
s.18, varied: SI 2013/1506 Reg.8
s.19, applied: 2013 c.32 s.89, SI 2013/645 Reg.9, SI 2013/1237 Sch.1, SI 2013/1506 Reg.3, Reg.17, Reg.19, Reg.27, Reg.29, SI 2013/1507 Reg.1
s.19, disapplied: SI 2013/1506 Reg.8
s.19, varied: SI 2013/1506 Reg.8
s.20, applied: 2013 c.32 Sch.9 para.1, Sch.9 para.18, SI 2013/645 Reg.9, SI 2013/1506 Reg.3, Reg.17, Reg.19, SI 2013/1507 Reg.1
s.20, disapplied: SI 2013/1506 Reg.8
s.20, varied: SI 2013/1506 Reg.8
s.21, applied: SI 2013/645 Reg.9, SI 2013/805 Sch.1, SI 2013/806 Sch.1, SI 2013/807 Sch.1, SI 2013/808 Sch.1, SI 2013/809 Sch.1, SI 2013/810 Sch.1, SI 2013/811 Sch.1, SI 2013/812 Sch.1, SI 2013/813 Sch.1, SI 2013/814 Sch.1, SI 2013/1506 Reg.3, Reg.17, Reg.19, SI 2013/1507 Reg.1
s.21, disapplied: SI 2013/1506 Reg.8
s.21, varied: SI 2013/1506 Reg.8
s.22, applied: SI 2013/645 Reg.9, SI 2013/805 Sch.1, SI 2013/806 Sch.1, SI 2013/807 Sch.1, SI 2013/808 Sch.1, SI 2013/809 Sch.1, SI 2013/810 Sch.1, SI 2013/811 Sch.1, SI 2013/812 Sch.1, SI 2013/813 Sch.1, SI 2013/814 Sch.1, SI 2013/1506 Reg.3, Reg.17, SI 2013/1507 Reg.1
s.22, disapplied: SI 2013/1506 Reg.8
s.22, varied: SI 2013/1506 Reg.8
s.23, applied: SI 2013/645 Reg.9, SI 2013/1506 Reg.3, Reg.17, Reg.19, SI 2013/1507 Reg.1
s.23, disapplied: SI 2013/1506 Reg.8
s.23, varied: SI 2013/1506 Reg.8
s.24, applied: SI 2013/645 Reg.9, SI 2013/1506 Reg.3, Reg.17, Reg.19, SI 2013/1507 Reg.1

s.24, disapplied: SI 2013/1506 Reg.8
s.24, varied: SI 2013/1506 Reg.8
s.24, enabling: SI 2013/1237
s.25, applied: SI 2013/645 Reg.9, SI 2013/1506 Reg.3, Reg.17, SI 2013/1507 Reg.1
s.25, disapplied: SI 2013/1506 Reg.8
s.25, varied: SI 2013/1506 Reg.8
s.25A, applied: SI 2013/645 Reg.9, SI 2013/1506 Reg.3, Reg.17, Reg.19, SI 2013/1507 Reg.1
s.25A, disapplied: SI 2013/1506 Reg.8
s.25A, varied: SI 2013/1506 Reg.8, Reg.19
s.26, applied: SI 2013/645 Reg.9, SI 2013/1506 Reg.3, Reg.17, Reg.19, SI 2013/1507 Reg.1
s.26, disapplied: SI 2013/1506 Reg.8
s.26, varied: SI 2013/1506 Reg.8
s.27, amended: 2013 c.32 Sch.12 para.7
s.27, applied: SI 2013/645 Reg.9, SI 2013/1506 Reg.3, Reg.17, Reg.19, SI 2013/1507 Reg.1
s.27A, amended: 2013 c.32 Sch.12 para.8
s.27A, applied: SI 2013/645 Reg.9, SI 2013/1506 Reg.3, Reg.17, Reg.19, SI 2013/1507 Reg.1
s.27A, varied: SI 2013/1506 Reg.19
s.28, amended: 2013 c.32 Sch.12 para.9, SI 2013/755 Sch.2 para.112
s.28, applied: SI 2013/645 Reg.9, SI 2013/1506 Reg.3, Reg.11, Reg.17, Reg.19, SI 2013/1507 Reg.1
s.29, applied: SI 2013/645 Reg.9, SI 2013/1506 Reg.3, SI 2013/1507 Reg.1
s.30, applied: SI 2013/645 Reg.9, SI 2013/1506 Reg.3, SI 2013/1507 Reg.1
s.31, applied: SI 2013/645 Reg.9, SI 2013/1506 Reg.3, SI 2013/1507 Reg.1
s.32, applied: SI 2013/645 Reg.9, SI 2013/1506 Reg.3, SI 2013/1507 Reg.1
s.33, applied: SI 2013/240 Art.12, SI 2013/645 Reg.9, SI 2013/1506 Reg.3, Reg.8, Reg.17, Reg.19, Reg.21, Reg.32, Reg.33, SI 2013/1507 Reg.1
s.33, disapplied: SI 2013/1506 Reg.8
s.33, varied: SI 2013/1506 Reg.8
s.34, applied: SI 2013/645 Reg.9, SI 2013/1506 Reg.3, Reg.17, Reg.19, SI 2013/1507 Reg.1
s.34, disapplied: SI 2013/1506 Reg.8
s.34, varied: SI 2013/1506 Reg.8
s.35, applied: SI 2013/645 Reg.9, SI 2013/1506 Reg.3, Reg.17, Reg.19, SI 2013/1507 Reg.1
s.35, disapplied: SI 2013/1506 Reg.8
s.35, varied: SI 2013/1506 Reg.8
s.36, applied: SI 2013/645 Reg.9, SI 2013/1506 Reg.3, Reg.17, Reg.19, SI 2013/1507 Reg.1
s.36, disapplied: SI 2013/1506 Reg.8
s.36, varied: SI 2013/1506 Reg.8
s.37, applied: SI 2013/645 Reg.9, SI 2013/1506 Reg.3, Reg.17, Reg.19, SI 2013/1507 Reg.1
s.37, disapplied: SI 2013/1506 Reg.8
s.37, varied: SI 2013/1506 Reg.8
s.38, amended: SI 2013/755 Sch.2 para.113
s.38, applied: SI 2013/645 Reg.9, SI 2013/1506 Reg.3, Reg.17, Reg.19, SI 2013/1507 Reg.1
s.38, disapplied: SI 2013/1506 Reg.8
s.38, varied: SI 2013/1506 Reg.8
s.39, applied: SI 2013/645 Reg.9, SI 2013/1506 Reg.3, Reg.17, Reg.19, SI 2013/1507 Reg.1
s.39, disapplied: SI 2013/1506 Reg.8
s.39, varied: SI 2013/1506 Reg.8
s.40, applied: SI 2013/645 Reg.9, SI 2013/1506 Reg.3, Reg.17, Reg.19, SI 2013/1507 Reg.1
s.40, disapplied: SI 2013/1506 Reg.8
s.40, varied: SI 2013/1506 Reg.8
s.41, applied: SI 2013/645 Reg.9, SI 2013/1506 Reg.3, Reg.17, Reg.19, SI 2013/1507 Reg.1
s.41, disapplied: SI 2013/1506 Reg.8
s.41, varied: SI 2013/1506 Reg.8
s.42, applied: SI 2013/645 Reg.9, SI 2013/1506 Reg.3, Reg.17, Reg.19, SI 2013/1507 Reg.1
s.42, disapplied: SI 2013/1506 Reg.8
s.42, varied: SI 2013/1506 Reg.8
s.43, applied: 2013 c.32 s.81, s.114, SI 2013/645 Reg.9, SI 2013/1506 Reg.3, SI 2013/1507 Reg.1
s.43, enabling: SI 2013/1507, SI 2013/1512, SI 2013/2987
s.43A, applied: SI 2013/645 Reg.9, SI 2013/1506 Reg.3, SI 2013/1507 Reg.1
s.44, amended: 2013 c.32 Sch.12 para.10
s.44, applied: SI 2013/645 Reg.9, SI 2013/1506 Reg.3, SI 2013/1507 Reg.1
s.44, repealed (in part): 2013 c.32 Sch.12 para.10, SI 2013/2042 Sch.1 para.2
s.45, applied: SI 2013/645 Reg.9, SI 2013/1506 Reg.3, SI 2013/1507 Reg.1
s.46, applied: SI 2013/645 Reg.9, SI 2013/1506 Reg.3, SI 2013/1507 Reg.1
s.46, varied: SI 2013/1506 Reg.29
s.47, amended: 2013 c.24 s.69
s.47, applied: SI 2013/645 Reg.9, SI 2013/1506 Reg.3, SI 2013/1507 Reg.1
s.47, repealed (in part): 2013 c.24 s.69
s.47, enabling: SI 2013/950, SI 2013/1667
s.48, applied: SI 2013/645 Reg.9, SI 2013/1506 Reg.3, SI 2013/1507 Reg.1
s.49, applied: SI 2013/645 Reg.9, SI 2013/1506 Reg.3, SI 2013/1507 Reg.1
s.49, enabling: SI 2013/448
s.50, amended: 2013 c.32 Sch.12 para.11
s.50, applied: SI 2013/449(b), SI 2013/448, SI 2013/645, SI 2013/645 Reg.9, SI 2013/1471, SI

2013/1506, SI 2013/1506 Reg.3, SI 2013/1507 Reg.1, SI 2013/1512, SI 2013/1667, SI 2013/2987
s.50, enabling: SI 2013/1667
s.51, applied: SI 2013/645 Reg.9, SI 2013/1506 Reg.3, SI 2013/1507 Reg.1
s.51A, amended: 2013 c.22 Sch.8 para.21, SI 2013/602 Sch.1 para.2
s.51A, applied: SI 2013/645 Reg.9, SI 2013/1506 Reg.3, SI 2013/1507 Reg.1
s.52, applied: SI 2013/645 Reg.9, SI 2013/1506 Reg.3, SI 2013/1507 Reg.1
s.52, enabling: SI 2013/1471
s.53, amended: 2013 c.32 Sch.12 para.12
s.53, applied: SI 2013/645 Reg.9, SI 2013/1506 Reg.3, SI 2013/1507 Reg.1, SI 2013/3104 Sch.1 para.20
s.54, applied: SI 2013/645 Reg.9, SI 2013/1506 Reg.3, SI 2013/1507 Reg.1
s.59, applied: SI 2013/1471 Reg.19
s.80, applied: SI 2013/645 Reg.9, SI 2013/1471 Reg.19, SI 2013/1506 Reg.3, SI 2013/1507 Reg.1
s.81, applied: SI 2013/645 Reg.9, SI 2013/1471 Reg.19, SI 2013/1506 Reg.3, SI 2013/1507 Reg.1
s.82, amended: 2013 c.32 Sch.12 para.13
s.82, applied: SI 2013/645 Reg.9, SI 2013/1471 Reg.19, SI 2013/1506 Reg.3, SI 2013/1507 Reg.1
s.82, enabling: SI 2013/449, SI 2013/645, SI 2013/950, SI 2013/1506, SI 2013/1507
s.84, applied: 2013 c.24 s.69
s.84, enabling: SI 2013/240
Sch.1, amended: 2013 c.32 Sch.12 para.14, SI 2013/448 Sch.1
Sch.2 para.1, amended: 2013 c.32 Sch.12 para.15
Sch.2 para.2, amended: 2013 c.32 Sch.12 para.15
Sch.2 para.2, applied: 2013 c.32 Sch.7 para.11
Sch.2 para.3, amended: 2013 c.32 Sch.12 para.15
Sch.2 para.4, amended: 2013 c.32 Sch.12 para.15
Sch.2 para.4A, added: 2013 c.32 Sch.12 para.15
Sch.2 para.5, amended: 2013 c.32 Sch.12 para.15
Sch.2 para.6, amended: 2013 c.32 Sch.12 para.15
Sch.3 para.1, enabling: SI 2013/449, SI 2013/645, SI 2013/950, SI 2013/1506, SI 2013/1512, SI 2013/2987
Sch.3 para.2, enabling: SI 2013/1506
Sch.3 para.3, enabling: SI 2013/449
Sch.3 para.4, enabling: SI 2013/1506
Sch.3 para.6, enabling: SI 2013/449, SI 2013/950, SI 2013/1506
Sch.3 para.8, enabling: SI 2013/645, SI 2013/1512
Sch.3 para.9, enabling: SI 2013/1512
Sch.3 para.10, enabling: SI 2013/1512
Sch.3 para.13, enabling: SI 2013/1506
Sch.3 para.14, enabling: SI 2013/645, SI 2013/1512, SI 2013/2987
Sch.3 para.15, enabling: SI 2013/449, SI 2013/645, SI 2013/1471, SI 2013/1506
Sch.3 para.16, enabling: SI 2013/449, SI 2013/645, SI 2013/1471, SI 2013/2987
Sch.3 para.20, enabling: SI 2013/645, SI 2013/1471

39. Consumer Credit Act 1974

see *Citifinancial Europe Plc v Rice* 2013 Hous. L.R. 23 (Sh Ct (Glasgow)), Sheriff AF Deutsch; see *Consolidated Finance Ltd v Collins* [2013] EWCA Civ 475, [2013] E.C.C. 21 (CA (Civ Div)), Arden, L.J.; see *Evans v Finance-U-Ltd* [2013] EWCA Civ 869, [2013] E.C.C. 26 (CA (Civ Div)), Mummery, L.J.; see *Jones v Link Financial Ltd* [2012] EWHC 2402 (QB), [2013] 1 W.L.R. 693 (QBD (Manchester)), Hamblen, J.; see *Santander UK Plc v Harrison* [2013] EWHC 199 (QB), [2013] Bus. L.R. 501 (QBD), Males, J.
applied: SI 2013/1881 Art.31, Art.51, Art.56, Art.60, SI 2013/1882 Art.2, Art.6, SI 2013/3029 Sch.9 para.35, SI 2013/3128 Art.4
referred to: SI 2013/3035 Sch.1
s.1, repealed (in part): SI 2013/1881 Art.20, Art.20
s.2, repealed (in part): SI 2013/1881 Art.20, Art.20
s.3, repealed (in part): SI 2013/1881 Art.20, Art.20
s.4, repealed (in part): SI 2013/1881 Art.20, Art.20
s.5, repealed (in part): SI 2013/1881 Art.20, Art.20
s.6, repealed (in part): SI 2013/1881 Art.20, Art.20
s.6A, applied: SI 2013/3128 Art.2
s.6A, repealed (in part): SI 2013/1881 Art.20, Art.20
s.7, repealed (in part): SI 2013/1881 Art.20, Art.20
s.8, amended: SI 2013/1881 Art.20
s.15, amended: SI 2013/1881 Art.20
s.16, repealed (in part): SI 2013/1881 Art.20, Art.20
s.16A, repealed (in part): SI 2013/1881 Art.20, Art.20
s.16B, repealed (in part): SI 2013/1881 Art.20, Art.20
s.16C, repealed (in part): SI 2013/1881 Art.20, Art.20
s.20, substituted: SI 2013/1881 Art.20
s.21, repealed (in part): SI 2013/1881 Art.20, Art.20
s.22, repealed (in part): SI 2013/1881 Art.20, Art.20
s.23, repealed (in part): SI 2013/1881 Art.20, Art.20
s.24, repealed (in part): SI 2013/1881 Art.20, Art.20
s.24A, applied: SI 2013/1881 Art.31
s.24A, repealed (in part): SI 2013/1881 Art.20, Art.20

s.25, amended: SI 2013/3115 Sch.2 para.32
s.25, repealed (in part): SI 2013/1881 Art.20, Art.20
s.25A, repealed (in part): SI 2013/1881 Art.20, Art.20
s.26, repealed (in part): SI 2013/1881 Art.20, Art.20
s.27, applied: SI 2013/1881 Art.31, Art.37, Art.38
s.27, repealed (in part): SI 2013/1881 Art.20, Art.20
s.27A, repealed (in part): SI 2013/1881 Art.20, Art.20
s.28, repealed (in part): SI 2013/1881 Art.20, Art.20
s.28A, repealed (in part): SI 2013/1881 Art.20, Art.20
s.28B, repealed (in part): SI 2013/1881 Art.20, Art.20
s.28C, repealed (in part): SI 2013/1881 Art.20, Art.20
s.29, repealed (in part): SI 2013/1881 Art.20, Art.20
s.30, applied: SI 2013/1881 Art.33
s.30, repealed (in part): SI 2013/1881 Art.20, Art.20
s.31, applied: SI 2013/1881 Art.35, Art.36
s.31, repealed (in part): SI 2013/1881 Art.20, Art.20
s.32, applied: SI 2013/1881 Art.37, Art.38
s.32, repealed (in part): SI 2013/1881 Art.20, Art.20
s.32A, applied: SI 2013/1881 Art.39, Art.40
s.32A, repealed (in part): SI 2013/1881 Art.20, Art.20
s.32B, repealed (in part): SI 2013/1881 Art.20, Art.20
s.33, repealed (in part): SI 2013/1881 Art.20, Art.20
s.33A, applied: SI 2013/1881 Art.41, Art.42, Art.47, Art.56
s.33A, repealed (in part): SI 2013/1881 Art.20, Art.20
s.33B, applied: SI 2013/1881 Art.47
s.33B, repealed (in part): SI 2013/1881 Art.20, Art.20
s.33C, repealed (in part): SI 2013/1881 Art.20, Art.20
s.33D, applied: SI 2013/1881 Art.41, Art.42
s.33D, repealed (in part): SI 2013/1881 Art.20, Art.20
s.33E, applied: SI 2013/1881 Art.41
s.33E, repealed (in part): SI 2013/1881 Art.20, Art.20
s.34, applied: SI 2013/1881 Art.35, Art.37, Art.41, Art.44
s.34, repealed (in part): SI 2013/1881 Art.20, Art.20
s.34, varied: SI 2013/1881 Art.44
s.34A, repealed (in part): SI 2013/1881 Art.20, Art.20
s.34Z, repealed (in part): SI 2013/1881 Art.20, Art.20
s.34ZA, applied: SI 2013/1881 Art.39, Art.40
s.34ZA, repealed (in part): SI 2013/1881 Art.20, Art.20
s.34ZA, varied: SI 2013/1881 Art.39
s.35, repealed (in part): SI 2013/1881 Art.20, Art.20
s.36, repealed (in part): SI 2013/1881 Art.20, Art.20
s.36A, applied: SI 2013/1881 Art.47
s.36A, repealed (in part): SI 2013/1881 Art.20, Art.20
s.36B, applied: SI 2013/1881 Art.43
s.36B, repealed (in part): SI 2013/1881 Art.20, Art.20
s.36C, applied: SI 2013/1881 Art.43
s.36C, repealed (in part): SI 2013/1881 Art.20, Art.20
s.36D, repealed (in part): SI 2013/1881 Art.20, Art.20
s.36E, applied: SI 2013/1881 Art.43
s.36E, repealed (in part): SI 2013/1881 Art.20, Art.20
s.36F, repealed (in part): SI 2013/1881 Art.20, Art.20
s.37, repealed (in part): SI 2013/1881 Art.20, Art.20
s.38, repealed (in part): SI 2013/1881 Art.20, Art.20
s.39, repealed (in part): SI 2013/1881 Art.20, Art.20
s.39A, applied: SI 2013/1881 Art.44, Art.45, Art.46, Art.47
s.39A, repealed (in part): SI 2013/1881 Art.20, Art.20
s.39A, varied: SI 2013/1881 Art.46
s.39B, applied: SI 2013/1881 Art.44, Art.47
s.39B, repealed (in part): SI 2013/1881 Art.20, Art.20
s.39C, applied: SI 2013/1881 Art.44, Art.47
s.39C, repealed (in part): SI 2013/1881 Art.20, Art.20
s.40, repealed (in part): SI 2013/1881 Art.20, Art.20
s.40, varied: SI 2013/1881 Art.48

s.40A, repealed (in part): SI 2013/1881 Art.20, Art.20
s.41, repealed (in part): SI 2013/1881 Art.20, Art.20
s.41, applied: SI 2013/1881 Art.32, Art.34, Art.36, Art.38, Art.40, Art.42, Art.45, Art.54, Art.55
s.41, repealed (in part): SI 2013/1881 Art.20, Art.20
s.41, varied: SI 2013/1881 Art.54
s.41A, repealed (in part): SI 2013/1881 Art.20, Art.20
s.41ZA, applied: SI 2013/1881 Art.54
s.41ZA, repealed (in part): SI 2013/1881 Art.20, Art.20
s.41ZA, varied: SI 2013/1881 Art.54
s.41ZB, applied: SI 2013/1881 Art.54
s.41ZB, repealed (in part): SI 2013/1881 Art.20, Art.20
s.41ZB, varied: SI 2013/1881 Art.54
s.42, repealed (in part): SI 2013/1881 Art.20, Art.20
s.43, repealed (in part): SI 2013/1881 Art.20, Art.20
s.44, repealed (in part): SI 2013/1881 Art.20, Art.20
s.45, repealed (in part): SI 2013/1881 Art.20, Art.20
s.47, repealed (in part): SI 2013/1881 Art.20, Art.20
s.49, amended: SI 2013/1882 Art.7
s.51, repealed (in part): SI 2013/1881 Art.20, Art.20
s.51A, repealed (in part): SI 2013/1881 Art.20, Art.20
s.51B, repealed: SI 2013/1881 Art.20
s.52, repealed (in part): SI 2013/1881 Art.20, Art.20
s.53, repealed (in part): SI 2013/1881 Art.20, Art.20
s.54, repealed (in part): SI 2013/1881 Art.20, Art.20
s.55A, repealed (in part): SI 2013/1881 Art.20, Art.20
s.55B, repealed (in part): SI 2013/1881 Art.20, Art.20
s.55C, amended: SI 2013/1881 Art.20
s.60, amended: SI 2013/1881 Art.20, SI 2013/1882 Art.7
s.60, applied: SI 2013/1881 Art.53
s.61A, amended: SI 2013/1881 Art.20
s.64, amended: SI 2013/1882 Art.7
s.64, applied: SI 2013/1881 Art.53
s.74, amended: SI 2013/1882 Art.7, SI 2013/3134 Sch.4 para.2
s.74, repealed (in part): SI 2013/1881 Art.20
s.74A, repealed (in part): SI 2013/1881 Art.20, Art.20
s.74B, repealed (in part): SI 2013/1881 Art.20, Art.20
s.75A, amended: SI 2013/1881 Art.20
s.77B, amended: SI 2013/1881 Art.20
s.81, repealed (in part): SI 2013/1881 Art.20
s.82, see *Santander UK Plc v Harrison* [2013] EWHC 199 (QB), [2013] Bus. L.R. 501 (QBD), Males, J.
s.82, amended: SI 2013/1881 Art.20
s.82, substituted: SI 2013/1881 Art.20
s.82A, see *Smith v 1st Credit (Finance) Ltd* [2012] EWHC 2600 (Ch), [2013] B.P.I.R. 129 (Ch D), Nicholas Strauss Q.C.
s.82A, repealed (in part): SI 2013/1881 Art.20, Art.20
s.86A, amended: SI 2013/1882 Art.7
s.93, amended: SI 2013/1881 Art.20
s.101, amended: SI 2013/1882 Art.7
s.101, applied: SI 2013/1881 Art.53
s.101, substituted: SI 2013/1882 Art.7
s.112, repealed (in part): SI 2013/1881 Art.20, Art.20
s.113, amended: SI 2013/1881 Art.20, SI 2013/1882 Art.7
s.114, amended: SI 2013/1881 Art.20
s.115, repealed (in part): SI 2013/1881 Art.20, Art.20
s.123, amended: SI 2013/1882 Art.7
s.126, see *Waterside Finance Ltd v Karim* [2012] EWHC 2999 (Ch), [2013] 1 P. & C.R. 21 (Ch D), Norris, J.
s.126, amended: SI 2013/1881 Art.20
s.140A, amended: SI 2013/1881 Art.20
s.140D, repealed (in part): SI 2013/1881 Art.20, Art.20
s.145, amended: SI 2013/1881 Art.20
s.146, repealed (in part): SI 2013/1881 Art.20, Art.20
s.147, repealed (in part): SI 2013/1881 Art.20, Art.20
s.148, repealed (in part): SI 2013/1881 Art.20, Art.20
s.148, varied: SI 2013/1881 Art.48A
s.149, repealed (in part): SI 2013/1881 Art.20, Art.20
s.149, varied: SI 2013/1881 Art.48B
s.150, repealed (in part): SI 2013/1881 Art.20, Art.20
s.151, repealed (in part): SI 2013/1881 Art.20, Art.20

s.152, repealed (in part): SI 2013/1881 Art.20, Art.20
s.155, amended: SI 2013/1881 Art.20
s.156, repealed (in part): SI 2013/1881 Art.20, Art.20
s.159, amended: SI 2013/1881 Art.20, SI 2013/1882 Art.7
s.160, amended: SI 2013/1881 Art.20, SI 2013/1882 Art.7
s.160, applied: SI 2013/1881 Art.53
s.160, substituted: SI 2013/1882 Art.7
s.160A, applied: SI 2013/1881 Art.56
s.160A, repealed (in part): SI 2013/1881 Art.20, Art.20
s.161, amended: SI 2013/1881 Art.20, SI 2013/1882 Art.7
s.161, repealed (in part): SI 2013/1881 Art.20
s.161, substituted: SI 2013/1881 Art.20
s.162, repealed (in part): SI 2013/1881 Art.20
s.162, varied: SI 2013/1882 Art.8
s.163, varied: SI 2013/1882 Art.8
s.164, varied: SI 2013/1882 Art.8
s.165, repealed (in part): SI 2013/1881 Art.20
s.165, varied: SI 2013/1882 Art.8
s.166, amended: SI 2013/1882 Art.7
s.167, repealed (in part): SI 2013/1881 Art.20
s.170, amended: SI 2013/1882 Art.7
s.171, repealed (in part): SI 2013/1881 Art.20
s.173, amended: SI 2013/1881 Art.20
s.174A, amended: SI 2013/1881 Art.20
s.174A, varied: SI 2013/1882 Art.8
s.178, amended: SI 2013/1882 Art.7
s.180, amended: SI 2013/1881 Art.20
s.181, amended: SI 2013/1881 Art.20, SI 2013/1882 Art.7
s.182, amended: SI 2013/1881 Art.20, SI 2013/1882 Art.7
s.182, repealed (in part): SI 2013/1881 Art.20
s.182, substituted: SI 2013/1882 Art.7
s.183, amended: SI 2013/1882 Art.7
s.183, repealed (in part): SI 2013/1881 Art.20
s.183, substituted: SI 2013/1882 Art.7
s.185, repealed (in part): SI 2013/1881 Art.20
s.188, amended: SI 2013/1882 Art.7
s.189, see *Jones v Link Financial Ltd* [2012] EWHC 2402 (QB), [2013] 1 W.L.R. 693 (QBD (Manchester)), Hamblen, J.
s.189, amended: SI 2013/1881 Art.20, SI 2013/1882 Art.7
s.189, substituted: SI 2013/1881 Art.20, SI 2013/1882 Art.7
s.189A, repealed (in part): SI 2013/1881 Art.20
s.190, repealed (in part): SI 2013/1881 Art.20
s.191, repealed (in part): SI 2013/1881 Art.20
Sch.1, amended: SI 2013/1881 Art.20
Sch.2 Part I, amended: SI 2013/1881 Art.20
Sch.2 Part II, amended: SI 2013/1881 Art.20
Sch.3 Part III para.5, repealed (in part): SI 2013/1881 Art.20
Sch.3 Part III para.6, repealed (in part): SI 2013/1881 Art.20
Sch.3 Part III para.7, repealed (in part): SI 2013/1881 Art.20
Sch.3 Part IV para.11, repealed (in part): SI 2013/1881 Art.20
Sch.3 Part X para.44, repealed (in part): SI 2013/1881 Art.20
Sch.3 Part X para.45, repealed (in part): SI 2013/1881 Art.20
Sch.3 Part X para.46, repealed (in part): SI 2013/1881 Art.20

40. Control of Pollution Act 1974

s.30, amended: SI 2013/755 Sch.2 para.115
s.60, applied: SI 2013/198 Art.15, SI 2013/586 Art.9, SI 2013/648 Art.12, SI 2013/675 Art.38, SI 2013/680 Art.9, SI 2013/1752 Art.6, SI 2013/1873 Art.8, SI 2013/2587 Art.46, SI 2013/2808 Art.33, SI 2013/2809 Art.30, SI 2013/3200 Art.15
s.61, applied: SI 2013/198 Art.15, SI 2013/586 Art.9, SI 2013/648 Art.12, SI 2013/675 Art.38, SI 2013/680 Art.9, SI 2013/1752 Art.6, SI 2013/1873 Art.8, SI 2013/1933 Art.40, SI 2013/1967 Art.31, SI 2013/2587 Art.46, SI 2013/2808 Art.33, SI 2013/2809 Art.30, Sch.1 para.4, SI 2013/3200 Art.15, SI 2013/3244 Art.63
s.61, disapplied: SI 2013/198 Art.15, SI 2013/586 Art.9, SI 2013/648 Art.12, SI 2013/675 Art.38, SI 2013/680 Art.9, SI 2013/1752 Art.6, SI 2013/1873 Art.8, SI 2013/1967 Art.31, SI 2013/2587 Art.46, SI 2013/2808 Art.33, SI 2013/3200 Art.15, SI 2013/3244 Art.63
s.62, amended: SI 2013/755 Sch.2 para.116
s.65, applied: SI 2013/198 Art.15, SI 2013/586 Art.9, SI 2013/648 Art.12, SI 2013/675 Art.38, SI 2013/680 Art.9, SI 2013/1752 Art.6, SI 2013/1873 Art.8, SI 2013/1933 Art.40, SI 2013/1967 Art.31, SI 2013/2587 Art.46, SI 2013/2808 Art.33, SI 2013/2809 Art.30, SI 2013/3200 Art.15, SI 2013/3244 Art.63
s.65, disapplied: SI 2013/198 Art.15, SI 2013/586 Art.9, SI 2013/648 Art.12, SI 2013/675 Art.38, SI 2013/680 Art.9, SI 2013/1752 Art.6, SI 2013/1873 Art.8, SI 2013/1967 Art.31, SI 2013/2587 Art.46, SI 2013/2808 Art.33, SI 2013/3200 Art.15, SI 2013/3244 Art.63
s.71, enabling: SI 2013/2036
s.104, enabling: SI 2013/2036

46. Friendly Societies Act 1974

s.12, amended: SI 2013/496 Sch.5 para.2
s.15A, amended: SI 2013/496 Sch.5 para.2
s.16, amended: SI 2013/496 Sch.5 para.2
s.18, amended: SI 2013/496 Sch.5 para.2
s.19, amended: SI 2013/496 Sch.5 para.2
s.20, amended: SI 2013/496 Sch.5 para.2
s.22, amended: 2013 c.22 Sch.9 para.84
s.24, amended: SI 2013/496 Sch.5 para.2
s.30A, amended: SI 2013/496 Sch.5 para.3
s.32, amended: SI 2013/496 Sch.5 para.4
s.32A, amended: SI 2013/496 Sch.5 para.5
s.39C, amended: SI 2013/496 Sch.5 para.6
s.41, amended: SI 2013/496 Sch.5 para.7
s.42, amended: SI 2013/496 Sch.5 para.8
s.43, amended: SI 2013/496 Sch.5 para.2, Sch.5 para.9
s.55, amended: SI 2013/496 Sch.5 para.2
s.65A, amended: SI 2013/496 Sch.5 para.10
s.76, amended: SI 2013/496 Sch.5 para.11
s.80, amended: 2013 c.22 Sch.9 para.84
s.81, amended: SI 2013/496 Sch.5 para.2
s.82, amended: SI 2013/496 Sch.5 para.2
s.84, amended: SI 2013/496 Sch.5 para.2
s.84A, amended: SI 2013/496 Sch.5 para.2
s.85, amended: SI 2013/496 Sch.5 para.2, Sch.5 para.12
s.86, amended: SI 2013/496 Sch.5 para.2
s.87, amended: SI 2013/496 Sch.5 para.13
s.90, amended: SI 2013/496 Sch.5 para.14
s.91, amended: SI 2013/496 Sch.5 para.2, Sch.5 para.15
s.93, amended: 2013 c.22 Sch.9 para.84, SI 2013/496 Sch.5 para.16
s.94, amended: SI 2013/496 Sch.5 para.2, Sch.5 para.17
s.95, amended: SI 2013/496 Sch.5 para.18
s.95A, amended: SI 2013/496 Sch.5 para.19
s.97, amended: SI 2013/496 Sch.5 para.20
s.98, amended: SI 2013/496 Sch.5 para.21
s.99, amended: SI 2013/496 Sch.5 para.2
s.101, amended: SI 2013/496 Sch.5 para.2, Sch.5 para.22
s.104A, amended: SI 2013/496 Sch.5 para.2
s.109, amended: SI 2013/496 Sch.5 para.2, Sch.5 para.23
s.110, amended: SI 2013/496 Sch.5 para.2, Sch.5 para.24
s.111, amended: SI 2013/496 Sch.5 para.2, Sch.5 para.25
Sch.2 Part I para.7, amended: SI 2013/496 Sch.5 para.2
Sch.2 Part II para.15, amended: SI 2013/496 Sch.5 para.2

53. Rehabilitation of Offenders Act 1974

see *A v B* [2013] I.R.L.R. 434 (EAT), Keith, J.; see *R. (on the application of T) v Chief Constable of Greater Manchester* [2013] EWCA Civ 25, [2013] 1 W.L.R. 2515 (CA (Civ Div)), Lord Dyson (M.R.)
applied: 2013 c.32 Sch.7 para.10
s.1, varied: SSI 2013/146 Art.2
s.3, amended: SSI 2013/146 Art.2
s.3, substituted: SSI 2013/146 Art.2
s.4, see *A v B* [2013] I.R.L.R. 434 (EAT), Keith, J.
s.4, disapplied: SSI 2013/50 Art.3, Art.4
s.4, referred to: SSI 2013/50 Art.3, Art.5
s.4, enabling: SI 2013/1198, SSI 2013/50, SSI 2013/204
s.5, amended: SSI 2013/146 Art.2
s.5, repealed (in part): SSI 2013/146 Art.2
s.7, see *A v B* [2013] I.R.L.R. 434 (EAT), Keith, J.
s.7, enabling: SI 2013/1198, SSI 2013/50, SSI 2013/204
s.8, amended: 2013 c.26 s.16
s.10, applied: SI 2013/1198, SSI 2013/50, SSI 2013/204
s.10, enabling: SI 2013/1198, SSI 2013/50, SSI 2013/204
Sch.2 para.4, enabling: SI 2013/1198
Sch.2 para.6, enabling: SI 2013/1198

55. National Theatre Act 1974

repealed: 2013 c.2 Sch.1 Part 6

1975

22. Oil Taxation Act 1975

applied: 2013 c.29 s.210
s.1, referred to: 2013 c.29 s.210
s.6, applied: 2013 c.29 s.84
s.8, applied: 2013 c.29 s.85
Sch.2 para.13B, amended: 2013 c.29 s.231
Sch.2 para.13C, amended: 2013 c.29 s.232
Sch.3 para.8, amended: 2013 c.29 Sch.31 para.3
Sch.5 para.2C, amended: 2013 c.29 Sch.31 para.4

23. Reservoirs Act 1975

applied: SI 2013/1677 Reg.3, Reg.7, Reg.8, Sch.1 para.7, Sch.3 para.2, Sch.6
s.A.1, applied: SI 2013/1896 Reg.3
s.A.1, enabling: SI 2013/1677, SI 2013/1896
s.1, amended: SI 2013/755 Sch.2 para.118
s.2, amended: SI 2013/755 Sch.2 para.119
s.2, applied: SI 2013/1677 Reg.7
s.2, enabling: SI 2013/1677
s.2A, amended: SI 2013/755 Sch.2 para.120
s.2B, amended: SI 2013/755 Sch.2 para.120
s.2B, applied: SI 2013/1590 Art.4, SI 2013/1896 Reg.4, Reg.7

s.2C, amended: SI 2013/755 Sch.2 para.120
s.2D, amended: SI 2013/755 Sch.2 para.120
s.2E, enabling: SI 2013/1896
s.3, applied: SI 2013/1677 Reg.8
s.3, enabling: SI 2013/1677
s.5, applied: SI 2013/1896
s.5, enabling: SI 2013/1677, SI 2013/1896
s.6, amended: SI 2013/1590 Art.4
s.6, applied: SI 2013/1677 Reg.5
s.7, applied: SI 2013/1677 Reg.4, Reg.10, SI 2013/1896 Reg.6
s.8, applied: SI 2013/1677 Reg.10, Reg.11
s.9, applied: SI 2013/1677 Reg.11, Sch.7 para.6
s.10, applied: SI 2013/1677 Reg.10, Reg.11, SI 2013/1896 Reg.6, Reg.7
s.10, enabling: SI 2013/1896
s.11, applied: SI 2013/1590 Art.4, SI 2013/1677 Reg.9, Reg.12, Sch.5
s.11, referred to: SI 2013/1677 Reg.9
s.11, enabling: SI 2013/1677
s.12, applied: SI 2013/1590 Art.4, SI 2013/1677 Reg.12, SI 2013/1896 Reg.6
s.12A, amended: SI 2013/755 Sch.2 para.121
s.12AA, applied: SI 2013/1677 Reg.10, Reg.12
s.13, applied: SI 2013/1677 Reg.3, Reg.7, Reg.10
s.14, applied: SI 2013/1677 Reg.5, Reg.10, Reg.11
s.15, applied: SI 2013/1677 Reg.10, Sch.1 para.8
s.16, applied: SI 2013/1677 Sch.1 para.9
s.19, applied: SI 2013/1676 r.2, SI 2013/1677 Reg.10, Reg.12
s.19, enabling: SI 2013/1676
s.19A, enabling: SI 2013/1896
s.20, applied: SI 2013/1677 Reg.10, Reg.11, Reg.12
s.20, enabling: SI 2013/1677
s.21, applied: SI 2013/1590 Art.4, SI 2013/1677 Reg.13
s.21, enabling: SI 2013/1677
s.21B, amended: SI 2013/755 Sch.2 para.122
s.21B, enabling: SI 2013/1677
s.22, amended: SI 2013/755 Sch.2 para.122
s.22A, amended: SI 2013/755 Sch.2 para.123
s.22A, substituted: SI 2013/755 Sch.2 para.123
s.27A, amended: SI 2013/755 Sch.2 para.124
Sch.1, amended: SI 2013/755 Sch.2 para.125

24. House of Commons Disqualification Act 1975

s.1, amended: SI 2013/602 Sch.2 para.10
Sch.1 Part I, amended: SI 2013/1036 Sch.1 para.218
Sch.1 Part II, amended: 2013 c.2 Sch.1 Part 10, 2013 c.22 Sch.8 para.22, 2013 c.24 Sch.4 para.23, 2013 c.32 Sch.12 para.55, SI 2013/252 Sch.1 Part 1, SI 2013/294 Sch.1, SI 2013/686 Sch.1 para.1, SI 2013/687 Sch.1 para.1, SI 2013/755 Sch.2 para.126, SI 2013/1465 Sch.1 Part 3, SI 2013/2042 Sch.1 para.4, SI 2013/2329 Sch.1 para.20
Sch.1 Part III, amended: 2013 c.19 s.21, 2013 c.22 Sch.8 para.22, Sch.14 para.13, 2013 c.24 Sch.20 para.2, 2013 c.32 Sch.12 para.55, SI 2013/602 Sch.2 para.10, SI 2013/755 Sch.2 para.126, SI 2013/2314 Art.7, SI 2013/2352 Sch.1 para.4

25. Northern Ireland Assembly Disqualification Act 1975

s.1, amended: SI 2013/602 Sch.2 para.11
Sch.1 Part I, amended: SI 2013/1036 Sch.1 para.219
Sch.1 Part II, amended: 2013 c.22 Sch.8 para.23, 2013 c.2 Sch.1 Part 10, 2013 c.24 Sch.4 para.24, 2013 c.32 Sch.12 para.56, SI 2013/252 Sch.1 Part 1, SI 2013/294 Sch.1, SI 2013/686 Sch.1 para.2, SI 2013/687 Sch.1 para.2, SI 2013/2329 Sch.1 para.21
Sch.1 Part III, amended: 2013 c.22 Sch.8 para.23, 2013 c.24 Sch.20 para.2, 2013 c.32 Sch.12 para.56, SI 2013/2352 Sch.1 para.5

26. Ministers of the Crown Act 1975

applied: 2013 c.15 s.2
s.1, enabling: SI 2013/537, SI 2013/1442, SI 2013/1721, SI 2013/2597
s.8, referred to: 2013 c.24 s.27

27. Ministerial and other Salaries Act 1975

s.1, amended: 2013 c.25 Sch.11 para.3
s.1A, amended: 2013 c.25 Sch.11 para.3

30. Local Government (Scotland) Act 1975

s.35, enabling: SSI 2013/113
s.37, amended: SSI 2013/113 Art.2
s.37, applied: SSI 2013/113
s.37, enabling: SSI 2013/113

33. Referendum Act 1975

applied: SI 2013/1677 Sch.1 para.4

41. Industrial and Provident Societies Act 1975

applied: SI 2013/496 Sch.1 para.5

47. Litigants in Person (Costs and Expenses) Act 1975

s.1, amended: 2013 c.22 Sch.9 para.103, Sch.10 para.35

63. Inheritance (Provision for Family and Dependants) Act 1975

s.5, applied: SI 2013/503 Reg.5
s.15, amended: 2013 c.22 Sch.10 para.36
s.15A, amended: 2013 c.22 Sch.10 para.36
s.15B, amended: 2013 c.22 Sch.10 para.36
s.15ZA, amended: 2013 c.22 Sch.10 para.36
s.25, amended: 2013 c.22 Sch.9 para.92
s.26, repealed (in part): 2013 c.22 Sch.11 para.210

71. Employment Protection Act 1975

s.97, repealed (in part): 2013 c.24 Sch.20 para.2

Sch.9 Part II para.1, repealed (in part): 2013 c.24 Sch.20 para.2
Sch.9 Part II para.2, repealed (in part): 2013 c.24 Sch.20 para.2
Sch.9 Part II para.3, repealed (in part): 2013 c.24 Sch.20 para.2
Sch.9 Part II para.4, repealed (in part): 2013 c.24 Sch.20 para.2
Sch.9 Part II para.5, repealed (in part): 2013 c.24 Sch.20 para.2
Sch.9 Part II para.6, repealed (in part): 2013 c.24 Sch.20 para.2
Sch.15 para.13, repealed: 2013 c.32 Sch.12 para.57
Sch.17 para.12, repealed (in part): 2013 c.24 Sch.20 para.2

72. Children Act 1975

s.50, applied: SI 2013/3029 Sch.9 para.30, SI 2013/3035 Sch.1
s.51, amended: SSI 2013/211 Sch.1 para.3

76. Local Land Charges Act 1975

s.5, disapplied: 2013 c.32 s.123
s.10, amended: 2013 c.22 Sch.9 para.52

1976

14. Fatal Accidents and Sudden Deaths Inquiry (Scotland) Act 1976

applied: 2013 c.32 s.85, Sch.10 para.3

30. Fatal Accidents Act 1976

s.1A, amended: SI 2013/510 Art.2
s.1A, enabling: SI 2013/510

35. Police Pensions Act 1976

applied: SI 2013/602 Sch.3 para.10, SSI 2013/86 Reg.10, SSI 2013/119 Art.2
referred to: 2013 c.22 Sch.8 para.10
s.1, amended: 2013 c.25 Sch.8 para.12
s.1, applied: 2013 c.25 Sch.5 para.22, Sch.6 para.9, SSI 2013/89, SSI 2013/119 Art.2, SSI 2013/184
s.1, enabling: SI 2013/487, SSI 2013/89, SSI 2013/184
s.7, amended: 2013 c.22 Sch.8 para.25, SI 2013/602 Sch.2 para.12
s.7, repealed (in part): 2013 c.22 Sch.8 para.25, SI 2013/602 Sch.2 para.12
s.11, amended: 2013 c.22 Sch.8 para.26, SI 2013/602 Sch.2 para.12
s.11, referred to: SI 2013/2318 Art.3
s.11, repealed (in part): 2013 c.22 Sch.8 para.26, SI 2013/602 Sch.2 para.12

55. Agriculture (Miscellaneous Provisions) Act 1976

s.4, amended: 2013 c.24 Sch.20 para.2

57. Local Government (Miscellaneous Provisions) Act 1976

s.44, amended: SI 2013/755 Sch.2 para.153

63. Bail Act 1976

s.3, see *R. (on the application of Shea) v Winchester Crown Court* [2013] EWHC 1050 (Admin), [2013] Lloyd's Rep. F.C. 346 (DC), Pitchford, L.J.
s.3, applied: SI 2013/1554 r.19_7, r.19_12, r.19_17
s.3AC, applied: SI 2013/1554 r.19_12
s.4, applied: SI 2013/1554 r.19_17
s.5, applied: SI 2013/1554 r.9_5, r.5_4, r.68_9, r.41_5, r.19_4
s.5B, applied: SI 2013/1554 r.19_6, r.19_7
s.5B, enabling: SI 2013/1554
s.6, applied: SI 2013/1554 r.19_17, r.62_5
s.7, applied: SI 2013/435 Sch.2 para.23, SI 2013/1554 r.18_2, r.37_11
s.8, see *R. (on the application of Shea) v Winchester Crown Court* [2013] EWHC 1050 (Admin), [2013] Lloyd's Rep. F.C. 346 (DC), Pitchford, L.J.
s.8, amended: SI 2013/602 Sch.2 para.13
s.8, applied: SI 2013/602 Sch.3 para.8
s.9, see *R. (on the application of Shea) v Winchester Crown Court* [2013] EWHC 1050 (Admin), [2013] Lloyd's Rep. F.C. 346 (DC), Pitchford, L.J.
s.9, applied: SI 2013/435 Sch.1 Part 7
Sch.1, referred to: SI 2013/1554 r.19_17
Sch.1 Part I, applied: SI 2013/1554 r.19_17
Sch.1 Part IA, applied: SI 2013/1554 r.19_17
Sch.1 Part II, applied: SI 2013/1554 r.19_17
Sch.1 Part IIA, applied: SI 2013/1554 r.19_7, r.19_17

76. Energy Act 1976

s.14, repealed: 2013 c.27 s.18
s.15, applied: SI 2013/2986
s.15, enabling: SI 2013/2986
s.17, enabling: SI 2013/2986
s.19, amended: 2013 c.27 s.18
s.19, repealed (in part): 2013 c.27 s.18

80. Rent (Agriculture) Act 1976

s.26, amended: 2013 c.22 Sch.9 para.52
s.28, amended: 2013 c.24 Sch.20 para.1
s.30, amended: SI 2013/755 Sch.2 para.154

85. National Insurance Surcharge Act 1976

repealed: 2013 c.2 Sch.1 Part 10

86. Fishery Limits Act 1976

s.1, enabling: SI 2013/3163

1977

3. Aircraft and Shipbuilding Industries Act 1977

s.1, repealed: SI 2013/687 Sch.1 para.3

s.2, repealed: SI 2013/687 Sch.1 para.3
s.3, repealed: SI 2013/687 Sch.1 para.3
s.4, repealed: SI 2013/687 Sch.1 para.3
s.4A, repealed: SI 2013/687 Sch.1 para.3
s.4B, repealed: SI 2013/687 Sch.1 para.3
s.5, repealed: SI 2013/687 Sch.1 para.3
s.6, repealed: SI 2013/687 Sch.1 para.3
s.7, repealed: SI 2013/687 Sch.1 para.3
s.8, repealed: SI 2013/687 Sch.1 para.3
s.9, repealed: SI 2013/687 Sch.1 para.3
s.10, repealed: SI 2013/687 Sch.1 para.3
s.11, repealed: SI 2013/687 Sch.1 para.3
s.12, repealed: SI 2013/687 Sch.1 para.3
s.13, repealed: SI 2013/687 Sch.1 para.3
s.14, repealed: SI 2013/687 Sch.1 para.3
s.15, repealed: SI 2013/687 Sch.1 para.3
s.16, repealed: SI 2013/687 Sch.1 para.3
s.17, applied: SI 2013/687 Art.4
s.17, repealed: SI 2013/687 Sch.1 para.3
s.18, applied: SI 2013/687 Art.4
s.18, repealed: SI 2013/687 Sch.1 para.3
s.19, repealed (in part): SI 2013/687 Sch.1 para.3
s.20, repealed (in part): SI 2013/687 Sch.1 para.3
s.20, substituted: SI 2013/687 Sch.1 para.3
s.40, repealed (in part): SI 2013/687 Sch.1 para.3
s.40, substituted: SI 2013/687 Sch.1 para.3
s.42, repealed: SI 2013/686 Sch.1 para.3
s.43, repealed: SI 2013/686 Sch.1 para.3
s.44, repealed: SI 2013/686 Sch.1 para.3
s.47, repealed: SI 2013/687 Sch.1 para.3
s.48, repealed: SI 2013/687 Sch.1 para.3
s.49, repealed: SI 2013/687 Sch.1 para.3
s.53, repealed: SI 2013/687 Sch.1 para.3
s.56, amended: SI 2013/686 Sch.1 para.3, SI 2013/687 Sch.1 para.3
s.56, repealed (in part): SI 2013/687 Sch.1 para.3
Sch.2 Part I, repealed: SI 2013/687 Sch.1 para.3
Sch.2 Part II para.1, repealed: SI 2013/687 Sch.1 para.3
Sch.2 Part II para.2, repealed: SI 2013/687 Sch.1 para.3
Sch.2 Part II para.3, repealed: SI 2013/687 Sch.1 para.3
Sch.2 Part II para.4, repealed: SI 2013/687 Sch.1 para.3
Sch.2 Part II para.5, repealed: SI 2013/687 Sch.1 para.3
Sch.3 para.1, repealed (in part): SI 2013/687 Sch.1 para.3
Sch.3 para.2, amended: SI 2013/686 Sch.1 para.3
Sch.3 para.2, repealed (in part): SI 2013/687 Sch.1 para.3
Sch.3 para.3, repealed (in part): SI 2013/687 Sch.1 para.3
Sch.3 para.4, repealed (in part): SI 2013/687 Sch.1 para.3
Sch.3 para.5, repealed (in part): SI 2013/687 Sch.1 para.3
Sch.3 para.6, repealed (in part): SI 2013/687 Sch.1 para.3
Sch.3 para.7, repealed (in part): SI 2013/687 Sch.1 para.3
Sch.3 para.8, repealed (in part): SI 2013/687 Sch.1 para.3
Sch.7 Part I para.1, repealed: SI 2013/686 Sch.1 para.3
Sch.7 Part I para.2, repealed: SI 2013/686 Sch.1 para.3
Sch.7 Part I para.3, repealed: SI 2013/686 Sch.1 para.3
Sch.7 Part I para.4, repealed: SI 2013/686 Sch.1 para.3
Sch.7 Part I para.5, repealed: SI 2013/686 Sch.1 para.3
Sch.7 Part II para.6, repealed: SI 2013/686 Sch.1 para.3
Sch.7 Part II para.7, repealed: SI 2013/686 Sch.1 para.3
Sch.7 Part II para.8, repealed: SI 2013/686 Sch.1 para.3
Sch.7 Part II para.9, repealed: SI 2013/686 Sch.1 para.3
Sch.7 Part II para.10, repealed: SI 2013/686 Sch.1 para.3
Sch.7 Part II para.11, repealed: SI 2013/686 Sch.1 para.3
Sch.7 Part III para.12, repealed: SI 2013/686 Sch.1 para.3
Sch.7 Part III para.13, repealed: SI 2013/686 Sch.1 para.3

37. Patents Act 1977

see *Actavis Group hf v Eli Lilly & Co* [2013] EWCA Civ 517, [2013] R.P.C. 37 (CA (Civ Div)), Longmore, L.J.; see *Tulane Education Fund, Re* [2013] EWCA Civ 890, [2013] Bus. L.R. 1225 (CA (Civ Div)), Sir Terence Etherton
varied: SI 2013/2602 Sch.1 para.1, Sch.1 para.2, Sch.1 para.3, Sch.1 para.4
s.1, see *Fisher-Rosemount Systems Inc's Patent Application* [2013] R.P.C. 4 (PO), H Jones; see *HTC Europe Co Ltd v Apple Inc* [2013] EWCA Civ 451, [2013] R.P.C. 30 (CA (Civ Div)), Richards, L.J.; see *Really Virtual Co Ltd v Comptroller-General of Patents* [2012] EWHC 1086 (Pat), [2013] R.P.C. 3 (Ch D (Patents Ct)), John Baldwin QC; see *Smith & Nephew Plc v Convatec Technologies Inc* [2012] EWCA Civ 1638, [2013] R.P.C. 9 (CA (Civ Div)), Arden, L.J.

s.1, varied: SI 2013/2602 Sch.1 para.5
s.5, varied: SI 2013/2602 Sch.1 para.6
s.22, varied: SI 2013/2602 Sch.1 para.7
s.23, varied: SI 2013/2602 Sch.1 para.7
s.32, varied: SI 2013/2602 Sch.1 para.8
s.40, varied: SI 2013/2602 Sch.1 para.9
s.41, amended: 2013 c.22 Sch.9 para.52
s.41, varied: SI 2013/2602 Sch.1 para.10
s.44, varied: SI 2013/2602 Sch.1 para.11
s.45, varied: SI 2013/2602 Sch.1 para.11
s.46, varied: SI 2013/2602 Sch.1 para.12
s.48, varied: SI 2013/2602 Sch.1 para.13
s.48A, varied: SI 2013/2602 Sch.1 para.13
s.48B, varied: SI 2013/2602 Sch.1 para.13
s.50, varied: SI 2013/2602 Sch.1 para.14
s.51, varied: SI 2013/2602 Sch.1 para.15
s.52, varied: SI 2013/2602 Sch.1 para.16
s.53, varied: SI 2013/2602 Sch.1 para.15
s.54, varied: SI 2013/2602 Sch.1 para.17
s.58, varied: SI 2013/2602 Sch.1 para.18
s.60, see *Merck Canada Inc v Sigma Pharmaceuticals Plc (Form of Order)* [2013] R.P.C. 2 (PCC), Judge Birss Q.C.; see *Nestec SA v Dualit Ltd* [2013] EWHC 923 (Pat), [2013] R.P.C. 32 (Ch D (Patents Ct)), Arnold, J.; see *Schutz (UK) Ltd v Werit UK Ltd* [2013] UKSC 16, [2013] 2 All E.R. 177 (SC), Lord Neuberger (President)
s.60, varied: SI 2013/2602 Sch.1 para.19
s.61, see *Merck Canada Inc v Sigma Pharmaceuticals Plc (Form of Order)* [2013] R.P.C. 2 (PCC), Judge Birss Q.C.
s.61, amended: 2013 c.22 Sch.9 para.52
s.61, varied: SI 2013/2602 Sch.1 para.20
s.62, varied: SI 2013/2602 Sch.1 para.21
s.63, varied: SI 2013/2602 Sch.1 para.22
s.68, see *Schutz (UK) Ltd v Werit UK Ltd* [2013] UKSC 16, [2013] 2 All E.R. 177 (SC), Lord Neuberger (President)
s.68, varied: SI 2013/2602 Sch.1 para.23
s.76A, varied: SI 2013/2602 Sch.1 para.24
s.90, enabling: SI 2013/538
s.93, amended: 2013 c.22 Sch.9 para.52
s.93, varied: SI 2013/2602 Sch.1 para.25
s.96, varied: SI 2013/2602 Sch.1 para.26
s.97, varied: SI 2013/2602 Sch.1 para.27
s.107, amended: 2013 c.22 Sch.9 para.52
s.107, varied: SI 2013/2602 Sch.1 para.28
s.109, varied: SI 2013/2602 Sch.1 para.29
s.118A, varied: SI 2013/2602 Sch.1 para.30
s.124, enabling: SI 2013/538, SI 2013/2602
s.124A, varied: SI 2013/2602 Sch.1 para.31
s.125A, varied: SI 2013/2602 Sch.1 para.32
s.126, varied: SI 2013/2602 Sch.1 para.33
s.128A, varied: SI 2013/2602 Sch.1 para.34
s.128B, see *Tulane Education Fund, Re* [2013] EWCA Civ 890, [2013] Bus. L.R. 1225 (CA (Civ Div)), Sir Terence Etherton
s.128B, varied: SI 2013/2602 Sch.1 para.34
s.130, see *Schutz (UK) Ltd v Werit UK Ltd* [2013] UKSC 16, [2013] 2 All E.R. 177 (SC), Lord Neuberger (President)
s.130, amended: 2013 c.22 Sch.9 para.27
s.130, varied: SI 2013/2602 Sch.1 para.35
s.132, enabling: SI 2013/2602
Sch.A1 para.1, varied: SI 2013/2602 Sch.1 para.36
Sch.A1 para.2, varied: SI 2013/2602 Sch.1 para.36
Sch.A1 para.3, varied: SI 2013/2602 Sch.1 para.36
Sch.A1 para.4, varied: SI 2013/2602 Sch.1 para.36
Sch.A1 para.5, varied: SI 2013/2602 Sch.1 para.36
Sch.A1 para.6, varied: SI 2013/2602 Sch.1 para.36
Sch.A1 para.7, varied: SI 2013/2602 Sch.1 para.36
Sch.A1 para.8, varied: SI 2013/2602 Sch.1 para.36
Sch.A1 para.9, varied: SI 2013/2602 Sch.1 para.36
Sch.A1 para.10, varied: SI 2013/2602 Sch.1 para.36
Sch.A1 para.11, varied: SI 2013/2602 Sch.1 para.36
Sch.A1 para.12, varied: SI 2013/2602 Sch.1 para.36
Sch.A2 para.1, varied: SI 2013/2602 Sch.1 para.36
Sch.A2 para.2, varied: SI 2013/2602 Sch.1 para.36
Sch.A2 para.3, see *International Stem Cell Corp v Comptroller General of Patents* [2013] EWHC 807 (Ch), [2013] 3 C.M.L.R. 14 (Ch D (Patents Ct)), Henry Carr QC
Sch.A2 para.3, varied: SI 2013/2602 Sch.1 para.36
Sch.A2 para.4, varied: SI 2013/2602 Sch.1 para.36
Sch.A2 para.5, varied: SI 2013/2602 Sch.1 para.36
Sch.A2 para.6, varied: SI 2013/2602 Sch.1 para.36
Sch.A2 para.7, varied: SI 2013/2602 Sch.1 para.36
Sch.A2 para.8, varied: SI 2013/2602 Sch.1 para.36
Sch.A2 para.9, varied: SI 2013/2602 Sch.1 para.36
Sch.A2 para.10, varied: SI 2013/2602 Sch.1 para.36
Sch.A2 para.11, varied: SI 2013/2602 Sch.1 para.36
Sch.4A para.1, varied: SI 2013/2602 Sch.1 para.37
Sch.4A para.2, varied: SI 2013/2602 Sch.1 para.37
Sch.4A para.3, varied: SI 2013/2602 Sch.1 para.37
Sch.4A para.4, varied: SI 2013/2602 Sch.1 para.37
Sch.4A para.5, see *Tulane Education Fund, Re* [2012] EWHC 932 (Pat), [2013] Bus. L.R. 53 (Ch D), Roger Wyand Q.C.; see *Tulane Education Fund, Re* [2013] EWCA Civ 890, [2013] Bus. L.R. 1225 (CA (Civ Div)), Sir Terence Etherton
Sch.4A para.5, varied: SI 2013/2602 Sch.1 para.37
Sch.4A para.6, varied: SI 2013/2602 Sch.1 para.37
Sch.4A para.7, varied: SI 2013/2602 Sch.1 para.37

38. Administration of Justice Act 1977
s.23, amended: 2013 c.22 Sch.9 para.52
Sch.3 para.4, repealed (in part): 2013 c.22 Sch.10 para.99

42. Rent Act 1977
Part V, applied: SI 2013/1169 r.26
s.65, amended: SI 2013/1036 Sch.1 para.13
s.65A, added: SI 2013/1036 Sch.1 para.14
s.65A, applied: SI 2013/1036 Sch.3 para.5
s.71, amended: SI 2013/1036 Sch.1 para.15
s.72, amended: SI 2013/1036 Sch.1 para.16
s.72A, amended: SI 2013/630 Reg.3, SI 2013/1036 Sch.1 para.17
s.75, amended: SI 2013/1036 Sch.1 para.18
s.77, amended: SI 2013/1036 Sch.1 para.19
s.78, amended: SI 2013/1036 Sch.1 para.20
s.79, amended: SI 2013/1036 Sch.1 para.21
s.79A, added: SI 2013/1036 Sch.1 para.22
s.80, amended: SI 2013/1036 Sch.1 para.23
s.81, amended: SI 2013/1036 Sch.1 para.24
s.81A, amended: SI 2013/1036 Sch.1 para.25
s.82, amended: SI 2013/1036 Sch.1 para.26
s.85, amended: SI 2013/1036 Sch.1 para.27
s.96, amended: 2013 c.22 Sch.9 para.52
s.103, amended: SI 2013/1036 Sch.1 para.28
s.104, amended: SI 2013/1036 Sch.1 para.29
s.106, amended: SI 2013/1036 Sch.1 para.30
s.107, amended: SI 2013/1036 Sch.1 para.31
s.122, amended: SI 2013/1036 Sch.1 para.32
s.132, amended: 2013 c.22 Sch.9 para.52
s.141, amended: 2013 c.22 Sch.9 para.52
Sch.10 para.1, substituted: SI 2013/1036 Sch.1 para.33
Sch.10 para.2, substituted: SI 2013/1036 Sch.1 para.33
Sch.10 para.2A, amended: SI 2013/1036 Sch.1 para.33
Sch.10 para.3, amended: SI 2013/1036 Sch.1 para.33
Sch.10 para.4, amended: SI 2013/1036 Sch.1 para.33
Sch.10 para.5, amended: SI 2013/1036 Sch.1 para.33
Sch.10 para.5A, added: SI 2013/1036 Sch.1 para.33
Sch.10 para.7, amended: SI 2013/1036 Sch.1 para.33
Sch.10 para.7A, amended: SI 2013/1036 Sch.1 para.33
Sch.10 para.7A, applied: 2013 c.25 Sch.5 para.7, Sch.6 para.2
Sch.10 para.8, amended: SI 2013/1036 Sch.1 para.33
Sch.10 para.9, amended: SI 2013/1036 Sch.1 para.33
Sch.11 Part I para.5A, amended: SI 2013/1036 Sch.1 para.34
Sch.11 Part I para.6, amended: SI 2013/1036 Sch.1 para.34
Sch.11 Part I para.6, applied: SI 2013/1169 r.28
Sch.11 Part I para.7, amended: SI 2013/1036 Sch.1 para.34
Sch.11 Part I para.8A, added: SI 2013/1036 Sch.1 para.34
Sch.11 Part I para.9, substituted: SI 2013/1036 Sch.1 para.34
Sch.11 Part I para.9B, amended: SI 2013/1036 Sch.1 para.34

43. Protection from Eviction Act 1977
s.1, applied: SI 2013/435 Sch.1 Part 7
s.8, amended: SI 2013/1036 Sch.1 para.35
s.9, repealed (in part): 2013 c.22 Sch.9 para.122

45. Criminal Law Act 1977
s.1, see *R. v Majeed (Mazhar)* [2012] EWCA Crim 1186, [2013] 1 W.L.R. 1041 (CA (Crim Div)), Lord Judge, L.C.J.
s.1, applied: SI 2013/435 Sch.1 para.3, Sch.2 para.3, SI 2013/1852 Sch.1 para.29
s.10, amended: 2013 c.22 Sch.9 para.28, Sch.9 para.76
s.38A, amended: SI 2013/602 Sch.2 para.14
s.39, applied: SI 2013/1554 r.4_4
s.48, enabling: SI 2013/1554
s.51, see *R. v Walter (Alexander)* [2012] EWCA Crim 3115, [2013] 2 Cr. App. R. (S.) 46 (CA (Crim Div)), Treacy, L.J.
s.51, applied: SI 2013/435 Sch.1 Part 7
s.54, applied: SI 2013/435 Sch.1 Part 7

49. National Health Service Act 1977
Part II, applied: SI 2013/335 Reg.42
s.16A, applied: SI 2013/3029 Sch.9 para.32, SI 2013/3035 Sch.1

1978

19. Oaths Act 1978
s.1, applied: SI 2013/1554 r.37_4
s.3, applied: SI 2013/1554 r.37_4
s.5, applied: SI 2013/1554 r.37_4, r.32_5
s.6, applied: SI 2013/1554 r.37_4

22. Domestic Proceedings and Magistrates Courts Act 1978
s.1, amended: 2013 c.22 Sch.11 para.67
s.6, amended: 2013 c.22 Sch.11 para.68
s.7, amended: 2013 c.22 Sch.11 para.69
s.19, amended: 2013 c.22 Sch.11 para.71

s.19, repealed (in part): 2013 c.22 Sch.11 para.71
s.20, amended: 2013 c.22 Sch.11 para.72, Sch.11 para.73
s.20A, amended: 2013 c.22 Sch.11 para.74
s.20ZA, amended: 2013 c.22 Sch.11 para.73
s.20ZA, repealed (in part): 2013 c.22 Sch.11 para.73
s.22, repealed: 2013 c.22 Sch.11 para.75
s.23, repealed (in part): 2013 c.22 Sch.11 para.76
s.25, amended: 2013 c.22 Sch.11 para.77
s.27, repealed: 2013 c.22 Sch.11 para.78
s.28, amended: 2013 c.22 Sch.11 para.79
s.29, repealed: 2013 c.22 Sch.11 para.80
s.30, amended: 2013 c.22 Sch.11 para.81
s.30, repealed (in part): 2013 c.22 Sch.11 para.81
s.31, repealed: 2013 c.22 Sch.11 para.82
s.32, amended: 2013 c.22 Sch.11 para.83
s.32, repealed (in part): 2013 c.22 Sch.11 para.83
s.35, amended: 2013 c.22 Sch.11 para.84
s.35, repealed (in part): 2013 c.22 Sch.11 para.84
s.88, amended: 2013 c.22 Sch.11 para.85
Sch.2 para.9, repealed: 2013 c.22 Sch.11 para.210

23. Judicature (Northern Ireland) Act 1978

s.25A, amended: 2013 c.22 s.22
s.56, disapplied: 2013 c.18 Sch.3 para.3
s.62, amended: 2013 c.18 Sch.2 para.7

25. Nuclear Safeguards and Electricity (Finance) Act 1978

s.2, amended: 2013 c.32 Sch.12 para.40
s.3, amended: 2013 c.32 Sch.12 para.41
s.3, applied: 2013 c.32 s.81

29. National Health Service (Scotland) Act 1978

applied: SI 2013/335 Reg.43, SI 2013/377 Reg.29
Part II, applied: SSI 2013/50 Sch.1 para.25
s.2, applied: 2013 asp 11 Sch.15 para.5, Sch.16 para.4
s.2, enabling: SSI 2013/334, SSI 2013/347, SSI 2013/355
s.2C, applied: SSI 2013/174 Reg.7
s.2CA, substituted: SSI 2013/292 Reg.8
s.10, amended: SSI 2013/220 Art.3
s.10, applied: 2013 asp 11 Sch.15 para.5, Sch.16 para.4, SSI 2013/174 Reg.5
s.10A, applied: 2013 asp 11 Sch.15 para.5, Sch.16 para.4
s.15, amended: SSI 2013/220 Art.4
s.17D, varied: SI 2013/160 Art.3
s.26, enabling: SSI 2013/355
s.46, applied: SI 2013/380 Reg.61, SI 2013/3029 Sch.1 para.19, Sch.1 para.20, Sch.6 para.21, Sch.7 para.10, SI 2013/3035 Sch.1
s.69, enabling: SSI 2013/191
s.70, enabling: SSI 2013/96
s.73, applied: SSI 2013/174 Reg.7
s.73, enabling: SSI 2013/96
s.74, enabling: SSI 2013/96
s.75A, amended: SSI 2013/177 Sch.1 para.2
s.75A, enabling: SSI 2013/327
s.75B, amended: SSI 2013/177 Sch.1 para.2, SSI 2013/292 Reg.8
s.75BA, added: SSI 2013/292 Reg.8
s.75BB, added: SSI 2013/292 Reg.8
s.98, applied: SSI 2013/292 Reg.10, Reg.11
s.105, enabling: SSI 2013/96, SSI 2013/191, SSI 2013/327, SSI 2013/334, SSI 2013/347, SSI 2013/355
s.106, enabling: SSI 2013/355
s.108, amended: SSI 2013/177 Sch.1 para.2
s.108, enabling: SSI 2013/96, SSI 2013/191, SSI 2013/327, SSI 2013/355
Sch.1 Part I para.2, enabling: SSI 2013/334
Sch.1 Part II para.10A, enabling: SSI 2013/334
Sch.1 Part II para.11, enabling: SSI 2013/334
Sch.11 para.2, enabling: SSI 2013/96
Sch.11 para.2A, enabling: SSI 2013/96

30. Interpretation Act 1978

applied: 2013 c.24 s.97
s.7, see *Freetown Ltd v Assethold Ltd* [2012] EWCA Civ 1657, [2013] 1 W.L.R. 701 (CA (Civ Div)), Sir Andrew Morritt (Chancellor); see *Freetown Ltd v Assethold Ltd* [2012] EWHC 1351 (QB), [2013] 1 W.L.R. 385 (QBD), Slade, J.; see *Syed (Curtailment of Leave: Notice), Re* [2013] UKUT 144 (IAC), [2013] Imm. A.R. 685 (UT (IAC)), Judge Spencer
s.7, applied: 2013 c.32 s.109, SI 2013/198 Art.19, SI 2013/233 Reg.16, SI 2013/359 Sch.1 para.17, SI 2013/533 Art.16, SI 2013/586 Art.17, SI 2013/648 Art.44, SI 2013/675 Art.41, SI 2013/767 Art.18, SI 2013/1662 Reg.27, SI 2013/1783 Reg.6, Sch.1 para.17, SI 2013/1933 Art.49, SI 2013/1967 Art.45, SI 2013/2808 Art.36, SI 2013/2809 Art.34, SI 2013/3113 Reg.4, SI 2013/3200 Art.33, SI 2013/3244 Art.65, SSI 2013/68 Reg.16, SSI 2013/95 Reg.16, SSI 2013/312 Reg.16
s.14A, added: 2013 c.24 s.59
s.14A, enabling: SI 2013/1753, SI 2013/2100
s.21, applied: SI 2013/359 Sch.1 para.19
Sch.1, added: SI 2013/602 Sch.2 para.15
Sch.1, amended: 2013 c.22 Sch.9 para.94, SI 2013/602 Sch.2 para.15
Sch.1, applied: SI 2013/1554 r.10_1
Sch.1, repealed (in part): SI 2013/602 Sch.2 para.15
Sch.2 Part I para.1, amended: 2013 c.24 s.59
Sch.2 Part II para.6, amended: SI 2013/602 Sch.2 para.15

34. Industrial and Provident Societies Act 1978

applied: SI 2013/496 Sch.1 para.5

36. House of Commons (Administration) Act 1978

s.2, amended: 2013 c.25 Sch.8 para.13

37. Protection of Children Act 1978

s.1, applied: SI 2013/435 Sch.1 Part 7

47. Civil Liability (Contribution) Act 1978

s.1, see *Hughes v Williams (Deceased)* [2012] EWHC 1078 (QB), [2013] R.T.R. 3 (QBD (Liverpool)), Blair, J.

s.1, applied: 2013 c.22 s.38

1979

2. Customs and Excise Management Act 1979

applied: 2013 c.32 Sch.6 para.6, SI 2013/1387 Reg.17, SI 2013/1964 Art.9, SI 2013/2012 Art.17

s.1, amended: 2013 c.29 s.225

s.13, applied: SI 2013/435 Sch.1 Part 7

s.16, applied: SI 2013/435 Sch.1 Part 7

s.50, applied: SI 2013/435 Sch.1 Part 7, SI 2013/1852 Sch.1 para.18

s.50, varied: SI 2013/2012 Art.17, SI 2013/3182 Art.12

s.68, applied: 2013 c.22 Sch.17 para.18, SI 2013/1852 Sch.1 para.19

s.68, varied: SI 2013/1964 Art.8, SI 2013/2012 Art.17, SI 2013/3182 Art.12

s.68A, applied: SI 2013/435 Sch.1 Part 7

s.77A, applied: SI 2013/2012 Art.18, SI 2013/3182 Art.13

s.77A, referred to: SI 2013/2012 Art.18, SI 2013/3182 Art.13

s.77A, varied: SI 2013/1964 Art.9

s.85, applied: SI 2013/435 Sch.1 Part 7

s.86, applied: SI 2013/435 Sch.1 Part 7

s.93, enabling: SI 2013/1229, SI 2013/3210

s.100G, enabling: SI 2013/3210

s.100H, enabling: SI 2013/3210

s.138, applied: SI 2013/1964 Art.9, SI 2013/2012 Art.18, SI 2013/3182 Art.13

s.139, amended: 2013 c.29 s.226

s.143, amended: 2013 c.29 s.227

s.145, applied: SI 2013/1964 Art.9, SI 2013/2012 Art.18, SI 2013/3182 Art.13

s.145, disapplied: 2013 c.7 Sch.2 para.1, Sch.2 para.2

s.146, applied: SI 2013/1964 Art.9, SI 2013/2012 Art.18, SI 2013/3182 Art.13

s.146A, applied: SI 2013/1964 Art.9, SI 2013/2012 Art.18, SI 2013/3182 Art.13

s.146A, disapplied: 2013 c.7 Sch.2 para.1, Sch.2 para.2

s.147, applied: SI 2013/1554 r.63_1, SI 2013/1964 Art.9, SI 2013/2012 Art.18, SI 2013/3182 Art.13

s.148, applied: SI 2013/1964 Art.9, SI 2013/2012 Art.18, SI 2013/3182 Art.13

s.150, applied: SI 2013/1964 Art.9, SI 2013/2012 Art.18, SI 2013/3182 Art.13

s.151, applied: SI 2013/1964 Art.9, SI 2013/2012 Art.18, SI 2013/3182 Art.13

s.152, applied: SI 2013/1964 Art.9, SI 2013/2012 Art.18, SI 2013/3182 Art.13

s.154, applied: SI 2013/1964 Art.9, SI 2013/2012 Art.18, SI 2013/3182 Art.13

s.155, applied: SI 2013/1964 Art.9, SI 2013/2012 Art.18, SI 2013/3182 Art.13

s.167, applied: 2013 c.22 Sch.17 para.18

s.168, applied: SI 2013/435 Sch.1 Part 7

s.170, see *R. v Varma (Aloke)* [2013] 1 A.C. 463 (SC), Lord Phillips, J.S.C. (President)

s.170, applied: 2013 c.22 Sch.17 para.18, SI 2013/435 Sch.1 Part 7, SI 2013/1852 Sch.1 para.20, SI 2013/2258 Sch.1 Part 1

s.170, varied: SI 2013/1964 Art.8, SI 2013/2012 Art.17, SI 2013/3182 Art.12

s.170B, applied: SI 2013/2258 Sch.1 Part 1

Sch.2A para.1, added: 2013 c.29 s.226

Sch.2A para.2, added: 2013 c.29 s.226

Sch.2A para.3, added: 2013 c.29 s.226

Sch.2A para.4, added: 2013 c.29 s.226

Sch.2A para.5, added: 2013 c.29 s.226

Sch.4 para.12, amended: 2013 c.24 Sch.21 para.2

3. Customs and Excise Duties (General Reliefs) Act 1979

applied: SI 2013/1964 Art.9

4. Alcoholic Liquor Duties Act 1979

applied: SI 2013/1964 Art.9

s.2, enabling: SI 2013/1229

s.5, amended: 2013 c.29 s.180

s.19, enabling: SI 2013/1229

s.36, amended: 2013 c.29 s.180

s.37, amended: 2013 c.29 s.180

s.62, amended: 2013 c.29 s.180

s.77, enabling: SI 2013/1195

Sch.1, amended: 2013 c.29 s.180

5. Hydrocarbon Oil Duties Act 1979

applied: SI 2013/1964 Art.9

s.2A, applied: SI 2013/2799

s.6, amended: 2013 c.29 s.179

s.8, amended: 2013 c.29 s.179

s.11, amended: 2013 c.29 s.179

s.14, amended: 2013 c.29 s.179

s.14A, amended: 2013 c.29 s.179

s.20AA, enabling: SI 2013/657

s.27, applied: SI 2013/2799

s.27, enabling: SI 2013/2799

Sch.1 para.2, amended: SI 2013/2799 Art.3
Sch.1 para.3, amended: SI 2013/2799 Art.4
Sch.1 para.3A, amended: SI 2013/2799 Art.5

10. Public Lending Right Act 1979

s.1, amended: SI 2013/2352 Sch.1 para.7
s.2, amended: SI 2013/2352 Sch.1 para.8
s.2, applied: SI 2013/2352 Art.6
s.2, repealed (in part): SI 2013/2352 Sch.1 para.8
s.3, amended: SI 2013/2352 Sch.1 para.9
s.3, applied: SI 2013/2352 Art.5
s.3, repealed (in part): SI 2013/2352 Sch.1 para.9
s.4, amended: SI 2013/2352 Sch.1 para.10
s.5, amended: SI 2013/2352 Sch.1 para.11
Sch.1 para.1, repealed: SI 2013/2352 Sch.1 para.12
Sch.1 para.1, substituted: SI 2013/2352 Sch.1 para.12
Sch.1 para.2, repealed: SI 2013/2352 Sch.1 para.12
Sch.1 para.2, substituted: SI 2013/2352 Sch.1 para.12
Sch.1 para.3, repealed: SI 2013/2352 Sch.1 para.12
Sch.1 para.3, substituted: SI 2013/2352 Sch.1 para.12
Sch.1 para.4, repealed: SI 2013/2352 Sch.1 para.12
Sch.1 para.4, substituted: SI 2013/2352 Sch.1 para.12
Sch.1 para.5, repealed: SI 2013/2352 Sch.1 para.12
Sch.1 para.5, substituted: SI 2013/2352 Sch.1 para.12
Sch.1 para.6, substituted: SI 2013/2352 Sch.1 para.12
Sch.1 para.7, repealed: SI 2013/2352 Sch.1 para.12
Sch.1 para.7, substituted: SI 2013/2352 Sch.1 para.12
Sch.1 para.8, amended: SI 2013/2352 Sch.1 para.12
Sch.1 para.8, substituted: SI 2013/2352 Sch.1 para.12

21. Forestry Act 1979

s.1, amended: SI 2013/755 Sch.2 para.156
s.2, amended: SI 2013/755 Sch.2 para.157

33. Land Registration (Scotland) Act 1979

s.16, varied: 2013 c.33 Sch.7 para.6

34. Credit Unions Act 1979

applied: SI 2013/386 Reg.12
amended: SI 2013/496 Sch.6 para.10
s.1, amended: SI 2013/496 Sch.6 para.2
s.1A, amended: SI 2013/496 Sch.6 para.3
s.1B, amended: SI 2013/496 Sch.6 para.4
s.3, amended: SI 2013/496 Sch.6 para.5
s.4, amended: SI 2013/496 Sch.6 para.6
s.5A, amended: SI 2013/496 Sch.6 para.7
s.7A, amended: SI 2013/496 Sch.6 para.8
s.11, applied: SI 2013/2589 Art.2
s.11, enabling: SI 2013/2589
s.16, amended: SI 2013/496 Sch.6 para.9
s.17, amended: SI 2013/496 Sch.6 para.11
s.18, amended: SI 2013/496 Sch.6 para.12
s.20, amended: SI 2013/496 Sch.6 para.13
s.21, amended: SI 2013/496 Sch.6 para.14
s.23, amended: SI 2013/496 Sch.6 para.15
s.31, amended: SI 2013/496 Sch.6 para.16
s.31A, amended: SI 2013/496 Sch.6 para.17
s.32, amended: SI 2013/496 Sch.6 para.18
Sch.1 para.7, amended: SI 2013/496 Sch.6 para.19
Sch.1 para.11, amended: SI 2013/496 Sch.6 para.19

38. Estate Agents Act 1979

s.1, amended: 2013 c.24 s.70
s.11A, amended: 2013 c.22 Sch.9 para.82
Sch.4 para.6, amended: 2013 c.22 Sch.9 para.82

41. Pneumoconiosis etc (Workers Compensation) Act 1979

s.1, enabling: SI 2013/690
s.7, applied: SI 2013/690
s.7, enabling: SI 2013/690

46. Ancient Monuments and Archaeological Areas Act 1979

applied: SI 2013/198 Art.6, SI 2013/1933 Art.15, SI 2013/1967 Art.14, SI 2013/2587 Art.23, SI 2013/3244 Art.20
s.1, applied: SI 2013/2727 Art.2

50. European Parliament (Pay and Pensions) Act 1979

s.1, applied: SI 2013/481 Art.6
s.4, amended: 2013 c.25 s.35
s.4, enabling: SI 2013/481

53. Charging Orders Act 1979

s.1, amended: 2013 c.22 Sch.9 para.52, Sch.10 para.38
s.1, applied: SI 2013/611 Reg.11
s.3, amended: 2013 c.22 Sch.9 para.52, Sch.10 para.38
s.3A, applied: SI 2013/491
s.3A, enabling: SI 2013/491
s.6, amended: 2013 c.22 Sch.9 para.52, Sch.10 para.38

1980

21. Competition Act 1980

s.11, amended: 2013 c.24 Sch.6 para.2
s.11A, amended: 2013 c.24 Sch.6 para.3
s.11C, amended: 2013 c.24 Sch.6 para.4
s.12, amended: 2013 c.24 Sch.6 para.5
s.16, amended: 2013 c.24 Sch.6 para.6
s.17, amended: 2013 c.24 Sch.6 para.7
s.33, amended: 2013 c.24 Sch.6 para.8

23. Consular Fees Act 1980

s.1, enabling: SI 2013/535, SI 2013/762, SI 2013/1720

26. British Aerospace Act 1980

s.10, repealed: SI 2013/687 Sch.1 para.4

27. Import of Live Fish (England and Wales) Act 1980

s.1, amended: SI 2013/755 Sch.2 para.158

43. Magistrates Courts Act 1980

applied: 2013 c.10 Sch.1 para.9, Sch.2 para.4, Sch.2 para.7, SI 2013/233 Reg.9, Reg.12, SI 2013/2033 Reg.39, Reg.41, SI 2013/2210 Reg.8, SI 2013/2996 Reg.22

s.1, applied: SI 2013/1554 r.7_1, r.2_4, r.37_8, r.18_2

s.2, applied: SI 2013/1554 r.37_1

s.6, applied: SI 2013/1554 r.14_1

s.8A, applied: SI 2013/1554 r.33_6, r.36_2

s.8B, applied: SI 2013/1554 r.34_3, r.35_3, r.35_4

s.8C, applied: SI 2013/1554 r.16_1

s.10, applied: SI 2013/1554 r.37_1

s.11, applied: SI 2013/1554 r.37_10, r.37_11

s.12, applied: SI 2013/1554 r.37_8

s.12A, applied: SI 2013/1554 r.37_8

s.13, applied: SI 2013/1554 r.37_11

s.14, applied: SI 2013/1554 r.37_1, r.37_11

s.17A, see *R. (on the application of Rahmdezfouli) v Wood Green Crown Court* [2013] EWHC 2998 (Admin), (2013) 177 J.P. 677 (DC), Moses, L.J.

s.17A, applied: SI 2013/1554 r.9_1

s.17B, applied: SI 2013/1554 r.9_1

s.17C, applied: SI 2013/1554 r.9_1

s.17D, applied: SI 2013/1554 r.9_1

s.17E, applied: SI 2013/1554 r.9_1

s.18, applied: SI 2013/1554 r.9_1

s.19, applied: SI 2013/1554 r.9_1

s.19, referred to: SI 2013/1554 r.9_10

s.20, applied: SI 2013/1554 r.9_1

s.20A, applied: SI 2013/1554 r.9_1

s.21, applied: SI 2013/1554 r.9_1

s.22, applied: SI 2013/1554 r.9_1, r.9_8, r.9_10

s.23, applied: SI 2013/1554 r.5_4, r.9_1

s.24, see *R. (on the application of W) v Caernarfon Youth Court* [2013] EWHC 1466 (Admin), (2013) 177 J.P. 534 (QBD (Admin)), Pitchford, L.J.

s.24, applied: SI 2013/1554 r.9_1

s.24A, applied: SI 2013/1554 r.9_1

s.24B, applied: SI 2013/1554 r.9_1

s.24C, applied: SI 2013/1554 r.9_1

s.24D, applied: SI 2013/1554 r.9_1

s.25, applied: SI 2013/1554 r.9_1

s.26, applied: SI 2013/1554 r.9_1

s.27, see *R. v J* [2013] EWCA Crim 569, [2013] 2 Cr. App. R. 10 (CA (Crim Div)), Sir John Thomas (President QBD)

s.27, applied: SI 2013/1554 r.37_11

s.27A, applied: SI 2013/1554 r.37_1

s.43B, applied: SI 2013/1554 r.19_6

s.46, applied: SI 2013/1554 r.2_4, SI 2013/1635 Reg.23

s.51, applied: SI 2013/1554 r.62_16

s.53, repealed (in part): 2013 c.22 Sch.10 para.99

s.54, applied: SI 2013/1554 r.62_16

s.54, repealed (in part): 2013 c.22 Sch.10 para.99

s.55, applied: SI 2013/1554 r.62_16

s.56, amended: 2013 c.22 Sch.10 para.99

s.57, amended: 2013 c.22 Sch.10 para.99

s.57A, repealed (in part): 2013 c.22 Sch.10 para.99

s.58, applied: SI 2013/483 Reg.46, SI 2013/1686 Reg.28

s.58, repealed (in part): 2013 c.22 Sch.10 para.40

s.59, amended: 2013 c.22 Sch.10 para.41

s.59, repealed (in part): 2013 c.22 Sch.10 para.41

s.59A, amended: 2013 c.22 Sch.10 para.42

s.59A, repealed (in part): 2013 c.22 Sch.10 para.42

s.59B, repealed: 2013 c.22 Sch.10 para.43

s.60, repealed (in part): 2013 c.22 Sch.10 para.44

s.61, amended: 2013 c.22 Sch.10 para.45

s.62, amended: 2013 c.22 Sch.10 para.46

s.62, repealed (in part): 2013 c.22 Sch.10 para.46

s.64, see *Chief Constable of Sussex v Taylor* [2013] EWHC 1616 (Admin), [2013] 5 Costs L.O. 692 (QBD (Admin)), Pitchford, L.J.; see *Patel v Camden LBC* [2013] EWHC 2459 (Admin), [2013] R.A. 439 (QBD (Admin)), Silber, J.

s.64, amended: 2013 c.22 Sch.10 para.47, Sch.10 para.99

s.64, repealed (in part): 2013 c.22 Sch.10 para.47, Sch.10 para.99

s.65, repealed: 2013 c.22 Sch.10 para.48

s.65A, repealed: 2013 c.22 Sch.10 para.48

s.66, repealed: 2013 c.22 Sch.10 para.48

s.67, repealed: 2013 c.22 Sch.10 para.48

s.68A, repealed: 2013 c.22 Sch.10 para.48

s.69, repealed: 2013 c.22 Sch.10 para.48

s.70, repealed: 2013 c.22 Sch.10 para.48

s.71, repealed: 2013 c.22 Sch.10 para.48

s.73, repealed: 2013 c.22 Sch.10 para.48

s.74, repealed: 2013 c.22 Sch.10 para.48

s.75, applied: SI 2013/1554 r.76_2

s.75, repealed (in part): 2013 c.22 Sch.10 para.48

s.75A, added: 2013 c.22 s.26

s.76, applied: SI 2013/1554 r.18_4, r.18_6, SI 2013/1894 Reg.29

s.76, repealed (in part): 2013 c.22 Sch.10 para.49

s.77, applied: SI 2013/1554 r.4_7

s.80, amended: 2013 c.22 Sch.10 para.49
s.80, applied: SI 2013/1554 r.18_4
s.82, see *R. (on the application of Lawson) v Westminster Magistrates' Court* [2013] EWHC 2434 (Admin), (2013) 177 J.P. 577 (DC), Treacy, L.J.
s.82, applied: SI 2013/1554 r.18_4
s.83, see *R. (on the application of Lawson) v Westminster Magistrates' Court* [2013] EWHC 2434 (Admin), (2013) 177 J.P. 577 (DC), Treacy, L.J.
s.83, applied: SI 2013/1554 r.18_6
s.84, see *R. (on the application of Lawson) v Westminster Magistrates' Court* [2013] EWHC 2434 (Admin), (2013) 177 J.P. 577 (DC), Treacy, L.J.
s.84, amended: 2013 c.22 Sch.16 para.25
s.85, amended: 2013 c.22 s.26
s.86, applied: SI 2013/1554 r.4_7, r.18_6
s.87, amended: 2013 c.22 Sch.9 para.52
s.89, amended: SI 2013/630 Reg.4
s.90, amended: SI 2013/630 Reg.4
s.90, applied: SSI 2013/189 Art.11
s.92, repealed (in part): 2013 c.22 Sch.10 para.49
s.93, repealed: 2013 c.22 Sch.10 para.49
s.94, repealed: 2013 c.22 Sch.10 para.49
s.94A, repealed: 2013 c.22 Sch.10 para.49
s.95, repealed: 2013 c.22 Sch.10 para.49
s.97, amended: 2013 c.22 Sch.10 para.99
s.97, applied: SI 2013/1554 Part 28, r.28_1, r.18_2, r.62_4, r.28_3, r.62_5, r.62_16
s.100, repealed (in part): 2013 c.22 Sch.10 para.49
s.106, applied: SI 2013/435 Sch.1 Part 7
s.108, applied: SI 2013/1554 r.76_6, r.63_1
s.109, applied: SI 2013/1554 r.76_1
s.111, applied: 2013 c.10 Sch.1 para.9, SI 2013/1387 Reg.8, Reg.19, Sch.2 para.9, SI 2013/1478 Reg.20, SI 2013/1554 r.64_1, r.64_2, r.64_3
s.111, repealed (in part): 2013 c.22 Sch.10 para.99
s.111A, amended: 2013 c.22 Sch.9 para.52, Sch.10 para.50
s.111A, repealed (in part): 2013 c.22 Sch.10 para.50
s.112, amended: 2013 c.22 Sch.10 para.51
s.119, applied: SI 2013/1554 r.41_5
s.121, applied: SI 2013/1554 r.37_1, r.62_16, r.64_3
s.121, repealed (in part): 2013 c.22 Sch.10 para.99
s.123, applied: SI 2013/1554 r.18_4, r.62_16
s.125, applied: SI 2013/1554 r.52_8, r.18_5
s.125A, applied: SI 2013/1554 r.52_8, r.18_5
s.125B, applied: SI 2013/1554 r.52_8, r.18_5
s.125D, applied: SI 2013/1554 r.52_8
s.127, applied: SI 2013/1554 r.7_2
s.127, disapplied: SI 2013/233 Reg.13, SI 2013/1554 r.62_16
s.128, applied: SI 2013/1554 r.5_4, r.18_3
s.136, applied: SI 2013/1554 r.18_3, r.18_6
s.139, amended: 2013 c.22 s.26
s.139A, added: 2013 c.22 s.26
s.142, see *DPP v Chajed* [2013] EWHC 188 (Admin), [2013] 2 Cr. App. R. 6 (DC), Laws, L.J.; see *R. (on the application of Klimeto) v Westminster Magistrates' Court* [2012] EWHC 2051 (Admin), [2013] 1 W.L.R. 420 (DC), Hughes, L.J.
s.142, applied: SI 2013/1554 r.42_4
s.144, amended: 2013 c.22 Sch.10 para.52
s.144, repealed (in part): 2013 c.22 Sch.10 para.99
s.145, repealed (in part): 2013 c.22 Sch.10 para.99
s.148, applied: SI 2013/1554 r.37_1
s.150, see *R. (on the application of Klimeto) v Westminster Magistrates' Court* [2012] EWHC 2051 (Admin), [2013] 1 W.L.R. 420 (DC), Hughes, L.J.
s.150, amended: 2013 c.22 Sch.10 para.99
s.150, applied: SI 2013/1554 r.37_1, r.32_9
Sch.3, applied: 2013 c.15 s.11, SI 2013/233 Reg.6, SI 2013/1389 Reg.50, SI 2013/1554 r.2_4, SI 2013/1635 Reg.23, SI 2013/1662 Reg.37
Sch.3 para.1, varied: SI 2013/2952 Reg.19
Sch.3 para.2, varied: SI 2013/2952 Reg.19
Sch.3 para.3, varied: SI 2013/2952 Reg.19
Sch.3 para.4, varied: SI 2013/2952 Reg.19
Sch.3 para.5, varied: SI 2013/2952 Reg.19
Sch.3 para.6, varied: SI 2013/2952 Reg.19
Sch.3 para.7, varied: SI 2013/2952 Reg.19
Sch.3 para.8, varied: SI 2013/2952 Reg.19
Sch.7 para.23, repealed: 2013 c.22 Sch.10 para.99
Sch.7 para.24, repealed: 2013 c.22 Sch.10 para.99
Sch.7 para.105, repealed: 2013 c.22 Sch.11 para.210
Sch.7 para.109, repealed: 2013 c.22 Sch.11 para.210
Sch.7 para.163, repealed: 2013 c.22 Sch.11 para.210
Sch.7 para.164, repealed: 2013 c.22 Sch.11 para.210

44. Education (Scotland) Act 1980

s.2, enabling: SSI 2013/175
s.14, applied: SSI 2013/194 r.82
s.36, amended: SSI 2013/211 Sch.1 para.4
s.44, amended: SSI 2013/211 Sch.1 para.4
s.49, applied: SI 2013/3029 Sch.4 para.18, Sch.4 para.19, Sch.9 para.16, Sch.9 para.23, Sch.9 para.24, Sch.10 para.53, SI 2013/3035 Sch.1
s.49, disapplied: SI 2013/377 Reg.28

s.49, enabling: SSI 2013/80
s.53, enabling: SSI 2013/64
s.56A, enabling: SSI 2013/305
s.56B, enabling: SSI 2013/305
s.56D, enabling: SSI 2013/305
s.66, applied: SSI 2013/50 Sch.4 para.18
s.73, applied: SI 2013/3029 Sch.4 para.18, Sch.4 para.19, Sch.9 para.16, Sch.9 para.23, Sch.9 para.24, Sch.10 para.53, Sch.11 para.10, SI 2013/3035 Sch.1
s.73, disapplied: SI 2013/377 Reg.28
s.73, enabling: SSI 2013/80
s.73A, amended: 2013 asp 12 Sch.1 para.1
s.73B, enabling: SSI 2013/80
s.73ZA, amended: 2013 asp 12 Sch.1 para.1
s.73ZA, applied: SI 2013/3029 Sch.9 para.16, Sch.10 para.53, SI 2013/3035 Sch.1
s.74, enabling: SSI 2013/80
s.102, applied: SSI 2013/50 Sch.1 para.7
s.131, amended: SSI 2013/211 Sch.1 para.4
s.135, amended: SSI 2013/211 Sch.2
s.135, applied: 2013 asp 11 Sch.2 para.17, SSI 2013/50 Sch.1 para.7

48. Finance Act 1980

Sch.17 Part III para.15, applied: 2013 c.29 s.84
Sch.17 Part III para.15, disapplied: 2013 c.29 s.84

51. Housing Act 1980

s.72, repealed: SI 2013/1036 Sch.1 para.37
s.86, amended: 2013 c.22 Sch.9 para.52
s.142, repealed (in part): SI 2013/1036 Sch.1 para.38

55. Law Reform (Miscellaneous Provisions) (Scotland) Act 1980

Sch.1 Part I, substituted: 2013 c.22 Sch.8 para.27

58. Limitation Act 1980

s.4A, applied: 2013 c.26 s.8
s.4A, referred to: 2013 c.26 s.8
s.9, see *Arca v Carlisle City Council* [2013] R.A. 248 (VT), Graham Zellick Q.C. (President); see *Smith v Nottingham City Council* [2013] R.A. 404 (VT), Graham Zellick Q.C. (President)
s.9, applied: 2013 c.15 s.2, s.3
s.27A, amended: 2013 c.22 Sch.8 para.28
s.27AB, added: SI 2013/2604 Art.4
s.27B, amended: 2013 c.22 Sch.8 para.28, SI 2013/2604 Art.4
s.32A, applied: 2013 c.26 s.8
s.35, see *Co-operative Group Ltd v Birse Developments Ltd* [2013] EWCA Civ 474, [2013] B.L.R. 383 (CA (Civ Div)), Longmore, L.J.; see *Insight Group Ltd v Kingston Smith (A Firm)* [2012] EWHC 3644 (QB), [2013] 3 All E.R. 518 (QBD), Leggatt, J.
s.35, amended: 2013 c.22 Sch.9 para.102

63. Overseas Development and Co-operation Act 1980

s.10, applied: SSI 2013/35 Reg.32
s.12, applied: SSI 2013/35 Reg.32

65. Local Government, Planning and Land Act 1980

s.2, repealed (in part): SSI 2013/119 Sch.1 para.7
s.166, applied: SI 2013/110
s.166, enabling: SI 2013/110
s.170, repealed (in part): SI 2013/687 Sch.1 para.5
s.185, amended: SI 2013/755 Sch.2 para.159
Sch.16 para.12, repealed: SI 2013/687 Sch.1 para.5

66. Highways Act 1980

see *Kind v Northumberland CC* [2012] EWHC 603 (Admin), [2013] 1 W.L.R. 743 (DC), Moore-Bick, L.J.
applied: SI 2013/198 Sch.3 para.1, SI 2013/680 Art.28, SI 2013/805 Sch.1, SI 2013/806 Sch.1, SI 2013/807 Sch.1, SI 2013/808 Sch.1, SI 2013/809 Sch.1, SI 2013/810 Sch.1, SI 2013/811 Sch.1, SI 2013/812 Sch.1, SI 2013/813 Sch.1, SI 2013/814 Sch.1, SI 2013/1873 Art.24, SI 2013/1933 Sch.12 para.3, SI 2013/3244 Sch.9 para.3
Part V, applied: SI 2013/805 Sch.1, SI 2013/806 Sch.1, SI 2013/807 Sch.1, SI 2013/808 Sch.1, SI 2013/809 Sch.1, SI 2013/810 Sch.1, SI 2013/811 Sch.1, SI 2013/812 Sch.1, SI 2013/813 Sch.1, SI 2013/814 Sch.1
s.10, enabling: SI 2013/189, SI 2013/348, SI 2013/764, SI 2013/1930, SI 2013/1960, SI 2013/2061, SI 2013/2172, SI 2013/2824
s.12, applied: SI 2013/675 Art.11, SI 2013/2808 Art.10
s.12, enabling: SI 2013/189, SI 2013/764, SI 2013/1930, SI 2013/2824
s.16, enabling: SI 2013/2060, SI 2013/2062, SI 2013/2173, SI 2013/2825
s.17, enabling: SI 2013/2060, SI 2013/2062, SI 2013/2173, SI 2013/2825
s.18, enabling: SI 2013/2173
s.19, enabling: SI 2013/2060, SI 2013/2062, SI 2013/2825
s.31, amended: 2013 c.27 s.13
s.31, applied: SI 2013/1774 Reg.2
s.31, enabling: SI 2013/1774
s.31A, applied: SI 2013/1774 Reg.5
s.31A, enabling: SI 2013/1774
s.41, see *Vernon Knight Associates v Cornwall Council* [2013] EWCA Civ 950, [2013] B.L.R. 519 (CA (Civ Div)), Lord Dyson (M.R.)
s.41, enabling: SI 2013/348, SI 2013/1960, SI 2013/2061, SI 2013/2172
s.58, applied: SI 2013/2808 Art.9
s.59, repealed (in part): 2013 c.22 Sch.9 para.87

s.64, applied: SI 2013/648 Art.9, SI 2013/1933 Art.3, SI 2013/2587 Art.4, SI 2013/2808 Art.8, SI 2013/3244 Art.4
s.79, amended: 2013 c.22 Sch.9 para.52
s.95A, amended: 2013 c.7 s.16
s.105B, amended: SI 2013/755 Sch.2 para.161
s.105B, repealed (in part): SI 2013/755 Sch.2 para.161
s.106, applied: SI 2013/39 Sch.1, SI 2013/50 Sch.1, SI 2013/818 Sch.1, SI 2013/1701 Sch.1
s.106, enabling: SI 2013/39, SI 2013/50, SI 2013/818, SI 2013/1701
s.107, amended: SI 2013/755 Sch.2 para.162
s.115, enabling: SI 2013/1384
s.118B, enabling: SI 2013/1760
s.119D, amended: SI 2013/755 Sch.2 para.163
s.120, amended: SI 2013/755 Sch.2 para.164
s.184, applied: SI 2013/2587 Art.4, SI 2013/2808 Art.8, SI 2013/3244 Art.4
s.254, amended: SI 2013/755 Sch.2 para.165
s.276, amended: SI 2013/755 Sch.2 para.166
s.278, applied: SI 2013/680 Art.18, SI 2013/2398 Sch.1
s.300, enabling: SI 2013/2987
s.308, amended: 2013 c.22 Sch.9 para.52
s.322, applied: SI 2013/1774 Reg.3
s.326, enabling: SI 2013/2173
s.329, amended: SI 2013/755 Sch.2 para.167
s.329, applied: SI 2013/533 Art.4
Sch.1 Part I para.3, amended: SI 2013/755 Sch.2 para.168
Sch.1 Part II para.11, amended: SI 2013/755 Sch.2 para.168
Sch.2 para.1, applied: SI 2013/50 Art.4, SI 2013/818 Art.1, SI 2013/1701 Art.4
Sch.4, referred to: SI 2013/675 Art.11, SI 2013/2060 Art.3, SI 2013/2062 Art.3, SI 2013/2825 Art.3

1981

14. Public Passenger Vehicles Act 1981
applied: SI 2013/1865 Reg.10, Reg.12
s.3, amended: SI 2013/1644 Sch.1
s.4B, applied: SI 2013/1865 Reg.8
s.5, amended: SI 2013/1644 Sch.1
s.5, enabling: SI 2013/2987
s.12, see *Grey (t/a citytax) v Swansea City and County Council* [2013] EWCA Civ 1057, [2013] P.T.S.R. 1366 (CA (Civ Div)), Richards, L.J.
s.12, amended: SI 2013/1644 Sch.1
s.14A, amended: SI 2013/1644 Sch.1
s.15, amended: SI 2013/1644 Sch.1
s.16, amended: SI 2013/1644 Sch.1
s.16, applied: SI 2013/1865 Reg.10
s.16, disapplied: SI 2013/1865 Reg.12
s.16, referred to: SI 2013/1865 Reg.10
s.16, enabling: SI 2013/1865
s.16A, amended: SI 2013/1644 Sch.1
s.17, amended: SI 2013/1644 Sch.1
s.17, applied: SI 2013/1865 Reg.10
s.17, referred to: SI 2013/1865 Reg.10
s.18, see *Grey (t/a citytax) v Swansea City and County Council* [2013] EWCA Civ 1057, [2013] P.T.S.R. 1366 (CA (Civ Div)), Richards, L.J.
s.18, amended: SI 2013/1644 Sch.1
s.19, amended: SI 2013/1644 Sch.1
s.20, amended: SI 2013/1644 Sch.1
s.21, amended: SI 2013/1644 Sch.1
s.25, applied: SI 2013/3244 Art.55
s.29, amended: SI 2013/1865 Reg.13
s.49A, amended: SI 2013/1644 Sch.1
s.50, amended: SI 2013/1644 Sch.1
s.52, amended: SI 2013/1644 Sch.1
s.52, enabling: SI 2013/2987
s.54, amended: SI 2013/1644 Sch.1, SI 2013/1865 Reg.13
s.54, applied: SI 2013/1865 Reg.12
s.54, enabling: SI 2013/1865
s.55, amended: SI 2013/1644 Sch.1
s.55, applied: SI 2013/1644 Art.7
s.56, amended: SI 2013/1644 Sch.1
s.56A, substituted: SI 2013/1644 Sch.1
s.57, amended: SI 2013/1644 Sch.1
s.57, enabling: SI 2013/2987
s.59, enabling: SI 2013/2987
s.60, enabling: SI 2013/1865, SI 2013/2987
s.61, applied: SI 2013/2987
s.65, applied: SI 2013/435 Sch.1 Part 7
s.82, amended: SI 2013/1644 Sch.1, SI 2013/1865 Reg.13
Sch.2A para.9, amended: SI 2013/1644 Sch.1
Sch.2A para.10, amended: SI 2013/1644 Sch.1
Sch.2A para.11, amended: SI 2013/1644 Sch.1
Sch.2A para.13, amended: SI 2013/1644 Sch.1
Sch.3 para.7A, amended: SI 2013/1644 Sch.1
Sch.3 para.7C, amended: SI 2013/1644 Sch.1

18. Disused Burial Grounds (Amendment) Act 1981
disapplied: SI 2013/2587 Art.7
s.8, amended: 2013 c.22 Sch.9 para.80

20. Judicial Pensions Act 1981
applied: 2013 c.25 Sch.5 para.8
s.11, applied: 2013 c.25 Sch.6 para.4
s.12, amended: 2013 c.22 Sch.14 para.13
s.16, amended: 2013 c.25 Sch.11 para.6
s.26, repealed: 2013 c.25 Sch.11 para.6
s.29ZA, added: 2013 c.25 Sch.8 para.14

s.33A, amended: SI 2013/3115 Sch.2 para.33
s.33ZA, enabling: SI 2013/484
Sch.1 Part III, applied: 2013 c.25 Sch.6 para.3
Sch.1 Part III, disapplied: 2013 c.25 Sch.5 para.8

22. Animal Health Act 1981

applied: SI 2013/2996 Reg.16
s.1, enabling: SI 2013/1241, SSI 2013/3, SSI 2013/21, SSI 2013/173, SSI 2013/337, SSI 2013/363
s.8, enabling: SSI 2013/3, SSI 2013/21, SSI 2013/173, SSI 2013/337, SSI 2013/363
s.8A, enabling: SSI 2013/173
s.15, enabling: SSI 2013/173
s.17, enabling: SSI 2013/173
s.21, amended: SI 2013/755 Sch.2 para.180
s.23, enabling: SSI 2013/173
s.35, enabling: SSI 2013/173
s.83, enabling: SSI 2013/3, SSI 2013/21, SSI 2013/173, SSI 2013/337, SSI 2013/363
s.88, varied: SSI 2013/3 Art.4
s.88, enabling: SSI 2013/3

29. Fisheries Act 1981

s.30, amended: 2013 asp 7 s.51
s.30, applied: SSI 2013/189 Art.1
s.30, enabling: SSI 2013/189

35. Finance Act 1981

s.107, amended: SI 2013/602 Sch.2 para.16

42. Indecent Displays (Control) Act 1981

s.1, applied: SI 2013/435 Sch.1 Part 7

45. Forgery and Counterfeiting Act 1981

s.1, applied: 2013 c.22 Sch.17 para.19, SI 2013/435 Sch.1 Part 7
s.2, applied: 2013 c.22 Sch.17 para.19, SI 2013/435 Sch.1 Part 7
s.3, applied: 2013 c.22 Sch.17 para.19, SI 2013/435 Sch.1 Part 7
s.4, applied: 2013 c.22 Sch.17 para.19, SI 2013/435 Sch.1 Part 7
s.5, applied: 2013 c.22 Sch.17 para.19, SI 2013/435 Sch.1 Part 7
s.14, applied: SI 2013/435 Sch.1 Part 7
s.15, applied: SI 2013/435 Sch.1 Part 7
s.16, applied: SI 2013/435 Sch.1 Part 7
s.175, applied: SI 2013/435 Sch.1 Part 7

47. Criminal Attempts Act 1981

s.1, applied: SI 2013/435 Sch.1 para.3, Sch.2 para.3, SI 2013/1852 Sch.1 para.2, Sch.1 para.7, Sch.1 para.13

49. Contempt of Court Act 1981

s.2, applied: SI 2013/1554 r.16_1
s.4, see *MXB v East Sussex Hospitals NHS Trust* [2012] EWHC 3279 (QB), (2013) 177 J.P. 31 (QBD), Tugendhat, J.; see *R. (on the application of Press Association) v Cambridge Crown Court* [2012] EWCA Crim 2434, [2013] 1 W.L.R. 1979 (CA (Crim Div)), Lord Judge, L.C.J.; see *R. v ITN News* [2013] EWCA Crim 773, [2013] 2 Cr. App. R. 22 (CA (Crim Div)), Lord Judge, L.C.J.
s.4, applied: SI 2013/1554 r.69_1, r.37_2, r.16_1
s.8, applied: SI 2013/1554 r.62_5
s.9, amended: 2013 c.22 s.31, s.32
s.9, applied: 2013 c.22 s.32, SI 2013/1554 r.62_5, r.16_1, r.16_10
s.9, disapplied: SI 2013/2786 Art.4
s.11, see *BBC, Applicants* [2013] CSIH 43, 2013 S.C. 533 (IH (1 Div)), The Lord President (Gill); see *BBC, Applicants* 2013 S.L.T. 324 (OH), Lord Glennie; see *C v Kemp* [2013] CSOH 56, 2013 S.L.T. 661 (OH), Lord Brailsford
s.11, applied: SI 2013/1554 r.37_2, r.16_1, r.69_1
s.12, applied: SI 2013/1554 r.16_1, r.62_4, r.62_5, r.63_1
s.14, see *Zuk v Zuk* [2012] EWCA Civ 1871, [2013] 2 F.L.R. 1466 (CA (Civ Div)), Thorpe, L.J.
s.14, amended: 2013 c.22 Sch.9 para.52, Sch.10 para.53
s.14, applied: SI 2013/1554 r.62_5, r.62_9
s.19, amended: SI 2013/294 Sch.1
Sch.1 para.7, amended: 2013 c.22 Sch.17 para.34
Sch.3, applied: SI 2013/1554 r.62_16

59. Matrimonial Homes (Family Protection) (Scotland) Act 1981

s.14, applied: SSI 2013/357 Art.3
s.18A, applied: SSI 2013/357 Art.3

61. British Nationality Act 1981

applied: 2013 c.22 s.55, SSI 2013/35 Reg.32
s.12, applied: SI 2013/617 Sch.4 para.2
s.24, applied: SI 2013/617 Sch.4 para.2
s.29, applied: SI 2013/617 Sch.4 para.2
s.34, applied: SI 2013/617 Sch.4 para.2
s.41, enabling: SI 2013/2541
s.42, applied: SI 2013/617 Sch.4 para.4
s.50, applied: SI 2013/617 Sch.4 para.2, Sch.5 para.2
Sch.3, applied: SI 2013/617 Sch.5 para.2

63. Betting and Gaming Duties Act 1981

s.20A, amended: 2013 c.29 s.184
s.20A, repealed (in part): 2013 c.29 s.184

64. New Towns Act 1981

s.10, applied: SI 2013/1488 Art.8
s.11, applied: SI 2013/1488 Art.8
Sch.4 Part III para.10, applied: SI 2013/1488 Art.8
Sch.4 Part IV para.12, amended: 2013 c.27 s.25
Sch.4 Part V para.16, amended: 2013 c.27 s.25

66. Compulsory Purchase (Vesting Declarations) Act 1981

applied: SI 2013/533 Art.7, SI 2013/648 Art.29, SI 2013/1203 Art.20, SI 2013/1873 Art.18, SI

2013/1933 Art.23, SI 2013/1967 Art.18, Sch.9 para.18, SI 2013/2587 Art.28, SI 2013/3244 Art.35
referred to: SI 2013/1203 Art.20, SI 2013/2809 Art.19
varied: SI 2013/680 Art.21, SI 2013/1203 Art.20, SI 2013/3244 Art.25
s.3, applied: SI 2013/1933 Art.23
s.3, varied: SI 2013/533 Art.7, SI 2013/648 Art.29, SI 2013/675 Art.24, SI 2013/680 Art.21, SI 2013/767 Art.5, SI 2013/1203 Art.20, SI 2013/1873 Art.18, SI 2013/1967 Art.18, SI 2013/2587 Art.28, SI 2013/2808 Art.22, SI 2013/2809 Art.19, SI 2013/3200 Art.21, SI 2013/3244 Art.25
s.4, applied: SI 2013/533 Art.13, SI 2013/648 Art.26, SI 2013/675 Art.21, Art.28, SI 2013/680 Art.19, SI 2013/767 Art.8, Art.15, SI 2013/1203 Art.17, SI 2013/1873 Art.15, SI 2013/1933 Art.27, Art.33, SI 2013/1967 Art.23, Art.29, SI 2013/2587 Art.32, Art.38, SI 2013/2808 Art.19, Art.25, SI 2013/2809 Art.16, Art.23, SI 2013/3200 Art.20, Art.25, SI 2013/3244 Art.28, Art.35
s.5, applied: SI 2013/1933 Art.23
s.5, varied: SI 2013/533 Art.7, SI 2013/648 Art.29, SI 2013/675 Art.24, SI 2013/680 Art.21, SI 2013/767 Art.5, SI 2013/1203 Art.20, SI 2013/1873 Art.18, SI 2013/1967 Art.18, SI 2013/2587 Art.28, SI 2013/2808 Art.22, SI 2013/2809 Art.19, SI 2013/3200 Art.21, SI 2013/3244 Art.25
s.7, applied: SI 2013/1933 Art.23
s.7, varied: SI 2013/533 Art.7, SI 2013/648 Art.29, SI 2013/675 Art.24, SI 2013/680 Art.21, SI 2013/767 Art.5, SI 2013/1203 Art.20, SI 2013/1873 Art.18, SI 2013/1967 Art.18, SI 2013/2587 Art.28, SI 2013/2808 Art.22, SI 2013/2809 Art.19, SI 2013/3200 Art.21, SI 2013/3244 Art.25

67. Acquisition of Land Act 1981
applied: SI 2013/198 Art.11, SI 2013/533 Art.6, SI 2013/1933 Art.22, SI 2013/1967 Art.17, SI 2013/2587 Art.27, SI 2013/3200 Art.20, SI 2013/3244 Art.24
s.2, referred to: SI 2013/1488 Art.8
s.5, amended: 2013 c.27 s.3
s.17, amended: 2013 c.27 s.25
s.17, applied: SI 2013/1488 Art.8
s.18, amended: 2013 c.27 s.25
s.18, applied: SI 2013/1488 Art.8
s.19, applied: SI 2013/1488 Art.8
s.19, varied: SI 2013/3244 Art.34
s.27, amended: 2013 c.27 s.25
Sch.1 para.2, applied: SI 2013/1488 Art.8
Sch.2 Part II para.2, varied: SI 2013/1873 Art.14
Sch.2 Part III para.3, varied: SI 2013/1873 Art.14
Sch.2 Part III para.4, varied: SI 2013/1873 Art.14
Sch.2 Part III para.5, varied: SI 2013/1873 Art.14
Sch.2 Part III para.6, varied: SI 2013/1873 Art.14
Sch.2 Part III para.7, varied: SI 2013/1873 Art.14
Sch.2 Part III para.8, varied: SI 2013/1873 Art.14
Sch.2 Part III para.9, varied: SI 2013/1873 Art.14
Sch.3 Part II para.4, amended: 2013 c.27 s.25
Sch.3 Part II para.4, applied: SI 2013/1488 Art.8
Sch.3 Part II para.5, amended: 2013 c.27 s.25
Sch.3 Part II para.5, applied: SI 2013/1488 Art.8
Sch.3 Part II para.6, applied: SI 2013/1488 Art.8

1982

10. Industrial Training Act 1982
applied: SI 2013/1893 Sch.2
s.11, applied: SI 2013/1397
s.11, referred to: SI 2013/1397
s.11, enabling: SI 2013/1397
s.12, applied: SI 2013/1397, SI 2013/1397 Art.14
s.12, enabling: SI 2013/1397

16. Civil Aviation Act 1982
s.4, disapplied: SI 2013/2620 Reg.3
s.8, applied: SI 2013/2870 Art.7
s.13, applied: SI 2013/2870 Art.12
s.23, amended: 2013 c.32 Sch.12 para.58
s.57, amended: SI 2013/602 Sch.2 para.17
s.60, enabling: SI 2013/2874, SI 2013/3169
s.61, applied: SI 2013/2870
s.61, enabling: SI 2013/2870, SI 2013/2874, SI 2013/3169
s.65, applied: SI 2013/2870 Art.12
s.69A, applied: SI 2013/2870 Art.12
s.75, applied: SI 2013/2870 Art.174
Sch.1 para.15, substituted: 2013 c.24 Sch.15 para.1

27. Civil Jurisdiction and Judgments Act 1982
s.5, amended: 2013 c.22 Sch.11 para.86
s.5, repealed (in part): 2013 c.22 Sch.11 para.86
s.5A, amended: 2013 c.22 Sch.11 para.86
s.5A, repealed (in part): 2013 c.22 Sch.11 para.86
s.6, repealed (in part): 2013 c.22 Sch.11 para.86
s.6A, repealed (in part): 2013 c.22 Sch.11 para.86
s.7, amended: 2013 c.22 Sch.11 para.86
s.12, enabling: SI 2013/3204
s.15, amended: 2013 c.22 Sch.11 para.86
s.18, amended: 2013 c.22 Sch.9 para.52, Sch.9 para.66, Sch.18 para.2, Sch.18 para.3
s.36, amended: 2013 c.22 Sch.11 para.86
s.48, amended: 2013 c.22 Sch.11 para.86
s.48, enabling: SI 2013/3204
s.50, amended: 2013 c.22 Sch.11 para.86

Sch.11 Part I para.2, repealed: 2013 c.22 Sch.10 para.99
Sch.12 Part I para.3, repealed: 2013 c.22 Sch.10 para.99
Sch.12 Part I para.7, repealed: 2013 c.22 Sch.10 para.99

30. Local Government (Miscellaneous Provisions) Act 1982
s.3, applied: SI 2013/394 Art.5
s.33, applied: SI 2013/648 Art.38
Sch.4, applied: SI 2013/394 Art.5

31. Firearms Act 1982
see *R. v Bewley (William)* [2012] EWCA Crim 1457, [2013] 1 W.L.R. 137 (CA (Crim Div)), Moses, L.J.
applied: SI 2013/449 Reg.3

36. Aviation Security Act 1982
Part IIA, amended: 2013 c.22 Sch.8 para.186
s.2, applied: SI 2013/435 Sch.1 Part 7
s.24AE, amended: 2013 c.22 Sch.8 para.186
s.24AI, amended: 2013 c.22 Sch.8 para.186
s.24AT, amended: SI 2013/602 Sch.2 para.18
s.31, amended: SI 2013/602 Sch.2 para.18

43. Local Government and Planning (Scotland) Act 1982
s.14, applied: SSI 2013/278 Sch.1

45. Civic Government (Scotland) Act 1982
s.3A, applied: SSI 2013/22
s.3A, enabling: SSI 2013/22
s.27A, referred to: SSI 2013/22 Art.3
s.27C, enabling: SSI 2013/22

53. Administration of Justice Act 1982
s.38, amended: 2013 c.22 Sch.9 para.52
Sch.3 Part IV para.8, repealed (in part): 2013 c.22 Sch.9 para.87

1983

2. Representation of the People Act 1983
applied: 2013 c.12 Sch.1 para.1
referred to: 2013 c.6 Sch.5 para.30, 2013 c.28 Sch.1
s.4, applied: 2013 asp 13 Sch.1 Part 1
s.4, referred to: SI 2013/794 Art.2
s.5, varied: 2013 asp 13 Sch.1 Part 2
s.6, varied: 2013 asp 13 Sch.1 Part 2
s.7, amended: 2013 c.6 Sch.4 para.2
s.7, applied: 2013 asp 14 Sch.2 para.1, 2013 c.6 Sch.5 para.25
s.7, varied: 2013 asp 13 Sch.1 Part 2
s.7A, amended: 2013 c.6 Sch.4 para.3
s.7A, applied: 2013 asp 14 Sch.2 para.1, 2013 c.6 Sch.5 para.25
s.7A, varied: 2013 asp 13 Sch.1 Part 2
s.7B, applied: 2013 asp 13 s.7
s.7B, varied: 2013 asp 13 Sch.1 Part 2
s.7C, amended: 2013 c.6 Sch.4 para.4
s.7C, varied: 2013 asp 13 Sch.1 Part 2
s.9, amended: 2013 c.6 Sch.4 para.5
s.9, applied: 2013 asp 13 s.2, SI 2013/3199 Reg.2
s.9A, amended: 2013 c.6 Sch.4 para.6
s.9A, varied: 2013 asp 13 Sch.1 Part 2
s.9B, amended: 2013 c.6 Sch.4 para.7
s.9B, applied: 2013 asp 13 s.4
s.9B, varied: 2013 asp 13 Sch.1 Part 2
s.9B, enabling: SI 2013/3198, SI 2013/3206
s.9C, amended: 2013 c.6 Sch.4 para.8
s.9C, varied: 2013 asp 13 Sch.1 Part 2
s.9D, added: 2013 c.6 s.4
s.9D, referred to: 2013 c.6 s.7
s.9E, added: 2013 c.6 s.5
s.9E, applied: 2013 c.6 Sch.5 para.10
s.9E, referred to: 2013 c.6 Sch.5 para.12, Sch.5 para.13
s.9E, enabling: SI 2013/3198, SI 2013/3206
s.10, amended: 2013 c.6 Sch.4 para.9
s.10, applied: 2013 asp 13 s.8, 2013 c.6 Sch.5 para.9, SI 2013/794 Art.2
s.10, disapplied: SI 2013/794 Art.4
s.10, repealed (in part): 2013 c.6 Sch.4 para.9
s.10, varied: 2013 asp 13 Sch.1 Part 2
s.10, enabling: SI 2013/1846
s.10A, amended: 2013 c.6 Sch.4 para.10
s.10A, applied: 2013 c.6 Sch.5 para.5
s.10A, referred to: SI 2013/794 Art.2
s.10A, repealed (in part): 2013 c.6 Sch.4 para.10
s.10A, varied: 2013 asp 13 Sch.1 Part 2, SI 2013/794 Art.2
s.10A, enabling: SI 2013/1846
s.10ZB, repealed (in part): 2013 c.6 s.23
s.10ZC, added: 2013 c.6 s.1
s.10ZC, applied: 2013 c.6 s.1, SI 2013/3206 Reg.14
s.10ZC, referred to: SI 2013/3198 Reg.14
s.10ZC, enabling: SI 2013/3198, SI 2013/3206
s.10ZD, added: 2013 c.6 Sch.1 para.1
s.10ZD, applied: 2013 c.6 Sch.1 para.2
s.10ZD, enabling: SI 2013/3198, SI 2013/3206
s.10ZE, added: 2013 c.6 Sch.1 para.1
s.10ZE, enabling: SI 2013/3198, SI 2013/3206
s.13, amended: 2013 c.6 Sch.4 para.11
s.13, applied: 2013 asp 14 Sch.2 para.13, Sch.2 para.51, 2013 c.6 Sch.5 para.30, SI 2013/794 Art.4, SI 2013/3197 Art.14, Art.24
s.13, disapplied: SI 2013/794 Art.4, SI 2013/3197 Art.14

s.13A, amended: 2013 c.6 s.16, Sch.1 para.3, Sch.4 para.12
s.13A, applied: 2013 asp 14 Sch.2 para.13, Sch.2 para.17, Sch.2 para.48, Sch.2 para.49, Sch.2 para.50, Sch.2 para.51
s.13A, varied: 2013 asp 13 Sch.1 Part 2
s.13AB, added: 2013 c.6 s.16
s.13AB, enabling: SI 2013/3198, SI 2013/3206
s.13B, amended: 2013 c.6 s.16, Sch.4 para.13
s.13B, applied: 2013 asp 14 Sch.2 para.13, Sch.2 para.48, Sch.2 para.49, Sch.2 para.50, Sch.2 para.51, Sch.2 para.56, Sch.3 para.13, Sch.3 para.19, Sch.3 para.21, Sch.3 para.22, Sch.3 para.23, Sch.3 para.24, Sch.3 para.26, Sch.3 para.28, Sch.3 para.36, Sch.3 para.37, Sch.3 para.40
s.13B, varied: 2013 asp 13 Sch.1 Part 2, 2013 asp 14 Sch.2 para.17
s.13BB, applied: 2013 asp 14 Sch.2 para.13, Sch.2 para.48, Sch.2 para.49, Sch.2 para.50, Sch.2 para.51, Sch.2 para.56, Sch.3 para.13, Sch.3 para.19, Sch.3 para.21, Sch.3 para.22, Sch.3 para.23, Sch.3 para.24, Sch.3 para.26, Sch.3 para.28, Sch.3 para.36, Sch.3 para.37, Sch.3 para.40
s.13BB, repealed (in part): 2013 c.6 Sch.4 para.14
s.13BB, varied: 2013 asp 14 Sch.2 para.17, SI 2013/794 Art.4
s.13D, varied: 2013 asp 13 Sch.1 Part 2
s.14, varied: 2013 asp 13 s.7A, Sch.1 Part 2
s.15, amended: 2013 c.6 Sch.4 para.15
s.15, applied: 2013 asp 14 Sch.2 para.8
s.15, varied: 2013 asp 13 s.7A, Sch.1 Part 2
s.16, varied: 2013 asp 13 s.7A, Sch.1 Part 2
s.17, varied: 2013 asp 13 s.7A, Sch.1 Part 2
s.18A, amended: SI 2013/3156 Art.9
s.18AA, added: SI 2013/3156 Art.9
s.18C, amended: 2013 c.6 s.17, SI 2013/3156 Art.9
s.18CA, added: SI 2013/3156 Art.9
s.18E, amended: SI 2013/3156 Art.9
s.18E, repealed (in part): SI 2013/3156 Art.9
s.29, amended: 2013 c.6 s.18
s.29A, added: 2013 c.6 s.18
s.37A, applied: SI 2013/2277
s.37A, enabling: SI 2013/2277
s.40, amended: 2013 c.6 s.15
s.41, applied: 2013 asp 14 s.5
s.49, amended: 2013 c.6 Sch.4 para.16
s.49, repealed (in part): 2013 c.6 Sch.4 para.16
s.52, varied: 2013 asp 13 Sch.1 Part 2
s.53, amended: 2013 c.6 Sch.2 para.5
s.53, applied: 2013 c.6 Sch.5 para.4, SI 2013/760, SI 2013/3197, SI 2013/3198, SI 2013/3206
s.53, enabling: SI 2013/760, SI 2013/1846, SI 2013/3198, SI 2013/3199, SI 2013/3206
s.54, amended: 2013 c.6 Sch.4 para.17
s.56, amended: 2013 c.6 s.16, Sch.4 para.18
s.56, applied: 2013 asp 14 Sch.2 para.13, Sch.2 para.17
s.56, varied: 2013 asp 13 Sch.1 Part 2
s.57, applied: SSI 2013/236 Art.2
s.57, varied: 2013 asp 13 Sch.1 Part 2, Sch.1 Part 4
s.57, enabling: SSI 2013/236
s.59, varied: 2013 asp 13 Sch.1 Part 2
s.62, amended: 2013 c.6 Sch.4 para.19
s.62, varied: 2013 asp 13 Sch.1 Part 2
s.63, varied: 2013 asp 13 Sch.1 Part 2
s.78, amended: 2013 c.22 Sch.9 para.52
s.86, amended: 2013 c.22 Sch.9 para.52
s.167, amended: 2013 c.22 Sch.9 para.52
s.185, applied: 2013 asp 14 Sch.7 para.18
s.200A, varied: SI 2013/242 Art.4
s.201, amended: 2013 c.6 s.2
s.201, applied: SI 2013/760, SI 2013/1599, SI 2013/1846, SI 2013/3114, SI 2013/3198, SI 2013/3199, SI 2013/3206
s.201, enabling: SI 2013/1599, SI 2013/1846, SI 2013/3198, SI 2013/3206
s.202, enabling: SI 2013/3198
Sch.ZA1, enabling: SI 2013/3198, SI 2013/3206
Sch.ZA1 para.1, added: 2013 c.6 Sch.3
Sch.ZA1 para.2, added: 2013 c.6 Sch.3
Sch.ZA1 para.2, referred to: 2013 c.6 Sch.5 para.13
Sch.ZA1 para.3, added: 2013 c.6 Sch.3
Sch.ZA1 para.3, referred to: 2013 c.6 Sch.5 para.13
Sch.ZA1 para.4, added: 2013 c.6 Sch.3
Sch.ZA1 para.5, added: 2013 c.6 Sch.3
Sch.ZA1 para.6, added: 2013 c.6 Sch.3
Sch.ZA1 para.7, added: 2013 c.6 Sch.3
Sch.ZA1 para.8, added: 2013 c.6 Sch.3
Sch.ZA1 para.9, added: 2013 c.6 Sch.3
Sch.ZA1 para.10, added: 2013 c.6 Sch.3
Sch.ZA1 para.11, added: 2013 c.6 Sch.3
Sch.ZA1 para.12, added: 2013 c.6 Sch.3
Sch.1 Part I para.1, amended: 2013 c.6 s.14
Sch.1 Part III para.19, amended: 2013 c.6 s.20
Sch.1 Part III para.24, enabling: SI 2013/3198, SI 2013/3206
Sch.1 Part III para.28, enabling: SI 2013/3198, SI 2013/3206
Sch.1 Part III para.30, amended: 2013 c.6 s.14
Sch.1 Part III para.31, substituted: 2013 c.6 s.21
Sch.1 Part III para.32, amended: 2013 c.6 s.21
Sch.1 Part III para.32, enabling: SI 2013/3198, SI 2013/3206

Sch.1 Part III para.37, amended: 2013 c.6 s.19
Sch.1 Part V para.56, amended: 2013 c.22 Sch.9 para.52
Sch.1 Part VI para.61, amended: 2013 c.6 s.14
Sch.1 Part VI para.63, amended: 2013 c.6 s.14
Sch.1 Part VI para.64, amended: 2013 c.6 s.14
Sch.2 para.1, amended: 2013 c.6 s.2, Sch.4 para.20
Sch.2 para.1, enabling: SI 2013/1846, SI 2013/3198, SI 2013/3206
Sch.2 para.1A, added: 2013 c.6 Sch.2 para.2
Sch.2 para.1A, applied: SI 2013/760 Reg.3
Sch.2 para.1A, referred to: 2013 c.6 Sch.5 para.4
Sch.2 para.1A, enabling: SI 2013/760, SI 2013/3198, SI 2013/3206
Sch.2 para.1B, added: 2013 c.6 Sch.4 para.20
Sch.2 para.3A, amended: 2013 c.6 Sch.4 para.20
Sch.2 para.3C, added: 2013 c.6 Sch.4 para.20
Sch.2 para.3C, referred to: 2013 c.6 Sch.5 para.12
Sch.2 para.3ZA, added: 2013 c.6 s.2
Sch.2 para.3ZA, enabling: SI 2013/3198, SI 2013/3206
Sch.2 para.5, amended: 2013 c.6 Sch.4 para.20
Sch.2 para.5, enabling: SI 2013/3198, SI 2013/3206
Sch.2 para.5A, enabling: SI 2013/3198, SI 2013/3206
Sch.2 para.5B, added: 2013 c.6 Sch.4 para.20
Sch.2 para.5B, enabling: SI 2013/3199
Sch.2 para.8B, added: 2013 c.6 s.2
Sch.2 para.8C, added: 2013 c.6 Sch.2 para.3
Sch.2 para.8C, enabling: SI 2013/3198, SI 2013/3206
Sch.2 para.10, referred to: SI 2013/3198 Reg.45, SI 2013/3206 Reg.47
Sch.2 para.10B, enabling: SI 2013/1846, SI 2013/3198, SI 2013/3206
Sch.2 para.11, enabling: SI 2013/3198, SI 2013/3206
Sch.2 para.12, enabling: SI 2013/3198, SI 2013/3206
Sch.2 para.13, amended: 2013 c.6 Sch.2 para.4
Sch.2 para.13, referred to: 2013 c.6 Sch.5 para.4
Sch.2 para.13, varied: 2013 c.6 s.13
Sch.2 para.13, enabling: SI 2013/760, SI 2013/3198, SI 2013/3206
Sch.4 para.9, amended: 2013 c.22 Sch.9 para.52
Sch.4A Part 2 para.7A, added: SI 2013/688 Art.2
Sch.4A Part 3 para.15, applied: SI 2013/688
Sch.4A Part 3 para.15, enabling: SI 2013/688
Sch.5 para.6, applied: 2013 asp 14 Sch.4 para.9

15. British Shipbuilders Act 1983
repealed: SI 2013/687 Sch.1 para.6

16. Level Crossings Act 1983
applied: SI 2013/1030 Art.6

18. Nuclear Material (Offences) Act 1983
s.2, applied: SI 2013/435 Sch.1 Part 7

20. Mental Health Act 1983
see *Coombs v Dorset NHS Primary Care Trust* [2013] EWCA Civ 471, [2013] 4 All E.R. 429 (CA (Civ Div)), Rix, L.J.; see *R. v Fletcher (Alan)* [2012] EWCA Crim 2777, [2013] M.H.L.R. 50 (CA (Crim Div)), Elias, L.J.; see *Secretary of State for Justice v MP* [2013] UKUT 25 (AAC), [2013] M.H.L.R. 154 (UT (AAC)), Judge Jacobs
applied: SI 2013/104 Reg.52, SI 2013/377 Reg.28, SI 2013/480 Reg.5, SI 2013/2537 Sch.1, SI 2013/3029 Reg.26, SI 2013/3035 Sch.1
Part II, applied: SI 2013/261 Reg.17
Part III, applied: SI 2013/1554 r.33_1
Part VII, applied: SI 2013/380 Reg.57, SI 2013/386 Reg.12
s.31, amended: 2013 c.22 Sch.9 para.52, Sch.9 para.112
s.35, applied: SI 2013/1554 r.42_8
s.36, applied: SI 2013/1554 r.42_8
s.37, see *DD v Durham CC* [2013] EWCA Civ 96, [2013] M.H.L.R. 85 (CA (Civ Div)), Sir John Thomas (President); see *MM v Nottinghamshire Healthcare NHS Trust* [2013] UKUT 107 (AAC), [2013] M.H.L.R. 161 (UT (AAC)), Judge Jacobs; see *R. v Ahmed (Imtiaz)* [2013] EWCA Crim 99, [2013] M.H.L.R. 65 (CA (Crim Div)), Elias, L.J.; see *R. v Ahmed (Mohammed Mokshud)* [2013] EWCA Crim 1393, (2013) 134 B.M.L.R. 20 (CA (Crim Div)), Pitchford, L.J.; see *R. v Fletcher (Alan)* [2012] EWCA Crim 2777, [2013] M.H.L.R. 50 (CA (Crim Div)), Elias, L.J.; see *R. v Searles (Ashley)* [2012] EWCA Crim 2685, [2013] M.H.L.R. 47 (CA (Crim Div)), Treacy, L.J.; see *RC v NHS Islington* [2013] UKUT 167 (AAC), [2013] M.H.L.R. 167 (UT (AAC)), Judge EAL Bano; see *Secretary of State for Justice v MP* [2013] UKUT 25 (AAC), [2013] M.H.L.R. 154 (UT (AAC)), Judge Jacobs
s.37, applied: SI 2013/1554 r.42_8, r.68_13, r.37_3
s.38, applied: SI 2013/1554 r.42_8
s.41, see *AC v Partnerships in Care Ltd* [2013] M.H.L.R. 52 (UT (AAC)), Judge Jacobs; see *R. v Ahmed (Imtiaz)* [2013] EWCA Crim 99, [2013] M.H.L.R. 65 (CA (Crim Div)), Elias, L.J.; see *R. v Ahmed (Mohammed Mokshud)* [2013] EWCA Crim 1393, (2013) 134 B.M.L.R. 20 (CA (Crim Div)), Pitchford, L.J.; see *R. v Fletcher (Alan)* [2012] EWCA Crim 2777, [2013] M.H.L.R. 50 (CA (Crim Div)), Elias, L.J.; see *R. v Jenkin (Shane William)* [2012] EWCA Crim 2557, [2013] 2 Cr. App. R. (S.) 15 (CA (Crim Div)), Lord Judge, L.C.J.; see *R. v Searles (Ashley)* [2012]

EWCA Crim 2685, [2013] M.H.L.R. 47 (CA (Crim Div)), Treacy, L.J.; see *RC v NHS Islington* [2013] UKUT 167 (AAC), [2013] M.H.L.R. 167 (UT (AAC)), Judge EAL Bano; see *Secretary of State for Justice v MP* [2013] UKUT 25 (AAC), [2013] M.H.L.R. 154 (UT (AAC)), Judge Jacobs
s.41, applied: SI 2013/435 Sch.1 para.3, Sch.2 para.3
s.45, applied: SI 2013/1554 r.76_6, r.63_1
s.45A, see *R. v Jenkin (Shane William)* [2012] EWCA Crim 2557, [2013] 2 Cr. App. R. (S.) 15 (CA (Crim Div)), Lord Judge, L.C.J.
s.45A, applied: SI 2013/376 Reg.19, SI 2013/377 Reg.31, SI 2013/379 Reg.63, Reg.96
s.45A, referred to: SI 2013/381 Sch.1 para.5
s.47, see *AC v Partnerships in Care Ltd* [2013] M.H.L.R. 52 (UT (AAC)), Judge Jacobs; see *DD v Durham CC* [2013] EWCA Civ 96, [2013] M.H.L.R. 85 (CA (Civ Div)), Sir John Thomas (President); see *R. v Ahmed (Imtiaz)* [2013] EWCA Crim 99, [2013] M.H.L.R. 65 (CA (Crim Div)), Elias, L.J.
s.47, applied: SI 2013/376 Reg.19, SI 2013/377 Reg.31, SI 2013/379 Reg.63, Reg.96
s.47, referred to: SI 2013/381 Sch.1 para.5
s.50, applied: SI 2013/376 Reg.19, SI 2013/377 Reg.31, SI 2013/379 Reg.63, Reg.96
s.117, see *R. (on the application of Sunderland City Council) v South Tyneside Council* [2012] EWCA Civ 1232, [2013] 1 All E.R. 394 (CA (Civ Div)), Lloyd, L.J.
s.117, applied: SI 2013/259 Reg.7, SI 2013/261 Sch.1 para.18
s.127, applied: SI 2013/435 Sch.1 Part 7
s.130A, enabling: SI 2013/261
s.139, see *Bank of Ireland v Colliers International UK Plc (In Administration)* [2012] EWHC 2942 (Ch), [2013] Ch. 422 (Ch D (Companies Ct)), David Richards, J.; see *DD v Durham CC* [2013] EWCA Civ 96, [2013] M.H.L.R. 85 (CA (Civ Div)), Sir John Thomas (President); see *TW v Enfield LBC* [2013] EWHC 1180 (QB), (2013) 132 B.M.L.R. 227 (QBD), Bean, J.
s.139, applied: SI 2013/160 Sch.1 para.3
s.141, repealed: 2013 c.8 s.1
s.145, see *An NHS Trust v A* [2013] EWHC 2442 (COP), [2013] Med. L.R. 561 (CP), Baker, J.
s.145, amended: 2013 c.8 Sch.1 para.1
s.146, amended: 2013 c.8 Sch.1 para.1
s.147, amended: 2013 c.8 Sch.1 para.1

29. Miscellaneous Financial Provisions Act 1983
Sch.2, amended: SI 2013/687 Sch.1 para.7

34. Mobile Homes Act 1983
applied: SI 2013/1469 Art.4, Art.6, SI 2013/1722 Art.1, SSI 2013/219 Art.4
s.1, amended: 2013 c.14 s.9, SI 2013/1722 Art.2
s.1, applied: SI 2013/1469 Art.3, Art.6, SSI 2013/188 Reg.3
s.1, disapplied: SI 2013/1469 Art.5
s.1, enabling: SSI 2013/188
s.2, amended: 2013 c.14 s.9, SI 2013/1722 Art.2, SI 2013/1723 Art.4
s.2, applied: SI 2013/1179 Sch.1, SI 2013/1469 Art.3, Art.6, SSI 2013/219 Art.4
s.2, disapplied: SI 2013/1469 Art.5
s.2A, applied: SI 2013/1723
s.2A, enabling: SI 2013/1723
s.2B, applied: SSI 2013/219
s.2B, enabling: SSI 2013/219
s.2C, added: 2013 c.14 s.9
s.2C, applied: SI 2013/981 Reg.11
s.2C, enabling: SI 2013/981
s.2D, added: 2013 c.14 s.9
s.2D, referred to: SI 2013/981 Reg.11
s.3, amended: 2013 c.14 s.10, SI 2013/1723 Art.4
s.3, applied: SI 2013/1469 Art.6
s.4, applied: SI 2013/1168 Art.2, SI 2013/1179 Sch.1
s.4, referred to: SI 2013/1723 Art.3
s.4, varied: SI 2013/1723 Art.3
s.5, amended: 2013 c.22 Sch.9 para.113, SI 2013/1036 Sch.1 para.39
Sch.1, disapplied: SI 2013/1168 Art.2
Sch.1 Part I, disapplied: SI 2013/1168 Art.2
Sch.1 Part I, applied: SI 2013/1469 Art.6
Sch.1 Part I para.1, amended: SI 2013/1723 Art.2
Sch.1 Part I para.2, amended: SI 2013/1723 Art.2
Sch.1 Part I para.3, amended: SI 2013/1723 Art.2
Sch.1 Part I para.3, disapplied: SI 2013/1469 Art.5
Sch.1 Part I para.3, amended: SI 2013/1723 Art.2
Sch.1 Part I para.3, disapplied: SI 2013/1469 Art.5
Sch.1 Part I para.4, amended: SSI 2013/219 Art.2
Sch.1 Part I para.4, applied: SSI 2013/219 Art.4
Sch.1 Part I para.4, amended: SI 2013/1723 Art.2
Sch.1 Part I para.4, applied: SI 2013/1179 Sch.1
Sch.1 Part I para.4, amended: SI 2013/1723 Art.2
Sch.1 Part I para.4, disapplied: SI 2013/1469 Art.5
Sch.1 Part I para.4, amended: SI 2013/1723 Art.2
Sch.1 Part I para.4, applied: SI 2013/1179 Sch.1
Sch.1 Part I para.4, disapplied: SI 2013/1469 Art.5
Sch.1 Part I para.5, amended: SSI 2013/219 Art.2
Sch.1 Part I para.5, applied: SSI 2013/219 Art.4
Sch.1 Part I para.5, amended: SI 2013/1723 Art.2
Sch.1 Part I para.5, applied: SI 2013/1179 Sch.1
Sch.1 Part I para.5, amended: SI 2013/1723 Art.2
Sch.1 Part I para.5, applied: SI 2013/1179 Sch.1
Sch.1 Part I para.5, disapplied: SI 2013/1469 Art.5

Sch.1 Part I para.5A, amended: SI 2013/1723 Art.2
Sch.1 Part I para.5A, applied: SI 2013/1169 r.48, SI 2013/1179 Sch.1
Sch.1 Part I para.6, amended: SSI 2013/219 Art.2
Sch.1 Part I para.6, applied: SSI 2013/219 Art.4
Sch.1 Part I para.6, repealed (in part): SSI 2013/219 Art.2
Sch.1 Part I para.6, amended: SI 2013/1723 Art.2
Sch.1 Part I para.6, applied: SI 2013/1169 r.48, SI 2013/1179 Sch.1
Sch.1 Part I para.6, disapplied: SI 2013/1469 Art.5
Sch.1 Part I para.6A, added: SI 2013/1723 Art.2
Sch.1 Part I para.6A, amended: SI 2013/1723 Art.2
Sch.1 Part I para.6B, added: SI 2013/1723 Art.2
Sch.1 Part I para.6B, amended: SI 2013/1723 Art.2
Sch.1 Part I para.7, substituted: SSI 2013/219 Art.2
Sch.1 Part I para.7, amended: SI 2013/1723 Art.2
Sch.1 Part I para.7A, added: 2013 c.14 s.10
Sch.1 Part I para.7A, amended: SI 2013/1723 Art.2
Sch.1 Part I para.7A, applied: SI 2013/981 Reg.3, Reg.8, Reg.9, Reg.10
Sch.1 Part I para.7B, added: 2013 c.14 s.10
Sch.1 Part I para.7B, amended: SI 2013/1723 Art.2
Sch.1 Part I para.7B, applied: SI 2013/981 Reg.3, Reg.4, Reg.7, Reg.8, Reg.9, Reg.10, SI 2013/1179 Sch.1
Sch.1 Part I para.7C, added: 2013 c.14 s.10
Sch.1 Part I para.7C, amended: SI 2013/1723 Art.2
Sch.1 Part I para.8, amended: SSI 2013/219 Art.2
Sch.1 Part I para.8, amended: 2013 c.14 s.10, SI 2013/1723 Art.2
Sch.1 Part I para.8, applied: SI 2013/1168 Art.2, SI 2013/1169 r.45
Sch.1 Part I para.8, referred to: SI 2013/1168 Art.2
Sch.1 Part I para.8, amended: SI 2013/1723 Art.2
Sch.1 Part I para.8, applied: SI 2013/1179 Sch.1
Sch.1 Part I para.8, disapplied: SI 2013/1469 Art.5
Sch.1 Part I para.8A, added: 2013 c.14 s.10
Sch.1 Part I para.8A, amended: SI 2013/1723 Art.2
Sch.1 Part I para.8A, applied: SI 2013/981 Reg.5, Reg.6, Reg.9
Sch.1 Part I para.8A, referred to: SI 2013/981 Reg.7
Sch.1 Part I para.8B, added: 2013 c.14 s.10
Sch.1 Part I para.8B, amended: SI 2013/1723 Art.2
Sch.1 Part I para.8B, applied: SI 2013/981 Reg.5, Reg.7, Reg.9, SI 2013/1179 Sch.1
Sch.1 Part I para.8C, added: 2013 c.14 s.10
Sch.1 Part I para.8C, amended: SI 2013/1723 Art.2
Sch.1 Part I para.9, substituted: SSI 2013/219 Art.2
Sch.1 Part I para.9, amended: 2013 c.14 s.10, SI 2013/1723 Art.2
Sch.1 Part I para.9, applied: SI 2013/1168 Art.2, SI 2013/1169 r.45
Sch.1 Part I para.9, amended: SI 2013/1723 Art.2
Sch.1 Part I para.10, substituted: SSI 2013/219 Art.2
Sch.1 Part I para.10, amended: SI 2013/1723 Art.2
Sch.1 Part I para.10, applied: SI 2013/1179 Sch.1
Sch.1 Part I para.10, amended: SI 2013/1723 Art.2
Sch.1 Part I para.11, added: SSI 2013/219 Art.2
Sch.1 Part I para.11, amended: SI 2013/1723 Art.2
Sch.1 Part I para.12, added: SSI 2013/219 Art.2
Sch.1 Part I para.12, amended: SI 2013/1723 Art.2
Sch.1 Part I para.13, added: SSI 2013/219 Art.2
Sch.1 Part I para.13, amended: SI 2013/1723 Art.2
Sch.1 Part I para.14, added: SSI 2013/219 Art.2
Sch.1 Part I para.14, amended: SI 2013/1723 Art.2
Sch.1 Part I para.15, added: SSI 2013/219 Art.2
Sch.1 Part I para.15, amended: SI 2013/1723 Art.2
Sch.1 Part I para.15, disapplied: SI 2013/1469 Art.5
Sch.1 Part I para.16, added: SSI 2013/219 Art.2
Sch.1 Part I para.16, amended: SI 2013/1723 Art.2
Sch.1 Part I para.16, disapplied: SI 2013/1469 Art.5
Sch.1 Part I para.17, added: SSI 2013/219 Art.2
Sch.1 Part I para.17, applied: SSI 2013/219 Art.4
Sch.1 Part I para.17, amended: 2013 c.14 s.11, SI 2013/1723 Art.2
Sch.1 Part I para.17, applied: SI 2013/1505 Reg.2
Sch.1 Part I para.17, amended: SI 2013/1723 Art.2
Sch.1 Part I para.18, added: SSI 2013/219 Art.2
Sch.1 Part I para.18, amended: 2013 c.14 s.11, SI 2013/1723 Art.2
Sch.1 Part I para.18, amended: SI 2013/1723 Art.2
Sch.1 Part I para.19, added: SSI 2013/219 Art.2
Sch.1 Part I para.19, amended: 2013 c.14 s.1, s.11, SI 2013/1723 Art.2
Sch.1 Part I para.19, amended: SI 2013/1723 Art.2
Sch.1 Part I para.19, disapplied: SI 2013/1469 Art.5
Sch.1 Part I para.19, referred to: SI 2013/1469 Art.5
Sch.1 Part I para.20, added: SSI 2013/219 Art.2
Sch.1 Part I para.20, amended: 2013 c.14 s.11, SI 2013/1723 Art.2
Sch.1 Part I para.20, amended: SI 2013/1723 Art.2
Sch.1 Part I para.20, disapplied: SI 2013/1469 Art.5
Sch.1 Part I para.21, added: SSI 2013/219 Art.2
Sch.1 Part I para.21, amended: SI 2013/1723 Art.2
Sch.1 Part I para.22, added: SSI 2013/219 Art.2
Sch.1 Part I para.22, applied: SSI 2013/219 Art.4
Sch.1 Part I para.22, amended: SI 2013/1723 Art.2
Sch.1 Part I para.23, added: SSI 2013/219 Art.2

Sch.1 Part I para.23, amended: SI 2013/1723 Art.2
Sch.1 Part I para.24, added: SSI 2013/219 Art.2
Sch.1 Part I para.24, amended: SI 2013/1723 Art.2
Sch.1 Part I para.25, added: SSI 2013/219 Art.2
Sch.1 Part I para.25, applied: SSI 2013/219 Art.4
Sch.1 Part I para.25, amended: SI 2013/1723 Art.2
Sch.1 Part I para.25A, added: 2013 c.14 s.11
Sch.1 Part I para.25A, amended: SI 2013/1723 Art.2
Sch.1 Part I para.25A, enabling: SI 2013/1505
Sch.1 Part I para.26, added: SSI 2013/219 Art.2
Sch.1 Part I para.26, amended: SI 2013/1723 Art.2
Sch.1 Part I para.26, applied: SI 2013/981 Reg.3
Sch.1 Part I para.26, amended: SI 2013/1723 Art.2
Sch.1 Part I para.26, applied: SI 2013/1179 Sch.1
Sch.1 Part I para.27, added: SSI 2013/219 Art.2
Sch.1 Part I para.27, amended: SI 2013/1723 Art.2
Sch.1 Part I para.28, added: SSI 2013/219 Art.2
Sch.1 Part I para.28, amended: SI 2013/1723 Art.2
Sch.1 Part I para.28, applied: SI 2013/1179 Sch.1
Sch.1 Part I para.29, added: SSI 2013/219 Art.2
Sch.1 Part I para.29, amended: SI 2013/1723 Art.2
Sch.1 Part I para.30, added: SSI 2013/219 Art.2
Sch.1 Part I para.31, added: SSI 2013/219 Art.2
Sch.1 Part I para.32, added: SSI 2013/219 Art.2
Sch.1 Part II, referred to: SI 2013/1179 Sch.1, SSI 2013/219 Art.4
Sch.1 Part II para.1, repealed (in part): SSI 2013/219 Art.3
Sch.1 Part II para.6, repealed (in part): SSI 2013/219 Art.3
Sch.1 Part II para.7, repealed (in part): SSI 2013/219 Art.3
Sch.1 Part III, amended: SI 2013/1723 Art.4
Sch.1 Part III paraA.1, added: 2013 c.14 s.10
Sch.1 Part III paraA.1, applied: SI 2013/981 Reg.3
Sch.1 Part III paraA.1, enabling: SI 2013/981
Sch.1 Part III para.1, amended: SI 2013/1723 Art.4
Sch.1 Part III para.2, amended: SI 2013/1723 Art.4

40. Education (Fees and Awards) Act 1983
s.1, enabling: SI 2013/1792, SSI 2013/80
s.2, enabling: SI 2013/1792

44. National Audit Act 1983
Sch.4 Part I, amended: SI 2013/687 Sch.1 para.8

47. National Heritage Act 1983
applied: SI 2013/2148 Art.5
disapplied: SI 2013/2146 Art.4
s.33, amended: 2013 c.24 Sch.17 para.1

54. Medical Act 1983
s.10A, applied: SI 2013/335 Reg.24
s.15, applied: SI 2013/335 Reg.24
s.15A, applied: SI 2013/335 Reg.24
s.17, amended: SI 2013/3036 Reg.2
s.21, applied: SI 2013/335 Reg.24
s.34J, applied: SI 2013/335 Reg.26
s.35CC, enabling: SI 2013/815
s.35D, applied: SI 2013/335 Reg.27
s.41A, see *Dutta v General Medical Council* [2013] EWHC 132 (Admin), (2013) 132 B.M.L.R. 212 (QBD (Admin)), Haddon-Cave, J.; see *Patel v General Medical Council* [2012] EWHC 3688 (Admin), [2013] 1 W.L.R. 2694 (QBD (Admin)), Eady, J.; see *Waghorn v General Medical Council* [2012] EWHC 3427 (Admin), [2013] 1 C.M.L.R. 45 (QBD (Admin)), Stuart-Smith, J.
s.41A, applied: SI 2013/335 Reg.27
s.44D, applied: SI 2013/335 Reg.24
s.45A, enabling: SI 2013/391
s.45E, applied: SI 2013/391
Sch.1 Part III para.19A, enabling: SI 2013/815
Sch.1 Part III para.19B, enabling: SI 2013/815
Sch.1 Part III para.19C, enabling: SI 2013/815
Sch.1 Part III para.19D, enabling: SI 2013/815
Sch.1 Part III para.19E, enabling: SI 2013/815
Sch.1 Part III para.23B, enabling: SI 2013/815
Sch.1 Part III para.24, applied: SI 2013/815
Sch.3B para.8, amended: 2013 c.22 Sch.9 para.110
Sch.4 para.1, applied: SI 2013/815
Sch.4 para.1, enabling: SI 2013/815
Sch.4 para.5A, applied: SI 2013/335 Reg.27

58. British Shipbuilders (Borrowing Powers) Act 1983
repealed: SI 2013/687 Sch.1 para.9

1984

22. Public Health (Control of Disease) Act 1984
s.2, applied: SI 2013/2196 Reg.2, SI 2013/2210 Reg.2, SI 2013/2493 Reg.2, SI 2013/2591 Reg.2, SI 2013/2952 Reg.21, SI 2013/2996 Reg.2
s.7, applied: SI 2013/2196 Reg.2, SI 2013/2210 Reg.2, SI 2013/2493 Reg.2, SI 2013/2952 Reg.21, SI 2013/2996 Reg.2

24. Dentists Act 1984
s.15, applied: SI 2013/335 Reg.34
s.27B, applied: SI 2013/335 Reg.34
s.27C, applied: SI 2013/335 Reg.34
s.28, applied: SI 2013/335 Reg.34
s.30, applied: SI 2013/335 Reg.34
s.32, applied: SI 2013/335 Reg.34
s.36A, applied: SSI 2013/50 Sch.4 para.4
Sch.2 Part I para.8, amended: SI 2013/3036 Reg.4

26. Inshore Fishing (Scotland) Act 1984
s.4, amended: 2013 asp 7 s.49
s.4, applied: SSI 2013/249 Art.3
s.4A, added: 2013 asp 7 s.49
s.4A, disapplied: SSI 2013/249 Art.3

s.6A, added: 2013 asp 7 s.50
s.10A, added: 2013 asp 7 s.50

27. Road Traffic Regulation Act 1984

see *R. (on the application of Attfield) v Barnet LBC* [2013] EWHC 2089 (Admin), [2013] P.T.S.R. 1559 (QBD (Admin)), Lang, J.
applied: SI 2013/586 Art.11, SI 2013/805 Sch.1, SI 2013/806 Sch.1, SI 2013/807 Sch.1, SI 2013/808 Sch.1, SI 2013/809 Sch.1, SI 2013/810 Sch.1, SI 2013/811 Sch.1, SI 2013/812 Sch.1, SI 2013/813 Sch.1, SI 2013/814 Sch.1, SI 2013/1481 Art.4, SI 2013/1485 Art.9, SI 2013/1781 Sch.1, SI 2013/1933 Art.38, Art.39, SI 2013/2183 Art.4, SI 2013/2293 Art.4, SI 2013/2389 Sch.1, SI 2013/2398 Sch.1, SI 2013/2399 Sch.1, SI 2013/2587 Art.18, Art.40, Art.41, Sch.7, SI 2013/2702 Art.7, SI 2013/2808 Art.11, Art.38, SI 2013/2809 Art.31, SI 2013/3244 Art.39, Art.40, SSI 2013/55 Art.4
referred to: SI 2013/2809 Art.31
enabling: SI 2013/56
s.1, applied: 2013 asp 8 s.5
s.1, enabling: SI 2013/394, SI 2013/656, SI 2013/780, SI 2013/791, SI 2013/1076, SI 2013/1208, SI 2013/1210, SI 2013/1480, SI 2013/1504, SI 2013/1649, SI 2013/1867, SI 2013/1988, SI 2013/3070, SI 2013/3173, SSI 2013/88, SSI 2013/207
s.2, enabling: SI 2013/394, SI 2013/656, SI 2013/780, SI 2013/791, SI 2013/1076, SI 2013/1208, SI 2013/1210, SI 2013/1480, SI 2013/1504, SI 2013/1649, SI 2013/1867, SI 2013/1988, SI 2013/3070, SI 2013/3173, SSI 2013/13, SSI 2013/15, SSI 2013/16, SSI 2013/17, SSI 2013/18, SSI 2013/27, SSI 2013/28, SSI 2013/30, SSI 2013/54, SSI 2013/55, SSI 2013/56, SSI 2013/57, SSI 2013/66, SSI 2013/88, SSI 2013/101, SSI 2013/102, SSI 2013/103, SSI 2013/104, SSI 2013/130, SSI 2013/132, SSI 2013/133, SSI 2013/134, SSI 2013/138, SSI 2013/140, SSI 2013/145, SSI 2013/158, SSI 2013/164, SSI 2013/165, SSI 2013/166, SSI 2013/167, SSI 2013/206, SSI 2013/207, SSI 2013/208, SSI 2013/209, SSI 2013/213, SSI 2013/223, SSI 2013/224, SSI 2013/231, SSI 2013/232, SSI 2013/233, SSI 2013/234, SSI 2013/235, SSI 2013/237, SSI 2013/240, SSI 2013/242, SSI 2013/243, SSI 2013/244, SSI 2013/245, SSI 2013/246, SSI 2013/248, SSI 2013/251, SSI 2013/255, SSI 2013/257, SSI 2013/263, SSI 2013/272, SSI 2013/273, SSI 2013/274, SSI 2013/275, SSI 2013/284, SSI 2013/285, SSI 2013/297, SSI 2013/298, SSI 2013/299, SSI 2013/300, SSI 2013/301, SSI 2013/306, SSI 2013/316, SSI 2013/329, SSI 2013/330, SSI 2013/331, SSI 2013/332, SSI 2013/338, SSI 2013/343, SSI 2013/352, SSI 2013/353, SSI 2013/358, SSI 2013/359, SSI 2013/360, SSI 2013/361
s.4, enabling: SI 2013/394, SI 2013/656, SI 2013/780, SI 2013/791, SI 2013/1649, SI 2013/1867, SI 2013/1988, SI 2013/3070, SI 2013/3173, SSI 2013/13, SSI 2013/15, SSI 2013/16, SSI 2013/17, SSI 2013/18, SSI 2013/27, SSI 2013/28, SSI 2013/30, SSI 2013/54, SSI 2013/55, SSI 2013/56, SSI 2013/57, SSI 2013/66, SSI 2013/101, SSI 2013/102, SSI 2013/103, SSI 2013/104, SSI 2013/130, SSI 2013/132, SSI 2013/133, SSI 2013/134, SSI 2013/138, SSI 2013/140, SSI 2013/145, SSI 2013/158, SSI 2013/165, SSI 2013/166, SSI 2013/167, SSI 2013/206, SSI 2013/208, SSI 2013/209, SSI 2013/213, SSI 2013/223, SSI 2013/224, SSI 2013/231, SSI 2013/232, SSI 2013/233, SSI 2013/234, SSI 2013/235, SSI 2013/237, SSI 2013/240, SSI 2013/242, SSI 2013/243, SSI 2013/244, SSI 2013/245, SSI 2013/246, SSI 2013/248, SSI 2013/251, SSI 2013/255, SSI 2013/257, SSI 2013/263, SSI 2013/272, SSI 2013/273, SSI 2013/274, SSI 2013/275, SSI 2013/285, SSI 2013/297, SSI 2013/298, SSI 2013/299, SSI 2013/300, SSI 2013/301, SSI 2013/306, SSI 2013/329, SSI 2013/330, SSI 2013/331, SSI 2013/332, SSI 2013/338, SSI 2013/343, SSI 2013/352, SSI 2013/353, SSI 2013/358, SSI 2013/359, SSI 2013/360, SSI 2013/361
s.6, enabling: SI 2013/2306
s.7, applied: SI 2013/2306
s.9, enabling: SI 2013/182, SI 2013/1062, SI 2013/1315
s.10, enabling: SI 2013/182, SI 2013/1062, SI 2013/1315
s.11, enabling: SI 2013/1062

28. County Courts Act 1984

Part I, amended: 2013 c.22 Sch.9 para.5
Part VI, amended: 2013 c.22 Sch.9 para.10
s.art I sA.1, added: 2013 c.22 s.17
s.1, repealed: 2013 c.22 s.17
s.2, applied: SI 2013/415 Art.5
s.2, repealed: 2013 c.22 s.17
s.2, enabling: SI 2013/415
s.3, amended: 2013 c.22 Sch.9 para.2
s.3, repealed (in part): 2013 c.22 Sch.9 para.2
s.4, amended: 2013 c.22 Sch.9 para.3, Sch.10 para.65
s.5, substituted: 2013 c.22 Sch.9 para.4
s.6, amended: 2013 c.22 Sch.9 para.5

s.6, repealed (in part): 2013 c.22 Sch.9 para.5
s.8, amended: 2013 c.22 Sch.9 para.6, Sch.13 para.37
s.8, repealed (in part): 2013 c.22 Sch.9 para.6
s.12, amended: 2013 c.22 Sch.9 para.7
s.13, amended: 2013 c.22 Sch.9 para.8
s.13, repealed (in part): 2013 c.22 Sch.9 para.8
s.14, amended: 2013 c.22 Sch.9 para.9
s.14, repealed (in part): 2013 c.22 Sch.9 para.9
s.15, amended: 2013 c.22 Sch.9 para.10
s.16, amended: 2013 c.22 Sch.9 para.10
s.17, amended: 2013 c.22 Sch.9 para.10
s.18, amended: 2013 c.22 Sch.9 para.10
s.21, see *Swan Housing Association Ltd v Gill* [2012] EWHC 3129 (QB), [2013] 1 W.L.R. 1253 (QBD), Eady, J.
s.21, amended: 2013 c.22 Sch.9 para.10
s.23, see *Ningbo Wentai Sports Equipment Co Ltd v Wang* [2013] F.S.R. 40 (PCC), Judge Birss Q.C.
s.23, amended: 2013 c.22 Sch.9 para.10
s.24, see *Ningbo Wentai Sports Equipment Co Ltd v Wang* [2013] F.S.R. 40 (PCC), Judge Birss Q.C.
s.24, amended: 2013 c.22 Sch.9 para.10
s.25, amended: 2013 c.22 Sch.9 para.10
s.26, repealed: 2013 c.22 Sch.9 para.10
s.27, amended: 2013 c.22 Sch.9 para.10
s.27, repealed (in part): 2013 c.22 Sch.9 para.10
s.28, repealed: 2013 c.22 Sch.9 para.10
s.30, amended: 2013 c.22 Sch.9 para.10
s.31, amended: 2013 c.22 Sch.9 para.10
s.31, repealed (in part): 2013 c.22 Sch.9 para.10
s.32, repealed: 2013 c.22 Sch.9 para.10
s.33, repealed: 2013 c.22 Sch.9 para.10
s.35, amended: 2013 c.22 Sch.9 para.10
s.36, amended: 2013 c.22 Sch.9 para.10
s.37, amended: 2013 c.22 Sch.9 para.10
s.37, repealed (in part): 2013 c.22 Sch.9 para.10
s.38, amended: 2013 c.22 Sch.9 para.10, Sch.10 para.66
s.40, see *Ningbo Wentai Sports Equipment Co Ltd v Wang* [2013] F.S.R. 40 (PCC), Judge Birss Q.C.
s.40, amended: 2013 c.22 Sch.9 para.10
s.40, repealed (in part): 2013 c.22 Sch.9 para.10, Sch.10 para.67
s.41, amended: 2013 c.22 Sch.9 para.10, Sch.10 para.67
s.42, amended: 2013 c.22 Sch.9 para.10
s.42, repealed (in part): 2013 c.22 Sch.10 para.67
s.45, amended: 2013 c.22 Sch.9 para.10
s.45, repealed (in part): 2013 c.22 Sch.9 para.10
s.46, amended: 2013 c.22 Sch.9 para.10
s.49, amended: 2013 c.22 Sch.9 para.10
s.52, amended: 2013 c.22 Sch.9 para.10
s.53, amended: 2013 c.22 Sch.9 para.10
s.54, amended: 2013 c.22 Sch.9 para.10
s.55, amended: 2013 c.22 Sch.9 para.10
s.55, repealed (in part): 2013 c.22 Sch.9 para.10
s.56, amended: 2013 c.22 Sch.9 para.10
s.57, amended: 2013 c.22 Sch.9 para.10, Sch.10 para.68
s.58, amended: 2013 c.22 Sch.9 para.10
s.59, repealed: 2013 c.22 Sch.9 para.10
s.60, amended: 2013 c.22 Sch.9 para.10
s.60A, amended: 2013 c.22 Sch.9 para.10
s.61, amended: 2013 c.22 Sch.9 para.10, Sch.10 para.69
s.62, amended: 2013 c.22 Sch.9 para.10
s.63, amended: 2013 c.22 Sch.9 para.10
s.63, repealed (in part): 2013 c.22 Sch.9 para.10
s.64, amended: 2013 c.22 Sch.9 para.10
s.65, amended: 2013 c.22 Sch.9 para.10
s.65, repealed (in part): 2013 c.22 Sch.9 para.10
s.66, amended: 2013 c.22 Sch.9 para.10, 2013 c.26 s.11
s.67, amended: 2013 c.22 Sch.9 para.10
s.68, amended: 2013 c.22 Sch.9 para.10
s.69, amended: 2013 c.22 Sch.9 para.10
s.70, amended: 2013 c.22 Sch.9 para.10
s.71, see *Gittins v Serco Home Affairs* [2012] EWHC 651 (Ch), [2013] 1 W.L.R. 1218 (Ch D (Leeds)), Judge Behrens
s.71, amended: 2013 c.22 Sch.9 para.10, Sch.10 para.70
s.72, amended: 2013 c.22 Sch.9 para.10
s.74, amended: 2013 c.22 Sch.9 para.10
s.74, varied: SI 2013/1169 r.13
s.76, amended: 2013 c.22 Sch.9 para.10
s.77, amended: 2013 c.22 Sch.9 para.10
s.78, amended: 2013 c.22 Sch.9 para.10
s.79, amended: 2013 c.22 Sch.9 para.10
s.80, amended: 2013 c.22 Sch.9 para.10
s.81, amended: 2013 c.22 Sch.9 para.10
s.82, amended: 2013 c.22 Sch.9 para.10
s.83, amended: 2013 c.22 Sch.9 para.10
s.84, amended: 2013 c.22 Sch.9 para.10
s.85, amended: 2013 c.22 Sch.9 para.10
s.85, applied: SI 2013/1894 Reg.29
s.87, amended: 2013 c.22 Sch.9 para.10
s.89, amended: 2013 c.22 Sch.9 para.10
s.90, amended: 2013 c.22 Sch.9 para.10
s.91, amended: 2013 c.22 Sch.9 para.10
s.92, amended: 2013 c.22 Sch.9 para.10
s.93, amended: 2013 c.22 Sch.9 para.10
s.94, amended: 2013 c.22 Sch.9 para.10
s.95, amended: 2013 c.22 Sch.9 para.10
s.96, amended: 2013 c.22 Sch.9 para.10
s.97, amended: 2013 c.22 Sch.9 para.10
s.98, amended: 2013 c.22 Sch.9 para.10

s.99, amended: 2013 c.22 Sch.9 para.10
s.100, amended: 2013 c.22 Sch.9 para.10
s.101, amended: 2013 c.22 Sch.9 para.10
s.102, amended: 2013 c.22 Sch.9 para.10
s.103, repealed (in part): 2013 c.22 Sch.9 para.10
s.104, amended: 2013 c.22 Sch.9 para.10
s.110, amended: 2013 c.22 Sch.9 para.10
s.111, amended: 2013 c.22 Sch.9 para.10
s.112, amended: 2013 c.22 Sch.9 para.10
s.112AA, repealed (in part): 2013 c.22 Sch.9 para.10
s.112C, amended: 2013 c.22 Sch.9 para.10
s.112D, amended: 2013 c.22 Sch.9 para.10
s.112E, amended: 2013 c.22 Sch.9 para.10
s.112F, amended: 2013 c.22 Sch.9 para.10
s.112G, amended: 2013 c.22 Sch.9 para.10
s.112I, amended: 2013 c.22 Sch.9 para.10
s.112L, amended: 2013 c.22 Sch.9 para.10
s.112M, amended: 2013 c.22 Sch.9 para.10
s.112N, amended: 2013 c.22 Sch.9 para.10
s.112N, repealed (in part): 2013 c.22 Sch.9 para.10
s.112Q, amended: 2013 c.22 Sch.9 para.10
s.112R, amended: 2013 c.22 Sch.9 para.10
s.112S, amended: 2013 c.22 Sch.9 para.10
s.112T, amended: 2013 c.22 Sch.9 para.10
s.112U, amended: 2013 c.22 Sch.9 para.10
s.112V, amended: 2013 c.22 Sch.9 para.10
s.112W, amended: 2013 c.22 Sch.9 para.10
s.112X, amended: 2013 c.22 Sch.9 para.10
s.112Y, amended: 2013 c.22 Sch.9 para.10
s.113, amended: 2013 c.22 Sch.9 para.10
s.114, amended: 2013 c.22 Sch.9 para.10
s.115, amended: 2013 c.22 Sch.9 para.10
s.117C, amended: 2013 c.22 Sch.9 para.10
s.117D, amended: 2013 c.22 Sch.9 para.10
s.117E, amended: 2013 c.22 Sch.9 para.10
s.117F, amended: 2013 c.22 Sch.9 para.10
s.117I, amended: 2013 c.22 Sch.9 para.10
s.117J, amended: 2013 c.22 Sch.9 para.10
s.117K, amended: 2013 c.22 Sch.9 para.10
s.117K, repealed (in part): 2013 c.22 Sch.9 para.10
s.117N, amended: 2013 c.22 Sch.9 para.10
s.117O, amended: 2013 c.22 Sch.9 para.10
s.117P, amended: 2013 c.22 Sch.9 para.10
s.117Q, amended: 2013 c.22 Sch.9 para.10
s.117R, amended: 2013 c.22 Sch.9 para.10
s.117T, amended: 2013 c.22 Sch.9 para.10
s.117T, repealed (in part): 2013 c.22 Sch.9 para.10
s.118, amended: 2013 c.22 Sch.9 para.10
s.118, repealed (in part): 2013 c.22 Sch.9 para.10
s.119, amended: 2013 c.22 Sch.9 para.10
s.120, amended: 2013 c.22 Sch.9 para.10
s.121, amended: 2013 c.22 Sch.9 para.10
s.122, amended: 2013 c.22 Sch.9 para.10
s.122, repealed: 2013 c.22 Sch.9 para.10
s.123, amended: 2013 c.22 Sch.9 para.10
s.124, amended: 2013 c.22 Sch.9 para.10
s.125, amended: 2013 c.22 Sch.9 para.10
s.126, amended: 2013 c.22 Sch.9 para.10
s.129, amended: 2013 c.22 Sch.9 para.10
s.130, amended: 2013 c.22 Sch.9 para.10
s.131, amended: 2013 c.22 Sch.9 para.10, Sch.10 para.71
s.132, amended: 2013 c.22 Sch.9 para.10, Sch.10 para.72
s.133, amended: 2013 c.22 Sch.9 para.10
s.135, see *R. v Ali (Khuram Shazad)* [2012] EWCA Crim 2298, [2013] 1 Cr. App. R. (S.) 126 (CA (Crim Div)), Aikens, L.J.
s.135, amended: 2013 c.22 Sch.9 para.10
s.136, amended: 2013 c.22 Sch.9 para.10
s.137, amended: 2013 c.22 Sch.9 para.10
s.138, amended: 2013 c.22 Sch.9 para.10
s.142, amended: 2013 c.22 Sch.9 para.10
s.143, amended: 2013 c.22 Sch.9 para.10
s.147, amended: 2013 c.22 Sch.9 para.10
Sch.1 para.1, amended: 2013 c.22 Sch.9 para.10
Sch.1 para.2, amended: 2013 c.22 Sch.9 para.10
Sch.2 Part V para.64, repealed: 2013 c.22 Sch.9 para.141
Sch.3 para.5A, added: 2013 c.22 Sch.9 para.10
Sch.3 para.7, amended: 2013 c.22 Sch.9 para.10

37. Child Abduction Act 1984

s.1, applied: SI 2013/435 Sch.1 Part 7
s.2, applied: SI 2013/435 Sch.1 Part 7

40. Animal Health and Welfare Act 1984

s.10, enabling: SI 2013/398, SI 2013/1241, SSI 2013/151

42. Matrimonial and Family Proceedings Act 1984

s.27, amended: 2013 c.22 Sch.11 para.88
s.31A, added: 2013 c.22 s.17
s.31B, added: 2013 c.22 s.17, Sch.10 para.1
s.31C, added: 2013 c.22 s.17, Sch.10 para.1
s.31D, added: 2013 c.22 s.17, Sch.10 para.1
s.31E, added: 2013 c.22 s.17, Sch.10 para.1
s.31F, added: 2013 c.22 s.17, Sch.10 para.1
s.31G, added: 2013 c.22 s.17, Sch.10 para.1
s.31H, added: 2013 c.22 s.17, Sch.10 para.1
s.31I, added: 2013 c.22 s.17, Sch.10 para.1
s.31J, added: 2013 c.22 s.17, Sch.10 para.1
s.31K, added: 2013 c.22 s.17, Sch.10 para.1
s.31L, added: 2013 c.22 s.17, Sch.10 para.1
s.31M, added: 2013 c.22 s.17, Sch.10 para.1
s.31N, added: 2013 c.22 s.17, Sch.10 para.1
s.31O, added: 2013 c.22 s.17, Sch.10 para.1
s.31P, added: 2013 c.22 s.17, Sch.10 para.1
s.32, amended: 2013 c.22 Sch.11 para.89
s.33, applied: SI 2013/415 Art.3

s.33, repealed: 2013 c.22 Sch.11 para.90
s.33, enabling: SI 2013/415
s.34, repealed: 2013 c.22 Sch.11 para.90
s.35, repealed: 2013 c.22 Sch.11 para.90
s.36, repealed: 2013 c.22 Sch.11 para.90
s.36A, repealed: 2013 c.22 Sch.11 para.90
s.36B, repealed: 2013 c.22 Sch.11 para.90
s.36C, repealed: 2013 c.22 Sch.11 para.90
s.36D, repealed: 2013 c.22 Sch.11 para.90
s.37, amended: 2013 c.22 Sch.11 para.91
s.38, amended: 2013 c.22 Sch.11 para.92
s.38, repealed (in part): 2013 c.22 Sch.11 para.92
s.39, amended: 2013 c.22 Sch.11 para.93
s.42, repealed: 2013 c.22 Sch.11 para.94
s.44, repealed: 2013 c.22 Sch.10 para.99
Sch.1 para.4, repealed: 2013 c.22 Sch.10 para.99
Sch.1 para.16, repealed: 2013 c.22 Sch.11 para.210
Sch.1 para.26, repealed: 2013 c.22 Sch.11 para.210

43. Finance Act 1984

s.117, repealed: 2013 c.2 Sch.1 Part 10

47. Repatriation of Prisoners Act 1984

Sch.1 Part 1 para.5, applied: SI 2013/480 Reg.5

51. Inheritance Tax Act 1984

s.3, applied: 2013 asp 11 Sch.2 para.15
s.18, amended: 2013 c.29 s.178
s.30, applied: 2013 c.29 s.155
s.31, applied: 2013 c.29 s.155
s.43, applied: SI 2013/2571 Sch.1 para.4
s.58, amended: 2013 c.29 s.86
s.58, varied: 2013 c.29 s.86
s.65, amended: 2013 c.29 s.175
s.65, applied: 2013 c.29 s.86
s.71A, amended: 2013 c.29 Sch.44 para.2
s.71B, amended: 2013 c.29 Sch.44 para.3
s.71D, amended: 2013 c.29 Sch.44 para.4
s.71E, amended: 2013 c.29 Sch.44 para.5
s.78, applied: 2013 c.29 s.155
s.89, see *Pitt v Holt* [2013] UKSC 26, [2013] 2 A.C. 108 (SC), Lord Neuberger, J.S.C.
s.89, amended: 2013 c.29 Sch.44 para.6
s.89A, amended: 2013 c.29 Sch.44 para.7
s.89B, amended: 2013 c.29 Sch.44 para.8, Sch.44 para.10
s.89C, added: 2013 c.29 Sch.44 para.10
s.157, amended: 2013 c.29 Sch.46 para.118
s.162, amended: 2013 c.29 Sch.36 para.2
s.162A, added: 2013 c.29 Sch.36 para.3
s.162B, added: 2013 c.29 Sch.36 para.3
s.162C, added: 2013 c.29 Sch.36 para.3
s.175A, added: 2013 c.29 Sch.36 para.4
s.221, applied: 2013 c.29 s.210
s.267, amended: 2013 c.29 s.177
s.267ZA, added: 2013 c.29 s.177
s.267ZB, added: 2013 c.29 s.177
s.272, amended: SI 2013/463 Art.2
Sch.3, amended: SI 2013/755 Sch.2 para.183

55. Building Act 1984

s.1, enabling: SI 2013/181, SI 2013/747, SI 2013/1105, SI 2013/1959, SI 2013/2621, SI 2013/2730
s.1A, enabling: SI 2013/2730
s.2, enabling: SI 2013/2730
s.2A, enabling: SI 2013/181, SI 2013/747
s.3, enabling: SI 2013/2730
s.8, enabling: SI 2013/747, SI 2013/1105, SI 2013/2621
s.14, applied: SI 2013/747, SI 2013/1105, SI 2013/1959, SI 2013/2621, SI 2013/2730
s.16, enabling: SI 2013/181, SI 2013/747
s.17, enabling: SI 2013/181, SI 2013/747
s.34, enabling: SI 2013/181, SI 2013/747, SI 2013/2730
s.47, applied: SI 2013/747 Reg.35, Reg.36
s.47, enabling: SI 2013/181, SI 2013/747, SI 2013/2730
s.49, enabling: SI 2013/181, SI 2013/747
s.50, applied: SI 2013/747 Reg.35, Reg.36
s.50, enabling: SI 2013/181
s.51, enabling: SI 2013/181, SI 2013/747
s.51A, applied: SI 2013/747 Reg.35, Reg.36
s.51A, enabling: SI 2013/181
s.54, applied: SI 2013/747 Reg.35, Reg.36
s.56, enabling: SI 2013/181
Sch.1 para.1, enabling: SI 2013/181, SI 2013/747, SI 2013/1105, SI 2013/1959, SI 2013/2621, SI 2013/2730
Sch.1 para.2, enabling: SI 2013/181, SI 2013/747
Sch.1 para.4, enabling: SI 2013/181, SI 2013/747, SI 2013/1105, SI 2013/1959, SI 2013/2621
Sch.1 para.4A, enabling: SI 2013/181, SI 2013/747, SI 2013/1105, SI 2013/2621
Sch.1 para.6, enabling: SI 2013/747
Sch.1 para.7, enabling: SI 2013/181, SI 2013/747, SI 2013/1105, SI 2013/1959, SI 2013/2621, SI 2013/2730
Sch.1 para.8, enabling: SI 2013/181, SI 2013/747, SI 2013/1105, SI 2013/2621, SI 2013/2730
Sch.1 para.10, enabling: SI 2013/181, SI 2013/747, SI 2013/1105, SI 2013/1959, SI 2013/2621, SI 2013/2730
Sch.1 para.11, enabling: SI 2013/1959

56. Foster Children (Scotland) Act 1984

s.7, amended: SSI 2013/211 Sch.1 para.5
s.13, amended: SSI 2013/211 Sch.1 para.5
s.21, amended: SSI 2013/211 Sch.1 para.5

58. Rent (Scotland) Act 1984

Sch.4 para.9, applied: 2013 c.25 Sch.5 para.9

60. Police and Criminal Evidence Act 1984

see *Hanningfield v Chief Constable of Essex* [2013] EWHC 243 (QB), [2013] 1 W.L.R. 3632 (QBD), Eady, J.; see *R. (on the application of Dulai) v Chelmsford Magistrates' Court* [2012] EWHC 1055 (Admin), [2013] 1 W.L.R. 220 (DC), Stanley Burnton, L.J.; see *R. v B* [2012] EWCA Crim 414, [2013] 1 W.L.R. 320 (CA (Crim Div)), Lord Judge, L.C.J.

applied: SI 2013/1542 Art.3, Art.4, Art.5, Art.6, Art.9, Art.12, Art.13, Art.14, Art.15, Art.18, SI 2013/1554 r.6_1

Part IV, applied: SI 2013/1542 Art.3, Art.12, Art.14

Part V, applied: SI 2013/1554 r.6_35

s.8, see *R. (on the application of Anand) v Revenue and Customs Commissioners* [2012] EWHC 2989 (Admin), [2013] C.P. Rep. 2 (DC), Pitchford, L.J.; see *R. v Zinga (Munaf Ahmed)* [2012] EWCA Crim 2357, [2013] Lloyd's Rep. F.C. 102 (CA (Crim Div)), Rafferty, L.J.

s.8, applied: SI 2013/1542 Art.8, Art.17, Sch.1 Part 1, Sch.2 Part 1, SI 2013/1554 r.6_1, r.6_30, SI 2013/2733 Art.9

s.8, varied: SI 2013/1542 Art.19, Sch.1 Part 2, Sch.2 Part 2

s.9, applied: SI 2013/1542 Sch.1 Part 1, Sch.2 Part 1

s.9, varied: SI 2013/1542 Sch.1 Part 2, Sch.2 Part 2

s.10, applied: SI 2013/1554 r.6_3

s.11, applied: SI 2013/1554 r.6_3

s.15, see *R. (on the application of Ahmed) v York Magistrates' Court* [2012] EWHC 3636 (Admin), (2013) 177 J.P. 233 (QBD (Admin)), Hickinbottom, J.; see *R. (on the application of Anand) v Revenue and Customs Commissioners* [2012] EWHC 2989 (Admin), [2013] C.P. Rep. 2 (DC), Pitchford, L.J.; see *R. (on the application of Van der Pijl) v Kingston Crown Court* [2012] EWHC 3745 (Admin), [2013] 1 W.L.R. 2706 (DC), Sir John Thomas (President); see *R. v Zinga (Munaf Ahmed)* [2012] EWCA Crim 2357, [2013] Lloyd's Rep. F.C. 102 (CA (Crim Div)), Rafferty, L.J.

s.15, applied: 2013 c.33 s.88, SI 2013/504 Reg.17, SI 2013/1542 Sch.1 Part 1, Sch.2 Part 1, SI 2013/1554 r.6_1, r.6_32

s.15, varied: SI 2013/1542 Sch.1 Part 2, Sch.2 Part 2

s.16, see *R. v Zinga (Munaf Ahmed)* [2012] EWCA Crim 2357, [2013] Lloyd's Rep. F.C. 102 (CA (Crim Div)), Rafferty, L.J.

s.16, applied: 2013 c.33 s.88, SI 2013/504 Reg.17, SI 2013/1542 Sch.1 Part 1, Sch.2 Part 1, SI 2013/1554 r.6_1, r.6_30, r.6_31, r.6_32

s.16, varied: SI 2013/1542 Sch.1 Part 2, Sch.2 Part 2

s.17, applied: SI 2013/1542 Sch.1 Part 1, Sch.2 Part 1

s.17, varied: SI 2013/1542 Sch.1 Part 2, Sch.2 Part 2

s.18, applied: SI 2013/1542 Sch.1 Part 1, Sch.2 Part 1

s.18, varied: SI 2013/1542 Art.10, Art.20, Sch.1 Part 2, Sch.2 Part 2

s.19, applied: SI 2013/1542 Art.9, Art.18, Sch.1 Part 1, Sch.2 Part 1

s.19, varied: SI 2013/1542 Sch.1 Part 2, Sch.2 Part 2

s.20, applied: SI 2013/1542 Sch.1 Part 1, Sch.2 Part 1

s.20, varied: SI 2013/1542 Sch.1 Part 2, Sch.2 Part 2

s.21, applied: SI 2013/1542 Art.9, Art.18, Sch.1 Part 1, Sch.2 Part 1

s.21, varied: SI 2013/1542 Sch.1 Part 2, Sch.2 Part 2

s.22, applied: SI 2013/1542 Sch.1 Part 1, Sch.2 Part 1

s.22, varied: SI 2013/1542 Art.11, Sch.1 Part 2, Sch.2 Part 2

s.23, applied: SI 2013/1554 r.6_30

s.24, see *Adler v Crown Prosecution Service* [2013] EWHC 1968 (Admin), (2013) 177 J.P. 558 (QBD (Admin)), Sir John Thomas (President QBD); see *Hanningfield v Chief Constable of Essex* [2013] EWHC 243 (QB), [2013] 1 W.L.R. 3632 (QBD), Eady, J.

s.24, applied: SI 2013/1542 Art.7, Art.16, Sch.1 Part 1, Sch.2 Part 1

s.24, varied: SI 2013/1542 Sch.1 Part 2, Sch.2 Part 2

s.28, see *Adler v Crown Prosecution Service* [2013] EWHC 1968 (Admin), (2013) 177 J.P. 558 (QBD (Admin)), Sir John Thomas (President QBD)

s.28, applied: SI 2013/1542 Sch.1 Part 1, Sch.2 Part 1

s.28, varied: SI 2013/1542 Sch.1 Part 2, Sch.2 Part 2

s.29, applied: SI 2013/1542 Sch.1 Part 1, Sch.2 Part 1

s.29, varied: SI 2013/1542 Sch.1 Part 2, Sch.2 Part 2

s.30, see *R. v Plunkett (Daniel Michael)* [2013] EWCA Crim 261, [2013] 1 W.L.R. 3121 (CA (Crim Div)), Sir John Thomas (President QBD)

s.30, applied: SI 2013/1542 Sch.1 Part 1, Sch.2 Part 1

s.30, varied: SI 2013/1542 Art.21, Sch.1 Part 2, Sch.2 Part 2
s.31, applied: SI 2013/1542 Sch.1 Part 1, Sch.2 Part 1
s.31, varied: SI 2013/1542 Sch.1 Part 2, Sch.2 Part 2
s.32, see *Hanningfield v Chief Constable of Essex* [2013] EWHC 243 (QB), [2013] 1 W.L.R. 3632 (QBD), Eady, J.
s.32, applied: SI 2013/1542 Sch.1 Part 1, Sch.2 Part 1
s.32, varied: SI 2013/1542 Sch.1 Part 2, Sch.2 Part 2
s.34, applied: SI 2013/1542 Sch.2 Part 1
s.34, varied: SI 2013/1542 Sch.2 Part 2
s.35, applied: SI 2013/1542 Sch.2 Part 1
s.35, varied: SI 2013/1542 Art.22, Sch.2 Part 2
s.36, applied: SI 2013/1542 Sch.2 Part 1
s.36, varied: SI 2013/1542 Art.23, Sch.2 Part 2
s.37, see *Hanningfield v Chief Constable of Essex* [2013] EWHC 243 (QB), [2013] 1 W.L.R. 3632 (QBD), Eady, J.
s.37, applied: SI 2013/1542 Sch.2 Part 1, SI 2013/1554 r.7_1
s.37, varied: SI 2013/1542 Sch.2 Part 2
s.37A, applied: SI 2013/1542 Sch.2 Part 1
s.37A, varied: SI 2013/1542 Sch.2 Part 2
s.37B, applied: SI 2013/1542 Sch.2 Part 1
s.37B, varied: SI 2013/1542 Sch.2 Part 2
s.38, applied: SI 2013/1542 Art.14, SI 2013/1554 r.7_1
s.38, referred to: SI 2013/1542 Art.12
s.39, applied: SI 2013/1542 Sch.2 Part 1
s.39, referred to: SI 2013/1542 Art.12
s.39, varied: SI 2013/1542 Art.3, Sch.2 Part 2
s.40, applied: SI 2013/1542 Sch.2 Part 1
s.40, varied: SI 2013/1542 Sch.2 Part 2
s.40A, applied: SI 2013/1542 Sch.2 Part 1
s.40A, varied: SI 2013/1542 Sch.2 Part 2
s.41, applied: SI 2013/1542 Sch.2 Part 1
s.41, referred to: SI 2013/1542 Art.12
s.41, varied: SI 2013/1542 Art.3, Art.24, Sch.2 Part 2
s.42, applied: SI 2013/1542 Sch.2 Part 1
s.42, referred to: SI 2013/1542 Art.12
s.42, varied: SI 2013/1542 Art.25, Sch.2 Part 2
s.43, applied: SI 2013/1542 Sch.2 Part 1
s.43, referred to: SI 2013/1542 Art.12
s.43, varied: SI 2013/1542 Art.3, Art.26, Sch.2 Part 2
s.44, applied: SI 2013/1542 Sch.2 Part 1
s.44, referred to: SI 2013/1542 Art.12
s.44, varied: SI 2013/1542 Art.3, Sch.2 Part 2
s.46, applied: SI 2013/1542 Sch.2 Part 1
s.46, varied: SI 2013/1542 Art.27, Sch.2 Part 2
s.46A, applied: SI 2013/1542 Sch.1 Part 1, Sch.2 Part 1
s.46A, varied: SI 2013/1542 Sch.1 Part 2, Sch.2 Part 2
s.47, applied: SI 2013/1554 r.19_6
s.50, applied: SI 2013/1542 Sch.2 Part 1
s.50, varied: SI 2013/1542 Art.28, Sch.2 Part 2
s.51, applied: SI 2013/1542 Sch.1 Part 1, Sch.2 Part 1
s.51, varied: SI 2013/1542 Sch.1 Part 2, Sch.2 Part 2
s.54, applied: SI 2013/1542 Sch.2 Part 1
s.54, varied: SI 2013/1542 Art.29, Sch.2 Part 2
s.54A, applied: SI 2013/1542 Sch.2 Part 1
s.54A, varied: SI 2013/1542 Sch.2 Part 2
s.55, applied: SI 2013/1542 Sch.2 Part 1
s.55, varied: SI 2013/1542 Art.30, Sch.2 Part 2
s.56, applied: SI 2013/1542 Sch.2 Part 1
s.56, varied: SI 2013/1542 Sch.2 Part 2
s.57, applied: SI 2013/1542 Sch.2 Part 1
s.57, varied: SI 2013/1542 Sch.2 Part 2
s.58, applied: SI 2013/1542 Sch.2 Part 1
s.58, varied: SI 2013/1542 Sch.2 Part 2
s.60, referred to: SI 2013/2685 Art.2
s.60A, referred to: SI 2013/2685 Art.2
s.62, applied: SI 2013/1542 Sch.2 Part 1
s.62, varied: SI 2013/1542 Sch.2 Part 2
s.63A, amended: 2013 c.22 Sch.8 para.186, SI 2013/602 Sch.2 para.19
s.63D, applied: SI 2013/1554 r.6_35, SI 2013/1813 Art.9
s.63D, referred to: SI 2013/1813 Art.2A, Art.10
s.63D, varied: SI 2013/1813 Art.10
s.63E, varied: SI 2013/1813 Art.10
s.63F, applied: SI 2013/1554 r.6_1, r.6_35, r.6_36, SI 2013/1813 Art.2A
s.63F, varied: SI 2013/1813 Art.10
s.63G, varied: SI 2013/1813 Art.10
s.63H, varied: SI 2013/1813 Art.10
s.63I, varied: SI 2013/1813 Art.10
s.63J, varied: SI 2013/1813 Art.10
s.63K, varied: SI 2013/1813 Art.10
s.63L, varied: SI 2013/1813 Art.10
s.63M, varied: SI 2013/1813 Art.10
s.63N, varied: SI 2013/1813 Art.10
s.63O, varied: SI 2013/1813 Art.10
s.63Q, varied: SI 2013/1813 Art.10
s.63R, applied: SI 2013/1542 Sch.2 Part 1, SI 2013/1554 r.6_1, r.6_35
s.63R, varied: SI 2013/1542 Art.31
s.63T, applied: SI 2013/1542 Sch.2 Part 1
s.63T, varied: SI 2013/1542 Art.31, SI 2013/1813 Art.10

s.63U, applied: SI 2013/1542 Sch.2 Part 1
s.63U, varied: SI 2013/1542 Art.31
s.64, applied: SI 2013/1542 Sch.2 Part 1
s.64, varied: SI 2013/1542 Art.31, Sch.2 Part 2
s.65, applied: SI 2013/1542 Sch.2 Part 1
s.65, varied: SI 2013/1542 Sch.2 Part 2
s.65A, amended: SI 2013/2774 Art.2
s.65A, applied: SI 2013/2774
s.65A, enabling: SI 2013/2774
s.66, applied: SI 2013/1554 r.6_30
s.66, referred to: SI 2013/2685 Art.2
s.67, applied: SI 2013/2685
s.67, enabling: SI 2013/2685
s.73, applied: SI 2013/1554 r.5_9, r.35_2
s.74, applied: SI 2013/1554 r.5_9
s.75, applied: SI 2013/1554 r.5_9
s.81, applied: SI 2013/1554 r.33_4
s.81, enabling: SI 2013/1554
s.107, applied: SI 2013/1542 Sch.1 Part 1, Sch.2 Part 1
s.107, varied: SI 2013/1542 Sch.1 Part 2, Sch.2 Part 2
s.113, enabling: SI 2013/2554
s.118, varied: SI 2013/1542 Art.3
Sch.1, see *R. (on the application of Van der Pijl) v Kingston Crown Court* [2012] EWHC 3745 (Admin), [2013] 1 W.L.R. 2706 (DC), Sir John Thomas (President)
Sch.1, applied: SI 2013/2733 Art.9
Sch.1 para.1, varied: SI 2013/1542 Sch.1 Part 2, Sch.2 Part 2
Sch.1 para.2, varied: SI 2013/1542 Sch.1 Part 2, Sch.2 Part 2
Sch.1 para.3, varied: SI 2013/1542 Sch.1 Part 2, Sch.2 Part 2
Sch.1 para.4, varied: SI 2013/1542 Sch.1 Part 2, Sch.2 Part 2
Sch.1 para.5, varied: SI 2013/1542 Sch.1 Part 2, Sch.2 Part 2
Sch.1 para.6, varied: SI 2013/1542 Sch.1 Part 2, Sch.2 Part 2
Sch.1 para.7, varied: SI 2013/1542 Sch.1 Part 2, Sch.2 Part 2
Sch.1 para.8, varied: SI 2013/1542 Sch.1 Part 2, Sch.2 Part 2
Sch.1 para.11, varied: SI 2013/1542 Sch.1 Part 2, Sch.2 Part 2
Sch.1 para.12, applied: SI 2013/1542 Art.8, Art.17
Sch.1 para.12, varied: SI 2013/1542 Sch.1 Part 2, Sch.2 Part 2
Sch.1 para.12A, varied: SI 2013/1542 Sch.1 Part 2, Sch.2 Part 2
Sch.1 para.13, varied: SI 2013/1542 Sch.1 Part 2, Sch.2 Part 2
Sch.1 para.14, varied: SI 2013/1542 Sch.1 Part 2, Sch.2 Part 2
Sch.1 para.15, varied: SI 2013/1542 Sch.1 Part 2, Sch.2 Part 2
Sch.1 para.16, varied: SI 2013/1542 Sch.1 Part 2, Sch.2 Part 2
Sch.1 para.17, varied: SI 2013/1542 Sch.1 Part 2, Sch.2 Part 2

1985

6. Companies Act 1985

s.6, enabling: SI 2013/1947
s.10, enabling: SI 2013/1947
s.12, enabling: SI 2013/1947
s.30, enabling: SI 2013/1947
s.43, enabling: SI 2013/1947
s.49, enabling: SI 2013/1947
s.51, enabling: SI 2013/1947
s.53, enabling: SI 2013/1947
s.54, enabling: SI 2013/1947
s.88, enabling: SI 2013/1947
s.117, enabling: SI 2013/1947
s.169, enabling: SI 2013/1947
s.169A, enabling: SI 2013/1947
s.190, enabling: SI 2013/1947
s.224, enabling: SI 2013/1947
s.225, enabling: SI 2013/1947
s.228, enabling: SI 2013/1947
s.242, enabling: SI 2013/1947
s.244, enabling: SI 2013/1947
s.266, enabling: SI 2013/1947
s.287, enabling: SI 2013/1947
s.288, enabling: SI 2013/1947
s.288A, enabling: SI 2013/1947
s.318, enabling: SI 2013/1947
s.325, enabling: SI 2013/1947
s.353, enabling: SI 2013/1947
s.363, enabling: SI 2013/1947
s.364, enabling: SI 2013/1947
s.391, enabling: SI 2013/1947
s.450, applied: 2013 c.22 Sch.17 para.20
s.466, amended: SI 2013/600 Sch.2 para.1
s.466, repealed (in part): SI 2013/600 Sch.2 para.1
s.652A, enabling: SI 2013/1947
s.652D, enabling: SI 2013/1947
s.691, enabling: SI 2013/1947
s.692, enabling: SI 2013/1947
s.694, enabling: SI 2013/1947
s.701, enabling: SI 2013/1947
s.702, enabling: SI 2013/1947
s.703P, enabling: SI 2013/1947
s.703Q, enabling: SI 2013/1947

s.706, enabling: SI 2013/1947
s.710B, enabling: SI 2013/1947
s.744, enabling: SI 2013/1947
Sch.9 Part II para.6, enabling: SI 2013/1947
Sch.13 Part IV para.27, enabling: SI 2013/1947
Sch.15D para.17, repealed (in part): SI 2013/1881 Sch.1 para.1
Sch.15D para.23, substituted: SI 2013/2329 Sch.1 para.22
Sch.15D para.24, amended: SI 2013/2329 Sch.1 para.22
Sch.15D para.26, amended: SI 2013/3134 Sch.4 para.3
Sch.15D para.28, amended: SI 2013/1881 Sch.1 para.1
Sch.15D para.29, repealed: 2013 c.33 Sch.10 para.1
Sch.15D para.50, repealed: SI 2013/2329 Sch.1 para.22
Sch.21A para.1, enabling: SI 2013/1947
Sch.21A para.4A, enabling: SI 2013/1947
Sch.21A para.7, enabling: SI 2013/1947
Sch.21A para.8, enabling: SI 2013/1947
Sch.21A para.9, enabling: SI 2013/1947

15. Hong Kong Act 1985
applied: 2013 c.22 s.55

23. Prosecution of Offences Act 1985
Part II, applied: SI 2013/1554 r.76_1
s.3, amended: 2013 c.22 Sch.8 para.30
s.9, applied: 2013 c.22 Sch.17 para.6
s.15, amended: 2013 c.22 Sch.17 para.35
s.16, see *Hunter v Newcastle Crown Court* [2013] EWHC 191 (Admin), [2013] 3 W.L.R. 918 (DC), Leveson, L.J.; see *R. v Smith (Ian) (Costs)* [2013] 3 Costs L.R. 516 (Sen Cts Costs Office), Costs Judge Campbell
s.16, applied: SI 2013/435 Sch.3 para.2, SI 2013/1554 r.76_1
s.17, applied: SI 2013/1554 r.8_1, r.76_1
s.18, applied: SI 2013/1554 r.76_1, r.76_5
s.19, see *R. (on the application of CPS) v Bolton Crown Court* [2012] EWHC 3570 (Admin), [2013] 1 W.L.R. 1880 (DC), Richards, L.J.
s.19, applied: SI 2013/1554 r.3_5, r.76_1
s.19, enabling: SI 2013/2526
s.19A, see *R. (on the application of CPS) v Bolton Crown Court* [2012] EWHC 3570 (Admin), [2013] 1 W.L.R. 1880 (DC), Richards, L.J.
s.19A, applied: SI 2013/435 Reg.27, SI 2013/1554 r.76_1, r.68_1, r.63_1, r.3_5
s.19B, see *R. v Applied Language Solutions Ltd (now Capita Translation and Interpreting Ltd)* [2013] EWCA Crim 326, [2013] 1 W.L.R. 3820 (CA (Crim Div)), Sir John Thomas (President QBD)
s.19B, applied: SI 2013/1554 r.76_1, r.68_1, r.63_1
s.20, enabling: SI 2013/2830
s.22, applied: SI 2013/1554 r.19_16
s.23, applied: SI 2013/1554 r.8_1, r.8_2, r.8_3
s.23A, applied: SI 2013/435 Sch.1 para.2, Sch.1 para.22, Sch.2 para.2, Sch.2 para.21, SI 2013/1554 r.8_1
s.29, enabling: SI 2013/2830

29. Enduring Powers of Attorney Act 1985
applied: SI 2013/380 Reg.57, SI 2013/3029 Sch.13 para.1, Sch.13 para.9, SI 2013/3035 Sch.1

37. Family Law (Scotland) Act 1985
s.8, see *R v C* 2013 Fam. L.R. 75 (Sh Ct (Tayside) (Alloa)), Sheriff D O'Carroll; see *W v W* [2013] CSOH 136, 2013 Fam. L.R. 85 (OH), Lord Tyre
s.8, applied: 2013 asp 11 Sch.1 para.4, Sch.1 para.5
s.14, see *R v C* 2013 Fam. L.R. 75 (Sh Ct (Tayside) (Alloa)), Sheriff D O'Carroll
s.14, applied: 2013 asp 11 Sch.1 para.4, Sch.1 para.5

38. Prohibition of Female Circumcision Act 1985
s.1, applied: SI 2013/435 Sch.1 Part 7

48. Food and Environment Protection Act 1985
s.9, see *R. v Frampton (Peter James)* [2012] EWCA Crim 2697, [2013] Env. L.R. 18 (CA (Crim Div)), Hallett, L.J.
s.9, applied: SI 2013/2258 Sch.1 Part 1

50. Representation of the People Act 1985
s.2, amended: 2013 c.6 Sch.4 para.21
s.3, enabling: SI 2013/3198, SI 2013/3206
s.15, applied: SI 2013/3156 Art.10
s.15, enabling: SI 2013/3114
s.16, repealed: 2013 c.6 s.15
s.29, amended: 2013 c.6 s.15

51. Local Government Act 1985
s.15, applied: SI 2013/2210 Reg.2
s.101, enabling: SI 2013/2986
Sch.8 para.15, applied: SI 2013/2196 Reg.2, SI 2013/2996 Reg.2

54. Finance Act 1985
s.97, repealed: 2013 c.2 Sch.1 Part 10
Sch.22 para.6, repealed: 2013 c.2 Sch.1 Part 10

60. Child Abduction and Custody Act 1985
s.10, enabling: SI 2013/3204
s.20, amended: SI 2013/1465 Sch.1 para.1, Sch.1 Part 3
s.24, enabling: SI 2013/3204
Sch.3 Part II para.5, amended: SI 2013/1465 Sch.1 para.1

Sch.3 Part II para.5, repealed (in part): SI 2013/1465 Sch.1 Part 3
Sch.3 Part II para.6, substituted: SI 2013/1465 Sch.1 para.1

61. Administration of Justice Act 1985
s.42, applied: SI 2013/534 Reg.13
s.51, repealed (in part): 2013 c.22 Sch.9 para.141
s.53, amended: 2013 c.22 Sch.9 para.52, Sch.10 para.73
Sch.7 para.7, repealed (in part): 2013 c.22 Sch.9 para.141

62. Oil and Pipelines Act 1985
referred to: 2013 c.32 s.129

66. Bankruptcy (Scotland) Act 1985
applied: SI 2013/1388 Sch.4 para.2, SSI 2013/318 Reg.20
s.1A, referred to: SSI 2013/318 Reg.21
s.2, varied: SI 2013/1388 Reg.19
s.5, applied: SSI 2013/318 Reg.6, Reg.10, Reg.15, Reg.24
s.5, referred to: SSI 2013/318 Reg.7, Reg.10
s.6, applied: SI 2013/1388 Reg.17
s.6, referred to: SSI 2013/318 Reg.4
s.6, varied: SI 2013/1388 Reg.19
s.7, repealed (in part): SSI 2013/225 Reg.19
s.8, applied: SSI 2013/318 Reg.17
s.9, applied: SSI 2013/318 Reg.18
s.9, referred to: SSI 2013/318 Reg.27, Reg.28
s.12, applied: SI 2013/1388 Reg.19
s.12, varied: SI 2013/1388 Reg.19
s.14, repealed (in part): SSI 2013/225 Reg.19
s.15, varied: SI 2013/1388 Reg.19
s.24, applied: SSI 2013/318 Reg.5
s.31B, applied: SI 2013/1554 r.60_4
s.33, referred to: SSI 2013/318 Reg.7
s.40, referred to: SSI 2013/318 Reg.24
s.55, referred to: SSI 2013/318 Reg.24
s.57, applied: SSI 2013/318 Reg.4
s.58A, applied: SSI 2013/318 Reg.4
s.69A, enabling: SSI 2013/318
s.70, varied: SI 2013/1388 Reg.19
s.72, applied: SSI 2013/318
s.72, enabling: SSI 2013/318
Sch.3 Part I para.6B, added: 2013 c.33 s.13
Sch.3 Part II para.9A, added: 2013 c.33 s.13
Sch.5 para.1, applied: SSI 2013/318 Reg.23
Sch.5 para.1A, applied: SSI 2013/318 Reg.23
Sch.5 para.2, applied: SSI 2013/318 Reg.15, Reg.24
Sch.5 para.5, enabling: SSI 2013/318

68. Housing Act 1985
applied: SI 2013/1179 Sch.1
Part V, applied: SI 2013/677 Art.3
s.22, applied: SI 2013/2898 Reg.21
s.27, applied: SI 2013/2356 Sch.2 para.21
s.32, applied: SI 2013/2898 Reg.19, Reg.22, Reg.23
s.34A, enabling: SI 2013/2898
s.43, applied: SI 2013/2898 Reg.19, Reg.22, Reg.23
s.82A, amended: 2013 c.22 Sch.9 para.52
s.110, amended: 2013 c.22 Sch.9 para.52
s.110, disapplied: 2013 c.3 s.5
s.122, applied: SI 2013/677 Art.3
s.125, applied: SI 2013/677 Art.3
s.125D, referred to: SI 2013/677 Art.3
s.125E, referred to: SI 2013/677 Art.3
s.126, applied: SI 2013/677 Art.3
s.127, applied: SI 2013/677 Art.3
s.131, applied: SI 2013/677 Art.2, Art.3
s.131, enabling: SI 2013/677
s.171A, applied: SI 2013/2898 Reg.21
s.171B, applied: SI 2013/2898 Reg.21
s.171C, applied: SI 2013/2898 Reg.21
s.171D, applied: SI 2013/2898 Reg.21
s.171E, applied: SI 2013/2898 Reg.21
s.171F, applied: SI 2013/2898 Reg.21
s.171G, applied: SI 2013/2898 Reg.21
s.171H, applied: SI 2013/2898 Reg.21
s.181, amended: 2013 c.22 Sch.9 para.52
s.269, amended: SI 2013/1036 Sch.1 para.41
s.269, applied: SI 2013/1179 Sch.1
s.269A, amended: SI 2013/1036 Sch.1 para.42
s.272, amended: 2013 c.22 Sch.9 para.52, SI 2013/1036 Sch.1 para.43
s.317, amended: SI 2013/1036 Sch.1 para.44
s.318, amended: SI 2013/1036 Sch.1 para.45
s.318, applied: SI 2013/1179 Sch.1
s.322, amended: SI 2013/1036 Sch.1 para.46
s.323, amended: SI 2013/1036 Sch.1 para.47
s.573, amended: SI 2013/755 Sch.2 para.184
Sch.3A, applied: SI 2013/2898 Reg.21
Sch.3A para.5, applied: SI 2013/2898 Reg.21
Sch.5 para.11, amended: SI 2013/1036 Sch.1 para.48
Sch.18 para.6, amended: 2013 c.22 Sch.9 para.52, Sch.9 para.88

69. Housing Associations Act 1985
s.1, referred to: SI 2013/3029 Sch.10 para.14, SI 2013/3035 Sch.1
s.84, amended: SI 2013/496 Sch.11 para.1
s.86, amended: SI 2013/496 Sch.11 para.1

70. Landlord and Tenant Act 1985
s.20, see *BDW Trading Ltd v South Anglia Housing Ltd* [2013] EWHC 2169 (Ch), [2013] L. & T.R. 25 (Ch D), Nicholas Strauss Q.C.; see *Peverel Properties Ltd v Hughes* [2013] L. & T.R. 6 (UT (Lands)), Judge Huskinson; see *Phillips v*

Francis [2012] EWHC 3650 (Ch), [2013] 1 W.L.R. 2343 (Ch D), Sir Andrew Morritt (Chancellor)
s.20, amended: SI 2013/1036 Sch.1 para.50
s.20C, amended: 2013 c.22 Sch.9 para.52, SI 2013/1036 Sch.1 para.52
s.20ZA, see *BDW Trading Ltd v South Anglia Housing Ltd* [2013] EWHC 2169 (Ch), [2013] L. & T.R. 25 (Ch D), Nicholas Strauss Q.C.; see *Daejan Investments Ltd v Benson* [2013] UKSC 14, [2013] 1 W.L.R. 854 (SC), Lord Neuberger (President); see *Phillips v Francis* [2012] EWHC 3650 (Ch), [2013] 1 W.L.R. 2343 (Ch D), Sir Andrew Morritt (Chancellor)
s.20ZA, amended: SI 2013/1036 Sch.1 para.51
s.20ZA, applied: SI 2013/1179 Sch.1
s.21A, amended: SI 2013/1036 Sch.1 para.53
s.27A, amended: SI 2013/1036 Sch.1 para.54
s.27A, applied: SI 2013/1179 Sch.1
s.29, amended: SI 2013/1036 Sch.1 para.55
s.29, applied: SI 2013/1169 r.29
s.38, see *Phillips v Francis* [2012] EWHC 3650 (Ch), [2013] 1 W.L.R. 2343 (Ch D), Sir Andrew Morritt (Chancellor)
s.38, amended: SI 2013/1036 Sch.1 para.56
Sch.1 para.8, amended: 2013 c.22 Sch.9 para.52, SI 2013/1036 Sch.1 para.57
Sch.1 para.8, applied: SI 2013/1179 Sch.1

1986

5. Agricultural Holdings Act 1986
see *Shirt v Shirt* [2012] EWCA Civ 1029, [2013] 1 F.L.R. 232 (CA (Civ Div)), Lord Neuberger (M.R.); see *Spencer v Secretary of State for Defence* [2012] EWCA Civ 1368, [2013] 1 All E.R. (Comm) 287 (CA (Civ Div)), Mummery, L.J.
applied: SI 2013/1169 r.43
s.26, applied: SI 2013/1169 r.27
s.27, amended: SI 2013/1036 Sch.1 para.204
s.28, applied: SI 2013/1169 r.27
s.39, applied: SI 2013/1169 r.16, r.26, r.27, r.29, r.41, r.42, r.43
s.39, referred to: SI 2013/1169 r.27
s.40, amended: SI 2013/1036 Sch.1 para.205
s.41, applied: SI 2013/1169 r.16, r.26, r.29, r.43
s.42, substituted: SI 2013/1036 Sch.1 para.206
s.44, applied: SI 2013/1169 r.27, r.41, r.43
s.53, see *Compton Beauchamp Estates Ltd v Spence* [2013] EWHC 1101 (Ch), [2013] 2 P. & C.R. 15 (Ch D), Morgan, J.
s.53, amended: SI 2013/1036 Sch.1 para.207
s.53, applied: SI 2013/1169 r.16, r.26, r.29, r.41
s.67, amended: SI 2013/1036 Sch.1 para.208
s.67, applied: SI 2013/1169 r.27
s.96, amended: 2013 c.22 Sch.9 para.56, SI 2013/1036 Sch.1 para.209
Sch.6 Part I para.3, applied: SI 2013/2607 Art.2
Sch.6 Part I para.4, enabling: SI 2013/2607
Sch.6 Part I para.5, amended: SI 2013/1036 Sch.1 para.210

14. Animals (Scientific Procedures) Act 1986
applied: SI 2013/2033 Reg.3, Reg.25
s.2B, referred to: SI 2013/509 Art.2
s.2C, applied: SI 2013/509 Art.2
s.8, enabling: SI 2013/509

31. Airports Act 1986
s.30, amended: SI 2013/610 Sch.1 para.1, Sch.2 para.1
s.36, varied: SI 2013/589 Art.3
s.37, varied: SI 2013/589 Art.3
s.38, varied: SI 2013/589 Art.3
s.39, varied: SI 2013/589 Art.3
s.40, varied: SI 2013/589 Art.3
s.40A, varied: SI 2013/589 Art.3
s.40B, varied: SI 2013/589 Art.3
s.41, varied: SI 2013/589 Art.3
s.42, varied: SI 2013/589 Art.3
s.43, varied: SI 2013/589 Art.3
s.44, varied: SI 2013/589 Art.3
s.44A, varied: SI 2013/589 Art.3
s.44B, varied: SI 2013/589 Art.3
s.45, varied: SI 2013/589 Art.3
s.46, varied: SI 2013/589 Art.3
s.47, varied: SI 2013/589 Art.3
s.48, varied: SI 2013/589 Art.3
s.49, varied: SI 2013/589 Art.3
s.50, varied: SI 2013/589 Art.3
s.51, varied: SI 2013/589 Art.3
s.52, varied: SI 2013/589 Art.3
s.53, varied: SI 2013/589 Art.3
s.54, varied: SI 2013/589 Art.3
s.55, varied: SI 2013/589 Art.3
s.56, varied: SI 2013/589 Art.3
s.69, amended: SI 2013/610 Sch.1 para.1

32. Drug Trafficking Offences Act 1986
s.26B, applied: SI 2013/435 Sch.1 Part 7
s.26C, applied: SI 2013/435 Sch.1 Part 7

33. Disabled Persons (Services, Consultation and Representation) Act 1986
s.7, amended: SI 2013/2341 Art.2

35. Protection of Military Remains Act 1986
s.1, applied: SSI 2013/155 Sch.5 para.14

41. Finance Act 1986
s.75, applied: 2013 asp 11 Sch.10 para.9, Sch.10 para.21
s.78, applied: SI 2013/460 Reg.3

s.80B, applied: SI 2013/1113 Reg.2
s.80B, enabling: SI 2013/1113
s.80C, applied: SI 2013/1382 Reg.4
s.89AA, applied: SI 2013/1382 Reg.4
s.90, amended: SI 2013/1401 Reg.3

44. Gas Act 1986

applied: 2013 c.12 Sch.1 para.1, 2013 c.28 Sch.1
Part I, applied: 2013 c.32 s.136, s.140, s.141
s.4A, applied: 2013 c.32 s.136, s.141
s.4AA, amended: 2013 c.32 s.138
s.4AA, applied: 2013 c.32 s.136, s.141
s.4AB, applied: 2013 c.32 s.136, s.141
s.4AB, repealed: 2013 c.32 s.138
s.4B, applied: 2013 c.32 s.136, s.141
s.4B, repealed (in part): 2013 c.32 s.138
s.5, applied: SI 2013/1726 Art.3
s.6A, applied: SI 2013/1726
s.6A, enabling: SI 2013/1726
s.7, applied: SI 2013/501 Reg.4, SI 2013/588 Reg.4
s.7A, applied: 2013 c.32 s.139, s.141, SI 2013/501 Reg.4, SI 2013/588 Reg.4
s.7B, amended: 2013 c.27 s.19
s.7B, applied: 2013 c.32 s.139
s.8, applied: 2013 c.32 s.139
s.15A, amended: 2013 c.22 Sch.9 para.52
s.23B, amended: 2013 c.24 Sch.6 para.16
s.23C, amended: 2013 c.24 Sch.6 para.17
s.23C, repealed (in part): 2013 c.24 Sch.6 para.17
s.23D, amended: 2013 c.24 Sch.6 para.18
s.23E, amended: 2013 c.24 Sch.6 para.19
s.23F, amended: 2013 c.24 Sch.6 para.20
s.23G, amended: 2013 c.24 Sch.6 para.21
s.27, amended: 2013 c.24 Sch.6 para.22
s.27A, amended: 2013 c.22 Sch.9 para.52
s.28, amended: 2013 c.24 Sch.14 para.2, 2013 c.32 Sch.14 para.1
s.28, repealed (in part): 2013 c.24 Sch.14 para.2
s.30A, amended: 2013 c.24 Sch.14 para.3, 2013 c.32 Sch.14 para.1
s.30A, applied: 2013 c.32 Sch.14 para.1
s.30B, applied: SI 2013/1389 Sch.3 para.4
s.30E, amended: 2013 c.32 Sch.14 para.1
s.30G, added: 2013 c.32 Sch.14 para.1
s.30G, applied: 2013 c.32 Sch.14 para.1
s.30H, added: 2013 c.32 Sch.14 para.1
s.30I, added: 2013 c.32 Sch.14 para.1
s.30J, added: 2013 c.32 Sch.14 para.1
s.30K, added: 2013 c.32 Sch.14 para.1
s.30L, added: 2013 c.32 Sch.14 para.1
s.30M, added: 2013 c.32 Sch.14 para.1
s.30N, added: 2013 c.32 Sch.14 para.1
s.30O, added: 2013 c.32 Sch.14 para.1
s.30O, applied: 2013 c.32 Sch.14 para.1
s.33AB, amended: 2013 c.22 Sch.9 para.52
s.36, enabling: SI 2013/1420
s.36A, amended: 2013 c.24 Sch.15 para.2
s.36A, disapplied: 2013 c.32 s.133
s.38, amended: 2013 c.32 Sch.14 para.1
s.41C, amended: 2013 c.32 s.143
s.41D, amended: 2013 c.24 Sch.6 para.23
s.41E, amended: 2013 c.24 Sch.6 para.24
s.41EA, amended: 2013 c.24 Sch.6 para.25
s.41EB, amended: 2013 c.24 Sch.6 para.26
s.41F, amended: 2013 c.24 Sch.6 para.27
s.48, amended: 2013 c.24 Sch.6 para.28
s.64, amended: 2013 c.32 Sch.14 para.1
Sch.4A, applied: 2013 c.24 Sch.4 para.48
Sch.4A para.1, amended: 2013 c.24 Sch.6 para.29
Sch.4A para.2, amended: 2013 c.24 Sch.6 para.29
Sch.4A para.3, amended: 2013 c.24 Sch.6 para.29
Sch.4A para.4, amended: 2013 c.24 Sch.6 para.29
Sch.4A para.4, repealed (in part): 2013 c.24 Sch.6 para.29
Sch.4A para.5, amended: 2013 c.24 Sch.6 para.29
Sch.4A para.6, amended: 2013 c.24 Sch.6 para.29
Sch.4A para.7, amended: 2013 c.24 Sch.6 para.29
Sch.4A para.8, amended: 2013 c.24 Sch.6 para.29
Sch.4A para.9, amended: 2013 c.24 Sch.6 para.29
Sch.4A para.10, amended: 2013 c.24 Sch.6 para.29
Sch.4A para.11, amended: 2013 c.24 Sch.6 para.29
Sch.4A para.12, amended: 2013 c.24 Sch.6 para.29
Sch.4A para.13, amended: 2013 c.24 Sch.6 para.29

45. Insolvency Act 1986

see *MK Airlines Ltd (In Liquidation), Re* [2012] EWHC 2764 (Ch), [2013] Bus. L.R. 243 (Ch D (Companies Ct)), Nicholas Strauss Q.C.; see *Schmitt v Deichmann* [2012] EWHC 62 (Ch), [2013] Ch. 61 (Ch D), Proudman, J.; see *Sun Legend Investments Ltd v Ho* [2013] B.P.I.R. 533 (CC (Birmingham)), District Judge Musgrave
applied: 2013 c.33 s.128, Sch.6 para.6, SI 2013/349 Reg.105, SI 2013/1046 r.34, r.36, r.57, r.73, r.96, r.98, r.100, r.102, r.108, r.111, r.124, r.143, r.146, r.148, r.150, r.151, r.153, r.154, r.155, r.157, r.162, r.167, r.180, r.182, r.183, r.185, r.186, r.190, r.191, r.193, r.195, r.205, SI 2013/1047 r.24, r.47, r.78, r.80, r.81, r.85, r.88, r.93, r.97, r.98, r.102, SI 2013/1388 Reg.17, Reg.18, SI 2013/3208 r.35, r.37, r.55, r.58, r.74, r.96, r.98, r.102, r.103, r.112, r.115, r.137, r.147, r.150, r.152, r.154, r.155, r.157, r.158, r.159, r.160, r.164, r.174, r.181, r.183, r.184, r.186, r.187, r.191, r.192, r.196, r.205, r.206, r.211
referred to: SI 2013/1046 r.2, r.98, SI 2013/1047 r.2, SI 2013/1388 Sch.4 para.1, SI 2013/3208 r.98, r.100, r.120, r.206

Part I, applied: 2013 c.24 s.93, SI 2013/1046 r.8, r.12, r.14, r.172, SI 2013/1047 r.6, r.9, SI 2013/3208 r.8, r.12, r.14, SSI 2013/174 Reg.14, Reg.16
Part II, applied: SI 2013/77 Art.4, SI 2013/689 Art.6, SI 2013/1046 r.172
Part III, applied: SI 2013/1046 r.172, SSI 2013/174 Reg.14, Reg.16
Part IV, applied: SI 2013/77 Art.4, SI 2013/349 Reg.105, Sch.7 para.29, SI 2013/689 Art.6, SI 2013/1046 r.172, SI 2013/2960 Sch.1 para.2, SSI 2013/174 Reg.14, Reg.16
Part V, applied: SI 2013/77 Art.4, SI 2013/689 Art.6, SI 2013/1046 r.172, SI 2013/1388 Reg.17, Reg.18, SSI 2013/174 Reg.14, Reg.16
Part VI, applied: SI 2013/1046 r.172
Part VII, applied: SI 2013/1046 r.172
Part VIIA, applied: 2013 c.32 Sch.7 para.10, SI 2013/349 Reg.105, Sch.7 para.29, SI 2013/1958 Sch.1 para.7, Sch.1 para.8, Sch.1 para.9, SI 2013/2960 Sch.1 para.2
Part VIII, applied: 2013 c.24 s.94
Part IX, applied: SI 2013/77 Art.4, SI 2013/689 Art.6
s.1, applied: SI 2013/2960 Sch.1 para.2
s.8, applied: SI 2013/2960 Sch.1 para.2
s.29, applied: SI 2013/2960 Sch.1 para.2
s.38, enabling: SI 2013/1947
s.53, amended: SI 2013/600 Sch.2 para.2
s.54, amended: SI 2013/600 Sch.2 para.2
s.62, amended: SI 2013/600 Sch.2 para.2
s.70, amended: SI 2013/600 Sch.2 para.2
s.98, applied: SI 2013/3208 r.55
s.117, amended: 2013 c.22 Sch.9 para.93
s.117, repealed (in part): 2013 c.22 Sch.9 para.93
s.117, enabling: SI 2013/415
s.121, varied: SI 2013/1388 Sch.2 Part 3
s.123, see *BNY Corporate Trustee Services Ltd v Eurosail-UK 2007-3BL Plc* [2013] UKSC 28, [2013] 1 W.L.R. 1408 (SC), Lord Hope, J.S.C.
s.123, applied: 2013 c.33 s.117
s.124, amended: SI 2013/496 Sch.11 para.2
s.124, applied: SI 2013/1046 r.79, SI 2013/1047 r.55, SI 2013/3208 r.79
s.124A, applied: 2013 c.33 s.117, SI 2013/1046 r.6, SI 2013/1047 r.4, SI 2013/1388 Reg.17, SI 2013/3208 r.6
s.124A, varied: SI 2013/1388 Sch.2 Part 3
s.124C, amended: SI 2013/496 Sch.11 para.2
s.125, applied: 2013 c.33 s.117
s.125, varied: SI 2013/1388 Sch.2 Part 3
s.125A, varied: SI 2013/1388 Sch.2 Part 3
s.126, varied: SI 2013/1388 Sch.2 Part 3
s.127, see *RC Brewery Ltd v Revenue and Customs Commissioners* [2013] EWHC 1184 (Ch), [2013] B.C.C. 718 (Ch D (Companies Ct)), Warren, J.; see *Revenue and Customs Commissioners v SED Essex Ltd* [2013] EWHC 1583 (Ch), [2013] B.V.C. 314 (Ch D), John Randall QC
s.127, varied: SI 2013/1388 Sch.2 Part 3
s.128, varied: SI 2013/1388 Sch.2 Part 3
s.129, varied: SI 2013/1388 Sch.2 Part 3
s.130, see *Bank of Ireland v Colliers International UK Plc (In Administration)* [2012] EWHC 2942 (Ch), [2013] Ch. 422 (Ch D (Companies Ct)), David Richards, J.; see *Gaardsoe v Optimal Wealth Management Ltd (in Liquidation)* [2012] EWHC 3266 (Ch), [2013] Ch. 298 (Ch D), John Martin Q.C.
s.130, varied: SI 2013/1388 Sch.2 Part 3
s.131, varied: SI 2013/1388 Sch.2 Part 3
s.132, varied: SI 2013/1388 Sch.2 Part 3
s.133, varied: SI 2013/1388 Sch.2 Part 3
s.134, varied: SI 2013/1388 Sch.2 Part 3
s.135, varied: SI 2013/1388 Sch.2 Part 3
s.136, varied: SI 2013/1388 Sch.2 Part 3
s.136A, varied: SI 2013/1388 Sch.2 Part 3
s.137, varied: SI 2013/1388 Sch.2 Part 3
s.137A, varied: SI 2013/1388 Sch.2 Part 3
s.138, varied: SI 2013/1388 Sch.2 Part 3
s.139, varied: SI 2013/1388 Sch.2 Part 3
s.141, varied: SI 2013/1388 Sch.2 Part 3
s.141A, varied: SI 2013/1388 Sch.2 Part 3
s.142, varied: SI 2013/1388 Sch.2 Part 3
s.143, varied: SI 2013/1388 Sch.2 Part 3
s.144, see *Joint Liquidators of the Scottish Coal Co Ltd, Petitioners* [2013] CSOH 124, 2013 S.L.T. 1055 (OH), Lord Hodge
s.144, varied: SI 2013/1388 Sch.2 Part 3
s.145, varied: SI 2013/1388 Sch.2 Part 3
s.146, varied: SI 2013/1388 Sch.2 Part 3
s.147, varied: SI 2013/1388 Sch.2 Part 3
s.153, varied: SI 2013/1388 Sch.2 Part 3
s.155, see *MG Rover Dealer Properties Ltd v Hunt* [2013] B.C.C. 698 (Ch D (Companies Ct)), Registrar Baister
s.155, varied: SI 2013/1388 Sch.2 Part 3
s.156, varied: SI 2013/1388 Sch.2 Part 3
s.157, varied: SI 2013/1388 Sch.2 Part 3
s.159, varied: SI 2013/1388 Sch.2 Part 3
s.160, varied: SI 2013/1388 Sch.2 Part 3
s.162, varied: SI 2013/1388 Sch.2 Part 3
s.163, varied: SI 2013/1388 Sch.2 Part 3
s.164, varied: SI 2013/1388 Sch.2 Part 3
s.167, varied: SI 2013/1388 Sch.2 Part 3
s.168, varied: SI 2013/1388 Sch.2 Part 3

s.169, see *Joint Liquidators of the Scottish Coal Co Ltd, Petitioners* [2013] CSOH 124, 2013 S.L.T. 1055 (OH), Lord Hodge
s.169, varied: SI 2013/1388 Sch.2 Part 3
s.170, varied: SI 2013/1388 Sch.2 Part 3
s.172, varied: SI 2013/1388 Sch.2 Part 3
s.174, varied: SI 2013/1388 Sch.2 Part 3
s.176A, applied: SI 2013/1046 r.20, r.33, r.64, r.68, r.97, r.99, r.200, SI 2013/1047 r.15, r.34, r.69, r.70, SI 2013/3208 r.20, r.34, r.65, r.69, r.97, r.99, r.201
s.178, see *Joint Liquidators of the Scottish Coal Co Ltd, Petitioners* [2013] CSOH 124, 2013 S.L.T. 1055 (OH), Lord Hodge
s.178, varied: SI 2013/1388 Sch.2 Part 3
s.179, varied: SI 2013/1388 Sch.2 Part 3
s.180, varied: SI 2013/1388 Sch.2 Part 3
s.181, varied: SI 2013/1388 Sch.2 Part 3
s.182, varied: SI 2013/1388 Sch.2 Part 3
s.186, varied: SI 2013/1388 Sch.2 Part 3
s.188, varied: SI 2013/1388 Sch.2 Part 3
s.189, varied: SI 2013/1388 Sch.2 Part 3
s.190, varied: SI 2013/1388 Sch.2 Part 3
s.192, varied: SI 2013/1388 Sch.2 Part 3
s.194, varied: SI 2013/1388 Sch.2 Part 3
s.195, varied: SI 2013/1388 Sch.2 Part 3
s.196, amended: 2013 c.22 Sch.9 para.52
s.196, varied: SI 2013/1388 Sch.2 Part 3
s.197, amended: 2013 c.22 Sch.9 para.93
s.197, varied: SI 2013/1388 Sch.2 Part 3
s.198, varied: SI 2013/1388 Sch.2 Part 3
s.199, varied: SI 2013/1388 Sch.2 Part 3
s.200, varied: SI 2013/1388 Sch.2 Part 3
s.206, varied: SI 2013/1388 Sch.2 Part 3
s.207, varied: SI 2013/1388 Sch.2 Part 3
s.208, varied: SI 2013/1388 Sch.2 Part 3
s.209, varied: SI 2013/1388 Sch.2 Part 3
s.210, varied: SI 2013/1388 Sch.2 Part 3
s.211, varied: SI 2013/1388 Sch.2 Part 3
s.212, see *Coniston Hotel (Kent) LLP (In Liquidation), Re* [2013] EWHC 93 (Ch), [2013] 2 B.C.L.C. 405 (Ch D (Companies Ct)), Norris, J.
s.212, applied: SI 2013/1388 Reg.18
s.212, varied: SI 2013/1388 Sch.2 Part 3
s.213, see *Bilta (UK) Ltd (In Liquidation) v Nazir* [2012] EWHC 2163 (Ch), [2013] 2 W.L.R. 825 (Ch D), Sir Andrew Morritt (Chancellor); see *Bilta (UK) Ltd (In Liquidation) v Nazir* [2013] EWCA Civ 968, [2013] 3 W.L.R. 1167 (CA (Civ Div)), Lord Dyson
s.213, applied: SI 2013/1388 Reg.18
s.213, varied: SI 2013/1388 Sch.2 Part 3
s.214, applied: SI 2013/1388 Reg.18
s.214, varied: SI 2013/1388 Sch.2 Part 3
s.215, applied: SI 2013/1388 Reg.18
s.215, varied: SI 2013/1388 Sch.2 Part 3
s.218, varied: SI 2013/1388 Sch.2 Part 3
s.219, varied: SI 2013/1388 Sch.2 Part 3
s.222, applied: SI 2013/1388 Sch.3 para.2
s.224, varied: SI 2013/1388 Sch.2 Part 3
s.229, varied: SI 2013/1388 Sch.2 Part 3
s.230, varied: SI 2013/1388 Sch.2 Part 3
s.230A, varied: SI 2013/1388 Sch.2 Part 3
s.231, applied: SI 2013/1046 r.20, r.32, SI 2013/1047 r.15, r.33, r.57, SI 2013/3208 r.20, r.33
s.231, varied: SI 2013/1388 Sch.2 Part 3
s.232, varied: SI 2013/1388 Sch.2 Part 3
s.233, applied: 2013 c.33 Sch.6 para.5
s.233, referred to: 2013 c.24 s.92, s.93
s.233, varied: 2013 c.33 Sch.6 para.3
s.234, see *Jackson v Cannons Law Practice LLP* [2013] B.P.I.R. 1020 (Ch D (Companies Ct)), Registrar Jones; see *Uniserve Ltd v Croxen* [2012] EWHC 1190 (Ch), [2013] B.C.C. 825 (Ch D), Sir Andrew Morritt (Chancellor)
s.234, applied: 2013 c.33 Sch.6 para.5
s.234, varied: 2013 c.33 Sch.6 para.3, SI 2013/1388 Sch.2 Part 3
s.235, applied: 2013 c.33 Sch.6 para.5, SI 2013/1046 r.15, r.109, SI 2013/1047 r.10, SI 2013/3208 r.15, r.113
s.235, varied: 2013 c.33 Sch.6 para.3, SI 2013/1388 Sch.2 Part 3
s.236, see *Jackson v Cannons Law Practice LLP* [2013] B.P.I.R. 1020 (Ch D (Companies Ct)), Registrar Jones
s.236, applied: 2013 c.33 Sch.6 para.5, SI 2013/1046 r.106, r.110, r.140, r.142, r.143, r.144, r.145, SI 2013/3208 r.110, r.114, r.144, r.146, r.147, r.148, r.149
s.236, referred to: SI 2013/1046 r.110, SI 2013/3208 r.114
s.236, varied: 2013 c.33 Sch.6 para.3, SI 2013/1388 Sch.2 Part 3
s.237, applied: 2013 c.33 Sch.6 para.5, SI 2013/1046 r.145, SI 2013/3208 r.149
s.237, varied: 2013 c.33 Sch.6 para.3, SI 2013/1388 Sch.2 Part 3
s.238, see *Bilta (UK) Ltd (In Liquidation) v Nazir* [2013] EWCA Civ 968, [2013] 3 W.L.R. 1167 (CA (Civ Div)), Lord Dyson; see *Ovenden Colbert Printers Ltd (In Liquidation), Re* [2013] EWHC 311 (Ch), [2013] 2 B.C.L.C. 388 (Ch D (Companies Ct)), Peter Smith, J.
s.238, applied: 2013 c.33 Sch.6 para.5
s.238, varied: 2013 c.33 Sch.6 para.3, SI 2013/1388 Sch.2 Part 3
s.239, applied: 2013 c.33 Sch.6 para.5

s.239, varied: 2013 c.33 Sch.6 para.3, SI 2013/1388 Sch.2 Part 3
s.240, applied: 2013 c.33 Sch.6 para.5
s.240, varied: 2013 c.33 Sch.6 para.3, SI 2013/1388 Sch.2 Part 3
s.241, varied: 2013 c.33 Sch.6 para.3, Sch.6 para.5, SI 2013/1388 Sch.2 Part 3
s.242, see *Joint Administrators of Prestonpans (Trading) Ltd, Petitioners* 2013 S.L.T. 138 (OH), Lord Malcolm; see *Liquidator of Letham Grange Development Co Ltd v Foxworth Investments Ltd* [2013] CSIH 13, 2013 S.L.T. 445 (IH (Ex Div)), Lady Paton
s.242, applied: 2013 c.33 Sch.6 para.5
s.242, varied: 2013 c.33 Sch.6 para.3, SI 2013/1388 Sch.2 Part 3
s.243, see *Joint Administrators of Prestonpans (Trading) Ltd, Petitioners* 2013 S.L.T. 138 (OH), Lord Malcolm
s.243, varied: 2013 c.33 Sch.6 para.3, Sch.6 para.5, SI 2013/1388 Sch.2 Part 3
s.244, applied: 2013 c.33 Sch.6 para.5
s.244, varied: 2013 c.33 Sch.6 para.3
s.245, applied: 2013 c.33 Sch.6 para.5
s.245, varied: 2013 c.33 Sch.6 para.3
s.246, applied: 2013 c.33 Sch.6 para.5
s.246, varied: 2013 c.33 Sch.6 para.3, SI 2013/1388 Sch.2 Part 3
s.246A, applied: SI 2013/1046 r.173, r.174, SI 2013/1047 r.24, SI 2013/3208 r.174
s.246A, varied: SI 2013/1388 Sch.2 Part 3
s.246B, applied: SI 2013/1046 r.164, SI 2013/1047 r.86, SI 2013/3208 r.166
s.246B, varied: SI 2013/1388 Sch.2 Part 3
s.251, varied: SI 2013/1388 Sch.2 Part 3
s.251A, applied: SI 2013/1394 Reg.5
s.253, repealed (in part): 2013 c.24 Sch.19 para.2
s.255, amended: 2013 c.24 Sch.19 para.3
s.256A, amended: 2013 c.24 Sch.19 para.4
s.263H, added: 2013 c.24 Sch.18
s.263I, added: 2013 c.24 Sch.18
s.263J, added: 2013 c.24 Sch.18
s.263K, added: 2013 c.24 Sch.18
s.263L, added: 2013 c.24 Sch.18
s.263M, added: 2013 c.24 Sch.18
s.263N, added: 2013 c.24 Sch.18
s.263O, added: 2013 c.24 Sch.18
s.264, repealed (in part): 2013 c.24 Sch.19 para.6
s.264, substituted: 2013 c.24 Sch.19 para.5
s.265, see *Akaydin, Re* [2013] B.P.I.R. 539 (Ch D), Registrar Baister; see *Anglo Irish Bank Corp Ltd v Flannery* [2012] EWHC 4090 (Ch), [2013] B.P.I.R. 165 (Ch D), Newey, J; see *Masters v Barclays Bank Plc* [2013] EWHC 2166 (Ch), [2013] B.P.I.R. 1058 (Ch D), Norris, J.
s.265, substituted: 2013 c.24 Sch.19 para.5, Sch.19 para.7
s.266, amended: 2013 c.24 Sch.19 para.8
s.266, substituted: 2013 c.24 Sch.19 para.5
s.267, see *Dunbar Assets Plc v Fowler* [2013] B.P.I.R. 46 (Ch D (Bankruptcy Ct)), Registrar Baister; see *Sun Legend Investments Ltd v Ho* [2013] B.P.I.R. 533 (CC (Birmingham)), District Judge Musgrave; see *Webster v Mackay* [2013] EWHC 2571 (Ch), [2013] B.P.I.R. 1136 (Ch D), Judge Purle Q.C.
s.267, substituted: 2013 c.24 Sch.19 para.5
s.268, substituted: 2013 c.24 Sch.19 para.5
s.269, substituted: 2013 c.24 Sch.19 para.5
s.270, substituted: 2013 c.24 Sch.19 para.5
s.271, see *Dunbar Assets Plc v Fowler* [2013] B.P.I.R. 46 (Ch D (Bankruptcy Ct)), Registrar Baister
s.271, substituted: 2013 c.24 Sch.19 para.5
s.271A, substituted: 2013 c.24 Sch.19 para.5
s.272, see *Gittins v Serco Home Affairs* [2012] EWHC 651 (Ch), [2013] 1 W.L.R. 1218 (Ch D (Leeds)), Judge Behrens
s.272, repealed: 2013 c.24 Sch.19 para.9
s.272, substituted: 2013 c.24 Sch.19 para.5
s.273, repealed: 2013 c.24 Sch.19 para.9
s.273, substituted: 2013 c.24 Sch.19 para.5
s.274, repealed: 2013 c.24 Sch.19 para.9
s.274, substituted: 2013 c.24 Sch.19 para.5
s.274A, repealed: 2013 c.24 Sch.19 para.9
s.274A, substituted: 2013 c.24 Sch.19 para.5
s.275, substituted: 2013 c.24 Sch.19 para.5
s.276, see *Bonney v Mirpuri* [2013] B.P.I.R. 412 (Ch D), Registrar Jones
s.276, substituted: 2013 c.24 Sch.19 para.5
s.277, substituted: 2013 c.24 Sch.19 para.5
s.278, see *Bramston v Haut* [2012] EWCA Civ 1637, [2013] 1 W.L.R. 1720 (CA (Civ Div)), Rix, L.J.
s.278, substituted: 2013 c.24 Sch.19 para.5
s.278, see *Bramston v Haut* [2012] EWCA Civ 1637, [2013] 1 W.L.R. 1720 (CA (Civ Div)), Rix, L.J.
s.278, amended: 2013 c.24 Sch.19 para.11
s.278, substituted: 2013 c.24 Sch.19 para.10
s.279, see *Bramston v Haut* [2012] EWCA Civ 1637, [2013] 1 W.L.R. 1720 (CA (Civ Div)), Rix, L.J.
s.279, repealed (in part): 2013 c.24 Sch.21 para.5
s.279, substituted: 2013 c.24 Sch.19 para.5

s.279, see *Bramston v Haut* [2012] EWCA Civ 1637, [2013] 1 W.L.R. 1720 (CA (Civ Div)), Rix, L.J.
s.279, amended: 2013 c.24 Sch.19 para.12
s.279, substituted: 2013 c.24 Sch.19 para.10
s.280, substituted: 2013 c.24 Sch.19 para.5
s.280, substituted: 2013 c.24 Sch.19 para.10
s.281, see *McRoberts v McRoberts* [2012] EWHC 2966 (Ch), [2013] 1 W.L.R. 1601 (Ch D), Hildyard, J; see *Templeton Insurance Ltd v Brunswick* [2012] EWHC 3319 (Ch), [2013] 3 Costs L.O. 429 (Ch D), Judge Simon Barker Q.C.
s.281, amended: 2013 c.22 Sch.10 para.74
s.281, substituted: 2013 c.24 Sch.19 para.5
s.281, see *McRoberts v McRoberts* [2012] EWHC 2966 (Ch), [2013] 1 W.L.R. 1601 (Ch D), Hildyard, J; see *Templeton Insurance Ltd v Brunswick* [2012] EWHC 3319 (Ch), [2013] 3 Costs L.O. 429 (Ch D), Judge Simon Barker Q.C.
s.281, substituted: 2013 c.24 Sch.19 para.10
s.281A, substituted: 2013 c.24 Sch.19 para.5
s.281A, substituted: 2013 c.24 Sch.19 para.10
s.282, see *1st Credit (Finance) Ltd v Carr* [2013] EWHC 2318 (Ch), [2013] B.P.I.R. 1012 (Ch D), Roth, J.; see *Sparkasse Bremen AG v Armutcu* [2012] EWHC 4026 (Ch), [2013] B.P.I.R. 210 (Ch D), Proudman, J.
s.282, substituted: 2013 c.24 Sch.19 para.5
s.282, see *1st Credit (Finance) Ltd v Carr* [2013] EWHC 2318 (Ch), [2013] B.P.I.R. 1012 (Ch D), Roth, J.; see *Sparkasse Bremen AG v Armutcu* [2012] EWHC 4026 (Ch), [2013] B.P.I.R. 210 (Ch D), Proudman, J.
s.282, amended: 2013 c.24 Sch.19 para.13
s.282, substituted: 2013 c.24 Sch.19 para.10
s.283, amended: 2013 c.24 Sch.19 para.14
s.284, amended: 2013 c.24 Sch.19 para.15
s.285, see *Bank of Ireland v Colliers International UK Plc (In Administration)* [2012] EWHC 2942 (Ch), [2013] Ch. 422 (Ch D (Companies Ct)), David Richards, J.; see *Consolidated Finance Ltd v Collins* [2013] EWCA Civ 475, [2013] E.C.C. 21 (CA (Civ Div)), Arden, L.J.; see *Evans v Finance-U-Ltd* [2013] EWCA Civ 869, [2013] E.C.C. 26 (CA (Civ Div)), Mummery, L.J.
s.285, amended: 2013 c.24 Sch.19 para.16
s.286, see *Consolidated Finance Ltd v Collins* [2013] EWCA Civ 475, [2013] E.C.C. 21 (CA (Civ Div)), Arden, L.J.
s.286, amended: 2013 c.24 Sch.19 para.17
s.286, repealed (in part): 2013 c.24 Sch.19 para.17
s.288, amended: 2013 c.24 Sch.19 para.18
s.290, amended: 2013 c.24 Sch.19 para.19
s.293, amended: 2013 c.24 Sch.19 para.20
s.295, amended: 2013 c.24 Sch.19 para.21
s.297, amended: 2013 c.24 Sch.19 para.22
s.297, repealed (in part): 2013 c.24 Sch.19 para.22
s.298, amended: 2013 c.24 Sch.19 para.23
s.299, amended: 2013 c.24 Sch.19 para.24
s.306B, applied: SI 2013/1554 r.60_4
s.310, applied: SI 2013/2356 Reg.84, SSI 2013/174 Reg.13
s.310A, applied: SI 2013/2356 Reg.84
s.320, see *Hunt v Conwy CBC* [2013] EWHC 1154 (Ch), [2013] B.P.I.R. 790 (Ch D), Sir William Blackburne
s.320, amended: 2013 c.24 Sch.19 para.25
s.321, amended: 2013 c.24 Sch.19 para.26
s.323, amended: 2013 c.24 Sch.19 para.27
s.334, amended: 2013 c.24 Sch.19 para.28
s.336, amended: 2013 c.24 Sch.19 para.29
s.337, amended: 2013 c.24 Sch.19 para.30
s.339, amended: 2013 c.24 Sch.19 para.31
s.340, amended: 2013 c.24 Sch.19 para.32
s.341, amended: 2013 c.24 Sch.19 para.33
s.342, amended: 2013 c.24 Sch.19 para.34
s.342A, amended: 2013 c.24 Sch.19 para.35
s.343, amended: 2013 c.24 Sch.19 para.36
s.344, amended: 2013 c.24 Sch.19 para.37
s.345, amended: 2013 c.24 Sch.19 para.38
s.346, amended: 2013 c.24 Sch.19 para.39
s.347, amended: 2013 c.24 Sch.19 para.40
s.348, amended: 2013 c.24 Sch.19 para.41
s.350, amended: 2013 c.24 Sch.19 para.42
s.351, amended: 2013 c.24 Sch.19 para.43
s.351, repealed (in part): 2013 c.24 Sch.19 para.43
s.354, amended: 2013 c.24 Sch.19 para.44
s.355, amended: 2013 c.24 Sch.19 para.45
s.356, amended: 2013 c.24 Sch.19 para.46
s.358, amended: 2013 c.24 Sch.19 para.47
s.359, amended: 2013 c.24 Sch.19 para.48
s.360, see *Consolidated Finance Ltd v Collins* [2013] EWCA Civ 475, [2013] E.C.C. 21 (CA (Civ Div)), Arden, L.J.
s.360, amended: 2013 c.24 Sch.19 para.49
s.360, applied: SI 2013/435 Sch.1 Part 7
s.364, amended: 2013 c.24 Sch.19 para.50
s.372, referred to: 2013 c.24 s.92, s.94
s.373, amended: 2013 c.22 Sch.9 para.52, Sch.9 para.93
s.374, amended: 2013 c.22 Sch.9 para.93
s.374, enabling: SI 2013/415
s.375, see *Appleyard v Wewelwala* [2012] EWHC 3302 (Ch), [2013] 1 W.L.R. 752 (Ch D), Briggs, J.; see *O'Donnell v Bank of Ireland* [2013] EWHC 489 (Ch), [2013] B.P.I.R. 1078 (Ch D), Newey, J.; see *Official Receiver v Cooksey* [2013] B.P.I.R. 526 (CC (Kingston on Thames)), District Judge

Stewart; see *Webster v Mackay* [2013] EWHC 2571 (Ch), [2013] B.P.I.R. 1136 (Ch D), Judge Purle Q.C.
s.375, amended: 2013 c.22 Sch.9 para.52
s.376, see *Bonney v Mirpuri* [2013] B.P.I.R. 412 (Ch D), Registrar Jones
s.376, amended: 2013 c.24 Sch.19 para.51
s.381, amended: 2013 c.24 Sch.19 para.52
s.383, amended: 2013 c.24 Sch.19 para.53
s.384, amended: 2013 c.24 Sch.19 para.54
s.385, see *Hunt v Conwy CBC* [2013] EWHC 1154 (Ch), [2013] B.P.I.R. 790 (Ch D), Sir William Blackburne
s.385, amended: 2013 c.24 Sch.19 para.55
s.386, see *Joint Liquidators of the Scottish Coal Co Ltd, Petitioners* [2013] CSOH 124, 2013 S.L.T. 1055 (OH), Lord Hodge
s.386, amended: 2013 c.33 s.13
s.386, applied: 2013 c.33 Sch.6 para.5, SI 2013/1047 r.46
s.386, varied: 2013 c.33 Sch.6 para.3
s.387, amended: 2013 c.24 Sch.19 para.56
s.387, applied: 2013 c.33 Sch.6 para.5
s.387, varied: 2013 c.33 Sch.6 para.3
s.388, varied: SI 2013/1388 Sch.2 Part 3
s.389, varied: 2013 c.33 Sch.6 para.3, Sch.6 para.5, SI 2013/1388 Sch.2 Part 3
s.389A, amended: 2013 c.24 Sch.19 para.57
s.390, amended: 2013 c.24 Sch.19 para.58
s.390, varied: 2013 c.33 Sch.6 para.3, Sch.6 para.5
s.391, applied: 2013 c.33 Sch.6 para.5
s.391, varied: 2013 c.33 Sch.6 para.3
s.398A, added: 2013 c.24 s.71
s.399, amended: 2013 c.22 Sch.9 para.93
s.411, applied: 2013 c.33 s.116, s.121, SI 2013/3208
s.411, enabling: SI 2013/1046, SI 2013/1047, SI 2013/2950, SI 2013/3208
s.412, enabling: SI 2013/2135
s.413, amended: 2013 c.22 Sch.9 para.93
s.413, applied: SI 2013/1046, SI 2013/2135, SI 2013/2950
s.414, applied: SI 2013/2302
s.414, enabling: SI 2013/1410, SI 2013/2302
s.415, amended: 2013 c.24 Sch.19 para.59
s.415, applied: SI 2013/2302
s.415, enabling: SI 2013/1410, SI 2013/2302
s.421A, amended: 2013 c.24 Sch.19 para.60
s.423, see *AC v DC (Financial Remedy: Effect of s.37 Avoidance Orders)* [2012] EWHC 2032 (Fam), [2013] 2 F.L.R. 1483 (Fam Div), Mostyn, J.; see *Fortress Value Recovery Fund I LLC v Blue Skye Special Opportunities Fund LP* [2013] EWHC 14 (Comm), [2013] 1 All E.R. (Comm) 973 (QBD (Comm)), Flaux, J.; see *Schmitt v Deichmann* [2012] EWHC 62 (Ch), [2013] Ch. 61 (Ch D), Proudman, J.; see *Simon Carves Ltd, Re* [2013] EWHC 685 (Ch), [2013] 2 B.C.L.C. 100 (Ch D), Sir William Blackburne; see *Williams v Taylor* [2012] EWCA Civ 1443, [2013] B.P.I.R. 133 (CA (Civ Div)), Ward, L.J.; see *Withers LLP v Harrison-Welch* [2012] EWHC 3077 (QB), [2013] B.P.I.R. 145 (QBD), Judge Shaun Spencer Q.C.
s.423, applied: 2013 c.33 Sch.6 para.5
s.423, varied: 2013 c.33 Sch.6 para.3
s.424, see *Simon Carves Ltd, Re* [2013] EWHC 685 (Ch), [2013] 2 B.C.L.C. 100 (Ch D), Sir William Blackburne
s.424, amended: 2013 c.24 Sch.19 para.61
s.424, applied: 2013 c.33 Sch.6 para.5
s.424, varied: 2013 c.33 Sch.6 para.3, Sch.6 para.5
s.425, applied: 2013 c.33 Sch.6 para.5
s.425, varied: 2013 c.33 Sch.6 para.3, Sch.6 para.5
s.429, amended: 2013 c.22 Sch.9 para.52
s.429, applied: SI 2013/349 Sch.7 para.29
s.430, applied: 2013 c.33 Sch.6 para.5
s.430, varied: 2013 c.33 Sch.6 para.3, SI 2013/1388 Sch.2 Part 3
s.431, applied: 2013 c.33 Sch.6 para.5, SI 2013/1046 r.150, SI 2013/1047 r.93, SI 2013/3208 r.154
s.431, varied: 2013 c.33 Sch.6 para.3, SI 2013/1388 Sch.2 Part 3
s.432, applied: 2013 c.33 Sch.6 para.5
s.432, varied: 2013 c.33 Sch.6 para.3, SI 2013/1388 Sch.2 Part 3
s.434C, varied: SI 2013/1388 Sch.2 Part 3
Sch.B1, applied: 2013 c.33 s.120, s.121, SI 2013/349 Reg.105, Sch.7 para.29, SI 2013/1046 r.8, r.12, r.14, r.133, SI 2013/1047 r.6, r.9, SI 2013/3208 r.8, r.12, r.14, SSI 2013/174 Reg.14, Reg.16
Sch.B1, referred to: SI 2013/1047 r.2
Sch.B1 Part 2 para.13, applied: 2013 c.33 s.123
Sch.B1 Part 3 para.14, applied: SI 2013/1046 r.6, r.10
Sch.B1 Part 6 para.40, applied: 2013 c.33 Sch.6 para.5
Sch.B1 Part 6 para.40, varied: 2013 c.33 Sch.6 para.3
Sch.B1 Part 6 para.41, applied: 2013 c.33 Sch.6 para.5
Sch.B1 Part 6 para.41, varied: 2013 c.33 Sch.6 para.3
Sch.B1 Part 6 para.42, varied: 2013 c.33 Sch.6 para.3, Sch.6 para.5

Sch.B1 Part 6 para.43, applied: 2013 c.33 Sch.6 para.5
Sch.B1 Part 6 para.43, varied: 2013 c.33 Sch.6 para.3
Sch.B1 Part 6 para.44, applied: 2013 c.33 Sch.6 para.5
Sch.B1 Part 6 para.44, varied: 2013 c.33 Sch.6 para.3
Sch.B1 Part 7 para.46, applied: SI 2013/1047 r.9
Sch.B1 Part 7 para.46, varied: 2013 c.33 Sch.6 para.3, Sch.6 para.5
Sch.B1 Part 7 para.47, applied: 2013 c.33 Sch.6 para.5, SI 2013/1046 r.18, r.109, SI 2013/1047 r.10, r.13
Sch.B1 Part 7 para.47, varied: 2013 c.33 Sch.6 para.3
Sch.B1 Part 7 para.48, applied: 2013 c.33 Sch.6 para.5, SI 2013/1046 r.15, r.18, SI 2013/1047 r.10, r.13
Sch.B1 Part 7 para.48, varied: 2013 c.33 Sch.6 para.3
Sch.B1 Part 7 para.49, applied: SI 2013/1046 r.17, r.20, r.21, SI 2013/1047 r.12, r.15, r.16
Sch.B1 Part 7 para.49, referred to: SI 2013/1046 r.20, r.21, SI 2013/1047 r.16
Sch.B1 Part 7 para.49, varied: 2013 c.33 Sch.6 para.3, Sch.6 para.5
Sch.B1 Part 7 para.51, applied: SI 2013/1047 r.23
Sch.B1 Part 7 para.54, applied: SI 2013/1046 r.32, SI 2013/1047 r.33
Sch.B1 Part 7 para.58, applied: SI 2013/1047 r.23
Sch.B1 Part 8 para.59, applied: 2013 c.33 Sch.6 para.5
Sch.B1 Part 8 para.59, varied: 2013 c.33 Sch.6 para.3
Sch.B1 Part 8 para.60, varied: 2013 c.33 Sch.6 para.3
Sch.B1 Part 8 para.61, applied: 2013 c.33 Sch.6 para.5
Sch.B1 Part 8 para.61, varied: 2013 c.33 Sch.6 para.3
Sch.B1 Part 8 para.62, applied: 2013 c.33 Sch.6 para.5, SI 2013/1046 r.22, SI 2013/1047 r.18
Sch.B1 Part 8 para.62, varied: 2013 c.33 Sch.6 para.3
Sch.B1 Part 8 para.63, varied: 2013 c.33 Sch.6 para.3, Sch.6 para.5
Sch.B1 Part 8 para.64, applied: 2013 c.33 Sch.6 para.5
Sch.B1 Part 8 para.64, varied: 2013 c.33 Sch.6 para.3
Sch.B1 Part 8 para.65, applied: 2013 c.33 Sch.6 para.5, SI 2013/1047 r.33
Sch.B1 Part 8 para.65, varied: 2013 c.33 Sch.6 para.3
Sch.B1 Part 8 para.66, applied: 2013 c.33 Sch.6 para.5
Sch.B1 Part 8 para.66, varied: 2013 c.33 Sch.6 para.3
Sch.B1 Part 8 para.67, applied: 2013 c.33 Sch.6 para.5
Sch.B1 Part 8 para.67, varied: 2013 c.33 Sch.6 para.3
Sch.B1 Part 8 para.68, varied: 2013 c.33 Sch.6 para.3, Sch.6 para.5
Sch.B1 Part 8 para.69, applied: 2013 c.33 Sch.6 para.5
Sch.B1 Part 8 para.69, varied: 2013 c.33 Sch.6 para.3
Sch.B1 Part 8 para.70, applied: 2013 c.33 Sch.6 para.5
Sch.B1 Part 8 para.70, varied: 2013 c.33 Sch.6 para.3
Sch.B1 Part 8 para.71, applied: 2013 c.33 Sch.6 para.5, SI 2013/1046 r.35, SI 2013/1047 r.35
Sch.B1 Part 8 para.71, varied: 2013 c.33 Sch.6 para.3
Sch.B1 Part 8 para.72, applied: 2013 c.33 Sch.6 para.5, SI 2013/1046 r.35, SI 2013/1047 r.35
Sch.B1 Part 8 para.72, varied: 2013 c.33 Sch.6 para.3
Sch.B1 Part 8 para.73, applied: 2013 c.33 Sch.6 para.5
Sch.B1 Part 8 para.73, varied: 2013 c.33 Sch.6 para.3
Sch.B1 Part 8 para.74, varied: 2013 c.33 Sch.6 para.3, Sch.6 para.5
Sch.B1 Part 8 para.75, varied: 2013 c.33 Sch.6 para.3, Sch.6 para.5
Sch.B1 Part 9 para.79, applied: SI 2013/1046 r.79, r.83, SI 2013/1047 r.55, r.59
Sch.B1 Part 9 para.79, varied: 2013 c.33 Sch.6 para.3, Sch.6 para.5
Sch.B1 Part 9 para.83, applied: SI 2013/1046 r.32, r.81, r.83, SI 2013/1047 r.15, r.33, r.49, r.57, r.59
Sch.B1 Part 9 para.84, applied: 2013 c.33 Sch.6 para.5, SI 2013/1046 r.82, r.83, SI 2013/1047 r.58, r.59
Sch.B1 Part 9 para.84, varied: 2013 c.33 Sch.6 para.3
Sch.B1 Part 9 para.85, applied: 2013 c.33 Sch.6 para.5
Sch.B1 Part 9 para.85, varied: 2013 c.33 Sch.6 para.3
Sch.B1 Part 9 para.86, applied: 2013 c.33 Sch.6 para.5

Sch.B1 Part 9 para.86, varied: 2013 c.33 Sch.6 para.3
Sch.B1 Part 10 para.87, varied: 2013 c.33 Sch.6 para.3, Sch.6 para.5
Sch.B1 Part 10 para.88, applied: SI 2013/1046 r.87
Sch.B1 Part 10 para.88, varied: 2013 c.33 Sch.6 para.3, Sch.6 para.5
Sch.B1 Part 10 para.89, applied: SI 2013/1046 r.88, SI 2013/1047 r.64
Sch.B1 Part 10 para.89, varied: 2013 c.33 Sch.6 para.3, Sch.6 para.5
Sch.B1 Part 10 para.90, varied: 2013 c.33 Sch.6 para.3
Sch.B1 Part 10 para.91, applied: 2013 c.33 s.127, SI 2013/1046 r.90, SI 2013/1047 r.65
Sch.B1 Part 10 para.91, varied: 2013 c.33 Sch.6 para.3, Sch.6 para.5
Sch.B1 Part 10 para.98, varied: 2013 c.33 Sch.6 para.3, Sch.6 para.5
Sch.B1 Part 10 para.99, applied: SI 2013/1046 r.36, r.38, SI 2013/1047 r.51
Sch.B1 Part 10 para.99, varied: 2013 c.33 Sch.6 para.3, Sch.6 para.5
Sch.B1 Part 11 para.100, varied: 2013 c.33 Sch.6 para.3
Sch.B1 Part 11 para.101, varied: 2013 c.33 Sch.6 para.3
Sch.B1 Part 11 para.102, varied: 2013 c.33 Sch.6 para.3
Sch.B1 Part 11 para.103, applied: 2013 c.33 s.127, SI 2013/1047 r.67
Sch.B1 Part 11 para.103, varied: 2013 c.33 Sch.6 para.3, Sch.6 para.5
Sch.B1 Part 11 para.104, applied: 2013 c.33 Sch.6 para.5
Sch.B1 Part 11 para.104, varied: 2013 c.33 Sch.6 para.3
Sch.B1 Part 11 para.106, applied: 2013 c.33 Sch.6 para.5
Sch.B1 Part 11 para.106, varied: 2013 c.33 Sch.6 para.3
Sch.B1 Part 11 para.107, applied: 2013 c.33 Sch.6 para.5, SI 2013/1046 r.20, SI 2013/1047 r.15
Sch.B1 Part 11 para.107, varied: 2013 c.33 Sch.6 para.3
Sch.B1 Part 11 para.108, applied: 2013 c.33 Sch.6 para.5
Sch.B1 Part 11 para.108, varied: 2013 c.33 Sch.6 para.3
Sch.B1 Part 11 para.109, applied: 2013 c.33 Sch.6 para.5
Sch.B1 Part 11 para.109, varied: 2013 c.33 Sch.6 para.3
Sch.B1 Part 11 para.110, varied: 2013 c.33 Sch.6 para.3, Sch.6 para.5
Sch.B1 Part 11 para.111, applied: 2013 c.33 Sch.6 para.5
Sch.B1 Part 11 para.111, varied: 2013 c.33 Sch.6 para.3
Sch.B1 Part 11 para.112, applied: 2013 c.33 Sch.6 para.5
Sch.B1 Part 11 para.112, varied: 2013 c.33 Sch.6 para.3
Sch.B1 Part 11 para.113, applied: 2013 c.33 Sch.6 para.5
Sch.B1 Part 11 para.113, varied: 2013 c.33 Sch.6 para.3
Sch.B1 Part 11 para.114, applied: 2013 c.33 Sch.6 para.5
Sch.B1 Part 11 para.114, varied: 2013 c.33 Sch.6 para.3
Sch.B1 Part 11 para.115, applied: 2013 c.33 Sch.6 para.5
Sch.B1 Part 11 para.115, varied: 2013 c.33 Sch.6 para.3
Sch.B1 Part 11 para.116, applied: 2013 c.33 Sch.6 para.5
Sch.B1 Part 11 para.116, varied: 2013 c.33 Sch.6 para.3
Sch.1B, applied: SI 2013/2960 Sch.1 para.2
Sch.1 para.1, varied: 2013 c.33 Sch.6 para.3, Sch.6 para.5
Sch.1 para.2, varied: 2013 c.33 Sch.6 para.3, Sch.6 para.5
Sch.1 para.3, varied: 2013 c.33 Sch.6 para.3, Sch.6 para.5
Sch.1 para.4, varied: 2013 c.33 Sch.6 para.3, Sch.6 para.5
Sch.1 para.5, varied: 2013 c.33 Sch.6 para.3, Sch.6 para.5
Sch.1 para.6, varied: 2013 c.33 Sch.6 para.3, Sch.6 para.5
Sch.1 para.7, varied: 2013 c.33 Sch.6 para.3, Sch.6 para.5
Sch.1 para.8, varied: 2013 c.33 Sch.6 para.3, Sch.6 para.5
Sch.1 para.9, varied: 2013 c.33 Sch.6 para.3, Sch.6 para.5
Sch.1 para.10, varied: 2013 c.33 Sch.6 para.3, Sch.6 para.5
Sch.1 para.11, varied: 2013 c.33 Sch.6 para.3, Sch.6 para.5
Sch.1 para.12, varied: 2013 c.33 Sch.6 para.3, Sch.6 para.5
Sch.1 para.13, varied: 2013 c.33 Sch.6 para.3, Sch.6 para.5

Sch.1 para.14, varied: 2013 c.33 Sch.6 para.3, Sch.6 para.5
Sch.1 para.15, varied: 2013 c.33 Sch.6 para.3, Sch.6 para.5
Sch.1 para.16, varied: 2013 c.33 Sch.6 para.3, Sch.6 para.5
Sch.1 para.17, varied: 2013 c.33 Sch.6 para.3, Sch.6 para.5
Sch.1 para.18, varied: 2013 c.33 Sch.6 para.3, Sch.6 para.5
Sch.1 para.19, varied: 2013 c.33 Sch.6 para.3, Sch.6 para.5
Sch.1 para.20, varied: 2013 c.33 Sch.6 para.3, Sch.6 para.5
Sch.1 para.21, varied: 2013 c.33 Sch.6 para.3, Sch.6 para.5
Sch.1 para.22, varied: 2013 c.33 Sch.6 para.3, Sch.6 para.5
Sch.1 para.23, varied: 2013 c.33 Sch.6 para.3, Sch.6 para.5
Sch.4A, applied: SI 2013/349 Reg.105, Sch.7 para.29
Sch.4ZB, applied: SI 2013/349 Reg.105, Sch.7 para.29
Sch.4 Part I para.1, varied: SI 2013/1388 Sch.2 para.3, Sch.2 Part 3
Sch.4 Part I para.2, varied: SI 2013/1388 Sch.2 para.3, Sch.2 Part 3
Sch.4 Part I para.3, varied: SI 2013/1388 Sch.2 para.3, Sch.2 Part 3
Sch.4 Part I para.3A, varied: SI 2013/1388 Sch.2 para.3, Sch.2 Part 3
Sch.4 Part II para.4, varied: SI 2013/1388 Sch.2 para.3, Sch.2 Part 3
Sch.4 Part II para.5, varied: SI 2013/1388 Sch.2 para.3, Sch.2 Part 3
Sch.4 Part III para.6, varied: SI 2013/1388 Sch.2 para.3, Sch.2 Part 3
Sch.4 Part III para.6A, varied: SI 2013/1388 Sch.2 para.3, Sch.2 Part 3
Sch.4 Part III para.7, varied: SI 2013/1388 Sch.2 para.3, Sch.2 Part 3
Sch.4 Part III para.8, varied: SI 2013/1388 Sch.2 para.3, Sch.2 Part 3
Sch.4 Part III para.9, varied: SI 2013/1388 Sch.2 para.3, Sch.2 Part 3
Sch.4 Part III para.10, varied: SI 2013/1388 Sch.2 para.3, Sch.2 Part 3
Sch.4 Part III para.11, varied: SI 2013/1388 Sch.2 para.3, Sch.2 Part 3
Sch.4 Part III para.12, varied: SI 2013/1388 Sch.2 para.3, Sch.2 Part 3
Sch.4 Part III para.13, varied: SI 2013/1388 Sch.2 para.3, Sch.2 Part 3
Sch.4A para.2, amended: 2013 c.24 Sch.19 para.63
Sch.4ZA Part I para.3, substituted: 2013 c.24 Sch.19 para.62
Sch.6, see *Joint Liquidators of the Scottish Coal Co Ltd, Petitioners* [2013] CSOH 124, 2013 S.L.T. 1055 (OH), Lord Hodge
Sch.6, applied: 2013 c.33 Sch.6 para.5
Sch.6 para.1, varied: 2013 c.33 Sch.6 para.3
Sch.6 para.2, varied: 2013 c.33 Sch.6 para.3
Sch.6 para.3, varied: 2013 c.33 Sch.6 para.3
Sch.6 para.3A, varied: 2013 c.33 Sch.6 para.3
Sch.6 para.3B, varied: 2013 c.33 Sch.6 para.3
Sch.6 para.3C, varied: 2013 c.33 Sch.6 para.3
Sch.6 para.3D, varied: 2013 c.33 Sch.6 para.3
Sch.6 para.4, varied: 2013 c.33 Sch.6 para.3
Sch.6 para.5, varied: 2013 c.33 Sch.6 para.3
Sch.6 para.5A, varied: 2013 c.33 Sch.6 para.3
Sch.6 para.5B, varied: 2013 c.33 Sch.6 para.3
Sch.6 para.5C, varied: 2013 c.33 Sch.6 para.3
Sch.6 para.6, varied: 2013 c.33 Sch.6 para.3
Sch.6 para.7, varied: 2013 c.33 Sch.6 para.3
Sch.6 para.8, varied: 2013 c.33 Sch.6 para.3
Sch.6 para.9, varied: 2013 c.33 Sch.6 para.3
Sch.6 para.10, varied: 2013 c.33 Sch.6 para.3
Sch.6 para.11, varied: 2013 c.33 Sch.6 para.3
Sch.6 para.12, varied: 2013 c.33 Sch.6 para.3
Sch.6 para.13, varied: 2013 c.33 Sch.6 para.3
Sch.6 para.14, amended: 2013 c.24 Sch.19 para.64
Sch.6 para.14, varied: 2013 c.33 Sch.6 para.3
Sch.6 para.15, varied: 2013 c.33 Sch.6 para.3
Sch.6 para.15A, varied: 2013 c.33 Sch.6 para.3
Sch.6 para.15B, added: 2013 c.33 s.13
Sch.6 para.15B, varied: 2013 c.33 Sch.6 para.3
Sch.6 para.15C, added: 2013 c.33 s.13
Sch.6 para.15C, varied: 2013 c.33 Sch.6 para.3
Sch.6 para.16, varied: 2013 c.33 Sch.6 para.3
Sch.8 para.27, applied: SI 2013/3208 r.150
Sch.9 para.2, amended: 2013 c.22 Sch.9 para.93
Sch.9 para.4A, added: 2013 c.24 Sch.19 para.65
Sch.9 para.4B, added: 2013 c.24 Sch.19 para.65
Sch.9 para.4C, added: 2013 c.24 Sch.19 para.65
Sch.9 para.24A, added: 2013 c.24 Sch.19 para.65
Sch.9 para.24B, added: 2013 c.24 Sch.19 para.65
Sch.9 para.24C, added: 2013 c.24 Sch.19 para.65
Sch.9 para.24D, added: 2013 c.24 Sch.19 para.65
Sch.10, amended: 2013 c.24 Sch.19 para.66
Sch.10, applied: 2013 c.33 Sch.6 para.5
Sch.10, varied: 2013 c.33 Sch.6 para.3, SI 2013/1388 Sch.2 Part 3

46. Company Directors Disqualification Act 1986

applied: 2013 c.32 Sch.7 para.10, SI 2013/349 Reg.105, Sch.7 para.29, SI 2013/1773 Reg.15, SI 2013/2960 Sch.1 para.2
s.1, applied: SI 2013/1773 Reg.10

s.9E, amended: 2013 c.33 s.67, Sch.8 para.8
s.22E, amended: SI 2013/496 Sch.11 para.3

47. Legal Aid (Scotland) Act 1986
applied: 2013 c.22 Sch.21 para.50, SSI 2013/200 Reg.24
referred to: SSI 2013/200 Reg.18
Part VA, applied: SSI 2013/200 Reg.7
Part VA, referred to: SSI 2013/200 Reg.18
s.4, amended: 2013 asp 3 s.23
s.4, referred to: SSI 2013/200 Reg.18
s.8, amended: 2013 asp 3 s.23, SSI 2013/137 Reg.3
s.8A, amended: 2013 asp 3 s.17, s.23, 2013 c.22 Sch.21 para.50
s.8A, applied: 2013 c.22 Sch.21 para.50
s.9, amended: 2013 asp 3 s.18, s.23
s.9, enabling: SSI 2013/200
s.9A, added: 2013 asp 3 s.18
s.9B, added: 2013 asp 3 s.18
s.11, amended: 2013 asp 3 s.19, s.23, SSI 2013/137 Reg.3
s.11, repealed (in part): 2013 asp 3 s.23
s.11A, added: 2013 asp 3 s.19
s.12, amended: 2013 asp 3 s.23
s.12, enabling: SSI 2013/142, SSI 2013/250
s.17, enabling: SSI 2013/142
s.21, amended: SI 2013/728 Art.2
s.25AA, amended: 2013 asp 3 s.21
s.25AB, amended: SI 2013/728 Art.2
s.25AC, added: 2013 asp 3 s.20
s.25AD, added: 2013 asp 3 s.20
s.28C, applied: SSI 2013/200 Reg.35
s.28D, applied: SSI 2013/200 Reg.19, Reg.30
s.28E, applied: SSI 2013/200 Reg.19, Reg.30
s.28F, applied: SSI 2013/200 Reg.19, Reg.30
s.28G, applied: SSI 2013/200 Reg.19, Reg.20, Reg.27, Reg.29, Reg.31
s.28H, applied: SSI 2013/200 Reg.19, Reg.20
s.28J, applied: SSI 2013/200 Reg.20
s.28K, applied: SSI 2013/200 Reg.14, Reg.16, Reg.17, Reg.29, Reg.34, Sch.2 para.7, Sch.2 para.15
s.28K, referred to: SSI 2013/200 Reg.18
s.28K, enabling: SSI 2013/200
s.28L, enabling: SSI 2013/200
s.29, applied: SSI 2013/150 Art.2
s.29, varied: SSI 2013/150 Art.19
s.31, applied: SSI 2013/200 Reg.35
s.31, enabling: SSI 2013/200
s.33, enabling: SSI 2013/92, SSI 2013/144, SSI 2013/250, SSI 2013/320
s.33A, amended: 2013 asp 3 s.23
s.33ZA, added: 2013 asp 3 s.22
s.36, amended: 2013 asp 3 s.23
s.36, enabling: SSI 2013/92, SSI 2013/200
s.37, amended: 2013 asp 3 s.23
s.37, applied: SSI 2013/200
s.38, amended: 2013 asp 3 s.15
s.42, applied: SSI 2013/200 Reg.11
s.42, enabling: SSI 2013/142, SSI 2013/200

49. Agriculture Act 1986
s.18, amended: SI 2013/755 Sch.2 para.185
Sch.1 Part III para.11, amended: SI 2013/1036 Sch.1 para.211

53. Building Societies Act 1986
applied: 2013 c.33 s.7
s.1, amended: 2013 c.33 Sch.9 para.4, SI 2013/496 Sch.8 para.2, Sch.8 para.3
s.1, repealed (in part): SI 2013/496 Sch.8 para.3
s.2, amended: SI 2013/496 Sch.8 para.2
s.3, amended: SI 2013/496 Sch.8 para.2
s.4, amended: SI 2013/496 Sch.8 para.2
s.5, amended: SI 2013/496 Sch.8 para.4
s.6, amended: SI 2013/496 Sch.8 para.5
s.7, amended: 2013 c.33 Sch.9 para.2, SI 2013/496 Sch.8 para.6
s.8, amended: SI 2013/496 Sch.8 para.7
s.9A, amended: SI 2013/496 Sch.8 para.8
s.9B, repealed: 2013 c.33 Sch.9 para.4
s.36, amended: SI 2013/496 Sch.8 para.9, Sch.8 para.10
s.36A, amended: SI 2013/496 Sch.8 para.9, Sch.8 para.11
s.37, amended: SI 2013/496 Sch.8 para.9, Sch.8 para.12
s.38, amended: SI 2013/496 Sch.8 para.9
s.39, amended: SI 2013/496 Sch.8 para.9
s.40, amended: SI 2013/496 Sch.8 para.9
s.41, amended: SI 2013/496 Sch.8 para.9
s.42, amended: SI 2013/496 Sch.8 para.9
s.42A, amended: SI 2013/496 Sch.8 para.9
s.42B, amended: SI 2013/496 Sch.8 para.9, Sch.8 para.13
s.42C, amended: SI 2013/496 Sch.8 para.9, Sch.8 para.14
s.43, amended: SI 2013/496 Sch.8 para.9
s.43A, amended: SI 2013/496 Sch.8 para.9
s.43B, amended: SI 2013/496 Sch.8 para.9
s.44, amended: SI 2013/496 Sch.8 para.9
s.45, amended: SI 2013/496 Sch.8 para.9
s.45A, amended: SI 2013/496 Sch.8 para.9
s.45AA, amended: SI 2013/496 Sch.8 para.9
s.46, amended: SI 2013/496 Sch.8 para.9
s.46A, amended: SI 2013/496 Sch.8 para.9, Sch.8 para.15
s.47, amended: SI 2013/496 Sch.8 para.9
s.48, amended: SI 2013/496 Sch.8 para.9
s.49, amended: SI 2013/496 Sch.8 para.9

s.50, amended: SI 2013/496 Sch.8 para.9
s.51, amended: SI 2013/496 Sch.8 para.9
s.52, amended: SI 2013/496 Sch.8 para.9, Sch.8 para.16
s.52A, amended: SI 2013/496 Sch.8 para.9
s.52B, amended: SI 2013/496 Sch.8 para.9, Sch.8 para.17
s.53, amended: SI 2013/496 Sch.8 para.9
s.53A, amended: SI 2013/496 Sch.8 para.9, Sch.8 para.18
s.54, amended: SI 2013/496 Sch.8 para.9, Sch.8 para.19
s.55, amended: SI 2013/496 Sch.8 para.9, Sch.8 para.20
s.56, amended: SI 2013/496 Sch.8 para.9, Sch.8 para.21
s.57, amended: SI 2013/496 Sch.8 para.9, Sch.8 para.22
s.59, amended: SI 2013/496 Sch.8 para.23
s.60, amended: 2013 c.33 Sch.9 para.10
s.61, amended: 2013 c.33 Sch.9 para.10, SI 2013/496 Sch.8 para.24
s.68, amended: 2013 c.33 Sch.9 para.10, SI 2013/496 Sch.8 para.25
s.69, amended: 2013 c.33 Sch.9 para.10, SI 2013/496 Sch.8 para.26
s.74, amended: 2013 c.33 Sch.9 para.5
s.76, amended: 2013 c.33 Sch.9 para.6, Sch.9 para.10, SI 2013/496 Sch.8 para.27
s.76, repealed (in part): 2013 c.33 Sch.9 para.6
s.78, amended: 2013 c.33 Sch.9 para.7
s.78C, amended: SI 2013/496 Sch.8 para.28
s.78D, amended: SI 2013/496 Sch.8 para.29
s.81, amended: 2013 c.33 Sch.9 para.11, SI 2013/496 Sch.8 para.30
s.87, amended: SI 2013/496 Sch.8 para.31
s.88, amended: SI 2013/496 Sch.8 para.32
s.89, amended: SI 2013/496 Sch.8 para.33
s.89A, amended: SI 2013/496 Sch.8 para.34
s.90D, amended: SI 2013/496 Sch.8 para.35
s.91, amended: SI 2013/496 Sch.8 para.36
s.93, amended: SI 2013/496 Sch.8 para.37
s.94, amended: SI 2013/496 Sch.8 para.38
s.95, amended: SI 2013/496 Sch.8 para.39
s.96, amended: SI 2013/496 Sch.8 para.40
s.97, amended: SI 2013/496 Sch.8 para.41
s.98, amended: SI 2013/496 Sch.8 para.42
s.100, amended: 2013 c.33 Sch.9 para.8, SI 2013/496 Sch.8 para.43
s.101, amended: SI 2013/496 Sch.8 para.44
s.103, amended: SI 2013/496 Sch.8 para.45
s.106, amended: SI 2013/496 Sch.8 para.46
s.107, amended: SI 2013/496 Sch.8 para.47
s.109, disapplied: SI 2013/460 Reg.3
s.111, amended: SI 2013/496 Sch.8 para.48
s.113, amended: SI 2013/496 Sch.8 para.49
s.115, amended: SI 2013/496 Sch.8 para.50
s.115A, added: 2013 c.33 Sch.9 para.9
s.115B, added: 2013 c.33 Sch.9 para.9
s.115C, added: 2013 c.33 Sch.9 para.9
s.116, amended: SI 2013/496 Sch.8 para.51
s.117, amended: 2013 c.33 Sch.9 para.15
s.117, repealed (in part): 2013 c.33 Sch.9 para.15
s.117A, added: 2013 c.33 Sch.9 para.16
s.119, amended: SI 2013/496 Sch.8 para.52, SI 2013/3115 Sch.2 para.34
s.119, repealed (in part): SI 2013/3115 Sch.2 para.34
Sch.2 Part I para.1, amended: SI 2013/496 Sch.8 para.53
Sch.2 Part I para.4, amended: SI 2013/496 Sch.8 para.53
Sch.2 Part I para.7, amended: 2013 c.33 Sch.9 para.7
Sch.2 Part I para.8, amended: 2013 c.33 Sch.9 para.7
Sch.2 Part I para.9, amended: SI 2013/496 Sch.8 para.53
Sch.2 Part I para.10, amended: SI 2013/496 Sch.8 para.53
Sch.2 Part I para.10A, amended: SI 2013/496 Sch.8 para.53
Sch.2 Part I para.11, amended: SI 2013/496 Sch.8 para.53
Sch.2 Part I para.15, amended: SI 2013/496 Sch.8 para.53
Sch.2 Part III para.20, amended: SI 2013/496 Sch.8 para.53
Sch.2 Part III para.20A, amended: 2013 c.33 Sch.9 para.12, SI 2013/496 Sch.8 para.53
Sch.2 Part III para.22B, amended: 2013 c.33 Sch.9 para.12
Sch.2 Part III para.23, amended: SI 2013/3115 Sch.2 para.35
Sch.2 Part III para.24, amended: 2013 c.33 Sch.9 para.12
Sch.2 Part III para.30, amended: SI 2013/496 Sch.8 para.53
Sch.2 Part III para.31, amended: SI 2013/496 Sch.8 para.53
Sch.2 Part III para.32, amended: 2013 c.33 Sch.9 para.12
Sch.2 Part III para.33, amended: 2013 c.33 Sch.9 para.12
Sch.2 Part III para.33A, amended: 2013 c.33 Sch.9 para.12
Sch.8A Part I para.2, amended: SI 2013/496 Sch.8 para.54

Sch.8A Part I para.3, amended: 2013 c.33 Sch.9 para.13, SI 2013/496 Sch.8 para.54
Sch.8A Part I para.4, amended: SI 2013/496 Sch.8 para.54
Sch.8A Part II para.7, amended: SI 2013/496 Sch.8 para.54
Sch.8A Part II para.8, amended: SI 2013/496 Sch.8 para.54
Sch.8A Part II para.9, amended: 2013 c.33 Sch.9 para.13, SI 2013/496 Sch.8 para.54
Sch.8A Part II para.10, amended: SI 2013/496 Sch.8 para.54
Sch.11 para.3, amended: SI 2013/496 Sch.8 para.55
Sch.11 para.4, amended: 2013 c.33 Sch.9 para.14, SI 2013/496 Sch.8 para.55
Sch.11 para.6, amended: SI 2013/496 Sch.8 para.55
Sch.11 para.6A, amended: SI 2013/496 Sch.8 para.55
Sch.11 para.7, amended: 2013 c.33 Sch.9 para.14, SI 2013/496 Sch.8 para.55
Sch.11 para.8, amended: 2013 c.33 Sch.9 para.14, SI 2013/496 Sch.8 para.55
Sch.14 Part I, amended: SI 2013/496 Sch.8 para.56
Sch.14 Part I para.1, amended: SI 2013/496 Sch.8 para.56
Sch.14 Part I para.3, amended: SI 2013/496 Sch.8 para.56
Sch.14 Part II para.6, amended: SI 2013/496 Sch.8 para.56
Sch.15 Part I para.3, amended: SI 2013/496 Sch.8 para.57
Sch.15 Part I para.4, amended: SI 2013/496 Sch.8 para.57
Sch.15 Part II para.21, amended: SI 2013/496 Sch.8 para.57
Sch.15 Part II para.29, amended: SI 2013/496 Sch.8 para.57
Sch.15 Part II para.31, amended: SI 2013/496 Sch.8 para.57
Sch.15 Part II para.32, amended: SI 2013/496 Sch.8 para.57
Sch.15 Part III para.48, amended: SI 2013/496 Sch.8 para.57
Sch.15 Part III para.55A, amended: SI 2013/496 Sch.8 para.57
Sch.15 Part III para.55C, amended: SI 2013/496 Sch.8 para.57
Sch.15 Part III para.55D, amended: SI 2013/496 Sch.8 para.57
Sch.15A Part I para.2, amended: SI 2013/496 Sch.8 para.58
Sch.15A Part I para.3, amended: SI 2013/496 Sch.8 para.58
Sch.15A Part II para.9A, amended: SI 2013/496 Sch.8 para.58
Sch.15A Part II para.10, amended: SI 2013/496 Sch.8 para.58
Sch.15A Part II para.11, amended: SI 2013/496 Sch.8 para.58
Sch.15A Part II para.15, amended: SI 2013/496 Sch.8 para.58
Sch.15A Part II para.18, repealed: 2013 c.33 Sch.9 para.4
Sch.15A Part II para.20, repealed: 2013 c.33 Sch.9 para.4
Sch.15A Part II para.21, amended: SI 2013/496 Sch.8 para.58
Sch.15A Part II para.23, amended: SI 2013/496 Sch.8 para.58
Sch.15A Part II para.24, amended: SI 2013/496 Sch.8 para.58
Sch.15A Part III para.31A, amended: SI 2013/496 Sch.8 para.58
Sch.15A Part III para.32, amended: SI 2013/496 Sch.8 para.58
Sch.15A Part III para.33, amended: SI 2013/496 Sch.8 para.58
Sch.15A Part III para.37, amended: SI 2013/496 Sch.8 para.58
Sch.15A Part III para.40, repealed: 2013 c.33 Sch.9 para.4
Sch.15A Part III para.42, repealed: 2013 c.33 Sch.9 para.4
Sch.15A Part III para.43, amended: SI 2013/496 Sch.8 para.58
Sch.15A Part III para.45, amended: SI 2013/496 Sch.8 para.58
Sch.15A Part III para.46, amended: SI 2013/496 Sch.8 para.58
Sch.16 Part I para.1, amended: SI 2013/496 Sch.8 para.59
Sch.16 Part II para.5, amended: SI 2013/496 Sch.8 para.59
Sch.16 Part III para.7, amended: SI 2013/496 Sch.8 para.59
Sch.16 Part III para.8, amended: SI 2013/496 Sch.8 para.59
Sch.16 Part III para.9, amended: SI 2013/496 Sch.8 para.59
Sch.17 Part I para.3, amended: SI 2013/496 Sch.8 para.60
Sch.17 Part I para.4, amended: SI 2013/496 Sch.8 para.60
Sch.17 Part IA para.5D, amended: SI 2013/496 Sch.8 para.60

Sch.17 Part II para.6, amended: SI 2013/496 Sch.8 para.60
Sch.17 Part II para.7, amended: SI 2013/496 Sch.8 para.60
Sch.17 Part II para.8, amended: SI 2013/496 Sch.8 para.60
Sch.20 para.16, repealed: 2013 c.33 Sch.9 para.17

55. Family Law Act 1986
Part I, referred to: SI 2013/104 Reg.69
Part III, referred to: SI 2013/104 Reg.69
s.55, amended: 2013 c.22 Sch.11 para.96
s.55A, see *E (Assisted Reproduction: Parent), Re* [2013] EWHC 1418 (Fam), [2013] 2 F.L.R. 1357 (Fam Div), Cobb, J.
s.55A, amended: 2013 c.22 Sch.11 para.97
s.56, amended: 2013 c.22 Sch.11 para.98
s.57, amended: 2013 c.22 Sch.11 para.99
s.60, repealed (in part): 2013 c.22 Sch.11 para.100
Sch.1 Part 1 para.24, repealed: 2013 c.22 Sch.11 para.210

56. Parliamentary Constituencies Act 1986
s.3, amended: 2013 c.6 s.6
s.3, referred to: 2013 c.6

61. Education (No.2) Act 1986
s.43, applied: SI 2013/1793 Reg.3

64. Public Order Act 1986
s.1, applied: SI 2013/435 Sch.1 Part 7
s.2, applied: SI 2013/435 Sch.1 Part 7
s.3, see *R. v Smith (Joseph Alexander)* [2013] EWCA Crim 11, [2013] 2 Cr. App. R. 5 (CA (Crim Div)), Pitchford L.J.
s.3, applied: SI 2013/435 Sch.1 Part 7
s.5, see *Gough v DPP* [2013] EWHC 3267 (Admin), (2013) 177 J.P. 669 (QBD (Admin)), Sir Brian Leveson (President, QBD); see *R. (on the application of Gavigan) v Enfield Magistrates' Court* [2013] EWHC 2805 (Admin), (2013) 177 J.P. 609 (DC), Aikens, L.J.
s.5, amended: 2013 c.22 s.57
s.6, amended: 2013 c.22 s.57
s.18, applied: SI 2013/435 Sch.1 Part 7
s.19, applied: SI 2013/435 Sch.1 Part 7
s.20, applied: SI 2013/435 Sch.1 Part 7
s.21, applied: SI 2013/435 Sch.1 Part 7
s.22, applied: SI 2013/435 Sch.1 Part 7
s.23, applied: SI 2013/435 Sch.1 Part 7
s.29JA, substituted: 2013 c.30 Sch.7 para.28
s.38, applied: SI 2013/435 Sch.1 Part 7

1987

4. Ministry of Defence Police Act 1987
s.1, amended: SI 2013/602 Sch.2 para.20
s.1, applied: SI 2013/602 Sch.3 para.6, SI 2013/1779 Art.3
s.2, amended: SI 2013/602 Sch.2 para.20
s.2, applied: SI 2013/602 Art.10
s.2A, amended: SI 2013/602 Sch.2 para.20
s.2A, applied: SI 2013/602 Art.7, Art.10, Sch.3 para.13
s.2B, amended: SI 2013/602 Sch.2 para.20
s.2C, amended: 2013 c.22 Sch.8 para.31
s.4A, amended: SI 2013/602 Sch.2 para.20
s.4B, amended: SI 2013/602 Sch.2 para.20

12. Petroleum Act 1987
s.21, applied: SI 2013/1758 Art.2, SI 2013/3188 Art.2
s.22, enabling: SI 2013/1758, SI 2013/3188
s.24, applied: SI 2013/1758(b), SI 2013/3188(b)

15. Reverter of Sites Act 1987
applied: SI 2013/1145(6), SI 2013/1221
s.1, applied: SI 2013/1145 Art.3, Art.4, SI 2013/1145(6), SI 2013/1221, SI 2013/1221 Art.3, SI 2013/1245, SI 2013/1245 Art.3, Art.4, SI 2013/2155, SI 2013/2155 Art.3, Art.4, SI 2013/3110 Sch.3 para.17
s.5, applied: SI 2013/2155
s.5, enabling: SI 2013/1145, SI 2013/1245, SI 2013/2155

18. Debtors (Scotland) Act 1987
applied: SSI 2013/318 Reg.13
s.64, applied: SSI 2013/318 Reg.13
s.71, applied: SSI 2013/318 Reg.14
s.75, enabling: SSI 2013/23

21. Pilotage Act 1987
s.1, amended: 2013 c.23 s.1
s.1A, amended: 2013 c.23 s.1
s.8, amended: 2013 c.23 s.2, s.3
s.8, repealed (in part): 2013 c.23 s.3
s.8A, added: 2013 c.23 s.3
s.8B, added: 2013 c.23 s.3
s.10, amended: 2013 c.23 s.2
s.15, amended: 2013 c.23 s.2, s.4
s.20, amended: 2013 c.23 s.2
s.31, amended: 2013 c.23 s.2

26. Housing (Scotland) Act 1987
s.69A, amended: SSI 2013/119 Sch.1 para.10
s.82, amended: SSI 2013/119 Sch.1 para.10
s.229, amended: SI 2013/496 Sch.11 para.4

31. Landlord and Tenant Act 1987
Part IV, applied: SI 2013/1179 Sch.1
s.8C, amended: SI 2013/1036 Sch.1 para.59
s.12A, amended: SI 2013/1036 Sch.1 para.60
s.12B, amended: SI 2013/1036 Sch.1 para.61
s.12C, amended: SI 2013/1036 Sch.1 para.62
s.13, amended: SI 2013/1036 Sch.1 para.63
s.14, amended: SI 2013/1036 Sch.1 para.64

s.17, amended: SI 2013/1036 Sch.1 para.65
s.20, amended: SI 2013/1036 Sch.1 para.66
s.21, amended: SI 2013/1036 Sch.1 para.67, Sch.1 para.68
s.22, amended: SI 2013/1036 Sch.1 para.67, Sch.1 para.69
s.23, amended: SI 2013/1036 Sch.1 para.67, Sch.1 para.70
s.24, amended: SI 2013/1036 Sch.1 para.67, Sch.1 para.71
s.24, applied: SI 2013/1179 Sch.1
s.24A, amended: SI 2013/1036 Sch.1 para.67
s.24B, amended: SI 2013/1036 Sch.1 para.67
s.30, amended: SI 2013/1036 Sch.1 para.72
s.31, amended: SI 2013/1036 Sch.1 para.73
s.34, amended: SI 2013/1036 Sch.1 para.74
s.35, see *Brickfield Properties Ltd v Botten* [2013] UKUT 133 (LC), [2013] 2 E.G.L.R. 70 (UT (Lands)), Judge Huskinson
s.35, amended: SI 2013/1036 Sch.1 para.75
s.35, enabling: SI 2013/1169
s.37, see *Shellpoint Trustees Ltd v Barnett* [2013] L. & T.R. 21 (UT (Lands)), Judge Gerald
s.37, amended: SI 2013/1036 Sch.1 para.76
s.39, amended: SI 2013/1036 Sch.1 para.77
s.40, amended: SI 2013/1036 Sch.1 para.78
s.52, amended: 2013 c.22 Sch.9 para.52, SI 2013/1036 Sch.1 para.79
s.60, amended: 2013 c.22 Sch.9 para.52
Sch.1 Part I para.4, amended: 2013 c.22 Sch.9 para.52
Sch.1 Part II para.9, amended: 2013 c.22 Sch.9 para.52

38. Criminal Justice Act 1987

applied: SI 2013/1554 r.6_1
s.2, see *R. (on the application of Rawlinson and Hunter Trustees) v Central Criminal Court* [2012] EWHC 2254 (Admin), [2013] 1 W.L.R. 1634 (DC), Sir John Thomas (President)
s.2, applied: 2013 c.22 Sch.3 para.5, SI 2013/1554 r.6_1, r.6_31
s.4, applied: SI 2013/435 Sch.1 para.2, Sch.1 para.22, Sch.2 para.2, Sch.2 para.21, SI 2013/614 Reg.22, SI 2013/1554 r.14_1
s.6, applied: SI 2013/435 Sch.1 para.2, Sch.1 para.22, Sch.2 para.2, Sch.2 para.21
s.7, applied: SI 2013/1554 r.15_1
s.9, applied: SI 2013/1554 r.35_3, r.74_1, r.35_4, r.34_3, r.36_2, r.66_1
s.10, applied: SI 2013/1554 r.15_1
s.11, applied: SI 2013/1554 r.16_1

41. Criminal Justice (Scotland) Act 1987

s.51, repealed: 2013 c.2 Sch.1 Part 2
s.52, repealed: 2013 c.2 Sch.1 Part 2
s.53, repealed: 2013 c.2 Sch.1 Part 2

42. Family Law Reform Act 1987

Sch.2 para.13, repealed: 2013 c.22 Sch.11 para.210
Sch.2 para.18, repealed: 2013 c.22 Sch.10 para.99
Sch.2 para.45, repealed: 2013 c.22 Sch.11 para.210
Sch.2 para.50, repealed: 2013 c.22 Sch.11 para.210
Sch.2 para.70, repealed: 2013 c.22 Sch.11 para.210
Sch.2 para.81, repealed: 2013 c.22 Sch.10 para.99
Sch.2 para.83, repealed: 2013 c.22 Sch.10 para.99
Sch.2 para.84, repealed: 2013 c.22 Sch.10 para.99
Sch.2 para.85, repealed: 2013 c.22 Sch.10 para.99
Sch.2 para.87, repealed: 2013 c.22 Sch.10 para.99
Sch.2 para.89, repealed (in part): 2013 c.22 Sch.11 para.210

43. Consumer Protection Act 1987

applied: SI 2013/1506 Reg.18
s.11, see *Imperial Tobacco Ltd, Petitioner* 2013 S.C. (U.K.S.C.) 153 (SC), Lord Hope, J.S.C. (Deputy President)
s.11, applied: SI 2013/1506 Reg.18, SI 2013/2327
s.11, enabling: SI 2013/2327
s.12, varied: SI 2013/1506 Reg.18

45. Parliamentary and other Pensions Act 1987

s.2, applied: SI 2013/2734 Reg.4
Sch.3 para.4, repealed: 2013 c.25 Sch.11 para.7

47. Abolition of Domestic Rates Etc (Scotland) Act 1987

Sch.2 para.7A, enabling: SI 2013/380

52. British Shipbuilders (Borrowing Powers) Act 1987

repealed: SI 2013/687 Sch.1 para.10

53. Channel Tunnel Act 1987

s.11, enabling: SI 2013/407

1988

1. Income and Corporation Taxes Act 1988

Part VII c.I, applied: SI 2013/765 Sch.2 para.4, SI 2013/3177 Sch.5 para.5, Sch.6 para.4
Part XIV c.IV, applied: SI 2013/2734 Sch.1 para.1
Part XVII c.IV, applied: 2013 c.29 s.29
s.266A, amended: 2013 c.29 Sch.46 para.16
s.273, applied: SI 2013/765 Sch.2 para.4
s.369, applied: SI 2013/3029 Sch.4 para.11, Sch.10 para.26, SI 2013/3035 Sch.1
s.552, amended: 2013 c.29 Sch.8 para.6, Sch.45 para.144
s.552B, amended: 2013 c.29 Sch.9 para.11
s.552ZB, added: 2013 c.29 Sch.9 para.10
s.552ZB, enabling: SI 2013/1820
s.590, applied: SI 2013/2734 Sch.1 para.1
s.590C, applied: SSI 2013/174 Reg.9, Reg.11, Reg.12

s.591, applied: SI 2013/2734 Sch.1 para.1
s.611A, referred to: SI 2013/2734 Sch.1 para.1
s.614, amended: 2013 c.29 Sch.46 para.28
s.615, referred to: SI 2013/2734 Sch.1 para.1
s.774, repealed: 2013 c.2 Sch.1 Part 10
s.812, repealed: 2013 c.2 Sch.1 Part 10
s.813, repealed: 2013 c.2 Sch.1 Part 10
s.814, repealed: 2013 c.2 Sch.1 Part 10
s.826, amended: 2013 c.29 Sch.18 para.1
s.843, amended: 2013 c.2 Sch.1 Part 10
Sch.15 Part A1 paraA.1, added: 2013 c.29 Sch.9 para.2
Sch.15 Part A1 paraA.2, added: 2013 c.29 Sch.9 para.2
Sch.15 Part A1 paraA.3, added: 2013 c.29 Sch.9 para.2
Sch.15 Part A1 paraA.3, applied: SI 2013/1820 Reg.2
Sch.15 Part A1 paraA.4, added: 2013 c.29 Sch.9 para.2
Sch.15 Part A1 paraA.5, added: 2013 c.29 Sch.9 para.2
Sch.15 Part A1 paraA.6, added: 2013 c.29 Sch.9 para.2
Sch.15 Part I paraB.1, added: 2013 c.29 Sch.9 para.3
Sch.15 Part I paraB.2, added: 2013 c.29 Sch.9 para.3
Sch.15 Part I paraB.3, added: 2013 c.29 Sch.9 para.3
Sch.15 Part I paraB.3, applied: SI 2013/1820 Reg.2, Reg.3, Reg.4, Reg.5
Sch.15 Part I paraB.3, enabling: SI 2013/1820
Sch.15 Part I para.17, amended: 2013 c.29 Sch.9 para.4
Sch.15 Part III para.25, amended: 2013 c.29 Sch.9 para.5
Sch.30 para.9, repealed: 2013 c.2 Sch.1 Part 10
Sch.30 para.14, repealed: 2013 c.2 Sch.1 Part 10
Sch.30 para.15, repealed: 2013 c.2 Sch.1 Part 10
Sch.30 para.19, repealed: 2013 c.2 Sch.1 Part 10
Sch.30 para.20, repealed: 2013 c.2 Sch.1 Part 10

4. Norfolk and Suffolk Broads Act 1988
s.25, varied: 2013 c.27 s.9

12. Merchant Shipping Act 1988
applied: SI 2013/1471 Reg.14

13. Coroners Act 1988
see *R. (on the application of Antoniou) v Central and North West London NHS Foundation Trust* [2013] EWHC 3055 (Admin), [2013] Med. L.R. 536 (DC), Aikens, L.J.; see *R. (on the application of Mousa) v Secretary of State for Defence* [2013] EWHC 1412 (Admin), [2013] H.R.L.R. 32 (DC), Sir John Thomas (President QBD)
applied: SI 2013/104 Reg.48
s.4A, amended: SI 2013/1874 Art.2
s.13, amended: SI 2013/1874 Art.2
Sch.1 para.2, applied: 2013 c.25 Sch.5 para.16

16. Farm Land and Rural Development Act 1988
s.2, amended: SI 2013/755 Sch.2 para.186

18. Matrimonial Proceedings (Transfers) Act 1988
s.1, amended: 2013 c.22 Sch.11 para.101

20. Dartford-Thurrock Crossing Act 1988
s.19, amended: 2013 c.22 Sch.8 para.186
s.33, amended: SI 2013/1970 Sch.1 para.28

28. Access to Medical Reports Act 1988
s.8, amended: 2013 c.22 Sch.9 para.52

32. Civil Evidence (Scotland) Act 1988
s.9, amended: SSI 2013/211 Sch.1 para.6

33. Criminal Justice Act 1988
see *Glatt v Sinclair* [2013] EWCA Civ 241, [2013] 1 W.L.R. 3602 (CA (Civ Div)), Maurice Kay, L.J.; see *R. v Bagnall (Darren John)* [2012] EWCA Crim 677, [2013] 1 W.L.R. 204 (CA (Crim Div)), Moses, L.J.; see *R. v Gangar (Shinder Singh)* [2012] EWCA Crim 1378, [2013] 1 W.L.R. 147 (CA (Crim Div)), Hughes, L.J.; see *Revenue and Customs Prosecutions Office v Johnson* [2012] EWCA Civ 1000, [2013] Lloyd's Rep. F.C. 1 (CA (Civ Div)), Pill, L.J.
applied: SI 2013/1554 r.56_1, r.29_26
Part IV, applied: SI 2013/1554 r.70_1
Part VI, applied: SI 2013/1554 r.56_1
s.32, applied: SI 2013/1554 r.29_1, r.37_4, r.29_26, SI 2013/1598 Art.2
s.36, applied: SI 2013/1554 r.70_1, r.65_3, r.74_1, r.74_2, SI 2013/2786 Art.5
s.39, see *R. v J* [2013] EWCA Crim 569, [2013] 2 Cr. App. R. 10 (CA (Crim Div)), Sir John Thomas (President QBD); see *R. v Nelson (Gary)* [2013] EWCA Crim 30, [2013] 1 W.L.R. 2861 (CA (Crim Div)), Rafferty, L.J. DBE
s.39, applied: SI 2013/435 Sch.1 Part 7
s.71, applied: SI 2013/435 Reg.4, Sch.1 para.14, Sch.2 para.26
s.72A, applied: SI 2013/1554 r.56_2
s.73, applied: SI 2013/1554 r.56_1
s.74A, applied: SI 2013/1554 r.56_3, r.56_5
s.74B, applied: SI 2013/1554 r.56_3
s.74C, applied: SI 2013/1554 r.56_3
s.93H, applied: SI 2013/1554 r.56_4
s.133, see *R. (on the application of Ali) v Secretary of State for Justice* [2013] EWHC 72 (Admin), [2013] 1 W.L.R. 3536 (DC), Beatson, L.J.
s.133, applied: SSI 2013/50 Sch.1 para.24
s.152, applied: SI 2013/1542 Art.14, SI 2013/1554 r.18_3
s.159, applied: SI 2013/1554 r.69_1, r.74_1, r.76_1

Sch.3 para.1, applied: SI 2013/1554 r.70_2
Sch.3 para.4, applied: SI 2013/1554 r.74_2
Sch.3 para.8, applied: SI 2013/1554 r.70_7
Sch.3 para.11, applied: SI 2013/1554 r.76_1
Sch.4, referred to: SI 2013/1554 r.56_1
Sch.15 para.111, repealed: 2013 c.2 Sch.1 Part 2

34. Legal Aid Act 1988
applied: SI 2013/534 Reg.6

36. Court of Session Act 1988
s.5, applied: SSI 2013/150 Art.2
s.5, enabling: SSI 2013/81, SSI 2013/111, SSI 2013/120, SSI 2013/162, SSI 2013/238, SSI 2013/294, SSI 2013/317, SSI 2013/346
s.8, applied: 2013 asp 3 s.14
s.8, repealed: 2013 asp 3 s.14
s.45, applied: 2013 c.19 s.3, s.8, 2013 c.33 s.12, s.82, Sch.4 para.7, SI 2013/442 Art.68, SI 2013/1389 Reg.13, Reg.38

39. Finance Act 1988
s.31, repealed: 2013 c.2 Sch.1 Part 10
s.58, repealed: 2013 c.2 Sch.1 Part 10
s.61, amended: 2013 c.2 Sch.1 Part 10
s.61, repealed (in part): 2013 c.2 Sch.1 Part 10
s.75, repealed: 2013 c.2 Sch.1 Part 10
s.119, repealed: 2013 c.2 Sch.1 Part 10
s.120, repealed: 2013 c.2 Sch.1 Part 10
s.122, repealed: 2013 c.2 Sch.1 Part 10
Sch.3 Part I para.13, repealed: 2013 c.2 Sch.1 Part 10

40. Education Reform Act 1988
s.127, applied: SI 2013/664 Art.4, SI 2013/1729 Art.4
s.128, applied: SI 2013/664, SI 2013/1729
s.128, enabling: SI 2013/664, SI 2013/1729
s.129, applied: SI 2013/1572 Art.2, SI 2013/2356 Sch.2 para.4, SI 2013/2490 Art.2
s.129, enabling: SI 2013/1572, SI 2013/2490
s.216, enabling: SI 2013/2992, SI 2013/2993
s.232, enabling: SI 2013/2993
Sch.6, referred to: SI 2013/3029 Sch.11 para.3, SI 2013/3035 Sch.1

41. Local Government Finance Act 1988
s.41, amended: 2013 c.27 s.29, s.30
s.41, applied: SI 2013/452 Sch.1 para.2
s.43, see *Kenya Aid Programme v Sheffield City Council* [2013] EWHC 54 (Admin), [2013] 3 W.L.R. 422 (DC), Treacy, L.J.; see *Public Safety Charitable Trust v Milton Keynes Council* [2013] EWHC 1237 (Admin), [2013] 2 E.G.L.R. 133 (QBD (Admin)), Sales, J.
s.43, applied: SI 2013/106 Reg.2, Reg.3, SI 2013/107 Sch.2 para.2, SI 2013/108 Reg.13, Reg.15, Reg.16, Reg.17, Reg.18, SI 2013/452 Sch.1 para.1, Sch.2 para.2, Sch.2 para.3, Sch.4 para.1, SI 2013/737 Sch.1 para.1
s.43, disapplied: SI 2013/106 Reg.2, Reg.3
s.43, enabling: SI 2013/371
s.44, enabling: SI 2013/15, SI 2013/371
s.45, applied: SI 2013/106 Reg.2, Reg.3, SI 2013/107 Sch.2 para.2, SI 2013/108 Reg.13, Reg.15, Reg.16, Reg.17, Reg.18, SI 2013/452 Sch.1 para.1, Sch.2 para.2, Sch.2 para.3, Sch.4 para.1, SI 2013/737 Sch.1 para.1
s.45A, amended: SI 2013/463 Art.3
s.47, applied: SI 2013/106 Reg.2, Reg.3, SI 2013/452 Sch.2 para.1, Sch.2 para.2, Sch.2 para.3, SI 2013/737 Sch.1 para.1
s.49, applied: SI 2013/106 Reg.2, Reg.3, SI 2013/737 Sch.1 para.1
s.52, amended: 2013 c.27 s.29, s.30
s.53, enabling: SI 2013/408, SI 2013/2887
s.54A, added: 2013 c.27 s.30
s.57A, applied: SI 2013/106 Reg.2
s.60, enabling: SI 2013/3046
s.62A, applied: SI 2013/1894 Reg.4
s.64, applied: SI 2013/107 Sch.2 para.2
s.66, see *Collection (Management) Ltd v Jackson (Valuation Officer)* [2013] UKUT 166 (LC), [2013] R.A. 311 (UT (Lands)), Judge Alice Robinson; see *Reeves (Listing Officer) v Northrop* [2013] EWCA Civ 362, [2013] 1 W.L.R. 2867 (CA (Civ Div)), Hughes, L.J.
s.66, amended: SI 2013/468 Art.2
s.66, enabling: SI 2013/468
s.74, applied: SI 2013/2356 Sch.2 para.2
s.75, applied: SI 2013/2356 Sch.2 para.2
s.97, applied: SI 2013/452 Reg.14
s.97, enabling: SI 2013/452
s.99, enabling: SI 2013/452, SI 2013/2974
s.140, enabling: SI 2013/547, SI 2013/2974
s.143, amended: 2013 c.27 s.30
s.143, applied: SI 2013/452, SI 2013/737
s.143, enabling: SI 2013/15, SI 2013/106, SI 2013/371, SI 2013/408, SI 2013/452, SI 2013/465, SI 2013/547, SI 2013/694, SI 2013/737, SI 2013/2887, SI 2013/2974
s.146, enabling: SI 2013/371
s.147, enabling: SI 2013/2986
Sch.4 Part II para.6, enabling: SI 2013/380
Sch.5 para.14, amended: SI 2013/755 Sch.2 para.187
Sch.7 Part I, applied: SI 2013/452 Sch.1 para.1
Sch.7B Part III para.6, applied: SI 2013/107 Reg.5, SI 2013/108 Reg.12, SI 2013/452 Reg.4, Reg.15, Sch.4 para.1
Sch.7B Part III para.6, enabling: SI 2013/452

Sch.7B Part III para.7, applied: SI 2013/107 Reg.5, SI 2013/108 Reg.12
Sch.7B Part III para.7, enabling: SI 2013/452
Sch.7B Part III para.8, applied: SI 2013/452
Sch.7B Part III para.8, enabling: SI 2013/452
Sch.7B Part IV, applied: SI 2013/737 Sch.1 para.2
Sch.7B Part IV para.9, applied: SI 2013/107 Reg.5, SI 2013/108 Reg.12, SI 2013/452 Sch.4 para.1
Sch.7B Part IV para.9, enabling: SI 2013/452
Sch.7B Part IV para.10, applied: SI 2013/107 Reg.5, SI 2013/108 Reg.12
Sch.7B Part IV para.10, enabling: SI 2013/452
Sch.7B Part IV para.11, enabling: SI 2013/452
Sch.7B Part V, applied: SI 2013/737 Sch.1 para.1, Sch.1 para.2
Sch.7B Part V para.13, applied: SI 2013/107 Reg.5, SI 2013/108 Reg.12
Sch.7B Part V para.16, applied: SI 2013/107 Reg.5, SI 2013/108 Reg.12
Sch.7B Part VII para.22, enabling: SI 2013/737
Sch.7B Part VII para.23, applied: SI 2013/107 Reg.5, SI 2013/108 Reg.12
Sch.7B Part VII para.25, enabling: SI 2013/737
Sch.7B Part VII para.26, applied: SI 2013/107 Reg.5, SI 2013/108 Reg.12
Sch.7B Part VII para.28, applied: SI 2013/107 Reg.5, SI 2013/108 Reg.12
Sch.7B Part VII para.28, enabling: SI 2013/737
Sch.7B Part VII para.30, applied: SI 2013/107 Reg.5, SI 2013/108 Reg.12
Sch.7B Part VIII para.32, enabling: SI 2013/106
Sch.7B Part VIII para.33, applied: SI 2013/107 Sch.2 para.2, SI 2013/108 Reg.13, SI 2013/452 Sch.1 para.1, Sch.4 para.1
Sch.7B Part VIII para.33, enabling: SI 2013/106
Sch.7B Part IX para.37, enabling: SI 2013/737
Sch.7B Part X para.39, applied: SI 2013/107, SI 2013/452, SI 2013/452 Reg.10, Sch.1 para.1, Sch.3
Sch.7B Part X para.39, enabling: SI 2013/107, SI 2013/452
Sch.7B Part X para.40, applied: SI 2013/108, SI 2013/452, SI 2013/452 Reg.10, Sch.1 para.1, Sch.3
Sch.7B Part X para.40, enabling: SI 2013/108, SI 2013/452
Sch.7B Part X para.41, enabling: SI 2013/452
Sch.7B Part X para.42, enabling: SI 2013/452
Sch.7B Part XI para.44, enabling: SI 2013/452
Sch.8 Part II para.4, enabling: SI 2013/3046
Sch.8 Part II para.6, enabling: SI 2013/3046
Sch.9 para.1, enabling: SI 2013/694
Sch.9 para.2, enabling: SI 2013/694
Sch.11 Part 1 paraA.19, enabling: SI 2013/465
Sch.11 Part 2 para.1, enabling: SI 2013/547
Sch.11 Part 2 para.5, enabling: SI 2013/547
Sch.11 Part 3 para.8, enabling: SI 2013/465, SI 2013/547
Sch.11 Part 3 para.11, enabling: SI 2013/465

43. Housing (Scotland) Act 1988
applied: SI 2013/449 Reg.3
s.2, applied: 2013 asp 11 Sch.6 para.2
s.18, amended: SSI 2013/137 Reg.4
s.30, applied: SSI 2013/20 Art.2
s.30A, applied: SSI 2013/20 Art.2, Art.3, Art.4
s.30B, applied: SSI 2013/20, SSI 2013/90
s.30B, enabling: SSI 2013/20, SSI 2013/90
s.32, applied: SSI 2013/20 Art.2
s.43, repealed (in part): SSI 2013/119 Sch.1 para.11
s.45, repealed (in part): SSI 2013/119 Sch.1 para.11
s.53, enabling: SSI 2013/20
s.66, applied: SI 2013/3029 Sch.10 para.41, SI 2013/3035 Sch.1

45. Firearms (Amendment) Act 1988
applied: SI 2013/602 Sch.3 para.1
s.6, applied: SI 2013/435 Sch.1 Part 7
s.12, applied: SI 2013/602 Sch.3 para.1
s.18B, amended: SI 2013/602 Sch.2 para.21

48. Copyright, Designs and Patents Act 1988
see *Scottish Premier League Ltd v Lisini Pub Management Co Ltd* [2013] CSOH 48, 2013 S.L.T. 629 (OH), Lord Woolman
applied: SI 2013/1782 Reg.13
Part I, applied: SI 2013/536, SI 2013/536 Art.2, Art.4, Art.5, SI 2013/1782 Reg.11, Reg.18
Part I c.III, applied: 2013 c.24 s.75
Part I c.IV, applied: SI 2013/1782 Reg.12
Part II, applied: SI 2013/536 Art.6, SI 2013/1782 Reg.11, Reg.23, Reg.26
Part II, disapplied: SI 2013/536 Art.7
Part II, referred to: SI 2013/536 Art.6
Part II c.II, amended: 2013 c.24 Sch.22 para.6
s.10A, added: SI 2013/1782 Reg.4
s.12, amended: SI 2013/1782 Reg.5
s.13A, amended: SI 2013/1782 Reg.6
s.18A, applied: SI 2013/536 Art.4
s.18A, disapplied: SI 2013/536 Art.4, Art.5
s.19, see *Football Association Premier League Ltd v QC Leisure* [2012] EWCA Civ 1708, [2013] Bus. L.R. 866 (CA (Civ Div)), Etherton, L.J.
s.19, disapplied: SI 2013/536 Art.4, Art.5
s.20, see *Football Association Premier League Ltd v British Sky Broadcasting Ltd* [2013] EWHC 2058 (Ch), [2013] E.C.D.R. 14 (Ch D), Arnold, J.; see *Football Association Premier League Ltd v QC Leisure* [2012] EWCA Civ 1708, [2013] Bus. L.R. 866 (CA (Civ Div)), Etherton, L.J.; see *ITV Broadcasting Ltd v TVCatchup Ltd (C-607/11)*

[2013] Bus. L.R. 1020 (ECJ (4th Chamber)), Judge Bay Larsen (President)
s.20, applied: SI 2013/536 Art.4
s.20, disapplied: SI 2013/536 Art.4, Art.5
s.26, disapplied: SI 2013/536 Art.4, Art.5
s.35, applied: SI 2013/158, SI 2013/1924
s.52, repealed: 2013 c.24 s.74
s.77, applied: SI 2013/1782 Reg.20
s.79, repealed (in part): 2013 c.24 s.74
s.80, applied: SI 2013/1782 Reg.20
s.107, applied: SI 2013/536 Art.4
s.107, disapplied: SI 2013/536 Art.4, Art.5
s.115, amended: 2013 c.22 Sch.9 para.72
s.116, amended: 2013 c.24 s.77
s.116A, added: 2013 c.24 s.77
s.116B, added: 2013 c.24 s.77
s.116C, added: 2013 c.24 s.77
s.116D, added: 2013 c.24 s.77
s.143, enabling: SI 2013/158, SI 2013/1924
s.158, enabling: SI 2013/536
s.159, enabling: SI 2013/536
s.170, substituted: 2013 c.24 s.76
s.180, applied: SI 2013/536 Art.6
s.180, varied: SI 2013/536 Art.6
s.182C, disapplied: SI 2013/536 Art.7
s.182CA, disapplied: SI 2013/536 Art.7
s.182D, amended: SI 2013/1782 Reg.7
s.182D, disapplied: SI 2013/536 Art.7
s.183, disapplied: SI 2013/536 Art.7
s.185, disapplied: SI 2013/536 Art.7
s.186, disapplied: SI 2013/536 Art.7
s.187, disapplied: SI 2013/536 Art.7
s.188, disapplied: SI 2013/536 Art.7
s.191, amended: SI 2013/1782 Reg.8
s.191B, applied: SI 2013/1782 Reg.25
s.191HA, added: SI 2013/1782 Reg.9
s.191HA, applied: SI 2013/1782 Reg.19, Reg.26
s.191HB, added: SI 2013/1782 Reg.9
s.191HB, applied: SI 2013/1782 Reg.19, Reg.26, Reg.27
s.192A, amended: SI 2013/1782 Reg.10
s.192A, applied: SI 2013/1782 Reg.25
s.198, disapplied: SI 2013/536 Art.7
s.205, amended: 2013 c.22 Sch.9 para.72
s.232, amended: 2013 c.22 Sch.9 para.72
s.252, amended: 2013 c.22 Sch.9 para.30
s.265, varied: SI 2013/2533 Sch.2 para.2
s.268, varied: SI 2013/2533 Sch.2 para.2
s.287, see *Ningbo Wentai Sports Equipment Co Ltd v Wang* [2013] F.S.R. 40 (PCC), Judge Birss Q.C.
s.287, repealed: 2013 c.22 Sch.9 para.30
s.288, repealed: 2013 c.22 Sch.9 para.30
s.289, repealed: 2013 c.22 Sch.9 para.30
s.291, repealed: 2013 c.22 Sch.9 para.30
s.304, enabling: SI 2013/2533
Sch.A1 para.1, added: 2013 c.24 Sch.22 para.1
Sch.A1 para.2, added: 2013 c.24 Sch.22 para.1
Sch.A1 para.3, added: 2013 c.24 Sch.22 para.1
Sch.A1 para.4, added: 2013 c.24 Sch.22 para.1
Sch.A1 para.5, added: 2013 c.24 Sch.22 para.1
Sch.A1 para.6, added: 2013 c.24 Sch.22 para.1
Sch.A1 para.7, added: 2013 c.24 Sch.22 para.1
Sch.A1 para.8, added: 2013 c.24 Sch.22 para.1
Sch.1 para.20, repealed: 2013 c.24 s.74
Sch.1 para.23, applied: SI 2013/1782 Reg.20
Sch.2 para.6, applied: SI 2013/158, SI 2013/1924
Sch.2A para.1, amended: 2013 c.24 Sch.22 para.3, Sch.22 para.4
Sch.2A para.1A, added: 2013 c.24 Sch.22 para.5
Sch.2A para.1A, amended: 2013 c.24 Sch.22 para.3
Sch.2A para.1B, added: 2013 c.24 Sch.22 para.5
Sch.2A para.1B, amended: 2013 c.24 Sch.22 para.3
Sch.2A para.1C, added: 2013 c.24 Sch.22 para.5
Sch.2A para.1C, amended: 2013 c.24 Sch.22 para.3
Sch.2A para.1D, added: 2013 c.24 Sch.22 para.5
Sch.2A para.1D, amended: 2013 c.24 Sch.22 para.3
Sch.2A para.2, amended: 2013 c.24 Sch.22 para.3
Sch.2A para.3, amended: 2013 c.24 Sch.22 para.3
Sch.2A para.4, amended: 2013 c.24 Sch.22 para.3
Sch.2A para.5, amended: 2013 c.24 Sch.22 para.3
Sch.2A para.6, amended: 2013 c.24 Sch.22 para.3
Sch.2A para.7, amended: 2013 c.24 Sch.22 para.3
Sch.2A para.8, amended: 2013 c.24 Sch.22 para.3
Sch.2A para.9, amended: 2013 c.24 Sch.22 para.3
Sch.2A para.10, amended: 2013 c.24 Sch.22 para.3
Sch.2A para.11, amended: 2013 c.24 Sch.22 para.3
Sch.2A para.12, amended: 2013 c.24 Sch.22 para.3
Sch.2A para.13, amended: 2013 c.24 Sch.22 para.3
Sch.2A para.14, amended: 2013 c.24 Sch.22 para.3
Sch.2A para.15, amended: 2013 c.24 Sch.22 para.3
Sch.2A para.16, amended: 2013 c.24 Sch.22 para.3
Sch.2A para.16, enabling: SI 2013/158, SI 2013/1924
Sch.2A para.17, amended: 2013 c.24 Sch.22 para.3
Sch.3 para.1, varied: SI 2013/2533 Sch.2 para.3
Sch.3 para.2, varied: SI 2013/2533 Sch.2 para.3
Sch.3 para.3, varied: SI 2013/2533 Sch.2 para.3
Sch.3 para.4, varied: SI 2013/2533 Sch.2 para.3
Sch.3 para.6, varied: SI 2013/2533 Sch.2 para.3
Sch.3 para.9, varied: SI 2013/2533 Sch.2 para.3
Sch.3 para.31, varied: SI 2013/2533 Sch.2 para.3
Sch.4, varied: SI 2013/2533 Sch.2 para.4

50. Housing Act 1988

Part I, applied: SI 2013/1169 r.26
s.1, amended: 2013 c.3 Sch.1 para.4
s.6, amended: SI 2013/1036 Sch.1 para.81
s.6A, amended: 2013 c.22 Sch.9 para.52
s.13, amended: SI 2013/1036 Sch.1 para.82
s.14, amended: SI 2013/1036 Sch.1 para.83
s.14A, amended: SI 2013/1036 Sch.1 para.84
s.14B, amended: SI 2013/1036 Sch.1 para.85
s.15A, added: 2013 c.3 s.6
s.22, amended: SI 2013/1036 Sch.1 para.86
s.23, amended: SI 2013/1036 Sch.1 para.87
s.36, amended: SI 2013/1036 Sch.1 para.88
s.40, amended: 2013 c.22 Sch.9 para.52, SI 2013/1036 Sch.1 para.89
s.41A, amended: SI 2013/630 Reg.6, SI 2013/1036 Sch.1 para.90
s.41B, amended: SI 2013/1036 Sch.1 para.91
s.42, amended: SI 2013/1036 Sch.1 para.92
s.42A, added: SI 2013/1036 Sch.1 para.93
s.45, amended: SI 2013/1036 Sch.1 para.94
s.129, applied: SI 2013/3029 Sch.10 para.41, SI 2013/3035 Sch.1
Sch.1 Part I para.8, enabling: SI 2013/38, SI 2013/1461
Sch.9 Part I para.4, amended: SI 2013/687 Sch.1 para.11

52. Road Traffic Act 1988

Part V, applied: SSI 2013/50 Sch.3 para.3, Sch.4 para.8
s.1, applied: SI 2013/435 Sch.1 Part 7
s.2, see *Elphinstone v Richardson* 2013 J.C. 29 (HCJ), Lord Carloway
s.2, applied: SI 2013/435 Sch.1 Part 7
s.3, applied: SI 2013/1565 Art.2
s.3A, see *Fleming (Jamie Anthony) v HM Advocate* 2013 S.C.L. 386 (HCJ), Lord Mackay of Drumadoon; see *Grant (Anthony Tallarn) v HM Advocate* [2013] HCJAC 11, 2013 S.C.L. 429 (HCJ), Lord Mackay of Drumadoon
s.3A, amended: 2013 c.22 Sch.22 para.2
s.3A, applied: SI 2013/435 Sch.1 Part 7
s.5A, added: 2013 c.22 s.56
s.6C, amended: 2013 c.22 Sch.22 para.3
s.6D, amended: 2013 c.22 Sch.22 para.4
s.7, see *Barclay v Richardson* 2013 J.C. 181 (HCJ), Lord Eassie; see *DPP v Chajed* [2013] EWHC 188 (Admin), [2013] 2 Cr. App. R. 6 (DC), Laws, L.J.
s.7, amended: 2013 c.22 Sch.22 para.5
s.10, amended: 2013 c.22 Sch.22 para.6
s.11, amended: 2013 c.22 s.56
s.13, enabling: SI 2013/2496
s.13A, enabling: SI 2013/2494
s.22A, applied: SI 2013/435 Sch.1 Part 7
s.31, enabling: SI 2013/2987
s.41, enabling: SI 2013/271
s.45, enabling: SI 2013/271
s.46, enabling: SI 2013/271
s.49, enabling: SI 2013/271
s.51, enabling: SI 2013/271
s.67, amended: SI 2013/602 Sch.2 para.22
s.73, amended: SI 2013/1644 Sch.1
s.73, repealed (in part): SI 2013/1644 Sch.1
s.89, enabling: SI 2013/1753
s.92, see *Golding v Secretary of State for Transport* [2013] EWHC 300 (Admin), [2013] R.T.R. 20 (QBD (Admin)), Kenneth Parker, J.
s.92, enabling: SI 2013/258
s.94, enabling: SI 2013/258, SI 2013/1013
s.101, enabling: SI 2013/2184
s.104, amended: 2013 c.22 Sch.9 para.126
s.105, enabling: SI 2013/258, SI 2013/1013, SI 2013/1753, SI 2013/2184
s.108, applied: SI 2013/22, SI 2013/22 Art.5
s.108, enabling: SI 2013/22, SI 2013/258
s.111, amended: SI 2013/1644 Sch.1
s.113, amended: SI 2013/1644 Sch.1
s.116, amended: SI 2013/1644 Sch.1
s.118, amended: SI 2013/1644 Sch.1
s.119, amended: SI 2013/1644 Sch.1
s.122, amended: SI 2013/1644 Sch.1
s.124, amended: 2013 c.22 Sch.8 para.32
s.144, amended: SI 2013/602 Sch.2 para.22
s.156, applied: SI 2013/2904
s.164, amended: SI 2013/1644 Sch.1
s.173, applied: SI 2013/435 Sch.1 Part 7
s.192, amended: 2013 c.22 Sch.22 para.7
s.195, amended: 2013 c.22 s.56
s.195, applied: SI 2013/258, SI 2013/271, SI 2013/1013, SI 2013/1753, SI 2013/2184, SI 2013/2494, SI 2013/2496, SI 2013/2904, SI 2013/2987

53. Road Traffic Offenders Act 1988

applied: SI 2013/1554 r.55_2
Part III, applied: SI 2013/1565 Art.2
s.15, amended: 2013 c.22 Sch.22 para.10
s.24, amended: 2013 c.22 Sch.22 para.11
s.25, applied: SI 2013/1554 r.37_15, r.55_2, r.4_7
s.27, applied: SI 2013/1554 r.55_2
s.30B, applied: SI 2013/1554 r.55_4
s.34, amended: 2013 c.22 Sch.22 para.12
s.34, applied: SI 2013/1554 r.55_1, r.55_2
s.34A, applied: SI 2013/372 Reg.9
s.34B, applied: SI 2013/372 Reg.9, Reg.11, SI 2013/1554 r.55_4
s.34B, referred to: SI 2013/372 Reg.10
s.34B, enabling: SI 2013/372
s.34BA, applied: SI 2013/372 Reg.9

s.34BA, enabling: SI 2013/372
s.34C, applied: SI 2013/372 Reg.6, Reg.9
s.34C, enabling: SI 2013/372
s.34E, applied: SI 2013/1554 r.55_4
s.35, applied: SI 2013/1554 r.55_1, r.55_2
s.39, applied: SI 2013/1554 r.63_2, r.64_2
s.40, applied: SI 2013/1554 r.63_2
s.47, applied: SI 2013/1554 r.5_4
s.51, enabling: SI 2013/1565
s.52, referred to: SI 2013/362 Reg.7
s.53, enabling: SI 2013/1569, SI 2013/1840
s.57, applied: SI 2013/1554 r.5_4
s.57A, applied: SI 2013/1554 r.5_4
s.71, applied: SI 2013/1554 r.5_4, r.4_7
s.88, applied: SI 2013/1565, SI 2013/1569, SI 2013/1840
s.89, amended: SI 2013/602 Sch.2 para.23
s.90B, enabling: SI 2013/2025
s.90E, applied: SI 2013/2025
s.90E, enabling: SI 2013/2025
Sch.1, amended: 2013 c.22 Sch.22 para.13
Sch.2 Part I, amended: 2013 c.22 s.56
Sch.3, amended: 2013 c.7 s.13, SI 2013/1565 Art.3

1989

6. Official Secrets Act 1989
applied: 2013 c.32 Sch.7 para.6, Sch.7 para.14, SI 2013/2356 Reg.95, SSI 2013/174 Reg.8
s.12, amended: 2013 c.22 Sch.8 para.36

14. Control of Pollution (Amendment) Act 1989
s.1, applied: SI 2013/2258 Sch.1 Part 1
s.5, applied: SI 2013/2258 Sch.1 Part 1
s.5C, amended: SI 2013/755 Sch.2 para.189
s.7, applied: SI 2013/2258 Sch.1 Part 1
s.9, amended: SI 2013/755 Sch.2 para.190

22. Road Traffic (Driver Licensing and Information Systems) Act 1989
Sch.5 para.8, amended: SI 2013/755 Sch.2 para.194

26. Finance Act 1989
s.91, repealed: 2013 c.2 Sch.1 Part 10
s.92, repealed (in part): 2013 c.2 Sch.1 Part 10
s.96, repealed (in part): 2013 c.2 Sch.1 Part 10
s.114, repealed: 2013 c.2 Sch.1 Part 10
s.160, repealed (in part): 2013 c.2 Sch.1 Part 10
s.162, repealed: 2013 c.2 Sch.1 Part 10

29. Electricity Act 1989
see *R. (on the application of Infinis Plc) v Gas and Electricity Markets Authority* [2013] EWCA Civ 70, [2013] J.P.L. 1037 (CA (Civ Div)), Sir James Munby (President, Fam); see *Sustainable Shetland v Scottish Ministers* [2013] CSOH 158, 2013 S.L.T. 1173 (OH), Lady Clark of Calton
applied: 2013 c.12 Sch.1 para.1, 2013 c.28 Sch.1, SI 2013/501 Reg.4, SI 2013/588 Reg.4, SI 2013/1873 Art.7
Part I, applied: 2013 c.32 s.39, s.59, s.64, s.136, s.140, s.141
s.3A, amended: 2013 c.32 s.65, s.138
s.3A, applied: 2013 c.32 s.39, s.53, s.136, s.141
s.3B, applied: 2013 c.32 s.39, s.53, s.136, s.141
s.3B, repealed: 2013 c.32 s.138
s.3C, amended: 2013 c.32 Sch.12 para.61
s.3C, applied: 2013 c.32 s.39, s.53, s.136, s.141
s.3D, applied: 2013 c.32 s.39, s.53, s.136, s.141
s.3D, repealed (in part): 2013 c.32 s.138
s.3E, applied: 2013 c.32 s.39
s.3F, applied: 2013 c.32 s.39
s.4, amended: 2013 c.32 s.147
s.4, applied: SI 2013/426 Art.3, SI 2013/1031 Art.3, SI 2013/2473 Art.3
s.4, disapplied: SI 2013/1011 Art.3
s.5, applied: SI 2013/680 Art.7, SI 2013/1011, SI 2013/1031, SI 2013/2473
s.5, enabling: SI 2013/426, SI 2013/1011, SI 2013/1031, SI 2013/2473
s.6, applied: 2013 c.32 s.24, s.26, s.32, s.34, s.37, s.40, s.41, s.139, s.141, Sch.2 para.13, Sch.2 para.19, SI 2013/343 Art.8, SI 2013/426 Art.4, SI 2013/586 Art.4, SI 2013/680 Art.4, Art.7, Sch.1 para.36, SI 2013/1011 Art.3, SI 2013/1031 Art.3, SI 2013/1119 Sch.1 para.4, SI 2013/1203 Art.6, SI 2013/2473 Art.3
s.6, referred to: 2013 c.32 s.45, s.49, s.50
s.6A, applied: SI 2013/175 Reg.34
s.6B, applied: SI 2013/175 Reg.34
s.6C, enabling: SI 2013/175
s.6D, applied: SI 2013/175 Reg.29
s.6D, enabling: SI 2013/175
s.6E, enabling: SI 2013/968
s.6F, added: 2013 c.32 s.147
s.6G, added: 2013 c.32 s.147
s.6H, added: 2013 c.32 s.147
s.7, applied: 2013 c.32 s.64, s.139
s.8A, applied: 2013 c.32 s.26, s.37, s.139, Sch.2 para.19
s.8A, referred to: 2013 c.32 s.45, s.49, s.50
s.11C, amended: 2013 c.24 Sch.6 para.31
s.11D, amended: 2013 c.24 Sch.6 para.32
s.11D, repealed (in part): 2013 c.24 Sch.6 para.32
s.11E, amended: 2013 c.24 Sch.6 para.33, 2013 c.32 s.138
s.11F, amended: 2013 c.24 Sch.6 para.34
s.11G, amended: 2013 c.24 Sch.6 para.35
s.11H, amended: 2013 c.24 Sch.6 para.36

s.15, amended: 2013 c.24 Sch.6 para.37
s.25, amended: 2013 c.24 Sch.14 para.5
s.25, applied: 2013 c.32 s.22, s.36, s.51, Sch.2 para.12
s.25, referred to: 2013 c.32 s.38
s.25, repealed (in part): 2013 c.24 Sch.14 para.5
s.27, applied: 2013 c.32 s.63
s.27A, amended: 2013 c.24 Sch.14 para.6, 2013 c.32 Sch.14 para.2
s.27A, applied: 2013 c.32 Sch.14 para.2
s.27B, applied: SI 2013/1389 Sch.3 para.4
s.27E, amended: 2013 c.32 Sch.14 para.2
s.27G, added: 2013 c.32 Sch.14 para.2
s.27G, applied: 2013 c.32 Sch.14 para.2
s.27H, added: 2013 c.32 Sch.14 para.2
s.27I, added: 2013 c.32 Sch.14 para.2
s.27J, added: 2013 c.32 Sch.14 para.2
s.27K, added: 2013 c.32 Sch.14 para.2
s.27L, added: 2013 c.32 Sch.14 para.2
s.27M, added: 2013 c.32 Sch.14 para.2
s.27N, added: 2013 c.32 Sch.14 para.2
s.27O, added: 2013 c.32 Sch.14 para.2
s.27O, applied: 2013 c.32 Sch.14 para.2
s.28, amended: 2013 c.32 s.138, Sch.14 para.2
s.32, enabling: SI 2013/768, SSI 2013/116
s.32A, enabling: SI 2013/768, SSI 2013/116
s.32C, enabling: SI 2013/768, SSI 2013/116
s.32D, applied: SI 2013/768, SSI 2013/116
s.32D, enabling: SI 2013/768, SSI 2013/116
s.32E, enabling: SI 2013/768, SSI 2013/116
s.32J, enabling: SI 2013/768, SSI 2013/116
s.32K, enabling: SI 2013/768, SSI 2013/116
s.32L, applied: SI 2013/768, SSI 2013/116
s.32LA, added: 2013 c.32 s.55
s.32LB, added: 2013 c.32 s.55
s.32M, amended: 2013 c.32 s.55
s.32N, added: 2013 c.32 s.56
s.32O, added: 2013 c.32 s.56
s.32P, added: 2013 c.32 s.56
s.32Q, added: 2013 c.32 s.56
s.32R, added: 2013 c.32 s.56
s.32S, added: 2013 c.32 s.56
s.32T, added: 2013 c.32 s.56
s.32U, added: 2013 c.32 s.56
s.32V, added: 2013 c.32 s.56
s.32W, added: 2013 c.32 s.56
s.32X, added: 2013 c.32 s.56
s.32Y, added: 2013 c.32 s.56
s.32Z, added: 2013 c.32 s.56
s.32Z1, added: 2013 c.32 s.56
s.32Z2, added: 2013 c.32 s.56
s.36, see *Sustainable Shetland v Scottish Ministers* [2013] CSOH 158, 2013 S.L.T. 1173 (OH), Lady Clark of Calton; see *William Grant & Sons Distillers Ltd v Scottish Ministers* 2013 S.C.L.R. 19 (OH), Lord Malcolm
s.36, applied: SSI 2013/304 Reg.5
s.36, disapplied: 2013 c.32 s.133
s.36, referred to: 2013 c.32 Sch.4 para.1, SI 2013/1570 Reg.3, Reg.4, Reg.6, Reg.7
s.36, enabling: SI 2013/495, SSI 2013/58
s.36C, added: 2013 c.27 s.20
s.36C, applied: SSI 2013/304 Reg.4
s.36C, referred to: SI 2013/1570 Reg.5
s.36C, enabling: SI 2013/1570, SSI 2013/304
s.37, applied: SSI 2013/264 Reg.4
s.37, disapplied: 2013 c.32 s.133, SSI 2013/264 Reg.3, Reg.6
s.37, enabling: SSI 2013/264
s.39B, amended: 2013 c.22 Sch.9 para.52
s.43, amended: 2013 c.24 Sch.14 para.7, Sch.15 para.3
s.43, disapplied: 2013 c.32 s.133
s.44A, amended: 2013 c.22 Sch.9 para.52
s.47ZA, referred to: 2013 c.32 s.38
s.49, enabling: SI 2013/1420
s.56A, amended: 2013 c.32 s.143
s.56B, amended: 2013 c.24 Sch.6 para.38
s.56C, amended: 2013 c.24 Sch.6 para.39, 2013 c.32 s.138, Sch.12 para.62
s.56C, repealed (in part): 2013 c.32 s.138
s.56CA, amended: 2013 c.24 Sch.6 para.40
s.56CB, amended: 2013 c.24 Sch.6 para.41
s.56D, amended: 2013 c.24 Sch.6 para.42
s.60, enabling: SI 2013/175, SI 2013/495, SI 2013/1570, SSI 2013/58, SSI 2013/264, SSI 2013/304
s.64, amended: 2013 c.24 Sch.6 para.43, 2013 c.32 s.147
s.106, amended: 2013 c.27 s.20, 2013 c.32 s.55, s.56, Sch.14 para.2
s.113, amended: 2013 c.32 s.56
Sch.2A para.5, applied: SI 2013/968, SI 2013/968 Art.2
Sch.2A para.5, varied: SI 2013/968 Art.2
Sch.2A para.5, enabling: SI 2013/968
Sch.4 para.3, amended: SI 2013/755 Sch.2 para.196
Sch.4 para.4, amended: SI 2013/755 Sch.2 para.196
Sch.4 para.6, see *Arnold White Estates Ltd v National Grid Electricity Transmission Plc* [2013] UKUT 5 (LC), [2013] R.V.R. 203 (UT (Lands)), George Bartlett Q.C.
Sch.4 para.6, applied: SI 2013/1987 r.4, r.11
Sch.4 para.9, applied: SI 2013/1987 r.4, r.11
Sch.5A, applied: 2013 c.24 Sch.4 para.48
Sch.5A para.1, amended: 2013 c.24 Sch.6 para.44

Sch.5A para.2, amended: 2013 c.24 Sch.6 para.44
Sch.5A para.3, amended: 2013 c.24 Sch.6 para.44
Sch.5A para.4, amended: 2013 c.24 Sch.6 para.44
Sch.5A para.4, repealed (in part): 2013 c.24 Sch.6 para.44
Sch.5A para.5, amended: 2013 c.24 Sch.6 para.44
Sch.5A para.6, amended: 2013 c.24 Sch.6 para.44
Sch.5A para.7, amended: 2013 c.24 Sch.6 para.44
Sch.5A para.8, amended: 2013 c.24 Sch.6 para.44
Sch.5A para.9, amended: 2013 c.24 Sch.6 para.44
Sch.5A para.10, amended: 2013 c.24 Sch.6 para.44
Sch.5A para.11, amended: 2013 c.24 Sch.6 para.44
Sch.5A para.12, amended: 2013 c.24 Sch.6 para.44
Sch.5A para.13, amended: 2013 c.24 Sch.6 para.44
Sch.6A, referred to: 2013 c.32 s.38
Sch.8 para.1, enabling: SI 2013/495, SSI 2013/58
Sch.8 para.2, varied: SSI 2013/304 Reg.6
Sch.8 para.3, applied: SI 2013/1570 Reg.8
Sch.8 para.4, applied: SI 2013/1570 Reg.8, SSI 2013/304 Reg.6
Sch.8 para.4, varied: SI 2013/1570 Reg.8
Sch.8 para.5A, applied: SI 2013/1570 Reg.8
Sch.8 para.5A, varied: SI 2013/1570 Reg.8
Sch.8 para.7A, applied: SI 2013/1570 Reg.8
Sch.8 para.7A, varied: SI 2013/1570 Reg.8
Sch.8 para.8, applied: SI 2013/1570 Reg.8
Sch.8 para.8, varied: SI 2013/1570 Reg.8
Sch.9 para.1, applied: SI 2013/1570 Reg.6
Sch.9 para.2, amended: SI 2013/755 Sch.2 para.197
Sch.16 para.11, repealed: 2013 c.32 Sch.12 para.30
Sch.16 para.22, repealed: 2013 c.27 s.18

33. Extradition Act 1989

applied: SI 2013/1554 r.2_1

36. Brunei (Appeals) Act 1989

s.1, enabling: SI 2013/246

37. Football Spectators Act 1989

s.11, applied: SI 2013/1568
s.11, enabling: SI 2013/1568
s.14, enabling: SI 2013/1709
s.14A, see *R. v Doyle (Ciaran)* [2012] EWCA Crim 995, [2013] 1 Cr. App. R. (S.) 36 (CA (Crim Div)), Hughes, L.J.
s.14A, applied: SI 2013/1554 r.50_1, r.63_1, r.68_1, r.74_1, r.68_3, r.68_4
s.14B, applied: SI 2013/9 Reg.9
s.14D, applied: SI 2013/9 Reg.9
s.14G, applied: SI 2013/9 Reg.9
s.14H, applied: SI 2013/9 Reg.9, SI 2013/1554 r.76_1
s.21B, applied: SI 2013/9 Reg.9
s.21D, applied: SI 2013/9 Reg.9
s.22, applied: SI 2013/1554 r.63_1
s.22A, referred to: SI 2013/1709
Sch.1 para.1, amended: 2013 c.22 Sch.22 para.15

38. Employment Act 1989

s.8, amended: SI 2013/630 Reg.7

40. Companies Act 1989

s.82, varied: SI 2013/442 Art.64
s.87, amended: SI 2013/2329 Sch.1 para.23
s.144, enabling: SI 2013/1947
s.155, amended: SI 2013/504 Reg.4, SI 2013/1908 Reg.2
s.155, enabling: SI 2013/504, SI 2013/1908
s.155A, added: SI 2013/504 Reg.4
s.155A, amended: SI 2013/1908 Reg.2
s.157, amended: SI 2013/504 Reg.4
s.157, applied: SI 2013/442 Art.65
s.158, amended: SI 2013/504 Reg.4, SI 2013/1908 Reg.2
s.158, enabling: SI 2013/504, SI 2013/1908
s.159, amended: SI 2013/504 Reg.4, SI 2013/1908 Reg.2
s.162, amended: SI 2013/504 Reg.4
s.162, applied: SI 2013/442 Art.66
s.163, amended: SI 2013/504 Reg.4
s.164, amended: SI 2013/504 Reg.4
s.165, amended: SI 2013/504 Reg.4
s.166, amended: SI 2013/504 Reg.4, SI 2013/1908 Reg.2
s.166, applied: SI 2013/442 Art.67, Art.68
s.167, amended: SI 2013/1908 Reg.2
s.167, applied: SI 2013/442 Art.67, Art.68
s.170A, added: SI 2013/504 Reg.4
s.170A, amended: SI 2013/1908 Reg.2
s.170B, added: SI 2013/504 Reg.4
s.174, enabling: SI 2013/504
s.175, amended: SI 2013/504 Reg.4
s.176, amended: SI 2013/1773 Sch.1 para.39
s.182A, added: SI 2013/504 Reg.4
s.182A, amended: SI 2013/1908 Reg.2
s.185, enabling: SI 2013/504, SI 2013/1908
s.186, enabling: SI 2013/504, SI 2013/1908
s.187, amended: SI 2013/504 Reg.4
s.187, enabling: SI 2013/504, SI 2013/1908
s.188, amended: SI 2013/504 Reg.4, SI 2013/1908 Reg.2
s.189A, added: SI 2013/1908 Reg.2
s.190, amended: SI 2013/504 Reg.4, SI 2013/1908 Reg.2
s.190, repealed (in part): SI 2013/1908 Reg.2
s.191, amended: SI 2013/504 Sch.1, SI 2013/1908 Reg.2
s.213, amended: SI 2013/504 Reg.4
Sch.10 Part II para.28, repealed: SI 2013/687 Sch.1 para.12

41. Children Act 1989

see *AI v MT (Alternate Dispute Resolution)* [2013] EWHC 100 (Fam), [2013] 2 F.L.R. 371 (Fam Div), Baker, J.; see *C (A Child) (Adoption: Assessment of Grandparents), Re* [2012] EWCA Civ 1787, [2013] 2 F.L.R. 59 (CA (Civ Div)), Thorpe, L.J.; see *G v G* [2012] EWHC 1979 (Fam), [2013] 1 F.L.R. 286 (Fam Div), Hedley, J.; see *HB v PB* [2013] EWHC 1956 (Fam), [2013] P.T.S.R. 1579 (Fam Div), Cobb, J.; see *JG (A Child) v Legal Services Commission* [2013] EWHC 804 (Admin), [2013] 2 F.L.R. 1174 (QBD (Admin)), Ryder, J.; see *R. (on the application of AA (Afghanistan)) v Secretary of State for the Home Department* [2013] UKSC 49, [2013] 1 W.L.R. 2224 (SC), Lord Neuberger (President); see *R. (on the application of ET) v Islington LBC* [2012] EWHC 3228 (Admin), [2013] 2 F.L.R. 347 (QBD (Admin)), Cranston, J.; see *R. (on the application of K) v Birmingham City Council* [2012] EWCA Civ 1432, [2013] 1 W.L.R. 1755 (CA (Civ Div)), Lord Dyson (M.R.); see *R. (on the application of KA (Nigeria)) v Essex CC* [2013] EWHC 43 (Admin), [2013] 1 W.L.R. 1163 (QBD (Admin)), Robin Purchas Q.C.

applied: SI 2013/104 Reg.26, SI 2013/349 Reg.116, SI 2013/480 Reg.5, SI 2013/898 Reg.48, SI 2013/1465 Art.13, SI 2013/3029 Sch.11 para.3, SI 2013/3035 Sch.1

referred to: SI 2013/104 Reg.65

Part I, referred to: SI 2013/104 Reg.69

Part II, referred to: SI 2013/104 Reg.69

Part III, applied: SI 2013/3029 Sch.11 para.4, SI 2013/3035 Sch.1

s.3, see *W (Children) (Direct Contact), Re* [2012] EWCA Civ 999, [2013] 1 F.L.R. 494 (CA (Civ Div)), Rix, L.J.

s.3, applied: SI 2013/376 Reg.4A, SI 2013/2094 Sch.1 para.18

s.11J, repealed (in part): 2013 c.22 Sch.11 para.103

s.14, amended: 2013 c.22 Sch.11 para.102, Sch.11 para.104

s.14F, see *Suffolk CC v Nottinghamshire CC* [2012] EWCA Civ 1640, [2013] P.T.S.R. 619 (CA (Civ Div)), Thorpe, L.J.

s.14F, applied: SI 2013/3029 Sch.9 para.30, Sch.10 para.62

s.14F, enabling: SI 2013/2091

s.15, applied: SI 2013/104 Reg.69, SI 2013/765 Reg.28, SI 2013/3029 Sch.9 para.30, SI 2013/3035 Sch.1

s.15, repealed (in part): 2013 c.22 Sch.11 para.105

s.17, see *R. (on the application of Kent CC) v HM Coroner for Kent (North-West District)* [2012] EWHC 2768 (Admin), (2013) 177 J.P. 82 (DC), Foskett, J.; see *R. (on the application of N) v Newham LBC* [2013] EWHC 2475 (Admin), [2013] B.L.G.R. 898 (QBD (Admin)), Swift, J.; see *R. (on the application of T (A Child)) v Newham LBC* [2013] EWHC 344 (Admin), (2013) 16 C.C.L. Rep. 259 (QBD (Admin)), John Powell, Q.C.

s.17, applied: SI 2013/376 Sch.10 para.17, SI 2013/377 Reg.28, SI 2013/3029 Sch.9 para.33, Sch.10 para.23, SI 2013/3035 Sch.1

s.17A, applied: SI 2013/471 Reg.11, Reg.20, Reg.33, SI 2013/480 Reg.24, SI 2013/483 Reg.10

s.22, see *Suffolk CC v Nottinghamshire CC* [2012] EWCA Civ 1640, [2013] P.T.S.R. 619 (CA (Civ Div)), Thorpe, L.J.

s.22, applied: SI 2013/461 Reg.26, SI 2013/1141 Sch.1 para.3, SI 2013/3177 Sch.5 para.2

s.22C, see *R. (on the application of X) v Tower Hamlets LBC* [2013] EWCA Civ 904, [2013] 4 All E.R. 237 (CA (Civ Div)), Maurice Kay, L.J. (VP, CA Civ); see *Sheffield City Council v Bradford MBC* [2013] 1 F.L.R. 1027 (Fam Div), Bodey, J.

s.22C, applied: SI 2013/379 Reg.37, SI 2013/3029 Reg.8, SI 2013/3035 Sch.1

s.22C, enabling: SI 2013/706, SI 2013/984, SI 2013/985, SI 2013/3239

s.23, applied: SI 2013/765 Reg.28, SI 2013/3029 Reg.8, Sch.9 para.31, SI 2013/3035 Sch.1

s.23A, applied: SI 2013/461 Reg.16

s.23A, enabling: SI 2013/706

s.23B, applied: SI 2013/376 Sch.10 para.17, SI 2013/461 Reg.16, SI 2013/3029 Sch.9 para.33, Sch.10 para.23, SI 2013/3035 Sch.1

s.23C, see *R. (on the application of Kebede) v Newcastle City Council* [2013] EWCA Civ 960, [2013] 3 F.C.R. 372 (CA (Civ Div)), Laws, L.J.

s.23C, applied: SI 2013/376 Sch.10 para.17, SI 2013/765 Reg.28, SI 2013/3029 Sch.9 para.33, Sch.9 para.34, Sch.10 para.23, Sch.10 para.24, SI 2013/3035 Sch.1

s.23D, enabling: SI 2013/706

s.23E, enabling: SI 2013/706

s.23ZA, enabling: SI 2013/706

s.23ZB, enabling: SI 2013/706

s.24, applied: SI 2013/160 Sch.1 para.4

s.24, referred to: SI 2013/160 Sch.1 para.4

s.24, applied: SI 2013/765 Reg.28

s.24A, applied: SI 2013/376 Sch.10 para.17, SI 2013/3029 Sch.9 para.33, Sch.10 para.23, SI 2013/3035 Sch.1

s.25, applied: SI 2013/235 Sch.3 para.3

s.25, enabling: SI 2013/663

s.26, enabling: SI 2013/706, SI 2013/984, SI 2013/985, SI 2013/3239
s.27, applied: SI 2013/261 Sch.1 para.19
s.31, see *A City Council v DC* [2013] EWHC 8 (Fam), [2013] 1 W.L.R. 3009 (Fam Div), Eleanor King, J.; see *AA (A Child) (Fact-finding Hearing), Re* [2012] EWHC 2647 (Fam), [2013] 1 F.L.R. 534 (Fam Div), Baker, J.; see *B (A Child) (Care Proceedings: Appeal), Re* [2013] UKSC 33, [2013] 1 W.L.R. 1911 (SC), Lord Neuberger, J.S.C.; see *B (Children) (Refusal to Grant Interim Order), Re* [2012] EWCA Civ 1275, [2013] 2 F.L.R. 153 (CA (Civ Div)), Hughes, L.J.; see *D (A Child) (Care Proceedings: Designated Local Authority), Re* [2012] EWCA Civ 627, [2013] Fam. 34 (CA (Civ Div)), Ward, L.J.; see *J (Children) (Care Proceedings: Threshold Criteria), Re* [2013] UKSC 9, [2013] 1 A.C. 680 (SC), Lord Hope, J.S.C. (Deputy President); see *K (A Child) (Post Adoption Placement Breakdown), Re* [2012] EWHC 4148 (Fam), [2013] 1 F.L.R. 1 (Fam Div (Coventry)), Judge Clifford Bellamy; see *M (A Child) (Fact-Finding Hearing: Burden of Proof), Re* [2012] EWCA Civ 1580, [2013] 2 F.L.R. 874 (CA (Civ Div)), Ward, L.J.; see *M (A Child) (Foreign Care Proceedings: Transfer),Re* [2013] EWHC 646 (Fam), [2013] Fam. 308 (Fam Div), Cobb, J.; see *P (A Child) (Care and Placement: Evidential Basis of Local Authority Case), Re* [2013] EWCA Civ 963, [2013] 3 F.C.R. 159 (CA (Civ Div)), Lloyd, L.J.; see *R. (on the application of ET) v Islington LBC* [2012] EWHC 3228 (Admin), [2013] 2 F.L.R. 347 (QBD (Admin)), Cranston, J.; see *R. (on the application of Kent CC) v HM Coroner for Kent (North-West District)* [2012] EWHC 2768 (Admin), (2013) 177 J.P. 82 (DC), Foskett, J.; see *S (Children) (Care and Placement Orders), Re* [2012] EWCA Civ 847, [2013] 1 F.L.R. 354 (CA (Civ Div)), Thorpe, L.J.; see *Sheffield City Council v Bradford MBC* [2013] 1 F.L.R. 1027 (Fam Div), Bodey, J.; see *Sutton LBC v G* [2012] EWHC 2604 (Fam), [2013] 1 F.L.R. 833 (Fam Div), Hogg, J.
s.31, amended: SI 2013/1465 Sch.1 para.2
s.31, applied: SI 2013/480 Reg.5, SI 2013/1407 Art.5, SSI 2013/99 Reg.3, Reg.4
s.31, referred to: SI 2013/1465 Art.13
s.31A, enabling: SI 2013/706, SI 2013/984, SI 2013/3239
s.36, applied: SSI 2013/99 Reg.4
s.36, referred to: SI 2013/1465 Art.13
s.38B, amended: 2013 c.22 Sch.11 para.106
s.41, applied: SI 2013/422 Reg.8
s.44B, amended: 2013 c.22 Sch.11 para.107
s.47, see *R. (on the application of ET) v Islington LBC* [2012] EWHC 3228 (Admin), [2013] 2 F.L.R. 347 (QBD (Admin)), Cranston, J.
s.47, applied: SI 2013/261 Sch.1 para.20
s.51, amended: SI 2013/1465 Sch.1 para.2
s.51, applied: SI 2013/1465 Art.10
s.51, enabling: SI 2013/706
s.59, applied: SI 2013/379 Reg.37, SI 2013/461 Reg.26, SI 2013/3029 Reg.8, Sch.9 para.31, SI 2013/3035 Sch.1
s.59, enabling: SI 2013/984
s.83, amended: 2013 c.22 Sch.11 para.108
s.85, referred to: SI 2013/160 Sch.1 para.4
s.85, varied: SI 2013/160 Sch.1 para.4
s.87D, enabling: SI 2013/523
s.92, amended: 2013 c.22 Sch.11 para.109
s.92, repealed (in part): 2013 c.22 Sch.11 para.109
s.92, enabling: SI 2013/421
s.93, repealed (in part): 2013 c.22 Sch.11 para.110
s.94, repealed: 2013 c.22 Sch.11 para.111
s.97, amended: 2013 c.22 Sch.10 para.75
s.97, repealed (in part): 2013 c.22 Sch.10 para.75
s.104, enabling: SI 2013/523, SI 2013/706, SI 2013/984, SI 2013/985, SI 2013/2091, SI 2013/3239
Sch.1, see *KS v ND (Schedule I: Appeal: Costs)* [2013] EWHC 464 (Fam), [2013] 2 F.L.R. 698 (Fam Div), Mostyn, J.
Sch.1, applied: SI 2013/104 Reg.69, SI 2013/765 Reg.28
Sch.1 para.1, amended: 2013 c.22 Sch.11 para.113
Sch.1 para.1, repealed (in part): 2013 c.22 Sch.11 para.113
Sch.1 para.5, repealed (in part): 2013 c.22 Sch.11 para.114
Sch.1 para.6A, amended: 2013 c.22 Sch.11 para.115
Sch.1 para.6A, repealed (in part): 2013 c.22 Sch.11 para.115
Sch.1 para.10, repealed (in part): 2013 c.22 Sch.11 para.116
Sch.1 para.11, amended: 2013 c.22 Sch.11 para.117
Sch.1 para.11, repealed (in part): 2013 c.22 Sch.11 para.117
Sch.1 para.12, amended: 2013 c.22 Sch.11 para.118
Sch.1 para.12, repealed (in part): 2013 c.22 Sch.11 para.118
Sch.1 para.13, amended: 2013 c.22 Sch.11 para.119
Sch.1 para.15, applied: SI 2013/3029 Sch.9 para.30, SI 2013/3035 Sch.1

Sch.2 Part II para.12E, enabling: SI 2013/706, SI 2013/984, SI 2013/3239
Sch.2 Part II para.12F, enabling: SI 2013/706, SI 2013/984, SI 2013/985
Sch.2 Part II para.19, applied: SSI 2013/99 Reg.3
Sch.2 Part III para.24, repealed (in part): 2013 c.22 Sch.11 para.120
Sch.8 para.3, amended: SI 2013/1465 Sch.1 para.2
Sch.11 Part I, enabling: SI 2013/421
Sch.11 Part I para.1, repealed: 2013 c.22 Sch.11 para.121
Sch.11 Part I para.2, repealed: 2013 c.22 Sch.11 para.121
Sch.11 Part I para.3, repealed: 2013 c.22 Sch.11 para.121
Sch.11 Part I para.4, repealed: 2013 c.22 Sch.11 para.121
Sch.11 Part II para.8, repealed (in part): 2013 c.22 Sch.10 para.99
Sch.13 para.42, repealed: 2013 c.22 Sch.11 para.210

42. Local Government and Housing Act 1989
s.4, applied: SI 2013/501 Reg.3, SI 2013/588 Reg.3
s.5, applied: SI 2013/501 Reg.3, SI 2013/588 Reg.3
s.13, amended: 2013 c.25 Sch.8 para.15
s.13, varied: SI 2013/218 Reg.6
s.14, amended: SSI 2013/211 Sch.1 para.7
s.14, repealed (in part): SSI 2013/211 Sch.2
s.15, applied: SI 2013/1050 Reg.5
s.15, disapplied: SI 2013/218 Reg.7
s.16, disapplied: SI 2013/218 Reg.7
Sch.1, disapplied: SI 2013/218 Reg.7
Sch.10 para.4, amended: SI 2013/1036 Sch.1 para.95
Sch.10 para.4A, added: SI 2013/1036 Sch.1 para.95
Sch.10 para.6, amended: SI 2013/1036 Sch.1 para.95
Sch.10 para.7, amended: SI 2013/1036 Sch.1 para.95
Sch.10 para.10, amended: SI 2013/1036 Sch.1 para.95
Sch.10 para.11, amended: SI 2013/1036 Sch.1 para.95
Sch.10 para.18, amended: SI 2013/1036 Sch.1 para.95
Sch.10 para.19, amended: SI 2013/1036 Sch.1 para.95

44. Opticians Act 1989
applied: SI 2013/2537 Sch.1
referred to: SI 2013/2537 Sch.1
s.13D, applied: SI 2013/2537 Sch.1
s.13D, referred to: SI 2013/2537 Sch.1
s.13F, applied: SI 2013/335 Reg.40, SI 2013/2537 Sch.1
s.13F, enabling: SI 2013/2537
s.13G, applied: SI 2013/2537 Sch.1
s.13H, applied: SI 2013/335 Reg.40, SI 2013/2537 Sch.1
s.13I, applied: SI 2013/335 Reg.40, SI 2013/2537 Sch.1
s.13L, applied: SI 2013/335 Reg.40, SI 2013/2537 Sch.1
s.23A, applied: SI 2013/2537 Sch.1
s.23C, enabling: SI 2013/2537
s.23D, enabling: SI 2013/2537
s.23E, enabling: SI 2013/2537
s.27, referred to: SI 2013/461 Reg.14
s.31A, enabling: SI 2013/2537
s.34, applied: SI 2013/2537

45. Prisons (Scotland) Act 1989
applied: SI 2013/3029 Reg.26, SI 2013/3035 Sch.1, SSI 2013/35 Sch.2 para.1
s.19, applied: SSI 2013/50 Sch.4 para.7
s.39, applied: SI 2013/378 Reg.13, SSI 2013/50 Sch.4 para.7

1990

5. Criminal Justice (International Co-operation) Act 1990
s.12, applied: SI 2013/435 Sch.1 Part 7
s.18, applied: SI 2013/435 Sch.1 Part 7

9. Planning (Listed Buildings and Conservation Areas) Act 1990
applied: SI 2013/2115 Reg.2, SI 2013/2148 Art.1, Art.5
disapplied: SI 2013/2146 Art.4
Part I c.V, varied: SI 2013/2148 Sch.1
s.1, amended: 2013 c.24 Sch.17 para.8
s.1, applied: SI 2013/2727 Art.2
s.1, varied: SI 2013/2148 Sch.1
s.2, varied: SI 2013/2148 Sch.1
s.3, varied: SI 2013/2148 Sch.1
s.4, varied: SI 2013/2148 Sch.1
s.5, varied: SI 2013/2148 Sch.1
s.6, amended: 2013 c.24 Sch.17 para.9
s.7, see *St Alkmund, Duffield, Re* [2013] Fam. 158 (Arches Ct), George Q.C. (Dean of Arches)
s.7, varied: SI 2013/2148 Sch.1
s.8, varied: SI 2013/2148 Sch.1
s.9, see *R. v Rance (Piers)* [2012] EWCA Crim 2023, [2013] 1 Cr. App. R. (S.) 123 (CA (Crim Div)), Moses, L.J.
s.9, varied: SI 2013/2148 Sch.1

s.10, varied: SI 2013/2148 Sch.1
s.10, enabling: SI 2013/1239
s.11, varied: SI 2013/2148 Sch.1
s.12, see *R. (on the application of Gray) v Southwark LBC* [2012] EWCA Civ 1738, [2013] Env. L.R. 22 (CA (Civ Div)), Pill, L.J.
s.12, varied: SI 2013/2148 Sch.1
s.13, varied: SI 2013/2148 Sch.1
s.14, varied: SI 2013/2148 Sch.1
s.15, varied: SI 2013/2148 Sch.1
s.16, see *St Alkmund, Duffield, Re* [2013] Fam. 158 (Arches Ct), George Q.C. (Dean of Arches)
s.16, varied: SI 2013/2148 Sch.1
s.17, varied: SI 2013/2148 Sch.1
s.18, varied: SI 2013/2148 Sch.1
s.19, varied: SI 2013/2148 Sch.1
s.20, applied: SI 2013/2115 Reg.3, SI 2013/2137 r.7
s.20, varied: SI 2013/2148 Sch.1
s.20A, varied: SI 2013/2148 Sch.1
s.21, varied: SI 2013/2148 Sch.1
s.21, enabling: SI 2013/2115
s.22, varied: SI 2013/2148 Sch.1
s.23, varied: SI 2013/2148 Sch.1
s.24, varied: SI 2013/2148 Sch.1
s.25, varied: SI 2013/2148 Sch.1
s.26, varied: SI 2013/2148 Sch.1
s.26A, added: 2013 c.24 s.60
s.26A, varied: SI 2013/2148 Sch.1
s.26B, added: 2013 c.24 s.60
s.26B, varied: SI 2013/2148 Sch.1
s.26C, added: 2013 c.24 s.60
s.26C, varied: SI 2013/2148 Sch.1
s.26D, added: 2013 c.24 s.60
s.26D, varied: SI 2013/2148 Sch.1
s.26E, added: 2013 c.24 s.60
s.26E, varied: SI 2013/2148 Sch.1
s.26F, added: 2013 c.24 s.60
s.26F, varied: SI 2013/2148 Sch.1
s.26G, added: 2013 c.24 s.60
s.26G, varied: SI 2013/2148 Sch.1
s.26H, added: 2013 c.24 s.61
s.26H, varied: SI 2013/2148 Sch.1
s.26I, added: 2013 c.24 s.61
s.26I, varied: SI 2013/2148 Sch.1
s.26J, added: 2013 c.24 s.61
s.26J, varied: SI 2013/2148 Sch.1
s.26K, added: 2013 c.24 s.61
s.26K, varied: SI 2013/2148 Sch.1
s.27, varied: SI 2013/2148 Sch.1
s.28, varied: SI 2013/2148 Sch.1
s.28A, added: 2013 c.24 s.60
s.28A, varied: SI 2013/2148 Sch.1
s.29, varied: SI 2013/2148 Sch.1
s.32, amended: 2013 c.24 Sch.17 para.10
s.32, varied: SI 2013/2148 Sch.1
s.32A, varied: SI 2013/2148 Sch.1
s.33, varied: SI 2013/2148 Sch.1
s.34, varied: SI 2013/2148 Sch.1
s.35, varied: SI 2013/2148 Sch.1
s.36, varied: SI 2013/2148 Sch.1
s.37, varied: SI 2013/2148 Sch.1
s.39, varied: SI 2013/2148 Sch.1
s.40, varied: SI 2013/2148 Sch.1
s.41, varied: SI 2013/2148 Sch.1
s.42, varied: SI 2013/2148 Sch.1
s.43, varied: SI 2013/2148 Sch.1
s.44, varied: SI 2013/2148 Sch.1
s.44A, varied: SI 2013/2148 Sch.1
s.45, varied: SI 2013/2148 Sch.1
s.46, varied: SI 2013/2148 Sch.1
s.51, varied: SI 2013/2148 Sch.1
s.52, varied: SI 2013/2148 Sch.1
s.60, varied: SI 2013/2148 Sch.1
s.61, varied: SI 2013/2148 Sch.1
s.62, amended: 2013 c.24 Sch.17 para.11
s.64, varied: SI 2013/2148 Sch.1
s.65, varied: SI 2013/2148 Sch.1
s.66, see *East Northamptonshire DC v Secretary of State for Communities and Local Government* [2013] EWHC 473 (Admin), [2013] 2 P. & C.R. 5 (QBD (Admin)), Lang, J.
s.66, varied: SI 2013/2148 Sch.1
s.67, varied: SI 2013/2148 Sch.1
s.69, applied: SI 2013/2727 Art.2
s.73, varied: SI 2013/2148 Sch.1
s.74, see *R. v Rance (Piers)* [2012] EWCA Crim 2023, [2013] 1 Cr. App. R. (S.) 123 (CA (Crim Div)), Moses, L.J.
s.74, amended: 2013 c.24 Sch.17 para.12
s.74, applied: SI 2013/2148 Art.5
s.75, amended: 2013 c.24 Sch.17 para.13
s.75, varied: SI 2013/2148 Sch.1
s.82, amended: 2013 c.24 Sch.17 para.14
s.82, varied: SI 2013/2148 Sch.1
s.82A, amended: 2013 c.24 Sch.17 para.15
s.86, varied: SI 2013/2148 Sch.1
s.87, varied: SI 2013/2148 Sch.1
s.88, amended: 2013 c.24 Sch.17 para.16
s.88, varied: SI 2013/2148 Sch.1
s.90, varied: SI 2013/2148 Sch.1
s.91, amended: SI 2013/755 Sch.2 para.205
s.92, amended: 2013 c.24 Sch.17 para.17
s.92, referred to: SI 2013/2148 Art.3
s.92, enabling: SI 2013/2148
s.93, amended: 2013 c.24 Sch.17 para.18
s.93, enabling: SI 2013/1239
Sch.1 para.1, varied: SI 2013/2148 Sch.1

Sch.1 para.2, varied: SI 2013/2148 Sch.1
Sch.1 para.3, varied: SI 2013/2148 Sch.1
Sch.2 para.1, varied: SI 2013/2148 Sch.1
Sch.2 para.2, varied: SI 2013/2148 Sch.1
Sch.2 para.3, varied: SI 2013/2148 Sch.1
Sch.2 para.4, varied: SI 2013/2148 Sch.1
Sch.2A para.1, added: 2013 c.24 Sch.16
Sch.2A para.1, varied: SI 2013/2148 Sch.1
Sch.2A para.2, added: 2013 c.24 Sch.16
Sch.2A para.2, varied: SI 2013/2148 Sch.1
Sch.2A para.3, added: 2013 c.24 Sch.16
Sch.2A para.3, varied: SI 2013/2148 Sch.1
Sch.2A para.4, added: 2013 c.24 Sch.16
Sch.2A para.4, varied: SI 2013/2148 Sch.1
Sch.3 para.1, amended: 2013 c.24 Sch.17 para.19
Sch.3 para.1, varied: SI 2013/2148 Sch.1
Sch.3 para.2, amended: 2013 c.24 Sch.17 para.19
Sch.3 para.2, varied: SI 2013/2148 Sch.1
Sch.3 para.3, amended: 2013 c.24 Sch.17 para.19
Sch.3 para.3, varied: SI 2013/2148 Sch.1
Sch.3 para.4, varied: SI 2013/2148 Sch.1
Sch.3 para.5, varied: SI 2013/2148 Sch.1
Sch.3 para.6, varied: SI 2013/2148 Sch.1
Sch.3 para.6A, varied: SI 2013/2148 Sch.1
Sch.3 para.7, varied: SI 2013/2148 Sch.1
Sch.3 para.8, varied: SI 2013/2148 Sch.1

10. Planning (Hazardous Substances) Act 1990

s.39, amended: SI 2013/755 Sch.2 para.206

16. Food Safety Act 1990

applied: SI 2013/479, SI 2013/2493 Reg.2, SI 2013/2750, SI 2013/2775, SI 2013/2996 Reg.2, SI 2013/3235, SSI 2013/217 Reg.8
s.3, varied: SI 2013/1768 Sch.1 para.1, SI 2013/2139 Sch.1 para.1, SI 2013/2196 Reg.8, SI 2013/2210 Reg.19, SI 2013/2493 Reg.8, SI 2013/2591 Reg.19, SI 2013/2750 Sch.14, SI 2013/2775 Sch.14, SSI 2013/217 Reg.8, SSI 2013/256 Reg.7, SSI 2013/266 Reg.17, SSI 2013/305 Sch.14
s.6, enabling: SI 2013/1768, SI 2013/2139, SI 2013/2750, SI 2013/2775, SI 2013/3235, SSI 2013/256, SSI 2013/266, SSI 2013/305
s.9, amended: SI 2013/2996 Reg.36, SI 2013/3049 Reg.5, SSI 2013/336 Reg.4
s.9, applied: SI 2013/2196 Reg.8, SI 2013/2210 Reg.18, SI 2013/2591 Reg.18, SI 2013/2996 Reg.25, Reg.29, SSI 2013/266 Reg.16
s.9, varied: SI 2013/2196 Reg.8, SI 2013/2493 Reg.8, SSI 2013/217 Reg.8
s.10, applied: SI 2013/2750 Reg.22, SI 2013/2775 Reg.22
s.10, varied: SI 2013/1768 Reg.7, SI 2013/2139 Reg.5, SI 2013/2591 Reg.7, SI 2013/2750 Reg.17, SI 2013/2775 Reg.17
s.16, enabling: SI 2013/466, SI 2013/545, SI 2013/804, SI 2013/1768, SI 2013/2139, SI 2013/2196, SI 2013/2210, SI 2013/2493, SI 2013/2591, SI 2013/2750, SI 2013/2775, SI 2013/2854, SI 2013/3235, SI 2013/3243, SSI 2013/83, SSI 2013/217, SSI 2013/256, SSI 2013/266, SSI 2013/305
s.17, enabling: SI 2013/466, SI 2013/545, SI 2013/804, SI 2013/1768, SI 2013/2139, SI 2013/2196, SI 2013/2210, SI 2013/2493, SI 2013/2591, SI 2013/2750, SI 2013/2775, SI 2013/3235, SI 2013/3243, SSI 2013/83, SSI 2013/217, SSI 2013/256, SSI 2013/266, SSI 2013/305
s.20, varied: SI 2013/1768 Sch.1 para.1, SI 2013/2139 Sch.1 para.1, SI 2013/2196 Reg.8, SI 2013/2210 Reg.19, SI 2013/2493 Reg.8, SI 2013/2591 Reg.19, SI 2013/2750 Sch.14, SI 2013/2775 Sch.14, SSI 2013/217 Reg.8, SSI 2013/256 Reg.7, SSI 2013/266 Reg.17, SSI 2013/305 Sch.14
s.21, varied: SI 2013/1768 Sch.1 para.1, SI 2013/2139 Sch.1 para.1, SI 2013/2196 Reg.8, SI 2013/2210 Reg.19, SI 2013/2493 Reg.8, SI 2013/2591 Reg.19, SI 2013/2750 Sch.14, SI 2013/2775 Sch.14, SSI 2013/217 Reg.8, SSI 2013/256 Reg.7, SSI 2013/266 Reg.17, SSI 2013/305 Sch.14
s.26, enabling: SI 2013/466, SI 2013/545, SI 2013/804, SI 2013/1768, SI 2013/2139, SI 2013/2196, SI 2013/2210, SI 2013/2493, SI 2013/2591, SI 2013/2750, SI 2013/2775, SI 2013/2854, SI 2013/3235, SSI 2013/83, SSI 2013/217, SSI 2013/256, SSI 2013/266, SSI 2013/305
s.27, enabling: SI 2013/264, SI 2013/479, SI 2013/3049, SSI 2013/84
s.29, applied: SI 2013/264 Reg.7, Reg.9, Reg.10, SI 2013/479 Reg.7, Reg.9, Reg.10, SI 2013/2996 Reg.15, SSI 2013/84 Reg.7, Reg.9, Reg.10
s.29, varied: SI 2013/1768 Sch.1 para.1, SI 2013/2139 Sch.1 para.1, SSI 2013/256 Reg.7
s.30, applied: SI 2013/264 Reg.10, SI 2013/479 Reg.10, SSI 2013/84 Reg.10
s.30, varied: SI 2013/1768 Sch.1 para.1, SI 2013/2139 Sch.1 para.1, SI 2013/2196 Reg.8, SI 2013/2210 Reg.19, SI 2013/2493 Reg.8, SI 2013/2591 Reg.19, SI 2013/2750 Sch.14, SI 2013/2775 Sch.14, SSI 2013/217 Reg.8, SSI 2013/256 Reg.7, SSI 2013/266 Reg.17, SSI 2013/305 Sch.14
s.30, enabling: SI 2013/264, SI 2013/479, SI 2013/3049, SSI 2013/84

s.31, enabling: SI 2013/264, SI 2013/479, SI 2013/3049, SSI 2013/84
s.32, see *R. (on the application of Dulai) v Chelmsford Magistrates' Court* [2012] EWHC 1055 (Admin), [2013] 1 W.L.R. 220 (DC), Stanley Burnton, L.J.
s.32, amended: SI 2013/1768 Sch.1 para.2
s.32, applied: SSI 2013/256 Reg.7
s.32, varied: SI 2013/2139 Sch.1 para.2
s.33, applied: SSI 2013/217 Reg.8
s.33, varied: SI 2013/1768 Sch.1 para.1, SI 2013/2139 Sch.1 para.1, SI 2013/2196 Reg.8, SI 2013/2210 Reg.19, SI 2013/2493 Reg.8, SI 2013/2591 Reg.19, SI 2013/2750 Sch.14, SI 2013/2775 Sch.14, SSI 2013/217 Reg.8, SSI 2013/256 Reg.7, SSI 2013/266 Reg.17, SSI 2013/305 Sch.14
s.34, applied: SI 2013/2210 Reg.19, SI 2013/2591 Reg.19, SSI 2013/256 Reg.7, SSI 2013/266 Reg.17
s.35, applied: SI 2013/2210 Reg.19, SI 2013/2591 Reg.19, SSI 2013/256 Reg.7, SSI 2013/266 Reg.17
s.35, varied: SI 2013/1768 Sch.1 para.1, SI 2013/2139 Sch.1 para.1, SI 2013/2196 Reg.8, SI 2013/2210 Reg.19, SI 2013/2493 Reg.8, SI 2013/2591 Reg.19, SI 2013/2750 Sch.14, SI 2013/2775 Sch.14, SSI 2013/217 Reg.8, SSI 2013/256 Reg.7, SSI 2013/266 Reg.17, SSI 2013/305 Sch.14
s.36, varied: SI 2013/1768 Sch.1 para.1, SI 2013/2139 Sch.1 para.1, SI 2013/2196 Reg.8, SI 2013/2210 Reg.19, SI 2013/2493 Reg.8, SI 2013/2591 Reg.19, SI 2013/2750 Sch.14, SI 2013/2775 Sch.14, SSI 2013/217 Reg.8, SSI 2013/256 Reg.7, SSI 2013/266 Reg.17, SSI 2013/305 Sch.14
s.36A, varied: SI 2013/2196 Reg.8, SI 2013/2210 Reg.19, SI 2013/2493 Reg.8, SI 2013/2591 Reg.19, SI 2013/2750 Sch.14, SI 2013/2775 Sch.14, SSI 2013/217 Reg.8, SSI 2013/256 Reg.7, SSI 2013/266 Reg.17, SSI 2013/305 Sch.14
s.37, varied: SI 2013/1768 Reg.8, SI 2013/2139 Reg.6, SI 2013/2591 Reg.8, SI 2013/2750 Reg.18, SI 2013/2775 Reg.18
s.39, varied: SI 2013/1768 Reg.9, SI 2013/2139 Reg.7, SI 2013/2750 Reg.18, SI 2013/2775 Reg.18
s.44, varied: SI 2013/1768 Sch.1 para.1, SI 2013/2139 Sch.1 para.1, SI 2013/2196 Reg.8, SI 2013/2210 Reg.19, SI 2013/2493 Reg.8, SI 2013/2591 Reg.19, SI 2013/2750 Sch.14, SI 2013/2775 Sch.14, SSI 2013/217 Reg.8, SSI 2013/256 Reg.7, SSI 2013/266 Reg.17, SSI 2013/305 Sch.14
s.48, applied: SI 2013/466, SI 2013/479, SI 2013/545, SI 2013/1768, SI 2013/2139, SI 2013/2196, SI 2013/2210, SI 2013/2493, SI 2013/2591, SI 2013/2750, SI 2013/2775, SI 2013/2854, SI 2013/3235, SI 2013/3243, SSI 2013/83, SSI 2013/84, SSI 2013/217, SSI 2013/256, SSI 2013/266, SSI 2013/305
s.48, enabling: SI 2013/264, SI 2013/466, SI 2013/479, SI 2013/545, SI 2013/804, SI 2013/1768, SI 2013/2139, SI 2013/2196, SI 2013/2210, SI 2013/2493, SI 2013/2591, SI 2013/2750, SI 2013/2775, SI 2013/3235, SI 2013/3243, SSI 2013/83, SSI 2013/84, SSI 2013/217, SSI 2013/256, SSI 2013/266, SSI 2013/305
s.48A, applied: SI 2013/264
s.49, enabling: SI 2013/264, SI 2013/479, SSI 2013/84
Sch.1 para.7, enabling: SI 2013/804

23. Access to Health Records Act 1990
applied: SI 2013/160 Sch.1 para.5
s.8, amended: 2013 c.22 Sch.9 para.52

29. Finance Act 1990
Sch.18 para.4, repealed: SI 2013/463 Art.2

35. Enterprise and New Towns (Scotland) Act 1990
s.2, applied: SI 2013/376 Reg.66, SI 2013/379 Reg.27, Reg.39, SI 2013/3029 Sch.1 para.3, Sch.2 para.5, Sch.6 para.5, Sch.7 para.8, Sch.7 para.10, Sch.9 para.18, Sch.10 para.39, SI 2013/3035 Sch.1
s.2, referred to: SI 2013/3029 Sch.9 para.18, SI 2013/3035 Sch.1
s.25, applied: 2013 asp 4 Sch.3
s.26, applied: 2013 asp 4 Sch.3

40. Law Reform (Miscellaneous Provisions) (Scotland) Act 1990
s.7, applied: SI 2013/349 Reg.105, Sch.7 para.29
s.26, amended: 2013 c.24 Sch.6 para.46
s.31, amended: 2013 c.24 Sch.6 para.47
s.40, amended: 2013 c.24 Sch.6 para.48
s.41, amended: 2013 c.24 Sch.6 para.49
s.41A, amended: 2013 c.24 Sch.6 para.50
s.44, amended: 2013 c.24 Sch.6 para.51

41. Courts and Legal Services Act 1990
s.1, amended: 2013 c.22 Sch.9 para.32, Sch.10 para.76
s.1, repealed (in part): 2013 c.22 Sch.9 para.32
s.9, repealed: 2013 c.22 Sch.10 para.76
s.10, repealed: 2013 c.22 Sch.10 para.76
s.11, amended: 2013 c.22 Sch.9 para.33, Sch.10 para.76
s.15, amended: 2013 c.22 Sch.9 para.34
s.58, see *Germany v Flatman* [2013] EWCA Civ 278, [2013] 1 W.L.R. 2676 (CA (Civ Div)), Mummery, L.J.
s.58, applied: 2013 c.22 s.40, SI 2013/689 Art.2, Art.3, Art.4, Art.5

s.58, enabling: SI 2013/689
s.58A, see *Walker v Burton* [2013] EWHC 811 (Ch), [2013] 3 Costs L.R. 469 (Ch D), Judge David Cooke
s.58A, applied: SI 2013/689
s.58AA, applied: SI 2013/262, SI 2013/609, SI 2013/609 Reg.3, Reg.5, Reg.8
s.58AA, enabling: SI 2013/609
s.58C, enabling: SI 2013/92, SI 2013/739
s.71, amended: 2013 c.22 Sch.9 para.35
s.71, applied: 2013 c.18 s.9, SI 2013/2537 Sch.1
s.74, repealed (in part): 2013 c.22 Sch.9 para.141, Sch.11 para.210
s.105, amended: SI 2013/1881 Sch.1 para.2
s.107, amended: SI 2013/1881 Sch.1 para.2
s.119, amended: SI 2013/1881 Sch.1 para.2
s.120, applied: SI 2013/609, SI 2013/689
s.120, enabling: SI 2013/609, SI 2013/689
Sch.10 para.40, repealed: SI 2013/686 Sch.1 para.4
Sch.11, amended: 2013 c.22 Sch.14 para.13
Sch.16 Part I para.23, repealed: 2013 c.22 Sch.11 para.210
Sch.18 para.49, amended: 2013 c.22 Sch.9 para.141

42. Broadcasting Act 1990

applied: 2013 c.22 Sch.15 para.3, SI 2013/243 Art.5
Part I, applied: 2013 asp 14 Sch.4 para.11
Part III, applied: 2013 asp 14 Sch.4 para.11
s.86, varied: SI 2013/243 Sch.1 para.2
s.104, varied: SI 2013/243 Sch.1 para.3
s.104B, varied: SI 2013/243 Sch.1 para.4
s.105, varied: SI 2013/243 Sch.1 para.5
s.106, varied: SI 2013/243 Sch.1 para.6
s.106ZA, varied: SI 2013/243 Sch.1 para.7
s.126, varied: SI 2013/243 Sch.1 para.8
s.180, repealed: 2013 c.24 Sch.21 para.2
s.202, amended: SI 2013/2217 Reg.3
Sch.2 Part II para.1, varied: SI 2013/243 Art.6, Sch.1 para.9
Sch.2 Part II para.2, varied: SI 2013/243 Art.6
Sch.2 Part II para.3, varied: SI 2013/243 Art.6, Sch.1 para.9
Sch.2 Part II para.4, varied: SI 2013/243 Art.6, Sch.1 para.9
Sch.2 Part II para.5, varied: SI 2013/243 Art.6
Sch.2 Part II para.5A, varied: SI 2013/243 Art.6
Sch.2 Part II para.6, varied: SI 2013/243 Art.6
Sch.18 Part II para.1, repealed: 2013 c.24 Sch.21 para.2
Sch.18 Part II para.2, repealed: 2013 c.24 Sch.21 para.2
Sch.18 Part II para.3, repealed: 2013 c.24 Sch.21 para.2
Sch.18 Part II para.4, repealed: 2013 c.24 Sch.21 para.2
Sch.18 Part II para.5, repealed: 2013 c.24 Sch.21 para.2
Sch.18 Part II para.6, repealed: 2013 c.24 Sch.21 para.2
Sch.18 Part II para.7, repealed: 2013 c.24 Sch.21 para.2
Sch.20 para.29, repealed (in part): 2013 c.22 Sch.10 para.99

43. Environmental Protection Act 1990

Part IIA, applied: SI 2013/648 Sch.2 para.3
Part VII, applied: SI 2013/755 Sch.7 para.3
s.30, amended: SI 2013/755 Sch.2 para.208
s.33, see *Mountpace Ltd v Haringey LBC* [2012] EWHC 698 (Admin), [2013] P.T.S.R. 664 (DC), Stanley Burnton, L.J.; see *R. (on the application of Thames Water Utilities Ltd) v Bromley Magistrates' Court* [2013] EWHC 472 (Admin), [2013] 1 W.L.R. 3641 (QBD (Admin)), Gross, L.J.
s.33, applied: SI 2013/2258 Sch.1 Part 1
s.33A, amended: SI 2013/755 Sch.2 para.209, SSI 2013/315 Art.3
s.33A, enabling: SSI 2013/315
s.33B, amended: 2013 c.22 Sch.16 para.9, SI 2013/755 Sch.2 para.210
s.33C, amended: SI 2013/755 Sch.2 para.211
s.34, see *Mountpace Ltd v Haringey LBC* [2012] EWHC 698 (Admin), [2013] P.T.S.R. 664 (DC), Stanley Burnton, L.J.; see *R. (on the application of Thames Water Utilities Ltd) v Bromley Magistrates' Court* [2013] EWHC 472 (Admin), [2013] 1 W.L.R. 3641 (QBD (Admin)), Gross, L.J.
s.34, applied: SI 2013/2258 Sch.1 Part 1
s.34A, amended: SI 2013/755 Sch.2 para.212
s.34B, amended: SI 2013/755 Sch.2 para.213
s.34B, applied: SI 2013/2258 Sch.1 Part 1
s.36, amended: SI 2013/755 Sch.2 para.214
s.73A, amended: SI 2013/755 Sch.2 para.215
s.78A, amended: SI 2013/755 Sch.2 para.216
s.78L, amended: SI 2013/755 Sch.2 para.217
s.78P, amended: 2013 c.22 Sch.9 para.52
s.78U, amended: SI 2013/755 Sch.2 para.218
s.79, applied: SI 2013/198 Art.15, SI 2013/586 Art.9, SI 2013/648 Art.12, SI 2013/675 Art.38, SI 2013/680 Art.9, SI 2013/1752 Art.6, SI 2013/1873 Art.8, SI 2013/1933 Art.40, SI 2013/1967 Art.31, SI 2013/2587 Art.46, SI 2013/2808 Art.33, SI 2013/2809 Art.30, SI 2013/3200 Art.15, SI 2013/3244 Art.63
s.82, applied: SI 2013/198 Art.15, SI 2013/586 Art.9, SI 2013/648 Art.12, SI 2013/675 Art.38, SI 2013/680 Art.9, SI 2013/689 Art.2, SI 2013/1752 Art.6, SI 2013/1873 Art.8, SI 2013/1933 Art.40, SI

2013/1967 Art.31, SI 2013/2587 Art.46, SI 2013/2808 Art.33, SI 2013/2809 Art.30, SI 2013/3200 Art.15, SI 2013/3244 Art.63
s.88, amended: SSI 2013/315 Art.3
s.88, enabling: SSI 2013/315
s.106, applied: SI 2013/648 Sch.2 para.4
s.128, repealed: SI 2013/755 Art.8
s.129, repealed: SI 2013/755 Art.8
s.130, repealed: SI 2013/755 Art.8
s.131, repealed: SI 2013/755 Art.8
s.132, repealed: SI 2013/755 Art.8
s.133, repealed: SI 2013/755 Art.8
s.134, applied: SI 2013/755 Sch.7 para.5
s.134, repealed: SI 2013/755 Art.8
s.140, applied: SSI 2013/349
s.140, enabling: SSI 2013/349
s.153, amended: SSI 2013/74 Art.2
s.153, repealed (in part): SSI 2013/74 Art.2
s.153, enabling: SSI 2013/74
Sch.6 para.1, repealed: SI 2013/755 Art.8
Sch.6 para.2, repealed: SI 2013/755 Art.8
Sch.6 para.3, repealed: SI 2013/755 Art.8
Sch.6 para.4, repealed: SI 2013/755 Art.8
Sch.6 para.5, repealed: SI 2013/755 Art.8
Sch.6 para.6, repealed: SI 2013/755 Art.8
Sch.6 para.7, repealed: SI 2013/755 Art.8
Sch.6 para.8, repealed: SI 2013/755 Art.8
Sch.6 para.9, repealed: SI 2013/755 Art.8
Sch.6 para.10, repealed: SI 2013/755 Art.8
Sch.6 para.11, repealed: SI 2013/755 Art.8
Sch.6 para.12, repealed: SI 2013/755 Art.8
Sch.6 para.13, repealed: SI 2013/755 Art.8
Sch.6 para.14, repealed: SI 2013/755 Art.8
Sch.6 para.15, repealed: SI 2013/755 Art.8
Sch.6 para.16, repealed: SI 2013/755 Art.8
Sch.6 para.17, repealed: SI 2013/755 Art.8
Sch.6 para.18, repealed: SI 2013/755 Art.8
Sch.6 para.19, repealed: SI 2013/755 Art.8
Sch.6 para.20, repealed: SI 2013/755 Art.8
Sch.6 para.21, repealed: SI 2013/755 Art.8
Sch.6 para.22, repealed: SI 2013/755 Art.8
Sch.6 para.23, repealed: SI 2013/755 Art.8
Sch.6 para.24, repealed: SI 2013/755 Art.8
Sch.6 para.25, repealed: SI 2013/755 Art.8
Sch.8, referred to: SI 2013/755 Sch.7 para.8
Sch.8 para.1, repealed: SI 2013/755 Art.8
Sch.8 para.2, repealed: SI 2013/755 Art.8
Sch.8 para.3, repealed: SI 2013/755 Art.8
Sch.8 para.4, repealed: SI 2013/755 Art.8
Sch.8 para.5, repealed: SI 2013/755 Art.8
Sch.8 para.6, repealed: SI 2013/755 Art.8
Sch.8 para.7, repealed: SI 2013/755 Art.8
Sch.8 para.8, repealed: SI 2013/755 Art.8
Sch.8 para.11, repealed: SI 2013/755 Art.8
Sch.9, referred to: SI 2013/755 Sch.7 para.8
Sch.9 para.1, repealed: SI 2013/755 Art.8
Sch.9 para.2, repealed: SI 2013/755 Art.8
Sch.9 para.3, repealed: SI 2013/755 Art.8
Sch.9 para.4, repealed: SI 2013/755 Art.8
Sch.9 para.5, repealed: SI 2013/755 Art.8
Sch.9 para.6, repealed: SI 2013/755 Art.8
Sch.9 para.7, repealed: SI 2013/755 Art.8
Sch.9 para.8, repealed: SI 2013/755 Art.8
Sch.9 para.9, repealed: SI 2013/755 Art.8
Sch.9 para.10, repealed: SI 2013/755 Art.8
Sch.9 para.11, repealed: SI 2013/755 Art.8
Sch.9 para.12, repealed: SI 2013/755 Art.8
Sch.9 para.13, repealed: SI 2013/755 Art.8
Sch.9 para.14, repealed: SI 2013/755 Art.8
Sch.9 para.15, repealed: SI 2013/755 Art.8
Sch.9 para.16, repealed: SI 2013/755 Art.8
Sch.9 para.17, repealed: SI 2013/755 Art.8

1991

5. Ministerial and other Pensions and Salaries Act 1991

s.1, repealed: 2013 c.25 Sch.11 para.7
s.3, repealed (in part): 2013 c.25 Sch.11 para.7
s.4, amended: 2013 c.25 Sch.11 para.2

17. Maintenance Enforcement Act 1991

s.1, amended: 2013 c.22 Sch.10 para.77
s.7, repealed: 2013 c.22 Sch.10 para.99
s.8, repealed: 2013 c.22 Sch.10 para.99
Sch.1 para.3, repealed: 2013 c.22 Sch.11 para.210
Sch.1 para.8, repealed: 2013 c.22 Sch.10 para.99
Sch.1 para.9, repealed: 2013 c.22 Sch.10 para.99
Sch.1 para.13, repealed: 2013 c.22 Sch.11 para.210
Sch.1 para.14, repealed: 2013 c.22 Sch.11 para.210
Sch.1 para.18, repealed: 2013 c.22 Sch.11 para.210
Sch.1 para.21, repealed: 2013 c.22 Sch.11 para.210
Sch.2 para.3, repealed: 2013 c.22 Sch.11 para.210
Sch.2 para.6, repealed: 2013 c.22 Sch.10 para.99
Sch.2 para.7, repealed: 2013 c.22 Sch.10 para.99
Sch.2 para.8, repealed: 2013 c.22 Sch.10 para.99
Sch.2 para.10, repealed: 2013 c.22 Sch.11 para.210
Sch.2 para.11, repealed (in part): 2013 c.22 Sch.10 para.99

22. New Roads and Street Works Act 1991

see *Thames Water Utilities Ltd v Transport for London* [2013] EWHC 187 (Admin), [2013] P.T.S.R. 627 (DC), Laws, L.J.
applied: SI 2013/805 Sch.1, SI 2013/806 Sch.1, SI 2013/807 Sch.1, SI 2013/808 Sch.1, SI 2013/809 Sch.1, SI 2013/810 Sch.1, SI 2013/811 Sch.1, SI 2013/812 Sch.1, SI 2013/813 Sch.1, SI 2013/814 Sch.1, SI 2013/1781 Sch.1, SI 2013/1933 Art.3, SI

2013/2389 Sch.1, SI 2013/2398 Sch.1, SI 2013/2399 Sch.1, SI 2013/2587 Art.4, SI 2013/2808 Art.8, SI 2013/2809 Art.10
referred to: SI 2013/805 Sch.1, SI 2013/806 Sch.1, SI 2013/807 Sch.1, SI 2013/808 Sch.1, SI 2013/809 Sch.1, SI 2013/810 Sch.1, SI 2013/811 Sch.1, SI 2013/812 Sch.1, SI 2013/813 Sch.1, SI 2013/814 Sch.1, SI 2013/1781 Sch.1, SI 2013/1933 Art.3, SI 2013/2399 Sch.1
Part I, applied: SI 2013/1203 Art.19
Part III, applied: SI 2013/198 Sch.3 para.2, Sch.3 para.7, SI 2013/533 Sch.1 para.1, Sch.1 para.2, SI 2013/648 Art.9, Art.36, Art.37, SI 2013/675 Art.32, Art.33, SI 2013/680 Art.28, SI 2013/767 Sch.4 para.5, SI 2013/805 Sch.1, SI 2013/806 Sch.1, SI 2013/807 Sch.1, SI 2013/808 Sch.1, SI 2013/809 Sch.1, SI 2013/810 Sch.1, SI 2013/811 Sch.1, SI 2013/812 Sch.1, SI 2013/813 Sch.1, SI 2013/814 Sch.1, SI 2013/1873 Art.23, Art.24, SI 2013/1933 Art.3, Sch.12 para.1, Sch.12 para.2, Sch.12 para.3, SI 2013/1967 Art.4, Sch.8 para.1, Sch.8 para.2, Sch.9 para.3, Sch.9 para.13, SI 2013/2587 Art.4, Art.44, SI 2013/2808 Art.8, Art.27, Art.28, Art.29, Sch.12 para.10, Sch.12 para.22, SI 2013/2809 Art.10, Sch.10 para.3, Sch.10 para.14, SI 2013/3200 Art.9, Sch.8 para.2, Sch.8 para.5, SI 2013/3244 Art.4, Sch.9 para.2, Sch.9 para.3, Sch.10 para.5
Part III, disapplied: SI 2013/1933 Sch.13 para.3
Part III, referred to: SI 2013/805 Sch.1, SI 2013/807 Sch.1, SI 2013/808 Sch.1, SI 2013/809 Sch.1, SI 2013/810 Sch.1, SI 2013/811 Sch.1, SI 2013/812 Sch.1, SI 2013/813 Sch.1, SI 2013/814 Sch.1, SI 2013/1781 Sch.1, SI 2013/2587 Art.4, SI 2013/2808 Art.8
s.3, applied: SI 2013/1933 Art.3
s.6, referred to: SI 2013/1781 Sch.1
s.48, applied: SI 2013/680 Art.10, SI 2013/1203 Art.13, SI 2013/1873 Art.9, SI 2013/3200 Art.10
s.48, referred to: SI 2013/2389 Sch.1, SI 2013/2399 Sch.1
s.48, varied: SI 2013/3244 Art.4
s.49, varied: SI 2013/3244 Art.4
s.50, applied: SI 2013/805 Sch.1, SI 2013/806 Sch.1, SI 2013/807 Sch.1, SI 2013/808 Sch.1, SI 2013/809 Sch.1, SI 2013/810 Sch.1, SI 2013/811 Sch.1, SI 2013/812 Sch.1, SI 2013/813 Sch.1, SI 2013/814 Sch.1, SI 2013/1781 Sch.1, SI 2013/2389 Sch.1, SI 2013/2398 Sch.1, SI 2013/2399 Sch.1
s.50, varied: SI 2013/3244 Art.4
s.51, applied: SI 2013/680 Art.10, SI 2013/1203 Art.13, SI 2013/1873 Art.9, SI 2013/3200 Art.10
s.51, varied: SI 2013/3244 Art.4
s.52, referred to: SI 2013/805 Sch.1, SI 2013/806 Sch.1, SI 2013/807 Sch.1, SI 2013/808 Sch.1, SI 2013/809 Sch.1, SI 2013/810 Sch.1, SI 2013/811 Sch.1, SI 2013/812 Sch.1, SI 2013/813 Sch.1, SI 2013/814 Sch.1, SI 2013/1781 Sch.1, SI 2013/2389 Sch.1, SI 2013/2398 Sch.1, SI 2013/2399 Sch.1
s.52, varied: SI 2013/3244 Art.4
s.53, applied: SI 2013/2389 Sch.1, SI 2013/2398 Sch.1
s.53, disapplied: SI 2013/805 Sch.1, SI 2013/806 Sch.1, SI 2013/807 Sch.1, SI 2013/808 Sch.1, SI 2013/809 Sch.1, SI 2013/810 Sch.1, SI 2013/811 Sch.1, SI 2013/812 Sch.1, SI 2013/813 Sch.1, SI 2013/814 Sch.1, SI 2013/1781 Sch.1, SI 2013/2389 Sch.1, SI 2013/2398 Sch.1, SI 2013/2399 Sch.1
s.53, repealed: SI 2013/2398 Sch.1
s.53, varied: SI 2013/3244 Art.4
s.53A, disapplied: SI 2013/2389 Sch.1
s.53A, varied: SI 2013/3244 Art.4
s.54, applied: SI 2013/675 Art.9, SI 2013/680 Art.10, SI 2013/805 Sch.1, SI 2013/806 Sch.1, SI 2013/807 Sch.1, SI 2013/808 Sch.1, SI 2013/809 Sch.1, SI 2013/810 Sch.1, SI 2013/811 Sch.1, SI 2013/812 Sch.1, SI 2013/813 Sch.1, SI 2013/814 Sch.1, SI 2013/1203 Art.13, SI 2013/1873 Art.9, SI 2013/1933 Art.3, SI 2013/1967 Art.4, SI 2013/2389 Sch.1, SI 2013/2398 Sch.1, SI 2013/2399 Sch.1, SI 2013/2587 Art.4, SI 2013/2808 Art.8, SI 2013/3200 Art.9, SI 2013/3244 Art.4
s.54, disapplied: SI 2013/805 Sch.1, SI 2013/806 Sch.1, SI 2013/807 Sch.1, SI 2013/808 Sch.1, SI 2013/809 Sch.1, SI 2013/810 Sch.1, SI 2013/811 Sch.1, SI 2013/812 Sch.1, SI 2013/813 Sch.1, SI 2013/814 Sch.1, SI 2013/1781 Sch.1, SI 2013/2389 Sch.1, SI 2013/2398 Sch.1, SI 2013/2399 Sch.1
s.54, referred to: SI 2013/1933 Art.3, SI 2013/2809 Art.10, SI 2013/3200 Art.9
s.54, repealed: SI 2013/2398 Sch.1
s.54, varied: SI 2013/1967 Art.4, SI 2013/2808 Art.8, SI 2013/2809 Art.10, SI 2013/3244 Art.4
s.55, applied: SI 2013/675 Art.9, SI 2013/680 Art.10, SI 2013/805 Sch.1, SI 2013/806 Sch.1, SI 2013/807 Sch.1, SI 2013/808 Sch.1, SI 2013/809 Sch.1, SI 2013/810 Sch.1, SI 2013/811 Sch.1, SI 2013/812 Sch.1, SI 2013/813 Sch.1, SI 2013/814 Sch.1, SI 2013/1203 Art.13, SI 2013/1873 Art.9, SI 2013/1933 Art.3, SI 2013/1967 Art.4, SI 2013/2389 Sch.1, SI 2013/2399 Sch.1, SI 2013/2587 Art.4, SI 2013/2808 Art.8, SI 2013/3200 Art.9, SI 2013/3244 Art.4

s.55, disapplied: SI 2013/805 Sch.1, SI 2013/806 Sch.1, SI 2013/807 Sch.1, SI 2013/808 Sch.1, SI 2013/809 Sch.1, SI 2013/810 Sch.1, SI 2013/811 Sch.1, SI 2013/812 Sch.1, SI 2013/813 Sch.1, SI 2013/814 Sch.1, SI 2013/1781 Sch.1, SI 2013/2389 Sch.1, SI 2013/2398 Sch.1, SI 2013/2399 Sch.1
s.55, referred to: SI 2013/1933 Art.3, SI 2013/2809 Art.10, SI 2013/3200 Art.9
s.55, repealed: SI 2013/2398 Sch.1
s.55, varied: SI 2013/1967 Art.4, SI 2013/2808 Art.8, SI 2013/2809 Art.10, SI 2013/3244 Art.4
s.56, applied: SI 2013/675 Art.9, SI 2013/680 Art.10, SI 2013/1203 Art.13, SI 2013/1873 Art.9
s.56, disapplied: SI 2013/805 Sch.1, SI 2013/806 Sch.1, SI 2013/807 Sch.1, SI 2013/808 Sch.1, SI 2013/809 Sch.1, SI 2013/810 Sch.1, SI 2013/811 Sch.1, SI 2013/812 Sch.1, SI 2013/813 Sch.1, SI 2013/814 Sch.1, SI 2013/1781 Sch.1, SI 2013/1933 Art.3, SI 2013/2389 Sch.1, SI 2013/2398 Sch.1, SI 2013/2399 Sch.1, SI 2013/2587 Art.4, SI 2013/2808 Art.8, SI 2013/3244 Art.4
s.56, referred to: SI 2013/3200 Art.9
s.56, repealed: SI 2013/2398 Sch.1
s.56, varied: SI 2013/3244 Art.4
s.56A, applied: SI 2013/675 Art.9, SI 2013/680 Art.10, SI 2013/805 Sch.1, SI 2013/806 Sch.1, SI 2013/807 Sch.1, SI 2013/808 Sch.1, SI 2013/809 Sch.1, SI 2013/810 Sch.1, SI 2013/811 Sch.1, SI 2013/812 Sch.1, SI 2013/813 Sch.1, SI 2013/814 Sch.1, SI 2013/1203 Art.13, SI 2013/1873 Art.9, SI 2013/2389 Sch.1, SI 2013/2399 Sch.1
s.56A, disapplied: SI 2013/1933 Art.3, SI 2013/2389 Sch.1, SI 2013/2587 Art.4, SI 2013/2808 Art.8, SI 2013/3244 Art.4
s.56A, varied: SI 2013/3244 Art.4
s.57, applied: SI 2013/675 Art.9, SI 2013/680 Art.10, SI 2013/805 Sch.1, SI 2013/806 Sch.1, SI 2013/807 Sch.1, SI 2013/808 Sch.1, SI 2013/809 Sch.1, SI 2013/810 Sch.1, SI 2013/811 Sch.1, SI 2013/812 Sch.1, SI 2013/813 Sch.1, SI 2013/814 Sch.1, SI 2013/1203 Art.13, SI 2013/1873 Art.9, SI 2013/1967 Art.4, SI 2013/2389 Sch.1, SI 2013/2399 Sch.1, SI 2013/2587 Art.4, SI 2013/2808 Art.8, SI 2013/3244 Art.4
s.57, disapplied: SI 2013/805 Sch.1, SI 2013/806 Sch.1, SI 2013/807 Sch.1, SI 2013/808 Sch.1, SI 2013/809 Sch.1, SI 2013/810 Sch.1, SI 2013/811 Sch.1, SI 2013/812 Sch.1, SI 2013/813 Sch.1, SI 2013/814 Sch.1, SI 2013/1781 Sch.1, SI 2013/2389 Sch.1, SI 2013/2398 Sch.1, SI 2013/2399 Sch.1
s.57, referred to: SI 2013/1933 Art.3, SI 2013/2809 Art.10, SI 2013/3200 Art.9
s.57, repealed: SI 2013/2398 Sch.1
s.57, varied: SI 2013/2808 Art.8, SI 2013/3244 Art.4
s.58, applied: SI 2013/675 Art.9, SI 2013/680 Art.10, SI 2013/805 Sch.1, SI 2013/806 Sch.1, SI 2013/807 Sch.1, SI 2013/808 Sch.1, SI 2013/809 Sch.1, SI 2013/810 Sch.1, SI 2013/811 Sch.1, SI 2013/812 Sch.1, SI 2013/813 Sch.1, SI 2013/814 Sch.1, SI 2013/1203 Art.13, SI 2013/1781 Sch.1, SI 2013/1873 Art.9, SI 2013/2389 Sch.1, SI 2013/2398 Sch.1, SI 2013/2399 Sch.1
s.58, disapplied: SI 2013/1933 Art.3, SI 2013/2587 Art.4, SI 2013/2808 Art.8, SI 2013/3244 Art.4
s.58, referred to: SI 2013/805 Sch.1, SI 2013/806 Sch.1, SI 2013/807 Sch.1, SI 2013/808 Sch.1, SI 2013/809 Sch.1, SI 2013/810 Sch.1, SI 2013/811 Sch.1, SI 2013/812 Sch.1, SI 2013/813 Sch.1, SI 2013/814 Sch.1
s.58, varied: SI 2013/675 Art.10, SI 2013/1781 Sch.1, SI 2013/3244 Art.4
s.58A, applied: SI 2013/675 Art.9, SI 2013/680 Art.10, SI 2013/805 Sch.1, SI 2013/806 Sch.1, SI 2013/807 Sch.1, SI 2013/808 Sch.1, SI 2013/809 Sch.1, SI 2013/810 Sch.1, SI 2013/811 Sch.1, SI 2013/812 Sch.1, SI 2013/813 Sch.1, SI 2013/814 Sch.1, SI 2013/1203 Art.13, SI 2013/1781 Sch.1, SI 2013/1873 Art.9, SI 2013/2389 Sch.1, SI 2013/2398 Sch.1, SI 2013/2399 Sch.1
s.58A, disapplied: SI 2013/2587 Art.4, SI 2013/2808 Art.8, SI 2013/3244 Art.4
s.58A, referred to: SI 2013/805 Sch.1, SI 2013/806 Sch.1, SI 2013/807 Sch.1, SI 2013/808 Sch.1, SI 2013/809 Sch.1, SI 2013/810 Sch.1, SI 2013/811 Sch.1, SI 2013/812 Sch.1, SI 2013/813 Sch.1, SI 2013/814 Sch.1
s.58A, varied: SI 2013/2398 Sch.1, SI 2013/3244 Art.4
s.59, applied: SI 2013/675 Art.9, SI 2013/680 Art.10, SI 2013/1203 Art.13, SI 2013/1873 Art.9, SI 2013/1967 Art.4, SI 2013/2587 Art.4, Art.44, SI 2013/2808 Art.8, SI 2013/3244 Art.4
s.59, referred to: SI 2013/1933 Art.3, SI 2013/2809 Art.10, SI 2013/3200 Art.9
s.59, varied: SI 2013/3244 Art.4
s.60, applied: SI 2013/675 Art.9, SI 2013/680 Art.10, SI 2013/1203 Art.13, SI 2013/1873 Art.9, SI 2013/1967 Art.4, SI 2013/2587 Art.4, Art.44, SI 2013/2808 Art.8, SI 2013/3244 Art.4
s.60, referred to: SI 2013/1933 Art.3, SI 2013/2809 Art.10, SI 2013/3200 Art.9
s.60, varied: SI 2013/3244 Art.4

s.61, applied: SI 2013/675 Art.9, SI 2013/680 Art.10, SI 2013/805 Sch.1, SI 2013/806 Sch.1, SI 2013/807 Sch.1, SI 2013/808 Sch.1, SI 2013/809 Sch.1, SI 2013/810 Sch.1, SI 2013/811 Sch.1, SI 2013/812 Sch.1, SI 2013/813 Sch.1, SI 2013/814 Sch.1, SI 2013/1203 Art.13, SI 2013/1781 Sch.1, SI 2013/1873 Art.9
s.61, varied: SI 2013/3244 Art.4
s.62, applied: SI 2013/675 Art.9, SI 2013/680 Art.10, SI 2013/805 Sch.1, SI 2013/806 Sch.1, SI 2013/807 Sch.1, SI 2013/808 Sch.1, SI 2013/809 Sch.1, SI 2013/810 Sch.1, SI 2013/811 Sch.1, SI 2013/812 Sch.1, SI 2013/813 Sch.1, SI 2013/814 Sch.1, SI 2013/1203 Art.13, SI 2013/1873 Art.9
s.62, varied: SI 2013/3244 Art.4
s.63, applied: SI 2013/675 Art.9, SI 2013/680 Art.10, SI 2013/805 Sch.1, SI 2013/806 Sch.1, SI 2013/807 Sch.1, SI 2013/808 Sch.1, SI 2013/809 Sch.1, SI 2013/810 Sch.1, SI 2013/811 Sch.1, SI 2013/812 Sch.1, SI 2013/813 Sch.1, SI 2013/814 Sch.1, SI 2013/1203 Art.13, SI 2013/1873 Art.9
s.63, varied: SI 2013/3244 Art.4
s.64, applied: SI 2013/675 Art.9, SI 2013/680 Art.10, SI 2013/805 Sch.1, SI 2013/806 Sch.1, SI 2013/807 Sch.1, SI 2013/808 Sch.1, SI 2013/809 Sch.1, SI 2013/810 Sch.1, SI 2013/811 Sch.1, SI 2013/812 Sch.1, SI 2013/813 Sch.1, SI 2013/814 Sch.1, SI 2013/1203 Art.13, SI 2013/1873 Art.9, SI 2013/2809 Art.10
s.64, varied: SI 2013/2398 Sch.1, SI 2013/3244 Art.4
s.65, applied: SI 2013/675 Art.9, SI 2013/680 Art.10, SI 2013/805 Sch.1, SI 2013/806 Sch.1, SI 2013/807 Sch.1, SI 2013/808 Sch.1, SI 2013/809 Sch.1, SI 2013/810 Sch.1, SI 2013/811 Sch.1, SI 2013/812 Sch.1, SI 2013/813 Sch.1, SI 2013/814 Sch.1, SI 2013/1203 Art.13, SI 2013/1873 Art.9, SI 2013/2398 Sch.1
s.65, referred to: SI 2013/3200 Art.9
s.65, varied: SI 2013/3244 Art.4
s.66, applied: SI 2013/675 Art.9, SI 2013/680 Art.10, SI 2013/1203 Art.13, SI 2013/1873 Art.9, SI 2013/2398 Sch.1
s.66, disapplied: SI 2013/805 Sch.1, SI 2013/806 Sch.1, SI 2013/807 Sch.1, SI 2013/808 Sch.1, SI 2013/809 Sch.1, SI 2013/810 Sch.1, SI 2013/811 Sch.1, SI 2013/812 Sch.1, SI 2013/813 Sch.1, SI 2013/814 Sch.1, SI 2013/1781 Sch.1, SI 2013/2389 Sch.1, SI 2013/2398 Sch.1, SI 2013/2399 Sch.1
s.66, repealed: SI 2013/2398 Sch.1
s.66, varied: SI 2013/3244 Art.4
s.67, applied: SI 2013/675 Art.9, SI 2013/680 Art.10, SI 2013/1203 Art.13, SI 2013/1873 Art.9
s.67, referred to: SI 2013/3200 Art.9
s.67, varied: SI 2013/3244 Art.4
s.68, applied: SI 2013/675 Art.9, SI 2013/680 Art.10, SI 2013/1203 Art.13, SI 2013/1873 Art.9, SI 2013/1967 Art.4, SI 2013/2587 Art.4, SI 2013/2808 Art.8, SI 2013/3244 Art.4
s.68, referred to: SI 2013/1933 Art.3, SI 2013/2809 Art.10, SI 2013/3200 Art.9
s.68, varied: SI 2013/3244 Art.4
s.69, applied: SI 2013/675 Art.9, SI 2013/680 Art.10, SI 2013/805 Sch.1, SI 2013/806 Sch.1, SI 2013/807 Sch.1, SI 2013/808 Sch.1, SI 2013/809 Sch.1, SI 2013/810 Sch.1, SI 2013/811 Sch.1, SI 2013/812 Sch.1, SI 2013/813 Sch.1, SI 2013/814 Sch.1, SI 2013/1203 Art.13, SI 2013/1873 Art.9, SI 2013/1967 Art.4, SI 2013/2389 Sch.1, SI 2013/2587 Art.4, SI 2013/2808 Art.8, SI 2013/3244 Art.4
s.69, referred to: SI 2013/1933 Art.3, SI 2013/2809 Art.10, SI 2013/3200 Art.9
s.69, varied: SI 2013/2398 Sch.1, SI 2013/3244 Art.4
s.70, applied: SI 2013/675 Art.9, SI 2013/680 Art.10, SI 2013/805 Sch.1, SI 2013/806 Sch.1, SI 2013/807 Sch.1, SI 2013/808 Sch.1, SI 2013/809 Sch.1, SI 2013/810 Sch.1, SI 2013/811 Sch.1, SI 2013/812 Sch.1, SI 2013/813 Sch.1, SI 2013/814 Sch.1, SI 2013/1203 Art.13, SI 2013/1873 Art.9, SI 2013/2389 Sch.1, SI 2013/2398 Sch.1
s.70, referred to: SI 2013/3200 Art.9
s.70, varied: SI 2013/3244 Art.4
s.71, applied: SI 2013/675 Art.9, SI 2013/680 Art.10, SI 2013/1203 Art.13, SI 2013/1873 Art.9
s.71, referred to: SI 2013/3200 Art.9
s.71, varied: SI 2013/3244 Art.4
s.72, applied: SI 2013/675 Art.9, SI 2013/680 Art.10, SI 2013/805 Sch.1, SI 2013/806 Sch.1, SI 2013/807 Sch.1, SI 2013/808 Sch.1, SI 2013/809 Sch.1, SI 2013/810 Sch.1, SI 2013/811 Sch.1, SI 2013/812 Sch.1, SI 2013/813 Sch.1, SI 2013/814 Sch.1, SI 2013/1203 Art.13, SI 2013/1873 Art.9, SI 2013/2587 Art.4, SI 2013/3244 Art.4
s.72, referred to: SI 2013/3200 Art.9
s.72, varied: SI 2013/3244 Art.4
s.73, applied: SI 2013/675 Art.9, SI 2013/680 Art.10, SI 2013/1203 Art.13, SI 2013/1873 Art.9
s.73, referred to: SI 2013/805 Sch.1, SI 2013/806 Sch.1, SI 2013/807 Sch.1, SI 2013/808 Sch.1, SI 2013/809 Sch.1, SI 2013/810 Sch.1, SI 2013/811 Sch.1, SI 2013/812 Sch.1, SI 2013/813 Sch.1, SI 2013/814 Sch.1, SI 2013/3200 Art.9
s.73, varied: SI 2013/3244 Art.4
s.73A, applied: SI 2013/675 Art.9, SI 2013/680 Art.10, SI 2013/1203 Art.13, SI 2013/1873 Art.9

s.73A, disapplied: SI 2013/1933 Art.3, SI 2013/2587 Art.4, SI 2013/2808 Art.8, SI 2013/3244 Art.4
s.73A, varied: SI 2013/1781 Sch.1, SI 2013/3244 Art.4
s.73B, applied: SI 2013/675 Art.9, SI 2013/680 Art.10, SI 2013/1203 Art.13, SI 2013/1873 Art.9
s.73B, disapplied: SI 2013/1933 Art.3, SI 2013/2587 Art.4, SI 2013/2808 Art.8, SI 2013/3244 Art.4
s.73B, varied: SI 2013/3244 Art.4
s.73C, applied: SI 2013/675 Art.9, SI 2013/680 Art.10, SI 2013/1203 Art.13, SI 2013/1873 Art.9
s.73C, disapplied: SI 2013/1933 Art.3, SI 2013/2587 Art.4, SI 2013/2808 Art.8, SI 2013/3244 Art.4
s.73C, varied: SI 2013/3244 Art.4
s.73D, applied: SI 2013/675 Art.9, SI 2013/680 Art.10, SI 2013/1203 Art.13, SI 2013/1873 Art.9
s.73D, varied: SI 2013/3244 Art.4
s.73E, applied: SI 2013/675 Art.9, SI 2013/680 Art.10, SI 2013/1203 Art.13, SI 2013/1873 Art.9
s.73E, varied: SI 2013/3244 Art.4
s.73F, applied: SI 2013/675 Art.9, SI 2013/680 Art.10, SI 2013/1203 Art.13, SI 2013/1873 Art.9
s.73F, varied: SI 2013/3244 Art.4
s.74, applied: SI 2013/675 Art.9, SI 2013/680 Art.10, SI 2013/805 Sch.1, SI 2013/806 Sch.1, SI 2013/807 Sch.1, SI 2013/808 Sch.1, SI 2013/809 Sch.1, SI 2013/810 Sch.1, SI 2013/811 Sch.1, SI 2013/812 Sch.1, SI 2013/813 Sch.1, SI 2013/814 Sch.1, SI 2013/1203 Art.13, SI 2013/1781 Sch.1, SI 2013/1873 Art.9, SI 2013/2389 Sch.1, SI 2013/2398 Sch.1, SI 2013/2399 Sch.1
s.74, referred to: SI 2013/805 Sch.1, SI 2013/806 Sch.1, SI 2013/807 Sch.1, SI 2013/808 Sch.1, SI 2013/809 Sch.1, SI 2013/810 Sch.1, SI 2013/811 Sch.1, SI 2013/812 Sch.1, SI 2013/813 Sch.1, SI 2013/814 Sch.1
s.74, varied: SI 2013/1781 Sch.1, SI 2013/3244 Art.4
s.74A, applied: SI 2013/675 Art.9, SI 2013/680 Art.10, SI 2013/805 Sch.1, SI 2013/806 Sch.1, SI 2013/807 Sch.1, SI 2013/808 Sch.1, SI 2013/809 Sch.1, SI 2013/810 Sch.1, SI 2013/811 Sch.1, SI 2013/812 Sch.1, SI 2013/813 Sch.1, SI 2013/814 Sch.1, SI 2013/1203 Art.13, SI 2013/1873 Art.9
s.74A, varied: SI 2013/3244 Art.4
s.74A, enabling: SI 2013/1147
s.74B, applied: SI 2013/675 Art.9, SI 2013/680 Art.10, SI 2013/1203 Art.13, SI 2013/1873 Art.9
s.74B, varied: SI 2013/3244 Art.4
s.75, applied: SI 2013/675 Art.9, SI 2013/680 Art.10, SI 2013/1203 Art.13, SI 2013/1873 Art.9, SI 2013/2587 Art.4, SI 2013/2808 Art.8, SI 2013/3244 Art.4
s.75, referred to: SI 2013/1933 Art.3, SI 2013/3200 Art.9
s.75, varied: SI 2013/3244 Art.4
s.76, applied: SI 2013/675 Art.9, SI 2013/680 Art.10, SI 2013/805 Sch.1, SI 2013/806 Sch.1, SI 2013/807 Sch.1, SI 2013/808 Sch.1, SI 2013/809 Sch.1, SI 2013/810 Sch.1, SI 2013/811 Sch.1, SI 2013/812 Sch.1, SI 2013/813 Sch.1, SI 2013/814 Sch.1, SI 2013/1203 Art.13, SI 2013/1873 Art.9, SI 2013/1967 Art.4, SI 2013/2587 Art.4, SI 2013/2808 Art.8, SI 2013/3244 Art.4
s.76, referred to: SI 2013/1933 Art.3, SI 2013/2809 Art.10, SI 2013/3200 Art.9
s.76, varied: SI 2013/3244 Art.4
s.77, applied: SI 2013/675 Art.9, SI 2013/680 Art.10, SI 2013/1203 Art.13, SI 2013/1873 Art.9, SI 2013/1967 Art.4, SI 2013/2587 Art.4, SI 2013/2808 Art.8, SI 2013/3244 Art.4
s.77, referred to: SI 2013/1933 Art.3, SI 2013/2809 Art.10, SI 2013/3200 Art.9
s.77, varied: SI 2013/3244 Art.4
s.78, applied: SI 2013/675 Art.9, SI 2013/680 Art.10, SI 2013/1203 Art.13, SI 2013/1873 Art.9
s.78, varied: SI 2013/3244 Art.4
s.78A, applied: SI 2013/675 Art.9, SI 2013/680 Art.10, SI 2013/1203 Art.13, SI 2013/1873 Art.9
s.78A, disapplied: SI 2013/2587 Art.4, SI 2013/2808 Art.8, SI 2013/3244 Art.4
s.78A, varied: SI 2013/3244 Art.4
s.79, applied: SI 2013/675 Art.9, SI 2013/680 Art.10, SI 2013/1203 Art.13, SI 2013/1873 Art.9
s.79, varied: SI 2013/3244 Art.4
s.80, applied: SI 2013/675 Art.9, SI 2013/680 Art.10, SI 2013/805 Sch.1, SI 2013/806 Sch.1, SI 2013/807 Sch.1, SI 2013/808 Sch.1, SI 2013/809 Sch.1, SI 2013/810 Sch.1, SI 2013/811 Sch.1, SI 2013/812 Sch.1, SI 2013/813 Sch.1, SI 2013/814 Sch.1, SI 2013/1203 Art.13, SI 2013/1873 Art.9
s.80, varied: SI 2013/3244 Art.4
s.81, applied: SI 2013/675 Art.9, SI 2013/680 Art.10, SI 2013/805 Sch.1, SI 2013/806 Sch.1, SI 2013/807 Sch.1, SI 2013/808 Sch.1, SI 2013/809 Sch.1, SI 2013/810 Sch.1, SI 2013/811 Sch.1, SI 2013/812 Sch.1, SI 2013/813 Sch.1, SI 2013/814 Sch.1, SI 2013/1203 Art.13, SI 2013/1873 Art.9, SI 2013/2389 Sch.1, SI 2013/2399 Sch.1
s.81, varied: SI 2013/3244 Art.4
s.82, applied: SI 2013/675 Art.9, SI 2013/680 Art.10, SI 2013/1203 Art.13, SI 2013/1873 Art.9
s.82, varied: SI 2013/3244 Art.4
s.83, applied: SI 2013/675 Art.9, SI 2013/680 Art.10, SI 2013/1203 Art.13, SI 2013/1873 Art.9

s.83, varied: SI 2013/3244 Art.4
s.84, applied: SI 2013/675 Art.9, SI 2013/680 Art.10, SI 2013/805 Sch.1, SI 2013/806 Sch.1, SI 2013/807 Sch.1, SI 2013/808 Sch.1, SI 2013/809 Sch.1, SI 2013/810 Sch.1, SI 2013/811 Sch.1, SI 2013/812 Sch.1, SI 2013/813 Sch.1, SI 2013/814 Sch.1, SI 2013/1203 Art.13, SI 2013/1873 Art.9
s.84, varied: SI 2013/3244 Art.4
s.85, applied: SI 2013/533 Sch.1 para.2, SI 2013/648 Art.32, Art.36, SI 2013/675 Art.9, Art.27, Art.32, SI 2013/680 Art.10, Art.24, SI 2013/805 Sch.1, SI 2013/806 Sch.1, SI 2013/807 Sch.1, SI 2013/808 Sch.1, SI 2013/809 Sch.1, SI 2013/810 Sch.1, SI 2013/811 Sch.1, SI 2013/812 Sch.1, SI 2013/813 Sch.1, SI 2013/814 Sch.1, SI 2013/1203 Art.13, Art.22, SI 2013/1873 Art.9, Art.21, SI 2013/1933 Art.26, Sch.12 para.2, SI 2013/1967 Art.22, SI 2013/2389 Sch.1, SI 2013/2399 Sch.1, SI 2013/2587 Art.31, SI 2013/2808 Art.24, Art.28, SI 2013/2809 Art.22, SI 2013/3200 Art.24, SI 2013/3244 Art.27, Sch.9 para.2
s.85, varied: SI 2013/3244 Art.4
s.86, applied: SI 2013/675 Art.9, SI 2013/680 Art.10, SI 2013/805 Sch.1, SI 2013/807 Sch.1, SI 2013/808 Sch.1, SI 2013/809 Sch.1, SI 2013/810 Sch.1, SI 2013/811 Sch.1, SI 2013/812 Sch.1, SI 2013/813 Sch.1, SI 2013/814 Sch.1, SI 2013/1203 Art.13, SI 2013/1781 Sch.1, SI 2013/1873 Art.9, SI 2013/2398 Sch.1
s.86, referred to: SI 2013/648 Art.9, SI 2013/805 Sch.1, SI 2013/806 Sch.1, SI 2013/807 Sch.1, SI 2013/808 Sch.1, SI 2013/809 Sch.1, SI 2013/810 Sch.1, SI 2013/811 Sch.1, SI 2013/812 Sch.1, SI 2013/813 Sch.1, SI 2013/814 Sch.1, SI 2013/1933 Art.3, SI 2013/2389 Sch.1, SI 2013/2399 Sch.1, SI 2013/2587 Art.4, SI 2013/2808 Art.8, SI 2013/2809 Art.10, SI 2013/3200 Art.9, SI 2013/3244 Art.4
s.86, varied: SI 2013/3244 Art.4
s.87, applied: SI 2013/675 Art.9, SI 2013/680 Art.10, SI 2013/1203 Art.13, SI 2013/1873 Art.9, SI 2013/1967 Art.4, SI 2013/2587 Art.4, SI 2013/2808 Art.8, SI 2013/3244 Art.4
s.87, referred to: SI 2013/1933 Art.3
s.87, varied: SI 2013/3244 Art.4
s.88, applied: SI 2013/675 Art.9, SI 2013/680 Art.10, SI 2013/1203 Art.13, SI 2013/1873 Art.9, SI 2013/2389 Sch.1, SI 2013/2399 Sch.1
s.88, referred to: SI 2013/805 Sch.1, SI 2013/806 Sch.1, SI 2013/807 Sch.1, SI 2013/808 Sch.1, SI 2013/809 Sch.1, SI 2013/810 Sch.1, SI 2013/811 Sch.1, SI 2013/812 Sch.1, SI 2013/813 Sch.1, SI 2013/814 Sch.1, SI 2013/1781 Sch.1, SI 2013/2398 Sch.1
s.88, varied: SI 2013/1781 Sch.1, SI 2013/3244 Art.4
s.89, applied: SI 2013/675 Art.9, SI 2013/680 Art.10, SI 2013/1203 Art.13, SI 2013/1873 Art.9, SI 2013/2389 Sch.1, SI 2013/2399 Sch.1
s.89, referred to: SI 2013/805 Sch.1, SI 2013/806 Sch.1, SI 2013/807 Sch.1, SI 2013/808 Sch.1, SI 2013/809 Sch.1, SI 2013/810 Sch.1, SI 2013/811 Sch.1, SI 2013/812 Sch.1, SI 2013/813 Sch.1, SI 2013/814 Sch.1, SI 2013/1781 Sch.1, SI 2013/2398 Sch.1
s.89, varied: SI 2013/1781 Sch.1, SI 2013/3244 Art.4
s.90, applied: SI 2013/675 Art.9, SI 2013/680 Art.10, SI 2013/1203 Art.13, SI 2013/1873 Art.9, SI 2013/2399 Sch.1
s.90, referred to: SI 2013/1781 Sch.1, SI 2013/2398 Sch.1
s.90, varied: SI 2013/2398 Sch.1, SI 2013/3244 Art.4
s.91, applied: SI 2013/675 Art.9, SI 2013/680 Art.10, SI 2013/1203 Art.13, SI 2013/1873 Art.9, SI 2013/2399 Sch.1
s.91, referred to: SI 2013/1781 Sch.1, SI 2013/2398 Sch.1
s.91, varied: SI 2013/3244 Art.4
s.92, applied: SI 2013/675 Art.9, SI 2013/680 Art.10, SI 2013/1203 Art.13, SI 2013/1873 Art.9
s.92, varied: SI 2013/3244 Art.4
s.93, applied: SI 2013/675 Art.9, SI 2013/680 Art.10, SI 2013/1203 Art.13, SI 2013/1873 Art.9, SI 2013/2389 Sch.1, SI 2013/2399 Sch.1, SI 2013/2587 Art.4, SI 2013/3244 Art.4
s.93, referred to: SI 2013/805 Sch.1, SI 2013/806 Sch.1, SI 2013/807 Sch.1, SI 2013/808 Sch.1, SI 2013/809 Sch.1, SI 2013/810 Sch.1, SI 2013/811 Sch.1, SI 2013/812 Sch.1, SI 2013/813 Sch.1, SI 2013/814 Sch.1, SI 2013/1781 Sch.1, SI 2013/2398 Sch.1
s.93, varied: SI 2013/1781 Sch.1, SI 2013/3244 Art.4
s.94, applied: SI 2013/675 Art.9, SI 2013/680 Art.10, SI 2013/1203 Art.13, SI 2013/1873 Art.9
s.94, varied: SI 2013/3244 Art.4
s.95, applied: SI 2013/675 Art.9, SI 2013/680 Art.10, SI 2013/1203 Art.13, SI 2013/1873 Art.9
s.95, varied: SI 2013/3244 Art.4
s.95A, applied: SI 2013/675 Art.9, SI 2013/680 Art.10, SI 2013/1203 Art.13, SI 2013/1873 Art.9
s.95A, varied: SI 2013/3244 Art.4
s.96, applied: SI 2013/675 Art.9, SI 2013/680 Art.10, SI 2013/805 Sch.1, SI 2013/806 Sch.1, SI

2013/807 Sch.1, SI 2013/808 Sch.1, SI 2013/809 Sch.1, SI 2013/810 Sch.1, SI 2013/811 Sch.1, SI 2013/812 Sch.1, SI 2013/813 Sch.1, SI 2013/814 Sch.1, SI 2013/1203 Art.13, SI 2013/1873 Art.9
s.96, varied: SI 2013/3244 Art.4
s.97, applied: SI 2013/675 Art.9, SI 2013/680 Art.10, SI 2013/1203 Art.13, SI 2013/1873 Art.9
s.97, varied: SI 2013/3244 Art.4
s.98, applied: SI 2013/675 Art.9, SI 2013/680 Art.10, SI 2013/805 Sch.1, SI 2013/806 Sch.1, SI 2013/807 Sch.1, SI 2013/808 Sch.1, SI 2013/809 Sch.1, SI 2013/810 Sch.1, SI 2013/811 Sch.1, SI 2013/812 Sch.1, SI 2013/813 Sch.1, SI 2013/814 Sch.1, SI 2013/1203 Art.13, SI 2013/1873 Art.9, SI 2013/2399 Sch.1
s.98, referred to: SI 2013/2389 Sch.1
s.98, varied: SI 2013/3244 Art.4
s.99, applied: SI 2013/675 Art.9, SI 2013/680 Art.10, SI 2013/805 Sch.1, SI 2013/806 Sch.1, SI 2013/807 Sch.1, SI 2013/808 Sch.1, SI 2013/809 Sch.1, SI 2013/810 Sch.1, SI 2013/811 Sch.1, SI 2013/812 Sch.1, SI 2013/813 Sch.1, SI 2013/814 Sch.1, SI 2013/1203 Art.13, SI 2013/1873 Art.9, SI 2013/2389 Sch.1, SI 2013/2399 Sch.1
s.99, referred to: SI 2013/2389 Sch.1
s.99, varied: SI 2013/3244 Art.4
s.100, applied: SI 2013/675 Art.9, SI 2013/680 Art.10, SI 2013/1203 Art.13, SI 2013/1873 Art.9
s.100, varied: SI 2013/3244 Art.4
s.101, applied: SI 2013/675 Art.9, SI 2013/680 Art.10, SI 2013/1203 Art.13, SI 2013/1873 Art.9
s.101, varied: SI 2013/3244 Art.4
s.102, applied: SI 2013/675 Art.9, SI 2013/680 Art.10, SI 2013/1203 Art.13, SI 2013/1873 Art.9
s.102, varied: SI 2013/3244 Art.4
s.103, applied: SI 2013/675 Art.9, SI 2013/680 Art.10, SI 2013/1203 Art.13, SI 2013/1873 Art.9
s.103, varied: SI 2013/3244 Art.4
s.104, applied: SI 2013/675 Art.9, SI 2013/680 Art.10, SI 2013/1203 Art.13, SI 2013/1873 Art.9
s.104, varied: SI 2013/3244 Art.4
s.105, applied: SI 2013/675 Art.9, SI 2013/680 Art.10, SI 2013/1203 Art.13, SI 2013/1873 Art.9
s.105, referred to: SI 2013/805 Sch.1, SI 2013/806 Sch.1, SI 2013/807 Sch.1, SI 2013/808 Sch.1, SI 2013/809 Sch.1, SI 2013/810 Sch.1, SI 2013/811 Sch.1, SI 2013/812 Sch.1, SI 2013/813 Sch.1, SI 2013/814 Sch.1
s.105, varied: SI 2013/3244 Art.4
s.106, applied: SI 2013/675 Art.9, SI 2013/680 Art.10, SI 2013/1203 Art.13, SI 2013/1873 Art.9
s.106, varied: SI 2013/2809 Art.13, SI 2013/3244 Art.4
s.112A, applied: SSI 2013/8 Reg.3
s.112A, referred to: SSI 2013/8 Reg.3
s.112A, enabling: SSI 2013/8
s.163, enabling: SSI 2013/8
s.163A, applied: SSI 2013/8
Sch.3A, disapplied: SI 2013/1933 Art.3, SI 2013/2587 Art.4, SI 2013/2808 Art.8, SI 2013/3244 Art.4
Sch.3A, referred to: SI 2013/805 Sch.1, SI 2013/806 Sch.1, SI 2013/807 Sch.1, SI 2013/808 Sch.1, SI 2013/809 Sch.1, SI 2013/810 Sch.1, SI 2013/811 Sch.1, SI 2013/812 Sch.1, SI 2013/813 Sch.1, SI 2013/814 Sch.1
Sch.3A para.1, varied: SI 2013/1781 Sch.1
Sch.3A para.2, varied: SI 2013/1781 Sch.1
Sch.3A para.3, varied: SI 2013/1781 Sch.1
Sch.3A para.4, varied: SI 2013/1781 Sch.1
Sch.3A para.5, varied: SI 2013/1781 Sch.1
Sch.3A para.6, varied: SI 2013/1781 Sch.1
Sch.4, applied: SI 2013/805 Sch.1, SI 2013/806 Sch.1, SI 2013/807 Sch.1, SI 2013/808 Sch.1, SI 2013/809 Sch.1, SI 2013/810 Sch.1, SI 2013/811 Sch.1, SI 2013/812 Sch.1, SI 2013/813 Sch.1, SI 2013/814 Sch.1, SI 2013/2389 Sch.1

27. Radioactive Material (Road Transport) Act 1991

s.1, amended: 2013 c.32 Sch.12 para.63
s.1, repealed (in part): 2013 c.32 Sch.12 para.63
s.2, repealed: 2013 c.32 Sch.12 para.63
s.3, repealed: 2013 c.32 Sch.12 para.63
s.4, repealed: 2013 c.32 Sch.12 para.63
s.5, repealed: 2013 c.32 Sch.12 para.63
s.6, repealed: 2013 c.32 Sch.12 para.63
s.7, repealed: 2013 c.32 Sch.12 para.63
s.8, repealed: 2013 c.32 Sch.12 para.63
s.9, repealed: 2013 c.32 Sch.12 para.63
Sch.1, repealed: 2013 c.32 Sch.12 para.63

28. Natural Heritage (Scotland) Act 1991

s.20, repealed: 2013 asp 5 Sch.4 para.1
s.21, repealed: 2013 asp 5 Sch.4 para.1
s.22, repealed: 2013 asp 5 Sch.4 para.1
s.24, repealed: 2013 asp 5 Sch.4 para.1
Sch.7 para.1, repealed: 2013 asp 5 Sch.4 para.1
Sch.7 para.2, repealed: 2013 asp 5 Sch.4 para.1
Sch.7 para.3, repealed: 2013 asp 5 Sch.4 para.1
Sch.7 para.4, repealed: 2013 asp 5 Sch.4 para.1
Sch.7 para.5, repealed: 2013 asp 5 Sch.4 para.1
Sch.7 para.6, repealed: 2013 asp 5 Sch.4 para.1
Sch.7 para.7, repealed: 2013 asp 5 Sch.4 para.1
Sch.8 para.1, repealed: 2013 asp 5 Sch.4 para.1
Sch.8 para.2, repealed: 2013 asp 5 Sch.4 para.1
Sch.8 para.3, repealed: 2013 asp 5 Sch.4 para.1
Sch.9 para.1, repealed: 2013 asp 5 Sch.4 para.1
Sch.9 para.2, repealed: 2013 asp 5 Sch.4 para.1
Sch.9 para.3, repealed: 2013 asp 5 Sch.4 para.1
Sch.9 para.4, repealed: 2013 asp 5 Sch.4 para.1

Sch.9 para.5, repealed: 2013 asp 5 Sch.4 para.1

29. Property Misdescriptions Act 1991

repealed: SI 2013/1575 Art.2

31. Finance Act 1991

s.27, repealed (in part): 2013 c.2 Sch.1 Part 10
s.46, repealed: 2013 c.2 Sch.1 Part 10
s.66, repealed: 2013 c.2 Sch.1 Part 10
s.75, repealed: 2013 c.2 Sch.1 Part 10
s.104, amended: 2013 c.29 Sch.31 para.11
s.105, repealed: 2013 c.29 Sch.31 para.5
s.106, repealed: 2013 c.29 Sch.31 para.5
s.108, repealed: 2013 c.29 Sch.31 para.8
s.116, amended: SI 2013/504 Reg.20
s.116, applied: SI 2013/1382 Reg.3
s.116, enabling: SI 2013/1382
s.117, amended: SI 2013/504 Reg.20
s.117, applied: SI 2013/1382 Reg.3
s.117, enabling: SI 2013/1382
Sch.6 para.4, repealed: 2013 c.2 Sch.1 Part 10

33. Agriculture and Forestry (Financial Provisions) Act 1991

s.1, repealed (in part): SI 2013/1881 Sch.1 para.3

40. Road Traffic Act 1991

applied: SSI 2013/312 Reg.2
s.49, applied: SI 2013/2399 Sch.1
s.49, varied: SI 2013/2389 Sch.1
s.66, applied: SSI 2013/68 Reg.4, SSI 2013/94 Reg.2, SSI 2013/95 Reg.4, SSI 2013/312 Reg.4
s.66, referred to: SSI 2013/69 Reg.2, SSI 2013/313 Reg.2
s.66, varied: SSI 2013/67 Sch.2 para.1, SSI 2013/93 Sch.2 para.1, SSI 2013/311 Sch.2 para.1
s.69, applied: SSI 2013/94 Reg.2
s.69, referred to: SSI 2013/69 Reg.2, SSI 2013/313 Reg.2
s.69, varied: SSI 2013/67 Sch.2 para.2, SSI 2013/93 Sch.2 para.2, SSI 2013/311 Sch.2 para.2
s.71, applied: SSI 2013/68 Reg.4, SSI 2013/95 Reg.4, SSI 2013/312 Reg.4
s.71, varied: SSI 2013/67 Sch.2 para.3, SSI 2013/93 Sch.2 para.3, SSI 2013/311 Sch.2 para.3
s.72, applied: SSI 2013/68 Reg.14, SSI 2013/95 Reg.14, SSI 2013/312 Reg.14
s.72, referred to: SSI 2013/68 Reg.3, SSI 2013/95 Reg.3, SSI 2013/312 Reg.3
s.73, applied: SI 2013/362 Reg.15, Reg.16, SSI 2013/68 Reg.6, Reg.9, SSI 2013/93 Art.6, SSI 2013/95 Reg.6, Reg.9, SSI 2013/312 Reg.6, Reg.9
s.73, varied: SSI 2013/67 Sch.2 para.4, SSI 2013/93 Sch.2 para.4, SSI 2013/311 Sch.2 para.4
s.73, enabling: SSI 2013/68, SSI 2013/95, SSI 2013/312
s.74, varied: SSI 2013/67 Sch.2 para.5, SSI 2013/93 Sch.2 para.5, SSI 2013/311 Sch.2 para.5
s.82, varied: SSI 2013/67 Sch.2 para.6, SSI 2013/93 Sch.2 para.6, SSI 2013/311 Sch.2 para.6
Sch.3, applied: SI 2013/362 Reg.25
Sch.3 para.1, amended: SI 2013/602 Sch.2 para.24
Sch.3 para.1, applied: SSI 2013/67, SSI 2013/93, SSI 2013/311
Sch.3 para.1, enabling: SSI 2013/67, SSI 2013/93, SSI 2013/311
Sch.3 para.2, amended: SI 2013/602 Sch.2 para.24, SSI 2013/119 Sch.1 para.13
Sch.3 para.2, applied: SSI 2013/67, SSI 2013/93, SSI 2013/311
Sch.3 para.2, enabling: SSI 2013/67, SSI 2013/93, SSI 2013/311
Sch.3 para.3, enabling: SSI 2013/67, SSI 2013/93, SSI 2013/311
Sch.6 para.1, varied: SSI 2013/67 Sch.2 para.7, SSI 2013/93 Sch.2 para.7, SSI 2013/311 Sch.2 para.7
Sch.6 para.2, applied: SSI 2013/68 Reg.4, SSI 2013/95 Reg.4, SSI 2013/312 Reg.4
Sch.6 para.2, varied: SSI 2013/67 Sch.2 para.7, SSI 2013/93 Sch.2 para.7, SSI 2013/311 Sch.2 para.7
Sch.6 para.3, varied: SSI 2013/67 Sch.2 para.7, SSI 2013/93 Sch.2 para.7, SSI 2013/311 Sch.2 para.7
Sch.6 para.4, varied: SSI 2013/67 Sch.2 para.7, SSI 2013/93 Sch.2 para.7, SSI 2013/311 Sch.2 para.7
Sch.6 para.5, applied: SSI 2013/68 Reg.14, SSI 2013/95 Reg.14, SSI 2013/312 Reg.14
Sch.6 para.5, referred to: SSI 2013/68 Reg.3, SSI 2013/95 Reg.3, SSI 2013/312 Reg.3
Sch.6 para.5, varied: SSI 2013/67 Sch.2 para.7, SSI 2013/93 Sch.2 para.7, SSI 2013/311 Sch.2 para.7
Sch.6 para.6, varied: SSI 2013/67 Sch.2 para.7, SSI 2013/93 Sch.2 para.7, SSI 2013/311 Sch.2 para.7
Sch.6 para.7, varied: SSI 2013/67 Sch.2 para.7, SSI 2013/93 Sch.2 para.7, SSI 2013/311 Sch.2 para.7
Sch.6 para.8, varied: SSI 2013/67 Sch.2 para.7, SSI 2013/93 Sch.2 para.7, SSI 2013/311 Sch.2 para.7
Sch.6 para.9, varied: SSI 2013/67 Sch.2 para.7, SSI 2013/93 Sch.2 para.7, SSI 2013/311 Sch.2 para.7
Sch.6 para.10, varied: SSI 2013/67 Sch.2 para.7, SSI 2013/93 Sch.2 para.7, SSI 2013/311 Sch.2 para.7

45. Coal Mining Subsidence Act 1991

s.36, amended: SI 2013/755 Sch.2 para.220

s.52, amended: SI 2013/755 Sch.2 para.221

48. Child Support Act 1991

applied: SI 2013/380 Sch.6 para.10, SI 2013/386 Reg.11
s.4, applied: SI 2013/1860 Art.3, SI 2013/2947 Art.4, Art.5
s.7, applied: SI 2013/1860 Art.3, SI 2013/2947 Art.4, Art.5
s.10, amended: 2013 c.22 Sch.11 para.123
s.14, enabling: SI 2013/1654
s.20, enabling: SI 2013/2380
s.28G, enabling: SI 2013/1517
s.32L, amended: 2013 c.22 Sch.11 para.124
s.42, enabling: SI 2013/1517
s.43, applied: SI 2013/380 Sch.6 para.10
s.43, enabling: SI 2013/380, SI 2013/1654
s.45, amended: 2013 c.22 Sch.11 para.125
s.45, repealed (in part): 2013 c.22 Sch.11 para.210
s.48, amended: 2013 c.22 Sch.11 para.126
s.51, enabling: SI 2013/1517
s.52, applied: SI 2013/1654, SI 2013/2380
s.52, enabling: SI 2013/1517, SI 2013/1654, SI 2013/2380
s.54, enabling: SI 2013/1517
s.55, enabling: SI 2013/1517
Sch.1 Part I para.3, enabling: SI 2013/1654
Sch.1 Part I para.4, applied: SI 2013/380 Sch.7 para.5
Sch.1 Part I para.5, enabling: SI 2013/630
Sch.1 Part I para.5A, varied: SI 2013/1654 Reg.2
Sch.1 Part I para.6, applied: SI 2013/380 Sch.7 para.4
Sch.1 Part I para.7, applied: SI 2013/380 Sch.7 para.4
Sch.1 Part I para.8, applied: SI 2013/380 Sch.7 para.4
Sch.1 Part I para.10, enabling: SI 2013/1517
Sch.1 Part I para.10A, enabling: SI 2013/1654
Sch.1 Part I para.10C, enabling: SI 2013/1517
Sch.4B Part I para.4, enabling: SI 2013/1654
Sch.4B Part I para.5, enabling: SI 2013/1654

53. Criminal Justice Act 1991

s.20A, amended: 2013 c.22 Sch.16 para.26
s.20A, applied: SI 2013/1554 r.37_10
s.24, amended: 2013 c.3 Sch.1 para.5, 2013 c.22 s.26, SI 2013/630 Reg.8
s.24, enabling: SI 2013/380, SI 2013/612
s.30, enabling: SI 2013/380, SI 2013/612
s.53, applied: SI 2013/435 Sch.1 para.2, Sch.1 para.22, Sch.2 para.2, Sch.2 para.21, SI 2013/1554 r.14_1
s.60, amended: 2013 c.22 Sch.11 para.127
s.90, applied: SI 2013/435 Sch.1 Part 7
Sch.6 para.5, applied: SI 2013/435 Sch.1 para.2, Sch.1 para.22, Sch.2 para.2, Sch.2 para.21

54. Deer Act 1991

s.8, amended: SI 2013/755 Sch.2 para.222

55. Agricultural Holdings (Scotland) Act 1991

s.13, applied: 2013 asp 11 Sch.19 para.13
s.14, applied: 2013 asp 11 Sch.19 para.13
s.15, applied: 2013 asp 11 Sch.19 para.13
s.31, applied: 2013 asp 11 Sch.19 para.13

59. Land Drainage Act 1991

applied: SI 2013/648 Art.47, SI 2013/1169 r.18
s.2, amended: SI 2013/755 Sch.2 para.317
s.3, amended: SI 2013/755 Sch.2 para.317
s.3, applied: SI 2013/819
s.3, enabling: SI 2013/819
s.4, amended: SI 2013/755 Sch.2 para.317
s.5, amended: SI 2013/755 Sch.2 para.317
s.6, amended: SI 2013/755 Sch.2 para.317
s.7, amended: SI 2013/755 Sch.2 para.317
s.9, amended: SI 2013/755 Sch.2 para.317
s.10, amended: SI 2013/755 Sch.2 para.317
s.11, amended: SI 2013/755 Sch.2 para.318
s.14A, amended: SI 2013/755 Sch.2 para.319
s.16, amended: SI 2013/755 Sch.2 para.320
s.18, amended: SI 2013/755 Sch.2 para.320
s.22, amended: SI 2013/755 Sch.2 para.321
s.23, amended: SI 2013/755 Sch.2 para.322
s.23, applied: SI 2013/1933 Art.4
s.23, disapplied: SI 2013/648 Art.47, SI 2013/2587 Art.6
s.28, amended: SI 2013/1036 Sch.1 para.213
s.30, amended: SI 2013/1036 Sch.1 para.214
s.31, amended: SI 2013/1036 Sch.1 para.215
s.32, amended: SI 2013/755 Sch.2 para.323
s.35, amended: SI 2013/755 Sch.2 para.324
s.36, amended: SI 2013/755 Sch.2 para.325
s.38, amended: SI 2013/755 Sch.2 para.325
s.39, amended: SI 2013/755 Sch.2 para.325
s.47, amended: SI 2013/755 Sch.2 para.325
s.54, applied: SI 2013/1894 Reg.4
s.56, amended: SI 2013/755 Sch.2 para.326
s.57, amended: SI 2013/755 Sch.2 para.326
s.58, amended: SI 2013/755 Sch.2 para.326
s.59, amended: SI 2013/755 Sch.2 para.327
s.61A, amended: SI 2013/755 Sch.2 para.328
s.61B, amended: SI 2013/755 Sch.2 para.329
s.61C, amended: SI 2013/755 Sch.2 para.330
s.61E, amended: SI 2013/755 Sch.2 para.331
s.61F, amended: SI 2013/755 Sch.2 para.332
s.67, amended: SI 2013/755 Sch.2 para.333
s.70, amended: SI 2013/755 Sch.2 para.334
s.72, amended: SI 2013/755 Sch.2 para.335
s.74, amended: SI 2013/755 Sch.2 para.336
Sch.1, applied: SI 2013/819 Sch.1

Sch.2 para.4, amended: SI 2013/755 Sch.2 para.337
Sch.2 para.5, amended: SI 2013/755 Sch.2 para.337
Sch.3 para.1, applied: SI 2013/819 Sch.1
Sch.3 para.2, applied: SI 2013/819
Sch.3 para.2, referred to: SI 2013/819
Sch.3 para.4, applied: SI 2013/819 Sch.1
Sch.3 para.5, applied: SI 2013/819 Art.1, Sch.1
Sch.4 para.1, amended: SI 2013/755 Sch.2 para.338
Sch.4 para.2, amended: SI 2013/755 Sch.2 para.338
Sch.4 para.3, amended: SI 2013/755 Sch.2 para.338
Sch.6 para.1, amended: SI 2013/755 Sch.2 para.339

62. Armed Forces Act 1991

s.21, amended: SI 2013/1465 Sch.1 para.3

65. Dangerous Dogs Act 1991

s.3, see *Adam (Derek) v HM Advocate* [2013] HCJAC 14, 2013 J.C. 221 (HCJ), Lord Menzies
s.3, applied: SI 2013/435 Sch.1 Part 7
s.4, applied: SI 2013/1554 r.76_1

1992

13. Further and Higher Education Act 1992

s.16, applied: SI 2013/3109 Reg.16, SI 2013/3110 Sch.3 para.8
s.16, enabling: SI 2013/374
s.16A, applied: SI 2013/374
s.17, enabling: SI 2013/374
s.18, applied: SI 2013/1793 Reg.3
s.20, enabling: SI 2013/375
s.21, enabling: SI 2013/375
s.22ZA, applied: SI 2013/375 Sch.2 para.6
s.26, applied: SI 2013/1673 Art.4, SI 2013/1724 Art.4, SI 2013/1727 Art.4, SI 2013/3045 Art.4
s.26, varied: SI 2013/1663 Art.4, SI 2013/3045 Art.4
s.27C, applied: SI 2013/1663, SI 2013/1663 Art.3, SI 2013/1673, SI 2013/1673 Art.3, SI 2013/1724, SI 2013/1724 Art.3, SI 2013/1727, SI 2013/1727 Art.3, SI 2013/3045, SI 2013/3045 Art.3
s.27C, enabling: SI 2013/1663, SI 2013/1673, SI 2013/1724, SI 2013/1727, SI 2013/3045
s.28, applied: SI 2013/375 Sch.1 para.4, SI 2013/3045 Art.5
s.28, referred to: SI 2013/1663 Art.5, SI 2013/3045 Art.5
s.28, enabling: SI 2013/1663, SI 2013/3045
s.33C, applied: SI 2013/3110 Sch.3 para.8
s.44, applied: SI 2013/1793 Reg.3
s.65, disapplied: SI 2013/377 Reg.28
s.69, enabling: SI 2013/1733
s.85B, applied: SI 2013/1793 Reg.3
s.85C, applied: SI 2013/1793 Reg.3
s.89, enabling: SI 2013/1733
s.90, applied: SI 2013/2356 Sch.2 para.14
Sch.4 Part 1 para.1, enabling: SI 2013/375
Sch.4 Part 3 para.13, enabling: SI 2013/375
Sch.4 Part 3 para.14, enabling: SI 2013/375
Sch.4 Part 3 para.15, enabling: SI 2013/375
Sch.4 Part 3 para.16, enabling: SI 2013/375
Sch.4 Part 3 para.17, enabling: SI 2013/375
Sch.4 Part 3 para.18, enabling: SI 2013/375
Sch.4 Part 3 para.19, enabling: SI 2013/375
Sch.4 Part 3 para.20, enabling: SI 2013/375
Sch.4 Part 3 para.21, enabling: SI 2013/375
Sch.4 Part 3 para.22, enabling: SI 2013/375
Sch.4 Part 3 para.23, enabling: SI 2013/375
Sch.4 Part 3 para.24, enabling: SI 2013/375
Sch.4 Part 3 para.25, enabling: SI 2013/375

14. Local Government Finance Act 1992

applied: SI 2013/3029 Sch.1 para.2, Sch.6 para.4, SI 2013/3035 Sch.1
Part I, applied: 2013 c.29 s.125, s.128, SI 2013/595 Art.9, SI 2013/596 Art.9
Part II, applied: 2013 c.29 s.125, s.128
s.1, referred to: SI 2013/3029 Sch.6 para.44
s.3, see *Listing Officer v Callear* [2012] EWHC 3697 (Admin), [2013] R.V.R. 34 (QBD (Admin)), Judge Shaun Spencer Q.C.; see *McLeod v Piggott (Listing Officer)* [2013] R.V.R. 101 (VT), R Hughes; see *Reeves (Listing Officer) v Northrop* [2013] EWCA Civ 362, [2013] 1 W.L.R. 2867 (CA (Civ Div)), Hughes, L.J.
s.3, amended: SI 2013/468 Art.3
s.3, enabling: SI 2013/468
s.6, applied: SI 2013/3029 Reg.9, SI 2013/3035 Sch.1
s.7, applied: SI 2013/3029 Reg.9, SI 2013/3035 Sch.1
s.9, applied: SI 2013/3029 Sch.1 para.3, SI 2013/3035 Sch.1
s.10, applied: SI 2013/2977 Reg.4
s.11, applied: SI 2013/2977 Reg.4, SI 2013/3029 Sch.1 para.40, Sch.6 para.46, SI 2013/3035 Sch.1
s.11A, applied: SI 2013/2977 Reg.4, SI 2013/3029 Sch.1 para.40, SI 2013/3035 Sch.1
s.11B, applied: SI 2013/2977 Reg.4, SI 2013/3029 Sch.1 para.40, SI 2013/3035 Sch.1
s.12, applied: SI 2013/3029 Sch.1 para.40, Sch.6 para.46, SI 2013/3035 Sch.1
s.13, amended: SI 2013/388 Sch.1 para.7

s.13, applied: SI 2013/2977 Reg.4, SI 2013/3029 Sch.1 para.40, Sch.6 para.46, Sch.10 para.40, SI 2013/3035 Sch.1
s.13, enabling: SI 2013/2977
s.13A, applied: SI 2013/111, SI 2013/112, SI 2013/3029, SI 2013/3029 Reg.11, Reg.16, Sch.1 para.8, Sch.9 para.45, Sch.12 para.11, SI 2013/3035, SI 2013/3035 Sch.1
s.13A, enabling: SI 2013/111, SI 2013/112, SI 2013/3029, SI 2013/3035
s.14A, enabling: SI 2013/501, SI 2013/588
s.14B, enabling: SI 2013/501, SI 2013/588
s.14C, enabling: SI 2013/501, SI 2013/588
s.14D, applied: SI 2013/501, SI 2013/588
s.16, applied: SI 2013/3029 Sch.12 para.10, SI 2013/3035 Sch.1
s.17, referred to: 2013 c.29 s.125, s.128
s.18, enabling: SI 2013/590
s.24, enabling: SI 2013/467
s.31A, see *R. (on the application of Buck) v Doncaster MBC* [2013] EWCA Civ 1190, [2013] B.L.G.R. 847 (CA (Civ Div)), Master of the Rolls
s.31A, amended: SI 2013/733 Art.2
s.32, amended: SI 2013/216 Reg.2
s.32, enabling: SI 2013/216
s.33, amended: SI 2013/216 Reg.3
s.33, enabling: SI 2013/216
s.43, amended: SI 2013/216 Reg.4
s.43, enabling: SI 2013/216
s.44, amended: SI 2013/216 Reg.5
s.44, enabling: SI 2013/216
s.52ZD, amended: SI 2013/733 Art.2
s.52ZF, amended: SI 2013/733 Art.2
s.52ZG, applied: SI 2013/2862 Art.2
s.52ZG, enabling: SI 2013/2862
s.52ZJ, amended: SI 2013/733 Art.2
s.52ZN, applied: SI 2013/2862 Art.2
s.52ZN, enabling: SI 2013/2862
s.52ZQ, amended: SI 2013/2597 Sch.1 para.6
s.52ZQ, applied: SI 2013/2597 Art.2
s.52ZQ, enabling: SI 2013/409
s.69, amended: SI 2013/733 Art.2
s.69, applied: SI 2013/2356 Sch.2 para.2
s.80, amended: SI 2013/388 Sch.1 para.7
s.80, enabling: SSI 2013/48, SSI 2013/49, SSI 2013/218, SSI 2013/239, SSI 2013/287
s.81, applied: SSI 2013/218 Reg.17, Reg.18
s.83, referred to: 2013 c.29 s.125, s.128
s.84, applied: SSI 2013/45 Reg.6, Sch.2 para.3
s.99, referred to: SSI 2013/200 Sch.1 para.7
s.113, amended: SI 2013/2597 Sch.1 para.6
s.113, enabling: SI 2013/62, SI 2013/63, SI 2013/276, SI 2013/409, SI 2013/467, SI 2013/501, SI 2013/570, SI 2013/588, SI 2013/590, SI 2013/612, SI 2013/725, SI 2013/2977, SI 2013/3181, SSI 2013/48, SSI 2013/49, SSI 2013/218, SSI 2013/239, SSI 2013/287
Sch.1, applied: SI 2013/3029 Sch.1 para.3, SI 2013/3035 Sch.1
Sch.1 para.2, enabling: SI 2013/638, SI 2013/1048
Sch.1 para.4, referred to: SI 2013/3029 Sch.1 para.3
Sch.1 para.9, enabling: SI 2013/639, SI 2013/725, SI 2013/1049
Sch.1A para.2, enabling: SI 2013/3181
Sch.1A para.4, enabling: SI 2013/276
Sch.1A para.9, enabling: SI 2013/215
Sch.1B para.2, enabling: SI 2013/3029
Sch.1B para.3, applied: SI 2013/3029 Reg.21, Reg.27
Sch.1B para.3, enabling: SI 2013/3029
Sch.1B para.4, enabling: SI 2013/3029
Sch.1B para.5, enabling: SI 2013/3029
Sch.1B para.6, applied: SI 2013/3035 Reg.2
Sch.1B para.6, enabling: SI 2013/112, SI 2013/3029, SI 2013/3035
Sch.1B para.7, enabling: SI 2013/111, SI 2013/3029
Sch.2 para.1, enabling: SI 2013/62, SI 2013/63, SI 2013/2977, SSI 2013/48, SSI 2013/49, SSI 2013/218, SSI 2013/239, SSI 2013/287
Sch.2 para.2, enabling: SI 2013/62, SI 2013/63, SI 2013/2977
Sch.2 para.4, enabling: SI 2013/62, SI 2013/2977
Sch.2 para.5, enabling: SI 2013/62
Sch.2 para.6, enabling: SI 2013/62
Sch.2 para.8, enabling: SI 2013/62
Sch.2 para.9, enabling: SI 2013/62
Sch.2 para.10, enabling: SI 2013/62
Sch.2 para.15, amended: SI 2013/388 Sch.1 para.7
Sch.2 para.15A, enabling: SI 2013/590
Sch.2 para.15B, applied: SI 2013/570
Sch.2 para.15B, enabling: SI 2013/570
Sch.2 para.15C, applied: SSI 2013/87 Reg.2, Reg.3
Sch.2 para.15C, enabling: SSI 2013/87
Sch.2 para.16, enabling: SI 2013/62
Sch.3 para.3, applied: SI 2013/501 Reg.11, SI 2013/588 Reg.15
Sch.3 para.6, enabling: SI 2013/570, SI 2013/590
Sch.4 para.1, enabling: SI 2013/380, SI 2013/570, SI 2013/612
Sch.4 para.6, enabling: SI 2013/380, SI 2013/612
Sch.4 para.11, amended: 2013 c.22 Sch.9 para.52
Sch.4 para.12, enabling: SI 2013/570
Sch.8 para.6, enabling: SI 2013/380, SI 2013/612
Sch.12 Part I para.1, enabling: SSI 2013/44, SSI 2013/107

Sch.12 Part I para.2, applied: SSI 2013/44, SSI 2013/107
Sch.12 Part II para.9, applied: SSI 2013/44 Art.3
Sch.12 Part II para.9, enabling: SSI 2013/44

23. Access to Neighbouring Land Act 1992

s.7, amended: 2013 c.22 Sch.9 para.53
s.8, amended: 2013 c.22 Sch.9 para.52

25. Prison Security Act 1992

s.1, applied: SI 2013/435 Sch.1 Part 7

31. Firearms (Amendment) Act 1992

applied: SI 2013/449 Reg.3

37. Further and Higher Education (Scotland) Act 1992

Part II, applied: SSI 2013/73 Sch.1
s.3, amended: 2013 asp 12 Sch.1 para.2
s.3, enabling: SSI 2013/179, SSI 2013/180, SSI 2013/181, SSI 2013/182, SSI 2013/183, SSI 2013/267, SSI 2013/268, SSI 2013/269, SSI 2013/270, SSI 2013/354
s.5, amended: 2013 asp 12 Sch.1 para.2
s.5, applied: SSI 2013/179, SSI 2013/180, SSI 2013/181, SSI 2013/182, SSI 2013/183, SSI 2013/267, SSI 2013/268, SSI 2013/269, SSI 2013/270, SSI 2013/354
s.12, amended: 2013 asp 12 Sch.1 para.2
s.12, applied: SI 2013/3029 Sch.9 para.16, Sch.10 para.53, SI 2013/3035 Sch.1
s.15A, added: 2013 asp 12 s.18
s.24, substituted: 2013 asp 12 s.7
s.25, applied: SSI 2013/179, SSI 2013/180, SSI 2013/181, SSI 2013/182, SSI 2013/183, SSI 2013/267, SSI 2013/268, SSI 2013/269, SSI 2013/270, SSI 2013/354
s.25, enabling: SSI 2013/179, SSI 2013/180, SSI 2013/181, SSI 2013/182, SSI 2013/183, SSI 2013/267, SSI 2013/268, SSI 2013/269, SSI 2013/270, SSI 2013/354
s.36, amended: 2013 asp 12 Sch.1 para.2
s.36, applied: SSI 2013/73 Sch.1
s.60, amended: 2013 asp 12 Sch.1 para.2
s.60, enabling: SSI 2013/179, SSI 2013/180, SSI 2013/181, SSI 2013/182, SSI 2013/183, SSI 2013/267, SSI 2013/268, SSI 2013/269, SSI 2013/270, SSI 2013/354
Sch.2 para.2, repealed: 2013 asp 12 Sch.1 para.2
Sch.2 para.3, substituted: 2013 asp 12 s.6
Sch.2 para.4, repealed: 2013 asp 12 Sch.1 para.2
Sch.2 para.5, amended: 2013 asp 12 Sch.1 para.2
Sch.2 para.5, repealed (in part): 2013 asp 12 Sch.1 para.2
Sch.2 para.5A, added: 2013 asp 12 Sch.1 para.2
Sch.2 para.5B, added: 2013 asp 12 Sch.1 para.2
Sch.2 para.5C, added: 2013 asp 12 Sch.1 para.2
Sch.2 para.6, repealed: 2013 asp 12 Sch.1 para.2
Sch.2 para.7, repealed: 2013 asp 12 Sch.1 para.2
Sch.2 para.8, repealed: 2013 asp 12 Sch.1 para.2
Sch.2 para.9, repealed: 2013 asp 12 Sch.1 para.2
Sch.2 para.10, repealed: 2013 asp 12 Sch.1 para.2
Sch.2 para.11, amended: 2013 asp 12 Sch.1 para.2
Sch.2 para.12, repealed: 2013 asp 12 Sch.1 para.2
Sch.2 para.16, amended: 2013 asp 12 Sch.1 para.2
Sch.2 para.16A, added: 2013 asp 12 Sch.1 para.2

40. Friendly Societies Act 1992

Part V, amended: SI 2013/496 Sch.9 para.16
s.1, amended: SI 2013/496 Sch.9 para.2, Sch.9 para.3
s.2, amended: SI 2013/496 Sch.9 para.2
s.3, amended: SI 2013/496 Sch.9 para.2
s.4, amended: SI 2013/496 Sch.9 para.2
s.5, amended: SI 2013/496 Sch.9 para.4
s.6, amended: SI 2013/496 Sch.9 para.5
s.11, amended: SI 2013/496 Sch.9 para.6
s.14, amended: SI 2013/496 Sch.9 para.7
s.20, amended: SI 2013/496 Sch.9 para.8
s.21, amended: SI 2013/496 Sch.9 para.9
s.22, amended: SI 2013/496 Sch.9 para.10
s.24, amended: SI 2013/496 Sch.9 para.11
s.25, amended: SI 2013/496 Sch.9 para.12
s.26, amended: SI 2013/496 Sch.9 para.13
s.29, amended: SI 2013/496 Sch.9 para.14
s.37, amended: SI 2013/496 Sch.9 para.15
s.52, amended: SI 2013/496 Sch.9 para.17
s.52, repealed (in part): SI 2013/496 Sch.9 para.17
s.54, amended: SI 2013/496 Sch.9 para.18
s.55, amended: SI 2013/496 Sch.9 para.19
s.58A, amended: SI 2013/496 Sch.9 para.20
s.62, amended: SI 2013/496 Sch.9 para.21
s.62A, amended: SI 2013/496 Sch.9 para.22
s.63A, amended: SI 2013/496 Sch.9 para.23
s.65, amended: SI 2013/496 Sch.9 para.24, Sch.9 para.25
s.66, amended: SI 2013/496 Sch.9 para.26
s.67, amended: SI 2013/496 Sch.9 para.27
s.74B, amended: SI 2013/496 Sch.9 para.28
s.74C, amended: SI 2013/496 Sch.9 para.29
s.76, amended: SI 2013/496 Sch.9 para.30
s.77, amended: SI 2013/496 Sch.9 para.31
s.78, amended: SI 2013/496 Sch.9 para.32
s.81, amended: SI 2013/496 Sch.9 para.33
s.82, amended: 2013 c.22 Sch.9 para.85
s.85, amended: SI 2013/496 Sch.9 para.34
s.86, amended: SI 2013/496 Sch.9 para.35
s.87, amended: SI 2013/496 Sch.9 para.36
s.88, amended: SI 2013/496 Sch.9 para.37
s.89, amended: SI 2013/496 Sch.9 para.38
s.90, amended: SI 2013/496 Sch.9 para.39
s.91, amended: SI 2013/496 Sch.9 para.40
s.93, amended: SI 2013/496 Sch.9 para.41

s.103, amended: SI 2013/496 Sch.9 para.42
s.104, amended: SI 2013/496 Sch.9 para.43
s.105A, amended: SI 2013/496 Sch.9 para.44
s.107, amended: SI 2013/496 Sch.9 para.45
s.111, amended: SI 2013/496 Sch.9 para.46
s.113, amended: SI 2013/496 Sch.9 para.47
s.114, amended: SI 2013/496 Sch.9 para.48
s.119, amended: 2013 c.22 Sch.9 para.85, SI 2013/496 Sch.9 para.49
s.119AB, amended: SI 2013/496 Sch.9 para.50
Sch.3 para.1, amended: SI 2013/496 Sch.9 para.51
Sch.3 para.2, amended: SI 2013/496 Sch.9 para.51
Sch.3 para.3, amended: SI 2013/496 Sch.9 para.51
Sch.3 para.6, amended: SI 2013/496 Sch.9 para.51
Sch.3 para.9, amended: SI 2013/496 Sch.9 para.51
Sch.3 para.11, amended: SI 2013/496 Sch.9 para.51
Sch.3 para.12, amended: SI 2013/496 Sch.9 para.51
Sch.4 para.2, amended: SI 2013/496 Sch.9 para.52
Sch.10 Part I para.3, amended: SI 2013/496 Sch.9 para.53
Sch.10 Part I para.4, amended: SI 2013/496 Sch.9 para.53
Sch.10 Part II para.24, amended: SI 2013/496 Sch.9 para.53
Sch.10 Part II para.32, amended: SI 2013/496 Sch.9 para.53
Sch.10 Part II para.34, amended: SI 2013/496 Sch.9 para.53
Sch.10 Part II para.35, amended: SI 2013/496 Sch.9 para.53
Sch.10 Part III para.54, amended: SI 2013/496 Sch.9 para.53
Sch.10 Part III para.62, amended: SI 2013/496 Sch.9 para.53
Sch.10 Part III para.64, amended: SI 2013/496 Sch.9 para.53
Sch.10 Part III para.65, amended: SI 2013/496 Sch.9 para.53
Sch.12 para.3, amended: SI 2013/496 Sch.9 para.54
Sch.14, amended: SI 2013/496 Sch.9 para.55
Sch.14 para.3, amended: SI 2013/496 Sch.9 para.55
Sch.14 para.7, amended: SI 2013/496 Sch.9 para.55
Sch.14 para.9, amended: SI 2013/496 Sch.9 para.55
Sch.14 para.10, amended: SI 2013/496 Sch.9 para.55
Sch.14 para.10A, amended: SI 2013/496 Sch.9 para.55
Sch.14 para.12, amended: SI 2013/496 Sch.9 para.55
Sch.14 para.14, amended: SI 2013/496 Sch.9 para.55
Sch.14 para.16, amended: SI 2013/496 Sch.9 para.55
Sch.15 Part I para.1, amended: SI 2013/496 Sch.9 para.56
Sch.15 Part I para.2, amended: SI 2013/496 Sch.9 para.56
Sch.15 Part I para.3, amended: SI 2013/496 Sch.9 para.56
Sch.15 Part I para.4, amended: SI 2013/496 Sch.9 para.56
Sch.15 Part I para.4ZA, added: SI 2013/496 Sch.9 para.56
Sch.15 Part II, amended: SI 2013/496 Sch.9 para.56
Sch.15 Part II para.5, amended: SI 2013/496 Sch.9 para.56
Sch.15 Part II para.6, amended: SI 2013/496 Sch.9 para.56
Sch.15 Part II para.7, amended: SI 2013/496 Sch.9 para.56
Sch.15 Part II para.8, amended: SI 2013/496 Sch.9 para.56
Sch.15 Part II para.9, amended: SI 2013/496 Sch.9 para.56
Sch.15 Part II para.10, amended: SI 2013/496 Sch.9 para.56
Sch.15 Part II para.11, amended: SI 2013/496 Sch.9 para.56
Sch.15 Part II para.11A, added: SI 2013/496 Sch.9 para.56
Sch.15 Part II para.11A, amended: SI 2013/496 Sch.9 para.56
Sch.15 Part II para.12, amended: SI 2013/496 Sch.9 para.56
Sch.15 Part II para.13, amended: SI 2013/496 Sch.9 para.56
Sch.15 Part II para.14, amended: SI 2013/496 Sch.9 para.56
Sch.15 Part II para.15, amended: SI 2013/496 Sch.9 para.56
Sch.15 Part II para.15A, amended: SI 2013/496 Sch.9 para.56
Sch.15 Part II para.16, amended: SI 2013/496 Sch.9 para.56
Sch.15 Part II para.16A, amended: SI 2013/496 Sch.9 para.56
Sch.15 Part II para.16B, amended: SI 2013/496 Sch.9 para.56
Sch.15 Part II para.17, amended: SI 2013/496 Sch.9 para.56

Sch.15 Part II para.18, amended: SI 2013/496 Sch.9 para.56

41. Charities Act 1992

s.58, amended: 2013 c.22 Sch.9 para.52

48. Finance (No.2) Act 1992

s.1, enabling: SI 2013/3210
s.47, repealed: 2013 c.2 Sch.1 Part 10
s.48, repealed: 2013 c.2 Sch.1 Part 10
s.49, repealed: 2013 c.2 Sch.1 Part 10
s.63, repealed: 2013 c.2 Sch.1 Part 10
Sch.11 para.1, repealed: 2013 c.2 Sch.1 Part 10
Sch.11 para.2, repealed: 2013 c.2 Sch.1 Part 10
Sch.11 para.3, repealed: 2013 c.2 Sch.1 Part 10
Sch.11 para.4, repealed: 2013 c.2 Sch.1 Part 10
Sch.11 para.5, repealed: 2013 c.2 Sch.1 Part 10
Sch.11 para.6, repealed: 2013 c.2 Sch.1 Part 10

51. Protection of Badgers Act 1992

s.10, amended: SI 2013/755 Sch.2 para.341

56. Maintenance Orders (Reciprocal Enforcement) Act 1992

Sch.1 Part I para.2, repealed (in part): 2013 c.22 Sch.11 para.210
Sch.1 Part II para.7, repealed: 2013 c.22 Sch.11 para.210
Sch.1 Part II para.9, repealed: 2013 c.22 Sch.11 para.210
Sch.1 Part II para.15, repealed: 2013 c.22 Sch.11 para.210

1993

8. Judicial Pensions and Retirement Act 1993

Part I, applied: 2013 c.25 Sch.5 para.10
s.1, amended: 2013 c.25 Sch.8 para.16
s.9A, enabling: SI 2013/484
s.10, amended: SI 2013/3115 Sch.2 para.36
s.11, amended: 2013 c.25 Sch.8 para.17
s.19, applied: 2013 c.25 Sch.5 para.10
s.26, amended: 2013 c.22 Sch.9 para.95, Sch.14 para.13
s.26, enabling: SSI 2013/2
s.29, enabling: SI 2013/484, SSI 2013/2
Sch.1 Part I, amended: 2013 c.22 Sch.14 para.13
Sch.1 Part I, referred to: 2013 c.25 s.39
Sch.1 Part II, amended: 2013 c.22 Sch.14 para.13, SI 2013/1036 Sch.1 para.222
Sch.5, amended: 2013 c.22 Sch.13 para.89, Sch.14 para.13, SI 2013/294 Sch.1, SI 2013/686 Sch.1 para.6, SI 2013/1036 Sch.1 para.223, SSI 2013/2 Art.2
Sch.6 para.47, repealed: SI 2013/686 Sch.1 para.6
Sch.7 para.5, amended: 2013 c.22 Sch.14 para.13
Sch.7 para.5, repealed (in part): 2013 c.22 Sch.13 para.89, SI 2013/294 Sch.1, SI 2013/686 Sch.1 para.6

11. Clean Air Act 1993

Part III, applied: SI 2013/447 Reg.2, SI 2013/2111 Reg.2
s.20, applied: SI 2013/462 Art.2, SI 2013/2112 Art.2
s.20, referred to: SI 2013/561 Art.2
s.20, enabling: SI 2013/447, SI 2013/562, SI 2013/2111
s.21, enabling: SI 2013/462, SI 2013/561, SI 2013/2112, SI 2013/3026
s.30, applied: SI 2013/2897
s.30, enabling: SI 2013/2897
s.31, amended: SI 2013/755 Sch.2 para.343
s.32, enabling: SI 2013/2897
s.36, amended: SI 2013/755 Sch.2 para.344
s.40, amended: SI 2013/755 Sch.2 para.345
s.63, enabling: SI 2013/2897

12. Radioactive Substances Act 1993

s.16, amended: 2013 c.32 Sch.12 para.67
s.17, amended: 2013 c.32 Sch.12 para.68
Sch.4 para.2, repealed: 2013 c.32 Sch.12 para.30

21. Osteopaths Act 1993

s.6, enabling: SI 2013/1026
s.10, amended: 2013 c.22 Sch.9 para.116
s.29, amended: 2013 c.22 Sch.9 para.116
s.29A, amended: 2013 c.22 Sch.9 para.116
s.35, applied: SI 2013/1026
s.35, enabling: SI 2013/1026
s.36, applied: SI 2013/1026

26. Bail (Amendment) Act 1993

s.1, applied: SI 2013/1554 r.19_9

28. Leasehold Reform, Housing and Urban Development Act 1993

Part I c.I, amended: SI 2013/1036 Sch.1 para.100
Part I c.II, amended: SI 2013/1036 Sch.1 para.106
Part I c.VI, amended: SI 2013/1036 Sch.1 para.116
s.24, amended: SI 2013/1036 Sch.1 para.101
s.25, amended: SI 2013/1036 Sch.1 para.102
s.27, amended: SI 2013/1036 Sch.1 para.103
s.33, amended: SI 2013/1036 Sch.1 para.104
s.38, amended: SI 2013/1036 Sch.1 para.105
s.48, amended: SI 2013/1036 Sch.1 para.107
s.51, amended: SI 2013/1036 Sch.1 para.108
s.60, amended: SI 2013/1036 Sch.1 para.109
s.62, amended: SI 2013/1036 Sch.1 para.110
s.69, amended: SI 2013/1036 Sch.1 para.111
s.70, amended: SI 2013/1036 Sch.1 para.112
s.71, amended: SI 2013/1036 Sch.1 para.113
s.73, amended: SI 2013/1036 Sch.1 para.114
s.75, amended: SI 2013/1036 Sch.1 para.115
s.87, applied: SI 2013/3192 Art.4, Art.5

s.88, amended: SI 2013/1036 Sch.1 para.117
s.90, amended: 2013 c.22 Sch.9 para.52, SI 2013/1036 Sch.1 para.118
s.91, amended: SI 2013/1036 Sch.1 para.119
s.93, amended: 2013 c.22 Sch.9 para.52, SI 2013/1036 Sch.1 para.120
s.94, amended: SI 2013/1036 Sch.1 para.121
s.101, amended: 2013 c.22 Sch.9 para.52, SI 2013/1036 Sch.1 para.122
Sch.1 Part II para.6, amended: SI 2013/1036 Sch.1 para.123
Sch.1 Part II para.7, amended: SI 2013/1036 Sch.1 para.123
Sch.2 para.8, amended: SI 2013/1036 Sch.1 para.124
Sch.5 para.2, amended: SI 2013/1036 Sch.1 para.125
Sch.5 para.3, amended: SI 2013/1036 Sch.1 para.125
Sch.8 para.4, amended: 2013 c.22 Sch.9 para.52
Sch.9 Part II para.4, amended: SI 2013/1036 Sch.1 para.126
Sch.9 Part III para.7, amended: SI 2013/1036 Sch.1 para.126
Sch.11 Part II para.6, amended: SI 2013/1036 Sch.1 para.127
Sch.13 Part II para.4A, amended: SI 2013/1036 Sch.1 para.128
Sch.13 Part II para.4B, amended: SI 2013/1036 Sch.1 para.128
Sch.14 para.2, amended: SI 2013/1036 Sch.1 para.129
Sch.14 para.4, amended: 2013 c.22 Sch.9 para.52, Sch.9 para.100

34. Finance Act 1993

s.67, repealed: 2013 c.2 Sch.1 Part 10
s.79, repealed (in part): 2013 c.2 Sch.1 Part 10
s.107, repealed (in part): 2013 c.2 Sch.1 Part 10
s.182, repealed (in part): 2013 c.2 Sch.1 Part 10
s.184, amended: SI 2013/636 Sch.1 para.3
s.205, repealed (in part): 2013 c.2 Sch.1 Part 10
Sch.6 para.10, repealed: 2013 c.2 Sch.1 Part 10
Sch.18 para.6, repealed: 2013 c.2 Sch.1 Part 10
Sch.23 Part VI, amended: 2013 c.2 Sch.1 Part 10

36. Criminal Justice Act 1993

s.70, amended: SI 2013/3115 Sch.2 para.37

39. National Lottery etc Act 1993

Part I, applied: SSI 2013/50 Sch.1 para.3, Sch.1 para.14, Sch.3 para.8
s.3A, amended: SI 2013/2329 Sch.1 para.2
s.3A, repealed (in part): SI 2013/2329 Sch.1 para.2
s.4A, repealed: SI 2013/2329 Sch.1 para.3
s.4B, amended: SI 2013/2329 Sch.1 para.4
s.4C, amended: SI 2013/2329 Sch.1 para.5
s.10C, amended: SI 2013/2329 Sch.1 para.6
s.10C, repealed (in part): SI 2013/2329 Sch.1 para.6
s.14, amended: SI 2013/2329 Sch.1 para.7
s.14, applied: SI 2013/2329 Art.6
s.20, amended: SI 2013/2329 Sch.1 para.8
s.23, applied: SI 2013/376 Reg.66
s.25, applied: 2013 asp 11 Sch.6 para.2, SI 2013/1098 Sch.1 para.3, Sch.1 para.5
s.31, amended: SI 2013/2329 Sch.1 para.9
Sch.2A para.1, amended: SI 2013/2329 Sch.1 para.10
Sch.2A para.1, repealed: SI 2013/2329 Sch.1 para.10
Sch.2A para.2, amended: SI 2013/2329 Sch.1 para.10
Sch.2A para.2, repealed: SI 2013/2329 Sch.1 para.10
Sch.2A para.3, amended: SI 2013/2329 Sch.1 para.10
Sch.2A para.3, repealed: SI 2013/2329 Sch.1 para.10
Sch.2A para.4, amended: SI 2013/2329 Sch.1 para.10
Sch.2A para.4, repealed: SI 2013/2329 Sch.1 para.10
Sch.2A para.5, amended: SI 2013/2329 Sch.1 para.10
Sch.2A para.5, repealed: SI 2013/2329 Sch.1 para.10
Sch.2A para.6, amended: SI 2013/2329 Sch.1 para.10
Sch.2A para.6, repealed: SI 2013/2329 Sch.1 para.10
Sch.2A para.6A, amended: SI 2013/2329 Sch.1 para.10
Sch.2A para.6A, repealed: SI 2013/2329 Sch.1 para.10
Sch.2A para.7, amended: SI 2013/2329 Sch.1 para.10
Sch.2A para.7, repealed: SI 2013/2329 Sch.1 para.10
Sch.2A para.8, amended: SI 2013/2329 Sch.1 para.10
Sch.2A para.8, repealed: SI 2013/2329 Sch.1 para.10
Sch.2A para.9, amended: SI 2013/2329 Sch.1 para.10
Sch.2A para.10, amended: SI 2013/2329 Sch.1 para.10
Sch.2A para.10, repealed: SI 2013/2329 Sch.1 para.10
Sch.2A para.11, amended: SI 2013/2329 Sch.1 para.10

Sch.2A para.11, applied: SI 2013/2329 Art.7
Sch.2A para.11, repealed: SI 2013/2329 Sch.1 para.10
Sch.2A para.12, amended: SI 2013/2329 Sch.1 para.10
Sch.2A para.12, repealed: SI 2013/2329 Sch.1 para.10
Sch.2A para.13, amended: SI 2013/2329 Sch.1 para.10
Sch.2A para.13, repealed: SI 2013/2329 Sch.1 para.10
Sch.2A para.14, amended: SI 2013/2329 Sch.1 para.10
Sch.2A para.14, repealed: SI 2013/2329 Sch.1 para.10
Sch.3A para.2, enabling: SI 2013/1098
Sch.3A para.3, enabling: SI 2013/1098

42. Cardiff Bay Barrage Act 1993

s.2, amended: SI 2013/755 Sch.2 para.347
s.3, amended: SI 2013/755 Sch.2 para.348
s.8, amended: SI 2013/755 Sch.2 para.349
s.9, amended: SI 2013/755 Sch.2 para.350
s.12, amended: SI 2013/755 Sch.2 para.351
s.14, amended: SI 2013/755 Sch.2 para.352
s.15, amended: SI 2013/755 Sch.2 para.353
s.16, amended: SI 2013/755 Sch.2 para.354
s.20, amended: SI 2013/755 Sch.2 para.355
s.26, amended: SI 2013/755 Sch.2 para.356
Sch.2 para.3, amended: SI 2013/755 Sch.2 para.357
Sch.2 para.11, amended: SI 2013/755 Sch.2 para.357
Sch.3 para.2, amended: SI 2013/755 Sch.2 para.358
Sch.3 para.4, amended: SI 2013/755 Sch.2 para.358
Sch.3 para.5, amended: SI 2013/755 Sch.2 para.358
Sch.3 para.7, amended: SI 2013/755 Sch.2 para.358
Sch.4 para.3, amended: SI 2013/755 Sch.2 para.359

43. Railways Act 1993

Part I, applied: SI 2013/680 Sch.7 para.19, SI 2013/1873 Sch.5 para.19, SI 2013/1967 Art.35, SI 2013/2809 Art.27, Art.39, SI 2013/3244 Sch.11 para.19
s.6, applied: SI 2013/339 Art.3
s.7, enabling: SI 2013/339
s.13, amended: 2013 c.24 Sch.6 para.70
s.13A, amended: 2013 c.24 Sch.6 para.71
s.13B, amended: 2013 c.24 Sch.6 para.72
s.14, amended: 2013 c.24 Sch.6 para.73
s.15, amended: 2013 c.24 Sch.6 para.74
s.15A, amended: 2013 c.24 Sch.6 para.75
s.15B, amended: 2013 c.24 Sch.6 para.76
s.15C, amended: 2013 c.24 Sch.6 para.77
s.16, amended: 2013 c.24 Sch.6 para.78
s.16A, applied: SI 2013/339 Art.16
s.16A, disapplied: SI 2013/339 Art.4
s.16B, enabling: SI 2013/339
s.17, applied: SI 2013/339 Art.5
s.18, applied: SI 2013/339 Art.5
s.20, enabling: SI 2013/339
s.22A, applied: SI 2013/339 Art.5
s.23, applied: SI 2013/339 Art.6
s.24, enabling: SI 2013/339
s.55, amended: 2013 c.24 Sch.14 para.12
s.57A, amended: 2013 c.24 Sch.14 para.13
s.67, amended: 2013 c.24 Sch.14 para.14, Sch.15 para.7
s.74, amended: 2013 c.24 Sch.6 para.79
s.74, repealed (in part): 2013 c.24 Sch.6 para.79
s.83, amended: 2013 c.24 Sch.6 para.80
s.122, applied: SI 2013/1967 Art.31
s.122, disapplied: SI 2013/1933 Art.40
s.143, enabling: SI 2013/339
s.145, amended: 2013 c.32 Sch.12 para.69, SI 2013/1881 Sch.1 para.5
s.145, repealed (in part): SI 2013/1575 Sch.1 para.1
s.151, enabling: SI 2013/339
Sch.4A, amended: 2013 c.24 Sch.6 para.81
Sch.4A para.8, amended: 2013 c.24 Sch.6 para.81
Sch.4A para.9, amended: 2013 c.24 Sch.6 para.81
Sch.4A para.10A, amended: 2013 c.24 Sch.6 para.81
Sch.4A para.11, amended: 2013 c.24 Sch.6 para.81
Sch.4A para.12, amended: 2013 c.24 Sch.6 para.81
Sch.4A para.13, amended: 2013 c.24 Sch.6 para.81
Sch.4A para.14, amended: 2013 c.24 Sch.6 para.81
Sch.4A para.15, amended: 2013 c.24 Sch.6 para.81

44. Crofters (Scotland) Act 1993

s.3, amended: 2013 asp 10 Sch.1 para.1
s.17, amended: 2013 asp 10 Sch.1 para.1
s.23, amended: 2013 asp 10 Sch.1 para.1
s.24, applied: 2013 asp 10 s.3, s.4
s.24, varied: 2013 asp 10 s.3
s.24A, added: 2013 asp 10 s.1
s.24B, added: 2013 asp 10 s.1
s.24B, amended: 2013 asp 10 s.3, s.5
s.24B, repealed (in part): 2013 asp 10 s.3, s.5
s.24C, added: 2013 asp 10 s.1
s.24C, amended: 2013 asp 10 s.3, s.5
s.24D, amended: 2013 asp 10 s.1, s.5
s.25, varied: 2013 asp 10 s.4
s.41, amended: 2013 asp 10 Sch.1 para.1
s.52A, varied: 2013 asp 10 s.4

46. Health Service Commissioners Act 1993
applied: SI 2013/160 Art.6, Art.8, SI 2013/235 Art.7, Sch.3 para.21

48. Pension Schemes Act 1993
applied: SI 2013/1893 Sch.2, SI 2013/2356 Reg.49, Reg.77, SI 2013/2734 Sch.2 para.10, Sch.2 para.24, SSI 2013/174 Reg.17, Reg.21, Reg.27
Part III, applied: SI 2013/527 Art.2
Part IV, applied: SSI 2013/174 Reg.5, Reg.18
Part IV c.II, applied: SSI 2013/174 Reg.5
Part IV c.III, applied: SI 2013/2356 Reg.88
Part IV c.IV, applied: SI 2013/2356 Reg.98, SI 2013/2734 Sch.2 para.6, Sch.2 para.20, Sch.3 para.15, Sch.3 para.23, SSI 2013/174 Reg.1, Reg.5
Part IV c.V, applied: SI 2013/2356 Reg.98, SI 2013/2734 Sch.2 para.6, Sch.2 para.20, SSI 2013/174 Reg.1, Reg.16, Reg.18
Part IV c.V, referred to: SSI 2013/174 Reg.1
Part IVA c.II, applied: SI 2013/2734 Sch.3 para.15, Sch.3 para.23
s.1, see *PI Consulting (Trustee Services) Ltd v Pensions Regulator* [2013] EWHC 3181 (Ch), [2013] Pens. L.R. 433 (Ch D), Morgan, J.
s.1, applied: SSI 2013/200 Sch.1 para.4
s.8, amended: 2013 c.30 Sch.4 para.19
s.8, applied: SI 2013/2734 Sch.2 para.12
s.9, applied: SSI 2013/174 Reg.17, Reg.21
s.12C, enabling: SI 2013/459
s.14, applied: SI 2013/2356 Reg.51, SSI 2013/174 Reg.3, Reg.10, Reg.14, Reg.17, Reg.21
s.15, applied: SSI 2013/174 Reg.17, Reg.21
s.15, varied: SI 2013/574 Art.5
s.17, amended: 2013 c.30 Sch.4 para.20
s.17, applied: SSI 2013/174 Reg.3, Reg.6, Reg 27
s.19, applied: SI 2013/2356 Reg.100
s.20, enabling: SI 2013/459
s.24D, amended: 2013 c.30 Sch.4 para.21
s.37, amended: 2013 c.30 Sch.4 para.22
s.37, enabling: SI 2013/459
s.38A, added: 2013 c.30 Sch.4 para.23
s.42A, applied: SI 2013/2734 Sch.6 para.2
s.45, applied: SI 2013/2734 Sch.6 para.3, Sch.8 para.11
s.47, amended: 2013 c.30 Sch.4 para.24
s.53, amended: 2013 c.22 Sch.9 para.52
s.55, applied: SI 2013/2356 Reg.18, Reg.97, SSI 2013/174 Reg.3, Reg.6
s.61, applied: SI 2013/2356 Reg.18, SSI 2013/174 Reg.16, Reg.18
s.71, amended: 2013 c.25 Sch.8 para.19
s.73, enabling: SI 2013/459
s.83, amended: 2013 c.25 Sch.8 para.20
s.84, amended: 2013 c.30 Sch.4 para.25
s.93, enabling: SI 2013/459
s.94, applied: SI 2013/2734 Sch.3 para.23
s.95, applied: SSI 2013/174 Reg.5
s.96, applied: SSI 2013/174 Reg.5
s.97, applied: SI 2013/2734 Sch.3 para.23, Sch.6 para.5
s.99, amended: 2013 c.30 Sch.7 para.32
s.101I, applied: SI 2013/2734 Sch.3 para.23, Sch.6 para.5
s.109, applied: SI 2013/573, SI 2013/573 Art.2
s.109, enabling: SI 2013/573
s.111A, enabling: SI 2013/2556
s.113, enabling: SI 2013/2734
s.115, amended: 2013 c.22 Sch.9 para.52
s.146, see *R. (on the application of Government Actuary's Department) v Pensions Ombudsman* [2013] EWCA Civ 901, [2013] I.C.R. 1215 (CA (Civ Div)), Lord Dyson (M.R.)
s.146, enabling: SI 2013/627
s.149, amended: SI 2013/504 Reg.21
s.150, amended: 2013 c.22 Sch.9 para.52
s.151, amended: 2013 c.22 Sch.9 para.52
s.152, amended: 2013 c.22 Sch.9 para.119
s.168, enabling: SI 2013/2734
s.181, see *PI Consulting (Trustee Services) Ltd v Pensions Regulator* [2013] EWHC 3181 (Ch), [2013] Pens. L.R. 433 (Ch D), Morgan, J.
s.181, enabling: SI 2013/459, SI 2013/627, SI 2013/2556, SI 2013/2734
s.182, enabling: SI 2013/459, SI 2013/627, SI 2013/2556, SI 2013/2734
s.183, enabling: SI 2013/459, SI 2013/2734
s.185, applied: SI 2013/459, SI 2013/627, SI 2013/2556, SI 2013/2734
s.185, repealed (in part): SI 2013/2042 Sch.1 para.15
s.185, enabling: SI 2013/459
Sch.3 para.1, amended: 2013 c.30 Sch.4 para.26
Sch.3 para.2, applied: SI 2013/2913 Art.2
Sch.3 para.2, enabling: SI 2013/2913
Sch.4, applied: 2013 c.33 Sch.6 para.5
Sch.4 para.1, varied: 2013 c.33 Sch.6 para.3
Sch.4 para.2, varied: 2013 c.33 Sch.6 para.3
Sch.4 para.3, varied: 2013 c.33 Sch.6 para.3
Sch.4 para.4, varied: 2013 c.33 Sch.6 para.3

49. Pension Schemes (Northern Ireland) Act 1993
s.145, amended: SI 2013/504 Reg.22

1994

9. Finance Act 1994

s.30, see *Ryanair Ltd v Revenue and Customs Commissioners* [2013] UKUT 176 (TCC), [2013] S.T.C. 1360 (UT (Tax)), Warren, J.
s.30, amended: 2013 c.29 s.185
s.33, enabling: SI 2013/493
s.38, amended: 2013 c.29 s.186
s.38, enabling: SI 2013/493
s.42, enabling: SI 2013/493
s.176, repealed (in part): 2013 c.2 Sch.1 Part 10
s.227B, amended: SI 2013/463 Art.7
s.230, amended: SI 2013/636 Sch.1 para.4
Sch.5A Part 2, amended: 2013 c.29 s.186
Sch.7A Part I para.3, amended: 2013 c.29 s.201
Sch.14 para.2, repealed: 2013 c.2 Sch.1 Part 10
Sch.14 para.4, repealed: 2013 c.2 Sch.1 Part 10
Sch.16 Part III para.5, repealed (in part): 2013 c.2 Sch.1 Part 10
Sch.17 para.1, repealed: 2013 c.2 Sch.1 Part 10
Sch.19 Part II para.38, repealed: 2013 c.2 Sch.1 Part 10
Sch.19 Part II para.39, repealed: 2013 c.2 Sch.1 Part 10
Sch.19 Part II para.40, repealed: 2013 c.2 Sch.1 Part 10

13. Intelligence Services Act 1994
applied: 2013 c.18 Sch.1 para.4
s.10, repealed: 2013 c.18 Sch.2 para.1
s.11, repealed (in part): 2013 c.18 Sch.2 para.1
Sch.3 para.1, repealed: 2013 c.18 Sch.2 para.1
Sch.3 para.2, repealed: 2013 c.18 Sch.2 para.1
Sch.3 para.3, repealed: 2013 c.18 Sch.2 para.1
Sch.3 para.4, repealed: 2013 c.18 Sch.2 para.1

15. Antarctic Act 1994
applied: 2013 c.15 s.13
s.3, amended: 2013 c.15 s.14
s.3, referred to: 2013 c.15 s.13
s.7, amended: 2013 c.15 s.14, s.16
s.8, amended: 2013 c.15 s.14, s.16
s.8A, added: 2013 c.15 s.16
s.8B, added: 2013 c.15 s.16
s.9, amended: 2013 c.15 s.14
s.10, amended: 2013 c.15 s.14, s.15
s.11, amended: 2013 c.15 s.14
s.12, amended: 2013 c.15 s.14, s.16
s.15, amended: 2013 c.15 s.15
s.16, amended: 2013 c.15 s.15
s.17, applied: 2013 c.15 s.11
s.19, applied: 2013 c.15 s.11
s.28, applied: 2013 c.15 s.11
s.29, applied: 2013 c.15 s.11
s.30, amended: 2013 c.15 s.15
s.31, amended: 2013 c.15 s.14, s.16
s.34, applied: 2013 c.15 s.18

17. Chiropractors Act 1994
s.10, amended: 2013 c.22 Sch.9 para.65
s.29, amended: 2013 c.22 Sch.9 para.65
s.29A, amended: 2013 c.22 Sch.9 para.65

19. Local Government (Wales) Act 1994
Sch.9 para.6, repealed: 2013 c.10 s.19

21. Coal Industry Act 1994
s.19, applied: SI 2013/3029 Sch.6 para.19, SI 2013/3035 Sch.1
s.59, amended: 2013 c.32 Sch.12 para.70, SI 2013/755 Sch.2 para.360, SI 2013/1882 Art.10

28. Merchant Shipping (Salvage and Pollution) Act 1994
Sch.2 para.7, repealed: 2013 c.22 Sch.9 para.141

30. Education Act 1994
s.20, applied: SI 2013/1793 Reg.3
s.21, amended: 2013 asp 12 Sch.1 para.3
s.22, applied: SI 2013/1793 Reg.3

31. Firearms (Amendment) Act 1994
applied: SI 2013/449 Reg.3

33. Criminal Justice and Public Order Act 1994
s.25, applied: SI 2013/1554 r.19_17
s.35, see *R. v D* [2013] EWCA Crim 465, [2013] 3 All E.R. 242 (CA (Crim Div)), Treacy, L.J.
s.35, applied: SI 2013/1554 r.37_3
s.51, see *R. v N* [2013] EWCA Crim 989, [2013] 1 W.L.R. 3900 (CA (Crim Div)), Sir John Thomas (President)
s.51, amended: 2013 c.22 Sch.17 para.36
s.51, applied: SI 2013/435 Sch.1 Part 7
s.75, applied: SI 2013/435 Sch.1 Part 7
s.102, amended: SI 2013/602 Sch.1 para.4
s.136, applied: 2013 c.22 s.55, Sch.21 para.41
s.136, varied: 2013 c.22 Sch.21 para.42
s.137, applied: 2013 c.22 s.55, Sch.21 para.41
s.137, varied: 2013 c.22 Sch.21 para.42
s.138, applied: 2013 c.22 s.55, Sch.21 para.41
s.138, varied: 2013 c.22 Sch.21 para.42, Sch.21 para.43
s.139, applied: 2013 c.22 s.55, Sch.21 para.41
s.139, varied: 2013 c.22 Sch.21 para.42
s.163, amended: SI 2013/602 Sch.1 para.4

36. Law of Property (Miscellaneous Provisions) Act 1994
s.17, amended: SI 2013/1036 Sch.1 para.224, SI 2013/2042 Sch.1 para.16

37. Drug Trafficking Act 1994
see *R. v Gangar (Shinder Singh)* [2012] EWCA Crim 1378, [2013] 1 W.L.R. 147 (CA (Crim Div)), Hughes, L.J.; see *R. v Y* [2012] EWCA Crim 2437, [2013] 1 W.L.R. 2014 (CA (Crim Div)), Sir John Thomas (President QBD); see *Sinclair v Dhillon* [2012] EWHC 3517 (Admin), [2013] Lloyd's Rep. F.C. 224 (QBD (Admin)), Haddon-Cave, J.

applied: SI 2013/1554 r.56_1
s.2, applied: SI 2013/435 Reg.4, Sch.1 para.14, Sch.2 para.26
s.3, applied: SI 2013/1554 r.56_2
s.10, applied: SI 2013/1554 r.56_5
s.11, applied: SI 2013/1554 r.56_1
s.13, applied: SI 2013/1554 r.56_3
s.14, applied: SI 2013/1554 r.56_3
s.15, applied: SI 2013/1554 r.56_3
s.22, applied: SI 2013/1554 r.56_6
s.49, applied: SI 2013/435 Sch.1 Part 7
s.50, applied: SI 2013/435 Sch.1 Part 7
s.51, applied: SI 2013/435 Sch.1 Part 7
s.52, applied: SI 2013/435 Sch.1 Part 7
s.53, applied: SI 2013/435 Sch.1 Part 7
s.55, applied: SI 2013/1554 r.56_4
s.58, applied: SI 2013/435 Sch.1 Part 7

39. Local Government etc (Scotland) Act 1994
s.2, applied: 2013 asp 3 s.9, SI 2013/192 Art.3, SI 2013/3029 Sch.1 para.19, Sch.1 para.20, Sch.2 para.6, Sch.3 para.5, Sch.6 para.21, Sch.7 para.10, SI 2013/3035 Sch.1, SSI 2013/347 Art.3
s.128, applied: SSI 2013/50 Sch.4 para.19, SSI 2013/150 Art.20, Art.21
s.129, applied: SSI 2013/150 Art.22
s.129, referred to: SSI 2013/150 Art.22
s.131, applied: SSI 2013/150 Art.21
s.134, applied: SSI 2013/150 Art.24
s.153, enabling: SSI 2013/34, SSI 2013/78
Sch.1 Part I, referred to: SSI 2013/347 Art.3
Sch.12 para.3, applied: SSI 2013/150 Art.23
Sch.12 para.7, applied: SSI 2013/150 Art.23

40. Deregulation and Contracting Out Act 1994
s.37, amended: 2013 c.32 Sch.12 para.71
s.69, enabling: SI 2013/502, SI 2013/695
s.70, applied: SI 2013/502, SI 2013/695
s.70, enabling: SI 2013/502, SI 2013/695
s.74, amended: SI 2013/1644 Sch.1
s.77, applied: SI 2013/502, SI 2013/695

1995

4. Finance Act 1995
s.5, enabling: SI 2013/1195
s.42, repealed (in part): 2013 c.2 Sch.1 Part 10
s.55, amended: 2013 c.29 Sch.9 para.6
s.55, applied: SI 2013/759 Art.2
s.55, enabling: SI 2013/759
s.57, repealed: 2013 c.2 Sch.1 Part 10
Sch.6 para.27, repealed: 2013 c.2 Sch.1 Part 10
Sch.17 Part III para.24, repealed: 2013 c.2 Sch.1 Part 10
Sch.17 Part III para.26, repealed: 2013 c.2 Sch.1 Part 10

6. Civil Evidence (Family Mediation) (Scotland) Act 1995
s.2, amended: SSI 2013/211 Sch.1 para.8
s.2, repealed (in part): SSI 2013/211 Sch.2

7. Requirements of Writing (Scotland) Act 1995
s.1, disapplied: SI 2013/1388 Reg.22

8. Agricultural Tenancies Act 1995
s.4, amended: SI 2013/1036 Sch.1 para.216

18. Jobseekers Act 1995
applied: SI 2013/378 Reg.39, Reg.41, Reg.42, Reg.68, SI 2013/381 Reg.1, SI 2013/386 Reg.32, SI 2013/480 Reg.6, SI 2013/628 Sch.1 para.22, SI 2013/983 Art.6, Art.7, Art.17, Art.18, SI 2013/1511 Art.11, SI 2013/1893 Sch.3 para.2, SI 2013/3029 Sch.1 para.11, Sch.1 para.16, Sch.9 para.9, Sch.10 para.9, SI 2013/3035 Sch.1, SSI 2013/148 Reg.6, SSI 2013/200 Sch.2 para.8
referred to: SI 2013/1511 Art.10
s.1, see *Saunderson v Secretary of State for Work and Pensions* 2013 S.L.T. 115 (IH (Ex Div)), Lord Eassie
s.1, applied: SI 2013/378 Reg.7, Reg.40, SI 2013/1179 Sch.2 para.2
s.1, referred to: SI 2013/276 Reg.7, SI 2013/378 Reg.40, Reg.46, Reg.47
s.2, applied: SI 2013/378 Reg.34, Reg.38, Reg.39, Reg.40, Reg.44, Reg.48
s.2, referred to: SI 2013/378 Reg.37
s.2, varied: SI 2013/378 Reg.69, Reg.75
s.2, enabling: SI 2013/378, SI 2013/2536
s.4, applied: 2013 c.16 Sch.1 para.1, SI 2013/378 Reg.48, Reg.49, Reg.50, Reg.51, Reg.64
s.4, enabling: SI 2013/378, SI 2013/443, SI 2013/1474, SI 2013/2536, SI 2013/3196
s.5, applied: SI 2013/378 Reg.37
s.5, enabling: SI 2013/378
s.6, applied: SI 2013/378 Reg.15
s.6, enabling: SI 2013/2536
s.6A, applied: SI 2013/378 Reg.15
s.6A, enabling: SI 2013/378
s.6B, applied: SI 2013/378 Reg.15, Reg.31
s.6B, disapplied: SI 2013/378 Reg.5
s.6B, enabling: SI 2013/378
s.6C, applied: SI 2013/378 Reg.15, Reg.21, SI 2013/2540 Reg.2
s.6C, disapplied: SI 2013/378 Reg.5
s.6D, applied: SI 2013/378 Reg.15, Reg.16, Reg.28
s.6D, disapplied: SI 2013/378 Reg.5
s.6D, enabling: SI 2013/378
s.6E, applied: SI 2013/378 Reg.15, Reg.28
s.6E, disapplied: SI 2013/378 Reg.5

s.6E, enabling: SI 2013/378
s.6F, applied: SI 2013/378 Reg.15
s.6F, disapplied: SI 2013/378 Reg.5
s.6F, enabling: SI 2013/378
s.6G, applied: SI 2013/378 Reg.15
s.6G, disapplied: SI 2013/378 Reg.5
s.6H, disapplied: SI 2013/378 Reg.5
s.6H, enabling: SI 2013/378, SI 2013/1508
s.6I, disapplied: SI 2013/378 Reg.5
s.6I, enabling: SI 2013/378
s.6J, applied: SI 2013/376 Sch.11 para.2, SI 2013/378 Reg.6, Reg.23, Reg.24, Reg.25, Reg.26, Reg.28, Reg.29, Reg.65, SI 2013/381 Reg.14, Reg.27, SI 2013/983 Art.17, Art.18
s.6J, disapplied: SI 2013/378 Reg.5
s.6J, referred to: SI 2013/378 Reg.28, Reg.46, Reg.47
s.6J, enabling: SI 2013/378, SI 2013/630
s.6K, applied: SI 2013/376 Sch.11 para.2, SI 2013/378 Reg.6, Reg.23, Reg.24, Reg.25, Reg.26, Reg.65, SI 2013/381 Reg.14, Reg.27, SI 2013/983 Art.17, Art.18
s.6K, disapplied: SI 2013/378 Reg.5
s.6K, referred to: SI 2013/378 Reg.46, Reg.47
s.6K, enabling: SI 2013/378
s.7, enabling: SI 2013/2536
s.8, enabling: SI 2013/443
s.12, enabling: SI 2013/276, SI 2013/378, SI 2013/443, SI 2013/1508, SI 2013/2536
s.13, enabling: SI 2013/443
s.14, applied: SI 2013/378 Reg.37
s.17, enabling: SI 2013/2536
s.17A, see *R. (on the application of Reilly) v Secretary of State for Work and Pensions* [2013] EWCA Civ 66, [2013] 1 W.L.R. 2239 (CA (Civ Div)), Pill, L.J.; see *R. (on the application of Reilly) v Secretary of State for Work and Pensions* [2013] UKSC 68, [2013] 3 W.L.R. 1276 (SC), Lord Neuberger (President)
s.17A, applied: 2013 c.17 s.1, SI 2013/276 Reg.3, SI 2013/2540 Reg.2, SI 2013/3029 Reg.2, SI 2013/3035 Sch.1
s.17A, enabling: SI 2013/276, SI 2013/2584
s.19, applied: SI 2013/386 Reg.32, Reg.33, SI 2013/983 Art.17, Art.18, Art.19, SI 2013/3029 Reg.2, SI 2013/3035 Sch.1
s.19A, applied: SI 2013/386 Reg.32, Reg.33, SI 2013/983 Art.17, Art.18, Art.19, SI 2013/3029 Reg.2, SI 2013/3035 Sch.1
s.19A, enabling: SI 2013/443
s.19B, applied: SI 2013/3029 Reg.2, SI 2013/3035 Sch.1
s.19B, enabling: SI 2013/443
s.19C, enabling: SI 2013/2536
s.20, enabling: SI 2013/2536
s.20E, enabling: SI 2013/276
s.26, applied: SI 2013/471 Reg.11, Reg.13, SI 2013/480 Reg.24, Reg.40
s.35, applied: SI 2013/378 Reg.3
s.35, varied: SI 2013/378 Reg.70
s.35, enabling: SI 2013/276, SI 2013/378, SI 2013/443, SI 2013/1474, SI 2013/1508, SI 2013/2536, SI 2013/2584, SI 2013/2722, SI 2013/3196
s.36, enabling: SI 2013/276, SI 2013/378, SI 2013/443, SI 2013/1474, SI 2013/1508, SI 2013/2536, SI 2013/2584, SI 2013/2722, SI 2013/3196
s.37, applied: SI 2013/378, SI 2013/2722
Sch.1, enabling: SI 2013/378
Sch.1 para.1, enabling: SI 2013/1508, SI 2013/2536
Sch.1 para.2, amended: SI 2013/630 Reg.10
Sch.1 para.4, applied: SI 2013/378 Reg.36, SI 2013/3029 Reg.2, Sch.13 para.2, SI 2013/3035 Sch.1
Sch.1 para.4, disapplied: SI 2013/378 Reg.36, SI 2013/381 Reg.48
Sch.1 para.8B, enabling: SI 2013/2722
Sch.1 para.12, enabling: SI 2013/2536
Sch.1 para.16, enabling: SI 2013/1508

21. Merchant Shipping Act 1995

see *Cosmotrade SA v Kairos Shipping Ltd* [2013] EWHC 1904 (Comm), [2013] 2 Lloyd's Rep. 535 (QBD (Comm)), Simon, J.
applied: SI 2013/1785 Reg.16, Reg.17
Part IX, applied: 2013 c.15 Sch.1 para.5, SI 2013/648 Art.62, SSI 2013/288 Art.8
s.18, enabling: SI 2013/1115
s.47, amended: 2013 c.23 s.10
s.85, enabling: SI 2013/1473, SI 2013/1785
s.86, applied: SI 2013/1473, SI 2013/1785, SI 2013/2944
s.86, enabling: SI 2013/1473, SI 2013/1785, SI 2013/2944
s.142, enabling: SI 2013/2944
s.145, applied: SI 2013/1785 Reg.17
s.193, amended: 2013 c.23 s.8
s.197, repealed (in part): 2013 c.23 s.9
s.197A, added: 2013 c.23 s.9
s.214, substituted: 2013 c.25 Sch.8 para.21
s.252, amended: 2013 c.23 s.11
s.255, applied: SSI 2013/46 Art.13
s.255C, amended: 2013 c.23 s.8
s.255C, repealed (in part): 2013 c.23 s.8
s.255F, repealed (in part): 2013 c.23 s.8
s.258, applied: SI 2013/1785 Reg.16
s.258, varied: SI 2013/1785 Reg.16

s.259, applied: SI 2013/1785 Reg.14, Reg.16
s.259, varied: SI 2013/1785 Reg.16
s.260, applied: SI 2013/1785 Reg.16
s.260, varied: SI 2013/1785 Reg.16
s.261, applied: SI 2013/1785 Reg.10, Reg.16
s.261, varied: SI 2013/1785 Reg.16
s.262, applied: SI 2013/1785 Reg.16
s.262, varied: SI 2013/1785 Reg.16
s.263, applied: SI 2013/1785 Reg.16
s.263, varied: SI 2013/1785 Reg.16
s.264, applied: SI 2013/1785 Reg.16
s.264, varied: SI 2013/1785 Reg.16
s.265, applied: SI 2013/1785 Reg.16
s.265, varied: SI 2013/1785 Reg.16
s.266, applied: SI 2013/1785 Reg.16
s.266, varied: SI 2013/1785 Reg.16
s.267, enabling: SI 2013/2882
s.284, referred to: SI 2013/1785 Reg.17
s.284, varied: SI 2013/1785 Reg.17, Reg.20
Sch.7, referred to: 2013 c.15 Sch.1 para.2
Sch.13 para.7, repealed (in part): 2013 c.22 Sch.9 para.141

23. Goods Vehicles (Licensing of Operators) Act 1995

s.1, amended: SI 2013/1644 Sch.1
s.2, enabling: SI 2013/1750, SI 2013/1753
s.5, amended: SI 2013/1644 Sch.1
s.7, amended: SI 2013/1644 Sch.1
s.8, amended: SI 2013/1644 Sch.1
s.9, amended: SI 2013/1644 Sch.1
s.10, amended: SI 2013/1644 Sch.1
s.11, amended: SI 2013/1644 Sch.1
s.12, amended: SI 2013/1644 Sch.1
s.13A, amended: SI 2013/1644 Sch.1
s.13C, amended: SI 2013/1644 Sch.1
s.14, amended: SI 2013/1644 Sch.1
s.16, amended: SI 2013/1644 Sch.1
s.17, amended: SI 2013/1644 Sch.1
s.18, amended: SI 2013/1644 Sch.1
s.19, amended: SI 2013/1644 Sch.1
s.20, amended: SI 2013/1644 Sch.1
s.21, amended: SI 2013/1644 Sch.1
s.22, amended: SI 2013/1644 Sch.1
s.23, amended: SI 2013/1644 Sch.1
s.24, amended: SI 2013/1644 Sch.1
s.25, amended: SI 2013/1644 Sch.1
s.26, amended: SI 2013/1644 Sch.1
s.27, amended: SI 2013/1644 Sch.1
s.28, amended: SI 2013/1644 Sch.1
s.29, amended: SI 2013/1644 Sch.1
s.30, amended: SI 2013/1644 Sch.1
s.31, amended: SI 2013/1644 Sch.1
s.32, amended: SI 2013/1644 Sch.1
s.34, amended: SI 2013/1644 Sch.1
s.35, amended: SI 2013/1644 Sch.1
s.36, amended: SI 2013/1644 Sch.1
s.37, amended: SI 2013/1644 Sch.1
s.42, amended: SI 2013/1644 Sch.1
s.43, amended: SI 2013/1644 Sch.1
s.44, amended: SI 2013/1644 Sch.1
s.45, amended: SI 2013/1644 Sch.1
s.48, amended: SI 2013/1644 Sch.1
s.49, amended: SI 2013/1644 Sch.1
s.57, applied: SI 2013/1750, SI 2013/1753
s.57, enabling: SI 2013/1750, SI 2013/1753
s.58, amended: SI 2013/1644 Sch.1
s.58, repealed (in part): SI 2013/1644 Sch.1
Sch.1A para.9, amended: SI 2013/1644 Sch.1
Sch.1A para.10, amended: SI 2013/1644 Sch.1
Sch.1A para.12, amended: SI 2013/1644 Sch.1
Sch.2 para.1, amended: SI 2013/1644 Sch.1
Sch.3 para.15, amended: SI 2013/1644 Sch.1
Sch.3 para.17, amended: SI 2013/1644 Sch.1
Sch.4 para.5, added: SI 2013/1644 Sch.1
Sch.5 para.2, amended: SI 2013/1644 Sch.1
Sch.5 para.3, amended: SI 2013/1644 Sch.1

25. Environment Act 1995

referred to: 2013 c.27 s.10
Part III, applied: SI 2013/2356 Sch.2 para.18
s.1, applied: SI 2013/1821 Art.5
s.4, amended: SI 2013/755 Sch.2 para.362
s.5, amended: SI 2013/755 Sch.2 para.364
s.5, substituted: SI 2013/755 Sch.2 para.363
s.6, amended: SI 2013/755 Sch.2 para.365
s.6, substituted: SI 2013/755 Sch.2 para.363
s.7, substituted: SI 2013/755 Sch.2 para.363
s.8, amended: SI 2013/755 Sch.2 para.366
s.8, substituted: SI 2013/755 Sch.2 para.363
s.9, amended: SI 2013/755 Sch.2 para.367
s.9, substituted: SI 2013/755 Sch.2 para.363
s.9A, added: SI 2013/755 Sch.2 para.368
s.9A, substituted: SI 2013/755 Sch.2 para.363
s.10, amended: SI 2013/755 Sch.2 para.369
s.10, substituted: SI 2013/755 Sch.2 para.363
s.12, applied: SI 2013/755 Art.9
s.12, repealed: SI 2013/755 Art.9
s.13, applied: SI 2013/755 Art.9
s.13, repealed: SI 2013/755 Art.9
s.37, amended: SI 2013/755 Sch.2 para.370
s.37, disapplied: SI 2013/1821 Art.6
s.38, amended: SI 2013/755 Sch.2 para.370
s.38, disapplied: SI 2013/1821 Art.6
s.39, amended: SI 2013/755 Sch.2 para.370
s.40, amended: SI 2013/755 Sch.2 para.370, Sch.2 para.371
s.40, applied: SI 2013/755 Sch.7 para.5, Sch.7 para.6, Sch.7 para.7
s.41, amended: SI 2013/755 Sch.2 para.370, Sch.2 para.372, SI 2013/1821 Art.16

s.41, applied: SI 2013/1821 Art.28, SI 2013/3113 Reg.59, Reg.65
s.41A, amended: SI 2013/755 Sch.2 para.370, SI 2013/1821 Art.17, SI 2013/3135 Reg.13
s.41A, applied: SI 2013/3135
s.41B, added: SI 2013/1821 Art.19
s.41B, amended: SI 2013/755 Sch.2 para.370
s.41B, applied: SI 2013/1821 Art.28
s.41B, disapplied: SI 2013/1821 Art.28
s.41C, added: SI 2013/1821 Art.19
s.41C, amended: SI 2013/755 Sch.2 para.370
s.42, amended: SI 2013/755 Sch.2 para.370, Sch.2 para.373, SI 2013/1821 Art.18, Art.20
s.42, applied: SI 2013/1821 Art.21, Art.28
s.42, disapplied: SI 2013/1821 Art.28
s.43, amended: SI 2013/755 Sch.2 para.370
s.44, amended: SI 2013/755 Sch.2 para.370
s.44, disapplied: SI 2013/1821 Art.6
s.45, amended: SI 2013/755 Sch.2 para.370
s.45, applied: SI 2013/1821 Art.7
s.46, amended: SI 2013/755 Sch.2 para.370
s.46, disapplied: SI 2013/1821 Art.10
s.46A, amended: SI 2013/755 Sch.2 para.370
s.47, amended: SI 2013/755 Sch.2 para.370
s.47, disapplied: SI 2013/1821 Art.8
s.48, amended: SI 2013/755 Sch.2 para.370
s.48, applied: 2013 asp 4 Sch.3
s.48, disapplied: SI 2013/1821 Art.8
s.49, amended: SI 2013/755 Sch.2 para.370
s.49, disapplied: SI 2013/1821 Art.8, Art.10
s.50, amended: SI 2013/755 Sch.2 para.370
s.50, disapplied: SI 2013/1821 Art.8
s.51, amended: SI 2013/755 Sch.2 para.370
s.51, disapplied: SI 2013/1821 Art.8
s.52, amended: SI 2013/755 Sch.2 para.370
s.52, disapplied: SI 2013/1821 Art.8
s.53, amended: SI 2013/755 Sch.2 para.370, Sch.2 para.374
s.53, applied: SI 2013/1821 Art.9
s.53, disapplied: SI 2013/1821 Art.9
s.54, amended: SI 2013/755 Sch.2 para.370
s.55, amended: SI 2013/755 Sch.2 para.370
s.56, amended: SI 2013/755 Sch.2 para.370, Sch.2 para.375, SI 2013/1821 Art.30, SI 2013/3113 Reg.94
s.66, amended: SI 2013/755 Sch.2 para.376
s.72, amended: SI 2013/755 Sch.2 para.376
s.80, amended: SI 2013/755 Sch.2 para.377
s.81, amended: SI 2013/755 Sch.2 para.378
s.87, amended: SI 2013/755 Sch.2 para.379
s.91, amended: SI 2013/755 Sch.2 para.380
s.93, applied: SI 2013/1857(b), SI 2013/1857(c), SI 2013/1857, SI 2013/1857(a)
s.93, referred to: SI 2013/1857(b)
s.93, enabling: SI 2013/1857
s.94, amended: SI 2013/755 Sch.2 para.381
s.94, enabling: SI 2013/1857
s.94A, enabling: SI 2013/1857
s.95, enabling: SI 2013/1857
s.96, applied: SI 2013/680 Art.15
s.108, amended: SI 2013/755 Sch.2 para.382
s.108, referred to: 2013 c.32 Sch.5 para.1
s.108, varied: SI 2013/1675 Reg.16
s.110, applied: SI 2013/2258 Sch.1 Part 1
s.111, amended: SI 2013/755 Sch.2 para.383
s.113, amended: SI 2013/755 Sch.2 para.384
s.115, amended: SI 2013/755 Sch.2 para.385
s.122, applied: SI 2013/755 Sch.7 para.7
Sch.1, applied: SI 2013/1821 Art.5
Sch.3 para.1, repealed: SI 2013/755 Art.9
Sch.3 para.2, repealed: SI 2013/755 Art.9
Sch.3 para.3, repealed: SI 2013/755 Art.9
Sch.3 para.4, repealed: SI 2013/755 Art.9
Sch.3 para.5, repealed: SI 2013/755 Art.9
Sch.3 para.6, repealed: SI 2013/755 Art.9
Sch.3 para.7, repealed: SI 2013/755 Art.9
Sch.7 para.4, amended: SI 2013/755 Sch.2 para.386
Sch.7 para.14, amended: SI 2013/755 Sch.2 para.386
Sch.14, applied: 2013 c.27 s.10
Sch.14, substituted: 2013 c.27 Sch.3 para.6
Sch.14 paraA.1, added: 2013 c.27 Sch.3 para.2
Sch.14 para.1, amended: 2013 c.27 Sch.3 para.3
Sch.14 para.2, amended: 2013 c.27 Sch.3 para.4
Sch.14 para.2A, added: 2013 c.27 Sch.3 para.5
Sch.14 para.2B, added: 2013 c.27 Sch.3 para.5
Sch.14 para.3, amended: 2013 c.27 Sch.3 para.6
Sch.14 para.3A, amended: 2013 c.27 Sch.3 para.7
Sch.14 para.4, amended: 2013 c.27 Sch.3 para.8
Sch.14 para.4, applied: 2013 c.27 s.10
Sch.14 para.6, applied: 2013 c.27 s.10
Sch.14 para.7, applied: 2013 c.27 s.10
Sch.14 para.12, amended: 2013 c.27 Sch.3 para.9
Sch.20 para.5, amended: SI 2013/755 Sch.2 para.387
Sch.22 para.7, repealed: 2013 c.32 Sch.12 para.30
Sch.22 para.8, repealed: 2013 c.32 Sch.12 para.30
Sch.22 para.9, repealed: 2013 c.32 Sch.12 para.30
Sch.23 Part I para.3, repealed: SI 2013/755 Art.9

26. Pensions Act 1995

disapplied: SI 2013/2734 Sch.2 para.27
s.10, amended: 2013 c.22 Sch.9 para.52
s.10, enabling: SI 2013/2734
s.22, applied: SI 2013/2734 Sch.8 para.3
s.23, applied: SI 2013/2734 Sch.8 para.3
s.35, applied: SI 2013/2734 Sch.3 para.13, Sch.3 para.28, Sch.3 para.30

s.37, applied: SI 2013/2734 Sch.4 para.8
s.40, applied: SI 2013/2734 Sch.3 para.32, Sch.3 para.33
s.41, applied: SI 2013/2734 Sch.3 para.5, Sch.3 para.24, Sch.3 para.25
s.41, enabling: SI 2013/2734
s.47, applied: SI 2013/2734 Sch.3 para.31
s.49, referred to: SI 2013/2356 Reg.69
s.49, enabling: SI 2013/2556
s.50, applied: SI 2013/2734 Sch.2 para.18
s.50, disapplied: SI 2013/2734 Sch.2 para.23
s.50, referred to: SSI 2013/174 Reg.11
s.68, enabling: SI 2013/459, SI 2013/1754
s.72A, applied: SI 2013/2734 Sch.8 para.15
s.75A, enabling: SI 2013/627
s.87, applied: SI 2013/2734 Sch.3 para.12
s.120, applied: SI 2013/627, SI 2013/1754, SI 2013/2556, SI 2013/2734
s.120, enabling: SI 2013/459
s.124, applied: SI 2013/2734 Reg.24
s.124, enabling: SI 2013/459, SI 2013/627, SI 2013/1754, SI 2013/2556, SI 2013/2734
s.170, repealed: 2013 c.25 Sch.11 para.7
s.174, enabling: SI 2013/459, SI 2013/627, SI 2013/1754, SI 2013/2556, SI 2013/2734

30. Landlord and Tenant (Covenants) Act 1995
s.8, amended: 2013 c.22 Sch.9 para.52
s.10, amended: 2013 c.22 Sch.9 para.52

35. Criminal Appeal Act 1995
s.9, applied: SI 2013/1554 r.68_1
s.11, applied: SI 2013/1554 r.63_1
s.22, amended: 2013 c.22 Sch.8 para.186

36. Children (Scotland) Act 1995
see *Glasgow City Council, Petitioner* [2013] CSOH 118, 2013 S.L.T. 917 (OH), Lady Wise
applied: SSI 2013/150 Art.2, Art.3, Art.4, Art.8, Art.11, Art.14, Art.19, Art.20
disapplied: SSI 2013/150 Art.2
referred to: SSI 2013/150 Art.2
Part II, applied: SI 2013/1465 Art.4, SSI 2013/150 Art.6, Art.7, Art.9, Art.13
Part II c.1, applied: SSI 2013/205 Reg.10
s.1, see *Midlothian Council v M* [2013] CSIH 71, 2013 Fam. L.R. 104 (IH (Ex Div)), Lord Clarke
s.1, referred to: SI 2013/376 Reg.4A
s.2, see *Midlothian Council v M* [2013] CSIH 71, 2013 Fam. L.R. 104 (IH (Ex Div)), Lord Clarke; see *W v C* 2013 Fam. L.R. 73 (Sh Ct (Lothian) (Edinburgh)), Sheriff J M Scott, QC
s.2, referred to: SI 2013/376 Reg.4A
s.3, amended: SSI 2013/211 Sch.1 para.9
s.11, see *M v S* [2013] CSOH 79, 2013 Fam. L.R. 52 (OH), Lord Brailsford; see *V v Locality Reporter Manager, Stirling* 2013 Fam. L.R. 69 (Sh Ct (Tayside) (Stirling)), Sheriff A W Robertson; see *W v C* 2013 Fam. L.R. 73 (Sh Ct (Lothian) (Edinburgh)), Sheriff J M Scott, QC
s.11, applied: SSI 2013/50 Sch.1 para.26
s.13, applied: SI 2013/3029 Sch.10 para.49, SI 2013/3035 Sch.1
s.17, amended: SSI 2013/211 Sch.1 para.9
s.17, applied: 2013 asp 13 s.7
s.17, enabling: SSI 2013/14, SSI 2013/149, SSI 2013/210
s.19, applied: SSI 2013/150 Art.12
s.22, amended: SSI 2013/137 Reg.5
s.22, applied: 2013 asp 1 s.1, s.8, s.11, SI 2013/3029 Sch.9 para.33, Sch.10 para.23, SI 2013/3035 Sch.1
s.23, applied: 2013 asp 1 s.1
s.24, applied: 2013 asp 1 s.1, s.3
s.25, applied: SSI 2013/205 Reg.9
s.26, applied: SI 2013/379 Reg.37, SI 2013/3029 Sch.9 para.31, SI 2013/3035 Sch.1
s.29, applied: SI 2013/376 Sch.10 para.17, SI 2013/3029 Sch.9 para.33, Sch.9 para.34, Sch.10 para.23, Sch.10 para.24, SI 2013/3035 Sch.1
s.30, applied: SI 2013/376 Sch.10 para.17, SI 2013/3029 Sch.9 para.33, Sch.10 para.23, SI 2013/3035 Sch.1
s.31, enabling: SSI 2013/210
s.33, amended: SI 2013/1465 Sch.1 Part 3, Sch.2 Part 2
s.33, repealed (in part): SI 2013/1465 Sch.2 Part 2
s.38, applied: SI 2013/1465 Art.10
s.41, applied: SSI 2013/150 Art.25
s.51, see *G v Authority Reporter, City of Aberdeen* [2013] CSIH 33, 2013 S.L.T. 538 (IH (2 Div)), The Lord Justice Clerk (Carloway); see *J, Appellant* 2013 S.L.T. (Sh Ct) 18 (Sh Ct (Glasgow)), Sheriff A D Miller
s.51, applied: SSI 2013/150 Art.13, SSI 2013/162 r.7
s.52, applied: SSI 2013/146 Art.2
s.53, amended: SSI 2013/119 Sch.1 para.15
s.54, applied: SSI 2013/150 Art.14
s.56, applied: SSI 2013/150 Art.15
s.57, see *NJ v Lord Advocate* [2013] CSOH 27, 2013 S.L.T. 347 (OH), Lord Brailsford
s.57, applied: SSI 2013/150 Art.16
s.59, applied: SSI 2013/150 Art.16
s.59, referred to: SSI 2013/150 Art.16
s.60, applied: SSI 2013/150 Art.16
s.60, referred to: SSI 2013/150 Art.16
s.61, applied: SSI 2013/150 Art.17
s.64, applied: SSI 2013/150 Art.18, Art.25
s.65, referred to: SSI 2013/150 Art.16
s.68, applied: SSI 2013/150 Art.19

s.70, applied: SI 2013/1465 Art.4, SSI 2013/150 Art.10, Art.11
s.70, repealed (in part): SI 2013/1465 Art.20
s.70, enabling: SSI 2013/6
s.74, applied: SI 2013/1465 Art.4
s.74, repealed: SI 2013/1465 Sch.2 Part 2
s.75, enabling: SSI 2013/205
s.82, applied: SI 2013/1465 Art.4
s.82, repealed (in part): SI 2013/1465 Sch.2 Part 2
s.83, applied: SI 2013/1465 Art.4
s.83, repealed (in part): SI 2013/1465 Sch.2 Part 2
s.85, see *G v Authority Reporter* 2013 S.L.T. (Sh Ct) 15 (Sh Ct (Tayside) (Alloa)), Sheriff Principal R A Dunlop, QC
s.85, applied: SSI 2013/150 Art.19
s.91, applied: SSI 2013/150 Art.2
s.91, enabling: SSI 2013/172
s.93, see *V v Locality Reporter Manager, Stirling* 2013 Fam. L.R. 69 (Sh Ct (Tayside) (Stirling)), Sheriff A W Robertson; see *W v Children's Reporter* 2013 S.L.T. (Sh Ct) 99 (Sh Ct (Glasgow)), Sheriff M Bovey, QC
s.93, amended: SI 2013/1465 Sch.1 para.5, Sch.2 Part 1, Sch.2 Part 2, SSI 2013/211 Sch.1 para.9, Sch.2
s.93, applied: SI 2013/377 Reg.28, SI 2013/1465 Art.4, SSI 2013/150 Art.9
s.101, applied: SSI 2013/50 Sch.4 para.20
s.105, amended: SI 2013/1465 Sch.2 Part 2
s.105, repealed (in part): SI 2013/1465 Sch.2 Part 2

38. Civil Evidence Act 1995

see *A&E Television Networks LLC v Discovery Communications Europe Ltd* [2013] EWHC 109 (Ch), [2013] E.T.M.R. 32 (Ch D), Peter Smith, J.
applied: SI 2013/1554 r.62_11
disapplied: SI 2013/1554 r.62_15
s.1, applied: SI 2013/1554 r.50_1
s.1, referred to: SI 2013/1554 r.62_11, r.50_1
s.2, applied: SI 2013/1554 r.62_11, r.50_6
s.2, disapplied: SI 2013/1554 r.61_8
s.5, applied: SI 2013/1554 r.62_15
s.5, referred to: SI 2013/1554 r.50_8
s.13, referred to: SI 2013/1554 r.62_11, r.50_1

39. Criminal Law (Consolidation) (Scotland) Act 1995

s.18, enabling: SSI 2013/4, SSI 2013/229
s.24, amended: 2013 c.22 s.55, Sch.21 para.45
s.24, applied: 2013 c.22 Sch.21 para.50
s.24, referred to: 2013 c.22 Sch.21 para.49
s.25, amended: 2013 c.22 Sch.21 para.46
s.25, referred to: 2013 c.22 Sch.21 para.49
s.25A, amended: 2013 c.22 Sch.21 para.47
s.25A, applied: 2013 c.22 Sch.21 para.50
s.25A, referred to: 2013 c.22 Sch.21 para.50
s.26, applied: 2013 c.22 Sch.21 para.49
s.26A, amended: 2013 c.22 s.55
s.26B, amended: 2013 c.22 s.55, Sch.21 para.48
s.44, applied: 2013 asp 14 Sch.5 para.11, 2013 c.33 s.87, SI 2013/971 Reg.26, SI 2013/1389 Reg.15

40. Criminal Procedure (Consequential Provisions) (Scotland) Act 1995

Sch.4 para.97, repealed (in part): SSI 2013/211 Sch.2

45. Gas Act 1995

s.6, enabling: SI 2013/2174

46. Criminal Procedure (Scotland) Act 1995

see *Brodie (George) v HM Advocate* 2013 J.C. 142 (HCJ), The Lord Justice General (Gill); see *Dunn v W* 2013 S.L.T. (Sh Ct) 2 (Sh Ct (Glasgow)), Sheriff J A Baird; see *Griffith (Javaughn) v HM Advocate* [2013] HCJAC 84, 2013 S.L.T. 944 (HCJ), Lord Eassie; see *HM Advocate v Cheung* 2013 S.L.T. (Sh Ct) 131 (Sh Ct (Tayside) (Alloa)), Sheriff A N Brown; see *I v Dunn* 2013 J.C. 82 (HCJ), Lady Paton; see *Singh (Sukhdev) v HM Advocate* [2013] HCJAC 69, 2013 S.C.C.R. 337 (HCJ), The Lord Justice Clerk (Carloway)
applied: SI 2013/1387 Reg.9, SI 2013/1478 Reg.21, SI 2013/3029 Reg.26, SI 2013/3035 Sch.1 Part X, applied: SI 2013/1387 Reg.9, SI 2013/1478 Reg.21
s.18, see *Lukstins (Indulis) v HM Advocate* 2013 J.C. 124 (HCJ), Lady Paton
s.18, applied: SSI 2013/35 Reg.13, SSI 2013/43 Reg.9
s.18E, amended: SSI 2013/211 Sch.1 para.10
s.18E, repealed (in part): SSI 2013/211 Sch.1 para.10
s.19, applied: SSI 2013/35 Reg.13, SSI 2013/43 Reg.9
s.19A, applied: SSI 2013/35 Reg.13, SSI 2013/43 Reg.9
s.19AA, applied: SSI 2013/35 Reg.13, SSI 2013/43 Reg.9
s.43, applied: SSI 2013/194 r.12, r.90, SSI 2013/205 Reg.12
s.44, amended: SI 2013/1465 Sch.3 para.2
s.44, applied: SSI 2013/205 Reg.11
s.44, enabling: SSI 2013/205
s.46, amended: SSI 2013/211 Sch.1 para.10
s.48, amended: SSI 2013/211 Sch.1 para.10
s.49, amended: SSI 2013/211 Sch.1 para.10
s.49, applied: SSI 2013/194 r.31, r.32, r.34, r.35, r.44, r.75, r.84
s.51, amended: SSI 2013/211 Sch.1 para.10
s.51, applied: SSI 2013/205 Reg.12

s.56, applied: SSI 2013/35 Reg.13
s.59A, applied: SI 2013/376 Reg.19, SI 2013/377 Reg.31, SI 2013/379 Reg.63, Reg.96
s.59A, referred to: SI 2013/381 Sch.1 para.5
s.70, amended: 2013 c.21 s.6
s.72, referred to: SSI 2013/72 r.5
s.112, applied: SI 2013/7 Art.13
s.121, applied: SI 2013/7 Art.14
s.134, referred to: SI 2013/1387 Reg.9, SI 2013/1478 Reg.21
s.136, applied: 2013 c.32 Sch.10 para.4, SI 2013/164 Reg.14, SI 2013/233 Reg.13, SI 2013/1478 Reg.22, SI 2013/1877 Reg.17
s.136, disapplied: 2013 asp 14 s.15, 2013 c.7 Sch.2 para.2, SI 2013/233 Reg.13
s.136, referred to: 2013 c.21 s.1
s.138, applied: SSI 2013/194 r.14
s.141, amended: 2013 c.21 s.6
s.182, applied: SI 2013/1387 Reg.9, SI 2013/1478 Reg.21
s.216, applied: SSI 2013/205 Reg.12
s.221, applied: SSI 2013/189 Art.11
s.222, applied: SSI 2013/189 Art.11
s.227ZJ, enabling: SSI 2013/6
s.230A, applied: SSI 2013/6 Reg.3, Reg.4
s.234CA, applied: SSI 2013/6 Reg.3, Reg.4
s.245A, enabling: SSI 2013/6
s.245C, enabling: SSI 2013/6
s.246, applied: SI 2013/335 Reg.4, Reg.9, SI 2013/349 Reg.106, Sch.7 para.15
s.262, amended: SSI 2013/211 Sch.1 para.10
s.285, amended: SSI 2013/119 Sch.1 para.16
s.288AA, see *Kapri v Lord Advocate* [2013] UKSC 48, [2013] 1 W.L.R. 2324 (SC), Lord Hope, J.S.C. (Deputy President)
s.288AA, applied: SI 2013/7 Art.7, Art.9, Art.13, Art.14
s.288AA, varied: SI 2013/7 Art.10
s.288ZA, applied: SI 2013/7 Art.8
s.288ZB, applied: SI 2013/7 Art.6
s.302, applied: SI 2013/335 Reg.4, Reg.9, SI 2013/349 Reg.106, Sch.2 para.3, Sch.4 para.31, Sch.5 para.21, Sch.7 para.15, SI 2013/898 Sch.1 para.23, Sch.4 para.31, Sch.5 para.19
s.302A, applied: SI 2013/335 Reg.4, Reg.9
s.305, enabling: SSI 2013/72, SSI 2013/196, SSI 2013/198
s.307, see *Murphy (Donna) v HM Advocate* 2013 J.C. 60 (HCJ), Lord Carloway
s.307, amended: 2013 c.22 s.55, SSI 2013/211 Sch.1 para.10, Sch.2
Sch.1, referred to: SI 2013/349 Reg.105, Sch.7 para.29
Sch.3, applied: SSI 2013/194 r.14
Sch.8 para.8, amended: SSI 2013/211 Sch.1 para.10

50. Disability Discrimination Act 1995
Part II, applied: 2013 c.22 Sch.4 para.4
s.58, applied: 2013 c.22 Sch.4 para.4

53. Criminal Injuries Compensation Act 1995
s.7A, applied: SSI 2013/50 Sch.1 para.22
s.7B, applied: SSI 2013/50 Sch.1 para.22
s.7C, applied: SSI 2013/50 Sch.1 para.22
s.7D, applied: SSI 2013/50 Sch.1 para.22

1996

6. Chemical Weapons Act 1996
s.20, enabling: SI 2013/1129

8. Finance Act 1996
s.42, amended: 2013 c.29 s.198
s.51, enabling: SI 2013/658
s.53, enabling: SI 2013/658
s.70, amended: SI 2013/755 Sch.2 para.389
s.153, repealed: 2013 c.2 Sch.1 Part 10
s.156, repealed: 2013 c.2 Sch.1 Part 10
Sch.5 Part VII para.35, amended: SI 2013/755 Sch.2 para.390
Sch.6 para.11, repealed: 2013 c.2 Sch.1 Part 10
Sch.7 para.20, repealed: 2013 c.2 Sch.1 Part 10
Sch.7 para.26, repealed: 2013 c.2 Sch.1 Part 10
Sch.14 para.26, repealed: 2013 c.2 Sch.1 Part 10
Sch.20 para.38, repealed: 2013 c.2 Sch.1 Part 10
Sch.21 para.19, repealed: 2013 c.2 Sch.1 Part 10
Sch.21 para.45, repealed: 2013 c.2 Sch.1 Part 10
Sch.21 para.46, repealed: 2013 c.2 Sch.1 Part 10
Sch.21 para.48, repealed: 2013 c.2 Sch.1 Part 10
Sch.36 para.1, repealed: 2013 c.2 Sch.1 Part 10
Sch.36 para.3, repealed (in part): 2013 c.2 Sch.1 Part 10
Sch.37 Part III para.11, repealed (in part): 2013 c.2 Sch.1 Part 10

14. Reserve Forces Act 1996
Part I, applied: 2013 c.12 Sch.1 para.1, Sch.2 para.1, 2013 c.28 Sch.1
Part III, applied: 2013 c.12 Sch.1 para.1, Sch.2 para.1, 2013 c.28 Sch.1
Part IV, applied: 2013 c.12 Sch.1 para.1, Sch.2 para.1, 2013 c.28 Sch.1
Part V, applied: 2013 c.12 Sch.1 para.1, Sch.2 para.1, 2013 c.28 Sch.1
s.1, applied: SI 2013/3104 Sch.2 para.30
s.4, applied: 2013 c.25 Sch.5 para.28, Sch.6 para.15
s.8, applied: 2013 c.25 Sch.5 para.28, Sch.6 para.15

16. Police Act 1996

s.2, applied: SSI 2013/39 Reg.9, SSI 2013/62 Reg.11
s.50, amended: 2013 c.25 Sch.8 para.23
s.50, enabling: SI 2013/1780, SI 2013/2793
s.51, amended: 2013 c.25 Sch.8 para.24
s.51, repealed (in part): 2013 c.25 Sch.8 para.24
s.52, amended: 2013 c.25 Sch.8 para.25
s.57, amended: 2013 c.22 Sch.8 para.39
s.59, amended: SI 2013/602 Sch.1 para.5
s.59, repealed (in part): 2013 c.22 Sch.8 para.40
s.60, amended: SI 2013/602 Sch.1 para.5
s.60, applied: SI 2013/3189, SSI 2013/86
s.60, enabling: SI 2013/3189, SSI 2013/86
s.61, referred to: SSI 2013/35 Reg.34
s.61, repealed (in part): 2013 c.22 Sch.8 para.41, SI 2013/602 Sch.1 para.5
s.62, amended: 2013 c.22 Sch.8 para.42, SI 2013/602 Sch.1 para.5, SSI 2013/119 Sch.1 para.17
s.62, referred to: SSI 2013/35 Reg.34
s.62, repealed (in part): 2013 c.22 Sch.8 para.42
s.63, amended: SI 2013/602 Sch.1 para.5
s.63, applied: SI 2013/281, SI 2013/1778, SI 2013/1780, SI 2013/2325, SI 2013/2793
s.63, repealed (in part): 2013 c.22 Sch.8 para.43
s.63, substituted: SI 2013/602 Sch.2 para.25
s.64, repealed (in part): 2013 c.22 Sch.8 para.44, SI 2013/602 Sch.1 para.5
s.88, amended: 2013 c.22 Sch.8 para.45
s.89, amended: SI 2013/602 Sch.2 para.25
s.90, repealed (in part): 2013 c.22 Sch.8 para.46
s.91, repealed (in part): 2013 c.22 Sch.8 para.47
s.97, amended: 2013 c.22 Sch.8 para.48
s.97, applied: SI 2013/602 Sch.3 para.5, SI 2013/2325 Reg.44
s.97, referred to: 2013 c.22 Sch.8 para.10
s.97, repealed (in part): 2013 c.22 Sch.8 para.48, SI 2013/602 Sch.2 para.25
s.98, amended: SI 2013/602 Sch.2 para.25
s.98, applied: SI 2013/602 Sch.3 para.18
s.99, amended: SI 2013/602 Sch.1 para.5
s.101, applied: SI 2013/602 Sch.3 para.5
Sch.1, referred to: 2013 c.22 Sch.3 para.19
Sch.4A para.2, applied: 2013 c.22 s.11
Sch.4A para.5, applied: 2013 c.22 s.11

17. Employment Tribunals Act 1996

applied: SI 2013/1893 Sch.2, SI 2013/3029 Sch.1 para.12, SI 2013/3035 Sch.1
s.1, enabling: SI 2013/1237
s.3A, amended: 2013 c.22 Sch.14 para.13
s.4, amended: 2013 c.24 s.11
s.4, applied: SI 2013/1237 Sch.1
s.4, enabling: SI 2013/1237
s.5, applied: SI 2013/1237 Sch.1
s.5A, amended: 2013 c.22 Sch.14 para.13
s.5B, amended: 2013 c.22 Sch.14 para.13
s.5D, amended: 2013 c.22 Sch.14 para.12, Sch.14 para.13
s.7, amended: 2013 c.22 Sch.9 para.52, 2013 c.24 Sch.1 para.3
s.7, enabling: SI 2013/1237, SI 2013/1948
s.7A, enabling: SI 2013/1237
s.7B, amended: 2013 c.22 Sch.14 para.13, 2013 c.24 Sch.1 para.4
s.7B, enabling: SI 2013/1237
s.9, amended: 2013 c.24 s.21
s.9, enabling: SI 2013/1237
s.10, amended: 2013 c.22 Sch.14 para.13
s.10, enabling: SI 2013/1237
s.10A, applied: SI 2013/1237 Sch.1
s.10A, enabling: SI 2013/1237
s.11, enabling: SI 2013/1237
s.12, enabling: SI 2013/1237
s.12A, added: 2013 c.24 s.16
s.13, amended: 2013 c.22 Sch.9 para.52, 2013 c.24 Sch.3 para.3
s.13, enabling: SI 2013/1237
s.13A, amended: 2013 c.24 Sch.3 para.3
s.13A, enabling: SI 2013/1237
s.13A, amended: 2013 c.24 s.21
s.14, amended: 2013 c.24 Sch.3 para.3
s.14, enabling: SI 2013/1671
s.15, amended: 2013 c.22 Sch.9 para.52, 2013 c.24 Sch.3 para.3
s.16, amended: SI 2013/630 Reg.11
s.17, amended: SI 2013/630 Reg.11
s.18, amended: 2013 c.24 s.9, Sch.1 para.5
s.18, repealed (in part): 2013 c.24 Sch.1 para.5
s.18A, added: 2013 c.24 s.7
s.18B, added: 2013 c.24 s.7
s.18C, added: 2013 c.24 Sch.1 para.6
s.19, enabling: SI 2013/1237
s.19A, amended: 2013 c.22 Sch.9 para.52, 2013 c.24 s.23, Sch.1 para.7
s.22, amended: 2013 c.22 Sch.14 para.11
s.22, applied: SI 2013/2191 Reg.6, SI 2013/2192 Reg.17
s.28, amended: 2013 c.24 s.12
s.30, amended: 2013 c.22 Sch.14 para.13, 2013 c.24 s.12
s.30, applied: SI 2013/1693
s.30, enabling: SI 2013/1693
s.33, applied: SI 2013/1237 Sch.1
s.34, enabling: SI 2013/1693
s.40, amended: 2013 c.24 Sch.1 para.8
s.41, amended: 2013 c.24 s.11, s.12, Sch.3 para.4
s.41, enabling: SI 2013/1237, SI 2013/1671, SI 2013/1948

s.42, amended: 2013 c.24 s.21, Sch.1 para.9

18. Employment Rights Act 1996

see *Benkharbouche v Embassy of Sudan* [2013] I.R.L.R. 918 (EAT), Langstaff, J. (President); see *R. (on the application of United Road Transport Union) v Secretary of State for Transport* [2013] EWCA Civ 962, [2013] I.R.L.R. 890 (CA (Civ Div)), Jackson, L.J.; see *Redfearn v United Kingdom (47335/06)* [2013] 3 Costs L.O. 402 (ECHR), Judge Garlicki (President)
applied: SI 2013/1893 Sch.2
Part XI, applied: SI 2013/503 Reg.5
s.11, amended: 2013 c.24 Sch.2 para.16
s.11, applied: SI 2013/1237 Reg.12
s.23, see *Abercrombie v Aga Rangemaster Ltd* [2013] EWCA Civ 1148, [2013] I.R.L.R. 953 (CA (Civ Div)), Sir Terence Etherton (Chancellor)
s.23, amended: 2013 c.24 Sch.2 para.17
s.28, see *Abercrombie v Aga Rangemaster Ltd* [2013] EWCA Civ 1148, [2013] I.R.L.R. 953 (CA (Civ Div)), Sir Terence Etherton (Chancellor); see *Abercrombie v Aga Rangemaster Ltd* [2013] I.C.R. 213 (EAT), Silber, J.
s.28, applied: SI 2013/3029 Sch.6 para.14, Sch.8 para.1, SI 2013/3035 Sch.1
s.28, referred to: SI 2013/378 Sch.1 para.1, SI 2013/3035 Sch.1
s.34, see *Abercrombie v Aga Rangemaster Ltd* [2013] EWCA Civ 1148, [2013] I.R.L.R. 953 (CA (Civ Div)), Sir Terence Etherton (Chancellor); see *Abercrombie v Aga Rangemaster Ltd* [2013] I.C.R. 213 (EAT), Silber, J.
s.34, amended: 2013 c.24 Sch.2 para.18
s.34, applied: SI 2013/3029 Sch.6 para.14, Sch.8 para.1, SI 2013/3035 Sch.1
s.34, referred to: SI 2013/378 Sch.1 para.1, SI 2013/3035 Sch.1
s.35, repealed (in part): 2013 c.24 Sch.20 para.2
s.43A, see *Onyango v Berkeley (t/a Berkeley Solicitors)* [2013] I.R.L.R. 338 (EAT), Judge Peter Clark
s.43A, applied: SI 2013/349 Sch.4 para.28, SI 2013/898 Sch.4 para.27
s.43B, amended: 2013 c.24 s.17
s.43C, see *Onyango v Berkeley (t/a Berkeley Solicitors)* [2013] I.R.L.R. 338 (EAT), Judge Peter Clark
s.43C, amended: 2013 c.24 s.18
s.43E, amended: 2013 c.24 s.18
s.43F, amended: 2013 c.24 s.18
s.43F, enabling: SI 2013/2213
s.43G, amended: 2013 c.24 s.18
s.43G, repealed (in part): 2013 c.24 s.18
s.43H, amended: 2013 c.24 s.18
s.43H, repealed (in part): 2013 c.24 s.18
s.43K, see *Abertawe Bro Morgannwg University Health Board v Ferguson* [2013] I.C.R. 1108 (EAT), Langstaff, J. (President)
s.43K, amended: 2013 c.24 s.20
s.43K, repealed (in part): 2013 c.24 s.20
s.43K, varied: 2013 c.24 s.20
s.43KA, amended: 2013 c.22 Sch.8 para.50
s.47B, see *Abertawe Bro Morgannwg University Health Board v Ferguson* [2013] I.C.R. 1108 (EAT), Langstaff, J. (President); see *Engel v Joint Committee for Parking and Traffic Regulation outside London (PATROL)* [2013] I.C.R. 1086 (EAT), Mitting, J.; see *Onyango v Berkeley (t/a Berkeley Solicitors)* [2013] I.R.L.R. 338 (EAT), Judge Peter Clark; see *Suhail v Herts Urgent Care* (2013) 130 B.M.L.R. 27 (EAT), Judge Serota Q.C.
s.47B, amended: 2013 c.24 s.19
s.47G, added: 2013 c.27 s.31
s.48, amended: 2013 c.24 s.19, Sch.2 para.19, 2013 c.27 s.31
s.49, amended: 2013 c.24 s.18
s.50, applied: SI 2013/3104 Sch.2 para.30
s.51, amended: 2013 c.24 Sch.2 para.20
s.54, amended: 2013 c.24 Sch.2 para.21
s.55, applied: SI 2013/3104 Sch.2 para.30
s.57, amended: 2013 c.24 Sch.2 para.22
s.57B, amended: 2013 c.24 Sch.2 para.24
s.57ZC, amended: 2013 c.24 Sch.2 para.23
s.60, amended: 2013 c.24 Sch.2 para.25
s.63, amended: 2013 c.24 Sch.2 para.26
s.63C, amended: 2013 c.24 Sch.2 para.27
s.63I, amended: 2013 c.24 Sch.2 para.28
s.64, applied: SI 2013/3029 Sch.6 para.14, Sch.8 para.1, SI 2013/3035 Sch.1
s.64, referred to: SI 2013/378 Sch.1 para.1, SI 2013/3035 Sch.1
s.68, applied: SI 2013/3029 Sch.6 para.14, Sch.8 para.1, SI 2013/3035 Sch.1
s.68, referred to: SI 2013/378 Sch.1 para.1, SI 2013/3035 Sch.1
s.70, amended: 2013 c.24 Sch.2 para.29
s.70, applied: SI 2013/3029 Sch.6 para.14, Sch.8 para.1, SI 2013/3035 Sch.1
s.70, referred to: SI 2013/378 Sch.1 para.1, SI 2013/3035 Sch.1
s.70A, amended: 2013 c.24 Sch.2 para.30
s.72, applied: SI 2013/1667 Reg.2, SI 2013/1667(a)
s.76, enabling: SI 2013/283
s.80, amended: 2013 c.24 Sch.2 para.31
s.80F, amended: SI 2013/283 Reg.2
s.80H, amended: 2013 c.24 Sch.2 para.32

s.86, applied: SI 2013/376 Reg.96, SI 2013/378 Reg.13
s.104G, added: 2013 c.27 s.31
s.108, amended: 2013 c.24 s.13, 2013 c.27 s.31
s.110, amended: 2013 c.22 Sch.9 para.52
s.111, amended: 2013 c.24 Sch.2 para.33
s.111A, added: 2013 c.24 s.14
s.112, applied: SI 2013/3029 Sch.6 para.14, SI 2013/3035 Sch.1
s.117, applied: SI 2013/3029 Sch.6 para.14, SI 2013/3035 Sch.1
s.118, applied: SI 2013/378 Sch.1 para.3
s.123, see *Optimum Group Services Plc v Muir* [2013] I.R.L.R. 339 (EAT (SC)), Lady Smith; see *Toni & Guys (St Paul's) Ltd v Georgiou* [2013] I.C.R. 1356 (EAT), Judge Peter Clark
s.123, amended: 2013 c.24 s.18
s.124, amended: SI 2013/1949 Art.2
s.127, applied: SI 2013/378 Sch.1 para.3
s.128, applied: SI 2013/1237 Sch.1
s.131, applied: SI 2013/1237 Sch.1
s.134A, amended: 2013 c.22 Sch.8 para.51
s.148, see *Dutton v Jones (t/a Llandow Metals)* [2013] I.C.R. 559 (EAT), Judge Hand Q.C.
s.148, applied: SI 2013/378 Reg.28
s.148, referred to: SI 2013/376 Reg.113
s.164, amended: 2013 c.24 Sch.2 para.34
s.194, amended: 2013 c.22 Sch.9 para.52
s.195, amended: 2013 c.22 Sch.9 para.52
s.200, applied: SI 2013/2325 Reg.44
s.201, amended: 2013 c.24 Sch.3 para.5
s.203, see *Toal v GB Oils Ltd* [2013] I.R.L.R. 696 (EAT), Mitting, J.
s.203, amended: 2013 c.24 s.23, Sch.1 para.10
s.205A, added: 2013 c.27 s.31
s.207B, added: 2013 c.24 Sch.2 para.35
s.209, enabling: SI 2013/1784
s.226, see *Dutton v Jones (t/a Llandow Metals)* [2013] I.C.R. 559 (EAT), Judge Hand Q.C.
s.226, amended: SI 2013/1949 Art.3
s.236, amended: 2013 c.24 s.20, 2013 c.27 s.31
s.236, applied: SI 2013/283
s.236, enabling: SI 2013/1784, SI 2013/2213

23. Arbitration Act 1996
Part I, disapplied: SI 2013/1169 r.4
s.82, amended: 2013 c.22 Sch.9 para.60
s.105, amended: 2013 c.22 Sch.9 para.60
Sch.3 para.32, repealed: SI 2013/686 Sch.1 para.7

25. Criminal Procedure and Investigations Act 1996
applied: SI 2013/1554 r.22_1, r.22_5, r.22_9, r.29_19, SI 2013/1813 Art.5, Art.7
disapplied: SI 2013/1554 r.22_9
referred to: SI 2013/1554 r.2_3
Part I, applied: SI 2013/1554 r.22_9
s.1, amended: 2013 c.22 Sch.17 para.37
s.2, referred to: SI 2013/1554 r.22_9
s.3, applied: SI 2013/1554 r.36_2, r.22_2, r.22_3, r.22_9
s.3, referred to: SI 2013/1554 r.22_9
s.5, applied: SI 2013/1554 r.22_4, r.22_9
s.5, referred to: SI 2013/1554 r.22_9
s.6, applied: SI 2013/1554 r.22_4, r.22_9
s.6A, see *Joseph Hill & Co Solicitors, Re* [2013] EWCA Crim 775, [2013] 2 Cr. App. R. 20 (CA (Crim Div)), Leveson, L.J.
s.6A, applied: SI 2013/1554 r.22_9
s.6A, referred to: SI 2013/1554 r.22_9
s.6C, applied: SI 2013/1554 r.22_4
s.6E, applied: SI 2013/1554 r.22_9
s.7, applied: SI 2013/1554 r.22_3, r.22_9
s.7A, applied: SI 2013/1554 r.22_3, r.22_9
s.8, applied: SI 2013/1554 r.22_5
s.11, applied: SI 2013/1554 r.22_9
s.12, applied: SI 2013/1554 r.22_9
s.13, applied: SI 2013/1554 r.22_9
s.14, applied: SI 2013/1554 r.22_6
s.15, applied: SI 2013/1554 r.22_6
s.17, applied: SI 2013/1554 r.22_7, r.62_9, r.22_8, r.62_16
s.18, applied: SI 2013/1554 r.62_9, r.62_16, r.22_8
s.19, applied: SI 2013/1554 r.62_16
s.19, enabling: SI 2013/1554
s.20, applied: SI 2013/1554 r.33_4
s.20, enabling: SI 2013/1554
s.23, applied: SI 2013/1813 Art.5, Art.7
s.25, applied: SI 2013/1813 Art.5, Art.7
s.28, amended: 2013 c.22 Sch.17 para.37
s.29, see *R. v Y* [2012] EWCA Crim 2437, [2013] 1 W.L.R. 2014 (CA (Crim Div)), Sir John Thomas (President QBD)
s.29, applied: SI 2013/1554 r.15_1
s.31, see *R. v Y* [2012] EWCA Crim 2437, [2013] 1 W.L.R. 2014 (CA (Crim Div)), Sir John Thomas (President QBD)
s.31, applied: SI 2013/1554 r.35_3, r.33_6, r.35_4, r.34_3, r.36_2
s.34, applied: SI 2013/1554 r.15_1
s.35, applied: SI 2013/1554 r.74_1, r.66_1
s.37, applied: SI 2013/1554 r.16_1
s.39, amended: 2013 c.22 Sch.17 para.37
s.40, applied: SI 2013/1554 r.35_3, r.33_6, r.35_4, r.34_3, r.36_2
s.41, applied: SI 2013/1554 r.16_1
s.54, applied: SI 2013/9 Reg.19, SI 2013/1554 r.40_1, r.40_4, r.40_5, r.40_6, r.40_7, r.40_8
s.54, referred to: SI 2013/1554 r.40_1, r.40_2, r.40_3, r.40_6
s.58, applied: SI 2013/1554 r.16_1, r.69_1

Sch.3 para.8, amended: 2013 c.22 Sch.17 para.37

27. Family Law Act 1996

applied: SI 2013/3174 Sch.4
Part IV, applied: SI 2013/503 Reg.5
Part IVA, applied: SI 2013/422 Reg.8, SSI 2013/357 Art.3
s.30, amended: 2013 c.3 Sch.1 para.6
s.33, applied: SI 2013/1554 r.19_17
s.45, amended: 2013 c.22 Sch.11 para.130
s.46, amended: 2013 c.22 Sch.11 para.131
s.47, amended: 2013 c.22 Sch.11 para.132
s.50, repealed: 2013 c.22 Sch.11 para.133
s.51, repealed: 2013 c.22 Sch.11 para.134
s.56, applied: SI 2013/3174 Sch.3 Part 3
s.57, amended: 2013 c.22 Sch.11 para.135
s.57, repealed (in part): 2013 c.22 Sch.11 para.135
s.59, repealed: 2013 c.22 Sch.11 para.136
s.61, repealed: 2013 c.22 Sch.11 para.137
s.63, amended: 2013 c.22 Sch.11 para.138
s.63M, amended: 2013 c.22 Sch.11 para.139
s.63M, repealed (in part): 2013 c.22 Sch.11 para.139
s.63N, repealed: 2013 c.22 Sch.11 para.140
s.63P, repealed: 2013 c.22 Sch.11 para.141
s.63S, amended: 2013 c.22 Sch.11 para.142
s.65, amended: 2013 c.22 Sch.11 para.143
Sch.5 para.1, amended: 2013 c.22 Sch.11 para.144
Sch.7 Part I para.1, amended: 2013 c.22 Sch.11 para.145
Sch.8 Part I para.7, repealed: 2013 c.13 Sch.2 para.4
Sch.8 Part III para.49, repealed: 2013 c.22 Sch.10 para.99

30. Community Care (Direct Payments) Act 1996

applied: SI 2013/480 Reg.40, SSI 2013/200 Sch.2 para.8

31. Defamation Act 1996

s.8, applied: 2013 c.26 s.12
s.14, amended: 2013 c.26 s.7
s.14, applied: 2013 c.26 s.3
s.15, see *MXB v East Sussex Hospitals NHS Trust* [2012] EWHC 3279 (QB), (2013) 177 J.P. 31 (QBD), Tugendhat, J.; see *Qadir v Associated Newspapers Ltd* [2012] EWHC 2606 (QB), [2013] E.M.L.R. 15 (QBD), Tugendhat, J.
s.15, amended: 2013 c.26 s.7
s.15, applied: 2013 c.26 s.3
Sch.1 Part II para.9, substituted: 2013 c.26 s.7
Sch.1 Part II para.10, substituted: 2013 c.26 s.7
Sch.1 Part II para.11A, added: 2013 c.26 s.7
Sch.1 Part II para.12, amended: 2013 c.26 s.7
Sch.1 Part II para.13, amended: 2013 c.26 s.7
Sch.1 Part II para.14, amended: 2013 c.26 s.7
Sch.1 Part II para.14A, added: 2013 c.26 s.7
Sch.1 Part II para.15, substituted: 2013 c.26 s.7
Sch.1 Part III para.16, substituted: 2013 c.26 s.7
Sch.1 Part III para.17, substituted: 2013 c.26 s.7

41. Hong Kong (War Wives and Widows) Act 1996

applied: 2013 c.22 s.55

42. Railway Heritage Act 1996

applied: SI 2013/64 Art.2
s.2, repealed: SI 2013/64 Art.2
s.3, amended: SI 2013/64 Art.2
s.4, amended: SI 2013/64 Art.2
s.5, amended: SI 2013/64 Art.2
s.6, amended: SI 2013/64 Art.2
s.7, amended: SI 2013/64 Art.2

43. Education (Scotland) Act 1996

s.3, applied: SI 2013/2216 Sch.1 para.13
s.21, applied: SI 2013/2216 Sch.1 para.13

52. Housing Act 1996

Part VI, applied: SI 2013/1467 Reg.3
Part VII, applied: SI 2013/1467 Reg.3
s.3, amended: SI 2013/496 Sch.11 para.5
s.4, amended: SI 2013/496 Sch.11 para.5
s.6, amended: SI 2013/496 Sch.11 para.5
s.45, amended: SI 2013/496 Sch.11 para.5
s.48, amended: SI 2013/496 Sch.11 para.5
s.81, amended: SI 2013/1036 Sch.1 para.130
s.95, amended: 2013 c.22 Sch.9 para.52
s.120, amended: SI 2013/630 Reg.12
s.121, amended: SI 2013/630 Reg.12
s.122, see *R. (on the application of Zacchaeus 2000 Trust) v Secretary of State for Work and Pensions* [2013] EWCA Civ 1202, [2013] P.T.S.R. 1427 (CA (Civ Div)), Sullivan, L.J.; see *R. (on the application of Zacchaeus 2000 Trust) v Secretary of State for Work and Pensions* [2013] EWHC 233 (Admin), [2013] P.T.S.R. 785 (QBD (Admin)), Underhill, J.
s.122, amended: SI 2013/630 Reg.12
s.122, applied: SI 2013/380 Reg.40, SI 2013/381 Sch.3 para.6, SI 2013/1510 Reg.2
s.122, enabling: SI 2013/382, SI 2013/666, SI 2013/1544, SI 2013/2827, SI 2013/2978
s.123, amended: SI 2013/630 Reg.12
s.138, amended: 2013 c.22 Sch.9 para.52
s.143N, amended: 2013 c.22 Sch.9 para.37
s.153E, amended: 2013 c.22 Sch.9 para.52
s.154, amended: 2013 c.22 Sch.9 para.52
s.155, amended: 2013 c.22 Sch.9 para.52
s.157, amended: 2013 c.22 Sch.9 para.52
s.158, amended: 2013 c.22 Sch.9 para.37
s.160A, amended: SI 2013/630 Reg.12
s.160ZA, amended: SI 2013/630 Reg.12
s.160ZA, enabling: SI 2013/1467
s.172, enabling: SI 2013/1467
s.175, applied: SI 2013/386 Reg.10

s.185, see *Konodyba v Kensington and Chelsea RLBC* [2012] EWCA Civ 982, [2013] P.T.S.R. 13 (CA (Civ Div)), Lord Neuberger (M.R.); see *Pryce v Southwark LBC* [2012] EWCA Civ 1572, [2013] 1 W.L.R. 996 (CA (Civ Div)), Pill, L.J.
s.185, amended: SI 2013/630 Reg.12
s.185, enabling: SI 2013/1467
s.203, amended: 2013 c.22 Sch.9 para.52
s.215, enabling: SI 2013/1467
s.231, amended: SI 2013/630 Reg.12
Sch.1 Part II para.9, amended: SI 2013/496 Sch.11 para.5
Sch.1 Part II para.12, amended: SI 2013/496 Sch.11 para.5
Sch.1 Part II para.15H, amended: SI 2013/496 Sch.11 para.5
Sch.2 para.3, applied: SI 2013/722 Art.3
Sch.2 para.7A, applied: SI 2013/722 Art.3
Sch.2 para.7B, applied: SI 2013/722 Art.3
Sch.2 para.7C, applied: SI 2013/722 Art.3
Sch.15 para.1, amended: 2013 c.22 Sch.9 para.37

53. Housing Grants, Construction and Regeneration Act 1996

s.3, amended: SI 2013/630 Reg.13, SI 2013/1788 Reg.2
s.3, repealed (in part): SI 2013/1788 Reg.2
s.30, enabling: SI 2013/276, SI 2013/552, SI 2013/3138
s.146, enabling: SI 2013/276, SI 2013/552, SI 2013/3138

55. Broadcasting Act 1996

applied: 2013 c.22 Sch.15 para.3
Part I, applied: 2013 asp 14 Sch.4 para.11
Part II, applied: 2013 asp 14 Sch.4 para.11
s.12, amended: SI 2013/2217 Reg.4
s.39, amended: SI 2013/2217 Reg.4
s.98, amended: SI 2013/2217 Reg.4
s.99, amended: SI 2013/2217 Reg.4
s.101A, amended: SI 2013/2217 Reg.4
s.101B, amended: SI 2013/2217 Reg.4
s.105, amended: SI 2013/2217 Reg.4

56. Education Act 1996

applied: SI 2013/1721 Art.2, SI 2013/1793 Reg.4, SI 2013/2356 Sch.2 Part 4
Part VI c.II, applied: SI 2013/3104 Sch.1 para.11
Part VI c.III, applied: SI 2013/1793 Reg.6
s.3, applied: SI 2013/1793 Reg.4
s.8, applied: SI 2013/1465 Art.13
s.13, see *R. (on the application of British Humanist Association) v Richmond upon Thames LBC* [2012] EWHC 3622 (Admin), [2013] 2 All E.R. 146 (QBD (Admin)), Sales, J.
s.13, applied: SI 2013/3104 Sch.2 para.8
s.15ZA, applied: SI 2013/3104 Sch.1 para.18
s.15ZC, applied: SI 2013/3104 Sch.1 para.18
s.18, applied: SI 2013/3104 Sch.2 para.7
s.19, applied: SI 2013/492 Reg.4, Reg.6, SI 2013/3104 Sch.2 para.21
s.19, enabling: SI 2013/3037
s.29, see *SM v Hackney Learning Trust* [2013] UKUT 78 (AAC), [2013] E.L.R. 321 (UT (AAC)), Judge Edward Jacobs
s.29, enabling: SI 2013/437, SI 2013/1255, SI 2013/2149, SI 2013/3110
s.32, applied: SI 2013/2155
s.316, see *Harrow LBC v AM* [2013] UKUT 157 (AAC), [2013] E.L.R. 351 (UT (AAC)), Judge Michael Mark
s.316, applied: SI 2013/1793 Reg.5
s.317, applied: SI 2013/1793 Reg.6, Reg.7
s.320, applied: SI 2013/377 Reg.28, SI 2013/3104 Sch.2 para.22
s.321, applied: SI 2013/3104 Sch.1 para.2
s.322, applied: SI 2013/261 Sch.1 para.21, SI 2013/3104 Sch.1 para.2
s.323, see *Buckinghamshire CC v HW* [2013] UKUT 470 (AAC), [2013] E.L.R. 519 (UT (AAC)), Judge Edward Jacobs
s.323, applied: SI 2013/3104 Sch.1 para.2
s.324, applied: SI 2013/492 Reg.4, Reg.5, Reg.6, SI 2013/1141 Sch.1 para.2, SI 2013/3104 Sch.1 para.2
s.325, applied: SI 2013/3104 Sch.1 para.2
s.326, applied: SI 2013/3104 Sch.1 para.2
s.326A, applied: SI 2013/3104 Sch.1 para.2
s.327, applied: SI 2013/3104 Sch.1 para.2
s.328, applied: SI 2013/3104 Sch.1 para.2
s.328A, applied: SI 2013/3104 Sch.1 para.2
s.329, see *Buckinghamshire CC v HW* [2013] UKUT 470 (AAC), [2013] E.L.R. 519 (UT (AAC)), Judge Edward Jacobs
s.329, applied: SI 2013/3104 Sch.1 para.2
s.329A, applied: SI 2013/3104 Sch.1 para.2
s.330, applied: SI 2013/3104 Sch.1 para.2
s.331, applied: SI 2013/3104 Sch.1 para.2
s.332A, applied: SI 2013/3104 Sch.1 para.5
s.336, amended: 2013 c.22 Sch.9 para.52
s.348, applied: SI 2013/3104 Sch.2 para.22
s.390, applied: SI 2013/3104 Sch.1 para.24
s.403, amended: SI 2013/594 Art.3
s.408, applied: SI 2013/437
s.408, enabling: SI 2013/437, SI 2013/3212
s.434, applied: SI 2013/1793 Reg.8
s.434, enabling: SI 2013/756
s.444, see *West Sussex CC v C* [2013] EWHC 1757 (Admin), (2013) 177 J.P. 567 (DC), Hallett, L.J.

s.444, applied: SI 2013/1983 Reg.3, Reg.8, Reg.14, Reg.18
s.444A, amended: SI 2013/1657 Art.2
s.444A, applied: SI 2013/1983 Reg.7, Reg.21
s.444A, enabling: SI 2013/1983
s.444B, amended: SI 2013/1657 Art.2
s.444B, enabling: SI 2013/757, SI 2013/1983
s.450, applied: SI 2013/1793 Reg.9
s.451, applied: SI 2013/1793 Reg.6
s.452, applied: SI 2013/1793 Reg.6
s.453, applied: SI 2013/1793 Reg.6
s.454, applied: SI 2013/1793 Reg.6
s.455, applied: SI 2013/1793 Reg.6
s.457, applied: SI 2013/1793 Reg.6
s.457, enabling: SI 2013/2731
s.460, applied: SI 2013/1793 Reg.6
s.462, referred to: SI 2013/1793 Reg.6
s.485, disapplied: SI 2013/377 Reg.28
s.496, applied: SI 2013/1721 Art.2
s.496, varied: SI 2013/1721 Art.3
s.497, see *R. (on the application of M) v Hounslow LBC* [2013] EWHC 579 (Admin), [2013] P.T.S.R. 942 (QBD (Admin)), Sales, J.; see *R. (on the application of McCormack) v St Edmund Campion Catholic School Governing Body* [2012] EWHC 3928 (Admin), [2013] E.L.R. 169 (QBD (Admin)), Beatson, J.
s.497, applied: SI 2013/1721 Art.2
s.497, varied: SI 2013/1721 Art.3
s.497A, applied: SI 2013/1721 Art.2, SI 2013/2356 Sch.2 para.1
s.497A, varied: SI 2013/1721 Art.3
s.497AA, applied: SI 2013/1721 Art.2
s.497AA, varied: SI 2013/1721 Art.3
s.497B, varied: SI 2013/1721 Art.3
s.507A, applied: SI 2013/3104 Sch.1 para.19
s.507B, amended: SI 2013/1721 Art.3
s.507B, applied: SI 2013/1721 Art.2, Art.4, SI 2013/3104 Sch.1 para.19
s.508A, applied: SI 2013/3104 Sch.1 para.10
s.508B, see *R. (on the application of M) v Hounslow LBC* [2013] EWHC 579 (Admin), [2013] P.T.S.R. 942 (QBD (Admin)), Sales, J.
s.508B, applied: SI 2013/1686 Reg.7, SI 2013/3104 Sch.1 para.10
s.508C, applied: SI 2013/1686 Reg.7, SI 2013/3104 Sch.1 para.10
s.508D, applied: SI 2013/3104 Sch.1 para.10
s.508E, applied: SI 2013/3104 Sch.1 para.10
s.508F, applied: SI 2013/3104 Sch.1 para.10
s.508G, applied: SI 2013/3104 Sch.1 para.10
s.508H, applied: SI 2013/3104 Sch.1 para.10
s.508I, applied: SI 2013/3104 Sch.1 para.10
s.509, applied: SI 2013/3104 Sch.1 para.10
s.509A, applied: SI 2013/3104 Sch.1 para.10
s.510, applied: SI 2013/3104 Sch.1 para.10
s.512, applied: SI 2013/2094 Sch.1 para.14
s.512A, enabling: SI 2013/3111
s.512ZB, applied: SI 2013/650 Art.2, Art.3, SI 2013/2021 Art.1, Art.2, SI 2013/2094 Sch.1 para.14
s.512ZB, enabling: SI 2013/650, SI 2013/2021
s.514, applied: SI 2013/3104 Sch.1 para.10
s.518, applied: SI 2013/3029 Sch.9 para.16, Sch.10 para.53, SI 2013/3035 Sch.1, SI 2013/3104 Sch.1 para.10
s.519, applied: SI 2013/1624 Reg.29, SI 2013/3104 Sch.5 para.14
s.519, enabling: SI 2013/1624
s.537, enabling: SI 2013/437, SI 2013/758, SI 2013/2912, SI 2013/3110
s.537A, applied: SI 2013/2094 Reg.3
s.537A, enabling: SI 2013/437, SI 2013/1193, SI 2013/1759, SI 2013/2094, SI 2013/3137, SI 2013/3212
s.543, applied: SI 2013/3109 Reg.16
s.551, enabling: SI 2013/756
s.554, enabling: SI 2013/548, SI 2013/549, SI 2013/920, SI 2013/1145, SI 2013/1221, SI 2013/1245, SI 2013/2155
s.555, applied: SI 2013/548(4), SI 2013/920(4), SI 2013/1145(4), SI 2013/549, SI 2013/1221, SI 2013/1245, SI 2013/2155
s.556, enabling: SI 2013/548, SI 2013/549, SI 2013/920, SI 2013/1145, SI 2013/1221, SI 2013/1245, SI 2013/2155
s.563, enabling: SI 2013/3212
s.568, enabling: SI 2013/650, SI 2013/2021
s.569, amended: SI 2013/1657 Art.2
s.569, enabling: SI 2013/437, SI 2013/756, SI 2013/757, SI 2013/758, SI 2013/1255, SI 2013/1624, SI 2013/1759, SI 2013/1983, SI 2013/2094, SI 2013/2149, SI 2013/2731, SI 2013/3137
s.570, varied: SI 2013/1721 Art.3
s.571, applied: SI 2013/1721 Art.2
s.571, varied: SI 2013/1721 Art.3
s.572, applied: SI 2013/1624 Reg.5
s.576, disapplied: SI 2013/2094 Sch.1 para.18
s.579, applied: SI 2013/2356 Sch.2 para.20
Sch.1 para.3, enabling: SI 2013/1624, SI 2013/3037
Sch.1 para.15, enabling: SI 2013/1624
Sch.31, applied: SI 2013/3104 Sch.1 para.24
Sch.36, referred to: SI 2013/1145 Art.5, SI 2013/1221 Art.6, SI 2013/2155 Art.5

61. Channel Tunnel Rail Link Act 1996

Sch.9 Part II para.6, repealed: 2013 c.2 Sch.1 Part 9

1997

5. Firearms (Amendment) Act 1997
applied: SI 2013/449 Reg.3
s.35A, amended: SI 2013/602 Sch.2 para.26

9. Planning (Listed Buildings and Conservation Areas) (Scotland) Act 1997
referred to: SSI 2013/156 Reg.17
s.11, applied: SSI 2013/156 Reg.1, Reg.24
s.17, applied: SSI 2013/156 Reg.1, Reg.17
s.18, applied: SSI 2013/156 Reg.1, Reg.17, Reg.24, Reg.29
s.18, referred to: SSI 2013/156 Reg.17
s.18, enabling: SSI 2013/156
s.19, applied: SSI 2013/156 Reg.1, Reg.18
s.19, enabling: SSI 2013/156
s.35, applied: SSI 2013/156 Reg.1, Reg.14
s.35, enabling: SSI 2013/156
s.36, enabling: SSI 2013/156
s.60, applied: SSI 2013/155 Reg.20, Reg.26
s.65, applied: SSI 2013/155 Reg.20, Reg.26
s.66, applied: SSI 2013/156 Reg.1, Reg.17
s.82, enabling: SSI 2013/156

12. Civil Procedure Act 1997
s.1, amended: 2013 c.22 Sch.9 para.67
s.1, applied: SI 2013/262, SI 2013/515, SI 2013/789, SI 2013/1412, SI 2013/1571, SI 2013/1695, SI 2013/1974, SI 2013/3112
s.2, amended: 2013 c.22 Sch.9 para.67
s.2, applied: SI 2013/262, SI 2013/515, SI 2013/1695, SI 2013/1974, SI 2013/3112
s.2, enabling: SI 2013/262, SI 2013/515, SI 2013/789, SI 2013/1412, SI 2013/1695, SI 2013/1974, SI 2013/3112
s.3, disapplied: 2013 c.18 Sch.3 para.3
s.3, referred to: 2013 c.18 Sch.3 para.3
Sch.1 para.3, amended: 2013 c.22 Sch.9 para.67
Sch.2 para.2, repealed (in part): 2013 c.22 Sch.9 para.141

16. Finance Act 1997
s.11, amended: 2013 c.29 s.183
s.12, enabling: SI 2013/1819
s.61, repealed: 2013 c.2 Sch.1 Part 10
s.96, applied: 2013 asp 11 Sch.10 para.10, Sch.10 para.22

20. British Nationality (Hong Kong) Act 1997
applied: 2013 c.22 s.55, SI 2013/617 Sch.4 para.2

22. Architects Act 1997
s.22, see *Dowland v Architects Registration Board* [2013] EWHC 893 (Admin), [2013] B.P.I.R. 566 (QBD (Admin)), Simon, J.
s.22, amended: 2013 c.22 Sch.9 para.61

32. Building Societies Act 1997
s.11, repealed: 2013 c.33 Sch.9 para.4

40. Protection from Harassment Act 1997
see *R. v Egan (Robert)* [2012] EWCA Crim 1240, [2013] 1 Cr. App. R. (S.) 42 (CA (Crim Div)), Moses, L.J.
applied: 2013 c.22 s.42
s.3, amended: 2013 c.22 Sch.9 para.39
s.3, applied: SI 2013/435 Sch.1 Part 7
s.3A, amended: 2013 c.22 Sch.9 para.52
s.4, applied: SI 2013/435 Sch.1 Part 7
s.5, see *R. v Smith (Mark John)* [2012] EWCA Crim 2566, [2013] 1 W.L.R. 1399 (CA (Crim Div)), Toulson, L.J.
s.5, applied: SI 2013/435 Sch.1 Part 7, SI 2013/1554 r.50_1
s.5A, see *R. v R* [2013] EWCA Crim 591, [2013] 2 Cr. App. R. 12 (CA (Crim Div)), McCombe, L.J.; see *R. v Smith (Mark John)* [2012] EWCA Crim 2566, [2013] 1 W.L.R. 1399 (CA (Crim Div)), Toulson, L.J.
s.5A, applied: SI 2013/9 Reg.9, SI 2013/1554 r.50_1
s.8, see *Vaickuviene v J Sainsbury Plc* [2013] CSIH 67, 2013 S.L.T. 1032 (IH (2 Div)), The Lord Justice Clerk (Carloway)
s.8, applied: SSI 2013/357 Art.3
s.8A, applied: SSI 2013/357 Art.3

42. Police (Health and Safety) Act 1997
s.5, amended: SI 2013/602 Sch.2 para.27

43. Crime (Sentences) Act 1997
Part II c.II, applied: SI 2013/9 Reg.12

44. Education Act 1997
s.30, applied: SI 2013/2216 Sch.1 para.13
s.42A, disapplied: SI 2013/709 Reg.3
s.42A, referred to: SI 2013/709 Reg.2
s.42A, varied: SI 2013/709 Reg.2
s.45, applied: SI 2013/1793 Reg.3, Reg.7
s.46, enabling: SI 2013/709
s.54, enabling: SI 2013/709

50. Police Act 1997
see *R. (on the application of T) v Chief Constable of Greater Manchester* [2013] EWCA Civ 25, [2013] 1 W.L.R. 2515 (CA (Civ Div)), Lord Dyson (M.R.)
applied: SSI 2013/50 Sch.3 para.12, SSI 2013/194 r.90
s.93, amended: 2013 c.22 s.55, Sch.8 para.56, Sch.21 para.2, SI 2013/602 Sch.1 para.6

s.94, amended: 2013 c.22 Sch.8 para.57, Sch.21 para.3, SI 2013/602 Sch.1 para.6
s.95, amended: SI 2013/602 Sch.1 para.6
s.97, amended: 2013 c.22 Sch.8 para.58
s.105, amended: SI 2013/602 Sch.1 para.6
s.107, amended: 2013 c.22 Sch.8 para.59, Sch.21 para.4, SI 2013/602 Sch.1 para.6
s.112, applied: SI 2013/1554 r.5_9
s.113A, amended: SI 2013/1200 Art.3, Art.4
s.113A, applied: SI 2013/1200, SI 2013/1394 Sch.2 para.2, SI 2013/1554 r.5_9, SSI 2013/50 Sch.3 para.12, SSI 2013/194 r.27
s.113A, enabling: SI 2013/1200
s.113B, see *R. (on the application of J) v Chief Constable of Devon and Cornwall* [2012] EWHC 2996 (Admin), (2013) 129 B.M.L.R. 94 (QBD (Admin)), Foskett, J.
s.113B, amended: 2013 c.22 Sch.8 para.60
s.113B, applied: SI 2013/335 Reg.4, Reg.9, Sch.1 para.2, SI 2013/1394 Sch.2 para.2, SI 2013/1554 r.5_9, SI 2013/1617 Reg.7, SI 2013/2668 Sch.1 para.2, Sch.1 para.3, Sch.1 para.4, Sch.4 para.4, Sch.4 para.9, Sch.5 para.11, SSI 2013/50 Sch.3 para.12
s.113B, repealed (in part): 2013 c.22 Sch.8 para.60
s.113B, enabling: SI 2013/1194, SI 2013/2669
s.113BA, applied: SI 2013/335 Reg.4, Reg.9, Sch.1 para.2, SI 2013/1394 Sch.2 para.2
s.113BA, referred to: SI 2013/2668 Sch.1 para.2, Sch.4 para.4, Sch.4 para.9, Sch.5 para.11
s.113BA, enabling: SI 2013/2669
s.113BB, applied: SI 2013/335 Reg.4, Reg.9, Sch.1 para.2, SI 2013/1394 Sch.2 para.2, SI 2013/1617 Reg.7
s.113BB, referred to: SI 2013/2668 Sch.1 para.2, Sch.4 para.4, Sch.4 para.9, Sch.5 para.11
s.113CA, applied: SSI 2013/50 Sch.3 para.12
s.113CB, applied: SSI 2013/50 Sch.3 para.12
s.116A, enabling: SI 2013/1194
s.120AD, enabling: SI 2013/1194
s.125, enabling: SI 2013/1194, SI 2013/2669
s.126, amended: SI 2013/602 Sch.1 para.6

53. Dangerous Dogs (Amendment) Act 1997
s.4, applied: SI 2013/1302 Art.2, SSI 2013/178 Art.3
s.4, enabling: SI 2013/1302, SSI 2013/178

58. Finance (No.2) Act 1997
s.17, repealed: 2013 c.2 Sch.1 Part 10
s.25, repealed (in part): 2013 c.2 Sch.1 Part 10
Sch.3 para.9, repealed: 2013 c.2 Sch.1 Part 10
Sch.4 Part II para.29, repealed: 2013 c.2 Sch.1 Part 10

64. Firearms (Amendment) (No.2) Act 1997
applied: SI 2013/449 Reg.3

66. Plant Varieties Act 1997
Sch.3 para.11, amended: 2013 c.22 Sch.9 para.120

1998

11. Bank of England Act 1998
s.2AA, added: SI 2013/3115 Sch.2 para.38
s.7, amended: 2013 c.33 s.137
s.7A, added: 2013 c.33 s.137
s.9H, applied: SI 2013/644 Art.3
s.9I, enabling: SI 2013/644
s.9L, enabling: SI 2013/644
s.9N, applied: SI 2013/644
s.17, amended: SI 2013/3115 Sch.2 para.38
s.40, applied: SI 2013/1189
s.41, substituted: SI 2013/3115 Sch.2 para.39
Sch.2 para.4, applied: SI 2013/1189 Art.3
Sch.2 para.5, enabling: SI 2013/1189
Sch.2 para.7, substituted: SI 2013/721 Art.2
Sch.2 para.8, enabling: SI 2013/721
Sch.2 para.10, applied: SI 2013/721, SI 2013/1189
Sch.2 para.11, applied: SI 2013/721, SI 2013/1189
Sch.2A para.5, amended: SI 2013/161 Art.12
Sch.2A para.9, amended: SI 2013/161 Art.12
Sch.2A para.9, substituted: SI 2013/161 Art.12
Sch.2A para.10, varied: SI 2013/1765 Art.2

17. Petroleum Act 1998
Part V, applied: SI 2013/1329 Reg.20, Reg.21
s.3, applied: SI 2013/1471 Reg.3
s.30, applied: 2013 c.29 s.80
s.38A, varied: 2013 c.29 s.86

18. Audit Commission Act 1998
applied: SI 2013/160 Art.4
s.5, amended: SI 2013/594 Art.4
s.10, amended: SI 2013/594 Art.4
s.17, amended: 2013 c.22 Sch.9 para.62
s.19, amended: SI 2013/594 Art.4
s.33, amended: SI 2013/594 Art.4
s.49, amended: SI 2013/594 Art.4
s.53, amended: SI 2013/594 Art.4
Sch.2 para.1A, substituted: SI 2013/594 Art.4

20. Late Payment of Commercial Debts (Interest) Act 1998
s.4, amended: SI 2013/395 Reg.2, SI 2013/908 Reg.2, SSI 2013/77 Reg.2, SSI 2013/131 Reg.2
s.5A, amended: SI 2013/395 Reg.3, SSI 2013/77 Reg.3

22. National Lottery Act 1998
Sch.1 Part III para.8, repealed: SI 2013/2329 Sch.1 para.25
Sch.1 Part III para.9, repealed: SI 2013/2329 Sch.1 para.25

Sch.1 Part III para.10, repealed: SI 2013/2329 Sch.1 para.25
Sch.1 Part III para.11, repealed: SI 2013/2329 Sch.1 para.25

29. Data Protection Act 1998

see *City and County of Swansea v Gayle* [2013] I.R.L.R. 768 (EAT), Langstaff, J. (President); see *Durham CC v D* [2012] EWCA Civ 1654, [2013] 1 W.L.R. 2305 (CA (Civ Div)), Maurice Kay, L.J. (VP, CA Civ); see *Halliday v Creation Consumer Finance Ltd* [2013] EWCA Civ 333, [2013] 3 C.M.L.R. 4 (CA (Civ Div)), Arden, L.J.; see *Santander UK Plc v Harrison* [2013] EWHC 199 (QB), [2013] Bus. L.R. 501 (QBD), Males, J.; see *Smeaton v Equifax Plc* [2013] EWCA Civ 108, [2013] 2 All E.R. 959 (CA (Civ Div)), Tomlinson, L.J.; see *South Lanarkshire Council v Scottish Information Commissioner* [2013] UKSC 55, [2013] 1 W.L.R. 2421 (SC), Lady Hale, J.S.C.
applied: 2013 c.22 Sch.7 para.1, 2013 c.28 Sch.1, SI 2013/164 Sch.1 para.6, SI 2013/486 Reg.32, SI 2013/1877 Sch.1 para.6
s.13, see *Halliday v Creation Consumer Finance Ltd* [2013] EWCA Civ 333, [2013] 3 C.M.L.R. 4 (CA (Civ Div)), Arden, L.J.; see *Smeaton v Equifax Plc* [2013] EWCA Civ 108, [2013] 2 All E.R. 959 (CA (Civ Div)), Tomlinson, L.J.
s.13, applied: 2013 c.22 s.42
s.15, amended: 2013 c.22 Sch.9 para.77
s.35, see *Durham CC v D* [2012] EWCA Civ 1654, [2013] 1 W.L.R. 2305 (CA (Civ Div)), Maurice Kay, L.J. (VP, CA Civ)
s.35, applied: SI 2013/373 Reg.20
s.55D, amended: 2013 c.22 Sch.9 para.52
s.56, amended: 2013 c.22 Sch.8 para.187, SI 2013/602 Sch.2 para.28, SI 2013/630 Reg.14
s.56, applied: SI 2013/602 Sch.3 para.2
s.63A, amended: 2013 c.18 Sch.2 para.2
s.75, amended: SI 2013/630 Reg.14

32. Police (Northern Ireland) Act 1998

s.27, amended: 2013 c.22 Sch.8 para.62
s.27, repealed (in part): 2013 c.22 Sch.8 para.62
s.60ZA, amended: 2013 c.22 s.11
s.60ZA, repealed (in part): 2013 c.22 s.11
s.61, amended: 2013 c.22 Sch.6 para.19
s.73, amended: SI 2013/602 Sch.2 para.29
Sch.3 para.8, amended: SI 2013/602 Sch.2 para.29

36. Finance Act 1998

s.30, repealed (in part): 2013 c.2 Sch.1 Part 10
s.32, enabling: SI 2013/157
s.62, repealed: 2013 c.2 Sch.1 Part 10
s.103, repealed: 2013 c.2 Sch.1 Part 10
s.104, repealed: 2013 c.2 Sch.1 Part 10
s.105, repealed: 2013 c.2 Sch.1 Part 10
s.106, repealed (in part): 2013 c.2 Sch.1 Part 10
s.153, repealed: 2013 c.2 Sch.1 Part 10
Sch.3 para.1, repealed: 2013 c.2 Sch.1 Part 10
Sch.3 para.2, repealed: 2013 c.2 Sch.1 Part 10
Sch.3 para.3, repealed: 2013 c.2 Sch.1 Part 10
Sch.3 para.4, repealed: 2013 c.2 Sch.1 Part 10
Sch.3 para.8, repealed: 2013 c.2 Sch.1 Part 10
Sch.3 para.11, repealed: 2013 c.2 Sch.1 Part 10
Sch.3 para.12, repealed: 2013 c.2 Sch.1 Part 10
Sch.3 para.13, repealed: 2013 c.2 Sch.1 Part 10
Sch.3 para.14, repealed: 2013 c.2 Sch.1 Part 10
Sch.3 para.15, repealed: 2013 c.2 Sch.1 Part 10
Sch.3 para.16, repealed: 2013 c.2 Sch.1 Part 10
Sch.3 para.17, repealed: 2013 c.2 Sch.1 Part 10
Sch.3 para.18, repealed: 2013 c.2 Sch.1 Part 10
Sch.3 para.19, repealed: 2013 c.2 Sch.1 Part 10
Sch.3 para.20, repealed: 2013 c.2 Sch.1 Part 10
Sch.3 para.21, repealed: 2013 c.2 Sch.1 Part 10
Sch.3 para.22, repealed: 2013 c.2 Sch.1 Part 10
Sch.3 para.23, repealed: 2013 c.2 Sch.1 Part 10
Sch.3 para.25, repealed: 2013 c.2 Sch.1 Part 10
Sch.3 para.26, repealed: 2013 c.2 Sch.1 Part 10
Sch.3 para.27, repealed: 2013 c.2 Sch.1 Part 10
Sch.3 para.28, repealed: 2013 c.2 Sch.1 Part 10
Sch.3 para.29, repealed: 2013 c.2 Sch.1 Part 10
Sch.3 para.30, repealed: 2013 c.2 Sch.1 Part 10
Sch.3 para.31, repealed: 2013 c.2 Sch.1 Part 10
Sch.3 para.32, repealed: 2013 c.2 Sch.1 Part 10
Sch.3 para.33, repealed: 2013 c.2 Sch.1 Part 10
Sch.3 para.34, repealed: 2013 c.2 Sch.1 Part 10
Sch.3 para.35, repealed: 2013 c.2 Sch.1 Part 10
Sch.3 para.36, repealed: 2013 c.2 Sch.1 Part 10
Sch.3 para.37, repealed: 2013 c.2 Sch.1 Part 10
Sch.3 para.38, repealed: 2013 c.2 Sch.1 Part 10
Sch.3 para.39, repealed: 2013 c.2 Sch.1 Part 10
Sch.3 para.41, repealed: 2013 c.2 Sch.1 Part 10
Sch.3 para.42, repealed: 2013 c.2 Sch.1 Part 10
Sch.3 para.43, repealed: 2013 c.2 Sch.1 Part 10
Sch.3 para.44, repealed: 2013 c.2 Sch.1 Part 10
Sch.3 para.45, repealed: 2013 c.2 Sch.1 Part 10
Sch.3 para.46, repealed: 2013 c.2 Sch.1 Part 10
Sch.3 para.47, repealed: 2013 c.2 Sch.1 Part 10
Sch.3 para.48, repealed: 2013 c.2 Sch.1 Part 10
Sch.7 para.1, amended: 2013 c.2 Sch.1 Part 10
Sch.7 para.2, repealed: 2013 c.2 Sch.1 Part 10
Sch.7 para.3, amended: 2013 c.2 Sch.1 Part 10
Sch.7 para.8, repealed: 2013 c.2 Sch.1 Part 10
Sch.7 para.12, repealed: 2013 c.2 Sch.1 Part 10
Sch.11 para.1, repealed: 2013 c.2 Sch.1 Part 10
Sch.11 para.2, repealed: 2013 c.2 Sch.1 Part 10
Sch.11 para.3, repealed: 2013 c.2 Sch.1 Part 10
Sch.11 para.4, repealed: 2013 c.2 Sch.1 Part 10
Sch.11 para.5, repealed: 2013 c.2 Sch.1 Part 10
Sch.18, disapplied: 2013 c.29 s.210

Sch.18 Part I para.1, amended: 2013 c.29 Sch.30 para.13
Sch.18 Part II para.8, amended: 2013 c.29 Sch.30 para.13
Sch.18 Part II para.10, amended: 2013 c.29 Sch.15 para.5, Sch.18 para.3
Sch.18 Part II para.18, amended: 2013 c.29 Sch.30 para.13
Sch.18 Part VI para.51A, amended: 2013 c.29 s.231
Sch.18 Part VI para.51B, amended: 2013 c.29 s.232
Sch.18 Part VI para.52, amended: 2013 c.29 Sch.15 para.6, Sch.18 para.4
Sch.18 Part IXA para.83A, amended: 2013 c.29 Sch.15 para.7
Sch.18 Part IXA para.83A, substituted: 2013 c.29 Sch.15 para.7
Sch.18 Part IXA para.83B, substituted: 2013 c.29 Sch.15 para.7
Sch.18 Part IXA para.83C, amended: 2013 c.29 Sch.15 para.7
Sch.18 Part IXA para.83C, substituted: 2013 c.29 Sch.15 para.7
Sch.18 Part IXA para.83D, substituted: 2013 c.29 Sch.15 para.7
Sch.18 Part IXA para.83E, substituted: 2013 c.29 Sch.15 para.7
Sch.18 Part IXA para.83F, substituted: 2013 c.29 Sch.15 para.7
Sch.18 Part X para.87, amended: SI 2013/636 Sch.1 para.5
Sch.18 Part IXD para.83S, amended: 2013 c.29 Sch.18 para.5
Sch.18 Part IXD para.83S, substituted: 2013 c.29 Sch.18 para.5
Sch.18 Part IXD para.83T, substituted: 2013 c.29 Sch.18 para.5
Sch.18 Part IXD para.83U, substituted: 2013 c.29 Sch.18 para.5
Sch.18 Part IXD para.83V, substituted: 2013 c.29 Sch.18 para.5
Sch.18 Part IXD para.83W, substituted: 2013 c.29 Sch.18 para.5
Sch.18 Part IXD para.83X, substituted: 2013 c.29 Sch.18 para.5

37. Crime and Disorder Act 1998

s.1, applied: SI 2013/9 Reg.9, SI 2013/435 Sch.1 Part 7
s.1B, amended: 2013 c.22 Sch.9 para.52, Sch.9 para.75
s.1C, applied: SI 2013/1554 r.50_1
s.1CA, applied: SI 2013/435 Sch.2 para.16
s.1D, applied: SI 2013/9 Reg.9, SI 2013/1554 r.50_1
s.1G, applied: SI 2013/9 Reg.9
s.1H, applied: SI 2013/9 Reg.9
s.2, applied: SI 2013/435 Sch.1 Part 7
s.4, applied: SI 2013/9 Reg.9
s.5, applied: SI 2013/261 Sch.1 para.22
s.8, applied: SI 2013/9 Reg.9, SI 2013/1554 r.50_1
s.9, applied: SI 2013/9 Reg.9, SI 2013/1554 r.50_1
s.10, amended: 2013 c.22 Sch.9 para.52
s.10, applied: SI 2013/9 Reg.9, SI 2013/1554 r.63_1
s.11, amended: 2013 c.22 Sch.11 para.147
s.12, amended: 2013 c.22 Sch.11 para.148
s.13, repealed: 2013 c.22 Sch.11 para.149
s.13B, amended: 2013 c.22 Sch.11 para.150, Sch.11 para.152, Sch.16 para.27
s.29, see *R. v Niewulis (Piotr)* [2013] EWCA Crim 556, [2013] 2 Cr. App. R. (S.) 83 (CA (Crim Div)), Davis, L.J.
s.29, applied: SI 2013/435 Sch.1 Part 7
s.30, applied: SI 2013/435 Sch.1 Part 7
s.31, see *R. (on the application of Dyer) v Watford Magistrates' Court* [2013] EWHC 547 (admin), (2013) 177 J.P. 265 (DC), Laws, L.J.
s.31, applied: SI 2013/435 Sch.1 Part 7
s.32, applied: SI 2013/435 Sch.1 Part 7
s.38, applied: SI 2013/261 Sch.1 para.23
s.50A, applied: SI 2013/1554 r.9_1
s.51, see *R. v Gul (Hamesh)* [2012] EWCA Crim 1761, [2013] 1 W.L.R. 1136 (CA (Crim Div)), Lord Judge, L.C.J.
s.51, applied: SI 2013/1103 Art.3, SI 2013/1554 r.14_1, r.8_1, r.9_1
s.51A, applied: SI 2013/1554 r.14_1, r.9_1
s.51B, applied: SI 2013/1554 r.9_1, r.9_6
s.51C, applied: SI 2013/1554 r.9_1, r.9_6
s.51D, applied: SI 2013/1554 r.14_1, r.9_1
s.51E, applied: SI 2013/1554 r.9_1
s.52, applied: SI 2013/1554 r.9_1
s.52A, applied: SI 2013/1554 r.9_2, r.16_1
s.57A, applied: SI 2013/1554 r.9_2, r.19_2
s.57B, applied: SI 2013/1554 r.9_2, r.19_2
s.57C, applied: SI 2013/1554 r.9_2
s.57D, applied: SI 2013/1554 r.9_2, r.37_10
s.57E, applied: SI 2013/1554 r.9_2, r.37_10
s.66C, applied: SI 2013/608 Art.2
s.66C, enabling: SI 2013/608
s.66G, applied: SI 2013/613
s.66G, enabling: SI 2013/613
s.115, amended: SI 2013/602 Sch.2 para.30
s.115, applied: SI 2013/1554 r.5_9

Sch.3 para.2, applied: SI 2013/435 Sch.1 para.2, Sch.1 para.22, Sch.2 para.2, Sch.2 para.21, SI 2013/1554 r.9_16
Sch.3 para.3, applied: SI 2013/1554 r.16_1
Sch.3 para.10, applied: SI 2013/435 Sch.1 para.22, Sch.2 para.21
Sch.3 para.13, applied: SI 2013/435 Sch.1 para.22, Sch.2 para.21
Sch.3 para.15, applied: SI 2013/435 Sch.1 para.22, Sch.2 para.21
Sch.8 para.42, repealed: 2013 c.22 Sch.10 para.99

38. Government of Wales Act 1998

s.105, disapplied: SI 2013/1821 Art.27
s.105, repealed: SI 2013/1821 Art.15
s.145, applied: SI 2013/1821 Art.26
s.147, repealed: SI 2013/1821 Art.11
s.154, amended: SI 2013/1821 Art.11, Art.15
Sch.4 Part III para.15, repealed: SI 2013/755 Sch.2 para.392
Sch.7 para.1, repealed: SI 2013/755 Sch.2 para.393
Sch.7 para.2, repealed: SI 2013/755 Sch.2 para.393
Sch.7 para.3, disapplied: SI 2013/1821 Art.27
Sch.7 para.3, repealed: SI 2013/1821 Art.15
Sch.7 para.4, disapplied: SI 2013/1821 Art.27
Sch.7 para.4, repealed: SI 2013/1821 Art.15
Sch.7 para.5, disapplied: SI 2013/1821 Art.27
Sch.7 para.5, repealed: SI 2013/1821 Art.15
Sch.7 para.6, disapplied: SI 2013/1821 Art.27
Sch.7 para.6, repealed: SI 2013/1821 Art.15
Sch.7 para.7, disapplied: SI 2013/1821 Art.27
Sch.7 para.7, repealed: SI 2013/1821 Art.15
Sch.7 para.8, disapplied: SI 2013/1821 Art.27
Sch.7 para.8, repealed: SI 2013/1821 Art.15
Sch.7 para.9, disapplied: SI 2013/1821 Art.27
Sch.7 para.9, repealed: SI 2013/1821 Art.15
Sch.7 para.10, disapplied: SI 2013/1821 Art.27
Sch.7 para.10, repealed: SI 2013/1821 Art.15
Sch.7 para.11, disapplied: SI 2013/1821 Art.27
Sch.7 para.11, repealed: SI 2013/1821 Art.15
Sch.12 para.23, repealed: 2013 c.8 Sch.1 para.3
Sch.17, referred to: SI 2013/1821 Art.26
Sch.17 Part I para.1, varied: SI 2013/1821 Art.26
Sch.17 Part I para.2, varied: SI 2013/1821 Art.26
Sch.17 Part I para.3, varied: SI 2013/1821 Art.26
Sch.17 Part I para.4, varied: SI 2013/1821 Art.26
Sch.17 Part I para.5, varied: SI 2013/1821 Art.26
Sch.17 Part I para.6, varied: SI 2013/1821 Art.26
Sch.17 Part I para.7, varied: SI 2013/1821 Art.26
Sch.17 Part I para.8, varied: SI 2013/1821 Art.26
Sch.17 Part I para.9, varied: SI 2013/1821 Art.26
Sch.17 Part I para.10, varied: SI 2013/1821 Art.26
Sch.17 Part I para.11, varied: SI 2013/1821 Art.26
Sch.17 Part II para.12, varied: SI 2013/1821 Art.26
Sch.17 Part II para.12A, varied: SI 2013/1821 Art.26
Sch.17 Part II para.13, varied: SI 2013/1821 Art.26
Sch.17 Part II para.14, varied: SI 2013/1821 Art.26
Sch.17 Part II para.14A, varied: SI 2013/1821 Art.26
Sch.17 Part III para.15, varied: SI 2013/1821 Art.26
Sch.17 Part III para.16, varied: SI 2013/1821 Art.26

39. National Minimum Wage Act 1998

applied: SI 2013/1893 Sch.2
s.1, enabling: SI 2013/1975
s.2, enabling: SI 2013/1975
s.3, enabling: SI 2013/1975
s.5, applied: SI 2013/1975
s.6, applied: SI 2013/1975
s.11, amended: 2013 c.24 Sch.2 para.37
s.11A, added: 2013 c.24 Sch.2 para.38
s.16, repealed (in part): 2013 c.24 Sch.20 para.2
s.16A, repealed (in part): 2013 c.24 Sch.20 para.2
s.19E, amended: 2013 c.22 Sch.9 para.52
s.24, amended: 2013 c.24 Sch.2 para.39
s.38, amended: 2013 c.22 Sch.9 para.52
s.39, amended: 2013 c.22 Sch.9 para.52
s.44, amended: SI 2013/1465 Sch.1 para.6
s.46, repealed (in part): 2013 c.24 Sch.20 para.2
s.47, amended: 2013 c.24 Sch.20 para.2
s.47, repealed (in part): 2013 c.24 Sch.20 para.2
s.49, amended: 2013 c.24 s.23, Sch.1 para.11
s.51, applied: SI 2013/1975
s.51, enabling: SI 2013/1975
s.55, amended: 2013 c.24 Sch.20 para.2
Sch.2 Part I para.1, repealed (in part): 2013 c.24 Sch.20 para.2
Sch.2 Part I para.2, repealed (in part): 2013 c.24 Sch.20 para.2, Sch.20 para.2
Sch.2 Part I para.3, repealed (in part): 2013 c.24 Sch.20 para.2
Sch.2 Part I para.4, repealed (in part): 2013 c.24 Sch.20 para.2
Sch.2 Part I para.5, repealed (in part): 2013 c.24 Sch.20 para.2
Sch.2 Part I para.6, repealed (in part): 2013 c.24 Sch.20 para.2
Sch.2 Part I para.7, repealed (in part): 2013 c.24 Sch.20 para.2
Sch.2 Part I para.8, repealed (in part): 2013 c.24 Sch.20 para.2
Sch.2 Part I para.9, repealed (in part): 2013 c.24 Sch.20 para.2
Sch.2 Part I para.10, repealed (in part): 2013 c.24 Sch.20 para.2

40. Criminal Justice (Terrorism and Conspiracy) Act 1998

s.5, applied: SI 2013/435 Sch.1 Part 7

41. Competition Act 1998

Commencement Orders: SI 2013/284 Art.2
applied: 2013 c.33 s.62, s.66, s.91
Part I, applied: 2013 c.24 s.46, s.52, Sch.4 para.16, Sch.4 para.30, 2013 c.33 s.61
Part I c.V, amended: 2013 c.24 Sch.5 para.30
Part I c.V, amended: 2013 c.24 Sch.5 para.35
s.1, varied: 2013 c.33 s.61
s.2, see *Deutsche Bank AG v Unitech Global Ltd* [2013] EWHC 2793 (Comm), [2013] 2 Lloyd's Rep. 629 (QBD (Comm)), Teare, J.; see *Tesco Stores Ltd v Office of Fair Trading* [2013] Comp. A.R. 23 (CAT), Lord Carlile of Berriew Q.C.
s.2, referred to: 2013 c.33 s.61
s.2, varied: 2013 c.33 s.61
s.3, varied: 2013 c.33 s.61
s.4, varied: 2013 c.33 s.61
s.5, varied: 2013 c.33 s.61
s.6, amended: 2013 c.24 Sch.5 para.2
s.6, varied: 2013 c.33 s.61
s.7, varied: 2013 c.33 s.61
s.8, amended: 2013 c.24 Sch.5 para.3
s.8, varied: 2013 c.33 s.61
s.9, varied: 2013 c.33 s.61
s.10, amended: 2013 c.24 Sch.5 para.4
s.10, varied: 2013 c.33 s.61
s.11, varied: 2013 c.33 s.61
s.12, varied: 2013 c.33 s.61
s.13, varied: 2013 c.33 s.61
s.14, varied: 2013 c.33 s.61
s.15, varied: 2013 c.33 s.61
s.16, varied: 2013 c.33 s.61
s.17, varied: 2013 c.33 s.61
s.18, see *Infederation Ltd v Google Inc* [2013] EWHC 2295 (Ch), [2013] U.K.C.L.R. 773 (Ch D), Roth, J.
s.18, referred to: 2013 c.33 s.61
s.18, varied: 2013 c.33 s.61
s.19, varied: 2013 c.33 s.61
s.20, varied: 2013 c.33 s.61
s.21, varied: 2013 c.33 s.61
s.22, varied: 2013 c.33 s.61
s.23, varied: 2013 c.33 s.61
s.24, varied: 2013 c.33 s.61
s.25, amended: 2013 c.24 Sch.5 para.5
s.25, varied: 2013 c.33 s.61
s.25A, added: 2013 c.24 s.42
s.25A, varied: 2013 c.33 s.61
s.26, amended: 2013 c.24 Sch.5 para.6, Sch.15 para.9
s.26, substituted: 2013 c.24 s.39
s.26, varied: 2013 c.33 s.61
s.26A, added: 2013 c.24 s.39
s.26A, varied: 2013 c.33 s.61
s.27, amended: 2013 c.24 Sch.5 para.7
s.27, varied: 2013 c.33 s.61
s.28, amended: 2013 c.24 Sch.5 para.8, Sch.13 para.2
s.28, varied: 2013 c.33 s.61
s.28A, amended: 2013 c.24 Sch.5 para.9, Sch.13 para.3
s.28A, varied: 2013 c.33 s.61
s.29, varied: 2013 c.33 s.61
s.30, varied: 2013 c.33 s.61
s.30A, amended: 2013 c.24 s.39
s.30A, varied: 2013 c.33 s.61
s.31, amended: 2013 c.24 Sch.5 para.10
s.31, varied: 2013 c.33 s.61
s.31A, amended: 2013 c.24 Sch.5 para.11
s.31A, varied: 2013 c.33 s.61
s.31B, amended: 2013 c.24 Sch.5 para.12
s.31B, varied: 2013 c.33 s.61
s.31C, amended: 2013 c.24 Sch.5 para.13
s.31C, varied: 2013 c.33 s.61
s.31D, amended: 2013 c.24 Sch.5 para.14
s.31D, applied: 2013 c.33 s.61
s.31D, varied: 2013 c.33 s.61
s.31E, amended: 2013 c.24 Sch.5 para.15
s.31E, varied: 2013 c.33 s.61
s.31F, added: 2013 c.24 s.45
s.31F, varied: 2013 c.33 s.61
s.32, amended: 2013 c.24 Sch.5 para.16
s.32, varied: 2013 c.33 s.61
s.33, amended: 2013 c.24 Sch.5 para.17
s.33, varied: 2013 c.33 s.61
s.34, amended: 2013 c.24 Sch.5 para.18
s.34, varied: 2013 c.33 s.61
s.35, amended: 2013 c.24 s.43, Sch.5 para.19
s.35, varied: 2013 c.33 s.61
s.36, amended: 2013 c.24 s.44, Sch.5 para.20
s.36, varied: 2013 c.33 s.61
s.37, amended: 2013 c.24 Sch.5 para.21
s.37, varied: 2013 c.33 s.61
s.38, amended: 2013 c.24 s.40, s.44, Sch.5 para.22, Sch.15 para.10
s.38, applied: 2013 c.33 s.61
s.38, varied: 2013 c.33 s.61
s.39, amended: 2013 c.24 Sch.5 para.23
s.39, varied: 2013 c.33 s.61
s.40, amended: 2013 c.24 Sch.5 para.24
s.40, varied: 2013 c.33 s.61
s.40A, added: 2013 c.24 s.40
s.40A, varied: 2013 c.33 s.61
s.40B, added: 2013 c.24 s.40
s.40B, applied: 2013 c.33 s.61

s.40B, varied: 2013 c.33 s.61
s.41, varied: 2013 c.33 s.61
s.42, amended: 2013 c.24 s.40
s.42, repealed (in part): 2013 c.24 s.40
s.42, varied: 2013 c.33 s.61
s.43, varied: 2013 c.33 s.61
s.44, amended: 2013 c.24 Sch.5 para.25
s.44, varied: 2013 c.33 s.61
s.45, amended: 2013 c.24 Sch.5 para.219
s.45, repealed: 2013 c.24 Sch.5 para.220
s.45, varied: 2013 c.33 s.61
s.46, amended: 2013 c.24 Sch.5 para.26, Sch.5 para.219
s.46, varied: 2013 c.33 s.61
s.47, amended: 2013 c.24 Sch.5 para.27, Sch.5 para.219
s.47, varied: 2013 c.33 s.61
s.47A, see *Albion Water Ltd v Dwr Cymru Cyfyngedig* [2013] CAT 16, [2013] Comp. A.R. 377 (CAT), Rose, J.; see *Albion Water Ltd v Dwr Cymru Cyfyngedig* [2013] CAT 6, [2013] Comp. A.R. 200 (CAT), Vivien Rose (Chairman); see *Bord Na Mona Horticulture Ltd v British Polythene Industries Plc* [2012] EWHC 3346 (Comm), [2013] U.K.C.L.R. 50 (QBD (Comm)), Flaux, J.; see *Deutsche Bahn AG v Morgan Advanced Materials Plc (formerly Morgan Crucible Co Plc)* [2013] CAT 18, [2013] Comp. A.R. 388 (CAT), Judge Marcus Smith Q.C.; see *Deutsche Bahn AG v Morgan Crucible Co Plc* [2012] EWCA Civ 1055, [2013] Bus. L.R. 125 (CA (Civ Div)), Mummery, L.J.; see *Emerson Electric Co v Mersen UK Portslade Ltd (formerly Le Carbone (Great Britain) Ltd)* [2012] EWCA Civ 1559, [2013] Bus. L.R. 342 (CA (Civ Div)), Mummery, L.J.; see *WH Newson Holding Ltd v IMI Plc* [2012] EWHC 3680 (Ch), [2013] Bus. L.R. 599 (Ch D), Roth, J.
s.47A, amended: 2013 c.24 Sch.5 para.28, Sch.5 para.219
s.47A, varied: 2013 c.33 s.61
s.47B, amended: 2013 c.24 Sch.5 para.219
s.47B, varied: 2013 c.33 s.61
s.48, amended: 2013 c.24 Sch.5 para.219
s.48, varied: 2013 c.33 s.61
s.49, amended: 2013 c.24 Sch.5 para.219
s.49, varied: 2013 c.33 s.61
s.50, amended: 2013 c.24 Sch.5 para.29
s.50, varied: 2013 c.33 s.61
s.51, amended: 2013 c.24 Sch.5 para.31
s.51, applied: 2013 c.24 Sch.4 para.30, 2013 c.33 s.61
s.51, varied: 2013 c.33 s.61
s.52, amended: 2013 c.24 Sch.5 para.32
s.52, applied: 2013 c.33 s.61
s.52, varied: 2013 c.33 s.61
s.53, varied: 2013 c.33 s.61
s.54, amended: 2013 c.24 s.51, Sch.5 para.33, Sch.15 para.11, 2013 c.33 s.67, Sch.8 para.9
s.54, applied: 2013 c.24 s.52, 2013 c.33 s.61
s.54, repealed (in part): 2013 c.24 Sch.15 para.11
s.54, varied: 2013 c.33 s.61
s.55, applied: 2013 c.33 s.62
s.55, varied: 2013 c.33 s.61
s.56, applied: 2013 c.33 s.62
s.56, varied: 2013 c.33 s.61
s.57, amended: 2013 c.24 Sch.5 para.34
s.57, applied: 2013 c.33 s.62
s.57, varied: 2013 c.33 s.61
s.58, amended: 2013 c.24 Sch.5 para.36
s.58, applied: 2013 c.33 s.62
s.58, varied: 2013 c.33 s.61
s.58A, amended: 2013 c.24 Sch.5 para.37
s.58A, varied: 2013 c.33 s.61
s.59, amended: 2013 c.24 Sch.5 para.38, Sch.5 para.221
s.59, varied: 2013 c.33 s.61
s.60, amended: 2013 c.24 Sch.5 para.39
s.60, varied: 2013 c.33 s.61
s.61, amended: 2013 c.24 Sch.5 para.40, Sch.13 para.4
s.62, amended: 2013 c.24 Sch.5 para.41, Sch.13 para.5
s.62A, amended: 2013 c.24 Sch.5 para.42, Sch.13 para.6
s.62B, amended: 2013 c.24 Sch.5 para.43
s.63, amended: 2013 c.24 Sch.5 para.44, Sch.13 para.7
s.65C, amended: 2013 c.24 Sch.5 para.45, Sch.13 para.8
s.65D, amended: 2013 c.24 Sch.5 para.46
s.65E, amended: 2013 c.24 Sch.5 para.47
s.65F, amended: 2013 c.24 Sch.5 para.48
s.65G, amended: 2013 c.24 Sch.5 para.49, Sch.13 para.9
s.65H, amended: 2013 c.24 Sch.5 para.50, Sch.13 para.10
s.65N, amended: 2013 c.24 Sch.5 para.51
s.75, enabling: SI 2013/294
s.75A, amended: 2013 c.24 Sch.5 para.52
s.76, enabling: SI 2013/284
Sch.1 Part I para.4, amended: 2013 c.24 Sch.5 para.53
Sch.1 Part I para.5, amended: 2013 c.24 Sch.5 para.53, Sch.15 para.12
Sch.2 Part III para.5, amended: 2013 c.24 Sch.5 para.54
Sch.3 para.9, amended: 2013 c.24 Sch.5 para.55

Sch.6A Part I para.1, amended: 2013 c.24 Sch.5 para.56
Sch.6A Part I para.2, amended: 2013 c.24 Sch.5 para.56
Sch.6A Part I para.3, amended: 2013 c.24 Sch.5 para.56
Sch.6A Part I para.4, amended: 2013 c.24 Sch.5 para.56
Sch.6A Part I para.5, amended: 2013 c.24 Sch.5 para.56
Sch.6A Part I para.6, amended: 2013 c.24 Sch.5 para.56
Sch.6A Part I para.7, amended: 2013 c.24 Sch.5 para.56
Sch.6A Part I para.8, amended: 2013 c.24 Sch.5 para.56
Sch.6A Part II para.10, amended: 2013 c.24 Sch.5 para.56
Sch.6A Part II para.11, amended: 2013 c.24 Sch.5 para.56
Sch.6A Part II para.12, amended: 2013 c.24 Sch.5 para.56
Sch.6A Part II para.13, amended: 2013 c.24 Sch.5 para.56
Sch.6A Part II para.14, amended: 2013 c.24 Sch.5 para.56
Sch.7 Part I para.1, repealed: 2013 c.24 Sch.5 para.222
Sch.7 Part I para.2, referred to: 2013 c.24 Sch.4 para.63
Sch.7 Part I para.2, repealed: 2013 c.24 Sch.5 para.222
Sch.7 Part I para.3, repealed: 2013 c.24 Sch.5 para.222
Sch.7 Part I para.4, repealed: 2013 c.24 Sch.5 para.222
Sch.7 Part I para.5, repealed: 2013 c.24 Sch.5 para.222
Sch.7 Part I para.6, repealed: 2013 c.24 Sch.5 para.222
Sch.7 Part I para.7, repealed: 2013 c.24 Sch.5 para.222
Sch.7 Part I para.7A, repealed: 2013 c.24 Sch.5 para.222
Sch.7 Part I para.8, repealed: 2013 c.24 Sch.5 para.222
Sch.7 Part I para.9, repealed: 2013 c.24 Sch.5 para.222
Sch.7 Part I para.10, repealed: 2013 c.24 Sch.5 para.222
Sch.7 Part I para.11, repealed: 2013 c.24 Sch.5 para.222
Sch.7 Part I para.12, repealed: 2013 c.24 Sch.5 para.222
Sch.7 Part I para.12A, repealed: 2013 c.24 Sch.5 para.222
Sch.7 Part I para.13, repealed: 2013 c.24 Sch.5 para.222
Sch.7 Part II para.14, repealed: 2013 c.24 Sch.5 para.222
Sch.7 Part II para.15, repealed: 2013 c.24 Sch.5 para.222
Sch.7 Part II para.16, repealed: 2013 c.24 Sch.5 para.222
Sch.7 Part II para.17, repealed: 2013 c.24 Sch.5 para.222
Sch.7 Part II para.18, repealed: 2013 c.24 Sch.5 para.222
Sch.7 Part II para.19, repealed: 2013 c.24 Sch.5 para.222
Sch.7 Part II para.19A, repealed: 2013 c.24 Sch.5 para.222
Sch.7 Part II para.20, repealed: 2013 c.24 Sch.5 para.222
Sch.7 Part II para.21, repealed: 2013 c.24 Sch.5 para.222
Sch.7 Part II para.22, repealed: 2013 c.24 Sch.5 para.222
Sch.7 Part III para.23, repealed: 2013 c.24 Sch.5 para.222
Sch.7 Part III para.24, repealed: 2013 c.24 Sch.5 para.222
Sch.7 Part III para.25, repealed: 2013 c.24 Sch.5 para.222
Sch.7 Part III para.26, repealed: 2013 c.24 Sch.5 para.222
Sch.7 Part III para.27, repealed: 2013 c.24 Sch.5 para.222
Sch.7 Part IV para.28, repealed: 2013 c.24 Sch.5 para.222
Sch.7 Part IV para.29, repealed: 2013 c.24 Sch.5 para.222
Sch.7 Part V para.30, repealed: 2013 c.24 Sch.5 para.222
Sch.7 Part V para.31, repealed: 2013 c.24 Sch.5 para.222
Sch.7 Part V para.32, repealed: 2013 c.24 Sch.5 para.222
Sch.7 Part V para.33, repealed: 2013 c.24 Sch.5 para.222
Sch.7 Part V para.34, repealed: 2013 c.24 Sch.5 para.222
Sch.7 Part V para.35, repealed: 2013 c.24 Sch.5 para.222
Sch.7 Part V para.36, repealed: 2013 c.24 Sch.5 para.222
Sch.7A para.1, repealed: 2013 c.24 Sch.5 para.223
Sch.7A para.2, repealed: 2013 c.24 Sch.5 para.223

Sch.7A para.3, repealed: 2013 c.24 Sch.5 para.223
Sch.7A para.4, repealed: 2013 c.24 Sch.5 para.223
Sch.7A para.5, repealed: 2013 c.24 Sch.5 para.223
Sch.7A para.6, repealed: 2013 c.24 Sch.5 para.223
Sch.7A para.7, repealed: 2013 c.24 Sch.5 para.223
Sch.8 Part I para.2, amended: 2013 c.24 Sch.5 para.57
Sch.8 Part I para.3, amended: 2013 c.24 Sch.5 para.57
Sch.8 Part I para.3A, amended: 2013 c.24 Sch.5 para.57
Sch.9 para.1, amended: 2013 c.24 Sch.5 para.58
Sch.9 para.1A, added: 2013 c.24 s.42
Sch.9 para.1A, amended: 2013 c.24 Sch.5 para.58
Sch.9 para.1A, applied: 2013 c.24 Sch.4 para.30
Sch.9 para.2, amended: 2013 c.24 Sch.5 para.58
Sch.9 para.3, amended: 2013 c.24 Sch.5 para.58
Sch.9 para.4, amended: 2013 c.24 Sch.5 para.58
Sch.9 para.5, amended: 2013 c.24 Sch.5 para.58
Sch.9 para.6, amended: 2013 c.24 Sch.5 para.58
Sch.9 para.7, amended: 2013 c.24 Sch.5 para.58
Sch.9 para.8, amended: 2013 c.24 Sch.5 para.58
Sch.9 para.9, amended: 2013 c.24 Sch.5 para.58
Sch.9 para.10, amended: 2013 c.24 Sch.5 para.58
Sch.9 para.11, amended: 2013 c.24 Sch.5 para.58
Sch.9 para.12, amended: 2013 c.24 Sch.5 para.58
Sch.9 para.13, amended: 2013 c.24 Sch.5 para.58
Sch.9 para.13A, added: 2013 c.24 s.42
Sch.9 para.13A, amended: 2013 c.24 Sch.5 para.58
Sch.9 para.13B, added: 2013 c.24 s.42
Sch.9 para.13B, amended: 2013 c.24 Sch.5 para.58
Sch.9 para.13C, added: 2013 c.24 s.42
Sch.9 para.13C, amended: 2013 c.24 Sch.5 para.58
Sch.9 para.14, amended: 2013 c.24 Sch.5 para.58

42. Human Rights Act 1998

see *A (A Child) (Disclosure of Third Party Information), Re* [2013] 2 A.C. 66 (SC), Lord Neuberger, J.S.C.; see *DD v Durham CC* [2013] EWCA Civ 96, [2013] M.H.L.R. 85 (CA (Civ Div)), Sir John Thomas (President); see *Donaldson v Scottish Legal Aid Board* 2013 S.L.T. 35 (OH), Lord Drummond Young; see *Izuazu (Article 8: New Rules: Nigeria), Re* [2013] UKUT 45 (IAC), [2013] Imm. A.R. 453 (UT (IAC)), Blake, J. (President); see *J v Commissioner of Police of the Metropolis* [2013] EWHC 32 (QB), [2013] 1 W.L.R. 2734 (QBD), Tugendhat, J.; see *Kerr v Northern Ireland Housing Executive* [2013] R.V.R. 137 (Lands Tr (NI)), Coghlin, L.J.; see *Mohan v Mohan* [2013] EWCA Civ 586, [2013] C.P. Rep. 36 (CA (Civ Div)), Thorpe, L.J.; see *R. (on the application of Chatting) v Viridian Housing* [2012] EWHC 3595 (Admin), [2013] H.R.L.R. 12 (QBD (Admin)), Nicholas Paines Q.C.; see *R. (on the application of Hodkin) v Registrar General of Births Deaths and Marriages* [2012] EWHC 3635 (Admin), [2013] P.T.S.R. 875 (QBD (Admin)), Ouseley, J.; see *R. (on the application of Modaresi) v Secretary of State for Health* [2013] UKSC 53, [2013] 4 All E.R. 318 (SC), Lord Neuberger (President); see *R. (on the application of Nicklinson) v Ministry of Justice* [2013] EWCA Civ 961, [2013] H.R.L.R. 36 (CA (Civ Div)), Lord Judge, L.C.J.; see *R. v Petherick (Rosie Lee)* [2012] EWCA Crim 2214, [2013] 1 W.L.R. 1102 (CA (Crim Div)), Hughes, L.J.; see *Ruddy v Chief Constable of Strathclyde* 2013 S.C. (U.K.S.C.) 126 (SC), Lord Hope, J.S.C. (Deputy President); see *Sims v Dacorum BC* [2013] EWCA Civ 12, [2013] C.P. Rep. 19 (CA (Civ Div)), Mummery, L.J.; see *Smart v Forensic Science Service Ltd* [2013] EWCA Civ 783, [2013] P.N.L.R. 32 (CA (Civ Div)), Moses, L.J.; see *Total Technology (Engineering) Ltd v Revenue and Customs Commissioners* [2013] S.T.C. 681 (UT (Tax)), Warren, J.

applied: SI 2013/1554 r.65_12, SI 2013/2325 Reg.24, Reg.83
s.4, amended: 2013 c.22 Sch.14 para.5
s.4, applied: SI 2013/1554 r.65_12
s.6, see *A (A Child) (Intractable Contact Dispute: Human Rights Violations), Re* [2013] EWCA Civ 1104, [2013] 3 F.C.R. 257 (CA (Civ Div)), Aikens L.J.; see *B (A Child) (Care Proceedings: Appeal), Re* [2013] UKSC 33, [2013] 1 W.L.R. 1911 (SC), Lord Neuberger, J.S.C.; see *G (A Child) (Care Proceedings: Welfare Evaluation), Re* [2013] EWCA Civ 965, [2013] 3 F.C.R. 293 (CA (Civ Div)), Longmore, L.J.; see *NJ v Lord Advocate* [2013] CSOH 27, 2013 S.L.T. 347 (OH), Lord Brailsford; see *Ogundimu (Article 8: New Rules: Nigeria), Re* [2013] UKUT 60 (IAC), [2013] Imm. A.R. 422 (UT (IAC)), Blake, J. (President); see *R. (on the application of S) v Secretary of State for Justice* [2012] EWHC 1810 (Admin), [2013] 1 W.L.R. 3079 (QBD (Admin)), Sales, J.; see *R. (on the application of Tajik) v City of Westminster Magistrates' Court* [2012] EWHC 3347 (Admin), [2013] 1 W.L.R. 2283 (DC), Moses, L.J.; see *Sarjantson v Chief Constable of Humberside* [2013] EWCA Civ 1252, [2013] 3 W.L.R. 1540 (CA (Civ Div)), Lord Dyson (M.R.); see *Shehadeh v Advocate General for Scotland* 2013 S.L.T. 205 (OH), Lord Doherty; see *South Lanarkshire Council v McKenna* 2013 S.C. 212 (IH (Ex Div)), Lord Clarke; see *Thurrock BC v West* [2012] EWCA Civ 1435, [2013] H.L.R. 5 (CA (Civ Div)), Hallett, L.J.

s.6, applied: 2013 c.19 Sch.1 para.18, 2013 c.32 s.63, 2013 c.33 s.120, Sch.4 para.14
Sch.1 Part I, applied: SI 2013/2325 Reg.24, Reg.83
Sch.4 para.4, amended: 2013 c.25 Sch.8 para.26

47. Northern Ireland Act 1998
applied: 2013 asp 14 Sch.4 para.1, 2013 c.12 Sch.1 para.1, 2013 c.28 Sch.1
s.37, amended: 2013 c.8 Sch.1 para.4
s.69B, amended: 2013 c.18 Sch.2 para.3
s.84, applied: SI 2013/3156
s.84, enabling: SI 2013/3156
Sch.2 para.20A, added: 2013 c.15 s.17
Sch.3 para.9, amended: 2013 c.22 Sch.8 para.63
Sch.13 para.5, repealed (in part): 2013 c.8 Sch.1 para.4

1999

3. Road Traffic (NHS Charges) Act 1999
s.7, enabling: SI 2013/2586
s.16, enabling: SI 2013/2586

8. Health Act 1999
s.31, applied: SI 2013/3104 Sch.1 para.7

14. Protection of Children Act 1999
s.9, amended: 2013 c.22 Sch.9 para.123

16. Finance Act 1999
s.46, repealed: 2013 c.2 Sch.1 Part 10
s.132, enabling: SI 2013/701, SI 2013/2259, SI 2013/2592
s.133, enabling: SI 2013/521, SI 2013/701, SI 2013/1844, SI 2013/2259
Sch.4 para.2, repealed: 2013 c.2 Sch.1 Part 10
Sch.4 para.3, repealed (in part): 2013 c.2 Sch.1 Part 10
Sch.4 para.5, repealed (in part): 2013 c.2 Sch.1 Part 10
Sch.4 para.6, repealed: 2013 c.2 Sch.1 Part 10
Sch.4 para.7, repealed (in part): 2013 c.2 Sch.1 Part 10
Sch.4 para.8, repealed: 2013 c.2 Sch.1 Part 10
Sch.4 para.9, repealed (in part): 2013 c.2 Sch.1 Part 10
Sch.4 para.10, repealed: 2013 c.2 Sch.1 Part 10
Sch.4 para.11, repealed: 2013 c.2 Sch.1 Part 10
Sch.4 para.12, repealed: 2013 c.2 Sch.1 Part 10
Sch.4 para.13, repealed (in part): 2013 c.2 Sch.1 Part 10
Sch.4 para.14, repealed (in part): 2013 c.2 Sch.1 Part 10
Sch.4 para.15, repealed (in part): 2013 c.2 Sch.1 Part 10
Sch.4 para.17, repealed (in part): 2013 c.2 Sch.1 Part 10
Sch.4 para.18, repealed (in part): 2013 c.2 Sch.1 Part 10
Sch.13 Part IV para.25A, added: SI 2013/1401 Reg.5

18. Adoption (Intercountry Aspects) Act 1999
s.1, enabling: SI 2013/985

22. Access to Justice Act 1999
Part I, applied: SI 2013/534 Reg.6, Reg.7, Reg.8
s.1, referred to: SI 2013/534 Reg.6
s.2, referred to: SI 2013/534 Reg.6
s.4, referred to: SI 2013/534 Reg.6
s.5, referred to: SI 2013/534 Reg.6
s.6, applied: SI 2013/534 Reg.7
s.8, referred to: SI 2013/534 Reg.6
s.9, applied: SI 2013/1179 Sch.2 para.2
s.10, applied: SI 2013/534 Reg.10
s.11, see *Nutting v Khaliq* [2012] EWCA Civ 1726, [2013] B.P.I.R. 340 (CA (Civ Div)), Mummery, L.J.
s.11, applied: SI 2013/1554 r.61_22
s.13, applied: SI 2013/534 Reg.11
s.14, applied: SI 2013/534 Reg.7, Reg.11, Reg.12
s.14, enabling: SI 2013/2804
s.16, applied: SI 2013/534 Reg.12
s.16, referred to: SI 2013/534 Reg.6
s.17A, applied: SI 2013/534 Reg.7
s.18, referred to: SI 2013/534 Reg.6
s.25, referred to: SI 2013/534 Reg.6
s.25, enabling: SI 2013/2804
s.45, repealed: 2013 c.2 Sch.1 Part 5
s.54, amended: 2013 c.22 Sch.9 para.52, Sch.10 para.79
s.55, amended: 2013 c.22 Sch.9 para.52, Sch.10 para.80
s.56, amended: 2013 c.22 Sch.9 para.52, Sch.10 para.81
s.57, amended: 2013 c.22 Sch.9 para.52, Sch.10 para.82
Sch.1, referred to: SI 2013/534 Reg.6
Sch.3, applied: SI 2013/534 Reg.7
Sch.4 para.1, referred to: SI 2013/534 Reg.6
Sch.4 para.11, referred to: SI 2013/534 Reg.6
Sch.4 para.12, referred to: SI 2013/534 Reg.6
Sch.10 para.22, repealed: 2013 c.22 Sch.10 para.99
Sch.10 para.33, repealed: 2013 c.22 Sch.10 para.99
Sch.10 para.34, repealed: 2013 c.22 Sch.10 para.99
Sch.11 para.26, repealed: 2013 c.22 Sch.10 para.99
Sch.11 para.27, repealed: 2013 c.22 Sch.10 para.99
Sch.13 para.73, repealed (in part): 2013 c.22 Sch.11 para.210
Sch.13 para.79, repealed: 2013 c.22 Sch.11 para.210
Sch.13 para.80, repealed: 2013 c.22 Sch.11 para.210

24. Pollution Prevention and Control Act 1999
referred to: SI 2013/362 Reg.26
s.2, amended: SI 2013/755 Sch.2 para.395
s.2, applied: SI 2013/390, SI 2013/766, SI 2013/971, SI 2013/1037, SI 2013/3135
s.2, enabling: SI 2013/390, SI 2013/766, SI 2013/971, SI 2013/1037, SI 2013/3135
s.3, amended: SI 2013/755 Sch.2 para.396
s.7, enabling: SI 2013/390, SI 2013/766, SI 2013/971, SI 2013/3135
Sch.1, enabling: SI 2013/390, SI 2013/766, SI 2013/1037, SI 2013/3135
Sch.1 Part I para.20, applied: SI 2013/123 Art.2, SI 2013/669 Art.2, SSI 2013/321 Art.2
Sch.1 Part I para.20, enabling: SI 2013/123, SI 2013/669, SI 2013/766, SSI 2013/321

26. Employment Relations Act 1999
s.11, see *Toal v GB Oils Ltd* [2013] I.R.L.R. 696 (EAT), Mitting, J.
s.11, amended: 2013 c.24 Sch.2 para.40
s.34, amended: 2013 c.24 s.15, s.22
s.38, enabling: SI 2013/278

27. Local Government Act 1999
Part I, applied: SI 2013/3104 Sch.1 para.20
s.15, applied: SI 2013/2356 Sch.2 para.1

29. Greater London Authority Act 1999
applied: 2013 c.12 Sch.1 para.1, 2013 c.28 Sch.1, SI 2013/973 Art.3
s.34A, applied: SI 2013/973 Art.3
s.34A, enabling: SI 2013/973
s.38, amended: 2013 c.27 s.28
s.86, amended: SI 2013/733 Art.3
s.99, amended: SI 2013/733 Art.3
s.100, amended: SI 2013/733 Art.3
s.101, amended: SI 2013/733 Art.3
s.102, amended: SI 2013/733 Art.3
s.103, amended: SI 2013/733 Art.3
s.191, amended: SI 2013/1644 Sch.3
s.194, amended: SI 2013/1644 Sch.3
s.195, amended: SI 2013/1644 Sch.3
s.235, amended: 2013 c.32 Sch.12 para.73
s.235, repealed (in part): SI 2013/1575 Sch.1 para.2
s.338, repealed (in part): SI 2013/2042 Sch.1 para.19
s.405, enabling: SI 2013/2986
s.406, enabling: SI 2013/2986
Sch.6 para.3, amended: SI 2013/3178 Reg.2
Sch.6 para.10, enabling: SI 2013/3178
Sch.28 para.10, varied: SI 2013/2277 Art.6

31. Contracts (Rights of Third Parties) Act 1999
s.2, amended: 2013 c.22 Sch.9 para.71

33. Immigration and Asylum Act 1999
Part VIII, applied: SI 2013/602 Art.3
s.4, applied: SI 2013/480 Reg.6
s.10, see *Ahmad (Removal of Children over 18: Pakistan), Re* [2013] Imm. A.R. 1 (UT (IAC)), Collins, J.; see *Patel v Secretary of State for the Home Department* [2013] UKSC 72, [2013] 3 W.L.R. 1517 (SC), Lord Mance, J.S.C.; see *RJ (India) v Secretary of State for the Home Department* [2012] EWCA Civ 1865, [2013] Imm. A.R. 407 (CA (Civ Div)), Laws, L.J.
s.10, disapplied: SI 2013/1460 Reg.6
s.20, amended: 2013 c.22 Sch.8 para.65, SI 2013/602 Sch.2 para.31
s.21, amended: 2013 c.22 Sch.8 para.66
s.21, repealed (in part): 2013 c.22 Sch.8 para.66
s.25, amended: 2013 c.22 Sch.9 para.90
s.43, amended: 2013 c.22 Sch.9 para.52, Sch.9 para.90
s.63, applied: SI 2013/1460 Reg.6
s.89, amended: 2013 c.22 Sch.9 para.90
s.92, amended: 2013 c.22 Sch.9 para.90
s.95, applied: SI 2013/480 Reg.6, SI 2013/3029 Sch.6 para.17, Sch.9 para.28, SI 2013/3035 Sch.1
s.98, applied: SI 2013/3029 Sch.6 para.17, Sch.9 para.28, SI 2013/3035 Sch.1
s.112, amended: 2013 c.22 Sch.9 para.90
s.115, applied: SI 2013/376 Reg.9, SI 2013/377 Reg.16, SI 2013/379 Reg.12, SI 2013/3029 Reg.28, Sch.13 para.5, SI 2013/3035 Sch.1
s.115, disapplied: SI 2013/377 Reg.16
s.115, enabling: SI 2013/1474, SI 2013/2536
Sch.8 para.3, applied: SI 2013/3029 Sch.6 para.17, SI 2013/3035 Sch.1
Sch.9, applied: SI 2013/3029 Sch.6 para.17, SI 2013/3035 Sch.1

2000

1. Northern Ireland Act 2000
applied: 2013 c.12 Sch.1 para.1, 2013 c.28 Sch.1

2. Representation of the People Act 2000
Sch.1 para.12, repealed (in part): 2013 c.6 Sch.4 para.22
Sch.4 para.1, enabling: SI 2013/3198
Sch.4 para.2, amended: 2013 c.6 s.21
Sch.4 para.3, applied: 2013 asp 14 Sch.2 para.2, SI 2013/3197 Art.17
Sch.4 para.4, enabling: SI 2013/3198, SI 2013/3206
Sch.4 para.5, applied: 2013 asp 14 Sch.2 para.51
Sch.4 para.6, amended: 2013 c.6 s.3
Sch.4 para.6, applied: 2013 c.6 Sch.5 para.18, SI 2013/3199 Reg.2

Sch.4 para.6, enabling: SI 2013/3198, SI 2013/3206
Sch.4 para.7, applied: 2013 asp 14 Sch.2 para.6, Sch.2 para.51
Sch.4 para.7B, enabling: SI 2013/1599, SI 2013/3198, SI 2013/3206
Sch.4 para.7E, added: 2013 c.6 s.22
Sch.4 para.7E, enabling: SI 2013/3198, SI 2013/3206
Sch.4 para.7F, added: 2013 c.6 s.22

5. Nuclear Safeguards Act 2000
applied: 2013 c.32 s.82
referred to: 2013 c.32 s.74, s.113
s.1, amended: 2013 c.32 Sch.12 para.43
s.2, amended: 2013 c.32 Sch.12 para.44
s.2, applied: 2013 c.32 s.97
s.3, amended: 2013 c.32 Sch.12 para.45
s.3, applied: 2013 c.32 s.81, s.114
s.4, referred to: 2013 c.32 Sch.12 para.46
s.4, repealed: 2013 c.32 Sch.12 para.46
s.5, amended: 2013 c.32 Sch.12 para.47
s.5, applied: 2013 c.32 s.81
s.6, amended: 2013 c.32 Sch.12 para.48
s.7, amended: 2013 c.32 Sch.12 para.49
s.12, referred to: 2013 c.32 Sch.12 para.46

6. Powers of Criminal Courts (Sentencing) Act 2000
see *R. v P* [2013] EWCA Crim 1143, [2013] 2 Cr. App. R. (S.) 63 (CA (Crim Div)), Treacy, L.J.
applied: SI 2013/1554 r.55_2
Part V c.II, applied: SI 2013/9 Reg.12
s.1, see *R. v L* [2012] EWCA Crim 1336, [2013] 1 Cr. App. R. (S.) 56 (CA (Crim Div)), Hallett, L.J.
s.1, amended: 2013 c.22 Sch.16 para.6
s.1, applied: SI 2013/435 Sch.1 para.15, Sch.2 para.2, SI 2013/1554 r.37_10, r.63_2
s.11, see *G v DPP* [2012] EWHC 3174 (Admin), [2013] M.H.L.R. 143 (DC), Pitchford, L.J.
s.11, applied: SI 2013/1554 r.33_1, r.42_8
s.12, see *R. v Varma (Aloke)* [2013] 1 A.C. 463 (SC), Lord Phillips, J.S.C. (President)
s.12, amended: 2013 c.3 Sch.1 para.8
s.82A, applied: SI 2013/1554 r.68_1
s.89, applied: SI 2013/1554 r.62_5, r.62_9
s.108, applied: SI 2013/1554 r.62_5, r.62_9
s.131, amended: 2013 c.22 Sch.16 para.8
s.131, varied: 2013 c.3 s.4
s.132, varied: 2013 c.3 s.4
s.133, amended: 2013 c.3 Sch.1 para.9
s.133, applied: SI 2013/1554 r.42_5
s.133, varied: 2013 c.3 s.4
s.140, applied: SI 2013/1554 r.42_10, r.56_5
s.141, applied: SI 2013/1554 r.76_2
s.142, amended: 2013 c.3 Sch.1 para.10
s.146, see *R. v Knight (Lewis)* [2012] EWCA Crim 3019, [2013] 2 Cr. App. R. (S.) 45 (CA (Crim Div)), Elias, L.J.
s.146, applied: SI 2013/1554 r.55_2
s.147, see *R. v Knight (Lewis)* [2012] EWCA Crim 3019, [2013] 2 Cr. App. R. (S.) 45 (CA (Crim Div)), Elias, L.J.
s.147, applied: SI 2013/1554 r.55_2
s.155, applied: SI 2013/435 Sch.2 para.16, SI 2013/1554 r.42_4
s.155, enabling: SI 2013/1554
Sch.1 Part 1A, applied: SI 2013/9 Reg.9
Sch.3, applied: SI 2013/1554 r.44_1
Sch.3 Part III para.10, applied: SI 2013/1554 r.63_1
Sch.5, applied: SI 2013/1554 r.44_1
Sch.7, applied: SI 2013/1554 r.44_1
Sch.8, applied: SI 2013/1554 r.44_1

7. Electronic Communications Act 2000
s.7, applied: 2013 c.32 Sch.8 para.10, SI 2013/378 Reg.3, SI 2013/1554 r.5_3
s.15, applied: SSI 2013/3 Art.3
s.15, referred to: SI 2013/377 Reg.9, SSI 2013/307 Reg.2

8. Financial Services and Markets Act 2000
see *Bieber v Teathers Ltd (In Liquidation)* [2012] EWCA Civ 1466, [2013] 1 B.C.L.C. 248 (CA (Civ Div)), Arden, L.J.; see *Financial Conduct Authority v Hobbs* [2013] EWCA Civ 918, [2013] Bus. L.R. 1290 (CA (Civ Div)), Rimer, L.J.; see *Santander UK Plc v Harrison* [2013] EWHC 199 (QB), [2013] Bus. L.R. 501 (QBD), Males, J.; see *Secretary of State for Business, Innovation and Skills v Chohan* [2013] EWHC 680 (Ch), [2013] Lloyd's Rep. F.C. 351 (Ch D (Companies Ct)), Hildyard, J.
applied: 2013 c.33 s.9, s.11, s.37, Sch.4 para.7, Sch.4 para.9, SI 2013/161 Art.5, SI 2013/418 Art.3, SI 2013/440 Art.1, SI 2013/441 Art.1, Art.14, Art.19, Art.21, SI 2013/442 Art.22, Art.70, SI 2013/478 Art.3, SI 2013/496 Sch.1 para.3, SI 2013/504 Reg.57, SI 2013/556 Art.2, SI 2013/655, SI 2013/655 Art.10, SI 2013/1635 Sch.1 para.2, SI 2013/1881 Art.46, Art.58, SI 2013/1882 Art.2, SI 2013/2356 Sch.2 para.7, SI 2013/3115 Reg.45, SI 2013/3128 Art.4, SSI 2013/50 Sch.2 para.1
referred to: SI 2013/161 Art.6, Art.7, SI 2013/441 Art.1, SI 2013/496 Sch.1 para.1
varied: SI 2013/1882 Art.3
Part IA c.1, added: 2013 c.33 s.2
Part IV, applied: SI 2013/452 Reg.16, SI 2013/472 Sch.2 para.92, SI 2013/2356 Sch.2 para.7
Part IV, referred to: SI 2013/1881 Art.47

Part IVA, applied: 2013 c.33 s.11, s.37, SI 2013/431 Reg.2, SI 2013/655 Art.10, SI 2013/1388 Reg.24, SI 2013/1635 Sch.1 para.2, SI 2013/1773 Reg.5, Reg.74, Reg.75, SI 2013/1881 Art.31
Part IVA, referred to: SI 2013/431 Reg.2, SI 2013/556 Art.3
Part V, applied: SI 2013/1635 Reg.29, SSI 2013/50 Sch.2 Part 2
Part VI, applied: SSI 2013/50 Sch.2 para.3
Part VII, applied: SI 2013/472 Sch.2 para.63
Part IX, applied: SI 2013/504 Reg.58, SI 2013/1773 Reg.70, SI 2013/3115 Reg.42
Part IXA c.4, applied: 2013 c.33 s.107, SI 2013/1635 Reg.7
Part IXB, applied: 2013 c.33 s.7
Part XI, applied: SI 2013/442 Art.19, SI 2013/1881 Art.58, SI 2013/3128 Art.4
Part XII, applied: SI 2013/1881 Art.59
Part XIIA, applied: SI 2013/165 Art.2
Part XIIA, added: 2013 c.33 s.133
Part XIV, applied: SI 2013/419 Art.3, SI 2013/504 Reg.10, SI 2013/1635 Reg.29, SI 2013/1881 Art.12, Art.44, Art.45, Art.58, SI 2013/3116 Art.4, SI 2013/3118 Reg.6
Part XIV, referred to: SI 2013/1881 Art.44, Art.45
Part XVII c.V, amended: SI 2013/1773 Sch.1 para.22
Part XXII, amended: 2013 c.33 s.134
Part XXVI, applied: SI 2013/1773 Reg.70
Part XXVIII, added: 2013 c.33 s.135
s.1A, amended: SI 2013/1773 Sch.1 para.2
s.1A, applied: SI 2013/419 Art.2, SI 2013/496 Sch.1 para.2, SI 2013/3116 Art.2, Art.3
s.1A, enabling: SI 2013/419, SI 2013/3116
s.1B, applied: 2013 c.33 s.101
s.1B, disapplied: SI 2013/1881 Art.61
s.1B, referred to: SI 2013/1635 Reg.3
s.1G, amended: SI 2013/655 Art.3
s.1G, applied: SI 2013/442 Art.7, SI 2013/1881 Art.65
s.1H, amended: SI 2013/655 Art.3, SI 2013/1881 Art.10, SI 2013/3115 Sch.2 para.2
s.1H, disapplied: SI 2013/1881 Art.11
s.1H, repealed (in part): SI 2013/1881 Art.10
s.1L, amended: SI 2013/1773 Sch.1 para.3
s.1L, applied: SI 2013/419 Art.2, SI 2013/3116 Art.2, Art.3
s.1L, varied: SI 2013/1882 Art.3
s.1L, enabling: SI 2013/419, SI 2013/3116
s.1N, applied: SI 2013/442 Art.5
s.1Q, amended: 2013 c.33 s.132
s.1Q, applied: SI 2013/442 Art.6, Art.7, SI 2013/1881 Art.65
s.1S, applied: SI 2013/496 Sch.1 para.2
s.2A, applied: SI 2013/419 Art.2, SI 2013/496 Sch.1 para.3, SI 2013/3116 Art.3
s.2A, enabling: SI 2013/419, SI 2013/3116
s.2B, amended: 2013 c.33 s.1
s.2B, applied: 2013 c.33 s.102, SI 2013/440 Art.2, SI 2013/496 Sch.1 para.3, SI 2013/3118 Reg.6
s.2C, applied: SI 2013/496 Sch.1 para.3
s.2D, applied: SI 2013/496 Sch.1 para.3
s.2E, applied: SI 2013/496 Sch.1 para.3
s.2F, applied: SI 2013/496 Sch.1 para.3
s.2G, applied: SI 2013/496 Sch.1 para.3
s.2H, applied: SI 2013/496 Sch.1 para.3
s.2H, substituted: 2013 c.33 s.130
s.2I, applied: SI 2013/496 Sch.1 para.3
s.2J, amended: 2013 c.33 s.1
s.2J, applied: 2013 c.33 s.102
s.2O, applied: SI 2013/496 Sch.1 para.3
s.3A, amended: 2013 c.33 s.135
s.3B, amended: 2013 c.33 s.130
s.3B, disapplied: SI 2013/1635 Reg.7
s.3D, applied: SI 2013/496 Sch.1 para.2, Sch.1 para.3
s.3E, applied: SI 2013/496 Sch.1 para.2, Sch.1 para.3
s.3I, amended: 2013 c.33 s.3, Sch.8 para.4
s.3I, applied: SI 2013/496 Sch.1 para.2, Sch.1 para.3
s.3I, varied: SI 2013/496 Sch.1 para.4
s.3J, applied: SI 2013/496 Sch.1 para.2, Sch.1 para.3
s.3K, applied: SI 2013/496 Sch.1 para.2, Sch.1 para.3
s.3M, amended: SI 2013/3115 Sch.2 para.3
s.3M, repealed (in part): SI 2013/3115 Sch.2 para.3
s.3M, varied: SI 2013/442 Art.69
s.9, applied: SI 2013/442 Art.5
s.10, applied: SI 2013/442 Art.6
s.20, applied: SI 2013/655 Art.10
s.20, disapplied: SI 2013/1773 Reg.76, Reg.78
s.21, see *Financial Services Authority v Asset L.I.Inc (t/a Asset Land Investment Inc)* [2013] EWHC 178 (Ch), [2013] 2 B.C.L.C. 480 (Ch D), Andrew Smith, J.
s.21, applied: SI 2013/1773 Reg.46, Reg.52, SI 2013/1881 Art.59
s.22, applied: 2013 c.33 s.11, s.37, SI 2013/244 Art.3, SI 2013/452 Reg.16, SI 2013/501 Reg.4, SI 2013/588 Reg.4, SI 2013/1046 r.10, SI 2013/1773 Reg.10, SI 2013/3208 r.204, SSI 2013/50 Sch.2 Part 2, SSI 2013/73 Sch.1
s.22, referred to: SI 2013/244 Art.3, SI 2013/380 Sch.6 para.8, SI 2013/503 Reg.19
s.22, enabling: SI 2013/655, SI 2013/1881

s.22A, applied: 2013 c.33 s.37
s.22A, enabling: SI 2013/556
s.23, applied: 2013 c.22 Sch.17 para.22
s.25, applied: 2013 c.22 Sch.17 para.22, SI 2013/1773 Reg.52
s.25, varied: SI 2013/1773 Reg.52
s.30, applied: SI 2013/1773 Reg.52
s.31, applied: SI 2013/440 Art.15, Art.21, SSI 2013/50 Sch.2 Part 2
s.34, applied: SI 2013/440 Art.15, Art.16
s.35, applied: SI 2013/440 Art.21, Art.22
s.38, applied: SI 2013/655 Art.10, SI 2013/1881 Art.59
s.39, amended: SI 2013/3115 Sch.2 para.4
s.39, applied: SI 2013/419 Art.2, SI 2013/1881 Art.59, SI 2013/3116 Art.3
s.39, enabling: SI 2013/419, SI 2013/3116
s.40, applied: SI 2013/440 Art.10
s.42, applied: SI 2013/441 Art.26, Art.27
s.43, applied: SI 2013/440 Art.3, Art.5, SI 2013/441 Art.11, Art.18, Art.26, Art.27, SSI 2013/50 Sch.2 para.1
s.44, applied: SI 2013/440 Art.3, Art.5, Art.6, SI 2013/441 Art.11, Art.18
s.45, applied: SI 2013/440 Art.3, SI 2013/441 Art.11, Art.18, SI 2013/472 Sch.2 para.92
s.45, referred to: SI 2013/440 Art.8
s.46, applied: SI 2013/440 Art.3, SI 2013/441 Art.11, Art.18
s.47, applied: SI 2013/440 Art.3, Art.9, SI 2013/441 Art.11, Art.18
s.48, applied: SI 2013/440 Art.4
s.52, applied: SI 2013/440 Art.10, SI 2013/441 Art.19, Art.21, Art.26, Art.27
s.53, applied: SI 2013/441 Art.20, Art.28
s.54, applied: SI 2013/441 Art.29
s.54A, applied: SI 2013/440 Art.11
s.54B, applied: SI 2013/440 Art.12
s.55A, applied: SI 2013/440 Art.10, SI 2013/655 Art.10, SI 2013/1881 Art.31, Art.59
s.55B, applied: SI 2013/1881 Art.59
s.55C, enabling: SI 2013/555
s.55E, applied: SI 2013/440 Art.2, SI 2013/655 Art.10, SI 2013/1881 Art.59
s.55F, applied: SI 2013/440 Art.2, SI 2013/655 Art.10, SI 2013/1881 Art.59
s.55G, amended: SI 2013/504 Reg.3
s.55H, amended: SI 2013/1773 Sch.1 para.4
s.55H, applied: SI 2013/440 Art.6, SI 2013/655 Art.8, SI 2013/1881 Art.31, Art.33, Art.59
s.55I, applied: SI 2013/440 Art.6, SI 2013/1881 Art.31, Art.33, Art.59
s.55J, amended: SI 2013/1773 Sch.1 para.5, SI 2013/3115 Sch.2 para.5
s.55J, applied: SI 2013/440 Art.8, SI 2013/655 Art.8, SI 2013/1773 Reg.6, Reg.55, Reg.68, SI 2013/1881 Art.59
s.55K, applied: SI 2013/440 Art.8, SI 2013/1773 Reg.6
s.55L, applied: SI 2013/440 Art.3, Art.5, Art.7, SI 2013/441 Art.26, Art.27, SI 2013/556 Art.10, SI 2013/655 Art.10, SI 2013/1773 Reg.6, Reg.22, Reg.55, Reg.68, SI 2013/1881 Art.11, Art.42, Art.56, Art.58, Art.59, SSI 2013/50 Sch.2 para.1
s.55M, applied: SI 2013/440 Art.3, Art.5, Art.7, SI 2013/441 Art.28, SI 2013/556 Art.11, SI 2013/1881 Art.11, Art.58, Art.59, SSI 2013/50 Sch.2 para.1
s.55O, applied: SI 2013/440 Art.3, SSI 2013/50 Sch.2 para.1
s.55P, applied: SI 2013/440 Art.4
s.55Q, applied: SI 2013/440 Art.9
s.55R, amended: SI 2013/3115 Sch.2 para.6
s.55R, applied: SI 2013/431 Reg.2
s.55R, referred to: SI 2013/431 Reg.2
s.55R, enabling: SI 2013/431
s.55U, disapplied: SI 2013/1881 Art.31, Art.33
s.55V, amended: SI 2013/1773 Sch.1 para.6, SI 2013/1797 Sch.1 para.1
s.55V, applied: SI 2013/440 Art.10, SI 2013/1881 Art.31, Art.32, Art.33, Art.58
s.55X, applied: SI 2013/441 Art.26, Art.27, SI 2013/1881 Art.32, Art.34, Art.36
s.55Y, applied: SI 2013/441 Art.28, SI 2013/1773 Reg.22, SI 2013/1881 Art.35, Art.37, Art.38, Art.39, Art.40, Art.41, Art.42
s.55Z, applied: SI 2013/440 Art.12, SI 2013/441 Art.29, SI 2013/655 Art.8, SI 2013/1881 Art.37, Art.38, Art.39, Art.40
s.55Z1, applied: SI 2013/440 Art.11
s.55Z2, amended: SI 2013/3115 Sch.2 para.7
s.55Z2A, added: SI 2013/3115 Sch.2 para.8
s.55Z3, disapplied: SI 2013/1881 Art.32, Art.34, Art.36, Art.38, Art.40, Art.42
s.56, see *Financial Conduct Authority v Hobbs* [2013] EWCA Civ 918, [2013] Bus. L.R. 1290 (CA (Civ Div)), Rimer, L.J.; see *Financial Conduct Authority v Hobbs* [2013] Lloyd's Rep. F.C. 460 (UT (Tax)), Judge Roger Berner
s.56, applied: SSI 2013/50 Sch.2 para.1
s.59, amended: 2013 c.33 s.18, Sch.3 para.1, SI 2013/1773 Sch.1 para.7
s.59, applied: SI 2013/440 Art.13, SI 2013/441 Art.2, SI 2013/556 Art.10, Art.11, SI 2013/1635 Reg.18, SSI 2013/50 Sch.2 para.1, Sch.2 Part 2
s.59, referred to: SI 2013/1635 Reg.18
s.59, repealed (in part): 2013 c.33 s.18
s.59A, amended: 2013 c.33 Sch.3 para.2

s.59ZA, added: 2013 c.33 s.19
s.60, amended: 2013 c.33 s.20
s.60, applied: SI 2013/440 Art.13
s.60A, added: 2013 c.33 s.21
s.61, amended: 2013 c.33 s.22, s.23
s.61, applied: SI 2013/440 Art.13
s.62, amended: 2013 c.33 s.23
s.62, applied: SI 2013/440 Art.13
s.62A, added: 2013 c.33 s.24
s.63, amended: 2013 c.33 s.25, Sch.3 para.3
s.63A, amended: 2013 c.33 s.28, Sch.3 para.4
s.63A, applied: SI 2013/441 Art.2, SI 2013/1635 Reg.18
s.63A, referred to: SI 2013/1635 Reg.18
s.63A, varied: SI 2013/441 Art.2
s.63B, applied: SI 2013/441 Art.2
s.63B, varied: SI 2013/441 Art.2
s.63C, applied: SI 2013/441 Art.2
s.63C, varied: SI 2013/441 Art.2
s.63D, disapplied: SI 2013/655 Art.9
s.63E, added: 2013 c.33 s.29
s.63F, added: 2013 c.33 s.29
s.63ZA, added: 2013 c.33 s.26
s.63ZB, added: 2013 c.33 s.26
s.63ZC, added: 2013 c.33 s.26
s.63ZD, added: 2013 c.33 s.27
s.63ZE, added: 2013 c.33 s.27
s.64, repealed: 2013 c.33 s.30
s.64A, added: 2013 c.33 s.30
s.64B, added: 2013 c.33 s.30
s.64C, added: 2013 c.33 s.31
s.65, disapplied: SI 2013/655 Art.9
s.65, repealed: 2013 c.33 s.30
s.66, amended: 2013 c.33 s.28, s.32, Sch.3 para.5, SI 2013/1773 Sch.1 para.8
s.66, applied: SI 2013/419 Art.2, SI 2013/441 Art.3, SI 2013/1882 Art.4, Art.6, SI 2013/3116 Art.2, Art.3
s.66, repealed (in part): 2013 c.33 s.32
s.66, varied: SI 2013/441 Art.3, SI 2013/1882 Art.3
s.66, enabling: SI 2013/419, SI 2013/3116
s.66A, added: 2013 c.33 s.32
s.66A, varied: SI 2013/1882 Art.3
s.66B, added: 2013 c.33 s.32
s.66B, varied: SI 2013/1882 Art.3
s.67, see *R. (on the application of Willford) v Financial Services Authority* [2013] EWCA Civ 674, [2013] C.P. Rep. 43 (CA (Civ Div)), Moore-Bick, L.J.
s.67, amended: 2013 c.33 Sch.3 para.6
s.67, applied: SI 2013/441 Art.3
s.67, varied: SI 2013/1882 Art.3
s.68, varied: SI 2013/1882 Art.3
s.69, amended: 2013 c.33 Sch.3 para.7
s.69, applied: SI 2013/441 Art.3, SI 2013/1635 Reg.29
s.70, applied: SI 2013/1635 Reg.29
s.71A, added: 2013 c.33 s.33
s.74, applied: SSI 2013/50 Sch.2 Part 2
s.77, applied: SSI 2013/50 Sch.2 para.3
s.85, applied: 2013 c.22 Sch.17 para.22
s.86, amended: SI 2013/1125 Reg.2, SI 2013/3115 Sch.2 para.9
s.88, applied: SI 2013/441 Art.4, SSI 2013/50 Sch.2 para.3, Sch.2 Part 2
s.88A, disapplied: SI 2013/441 Art.4
s.89P, applied: SSI 2013/50 Sch.2 para.3, Sch.2 Part 2
s.90ZA, amended: SI 2013/1388 Reg.3
s.103A, amended: 2013 c.33 Sch.1 para.2, Sch.1 para.3
s.103A, applied: SI 2013/442 Art.9, Art.10, Art.11
s.105, amended: 2013 c.33 Sch.1 para.2
s.106, amended: 2013 c.33 Sch.1 para.2, Sch.1 para.4
s.106B, added: 2013 c.33 Sch.1 para.5
s.107, amended: 2013 c.33 Sch.1 para.2, Sch.1 para.6
s.107, applied: SI 2013/442 Art.9
s.109, applied: SI 2013/442 Art.8
s.109, substituted: 2013 c.33 Sch.1 para.7
s.109A, added: 2013 c.33 Sch.1 para.8
s.110, amended: 2013 c.33 Sch.1 para.2, Sch.1 para.9
s.111, amended: 2013 c.33 Sch.1 para.10
s.111, applied: SI 2013/442 Art.9
s.112, amended: 2013 c.33 Sch.1 para.2, Sch.1 para.11
s.112, applied: SI 2013/442 Art.10
s.112A, amended: 2013 c.33 Sch.1 para.12
s.112ZA, amended: 2013 c.33 Sch.1 para.2
s.113, amended: 2013 c.33 Sch.1 para.2
s.113, applied: SI 2013/442 Art.11
s.114, amended: 2013 c.33 Sch.1 para.2
s.114A, amended: 2013 c.33 Sch.1 para.2
s.119, applied: SI 2013/441 Art.11, Art.28
s.133, amended: 2013 c.22 Sch.9 para.83, 2013 c.33 s.4, SI 2013/1388 Reg.3
s.133, applied: SI 2013/442 Art.14
s.133, varied: SI 2013/442 Art.12, Art.13, SI 2013/1635 Reg.31, SI 2013/1881 Art.55, SI 2013/1882 Art.3
s.133, enabling: SI 2013/606
s.133A, varied: SI 2013/442 Art.12, Art.13
s.133B, varied: SI 2013/1635 Reg.31
s.137A, applied: SI 2013/1773 Reg.44, SI 2013/1881 Art.63, Art.64

s.137C, amended: 2013 c.33 s.131
s.137C, applied: SI 2013/3128 Art.4
s.138A, amended: 2013 c.33 Sch.3 para.8, SI 2013/1388 Reg.3
s.138A, applied: SI 2013/161 Art.9, Art.10
s.138B, applied: SI 2013/161 Art.9
s.138B, disapplied: SI 2013/161 Art.9
s.138D, see *Bate v Aviva Insurance UK Ltd* [2013] EWHC 1687 (Comm), [2013] Lloyd's Rep. I.R. 492 (QBD (Comm)), Judge Mackie, Q.C.
s.138D, amended: 2013 c.33 Sch.3 para.9
s.138H, applied: SI 2013/161 Art.3, SI 2013/1881 Art.64
s.138I, applied: SI 2013/1797 Reg.6, SI 2013/1881 Art.61
s.138I, disapplied: 2013 c.33 Sch.4 para.9, SI 2013/161 Art.8, SI 2013/496 Sch.1 para.6, SI 2013/655 Art.9, SI 2013/1881 Art.61
s.138I, varied: SI 2013/1797 Reg.6, SI 2013/1881 Art.61
s.138J, applied: SI 2013/442 Art.70, SI 2013/1797 Reg.6, SI 2013/1881 Art.62
s.138J, disapplied: SI 2013/644 Art.3, SI 2013/1881 Art.62
s.138J, varied: SI 2013/1797 Reg.6, SI 2013/1881 Art.62
s.138K, applied: SI 2013/1797 Reg.6
s.138K, disapplied: SI 2013/161 Art.8
s.138K, varied: SI 2013/1797 Reg.6
s.138L, applied: SI 2013/1797 Reg.6
s.138L, varied: SI 2013/1797 Reg.6
s.139A, applied: SI 2013/496 Sch.1 para.2, Sch.1 para.8, Sch.1 para.9, Sch.1 para.10
s.139A, disapplied: SI 2013/655 Art.9
s.139B, applied: SI 2013/496 Sch.1 para.8
s.140A, amended: 2013 c.33 Sch.3 para.10
s.140A, applied: SI 2013/496 Sch.1 para.6, Sch.1 para.7, Sch.1 para.9, Sch.1 para.10
s.140A, repealed (in part): 2013 c.33 Sch.3 para.10
s.142A, added: 2013 c.33 s.4
s.142B, added: 2013 c.33 s.4
s.142C, added: 2013 c.33 s.4
s.142D, added: 2013 c.33 s.4
s.142E, added: 2013 c.33 s.4
s.142F, added: 2013 c.33 s.4
s.142G, added: 2013 c.33 s.4
s.142G, applied: 2013 c.33 s.8, s.9, s.10
s.142H, added: 2013 c.33 s.4
s.142I, added: 2013 c.33 s.4
s.142J, added: 2013 c.33 s.4
s.142K, added: 2013 c.33 s.4
s.142L, added: 2013 c.33 s.4
s.142M, added: 2013 c.33 s.4
s.142N, added: 2013 c.33 s.4
s.142O, added: 2013 c.33 s.4
s.142P, added: 2013 c.33 s.4
s.142Q, added: 2013 c.33 s.4
s.142R, added: 2013 c.33 s.4
s.142S, added: 2013 c.33 s.4
s.142T, added: 2013 c.33 s.4
s.142U, added: 2013 c.33 s.4
s.142V, added: 2013 c.33 s.4
s.142W, added: 2013 c.33 s.4
s.142W, disapplied: 2013 c.33 s.7
s.142X, added: 2013 c.33 s.4
s.142X, disapplied: 2013 c.33 s.7
s.142Y, added: 2013 c.33 s.4
s.142Y, applied: 2013 c.33 s.7
s.142Y, disapplied: 2013 c.33 s.7
s.142Z, added: 2013 c.33 s.4
s.142Z1, added: 2013 c.33 s.4
s.148, applied: SI 2013/161 Art.9, Art.10
s.155, applied: SI 2013/1881 Art.61, Art.62
s.165, amended: SI 2013/1773 Sch.1 para.9
s.165, applied: SI 2013/442 Art.15, SI 2013/1773 Reg.71, SI 2013/3128 Art.4
s.165, varied: SI 2013/1635 Reg.13, SI 2013/1881 Art.12, Art.50, SI 2013/1882 Art.3, SI 2013/3115 Reg.14, SI 2013/3128 Art.4
s.165A, applied: SI 2013/442 Art.16
s.165A, varied: SI 2013/1635 Reg.13, SI 2013/3128 Art.4
s.165B, applied: SI 2013/442 Art.17
s.165B, varied: SI 2013/1635 Reg.13, SI 2013/3128 Art.4
s.165C, varied: SI 2013/1635 Reg.13, SI 2013/3128 Art.4
s.166, applied: SI 2013/442 Art.18, SI 2013/1773 Reg.71
s.166, varied: SI 2013/1635 Reg.13, SI 2013/3115 Reg.14, SI 2013/3128 Art.4
s.166A, varied: SI 2013/1635 Reg.13, SI 2013/3128 Art.4
s.167, applied: SI 2013/442 Art.19, SI 2013/1773 Reg.71
s.167, varied: SI 2013/1635 Reg.13, SI 2013/1881 Art.12, SI 2013/1882 Art.3, SI 2013/3115 Reg.14, SI 2013/3128 Art.4
s.168, amended: SI 2013/1773 Sch.1 para.10
s.168, applied: SI 2013/419 Art.2, SI 2013/442 Art.19, SI 2013/3116 Art.2, Art.3
s.168, varied: SI 2013/442 Art.19, SI 2013/1635 Reg.13, SI 2013/1773 Reg.52, Reg.53, SI 2013/1881 Art.50, SI 2013/1882 Art.3, SI 2013/3128 Art.4
s.168, enabling: SI 2013/419, SI 2013/3116
s.169, applied: SI 2013/442 Art.20, SI 2013/1773 Reg.71

s.169, varied: SI 2013/1635 Reg.13, SI 2013/3128 Art.4
s.169A, applied: SI 2013/442 Art.20
s.169A, varied: SI 2013/1635 Reg.13, SI 2013/3128 Art.4
s.170, applied: SI 2013/442 Art.19, SI 2013/1773 Reg.71
s.170, varied: SI 2013/1635 Reg.13, SI 2013/3115 Reg.14, SI 2013/3128 Art.4
s.171, applied: SI 2013/1773 Reg.71
s.171, varied: SI 2013/1635 Reg.13, SI 2013/3115 Reg.14, SI 2013/3128 Art.4
s.172, varied: SI 2013/1635 Reg.13, SI 2013/3128 Art.4
s.173, varied: SI 2013/1635 Reg.13, SI 2013/3128 Art.4
s.174, applied: SI 2013/1773 Reg.71
s.174, varied: SI 2013/1635 Reg.13, SI 2013/3128 Art.4
s.175, applied: SI 2013/442 Art.15, SI 2013/1773 Reg.71, SI 2013/3128 Art.4
s.175, varied: SI 2013/1635 Reg.13, SI 2013/3115 Reg.14, SI 2013/3128 Art.4
s.176, applied: SI 2013/442 Art.21, SI 2013/1773 Reg.71
s.176, varied: SI 2013/1635 Reg.13, SI 2013/3115 Reg.14, SI 2013/3128 Art.4
s.176A, applied: SI 2013/1773 Reg.71
s.176A, varied: SI 2013/3115 Reg.14, SI 2013/3128 Art.4
s.177, applied: SI 2013/1773 Reg.71
s.177, varied: SI 2013/3115 Reg.14, SI 2013/3128 Art.4
s.178, applied: SI 2013/442 Art.23, Art.25, Art.29
s.180, applied: SI 2013/442 Art.24, Art.25
s.183, enabling: SI 2013/1773
s.184, amended: SI 2013/3115 Sch.2 para.10
s.185, applied: SI 2013/442 Art.25
s.186, amended: SI 2013/3115 Sch.2 para.11
s.188, amended: SI 2013/3115 Sch.2 para.12
s.188, applied: SI 2013/442 Art.25
s.188, enabling: SI 2013/1773
s.189, applied: SI 2013/441 Art.19, Art.21, Art.30, SI 2013/442 Art.25, Art.26
s.190, amended: SI 2013/3115 Sch.2 para.13
s.190, applied: SI 2013/442 Art.27
s.191, applied: SI 2013/442 Art.26
s.191A, applied: SI 2013/441 Art.19, Art.21, Art.30, SI 2013/442 Art.25
s.191B, applied: SI 2013/442 Art.28
s.191D, applied: SI 2013/442 Art.29
s.191F, applied: SI 2013/442 Art.30
s.191G, amended: SI 2013/3115 Sch.2 para.14
s.192B, applied: SI 2013/165 Art.2, SI 2013/556 Art.10, Art.11
s.192B, referred to: SI 2013/165 Art.2
s.192B, enabling: SI 2013/165
s.192C, applied: SI 2013/556 Art.10, Art.11
s.192K, amended: 2013 c.33 s.133
s.193, amended: SI 2013/1773 Sch.1 para.11
s.194, amended: SI 2013/1773 Sch.1 para.12
s.194, applied: SI 2013/441 Art.5, SI 2013/1881 Art.11
s.194, repealed (in part): SI 2013/1881 Art.10
s.194, varied: SI 2013/1882 Art.3
s.194A, applied: SI 2013/441 Art.6
s.194B, added: SI 2013/3115 Sch.2 para.15
s.195, applied: SI 2013/441 Art.7
s.195A, amended: SI 2013/1773 Sch.1 para.13, SI 2013/1797 Sch.1 para.1
s.195A, applied: SI 2013/441 Art.6
s.196, applied: SI 2013/440 Art.3, Art.4, Art.7, SI 2013/441 Art.11, Art.18, SI 2013/556 Art.10, Art.11
s.197, applied: SI 2013/441 Art.20
s.198, applied: SI 2013/441 Art.8
s.199, amended: SI 2013/1773 Sch.1 para.14, SI 2013/3115 Sch.2 para.16
s.199, applied: SI 2013/441 Art.9
s.199, varied: SI 2013/1882 Art.3
s.200, applied: SI 2013/440 Art.7, SI 2013/441 Art.10, Art.20
s.200, varied: SI 2013/440 Art.7
s.203, repealed (in part): SI 2013/1881 Art.10, Art.10
s.203, varied: SI 2013/1881 Art.11
s.204, repealed (in part): SI 2013/1881 Art.10, Art.10
s.204, varied: SI 2013/1881 Art.11
s.204A, amended: SI 2013/1773 Sch.1 para.15
s.204A, applied: SI 2013/419 Art.3, SI 2013/441 Art.11, SI 2013/3116 Art.2, Art.3
s.204A, varied: SI 2013/441 Art.11, SI 2013/1882 Art.3
s.204A, enabling: SI 2013/419, SI 2013/3116
s.205, applied: SI 2013/441 Art.11, SI 2013/1773 Reg.71, SI 2013/1882 Art.4, Art.6
s.206, applied: SI 2013/441 Art.11, SI 2013/1773 Reg.71, SI 2013/1881 Art.47, SI 2013/1882 Art.4, Art.6
s.206A, applied: SI 2013/441 Art.11, Art.23, SI 2013/1882 Art.4, Art.6
s.207, applied: SI 2013/441 Art.11, SI 2013/1773 Reg.71, SI 2013/1881 Art.44
s.208, applied: SI 2013/1773 Reg.71
s.208, disapplied: SI 2013/1881 Art.45
s.209, applied: SI 2013/1773 Reg.71

s.210, applied: SI 2013/441 Art.11, SI 2013/504 Reg.10, SI 2013/1635 Reg.29, SI 2013/1773 Reg.71, SI 2013/1881 Art.44
s.210, disapplied: SI 2013/1881 Art.47
s.211, applied: SI 2013/504 Reg.10, SI 2013/1635 Reg.29, SI 2013/1773 Reg.71
s.212, amended: 2013 c.33 s.16
s.212, applied: SI 2013/442 Art.31
s.213, see *Billingsley v UPS Ltd* [2013] R.T.R. 30 (QBD), Judge Oliver-Jones Q.C.
s.213, applied: SI 2013/598 Art.2, Art.3, SI 2013/1881 Art.59
s.213, enabling: SI 2013/598, SI 2013/1773
s.214, enabling: SI 2013/1773
s.218B, added: 2013 c.33 s.15
s.224, enabling: SI 2013/1773
s.224ZA, added: 2013 c.33 s.14
s.225, applied: SSI 2013/50 Sch.2 para.2, Sch.2 Part 2
s.226, applied: SI 2013/1881 Art.11
s.226, referred to: SI 2013/1881 Art.11
s.226A, applied: SI 2013/1881 Art.11
s.226A, repealed: SI 2013/1881 Art.10
s.227, amended: SI 2013/1881 Art.10
s.228, amended: SI 2013/1881 Art.10
s.229, see *Clark v In Focus Asset Management & Tax Solutions Ltd* [2012] EWHC 3669 (QB), [2013] P.N.L.R. 14 (QBD), Cranston, J.
s.229, amended: SI 2013/1881 Art.10
s.229, repealed (in part): SI 2013/1881 Art.10
s.230, amended: SI 2013/1881 Art.10
s.234A, applied: SI 2013/1881 Art.11
s.234A, repealed: SI 2013/1881 Art.10
s.234C, amended: 2013 c.33 s.68
s.234C, applied: SI 2013/3191, SI 2013/3191 Art.2
s.234C, enabling: SI 2013/3191
s.234D, amended: SI 2013/1881 Art.10
s.234H, repealed: 2013 c.33 Sch.8 para.2
s.234I, added: 2013 c.33 Sch.8 para.3
s.234J, added: 2013 c.33 Sch.8 para.3
s.234K, added: 2013 c.33 Sch.8 para.3
s.234L, added: 2013 c.33 Sch.8 para.3
s.234M, added: 2013 c.33 Sch.8 para.3
s.234N, added: 2013 c.33 Sch.8 para.3
s.234O, added: 2013 c.33 Sch.8 para.3
s.235A, added: SI 2013/1388 Reg.3
s.235A, applied: SI 2013/1388 Reg.17
s.237, amended: SI 2013/1388 Reg.3, SI 2013/1773 Sch.1 para.16
s.237, applied: SSI 2013/50 Sch.2 Part 2
s.237, referred to: SI 2013/1773 Reg.10
s.238, amended: SI 2013/1388 Reg.3
s.238, applied: SI 2013/1773 Reg.46, Reg.53
s.241, amended: SI 2013/636 Sch.1 para.6
s.242, applied: SI 2013/1773 Reg.54
s.243, applied: SSI 2013/50 Sch.2 para.1
s.249, amended: SI 2013/1388 Reg.3
s.249, applied: SI 2013/441 Art.12
s.249, referred to: SI 2013/441 Art.14, Art.19
s.249, varied: SI 2013/441 Art.12
s.251, applied: SSI 2013/50 Sch.2 para.1
s.257, applied: SSI 2013/50 Sch.2 para.1
s.258A, amended: SI 2013/1388 Reg.3
s.259, amended: SI 2013/1388 Reg.3
s.261B, amended: SI 2013/1388 Reg.3
s.261C, added: SI 2013/1388 Reg.3
s.261C, applied: SI 2013/1773 Reg.54
s.261D, added: SI 2013/1388 Reg.3
s.261D, amended: SI 2013/1773 Sch.1 para.17
s.261D, applied: SSI 2013/50 Sch.2 para.1
s.261E, added: SI 2013/1388 Reg.3
s.261F, added: SI 2013/1388 Reg.3
s.261G, added: SI 2013/1388 Reg.3
s.261H, added: SI 2013/1388 Reg.3
s.261I, added: SI 2013/1388 Reg.3
s.261J, added: SI 2013/1388 Reg.3
s.261K, added: SI 2013/1388 Reg.3
s.261L, added: SI 2013/1388 Reg.3
s.261M, added: SI 2013/1388 Reg.3
s.261N, added: SI 2013/1388 Reg.3
s.261O, added: SI 2013/1388 Reg.3
s.261P, added: SI 2013/1388 Reg.3
s.261Q, added: SI 2013/1388 Reg.3
s.261Q, applied: SSI 2013/50 Sch.2 para.1
s.261R, added: SI 2013/1388 Reg.3
s.261S, added: SI 2013/1388 Reg.3
s.261T, added: SI 2013/1388 Reg.3
s.261U, added: SI 2013/1388 Reg.3
s.261V, added: SI 2013/1388 Reg.3
s.261W, added: SI 2013/1388 Reg.3
s.261X, added: SI 2013/1388 Reg.3
s.261X, applied: SSI 2013/50 Sch.2 para.1
s.261Y, added: SI 2013/1388 Reg.3
s.261Z, added: SI 2013/1388 Reg.3
s.261Z1, added: SI 2013/1388 Reg.3
s.261Z2, added: SI 2013/1388 Reg.3
s.261Z3, added: SI 2013/1388 Reg.3
s.261Z4, added: SI 2013/1388 Reg.3
s.261Z5, added: SI 2013/1388 Reg.3
s.262, enabling: SI 2013/1773
s.270, amended: SI 2013/1388 Reg.3
s.270, applied: SI 2013/1773 Sch.1 para.45, SSI 2013/50 Sch.2 para.1
s.270, repealed: SI 2013/1773 Sch.1 para.18
s.271, repealed: SI 2013/1773 Sch.1 para.18
s.272, amended: SI 2013/1388 Reg.3, SI 2013/1773 Sch.1 para.19

s.272, applied: SI 2013/1773 Reg.54, Sch.1 para.45, SSI 2013/50 Sch.2 para.1
s.272, repealed (in part): SI 2013/1773 Sch.1 para.19
s.277, amended: SI 2013/1773 Sch.1 para.20
s.277, applied: SI 2013/1773 Sch.1 para.45
s.277A, added: SI 2013/1773 Sch.1 para.21
s.277A, applied: SI 2013/1773 Sch.1 para.45
s.278, amended: SI 2013/1773 Sch.1 para.23
s.279, amended: SI 2013/1773 Sch.1 para.24
s.280, amended: SI 2013/1773 Sch.1 para.25
s.281, amended: SI 2013/1773 Sch.1 para.26
s.283A, amended: SI 2013/1388 Reg.3
s.285, amended: SI 2013/504 Reg.3
s.285, applied: 2013 c.33 s.115, SI 2013/442 Art.32
s.285, disapplied: SI 2013/504 Reg.52
s.285, referred to: 2013 c.33 s.112
s.285A, amended: SI 2013/504 Reg.3
s.286, applied: SI 2013/504(c)
s.286, enabling: SI 2013/504, SI 2013/1908
s.288, amended: SI 2013/504 Reg.3
s.288, applied: SI 2013/442 Art.33, SI 2013/504 Reg.52
s.289, amended: SI 2013/504 Reg.3
s.289, applied: SI 2013/442 Art.33
s.290, amended: SI 2013/504 Reg.3
s.290, applied: SI 2013/442 Art.32, Art.34, SSI 2013/50 Sch.2 para.1
s.290, referred to: SI 2013/442 Art.38
s.290A, amended: SI 2013/504 Reg.3
s.290A, referred to: SI 2013/442 Art.38
s.290ZA, added: SI 2013/504 Reg.3
s.290ZA, applied: SSI 2013/50 Sch.2 para.1
s.292, amended: SI 2013/504 Reg.3
s.292, applied: SI 2013/442 Art.32, Art.34, SI 2013/504 Reg.53, SSI 2013/50 Sch.2 para.1
s.293, applied: SI 2013/442 Art.35
s.293A, applied: SI 2013/419 Art.2
s.293A, enabling: SI 2013/419
s.294, applied: SI 2013/161 Art.9, Art.10
s.296, applied: SI 2013/419 Art.4, SI 2013/442 Art.36, SSI 2013/50 Sch.2 para.1
s.296, enabling: SI 2013/419
s.296A, amended: SI 2013/504 Reg.3
s.296A, applied: SI 2013/504 Reg.52, SSI 2013/50 Sch.2 para.1
s.297, amended: SI 2013/504 Reg.3
s.297, applied: SI 2013/419 Art.4, SI 2013/442 Art.37
s.297, disapplied: SI 2013/504 Reg.52
s.297, enabling: SI 2013/419
s.298, applied: SI 2013/442 Art.38
s.299, applied: SI 2013/442 Art.39
s.300A, applied: SI 2013/442 Art.40
s.300A, disapplied: SI 2013/504 Reg.52
s.300B, applied: SI 2013/442 Art.41
s.300B, disapplied: SI 2013/504 Reg.52
s.300C, applied: SI 2013/442 Art.42
s.300C, disapplied: SI 2013/504 Reg.52
s.300D, applied: SI 2013/442 Art.42
s.300D, disapplied: SI 2013/504 Reg.52
s.300E, amended: SI 2013/504 Reg.3
s.300E, disapplied: SI 2013/504 Reg.52
s.301, applied: SI 2013/442 Art.43
s.301A, amended: SI 2013/1908 Reg.5
s.301E, amended: SI 2013/3115 Sch.2 para.17
s.301M, amended: SI 2013/3115 Sch.2 para.18
s.312E, applied: SI 2013/419 Art.4
s.312E, disapplied: SI 2013/441 Art.13
s.312E, enabling: SI 2013/419
s.312F, disapplied: SI 2013/441 Art.13
s.312G, disapplied: SI 2013/441 Art.13
s.312H, disapplied: SI 2013/441 Art.13
s.312I, disapplied: SI 2013/441 Art.13
s.313, amended: SI 2013/504 Reg.3
s.313D, amended: SI 2013/3115 Sch.2 para.19
s.320, applied: SI 2013/442 Art.44
s.321, applied: SI 2013/441 Art.19, Art.21, Art.31
s.327, applied: SI 2013/1881 Art.12, Art.59, SSI 2013/50 Sch.2 Part 2
s.328, amended: SI 2013/1881 Art.10
s.329, applied: SSI 2013/50 Sch.2 para.1
s.339B, added: 2013 c.33 s.134
s.339C, added: 2013 c.33 s.134
s.342, amended: SI 2013/3115 Sch.2 para.20
s.342, applied: SI 2013/441 Art.14
s.343, amended: SI 2013/3115 Sch.2 para.21
s.345, applied: SI 2013/441 Art.14, Art.19, Art.21
s.345, referred to: SI 2013/441 Art.19
s.345, varied: SI 2013/441 Art.14
s.345B, applied: SI 2013/441 Art.14
s.346, applied: 2013 c.22 Sch.17 para.22
s.347, amended: 2013 c.33 s.34, Sch.3 para.11, SI 2013/1388 Reg.3
s.348, amended: 2013 c.33 Sch.8 para.5
s.348, applied: SI 2013/3115 Reg.10
s.348, referred to: SI 2013/3115 Reg.17
s.348, varied: SI 2013/1635 Reg.11
s.349, varied: SI 2013/1635 Reg.11
s.349, enabling: SI 2013/1773, SI 2013/3115
s.351A, amended: SI 2013/1388 Reg.3
s.352, varied: SI 2013/1635 Reg.11
s.353, repealed (in part): SI 2013/1881 Art.10
s.354A, amended: 2013 c.33 Sch.8 para.6
s.355, applied: SI 2013/442 Art.47, Art.48, Art.49, Art.56
s.358, applied: SI 2013/442 Art.45

s.359, applied: SI 2013/418 Art.2
s.361, applied: SI 2013/442 Art.46
s.362, applied: SI 2013/442 Art.47
s.362A, see *Ceart Risk Services Ltd, Re* [2012] EWHC 1178 (Ch), [2013] Bus. L.R. 116 (Ch D (Companies Ct)), Arnold, J.
s.362A, applied: SI 2013/442 Art.48
s.363, applied: SI 2013/442 Art.49
s.364, applied: SI 2013/442 Art.50
s.365, applied: SI 2013/442 Art.51
s.366, applied: SI 2013/442 Art.52
s.367, applied: SI 2013/418 Art.2
s.369, applied: SI 2013/442 Art.53, Art.54
s.369A, applied: SI 2013/442 Art.54
s.370, applied: SI 2013/442 Art.55, SI 2013/1388 Reg.17
s.371, applied: SI 2013/442 Art.56
s.372, applied: SI 2013/418 Art.2
s.373, applied: SI 2013/442 Art.57
s.374, applied: SI 2013/442 Art.58
s.375, applied: SI 2013/442 Art.59
s.376, amended: 2013 c.33 Sch.10 para.2
s.376, applied: SI 2013/442 Art.60
s.380, see *Financial Services Authority v Sinaloa Gold Plc* [2013] UKSC 11, [2013] 2 A.C. 28 (SC), Lord Neuberger (President)
s.380, amended: 2013 c.33 Sch.10 para.3, SI 2013/1773 Sch.1 para.27
s.380, applied: SI 2013/419 Art.5, SI 2013/441 Art.15, SI 2013/3116 Art.2, Art.3, Art.4
s.380, varied: SI 2013/441 Art.15, Art.18, SI 2013/1635 Reg.24, SI 2013/1882 Art.3
s.380, enabling: SI 2013/419, SI 2013/3116
s.381, varied: SI 2013/1635 Reg.24
s.382, amended: 2013 c.33 Sch.10 para.3, SI 2013/1773 Sch.1 para.28
s.382, applied: SI 2013/419 Art.5, SI 2013/441 Art.16, SI 2013/1046 r.148, SI 2013/3116 Art.2, Art.3, Art.4, SI 2013/3208 r.152
s.382, varied: SI 2013/441 Art.16, Art.18, SI 2013/1635 Reg.24, SI 2013/1882 Art.3
s.382, enabling: SI 2013/419, SI 2013/3116
s.383, varied: SI 2013/1635 Reg.24
s.384, amended: 2013 c.33 Sch.10 para.3, SI 2013/1773 Sch.1 para.29
s.384, applied: SI 2013/419 Art.5, SI 2013/441 Art.17, SI 2013/1881 Art.58, SI 2013/3116 Art.2, Art.3, Art.4
s.384, varied: SI 2013/441 Art.17, Art.18, SI 2013/1635 Reg.24, SI 2013/1882 Art.3
s.384, enabling: SI 2013/419, SI 2013/3116
s.385, applied: SI 2013/441 Art.17
s.385, varied: SI 2013/1882 Art.3
s.386, varied: SI 2013/1882 Art.3
s.387, amended: 2013 c.33 Sch.3 para.12
s.387, varied: SI 2013/1635 Reg.30
s.388, amended: 2013 c.33 Sch.3 para.13
s.388, applied: SI 2013/504 Reg.56, SI 2013/1881 Art.52, Art.58
s.388, varied: SI 2013/1635 Reg.30, SI 2013/1881 Art.52
s.389, see *Financial Conduct Authority v Hobbs* [2013] EWCA Civ 918, [2013] Bus. L.R. 1290 (CA (Civ Div)), Rimer, L.J.
s.389, applied: SI 2013/504 Reg.56
s.390, applied: SI 2013/441 Art.22
s.390, varied: SI 2013/1635 Reg.30
s.391, amended: 2013 c.33 s.4, SI 2013/1388 Reg.3, SI 2013/3115 Sch.2 para.22
s.391, applied: SI 2013/442 Art.7, SI 2013/504 Reg.56, SI 2013/1881 Art.65
s.391, disapplied: SI 2013/441 Art.33
s.391, varied: SI 2013/1635 Reg.30, SI 2013/1773 Reg.20, Reg.64, SI 2013/1882 Art.3
s.391A, added: SI 2013/3115 Sch.2 para.23
s.392, amended: 2013 c.33 s.4, SI 2013/1388 Reg.3
s.392, varied: SI 2013/1635 Reg.30, SI 2013/1882 Art.3
s.393, applied: SI 2013/504 Reg.10, Reg.56, SI 2013/1635 Reg.29
s.394, applied: SI 2013/441 Art.25, SI 2013/504 Reg.56
s.395, amended: 2013 c.33 Sch.3 para.14, SI 2013/1388 Reg.3
s.395, varied: SI 2013/1635 Reg.30
s.397, applied: 2013 c.22 Sch.17 para.22
s.397, varied: SI 2013/1881 Art.50
s.398, amended: SI 2013/1773 Sch.1 para.30
s.398, applied: 2013 c.22 Sch 17 para.22, SI 2013/3115 Reg.45
s.398, varied: SI 2013/1881 Art.50
s.399, varied: SI 2013/1881 Art.50
s.400, applied: SI 2013/504 Reg.57
s.400, varied: SI 2013/1881 Art.50
s.401, applied: SI 2013/441 Art.34, SI 2013/504 Reg.57
s.401, repealed (in part): SI 2013/1881 Art.10
s.401, varied: SI 2013/1881 Art.50, SI 2013/1882 Art.3
s.402, applied: SI 2013/418 Art.3
s.402, varied: SI 2013/1881 Art.49, Art.50
s.403, applied: SI 2013/504 Reg.57
s.403, varied: SI 2013/1881 Art.50
s.404E, amended: SI 2013/1881 Art.10
s.404E, disapplied: SI 2013/1881 Art.11
s.404E, repealed (in part): SI 2013/1881 Art.10
s.404F, applied: SI 2013/1881 Art.58

s.415, applied: SI 2013/496 Sch.1 para.2
s.415B, amended: 2013 c.33 Sch.3 para.15
s.417, amended: 2013 c.33 s.4, SI 2013/504 Reg.3, SI 2013/1773 Sch.1 para.31, SI 2013/3115 Sch.2 para.24
s.418, amended: SI 2013/1797 Sch.1 para.1
s.418, repealed (in part): SI 2013/1797 Sch.2 para.1
s.422, amended: SI 2013/3115 Sch.2 para.25
s.422A, amended: SI 2013/3115 Sch.2 para.26
s.424A, applied: 2013 c.33 s.11, s.37
s.425, amended: SI 2013/1773 Sch.1 para.32, SI 2013/3115 Sch.2 para.27
s.425A, amended: SI 2013/655 Art.3, SI 2013/3115 Sch.2 para.28
s.426, applied: SI 2013/440 Art.1, SI 2013/441 Art.1
s.426, enabling: SI 2013/3128
s.428, enabling: SI 2013/165, SI 2013/431, SI 2013/504, SI 2013/555, SI 2013/556, SI 2013/598, SI 2013/655, SI 2013/1773, SI 2013/1881, SI 2013/1908, SI 2013/3115
s.429, amended: 2013 c.33 s.136
s.429, applied: SI 2013/555, SI 2013/598
Sch.1ZA, applied: SI 2013/496 Sch.1 para.2
Sch.1ZB, applied: SI 2013/496 Sch.1 para.3
Sch.1 Part I para.7, applied: SI 2013/442 Art.61, Art.62
Sch.1 Part I para.8, applied: SI 2013/442 Art.61
Sch.1 Part I para.10, applied: SI 2013/442 Art.3
Sch.1A Part I, substituted: SI 2013/1881 Art.10
Sch.1A Part I para.7, repealed (in part): SI 2013/1881 Art.10
Sch.1A Part I para.8, repealed (in part): SI 2013/1881 Art.10
Sch.1A Part I para.10, amended: SI 2013/1881 Art.10
Sch.1A Part I para.10, repealed (in part): SI 2013/1881 Art.10
Sch.1A Part II para.13, repealed: SI 2013/1881 Art.10
Sch.1ZA Part 1 para.8, amended: 2013 c.33 s.4, Sch.3 para.16, Sch.8 para.7, SI 2013/1388 Reg.3
Sch.1ZA Part 1 para.8, applied: SI 2013/161 Art.3, SI 2013/1881 Art.64
Sch.1ZA Part 1 para.8, varied: SI 2013/161 Art.3
Sch.1ZA Part 1 para.10, varied: SI 2013/161 Art.7
Sch.1ZA Part 1 para.11, amended: 2013 c.33 s.131
Sch.1ZA Part 1 para.11, applied: SI 2013/442 Art.3
Sch.1ZA Part 1 para.11, varied: SI 2013/442 Art.3
Sch.1ZA Part 2 para.16, varied: SI 2013/161 Art.7
Sch.1ZA Part 3, applied: SI 2013/1881 Art.46
Sch.1ZA Part 3 para.19, varied: SI 2013/442 Art.4, SI 2013/1635 Reg.7
Sch.1ZA Part 3 para.20, amended: 2013 c.33 Sch.10 para.4
Sch.1ZA Part 3 para.20, applied: SI 2013/418 Art.2, Art.3, SI 2013/1773 Reg.71
Sch.1ZA Part 3 para.20, varied: SI 2013/1635 Reg.7
Sch.1ZA Part 3 para.20, enabling: SI 2013/418
Sch.1ZA Part 3 para.21, applied: SI 2013/1773 Reg.71
Sch.1ZA Part 3 para.21, varied: SI 2013/1635 Reg.7
Sch.1ZA Part 3 para.22, varied: SI 2013/1635 Reg.7
Sch.1ZA Part 3 para.23, amended: 2013 c.33 Sch.8 para.7, SI 2013/1773 Sch.1 para.33
Sch.1ZA Part 3 para.23, applied: SI 2013/419 Art.6, SI 2013/496 Sch.1 para.6, SI 2013/1635 Reg.7, SI 2013/3116 Art.2, Art.3
Sch.1ZA Part 3 para.23, varied: SI 2013/1635 Reg.7
Sch.1ZA Part 3 para.23, enabling: SI 2013/419, SI 2013/3116
Sch.1ZA Part 4 para.25, amended: 2013 c.33 s.109
Sch.1ZA Part 4 para.25, applied: SI 2013/1635 Reg.8
Sch.1ZA Part 4 para.25, varied: SI 2013/161 Art.7
Sch.1ZB Part 1 para.15, amended: SI 2013/161 Art.12
Sch.1ZB Part 1 para.16, amended: 2013 c.33 s.4, Sch.3 para.17
Sch.1ZB Part 1 para.16, applied: SI 2013/161 Art.3
Sch.1ZB Part 1 para.16, repealed (in part): 2013 c.33 Sch.3 para.17
Sch.1ZB Part 1 para.19, amended: 2013 c.33 s.5, s.130
Sch.1ZB Part 1 para.20, amended: 2013 c.33 s.130
Sch.1ZB Part 3 para.28, applied: SI 2013/418 Art.3
Sch.1ZB Part 3 para.28, enabling: SI 2013/418
Sch.1ZB Part 3 para.31, applied: SI 2013/419 Art.6, SI 2013/496 Sch.1 para.7, SI 2013/3116 Art.3
Sch.1ZB Part 3 para.31, enabling: SI 2013/419, SI 2013/3116
Sch.1ZB Part 4 para.33, amended: 2013 c.33 s.109
Sch.2, applied: 2013 c.33 s.11, s.37, SI 2013/452 Reg.16, SI 2013/501 Reg.4, SI 2013/588 Reg.4, SI 2013/3208 r.204
Sch.2, referred to: SI 2013/244 Art.3, SI 2013/380 Sch.6 para.8, SI 2013/503 Reg.19

Sch.2 Part IIA para.24C, amended: SI 2013/1881 Art.10
Sch.2 Part IIA para.24C, repealed (in part): SI 2013/1881 Art.10
Sch.2 Part III para.25, enabling: SI 2013/655, SI 2013/1881
Sch.2 Part III para.26, applied: SI 2013/655, SI 2013/1881
Sch.3, applied: SI 2013/440 Art.15, SI 2013/1773 Reg.49, Reg.54
Sch.3 Part I para.1, amended: SI 2013/1773 Sch.1 para.34, SI 2013/3115 Sch.2 para.29
Sch.3 Part I para.2, amended: SI 2013/1162 Reg.12
Sch.3 Part I para.2, repealed: SI 2013/3115 Sch.2 para.29
Sch.3 Part I para.3, applied: SI 2013/440 Art.21
Sch.3 Part I para.4E, added: SI 2013/1773 Sch.1 para.34
Sch.3 Part I para.5, amended: SI 2013/1773 Sch.1 para.34, SI 2013/1797 Sch.1 para.1, SI 2013/3115 Sch.2 para.29
Sch.3 Part I para.5, applied: SI 2013/2356 Sch.2 para.7
Sch.3 Part I para.5A, amended: SI 2013/1773 Sch.1 para.34
Sch.3 Part I para.7A, amended: SI 2013/1773 Sch.1 para.34, SI 2013/1797 Sch.1 para.1
Sch.3 Part I para.10A, amended: SI 2013/1773 Sch.1 para.34, SI 2013/1797 Sch.1 para.1
Sch.3 Part I para.11D, added: SI 2013/1773 Sch.1 para.34
Sch.3 Part II para.12, applied: SI 2013/440 Art.17, SI 2013/2356 Sch.2 para.7
Sch.3 Part II para.12, referred to: SI 2013/440 Art.18
Sch.3 Part II para.13, amended: SI 2013/1773 Sch.1 para.34
Sch.3 Part II para.13, applied: SI 2013/440 Art.15, Art.17
Sch.3 Part II para.13, enabling: SI 2013/439, SI 2013/1773, SI 2013/1797, SI 2013/3115
Sch.3 Part II para.14, amended: SI 2013/1773 Sch.1 para.34, SI 2013/1797 Sch.1 para.1
Sch.3 Part II para.14, applied: SI 2013/440 Art.15, Art.18
Sch.3 Part II para.14, referred to: SI 2013/440 Art.18
Sch.3 Part II para.14, enabling: SI 2013/1773, SI 2013/3115
Sch.3 Part II para.15, applied: SI 2013/2356 Sch.2 para.7
Sch.3 Part II para.15, repealed (in part): SI 2013/1881 Art.10
Sch.3 Part II para.17, enabling: SI 2013/439, SI 2013/1773, SI 2013/3115
Sch.3 Part II para.18, enabling: SI 2013/3115
Sch.3 Part III, amended: SI 2013/1773 Sch.1 para.34
Sch.3 Part III para.18A, applied: SI 2013/440 Art.19, Art.20, SI 2013/441 Art.32
Sch.3 Part III para.19, amended: SI 2013/1773 Sch.1 para.34, SI 2013/1797 Sch.1 para.1, SI 2013/3115 Sch.2 para.29
Sch.3 Part III para.19, applied: SI 2013/440 Art.19, SI 2013/441 Art.19, Art.21, Art.32
Sch.3 Part III para.19, referred to: SI 2013/440 Art.19
Sch.3 Part III para.20, amended: SI 2013/1773 Sch.1 para.34, SI 2013/1797 Sch.1 para.1, SI 2013/3115 Sch.2 para.29
Sch.3 Part III para.20, applied: SI 2013/440 Art.20
Sch.3 Part III para.20C, added: SI 2013/1773 Sch.1 para.34
Sch.3 Part III para.20C, amended: SI 2013/1797 Sch.1 para.1
Sch.3 Part III para.20ZA, amended: SI 2013/3115 Sch.2 para.29
Sch.3 Part III para.22, enabling: SI 2013/1773, SI 2013/1797, SI 2013/3115
Sch.3 Part III para.23, repealed: SI 2013/1881 Art.10
Sch.3 Part III para.24, amended: SI 2013/3115 Sch.2 para.29
Sch.3 Part III para.29, added: SI 2013/1773 Sch.1 para.34
Sch.4, applied: SI 2013/440 Art.21
Sch.4 para.3, applied: SI 2013/440 Art.23
Sch.4 para.3A, enabling: SI 2013/439
Sch.4 para.5, applied: SI 2013/440 Art.23
Sch.5 para.2, amended: SI 2013/1773 Sch.1 para.35
Sch.6, applied: SI 2013/161 Art.8
Sch.6 Part I para.1, amended: SI 2013/555 Art.2
Sch.6 Part I para.1, substituted: SI 2013/555 Art.2
Sch.6 Part I para.1A, amended: SI 2013/555 Art.2
Sch.6 Part I para.1A, substituted: SI 2013/555 Art.2
Sch.6 Part I para.2, amended: SI 2013/555 Art.2
Sch.6 Part I para.2, substituted: SI 2013/555 Art.2
Sch.6 Part I para.2A, amended: SI 2013/555 Art.2
Sch.6 Part I para.2A, substituted: SI 2013/555 Art.2
Sch.6 Part I para.3, amended: SI 2013/555 Art.2
Sch.6 Part I para.3, substituted: SI 2013/555 Art.2
Sch.6 Part I para.4, amended: SI 2013/555 Art.2
Sch.6 Part I para.4, substituted: SI 2013/555 Art.2
Sch.6 Part I para.5, amended: SI 2013/555 Art.2

Sch.6 Part I para.5, substituted: SI 2013/555 Art.2
Sch.6 Part 1B para.2A, amended: SI 2013/555 Art.2
Sch.6 Part 1B para.2B, amended: SI 2013/555 Art.2, SI 2013/1773 Sch.1 para.36, SI 2013/1797 Sch.1 para.1
Sch.6 Part 1B para.2C, amended: SI 2013/555 Art.2, SI 2013/1881 Art.10
Sch.6 Part 1B para.2D, amended: SI 2013/555 Art.2, SI 2013/1881 Art.10
Sch.6 Part 1B para.2E, amended: SI 2013/555 Art.2
Sch.6 Part 1B para.2F, amended: SI 2013/555 Art.2, SI 2013/1881 Art.10
Sch.6 Part 1B para.2G, added: SI 2013/1881 Art.10
Sch.6 Part 1B para.2G, amended: SI 2013/555 Art.2
Sch.6 Part 1C para.3A, amended: SI 2013/555 Art.2
Sch.6 Part 1C para.3B, amended: SI 2013/555 Art.2
Sch.6 Part 1C para.3C, amended: SI 2013/555 Art.2
Sch.6 Part 1C para.3D, amended: SI 2013/555 Art.2
Sch.6 Part 1C para.3E, amended: SI 2013/555 Art.2
Sch.6 Part 1D para.4A, amended: SI 2013/555 Art.2
Sch.6 Part 1D para.4B, amended: SI 2013/555 Art.2
Sch.6 Part 1D para.4C, amended: SI 2013/555 Art.2
Sch.6 Part 1D para.4D, amended: SI 2013/555 Art.2
Sch.6 Part 1D para.4E, amended: SI 2013/555 Art.2
Sch.6 Part 1D para.4F, amended: SI 2013/555 Art.2
Sch.6 Part 1E para.5A, amended: SI 2013/555 Art.2
Sch.6 Part 1E para.5B, amended: SI 2013/555 Art.2
Sch.6 Part 1E para.5C, amended: SI 2013/555 Art.2
Sch.6 Part 1E para.5D, amended: SI 2013/555 Art.2
Sch.6 Part 1E para.5E, amended: SI 2013/555 Art.2
Sch.6 Part 1E para.5F, amended: SI 2013/555 Art.2
Sch.6 Part 1F para.6A, amended: SI 2013/555 Art.2
Sch.6 Part 1G para.7A, amended: SI 2013/555 Art.2
Sch.6 Part II para.6, amended: SI 2013/555 Art.2
Sch.6 Part II para.6, substituted: SI 2013/555 Art.2
Sch.6 Part II para.7, amended: SI 2013/555 Art.2
Sch.6 Part II para.7, substituted: SI 2013/555 Art.2
Sch.6 Part III para.8, amended: SI 2013/555 Art.2
Sch.6 Part III para.9, amended: SI 2013/555 Art.2
Sch.11A Part II para.8, amended: SI 2013/3115 Sch.2 para.30
Sch.12, referred to: SI 2013/442 Art.9
Sch.12 Part I para.1, amended: 2013 c.33 Sch.1 para.2
Sch.12 Part I para.2, applied: SI 2013/442 Art.9
Sch.12 Part I para.3, applied: SI 2013/442 Art.9
Sch.12 Part I para.4, applied: SI 2013/442 Art.9
Sch.12 Part I para.5, applied: SI 2013/442 Art.9
Sch.12 Part I para.5A, applied: SI 2013/442 Art.9
Sch.12 Part II para.7, amended: 2013 c.33 Sch.1 para.2
Sch.12 Part II para.8, applied: SI 2013/442 Art.9
Sch.12 Part II para.9, amended: 2013 c.33 Sch.1 para.2
Sch.12 Part II para.9, applied: SI 2013/442 Art.9
Sch.12 Part IIA para.9A, applied: SI 2013/442 Art.9
Sch.12 Part IIB para.9B, added: 2013 c.33 Sch.1 para.13
Sch.12 Part IIB para.9C, added: 2013 c.33 Sch.1 para.13
Sch.12 Part IIB para.9D, added: 2013 c.33 Sch.1 para.13
Sch.12 Part III para.10, applied: SI 2013/442 Art.9
Sch.15 Part I, applied: SI 2013/1389 Reg.9
Sch.15 Part I para.1, varied: SI 2013/3128 Art.4
Sch.15 Part I para.2, varied: SI 2013/3128 Art.4
Sch.15 Part I para.3, varied: SI 2013/3128 Art.4
Sch.15 Part I para.4, varied: SI 2013/3128 Art.4
Sch.15 Part I para.5, varied: SI 2013/3128 Art.4
Sch.15 Part I para.6, varied: SI 2013/3128 Art.4
Sch.15 Part I para.7, varied: SI 2013/3128 Art.4
Sch.16 para.1, repealed: SI 2013/1881 Art.10
Sch.16 para.1, varied: SI 2013/1881 Art.11
Sch.16 para.2, repealed: SI 2013/1881 Art.10
Sch.16 para.2, varied: SI 2013/1881 Art.11
Sch.16 para.3, repealed: SI 2013/1881 Art.10
Sch.16 para.3, varied: SI 2013/1881 Art.11
Sch.16 para.4, repealed: SI 2013/1881 Art.10
Sch.16 para.4, varied: SI 2013/1881 Art.11
Sch.16 para.5, repealed: SI 2013/1881 Art.10
Sch.16 para.5, varied: SI 2013/1881 Art.11
Sch.17, applied: SSI 2013/50 Sch.2 para.2, Sch.2 Part 2

Sch.17 Part II para.3, amended: SI 2013/1881 Art.10
Sch.17 Part II para.7, amended: SI 2013/1881 Art.10
Sch.17 Part II para.9, amended: SI 2013/1881 Art.10
Sch.17 Part II para.10, amended: SI 2013/1881 Art.10
Sch.17 Part II para.11, amended: SI 2013/1881 Art.10
Sch.17 Part IIIA para.16A, repealed: SI 2013/1881 Art.10
Sch.17 Part IIIA para.16B, repealed: SI 2013/1881 Art.10
Sch.17 Part IIIA para.16C, repealed: SI 2013/1881 Art.10
Sch.17 Part IIIA para.16D, amended: 2013 c.22 Sch.9 para.52
Sch.17 Part IIIA para.16D, repealed: SI 2013/1881 Art.10
Sch.17 Part IIIA para.16E, repealed: SI 2013/1881 Art.10
Sch.17 Part IIIA para.16F, repealed: SI 2013/1881 Art.10
Sch.17 Part IIIA para.16G, repealed: SI 2013/1881 Art.10
Sch.17 Part III para.16, amended: 2013 c.22 Sch.9 para.52
Sch.17A Part 2 para.10, amended: 2013 c.33 Sch.10 para.5
Sch.17A Part 2 para.10, applied: SI 2013/442 Art.70
Sch.17A Part 2 para.11, amended: SI 2013/504 Reg.3
Sch.17A Part 2 para.14, applied: SI 2013/419 Art.4
Sch.17A Part 2 para.14, enabling: SI 2013/419
Sch.17A Part 2 para.17, referred to: SI 2013/165 Art.2
Sch.17A Part 2 para.17, enabling: SI 2013/165
Sch.17A Part 2 para.18, amended: SI 2013/504 Reg.3
Sch.17A Part 2 para.19, amended: SI 2013/504 Reg.3
Sch.17A Part 2 para.23, amended: SI 2013/504 Reg.3
Sch.17A Part 2 para.26, applied: SI 2013/419 Art.5
Sch.17A Part 2 para.26, enabling: SI 2013/419
Sch.17A Part 2 para.30, applied: SI 2013/419 Art.4
Sch.17A Part 2 para.30, enabling: SI 2013/419
Sch.17A Part 3 para.34, amended: SI 2013/504 Reg.3
Sch.17A Part 3 para.35, amended: SI 2013/504 Reg.3
Sch.17A Part 4 para.36, amended: SI 2013/504 Reg.3
Sch.17A Part 4 para.36, applied: SI 2013/419 Art.6
Sch.17A Part 4 para.36, enabling: SI 2013/419
Sch.22, applied: SI 2013/1046 r.10

12. Limited Liability Partnerships Act 2000

applied: SI 2013/2605 Art.23, Art.57
s.8, applied: SI 2013/1389 Sch.2 para.3
s.15, applied: SI 2013/415
s.15, enabling: SI 2013/618, SI 2013/2005
s.17, applied: SI 2013/415, SI 2013/2005
s.17, enabling: SI 2013/618
s.18, referred to: SI 2013/486 Reg.8, Reg.20

14. Care Standards Act 2000

Part II, applied: SI 2013/1394 Reg.34, Reg.35, Sch.2 para.2, Sch.10 para.3, Sch.10 para.5
s.1, enabling: SI 2013/1394
s.3, referred to: SI 2013/2730 Reg.1, Reg.6
s.4, referred to: SI 2013/2668 Sch.3 para.17
s.4, enabling: SI 2013/499
s.11, see *Waghorn v Care Quality Commission* [2012] EWHC 1816 (Admin), [2013] Med. L.R. 80 (QBD (Admin)), Cox, J.
s.11, applied: SI 2013/253 Reg.2
s.11, disapplied: SI 2013/1394 Sch.10 para.8
s.11, varied: SI 2013/1394 Sch.7 para.1
s.11, enabling: SI 2013/1394, SI 2013/2668, SI 2013/3239
s.12, applied: SI 2013/253 Reg.2
s.12, disapplied: SI 2013/1394 Sch.10 para.8
s.12, varied: SI 2013/1394 Sch.7 para.2
s.12, enabling: SI 2013/225, SI 2013/1394, SI 2013/2668, SI 2013/3239
s.13, varied: SI 2013/1394 Sch.7 para.3
s.14, applied: SI 2013/253 Reg.2, SI 2013/2668 Reg.22
s.14, varied: SI 2013/253 Sch.1 para.1, SI 2013/1394 Sch.7 para.4
s.14, enabling: SI 2013/1394, SI 2013/2668
s.15, applied: SI 2013/253 Reg.2
s.15, enabling: SI 2013/1394, SI 2013/2668
s.16, applied: SI 2013/253 Reg.2, SI 2013/1394 Sch.10 para.8
s.16, varied: SI 2013/253 Sch.1 para.2
s.16, enabling: SI 2013/523, SI 2013/1394, SI 2013/2668, SI 2013/3239
s.17, varied: SI 2013/1394 Sch.7 para.5
s.19, applied: SI 2013/1394 Sch.10 para.6
s.19, varied: SI 2013/1394 Sch.7 para.6
s.20, varied: SI 2013/1394 Sch.7 para.7
s.21, varied: SI 2013/1394 Sch.7 para.8
s.22, applied: SI 2013/253 Reg.2, SI 2013/706, SI 2013/984
s.22, varied: SI 2013/253 Sch.1 para.3

s.22, enabling: SI 2013/225, SI 2013/499, SI 2013/706, SI 2013/984, SI 2013/1394, SI 2013/2668, SI 2013/3239
s.22A, varied: SI 2013/1394 Sch.7 para.9
s.22B, varied: SI 2013/1394 Sch.7 para.10
s.23, see *R. (on the application of X) v Tower Hamlets LBC* [2013] EWCA Civ 904, [2013] 4 All E.R. 237 (CA (Civ Div)), Maurice Kay, L.J. (VP, CA Civ)
s.23, applied: SI 2013/253 Reg.2, SI 2013/1394 Reg.31
s.23, varied: SI 2013/253 Sch.1 para.4
s.24, varied: SI 2013/1394 Sch.7 para.11
s.24A, varied: SI 2013/1394 Sch.7 para.12
s.25, applied: SI 2013/253 Reg.2
s.25, enabling: SI 2013/499
s.26, varied: SI 2013/1394 Sch.7 para.13
s.28, varied: SI 2013/1394 Sch.7 para.14
s.30A, applied: SI 2013/253 Reg.2
s.30A, varied: SI 2013/253 Sch.1 para.5, SI 2013/1394 Sch.7 para.15
s.31, applied: SI 2013/253 Reg.2
s.31, varied: SI 2013/253 Sch.1 para.6, SI 2013/1394 Sch.7 para.16
s.31, enabling: SI 2013/523, SI 2013/1394
s.32, varied: SI 2013/1394 Sch.7 para.17
s.33, applied: SI 2013/253 Reg.2
s.33, varied: SI 2013/253 Sch.1 para.7
s.34, applied: SI 2013/253 Reg.2
s.34, varied: SI 2013/253 Sch.1 para.8
s.35, applied: SI 2013/253 Reg.2
s.35, varied: SI 2013/253 Sch.1 para.9
s.35, enabling: SI 2013/1394
s.36, applied: SI 2013/253 Reg.2, SI 2013/2668 Reg.17
s.36, enabling: SI 2013/446, SI 2013/2668, SI 2013/3239
s.37, varied: SI 2013/1394 Sch.7 para.18
s.42, applied: SI 2013/253 Reg.2, SI 2013/2903 Reg.5
s.42, enabling: SI 2013/253, SI 2013/1394
s.118, enabling: SI 2013/225, SI 2013/446, SI 2013/499, SI 2013/523, SI 2013/706, SI 2013/984, SI 2013/1394, SI 2013/2668, SI 2013/3239
Sch.2A para.15, amended: SI 2013/755 Sch.2 para.397

17. Finance Act 2000

Sch.6, disapplied: 2013 c.29 Sch.42 para.1
Sch.6 Part II para.4, amended: 2013 c.29 Sch.42 para.1, Sch.42 para.3
Sch.6 Part II para.5, amended: 2013 c.29 Sch.42 para.4
Sch.6 Part II para.5, applied: 2013 c.29 Sch.42 para.20
Sch.6 Part II para.6, amended: 2013 c.29 Sch.42 para.1, Sch.42 para.5
Sch.6 Part II para.6, repealed (in part): 2013 c.29 Sch.42 para.1
Sch.6 Part II para.14, amended: 2013 c.29 Sch.42 para.1, Sch.42 para.6
Sch.6 Part II para.14, applied: 2013 c.29 Sch.42 para.20
Sch.6 Part II para.14, repealed (in part): 2013 c.29 Sch.42 para.1, Sch.42 para.6
Sch.6 Part II para.15, amended: 2013 c.29 Sch.42 para.1, Sch.42 para.7
Sch.6 Part II para.15, repealed (in part): 2013 c.29 Sch.42 para.1
Sch.6 Part II para.15A, repealed: 2013 c.29 Sch.42 para.1
Sch.6 Part II para.16, enabling: SI 2013/232
Sch.6 Part II para.17, amended: 2013 c.29 Sch.42 para.8
Sch.6 Part II para.17, applied: 2013 c.29 Sch.42 para.20
Sch.6 Part II para.17, repealed (in part): 2013 c.29 Sch.42 para.8
Sch.6 Part II para.21, amended: 2013 c.29 Sch.42 para.9
Sch.6 Part II para.21, repealed (in part): 2013 c.29 Sch.42 para.1
Sch.6 Part II para.22, enabling: SI 2013/713
Sch.6 Part II para.23, enabling: SI 2013/713
Sch.6 Part II para.24, repealed (in part): 2013 c.29 Sch.42 para.1
Sch.6 Part II para.24A, added: 2013 c.29 Sch.42 para.10
Sch.6 Part II para.24B, added: 2013 c.29 Sch.42 para.10
Sch.6 Part II para.24B, enabling: SI 2013/713, SI 2013/1716
Sch.6 Part II para.24C, added: 2013 c.29 Sch.42 para.10
Sch.6 Part II para.24D, added: 2013 c.29 Sch.42 para.10
Sch.6 Part II para.24D, enabling: SI 2013/713, SI 2013/1716
Sch.6 Part III para.26, repealed (in part): 2013 c.29 Sch.42 para.1
Sch.6 Part III para.28A, repealed: 2013 c.29 Sch.42 para.1
Sch.6 Part III para.29, repealed (in part): 2013 c.29 Sch.42 para.1
Sch.6 Part III para.34, amended: 2013 c.29 Sch.42 para.1
Sch.6 Part III para.38A, added: 2013 c.29 Sch.42 para.11

Sch.6 Part III para.39, amended: 2013 c.29 Sch.42 para.1, Sch.42 para.12
Sch.6 Part IV para.40, amended: 2013 c.29 Sch.42 para.1
Sch.6 Part IV para.40, repealed (in part): 2013 c.29 Sch.42 para.1
Sch.6 Part IV para.42, amended: 2013 c.29 s.199, Sch.42 para.13
Sch.6 Part IV para.42, repealed (in part): 2013 c.29 Sch.42 para.1
Sch.6 Part IV para.42A, added: 2013 c.29 Sch.42 para.14
Sch.6 Part IV para.42A, amended: 2013 c.29 Sch.42 para.1, Sch.42 para.23, Sch.42 para.24
Sch.6 Part IV para.42A, repealed (in part): 2013 c.29 Sch.42 para.1, Sch.42 para.1
Sch.6 Part IV para.42B, added: 2013 c.29 Sch.42 para.14
Sch.6 Part IV para.42B, repealed: 2013 c.29 Sch.42 para.1
Sch.6 Part IV para.42C, added: 2013 c.29 Sch.42 para.14
Sch.6 Part IV para.42C, repealed: 2013 c.29 Sch.42 para.1
Sch.6 Part IV para.42D, added: 2013 c.29 Sch.42 para.14
Sch.6 Part IV para.42D, repealed: 2013 c.29 Sch.42 para.1
Sch.6 Part IV para.44, enabling: SI 2013/713
Sch.6 Part IV para.50, enabling: SI 2013/505
Sch.6 Part IV para.52D, enabling: SI 2013/508
Sch.6 Part IV para.52E, enabling: SI 2013/508
Sch.6 Part IV para.52F, enabling: SI 2013/508
Sch.6 Part V para.55, amended: 2013 c.29 Sch.42 para.15
Sch.6 Part VI para.62, amended: 2013 c.29 Sch.42 para.16
Sch.6 Part VI para.62, repealed (in part): 2013 c.29 Sch.42 para.1
Sch.6 Part VI para.62, enabling: SI 2013/713
Sch.6 Part X para.120, referred to: SI 2013/1119 Art.24, Art.25
Sch.6 Part XIII para.146, amended: 2013 c.29 Sch.42 para.17
Sch.6 Part XIII para.146, applied: SI 2013/232
Sch.6 Part XIII para.146, enabling: SI 2013/505, SI 2013/508, SI 2013/713
Sch.6 Part XIV para.147, amended: 2013 c.29 Sch.42 para.18
Sch.6 Part XIV para.152A, added: 2013 c.29 Sch.42 para.19
Sch.6 Part XIV para.152B, added: 2013 c.29 Sch.42 para.19
Sch.22 Part IV para.29, enabling: SI 2013/5, SI 2013/2245
Sch.22 Part IV para.31, enabling: SI 2013/5, SI 2013/2245
Sch.22 Part IV para.36, enabling: SI 2013/5, SI 2013/2245
Sch.22 Part VI para.51, amended: SI 2013/2819 Reg.35
Sch.22 Part VI para.51, repealed (in part): SI 2013/2819 Reg.35
Sch.30 para.4, repealed (in part): 2013 c.2 Sch.1 Part 10
Sch.30 para.10, repealed: 2013 c.2 Sch.1 Part 10
Sch.30 para.14, repealed: 2013 c.2 Sch.1 Part 10
Sch.30 para.18, repealed: 2013 c.2 Sch.1 Part 10
Sch.30 para.26, repealed: 2013 c.2 Sch.1 Part 10

19. Child Support, Pensions and Social Security Act 2000

applied: SI 2013/386 Reg.7, Reg.18
s.1, disapplied: SI 2013/630
s.83, repealed (in part): 2013 c.22 Sch.11 para.210
Sch.7, applied: SI 2013/386 Reg.7, Reg.18
Sch.8 para.2, repealed: 2013 c.22 Sch.10 para.99
Sch.8 para.10, repealed: 2013 c.22 Sch.11 para.210

20. Government Resources and Accounts Act 2000

s.2, applied: 2013 c.28 s.5
s.4A, applied: SI 2013/488, SI 2013/3187
s.4A, enabling: SI 2013/488, SI 2013/3187
s.6, varied: SI 2013/148 Art.2
s.10, applied: SI 2013/1796, SI 2013/1796 Art.2
s.10, enabling: SI 2013/1796
s.22, applied: SI 2013/148
s.22, enabling: SI 2013/148

21. Learning and Skills Act 2000

s.33E, applied: SI 2013/1793 Reg.13
s.39, applied: SI 2013/375 Sch.1 para.2
s.145, amended: 2013 c.22 Sch.9 para.52

22. Local Government Act 2000

Part 1A, applied: SI 2013/643 Art.2
s.9D, enabling: SI 2013/2190
s.9DA, enabling: SI 2013/218, SI 2013/2190
s.9F, applied: SI 2013/218 Reg.30
s.9FA, applied: SI 2013/218 Reg.30
s.9FA, varied: SI 2013/218 Reg.30
s.9FF, amended: SI 2013/594 Art.5
s.9FF, repealed (in part): SI 2013/594 Art.5
s.9HE, amended: SI 2013/2597 Sch.1 para.7
s.9HE, applied: SI 2013/2597 Art.2
s.9J, enabling: SI 2013/218
s.9JA, applied: SI 2013/643 Art.2
s.9JA, enabling: SI 2013/218
s.9MG, amended: SI 2013/2597 Sch.1 para.7
s.9MG, applied: SI 2013/2597 Art.2
s.13, enabling: SI 2013/2438, SI 2013/2902

s.21, applied: SI 2013/1050 Reg.14
s.21A, applied: SI 2013/1050 Reg.12
s.77, amended: 2013 c.22 Sch.9 para.52
s.86, enabling: SI 2013/2969
s.87, enabling: SI 2013/2969
s.93, applied: SI 2013/3029 Sch.5 para.21, SI 2013/3035 Sch.1
s.105, amended: SI 2013/2597 Sch.1 para.7
s.105, enabling: SI 2013/218, SI 2013/2190, SI 2013/2438, SI 2013/2902, SI 2013/2969
Sch.1 para.8, applied: SI 2013/1050 Reg.5
Sch.1 para.9, applied: SI 2013/1050 Reg.5

23. Regulation of Investigatory Powers Act 2000
see *An Informer v Chief Constable* [2012] EWCA Civ 197, [2013] Q.B. 579 (CA (Civ Div)), Pill, L.J.
applied: SI 2013/602 Sch.3 para.3, SI 2013/1554 r.6_1
Part I, applied: 2013 c.22 Sch.7 para.1, SI 2013/164 Sch.1 para.6, SI 2013/1877 Sch.1 para.6
s.5, applied: SI 2013/602 Sch.3 para.11
s.6, amended: 2013 c.22 Sch.8 para.78, SI 2013/602 Sch.2 para.33
s.6, repealed (in part): SI 2013/602 Sch.2 para.33
s.17, applied: 2013 c.18 s.6
s.17, repealed (in part): 2013 c.22 Sch.8 para.79, SI 2013/602 Sch.2 para.33
s.18, amended: 2013 c.18 s.16, Sch.2 para.11
s.19, repealed (in part): 2013 c.22 Sch.8 para.80, SI 2013/602 Sch.2 para.33
s.21, referred to: SI 2013/1554 r.6_27
s.22, amended: SI 2013/602 Sch.2 para.33
s.22, applied: SI 2013/1554 r.6_27
s.22, repealed (in part): SI 2013/602 Sch.2 para.33
s.23, amended: SI 2013/602 Sch.2 para.33
s.23, repealed (in part): SI 2013/602 Sch.2 para.33
s.23A, amended: SI 2013/602 Sch.2 para.33
s.23A, applied: SI 2013/1554 r.6_1, r.6_27, r.6_28
s.23B, applied: SI 2013/1554 r.6_27
s.25, amended: 2013 c.22 Sch.8 para.81
s.25, repealed (in part): SI 2013/602 Sch.2 para.33
s.26, see *J v Commissioner of Police of the Metropolis* [2013] EWHC 32 (QB), [2013] 1 W.L.R. 2734 (QBD), Tugendhat, J.
s.26, referred to: SI 2013/1554 r.6_27
s.28, see *R. v Plunkett (Daniel Michael)* [2013] EWCA Crim 261, [2013] 1 W.L.R. 3121 (CA (Crim Div)), Sir John Thomas (President QBD)
s.28, applied: SI 2013/1554 r.6_27
s.29, applied: SI 2013/1554 r.6_27, SI 2013/2788 Art.3, Art.4, Art.17
s.29, referred to: SI 2013/2788 Art.3, Art.4, Art.5
s.29, repealed (in part): SI 2013/602 Sch.2 para.33
s.29, enabling: SI 2013/2788
s.30, see *J v Commissioner of Police of the Metropolis* [2013] EWHC 32 (QB), [2013] 1 W.L.R. 2734 (QBD), Tugendhat, J.
s.30, enabling: SI 2013/2788
s.32, amended: 2013 c.22 s.55, Sch.8 para.82, Sch.21 para.6, SI 2013/602 Sch.2 para.33
s.32A, applied: SI 2013/1554 r.6_1, r.6_27, r.6_28
s.32B, applied: SI 2013/1554 r.6_27
s.33, amended: 2013 c.22 Sch.8 para.83, Sch.21 para.7, SI 2013/602 Sch.2 para.33
s.33, repealed (in part): SI 2013/602 Sch.2 para.33
s.34, amended: 2013 c.22 Sch.8 para.84, Sch.21 para.8, SI 2013/602 Sch.2 para.33
s.35, amended: 2013 c.22 Sch.8 para.85, Sch.21 para.9
s.36, amended: 2013 c.22 Sch.8 para.86, Sch.21 para.10, SI 2013/602 Sch.2 para.33
s.37, amended: 2013 c.22 Sch.8 para.87, Sch.21 para.11
s.40, amended: 2013 c.22 Sch.8 para.88, Sch.21 para.12
s.43, referred to: SI 2013/2788 Art.5
s.43, varied: SI 2013/2788 Art.3
s.43, enabling: SI 2013/2788
s.45, amended: SI 2013/602 Sch.2 para.33
s.45, repealed (in part): SI 2013/602 Sch.2 para.33
s.46, amended: 2013 c.22 Sch.8 para.89, Sch.21 para.13
s.49, amended: 2013 c.22 Sch.8 para.90, SI 2013/602 Sch.2 para.33
s.51, amended: 2013 c.22 Sch.8 para.91, SI 2013/602 Sch.2 para.33
s.51, repealed (in part): SI 2013/602 Sch.2 para.33
s.54, amended: 2013 c.22 Sch.8 para.92, SI 2013/602 Sch.2 para.33
s.55, amended: 2013 c.22 Sch.8 para.93
s.55, repealed (in part): SI 2013/602 Sch.2 para.33
s.56, amended: 2013 c.22 Sch.8 para.94, SI 2013/602 Sch.2 para.33
s.58, amended: SI 2013/602 Sch.2 para.33
s.58, repealed (in part): 2013 c.22 Sch.8 para.95, SI 2013/602 Sch.2 para.33
s.59A, added: 2013 c.18 s.5
s.60, amended: 2013 c.18 Sch.2 para.4
s.65, see *J v Commissioner of Police of the Metropolis* [2013] EWHC 32 (QB), [2013] 1 W.L.R. 2734 (QBD), Tugendhat, J.
s.65, amended: 2013 c.22 Sch.8 para.96, SI 2013/602 Sch.2 para.33
s.65, repealed (in part): SI 2013/602 Sch.2 para.33
s.68, amended: SI 2013/602 Sch.2 para.33
s.68, repealed (in part): 2013 c.22 Sch.8 para.97, SI 2013/602 Sch.2 para.33
s.76A, amended: 2013 c.22 Sch.8 para.98

s.76A, applied: 2013 c.22 Sch.4 para.2
s.76A, repealed (in part): SI 2013/602 Sch.2 para.33
s.78, enabling: SI 2013/2788
s.81, amended: SI 2013/602 Sch.2 para.33
Sch.A1 Part I para.6, amended: 2013 c.22 Sch.9 para.125
Sch.1 Part I para.2, substituted: 2013 c.22 Sch.8 para.99
Sch.1 Part I para.2A, repealed: SI 2013/602 Sch.2 para.33
Sch.1 Part I para.20H, added: 2013 c.32 Sch.12 para.74
Sch.1 Part II para.28F, added: SI 2013/755 Sch.2 para.398
Sch.2 para.2, amended: 2013 c.22 Sch.8 para.100, SI 2013/602 Sch.2 para.33
Sch.2 para.4, amended: 2013 c.22 Sch.8 para.100, SI 2013/602 Sch.2 para.33
Sch.2 para.5, amended: 2013 c.22 Sch.8 para.100, SI 2013/602 Sch.2 para.33
Sch.2 para.6, amended: 2013 c.22 Sch.8 para.100, SI 2013/602 Sch.2 para.33
Sch.2 para.6, repealed (in part): SI 2013/602 Sch.2 para.33

26. Postal Services Act 2000

applied: SI 2013/1783 Reg.25
referred to: SI 2013/1384 Art.4, Art.9, SI 2013/2808 Art.11
s.77, amended: SI 2013/1970 Sch.1 para.27
s.125, referred to: SI 2013/3173 Art.4, SSI 2013/63 r.19, SSI 2013/88 Art.5

35. Children (Leaving Care) Act 2000

s.6, applied: SI 2013/3029 Reg.6, SI 2013/3035 Sch.1

36. Freedom of Information Act 2000

see *R. (on the application of Evans) v Attorney General* [2013] EWHC 1960 (Admin), [2013] 3 W.L.R. 1631 (DC), Lord Judge, L.C.J.
applied: 2013 c.32 Sch.9 para.16, SI 2013/1119 Sch.2 para.2, SI 2013/1977 Reg.2
s.11A, applied: SI 2013/1977 Reg.2
s.11B, enabling: SI 2013/1977
s.19, applied: SI 2013/1977 Reg.2
s.23, amended: 2013 c.18 Sch.2 para.5, 2013 c.22 Sch.8 para.102
s.39, see *R. (on the application of Evans) v Attorney General* [2013] EWHC 1960 (Admin), [2013] 3 W.L.R. 1631 (DC), Lord Judge, L.C.J.
s.39, applied: 2013 c.32 Sch.9 para.16
s.44, applied: 2013 c.32 Sch.9 para.22
s.84, amended: 2013 c.22 Sch.8 para.103
Sch.1 Part I para.1, substituted: 2013 c.24 Sch.4 para.25
Sch.1 Part I para.1ZA, added: 2013 c.24 Sch.4 para.25
Sch.1 Part I para.2, amended: 2013 c.18 Sch.2 para.5
Sch.1 Part I para.3, amended: 2013 c.18 Sch.2 para.5
Sch.1 Part I para.6, referred to: SI 2013/1119 Sch.2 para.2
Sch.1 Part II para.7, referred to: SI 2013/1119 Sch.2 para.16
Sch.1 Part II para.8, referred to: SI 2013/1119 Sch.2 para.16
Sch.1 Part II para.9, referred to: SI 2013/1119 Sch.2 para.16
Sch.1 Part II para.10, referred to: SI 2013/1119 Sch.2 para.16
Sch.1 Part II para.11, referred to: SI 2013/1119 Sch.2 para.16
Sch.1 Part IV, referred to: SI 2013/1119 Art.19
Sch.1 Part V para.64, referred to: SI 2013/1119 Sch.2 para.2
Sch.1 Part VI, amended: 2013 c.19 s.21, 2013 c.22 Sch.8 para.104, 2013 c.24 Sch.20 para.2, 2013 c.2 Sch.1 Part 10, 2013 c.32 Sch.12 para.75, 2013 c.33 Sch.4 para.15, SI 2013/64 Art.4, SI 2013/252 Sch.1 Part 1, SI 2013/687 Sch.1 para.14, SI 2013/755 Sch.2 para.399, SI 2013/783 Art.7, SI 2013/1644 Sch.1, SI 2013/2042 Sch.1 para.22, SI 2013/2329 Sch.1 para.26, SI 2013/2352 Sch.1 para.13
Sch.1 Part VI, referred to: SI 2013/1119 Sch.2 para.10

37. Countryside and Rights of Way Act 2000

s.1, amended: SI 2013/755 Sch.2 para.401
s.2, referred to: SI 2013/1798 Reg.3
s.4, amended: SI 2013/755 Sch.2 para.402
s.5, enabling: SI 2013/1798
s.10, amended: SI 2013/514 Reg.2
s.10, applied: SI 2013/1798 Reg.2
s.10, enabling: SI 2013/514
s.11, enabling: SI 2013/1798
s.20, amended: SI 2013/755 Sch.2 para.402
s.21, amended: SI 2013/755 Sch.2 para.403
s.26, amended: SI 2013/755 Sch.2 para.404
s.33, amended: SI 2013/755 Sch.2 para.405
s.33, repealed (in part): SI 2013/755 Sch.2 para.405
s.44, enabling: SI 2013/1798
s.45, enabling: SI 2013/514, SI 2013/1798
s.58, amended: SI 2013/755 Sch.2 para.406
s.61, amended: SI 2013/755 Sch.2 para.406
s.82, amended: SI 2013/755 Sch.2 para.407
s.83, amended: SI 2013/755 Sch.2 para.408
s.84, amended: SI 2013/755 Sch.2 para.408

s.86, amended: SI 2013/755 Sch.2 para.408
s.86, applied: SI 2013/2356 Sch.2 para.23
s.90, amended: SI 2013/755 Sch.2 para.408
s.91, amended: SI 2013/755 Sch.2 para.408
s.92, amended: SI 2013/755 Sch.2 para.409
Sch.1 Part II para.14, amended: SI 2013/755 Sch.2 para.410
Sch.6 Part I para.3, repealed: 2013 c.27 s.13
Sch.6 Part I para.12, amended: SI 2013/755 Sch.2 para.411
Sch.6 Part I para.16, amended: SI 2013/755 Sch.2 para.411
Sch.13 para.6, amended: SI 2013/755 Sch.2 para.412

41. Political Parties, Elections and Referendums Act 2000

Part VII, referred to: SI 2013/242 Art.4
s.7, amended: 2013 c.6 s.22
s.7, applied: SI 2013/760, SI 2013/1514, SI 2013/1599, SI 2013/1846, SI 2013/2064, SI 2013/2876, SI 2013/2893, SI 2013/3114, SI 2013/3156, SI 2013/3198, SI 2013/3199, SI 2013/3206
s.20A, repealed: 2013 c.6 s.23
s.48, amended: 2013 c.22 Sch.9 para.121
s.64, applied: 2013 asp 14 Sch.4 para.3
s.71I, applied: 2013 asp 14 Sch.4 para.49
s.77, amended: 2013 c.22 Sch.9 para.121
s.77, varied: 2013 asp 14 Sch.4 para.15
s.92, amended: 2013 c.22 Sch.9 para.121
s.108, applied: SI 2013/242 Art.4
s.112, disapplied: SI 2013/242 Art.4
s.115, amended: 2013 c.22 Sch.9 para.121
s.127, applied: SI 2013/242 Art.4
s.127, varied: SI 2013/242 Art.4
Sch.1 para.14, disapplied: 2013 asp 14 s.29
Sch.1 para.14, varied: 2013 asp 14 s.28
Sch.1 para.20, applied: 2013 asp 14 s.27
Sch.6 para.2, applied: 2013 asp 14 Sch.4 para.3, Sch.4 para.40
Sch.6 para.3, applied: 2013 asp 14 Sch.4 para.42
Sch.6A para.2, applied: 2013 asp 14 Sch.4 para.55
Sch.6A para.3, applied: 2013 asp 14 Sch.4 para.60
Sch.6A para.5, applied: 2013 asp 14 Sch.4 para.57
Sch.6A para.6, applied: 2013 asp 14 Sch.4 para.57
Sch.6A para.7, applied: 2013 asp 14 Sch.4 para.57
Sch.12 para.1, applied: 2013 asp 14 Sch.4 para.12, Sch.4 para.32, SI 2013/242 Art.4
Sch.12 para.1, varied: SI 2013/242 Art.4
Sch.13 Part I para.1, disapplied: SI 2013/242 Art.4
Sch.19B para.14, applied: 2013 asp 14 Sch.5 para.13
Sch.19C Part I para.2, amended: 2013 c.22 Sch.9 para.121
Sch.19C Part II para.6, amended: 2013 c.22 Sch.9 para.121
Sch.19C Part II para.9, amended: 2013 c.22 Sch.9 para.121
Sch.19C Part III para.13, amended: 2013 c.22 Sch.9 para.121
Sch.19C Part VI para.25, applied: 2013 asp 14 Sch.6 para.26
Sch.19C Part VI para.28, amended: SI 2013/602 Sch.2 para.34

43. Criminal Justice and Court Services Act 2000

s.71, amended: 2013 c.22 Sch.8 para.105, SI 2013/602 Sch.2 para.35

2001

2. Capital Allowances Act 2001

applied: SI 2013/2242 Art.4
Part 2, applied: 2013 c.29 s.73
Part 2 c.16A, applied: 2013 c.29 Sch.26 para.13
Part 2 c.5, applied: 2013 c.29 s.73
s.1, amended: 2013 c.29 Sch.4 para.46
s.11, varied: 2013 c.29 s.73
s.12, varied: 2013 c.29 s.73
s.13, varied: 2013 c.29 s.73
s.13A, varied: 2013 c.29 s.73
s.13B, varied: 2013 c.29 s.73
s.14, varied: 2013 c.29 s.73
s.15, varied: 2013 c.29 s.73
s.16, varied: 2013 c.29 s.73
s.17, varied: 2013 c.29 s.73
s.17A, varied: 2013 c.29 s.73
s.17B, varied: 2013 c.29 s.73
s.18, amended: 2013 c.29 Sch.18 para.21
s.18, varied: 2013 c.29 s.73
s.19, varied: 2013 c.29 s.73
s.20, varied: 2013 c.29 s.73
s.21, varied: 2013 c.29 s.73
s.22, varied: 2013 c.29 s.73
s.23, varied: 2013 c.29 s.73
s.24, varied: 2013 c.29 s.73
s.25, varied: 2013 c.29 s.73
s.26, amended: 2013 c.29 Sch.32 para.3
s.26, varied: 2013 c.29 s.73
s.27, varied: 2013 c.29 s.73
s.28, varied: 2013 c.29 s.73
s.29, varied: 2013 c.29 s.73
s.30, varied: 2013 c.29 s.73
s.31, varied: 2013 c.29 s.73
s.32, varied: 2013 c.29 s.73
s.33, varied: 2013 c.29 s.73
s.33A, varied: 2013 c.29 s.73
s.33B, varied: 2013 c.29 s.73

s.34, varied: 2013 c.29 s.73
s.34A, varied: 2013 c.29 s.73
s.35, varied: 2013 c.29 s.73
s.36, varied: 2013 c.29 s.73
s.37, varied: 2013 c.29 s.73
s.38, varied: 2013 c.29 s.73
s.38A, varied: 2013 c.29 s.73
s.38B, varied: 2013 c.29 s.73
s.38ZA, added: 2013 c.29 Sch.5 para.5
s.38ZA, varied: 2013 c.29 s.73
s.39, varied: 2013 c.29 s.73
s.40, varied: 2013 c.29 s.73
s.41, varied: 2013 c.29 s.73
s.42, varied: 2013 c.29 s.73
s.43, varied: 2013 c.29 s.73
s.44, varied: 2013 c.29 s.73
s.45, varied: 2013 c.29 s.73
s.45A, varied: 2013 c.29 s.73
s.45A, enabling: SI 2013/1763
s.45AA, amended: 2013 c.29 s.67
s.45AA, varied: 2013 c.29 s.73
s.45B, varied: 2013 c.29 s.73
s.45C, varied: 2013 c.29 s.73
s.45D, amended: 2013 c.29 s.68
s.45D, varied: 2013 c.29 s.73
s.45DA, varied: 2013 c.29 s.73
s.45DB, varied: 2013 c.29 s.73
s.45E, amended: 2013 c.29 s.69
s.45E, varied: 2013 c.29 s.73
s.45F, varied: 2013 c.29 s.73
s.45G, varied: 2013 c.29 s.73
s.45H, varied: 2013 c.29 s.73
s.45H, enabling: SI 2013/1762
s.45I, varied: 2013 c.29 s.73
s.45J, varied: 2013 c.29 s.73
s.45K, varied: 2013 c.29 s.73
s.45L, varied: 2013 c.29 s.73
s.45M, varied: 2013 c.29 s.73
s.45N, varied: 2013 c.29 s.73
s.46, see *MGF (Trench Construction Systems) Ltd v Revenue and Customs Commissioners* [2013] S.F.T.D. 281 (FTT (Tax)), Judge Jonathan Cannan
s.46, amended: 2013 c.29 s.68, s.70
s.46, varied: 2013 c.29 s.73
s.47, varied: 2013 c.29 s.73
s.48, varied: 2013 c.29 s.73
s.49, varied: 2013 c.29 s.73
s.50, varied: 2013 c.29 s.73
s.51, varied: 2013 c.29 s.73
s.51A, applied: 2013 c.29 Sch.1 para.1, Sch.1 para.2, Sch.1 para.3, Sch.1 para.4
s.51A, varied: 2013 c.29 s.7, s.73
s.51B, varied: 2013 c.29 s.73
s.51C, varied: 2013 c.29 s.73
s.51D, varied: 2013 c.29 s.73
s.51E, varied: 2013 c.29 s.73
s.51F, varied: 2013 c.29 s.73
s.51G, varied: 2013 c.29 s.73
s.51H, varied: 2013 c.29 s.73
s.51I, varied: 2013 c.29 s.73
s.51J, varied: 2013 c.29 s.73
s.51K, applied: 2013 c.29 Sch.1 para.5
s.51K, varied: 2013 c.29 s.73
s.51L, varied: 2013 c.29 s.73
s.51M, applied: 2013 c.29 Sch.1 para.5
s.51M, varied: 2013 c.29 s.73
s.51N, applied: 2013 c.29 Sch.1 para.5
s.51N, varied: 2013 c.29 s.73
s.52, varied: 2013 c.29 s.73
s.52A, varied: 2013 c.29 s.73
s.53, varied: 2013 c.29 s.73
s.54, varied: 2013 c.29 s.73
s.55, varied: 2013 c.29 s.73
s.56, varied: 2013 c.29 s.73
s.56A, varied: 2013 c.29 s.73
s.57, amended: 2013 c.29 Sch.32 para.4
s.57, varied: 2013 c.29 s.73
s.58, varied: 2013 c.29 s.73
s.59, amended: 2013 c.29 Sch.4 para.47, Sch.5 para.5
s.59, varied: 2013 c.29 s.73
s.60, applied: 2013 c.29 s.73
s.60, varied: 2013 c.29 s.73
s.61, varied: 2013 c.29 s.73
s.62, varied: 2013 c.29 s.73
s.62A, varied: 2013 c.29 s.73
s.63, varied: 2013 c.29 s.73
s.64, varied: 2013 c.29 s.73
s.64A, varied: 2013 c.29 s.73
s.65, varied: 2013 c.29 s.73
s.66, varied: 2013 c.29 s.73
s.66A, added: 2013 c.29 Sch.4 para.48
s.66A, varied: 2013 c.29 s.73
s.67, varied: 2013 c.29 s.73
s.68, varied: 2013 c.29 s.73
s.69, varied: 2013 c.29 s.73
s.70, varied: 2013 c.29 s.73
s.70A, varied: 2013 c.29 s.73
s.70B, varied: 2013 c.29 s.73
s.70C, varied: 2013 c.29 s.73
s.70D, varied: 2013 c.29 s.73
s.70DA, varied: 2013 c.29 s.73
s.70E, varied: 2013 c.29 s.73
s.70F, varied: 2013 c.29 s.73
s.70G, varied: 2013 c.29 s.73
s.70H, varied: 2013 c.29 s.73
s.70I, varied: 2013 c.29 s.73
s.70J, varied: 2013 c.29 s.73

s.70K, varied: 2013 c.29 s.73
s.70L, varied: 2013 c.29 s.73
s.70M, varied: 2013 c.29 s.73
s.70N, varied: 2013 c.29 s.73
s.70O, varied: 2013 c.29 s.73
s.70P, varied: 2013 c.29 s.73
s.70Q, varied: 2013 c.29 s.73
s.70R, varied: 2013 c.29 s.73
s.70S, varied: 2013 c.29 s.73
s.70T, varied: 2013 c.29 s.73
s.70U, varied: 2013 c.29 s.73
s.70V, varied: 2013 c.29 s.73
s.70W, varied: 2013 c.29 s.73
s.70X, varied: 2013 c.29 s.73
s.70Y, varied: 2013 c.29 s.73
s.70YA, varied: 2013 c.29 s.73
s.70YB, varied: 2013 c.29 s.73
s.70YC, varied: 2013 c.29 s.73
s.70YD, varied: 2013 c.29 s.73
s.70YE, varied: 2013 c.29 s.73
s.70YF, varied: 2013 c.29 s.73
s.70YG, varied: 2013 c.29 s.73
s.70YH, varied: 2013 c.29 s.73
s.70YI, varied: 2013 c.29 s.73
s.70YJ, varied: 2013 c.29 s.73
s.71, varied: 2013 c.29 s.73
s.72, varied: 2013 c.29 s.73
s.73, varied: 2013 c.29 s.73
s.74, varied: 2013 c.29 s.73
s.75, varied: 2013 c.29 s.73
s.76, varied: 2013 c.29 s.73
s.77, varied: 2013 c.29 s.73
s.78, varied: 2013 c.29 s.73
s.79, varied: 2013 c.29 s.73
s.80, varied: 2013 c.29 s.73
s.81, varied: 2013 c.29 s.73
s.82, varied: 2013 c.29 s.73
s.83, varied: 2013 c.29 s.73
s.84, varied: 2013 c.29 s.73
s.85, varied: 2013 c.29 s.73
s.86, varied: 2013 c.29 s.73
s.87, varied: 2013 c.29 s.73
s.88, varied: 2013 c.29 s.73
s.89, varied: 2013 c.29 s.73
s.90, varied: 2013 c.29 s.73
s.91, varied: 2013 c.29 s.73
s.92, varied: 2013 c.29 s.73
s.93, varied: 2013 c.29 s.73
s.94, varied: 2013 c.29 s.73
s.95, varied: 2013 c.29 s.73
s.96, varied: 2013 c.29 s.73
s.97, varied: 2013 c.29 s.73
s.98, varied: 2013 c.29 s.73
s.99, varied: 2013 c.29 s.73
s.100, varied: 2013 c.29 s.73
s.101, varied: 2013 c.29 s.73
s.102, varied: 2013 c.29 s.73
s.103, varied: 2013 c.29 s.73
s.104, varied: 2013 c.29 s.73
s.104A, varied: 2013 c.29 s.73
s.104AA, amended: 2013 c.29 s.68
s.104AA, varied: 2013 c.29 s.73
s.104B, varied: 2013 c.29 s.73
s.104C, varied: 2013 c.29 s.73
s.104D, varied: 2013 c.29 s.73
s.104E, varied: 2013 c.29 s.73
s.104F, varied: 2013 c.29 s.73
s.104G, varied: 2013 c.29 s.73
s.105, varied: 2013 c.29 s.73
s.106, varied: 2013 c.29 s.73
s.107, varied: 2013 c.29 s.73
s.108, varied: 2013 c.29 s.73
s.109, varied: 2013 c.29 s.73
s.110, varied: 2013 c.29 s.73
s.111, varied: 2013 c.29 s.73
s.112, varied: 2013 c.29 s.73
s.113, varied: 2013 c.29 s.73
s.114, varied: 2013 c.29 s.73
s.115, varied: 2013 c.29 s.73
s.116, varied: 2013 c.29 s.73
s.117, varied: 2013 c.29 s.73
s.118, varied: 2013 c.29 s.73
s.119, varied: 2013 c.29 s.73
s.120, varied: 2013 c.29 s.73
s.121, varied: 2013 c.29 s.73
s.122, varied: 2013 c.29 s.73
s.123, varied: 2013 c.29 s.73
s.124, varied: 2013 c.29 s.73
s.125, varied: 2013 c.29 s.73
s.126, varied: 2013 c.29 s.73
s.127, varied: 2013 c.29 s.73
s.128, varied: 2013 c.29 s.73
s.129, varied: 2013 c.29 s.73
s.130, varied: 2013 c.29 s.73
s.131, varied: 2013 c.29 s.73
s.132, varied: 2013 c.29 s.73
s.133, varied: 2013 c.29 s.73
s.134, varied: 2013 c.29 s.73
s.135, varied: 2013 c.29 s.73
s.136, varied: 2013 c.29 s.73
s.137, varied: 2013 c.29 s.73
s.138, varied: 2013 c.29 s.73
s.139, varied: 2013 c.29 s.73
s.140, varied: 2013 c.29 s.73
s.141, varied: 2013 c.29 s.73
s.142, varied: 2013 c.29 s.73
s.143, varied: 2013 c.29 s.73
s.144, varied: 2013 c.29 s.73

s.145, varied: 2013 c.29 s.73
s.146, varied: 2013 c.29 s.73
s.147, varied: 2013 c.29 s.73
s.148, varied: 2013 c.29 s.73
s.149, varied: 2013 c.29 s.73
s.150, varied: 2013 c.29 s.73
s.151, varied: 2013 c.29 s.73
s.152, varied: 2013 c.29 s.73
s.153, varied: 2013 c.29 s.73
s.154, varied: 2013 c.29 s.73
s.155, varied: 2013 c.29 s.73
s.156, varied: 2013 c.29 s.73
s.157, varied: 2013 c.29 s.73
s.158, varied: 2013 c.29 s.73
s.159, varied: 2013 c.29 s.73
s.160, varied: 2013 c.29 s.73
s.161, varied: 2013 c.29 s.73
s.161A, varied: 2013 c.29 s.73
s.161B, varied: 2013 c.29 s.73
s.161C, amended: 2013 c.29 Sch.32 para.5
s.161C, varied: 2013 c.29 s.73
s.161D, varied: 2013 c.29 s.73
s.162, varied: 2013 c.29 s.73
s.163, amended: 2013 c.29 s.90
s.163, varied: 2013 c.29 s.73
s.164, amended: 2013 c.29 s.91, Sch.32 para.6
s.164, varied: 2013 c.29 s.73
s.165, amended: 2013 c.29 Sch.32 para.7
s.165, varied: 2013 c.29 s.73
s.165A, added: 2013 c.29 Sch.32 para.2
s.165A, varied: 2013 c.29 s.73
s.165B, added: 2013 c.29 Sch.32 para.2
s.165B, varied: 2013 c.29 s.73
s.165C, added: 2013 c.29 Sch.32 para.2
s.165C, varied: 2013 c.29 s.73
s.165D, added: 2013 c.29 Sch.32 para.2
s.165D, varied: 2013 c.29 s.73
s.165E, added: 2013 c.29 Sch.32 para.2
s.165E, varied: 2013 c.29 s.73
s.166, varied: 2013 c.29 s.73
s.167, varied: 2013 c.29 s.73
s.168, varied: 2013 c.29 s.73
s.169, varied: 2013 c.29 s.73
s.170, varied: 2013 c.29 s.73
s.171, varied: 2013 c.29 s.73
s.172, varied: 2013 c.29 s.73
s.172A, varied: 2013 c.29 s.73
s.173, varied: 2013 c.29 s.73
s.174, varied: 2013 c.29 s.73
s.175, varied: 2013 c.29 s.73
s.175A, varied: 2013 c.29 s.73
s.176, varied: 2013 c.29 s.73
s.177, varied: 2013 c.29 s.73
s.178, varied: 2013 c.29 s.73
s.179, varied: 2013 c.29 s.73
s.180, varied: 2013 c.29 s.73
s.180A, varied: 2013 c.29 s.73
s.181, varied: 2013 c.29 s.73
s.182, varied: 2013 c.29 s.73
s.182A, varied: 2013 c.29 s.73
s.183, varied: 2013 c.29 s.73
s.184, varied: 2013 c.29 s.73
s.185, varied: 2013 c.29 s.73
s.186, varied: 2013 c.29 s.73
s.186A, varied: 2013 c.29 s.73
s.187, varied: 2013 c.29 s.73
s.187A, varied: 2013 c.29 s.73
s.187B, varied: 2013 c.29 s.73
s.188, varied: 2013 c.29 s.73
s.189, varied: 2013 c.29 s.73
s.190, varied: 2013 c.29 s.73
s.191, varied: 2013 c.29 s.73
s.192, varied: 2013 c.29 s.73
s.192A, varied: 2013 c.29 s.73
s.193, varied: 2013 c.29 s.73
s.194, varied: 2013 c.29 s.73
s.195, varied: 2013 c.29 s.73
s.195A, varied: 2013 c.29 s.73
s.195B, varied: 2013 c.29 s.73
s.196, varied: 2013 c.29 s.73
s.197, varied: 2013 c.29 s.73
s.198, varied: 2013 c.29 s.73
s.199, varied: 2013 c.29 s.73
s.200, varied: 2013 c.29 s.73
s.201, varied: 2013 c.29 s.73
s.202, varied: 2013 c.29 s.73
s.203, varied: 2013 c.29 s.73
s.204, varied: 2013 c.29 s.73
s.205, varied: 2013 c.29 s.73
s.206, varied: 2013 c.29 s.73
s.207, varied: 2013 c.29 s.73
s.208, varied: 2013 c.29 s.73
s.208A, varied: 2013 c.29 s.73
s.209, varied: 2013 c.29 s.73
s.210, varied: 2013 c.29 s.73
s.211, varied: 2013 c.29 s.73
s.212, varied: 2013 c.29 s.73
s.212A, substituted: 2013 c.29 Sch.26 para.4
s.212A, varied: 2013 c.29 s.73
s.212B, amended: 2013 c.29 Sch.26 para.2, Sch.26 para.5
s.212B, substituted: 2013 c.29 Sch.26 para.4
s.212B, varied: 2013 c.29 s.73
s.212C, amended: 2013 c.29 Sch.26 para.6
s.212C, substituted: 2013 c.29 Sch.26 para.4
s.212C, varied: 2013 c.29 s.73
s.212D, substituted: 2013 c.29 Sch.26 para.4
s.212D, varied: 2013 c.29 s.73

s.212E, substituted: 2013 c.29 Sch.26 para.4
s.212E, varied: 2013 c.29 s.73
s.212F, substituted: 2013 c.29 Sch.26 para.4
s.212F, varied: 2013 c.29 s.73
s.212G, substituted: 2013 c.29 Sch.26 para.4
s.212G, varied: 2013 c.29 s.73
s.212H, substituted: 2013 c.29 Sch.26 para.4
s.212H, varied: 2013 c.29 s.73
s.212I, amended: 2013 c.29 Sch.26 para.7
s.212I, substituted: 2013 c.29 Sch.26 para.4
s.212I, varied: 2013 c.29 s.73
s.212J, amended: 2013 c.29 Sch.26 para.8
s.212J, substituted: 2013 c.29 Sch.26 para.4
s.212J, varied: 2013 c.29 s.73
s.212K, amended: 2013 c.29 Sch.26 para.9
s.212K, substituted: 2013 c.29 Sch.26 para.4
s.212K, varied: 2013 c.29 s.73
s.212L, substituted: 2013 c.29 Sch.26 para.4
s.212L, varied: 2013 c.29 s.73
s.212LA, added: 2013 c.29 Sch.26 para.3
s.212LA, substituted: 2013 c.29 Sch.26 para.4
s.212LA, varied: 2013 c.29 s.73
s.212M, substituted: 2013 c.29 Sch.26 para.4
s.212M, varied: 2013 c.29 s.73
s.212N, amended: 2013 c.29 Sch.26 para.10
s.212N, substituted: 2013 c.29 Sch.26 para.4
s.212N, varied: 2013 c.29 s.73
s.212O, substituted: 2013 c.29 Sch.26 para.4
s.212O, varied: 2013 c.29 s.73
s.212P, amended: 2013 c.29 Sch.26 para.11
s.212P, substituted: 2013 c.29 Sch.26 para.4
s.212P, varied: 2013 c.29 s.73
s.212Q, amended: 2013 c.29 Sch.26 para.12
s.212Q, substituted: 2013 c.29 Sch.26 para.4
s.212Q, varied: 2013 c.29 s.73
s.212R, substituted: 2013 c.29 Sch.26 para.4
s.212R, varied: 2013 c.29 s.73
s.212S, substituted: 2013 c.29 Sch.26 para.4
s.212S, varied: 2013 c.29 s.73
s.212T, varied: 2013 c.29 s.73
s.212U, varied: 2013 c.29 s.73
s.213, varied: 2013 c.29 s.73
s.214, varied: 2013 c.29 s.73
s.215, varied: 2013 c.29 s.73
s.216, varied: 2013 c.29 s.73
s.217, varied: 2013 c.29 s.73
s.218, varied: 2013 c.29 s.73
s.218A, varied: 2013 c.29 s.73
s.218ZA, varied: 2013 c.29 s.73
s.219, varied: 2013 c.29 s.73
s.220, varied: 2013 c.29 s.73
s.221, varied: 2013 c.29 s.73
s.222, varied: 2013 c.29 s.73
s.223, varied: 2013 c.29 s.73
s.224, varied: 2013 c.29 s.73
s.225, varied: 2013 c.29 s.73
s.226, varied: 2013 c.29 s.73
s.227, varied: 2013 c.29 s.73
s.228, varied: 2013 c.29 s.73
s.228A, varied: 2013 c.29 s.73
s.228B, varied: 2013 c.29 s.73
s.228C, varied: 2013 c.29 s.73
s.228D, varied: 2013 c.29 s.73
s.228E, varied: 2013 c.29 s.73
s.228F, varied: 2013 c.29 s.73
s.228G, varied: 2013 c.29 s.73
s.228H, varied: 2013 c.29 s.73
s.228J, varied: 2013 c.29 s.73
s.228K, varied: 2013 c.29 s.73
s.228L, varied: 2013 c.29 s.73
s.228M, varied: 2013 c.29 s.73
s.228MA, varied: 2013 c.29 s.73
s.228MB, varied: 2013 c.29 s.73
s.228MC, varied: 2013 c.29 s.73
s.229, varied: 2013 c.29 s.73
s.229A, varied: 2013 c.29 s.73
s.230, varied: 2013 c.29 s.73
s.231, varied: 2013 c.29 s.73
s.232, varied: 2013 c.29 s.73
s.233, varied: 2013 c.29 s.73
s.234, varied: 2013 c.29 s.73
s.235, varied: 2013 c.29 s.73
s.236, varied: 2013 c.29 s.73
s.237, varied: 2013 c.29 s.73
s.238, varied: 2013 c.29 s.73
s.239, varied: 2013 c.29 s.73
s.240, varied: 2013 c.29 s.73
s.241, varied: 2013 c.29 s.73
s.242, varied: 2013 c.29 s.73
s.243, varied: 2013 c.29 s.73
s.244, varied: 2013 c.29 s.73
s.245, varied: 2013 c.29 s.73
s.246, varied: 2013 c.29 s.73
s.247, varied: 2013 c.29 s.73
s.248, varied: 2013 c.29 s.73
s.249, varied: 2013 c.29 s.73
s.250, varied: 2013 c.29 s.73
s.250A, varied: 2013 c.29 s.73
s.251, varied: 2013 c.29 s.73
s.252, varied: 2013 c.29 s.73
s.253, varied: 2013 c.29 s.73
s.254, varied: 2013 c.29 s.73
s.255, varied: 2013 c.29 s.73
s.256, varied: 2013 c.29 s.73
s.257, varied: 2013 c.29 s.73
s.257A, varied: 2013 c.29 s.73
s.258, varied: 2013 c.29 s.73
s.259, varied: 2013 c.29 s.73

s.260, varied: 2013 c.29 s.73
s.261, varied: 2013 c.29 s.73
s.261A, varied: 2013 c.29 s.73
s.262, varied: 2013 c.29 s.73
s.262A, varied: 2013 c.29 s.73
s.263, varied: 2013 c.29 s.73
s.264, varied: 2013 c.29 s.73
s.265, varied: 2013 c.29 s.73
s.266, varied: 2013 c.29 s.73
s.267, varied: 2013 c.29 s.73
s.267A, varied: 2013 c.29 s.73
s.268, varied: 2013 c.29 s.73
s.268A, varied: 2013 c.29 s.73
s.268B, varied: 2013 c.29 s.73
s.268C, varied: 2013 c.29 s.73
s.268D, amended: 2013 c.29 s.72
s.268D, varied: 2013 c.29 s.73
s.268E, varied: 2013 c.29 s.73
s.269, varied: 2013 c.29 s.73
s.270, varied: 2013 c.29 s.73
s.395, amended: 2013 c.29 s.92, Sch.32 para.10
s.403, amended: 2013 c.29 s.92
s.416, amended: 2013 c.29 s.92
s.416, substituted: 2013 c.29 s.92
s.416B, amended: 2013 c.29 s.92
s.416ZA, added: 2013 c.29 s.92
s.416ZB, added: 2013 c.29 s.92
s.416ZC, added: 2013 c.29 Sch.32 para.9
s.416ZD, added: 2013 c.29 Sch.32 para.9
s.416ZE, added: 2013 c.29 Sch.32 para.9
s.538, amended: 2013 c.29 s.73
s.542, amended: 2013 c.2 Sch.1 Part 10
Sch.A1 Part 1 para.3, amended: SI 2013/464 Art.2
Sch.A1 Part 1 para.3, enabling: SI 2013/464
Sch.A1 Part 1 para.11, amended: 2013 c.29 Sch.18 para.6

9. Finance Act 2001
s.81, repealed: 2013 c.2 Sch.1 Part 10
Sch.27 para.7, repealed: 2013 c.2 Sch.1 Part 10

12. Private Security Industry Act 2001
applied: SSI 2013/50 Sch.4 para.6, SSI 2013/73 Sch.1
s.8, applied: SSI 2013/50 Sch.3 para.3
s.11, applied: SSI 2013/50 Sch.1 para.20
Sch.2 Part 1 para.4A, amended: SI 2013/1465 Sch.1 para.7

15. Health and Social Care Act 2001
s.57, applied: SI 2013/471 Reg.11, Reg.20, Reg.33, SI 2013/480 Reg.24, Reg.40, SI 2013/483 Reg.10, SI 2013/628 Sch.1 para.23, SI 2013/3029 Sch.5 para.28, Sch.9 para.59, Sch.10 para.60, SI 2013/3035 Sch.1
s.57, referred to: SI 2013/377 Reg.28
s.57, enabling: SI 2013/2270
s.64, enabling: SI 2013/2270

16. Criminal Justice and Police Act 2001
s.3, enabling: SI 2013/1165, SI 2013/1579
s.10A, enabling: SI 2013/1579
s.66, repealed (in part): SI 2013/1575 Sch.1 para.5
s.97, repealed (in part): 2013 c.22 Sch.8 para.107
Sch.1 Part 1 para.18A, repealed: SI 2013/1881 Sch.1 para.7
Sch.1 Part 1 para.53, repealed: SI 2013/1575 Sch.1 para.6
Sch.2 Part 2 para.20, repealed: SI 2013/1575 Sch.1 para.7

17. International Criminal Court Act 2001
s.51, applied: SI 2013/1852 Sch.1 para.25
s.52, applied: SI 2013/1852 Sch.1 para.25

24. Anti-terrorism, Crime and Security Act 2001
s.17, referred to: 2013 c.32 Sch.9 para.19
s.18, applied: 2013 c.32 Sch.9 para.19
s.74, amended: SI 2013/602 Sch.2 para.37
s.77, amended: 2013 c.32 Sch.12 para.32
s.77, applied: 2013 c.32 s.114, SI 2013/190
s.77, enabling: SI 2013/190
s.79, applied: 2013 c.32 Sch.9 para.23
s.80, amended: 2013 c.32 Sch.12 para.33
s.80, applied: 2013 c.32 s.81, s.101, Sch.9 para.23
s.100, amended: SI 2013/602 Sch.2 para.37
s.100, applied: SI 2013/602 Sch.3 para.15
Sch.1 Part 4 para.10, amended: SI 2013/602 Sch.2 para.37

2002

1. International Development Act 2002
applied: 2013 c.12 Sch.1 para.1, 2013 c.28 Sch.1, SSI 2013/35 Reg.32, SSI 2013/76 Reg.2
s.11, applied: SI 2013/1771, SI 2013/1771 Art.3, SI 2013/3175, SI 2013/3175 Art.3, SI 2013/3230, SI 2013/3230 Art.3
s.11, referred to: SI 2013/1771, SI 2013/3175
s.11, enabling: SI 2013/1771, SI 2013/3175, SI 2013/3230

8. British Overseas Territories Act 2002
applied: 2013 c.22 s.55

9. Land Registration Act 2002
applied: SI 2013/503 Reg.22
s.27, see *Fitzwilliam v Richall Holdings Services Ltd* [2013] EWHC 86 (Ch), [2013] 1 P. & C.R. 19 (Ch D), Newey, J.
s.27, applied: SI 2013/3174 Art.4
s.41, applied: SI 2013/3174 Sch.3 Part 1, Sch.4
s.64, applied: SI 2013/3174 Sch.3 Part 1
s.73, amended: SI 2013/1036 Sch.1 para.226
s.73, applied: SI 2013/1169 r.28

s.75, amended: 2013 c.22 Sch.9 para.52
s.76, amended: 2013 c.22 Sch.9 para.52
s.100, enabling: SI 2013/1627
s.102, applied: SI 2013/3174
s.102, enabling: SI 2013/3174
s.107, repealed: SI 2013/1036 Sch.1 para.227
s.108, amended: SI 2013/1036 Sch.1 para.228
s.108, applied: SI 2013/1169 r.29
s.109, repealed: SI 2013/1036 Sch.1 para.229
s.110, amended: SI 2013/1036 Sch.1 para.230
s.110, applied: SI 2013/1169 r.12, r.37, r.38, r.39
s.110, enabling: SI 2013/1169
s.111, amended: SI 2013/1036 Sch.1 para.231
s.111, applied: SI 2013/1036 Sch.3 para.4
s.112, amended: SI 2013/1036 Sch.1 para.232
s.113, repealed: SI 2013/1036 Sch.1 para.233
s.114, repealed: SI 2013/1036 Sch.1 para.234
s.127, applied: SI 2013/3174
s.128, amended: SI 2013/1036 Sch.1 para.235
s.128, repealed (in part): SI 2013/1036 Sch.1 para.235
s.128, enabling: SI 2013/3174
s.132, amended: 2013 c.22 Sch.9 para.52, SI 2013/1036 Sch.1 para.236
Sch.5 para.4, amended: SI 2013/1036 Sch.1 para.237
Sch.5 para.4, repealed (in part): SI 2013/1036 Sch.1 para.237
Sch.9 para.1, repealed: SI 2013/1036 Sch.1 para.238
Sch.9 para.2, repealed: SI 2013/1036 Sch.1 para.238
Sch.9 para.3, repealed: SI 2013/1036 Sch.1 para.238
Sch.9 para.4, repealed: SI 2013/1036 Sch.1 para.238
Sch.9 para.5, repealed: SI 2013/1036 Sch.1 para.238
Sch.9 para.6, repealed: SI 2013/1036 Sch.1 para.238
Sch.9 para.7, repealed: SI 2013/1036 Sch.1 para.238
Sch.9 para.8, repealed: SI 2013/1036 Sch.1 para.238
Sch.9 para.9, repealed: SI 2013/1036 Sch.1 para.238

11. Office of Communications Act 2002

Sch.1 para.18, substituted: 2013 c.24 Sch.15 para.40

15. Commonhold and Leasehold Reform Act 2002

see *Phillips v Francis* [2012] EWHC 3650 (Ch), [2013] 1 W.L.R. 2343 (Ch D), Sir Andrew Morritt (Chancellor)
referred to: SI 2013/3174 Sch.3 Part 1
Part 2 c.5, amended: SI 2013/1036 Sch.1 para.140
s.9, applied: SI 2013/3174 Sch.3 Part 1
s.58, applied: SI 2013/3174 Sch.3 Part 1
s.66, amended: 2013 c.22 Sch.9 para.52
s.79, see *Avon Freeholds Ltd v Regent Court RTM Co Ltd* [2013] UKUT 213 (LC), [2013] L. & T.R. 23 (UT (Lands)), Sir Keith Lindblom (President)
s.79, amended: SI 2013/1036 Sch.1 para.132
s.84, see *Corscombe Close Block 8 RTM Co Ltd v Roseleb Ltd* [2013] UKUT 81 (LC), [2013] L. & T.R. 16 (UT (Lands)), Judge Mole Q.C.
s.84, amended: SI 2013/1036 Sch.1 para.133
s.85, amended: SI 2013/1036 Sch.1 para.134
s.88, amended: SI 2013/1036 Sch.1 para.135
s.94, amended: SI 2013/1036 Sch.1 para.136
s.99, amended: SI 2013/1036 Sch.1 para.137
s.107, amended: 2013 c.22 Sch.9 para.52
s.112, see *Gala Unity Ltd v Ariadne Road RTM Co Ltd* [2012] EWCA Civ 1372, [2013] 1 W.L.R. 988 (CA (Civ Div)), Arden, L.J.
s.112, amended: SI 2013/1036 Sch.1 para.138
s.159, amended: SI 2013/1036 Sch.1 para.139
s.168, amended: SI 2013/1036 Sch.1 para.141
s.172, amended: SI 2013/1036 Sch.1 para.142
s.175, repealed (in part): SI 2013/1036 Sch.1 para.143
s.176A, added: SI 2013/1036 Sch.1 para.144
s.176B, added: SI 2013/1036 Sch.1 para.144
s.176B, applied: SI 2013/1036 Sch.3 para.4
s.176C, added: SI 2013/1036 Sch.1 para.144
Sch.6 para.5, amended: SI 2013/1036 Sch.1 para.145
Sch.7 para.8, amended: SI 2013/1036 Sch.1 para.146
Sch.11 Part 1 para.3, amended: SI 2013/1036 Sch.1 para.147
Sch.11 Part 1 para.3, applied: SI 2013/1179 Sch.1
Sch.11 Part 1 para.5, amended: SI 2013/1036 Sch.1 para.147
Sch.11 Part 1 para.5, applied: SI 2013/1179 Sch.1
Sch.11 Part 1 para.6, amended: SI 2013/1036 Sch.1 para.147
Sch.11 Part 2 para.11, amended: 2013 c.22 Sch.9 para.69
Sch.12 para.1, amended: SI 2013/1036 Sch.1 para.148

17. National Health Service Reform and Health Care Professions Act 2002

s.25, referred to: SI 2013/1617 Reg.11, Reg.14

23. Finance Act 2002

s.88, repealed (in part): 2013 c.2 Sch.1 Part 10
s.136, enabling: SI 2013/521
Sch.23 Part 3 para.26, enabling: SI 2013/1843

24. European Parliamentary Elections Act 2002

s.2, enabling: SI 2013/2876
s.4, enabling: SI 2013/2063
s.6, enabling: SI 2013/2064, SI 2013/2876, SI 2013/2893
s.7, referred to: 2013 c.6 Sch.5 para.14
s.7, enabling: SI 2013/1599, SI 2013/2876, SI 2013/2893, SI 2013/3114
s.10, amended: SI 2013/2876 Reg.3
s.13, applied: SI 2013/1599, SI 2013/2876, SI 2013/2893, SI 2013/3114

26. Justice (Northern Ireland) Act 2002

s.3, applied: SI 2013/2192 Reg.17
s.5A, amended: SI 2013/602 Sch.2 para.38
Sch.1, applied: SI 2013/1674 Reg.21

28. Export Control Act 2002

s.1, enabling: SI 2013/340, SI 2013/428, SI 2013/1964, SI 2013/2012, SI 2013/3182
s.2, enabling: SI 2013/340, SI 2013/428, SI 2013/1964, SI 2013/2012, SI 2013/3182
s.3, enabling: SI 2013/340, SI 2013/1964, SI 2013/2012, SI 2013/3182
s.4, enabling: SI 2013/340, SI 2013/428, SI 2013/1964, SI 2013/2012, SI 2013/3182
s.5, enabling: SI 2013/340, SI 2013/428, SI 2013/1964, SI 2013/2012, SI 2013/3182
s.6, enabling: SI 2013/2012
s.7, enabling: SI 2013/340, SI 2013/428, SI 2013/1964, SI 2013/3182
s.11, applied: SI 2013/1964 Art.1, SI 2013/2012 Art.1, SI 2013/3182 Art.1

29. Proceeds of Crime Act 2002

see *Chief Constable of Sussex v Taylor* [2013] EWHC 1616 (Admin), [2013] 5 Costs L.O. 692 (QBD (Admin)), Pitchford, L.J.; see *Practice Direction (Costs in Criminal Proceedings)* [2013] EWCA Crim 1632, [2013] 1 W.L.R. 3255 (Sen Cts), Lord Thomas L.C.J.; see *R. v Gangar (Shinder Singh)* [2012] EWCA Crim 1378, [2013] 1 W.L.R. 147 (CA (Crim Div)), Hughes, L.J.; see *R. v Jawad (Mohid)* [2013] EWCA Crim 644, [2013] 1 W.L.R. 3861 (CA (Crim Div)), Hughes, L.J.; see *R. v Kenny (Mark)* [2013] EWCA Crim 1, [2013] Q.B. 896 (CA (Crim Div)), Gross, L.J.; see *R. v Varma (Aloke)* [2013] 1 A.C. 463 (SC), Lord Phillips, J.S.C. (President); see *R. v Waya (Terry)* [2013] 1 A.C. 294 (SC), Lord Phillips, J.S.C.; see *Revenue and Customs Prosecutions Office v Johnson* [2012] EWCA Civ 1000, [2013] Lloyd's Rep. F.C. 1 (CA (Civ Div)), Pill, L.J.; see *Shah v HSBC Private Bank (UK) Ltd* [2012] EWHC 1283 (QB), [2013] 1 All E.R. (Comm) 72 (QBD), Supperstone, J.; see *Sinclair v Dhillon* [2012] EWHC 3517 (Admin), [2013] Lloyd's Rep. F.C. 224 (QBD (Admin)), Haddon-Cave, J.; see *Sumal & Sons (Properties) Ltd v Newham LBC* [2012] EWCA Crim 1840, [2013] 1 W.L.R. 2078 (CA (Crim Div)), Davis, L.J.
applied: 2013 c.22 s.1, s.7, Sch.3 para.3, Sch.3 para.5, SI 2013/1554 r.6_1, r.58_1, SI 2013/2605 Art.5, Art.39
Part 2, applied: 2013 c.22 s.47, SI 2013/435 Reg.4, Sch.1 para.14, Sch.2 para.26, SI 2013/1046 r.148, SI 2013/1554 r.76_1, r.71_1, r.71_2, r.71_4, r.57_2, r.71_5, r.57_3, r.71_8, r.71_9, r.71_10, r.57_8, r.57_9, r.57_14, SI 2013/2605 Art.19, Art.26, Art.31, SI 2013/3208 r.152
Part 3, applied: 2013 c.22 s.7, Sch.7 para.6, SI 2013/1046 r.148, SI 2013/2605 Art.53, Art.60, Art.65, SI 2013/3208 r.152
Part 4, applied: SI 2013/1046 r.148, SI 2013/2605 Art.19, Art.26, Art.31, SI 2013/3208 r.152
Part 5, applied: 2013 c.22 s.7, Sch.7 para.6, Sch.7 para.8, SSI 2013/76 Reg.2
Part 5 c.2, applied: 2013 c.22 Sch.25 para.7, SSI 2013/50 Sch.1 para.19
Part 5 c.3, applied: 2013 c.29 s.224, Sch.48 para.22, SSI 2013/50 Sch.1 para.19
Part 5 c.4, applied: 2013 c.22 Sch.25 para.7
Part 6, applied: 2013 c.22 s.7
Part 8, applied: 2013 c.22 s.49, SI 2013/1554 r.6_1, SSI 2013/50 Sch.1 para.19, SSI 2013/76 Reg.2
Part 8, referred to: SI 2013/2326 Art.2
Part 8 c.1, applied: 2013 c.22 s.47
Part 8 c.2, applied: 2013 c.22 s.47, 2013 c.29 s.224, Sch.48 para.22, SI 2013/2605 Art.35
Part 8 c.3, applied: 2013 c.29 s.224, Sch.48 para.22, SI 2013/2605 Art.69
Part 8 c.4, applied: 2013 c.22 s.47
s.2A, amended: 2013 c.22 Sch.8 para.109
s.2B, amended: 2013 c.22 Sch.8 para.110
s.2B, repealed (in part): 2013 c.22 Sch.8 para.110
s.3, amended: 2013 c.22 Sch.8 para.111
s.6, see *R. v Bestel (Jean Pierre)* [2013] EWCA Crim 1305, [2013] 2 Cr. App. R. 30 (CA (Crim Div)), Pitchford, L.J.; see *R. v Hursthouse (Susan Ann)* [2013] EWCA Crim 517, [2013] W.T.L.R. 887 (CA (Crim Div)), Treacy, L.J.; see *R. v Varma (Aloke)* [2013] 1 A.C. 463 (SC), Lord Phillips, J.S.C. (President)
s.6, amended: 2013 c.3 Sch.1 para.12
s.6, applied: SI 2013/1554 r.58_7
s.7, see *R. v Lee (Paul)* [2013] EWCA Crim 657, [2013] Lloyd's Rep. F.C. 453 (CA (Crim Div)), Hughes, L.J.
s.7, amended: 2013 c.3 Sch.1 para.13
s.13, see *R. v Jawad (Mohid)* [2013] EWCA Crim 644, [2013] 1 W.L.R. 3861 (CA (Crim Div)),

Hughes, L.J.; see *R. v Varma (Aloke)* [2013] 1 A.C. 463 (SC), Lord Phillips, J.S.C. (President)
s.13, amended: 2013 c.3 Sch.1 para.14
s.14, amended: 2013 c.3 Sch.1 para.15
s.14, applied: SI 2013/1554 r.58_2
s.15, amended: 2013 c.3 Sch.1 para.16
s.16, applied: SI 2013/1554 r.58_1
s.18, applied: SI 2013/1554 r.58_1
s.19, amended: 2013 c.3 Sch.1 para.17
s.19, applied: SI 2013/1554 r.58_3
s.20, amended: 2013 c.3 Sch.1 para.18
s.20, applied: SI 2013/1554 r.58_3
s.21, amended: 2013 c.3 Sch.1 para.19
s.21, applied: SI 2013/1554 r.58_3
s.22, applied: SI 2013/1554 r.58_4
s.23, see *R. v Bestel (Jean Pierre)* [2013] EWCA Crim 1305, [2013] 2 Cr. App. R. 30 (CA (Crim Div)), Pitchford, L.J.
s.23, applied: SI 2013/1554 r.58_5
s.24, applied: SI 2013/1554 r.58_6
s.25, applied: SI 2013/1554 r.58_6
s.28, applied: SI 2013/1554 r.58_7, r.58_8, r.58_11
s.29, applied: SI 2013/1554 r.58_7, r.58_11
s.30, applied: SI 2013/1554 r.58_8, r.58_11
s.31, applied: SI 2013/1554 r.71_8, r.72_1, r.72_3
s.32, amended: 2013 c.3 Sch.1 para.20
s.33, amended: 2013 c.3 Sch.1 para.21
s.39, applied: SI 2013/1554 r.58_9
s.41, see *Crown Prosecution Service v Eastenders Group* [2012] EWCA Crim 2436, [2013] 1 W.L.R. 1494 (CA (Crim Div)), Laws, L.J.
s.41, amended: 2013 c.22 s.46
s.41, applied: SI 2013/471 Reg.11, Reg.20, Reg.33, SI 2013/483 Reg.10, SI 2013/1554 r.59_1, r.59_2, r.59_3, r.59_4, r.59_5
s.41, repealed (in part): 2013 c.22 s.46
s.41A, amended: 2013 c.22 Sch.8 para.112, Sch.21 para.15
s.42, applied: SI 2013/1554 r.59_1, r.61_14, r.59_3, r.59_4, r.59_5
s.43, applied: SI 2013/1554 r.73_1, r.73_2, r.73_3, r.73_4, r.73_5, r.73_6, r.73_7
s.47A, amended: 2013 c.22 s.55
s.47C, amended: 2013 c.22 Sch.21 para.16
s.47G, amended: 2013 c.22 Sch.21 para.17
s.47M, amended: 2013 c.22 Sch.21 para.18
s.48, see *Crown Prosecution Service v Eastenders Group* [2012] EWCA Crim 2436, [2013] 1 W.L.R. 1494 (CA (Crim Div)), Laws, L.J.
s.48, applied: SI 2013/1554 r.60_1, r.60_5, r.60_6, r.60_7, r.60_8
s.49, applied: SI 2013/1554 r.60_2, r.60_6
s.50, applied: SI 2013/1554 r.58_4, r.58_5, r.60_1, r.60_5, r.60_6, r.60_7, r.58_6, r.60_8
s.51, applied: SI 2013/1554 r.60_2
s.55, amended: 2013 c.3 Sch.1 para.22, 2013 c.22 Sch.8 para.113
s.55, applied: SI 2013/1554 r.60_1, r.60_5, r.60_6
s.58, applied: SI 2013/1554 r.61_1
s.59, applied: SI 2013/1554 r.61_1
s.62, applied: SI 2013/1554 r.60_3
s.63, applied: SI 2013/1554 r.60_3, r.60_4
s.65, applied: SI 2013/1554 r.73_1, r.73_2, r.73_3, r.73_4, r.73_5, r.73_6, r.73_7
s.67, applied: SI 2013/1554 r.58_12
s.68, applied: SI 2013/1554 r.59_1, r.60_1, r.59_4, r.60_2
s.72, amended: 2013 c.22 Sch.8 para.114, Sch.21 para.19
s.72, applied: SI 2013/1554 r.58_10
s.73, applied: SI 2013/1554 r.58_11
s.85, amended: 2013 c.22 Sch.17 para.38
s.85, applied: SI 2013/1554 r.72_3
s.89, enabling: SI 2013/24
s.90, enabling: SI 2013/24
s.91, enabling: SI 2013/1554
s.120A, amended: 2013 c.22 Sch.8 para.115, Sch.21 para.20
s.127A, amended: 2013 c.22 s.55
s.127C, amended: 2013 c.22 Sch.21 para.21
s.127G, amended: 2013 c.22 Sch.21 para.22
s.127M, amended: 2013 c.22 Sch.21 para.23
s.139, amended: 2013 c.22 Sch.8 para.116, SSI 2013/119 Sch.1 para.19
s.190A, amended: 2013 c.22 Sch.8 para.117, Sch.21 para.24
s.195A, amended: 2013 c.22 s.55
s.195C, amended: 2013 c.22 Sch.21 para.25
s.195G, amended: 2013 c.22 Sch.21 para.26
s.195M, amended: 2013 c.22 Sch.21 para.27
s.195S, amended: 2013 c.22 Sch.8 para.118
s.203, amended: 2013 c.22 Sch.8 para.119
s.220, amended: 2013 c.22 Sch.8 para.120
s.280, amended: 2013 c.22 Sch.18 para.5
s.282A, added: 2013 c.22 s.48
s.282A, applied: 2013 c.22 Sch.25 para.4
s.282B, added: 2013 c.22 Sch.18 para.6
s.282B, applied: 2013 c.22 Sch.25 para.4
s.282C, added: 2013 c.22 Sch.18 para.6
s.282C, applied: 2013 c.22 Sch.25 para.4
s.282D, added: 2013 c.22 Sch.18 para.6
s.282D, applied: 2013 c.22 Sch.25 para.4
s.282D, enabling: SSI 2013/162
s.282E, added: 2013 c.22 Sch.18 para.6
s.282F, added: 2013 c.22 Sch.18 para.6
s.282F, applied: 2013 c.22 Sch.25 para.4

s.286, see *Serious Organised Crime Agency v Perry* [2013] 1 A.C. 182 (SC), Lord Phillips, J.S.C.
s.286, repealed: 2013 c.22 s.48
s.289, amended: 2013 c.29 Sch.48 para.2
s.290, amended: 2013 c.29 Sch.48 para.3
s.291, amended: 2013 c.29 Sch.48 para.4
s.292, amended: 2013 c.29 Sch.48 para.5
s.294, amended: 2013 c.29 Sch.48 para.6
s.295, amended: 2013 c.29 Sch.48 para.7
s.296, amended: 2013 c.29 Sch.48 para.8
s.297, amended: 2013 c.29 Sch.48 para.9
s.297A, amended: 2013 c.22 Sch.21 para.28
s.297F, amended: 2013 c.22 Sch.21 para.29
s.302, amended: 2013 c.29 Sch.48 para.10, SSI 2013/119 Sch.1 para.19
s.302, applied: SI 2013/1554 r.58_10
s.308, see *Executive Jet Support Ltd v Serious Organised Crime Agency* [2012] EWHC 2737 (QB), [2013] 1 W.L.R. 1433 (QBD), Griffith Williams, J.; see *Serious Organised Crime Agency v O'Docherty* [2013] EWCA Civ 518, [2013] C.P. Rep. 35 (CA (Civ Div)), Mummery, L.J.
s.308, amended: 2013 c.3 Sch.1 para.23
s.316, see *Serious Organised Crime Agency v Perry* [2013] 1 A.C. 182 (SC), Lord Phillips, J.S.C.
s.316, amended: 2013 c.22 s.48, Sch.8 para.121
s.316, applied: 2013 c.22 Sch.25 para.4
s.316, referred to: SI 2013/1554 r.6_1
s.317, amended: 2013 c.22 Sch.8 para.122
s.317, applied: SSI 2013/50 Sch.1 para.19
s.318, amended: 2013 c.22 Sch.8 para.123
s.319, amended: 2013 c.22 Sch.8 para.124
s.321, amended: 2013 c.22 Sch.8 para.125
s.321, applied: SSI 2013/50 Sch.1 para.19
s.322, amended: 2013 c.22 Sch.8 para.126
s.322, applied: SSI 2013/50 Sch.1 para.19
s.324, amended: 2013 c.22 Sch.8 para.127
s.325, amended: 2013 c.22 Sch.8 para.128
s.327, applied: 2013 c.22 Sch.17 para.23, SI 2013/435 Sch.1 Part 7, SI 2013/2258 Sch.1 Part 1, SI 2013/2605 Art.23, Art.57
s.328, see *Dare v Crown Prosecution Service* [2012] EWHC 2074 (Admin), (2013) 177 J.P. 37 (QBD (Admin)), Bean, J.
s.328, applied: 2013 c.22 Sch.17 para.23, SI 2013/435 Sch.1 Part 7, SI 2013/2258 Sch.1 Part 1, SI 2013/2605 Art.23, Art.57
s.329, applied: 2013 c.22 Sch.17 para.23, SI 2013/435 Sch.1 Part 7, SI 2013/2605 Art.23, Art.57
s.330, amended: 2013 c.22 Sch.8 para.129
s.330, applied: 2013 c.22 Sch.17 para.23, SI 2013/435 Sch.1 Part 7, SI 2013/2258 Sch.1 Part 1
s.331, amended: 2013 c.22 Sch.8 para.130
s.331, applied: SI 2013/435 Sch.1 Part 7, SI 2013/2258 Sch.1 Part 1
s.332, amended: 2013 c.22 Sch.8 para.131
s.332, applied: SI 2013/435 Sch.1 Part 7, SI 2013/2258 Sch.1 Part 1
s.333, see *Shah v HSBC Private Bank (UK) Ltd* [2012] EWHC 1283 (QB), [2013] 1 All E.R. (Comm) 72 (QBD), Supperstone, J.
s.333, applied: SI 2013/435 Sch.1 Part 7
s.333A, amended: 2013 c.22 Sch.8 para.132
s.333A, applied: 2013 c.22 Sch.17 para.23, SI 2013/2605 Art.5, Art.39
s.336, amended: 2013 c.22 Sch.8 para.133
s.339, applied: SI 2013/435 Sch.1 Part 7
s.339ZA, amended: 2013 c.22 Sch.8 para.134
s.340, amended: 2013 c.22 Sch.8 para.135
s.341, amended: 2013 c.22 Sch.19 para.2, Sch.19 para.25
s.341, applied: 2013 c.22 s.1, SSI 2013/50 Sch.1 para.19
s.341A, added: 2013 c.22 Sch.19 para.3
s.342, see *Shah v HSBC Private Bank (UK) Ltd* [2012] EWHC 1283 (QB), [2013] 1 All E.R. (Comm) 72 (QBD), Supperstone, J.
s.342, applied: SI 2013/1554 r.6_22
s.343, applied: SI 2013/1554 r.6_1
s.345, amended: 2013 c.22 Sch.19 para.4
s.345, applied: SI 2013/1554 r.6_1, r.6_22
s.346, amended: 2013 c.22 Sch.19 para.5
s.347, applied: SI 2013/1554 r.6_1
s.348, applied: SI 2013/1554 r.6_3
s.351, amended: 2013 c.22 Sch.8 para.136, Sch.21 para.30, 2013 c.29 Sch.48 para.11
s.351, applied: SI 2013/1554 r.6_1
s.351, enabling: SI 2013/1554
s.352, amended: 2013 c.22 Sch.8 para.137, Sch.19 para.6, Sch.21 para.31, 2013 c.29 Sch.48 para.12
s.352, repealed (in part): 2013 c.29 Sch.48 para.12
s.353, amended: 2013 c.22 Sch.8 para.138, Sch.19 para.7, Sch.21 para.32, 2013 c.29 Sch.48 para.13
s.353, repealed (in part): 2013 c.29 Sch.48 para.13
s.356, amended: 2013 c.22 Sch.21 para.33
s.357, see *Serious Organised Crime Agency v Perry* [2013] 1 A.C. 182 (SC), Lord Phillips, J.S.C.
s.357, amended: 2013 c.22 Sch.8 para.139, Sch.19 para.8, Sch.21 para.34
s.357, applied: SI 2013/1554 r.6_1, r.6_17
s.358, amended: 2013 c.22 Sch.19 para.9
s.359, applied: SI 2013/2605 Art.19
s.361, applied: SI 2013/1554 r.6_3

s.362, amended: 2013 c.22 Sch.8 para.140
s.362, applied: SI 2013/1554 r.6_1
s.362, enabling: SI 2013/1554
s.363, amended: 2013 c.22 Sch.19 para.10
s.363, applied: SI 2013/1554 r.6_1
s.363, repealed (in part): 2013 c.22 Sch.19 para.10
s.365, amended: 2013 c.22 Sch.19 para.11
s.366, applied: SI 2013/2605 Art.26
s.369, amended: 2013 c.22 Sch.8 para.141, Sch.21 para.35, 2013 c.29 Sch.48 para.14
s.369, applied: SI 2013/1554 r.6_1
s.369, enabling: SI 2013/1554
s.370, amended: 2013 c.22 Sch.19 para.12
s.370, applied: SI 2013/1554 r.6_1, r.6_22
s.370, repealed (in part): 2013 c.22 Sch.19 para.12
s.371, amended: 2013 c.22 Sch.19 para.13
s.371, applied: SI 2013/1554 r.6_1
s.372, applied: SI 2013/1554 r.6_1
s.373, applied: SI 2013/1554 r.6_1
s.374, applied: SI 2013/1554 r.6_1
s.375, amended: 2013 c.22 Sch.8 para.142, Sch.21 para.36, 2013 c.29 Sch.48 para.15
s.375, applied: SI 2013/1554 r.6_1
s.375, enabling: SI 2013/1554
s.375A, added: 2013 c.22 Sch.19 para.26
s.375B, added: 2013 c.22 Sch.19 para.26
s.375C, added: 2013 c.29 Sch.48 para.16
s.377, amended: 2013 c.22 Sch.8 para.143, Sch.21 para.37, 2013 c.29 Sch.48 para.17
s.377, applied: SI 2013/1554 r.6_14
s.377A, applied: SI 2013/1554 r.6_14
s.378, amended: 2013 c.22 s.55, Sch.8 para.144, Sch.19 para.27, Sch.19 para.29, Sch.19 para.30, 2013 c.29 Sch.48 para.18
s.380, amended: 2013 c.22 Sch.19 para.14
s.381, amended: 2013 c.22 Sch.19 para.15
s.387, amended: 2013 c.22 Sch.19 para.16
s.388, amended: 2013 c.22 Sch.19 para.17
s.391, amended: 2013 c.22 Sch.19 para.18
s.392, amended: 2013 c.22 Sch.19 para.19
s.393, applied: SI 2013/2605 Art.53
s.397, amended: 2013 c.22 Sch.19 para.20
s.397, repealed (in part): 2013 c.22 Sch.19 para.20
s.399, amended: 2013 c.22 Sch.19 para.21
s.400, applied: SI 2013/2605 Art.60
s.404, amended: 2013 c.22 Sch.19 para.22
s.404, repealed (in part): 2013 c.22 Sch.19 para.22
s.405, amended: 2013 c.22 Sch.19 para.23
s.408A, added: 2013 c.22 Sch.19 para.28
s.408B, added: 2013 c.22 Sch.19 para.28
s.408C, added: 2013 c.29 Sch.48 para.19
s.412, amended: 2013 c.22 Sch.21 para.38, 2013 c.29 Sch.48 para.20
s.415, referred to: SI 2013/2605 Art.23, Art.57
s.416, amended: 2013 c.22 Sch.8 para.145
s.438, amended: 2013 c.22 Sch.8 para.146
s.439, amended: 2013 c.22 Sch.8 para.147
s.441, applied: 2013 c.22 Sch.7 para.6
s.443, amended: 2013 c.22 Sch.8 para.148
s.444, amended: 2013 c.22 Sch.8 para.149
s.444, enabling: SI 2013/2604
s.445, amended: 2013 c.22 Sch.8 para.150
s.445, enabling: SI 2013/2605
s.446, enabling: SSI 2013/293, SSI 2013/294, SSI 2013/317
s.449, amended: 2013 c.22 Sch.8 para.151
s.459, amended: 2013 c.22 s.46
s.459, enabling: SI 2013/24, SI 2013/2604, SI 2013/2605
Sch.4 para.9B, repealed: SI 2013/1881 Sch.1 para.8
Sch.7A para.1, added: 2013 c.22 s.48
Sch.7A para.2, added: 2013 c.22 s.48
Sch.7A para.3, added: 2013 c.22 s.48
Sch.7A para.4, added: 2013 c.22 s.48
Sch.7A para.5, added: 2013 c.22 s.48
Sch.7A para.6, added: 2013 c.22 s.48
Sch.7A para.7, added: 2013 c.22 s.48
Sch.7A para.8, added: 2013 c.22 s.48
Sch.8, amended: 2013 c.22 Sch.8 para.152
Sch.9, applied: SI 2013/2605 Art.2, Art.36
Sch.9 Part 1 para.1, amended: SI 2013/3115 Sch.2 para.41
Sch.9 Part 1 para.3, amended: SI 2013/3115 Sch.2 para.41
Sch.9 Part 3 para.5, applied: SI 2013/2605 Art.2, Art.36

30. Police Reform Act 2002

Part 2, applied: SI 2013/1778 Reg.2, SI 2013/1779 Art.3, Art.4
s.9, amended: 2013 c.22 Sch.8 para.153
s.9, varied: SI 2013/2325 Reg.5
s.10, amended: 2013 c.22 Sch.6 para.9
s.10, repealed (in part): 2013 c.22 Sch.6 para.9
s.11, amended: 2013 c.22 Sch.6 para.10
s.11, repealed (in part): 2013 c.22 Sch.6 para.10
s.15, amended: 2013 c.22 Sch.6 para.11
s.15, repealed (in part): 2013 c.22 Sch.6 para.11
s.16, amended: 2013 c.22 Sch.6 para.12
s.16A, repealed: 2013 c.22 Sch.6 para.13
s.17, repealed (in part): 2013 c.22 Sch.6 para.14
s.19, varied: SI 2013/2325 Reg.5
s.22, varied: SI 2013/2325 Reg.5
s.24, applied: SI 2013/281, SI 2013/1778, SI 2013/2325
s.24, varied: SI 2013/2325 Reg.5
s.26, applied: SI 2013/1779
s.26, enabling: SI 2013/1779

s.26A, applied: SI 2013/2325 Reg.3
s.26A, repealed: 2013 c.22 Sch.6 para.15
s.26B, repealed: 2013 c.22 Sch.6 para.15
s.26C, added: 2013 c.22 s.11
s.26C, enabling: SI 2013/2325
s.27, varied: SI 2013/2325 Reg.5
s.28A, applied: SI 2013/1778 Reg.2
s.28A, enabling: SI 2013/1778
s.29, amended: 2013 c.22 Sch.6 para.16
s.82, amended: SI 2013/602 Sch.2 para.39
s.82, enabling: SI 2013/122
s.103, repealed (in part): SI 2013/602 Sch.2 para.39
s.105, enabling: SI 2013/1779, SI 2013/2325
Sch.2 para.1, varied: SI 2013/2325 Reg.5
Sch.2 para.2, varied: SI 2013/2325 Reg.5
Sch.2 para.3, varied: SI 2013/2325 Reg.5
Sch.2 para.4, varied: SI 2013/2325 Reg.5
Sch.2 para.5, varied: SI 2013/2325 Reg.5
Sch.2 para.6, amended: SI 2013/602 Sch.2 para.39
Sch.2 para.6, varied: SI 2013/2325 Reg.5
Sch.2 para.7, varied: SI 2013/2325 Reg.5
Sch.2 para.8, varied: SI 2013/2325 Reg.5
Sch.2 para.9, varied: SI 2013/2325 Reg.5
Sch.2 para.10, varied: SI 2013/2325 Reg.5
Sch.2 para.11, varied: SI 2013/2325 Reg.5
Sch.2 para.12, varied: SI 2013/2325 Reg.5
Sch.2 para.13, varied: SI 2013/2325 Reg.5
Sch.2 para.14, varied: SI 2013/2325 Reg.5
Sch.2 para.15, varied: SI 2013/2325 Reg.5
Sch.2 para.16, varied: SI 2013/2325 Reg.5
Sch.2 para.17, varied: SI 2013/2325 Reg.5
Sch.2 para.18, varied: SI 2013/2325 Reg.5
Sch.3 Part 3 para.16, amended: 2013 c.22 Sch.6 para.17
Sch.3 Part 3 para.17, amended: 2013 c.22 Sch.6 para.17
Sch.3 Part 3 para.19F, amended: 2013 c.22 Sch.8 para.153
Sch.3 Part 3 para.19F, applied: SI 2013/281 Reg.2, Reg.3
Sch.3 Part 3 para.19F, enabling: SI 2013/281

32. Education Act 2002

Part 1 c.1, applied: SI 2013/473, SI 2013/1553
s.1, applied: SI 2013/473
s.2, enabling: SI 2013/473, SI 2013/1553
s.4, applied: SI 2013/473, SI 2013/1553
s.12, applied: SI 2013/3104 Sch.1 para.20
s.14, applied: SI 2013/1553 Art.2, SI 2013/3029 Sch.9 para.16, Sch.10 para.53, SI 2013/3035 Sch.1
s.14, disapplied: SI 2013/377 Reg.28
s.19, enabling: SI 2013/1624, SI 2013/2124, SI 2013/2127, SI 2013/2688
s.21, enabling: SI 2013/1624
s.23, enabling: SI 2013/1624, SI 2013/2124, SI 2013/2127
s.24, applied: SI 2013/3104 Reg.22, SI 2013/3109 Reg.16, SI 2013/3110 Sch.3 para.8
s.24, enabling: SI 2013/1624, SI 2013/3104
s.27, applied: SI 2013/3104 Sch.1 para.20, Sch.5 para.25
s.29, applied: SI 2013/1793 Reg.6
s.30, enabling: SI 2013/437, SI 2013/1561
s.34, enabling: SI 2013/1624
s.35, applied: SI 2013/1624 Reg.19
s.35, enabling: SI 2013/1940
s.36, applied: SI 2013/1624 Reg.19
s.36, enabling: SI 2013/1940
s.44, applied: SI 2013/3104 Sch.1 para.20
s.51A, applied: SI 2013/1624 Reg.19
s.52, applied: SI 2013/1793 Reg.8
s.78, referred to: SI 2013/3109 Sch.1 para.17
s.80, referred to: SI 2013/3109 Sch.1 para.17
s.84, amended: SI 2013/2092 Art.2, SI 2013/2093 Art.2
s.84, applied: SI 2013/2230 Art.2, Art.3
s.84, enabling: SI 2013/2092, SI 2013/2093, SI 2013/2230
s.85, amended: SI 2013/2092 Art.3
s.86, enabling: SI 2013/2092
s.87, applied: SI 2013/1513, SI 2013/3104 Sch.1 para.23
s.87, enabling: SI 2013/1513, SI 2013/2232
s.90, applied: SI 2013/3109 Reg.16
s.91, enabling: SI 2013/1487
s.96, applied: SI 2013/1487, SI 2013/2092, SI 2013/2093, SI 2013/2232
s.102, applied: SI 2013/433 Art.2
s.103, applied: SI 2013/433 Art.2, SI 2013/434 Art.2
s.108, enabling: SI 2013/433, SI 2013/434
s.116B, applied: SI 2013/3048 Sch.2 para.14
s.116D, applied: SI 2013/1793 Reg.13
s.117, applied: SI 2013/434
s.120, applied: SI 2013/1932
s.121, referred to: SI 2013/1932
s.122, enabling: SI 2013/1932
s.123, enabling: SI 2013/1932
s.124, enabling: SI 2013/1932
s.125, applied: SI 2013/1932
s.126, applied: SI 2013/1932
s.136, enabling: SI 2013/1976
s.141F, applied: SI 2013/1554 r.16_1, r.16_5
s.175, applied: SI 2013/3104 Sch.1 para.6
s.181, applied: SI 2013/3029 Sch.9 para.16, Sch.10 para.53, SI 2013/3035 Sch.1
s.207, enabling: SI 2013/492
s.210, applied: SI 2013/2092, SI 2013/2093

s.210, enabling: SI 2013/433, SI 2013/434, SI 2013/437, SI 2013/492, SI 2013/1513, SI 2013/1553, SI 2013/1561, SI 2013/1624, SI 2013/1940, SI 2013/2124, SI 2013/2127, SI 2013/2230, SI 2013/2232, SI 2013/2688
Sch.21 para.22, amended: SI 2013/2042 Sch.1 para.23

38. Adoption and Children Act 2002
see *G v G* [2012] EWHC 1979 (Fam), [2013] 1 F.L.R. 286 (Fam Div), Hedley, J.
applied: SI 2013/3029 Reg.8, SI 2013/3035 Sch.1
s.2, applied: SI 2013/765 Reg.28, SI 2013/3029 Sch.9 para.30, Sch.10 para.61, SI 2013/3035 Sch.1
s.2, enabling: SI 2013/2091
s.3, applied: SI 2013/765 Reg.28, SI 2013/3029 Sch.9 para.30, Sch.10 para.61, SI 2013/3035 Sch.1
s.4, applied: SI 2013/261 Sch.1 para.24, SI 2013/765 Reg.28, SI 2013/3029 Sch.9 para.30, Sch.10 para.61, SI 2013/3035 Sch.1
s.4, enabling: SI 2013/985, SI 2013/2091
s.9, enabling: SI 2013/985
s.11, enabling: SI 2013/985
s.12, enabling: SI 2013/985
s.13, amended: 2013 c.22 Sch.11 para.152
s.45, enabling: SI 2013/985
s.46, amended: SI 2013/1465 Sch.1 para.9
s.54, enabling: SI 2013/985
s.55, repealed (in part): 2013 c.22 Sch.11 para.153
s.60, amended: 2013 c.22 Sch.11 para.154
s.83, enabling: SI 2013/985
s.87, enabling: SI 2013/1801
s.92, amended: 2013 c.22 Sch.11 para.155
s.94, enabling: SI 2013/985
s.95, amended: 2013 c.22 Sch.11 para.156
s.100, repealed: 2013 c.22 Sch.11 para.210
s.101, amended: 2013 c.22 Sch.11 para.157
s.140, enabling: SI 2013/985, SI 2013/1801, SI 2013/2091
s.141, repealed (in part): 2013 c.22 Sch.11 para.158
s.141, enabling: SI 2013/3204
s.142, enabling: SI 2013/985, SI 2013/1801, SI 2013/2091
s.144, amended: 2013 c.22 Sch.11 para.159
Sch.1 para.3, referred to: SI 2013/1801 Art.3
Sch.3 para.37, repealed: 2013 c.22 Sch.10 para.99
Sch.3 para.38, repealed: 2013 c.22 Sch.10 para.99
Sch.3 para.39, repealed (in part): 2013 c.22 Sch.10 para.99
Sch.3 para.75, repealed: 2013 c.22 Sch.11 para.210

40. Enterprise Act 2002
applied: 2013 c.33 s.91
referred to: SI 2013/1582 Sch.1 para.1
Part 1, applied: SI 2013/783 Art.2, Art.4
Part 1, amended: 2013 c.24 Sch.5 para.60
Part 3, applied: 2013 c.24 Sch.4 para.56
Part 3 c.4, amended: 2013 c.24 Sch.5 para.127
Part 4, applied: 2013 c.24 s.52, Sch.4 para.16, Sch.4 para.57, 2013 c.33 s.59, s.66
Part 4 c.3, substituted: 2013 c.24 Sch.5 para.193
Part 8, applied: SI 2013/478 Art.3
Part 9, applied: 2013 c.19 s.18
Part 9, referred to: 2013 c.33 s.91
s.1, amended: 2013 c.24 Sch.5 para.65
s.1, repealed: 2013 c.24 Sch.5 para.229
s.2, amended: 2013 c.24 Sch.5 para.65
s.2, repealed: 2013 c.24 Sch.5 para.229
s.3, amended: 2013 c.24 Sch.5 para.65
s.3, repealed: 2013 c.24 Sch.5 para.229
s.4, amended: 2013 c.24 Sch.5 para.65
s.4, repealed: 2013 c.24 Sch.5 para.229
s.5, amended: 2013 c.24 Sch.5 para.60, Sch.5 para.65
s.6, amended: 2013 c.24 Sch.5 para.61, Sch.5 para.65
s.7, amended: 2013 c.24 Sch.5 para.62, Sch.5 para.65
s.8, amended: 2013 c.24 Sch.5 para.65
s.8, repealed: 2013 c.24 Sch.5 para.63
s.8A, added: SI 2013/783 Art.3
s.8A, amended: 2013 c.24 Sch.5 para.65
s.9, amended: 2013 c.24 Sch.5 para.65
s.10, amended: 2013 c.24 Sch.5 para.65
s.11, amended: 2013 c.24 Sch.5 para.64, Sch.5 para.65
s.14, amended: 2013 c.24 s.48
s.16, amended: 2013 c.22 Sch.9 para.81
s.22, see *Ryanair Holdings Plc v Office of Fair Trading* [2012] EWCA Civ 643, [2013] Bus. L.R. 214 (CA (Civ Div)), Sir Andrew Morritt (Chancellor)
s.22, amended: 2013 c.24 Sch.5 para.67, Sch.8 para.2
s.23, amended: 2013 c.24 Sch.5 para.68
s.23, varied: SI 2013/1582 Sch.1 para.7
s.24, amended: 2013 c.24 Sch.5 para.69
s.24, varied: SI 2013/1582 Sch.1 para.7
s.25, amended: 2013 c.24 Sch.5 para.70, Sch.15 para.16
s.25, varied: SI 2013/1582 Sch.1 para.7
s.26, varied: SI 2013/1582 Sch.1 para.7
s.28, amended: 2013 c.24 Sch.5 para.71
s.31, repealed: 2013 c.24 Sch.15 para.17
s.32, amended: 2013 c.24 Sch.15 para.18
s.32, repealed (in part): 2013 c.24 Sch.15 para.18
s.33, amended: 2013 c.24 Sch.5 para.72, Sch.8 para.3

s.34A, amended: 2013 c.24 Sch.5 para.73, Sch.15 para.19
s.34A, repealed (in part): 2013 c.24 Sch.15 para.19
s.34B, repealed: 2013 c.24 Sch.15 para.20
s.34C, added: 2013 c.24 Sch.5 para.74
s.34C, applied: 2013 c.24 Sch.4 para.47
s.34ZA, added: 2013 c.24 Sch.8 para.4
s.34ZB, added: 2013 c.24 Sch.8 para.4
s.34ZC, added: 2013 c.24 Sch.8 para.4
s.35, amended: 2013 c.24 Sch.5 para.75
s.35, applied: 2013 c.24 Sch.4 para.56
s.36, amended: 2013 c.24 Sch.5 para.76
s.36, applied: 2013 c.24 Sch.4 para.56
s.37, amended: 2013 c.24 Sch.5 para.77
s.37, applied: 2013 c.24 Sch.4 para.47
s.37, repealed (in part): 2013 c.24 Sch.5 para.77
s.38, amended: 2013 c.24 Sch.5 para.78
s.38, repealed (in part): 2013 c.24 Sch.5 para.78
s.39, amended: 2013 c.24 Sch.5 para.79, Sch.8 para.5
s.40, amended: 2013 c.24 Sch.5 para.80
s.41, amended: 2013 c.24 Sch.5 para.81
s.41A, added: 2013 c.24 Sch.8 para.6
s.41B, added: 2013 c.24 Sch.8 para.6
s.42, amended: 2013 c.24 Sch.5 para.82, Sch.15 para.21
s.42, repealed (in part): 2013 c.24 Sch.15 para.21
s.43, amended: 2013 c.24 Sch.5 para.83
s.44, amended: 2013 c.24 Sch.5 para.84
s.45, amended: 2013 c.24 Sch.5 para.85
s.46, amended: 2013 c.24 Sch.5 para.86, Sch.15 para.22
s.46A, amended: 2013 c.24 Sch.5 para.87
s.46B, amended: 2013 c.24 Sch.15 para.23
s.46B, repealed (in part): 2013 c.24 Sch.15 para.23
s.46C, repealed: 2013 c.24 Sch.15 para.24
s.46D, added: 2013 c.24 Sch.5 para.88
s.46D, applied: 2013 c.24 Sch.4 para.47
s.47, amended: 2013 c.24 Sch.5 para.89
s.47, applied: 2013 c.24 Sch.4 para.56
s.48, amended: 2013 c.24 Sch.5 para.90
s.48, applied: 2013 c.24 Sch.4 para.47
s.49, amended: 2013 c.24 Sch.5 para.91, Sch.15 para.25
s.50, amended: 2013 c.24 Sch.5 para.92
s.51, amended: 2013 c.24 Sch.5 para.93
s.52, amended: 2013 c.24 Sch.5 para.94
s.53, amended: 2013 c.24 Sch.5 para.95
s.54, amended: 2013 c.24 Sch.5 para.96
s.55, amended: 2013 c.24 Sch.5 para.97
s.56, amended: 2013 c.24 Sch.5 para.98
s.57, amended: 2013 c.24 Sch.5 para.99
s.58, amended: 2013 c.24 Sch.5 para.100
s.59, amended: 2013 c.24 Sch.5 para.101, Sch.15 para.26
s.59, repealed (in part): 2013 c.24 Sch.15 para.26
s.60, amended: 2013 c.24 Sch.5 para.102
s.61, amended: 2013 c.24 Sch.5 para.103
s.62, amended: 2013 c.24 Sch.5 para.104
s.62A, added: 2013 c.24 Sch.5 para.105
s.62A, applied: 2013 c.24 Sch.4 para.47
s.63, amended: 2013 c.24 Sch.5 para.106
s.63, applied: 2013 c.24 Sch.4 para.56
s.64, amended: 2013 c.24 Sch.5 para.107, Sch.15 para.27
s.64, applied: 2013 c.24 Sch.4 para.47
s.65, amended: 2013 c.24 Sch.5 para.108
s.66, amended: 2013 c.24 Sch.5 para.109
s.67, amended: 2013 c.24 Sch.5 para.110, Sch.15 para.28
s.68, amended: 2013 c.24 Sch.5 para.111, Sch.15 para.29
s.71, repealed: 2013 c.24 s.30
s.72, amended: 2013 c.24 s.30, Sch.5 para.112, Sch.7 para.5
s.72, repealed (in part): 2013 c.24 s.30, Sch.7 para.5
s.73, amended: 2013 c.24 Sch.5 para.113
s.73A, added: 2013 c.24 Sch.8 para.7
s.73B, added: 2013 c.24 Sch.8 para.7
s.74, amended: 2013 c.24 Sch.5 para.114
s.75, amended: 2013 c.24 Sch.5 para.115
s.76, amended: 2013 c.24 Sch.5 para.116
s.77, amended: 2013 c.24 Sch.5 para.117, Sch.15 para.30
s.78, amended: 2013 c.24 Sch.5 para.118, Sch.15 para.31
s.79, amended: 2013 c.24 Sch.5 para.119
s.80, amended: 2013 c.24 Sch.5 para.120, Sch.7 para.2
s.80, repealed (in part): 2013 c.24 Sch.7 para.2
s.81, amended: 2013 c.24 Sch.5 para.121, Sch.7 para.3
s.81, repealed (in part): 2013 c.24 Sch.7 para.3
s.82, amended: 2013 c.24 Sch.5 para.122
s.83, amended: 2013 c.24 Sch.5 para.123
s.83, repealed (in part): 2013 c.24 Sch.5 para.123
s.84, amended: 2013 c.24 Sch.5 para.124
s.84, repealed (in part): 2013 c.24 Sch.5 para.124
s.85, amended: 2013 c.24 Sch.5 para.125
s.89, amended: 2013 c.24 Sch.15 para.32
s.91, amended: 2013 c.24 Sch.5 para.126
s.92, amended: 2013 c.24 Sch.5 para.128
s.92, repealed (in part): 2013 c.24 Sch.5 para.128
s.93, amended: 2013 c.24 Sch.5 para.129, Sch.15 para.33
s.93, repealed (in part): 2013 c.24 Sch.5 para.129

s.94, amended: 2013 c.24 Sch.5 para.130, Sch.15 para.34
s.94, repealed (in part): 2013 c.24 Sch.5 para.130
s.94A, added: 2013 c.24 s.31
s.94B, added: 2013 c.24 s.31
s.95, amended: 2013 c.24 Sch.5 para.131
s.96, amended: 2013 c.24 Sch.5 para.132, Sch.8 para.8
s.96, repealed (in part): 2013 c.24 Sch.8 para.8
s.97, repealed: 2013 c.24 Sch.8 para.9
s.98, repealed: 2013 c.24 Sch.8 para.9
s.99, amended: 2013 c.24 Sch.5 para.133, Sch.8 para.10, Sch.15 para.35
s.99, repealed (in part): 2013 c.24 Sch.15 para.35
s.100, amended: 2013 c.24 Sch.5 para.134, Sch.8 para.11
s.100, repealed (in part): 2013 c.24 Sch.8 para.11
s.101, amended: 2013 c.24 Sch.8 para.12
s.101, repealed (in part): 2013 c.24 Sch.8 para.12
s.103, amended: 2013 c.24 s.32
s.104, amended: 2013 c.24 Sch.5 para.135
s.104, repealed (in part): 2013 c.24 Sch.5 para.135
s.104A, amended: 2013 c.24 Sch.5 para.136
s.105, amended: 2013 c.24 Sch.5 para.137
s.106, amended: 2013 c.24 Sch.5 para.138
s.106, repealed (in part): 2013 c.24 Sch.5 para.138
s.106A, amended: 2013 c.24 Sch.5 para.139
s.106B, amended: 2013 c.24 Sch.5 para.140
s.107, amended: 2013 c.24 Sch.5 para.141, Sch.15 para.36
s.107, repealed (in part): 2013 c.24 Sch.5 para.141, Sch.15 para.36
s.108, amended: 2013 c.24 Sch.5 para.142
s.109, amended: 2013 c.24 s.29, Sch.5 para.143
s.110, amended: 2013 c.24 Sch.5 para.144
s.110, repealed (in part): 2013 c.24 s.29
s.110A, added: 2013 c.24 s.29
s.110B, added: 2013 c.24 s.29
s.111, amended: 2013 c.24 s.29, Sch.5 para.145
s.112, amended: 2013 c.24 Sch.5 para.146
s.113, amended: 2013 c.24 Sch.5 para.147
s.114, amended: 2013 c.24 Sch.5 para.148
s.115, amended: 2013 c.24 Sch.5 para.149
s.116, amended: 2013 c.24 Sch.5 para.150
s.117, amended: 2013 c.24 Sch.5 para.151
s.118, amended: 2013 c.24 Sch.5 para.152
s.119, amended: 2013 c.24 Sch.5 para.153
s.119B, amended: 2013 c.24 Sch.5 para.154
s.120, see *Akzo Nobel NV v Competition Commission* [2013] CAT 13, [2013] Comp. A.R. 326 (CAT), Norris, J.; see *Ryanair Holdings Plc v Competition Commission* [2013] Comp. A.R. 18 (CAT), Marcus Smith Q.C.
s.120, amended: 2013 c.24 s.31, Sch.5 para.155
s.121, amended: 2013 c.24 Sch.5 para.156
s.122, see *Ryanair Holdings Plc v Office of Fair Trading* [2012] EWCA Civ 643, [2013] Bus. L.R. 214 (CA (Civ Div)), Sir Andrew Morritt (Chancellor)
s.122, amended: 2013 c.24 Sch.5 para.157
s.123, amended: 2013 c.24 Sch.5 para.158
s.124, amended: 2013 c.24 s.31, Sch.8 para.13
s.130, amended: 2013 c.24 Sch.5 para.159, Sch.15 para.37
s.130A, added: 2013 c.24 Sch.12 para.1
s.130A, amended: 2013 c.24 Sch.12 para.8, Sch.12 para.9
s.130A, applied: 2013 c.24 Sch.4 para.29
s.130A, varied: 2013 c.33 s.59
s.131, see *Association of Convenience Stores v Office of Fair Trading* [2013] Comp. A.R. 1 (CAT), Vivien Rose (Chairman)
s.131, amended: 2013 c.24 s.33, Sch.5 para.163, Sch.10 para.2, Sch.12 para.8, Sch.12 para.9
s.131, applied: 2013 c.24 Sch.4 para.29
s.131, varied: 2013 c.33 s.59
s.131A, added: 2013 c.24 Sch.12 para.2
s.131A, amended: 2013 c.24 Sch.12 para.8, Sch.12 para.9
s.131A, applied: 2013 c.24 Sch.4 para.29
s.131A, varied: 2013 c.33 s.59
s.131B, added: 2013 c.24 Sch.12 para.2
s.131B, amended: 2013 c.24 Sch.12 para.8, Sch.12 para.9
s.131B, varied: 2013 c.33 s.59
s.131C, added: 2013 c.24 Sch.12 para.2
s.131C, amended: 2013 c.24 Sch.12 para.8, Sch.12 para.9
s.131C, varied: 2013 c.33 s.59
s.132, amended: 2013 c.24 s.34, Sch.5 para.164, Sch.10 para.3, Sch.12 para.8, Sch.12 para.9, Sch.12 para.10
s.132, varied: 2013 c.33 s.59
s.133, amended: 2013 c.24 Sch.5 para.165, Sch.9 para.2, Sch.12 para.8, Sch.12 para.9
s.133, varied: 2013 c.33 s.59
s.133A, added: 2013 c.24 Sch.5 para.166
s.133A, amended: 2013 c.24 Sch.12 para.8, Sch.12 para.9
s.133A, varied: 2013 c.33 s.59
s.134, amended: 2013 c.24 Sch.5 para.167, Sch.9 para.3, Sch.12 para.8, Sch.12 para.9
s.134, applied: 2013 c.24 Sch.4 para.57
s.134, varied: 2013 c.33 s.59
s.135, amended: 2013 c.24 Sch.5 para.168, Sch.10 para.4, Sch.12 para.8, Sch.12 para.9
s.135, repealed (in part): 2013 c.24 Sch.12 para.11
s.135, varied: 2013 c.33 s.59

s.136, amended: 2013 c.24 Sch.5 para.169, Sch.12 para.8, Sch.12 para.9, 2013 c.33 s.67, Sch.8 para.10
s.136, repealed (in part): 2013 c.24 Sch.5 para.169
s.136, varied: 2013 c.33 s.59
s.137, amended: 2013 c.24 Sch.5 para.170, Sch.12 para.3, Sch.12 para.8, Sch.12 para.9
s.137, varied: 2013 c.33 s.59
s.138, amended: 2013 c.24 Sch.5 para.171, Sch.9 para.4, Sch.12 para.4, Sch.12 para.8, Sch.12 para.9
s.138, varied: 2013 c.33 s.59
s.138A, added: 2013 c.24 Sch.12 para.5
s.138A, amended: 2013 c.24 Sch.12 para.8, Sch.12 para.9
s.138A, varied: 2013 c.33 s.59
s.138B, added: 2013 c.24 Sch.12 para.5
s.138B, amended: 2013 c.24 Sch.12 para.8, Sch.12 para.9
s.138B, varied: 2013 c.33 s.59
s.139, amended: 2013 c.24 s.35, Sch.5 para.172, Sch.12 para.8
s.139, varied: 2013 c.33 s.59
s.140, amended: 2013 c.24 Sch.5 para.173, Sch.10 para.5, Sch.12 para.8
s.140, varied: 2013 c.33 s.59
s.140A, added: 2013 c.24 s.35
s.140A, amended: 2013 c.24 Sch.12 para.8
s.140A, applied: 2013 c.24 Sch.4 para.29
s.140A, varied: 2013 c.33 s.59
s.140B, added: 2013 c.24 Sch.10 para.6
s.140B, amended: 2013 c.24 Sch.12 para.8
s.140B, varied: 2013 c.33 s.59
s.141, amended: 2013 c.24 Sch.5 para.174, Sch.9 para.5, Sch.10 para.7, Sch.12 para.8
s.141, applied: 2013 c.24 Sch.4 para.57
s.141, substituted: 2013 c.24 Sch.10 para.7
s.141, varied: 2013 c.33 s.59
s.141A, added: 2013 c.24 s.35
s.141A, amended: 2013 c.24 Sch.12 para.8
s.141A, applied: 2013 c.24 Sch.4 para.57
s.141A, varied: 2013 c.33 s.59
s.141B, added: 2013 c.24 s.35
s.141B, amended: 2013 c.24 Sch.12 para.8
s.141B, varied: 2013 c.33 s.59
s.142, amended: 2013 c.24 Sch.5 para.175, Sch.10 para.8, Sch.12 para.8
s.142, varied: 2013 c.33 s.59
s.143, amended: 2013 c.24 Sch.5 para.176, Sch.10 para.9, Sch.12 para.8
s.143, repealed (in part): 2013 c.24 Sch.10 para.9
s.143, substituted: 2013 c.24 Sch.10 para.9
s.143, varied: 2013 c.33 s.59
s.143A, added: 2013 c.24 Sch.10 para.10
s.143A, amended: 2013 c.24 Sch.12 para.8
s.143A, varied: 2013 c.33 s.59
s.144, amended: 2013 c.24 Sch.5 para.177, Sch.10 para.11, Sch.12 para.6, Sch.12 para.8
s.144, varied: 2013 c.33 s.59
s.145, amended: 2013 c.24 Sch.5 para.178, Sch.10 para.12, Sch.12 para.8
s.145, varied: 2013 c.33 s.59
s.146, amended: 2013 c.24 Sch.5 para.179, Sch.10 para.13, Sch.12 para.8
s.146, varied: 2013 c.33 s.59
s.146A, added: 2013 c.24 Sch.10 para.14
s.146A, amended: 2013 c.24 Sch.12 para.8
s.146A, varied: 2013 c.33 s.59
s.147, amended: 2013 c.24 Sch.5 para.180, Sch.9 para.6, Sch.10 para.15, Sch.12 para.8
s.147, varied: 2013 c.33 s.59
s.147A, added: 2013 c.24 Sch.10 para.16
s.147A, amended: 2013 c.24 Sch.12 para.8
s.147A, varied: 2013 c.33 s.59
s.148, amended: 2013 c.24 Sch.5 para.181, Sch.12 para.8
s.148, repealed (in part): 2013 c.24 Sch.10 para.17
s.148, substituted: 2013 c.24 Sch.10 para.17
s.148, varied: 2013 c.33 s.59
s.148A, added: 2013 c.24 Sch.10 para.18
s.148A, amended: 2013 c.24 Sch.12 para.8
s.148A, varied: 2013 c.33 s.59
s.149, amended: 2013 c.24 Sch.5 para.182, Sch.10 para.19, Sch.12 para.8
s.149, varied: 2013 c.33 s.59
s.150, amended: 2013 c.24 Sch.5 para.183, Sch.10 para.20, Sch.12 para.8
s.150, varied: 2013 c.33 s.59
s.151, amended: 2013 c.24 Sch.5 para.184, Sch.10 para.21, Sch.12 para.8
s.151, substituted: 2013 c.24 Sch.10 para.21
s.151, varied: 2013 c.33 s.59
s.152, amended: 2013 c.24 Sch.5 para.185, Sch.12 para.8
s.152, repealed (in part): 2013 c.24 Sch.10 para.22
s.152, varied: 2013 c.33 s.59
s.153, amended: 2013 c.24 Sch.5 para.186, Sch.12 para.8
s.153, varied: 2013 c.33 s.59
s.154, see *John Lewis Plc v Office of Fair Trading* [2013] CAT 7, [2013] Comp. A.R. 301 (CAT), Vivien Rose (Chairman)
s.154, amended: 2013 c.24 Sch.5 para.187, Sch.9 para.7, Sch.12 para.8
s.154, applied: 2013 c.24 Sch.4 para.29
s.154, varied: 2013 c.33 s.59
s.155, amended: 2013 c.24 Sch.5 para.188, Sch.10 para.23, Sch.12 para.8
s.155, varied: 2013 c.33 s.59

s.156, amended: 2013 c.24 Sch.5 para.189, Sch.9 para.8, Sch.12 para.8, Sch.12 para.12
s.156, varied: 2013 c.33 s.59
s.157, amended: 2013 c.24 s.37, Sch.10 para.24, Sch.12 para.8
s.157, varied: 2013 c.33 s.59
s.158, amended: 2013 c.24 s.37, Sch.10 para.25, Sch.12 para.8
s.158, varied: 2013 c.33 s.59
s.159, amended: 2013 c.24 Sch.5 para.190, Sch.10 para.26, Sch.12 para.8
s.159, varied: 2013 c.33 s.59
s.160, amended: 2013 c.24 Sch.5 para.191, Sch.10 para.27, Sch.12 para.8
s.160, varied: 2013 c.33 s.59
s.161, amended: 2013 c.24 Sch.5 para.192, Sch.10 para.28, Sch.12 para.8
s.161, disapplied: 2013 c.19 s.21
s.161, varied: 2013 c.33 s.59
s.162, see *John Lewis Plc v Office of Fair Trading* [2013] CAT 7, [2013] Comp. A.R. 301 (CAT), Vivien Rose (Chairman)
s.162, amended: 2013 c.24 Sch.5 para.194, Sch.12 para.8
s.162, repealed (in part): 2013 c.24 Sch.5 para.194
s.162, varied: 2013 c.33 s.59
s.163, amended: 2013 c.24 Sch.5 para.195, Sch.12 para.8
s.163, substituted: 2013 c.24 Sch.5 para.195
s.163, varied: 2013 c.33 s.59
s.164, amended: 2013 c.24 Sch.12 para.8
s.164, varied: 2013 c.33 s.59
s.165, amended: 2013 c.24 Sch.12 para.8
s.165, varied: 2013 c.33 s.59
s.166, amended: 2013 c.24 Sch.5 para.196, Sch.12 para.8
s.166, applied: 2013 c.33 s.59
s.166, referred to: 2013 c.33 s.59
s.166, varied: 2013 c.33 s.59
s.167, see *John Lewis Plc v Office of Fair Trading* [2013] CAT 7, [2013] Comp. A.R. 301 (CAT), Vivien Rose (Chairman)
s.167, amended: 2013 c.24 Sch.5 para.197, Sch.12 para.8
s.167, repealed (in part): 2013 c.24 Sch.5 para.197
s.167, varied: 2013 c.33 s.59
s.168, amended: 2013 c.24 Sch.5 para.198, Sch.12 para.8
s.168, varied: 2013 c.33 s.59
s.169, amended: 2013 c.24 Sch.5 para.199, Sch.10 para.29, Sch.12 para.8, Sch.12 para.13
s.169, applied: 2013 c.24 Sch.4 para.29
s.169, repealed (in part): 2013 c.24 Sch.5 para.199
s.169, varied: 2013 c.33 s.59
s.170, amended: 2013 c.24 Sch.5 para.200, Sch.12 para.8
s.170, repealed (in part): 2013 c.24 Sch.5 para.200
s.170, varied: 2013 c.33 s.59
s.171, amended: 2013 c.24 Sch.5 para.201, Sch.12 para.8
s.171, applied: 2013 c.33 s.59
s.171, referred to: 2013 c.33 s.59
s.171, repealed (in part): 2013 c.24 Sch.5 para.201
s.171, varied: 2013 c.33 s.59
s.172, amended: 2013 c.24 Sch.5 para.202, Sch.10 para.30, Sch.12 para.8, Sch.12 para.14
s.172, repealed (in part): 2013 c.24 Sch.10 para.30
s.172, varied: 2013 c.33 s.59
s.173, amended: 2013 c.24 Sch.5 para.203, Sch.12 para.8
s.173, varied: 2013 c.33 s.59
s.174, amended: 2013 c.24 s.36, Sch.5 para.204, Sch.12 para.8
s.174, substituted: 2013 c.24 s.36
s.174, varied: 2013 c.33 s.59
s.174A, added: 2013 c.24 Sch.11 para.1
s.174A, amended: 2013 c.24 Sch.12 para.8
s.174A, varied: 2013 c.33 s.59
s.174B, added: 2013 c.24 Sch.11 para.1
s.174B, amended: 2013 c.24 Sch.12 para.8
s.174B, varied: 2013 c.33 s.59
s.174C, added: 2013 c.24 Sch.11 para.1
s.174C, amended: 2013 c.24 Sch.12 para.8
s.174C, varied: 2013 c.33 s.59
s.174D, added: 2013 c.24 Sch.11 para.1
s.174D, amended: 2013 c.24 Sch.12 para.8
s.174D, varied: 2013 c.33 s.59
s.174E, added: 2013 c.24 Sch.11 para.1
s.174E, amended: 2013 c.24 Sch.12 para.8
s.174E, varied: 2013 c.33 s.59
s.175, amended: 2013 c.24 Sch.12 para.8
s.175, repealed: 2013 c.24 Sch.11 para.3
s.175, varied: 2013 c.33 s.59
s.176, amended: 2013 c.24 Sch.12 para.8
s.176, repealed: 2013 c.24 Sch.11 para.4
s.176, varied: 2013 c.33 s.59
s.177, amended: 2013 c.24 Sch.5 para.205, Sch.10 para.31, Sch.12 para.8
s.177, varied: 2013 c.33 s.59
s.178, amended: 2013 c.24 Sch.5 para.206, Sch.12 para.8
s.178, varied: 2013 c.33 s.59
s.179, see *Association of Convenience Stores v Office of Fair Trading* [2013] Comp. A.R. 1 (CAT), Vivien Rose (Chairman); see *John Lewis Plc v Office of Fair Trading* [2013] CAT 7, [2013] Comp. A.R. 301 (CAT), Vivien Rose (Chairman)

s.179, amended: 2013 c.24 Sch.5 para.207, Sch.11 para.5, Sch.12 para.8, Sch.12 para.15
s.179, varied: 2013 c.33 s.59
s.180, amended: 2013 c.24 Sch.12 para.8
s.180, varied: 2013 c.33 s.59
s.181, amended: 2013 c.24 Sch.11 para.6, Sch.12 para.8, Sch.12 para.16
s.181, varied: 2013 c.33 s.59
s.182, amended: 2013 c.24 Sch.12 para.8
s.182, varied: 2013 c.33 s.59
s.183, amended: 2013 c.24 Sch.5 para.208, Sch.10 para.32, Sch.12 para.8
s.183, varied: 2013 c.33 s.59
s.184, amended: 2013 c.24 Sch.5 para.209, Sch.9 para.9, Sch.10 para.33, Sch.12 para.8, Sch.12 para.17
s.184, varied: 2013 c.33 s.59
s.185, repealed: 2013 c.24 Sch.5 para.225
s.186, repealed. 2013 c.24 Sch.5 para.225
s.187, repealed: 2013 c.24 Sch.5 para.225
s.188, amended: 2013 c.24 s.47
s.188, applied: 2013 c.24 s.47
s.188, repealed (in part): 2013 c.24 s.47
s.188A, added: 2013 c.24 s.47
s.188B, added: 2013 c.24 s.47
s.190, amended: 2013 c.24 Sch.5 para.210
s.190A, added: 2013 c.24 s.47
s.192, amended: 2013 c.24 Sch.5 para.211
s.193, amended: 2013 c.24 Sch.5 para.212
s.194, amended: 2013 c.24 s.48, Sch.5 para.213
s.195, amended: 2013 c.24 Sch.5 para.214
s.196, amended: 2013 c.24 Sch.5 para.215
s.201, amended: 2013 c.24 Sch.5 para.216
s.211, applied: SI 2013/761, SI 2013/761 Art.2
s.211, enabling: SI 2013/761
s.212, applied: SI 2013/3168 Art.2
s.212, enabling: SI 2013/3168
s.213, applied: SI 2013/478 Art.2
s.213, enabling: SI 2013/478
s.214, amended: SI 2013/783 Art.9
s.215, amended: 2013 c.22 Sch.9 para.81
s.238, applied: SI 2013/783 Art.4
s.241, amended: 2013 c.24 s.55
s.241, applied: SI 2013/783 Art.4, SI 2013/1808 Art.2
s.241, enabling: SI 2013/1808
s.247, repealed (in part): SI 2013/1575 Sch.1 para.9
s.249, varied: SI 2013/1582 Sch.1 para.7
s.273, amended: 2013 c.24 Sch.5 para.217
s.277, enabling: SI 2013/478
Sch.1 para.1, repealed: 2013 c.24 Sch.5 para.229
Sch.1 para.2, repealed: 2013 c.24 Sch.5 para.229
Sch.1 para.3, repealed: 2013 c.24 Sch.5 para.229
Sch.1 para.4, repealed: 2013 c.24 Sch.5 para.229
Sch.1 para.5, repealed: 2013 c.24 Sch.5 para.229
Sch.1 para.6, repealed: 2013 c.24 Sch.5 para.229
Sch.1 para.7, repealed: 2013 c.24 Sch.5 para.229
Sch.1 para.8, repealed: 2013 c.24 Sch.5 para.229
Sch.1 para.9, repealed: 2013 c.24 Sch.5 para.229
Sch.1 para.10, repealed: 2013 c.24 Sch.5 para.229
Sch.1 para.11, repealed: 2013 c.24 Sch.5 para.229
Sch.1 para.12, repealed: 2013 c.24 Sch.5 para.229
Sch.1 para.13, see *Association of Convenience Stores v Office of Fair Trading* [2013] Comp. A.R. 1 (CAT), Vivien Rose (Chairman)
Sch.1 para.13, repealed: 2013 c.24 Sch.5 para.229
Sch.1 para.14, repealed: 2013 c.24 Sch.5 para.229
Sch.1 para.15, repealed: 2013 c.24 Sch.5 para.229
Sch.1 para.16, repealed: 2013 c.24 Sch.5 para.229
Sch.3 Part 1 para.1, varied: SI 2013/1582 Sch.1 para.7
Sch.3 Part 1 para.2, varied: SI 2013/1582 Sch.1 para.7
Sch.3 Part 1 para.3, varied: SI 2013/1582 Sch.1 para.7
Sch.3 Part 1 para.4, varied: SI 2013/1582 Sch.1 para.7
Sch.3 Part 1 para.5, varied: SI 2013/1582 Sch.1 para.7
Sch.3 Part 1 para.6, varied: SI 2013/1582 Sch.1 para.7
Sch.3 Part 1 para.7, varied: SI 2013/1582 Sch.1 para.7
Sch.3 Part 1 para.8, varied: SI 2013/1582 Sch.1 para.7
Sch.3 Part 1 para.9, varied: SI 2013/1582 Sch.1 para.7
Sch.3 Part 1 para.10, varied: SI 2013/1582 Sch.1 para.7
Sch.3 Part 1 para.11, varied: SI 2013/1582 Sch.1 para.7
Sch.3 Part 1 para.12, varied: SI 2013/1582 Sch.1 para.7
Sch.3 Part 2 para.13, repealed: 2013 c.24 Sch.5 para.226
Sch.3 Part 2 para.13, varied: SI 2013/1582 Sch.1 para.7
Sch.3 Part 2 para.14, repealed: 2013 c.24 Sch.5 para.226
Sch.3 Part 2 para.14, varied: SI 2013/1582 Sch.1 para.7
Sch.3 Part 2 para.15, repealed: 2013 c.24 Sch.5 para.226
Sch.3 Part 2 para.15, varied: SI 2013/1582 Sch.1 para.7
Sch.3 Part 2 para.16, repealed: 2013 c.24 Sch.5 para.226

Sch.3 Part 2 para.16, varied: SI 2013/1582 Sch.1 para.7
Sch.3 Part 3 para.17, varied: SI 2013/1582 Sch.1 para.7
Sch.3 Part 3 para.18, varied: SI 2013/1582 Sch.1 para.7
Sch.4 Part 2 para.10A, added: 2013 c.24 s.48
Sch.4 Part 2 para.22, amended: 2013 c.24 Sch.5 para.66
Sch.4 Part 2 para.25, amended: 2013 c.22 Sch.9 para.81
Sch.7 para.1, repealed: 2013 c.24 Sch.7 para.4
Sch.7 para.2, amended: 2013 c.24 Sch.5 para.160, Sch.7 para.4
Sch.7 para.3, amended: 2013 c.24 Sch.5 para.160
Sch.7 para.4, amended: 2013 c.24 Sch.5 para.160
Sch.7 para.5, amended: 2013 c.24 Sch.5 para.160
Sch.7 para.7, amended: 2013 c.24 Sch.5 para.160, Sch.15 para.38
Sch.7 para.8, amended: 2013 c.24 Sch.5 para.160, Sch.15 para.38
Sch.7 para.10, amended: 2013 c.24 Sch.5 para.160
Sch.7 para.11, amended: 2013 c.24 Sch.5 para.160
Sch.8 para.8, amended: 2013 c.24 Sch.5 para.161
Sch.8 para.15, repealed: 2013 c.24 s.50
Sch.8 para.17, amended: 2013 c.24 s.50
Sch.8 para.18, amended: 2013 c.24 s.50
Sch.8 para.19, amended: 2013 c.24 Sch.5 para.161
Sch.8 para.20C, added: 2013 c.24 s.49
Sch.8 para.24, amended: 2013 c.24 Sch.5 para.161
Sch.8 para.24, repealed (in part): 2013 c.24 Sch.5 para.161
Sch.10 para.2, amended: 2013 c.24 Sch.5 para.162
Sch.11 para.1, repealed: 2013 c.24 Sch.5 para.227
Sch.11 para.2, repealed: 2013 c.24 Sch.5 para.227
Sch.11 para.3, repealed: 2013 c.24 Sch.5 para.227
Sch.11 para.4, repealed: 2013 c.24 Sch.5 para.227
Sch.11 para.5, repealed: 2013 c.24 Sch.5 para.227
Sch.11 para.6, repealed: 2013 c.24 Sch.5 para.227
Sch.11 para.7, repealed: 2013 c.24 Sch.5 para.227
Sch.11 para.8, repealed: 2013 c.24 Sch.5 para.227
Sch.11 para.9, repealed: 2013 c.24 Sch.5 para.227
Sch.11 para.10, repealed: 2013 c.24 Sch.5 para.227
Sch.11 para.11, repealed: 2013 c.24 Sch.5 para.227
Sch.11 para.12, repealed: 2013 c.24 Sch.5 para.227
Sch.12, repealed: 2013 c.24 Sch.5 para.228
Sch.14, amended: 2013 c.19 s.21, SI 2013/1575 Sch.1 para.10
Sch.15, amended: 2013 c.19 s.21, 2013 c.24 Sch.15 para.39, SI 2013/1575 Sch.1 para.11
Sch.24 para.21, repealed: SI 2013/294 Sch.1
Sch.25 para.7, repealed: SI 2013/294 Sch.1

41. Nationality, Immigration and Asylum Act 2002

s.82, see *Ahmadi (S.47 Decision: Validity: Sapkota: Afghanistan), Re* [2013] EWCA Civ 512, [2013] 4 All E.R. 442 (CA (Civ Div)), Sullivan, L.J.; see *EG (UT Rule 17: Withdrawal: Rule 24: Scope: Ethiopia), Re* [2013] UKUT 143 (IAC), [2013] Imm. A.R. 670 (UT (IAC)), Judge Eshun; see *Khanum (Paragraph 353B), Re* [2013] UKUT 311 (IAC), [2013] Imm. A.R. 858 (UT (IAC)), CMG Ockelton (Vice President); see *ST (Child Asylum Seekers: Sri Lanka), Re* [2013] UKUT 292 (IAC), [2013] Imm. A.R. 813 (UT (IAC)), Blake, J. (President)
s.82, applied: SI 2013/617 Sch.3 para.1, SI 2013/749 Sch.1 para.1, SI 2013/1460 Reg.6
s.84, see *EG (UT Rule 17: Withdrawal: Rule 24: Scope: Ethiopia), Re* [2013] UKUT 143 (IAC), [2013] Imm. A.R. 670 (UT (IAC)), Judge Eshun; see *Khanum (Paragraph 353B), Re* [2013] UKUT 311 (IAC), [2013] Imm. A.R. 858 (UT (IAC)), CMG Ockelton (Vice President)
s.84, amended: 2013 c.22 s.51
s.88A, amended: 2013 c.22 s.52
s.88A, repealed (in part): 2013 c.22 s.52
s.92, see *R. (on the application of EM (Eritrea)) v Secretary of State for the Home Department* [2012] EWCA Civ 1336, [2013] 1 W.L.R. 576 (CA (Civ Div)), Richards, L.J.; see *R. (on the application of GI (Sudan)) v Secretary of State for the Home Department* [2012] EWCA Civ 867, [2013] Q.B. 1008 (CA (Civ Div)), Laws, L.J.; see *R. (on the application of Nirula) v First-tier Tribunal* [2012] EWCA Civ 1436, [2013] 1 W.L.R. 1090 (CA (Civ Div)), Longmore, L.J.
s.92, amended: 2013 c.22 s.53
s.97A, amended: 2013 c.22 s.54
s.97B, added: 2013 c.22 s.53
s.99, amended: 2013 c.22 s.51
s.104, see *EG (UT Rule 17: Withdrawal: Rule 24: Scope: Ethiopia), Re* [2013] UKUT 143 (IAC), [2013] Imm. A.R. 670 (UT (IAC)), Judge Eshun
s.104, applied: SI 2013/765 Reg.8
s.105, enabling: SI 2013/793
s.109, enabling: SI 2013/3032
s.112, enabling: SI 2013/793

2003

1. Income Tax (Earnings and Pensions) Act 2003

applied: 2013 c.29 Sch.45 para.26
Part 2, applied: SI 2013/628 Reg.3
Part 2 c.5, amended: 2013 c.29 Sch.46 para.7
Part 2 c.5, amended: 2013 c.29 Sch.46 para.9
Part 2 c.8, applied: SI 2013/376 Reg.77

Part 2 c.9, applied: SI 2013/376 Reg.77
Part 3 c.10, applied: SI 2013/376 Reg.55
Part 3 c.11, applied: SI 2013/376 Reg.55
Part 3 c.2, applied: SI 2013/376 Reg.55
Part 3 c.3, applied: SI 2013/376 Reg.55
Part 3 c.4, applied: SI 2013/376 Reg.55
Part 3 c.5, applied: SI 2013/376 Reg.55
Part 3 c.6, applied: SI 2013/376 Reg.55
Part 3 c.7, applied: SI 2013/376 Reg.55
Part 3 c.8, applied: SI 2013/376 Reg.55
Part 3 c.9, applied: SI 2013/376 Reg.55
Part 4, applied: SI 2013/376 Reg.55
Part 5 c.2, applied: SI 2013/376 Reg.55
Part 9, applied: SI 2013/628 Reg.3
Part 10, applied: SI 2013/628 Reg.3
Part 12, applied: SI 2013/376 Reg.55
s.7, referred to: 2013 c.29 Sch.45 para.26, SI 2013/376 Reg.55
s.15, amended: 2013 c.29 Sch.6 para.2, Sch.45 para.58
s.19, amended: 2013 c.29 Sch.23 para.2
s.22, amended: 2013 c.29 Sch.45 para.59, Sch.46 para.7
s.23, amended: 2013 c.29 Sch.45 para.60, Sch.46 para.8
s.24, amended: 2013 c.29 Sch.45 para.61
s.26, amended: 2013 c.29 Sch.45 para.62, Sch.46 para.9
s.26A, added: 2013 c.29 Sch.46 para.10
s.27, amended: 2013 c.29 Sch.45 para.149
s.33, applied: SSI 2013/45
s.41C, amended: 2013 c.29 Sch.46 para.11
s.41ZA, added: 2013 c.29 Sch.6 para.3
s.49, amended: 2013 c.29 s.22
s.56, amended: 2013 c.29 Sch.46 para.30
s.61G, amended: 2013 c.29 Sch.46 para.31
s.139, amended: 2013 c.29 s.23
s.140, amended: 2013 c.29 s.23
s.140, repealed (in part): 2013 c.29 s.23
s.150, amended: SI 2013/3033 Art.2
s.155, amended: SI 2013/3033 Art.3
s.161, amended: SI 2013/3033 Art.4
s.170, enabling: SI 2013/3033
s.221, amended: 2013 c.29 Sch.23 para.4
s.222, amended: 2013 c.29 Sch.23 para.4
s.223, amended: 2013 c.29 Sch.23 para.4
s.224, amended: 2013 c.29 Sch.23 para.4
s.225, amended: 2013 c.29 Sch.23 para.4
s.226, amended: 2013 c.29 Sch.23 para.4
s.226A, added: 2013 c.29 Sch.23 para.3
s.226A, amended: 2013 c.29 Sch.23 para.4
s.226B, added: 2013 c.29 Sch.23 para.3
s.226B, amended: 2013 c.29 Sch.23 para.4
s.226C, added: 2013 c.29 Sch.23 para.3
s.226C, amended: 2013 c.29 Sch.23 para.4
s.226D, added: 2013 c.29 Sch.23 para.3
s.226D, amended: 2013 c.29 Sch.23 para.4
s.232, amended: 2013 c.29 Sch.45 para.63
s.270A, amended: SI 2013/513 Art.2
s.270A, enabling: SI 2013/513
s.271, amended: 2013 c.29 Sch.46 para.12
s.293B, added: 2013 c.29 s.10
s.308, amended: 2013 c.29 s.11
s.318A, amended: SI 2013/513 Art.2
s.318B, amended: 2013 c.29 s.12
s.318D, amended: SI 2013/630 Reg.16
s.318D, enabling: SI 2013/513
s.326A, amended: SI 2013/1133 Art.2
s.326A, enabling: SI 2013/1133
s.326B, added: 2013 c.29 Sch.23 para.37
s.328, amended: 2013 c.29 Sch.46 para.32
s.329, amended: 2013 c.29 Sch.45 para.64
s.337, applied: 2013 c.29 Sch.45 para.26
s.338, applied: 2013 c.29 Sch.45 para.26
s.340, applied: 2013 c.29 Sch.45 para.26
s.341, amended: 2013 c.29 Sch.46 para.33
s.342, amended: 2013 c.29 Sch.46 para.34
s.342, applied: 2013 c.29 Sch.45 para.26
s.343, amended: SI 2013/1126 Art.2
s.343, enabling: SI 2013/1126
s.370, amended: 2013 c.29 Sch.46 para.35
s.376, amended: 2013 c.29 Sch.46 para.36
s.378, amended: 2013 c.29 Sch.46 para.37
s.378, repealed (in part): 2013 c.29 Sch.46 para.37
s.394, amended: 2013 c.29 Sch.45 para.65
s.394A, added: 2013 c.29 Sch.45 para.125
s.413, amended: 2013 c.29 Sch.46 para.38
s.413A, amended: SI 2013/234 Art.3
s.421E, amended: 2013 c.29 Sch.45 para.66
s.428, amended: 2013 c.29 Sch.23 para.5
s.431, amended: 2013 c.29 Sch.23 para.6
s.437, amended: 2013 c.29 Sch.23 para.7
s.446B, amended: 2013 c.29 Sch.23 para.8
s.446T, amended: 2013 c.29 Sch.23 para.9
s.446V, amended: 2013 c.29 Sch.23 para.10
s.452, amended: 2013 c.29 Sch.23 para.11
s.474, amended: 2013 c.29 Sch.45 para.67
s.479, amended: 2013 c.29 Sch.23 para.12
s.498, amended: 2013 c.29 Sch.2 para.2, Sch.2 para.19
s.519, amended: 2013 c.29 Sch.2 para.21
s.524, amended: 2013 c.29 Sch.2 para.14, Sch.2 para.26
s.531, amended: 2013 c.29 Sch.23 para.13
s.532, amended: 2013 c.29 Sch.23 para.14, Sch.2 para.94
s.554N, amended: 2013 c.29 Sch.23 para.15
s.554O, amended: SI 2013/1881 Sch.1 para.9

s.554Z4, amended: 2013 c.29 Sch.45 para.68
s.554Z4A, added: 2013 c.29 Sch.45 para.126
s.554Z6, amended: 2013 c.29 Sch.45 para.69
s.554Z9, amended: 2013 c.29 Sch.45 para.70, Sch.46 para.13
s.554Z10, amended: 2013 c.29 Sch.45 para.71, Sch.46 para.14
s.554Z11A, added: 2013 c.29 Sch.45 para.127
s.554Z12, amended: 2013 c.29 Sch.45 para.128
s.572A, added: 2013 c.29 Sch.45 para.129
s.575, amended: 2013 c.29 Sch.45 para.72
s.576A, applied: 2013 c.29 Sch.45 para.158
s.576A, substituted: 2013 c.29 Sch.45 para.116
s.579CA, applied: 2013 c.29 Sch.45 para.158
s.579CA, substituted: 2013 c.29 Sch.45 para.117
s.639, referred to: SI 2013/379 Reg.68
s.660, amended: SI 2013/630 Reg.16
s.675, amended: SI 2013/630 Reg.16
s.677, amended: 2013 c.29 s.13
s.681A, amended: 2013 c.29 Sch.46 para.39
s.683, amended: 2013 c.29 Sch.45 para.130
s.684, enabling: SI 2013/521, SI 2013/2300
s.690, amended: 2013 c.29 Sch.45 para.73, Sch.46 para.15
Sch.1 Part 2, amended: 2013 c.29 Sch.45 para.105
Sch.2, referred to: 2013 c.29 Sch.2 para.38, Sch.2 para.58, Sch.2 para.89, Sch.2 para.90, Sch.2 para.93
Sch.2 Part 2 para.8, repealed (in part): 2013 c.29 Sch.46 para.40
Sch.2 Part 3 para.13, amended: 2013 c.29 Sch.2 para.34
Sch.2 Part 3 para.14, amended: 2013 c.29 Sch.2 para.35
Sch.2 Part 3 para.14, repealed (in part): 2013 c.29 Sch.2 para.35
Sch.2 Part 3 para.19, repealed: 2013 c.29 Sch.2 para.36
Sch.2 Part 3 para.20, repealed: 2013 c.29 Sch.2 para.36
Sch.2 Part 3 para.21, repealed: 2013 c.29 Sch.2 para.36
Sch.2 Part 3 para.22, repealed: 2013 c.29 Sch.2 para.36
Sch.2 Part 3 para.23, repealed: 2013 c.29 Sch.2 para.36
Sch.2 Part 3 para.24, repealed: 2013 c.29 Sch.2 para.36
Sch.2 Part 4 para.25, amended: 2013 c.29 Sch.2 para.47
Sch.2 Part 4 para.30, repealed: 2013 c.29 Sch.2 para.48
Sch.2 Part 4 para.31, repealed: 2013 c.29 Sch.2 para.48
Sch.2 Part 4 para.32, amended: 2013 c.29 Sch.2 para.3
Sch.2 Part 4 para.32, repealed: 2013 c.29 Sch.2 para.48
Sch.2 Part 4 para.33, repealed: 2013 c.29 Sch.2 para.48
Sch.2 Part 5 para.35, repealed (in part): 2013 c.29 Sch.2 para.49
Sch.2 Part 5 para.37, amended: 2013 c.29 Sch.2 para.20
Sch.2 Part 6 para.43, amended: 2013 c.29 Sch.2 para.50
Sch.2 Part 6 para.52, amended: 2013 c.29 Sch.2 para.79
Sch.2 Part 7 para.59, repealed (in part): 2013 c.29 Sch.2 para.51
Sch.2 Part 8 para.62, amended: 2013 c.29 Sch.2 para.83
Sch.2 Part 8 para.62, applied: 2013 c.29 Sch.2 para.86
Sch.2 Part 8 para.63, amended: 2013 c.29 Sch.2 para.87
Sch.2 Part 8 para.64, repealed: 2013 c.29 Sch.2 para.88
Sch.2 Part 8 para.68, amended: 2013 c.29 Sch.2 para.84, Sch.2 para.90
Sch.2 Part 8 para.68, referred to: 2013 c.29 Sch.2 para.90
Sch.2 Part 8 para.68, repealed (in part): 2013 c.29 Sch.2 para.90
Sch.2 Part 8 para.69, amended: 2013 c.29 Sch.2 para.85
Sch.2 Part 9 para.70, amended: 2013 c.29 Sch.2 para.92
Sch.2 Part 9 para.75, amended: 2013 c.29 Sch.2 para.52, Sch.2 para.80
Sch.2 Part 9 para.78, repealed: 2013 c.29 Sch.2 para.93
Sch.2 Part 10 para.84, amended: 2013 c.29 Sch.2 para.53
Sch.2 Part 10 para.84, repealed (in part): 2013 c.29 Sch.2 para.53
Sch.2 Part 11 para.92, amended: 2013 c.29 Sch.2 para.55
Sch.2 Part 11 para.98, repealed: 2013 c.29 Sch.2 para.5
Sch.2 Part 11 para.99, amended: 2013 c.29 Sch.2 para.56
Sch.2 Part 11 para.100, amended: 2013 c.29 Sch.2 para.6, Sch.2 para.37, Sch.2 para.57
Sch.3, referred to: 2013 c.29 Sch.2 para.43, Sch.2 para.67
Sch.3 Part 2 para.6, amended: 2013 c.29 Sch.46 para.41

Sch.3 Part 2 para.6, repealed (in part): 2013 c.29 Sch.46 para.41
Sch.3 Part 3 para.9, amended: 2013 c.29 Sch.2 para.40
Sch.3 Part 3 para.11, repealed: 2013 c.29 Sch.2 para.41
Sch.3 Part 3 para.12, repealed: 2013 c.29 Sch.2 para.41
Sch.3 Part 3 para.13, repealed: 2013 c.29 Sch.2 para.41
Sch.3 Part 3 para.14, repealed: 2013 c.29 Sch.2 para.41
Sch.3 Part 3 para.15, repealed: 2013 c.29 Sch.2 para.41
Sch.3 Part 3 para.16, repealed: 2013 c.29 Sch.2 para.41
Sch.3 Part 4 para.17, amended: 2013 c.29 Sch.2 para.60
Sch.3 Part 4 para.21, repealed: 2013 c.29 Sch.2 para.61
Sch.3 Part 6 para.27, amended: 2013 c.29 Sch.2 para.8
Sch.3 Part 6 para.28, amended: 2013 c.29 Sch.2 para.62
Sch.3 Part 6 para.30, amended: 2013 c.29 Sch.2 para.9
Sch.3 Part 6 para.31, repealed: 2013 c.29 Sch.2 para.10
Sch.3 Part 6 para.33, repealed: 2013 c.29 Sch.2 para.11
Sch.3 Part 6 para.34, amended: 2013 c.29 Sch.2 para.12, Sch.2 para.23
Sch.3 Part 6 para.37, amended: 2013 c.29 Sch.2 para.24
Sch.3 Part 7 para.38, amended: 2013 c.29 Sch.2 para.25
Sch.3 Part 7 para.39, amended: 2013 c.29 Sch.2 para.63
Sch.3 Part 9 para.48, amended: 2013 c.29 Sch.2 para.65
Sch.3 Part 9 para.49, amended: 2013 c.29 Sch.2 para.13, Sch.2 para.42, Sch.2 para.66
Sch.4, referred to: 2013 c.29 Sch.2 para.77
Sch.4 Part 2 para.6, amended: 2013 c.29 Sch.2 para.68
Sch.4 Part 3 para.10, amended: 2013 c.29 Sch.2 para.44
Sch.4 Part 3 para.11, amended: 2013 c.29 Sch.2 para.44
Sch.4 Part 3 para.13, amended: 2013 c.29 Sch.2 para.44
Sch.4 Part 4 para.15, amended: 2013 c.29 Sch.2 para.70
Sch.4 Part 4 para.19, repealed: 2013 c.29 Sch.2 para.71
Sch.4 Part 5 para.21, amended: 2013 c.29 Sch.2 para.28
Sch.4 Part 5 para.22, amended: 2013 c.29 Sch.2 para.72
Sch.4 Part 5 para.25A, added: 2013 c.29 Sch.2 para.29
Sch.4 Part 6 para.26, amended: 2013 c.29 Sch.2 para.30
Sch.4 Part 6 para.27, amended: 2013 c.29 Sch.2 para.73
Sch.4 Part 8 para.35A, repealed: 2013 c.29 Sch.2 para.15
Sch.4 Part 8 para.36, amended: 2013 c.29 Sch.2 para.75
Sch.4 Part 8 para.37, amended: 2013 c.29 Sch.2 para.76
Sch.5 Part 4 para.27, repealed (in part): 2013 c.29 Sch.46 para.42
Sch.5 Part 6 para.39, amended: 2013 c.29 Sch.2 para.31

5. Community Care (Delayed Discharges etc.) Act 2003

s.1, amended: SI 2013/2341 Art.3

7. European Parliament (Representation) Act 2003

s.17, applied: SI 2013/2876
s.17, enabling: SI 2013/2876
s.18, applied: SI 2013/2876
s.18, enabling: SI 2013/2876

14. Finance Act 2003

Part 4, applied: 2013 c.29 s.194
s.45, see *DV3 RS Limited Partnership v Revenue and Customs Commissioners* [2013] EWCA Civ 907, [2013] S.T.C. 2150 (CA (Civ Div)), Maurice Kay, L.J. (VP, CA Civ); see *DV3 RS Limited Partnership v Revenue and Customs Commissioners* [2013] S.T.C. 430 (UT (Tax)), Henderson, J.
s.45, amended: 2013 c.29 s.194
s.45, applied: 2013 c.29 s.194
s.45, referred to: 2013 c.29 Sch.39 para.11
s.45, substituted: 2013 c.29 Sch.39 para.2
s.57A, amended: 2013 c.29 Sch.39 para.4
s.66, applied: 2013 c.29 s.153
s.71A, applied: 2013 c.29 s.157
s.72, applied: 2013 c.29 s.157
s.76, applied: 2013 c.29 s.194
s.77, amended: 2013 c.29 Sch.39 para.5
s.79, amended: 2013 c.29 Sch.39 para.6
s.79, repealed (in part): 2013 c.29 Sch.39 para.6
s.81, amended: 2013 c.29 Sch.40 para.3
s.81ZA, added: 2013 c.29 Sch.40 para.4
s.81ZA, amended: 2013 c.29 Sch.40 para.9

s.85, amended: 2013 c.29 Sch.40 para.5
s.86, amended: 2013 c.29 Sch.40 para.6
s.87, amended: 2013 c.29 Sch.41 para.4
s.116, applied: 2013 c.29 s.113
s.116, varied: 2013 c.29 s.114
s.117, see *Pollen Estate Trustee Co Ltd v Revenue and Customs Commissioners* [2013] EWCA Civ 753, [2013] 1 W.L.R. 3785 (CA (Civ Div)), Laws, L.J.
s.117, applied: 2013 c.29 s.157
s.119, amended: 2013 c.29 Sch.39 para.7, Sch.41 para.5
s.122, amended: 2013 c.29 Sch.39 para.8, Sch.40 para.7
s.153, amended: 2013 c.2 Sch.1 Part 10
s.204, enabling: SI 2013/701
s.207, amended: 2013 c.2 Sch.1 Part 10
Sch.2A para.1, added: 2013 c.29 Sch.39 para.3
Sch.2A para.2, added: 2013 c.29 Sch.39 para.3
Sch.2A para.3, added: 2013 c.29 Sch.39 para.3
Sch.2A para.4, added: 2013 c.29 Sch.39 para.3
Sch.2A para.5, added: 2013 c.29 Sch.39 para.3
Sch.2A para.6, added: 2013 c.29 Sch.39 para.3
Sch.2A para.7, added: 2013 c.29 Sch.39 para.3
Sch.2A para.8, added: 2013 c.29 Sch.39 para.3
Sch.2A para.9, added: 2013 c.29 Sch.39 para.3
Sch.2A para.10, added: 2013 c.29 Sch.39 para.3
Sch.2A para.11, added: 2013 c.29 Sch.39 para.3
Sch.2A para.12, added: 2013 c.29 Sch.39 para.3
Sch.2A para.13, added: 2013 c.29 Sch.39 para.3
Sch.2A para.14, added: 2013 c.29 Sch.39 para.3
Sch.2A para.15, added: 2013 c.29 Sch.39 para.3
Sch.2A para.16, added: 2013 c.29 Sch.39 para.3
Sch.2A para.17, added: 2013 c.29 Sch.39 para.3
Sch.2A para.18, added: 2013 c.29 Sch.39 para.3
Sch.2A para.19, added: 2013 c.29 Sch.39 para.3
Sch.2A para.20, added: 2013 c.29 Sch.39 para.3
Sch.2A para.21, added: 2013 c.29 Sch.39 para.3
Sch.4A para.2, amended: 2013 c.29 Sch.40 para.2
Sch.4A para.5, substituted: 2013 c.29 Sch.40 para.2
Sch.4A para.5A, added: 2013 c.29 Sch.40 para.2
Sch.4A para.5B, added: 2013 c.29 Sch.40 para.2
Sch.4A para.5C, added: 2013 c.29 Sch.40 para.2
Sch.4A para.5D, added: 2013 c.29 Sch.40 para.2
Sch.4A para.5E, added: 2013 c.29 Sch.40 para.2
Sch.4A para.5F, added: 2013 c.29 Sch.40 para.2
Sch.4A para.5G, added: 2013 c.29 Sch.40 para.2
Sch.4A para.5H, added: 2013 c.29 Sch.40 para.2
Sch.4A para.5I, added: 2013 c.29 Sch.40 para.2
Sch.4A para.5J, added: 2013 c.29 Sch.40 para.2
Sch.4A para.5K, added: 2013 c.29 Sch.40 para.2
Sch.4A para.6A, added: 2013 c.29 Sch.40 para.2
Sch.4A para.6A, amended: 2013 c.29 Sch.40 para.9
Sch.4A para.6A, repealed (in part): 2013 c.29 Sch.40 para.9
Sch.4A para.6B, added: 2013 c.29 Sch.40 para.2
Sch.4A para.6B, repealed (in part): 2013 c.29 Sch.40 para.9
Sch.4A para.6C, added: 2013 c.29 Sch.40 para.2
Sch.4A para.6C, amended: 2013 c.29 Sch.40 para.9
Sch.4A para.6D, added: 2013 c.29 Sch.40 para.2
Sch.4A para.6D, amended: 2013 c.29 Sch.40 para.9
Sch.4A para.6D, repealed (in part): 2013 c.29 Sch.40 para.9
Sch.4A para.6E, added: 2013 c.29 Sch.40 para.2
Sch.4A para.6E, amended: 2013 c.29 Sch.40 para.9
Sch.4A para.6F, added: 2013 c.29 Sch.40 para.2
Sch.4A para.6F, amended: 2013 c.29 Sch.40 para.9
Sch.4A para.6G, added: 2013 c.29 Sch.40 para.2
Sch.4A para.6G, amended: 2013 c.29 Sch.40 para.9
Sch.4A para.6H, added: 2013 c.29 Sch.40 para.2
Sch.4A para.6H, amended: 2013 c.29 Sch.40 para.9
Sch.4A para.9, amended: 2013 c.29 Sch.40 para.2
Sch.6B para.7, amended: 2013 c.29 Sch.39 para.9
Sch.7 Part 1 para.2, amended: SI 2013/234 Art.8
Sch.7 Part 1 para.2A, added: SI 2013/234 Art.7
Sch.7 Part 1 para.2B, added: SI 2013/234 Art.7
Sch.9 para.1, amended: SI 2013/602 Sch.2 para.40
Sch.10 Part 1 para.6, applied: 2013 c.29 s.194
Sch.10 Part 6 para.34A, amended: 2013 c.29 s.231
Sch.11A, applied: 2013 c.29 s.210
Sch.11A para.1, applied: 2013 c.29 s.210
Sch.11A para.1, varied: 2013 c.29 Sch.33 para.28, Sch.33 para.31, Sch.33 para.34
Sch.11A para.2, varied: 2013 c.29 Sch.33 para.28, Sch.33 para.31, Sch.33 para.34
Sch.11A para.3, varied: 2013 c.29 Sch.33 para.28, Sch.33 para.31, Sch.33 para.34
Sch.11A para.3A, varied: 2013 c.29 Sch.33 para.28, Sch.33 para.31, Sch.33 para.34
Sch.11A para.4, varied: 2013 c.29 Sch.33 para.28, Sch.33 para.31, Sch.33 para.34
Sch.11A para.5, varied: 2013 c.29 Sch.33 para.28, Sch.33 para.31, Sch.33 para.34
Sch.11A para.6, varied: 2013 c.29 Sch.33 para.28, Sch.33 para.31, Sch.33 para.34
Sch.11A para.7, varied: 2013 c.29 Sch.33 para.28, Sch.33 para.31, Sch.33 para.34
Sch.11A para.8, varied: 2013 c.29 Sch.33 para.28, Sch.33 para.31, Sch.33 para.34

Sch.11A para.9, varied: 2013 c.29 Sch.33 para.28, Sch.33 para.31, Sch.33 para.34
Sch.11A para.10, varied: 2013 c.29 Sch.33 para.28, Sch.33 para.31, Sch.33 para.34
Sch.11A para.11, varied: 2013 c.29 Sch.33 para.28, Sch.33 para.31, Sch.33 para.34
Sch.11A para.12, varied: 2013 c.29 Sch.33 para.28, Sch.33 para.31, Sch.33 para.34
Sch.11A para.13, varied: 2013 c.29 Sch.33 para.28, Sch.33 para.31, Sch.33 para.34
Sch.11A para.14, varied: 2013 c.29 Sch.33 para.28, Sch.33 para.31, Sch.33 para.34
Sch.11A para.15, varied: 2013 c.29 Sch.33 para.28, Sch.33 para.31, Sch.33 para.34
Sch.12 Part 1 para.1, varied: 2013 c.29 s.165
Sch.12 Part 1 para.1A, varied: 2013 c.29 s.165
Sch.12 Part 1 para.2, varied: 2013 c.29 s.165
Sch.12 Part 1 para.3, varied: 2013 c.29 s.165
Sch.12 Part 2 para.4, varied: 2013 c.29 s.165
Sch.12 Part 2 para.5, amended: 2013 c.22 Sch.9 para.52
Sch.12 Part 2 para.5, varied: 2013 c.29 s.165
Sch.12 Part 2 para.6, varied: 2013 c.29 s.165
Sch.12 Part 2 para.7, varied: 2013 c.29 s.165
Sch.17A para.3, amended: 2013 c.29 Sch.41 para.2
Sch.17A para.3, applied: 2013 c.29 Sch.41 para.8
Sch.17A para.3A, added: 2013 c.29 Sch.41 para.3
Sch.17A para.3A, referred to: 2013 c.29 Sch.41 para.8
Sch.17A para.12A, amended: 2013 c.29 Sch.41 para.6
Sch.17A para.12B, amended: 2013 c.29 Sch.39 para.10
Sch.17A para.14, repealed: 2013 c.29 Sch.41 para.7
Sch.17A para.15, repealed: 2013 c.29 Sch.41 para.7
Sch.17A para.19, amended: 2013 c.29 Sch.41 para.6

17. Licensing Act 2003

s.34, see *Taylor v Manchester City Council* [2012] EWHC 3467 (Admin), [2013] 2 All E.R. 490 (QBD (Admin)), Hickinbottom, J.
s.34, enabling: SI 2013/432
s.41A, enabling: SI 2013/432
s.54, enabling: SI 2013/432
s.84, enabling: SI 2013/432
s.86A, enabling: SI 2013/432
s.91, enabling: SI 2013/432
s.193, enabling: SI 2013/432
s.197, applied: SI 2013/1578
s.197, enabling: SI 2013/1578
Sch.1 Part 1 para.2, amended: SI 2013/1578 Art.2
Sch.1 Part 1 para.4, enabling: SI 2013/1578
Sch.1 Part 3 para.16, amended: SI 2013/1578 Art.3
Sch.1 Part 3 para.17, amended: SI 2013/1578 Art.4

20. Railways and Transport Safety Act 2003

s.24, amended: SI 2013/602 Sch.2 para.41
s.24, applied: SI 2013/602 Sch.3 para.7
s.25, amended: SI 2013/602 Sch.2 para.41
s.25, applied: SI 2013/602 Sch.3 para.7
s.63, amended: SI 2013/602 Sch.2 para.41
s.64, amended: SI 2013/602 Sch.2 para.41
s.67, amended: SI 2013/602 Sch.2 para.41
s.78, applied: SI 2013/2787 Reg.6
s.79, applied: SI 2013/2787 Reg.6
s.83, referred to: 2013 c.22 Sch.22 para.8, Sch.22 para.14
s.92, applied: SI 2013/2787 Reg.6
s.93, applied: SI 2013/2787 Reg.6
s.94, applied: SI 2013/2787 Reg.6
s.96, referred to: 2013 c.22 Sch.22 para.8, Sch.22 para.14
Sch.1 para.7, substituted: 2013 c.24 Sch.15 para.41
Sch.4 Part 1 para.7, amended: SI 2013/602 Sch.2 para.41

21. Communications Act 2003

applied: SI 2013/243 Art.5
referred to: SI 2013/656 Art.4, SI 2013/791 Art.6, SI 2013/1867 Art.6, SI 2013/1988 Art.5
s.16, applied: SI 2013/1163 Sch.1
s.94, amended: 2013 c.24 Sch.14 para.17
s.96A, amended: 2013 c.24 Sch.14 para.18
s.109, amended: 2013 c.27 s.9
s.109, applied: 2013 c.27 s.9, SI 2013/1403
s.109, enabling: SI 2013/1403
s.124Q, amended: 2013 c.22 Sch.9 para.52
s.192, amended: 2013 c.24 Sch.15 para.43
s.193, amended: 2013 c.24 Sch.6 para.98, Sch.15 para.44
s.193A, added: 2013 c.24 s.54
s.194, repealed: 2013 c.24 Sch.6 para.99
s.195, amended: 2013 c.24 Sch.15 para.45
s.197, amended: 2013 c.24 Sch.6 para.100
s.245, varied: SI 2013/243 Sch.1 para.11
s.253, varied: SI 2013/243 Sch.1 para.12
s.253A, varied: SI 2013/243 Sch.1 para.12
s.262, enabling: SI 2013/243
s.314, varied: SI 2013/243 Sch.1 para.13
s.355, varied: SI 2013/243 Sch.1 para.13
s.356, varied: SI 2013/243 Sch.1 para.13
s.362, amended: SI 2013/2217 Reg.7
s.367, repealed: 2013 c.24 Sch.21 para.2
s.371, amended: 2013 c.24 Sch.15 para.46
s.393, repealed (in part): 2013 c.24 Sch.21 para.2
s.402, enabling: SI 2013/1403
s.403, applied: SI 2013/3108
s.404, repealed (in part): 2013 c.24 Sch.21 para.2

s.411, applied: 2013 c.27 s.36
Sch.12 Part 2 para.18, disapplied: SI 2013/242 Art.4
Sch.17 para.39, repealed: 2013 c.24 Sch.21 para.2
Sch.17 para.168, amended: 2013 c.10 s.19

26. Local Government Act 2003
s.11, enabling: SI 2013/476, SI 2013/1751
s.21, enabling: SI 2013/476
s.31, applied: SI 2013/259 Reg.7
s.42, enabling: SI 2013/2265
s.47, enabling: SI 2013/2265
s.48, enabling: SI 2013/2265
s.49, enabling: SI 2013/2265
s.105, applied: SI 2013/2356 Sch.2 para.22
s.123, enabling: SI 2013/476, SI 2013/1751

28. Legal Deposit Libraries Act 2003
applied: SI 2013/777 Reg.13
s.1, applied: SI 2013/777 Reg.14, Reg.15, Reg.16
s.1, enabling: SI 2013/777
s.2, enabling: SI 2013/777
s.6, enabling: SI 2013/777
s.7, applied: SI 2013/777
s.7, enabling: SI 2013/777
s.10, applied: SI 2013/777, SI 2013/777 Reg.13, Reg.18
s.10, enabling: SI 2013/777
s.11, applied: SI 2013/777
s.11, enabling: SI 2013/777

32. Crime (International Co-operation) Act 2003
s.3, applied: SI 2013/1554 r.4_4, r.32_1
s.4, applied: SI 2013/1554 r.4_4, r.32_2
s.4A, applied: SI 2013/1554 r.4_4
s.4B, applied: SI 2013/1554 r.4_4
s.7, see *Crown Prosecution Service v Gohil* [2012] EWCA Civ 1550, [2013] Fam. 276 (CA (Civ Div)), Lord Dyson (M.R.)
s.7, applied: SI 2013/1554 r.32_3
s.8, applied: SI 2013/1554 r.32_3
s.13, see *Ismail v Secretary of State for the Home Department* [2013] EWHC 663 (Admin), [2013] Lloyd's Rep. F.C. 329 (QBD (Admin)), Goldring, L.J.; see *R. (on the application of Omar) v Secretary of State for Foreign and Commonwealth Affairs* [2012] EWHC 1737 (Admin), [2013] 1 All E.R. 161 (QBD (Admin)), Sir John Thomas (President)
s.13, applied: 2013 c.22 s.8, SI 2013/2733 Art.3, Art.4, Art.5, Art.9, Art.10
s.14, applied: SI 2013/2733 Art.3, Art.4
s.15, applied: SI 2013/1554 r.32_4, r.32_5, SI 2013/2733 Art.3, Art.4, Art.6, Art.8
s.16, applied: SI 2013/2733 Art.5, Art.9, Art.11
s.17, applied: SI 2013/2733 Art.5, Art.9, Art.10, Art.11
s.18, amended: SI 2013/602 Sch.2 para.42
s.19, applied: SI 2013/2733 Art.3, Art.7, Art.9, Art.11
s.21, applied: SI 2013/1554 r.32_10
s.27, applied: 2013 c.22 s.8
s.27, enabling: SI 2013/2733
s.29, enabling: SI 2013/1598
s.30, applied: SI 2013/1554 r.32_6, r.32_7
s.30, referred to: SI 2013/1554 r.32_6
s.31, applied: SI 2013/296 Art.3, SI 2013/1554 r.32_6, r.32_8
s.31, referred to: SI 2013/1554 r.32_6
s.47, applied: SI 2013/296 Art.3
s.48, applied: SI 2013/296 Art.3
s.50, applied: SI 2013/296
s.51, amended: SI 2013/602 Sch.2 para.42
s.51, applied: SI 2013/296 Art.3
s.51, enabling: SI 2013/296
s.56, disapplied: SI 2013/1554 r.55_5
s.56, referred to: SI 2013/1554 r.55_5
s.57, applied: SI 2013/1554 r.55_5
s.57, disapplied: SI 2013/1554 r.55_5
s.59, applied: SI 2013/1554 r.55_5
s.60, applied: SI 2013/1554 r.55_5
s.63, applied: SI 2013/1554 r.55_5
s.84, amended: SI 2013/602 Sch.2 para.42
Sch.1, applied: SI 2013/1554 r.32_4, r.32_5
Sch.1 para.6, applied: SI 2013/1554 r.32_5, SI 2013/2733 Art.3, Art.8
Sch.2 Part 1, applied: SI 2013/1554 r.32_6, r.32_7
Sch.2 Part 2, applied: SI 2013/1554 r.32_6, r.32_8
Sch.2 Part 2 para.15, applied: SI 2013/296 Art.3
Sch.3 Part 1 para.3, amended: 2013 c.22 Sch.22 para.16

38. Anti-social Behaviour Act 2003
s.2, applied: SI 2013/9 Reg.9
s.5, applied: SI 2013/9 Reg.9
s.6, applied: SI 2013/9 Reg.9
s.13, amended: 2013 c.22 Sch.9 para.52
s.20, applied: SI 2013/9 Reg.9
s.22, applied: SI 2013/9 Reg.9
s.23, enabling: SI 2013/1657
s.26, applied: SI 2013/9 Reg.9
s.26A, amended: 2013 c.22 Sch.9 para.52
s.26B, amended: 2013 c.22 Sch.9 para.52
s.26C, amended: 2013 c.22 Sch.9 para.52
s.28, amended: 2013 c.22 Sch.9 para.52
s.28, applied: SI 2013/9 Reg.9
s.94, enabling: SI 2013/1657

39. Courts Act 2003
s.1, amended: 2013 c.22 Sch.9 para.40, Sch.10 para.84
s.8, applied: SI 2013/1777, SI 2013/1878
s.8, enabling: SI 2013/1777, SI 2013/1878

s.10, amended: 2013 c.22 Sch.13 para.39
s.10, applied: SI 2013/1674 Reg.6
s.18, amended: 2013 c.22 Sch.10 para.85
s.19, amended: 2013 c.22 Sch.10 para.86
s.24, amended: 2013 c.22 Sch.13 para.38
s.26, repealed (in part): 2013 c.22 Sch.10 para.99
s.28, amended: 2013 c.22 Sch.10 para.87
s.28, repealed (in part): 2013 c.22 Sch.10 para.87
s.30, repealed (in part): 2013 c.22 Sch.10 para.88
s.34, amended: 2013 c.22 Sch.10 para.89
s.36A, added: 2013 c.22 s.26
s.41, repealed (in part): 2013 c.22 Sch.8 para.189
s.49, repealed (in part): 2013 c.22 Sch.10 para.99
s.59, amended: 2013 c.22 Sch.9 para.40
s.64, amended: 2013 c.22 Sch.9 para.40, Sch.13 para.89
s.66, amended: 2013 c.22 Sch.14 para.4
s.66, applied: SI 2013/1554 r.6_1
s.66, repealed (in part): 2013 c.22 Sch.10 para.90
s.69, applied: SI 2013/1554(a)
s.69, enabling: SI 2013/2525, SI 2013/3183
s.72, applied: SI 2013/2525, SI 2013/3183
s.75, amended: 2013 c.22 Sch.10 para.91
s.75, referred to: SI 2013/2786 Art.5
s.75, enabling: SI 2013/530, SI 2013/1472, SI 2013/3204
s.76, amended: 2013 c.22 Sch.10 para.92
s.76, repealed (in part): 2013 c.22 Sch.10 para.92
s.76, enabling: SI 2013/530, SI 2013/1472, SI 2013/3204
s.77, amended: 2013 c.22 Sch.10 para.93
s.77, repealed (in part): 2013 c.22 Sch.10 para.93
s.79, applied: SI 2013/530, SI 2013/1472, SI 2013/3204
s.81, amended: 2013 c.22 Sch.9 para.40, Sch.10 para.94
s.85, applied: 2013 c.18 Sch.3 para.3
s.92, amended: 2013 c.22 Sch.9 para.40, Sch.10 para.95
s.92, applied: SI 2013/734, SI 2013/1046 r.195, SI 2013/1407, SI 2013/1408, SI 2013/1409, SI 2013/1410, SI 2013/2302, SI 2013/3208 r.196
s.92, enabling: SI 2013/734, SI 2013/1407, SI 2013/1408, SI 2013/1409, SI 2013/1410, SI 2013/2302
s.98, amended: 2013 c.22 Sch.9 para.40
s.108, enabling: SI 2013/1407, SI 2013/1409, SI 2013/1410, SI 2013/1777, SI 2013/1878
s.111, amended: 2013 c.22 s.27
Sch.5 Part 1 para.2, amended: 2013 c.3 Sch.1 para.25
Sch.5 Part 3 para.7A, amended: 2013 c.3 Sch.1 para.26
Sch.5 Part 3 para.9A, added: 2013 c.22 s.27
Sch.5 Part 3A para.9A, amended: 2013 c.22 s.27
Sch.5 Part 3A para.9A, substituted: 2013 c.22 s.27
Sch.5 Part 3A para.9B, amended: 2013 c.22 s.27
Sch.5 Part 3A para.9C, amended: 2013 c.22 s.27
Sch.5 Part 3A para.9C, repealed (in part): 2013 c.22 s.27
Sch.5 Part 3 para.10, amended: SI 2013/630 Reg.17
Sch.5 Part 4 para.12, applied: SI 2013/1554 r.52_4
Sch.5 Part 4 para.13, amended: 2013 c.3 Sch.1 para.27, 2013 c.22 s.26
Sch.5 Part 6 para.22, applied: SI 2013/1554 r.52_4
Sch.5 Part 8 para.31, applied: SI 2013/1554 r.52_4
Sch.5 Part 9 para.37, applied: SI 2013/1554 r.52_4
Sch.5 Part 10 para.48, amended: 2013 c.22 Sch.16 para.28
Sch.6 para.2, amended: 2013 c.22 Sch.16 para.28, SI 2013/630 Reg.17
Sch.7 para.8, amended: 2013 c.22 Sch.9 para.40
Sch.8 para.69, repealed: 2013 c.22 Sch.11 para.210
Sch.8 para.85, repealed: 2013 c.22 Sch.11 para.210
Sch.8 para.88, repealed: 2013 c.22 Sch.11 para.210
Sch.8 para.89, repealed: 2013 c.22 Sch.11 para.210
Sch.8 para.90, repealed: 2013 c.22 Sch.11 para.210
Sch.8 para.92, repealed (in part): 2013 c.22 Sch.11 para.210
Sch.8 para.98, repealed: 2013 c.22 Sch.10 para.99
Sch.8 para.99, repealed: 2013 c.22 Sch.10 para.99
Sch.8 para.100, repealed: 2013 c.22 Sch.10 para.99
Sch.8 para.101, repealed: 2013 c.22 Sch.10 para.99
Sch.8 para.102, repealed: 2013 c.22 Sch.10 para.99
Sch.8 para.103, repealed: 2013 c.22 Sch.10 para.99
Sch.8 para.143, repealed: 2013 c.22 Sch.10 para.99
Sch.8 para.151, repealed: 2013 c.22 Sch.11 para.210
Sch.8 para.152, repealed: 2013 c.22 Sch.11 para.210
Sch.8 para.153, repealed: 2013 c.22 Sch.11 para.210
Sch.8 para.154, repealed (in part): 2013 c.22 Sch.11 para.210
Sch.8 para.155, repealed (in part): 2013 c.22 Sch.11 para.210
Sch.8 para.157, repealed: 2013 c.22 Sch.11 para.210
Sch.8 para.158, repealed (in part): 2013 c.22 Sch.11 para.210
Sch.8 para.159, repealed: 2013 c.22 Sch.11 para.210
Sch.8 para.160, repealed: 2013 c.22 Sch.11 para.210
Sch.8 para.161, repealed: 2013 c.22 Sch.11 para.210

Sch.8 para.162, repealed: 2013 c.22 Sch.11 para.210
Sch.8 para.163, repealed: 2013 c.22 Sch.11 para.210
Sch.8 para.169, repealed: 2013 c.22 Sch.11 para.210
Sch.8 para.170, repealed: 2013 c.22 Sch.11 para.210
Sch.8 para.193, repealed: 2013 c.22 Sch.11 para.210
Sch.8 para.194, repealed: 2013 c.22 Sch.11 para.210
Sch.8 para.195, repealed (in part): 2013 c.22 Sch.11 para.210
Sch.8 para.196, repealed (in part): 2013 c.22 Sch.11 para.210
Sch.8 para.208, repealed (in part): 2013 c.22 Sch.10 para.99
Sch.8 para.210, repealed: 2013 c.22 Sch.10 para.99
Sch.8 para.211, repealed (in part): 2013 c.22 Sch.10 para.99
Sch.8 para.214, repealed: 2013 c.22 Sch.10 para.99
Sch.8 para.215, repealed: 2013 c.22 Sch.10 para.99
Sch.8 para.216, repealed: 2013 c.22 Sch.10 para.99
Sch.8 para.217, repealed: 2013 c.22 Sch.10 para.99
Sch.8 para.228, repealed: 2013 c.22 Sch.10 para.99
Sch.8 para.229, repealed: 2013 c.22 Sch.10 para.99
Sch.8 para.268, repealed: 2013 c.22 Sch.11 para.210
Sch.8 para.269, repealed: 2013 c.22 Sch.11 para.210
Sch.8 para.336, repealed: 2013 c.22 Sch.11 para.210
Sch.8 para.338, repealed: 2013 c.22 Sch.11 para.210
Sch.8 para.349, repealed: 2013 c.22 Sch.10 para.99
Sch.8 para.412, repealed: 2013 c.22 Sch.11 para.210

41. Extradition Act 2003

see *Edwards v United States* [2013] EWHC 1906 (Admin), [2013] 4 All E.R. 871 (QBD (Admin)), Laws, L.J.; see *Kapri v Lord Advocate* [2013] UKSC 48, [2013] 1 W.L.R. 2324 (SC), Lord Hope, J.S.C. (Deputy President); see *R. (on the application of HH) v Westminster City Magistrates' Court* [2013] 1 A.C. 338 (SC), Lord Hope, J.S.C.; see *R. (on the application of Klimeto) v Westminster Magistrates' Court* [2012] EWHC 2051 (Admin), [2013] 1 W.L.R. 420 (DC), Hughes, L.J.; see *South Africa v Dewani* [2012] EWHC 842 (Admin), [2013] 1 W.L.R. 82 (DC), Sir John Thomas (President)
applied: SI 2013/614 Reg.16, Reg.17, SI 2013/1598 Art.2
Part 1, applied: SI 2013/1554 r.17_1, r.17_3, r.76_1, r.17_4, r.76_4, r.17_5, r.17_15, r.76_5, r.17_16
Part 2, applied: SI 2013/1554 r.17_1, r.17_3, r.17_4, r.17_5, r.17_8, r.76_1, r.76_4, r.17_10, r.17_15, r.17_16, r.76_5
s.1, enabling: SI 2013/1583
s.6, applied: SI 2013/1554 r.17_5, r.17_16
s.9, see *R. (on the application of Klimeto) v Westminster Magistrates' Court* [2012] EWHC 2051 (Admin), [2013] 1 W.L.R. 420 (DC), Hughes, L.J.
s.9, applied: SI 2013/1554 r.17_15
s.10, applied: SI 2013/1554 r.17_15
s.11, see *Pomiechowski v Poland* [2012] EWHC 3161 (Admin), [2013] 1 W.L.R. 2653 (QBD (Admin)), Burnett, J.
s.11, amended: 2013 c.22 Sch.20 para.2
s.19B, added: 2013 c.22 Sch.20 para.3
s.19C, added: 2013 c.22 Sch.20 para.3
s.19D, added: 2013 c.22 Sch.20 para.3
s.19E, added: 2013 c.22 Sch.20 para.3
s.19F, added: 2013 c.22 Sch.20 para.3
s.19F, applied: SI 2013/2388 Art.3
s.19F, enabling: SI 2013/2388
s.30, amended: 2013 c.22 Sch.20 para.17
s.30A, added: 2013 c.22 Sch.20 para.17
s.33B, added: 2013 c.22 Sch.20 para.19
s.33ZA, added: 2013 c.22 Sch.20 para.18
s.34, substituted: 2013 c.22 Sch.20 para.20
s.35, see *Criminal Court of Lisbon v K* 2013 S.L.T. (Sh Ct) 135 (Sh Ct (Lothian) (Edinburgh)), Sheriff F R Crowe
s.35, applied: SI 2013/1554 r.17_16
s.36, see *Criminal Court of Lisbon v K* 2013 S.L.T. (Sh Ct) 135 (Sh Ct (Lothian) (Edinburgh)), Sheriff F R Crowe
s.36, amended: 2013 c.22 Sch.20 para.21
s.36, applied: SI 2013/1554 r.17_16
s.36A, added: 2013 c.22 Sch.20 para.21
s.37, applied: SI 2013/1554 r.17_16
s.45, applied: SI 2013/1554 r.17_5
s.46, applied: SI 2013/1554 r.17_16
s.47, applied: SI 2013/1554 r.17_16
s.60, applied: SI 2013/1554 r.76_1
s.61, applied: SI 2013/1554 r.76_1
s.67, applied: SI 2013/1554 r.17_2
s.69, enabling: SI 2013/1583
s.70, amended: 2013 c.22 Sch.20 para.11
s.70, applied: SI 2013/1583 Art.1
s.71, enabling: SI 2013/1583
s.73, applied: SI 2013/1583 Art.1
s.73, enabling: SI 2013/1583
s.74, applied: SI 2013/1554 r.17_16

s.74, enabling: SI 2013/1583
s.79, amended: 2013 c.22 Sch.20 para.5
s.83A, added: 2013 c.22 Sch.20 para.6
s.83B, added: 2013 c.22 Sch.20 para.6
s.83C, added: 2013 c.22 Sch.20 para.6
s.83D, added: 2013 c.22 Sch.20 para.6
s.83E, added: 2013 c.22 Sch.20 para.6
s.83E, applied: SI 2013/2388 Art.3
s.83E, enabling: SI 2013/2388
s.84, applied: SI 2013/1554 r.17_15
s.84, enabling: SI 2013/1583
s.86, applied: SI 2013/1554 r.17_15
s.86, enabling: SI 2013/1583
s.107, amended: 2013 c.22 Sch.20 para.23
s.107A, added: 2013 c.22 Sch.20 para.23
s.108, amended: 2013 c.22 Sch.20 para.12
s.109, varied: SI 2013/2384 Art.3
s.112, amended: 2013 c.22 Sch.20 para.24
s.112A, added: 2013 c.22 Sch.20 para.24
s.115B, added: 2013 c.22 Sch.20 para.25
s.116, see *H v Lord Advocate* [2013] 1 A.C. 413 (SC), Lord Hope (Deputy President)
s.116, substituted: 2013 c.22 Sch.20 para.26
s.117, amended: 2013 c.22 Sch.20 para.13
s.117, applied: SI 2013/1554 r.17_16
s.118, see *R. (on the application of Tajik) v City of Westminster Magistrates' Court* [2012] EWHC 3347 (Admin), [2013] 1 W.L.R. 2283 (DC), Moses, L.J.
s.118, amended: 2013 c.22 Sch.20 para.27
s.118, applied: SI 2013/1554 r.17_16
s.118A, added: 2013 c.22 Sch.20 para.27
s.118B, added: 2013 c.22 Sch.20 para.28
s.127, applied: SI 2013/1554 r.17_9, r.17_11
s.133, applied: SI 2013/1554 r.76_1
s.134, applied: SI 2013/1554 r.76_1
s.139, applied: SI 2013/1554 r.17_2
s.177, applied: 2013 c.22 Sch.20 para.8, Sch.20 para.29
s.178, applied: 2013 c.22 Sch.20 para.8, Sch.20 para.29
s.180, applied: SI 2013/1554 r.17_16
s.181, applied: SI 2013/1554 r.17_16
s.187, applied: SI 2013/1554 r.17_16
s.194, applied: SI 2013/1583 Art.1
s.202, applied: SI 2013/1554 r.17_15
s.205, applied: SI 2013/1554 r.17_15
s.206A, applied: SI 2013/1554 r.17_3
s.206B, applied: SI 2013/1554 r.17_3
s.206C, applied: SI 2013/1554 r.17_3
s.222, applied: 2013 c.22 Sch.20 para.8, Sch.20 para.29
s.223, applied: SI 2013/1583
s.223, enabling: SI 2013/1583, SI 2013/2388

43. Health and Social Care (Community Health and Standards) Act 2003

s.153, enabling: SI 2013/282, SSI 2013/53
s.155, amended: 2013 c.22 Sch.9 para.52
s.157, enabling: SI 2013/2586
s.168, enabling: SSI 2013/53
s.195, applied: SI 2013/282, SI 2013/2586
s.195, enabling: SI 2013/282, SI 2013/2586, SSI 2013/53

44. Criminal Justice Act 2003

Commencement Orders: 2013 c.24 Sch.20 para.2; SI 2013/1103 Art.2, Art.3, Art.4
see *R. (on the application of Modhej) v Secretary of State for Justice* [2012] EWCA Civ 957, [2013] 1 W.L.R. 801 (CA (Civ Div)), Lord Judge, L.C.J.; see *R. v B* [2012] EWCA Crim 414, [2013] 1 W.L.R. 320 (CA (Crim Div)), Lord Judge, L.C.J.; see *R. v Garg (Sudhanshu)* [2012] EWCA Crim 2520, [2013] 2 Cr. App. R. (S.) 30 (CA (Crim Div)), Lord Judge, L.C.J.; see *R. v Reeves (Danielle Catherine)* [2012] EWCA Crim 2613, [2013] 2 Cr. App. R. (S.) 21 (CA (Crim Div)), Treacy, L.J.; see *R. v Riat (Jaspal)* [2012] EWCA Crim 1509, [2013] 1 W.L.R. 2592 (CA (Crim Div)), Hughes, L.J.; see *R. v Terry (Paul Graham)* [2012] EWCA Crim 1411, [2013] 1 Cr. App. R. (S.) 51 (CA (Crim Div)), Moses, L.J.
applied: SI 2013/1554 r.41_10, r.29_26
disapplied: SI 2013/1554 r.22_9
Part 9, applied: SI 2013/1554 r.74_1
Part 10, applied: SI 2013/1554 r.41_11, SI 2013/2786 Art.5, Art.9
Part 12, applied: SI 2013/1554 r.33_1
Part 12 c.6, applied: SI 2013/9 Reg.12
s.16, applied: SI 2013/1554 r.19_8
s.22, applied: SI 2013/1554 r.19_8
s.23A, applied: SI 2013/615 Art.2
s.23A, enabling: SI 2013/615
s.25, applied: SI 2013/801
s.25, enabling: SI 2013/801
s.29, amended: 2013 c.22 Sch.8 para.187
s.29, applied: SI 2013/1554 r.2_4, r.7_1, r.37_8
s.30, applied: SI 2013/1554 r.7_1, r.7_2
s.44, applied: SI 2013/1554 r.15_1
s.47, applied: SI 2013/1554 r.74_1, r.66_1
s.51, applied: SI 2013/1554 r.37_4, r.29_1, r.29_26
s.52, applied: SI 2013/1554 r.29_1
s.58, see *R. v M* [2012] EWCA Crim 2293, [2013] 1 W.L.R. 1083 (CA (Crim Div)), Lord Judge, L.C.J.; see *R. v Mian (Yousaf)* [2012] EWCA Crim 792, [2013] 1 W.L.R. 772 (CA (Crim Div)), Rix, L.J.
s.58, applied: SI 2013/1554 r.67_1, r.67_2
s.71, applied: SI 2013/1554 r.16_1

s.76, see *R. v B* [2012] EWCA Crim 414, [2013] 1 W.L.R. 320 (CA (Crim Div)), Lord Judge, L.C.J.
s.76, applied: SI 2013/1554 r.74_1
s.77, applied: SI 2013/1554 r.41_13, r.14_1, r.41_14, r.41_15
s.80, applied: SI 2013/1554 r.41_3, r.41_4, r.41_10, r.41_11
s.82, applied: SI 2013/1554 r.16_1, r.41_8, r.41_9
s.88, applied: SI 2013/1554 r.41_5
s.89, applied: SI 2013/1554 r.41_5, r.41_6
s.90, applied: SI 2013/1554 r.41_7
s.98, see *R. v D* [2011] EWCA Crim 1474, [2013] 1 W.L.R. 676 (CA (Crim Div)), Hughes, LJ. (V-P); see *R. v Sule (Sahid)* [2012] EWCA Crim 1130, [2013] 1 Cr. App. R. 3 (CA (Crim Div)), Stanley Burton, L.J.
s.98, applied: SI 2013/1554 r.35_1
s.100, see *R. v Dizaei (Jamshid Ali)* [2013] EWCA Crim 88, [2013] 1 W.L.R. 2257 (CA (Crim Div)), Lord Judge, L.C.J.
s.100, applied: SI 2013/1554 r.35_1
s.101, see *R. v D* [2011] EWCA Crim 1474, [2013] 1 W.L.R. 676 (CA (Crim Div)), Hughes, LJ. (V-P); see *R. v Dizaei (Jamshid Ali)* [2013] EWCA Crim 88, [2013] 1 W.L.R. 2257 (CA (Crim Div)), Lord Judge, L.C.J.
s.101, applied: SI 2013/1554 r.35_1
s.102, applied: SI 2013/1554 r.35_1
s.103, see *R. v D* [2011] EWCA Crim 1474, [2013] 1 W.L.R. 676 (CA (Crim Div)), Hughes, LJ. (V-P)
s.103, applied: SI 2013/1554 r.35_1
s.104, applied: SI 2013/1554 r.35_1
s.105, applied: SI 2013/1554 r.35_1
s.106, applied: SI 2013/1554 r.35_1
s.107, applied: SI 2013/1554 r.35_5
s.111, applied: SI 2013/1554 r.35_4
s.114, see *R. v Riat (Jaspal)* [2012] EWCA Crim 1509, [2013] 1 W.L.R. 2592 (CA (Crim Div)), Hughes, L.J.; see *R. v Turner (Simon Paul)* [2012] EWCA Crim 1786, [2013] 1 Cr. App. R. 25 (CA (Crim Div)), Lord Judge, L.C.J.
s.114, applied: SI 2013/1554 r.34_1, r.34_2, SI 2013/1852 Art.19
s.115, applied: SI 2013/1554 r.34_1
s.116, see *R. v Riat (Jaspal)* [2012] EWCA Crim 1509, [2013] 1 W.L.R. 2592 (CA (Crim Div)), Hughes, L.J.; see *R. v Rowley (William)* [2012] EWCA Crim 1434, [2013] 1 W.L.R. 895 (CA (Crim Div)), Moore-Bick, L.J.
s.116, applied: SI 2013/1554 r.29_19, r.34_2, SI 2013/1852 Art.19
s.117, see *Grazette v DPP* [2012] EWHC 3863 (Admin), (2013) 177 J.P. 259 (DC), Moses, L.J.
s.117, applied: SI 2013/1554 r.34_2
s.118, applied: SI 2013/1554 r.34_2
s.119, applied: SI 2013/1554 r.34_2
s.120, applied: SI 2013/1554 r.34_2
s.121, applied: SI 2013/1554 r.34_2
s.127, applied: SI 2013/1554 r.33_3, r.34_2
s.132, applied: SI 2013/1554 r.34_2, r.34_4
s.132, enabling: SI 2013/1554
s.133, applied: SI 2013/1554 r.27_4
s.139, applied: SI 2013/1554 r.37_4
s.148, amended: 2013 c.22 Sch.16 para.3
s.150, substituted: 2013 c.22 Sch.16 para.23
s.151, amended: 2013 c.3 Sch.1 para.29
s.154, applied: 2013 c.22 s.28, 2013 c.33 s.36
s.154, referred to: 2013 c.22 Sch.16 para.30, 2013 c.32 s.75, s.102, s.103, s.105, Sch.8 para.7, Sch.8 para.17, Sch.9 para.6, Sch.10 para.13, 2013 c.33 s.90, Sch.5 para.14, SI 2013/3182 Art.12
s.156, see *R. v Nichols (Andrew Alan)* [2012] EWCA Crim 2650, [2013] 2 Cr. App. R. (S.) 10 (CA (Crim Div)), Rafferty, L.J.
s.156, applied: SI 2013/1554 r.37_10
s.157, applied: SI 2013/1554 r.42_8
s.159, applied: SI 2013/1554 r.37_10
s.161A, amended: 2013 c.3 Sch.1 para.30
s.162, amended: 2013 c.22 Sch.16 para.24
s.162, applied: SI 2013/1554 r.37_10
s.174, applied: SI 2013/1554 r.5_4, r.37_10
s.174, enabling: SI 2013/1554
s.177, see *R. (on the application of Dragoman) v Camberwell Green Magistrates' Court* [2012] EWHC 4105 (Admin), (2013) 177 J.P. 372 (DC), Sir John Thomas (President)
s.177, amended: 2013 c.22 Sch.16 para.2, Sch.16 para.12
s.177, referred to: SI 2013/1554 r.42_2
s.177, repealed (in part): 2013 c.22 Sch.16 para.12
s.190, amended: 2013 c.22 Sch.16 para.13
s.190, applied: SI 2013/1554 r.42_2
s.190, repealed (in part): 2013 c.22 Sch.16 para.13
s.192, amended: 2013 c.22 Sch.16 para.14
s.197, amended: 2013 c.22 Sch.16 para.15
s.207, applied: SI 2013/1554 r.42_8
s.215, amended: 2013 c.22 Sch.16 para.16
s.215, applied: SI 2013/1554 r.42_2
s.215A, added: 2013 c.22 Sch.16 para.17
s.218, amended: 2013 c.22 Sch.16 para.18
s.258, applied: SI 2013/1554 r.62_5, r.62_9
s.269, applied: SI 2013/1554 r.68_1
s.274, applied: SI 2013/1554 r.68_1, r.68_2
s.280, referred to: 2013 c.33 s.90, s.93
s.281, applied: SI 2013/1460 Reg.15
s.281, referred to: 2013 c.5 s.4, 2013 c.22 Sch.4 para.3, Sch.5 para.24, 2013 c.32 s.75, s.99, Sch.8 para.18

s.282, referred to: 2013 c.22 Sch.7 para.10
s.329, see *Bank of Ireland v Colliers International UK Plc (In Administration)* [2012] EWHC 2942 (Ch), [2013] Ch. 422 (Ch D (Companies Ct)), David Richards, J.
s.329, amended: 2013 c.22 Sch.9 para.52
s.330, applied: SI 2013/801
s.330, enabling: SI 2013/1103
s.336, enabling: SI 2013/1103
Sch.8, applied: SI 2013/1554 r.44_1
Sch.8 Part 1 para.3, amended: 2013 c.22 Sch.16 para.19
Sch.8 Part 2 para.9, amended: 2013 c.22 Sch.16 para.22
Sch.8 Part 2 para.9, applied: SI 2013/1554 r.63_1
Sch.8 Part 3 para.13, applied: SI 2013/1554 r.63_1
Sch.9 Part 1 para.1, amended: 2013 c.22 Sch.16 para.20
Sch.9 Part 2 para.3, amended: 2013 c.22 Sch.16 para.20
Sch.9 Part 2 para.4, amended: 2013 c.22 Sch.16 para.20
Sch.9 Part 3 para.13, amended: 2013 c.22 Sch.16 para.20
Sch.12, applied: SI 2013/1554 r.44_1
Sch.12 Part 3 para.15, amended: 2013 c.22 Sch.16 para.21
Sch.13 Part 1 para.1, amended: 2013 c.22 Sch.16 para.20
Sch.13 Part 2 para.6, amended: 2013 c.22 Sch.16 para.20
Sch.13 Part 2 para.9, amended: 2013 c.22 Sch.16 para.20
Sch.13 Part 3 para.17, amended: 2013 c.22 Sch.16 para.20
Sch.22 para.14, applied: SI 2013/1554 r.68_1, r.68_2
Sch.25 para.28, repealed (in part): 2013 c.24 Sch.20 para.2

2004

5. Planning and Compulsory Purchase Act 2004

Part 2, applied: SI 2013/2148 Art.4
s.13, varied: SI 2013/2148 Sch.2 para.1, Sch.2 para.2, Sch.2 para.3, Sch.2 para.4
s.14, varied: SI 2013/2148 Sch.2 para.1, Sch.2 para.2, Sch.2 para.3, Sch.2 para.4
s.15, varied: SI 2013/2148 Sch.2 para.1, Sch.2 para.2, Sch.2 para.3, Sch.2 para.4
s.16, varied: SI 2013/2148 Sch.2 para.1, Sch.2 para.2, Sch.2 para.3, Sch.2 para.4
s.17, varied: SI 2013/2148 Sch.2 para.1, Sch.2 para.2, Sch.2 para.3, Sch.2 para.4
s.18, varied: SI 2013/2148 Sch.2 para.1, Sch.2 para.2, Sch.2 para.3, Sch.2 para.4
s.19, varied: SI 2013/2148 Sch.2 para.1, Sch.2 para.2, Sch.2 para.3, Sch.2 para.4
s.20, varied: SI 2013/2148 Sch.2 para.1, Sch.2 para.2, Sch.2 para.3, Sch.2 para.4
s.21, varied: SI 2013/2148 Sch.2 para.1, Sch.2 para.2, Sch.2 para.3, Sch.2 para.4
s.22, varied: SI 2013/2148 Sch.2 para.1, Sch.2 para.2, Sch.2 para.3, Sch.2 para.4
s.23, varied: SI 2013/2148 Sch.2 para.1, Sch.2 para.2, Sch.2 para.3, Sch.2 para.4
s.24, see *University of Bristol v North Somerset Council* [2013] EWHC 231 (Admin), [2013] J.P.L. 940 (QBD (Admin)), Judge Alice Robinson
s.24, varied: SI 2013/2148 Sch.2 para.1, Sch.2 para.2, Sch.2 para.3, Sch.2 para.4
s.25, varied: SI 2013/2148 Sch.2 para.1, Sch.2 para.2, Sch.2 para.3, Sch.2 para.4
s.26, varied: SI 2013/2148 Sch.2 para.1, Sch.2 para.2, Sch.2 para.3, Sch.2 para.4
s.27, varied: SI 2013/2148 Sch.2 para.1, Sch.2 para.2, Sch.2 para.3, Sch.2 para.4
s.28, varied: SI 2013/2148 Sch.2 para.1, Sch.2 para.2, Sch.2 para.3, Sch.2 para.4
s.29, varied: SI 2013/2148 Sch.2 para.1, Sch.2 para.2, Sch.2 para.3, Sch.2 para.4
s.30, varied: SI 2013/2148 Sch.2 para.1, Sch.2 para.2, Sch.2 para.3, Sch.2 para.4
s.31, varied: SI 2013/2148 Sch.2 para.1, Sch.2 para.2, Sch.2 para.3, Sch.2 para.4
s.32, varied: SI 2013/2148 Sch.2 para.1, Sch.2 para.2, Sch.2 para.3, Sch.2 para.4
s.33, varied: SI 2013/2148 Sch.2 para.1, Sch.2 para.2, Sch.2 para.3, Sch.2 para.4
s.33A, see *University of Bristol v North Somerset Council* [2013] EWHC 231 (Admin), [2013] J.P.L. 940 (QBD (Admin)), Judge Alice Robinson
s.33A, varied: SI 2013/2148 Sch.2 para.1, Sch.2 para.2, Sch.2 para.3, Sch.2 para.4
s.34, varied: SI 2013/2148 Sch.2 para.1, Sch.2 para.2, Sch.2 para.3, Sch.2 para.4
s.35, varied: SI 2013/2148 Sch.2 para.1, Sch.2 para.2, Sch.2 para.3, Sch.2 para.4
s.36, varied: SI 2013/2148 Sch.2 para.1, Sch.2 para.2, Sch.2 para.3, Sch.2 para.4
s.37, varied: SI 2013/2148 Sch.2 para.1, Sch.2 para.2, Sch.2 para.3, Sch.2 para.4
s.38A, enabling: SI 2013/798
s.54, enabling: SI 2013/1238
s.59, amended: 2013 c.27 Sch.1 para.12
s.116, enabling: SI 2013/2148

s.122, enabling: SI 2013/1238
Sch.8 para.1, applied: SI 2013/427 Art.3, SI 2013/629 Art.3, SI 2013/933 Art.3, SI 2013/934 Art.3, SI 2013/935 Art.3

6. Child Trust Funds Act 2004
s.3, enabling: SI 2013/263, SI 2013/1744
s.7, enabling: SI 2013/1744
s.12, enabling: SI 2013/263
s.15, enabling: SI 2013/263
s.28, enabling: SI 2013/263, SI 2013/1744

7. Gender Recognition Act 2004
applied: 2013 c.30 Sch.4 para.11, Sch.4 para.12, Sch.4 para.13, Sch.4 para.15
s.2, amended: 2013 c.30 Sch.5 para.16
s.3, amended: 2013 c.30 Sch.5 para.2, Sch.5 para.18
s.3A, added: 2013 c.30 Sch.5 para.17
s.3B, added: 2013 c.30 Sch.5 para.19
s.4, amended: 2013 c.30 Sch.5 para.3
s.4A, added: 2013 c.30 Sch.5 para.4
s.4B, added: 2013 c.30 Sch.5 para.4
s.5, amended: 2013 c.30 Sch.5 para.4
s.5A, amended: 2013 c.30 Sch.5 para.4
s.5B, added: 2013 c.30 Sch.5 para.5
s.6, amended: 2013 c.30 Sch.5 para.6
s.6, substituted: 2013 c.30 Sch.5 para.6
s.6, amended: 2013 c.30 Sch.5 para.5
s.7, amended: 2013 c.30 Sch.5 para.7
s.7, enabling: SI 2013/2302
s.7, amended: 2013 c.30 Sch.5 para.5
s.8, amended: 2013 c.22 Sch.11 para.160, 2013 c.30 Sch.5 para.8
s.8, amended: 2013 c.30 Sch.5 para.5
s.10, amended: 2013 c.30 Sch.5 para.9
s.11A, added: 2013 c.30 Sch.5 para.10
s.11B, added: 2013 c.30 Sch.5 para.11
s.21, amended: 2013 c.30 Sch.5 para.12
s.22, amended: 2013 c.30 Sch.5 para.13
s.25, amended: 2013 c.30 Sch.5 para.14
Sch.1, amended: SI 2013/2042 Sch.1 para.28
Sch.1 para.4, amended: 2013 c.30 Sch.5 para.20
Sch.1 para.6, amended: SI 2013/2042 Sch.1 para.28
Sch.1 para.9, amended: SI 2013/2042 Sch.1 para.28
Sch.3 Part 1 para.11A, added: 2013 c.30 Sch.5 para.9

8. Higher Education Act 2004
s.24, enabling: SI 2013/3106
s.28, enabling: SI 2013/1792
s.47, enabling: SI 2013/1792, SI 2013/3106

10. Age-Related Payments Act 2004
s.6, applied: SI 2013/2980 Reg.5
s.7, amended: SI 2013/1442 Art.3
s.7, applied: SI 2013/1442 Art.2, SI 2013/2980
s.7, enabling: SI 2013/2980

11. Gangmasters (Licensing) Act 2004
s.6, applied: SI 2013/2216 Reg.2
s.6, enabling: SI 2013/2216

12. Finance Act 2004
applied: SI 2013/2356 Reg.17, Reg.18, Reg.25, Reg.26, Reg.28, Reg.29, Reg.34, Reg.87, SSI 2013/174 Reg.11, Reg.15, Reg.23
Part 4, applied: 2013 c.29 Sch.22 para.1, SSI 2013/174 Reg.1, Reg.5, Reg.10, Reg.12, Reg.13, Reg.14, Reg.17
Part 4 c.2, applied: SSI 2013/174 Reg.5, Reg.16
Part 7, applied: SI 2013/2571 Reg.4, SI 2013/2892 Reg.12
s.62, enabling: SI 2013/620
s.75, enabling: SI 2013/620
s.150, amended: 2013 c.29 s.53
s.150, enabling: SI 2013/2259
s.153, applied: 2013 c.29 Sch.22 para.1, SI 2013/376 Sch.10 para.10, SI 2013/2734 Sch.1 para.2, Sch.6 para.8
s.158, amended: SI 2013/1114 Art.2
s.164, applied: SI 2013/2356 Reg.34
s.164, enabling: SI 2013/1818
s.165, amended: 2013 c.29 s.50
s.166, applied: SI 2013/2356 Reg.34
s.167, amended: 2013 c.29 s.50
s.168, applied: SI 2013/2356 Reg.34
s.169, amended: 2013 c.29 s.53
s.169, applied: SI 2013/2356 Reg.96
s.169, enabling: SI 2013/2259
s.185G, amended: 2013 c.29 Sch.46 para.120
s.188, applied: SI 2013/765 Sch.2 para.3, Sch.2 para.4, SI 2013/3177 Sch.5 para.4, Sch.5 para.5, Sch.6 para.3, Sch.6 para.4
s.188, repealed (in part): 2013 c.29 s.52
s.190, repealed (in part): 2013 c.29 s.52
s.196, repealed (in part): 2013 c.29 s.52
s.202, repealed (in part): 2013 c.29 s.52
s.205, amended: 2013 c.29 Sch.46 para.121
s.205, applied: SSI 2013/174 Reg.16, Reg.18
s.205A, amended: 2013 c.29 Sch.46 para.122
s.205A, applied: SSI 2013/174 Reg.9
s.206, amended: 2013 c.29 Sch.46 para.123
s.206, applied: SI 2013/2356 Reg.17, SSI 2013/174 Reg.9, Reg.23
s.207, amended: 2013 c.29 Sch.46 para.124
s.208, amended: 2013 c.29 Sch.46 para.125
s.209, amended: 2013 c.29 Sch.46 para.126
s.214, applied: SSI 2013/174 Reg.9
s.216, applied: SSI 2013/174 Reg.9
s.217, amended: 2013 c.29 Sch.46 para.127
s.218, amended: 2013 c.29 s.48, Sch.22 para.6

s.219, amended: 2013 c.29 Sch.22 para.7
s.228, amended: 2013 c.29 s.49
s.228, applied: SI 2013/2356 Reg.56
s.229, applied: SSI 2013/174 Reg.11
s.230, applied: 2013 c.29 Sch.22 para.1
s.231, applied: 2013 c.29 Sch.22 para.1
s.232, applied: 2013 c.29 Sch.22 para.1
s.233, applied: 2013 c.29 Sch.22 para.1
s.233, repealed (in part): 2013 c.29 s.52
s.234, applied: 2013 c.29 Sch.22 para.1
s.235, applied: 2013 c.29 Sch.22 para.1
s.236, applied: 2013 c.29 Sch.22 para.1
s.236A, applied: 2013 c.29 Sch.22 para.1
s.237, applied: 2013 c.29 Sch.22 para.1
s.237A, amended: 2013 c.29 Sch.46 para.128
s.237A, applied: SSI 2013/174 Reg.9
s.237B, amended: 2013 c.29 Sch.46 para.129
s.237B, applied: SI 2013/2356 Reg.86, SSI 2013/174 Reg.9
s.237B, referred to: SSI 2013/174 Reg.9
s.237D, applied: SSI 2013/174 Reg.9
s.237E, applied: SSI 2013/174 Reg.9
s.239, amended: 2013 c.29 Sch.46 para.130
s.241, applied: SSI 2013/174 Reg.14
s.242, amended: 2013 c.29 Sch.46 para.131
s.251, enabling: SI 2013/1741, SI 2013/1742, SI 2013/2259
s.254, enabling: SI 2013/1111
s.256, referred to: SSI 2013/174 Reg.2
s.260, repealed (in part): SI 2013/1114 Art.5
s.273ZA, enabling: SI 2013/605, SI 2013/1810
s.275, applied: SI 2013/2356 Reg.17
s.280, amended: 2013 c.29 s.53
s.281, enabling: SI 2013/1114
s.282, enabling: SI 2013/1114, SI 2013/1742, SI 2013/1818, SI 2013/2259
s.306, enabling: SI 2013/2571, SI 2013/2595
s.308, applied: SI 2013/2592 Reg.2, SI 2013/2595 Reg.1
s.308, enabling: SI 2013/2592
s.309, applied: 2013 c.29 Sch.33 para.25
s.310, applied: 2013 c.29 Sch.33 para.25
s.312B, added: 2013 c.29 s.223
s.312B, enabling: SI 2013/2592
s.313, applied: 2013 c.29 Sch.33 para.25
s.313, enabling: SI 2013/2592
s.313ZA, enabling: SI 2013/2592
s.313ZB, added: 2013 c.29 s.223
s.313ZB, enabling: SI 2013/2592
s.317, enabling: SI 2013/2571, SI 2013/2592, SI 2013/2595
s.318, amended: 2013 c.29 Sch.35 para.2
s.318, enabling: SI 2013/2592
Sch.11 Part 1 para.4, enabling: SI 2013/620
Sch.11 Part 2 para.8, enabling: SI 2013/620
Sch.11 Part 3 para.12, enabling: SI 2013/620
Sch.24 para.3, repealed (in part): 2013 c.29 Sch.29 para.11
Sch.28, applied: SSI 2013/174 Reg.19
Sch.28 Part 1 para.2, amended: 2013 c.29 s.51
Sch.28 Part 1 para.2, enabling: SI 2013/1111
Sch.28 Part 2 para.15, applied: SSI 2013/174 Reg.13, Reg.15, Reg.17
Sch.29 Part 1 para.1, amended: 2013 c.29 s.51
Sch.29 Part 1 para.1, applied: SSI 2013/174 Reg.14
Sch.29 Part 1 para.2, amended: 2013 c.29 Sch.22 para.8
Sch.29 Part 1 para.2, applied: SSI 2013/174 Reg.10, Reg.14
Sch.29 Part 1 para.5, amended: 2013 c.29 s.52
Sch.29 Part 1 para.7, applied: SI 2013/2356 Reg.81, SI 2013/3029 Sch.1 para.16, SI 2013/3035 Sch.1, SSI 2013/174 Reg.6
Sch.29 Part 1 para.8, amended: 2013 c.29 Sch.22 para.8
Sch.29 Part 2 para.14, applied: SSI 2013/174 Reg.9
Sch.29 Part 2 para.20, applied: SSI 2013/174 Reg.6
Sch.29A Part 3 para.15, amended: SI 2013/636 Sch.1 para.7
Sch.34, applied: 2013 c.29 Sch.22 para.1
Sch.34 para.13, applied: 2013 c.29 Sch.22 para.1
Sch.34 para.18, applied: 2013 c.29 Sch.22 para.1
Sch.36 Part 1 para.1, applied: SI 2013/2734 Sch.1 para.2
Sch.36 Part 2 para.7, disapplied: 2013 c.29 Sch.22 para.1, SI 2013/1741 Reg.4
Sch.36 Part 2 para.12, applied: 2013 c.29 Sch.22 para.1
Sch.36 Part 2 para.12, disapplied: 2013 c.29 Sch.22 para.1, SI 2013/1741 Reg.4
Sch.36 Part 2 para.12, varied: 2013 c.29 Sch.22 para.1
Sch.36 Part 2 para.14, applied: 2013 c.29 Sch.22 para.1
Sch.36 Part 2 para.14, repealed (in part): 2013 c.29 s.52
Sch.36 Part 2 para.17A, varied: 2013 c.29 Sch.22 para.1
Sch.36 Part 3 para.34, amended: SI 2013/1114 Art.3

15. Carers (Equal Opportunities) Act 2004

s.3, applied: SI 2013/261 Sch.1 para.25

17. Health Protection Agency Act 2004

referred to: SI 2013/160 Art.8
Sch.1 para.22, applied: SI 2013/160 Art.8

Sch.1 para.23, applied: SI 2013/160 Art.8
Sch.1 para.24, applied: SI 2013/160 Art.8
Sch.1 para.25, applied: SI 2013/160 Art.8
Sch.1 para.26, applied: SI 2013/160 Art.8
Sch.1 para.27, applied: SI 2013/160 Art.8

19. Asylum and Immigration (Treatment of Claimants, etc.) Act 2004

s.4, applied: SI 2013/470 Art.4, Art.6, SI 2013/817 Reg.3
s.19, enabling: SI 2013/226
s.20, applied: SI 2013/226
s.42, applied: SI 2013/749

20. Energy Act 2004

applied: SI 2013/1046 r.36, r.146, SI 2013/1047 r.47, r.102, SI 2013/1203 Sch.1 para.9
referred to: SI 2013/1046 r.2, SI 2013/1047 r.2
s.14, amended: 2013 c.32 Sch.12 para.78, SI 2013/755 Sch.2 para.426
s.56, applied: SI 2013/602 Art.10
s.59, amended: SI 2013/602 Sch.2 para.44
s.59A, amended: 2013 c.22 Sch.8 para.155
s.62, amended: SI 2013/602 Sch.2 para.44
s.64, amended: SI 2013/602 Sch.2 para.44
s.65, amended: SI 2013/602 Sch.2 para.44
s.66, amended: SI 2013/602 Sch.2 para.44
s.68, amended: SI 2013/602 Sch.2 para.44
s.68, repealed (in part): SI 2013/602 Sch.2 para.44
s.76, applied: 2013 c.32 s.116
s.78, repealed (in part): 2013 c.32 Sch.12 para.30
s.105, applied: SI 2013/343 Art.10, Sch.1 para.16, SI 2013/1203 Art.9, Sch.1 para.18, Sch.2 para.19, SI 2013/1734 Art.7, Sch.1 para.22
s.106, applied: SI 2013/1203 Sch.2 para.3, SI 2013/1734 Sch.2 para.3
s.108, applied: SI 2013/1203 Sch.2 para.3, SI 2013/1734 Sch.2 para.3
s.124, applied: SI 2013/816
s.124, enabling: SI 2013/816
s.125A, enabling: SI 2013/816
s.125B, enabling: SI 2013/816
s.126, enabling: SI 2013/816
s.127, enabling: SI 2013/816
s.129, enabling: SI 2013/816
s.132, enabling: SI 2013/816
s.137, amended: 2013 c.32 s.65
s.146, amended: 2013 c.32 s.65
s.154, amended: 2013 c.32 s.48
s.154, applied: SI 2013/1046 r.205
s.155, amended: 2013 c.32 s.48
s.155, applied: SI 2013/1046 r.205
s.156, applied: SI 2013/1046 r.8, r.205
s.156, referred to: SI 2013/1046 r.8, r.90, SI 2013/1047 r.6, r.65
s.157, applied: SI 2013/1046 r.13, r.205
s.158, applied: SI 2013/1046 r.6, r.33, r.205, SI 2013/1047 r.34
s.158, referred to: SI 2013/1046 r.20, SI 2013/1047 r.15
s.159, applied: SI 2013/1046 r.205
s.159, enabling: SI 2013/1046, SI 2013/1047, SI 2013/2950
s.160, applied: SI 2013/1046 r.205
s.161, applied: SI 2013/1046 r.205
s.162, applied: SI 2013/1046 r.205
s.163, applied: SI 2013/1046 r.14, r.205, SI 2013/1047 r.9
s.164, applied: SI 2013/1046 r.6, r.8, r.12, r.14, r.205, SI 2013/1047 r.6, r.9
s.165, applied: SI 2013/1046 r.205
s.166, applied: SI 2013/1046 r.205
s.167, applied: SI 2013/1046 r.205
s.168, applied: SI 2013/1046 r.205
s.169, applied: SI 2013/1046 r.205
s.170, applied: SI 2013/1046 r.205
s.171, applied: SI 2013/1046 r.205
s.172, referred to: 2013 c.32 s.38
s.173, amended: 2013 c.24 Sch.6 para.102
s.173, applied: SI 2013/2429 Art.3, Art.4
s.173, enabling: SI 2013/2429
s.174, amended: 2013 c.24 Sch.6 para.103
s.174, repealed (in part): 2013 c.24 Sch.6 para.103
s.175, amended: 2013 c.24 Sch.6 para.104
s.176, repealed: 2013 c.24 Sch.6 para.105
s.177, repealed: 2013 c.24 Sch.6 para.106
s.188, enabling: SI 2013/495, SI 2013/1138, SI 2013/1986
s.192, enabling: SI 2013/816
Sch.2 para.4, amended: 2013 c.32 Sch.12 para.79, SI 2013/755 Sch.2 para.427
Sch.2 para.5, amended: 2013 c.32 Sch.12 para.79, SI 2013/755 Sch.2 para.427
Sch.3 para.2, amended: 2013 c.32 Sch.12 para.80, SI 2013/755 Sch.2 para.428
Sch.3 para.3, amended: 2013 c.32 Sch.12 para.80, SI 2013/755 Sch.2 para.428
Sch.20, applied: SI 2013/1046 r.205, SI 2013/1047 r.2
Sch.20, referred to: SI 2013/1047 r.2, r.6, r.9
Sch.20 Part 1 para.1, varied: SI 2013/1046 r.2, r.8, r.12, r.14
Sch.20 Part 1 para.2, varied: SI 2013/1046 r.2, r.8, r.12, r.14
Sch.20 Part 2 para.3, varied: SI 2013/1046 r.2, r.8, r.12, r.14
Sch.20 Part 2 para.4, varied: SI 2013/1046 r.2, r.8, r.12, r.14
Sch.20 Part 2 para.5, varied: SI 2013/1046 r.2, r.8, r.12, r.14

Sch.20 Part 2 para.6, varied: SI 2013/1046 r.2, r.8, r.12, r.14
Sch.20 Part 2 para.7, varied: SI 2013/1046 r.2, r.8, r.12, r.14
Sch.20 Part 2 para.8, varied: SI 2013/1046 r.2, r.8, r.12, r.14
Sch.20 Part 2 para.9, varied: SI 2013/1046 r.2, r.8, r.12, r.14
Sch.20 Part 2 para.10, varied: SI 2013/1046 r.2, r.8, r.12, r.14
Sch.20 Part 2 para.11, varied: SI 2013/1046 r.2, r.8, r.12, r.14
Sch.20 Part 2 para.12, varied: SI 2013/1046 r.2, r.8, r.12, r.14
Sch.20 Part 2 para.13, varied: SI 2013/1046 r.2, r.8, r.12, r.14
Sch.20 Part 2 para.14, varied: SI 2013/1046 r.2, r.8, r.12, r.14
Sch.20 Part 2 para.15, varied: SI 2013/1046 r.2, r.8, r.12, r.14
Sch.20 Part 2 para.16, varied: SI 2013/1046 r.2, r.8, r.12, r.14
Sch.20 Part 2 para.17, varied: SI 2013/1046 r.2, r.8, r.12, r.14
Sch.20 Part 2 para.18, varied: SI 2013/1046 r.2, r.8, r.12, r.14
Sch.20 Part 2 para.19, varied: SI 2013/1046 r.2, r.8, r.12, r.14
Sch.20 Part 2 para.20, varied: SI 2013/1046 r.2, r.8, r.12, r.14
Sch.20 Part 2 para.21, varied: SI 2013/1046 r.2, r.8, r.12, r.14
Sch.20 Part 2 para.22, varied: SI 2013/1046 r.2, r.8, r.12, r.14
Sch.20 Part 2 para.23, varied: SI 2013/1046 r.2, r.8, r.12, r.14
Sch.20 Part 2 para.24, varied: SI 2013/1046 r.2, r.8, r.12, r.14
Sch.20 Part 2 para.25, varied: SI 2013/1046 r.2, r.8, r.12, r.14
Sch.20 Part 2 para.26, varied: SI 2013/1046 r.2, r.8, r.12, r.14
Sch.20 Part 2 para.27, varied: SI 2013/1046 r.2, r.8, r.12, r.14
Sch.20 Part 2 para.28, varied: SI 2013/1046 r.2, r.8, r.12, r.14
Sch.20 Part 2 para.29, varied: SI 2013/1046 r.2, r.8, r.12, r.14
Sch.20 Part 2 para.30, varied: SI 2013/1046 r.2, r.8, r.12, r.14
Sch.20 Part 2 para.31, varied: SI 2013/1046 r.2, r.8, r.12, r.14
Sch.20 Part 2 para.32, varied: SI 2013/1046 r.2, r.8, r.12, r.14
Sch.20 Part 3 para.33, varied: SI 2013/1046 r.2, r.8, r.12, r.14
Sch.20 Part 3 para.34, varied: SI 2013/1046 r.2, r.8, r.12, r.14
Sch.20 Part 3 para.35, varied: SI 2013/1046 r.2, r.8, r.12, r.14
Sch.20 Part 3 para.36, varied: SI 2013/1046 r.2, r.8, r.12, r.14
Sch.20 Part 3 para.37, varied: SI 2013/1046 r.2, r.8, r.12, r.14
Sch.20 Part 3 para.38, varied: SI 2013/1046 r.2, r.8, r.12, r.14
Sch.20 Part 3 para.39, varied: SI 2013/1046 r.2, r.8, r.12, r.14
Sch.20 Part 3 para.40, varied: SI 2013/1046 r.2, r.8, r.12, r.14
Sch.20 Part 4 para.41, varied: SI 2013/1046 r.2, r.8, r.12, r.14
Sch.20 Part 4 para.42, varied: SI 2013/1046 r.2, r.8, r.12, r.14
Sch.20 Part 4 para.43, varied: SI 2013/1046 r.2, r.8, r.12, r.14
Sch.20 Part 4 para.44, varied: SI 2013/1046 r.2, r.8, r.12, r.14
Sch.20 Part 4 para.45, varied: SI 2013/1046 r.2, r.8, r.12, r.14
Sch.20 Part 4 para.46, varied: SI 2013/1046 r.2, r.8, r.12, r.14
Sch.20 Part 4 para.47, varied: SI 2013/1046 r.2, r.8, r.12, r.14
Sch.21, applied: SI 2013/1046 r.205
Sch.22, applied: 2013 c.24 Sch.4 para.48
Sch.22 para.1, amended: 2013 c.24 Sch.6 para.107
Sch.22 para.2, amended: 2013 c.24 Sch.6 para.107
Sch.22 para.3, amended: 2013 c.24 Sch.6 para.107
Sch.22 para.4, amended: 2013 c.24 Sch.6 para.107
Sch.22 para.5, amended: 2013 c.24 Sch.6 para.107
Sch.22 para.5, repealed (in part): 2013 c.24 Sch.6 para.107
Sch.22 para.6, amended: 2013 c.24 Sch.6 para.107
Sch.22 para.7, amended: 2013 c.24 Sch.6 para.107
Sch.22 para.8, amended: 2013 c.24 Sch.6 para.107
Sch.22 para.9, amended: 2013 c.24 Sch.6 para.107
Sch.22 para.10, amended: 2013 c.24 Sch.6 para.107
Sch.22 para.11, amended: 2013 c.24 Sch.6 para.107
Sch.22 para.12, amended: 2013 c.24 Sch.6 para.107
Sch.22 para.13, amended: 2013 c.24 Sch.6 para.107
Sch.22 para.15, amended: 2013 c.24 Sch.6 para.107

21. Fire and Rescue Services Act 2004

applied: SI 2013/378 Reg.44, Sch.1 para.6, SI 2013/2356 Sch.2 para.5
s.2, applied: SI 2013/3029 Sch.3 para.3, Sch.8 para.9, SI 2013/3035 Sch.1
s.4, applied: SI 2013/3029 Sch.3 para.3, SI 2013/3035 Sch.1
s.5A, applied: SI 2013/2356 Reg.31
s.28, applied: SI 2013/1120 Art.2, SI 2013/3155 Art.2
s.28, enabling: SI 2013/1120, SI 2013/3155
s.34, amended: 2013 c.25 Sch.8 para.27, SI 2013/602 Sch.1 para.7
s.34, applied: 2013 c.25 Sch.5 para.21, Sch.6 para.8, SI 2013/704, SI 2013/735, SI 2013/1393, SI 2013/1577, SSI 2013/129, SSI 2013/186
s.34, enabling: SI 2013/704, SI 2013/735, SI 2013/1393, SI 2013/1577, SSI 2013/129, SSI 2013/186
s.35, amended: SI 2013/602 Sch.1 para.7
s.44, applied: SI 2013/602 Art.17, Art.21
s.45, applied: SI 2013/602 Art.17, Art.21
s.45, referred to: SI 2013/602 Art.17
s.46, applied: SI 2013/602 Art.17, Art.21
s.60, enabling: SI 2013/704, SI 2013/735, SI 2013/1393, SI 2013/1577, SSI 2013/129, SSI 2013/186
s.62, enabling: SI 2013/735, SI 2013/1577

23. Public Audit (Wales) Act 2004
s.32, amended: 2013 c.22 Sch.9 para.124
s.39, applied: SI 2013/217
s.39, enabling: SI 2013/217
s.58, enabling: SI 2013/217

24. Employment Relations Act 2004
s.47, repealed (in part): 2013 c.24 Sch.20 para.2
Sch.1 para.1, repealed (in part): 2013 c.24 Sch.20 para.2

25. Horserace Betting and Olympic Lottery Act 2004
s.9, amended: 2013 c.22 Sch.9 para.52
s.14, applied: SI 2013/207 Art.6
s.21, amended: SI 2013/2329 Sch.1 para.27
s.22, amended: SI 2013/2329 Sch.1 para.27
s.26, amended: SI 2013/2329 Sch.1 para.27
s.31, amended: SI 2013/2329 Sch.1 para.27
s.32, enabling: SI 2013/207
Sch.5 Part 2 para.14, applied: SI 2013/207 Art.5

28. Domestic Violence, Crime and Victims Act 2004
s.5, applied: SI 2013/435 Sch.1 Part 7
s.17, applied: SI 2013/1554 r.15_1
s.32, applied: SI 2013/2907
s.33, applied: SI 2013/2907
s.33, enabling: SI 2013/2907
s.37, enabling: SI 2013/2907
s.55, applied: SI 2013/2853 Art.2
s.55, repealed: SI 2013/2853 Art.2
Sch.9 para.13, amended: 2013 c.22 Sch.8 para.186

30. Human Tissue Act 2004
applied: SI 2013/1629 Reg.14

31. Children Act 2004
Commencement Orders: SI 2013/2247 Art.2
s.10, applied: SI 2013/261 Sch.1 para.26
s.11, amended: 2013 c.22 s.8
s.11, applied: SI 2013/261 Sch.1 para.27
s.14, enabling: SI 2013/2299
s.15A, applied: SI 2013/2299 Reg.2
s.15A, enabling: SI 2013/2299
s.28, amended: 2013 c.22 s.8
s.66, enabling: SI 2013/2299
s.67, enabling: SI 2013/2247

32. Armed Forces (Pensions and Compensation) Act 2004
applied: SI 2013/3029 Sch.2 para.5, Sch.2 para.6
s.1, amended: 2013 c.25 Sch.8 para.28
s.1, applied: 2013 c.25 Sch.5 para.29, Sch.6 para.16, Sch.6 para.17
s.1, enabling: SI 2013/436, SI 2013/591, SI 2013/796, SI 2013/2914, SI 2013/3021, SI 2013/3233
s.10, applied: SI 2013/796, SI 2013/3233
s.10, enabling: SI 2013/591, SI 2013/796, SI 2013/2914, SI 2013/3021, SI 2013/3233

33. Civil Partnership Act 2004
see *Walker v Innospec Ltd* [2013] Pens. L.R. 21 (ET), Judge Russell
applied: 2013 asp 11 Sch.1 para.5, SI 2013/3174 Art.3, Art.4
referred to: 2013 c.30 s.15
Part 5 c.1, applied: 2013 c.30 s.9
s.1, amended: 2013 c.30 Sch.7 para.34
s.4, amended: 2013 c.30 Sch.7 para.35
s.6A, enabling: SI 2013/2294
s.37, amended: 2013 c.22 Sch.11 para.162
s.44, applied: SI 2013/104 Reg.25
s.46, amended: 2013 c.22 Sch.11 para.163
s.58, amended: 2013 c.22 Sch.11 para.164
s.66, amended: 2013 c.22 Sch.11 para.165
s.66, repealed (in part): 2013 c.22 Sch.11 para.165
s.113, applied: SSI 2013/357 Art.3
s.210, amended: 2013 c.30 Sch.7 para.36
s.210, applied: 2013 c.30 s.9
s.211, applied: 2013 c.30 s.9
s.213, amended: 2013 c.30 Sch.2 para.5
s.220, amended: 2013 c.22 Sch.11 para.166
s.222, amended: 2013 c.13 Sch.2 para.3
s.222, repealed (in part): 2013 c.13 Sch.2 para.3
s.241, enabling: SI 2013/2872
s.244, enabling: SI 2013/2872
s.258, enabling: SI 2013/2294

Sch.1 Part 2 para.6, amended: 2013 c.22 Sch.11 para.167
Sch.1 Part 2 para.7, amended: 2013 c.22 Sch.11 para.167
Sch.2 Part 4 para.15, amended: 2013 c.22 Sch.11 para.168
Sch.2 Part 4 para.15, repealed (in part): 2013 c.22 Sch.11 para.168
Sch.5, applied: 2013 asp 11 Sch.1 para.5
Sch.5 Part 1, applied: SI 2013/3177 Sch.5 para.1, Sch.6 para.1
Sch.5 Part 1 para.1, amended: 2013 c.22 Sch.11 para.177
Sch.5 Part 1 para.2, amended: 2013 c.22 Sch.11 para.177
Sch.5 Part 1 para.3, amended: 2013 c.22 Sch.11 para.177
Sch.5 Part 1 para.4, amended: 2013 c.22 Sch.11 para.177
Sch.5 Part 1 para.5, amended: 2013 c.22 Sch.11 para.177
Sch.5 Part 2 para.6, amended: 2013 c.22 Sch.11 para.177
Sch.5 Part 2 para.7, amended: 2013 c.22 Sch.11 para.177
Sch.5 Part 2 para.8, amended: 2013 c.22 Sch.11 para.177
Sch.5 Part 2 para.9, amended: 2013 c.22 Sch.11 para.177
Sch.5 Part 3 para.10, amended: 2013 c.22 Sch.11 para.177
Sch.5 Part 3 para.11, amended: 2013 c.22 Sch.11 para.177
Sch.5 Part 3 para.12, amended: 2013 c.22 Sch.11 para.177
Sch.5 Part 3 para.13, amended: 2013 c.22 Sch.11 para.177
Sch.5 Part 3 para.14, amended: 2013 c.22 Sch.11 para.177
Sch.5 Part 4A para.19A, amended: 2013 c.22 Sch.11 para.177
Sch.5 Part 4A para.19B, amended: 2013 c.22 Sch.11 para.177
Sch.5 Part 4A para.19C, amended: 2013 c.22 Sch.11 para.177
Sch.5 Part 4A para.19D, amended: 2013 c.22 Sch.11 para.177
Sch.5 Part 4A para.19E, amended: 2013 c.22 Sch.11 para.177
Sch.5 Part 4A para.19F, amended: 2013 c.22 Sch.11 para.177
Sch.5 Part 4 para.15, amended: 2013 c.22 Sch.11 para.177
Sch.5 Part 4 para.16, amended: 2013 c.22 Sch.11 para.177
Sch.5 Part 4 para.17, amended: 2013 c.22 Sch.11 para.177
Sch.5 Part 4 para.18, amended: 2013 c.22 Sch.11 para.177
Sch.5 Part 4 para.19, amended: 2013 c.22 Sch.11 para.177
Sch.5 Part 5 para.20, amended: 2013 c.22 Sch.11 para.177
Sch.5 Part 5 para.21, amended: 2013 c.22 Sch.11 para.177
Sch.5 Part 5 para.22, amended: 2013 c.22 Sch.11 para.177
Sch.5 Part 5 para.23, amended: 2013 c.22 Sch.11 para.177
Sch.5 Part 6, applied: SI 2013/3177 Sch.5 para.1, Sch.6 para.1
Sch.5 Part 6 para.24, amended: 2013 c.22 Sch.11 para.177
Sch.5 Part 6 para.25, amended: 2013 c.22 Sch.11 para.177
Sch.5 Part 6 para.25, applied: SI 2013/503 Reg.5
Sch.5 Part 6 para.26, amended: 2013 c.22 Sch.11 para.177
Sch.5 Part 6 para.26, applied: SI 2013/503 Reg.5
Sch.5 Part 6 para.27, amended: 2013 c.22 Sch.11 para.177
Sch.5 Part 6 para.28, amended: 2013 c.22 Sch.11 para.177
Sch.5 Part 6 para.29, amended: 2013 c.22 Sch.11 para.177
Sch.5 Part 7, applied: SI 2013/3177 Sch.5 para.1, Sch.6 para.1
Sch.5 Part 7 para.30, amended: 2013 c.22 Sch.11 para.177
Sch.5 Part 7 para.31, amended: 2013 c.22 Sch.11 para.177
Sch.5 Part 7 para.32, amended: 2013 c.22 Sch.11 para.177
Sch.5 Part 7 para.33, amended: 2013 c.22 Sch.11 para.177
Sch.5 Part 7 para.34, amended: 2013 c.22 Sch.11 para.177
Sch.5 Part 7 para.34A, amended: 2013 c.22 Sch.11 para.177
Sch.5 Part 7 para.34B, amended: 2013 c.22 Sch.11 para.177
Sch.5 Part 7 para.35, amended: 2013 c.22 Sch.11 para.177
Sch.5 Part 7 para.36, amended: 2013 c.22 Sch.11 para.177
Sch.5 Part 7 para.37, amended: 2013 c.22 Sch.11 para.177

Sch.5 Part 8 para.38, amended: 2013 c.22 Sch.11 para.177
Sch.5 Part 8 para.38A, amended: 2013 c.22 Sch.11 para.177
Sch.5 Part 8 para.38B, amended: 2013 c.22 Sch.11 para.177
Sch.5 Part 9 para.39, amended: 2013 c.22 Sch.11 para.177
Sch.5 Part 9 para.40, amended: 2013 c.22 Sch.11 para.177
Sch.5 Part 9 para.41, amended: 2013 c.22 Sch.11 para.177
Sch.5 Part 9 para.42, amended: 2013 c.22 Sch.11 para.177
Sch.5 Part 9 para.43, amended: 2013 c.22 Sch.11 para.177
Sch.5 Part 9 para.44, amended: 2013 c.22 Sch.11 para.177
Sch.5 Part 9 para.45, amended: 2013 c.22 Sch.11 para.177
Sch.5 Part 10 para.46, amended: 2013 c.22 Sch.11 para.177
Sch.5 Part 10 para.47, amended: 2013 c.22 Sch.11 para.177
Sch.5 Part 10 para.48, amended: 2013 c.22 Sch.11 para.177
Sch.5 Part 10 para.49, amended: 2013 c.22 Sch.11 para.177
Sch.5 Part 11 para.50, amended: 2013 c.22 Sch.11 para.177
Sch.5 Part 11 para.51, amended: 2013 c.22 Sch.11 para.177
Sch.5 Part 11 para.52, amended: 2013 c.22 Sch.11 para.177
Sch.5 Part 11 para.53, amended: 2013 c.22 Sch.11 para.177
Sch.5 Part 11 para.54, amended: 2013 c.22 Sch.11 para.177
Sch.5 Part 11 para.55, amended: 2013 c.22 Sch.11 para.177
Sch.5 Part 11 para.56, amended: 2013 c.22 Sch.11 para.177
Sch.5 Part 11 para.57, amended: 2013 c.22 Sch.11 para.177
Sch.5 Part 11 para.58, amended: 2013 c.22 Sch.11 para.177
Sch.5 Part 11 para.59, amended: 2013 c.22 Sch.11 para.177
Sch.5 Part 11 para.60, amended: 2013 c.22 Sch.11 para.177
Sch.5 Part 11 para.61, amended: 2013 c.22 Sch.11 para.177
Sch.5 Part 11 para.62, amended: 2013 c.22 Sch.11 para.177
Sch.5 Part 12 para.63, amended: 2013 c.22 Sch.11 para.170, Sch.11 para.177
Sch.5 Part 12 para.64, amended: 2013 c.22 Sch.11 para.171, Sch.11 para.177
Sch.5 Part 12 para.64, repealed (in part): 2013 c.22 Sch.11 para.171
Sch.5 Part 12 para.65, amended: 2013 c.22 Sch.11 para.172, Sch.11 para.177
Sch.5 Part 12 para.65, repealed (in part): 2013 c.22 Sch.11 para.172
Sch.5 Part 13 para.66, amended: 2013 c.22 Sch.11 para.177
Sch.5 Part 13 para.67, amended: 2013 c.22 Sch.11 para.177
Sch.5 Part 13 para.68, amended: 2013 c.22 Sch.11 para.177
Sch.5 Part 13 para.69, amended: 2013 c.22 Sch.11 para.173, Sch.11 para.177
Sch.5 Part 13 para.70, amended: 2013 c.22 Sch.11 para.177
Sch.5 Part 13 para.70, repealed: 2013 c.22 Sch.11 para.174
Sch.5 Part 13 para.71, amended: 2013 c.22 Sch.11 para.177
Sch.5 Part 13 para.72, amended: 2013 c.22 Sch.11 para.177
Sch.5 Part 13 para.73, amended: 2013 c.22 Sch.11 para.175, Sch.11 para.177
Sch.5 Part 13 para.73, repealed (in part): 2013 c.22 Sch.11 para.175
Sch.5 Part 14 para.74, amended: 2013 c.22 Sch.11 para.177
Sch.5 Part 14 para.75, amended: 2013 c.22 Sch.11 para.177
Sch.5 Part 14 para.76, amended: 2013 c.22 Sch.11 para.177
Sch.5 Part 14 para.77, amended: 2013 c.22 Sch.11 para.177
Sch.5 Part 14 para.78, amended: 2013 c.22 Sch.11 para.177
Sch.5 Part 14 para.79, amended: 2013 c.22 Sch.11 para.177
Sch.5 Part 14 para.79A, amended: 2013 c.22 Sch.11 para.177
Sch.5 Part 14 para.80, amended: 2013 c.22 Sch.11 para.176, Sch.11 para.177
Sch.6 Part 1 para.1, amended: 2013 c.22 Sch.11 para.179, Sch.11 para.200
Sch.6 Part 1 para.2, amended: 2013 c.22 Sch.11 para.200
Sch.6 Part 1 para.3, amended: 2013 c.22 Sch.11 para.200
Sch.6 Part 1 para.4, amended: 2013 c.22 Sch.11 para.200

Sch.6 Part 1 para.5, amended: 2013 c.22 Sch.11 para.200
Sch.6 Part 1 para.6, amended: 2013 c.22 Sch.11 para.200
Sch.6 Part 1 para.7, amended: 2013 c.22 Sch.11 para.200
Sch.6 Part 1 para.8, amended: 2013 c.22 Sch.11 para.200
Sch.6 Part 1 para.8, repealed: 2013 c.22 Sch.11 para.180
Sch.6 Part 2 para.9, amended: 2013 c.22 Sch.11 para.181, Sch.11 para.200
Sch.6 Part 2 para.10, amended: 2013 c.22 Sch.11 para.200
Sch.6 Part 2 para.11, amended: 2013 c.22 Sch.11 para.200
Sch.6 Part 2 para.12, amended: 2013 c.22 Sch.11 para.200
Sch.6 Part 2 para.13, amended: 2013 c.22 Sch.11 para.200
Sch.6 Part 2 para.14, amended: 2013 c.22 Sch.11 para.200
Sch.6 Part 3 para.15, amended: 2013 c.22 Sch.11 para.182, Sch.11 para.200
Sch.6 Part 3 para.16, amended: 2013 c.22 Sch.11 para.200
Sch.6 Part 3 para.17, amended: 2013 c.22 Sch.11 para.200
Sch.6 Part 3 para.18, amended: 2013 c.22 Sch.11 para.200
Sch.6 Part 3 para.19, amended: 2013 c.22 Sch.11 para.200
Sch.6 Part 4 para.20, amended: 2013 c.22 Sch.11 para.183, Sch.11 para.200
Sch.6 Part 4 para.20, repealed (in part): 2013 c.22 Sch.11 para.183
Sch.6 Part 4 para.21, amended: 2013 c.22 Sch.11 para.200
Sch.6 Part 4 para.22, amended: 2013 c.22 Sch.11 para.200
Sch.6 Part 4 para.23, amended: 2013 c.22 Sch.11 para.200
Sch.6 Part 4 para.23, repealed: 2013 c.22 Sch.11 para.184
Sch.6 Part 4 para.24, amended: 2013 c.22 Sch.11 para.185, Sch.11 para.200
Sch.6 Part 4 para.24, repealed (in part): 2013 c.22 Sch.11 para.185
Sch.6 Part 4 para.25, amended: 2013 c.22 Sch.11 para.200
Sch.6 Part 4 para.25, repealed (in part): 2013 c.22 Sch.11 para.186
Sch.6 Part 5 para.26, amended: 2013 c.22 Sch.11 para.200
Sch.6 Part 5 para.27, amended: 2013 c.22 Sch.11 para.200
Sch.6 Part 5 para.28, amended: 2013 c.22 Sch.11 para.200
Sch.6 Part 5 para.29, amended: 2013 c.22 Sch.11 para.187, Sch.11 para.200
Sch.6 Part 6 para.30, amended: 2013 c.22 Sch.11 para.188, Sch.11 para.200
Sch.6 Part 6 para.31, amended: 2013 c.22 Sch.11 para.189, Sch.11 para.200
Sch.6 Part 6 para.32, amended: 2013 c.22 Sch.11 para.200
Sch.6 Part 6 para.33, amended: 2013 c.22 Sch.11 para.200
Sch.6 Part 6 para.34, amended: 2013 c.22 Sch.11 para.200
Sch.6 Part 6 para.35, amended: 2013 c.22 Sch.11 para.190, Sch.11 para.200
Sch.6 Part 6 para.36, amended: 2013 c.22 Sch.11 para.200
Sch.6 Part 6 para.36, repealed: 2013 c.22 Sch.11 para.191
Sch.6 Part 6 para.37, amended: 2013 c.22 Sch.11 para.192, Sch.11 para.200
Sch.6 Part 6 para.37, repealed (in part): 2013 c.22 Sch.11 para.192
Sch.6 Part 6 para.38, amended: 2013 c.22 Sch.11 para.193, Sch.11 para.200
Sch.6 Part 6 para.39, amended: 2013 c.22 Sch.11 para.194, Sch.11 para.200
Sch.6 Part 6 para.40, amended: 2013 c.22 Sch.11 para.195, Sch.11 para.200
Sch.6 Part 6 para.41, amended: 2013 c.22 Sch.11 para.200
Sch.6 Part 6 para.41, repealed: 2013 c.22 Sch.11 para.196
Sch.6 Part 6 para.42, amended: 2013 c.22 Sch.11 para.200
Sch.6 Part 6 para.42, repealed: 2013 c.22 Sch.11 para.196
Sch.6 Part 7 para.43, amended: 2013 c.22 Sch.11 para.200
Sch.6 Part 7 para.44, amended: 2013 c.22 Sch.11 para.197, Sch.11 para.200
Sch.6 Part 7 para.44, repealed (in part): 2013 c.22 Sch.11 para.197
Sch.6 Part 8 para.45, amended: 2013 c.22 Sch.11 para.200
Sch.6 Part 8 para.46, amended: 2013 c.22 Sch.11 para.198, Sch.11 para.200
Sch.6 Part 8 para.46, repealed (in part): 2013 c.22 Sch.11 para.198
Sch.6 Part 8 para.47, amended: 2013 c.22 Sch.11 para.199, Sch.11 para.200

Sch.6 Part 8 para.47, repealed (in part): 2013 c.22 Sch.11 para.199
Sch.6 Part 8 para.48, amended: 2013 c.22 Sch.11 para.200
Sch.7 Part 3 para.19, amended: 2013 c.22 Sch.11 para.201
Sch.23 Part 2 para.4, applied: SI 2013/227
Sch.23 Part 2 para.4, enabling: SI 2013/227
Sch.25 para.3, repealed: 2013 c.25 Sch.11 para.7
Sch.27 para.22, repealed (in part): 2013 c.22 Sch.10 para.99
Sch.27 para.64, repealed: 2013 c.22 Sch.10 para.99
Sch.27 para.65, repealed: 2013 c.22 Sch.10 para.99
Sch.27 para.91, repealed: 2013 c.22 Sch.11 para.210
Sch.27 para.92, repealed: 2013 c.22 Sch.11 para.210
Sch.27 para.93, repealed: 2013 c.22 Sch.11 para.210
Sch.27 para.94, repealed: 2013 c.22 Sch.11 para.210
Sch.27 para.96, repealed: 2013 c.22 Sch.11 para.210
Sch.28 Part 4 para.61, repealed: SSI 2013/211 Sch.2

34. Housing Act 2004

see *Superstrike Ltd v Rodrigues* [2013] EWCA Civ 669, [2013] 1 W.L.R. 3848 (CA (Civ Div)), Lloyd, L.J.
applied: SI 2013/1179 Sch.1
Part 7, added: SI 2013/1036 Sch.1 para.176
s.22, amended: SI 2013/1036 Sch.1 para.150
s.22, applied: SI 2013/1179 Sch.1
s.34, amended: SI 2013/1036 Sch.1 para.151
s.45, amended: SI 2013/1036 Sch.1 para.152
s.62, amended: SI 2013/1036 Sch.1 para.153
s.62, applied: SI 2013/1179 Sch.1
s.72, amended: SI 2013/1036 Sch.1 para.154
s.73, amended: SI 2013/630 Reg.18, SI 2013/1036 Sch.1 para.155, SI 2013/1788 Reg.3
s.74, see *Parker v Waller* [2013] J.P.L. 568 (UT (Lands)), George Bartlett Q.C. (President)
s.74, amended: SI 2013/630 Reg.18, SI 2013/1788 Reg.3
s.86, amended: SI 2013/1036 Sch.1 para.156
s.86, applied: SI 2013/1179 Sch.1
s.95, see *Sumal & Sons (Properties) Ltd v Newham LBC* [2012] EWCA Crim 1840, [2013] 1 W.L.R. 2078 (CA (Crim Div)), Davis, L.J.
s.95, amended: SI 2013/1036 Sch.1 para.157
s.96, see *Sumal & Sons (Properties) Ltd v Newham LBC* [2012] EWCA Crim 1840, [2013] 1 W.L.R. 2078 (CA (Crim Div)), Davis, L.J.
s.96, amended: SI 2013/630 Reg.18, SI 2013/1036 Sch.1 para.158, SI 2013/1788 Reg.3
s.97, amended: SI 2013/630 Reg.18, SI 2013/1788 Reg.3
s.102, amended: SI 2013/1036 Sch.1 para.159
s.103, amended: SI 2013/1036 Sch.1 para.160
s.105, amended: SI 2013/1036 Sch.1 para.161
s.110, amended: SI 2013/1036 Sch.1 para.162
s.114, amended: SI 2013/1036 Sch.1 para.163
s.120, amended: SI 2013/1036 Sch.1 para.164
s.126, amended: SI 2013/1036 Sch.1 para.165
s.126, applied: SI 2013/1179 Sch.1
s.130, amended: SI 2013/1036 Sch.1 para.166
s.133, amended: SI 2013/1036 Sch.1 para.167
s.134, see *Braithwaite v Secretary of State for Communities and Local Government* [2012] EWHC 2835 (Admin), [2013] J.P.L. 312 (QBD (Admin)), Kenneth Parker, J.
s.134, amended: SI 2013/1036 Sch.1 para.168
s.138, amended: SI 2013/1036 Sch.1 para.169
s.138, applied: SI 2013/1179 Sch.1
s.143, amended: SI 2013/1036 Sch.1 para.170
s.144, amended: SI 2013/1036 Sch.1 para.171
s.181, amended: SI 2013/1036 Sch.1 para.172
s.214, amended: 2013 c.22 Sch.9 para.52
s.215, see *Superstrike Ltd v Rodrigues* [2013] EWCA Civ 669, [2013] 1 W.L.R. 3848 (CA (Civ Div)), Lloyd, L.J.
s.215, amended: 2013 c.22 Sch.9 para.52
s.229, amended: SI 2013/1036 Sch.1 para.173
s.229, enabling: SI 2013/1723
s.230, amended: 2013 c.14 s.7, SI 2013/1036 Sch.1 para.174
s.231, amended: SI 2013/1036 Sch.1 para.175
s.231A, applied: SI 2013/1036 Sch.3 para.4
s.244, amended: SI 2013/1036 Sch.1 para.177
s.250, applied: SI 2013/1723
s.250, enabling: SI 2013/1723
s.255, amended: SI 2013/1036 Sch.1 para.178
s.256, amended: SI 2013/1036 Sch.1 para.179
s.261, amended: SI 2013/1036 Sch.1 para.180
Sch.1 Part 3, amended: SI 2013/1036 Sch.1 para.181
Sch.1 Part 3 para.10, amended: SI 2013/1036 Sch.1 para.181
Sch.1 Part 3 para.10, applied: SI 2013/1179 Sch.1
Sch.1 Part 3 para.13, amended: SI 2013/1036 Sch.1 para.181
Sch.1 Part 3 para.13, applied: SI 2013/1179 Sch.1
Sch.1 Part 3 para.14, amended: SI 2013/1036 Sch.1 para.181
Sch.1 Part 3 para.15, amended: SI 2013/1036 Sch.1 para.181

Sch.1 Part 3 para.18, amended: SI 2013/1036 Sch.1 para.181
Sch.2 Part 3, amended: SI 2013/1036 Sch.1 para.182
Sch.2 Part 3 para.7, amended: SI 2013/1036 Sch.1 para.182
Sch.2 Part 3 para.7, applied: SI 2013/1179 Sch.1
Sch.2 Part 3 para.9, amended: SI 2013/1036 Sch.1 para.182
Sch.2 Part 3 para.9, applied: SI 2013/1179 Sch.1
Sch.2 Part 3 para.10, amended: SI 2013/1036 Sch.1 para.182
Sch.2 Part 3 para.11, amended: SI 2013/1036 Sch.1 para.182
Sch.2 Part 3 para.13, amended: SI 2013/1036 Sch.1 para.182
Sch.3 Part 3 para.8, amended: SI 2013/1036 Sch.1 para.183
Sch.3 Part 3 para.11, amended: SI 2013/1036 Sch.1 para.183
Sch.3 Part 3 para.11, applied: SI 2013/1179 Sch.1
Sch.3 Part 3 para.14, amended: SI 2013/1036 Sch.1 para.183
Sch.5 Part 3 para.31, amended: SI 2013/1036 Sch.1 para.184
Sch.5 Part 3 para.31, applied: SI 2013/1179 Sch.1
Sch.5 Part 3 para.32, amended: SI 2013/1036 Sch.1 para.184
Sch.5 Part 3 para.32, applied: SI 2013/1179 Sch.1
Sch.5 Part 3 para.33, amended: SI 2013/1036 Sch.1 para.184
Sch.5 Part 3 para.34, amended: SI 2013/1036 Sch.1 para.184
Sch.6 Part 3 para.24, amended: SI 2013/1036 Sch.1 para.185
Sch.6 Part 3 para.24, applied: SI 2013/1179 Sch.1
Sch.6 Part 3 para.24, referred to: SI 2013/1179 Sch.1
Sch.6 Part 3 para.25, amended: SI 2013/1036 Sch.1 para.185
Sch.6 Part 3 para.26, amended: SI 2013/1036 Sch.1 para.185
Sch.6 Part 3 para.28, amended: SI 2013/1036 Sch.1 para.185
Sch.6 Part 3 para.28, applied: SI 2013/1179 Sch.1
Sch.6 Part 3 para.29, amended: SI 2013/1036 Sch.1 para.185
Sch.6 Part 3 para.30, amended: SI 2013/1036 Sch.1 para.185
Sch.6 Part 3 para.32, amended: SI 2013/1036 Sch.1 para.185
Sch.6 Part 3 para.32, applied: SI 2013/1179 Sch.1
Sch.6 Part 3 para.33, amended: SI 2013/1036 Sch.1 para.185
Sch.6 Part 3 para.34, amended: SI 2013/1036 Sch.1 para.185
Sch.7 Part 1 para.1, amended: SI 2013/1036 Sch.1 para.186
Sch.7 Part 1 para.2, amended: SI 2013/1036 Sch.1 para.186
Sch.7 Part 1 para.5, amended: SI 2013/1036 Sch.1 para.186
Sch.7 Part 2 para.9, amended: SI 2013/1036 Sch.1 para.186
Sch.7 Part 2 para.10, amended: SI 2013/1036 Sch.1 para.186
Sch.7 Part 2 para.14, amended: SI 2013/1036 Sch.1 para.186
Sch.7 Part 3 para.22, amended: SI 2013/1036 Sch.1 para.186
Sch.7 Part 4 para.26, amended: SI 2013/1036 Sch.1 para.186
Sch.7 Part 4 para.26, applied: SI 2013/1179 Sch.1
Sch.7 Part 4 para.27, amended: SI 2013/1036 Sch.1 para.186
Sch.7 Part 4 para.28, amended: SI 2013/1036 Sch.1 para.186
Sch.7 Part 4 para.30, amended: SI 2013/1036 Sch.1 para.186
Sch.7 Part 4 para.30, applied: SI 2013/1179 Sch.1
Sch.7 Part 4 para.31, amended: SI 2013/1036 Sch.1 para.186
Sch.7 Part 4 para.32, amended: SI 2013/1036 Sch.1 para.186
Sch.7 Part 4 para.34, amended: SI 2013/1036 Sch.1 para.186
Sch.7 Part 4 para.34, applied: SI 2013/1179 Sch.1
Sch.7 Part 4 para.35, amended: SI 2013/1036 Sch.1 para.186
Sch.7 Part 4 para.36, amended: SI 2013/1036 Sch.1 para.186
Sch.13 para.1, amended: SI 2013/1036 Sch.1 para.187
Sch.13 para.3, amended: 2013 c.14 s.7
Sch.13 para.5, amended: 2013 c.22 Sch.9 para.52
Sch.13 para.8, amended: 2013 c.14 s.7
Sch.13 para.13, amended: 2013 c.22 Sch.9 para.52, Sch.9 para.89
Sch.14 para.4, applied: SI 2013/1601 Reg.2
Sch.14 para.4, enabling: SI 2013/1601

35. Pensions Act 2004

applied: 2013 c.25 s.17, SI 2013/2356 Reg.17
Part 3, applied: SI 2013/2734 Reg.24, Sch.3 para.6, Sch.3 para.9, Sch.3 para.10
Part 3, disapplied: SI 2013/2734 Reg.24
s.11, amended: 2013 c.25 Sch.4 para.2
s.13, amended: 2013 c.25 Sch.4 para.3
s.14A, added: 2013 c.25 Sch.4 para.4

s.17, amended: 2013 c.25 Sch.4 para.5
s.70, amended: 2013 c.25 Sch.4 para.6
s.70A, added: 2013 c.25 Sch.4 para.7
s.71, amended: 2013 c.25 Sch.4 para.8
s.72, amended: 2013 c.25 Sch.4 para.9
s.73, amended: 2013 c.25 Sch.4 para.10
s.89, amended: 2013 c.25 Sch.4 para.11
s.89A, added: 2013 c.25 Sch.4 para.12
s.90, amended: 2013 c.25 Sch.4 para.13
s.90A, added: 2013 c.25 Sch.4 para.14
s.91, amended: 2013 c.25 Sch.4 para.15
s.91, enabling: SI 2013/2316, SI 2013/2869
s.92, amended: 2013 c.25 Sch.4 para.16
s.93, amended: 2013 c.25 Sch.4 para.17
s.103, see *Trustees of the Lehman Brothers Pension Scheme v Pensions Regulator* [2013] EWCA Civ 751, [2013] 4 All E.R. 744 (CA (Civ Div)), Arden, L.J.
s.103, amended: 2013 c.22 Sch.9 para.52
s.143, enabling: SI 2013/627
s.143A, enabling: SI 2013/627
s.154, amended: 2013 c.25 Sch.4 para.18
s.170, enabling: SI 2013/627
s.177, varied: SI 2013/105 Art.3
s.178, applied: SI 2013/105
s.178, varied: SI 2013/105 Art.2
s.178, enabling: SI 2013/105
s.203, enabling: SI 2013/627
s.207, enabling: SI 2013/627
s.217, amended: 2013 c.22 Sch.9 para.52
s.218, amended: 2013 c.22 Sch.9 para.52
s.223, applied: SI 2013/2734 Sch.3 para.8
s.224, applied: SI 2013/2734 Reg.15, Sch.4 para.1, Sch.4 para.2, Sch.4 para.4
s.224, referred to: SI 2013/2734 Sch.3 para.9, Sch.3 para.10
s.226, applied: SI 2013/2734 Sch.3 para.11, Sch.4 para.5
s.227, applied: SI 2013/2734 Sch.3 para.6, Sch.3 para.12
s.231, applied: SI 2013/2734 Reg.9, Sch.4 para.6
s.231A, applied: SI 2013/2734 Sch.3 para.14
s.248A, added: 2013 c.25 Sch.4 para.19
s.249A, amended: 2013 c.25 Sch.4 para.20
s.249B, added: 2013 c.25 Sch.4 para.21
s.288, applied: SI 2013/2734 Sch.1 para.1
s.289, applied: SI 2013/2734 Sch.1 para.1
s.307, enabling: SI 2013/627
s.315, enabling: SI 2013/105, SI 2013/627, SI 2013/1754
s.317, applied: SI 2013/627, SI 2013/1754
s.318, amended: 2013 c.25 Sch.4 para.22
s.318, enabling: SI 2013/627, SI 2013/1754
Sch.3, amended: SI 2013/504 Reg.23
Sch.7 para.23, enabling: SI 2013/627
Sch.7 para.24, enabling: SI 2013/627
Sch.7 para.25, enabling: SI 2013/627
Sch.7 para.25A, enabling: SI 2013/627, SI 2013/1754
Sch.7 para.26, applied: SI 2013/105 Art.4
Sch.7 para.26, enabling: SI 2013/105, SI 2013/627
Sch.7 para.27, enabling: SI 2013/105
Sch.7 para.31, enabling: SI 2013/627
Sch.8, amended: SI 2013/504 Reg.23

36. Civil Contingencies Act 2004

s.2, enabling: SSI 2013/247
s.14, applied: SSI 2013/247
s.17, enabling: SSI 2013/247
s.25, repealed: SI 2013/2042 Sch.1 para.29
Sch.1 Part 1 para.12A, added: SI 2013/755 Sch.2 para.429
Sch.1 Part 2 para.14, substituted: SSI 2013/119 Sch.3 para.1
Sch.1 Part 2 para.15, substituted: SSI 2013/119 Sch.3 para.1
Sch.1 Part 3 para.29B, added: 2013 c.32 Sch.12 para.81

2005

4. Constitutional Reform Act 2005

s.3, amended: 2013 c.22 Sch.14 para.13
s.7, amended: 2013 c.22 Sch.9 para.42, Sch.10 para.97
s.16, disapplied: SI 2013/2192 Reg.3
s.23, amended: 2013 c.22 Sch.13 para.2
s.26, amended: 2013 c.22 Sch.13 para.3, Sch.13 para.7
s.26, applied: SI 2013/2193 Reg.4, Reg.10, Reg.23
s.27, amended: 2013 c.22 Sch.13 para.4, Sch.13 para.7, Sch.13 para.9
s.27, applied: SI 2013/2193 Reg.18, Reg.19, Reg.20
s.27, repealed (in part): 2013 c.22 Sch.13 para.7
s.27A, added: 2013 c.22 Sch.13 para.5
s.27A, applied: SI 2013/2193
s.27A, enabling: SI 2013/2193
s.27B, added: 2013 c.22 Sch.13 para.6
s.28, repealed: 2013 c.22 Sch.13 para.7
s.29, repealed: 2013 c.22 Sch.13 para.7
s.30, repealed: 2013 c.22 Sch.13 para.7
s.31, repealed: 2013 c.22 Sch.13 para.7
s.48, amended: 2013 c.22 s.29, s.30
s.49, amended: 2013 c.22 s.29
s.51A, added: 2013 c.22 s.30
s.51B, added: 2013 c.22 s.30
s.51C, added: 2013 c.22 s.30

s.51C, applied: SI 2013/2532 Reg.3
s.51D, added: 2013 c.22 s.30
s.51D, enabling: SI 2013/2532
s.51E, added: 2013 c.22 s.30
s.52, applied: SI 2013/2302
s.52, enabling: SI 2013/2302
s.60, repealed (in part): 2013 c.22 Sch.13 para.7
s.63, amended: 2013 c.22 Sch.13 para.10
s.66, amended: 2013 c.22 Sch.13 para.55
s.67, amended: 2013 c.22 Sch.13 para.56
s.69, amended: 2013 c.22 Sch.13 para.57
s.69, applied: SI 2013/2192 Reg.10, Reg.16
s.70, amended: 2013 c.22 Sch.13 para.58, Sch.13 para.82
s.70, applied: SI 2013/2192 Reg.4, Reg.5, Reg.6, Reg.7, Reg.8, Reg.11, Reg.12, Reg.13, Reg.14
s.70, repealed (in part): 2013 c.22 Sch.13 para.58
s.71, repealed: 2013 c.22 Sch.13 para.53
s.71, substituted: 2013 c.22 Sch.13 para.82
s.71A, repealed: 2013 c.22 Sch.13 para.53
s.71B, repealed: 2013 c.22 Sch.13 para.53
s.72, repealed: 2013 c.22 Sch.13 para.53
s.73, repealed: 2013 c.22 Sch.13 para.53
s.74, repealed: 2013 c.22 Sch.13 para.53
s.75, repealed: 2013 c.22 Sch.13 para.53
s.75A, amended: 2013 c.22 Sch.13 para.59
s.75B, amended: 2013 c.22 Sch.13 para.60
s.75B, applied: SI 2013/2192 Reg.4, Reg.17, Reg.18, Reg.19, Reg.20
s.75C, repealed: 2013 c.22 Sch.13 para.53
s.75D, repealed: 2013 c.22 Sch.13 para.53
s.75E, repealed: 2013 c.22 Sch.13 para.53
s.75F, repealed: 2013 c.22 Sch.13 para.53
s.75G, repealed: 2013 c.22 Sch.13 para.53
s.76, amended: 2013 c.22 Sch.13 para.61
s.78, amended: 2013 c.22 Sch.13 para.62
s.78, applied: SI 2013/2192 Reg.28
s.79, amended: 2013 c.22 Sch.13 para.63
s.79, applied: SI 2013/2192 Reg.4, Reg.23, Reg.24, Reg.25, Reg.26
s.80, repealed: 2013 c.22 Sch.13 para.53
s.81, repealed: 2013 c.22 Sch.13 para.53
s.82, repealed: 2013 c.22 Sch.13 para.53
s.83, repealed: 2013 c.22 Sch.13 para.53
s.84, repealed: 2013 c.22 Sch.13 para.53
s.85, amended: 2013 c.22 Sch.13 para.64, Sch.14 para.3
s.86, amended: 2013 c.22 Sch.13 para.65
s.87, amended: 2013 c.22 Sch.13 para.66
s.87, applied: SI 2013/2192 Reg.34, Reg.43, Reg.48
s.88, amended: 2013 c.22 Sch.13 para.67
s.88, applied: SI 2013/2192 Reg.30, Reg.31, Reg.32, Reg.40, Reg.41
s.88, repealed (in part): 2013 c.22 Sch.13 para.67
s.89, repealed: 2013 c.22 Sch.13 para.53
s.90, repealed: 2013 c.22 Sch.13 para.53
s.91, repealed: 2013 c.22 Sch.13 para.53
s.92, repealed: 2013 c.22 Sch.13 para.53
s.93, repealed: 2013 c.22 Sch.13 para.53
s.94, applied: SI 2013/2192, SI 2013/2192 Reg.36, Reg.48
s.94, substituted: 2013 c.22 Sch.13 para.68
s.94, enabling: SI 2013/2192
s.94A, amended: 2013 c.22 Sch.13 para.40
s.94AA, added: 2013 c.22 Sch.14 para.3
s.94B, amended: 2013 c.22 Sch.13 para.48
s.94C, added: 2013 c.22 Sch.13 para.53
s.94C, applied: SI 2013/2192
s.94C, enabling: SI 2013/2192
s.95, amended: 2013 c.22 Sch.13 para.69
s.96, repealed: 2013 c.22 Sch.13 para.53
s.97, amended: 2013 c.22 Sch.13 para.70
s.97, repealed (in part): 2013 c.22 Sch.13 para.70
s.99, amended: 2013 c.22 Sch.13 para.71
s.100, amended: 2013 c.22 Sch.13 para.72
s.101, amended: 2013 c.22 Sch.13 para.73
s.102, amended: 2013 c.22 Sch.13 para.74
s.103, amended: 2013 c.22 Sch.13 para.75
s.104, amended: 2013 c.22 Sch.13 para.76
s.105, amended: 2013 c.22 Sch.13 para.77
s.107, amended: SI 2013/602 Sch.2 para.45
s.108, applied: SI 2013/1674 Reg.7, Reg.17
s.109, referred to: SI 2013/362 Reg.16, SI 2013/1237 Reg.5, SI 2013/2192 Reg.11, Reg.46
s.110, applied: SI 2013/1674 Reg.22
s.110, varied: SI 2013/1674 Reg.22
s.111, applied: SI 2013/1674 Reg.19, Reg.22, Reg.23
s.112, applied: SI 2013/1674 Reg.22
s.113, applied: SI 2013/1674 Reg.19, Reg.22
s.115, enabling: SI 2013/1674
s.118, applied: SI 2013/1674 Reg.3
s.120, enabling: SI 2013/1674
s.121, enabling: SI 2013/1674
s.122, amended: 2013 c.22 Sch.13 para.26
s.137A, added: 2013 c.22 Sch.13 para.11
s.139, amended: 2013 c.22 Sch.13 para.7
s.144, amended: 2013 c.22 Sch.13 para.7, Sch.13 para.27, Sch.13 para.78
s.144, applied: SI 2013/2191, SI 2013/2192, SI 2013/2193
Sch.4 Part 1 para.71, repealed (in part): 2013 c.22 Sch.13 para.34, Sch.13 para.89
Sch.4 Part 1 para.89, repealed: SI 2013/686 Sch.1 para.8
Sch.4 Part 1 para.101, repealed: 2013 c.22 Sch.10 para.99

Sch.4 Part 1 para.161, repealed: 2013 c.22 Sch.9 para.141
Sch.4 Part 1 para.162, repealed (in part): 2013 c.22 Sch.9 para.141
Sch.4 Part 1 para.163, repealed: 2013 c.22 Sch.9 para.141
Sch.4 Part 1 para.166, repealed: 2013 c.22 Sch.9 para.141
Sch.4 Part 1 para.171, repealed: 2013 c.22 Sch.11 para.210
Sch.4 Part 1 para.172, repealed: 2013 c.22 Sch.11 para.210
Sch.4 Part 1 para.173, repealed: 2013 c.22 Sch.11 para.210
Sch.4 Part 1 para.174, repealed: 2013 c.22 Sch.11 para.210
Sch.4 Part 1 para.200, repealed: 2013 c.22 Sch.9 para.141
Sch.4 Part 1 para.201, repealed: 2013 c.22 Sch.9 para.141
Sch.4 Part 1 para.205, repealed: 2013 c.22 Sch.11 para.210
Sch.4 Part 1 para.206, repealed: 2013 c.22 Sch.11 para.210
Sch.4 Part 1 para.210, repealed: 2013 c.22 Sch.11 para.210
Sch.4 Part 1 para.213, repealed: 2013 c.22 Sch.10 para.99
Sch.4 Part 1 para.253, repealed: 2013 c.22 Sch.11 para.210
Sch.4 Part 1 para.254, repealed: 2013 c.22 Sch.11 para.210
Sch.4 Part 1 para.344, repealed (in part): 2013 c.22 Sch.10 para.99
Sch.7 para.2, amended: 2013 c.22 Sch.13 para.79
Sch.7 para.4, amended: 2013 c.22 Sch.13 para.32, Sch.13 para.35, Sch.13 para.36, Sch.13 para.37, Sch.13 para.38, 2013 c.25 Sch.8 para.29, 2013 c.30 s.8, SI 2013/686 Sch.1 para.8, SI 2013/1036 Sch.1 para.240
Sch.8 Part 1 para.1, repealed: 2013 c.22 Sch.13 para.7
Sch.8 Part 1 para.2, repealed: 2013 c.22 Sch.13 para.7
Sch.8 Part 1 para.3, repealed: 2013 c.22 Sch.13 para.7
Sch.8 Part 1 para.4, repealed: 2013 c.22 Sch.13 para.7
Sch.8 Part 1 para.5, repealed: 2013 c.22 Sch.13 para.7
Sch.8 Part 1 para.6, repealed: 2013 c.22 Sch.13 para.7
Sch.8 Part 1 para.7, repealed: 2013 c.22 Sch.13 para.7
Sch.8 Part 1 para.8, repealed: 2013 c.22 Sch.13 para.7
Sch.8 Part 1 para.9, repealed: 2013 c.22 Sch.13 para.7
Sch.8 Part 2 para.10, repealed: 2013 c.22 Sch.13 para.7
Sch.8 Part 2 para.11, repealed: 2013 c.22 Sch.13 para.7
Sch.8 Part 2 para.12, repealed: 2013 c.22 Sch.13 para.7
Sch.8 Part 3 para.13, amended: 2013 c.22 Sch.13 para.7
Sch.8 Part 3 para.14, amended: 2013 c.22 Sch.13 para.7
Sch.9 Part 1 para.29, repealed: SI 2013/686 Sch.1 para.8
Sch.11 Part 3 para.6, amended: SI 2013/294 Sch.1
Sch.12, referred to: SI 2013/2191 Reg.19
Sch.12 Part 1, applied: SI 2013/2191 Reg.8
Sch.12 Part 1 para.1, amended: 2013 c.22 Sch.13 para.17
Sch.12 Part 1 para.1, applied: SI 2013/2191 Sch.1
Sch.12 Part 1 para.1, enabling: SI 2013/2191
Sch.12 Part 1 para.2, referred to: SI 2013/2191 Sch.1
Sch.12 Part 1 para.2, repealed (in part): 2013 c.22 Sch.13 para.18
Sch.12 Part 1 para.3A, added: 2013 c.22 Sch.13 para.19
Sch.12 Part 1 para.3B, added: 2013 c.22 Sch.13 para.19
Sch.12 Part 1 para.3B, enabling: SI 2013/2191
Sch.12 Part 1 para.3C, added: 2013 c.22 Sch.13 para.19
Sch.12 Part 1 para.3C, enabling: SI 2013/2191
Sch.12 Part 1 para.4, repealed: 2013 c.22 Sch.13 para.18
Sch.12 Part 1 para.5, repealed: 2013 c.22 Sch.13 para.18
Sch.12 Part 1 para.6, repealed: 2013 c.22 Sch.13 para.18
Sch.12 Part 1 para.6A, enabling: SI 2013/2191
Sch.12 Part 1 para.7, substituted: 2013 c.22 Sch.13 para.20
Sch.12 Part 1 para.8, substituted: 2013 c.22 Sch.13 para.20
Sch.12 Part 1 para.9, substituted: 2013 c.22 Sch.13 para.20
Sch.12 Part 1 para.10, substituted: 2013 c.22 Sch.13 para.20
Sch.12 Part 1 para.11, amended: 2013 c.22 Sch.13 para.21, Sch.13 para.82
Sch.12 Part 1 para.11, applied: SI 2013/2191 Reg.16

Sch.12 Part 1 para.11, enabling: SI 2013/2191
Sch.12 Part 1 para.13, substituted: 2013 c.22 Sch.13 para.22
Sch.12 Part 1 para.13, enabling: SI 2013/2191
Sch.12 Part 1 para.14, amended: 2013 c.22 Sch.13 para.23
Sch.12 Part 1 para.14, enabling: SI 2013/2191
Sch.12 Part 1 para.17A, added: 2013 c.22 Sch.13 para.24
Sch.12 Part 1 para.17A, enabling: SI 2013/2191
Sch.12 Part 2 para.20, amended: 2013 c.22 Sch.13 para.25, Sch.13 para.80
Sch.12 Part 2 para.20, applied: SI 2013/2191 Reg.7, Reg.8
Sch.12 Part 2 para.27, amended: 2013 c.22 Sch.13 para.80
Sch.14, referred to: SI 2013/2191 Reg.8, Reg.13, SI 2013/2192 Reg.4, Reg.11, Reg.23
Sch.14 Part 1, amended: 2013 c.22 Sch.13 para.29, SI 2013/294 Sch.1
Sch.14 Part 1, referred to: SI 2013/2192 Reg.29, Reg.37
Sch.14 Part 2, amended: 2013 c.22 Sch.13 para.41, Sch.13 para.89, Sch.14 para.3
Sch.14 Part 2, referred to: SI 2013/2192 Reg.29, Reg.37
Sch.14 Part 3, amended: 2013 c.22 Sch.13 para.49, Sch.14 para.13, SI 2013/686 Sch.1 para.8, SI 2013/1036 Sch.1 para.241
Sch.14 Part 3, referred to: SI 2013/2191 Reg.6, SI 2013/2192 Reg.29, Reg.37

5. Income Tax (Trading and Other Income) Act 2005

applied: 2013 c.29 Sch.45 para.26, SI 2013/628 Reg.3
Part 2, applied: SI 2013/2819 Reg.17
Part 2 c.2, applied: SI 2013/2819 Reg.17
Part 3, applied: SI 2013/2819 Reg.17
Part 3 c.3, applied: SI 2013/2819 Reg.17
Part 4 c.10, applied: SI 2013/2819 Reg.31
Part 4 c.2, applied: SI 2013/2819 Reg.14, SI 2013/3209 Reg.5
Part 4 c.2A, disapplied: 2013 c.29 Sch.12 para.18
Part 5, applied: SI 2013/376 Reg.66
s.6, amended: 2013 c.29 Sch.45 para.75
s.17, amended: 2013 c.29 Sch.45 para.76
s.25, amended: 2013 c.29 Sch.4 para.3
s.25A, added: 2013 c.29 Sch.4 para.4
s.31, amended: 2013 c.29 s.78, Sch.4 para.49, Sch.5 para.3
s.31A, added: 2013 c.29 Sch.4 para.5
s.31B, added: 2013 c.29 Sch.4 para.5
s.31C, added: 2013 c.29 Sch.4 para.5
s.31D, added: 2013 c.29 Sch.4 para.5
s.31E, added: 2013 c.29 Sch.4 para.5
s.31F, added: 2013 c.29 Sch.4 para.5
s.32A, added: 2013 c.29 Sch.4 para.7
s.33A, added: 2013 c.29 Sch.4 para.8
s.38, amended: 2013 c.29 Sch.4 para.9
s.49, applied: 2013 c.29 s.68
s.51A, added: 2013 c.29 Sch.4 para.10
s.55A, substituted: 2013 c.29 Sch.4 para.11
s.56, amended: 2013 c.29 Sch.4 para.50
s.56A, added: 2013 c.29 Sch.4 para.13
s.57B, added: 2013 c.29 Sch.4 para.14
s.58, amended: 2013 c.29 Sch.4 para.15
s.61, amended: 2013 c.29 Sch.28 para.2
s.72, amended: 2013 c.29 Sch.4 para.16
s.94A, amended: 2013 c.29 Sch.4 para.17
s.94B, added: 2013 c.29 Sch.5 para.2
s.94C, added: 2013 c.29 Sch.5 para.2
s.94D, added: 2013 c.29 Sch.5 para.2
s.94E, added: 2013 c.29 Sch.5 para.2
s.94F, added: 2013 c.29 Sch.5 para.2
s.94G, added: 2013 c.29 Sch.5 para.2
s.94H, added: 2013 c.29 Sch.5 para.2
s.94I, added: 2013 c.29 Sch.5 para.2
s.95A, added: 2013 c.29 Sch.4 para.19
s.96A, added: 2013 c.29 Sch.4 para.20
s.97A, added: 2013 c.29 Sch.4 para.21
s.97B, added: 2013 c.29 Sch.4 para.21
s.105, amended: 2013 c.29 Sch.4 para.22
s.106A, added: 2013 c.29 Sch.4 para.23
s.106B, added: 2013 c.29 Sch.4 para.23
s.106C, added: 2013 c.29 Sch.4 para.23
s.106D, added: 2013 c.29 Sch.4 para.23
s.106E, added: 2013 c.29 Sch.4 para.23
s.111A, added: 2013 c.29 Sch.4 para.24
s.130A, added: 2013 c.29 Sch.4 para.25
s.144A, added: 2013 c.29 Sch.4 para.26
s.148K, added: 2013 c.29 Sch.4 para.28
s.148ZA, added: 2013 c.29 Sch.4 para.27
s.154A, amended: 2013 c.29 Sch.46 para.44
s.160, applied: 2013 c.29 Sch.4 para.57
s.160, repealed: 2013 c.29 Sch.4 para.51
s.172AA, added: 2013 c.29 Sch.4 para.29
s.188A, added: 2013 c.29 Sch.4 para.30
s.191A, added: 2013 c.29 Sch.4 para.31
s.221A, added: 2013 c.29 Sch.4 para.32
s.225N, amended: 2013 c.29 Sch.31 para.1, Sch.31 para.14
s.225N, repealed (in part): 2013 c.29 Sch.31 para.6, Sch.31 para.14
s.225N, substituted: 2013 c.29 Sch.31 para.14
s.225O, repealed: 2013 c.29 Sch.31 para.6
s.225P, repealed: 2013 c.29 Sch.31 para.15
s.225Q, repealed: 2013 c.29 Sch.31 para.15
s.225R, amended: 2013 c.29 Sch.31 para.1, Sch.31 para.16

s.225R, substituted: 2013 c.29 Sch.31 para.16
s.225T, repealed: 2013 c.29 Sch.31 para.9
s.225V, added: 2013 c.29 Sch.31 para.22
s.225ZAA, added: 2013 c.29 Sch.4 para.33
s.225ZH, added: 2013 c.29 Sch.4 para.34
s.227A, added: 2013 c.29 Sch.4 para.36
s.229, amended: 2013 c.29 Sch.4 para.52
s.238, applied: 2013 c.29 Sch.4 para.57
s.238, repealed: 2013 c.29 Sch.4 para.52
s.239, applied: 2013 c.29 Sch.4 para.57
s.239, repealed: 2013 c.29 Sch.4 para.52
s.239A, added: 2013 c.29 Sch.4 para.37
s.239B, added: 2013 c.29 Sch.4 para.37
s.240A, added: 2013 c.29 Sch.4 para.38
s.240B, added: 2013 c.29 Sch.4 para.38
s.240C, added: 2013 c.29 Sch.4 para.38
s.240D, added: 2013 c.29 Sch.4 para.38
s.240E, added: 2013 c.29 Sch.4 para.38
s.243, amended: 2013 c.29 Sch.45 para.77
s.246, amended: 2013 c.29 Sch.4 para.39
s.254, amended: 2013 c.29 Sch.4 para.39, Sch.5 para.4
s.270, amended: 2013 c.29 Sch.45 para.81
s.274, amended: 2013 c.29 s.78
s.292, amended: 2013 c.29 Sch.28 para.3
s.365, amended: 2013 c.29 Sch.12 para.2
s.365, repealed (in part): 2013 c.29 Sch.12 para.2, SI 2013/2819 Reg.36
s.368, amended: 2013 c.29 Sch.45 para.83
s.368A, added: 2013 c.29 Sch.45 para.132
s.370A, added: 2013 c.29 Sch.11 para.6
s.372, disapplied: SI 2013/460 Reg.3
s.380, amended: 2013 c.29 Sch.11 para.7
s.381A, added: 2013 c.29 Sch.12 para.3
s.381B, added: 2013 c.29 Sch.12 para.3
s.381C, added: 2013 c.29 Sch.12 para.3
s.381D, added: 2013 c.29 Sch.12 para.3
s.381E, added: 2013 c.29 Sch.12 para.3
s.385A, added: 2013 c.29 Sch.23 para.16
s.397, amended: 2013 c.29 Sch.29 para.13, SI 2013/2819 Reg.36
s.397, disapplied: SI 2013/2819 Reg.12
s.397A, amended: 2013 c.29 Sch.29 para.14, SI 2013/2819 Reg.36
s.397A, disapplied: SI 2013/2819 Reg.12
s.397A, repealed (in part): 2013 c.29 Sch.29 para.14
s.397B, repealed: 2013 c.29 Sch.29 para.15
s.399, amended: SI 2013/2819 Reg.36
s.399, disapplied: SI 2013/2819 Reg.12
s.400, disapplied: SI 2013/2819 Reg.12
s.400, repealed (in part): SI 2013/2819 Reg.36
s.401C, added: 2013 c.29 Sch.45 para.133
s.408A, added: 2013 c.29 Sch.45 para.134
s.410, amended: SI 2013/2819 Reg.36
s.413A, added: 2013 c.29 Sch.45 para.135
s.415, amended: SI 2013/463 Art.8
s.417, amended: 2013 c.29 Sch.30 para.14
s.420A, added: 2013 c.29 Sch.45 para.136
s.459, amended: 2013 c.29 Sch.46 para.45
s.463A, added: 2013 c.29 Sch.9 para.8
s.463B, added: 2013 c.29 Sch.9 para.8
s.463C, added: 2013 c.29 Sch.9 para.8
s.463D, added: 2013 c.29 Sch.9 para.8
s.463E, added: 2013 c.29 Sch.9 para.8
s.465, amended: 2013 c.29 Sch.45 para.84, Sch.45 para.150
s.465B, added: 2013 c.29 Sch.45 para.140
s.467, amended: 2013 c.29 Sch.45 para.85
s.468, amended: 2013 c.29 Sch.45 para.141, Sch.46 para.46
s.473A, applied: 2013 c.29 Sch.8 para.7
s.476, amended: 2013 c.29 Sch.8 para.2
s.485, amended: 2013 c.29 Sch.9 para.9
s.514, amended: 2013 c.29 Sch.45 para.142
s.520, amended: SI 2013/636 Sch.1 para.8
s.528, amended: 2013 c.29 Sch.45 para.86
s.528, substituted: 2013 c.29 Sch.8 para.3
s.528A, amended: 2013 c.29 Sch.45 para.87
s.529, repealed: 2013 c.29 Sch.8 para.4
s.536, amended: 2013 c.29 Sch.8 para.5, Sch.45 para.88
s.541, amended: 2013 c.29 Sch.45 para.143
s.547, repealed: SI 2013/2819 Reg.36
s.548, repealed: SI 2013/2819 Reg.36
s.549, repealed: SI 2013/2819 Reg.36
s.550, repealed: SI 2013/2819 Reg.36
s.555, repealed: 2013 c.29 Sch.12 para.13
s.556, repealed: 2013 c.29 Sch.12 para.13
s.557, repealed: 2013 c.29 Sch.12 para.13
s.558, repealed: 2013 c.29 Sch.12 para.13
s.559, repealed: 2013 c.29 Sch.12 para.13
s.560, repealed: 2013 c.29 Sch.12 para.13
s.561, repealed: 2013 c.29 Sch.12 para.13
s.562, repealed: 2013 c.29 Sch.12 para.13
s.563, repealed: 2013 c.29 Sch.12 para.13
s.564, repealed: 2013 c.29 Sch.12 para.13
s.565, repealed: 2013 c.29 Sch.12 para.13
s.566, repealed: 2013 c.29 Sch.12 para.13
s.567, repealed: 2013 c.29 Sch.12 para.13
s.568, repealed: 2013 c.29 Sch.12 para.13
s.569, amended: 2013 c.29 Sch.46 para.47
s.569, repealed: 2013 c.29 Sch.12 para.13
s.577, amended: 2013 c.29 Sch.45 para.89
s.636, amended: 2013 c.29 Sch.46 para.48
s.648, amended: 2013 c.29 Sch.46 para.49
s.651, amended: 2013 c.29 Sch.46 para.50
s.664, amended: 2013 c.29 Sch.46 para.51

s.687, amended: 2013 c.29 Sch.12 para.13
s.689A, added: 2013 c.29 Sch.45 para.137
s.694, enabling: SI 2013/267, SI 2013/605, SI 2013/623, SI 2013/1743
s.695, enabling: SI 2013/605, SI 2013/623, SI 2013/1743
s.695A, enabling: SI 2013/605, SI 2013/1743
s.696, enabling: SI 2013/623
s.701, enabling: SI 2013/605, SI 2013/623, SI 2013/1743
s.715, amended: 2013 c.29 Sch.46 para.52
s.771, amended: 2013 c.29 Sch.46 para.53
s.786, amended: 2013 c.29 Sch.4 para.40
s.805, amended: 2013 c.29 Sch.4 para.42
s.806, amended: SI 2013/1465 Sch.1 para.10
s.806, repealed (in part): SI 2013/1465 Sch.1 para.10
s.820, substituted: 2013 c.29 Sch.4 para.43
s.832, amended: 2013 c.29 Sch.45 para.90
s.832A, applied: 2013 c.29 Sch.45 para.158
s.832A, substituted: 2013 c.29 Sch.45 para.118
s.839, amended: SI 2013/2819 Reg.36
s.849, amended: 2013 c.29 Sch.45 para.78
s.852, amended: 2013 c.29 Sch.45 para.79
s.854, amended: 2013 c.29 Sch.45 para.80
Sch.1 Part 1 para.310, repealed: 2013 c.2 Sch.1 Part 10
Sch.1 Part 1 para.326, repealed: 2013 c.2 Sch.1 Part 10
Sch.1 Part 2 para.435, repealed: 2013 c.29 Sch.12 para.13
Sch.1 Part 2 para.457, repealed (in part): 2013 c.2 Sch.1 Part 10
Sch.1 Part 2 para.458, repealed (in part): 2013 c.2 Sch.1 Part 10
Sch.2 Part 5 para.95, repealed: 2013 c.29 Sch.12 para.13
Sch.4 Part 2, amended: 2013 c.29 Sch.45 para.106, Sch.4 para.53, Sch.12 para.13

7. Finance Act 2005

s.28, amended: 2013 c.29 Sch.45 para.151
s.30, amended: 2013 c.29 Sch.45 para.151, Sch.46 para.133
s.30, repealed (in part): 2013 c.29 Sch.45 para.151
s.31, amended: 2013 c.29 Sch.45 para.151
s.32, amended: 2013 c.29 Sch.45 para.151
s.34, amended: 2013 c.29 Sch.44 para.15
s.35, amended: 2013 c.29 Sch.44 para.16
s.38, substituted: 2013 c.29 Sch.44 para.17
s.41, amended: 2013 c.29 Sch.45 para.151
s.41, repealed (in part): 2013 c.29 Sch.45 para.151
s.102, enabling: SI 2013/1117
Sch.1A para.1, added: 2013 c.29 Sch.44 para.19
Sch.1A para.2, added: 2013 c.29 Sch.44 para.19
Sch.1A para.3, added: 2013 c.29 Sch.44 para.19
Sch.1A para.4, added: 2013 c.29 Sch.44 para.19
Sch.1A para.5, added: 2013 c.29 Sch.44 para.19
Sch.1A para.6, added: 2013 c.29 Sch.44 para.19
Sch.1A para.7, added: 2013 c.29 Sch.44 para.19
Sch.1A para.8, added: 2013 c.29 Sch.44 para.19

9. Mental Capacity Act 2005

see *A Local Authority v K* [2013] EWHC 242 (COP), (2013) 130 B.M.L.R. 195 (CP), Cobb, J.; see *An NHS Trust v DE* [2013] EWHC 2562 (Fam), [2013] 3 F.C.R. 343 (CP), Eleanor King, J.; see *L (Vulnerable Adults with Capacity: Court's Jurisdiction), Re* [2012] EWCA Civ 253, [2013] Fam. 1 (CA (Civ Div)), Maurice Kay, L.J.; see *M, Re* [2013] W.T.L.R. 681 (CP), Senior Judge Denzil Lush; see *NT v FS* [2013] EWHC 684 (COP), [2013] W.T.L.R. 867 (CP), Judge Behrens; see *Sedge v Prime* [2012] EWHC 3460 (QB), (2013) 129 B.M.L.R. 37 (QBD), John Leighton Williams Q.C.; see *XCC v AA* [2012] EWHC 2183 (COP), [2013] 2 All E.R. 988 (CP), Parker, J.; see *York City Council v C* [2013] Med. L.R. 26 (CP), Hedley, J.; see *ZH v Commissioner of Police of the Metropolis* [2013] EWCA Civ 69, [2013] 1 W.L.R. 3021 (CA (Civ Div)), Lord Dyson (M.R.)
applied: SI 2013/380 Reg.57, SI 2013/386 Reg.12, SI 2013/3029 Sch.13 para.1, Sch.13 para.9, SI 2013/3035 Sch.1, SI 2013/3208 r.124
Part 1, applied: SI 2013/380 Reg.57, SI 2013/386 Reg.12
s.4, see *An NHS Trust v DE* [2013] EWHC 2562 (Fam), [2013] 3 F.C.R. 343 (CP), Eleanor King, J.; see *NT v FS* [2013] EWHC 684 (COP), [2013] W.T.L.R. 867 (CP), Judge Behrens; see *SB (A Patient) (Capacity to Consent to Termination), Re* [2013] EWHC 1417 (COP), [2013] 3 F.C.R. 384 (CP), Holman, J.; see *XCC v AA* [2012] EWHC 2183 (COP), [2013] 2 All E.R. 988 (CP), Parker, J.; see *York City Council v C* [2013] Med. L.R. 26 (CP), Hedley, J.
s.4, referred to: SI 2013/1617 Reg.2
s.21A, applied: SI 2013/480 Reg.5
s.46, see *A Local Authority v K* [2013] EWHC 242 (COP), (2013) 130 B.M.L.R. 195 (CP), Cobb, J.
s.46, amended: 2013 c.22 Sch.14 para.5
s.46, repealed (in part): 2013 c.22 Sch.14 para.5
s.54, applied: SI 2013/2302
s.54, enabling: SI 2013/2302
s.58, enabling: SI 2013/506, SI 2013/1748
s.64, enabling: SI 2013/1748
s.65, enabling: SI 2013/506, SI 2013/1748
Sch.A1 Part 1 para.2, applied: SI 2013/480 Reg.5
Sch.A1 Part 10, applied: SI 2013/480 Reg.5
Sch.1, enabling: SI 2013/506

Sch.1 Part 2 para.6, applied: SI 2013/506 Reg.13

10. Public Services Ombudsman (Wales) Act 2005

Sch.3, amended: SI 2013/755 Sch.2 para.430

11. Commissioners for Revenue and Customs Act 2005

s.2, applied: SSI 2013/76 Reg.2
s.6, applied: 2013 c.29 Sch.48 para.22
s.7, applied: 2013 c.29 Sch.48 para.22
s.18, applied: 2013 c.29 s.80
s.20, amended: 2013 c.22 Sch.8 para.156
s.25, amended: 2013 c.22 Sch.9 para.68
s.27, amended: SI 2013/602 Sch.2 para.46
s.36, applied: SI 2013/1554 r.8_1
s.40, amended: 2013 c.22 Sch.8 para.186
s.41, amended: 2013 c.22 Sch.8 para.187
Sch.2 Part 1, repealed: 2013 c.29 Sch.48 para.21
Sch.2 Part 1 para.13, repealed: 2013 c.29 Sch.48 para.21
Sch.2 Part 1 para.13A, repealed: 2013 c.29 Sch.48 para.21

12. Inquiries Act 2005

applied: SI 2013/1616 r.24

14. Railways Act 2005

s.22, applied: SI 2013/339 Art.12
s.22, disapplied: SI 2013/339 Art.7
s.23, applied: SI 2013/339 Art.12
s.23, disapplied: SI 2013/339 Art.7
s.24, applied: SI 2013/339 Art.12
s.24, disapplied: SI 2013/339 Art.7
s.25, applied: SI 2013/339 Art.10, Art.15
s.25, disapplied: SI 2013/2587 Art.3
s.25, enabling: SI 2013/339
s.26, applied: SI 2013/339 Art.13
s.26, disapplied: SI 2013/339 Art.8
s.27, applied: SI 2013/339 Art.13
s.27, disapplied: SI 2013/339 Art.8
s.28, applied: SI 2013/339 Art.13
s.28, disapplied: SI 2013/339 Art.8
s.29, applied: SI 2013/339 Art.14
s.29, disapplied: SI 2013/339 Art.9
s.30, applied: SI 2013/339 Art.14
s.30, disapplied: SI 2013/339 Art.9
s.31, applied: SI 2013/339 Art.14
s.31, disapplied: SI 2013/339 Art.9
s.38, enabling: SI 2013/339
s.46, enabling: SI 2013/3269
Sch.3 para.1, amended: 2013 c.32 Sch.12 para.83
Sch.3 para.1, applied: 2013 c.32 s.84
Sch.3 para.2, amended: 2013 c.32 Sch.12 para.84
Sch.3 para.2, applied: SI 2013/950
Sch.3 para.4, amended: 2013 c.32 Sch.12 para.85
Sch.3 para.4, applied: 2013 c.32 s.90

16. Clean Neighbourhoods and Environment Act 2005

s.54, enabling: SI 2013/2854

18. Education Act 2005

Part 1, applied: SI 2013/548 Sch.1 para.3, SI 2013/549 Sch.1 para.3, SI 2013/920 Sch.1 para.3, SI 2013/1145 Sch.1 para.3, SI 2013/1221 Sch.1 para.3, SI 2013/1245 Sch.1 para.3, SI 2013/2155 Sch.1 para.2
s.5, applied: SI 2013/3104 Sch.2 para.9
s.19, applied: SI 2013/541, SI 2013/3159
s.19, enabling: SI 2013/541, SI 2013/3159

19. Gambling Act 2005

see *Clockfair Ltd v Sandwell MBC* [2012] EWHC 1857 (Admin), [2013] P.T.S.R. 675 (QBD (Admin)), Lloyd Jones, J.
applied: SI 2013/3134 Reg.6
s.23, amended: SI 2013/602 Sch.2 para.49
s.24, amended: SI 2013/602 Sch.2 para.49
s.25, amended: SI 2013/602 Sch.2 para.49
s.30, amended: SI 2013/2329 Sch.1 para.12
s.31, repealed: SI 2013/2329 Sch.1 para.13
s.157, amended: SI 2013/602 Sch.1 para.8
Sch.3 para.2, repealed: SI 2013/2329 Sch.1 para.14
Sch.4 para.8, amended: SI 2013/2329 Sch.1 para.15
Sch.6 Part 1, amended: SI 2013/2329 Sch.1 para.16
Sch.6 Part 2, amended: 2013 c.22 Sch.8 para.166

22. Finance (No.2) Act 2005

s.7, amended: 2013 c.29 Sch.46 para.135
s.17, enabling: SI 2013/1772, SI 2013/2994
s.18, amended: 2013 c.29 Sch.46 para.136
s.18, enabling: SI 2013/1772, SI 2013/2994

2006

3. Equality Act 2006

applied: SI 2013/1893 Sch.2
s.7, amended: 2013 c.24 s.64
s.9, amended: 2013 c.24 s.64
s.10, repealed (in part): 2013 c.24 s.64
s.12, amended: 2013 c.24 s.64
s.13, amended: 2013 c.24 s.64
s.16, amended: 2013 c.24 s.64
s.17, amended: 2013 c.24 s.64
s.19, repealed: 2013 c.24 s.64
s.21, amended: 2013 c.22 Sch.9 para.52
s.22, amended: 2013 c.22 Sch.9 para.52
s.24, amended: 2013 c.22 Sch.9 para.52
s.27, repealed: 2013 c.24 s.64
s.28, amended: 2013 c.24 s.23
s.32, amended: 2013 c.22 Sch.9 para.52
s.39, amended: 2013 c.24 s.64
Sch.1 Part 3 para.39, amended: 2013 c.24 s.64

Sch.1 Part 5 para.52, amended: 2013 c.24 s.64
Sch.1 Part 5 para.52, repealed (in part): 2013 c.24 s.64
Sch.2 para.11, amended: 2013 c.22 Sch.9 para.52
Sch.2 para.12, amended: 2013 c.22 Sch.9 para.52
Sch.2 para.14, amended: 2013 c.18 Sch.2 para.6

13. Immigration, Asylum and Nationality Act 2006

s.4, amended: 2013 c.22 s.52
s.4, referred to: 2013 c.22 s.52
s.16, referred to: 2013 c.5 s.4
s.17, amended: 2013 c.22 Sch.9 para.52
s.17, referred to: 2013 c.5 s.4
s.19, referred to: 2013 c.5 s.4
s.36, amended: SI 2013/602 Sch.2 para.50
s.39, amended: 2013 c.22 Sch.8 para.186, SI 2013/602 Sch.2 para.50
s.47, see *Adamally (Section 47 Removal Decisions: Tribunal Procedures), Re* [2013] Imm. A.R. 306 (UT (IAC)), CMG Ockelton (Vice President); see *Ahmadi (S.47 Decision: Validity: Sapkota: Afghanistan), Re* [2013] EWCA Civ 512, [2013] 4 All E.R. 442 (CA (Civ Div)), Sullivan, L.J.; see *Patel v Secretary of State for the Home Department* [2012] EWCA Civ 741, [2013] 1 W.L.R. 63 (CA (Civ Div)), Lord Neuberger (M.R.); see *Patel v Secretary of State for the Home Department* [2013] UKSC 72, [2013] 3 W.L.R. 1517 (SC), Lord Mance, J.S.C.
s.47, amended: 2013 c.22 s.51
s.47, disapplied: SI 2013/1460 Reg.6
s.51, applied: SI 2013/617 Reg.9
s.51, enabling: SI 2013/249, SI 2013/617, SI 2013/749
s.52, applied: SI 2013/249, SI 2013/617 Reg.9
s.52, enabling: SI 2013/249, SI 2013/617, SI 2013/749
s.62, applied: 2013 c.22 s.52

14. Consumer Credit Act 2006

s.2, repealed (in part): SI 2013/1881 Sch.1 para.10
s.3, repealed: SI 2013/1881 Sch.1 para.10
s.4, repealed: SI 2013/1881 Sch.1 para.10
s.5, repealed (in part): SI 2013/1881 Sch.1 para.10
s.22, repealed (in part): SI 2013/1881 Sch.1 para.10
s.24, repealed (in part): SI 2013/1881 Sch.1 para.10
s.25, repealed (in part): SI 2013/1881 Sch.1 para.10
s.26, repealed: SI 2013/1881 Sch.1 para.10
s.27, repealed (in part): SI 2013/1881 Sch.1 para.10
s.28, repealed: SI 2013/1881 Sch.1 para.10
s.29, repealed: SI 2013/1881 Sch.1 para.10
s.30, repealed: SI 2013/1881 Sch.1 para.10
s.31, repealed: SI 2013/1881 Sch.1 para.10
s.32, repealed: SI 2013/1881 Sch.1 para.10
s.33, repealed: SI 2013/1881 Sch.1 para.10
s.34, repealed: SI 2013/1881 Sch.1 para.10
s.35, repealed: SI 2013/1881 Sch.1 para.10
s.36, repealed: SI 2013/1881 Sch.1 para.10
s.37, repealed: SI 2013/1881 Sch.1 para.10
s.38, repealed: SI 2013/1881 Sch.1 para.10
s.39, repealed: SI 2013/1881 Sch.1 para.10
s.40, repealed: SI 2013/1881 Sch.1 para.10
s.41, repealed: SI 2013/1881 Sch.1 para.10
s.42, repealed: SI 2013/1881 Sch.1 para.10
s.43, repealed: SI 2013/1881 Sch.1 para.10
s.44, repealed: SI 2013/1881 Sch.1 para.10
s.45, repealed: SI 2013/1881 Sch.1 para.10
s.46, repealed: SI 2013/1881 Sch.1 para.10
s.47, repealed: SI 2013/1881 Sch.1 para.10
s.48, repealed: SI 2013/1881 Sch.1 para.10
s.49, repealed: SI 2013/1881 Sch.1 para.10
s.50, repealed: SI 2013/1881 Sch.1 para.10
s.51, repealed (in part): SI 2013/1881 Sch.1 para.10
s.52, repealed: SI 2013/1881 Sch.1 para.10
s.53, repealed: SI 2013/1881 Sch.1 para.10
s.54, repealed: SI 2013/1881 Sch.1 para.10
s.59, repealed: SI 2013/1881 Sch.1 para.10
s.60, repealed: SI 2013/1881 Sch.1 para.10
s.61, repealed (in part): SI 2013/1881 Sch.1 para.10
s.62, repealed: SI 2013/1881 Sch.1 para.10
s.65, repealed: SI 2013/1881 Sch.1 para.10
Sch.2, repealed: SI 2013/1881 Sch.1 para.10
Sch.3 para.18, repealed: SI 2013/1881 Sch.1 para.10
Sch.3 para.19, repealed: SI 2013/1881 Sch.1 para.10
Sch.3 para.20, repealed: SI 2013/1881 Sch.1 para.10
Sch.3 para.21, repealed: SI 2013/1881 Sch.1 para.10
Sch.3 para.22, repealed: SI 2013/1881 Sch.1 para.10
Sch.3 para.23, repealed: SI 2013/1881 Sch.1 para.10
Sch.3 para.24, repealed: SI 2013/1881 Sch.1 para.10
Sch.3 para.25, repealed: SI 2013/1881 Sch.1 para.10

15. Identity Cards Act 2006

s.25, applied: SI 2013/435 Sch.1 Part 7

16. Natural Environment and Rural Communities Act 2006

s.32, amended: SI 2013/755 Sch.2 para.432
s.42, amended: SI 2013/755 Sch.2 para.433

s.43, amended: SI 2013/1506 Sch.5 para.2

21. Childcare Act 2006

Part 1, applied: SI 2013/3029 Sch.1 para.19, Sch.6 para.21
Part 3, applied: SI 2013/3029 Sch.1 para.19, Sch.6 para.21
Part 3 c.2, applied: SI 2013/3029 Sch.1 para.19, Sch.6 para.21, SI 2013/3035 Sch.1
Part 3 c.3, applied: SI 2013/3029 Sch.1 para.19, Sch.6 para.21, SI 2013/3035 Sch.1
s.6, amended: SI 2013/630 Reg.19
s.7, applied: SI 2013/3193 Reg.3, Reg.4
s.7, enabling: SI 2013/3193
s.18, applied: SI 2013/3029 Sch.1 para.19, Sch.6 para.21
s.18, referred to: SI 2013/3029 Sch.1 para.19, Sch.6 para.21, SI 2013/3035 Sch.1
s.22, amended: SI 2013/1788 Reg.4
s.26, enabling: SI 2013/2274
s.34, applied: SI 2013/3029 Sch.1 para.19, Sch.6 para.21
s.34, referred to: SI 2013/3029 Sch.1 para.19, Sch.6 para.21, SI 2013/3035 Sch.1
s.40, applied: SI 2013/3193 Reg.2
s.53, applied: SI 2013/3029 Sch.1 para.19, Sch.6 para.21
s.53, referred to: SI 2013/3029 Sch.1 para.19, Sch.6 para.21, SI 2013/3035 Sch.1
s.72, amended: 2013 c.22 Sch.11 para.203
s.79, amended: 2013 c.22 Sch.11 para.204
s.79, repealed (in part): 2013 c.22 Sch.11 para.204
s.83, amended: SI 2013/630 Reg.19
s.98F, amended: 2013 c.22 Sch.11 para.205
s.98F, repealed (in part): 2013 c.22 Sch.11 para.205
s.104, enabling: SI 2013/3193
Sch.1 para.10, applied: SI 2013/3035 Sch.1
Sch.2 para.2, repealed: 2013 c.22 Sch.10 para.99

22. Electoral Administration Act 2006

Commencement Orders: 2013 c.6 s.23
s.1, repealed: 2013 c.6 s.23
s.2, repealed: 2013 c.6 s.23
s.3, repealed: 2013 c.6 s.23
s.3A, repealed: 2013 c.6 s.23
s.4, repealed: 2013 c.6 s.23
s.5, repealed: 2013 c.6 s.23
s.6, repealed: 2013 c.6 s.23
s.7, repealed: 2013 c.6 s.23
s.8, repealed: 2013 c.6 s.23
s.77, repealed (in part): 2013 c.6 s.23
Sch.1 Part 1 para.4, repealed (in part): 2013 c.6 Sch.4 para.23
Sch.1 Part 1 para.5, repealed (in part): 2013 c.6 Sch.4 para.23
Sch.1 Part 1 para.6, repealed (in part): 2013 c.6 Sch.4 para.23
Sch.1 Part 7 para.107, amended: 2013 c.6 s.18

23. National Lottery Act 2006

s.6, amended: SI 2013/2329 Sch.1 para.28

25. Finance Act 2006

s.173, see *Revenue and Customs Commissioners v Ben Nevis (Holdings) Ltd* [2013] EWCA Civ 578, [2013] S.T.C. 1579 (CA (Civ Div)), Jackson, L.J.
s.173, applied: SI 2013/3145, SI 2013/3146, SI 2013/3147, SI 2013/3148, SI 2013/3149, SI 2013/3151, SI 2013/3152, SI 2013/3153, SI 2013/3154
s.173, enabling: SI 2013/3144, SI 2013/3145, SI 2013/3146, SI 2013/3147, SI 2013/3148, SI 2013/3149, SI 2013/3151, SI 2013/3152, SI 2013/3153, SI 2013/3154
Sch.23 para.21, repealed: 2013 c.29 s.51
Sch.25 para.4, repealed: 2013 c.29 Sch.41 para.6
Sch.25 para.5, repealed: 2013 c.29 Sch.41 para.6
Sch.25 para.7, repealed: 2013 c.29 Sch.41 para.7
Sch.25 para.8, repealed: 2013 c.29 Sch.41 para.7
Sch.25 para.9, repealed (in part): 2013 c.29 Sch.41 para.7

26. Commons Act 2006

see *R. (on the application of Barnsley MBC) v Secretary of State for Communities and Local Government* [2012] EWHC 1366 (Admin), [2013] P.T.S.R. 23 (QBD (Admin)), Foskett, J.
applied: SI 2013/3244 Art.61
Part 1, applied: SI 2013/2959 Art.3, Art.8, Sch.1 para.6, SI 2013/3244 Art.61
s.15, see *R. (on the application of Barkas) v North Yorkshire CC* [2012] EWCA Civ 1373, [2013] 1 W.L.R. 1521 (CA (Civ Div)), Richards, L.J.; see *R. (on the application of Newhaven Port and Properties Ltd) v East Sussex CC* [2013] EWCA Civ 276, [2013] 3 W.L.R. 1389 (CA (Civ Div)), Richards, L.J.; see *R. (on the application of Newhaven Port and Properties Ltd) v Secretary of State for the Environment, Food and Rural Affairs* [2013] EWCA Civ 673, [2013] 3 W.L.R. 1433 (CA (Civ Div)), Lloyd, L.J.
s.15, amended: 2013 c.27 s.14
s.15, applied: 2013 c.27 s.16, SI 2013/2587 Art.5
s.15, referred to: SI 2013/1488 Art.8
s.15A, added: 2013 c.27 s.15
s.15A, applied: SI 2013/1774 Reg.2, Reg.3, Reg.5
s.15A, enabling: SI 2013/1774
s.15B, added: 2013 c.27 s.15
s.15B, applied: SI 2013/1774 Reg.5
s.15B, enabling: SI 2013/1774
s.15C, added: 2013 c.27 s.16
s.24, amended: 2013 c.27 s.17

s.24, repealed (in part): 2013 c.27 s.17
s.26, enabling: SI 2013/2959
s.27, applied: SI 2013/2959
s.29, enabling: SI 2013/2959
s.30, enabling: SI 2013/2959
s.31, applied: SI 2013/2959
s.31, enabling: SI 2013/2959
s.34, amended: 2013 c.22 Sch.9 para.52
s.35, enabling: SI 2013/2959
s.41, amended: 2013 c.22 Sch.9 para.70
s.46, amended: 2013 c.22 Sch.9 para.52
s.59, amended: 2013 c.27 s.16
s.59, enabling: SI 2013/2959
Sch.1A, added: 2013 c.27 Sch.4
Sch.1A, referred to: 2013 c.27 s.16
Sch.1 para.1, amended: SI 2013/755 Sch.2 para.434
Sch.2, applied: SI 2013/3244 Art.61
Sch.2 para.2, applied: SI 2013/2587 Art.5
Sch.2 para.3, applied: SI 2013/2587 Art.5
Sch.2 para.4, applied: SI 2013/2587 Art.5
Sch.2 para.5, applied: SI 2013/2587 Art.5
Sch.2 para.6, applied: SI 2013/2587 Art.5
Sch.2 para.7, applied: SI 2013/2587 Art.5
Sch.2 para.8, applied: SI 2013/2587 Art.5
Sch.2 para.9, applied: SI 2013/2587 Art.5
Sch.2 para.10, applied: SI 2013/2587 Art.5
Sch.2 para.11, applied: SI 2013/2587 Art.5
Sch.2 para.12, applied: SI 2013/2587 Art.5
Sch.2 para.13, applied: SI 2013/2587 Art.5
Sch.2 para.14, applied: SI 2013/2587 Art.5

28. Health Act 2006

Commencement Orders: SI 2013/1112 Art.2
s.17, enabling: SI 2013/373
s.18, amended: SI 2013/602 Sch.2 para.51
s.18, enabling: SI 2013/373
s.20, applied: SI 2013/373 Reg.17, Reg.18
s.20, disapplied: SI 2013/373 Reg.18
s.20, enabling: SI 2013/373
s.24, applied: SI 2013/373
s.79, enabling: SI 2013/373
s.83, enabling: SI 2013/1112

29. Compensation Act 2006

s.8, amended: 2013 c.22 Sch.9 para.52
s.13, amended: 2013 c.33 s.139
s.13, repealed (in part): 2013 c.33 s.139
Sch.1 para.7, substituted: 2013 c.33 s.140
Sch.1 para.8, amended: 2013 c.33 s.139
Sch.1 para.9, amended: 2013 c.33 s.139
Sch.1 para.10, amended: 2013 c.33 s.139
Sch.1 para.11, amended: 2013 c.33 s.139
Sch.1 para.14, amended: 2013 c.33 s.139
Sch.1 para.16, added: 2013 c.33 s.139

30. Commissioner for Older People (Wales) Act 2006

Sch.2, amended: SI 2013/755 Sch.2 para.435

32. Government of Wales Act 2006

s.13, applied: SI 2013/1514
s.13, enabling: SI 2013/1514
s.18, amended: 2013 c.8 Sch.1 para.5
s.18, repealed (in part): 2013 c.8 Sch.1 para.5
s.63, applied: SI 2013/64, SI 2013/2042, SI 2013/2314, SI 2013/2329, SI 2013/2352
s.148, amended: SI 2013/755 Sch.2 para.437
s.148, repealed (in part): SI 2013/755 Sch.2 para.437
s.150, applied: SI 2013/1821
s.150, enabling: SI 2013/1821
s.152, amended: SI 2013/755 Sch.2 para.438
s.157, enabling: SI 2013/1821
s.158, applied: SI 2013/123 Art.1
Sch.7 Part 1 para.4, amended: 2013 c.32 Sch.12 para.90
Sch.9 Part 5 para.32, enabling: SI 2013/1237
Sch.10 para.13, repealed: 2013 c.8 Sch.1 para.5
Sch.11 para.35, applied: SI 2013/1657

33. Northern Ireland (Miscellaneous Provisions) Act 2006

s.14, amended: SI 2013/320 Art.2
s.14, applied: SI 2013/320
s.14, enabling: SI 2013/320
Sch.4 Part 1 para.8, repealed: 2013 c.6 s.23

35. Fraud Act 2006

s.1, applied: 2013 c.22 Sch.17 para.25, SI 2013/2258 Sch.1 Part 1
s.2, see *R. v Gilbert (Stephanie Rae)* [2012] EWCA Crim 2392, [2013] Lloyd's Rep. F.C. 109 (CA (Crim Div)), Lord Judge, L.C.J.
s.2, applied: SI 2013/435 Sch.1 Part 7
s.3, applied: SI 2013/435 Sch.1 Part 7
s.4, applied: SI 2013/435 Sch.1 Part 7
s.5, applied: SI 2013/435 Sch.1 Part 7
s.6, applied: 2013 c.22 Sch.17 para.25, SI 2013/435 Sch.1 Part 7
s.7, applied: 2013 c.22 Sch.17 para.25, SI 2013/435 Sch.1 Part 7
s.9, applied: SI 2013/435 Sch.1 Part 7
s.11, applied: 2013 c.22 Sch.17 para.25, SI 2013/435 Sch.1 Part 7

40. Education and Inspections Act 2006

applied: SI 2013/3110 Sch.4 para.3
Part 2, applied: SI 2013/3104 Sch.1 para.10
s.7, see *R. (on the application of British Humanist Association) v Richmond upon Thames LBC* [2012] EWHC 3622 (Admin), [2013] 2 All E.R. 146 (QBD (Admin)), Sales, J.
s.7, applied: SI 2013/3109 Reg.4, Reg.13, Reg.16, Reg.24
s.7, referred to: SI 2013/3109 Reg.2

s.7, varied: SI 2013/3109 Sch.4 para.2
s.7, enabling: SI 2013/3109
s.10, see *R. (on the application of British Humanist Association) v Richmond upon Thames LBC* [2012] EWHC 3622 (Admin), [2013] 2 All E.R. 146 (QBD (Admin)), Sales, J.
s.10, applied: SI 2013/3109 Reg.3, Reg.8, Reg.10, Reg.13, Reg.16, Reg.24, Sch.1 para.5
s.10, referred to: SI 2013/3109 Reg.2
s.10, varied: SI 2013/3109 Sch.4 para.2
s.10, enabling: SI 2013/3109
s.11, see *R. (on the application of British Humanist Association) v Richmond upon Thames LBC* [2012] EWHC 3622 (Admin), [2013] 2 All E.R. 146 (QBD (Admin)), Sales, J.
s.11, applied: SI 2013/3109 Reg.3, Reg.9, Reg.10, Reg.13, Reg.16, Reg.24
s.11, referred to: SI 2013/3109 Reg.2
s.11, varied: SI 2013/3109 Sch.4 para.3
s.11, enabling: SI 2013/3109
s.11A, referred to: SI 2013/3109 Reg.2
s.12, referred to: SI 2013/3109 Reg.2
s.13, enabling: SI 2013/3109
s.15, applied: SI 2013/1624 Reg.19, SI 2013/3109 Reg.3, Reg.12, Reg.13, Sch.2 para.9
s.15, referred to: SI 2013/3109 Reg.2
s.15, enabling: SI 2013/2655, SI 2013/3109
s.16, applied: SI 2013/1624 Reg.19
s.18, enabling: SI 2013/3110
s.19, enabling: SI 2013/3110
s.21, enabling: SI 2013/3110
s.22, enabling: SI 2013/3110
s.23, enabling: SI 2013/3110
s.24, enabling: SI 2013/3110
s.60, applied: SI 2013/3104 Sch.1 para.9
s.60A, applied: SI 2013/3104 Sch.1 para.9
s.63, applied: SI 2013/3104 Sch.1 para.9
s.64, applied: SI 2013/3104 Sch.1 para.9
s.65, applied: SI 2013/3104 Sch.1 para.9
s.66, applied: SI 2013/3104 Sch.1 para.9
s.67, applied: SI 2013/1624 Reg.7, Reg.9
s.89, applied: SI 2013/1793 Reg.12
s.92, applied: SI 2013/1793 Reg.12
s.106, enabling: SI 2013/757
s.114, enabling: SI 2013/245, SI 2013/542, SI 2013/787, SI 2013/1118, SI 2013/1448, SI 2013/1717, SI 2013/2596, SI 2013/2871, SI 2013/3158
s.147, enabling: SI 2013/523
s.151, enabling: SI 2013/523
s.155, enabling: SI 2013/523
s.181, enabling: SI 2013/757, SI 2013/3109, SI 2013/3110
s.183, enabling: SI 2013/3109, SI 2013/3110
Sch.2, applied: SI 2013/3104 Sch.1 para.10, SI 2013/3109 Reg.24
Sch.2 Part 1, applied: SI 2013/3109 Reg.21
Sch.2 Part 1 para.1, varied: SI 2013/3109 Sch.3 para.1
Sch.2 Part 1 para.2, varied: SI 2013/3109 Sch.3 para.2
Sch.2 Part 1 para.5, applied: SI 2013/3109 Reg.21
Sch.2 Part 1 para.5, varied: SI 2013/3109 Sch.3 para.3
Sch.2 Part 1 para.5, enabling: SI 2013/3109
Sch.2 Part 2 para.5A, applied: SI 2013/3109 Reg.5
Sch.2 Part 2 para.7A, applied: SI 2013/3109 Reg.5
Sch.2 Part 2 para.8, applied: SI 2013/3109 Reg.7, Reg.13, Reg.14, Reg.16, Reg.20
Sch.2 Part 2 para.8, varied: SI 2013/3109 Sch.3 para.4, Sch.4 para.3, Sch.4 para.4, Sch.4 para.5, Sch.4 para.6
Sch.2 Part 2 para.8, enabling: SI 2013/3109
Sch.2 Part 2 para.9, applied: SI 2013/3109 Reg.20
Sch.2 Part 2 para.10, applied: SI 2013/3109 Reg.7, Reg.13, Reg.17, Reg.20
Sch.2 Part 2 para.10, enabling: SI 2013/3109
Sch.2 Part 2 para.11, applied: SI 2013/3109 Reg.20
Sch.2 Part 2 para.13, applied: SI 2013/3109 Reg.17, Reg.20
Sch.2 Part 2 para.13, varied: SI 2013/3109 Sch.3 para.4
Sch.2 Part 2 para.13, enabling: SI 2013/3109
Sch.2 Part 2 para.14, applied: SI 2013/3109 Reg.18, Reg.23
Sch.2 Part 2 para.14, varied: SI 2013/3109 Sch.3 para.5
Sch.2 Part 2 para.14, enabling: SI 2013/3109
Sch.2 Part 2 para.15, applied: SI 2013/3109 Reg.19
Sch.2 Part 2 para.15, enabling: SI 2013/3109
Sch.2 Part 2 para.19, applied: SI 2013/3109 Reg.15, Reg.20
Sch.2 Part 2 para.19, enabling: SI 2013/3109
Sch.2 Part 2 para.20, enabling: SI 2013/3109
Sch.2 Part 3 para.21, applied: SI 2013/3109 Reg.20, Reg.21, Reg.22, Reg.23
Sch.2 Part 3 para.21, disapplied: SI 2013/3109 Reg.21
Sch.2 Part 3 para.21, enabling: SI 2013/3109

41. National Health Service Act 2006

see *Coombs v Dorset NHS Primary Care Trust* [2013] EWCA Civ 471, [2013] 4 All E.R. 429 (CA (Civ Div)), Rix, L.J.
applied: SI 2013/160 Art.9, SI 2013/235 Sch.3 para.19, Sch.3 para.20, Sch.3 para.23, SI 2013/261 Reg.7, SI 2013/349 Reg.89, Reg.91, Reg.92,

Reg.115, Sch.7 para.26, Sch.9 para.1, Sch.9 para.3, Sch.9 para.14, Sch.9 para.15, SI 2013/363 Sch.1 para.10, SI 2013/377 Reg.29, SI 2013/461 Reg.2, Reg.8, Reg.15, Reg.16, SI 2013/469 Sch.1, SI 2013/1617 Reg.3, Reg.4, Reg.5, SI 2013/2269 Reg.16
referred to: SI 2013/349 Sch.9 para.1, SI 2013/2269 Reg.9
Part 4, applied: SI 2013/335 Reg.42, SI 2013/363 Sch.1 para.21, Sch.2 para.19, SI 2013/2677 Reg.5
Part 5, applied: SI 2013/364 Sch.1 para.15, Sch.2 para.15, SI 2013/2677 Reg.5
Part 6, applied: SI 2013/365 Reg.20
Part 7, applied: SI 2013/257 Reg.1, SI 2013/349 Reg.106, Sch.2 para.5, SI 2013/500 Reg.1
Part 7 c.1, applied: SI 2013/349 Reg.62, Sch.2 para.26
Part 7 c.2, applied: SI 2013/349 Sch.9 para.15
Part 7 c.6, applied: SI 2013/349 Reg.11, Reg.76, Sch.9 para.13
Part 9, applied: SI 2013/349 Reg.95, Sch.7 para.17
s.1F, applied: SI 2013/349 Sch.4 para.33, Sch.5 para.23, Sch.7 para.16
s.2, applied: SI 2013/261 Sch.1 para.1, SI 2013/349 Reg.117, SI 2013/351 Reg.2, SI 2013/2214 Reg.5, Reg.6
s.2A, amended: 2013 c.32 Sch.12 para.91
s.2A, applied: SI 2013/351 Reg.7, Reg.8
s.2B, applied: SI 2013/259 Reg.7, SI 2013/351 Reg.4, Reg.6, Reg.7, Reg.9
s.3, applied: SI 2013/259 Reg.7, SI 2013/261 Reg.2, Sch.1 para.2, SI 2013/350 Reg.2, SI 2013/351 Reg.7
s.3, disapplied: SI 2013/350 Reg.2
s.3, enabling: SI 2013/350, SI 2013/2891
s.3A, applied: SI 2013/259 Reg.7, SI 2013/261 Reg.2, Sch.1 para.3, SI 2013/351 Reg.7
s.3B, applied: SI 2013/259 Reg.7, Reg.8
s.3B, enabling: SI 2013/261
s.4, applied: SI 2013/259 Reg.7
s.5, applied: SI 2013/380 Reg.61, SI 2013/3035 Sch.1
s.6, applied: SI 2013/378 Reg.41, SI 2013/379 Reg.91
s.6A, amended: SI 2013/2269 Reg.7
s.6A, applied: SI 2013/261 Reg.3, Reg.4, Reg.6, Reg.7, Reg.8
s.6B, applied: SI 2013/261 Reg.3, Reg.4, Reg.6, Reg.8
s.6BA, added: SI 2013/2269 Reg.7
s.6BA, applied: SI 2013/261 Reg.3, Reg.4, Reg.6, SI 2013/2269 Reg.14
s.6BB, added: SI 2013/2269 Reg.7
s.6BB, applied: SI 2013/261 Reg.3, Reg.4, Reg.6
s.6C, applied: SI 2013/259 Reg.7
s.6C, enabling: SI 2013/351
s.6D, enabling: SI 2013/261
s.6E, enabling: SI 2013/2891
s.7, applied: SI 2013/469
s.7, enabling: SI 2013/261, SI 2013/349, SI 2013/469
s.7A, applied: SI 2013/259 Reg.7, SI 2013/261 Sch.1 para.4
s.8, enabling: SI 2013/261, SI 2013/349
s.9, applied: SI 2013/257 Reg.1, SI 2013/349 Reg.103, Reg.109, Sch.7 para.22, Sch.7 para.23
s.12, applied: SI 2013/351 Reg.2, SI 2013/378 Reg.41, SI 2013/379 Reg.91
s.12A, applied: SI 2013/3029 Sch.5 para.28, Sch.9 para.59, Sch.10 para.60, SI 2013/3035 Sch.1
s.12A, repealed (in part): SI 2013/1563 Art.2
s.12A, enabling: SI 2013/1617, SI 2013/2354
s.12B, applied: SI 2013/3029 Sch.5 para.28, Sch.9 para.59, Sch.10 para.60, SI 2013/3035 Sch.1
s.12B, enabling: SI 2013/1617, SI 2013/2354
s.12C, applied: SI 2013/3029 Sch.5 para.28, Sch.9 para.59, Sch.10 para.60, SI 2013/3035 Sch.1
s.12C, repealed (in part): SI 2013/1563 Art.2
s.12C, enabling: SI 2013/1563
s.12D, applied: SI 2013/3029 Sch.9 para.59, Sch.10 para.60, SI 2013/3035 Sch.1
s.12ZA, applied: SI 2013/261 Sch.1 para.5
s.13A, applied: SI 2013/474 Reg.2
s.13D, applied: SI 2013/257 Reg.3, SI 2013/500 Reg.3
s.13E, applied: SI 2013/257 Reg.3, SI 2013/474 Reg.2, SI 2013/500 Reg.3
s.13G, applied: SI 2013/349 Reg.18
s.13I, applied: SI 2013/349 Reg.18
s.13K, applied: SI 2013/349 Reg.18
s.13N, applied: SI 2013/500 Reg.3
s.13P, applied: SI 2013/349 Reg.18
s.14, enabling: SI 2013/261
s.14A, applied: SI 2013/124 Art.2, SI 2013/350 Reg.2
s.14A, enabling: SI 2013/124
s.14D, applied: SI 2013/379 Reg.37
s.14D, applied: SI 2013/488 Sch.1, SI 2013/3035 Sch.1
s.14P, applied: SI 2013/474 Reg.4
s.14Q, applied: SI 2013/257 Reg.3, SI 2013/500 Reg.3
s.14R, applied: SI 2013/257 Reg.3, SI 2013/500 Reg.3
s.14T, applied: SI 2013/351 Reg.7
s.14W, applied: SI 2013/261 Sch.1 para.6
s.14Z1, applied: SI 2013/500 Reg.3
s.14Z2, applied: SI 2013/261 Sch.1 para.7

s.14Z4, enabling: SI 2013/261
s.18, applied: SI 2013/3029 Sch.9 para.32, SI 2013/3035 Sch.1
s.19, enabling: SI 2013/261
s.25, applied: SI 2013/59, SI 2013/261 Reg.15, SI 2013/488 Sch.1, SI 2013/531, SI 2013/1698, SI 2013/2375, SI 2013/2376, SI 2013/2677 Reg.4
s.25, enabling: SI 2013/4, SI 2013/59, SI 2013/531, SI 2013/593, SI 2013/1698, SI 2013/2375, SI 2013/2376, SI 2013/2378
s.28, applied: SI 2013/260, SI 2013/295, SI 2013/1197
s.28, enabling: SI 2013/235, SI 2013/260, SI 2013/295, SI 2013/647, SI 2013/1197
s.30, applied: SI 2013/261 Reg.15, SI 2013/488 Sch.1
s.51, applied: SI 2013/488 Sch.1
s.65D, applied: SI 2013/838
s.65D, enabling: SI 2013/838
s.65F, see *R. (on the application of Lewisham LBC) v Secretary of State for Health* [2013] EWHC 2381 (Admin), [2013] P.T.S.R. 1298 (QBD (Admin)), Silber, J.
s.65F, applied: SI 2013/218 Reg.24, Reg.26, Reg.27
s.65F, referred to: SI 2013/1483 Art.2
s.65I, see *R. (on the application of Lewisham LBC) v Secretary of State for Health* [2013] EWHC 2381 (Admin), [2013] P.T.S.R. 1298 (QBD (Admin)), Silber, J.
s.65I, applied: SI 2013/218 Reg.24, Reg.26, Reg.27, SI 2013/2378
s.65I, referred to: SI 2013/2671 Art.2
s.65J, enabling: SI 2013/1483, SI 2013/2671
s.71, applied: SI 2013/497
s.71, enabling: SI 2013/497
s.73A, enabling: SI 2013/261
s.73B, enabling: SI 2013/261
s.75, applied: SI 2013/2356 Reg.4, SI 2013/3104 Sch.1 para.7
s.75, enabling: SI 2013/261, SI 2013/1617
s.77, applied: SI 2013/2356 Reg.4
s.80, applied: SI 2013/261 Sch.1 para.8
s.83, applied: SI 2013/257 Reg.11, SI 2013/259 Reg.7, SI 2013/350 Reg.2, SI 2013/500 Reg.11, SI 2013/1617 Reg.8
s.83, enabling: SI 2013/363
s.84, applied: SI 2013/1617 Reg.8
s.85, enabling: SI 2013/363
s.86, enabling: SI 2013/363
s.87, applied: SI 2013/349 Reg.92, Sch.9 para.14
s.88, enabling: SI 2013/363, SI 2013/2194
s.89, enabling: SI 2013/363
s.90, amended: 2013 c.22 Sch.9 para.52
s.90, enabling: SI 2013/363
s.91, enabling: SI 2013/335, SI 2013/363
s.92, applied: SI 2013/160 Sch.1 para.5, SI 2013/1617 Reg.8
s.93, enabling: SI 2013/363
s.94, amended: 2013 c.22 Sch.9 para.52
s.94, enabling: SI 2013/363
s.97, enabling: SI 2013/363
s.98A, applied: SI 2013/261 Sch.1 para.9
s.99, applied: SI 2013/259 Reg.7
s.102, enabling: SI 2013/364
s.103, applied: SI 2013/469 Reg.2, Sch.1
s.104, enabling: SI 2013/364
s.105, amended: 2013 c.22 Sch.9 para.52
s.105, enabling: SI 2013/364
s.106, applied: SI 2013/469 Sch.1
s.106, enabling: SI 2013/335
s.107, applied: SI 2013/160 Sch.1 para.5
s.108, enabling: SI 2013/364
s.109, amended: 2013 c.22 Sch.9 para.52
s.109, applied: SI 2013/469 Reg.2, Sch.1
s.109, enabling: SI 2013/364
s.111, applied: SI 2013/259 Reg.7
s.112, applied: SI 2013/469 Sch.1
s.115, applied: SI 2013/259 Reg.7
s.115, enabling: SI 2013/365, SI 2013/2555
s.116, enabling: SI 2013/365, SI 2013/2555
s.118, enabling: SI 2013/365
s.119, enabling: SI 2013/365
s.121, enabling: SI 2013/365
s.122, amended: 2013 c.22 Sch.9 para.52
s.122, enabling: SI 2013/365
s.123, enabling: SI 2013/335
s.125A, applied: SI 2013/261 Sch.1 para.10
s.126, applied: SI 2013/259 Reg.7, SI 2013/349 Sch.7 para.26
s.126, enabling: SI 2013/349
s.127, applied: SI 2013/349 Sch.7 para.26
s.127, referred to: SI 2013/349 Reg.89
s.128A, applied: SI 2013/349 Reg.3
s.128A, enabling: SI 2013/349
s.129, applied: SI 2013/349 Reg.6
s.129, disapplied: SI 2013/349 Reg.23, Reg.24, Reg.25, Reg.26, Reg.27, Reg.28, Reg.29, Sch.2 para.8
s.129, referred to: SI 2013/349 Reg.13, Reg.15, Reg.17, Reg.18, Reg.20
s.129, enabling: SI 2013/349
s.130, enabling: SI 2013/349
s.131, applied: SI 2013/349 Sch.2 para.12
s.132, enabling: SI 2013/349
s.136, enabling: SI 2013/349
s.139, amended: 2013 c.22 Sch.9 para.52
s.139, enabling: SI 2013/349

s.140, enabling: SI 2013/349
s.142, enabling: SI 2013/349
s.143, enabling: SI 2013/349
s.145, enabling: SI 2013/349
s.148, enabling: SI 2013/349
s.150A, enabling: SI 2013/349
s.151, applied: SI 2013/349 Reg.35, Reg.76, Reg.78, Reg.79, Reg.82, Reg.88
s.151, referred to: SI 2013/349 Reg.105, Sch.7 para.29, SI 2013/461 Reg.21
s.151, enabling: SI 2013/349
s.152, applied: SI 2013/349 Reg.76, Reg.82, Reg.88
s.154, applied: SI 2013/349 Reg.76, Reg.83, Reg.88
s.154, enabling: SI 2013/349
s.155, applied: SI 2013/349 Reg.83, Reg.88
s.157, applied: SI 2013/349 Reg.82, Reg.83, Reg.84, Reg.85
s.157, referred to: SI 2013/349 Reg.84
s.158, applied: SI 2013/349 Reg.82, Reg.84
s.159, applied: SI 2013/461 Reg.21
s.159, varied: SI 2013/349 Reg.87
s.159, enabling: SI 2013/349
s.160, enabling: SI 2013/349
s.161, enabling: SI 2013/349
s.162, enabling: SI 2013/349
s.163, enabling: SI 2013/349
s.164, applied: SI 2013/349 Reg.89, Reg.90, Reg.93
s.164, enabling: SI 2013/349
s.165, applied: SI 2013/349 Reg.89
s.168A, applied: SI 2013/349 Reg.101
s.169, enabling: SI 2013/349
s.172, applied: SI 2013/1617 Reg.8
s.172, enabling: SI 2013/475
s.175, applied: SI 2013/2269 Reg.13, Reg.14
s.176, applied: SI 2013/1617 Reg.8
s.176, enabling: SI 2013/364, SI 2013/475, SI 2013/711
s.177, applied: SI 2013/469 Sch.1
s.177, enabling: SI 2013/364
s.179, applied: SI 2013/1617 Reg.8
s.179, enabling: SI 2013/461
s.180, applied: SI 2013/461 Reg.8, Reg.21, Reg.27
s.180, enabling: SI 2013/461, SI 2013/1856
s.181, applied: SI 2013/461 Reg.21, Reg.22
s.181, enabling: SI 2013/461
s.182, enabling: SI 2013/461, SI 2013/475, SI 2013/1600
s.183, amended: SI 2013/2269 Reg.8
s.183, enabling: SI 2013/475, SI 2013/1600
s.184, enabling: SI 2013/475, SI 2013/1600
s.185, enabling: SI 2013/365
s.186, enabling: SI 2013/365
s.186A, enabling: SI 2013/351
s.188, enabling: SI 2013/475
s.213, enabling: SI 2013/132
s.217, enabling: SI 2013/132
s.222, applied: SI 2013/261 Sch.1 para.11
s.223B, applied: SI 2013/259 Reg.7, Reg.8
s.223G, applied: SI 2013/259 Reg.7
s.223H, referred to: SI 2013/474 Reg.4
s.223I, applied: SI 2013/474 Reg.4
s.223J, applied: SI 2013/474 Reg.4
s.223K, applied: SI 2013/474 Reg.4, Reg.5, Reg.6
s.223K, referred to: SI 2013/474 Reg.2, Reg.3
s.223K, enabling: SI 2013/474
s.236, applied: SI 2013/261 Reg.17
s.236, enabling: SI 2013/261
s.244, enabling: SI 2013/218
s.245, enabling: SI 2013/218
s.246, applied: SI 2013/218 Reg.30
s.247, enabling: SI 2013/218
s.252A, applied: SI 2013/261 Sch.1 para.12
s.256, amended: SI 2013/2341 Art.4
s.256, applied: SI 2013/261 Sch.1 para.13
s.257, applied: SI 2013/261 Sch.1 para.14
s.259, enabling: SI 2013/363
s.261, enabling: SI 2013/2881
s.262, enabling: SI 2013/2881
s.263, applied: SI 2013/2881
s.263, enabling: SI 2013/2881
s.264, applied: SI 2013/2881
s.264, enabling: SI 2013/2881
s.265, applied: SI 2013/2881
s.265, enabling: SI 2013/2881
s.266, enabling: SI 2013/2881
s.269, applied: SI 2013/261 Reg.9
s.269, enabling: SI 2013/261
s.272, applied: SI 2013/350, SI 2013/351, SI 2013/1563
s.272, enabling: SI 2013/4, SI 2013/59, SI 2013/132, SI 2013/218, SI 2013/235, SI 2013/260, SI 2013/261, SI 2013/295, SI 2013/335, SI 2013/349, SI 2013/350, SI 2013/351, SI 2013/363, SI 2013/364, SI 2013/365, SI 2013/461, SI 2013/469, SI 2013/474, SI 2013/475, SI 2013/497, SI 2013/531, SI 2013/569, SI 2013/593, SI 2013/647, SI 2013/679, SI 2013/711, SI 2013/1197, SI 2013/1441, SI 2013/1600, SI 2013/1617, SI 2013/1698, SI 2013/1856, SI 2013/2194, SI 2013/2354, SI 2013/2375, SI 2013/2376, SI 2013/2378, SI 2013/2555, SI 2013/2881, SI 2013/2891
s.273, enabling: SI 2013/4, SI 2013/59, SI 2013/235, SI 2013/260, SI 2013/261, SI 2013/295, SI 2013/469, SI 2013/593, SI 2013/647, SI

2013/679, SI 2013/1197, SI 2013/1698, SI 2013/2375, SI 2013/2376, SI 2013/2378
s.274, enabling: SI 2013/461, SI 2013/1856
Sch.1, applied: SI 2013/259 Reg.7, SI 2013/3035 Sch.1
Sch.1 para.7A, applied: SI 2013/259 Reg.7, SI 2013/351 Reg.3
Sch.1 para.7B, applied: SI 2013/218 Reg.9, SI 2013/259 Reg.7
Sch.1 para.7B, enabling: SI 2013/218
Sch.1 para.8, applied: SI 2013/351 Reg.6
Sch.1 para.9, applied: SI 2013/259 Reg.7, SI 2013/261 Sch.1 para.15, SI 2013/3029 Sch.1 para.19, Sch.1 para.20, Sch.6 para.21, Sch.7 para.10, SI 2013/3035 Sch.1
Sch.1 para.10, applied: SI 2013/261 Sch.1 para.15, SI 2013/380 Reg.61, SI 2013/3029 Sch.1 para.20, Sch.7 para.10
Sch.1 para.13, applied: SI 2013/259 Reg.7, SI 2013/261 Sch.1 para.16
Sch.1A Part 2 para.16, applied: SI 2013/261 Sch.1 para.17
Sch.4 Part 1 para.5, enabling: SI 2013/531, SI 2013/593
Sch.4 Part 1 para.7, enabling: SI 2013/531
Sch.4 Part 1 para.10, enabling: SI 2013/679, SI 2013/1441
Sch.4 Part 2 para.18, applied: SI 2013/378 Reg.41, SI 2013/379 Reg.91
Sch.4 Part 3 para.28, enabling: SI 2013/2378
Sch.5 para.1, applied: SI 2013/569
Sch.5 para.1, enabling: SI 2013/569
Sch.11, applied: SI 2013/349 Sch.9 para.15
Sch.11 para.1, enabling: SI 2013/349
Sch.12 para.2, applied: SI 2013/349 Reg.99
Sch.12 para.2, enabling: SI 2013/349
Sch.12 para.3, amended: 2013 c.22 Sch.9 para.52
Sch.12 para.3, enabling: SI 2013/349
Sch.15 para.3, applied: SI 2013/160 Art.4
Sch.15 para.4, applied: SI 2013/160 Art.4
Sch.15 para.5, applied: SI 2013/160 Art.4
Sch.15 para.8, applied: SI 2013/160 Art.4
Sch.17, applied: SI 2013/218 Reg.30

42. National Health Service (Wales) Act 2006
applied: SI 2013/335 Reg.43, SI 2013/377 Reg.29, SI 2013/898 Reg.41, Reg.42, SI 2013/2269 Reg.12, Reg.14, Reg.16
s.5, applied: SI 2013/380 Reg.61, SI 2013/3029 Sch.1 para.19, Sch.6 para.21, Sch.7 para.10, SI 2013/3035 Sch.1
s.6, applied: SI 2013/378 Reg.41, SI 2013/379 Reg.91
s.6A, amended: SI 2013/2269 Reg.10
s.6BA, added: SI 2013/2269 Reg.10
s.6BB, added: SI 2013/2269 Reg.10
s.10, applied: SI 2013/378 Reg.41, SI 2013/379 Reg.91
s.11, applied: SI 2013/379 Reg.37, SI 2013/3029 Sch.9 para.32, SI 2013/3035 Sch.1
s.11, enabling: SI 2013/2918
s.15, enabling: SI 2013/898
s.18, applied: SI 2013/2729
s.18, enabling: SI 2013/2729
s.33, applied: SI 2013/2356 Reg.4
s.45, applied: SI 2013/898 Sch.6 para.9
s.46, enabling: SI 2013/683
s.48, amended: 2013 c.22 Sch.9 para.52
s.52, amended: 2013 c.22 Sch.9 para.52
s.62, amended: 2013 c.22 Sch.9 para.52
s.66, amended: 2013 c.22 Sch.9 para.52
s.71, enabling: SI 2013/543, SI 2013/684
s.80, applied: SI 2013/898 Sch.5 para.1, Sch.6 para.2
s.80, enabling: SI 2013/898
s.81, applied: SI 2013/898 Reg.41
s.83, enabling: SI 2013/898
s.84, enabling: SI 2013/898
s.86, enabling: SI 2013/898
s.88, applied: SI 2013/898 Reg.41
s.88, enabling: SI 2013/898
s.89, applied: SI 2013/898 Reg.41
s.97, amended: 2013 c.22 Sch.9 para.52
s.104, enabling: SI 2013/898
s.107, applied: SI 2013/898 Reg.40
s.107, enabling: SI 2013/898
s.108, applied: SI 2013/898 Reg.38, Reg.40
s.110, applied: SI 2013/898 Reg.36, Reg.38, Reg.40
s.110, enabling: SI 2013/898
s.111, applied: SI 2013/898 Reg.36
s.113, applied: SI 2013/898 Reg.34, Reg.36, Reg.38
s.114, applied: SI 2013/898 Reg.38
s.115, enabling: SI 2013/898
s.116, enabling: SI 2013/898
s.118, enabling: SI 2013/898
s.121, applied: SI 2013/898 Sch.4 para.37, Sch.5 para.25
s.124, applied: SI 2013/2269 Reg.13, Reg.14
s.125, enabling: SI 2013/544
s.128, enabling: SI 2013/543, SI 2013/684
s.129, enabling: SI 2013/543, SI 2013/684
s.130, enabling: SI 2013/543, SI 2013/684
s.131, amended: SI 2013/2269 Reg.11
s.131, enabling: SI 2013/684
s.203, enabling: SI 2013/543, SI 2013/544, SI 2013/683, SI 2013/684, SI 2013/2918
s.204, enabling: SI 2013/2729, SI 2013/2918

s.205, enabling: SI 2013/898
Sch.1, applied: SI 2013/3029 Sch.1 para.19, Sch.6 para.21, Sch.7 para.10, SI 2013/3035 Sch.1
Sch.1 para.5, applied: SI 2013/3029 Sch.1 para.20
Sch.1 para.10, applied: SI 2013/380 Reg.61
Sch.2 Part 2 para.11, enabling: SI 2013/2918
Sch.2 Part 2 para.12, enabling: SI 2013/2918
Sch.3 Part 1 para.5, enabling: SI 2013/2729
Sch.3 Part 2 para.18, applied: SI 2013/378 Reg.41, SI 2013/379 Reg.91
Sch.7 para.3, amended: 2013 c.22 Sch.9 para.52
Sch.11, applied: SI 2013/218 Reg.30

43. National Health Service (Consequential Provisions) Act 2006

s.4, enabling: SI 2013/295
Sch.1 para.170, repealed (in part): SI 2013/594 Art.8
Sch.1 para.183, repealed: SI 2013/594 Art.8
Sch.2 Part 2 para.8, enabling: SI 2013/295

46. Companies Act 2006

see *Fort Gilkicker Ltd, Re* [2013] EWHC 348 (Ch), [2013] Ch. 551 (Ch D (Companies Ct)), Briggs, J.; see *Joint Liquidators of the Scottish Coal Co Ltd, Petitioners* [2013] CSOH 124, 2013 S.L.T. 1055 (OH), Lord Hodge; see *Liberty Mercian Ltd v Cuddy Civil Engineering Ltd* [2013] EWHC 2688 (TCC), [2013] T.C.L.R. 9 (QBD (TCC)), Ramsey, J.
applied: 2013 c.32 Sch.2 para.5, 2013 c.33 Sch.4 para.7, SI 2013/1046 r.34, SI 2013/1973 Reg.9, SI 2013/2605 Art.23, Art.57, SI 2013/3008 Reg.3, SI 2013/3208 r.35
disapplied: SI 2013/3008 Reg.3
Part 10 c.4, applied: 2013 c.24 s.5
Part 10 c.4A, applied: 2013 c.24 s.5
Part 10 c.4A, disapplied: 2013 c.24 s.82
Part 15, applied: 2013 c.24 s.5
Part 15 c.7, amended: SI 2013/1970 Reg.10
Part 16, applied: 2013 c.24 s.5
Part 16, disapplied: 2013 c.33 Sch.4 para.8
Part 31, applied: SSI 2013/174 Reg.16
s.30, applied: SI 2013/442 Art.52
s.31, applied: SSI 2013/174 Reg.14
s.48, applied: SI 2013/1047 r.77
s.104, applied: SI 2013/898 Reg.33
s.107, applied: SI 2013/898 Reg.34
s.108, applied: SI 2013/898 Reg.34
s.146, amended: SI 2013/1970 Sch.1 para.2
s.146, applied: SI 2013/1973 Reg.4
s.180, amended: 2013 c.24 s.81
s.190, amended: 2013 c.24 s.81
s.215, amended: 2013 c.24 s.81
s.226A, added: 2013 c.24 s.80
s.226B, added: 2013 c.24 s.80
s.226C, added: 2013 c.24 s.80
s.226D, added: 2013 c.24 s.80
s.226D, varied: 2013 c.24 s.82
s.226E, added: 2013 c.24 s.80
s.226F, added: 2013 c.24 s.80
s.323, applied: SI 2013/1047 r.20, r.77
s.382, amended: SI 2013/3008 Reg.4
s.382, referred to: SI 2013/532 Reg.49
s.383, amended: SI 2013/3008 Reg.4
s.384, amended: SI 2013/2005 Reg.2
s.384A, added: SI 2013/3008 Reg.4
s.384B, added: SI 2013/3008 Reg.4
s.385, applied: 2013 c.24 s.5
s.393, amended: SI 2013/3008 Reg.5
s.396, amended: SI 2013/3008 Reg.5
s.396, enabling: SI 2013/3008
s.409, enabling: SI 2013/2005
s.414, amended: SI 2013/3008 Reg.5
s.414A, added: SI 2013/1970 Reg.3
s.414B, added: SI 2013/1970 Reg.3
s.414C, added: SI 2013/1970 Reg.3
s.414D, added: SI 2013/1970 Reg.3
s.414E, added: SI 2013/1970 Reg.3
s.415, applied: 2013 c.24 s.5
s.415A, amended: SI 2013/1970 Reg.4
s.416, repealed (in part): SI 2013/1970 Reg.6
s.416, enabling: SI 2013/1970
s.417, repealed: SI 2013/1970 Reg.5
s.421, amended: 2013 c.24 s.79
s.421, enabling: SI 2013/1981
s.422A, added: 2013 c.24 s.79
s.422A, applied: SI 2013/1981 Reg.4
s.422A, enabling: SI 2013/1981
s.423, amended: SI 2013/1970 Sch.1 para.3
s.423, applied: SI 2013/1973 Reg.6, Reg.7
s.423, referred to: SI 2013/1973 Reg.4, Reg.9
s.426, amended: SI 2013/1970 Reg.10
s.426, applied: SI 2013/1973 Reg.5
s.426, repealed (in part): SI 2013/1970 Reg.10
s.426, enabling: SI 2013/1973
s.426A, added: SI 2013/1970 Reg.12
s.427, repealed: SI 2013/1970 Reg.11
s.428, repealed: SI 2013/1970 Reg.11
s.429, repealed: SI 2013/1970 Reg.13
s.430, amended: 2013 c.24 s.81
s.431, amended: SI 2013/1970 Sch.1 para.4
s.432, amended: SI 2013/1970 Sch.1 para.5
s.433, amended: SI 2013/1970 Sch.1 para.6
s.434, repealed (in part): SI 2013/1970 Sch.1 para.7
s.435, repealed (in part): SI 2013/1970 Sch.1 para.8
s.437, applied: 2013 c.24 s.6
s.439, amended: 2013 c.24 s.79

s.439A, added: 2013 c.24 s.79
s.439A, varied: 2013 c.24 s.82
s.440, amended: 2013 c.24 s.81
s.442, applied: SI 2013/1973 Reg.5
s.444, amended: SI 2013/3008 Reg.6
s.444, applied: SI 2013/3008 Reg.2
s.445, amended: SI 2013/1970 Sch.1 para.9
s.446, amended: SI 2013/1970 Sch.1 para.10
s.447, amended: SI 2013/1970 Sch.1 para.11
s.448, amended: SI 2013/2005 Reg.2
s.454, amended: SI 2013/1970 Sch.1 para.12
s.454, enabling: SI 2013/1971, SI 2013/2224
s.455, amended: SI 2013/1970 Sch.1 para.13
s.456, amended: SI 2013/1970 Sch.1 para.14
s.456, repealed (in part): SI 2013/1970 Sch.1 para.14
s.457, amended: SI 2013/1970 Sch.1 para.15
s.459, amended: SI 2013/1970 Sch.1 para.16
s.463, amended: SI 2013/1970 Sch.1 para.17
s.463, repealed (in part): SI 2013/1970 Sch.1 para.17
s.467, amended: SI 2013/2005 Reg.2
s.468, enabling: SI 2013/1970, SI 2013/2005, SI 2013/3008
s.469, amended: SI 2013/3008 Reg.7
s.471, amended: SI 2013/1970 Sch.1 para.18, SI 2013/3008 Reg.7
s.471, repealed (in part): SI 2013/1970 Sch.1 para.18
s.472, amended: SI 2013/3008 Reg.7
s.472A, amended: SI 2013/636 Sch.1 para.9
s.473, applied: SI 2013/1970, SI 2013/1981, SI 2013/2005, SI 2013/3008
s.473, enabling: SI 2013/1970
s.474, amended: SI 2013/636 Sch.1 para.9, SI 2013/2005 Reg.2, SI 2013/3008 Reg.7
s.484, applied: SI 2013/2005
s.484, enabling: SI 2013/2005
s.493, amended: SI 2013/1970 Sch.1 para.19
s.494, amended: SI 2013/1970 Sch.1 para.20
s.495, amended: SI 2013/3008 Reg.8
s.495, applied: SI 2013/1973 Reg.5
s.496, amended: SI 2013/1970 Sch.1 para.21
s.496, applied: SI 2013/1973 Reg.5
s.497, applied: SI 2013/1973 Reg.5
s.497A, amended: SI 2013/636 Sch.1 para.9
s.497A, repealed (in part): SI 2013/636 Sch.1 para.9
s.498, amended: SI 2013/1970 Sch.1 para.22
s.538A, amended: SI 2013/636 Sch.1 para.9
s.538A, repealed (in part): SI 2013/636 Sch.1 para.9
s.539, amended: SI 2013/636 Sch.1 para.9, SI 2013/2005 Reg.2
s.658, applied: 2013 c.22 Sch.17 para.24
s.680, applied: 2013 c.22 Sch.17 para.24
s.691, amended: SI 2013/999 Reg.3
s.692, amended: SI 2013/999 Reg.4
s.693, amended: SI 2013/999 Reg.6
s.693A, added: SI 2013/999 Reg.7
s.694, amended: SI 2013/999 Reg.5, Reg.8
s.697, amended: SI 2013/999 Reg.5
s.700, amended: SI 2013/999 Reg.5
s.704, amended: SI 2013/999 Reg.9
s.712, amended: SI 2013/999 Reg.10
s.713, amended: SI 2013/999 Reg.11
s.720A, added: SI 2013/999 Reg.12
s.720B, added: SI 2013/999 Reg.12
s.723, amended: SI 2013/999 Reg.13
s.724, amended: SI 2013/999 Reg.14
s.724, repealed (in part): SI 2013/999 Reg.14
s.729, repealed (in part): SI 2013/999 Reg.15
s.737, applied: SI 2013/999
s.737, enabling: SI 2013/999
s.783, applied: 2013 c.33 s.113
s.784, applied: SI 2013/632
s.784, enabling: SI 2013/632, SI 2013/1773
s.785, enabling: SI 2013/632, SI 2013/1773
s.788, enabling: SI 2013/632
s.789, applied: SI 2013/632
s.837, repealed (in part): SI 2013/1970 Sch.1 para.23
s.855, amended: SI 2013/636 Sch.1 para.9
s.859A, added: SI 2013/600 Sch.1
s.859B, added: SI 2013/600 Sch.1
s.859C, added: SI 2013/600 Sch.1
s.859D, added: SI 2013/600 Sch.1
s.859E, added: SI 2013/600 Sch.1
s.859F, added: SI 2013/600 Sch.1
s.859G, added: SI 2013/600 Sch.1
s.859H, added: SI 2013/600 Sch.1
s.859I, added: SI 2013/600 Sch.1
s.859J, added: SI 2013/600 Sch.1
s.859K, added: SI 2013/600 Sch.1
s.859K, applied: SI 2013/618 Reg.8
s.859L, added: SI 2013/600 Sch.1
s.859L, applied: SI 2013/618 Reg.8
s.859M, added: SI 2013/600 Sch.1
s.859N, added: SI 2013/600 Sch.1
s.859O, added: SI 2013/600 Sch.1
s.859O, applied: SI 2013/618 Reg.8
s.859P, added: SI 2013/600 Sch.1
s.859Q, added: SI 2013/600 Sch.1
s.860, repealed: SI 2013/600 Reg.3
s.861, repealed: SI 2013/600 Reg.3
s.862, repealed: SI 2013/600 Reg.3
s.863, repealed: SI 2013/600 Reg.3
s.864, repealed: SI 2013/600 Reg.3

s.865, repealed: SI 2013/600 Reg.3
s.866, repealed: SI 2013/600 Reg.3
s.867, repealed: SI 2013/600 Reg.3
s.868, repealed: SI 2013/600 Reg.3
s.869, repealed: SI 2013/600 Reg.3
s.870, repealed: SI 2013/600 Reg.3
s.871, repealed: SI 2013/600 Reg.3
s.872, repealed: SI 2013/600 Reg.3
s.873, repealed: SI 2013/600 Reg.3
s.874, repealed: SI 2013/600 Reg.3
s.875, repealed: SI 2013/600 Reg.3
s.876, repealed: SI 2013/600 Reg.3
s.877, repealed: SI 2013/600 Reg.3
s.878, repealed: SI 2013/600 Reg.3
s.879, repealed: SI 2013/600 Reg.3
s.880, repealed: SI 2013/600 Reg.3
s.881, repealed: SI 2013/600 Reg.3
s.882, repealed: SI 2013/600 Reg.3
s.883, repealed: SI 2013/600 Reg.3
s.884, repealed: SI 2013/600 Reg.3
s.885, repealed: SI 2013/600 Reg.3
s.886, repealed: SI 2013/600 Reg.3
s.887, repealed: SI 2013/600 Reg.3
s.888, repealed: SI 2013/600 Reg.3
s.889, repealed: SI 2013/600 Reg.3
s.890, repealed: SI 2013/600 Reg.3
s.891, repealed: SI 2013/600 Reg.3
s.892, repealed: SI 2013/600 Reg.3
s.893, amended: SI 2013/600 Sch.2 para.3
s.894, applied: SI 2013/600
s.894, enabling: SI 2013/600
s.993, see *R. v Mackey (Karen Lesley)* [2012] EWCA Crim 2205, [2013] 1 Cr. App. R. (S.) 100 (CA (Crim Div)), Gross, L.J.
s.993, applied: 2013 c.22 Sch.17 para.24
s.1040, applied: SI 2013/3008 Reg.3
s.1043, applied: SI 2013/1046 r.2, SI 2013/1047 r.2, SI 2013/3208 r.2
s.1043, enabling: SI 2013/1972
s.1046, applied: SI 2013/1046 r.2, SI 2013/3208 r.2
s.1049, amended: SI 2013/1970 Sch.1 para.24
s.1050, amended: SI 2013/1970 Sch.1 para.25
s.1061, applied: SI 2013/3200 Sch.8 Part 3
s.1062, applied: SI 2013/3200 Sch.8 Part 3
s.1076, amended: SI 2013/600 Sch.2 para.3
s.1081, amended: SI 2013/600 Sch.2 para.3
s.1087, repealed (in part): SI 2013/600 Sch.2 para.3
s.1096, amended: SI 2013/600 Sch.2 para.3
s.1105, amended: SI 2013/600 Sch.2 para.3
s.1136, amended: SI 2013/600 Sch.2 para.3
s.1139, applied: SI 2013/1554 r.4_4
s.1156, amended: 2013 c.22 Sch.9 para.43
s.1156, applied: SI 2013/415
s.1156, repealed (in part): 2013 c.22 Sch.9 para.43
s.1156, enabling: SI 2013/415
s.1159, applied: SI 2013/452 Reg.16, SSI 2013/50 Sch.3 para.6
s.1161, referred to: 2013 c.32 s.45
s.1162, applied: SI 2013/532 Sch.2 para.14
s.1173, amended: SI 2013/3115 Sch.2 para.42
s.1183, amended: 2013 c.22 Sch.9 para.52
s.1210, amended: SI 2013/3115 Sch.2 para.42
s.1212, applied: SI 2013/1831 Reg.9
s.1219, applied: SI 2013/1672 Reg.8
s.1239, referred to: SI 2013/1672 Reg.6
s.1239, enabling: SI 2013/1672
s.1242, amended: SI 2013/1672 Reg.14
s.1242, applied: SI 2013/1672 Reg.12
s.1243, applied: SI 2013/1672 Reg.12
s.1244, applied: SI 2013/1672 Reg.12
s.1246, enabling: SI 2013/1672
s.1253, amended: SI 2013/1672 Reg.15
s.1278, repealed (in part): SI 2013/1773 Sch.1 para.42
s.1290, applied: SI 2013/600, SI 2013/632, SI 2013/999, SI 2013/1970, SI 2013/1981, SI 2013/2005, SI 2013/3008
s.1292, applied: SI 2013/1970
s.1292, enabling: SI 2013/600, SI 2013/632, SI 2013/1672, SI 2013/1947, SI 2013/1970, SI 2013/1981, SI 2013/2005, SI 2013/3008
s.1296, enabling: SI 2013/1947
s.1300, enabling: SI 2013/1947
Sch.2 Part 2 para.25, repealed (in part): SI 2013/1881 Sch.1 para.11
Sch.2 Part 2 para.31, amended: SI 2013/2329 Sch.1 para.29
Sch.2 Part 2 para.32, amended: SI 2013/2329 Sch.1 para.29
Sch.2 Part 2 para.34, amended: SI 2013/3134 Sch.4 para.6
Sch.2 Part 2 para.37, amended: SI 2013/1882 Art.10
Sch.8, amended: 2013 c.24 s.81, SI 2013/600 Sch.2 para.3, SI 2013/1970 Sch.1 para.26
Sch.10 Part 2 para.13, amended: SI 2013/1672 Reg.16
Sch.10 Part 3 para.22, applied: SI 2013/1672 Reg.8
Sch.10 Part 3 para.23A, amended: SI 2013/1672 Reg.16
Sch.10 Part 3 para.25, amended: SI 2013/1672 Reg.16
Sch.11A Part 2 para.39, repealed (in part): SI 2013/1881 Sch.1 para.11

Sch.11A Part 2 para.46, amended: SI 2013/2329 Sch.1 para.29
Sch.11A Part 2 para.47, amended: SI 2013/2329 Sch.1 para.29
Sch.11A Part 2 para.49, amended: SI 2013/3134 Sch.4 para.6
Sch.11A Part 2 para.52, amended: SI 2013/1882 Art.10
Sch.12 para.2, amended: SI 2013/1672 Reg.17
Sch.12 para.3, amended: SI 2013/1672 Reg.17

48. Police and Justice Act 2006

Commencement Orders: SI 2013/592 Art.2
s.1, repealed: 2013 c.22 Sch.8 para.168
s.13, amended: 2013 c.22 Sch.8 para.169
s.13, repealed (in part): SI 2013/602 Sch.2 para.54
s.27, amended: 2013 c.22 Sch.9 para.44
s.49, enabling: SI 2013/592
s.53, enabling: SI 2013/592
Sch.1 Part 1 para.1, repealed: 2013 c.22 Sch.8 para.170
Sch.1 Part 1 para.2, repealed: 2013 c.22 Sch.8 para.170
Sch.1 Part 1 para.3, amended: SI 2013/602 Sch.2 para.54
Sch.1 Part 1 para.3, repealed (in part): 2013 c.22 Sch.8 para.170, SI 2013/602 Sch.2 para.54
Sch.1 Part 1 para.4, amended: SI 2013/602 Sch.2 para.54
Sch.1 Part 1 para.4, repealed: 2013 c.22 Sch.8 para.170
Sch.1 Part 1 para.5, repealed: 2013 c.22 Sch.8 para.170
Sch.1 Part 1 para.6, amended: SI 2013/602 Sch.2 para.54
Sch.1 Part 1 para.6, repealed: 2013 c.22 Sch.8 para.170
Sch.1 Part 2 para.7, repealed: 2013 c.22 Sch.8 para.170
Sch.1 Part 2 para.8, repealed: 2013 c.22 Sch.8 para.170
Sch.1 Part 2 para.9, repealed: 2013 c.22 Sch.8 para.170
Sch.1 Part 2 para.10, repealed: 2013 c.22 Sch.8 para.170
Sch.1 Part 2 para.11, repealed: 2013 c.22 Sch.8 para.170
Sch.1 Part 2 para.12, repealed: 2013 c.22 Sch.8 para.170
Sch.1 Part 2 para.13, repealed: 2013 c.22 Sch.8 para.170
Sch.1 Part 2 para.14, repealed: 2013 c.22 Sch.8 para.170
Sch.1 Part 2 para.15, repealed: 2013 c.22 Sch.8 para.170
Sch.1 Part 2 para.16, repealed: 2013 c.22 Sch.8 para.170
Sch.1 Part 2 para.17, repealed: 2013 c.22 Sch.8 para.170
Sch.1 Part 2 para.18, repealed: 2013 c.22 Sch.8 para.170
Sch.1 Part 2 para.19, repealed: 2013 c.22 Sch.8 para.170
Sch.1 Part 2 para.20, repealed: 2013 c.22 Sch.8 para.170
Sch.1 Part 2 para.21, repealed: 2013 c.22 Sch.8 para.170
Sch.1 Part 2 para.22, repealed: 2013 c.22 Sch.8 para.170
Sch.1 Part 2 para.23, repealed: 2013 c.22 Sch.8 para.170
Sch.1 Part 2 para.24, repealed: 2013 c.22 Sch.8 para.170
Sch.1 Part 2 para.25, repealed: 2013 c.22 Sch.8 para.170
Sch.1 Part 2 para.26, repealed: 2013 c.22 Sch.8 para.170
Sch.1 Part 2 para.27, repealed: 2013 c.22 Sch.8 para.170
Sch.1 Part 3 para.28, repealed: 2013 c.22 Sch.8 para.170
Sch.1 Part 3 para.29, repealed: 2013 c.22 Sch.8 para.170
Sch.1 Part 3 para.30, repealed: 2013 c.22 Sch.8 para.170
Sch.1 Part 3 para.31, repealed: 2013 c.22 Sch.8 para.170
Sch.1 Part 3 para.32, repealed: 2013 c.22 Sch.8 para.170
Sch.1 Part 4 para.33, repealed: 2013 c.22 Sch.8 para.170
Sch.1 Part 4 para.34, repealed: 2013 c.22 Sch.8 para.170
Sch.1 Part 4 para.35, amended: SI 2013/602 Sch.2 para.54
Sch.1 Part 4 para.35, repealed (in part): 2013 c.22 Sch.8 para.170, SI 2013/602 Sch.2 para.54
Sch.1 Part 4 para.36, repealed: 2013 c.22 Sch.8 para.170
Sch.1 Part 5 para.37, repealed: 2013 c.22 Sch.8 para.170
Sch.1 Part 5 para.38, repealed: 2013 c.22 Sch.8 para.170
Sch.1 Part 5 para.39, repealed: 2013 c.22 Sch.8 para.170
Sch.1 Part 5 para.40, repealed: 2013 c.22 Sch.8 para.170
Sch.1 Part 5 para.41, repealed: 2013 c.22 Sch.8 para.170

Sch.1 Part 5 para.42, repealed: 2013 c.22 Sch.8 para.170
Sch.1 Part 5 para.43, repealed: 2013 c.22 Sch.8 para.170
Sch.1 Part 5 para.44, repealed: 2013 c.22 Sch.8 para.170
Sch.1 Part 5 para.45, repealed: 2013 c.22 Sch.8 para.170
Sch.1 Part 5 para.46, repealed: 2013 c.22 Sch.8 para.170
Sch.1 Part 6 para.47, repealed: 2013 c.22 Sch.8 para.170
Sch.1 Part 6 para.48, amended: SI 2013/602 Sch.2 para.54
Sch.1 Part 6 para.48, repealed (in part): 2013 c.22 Sch.8 para.170, SI 2013/602 Sch.2 para.54
Sch.1 Part 7 para.49, repealed: 2013 c.22 Sch.8 para.170
Sch.1 Part 7 para.50, repealed: 2013 c.22 Sch.8 para.170
Sch.1 Part 7 para.51, repealed: 2013 c.22 Sch.8 para.170
Sch.1 Part 7 para.52, repealed: 2013 c.22 Sch.8 para.170
Sch.1 Part 7 para.53, repealed: 2013 c.22 Sch.8 para.170
Sch.1 Part 7 para.54, repealed: 2013 c.22 Sch.8 para.170
Sch.1 Part 7 para.55, repealed: 2013 c.22 Sch.8 para.170
Sch.1 Part 7 para.56, repealed: 2013 c.22 Sch.8 para.170
Sch.1 Part 7 para.57, repealed: 2013 c.22 Sch.8 para.170
Sch.1 Part 7 para.58, repealed: 2013 c.22 Sch.8 para.170
Sch.1 Part 7 para.59, repealed: 2013 c.22 Sch.8 para.170
Sch.1 Part 7 para.60, repealed: 2013 c.22 Sch.8 para.170
Sch.1 Part 7 para.61, repealed: 2013 c.22 Sch.8 para.170
Sch.1 Part 7 para.62, repealed: 2013 c.22 Sch.8 para.170
Sch.1 Part 7 para.63, repealed: 2013 c.22 Sch.8 para.170
Sch.1 Part 7 para.64, repealed: 2013 c.22 Sch.8 para.170
Sch.1 Part 7 para.65, repealed: 2013 c.22 Sch.8 para.170
Sch.1 Part 7 para.66, repealed: 2013 c.22 Sch.8 para.170
Sch.1 Part 7 para.67, repealed: 2013 c.22 Sch.8 para.170
Sch.1 Part 7 para.68, repealed: 2013 c.22 Sch.8 para.170
Sch.1 Part 7 para.69, repealed: 2013 c.22 Sch.8 para.170
Sch.1 Part 7 para.70, repealed: 2013 c.22 Sch.8 para.170
Sch.1 Part 7 para.71, repealed: 2013 c.22 Sch.8 para.170
Sch.1 Part 7 para.72, repealed: 2013 c.22 Sch.8 para.170
Sch.1 Part 7 para.73, repealed: 2013 c.22 Sch.8 para.170
Sch.1 Part 7 para.74, repealed: 2013 c.22 Sch.8 para.170
Sch.1 Part 7 para.75, repealed: 2013 c.22 Sch.8 para.170
Sch.1 Part 7 para.76, repealed: 2013 c.22 Sch.8 para.170
Sch.1 Part 7 para.77, repealed: 2013 c.22 Sch.8 para.170
Sch.1 Part 7 para.78, repealed: 2013 c.22 Sch.8 para.170
Sch.1 Part 7 para.79, repealed: 2013 c.22 Sch.8 para.170
Sch.1 Part 7 para.80, repealed: 2013 c.22 Sch.8 para.170
Sch.1 Part 7 para.81, repealed: 2013 c.22 Sch.8 para.170
Sch.1 Part 7 para.82, repealed: 2013 c.22 Sch.8 para.170
Sch.1 Part 7 para.83, repealed: 2013 c.22 Sch.8 para.170
Sch.1 Part 7 para.84, repealed: 2013 c.22 Sch.8 para.170
Sch.1 Part 7 para.85, repealed: 2013 c.22 Sch.8 para.170
Sch.1 Part 7 para.86, repealed: 2013 c.22 Sch.8 para.170
Sch.1 Part 7 para.87, repealed: 2013 c.22 Sch.8 para.170
Sch.1 Part 7 para.88, repealed: 2013 c.22 Sch.8 para.170
Sch.1 Part 7 para.89, repealed: 2013 c.22 Sch.8 para.170
Sch.1 Part 7 para.90, repealed: 2013 c.22 Sch.8 para.170
Sch.1 Part 7 para.91, repealed: 2013 c.22 Sch.8 para.170
Sch.1 Part 7 para.92, repealed: 2013 c.22 Sch.8 para.170
Sch.13 Part 1 para.4, repealed: 2013 c.22 Sch.20 para.9
Sch.13 Part 1 para.5, repealed: 2013 c.22 Sch.20 para.9

Sch.13 Part 1 para.6, repealed: 2013 c.22 Sch.20 para.9

49. Road Safety Act 2006

Commencement Orders: SI 2013/1012 Art.2; 2013 c.32 Sch.12 para.92
s.49A, amended: SI 2013/602 Sch.2 para.55
s.57, repealed: 2013 c.32 Sch.12 para.92
s.61, enabling: SI 2013/1012
Sch.3 para.20, referred to: SI 2013/1644 Sch.1

51. Legislative and Regulatory Reform Act 2006

Part 1, applied: SI 2013/251
s.1, enabling: SI 2013/103, SI 2013/251
s.2, enabling: SI 2013/103
s.3, applied: SI 2013/103, SI 2013/251
s.13, applied: SI 2013/103, SI 2013/251
s.14, applied: SI 2013/103, SI 2013/251
s.15, applied: SI 2013/103, SI 2013/251
s.17, applied: SI 2013/103, SI 2013/251

52. Armed Forces Act 2006

applied: SI 2013/602 Sch.3 para.9, SI 2013/2603 Art.2
Part 2 c.3, applied: SI 2013/1852 Art.3
Part 4, applied: SI 2013/1852 Art.25
s.20, applied: SI 2013/2787 Reg.6
s.20A, applied: SI 2013/2787 Reg.6
s.20A, enabling: SI 2013/2787
s.42, applied: SI 2013/2787 Reg.6
s.67, applied: SI 2013/1852 Art.6
s.70, applied: SI 2013/1852 Art.6
s.90, applied: SI 2013/1852 Art.6
s.93F, applied: SI 2013/2787 Reg.6
s.93F, enabling: SI 2013/2787
s.98, applied: SI 2013/1852 Art.6
s.99, applied: SI 2013/1852 Art.6
s.100, applied: SI 2013/1852 Art.6
s.101, applied: SI 2013/1852 Art.6
s.102, applied: SI 2013/1852 Art.6
s.104, applied: SI 2013/1852 Art.6
s.105, applied: SI 2013/1852 Art.22, Art.25
s.107, applied: SI 2013/1852 Art.20, Art.22, Art.25
s.107, referred to: SI 2013/1852 Art.25
s.108, applied: SI 2013/1852 Art.22
s.112, applied: SI 2013/1852 Art.22
s.112, enabling: SI 2013/2527
s.116, applied: SI 2013/602 Sch.3 para.9
s.116, disapplied: SI 2013/1852 Art.7
s.119, applied: SI 2013/602 Sch.3 para.9
s.121, applied: SI 2013/1852 Art.7
s.122, applied: SI 2013/1852 Art.7
s.125, applied: SI 2013/1852 Art.7
s.151, enabling: SI 2013/2527
s.153, enabling: SI 2013/2527
s.155, enabling: SI 2013/1851
s.163, applied: SI 2013/1852 Art.7, Art.19, SI 2013/2524
s.163, enabling: SI 2013/1851, SI 2013/2527
s.166, applied: SI 2013/1852 Art.3
s.166, varied: SI 2013/1852 Art.3
s.178, amended: 2013 c.22 Sch.16 para.32
s.182, amended: 2013 c.22 Sch.16 para.33, Sch.16 para.37
s.183, amended: 2013 c.22 Sch.16 para.37
s.266, amended: 2013 c.22 Sch.16 para.38
s.267, amended: SI 2013/3234 Art.2
s.270, amended: 2013 c.22 Sch.16 para.34
s.270A, amended: 2013 c.3 Sch.1 para.31
s.284, amended: 2013 c.22 Sch.16 para.36
s.288, enabling: SI 2013/2527
s.322, enabling: SI 2013/1761
s.323, enabling: SI 2013/1852, SI 2013/3234, SSI 2013/233
s.365, disapplied: SI 2013/1852 Art.27
s.367, applied: SI 2013/2094 Sch.1 para.18
s.373, applied: SI 2013/1851, SI 2013/1852, SI 2013/2787, SI 2013/3234
s.374, applied: SI 2013/378 Reg.28, SI 2013/386 Reg.10
s.375, amended: SI 2013/602 Sch.2 para.56
s.382, enabling: SI 2013/2603
Sch.1 Part 1 para.9A, added: 2013 c.22 Sch.22 para.17

2007

3. Income Tax Act 2007

applied: SI 2013/378 Reg.62
Part 11 c.2, repealed: 2013 c.29 Sch.29 para.18
Part 11 c.3, repealed: 2013 c.29 Sch.29 para.18
Part 12, applied: SI 2013/2819 Reg.31
Part 12 c.2, applied: SI 2013/2819 Reg.14
s.2, amended: 2013 c.29 s.15, Sch.29 para.17
s.2, repealed (in part): 2013 c.29 Sch.29 para.17, SI 2013/2819 Reg.37
s.10, amended: 2013 c.29 s.3, SI 2013/3088 Art.2
s.12, amended: SI 2013/3088 Art.2
s.14, amended: SI 2013/2819 Reg.37
s.21, applied: 2013 c.29 s.3
s.21, enabling: SI 2013/3088
s.23, amended: 2013 c.29 Sch.3 para.2
s.23, applied: 2013 c.29 s.16, SI 2013/2819 Reg.18
s.24, amended: 2013 c.29 s.15, SI 2013/2819 Reg.37
s.24A, added: 2013 c.29 Sch.3 para.1
s.24A, applied: 2013 c.29 Sch.3 para.4, Sch.3 para.5
s.29, amended: 2013 c.29 s.56

s.32, amended: 2013 c.29 s.56
s.35, amended: 2013 c.29 s.2, SI 2013/3088 Art.3
s.35, applied: 2013 c.29 s.2, SI 2013/378 Reg.62, Reg.63, SI 2013/379 Reg.84, SI 2013/3029 Sch.1 para.13, Sch.1 para.24, Sch.6 para.15, Sch.6 para.19, Sch.6 para.25, SI 2013/3035 Sch.1
s.36, amended: SI 2013/3088 Art.3
s.36, applied: SI 2013/3029 Sch.1 para.13, Sch.1 para.24, Sch.6 para.19, Sch.6 para.25, SI 2013/3035 Sch.1
s.37, amended: SI 2013/3088 Art.3
s.37, applied: SI 2013/3029 Sch.1 para.13, Sch.1 para.24, Sch.6 para.15, Sch.6 para.19, Sch.6 para.25, SI 2013/3035 Sch.1
s.38, amended: SI 2013/3088 Art.3
s.38, applied: SI 2013/378 Reg.62, Reg.63, SI 2013/379 Reg.84
s.39, applied: SI 2013/378 Reg.62, Reg.63, SI 2013/379 Reg.84
s.40, applied: SI 2013/378 Reg.62, Reg.63, SI 2013/379 Reg.84
s.43, amended: SI 2013/3088 Art.3
s.45, amended: 2013 c.2 Sch.1 Part 10, SI 2013/3088 Art.3
s.46, amended: 2013 c.2 Sch.1 Part 10, SI 2013/3088 Art.3
s.47, amended: 2013 c.2 Sch.1 Part 10
s.48, amended: 2013 c.2 Sch.1 Part 10
s.57, amended: 2013 c.2 Sch.1 Part 10
s.57, disapplied: 2013 c.29 s.2
s.57, enabling: SI 2013/3088
s.64, see *R. (on the application of Rouse) v Revenue and Customs Commissioners* [2013] UKUT 383 (TCC), [2013] B.T.C. 1973 (UT (Tax)), Warren, J.
s.64, amended: 2013 c.29 Sch.4 para.54
s.65, amended: 2013 c.29 Sch.3 para.2
s.72, amended: 2013 c.29 Sch.4 para.54
s.73, amended: 2013 c.29 Sch.3 para.2
s.74E, added: 2013 c.29 Sch.4 para.54
s.121, amended: 2013 c.29 Sch.3 para.2
s.129, amended: 2013 c.29 Sch.3 para.2
s.133, amended: 2013 c.29 Sch.3 para.2
s.148, amended: 2013 c.29 Sch.3 para.2
s.257DG, amended: 2013 c.29 s.56
s.335, amended: 2013 c.29 Sch.27 para.2
s.335A, added: 2013 c.29 Sch.27 para.3
s.340, enabling: SI 2013/417
s.341, enabling: SI 2013/417
s.357, amended: 2013 c.29 Sch.27 para.4
s.361, amended: 2013 c.29 Sch.27 para.5
s.361, repealed (in part): 2013 c.29 Sch.27 para.5
s.383, amended: 2013 c.29 Sch.4 para.55
s.384B, added: 2013 c.29 Sch.4 para.55
s.447, amended: 2013 c.29 s.15
s.448, amended: 2013 c.29 s.15
s.449, amended: 2013 c.29 s.15
s.449, applied: SI 2013/2819 Reg.19
s.450, amended: 2013 c.29 s.15
s.450, applied: SI 2013/2819 Reg.19
s.451, amended: 2013 c.29 s.15
s.452, amended: 2013 c.29 s.15
s.462, repealed (in part): SI 2013/2819 Reg.37
s.465, amended: 2013 c.29 Sch.46 para.55
s.475, amended: 2013 c.29 Sch.45 para.103, Sch.46 para.56
s.475, referred to: 2013 c.29 Sch.45 para.41
s.476, amended: 2013 c.29 Sch.46 para.57
s.479, disapplied: SI 2013/2819 Reg.12
s.494, disapplied: SI 2013/2819 Reg.12
s.495, disapplied: SI 2013/2819 Reg.12
s.496B, disapplied: SI 2013/2819 Reg.12
s.504, repealed: SI 2013/2819 Reg.37
s.504A, repealed: SI 2013/2819 Reg.37
s.505, repealed: SI 2013/2819 Reg.37
s.532, amended: SI 2013/2819 Reg.37
s.564B, amended: SI 2013/1881 Sch.1 para.12
s.564B, varied: 2013 asp 11 Sch.7 para.25
s.564S, applied: 2013 asp 11 Sch.8 para.6
s.565, repealed: 2013 c.29 Sch.29 para.18
s.566, repealed: 2013 c.29 Sch.29 para.18
s.567, repealed: 2013 c.29 Sch.29 para.18
s.568, repealed: 2013 c.29 Sch.29 para.18
s.569, repealed: 2013 c.29 Sch.29 para.18
s.570, repealed: 2013 c.29 Sch.29 para.18
s.571, repealed: 2013 c.29 Sch.29 para.18
s.577, repealed (in part): 2013 c.2 Sch.1 Part 10
s.596, amended: 2013 c.29 s.76
s.596, repealed (in part): 2013 c.29 Sch.12 para.15, Sch.29 para.18
s.597, repealed: 2013 c.29 Sch.12 para.15
s.598, repealed: 2013 c.29 Sch.12 para.15
s.599, repealed: 2013 c.29 Sch.12 para.15
s.600, repealed: 2013 c.29 Sch.12 para.15
s.601, repealed: 2013 c.29 Sch.12 para.15
s.602, repealed: 2013 c.29 Sch.12 para.15
s.603, repealed: 2013 c.29 Sch.12 para.15
s.604, repealed: 2013 c.29 Sch.12 para.15
s.605, repealed: 2013 c.29 Sch.12 para.15
s.606, repealed (in part): 2013 c.29 Sch.12 para.15, Sch.29 para.18
s.607, repealed: 2013 c.29 Sch.12 para.15
s.608, repealed: 2013 c.29 Sch.12 para.15
s.609, repealed: 2013 c.29 Sch.12 para.15
s.610, repealed: 2013 c.29 Sch.12 para.15
s.611, repealed: 2013 c.29 Sch.12 para.15
s.614ZA, added: 2013 c.29 Sch.29 para.1
s.614ZB, added: 2013 c.29 Sch.29 para.1

s.614ZC, added: 2013 c.29 Sch.29 para.1
s.614ZD, added: 2013 c.29 Sch.29 para.1
s.643, amended: 2013 c.29 Sch.46 para.58
s.647, amended: 2013 c.29 Sch.29 para.19
s.658, amended: 2013 c.29 Sch.29 para.20
s.718, amended: 2013 c.29 Sch.10 para.2, Sch.46 para.59
s.718, repealed (in part): 2013 c.29 Sch.10 para.2
s.720, amended: 2013 c.29 Sch.10 para.3, Sch.46 para.60
s.721, amended: 2013 c.29 Sch.10 para.10, Sch.46 para.61
s.721, repealed (in part): 2013 c.29 Sch.10 para.10
s.724, amended: 2013 c.29 Sch.10 para.11
s.725, amended: 2013 c.29 Sch.10 para.12
s.725, varied: 2013 c.29 Sch.10 para.12
s.726, amended: 2013 c.29 Sch.10 para.13, Sch.45 para.91, Sch.46 para.19
s.727, amended: 2013 c.29 Sch.10 para.4, Sch.46 para.62
s.728, amended: 2013 c.29 Sch.10 para.14, Sch.46 para.63
s.728, repealed (in part): 2013 c.29 Sch.10 para.14
s.730, amended: 2013 c.29 Sch.10 para.15, Sch.45 para.91, Sch.46 para.20
s.731, amended: 2013 c.29 Sch.10 para.5
s.732, amended: 2013 c.29 Sch.46 para.64
s.735, amended: 2013 c.29 Sch.45 para.91, Sch.46 para.21
s.736, amended: 2013 c.29 Sch.10 para.6
s.742A, added: 2013 c.29 Sch.10 para.7
s.743, amended: 2013 c.29 Sch.10 para.16
s.743, repealed (in part): 2013 c.29 Sch.10 para.16
s.744, amended: 2013 c.29 Sch.10 para.17
s.745, amended: 2013 c.29 Sch.10 para.18
s.746, amended: 2013 c.29 Sch.10 para.19
s.749, amended: 2013 c.29 Sch.46 para.65
s.751, amended: 2013 c.29 Sch.10 para.8
s.809A, amended: 2013 c.29 Sch.46 para.2
s.809B, amended: 2013 c.29 Sch.45 para.152, Sch.46 para.3
s.809B, repealed (in part): 2013 c.29 Sch.46 para.3
s.809CZB, amended: SI 2013/2819 Reg.37
s.809D, amended: 2013 c.29 Sch.45 para.152, Sch.46 para.4
s.809E, amended: 2013 c.29 Sch.45 para.152, Sch.46 para.5
s.809F, amended: 2013 c.29 Sch.46 para.22
s.809K, amended: 2013 c.29 s.21
s.809Q, amended: 2013 c.29 Sch.6 para.5
s.809RA, added: 2013 c.29 Sch.6 para.6
s.809RB, added: 2013 c.29 Sch.6 para.6
s.809RC, added: 2013 c.29 Sch.6 para.6
s.809RD, added: 2013 c.29 Sch.6 para.6
s.809UA, added: 2013 c.29 s.21
s.809X, amended: 2013 c.29 Sch.7 para.2
s.809Y, amended: 2013 c.29 Sch.7 para.3
s.809YD, amended: 2013 c.29 Sch.46 para.23
s.809YF, added: 2013 c.29 Sch.7 para.4
s.809Z, amended: 2013 c.29 Sch.7 para.5
s.809Z, repealed (in part): 2013 c.29 Sch.7 para.5
s.809Z1, repealed: 2013 c.29 Sch.7 para.6
s.809Z4, amended: 2013 c.29 Sch.7 para.7
s.809Z4, applied: 2013 c.29 Sch.7 para.11
s.809Z4, repealed (in part): 2013 c.29 Sch.7 para.7
s.809Z6, amended: 2013 c.29 Sch.7 para.8
s.809Z7, amended: 2013 c.29 Sch.46 para.24
s.809Z9, amended: 2013 c.29 s.21
s.810, amended: 2013 c.29 Sch.45 para.152
s.812, amended: 2013 c.29 Sch.46 para.66
s.812A, added: 2013 c.29 Sch.45 para.138
s.825, amended: SI 2013/2819 Reg.37
s.825, repealed (in part): SI 2013/2819 Reg.37
s.829, repealed: 2013 c.29 Sch.45 para.152
s.830, repealed: 2013 c.29 Sch.45 para.152
s.831, repealed: 2013 c.29 Sch.45 para.152
s.832, repealed: 2013 c.29 Sch.45 para.152
s.834, amended: 2013 c.29 Sch.46 para.67
s.847, repealed (in part): SI 2013/2819 Reg.37
s.848, repealed (in part): SI 2013/2819 Reg.37
s.858, amended: 2013 c.29 Sch.46 para.68
s.859, amended: 2013 c.29 Sch.46 para.69
s.860, amended: 2013 c.29 Sch.46 para.70
s.861, amended: 2013 c.29 Sch.46 para.71
s.873, amended: SI 2013/2819 Reg.37
s.874, amended: 2013 c.29 Sch.11 para.2, Sch.11 para.5
s.874, applied: SI 2013/3209 Reg.6
s.875, amended: 2013 c.29 Sch.11 para.3
s.878, amended: 2013 c.29 Sch.11 para.4
s.878, disapplied: SI 2013/3209 Reg.9
s.885, disapplied: SI 2013/3209 Reg.9
s.886, amended: SI 2013/504 Reg.24
s.889, applied: SI 2013/3209 Reg.6
s.889, disapplied: SI 2013/460 Reg.3
s.899, amended: SI 2013/2819 Reg.37
s.904, amended: SI 2013/2819 Reg.37
s.918, amended: 2013 c.29 Sch.29 para.21
s.919, amended: 2013 c.29 Sch.29 para.22
s.920, repealed: 2013 c.29 Sch.29 para.23
s.921, amended: 2013 c.29 Sch.29 para.24
s.922, repealed: 2013 c.29 Sch.29 para.25
s.923, repealed: 2013 c.29 Sch.29 para.25
s.923C, repealed: 2013 c.29 Sch.29 para.25
s.924, repealed: 2013 c.29 Sch.29 para.25
s.925, repealed: 2013 c.29 Sch.29 para.25
s.925A, amended: 2013 c.29 Sch.29 para.26
s.925B, repealed: 2013 c.29 Sch.29 para.27

s.925C, amended: 2013 c.29 Sch.29 para.28
s.926, repealed (in part): 2013 c.29 Sch.29 para.29
s.939, amended: 2013 c.29 Sch.11 para.8
s.941, applied: SI 2013/2819 Reg.30, Reg.31
s.941, repealed: SI 2013/2819 Reg.37
s.942, repealed: SI 2013/2819 Reg.37
s.943, repealed: SI 2013/2819 Reg.37
s.943A, repealed: SI 2013/2819 Reg.37
s.943B, repealed: SI 2013/2819 Reg.37
s.943C, repealed: SI 2013/2819 Reg.37
s.943D, repealed: SI 2013/2819 Reg.37
s.964, repealed (in part): SI 2013/2819 Reg.37
s.966, disapplied: 2013 c.29 s.8, s.9
s.966, enabling: SI 2013/605
s.970, enabling: SI 2013/605
s.973, amended: 2013 c.29 Sch.19 para.12
s.974, amended: 2013 c.29 Sch.19 para.12
s.975, amended: 2013 c.29 Sch.11 para.9, SI 2013/2819 Reg.37
s.975, repealed (in part): SI 2013/2819 Reg.37
s.975A, added: 2013 c.29 Sch.11 para.10
s.989, amended: 2013 c.29 Sch.45 para.107
s.989, applied: SI 2013/1962 Reg.4
s.991, amended: 2013 c.33 Sch.10 para.6
s.1025, repealed (in part): SI 2013/2819 Reg.37
Sch.1 Part 2 para.254, repealed (in part): 2013 c.2 Sch.1 Part 10
Sch.1 Part 2 para.310, repealed: 2013 c.29 Sch.12 para.15
Sch.1 Part 2 para.335, repealed (in part): 2013 c.29 Sch.29 para.30
Sch.1 Part 2 para.359, repealed: 2013 c.2 Sch.1 Part 10
Sch.1 Part 2 para.541, repealed: SI 2013/2819 Reg.41
Sch.1 Part 2 para.542, repealed: SI 2013/2819 Reg.41
Sch.1 Part 2 para.543, repealed: 2013 c.29 Sch.12 para.15
Sch.1 Part 2 para.544, repealed: 2013 c.29 Sch.12 para.15
Sch.2 Part 12 para.108, repealed: 2013 c.29 Sch.29 para.31
Sch.2 Part 12 para.109, repealed: 2013 c.29 Sch.29 para.31
Sch.2 Part 12 para.110, repealed: 2013 c.29 Sch.29 para.31
Sch.2 Part 12 para.111, repealed: 2013 c.29 Sch.29 para.31
Sch.2 Part 12 para.112, repealed: 2013 c.29 Sch.12 para.15
Sch.2 Part 12 para.113, repealed: 2013 c.29 Sch.12 para.15
Sch.2 Part 12 para.114, repealed: 2013 c.29 Sch.12 para.15
Sch.2 Part 12 para.115, repealed: 2013 c.29 Sch.12 para.15
Sch.2 Part 12 para.116, repealed: 2013 c.29 Sch.12 para.15
Sch.2 Part 12 para.117, repealed: 2013 c.29 Sch.12 para.15
Sch.2 Part 12 para.118, repealed: 2013 c.29 Sch.12 para.15
Sch.2 Part 12 para.119, repealed: 2013 c.29 Sch.12 para.15
Sch.2 Part 12 para.120, repealed: 2013 c.29 Sch.12 para.15
Sch.2 Part 12 para.121, repealed: 2013 c.29 Sch.12 para.15
Sch.2 Part 12 para.122, repealed: 2013 c.29 Sch.12 para.15
Sch.2 Part 12 para.123, repealed: 2013 c.29 Sch.12 para.15
Sch.2 Part 12 para.124, repealed: 2013 c.29 Sch.12 para.15
Sch.2 Part 15 para.167, repealed: SI 2013/2819 Reg.37
Sch.2 Part 15 para.168, repealed: SI 2013/2819 Reg.37
Sch.4, amended: 2013 c.29 Sch.12 para.15, Sch.29 para.32, Sch.45 para.108, SI 2013/2819 Reg.37

6. Justice and Security (Northern Ireland) Act 2007

applied: 2013 c.12 Sch.1 para.1, 2013 c.28 Sch.1
s.9, applied: SI 2013/1619, SI 2013/1619 Art.2
s.9, enabling: SI 2013/1619
s.34, applied: SI 2013/1128, SI 2013/1128 Art.2
s.34, enabling: SI 2013/1128
s.36, enabling: SI 2013/1128

11. Finance Act 2007

Sch.14 para.22, repealed: 2013 c.29 Sch.12 para.14
Sch.14 para.23, repealed: 2013 c.29 Sch.12 para.14
Sch.24 Part 1 para.1, amended: 2013 c.29 Sch.34 para.6
Sch.24 Part 1 para.1, varied: SI 2013/938 Reg.15
Sch.24 Part 1 para.1A, varied: SI 2013/938 Reg.15
Sch.24 Part 1 para.2, varied: SI 2013/938 Reg.15
Sch.24 Part 1 para.3, applied: 2013 c.29 Sch.21 para.10, SI 2013/1618 Art.1
Sch.24 Part 2 para.4, varied: SI 2013/938 Reg.15
Sch.24 Part 2 para.4A, varied: SI 2013/938 Reg.15
Sch.24 Part 2 para.4C, varied: SI 2013/938 Reg.15
Sch.24 Part 2 para.5, varied: SI 2013/938 Reg.15
Sch.24 Part 2 para.6, varied: SI 2013/938 Reg.15
Sch.24 Part 2 para.7, varied: SI 2013/938 Reg.15
Sch.24 Part 2 para.8, varied: SI 2013/938 Reg.15
Sch.24 Part 2 para.9, varied: SI 2013/938 Reg.15
Sch.24 Part 2 para.11, varied: SI 2013/938 Reg.15

Sch.24 Part 2 para.12, varied: SI 2013/938 Reg.15
Sch.24 Part 3 para.13, amended: 2013 c.29 Sch.50 para.1
Sch.24 Part 3 para.13, varied: SI 2013/938 Reg.15
Sch.24 Part 4 para.18, varied: SI 2013/938 Reg.15
Sch.24 Part 4 para.19, varied: SI 2013/938 Reg.15
Sch.24 Part 4 para.20, varied: SI 2013/938 Reg.15
Sch.24 Part 4 para.21, varied: SI 2013/938 Reg.15
Sch.24 Part 5 para.21A, varied: SI 2013/938 Reg.15
Sch.24 Part 5 para.21A, enabling: SI 2013/1618
Sch.24 Part 5 para.21B, varied: SI 2013/938 Reg.15
Sch.24 Part 5 para.24, varied: SI 2013/938 Reg.15
Sch.24 Part 5 para.25, varied: SI 2013/938 Reg.15
Sch.24 Part 5 para.26, varied: SI 2013/938 Reg.15
Sch.24 Part 5 para.27, varied: SI 2013/938 Reg.15
Sch.24 Part 5 para.28, amended: 2013 c.29 Sch.15 para.8, Sch.18 para.7
Sch.24 Part 5 para.29, varied: SI 2013/938 Reg.15
Sch.24 Part 5 para.30, varied: SI 2013/938 Reg.15
Sch.24 Part 5 para.31, varied: SI 2013/938 Reg.15

12. Mental Health Act 2007
Sch.1 Part 1 para.16, repealed: 2013 c.8 Sch.1 para.6
Sch.3 para.33, repealed: 2013 c.8 Sch.1 para.6

16. Parliament (Joint Departments) Act 2007
s.3, amended: 2013 c.25 Sch.8 para.30

19. Corporate Manslaughter and Corporate Homicide Act 2007
s.6, amended: SI 2013/602 Sch.1 para.9
s.7, amended: SI 2013/1465 Sch.1 para.11
s.13, amended: 2013 c.22 Sch.8 para.174, SI 2013/602 Sch.2 para.57
s.13, repealed (in part): SI 2013/602 Sch.2 para.57
s.25, amended: 2013 c.32 Sch.12 para.93
Sch.1, amended: 2013 c.22 Sch.8 para.175

20. Forced Marriage (Civil Protection) Act 2007
s.1, amended: 2013 c.22 Sch.11 para.210
s.2, applied: SSI 2013/357 Art.3
Sch.1 Part 1 para.1, applied: SSI 2013/357 Art.3
Sch.2 Part 1 para.3, repealed (in part): 2013 c.22 Sch.11 para.210

21. Offender Management Act 2007
Commencement Orders: SI 2013/1963 Art.2
s.5, applied: SI 2013/488 Sch.1, SI 2013/2356 Sch.2 para.9
s.13, applied: SI 2013/3029 Reg.26, SI 2013/3035 Sch.1
s.41, enabling: SI 2013/1963

28. Local Government and Public Involvement in Health Act 2007
applied: 2013 c.12 Sch.1 para.1, 2013 c.28 Sch.1
s.8, applied: SI 2013/595, SI 2013/596
s.10, enabling: SI 2013/595, SI 2013/596
s.11, enabling: SI 2013/595, SI 2013/596
s.12, enabling: SI 2013/595, SI 2013/596
s.13, enabling: SI 2013/595, SI 2013/596
s.15, enabling: SI 2013/595, SI 2013/596
s.92, applied: SI 2013/220
s.92, enabling: SI 2013/220, SI 2013/221
s.104, amended: SI 2013/594 Art.6
s.104, repealed (in part): SI 2013/594 Art.6
s.116, applied: SI 2013/301 Reg.6, Reg.12, Reg.21
s.116A, applied: SI 2013/301 Reg.6, Reg.12, Reg.21
s.116B, applied: SI 2013/474 Reg.2
s.221, applied: SI 2013/218 Reg.21, SI 2013/351 Reg.12
s.221, referred to: SI 2013/218 Reg.21
s.225, applied: SI 2013/349 Reg.11, Reg.47, Sch.7 para.1, SI 2013/351 Reg.12, Reg.13, Reg.14
s.225, enabling: SI 2013/351
s.229, enabling: SI 2013/351
s.240, applied: SI 2013/351, SI 2013/595, SI 2013/596
s.240, enabling: SI 2013/351
Sch.3 para.23, repealed (in part): SI 2013/3005 Art.2
Sch.3 para.24, repealed (in part): SI 2013/3005 Art.2
Sch.3 para.25, repealed (in part): SI 2013/3005 Art.2

29. Legal Services Act 2007
see *R. (on the application of Prudential Plc) v Special Commissioner of Income Tax* [2013] UKSC 1, [2013] 2 A.C. 185 (SC), Lord Neuberger, J.S.C.
applied: SI 2013/1169 r.14
s.57, amended: 2013 c.24 Sch.6 para.109
s.58, amended: 2013 c.24 Sch.6 para.110
s.59, amended: 2013 c.24 Sch.6 para.111
s.60, amended: 2013 c.24 Sch.6 para.112
s.61, amended: 2013 c.24 Sch.6 para.113
s.66, amended: 2013 c.24 Sch.6 para.114
s.67, amended: 2013 c.24 Sch.6 para.115
s.141, amended: 2013 c.22 Sch.9 para.52
s.169, amended: 2013 c.22 Sch.8 para.187, SI 2013/602 Sch.2 para.58
s.174A, added: 2013 c.33 s.140
s.194, amended: 2013 c.22 Sch.9 para.101
s.195, repealed (in part): SI 2013/1881 Sch.1 para.13
s.206, amended: 2013 c.33 s.140
s.207, amended: 2013 c.24 Sch.6 para.116, SI 2013/2042 Sch.1 para.39
Sch.3 para.1, amended: 2013 c.22 Sch.10 para.98
Sch.4 Part 2, amended: 2013 c.24 Sch.6 para.117

Sch.4 Part 2 para.5, amended: 2013 c.24 Sch.6 para.117
Sch.4 Part 2 para.6, amended: 2013 c.24 Sch.6 para.117
Sch.4 Part 2 para.15, amended: 2013 c.24 Sch.6 para.117
Sch.6 para.3, amended: 2013 c.24 Sch.6 para.118
Sch.6 para.5, amended: 2013 c.24 Sch.6 para.118
Sch.6 para.8, amended: 2013 c.24 Sch.6 para.118
Sch.6 para.9, amended: 2013 c.24 Sch.6 para.118
Sch.6 para.11, amended: 2013 c.24 Sch.6 para.118
Sch.6 para.17, amended: 2013 c.24 Sch.6 para.118
Sch.7 para.3, amended: 2013 c.24 Sch.6 para.119
Sch.7 para.5, amended: 2013 c.24 Sch.6 para.119
Sch.8 Part 1 para.3, amended: 2013 c.24 Sch.6 para.120
Sch.8 Part 1 para.5, amended: 2013 c.24 Sch.6 para.120
Sch.8 Part 2 para.14, amended: 2013 c.24 Sch.6 para.120
Sch.8 Part 2 para.16, amended: 2013 c.24 Sch.6 para.120
Sch.9 para.3, amended: 2013 c.24 Sch.6 para.121
Sch.9 para.4, amended: 2013 c.24 Sch.6 para.121
Sch.10 Part 1, amended: 2013 c.24 Sch.6 para.122
Sch.10 Part 1 para.3, amended: 2013 c.24 Sch.6 para.122
Sch.10 Part 1 para.4, amended: 2013 c.24 Sch.6 para.122
Sch.10 Part 1 para.13, amended: 2013 c.24 Sch.6 para.122
Sch.10 Part 2 para.19, amended: 2013 c.24 Sch.6 para.122
Sch.10 Part 2 para.20, amended: 2013 c.24 Sch.6 para.122
Sch.16 Part 1 para.69, repealed (in part): 2013 c.22 Sch.9 para.141
Sch.21 para.130, repealed: 2013 c.2 Sch.1 Part 5
Sch.21 para.144, repealed (in part): 2013 c.22 Sch.10 para.99
Sch.24, amended: 2013 c.24 Sch.6 para.123

2008

2. Banking (Special Provisions) Act 2008
applied: SI 2013/9 Reg.9, SI 2013/614 Reg.12
s.11, amended: 2013 c.33 Sch.9 para.4
s.15, amended: SI 2013/3115 Sch.2 para.43
s.15, repealed (in part): SI 2013/3115 Sch.2 para.43

4. Criminal Justice and Immigration Act 2008
Commencement Orders: SI 2013/616 Art.2
s.1, applied: SI 2013/1554 r.42_2
s.7, referred to: SI 2013/1554 r.42_2
s.76, amended: 2013 c.22 s.43
s.84, applied: SI 2013/1554 r.52_10
s.85, applied: SI 2013/1554 r.52_10
s.100, applied: SI 2013/9 Reg.9
s.101, applied: SI 2013/9 Reg.9
s.103, applied: SI 2013/9 Reg.9
s.104, applied: SI 2013/9 Reg.9
s.106, applied: SI 2013/9 Reg.9
s.153, enabling: SI 2013/616
Sch.2, applied: SI 2013/1554 r.44_1
Sch.19, referred to: SI 2013/1554 r.52_10

6. Child Maintenance and Other Payments Act 2008
Commencement Orders: SI 2013/1654; SI 2013/1860 Art.2, Art.3; SI 2013/2947 Art.2, Art.3
s.16, disapplied: SI 2013/2947 Art.3
s.17, disapplied: SI 2013/2947 Art.3
s.18, disapplied: SI 2013/2947 Art.3
s.46, enabling: SI 2013/670
s.49, enabling: SI 2013/2380
s.50, enabling: SI 2013/2380
s.53, applied: SI 2013/2380
s.53, enabling: SI 2013/670, SI 2013/2380
s.55, applied: SI 2013/670
s.55, enabling: SI 2013/1517
s.57, disapplied: SI 2013/2947 Art.3
s.57, enabling: SI 2013/1517
s.58, disapplied: SI 2013/2947 Art.3
s.62, enabling: SI 2013/1860, SI 2013/2947
Sch.4, disapplied: SI 2013/2947 Art.3
Sch.5 para.1, applied: SI 2013/2947 Art.3, Art.5
Sch.7 para.1, disapplied: SI 2013/2947 Art.3
Sch.8, disapplied: SI 2013/2947 Art.3

9. Finance Act 2008
s.21, enabling: SI 2013/1097, SI 2013/3103
s.77, repealed (in part): 2013 c.29 s.68
s.105, repealed: 2013 c.29 Sch.31 para.12
s.122, enabling: SI 2013/1114
s.127, applied: SI 2013/1894 Reg.4, Reg.28, Reg.29
s.147, repealed: 2013 c.29 s.188
s.160, applied: SI 2013/234
s.160, enabling: SI 2013/234
Sch.1 Part 1 para.23, repealed: SI 2013/2819 Reg.41
Sch.12 Part 2 para.25, repealed: SI 2013/2819 Reg.41
Sch.12 Part 2 para.26, repealed: 2013 c.29 Sch.29 para.33
Sch.12 Part 2 para.27, repealed (in part): 2013 c.29 Sch.29 para.33
Sch.12 Part 2 para.28, repealed (in part): 2013 c.29 Sch.29 para.33

Sch.12 Part 2 para.29, repealed (in part): 2013 c.29 Sch.29 para.33
Sch.12 Part 2 para.30, repealed: 2013 c.29 Sch.29 para.33
Sch.23 para.1, repealed: 2013 c.29 Sch.29 para.33
Sch.23 para.2, repealed: 2013 c.29 Sch.29 para.33
Sch.23 para.3, repealed: 2013 c.29 Sch.29 para.33
Sch.23 para.4, repealed: 2013 c.29 Sch.29 para.33
Sch.23 para.6, repealed: 2013 c.29 Sch.29 para.33
Sch.23 para.7, repealed: 2013 c.29 Sch.29 para.33
Sch.23 para.9, repealed: 2013 c.29 Sch.29 para.33
Sch.23 para.10, repealed: 2013 c.29 Sch.29 para.33
Sch.23 para.11, repealed: 2013 c.29 Sch.29 para.33
Sch.36 Part 1, applied: SI 2013/1114 Art.1, SI 2013/1741 Reg.11
Sch.36 Part 1 para.1, varied: SI 2013/938 Reg.5
Sch.36 Part 1 para.2, varied: SI 2013/938 Reg.5
Sch.36 Part 1 para.3, varied: SI 2013/938 Reg.5
Sch.36 Part 1 para.4, varied: SI 2013/938 Reg.5
Sch.36 Part 1 para.5, varied: SI 2013/938 Reg.5
Sch.36 Part 1 para.5A, varied: SI 2013/938 Reg.5
Sch.36 Part 1 para.6, varied: SI 2013/938 Reg.5
Sch.36 Part 1 para.7, varied: SI 2013/938 Reg.5
Sch.36 Part 1 para.8, varied: SI 2013/938 Reg.5
Sch.36 Part 1 para.9, varied: SI 2013/938 Reg.5
Sch.36 Part 2 para.10, varied: SI 2013/938 Reg.5
Sch.36 Part 2 para.10A, varied: SI 2013/938 Reg.5
Sch.36 Part 2 para.11, varied: SI 2013/938 Reg.5
Sch.36 Part 2 para.12, varied: SI 2013/938 Reg.5
Sch.36 Part 2 para.12A, amended: 2013 c.29 Sch.34 para.2
Sch.36 Part 2 para.12A, varied: SI 2013/938 Reg.5
Sch.36 Part 2 para.12B, varied: SI 2013/938 Reg.5
Sch.36 Part 2 para.13, varied: SI 2013/938 Reg.5
Sch.36 Part 2 para.14, varied: SI 2013/938 Reg.5
Sch.36 Part 3 para.15, varied: SI 2013/938 Reg.5
Sch.36 Part 3 para.16, varied: SI 2013/938 Reg.5
Sch.36 Part 3 para.17, varied: SI 2013/938 Reg.5
Sch.36 Part 4 para.18, varied: SI 2013/938 Reg.5
Sch.36 Part 4 para.19, varied: SI 2013/938 Reg.5
Sch.36 Part 4 para.20, varied: SI 2013/938 Reg.5
Sch.36 Part 4 para.21, varied: SI 2013/938 Reg.5
Sch.36 Part 4 para.21A, varied: SI 2013/938 Reg.5
Sch.36 Part 4 para.21B, added: 2013 c.29 Sch.34 para.3
Sch.36 Part 4 para.21B, varied: SI 2013/938 Reg.5
Sch.36 Part 4 para.22, varied: SI 2013/938 Reg.5
Sch.36 Part 4 para.23, varied: SI 2013/938 Reg.5
Sch.36 Part 4 para.24, varied: SI 2013/938 Reg.5
Sch.36 Part 4 para.25, varied: SI 2013/938 Reg.5
Sch.36 Part 4 para.26, varied: SI 2013/938 Reg.5
Sch.36 Part 4 para.27, varied: SI 2013/938 Reg.5
Sch.36 Part 4 para.28, varied: SI 2013/938 Reg.5
Sch.36 Part 5 para.29, varied: SI 2013/938 Reg.5
Sch.36 Part 5 para.30, varied: SI 2013/938 Reg.5
Sch.36 Part 5 para.31, varied: SI 2013/938 Reg.5
Sch.36 Part 5 para.32, varied: SI 2013/938 Reg.5
Sch.36 Part 5 para.33, varied: SI 2013/938 Reg.5
Sch.36 Part 6 para.34, varied: SI 2013/938 Reg.5
Sch.36 Part 6 para.34A, varied: SI 2013/938 Reg.5
Sch.36 Part 6 para.34B, amended: 2013 c.29 s.54
Sch.36 Part 6 para.34B, varied: SI 2013/938 Reg.5
Sch.36 Part 6 para.34B, enabling: SI 2013/2259
Sch.36 Part 6 para.34C, amended: 2013 c.29 s.54
Sch.36 Part 6 para.34C, varied: SI 2013/938 Reg.5
Sch.36 Part 6 para.35, varied: SI 2013/938 Reg.5
Sch.36 Part 6 para.36, varied: SI 2013/938 Reg.5
Sch.36 Part 6 para.37, amended: 2013 c.29 Sch.34 para.4
Sch.36 Part 6 para.37, varied: SI 2013/938 Reg.5
Sch.36 Part 6 para.37A, varied: SI 2013/938 Reg.5
Sch.36 Part 6 para.37B, varied: SI 2013/938 Reg.5
Sch.36 Part 6 para.38, varied: SI 2013/938 Reg.5
Sch.36 Part 7 para.39, varied: SI 2013/938 Reg.5
Sch.36 Part 7 para.40, varied: SI 2013/938 Reg.5
Sch.36 Part 7 para.40A, varied: SI 2013/938 Reg.5
Sch.36 Part 7 para.41, varied: SI 2013/938 Reg.5
Sch.36 Part 7 para.42, varied: SI 2013/938 Reg.5
Sch.36 Part 7 para.43, varied: SI 2013/938 Reg.5
Sch.36 Part 7 para.44, varied: SI 2013/938 Reg.5
Sch.36 Part 7 para.45, varied: SI 2013/938 Reg.5
Sch.36 Part 7 para.46, varied: SI 2013/938 Reg.5
Sch.36 Part 7 para.47, varied: SI 2013/938 Reg.5
Sch.36 Part 7 para.48, varied: SI 2013/938 Reg.5
Sch.36 Part 7 para.49, varied: SI 2013/938 Reg.5
Sch.36 Part 7 para.49A, varied: SI 2013/938 Reg.5
Sch.36 Part 7 para.49B, varied: SI 2013/938 Reg.5
Sch.36 Part 7 para.49C, varied: SI 2013/938 Reg.5
Sch.36 Part 7 para.50, varied: SI 2013/938 Reg.5
Sch.36 Part 7 para.51, varied: SI 2013/938 Reg.5
Sch.36 Part 7 para.52, varied: SI 2013/938 Reg.5
Sch.36 Part 8 para.53, varied: SI 2013/938 Reg.5
Sch.36 Part 8 para.54, varied: SI 2013/938 Reg.5
Sch.36 Part 8 para.55, varied: SI 2013/938 Reg.5
Sch.36 Part 9 para.56, varied: SI 2013/938 Reg.5
Sch.36 Part 9 para.57, varied: SI 2013/938 Reg.5
Sch.36 Part 9 para.58, varied: SI 2013/938 Reg.5
Sch.36 Part 9 para.59, varied: SI 2013/938 Reg.5
Sch.36 Part 9 para.60, varied: SI 2013/938 Reg.5
Sch.36 Part 9 para.61, varied: SI 2013/938 Reg.5
Sch.36 Part 9 para.61A, varied: SI 2013/938 Reg.5
Sch.36 Part 9 para.62, varied: SI 2013/938 Reg.5
Sch.36 Part 9 para.63, amended: 2013 c.29 Sch.34 para.5
Sch.36 Part 9 para.63, varied: SI 2013/938 Reg.5
Sch.36 Part 9 para.64, varied: SI 2013/938 Reg.5
Sch.36 Part 10 para.65, varied: SI 2013/938 Reg.5
Sch.36 Part 10 para.66, varied: SI 2013/938 Reg.5

d: SI 2013/648 Art.28, SI 2013/675
13/1203 Art.19, SI 2013/1873 Art.17,
8 Art.21, SI 2013/2809 Art.18
led (in part): 2013 c.27 s.23
ded: 2013 c.27 s.27
ed: SI 2013/2808 Art.7
aled (in part): 2013 c.27 s.27
abling: SI 2013/343, SI 2013/1203, SI
, SI 2013/1873
bling: SI 2013/520
lied: SI 2013/648 Art.25, SI 2013/675
rt.28, Art.29, SI 2013/1203 Art.19, SI
8 Art.25, Art.26, SI 2013/2809 Art.18,
rt.24, SI 2013/3200 Art.25, Art.26
lied: SI 2013/343 Art.7, SI 2013/586
13/680 Art.7
d: SI 2013/586 Art.9, SI 2013/648

o: SI 2013/648 Art.25
2013 c.22 Sch.9 para.52
2013/2948
2013/2948
13/982
3/982
13/982
3/982
82
2

2013/3221
013/520, SI
883, SI

938

Sch.5 Part 1 para.14, enabling: SI 2013/675, SI 2013/2808, SI 2013/2809
Sch.5 Part 1 para.15, enabling: SI 2013/675, SI 2013/2808, SI 2013/2809
Sch.5 Part 1 para.16, enabling: SI 2013/675, SI 2013/2808, SI 2013/2809
Sch.5 Part 1 para.17, enabling: SI 2013/675, SI 2013/2808, SI 2013/2809
Sch.5 Part 1 para.19, enabling: SI 2013/675
Sch.5 Part 1 para.20, enabling: SI 2013/675
Sch.5 Part 1 para.23, enabling: SI 2013/675
Sch.5 Part 1 para.24, enabling: SI 2013/675, SI 2013/2808, SI 2013/2809
Sch.5 Part 1 para.26, enabling: SI 2013/675, SI 2013/2808, SI 2013/2809
Sch.5 Part 1 para.36, enabling: SI 2013/675, SI 2013/2808, SI 2013/2809
Sch.5 Part 1 para.37, enabling: SI 2013/675, SI 2013/2808, SI 2013/2809
Sch.6 para.2, enabling: SI 2013/522
Sch.6 para.4, enabling: SI 2013/522
Sch.8 para.2, amended: SI 2013/755 Sch.2 para.440
Sch.12 para.12, repealed: 2013 c.27 s.24
Sch.12 para.13, repealed: 2013 c.27 s.24
Sch.12 para.18, amended: 2013 c.27 s.23
Sch.12 para.24, amended: 2013 c.22 Sch.9 para.52

30. Pensions Act 2008
disapplied: SSI 2013/174 Reg.6
s.3, amended: SI 2013/667 Art.2
s.3, applied: SI 2013/667, SI 2013/667 Art.3, SSI 2013/174 Reg.5, Reg.6
s.3, enabling: SI 2013/2556
s.4, enabling: SI 2013/2556
s.5, amended: SI 2013/667 Art.2
s.5, applied: SI 2013/667, SI 2013/667 Art.3, SSI 2013/174 Reg.5, Reg.6
s.5, enabling: SI 2013/2556
s.8, applied: SI 2013/2734 Reg.17, SSI 2013/174 Reg.6
s.8, enabling: SI 2013/2556
s.10, enabling: SI 2013/2556
s.11, enabling: SI 2013/2556
s.13, amended: SI 2013/667 Art.2
s.13, applied: SI 2013/667, SI 2013/667 Art.3
s.13, referred to: SI 2013/667 Art.3
s.14, enabling: SI 2013/667
s.15, enabling: SI 2013/2556
s.15A, enabling: SI 2013/667
s.17, enabling: SI 2013/2328
s.23, enabling: SI 2013/2556
s.33, enabling: SI 2013/2556
37, enabling: SI 2013/2556
2, amended: 2013 c.22 Sch.9 para.52

Sch.36 Part 10 para.67, varied: SI 2013/938 Reg.5
Sch.36 Part 10 para.68, varied: SI 2013/938 Reg.5
Sch.36 Part 10 para.69, varied: SI 2013/938 Reg.5
Sch.36 Part 10 para.70, varied: SI 2013/938 Reg.5
Sch.36 Part 10 para.71, varied: SI 2013/938 Reg.5
Sch.36 Part 10 para.72, varied: SI 2013/938 Reg.5
Sch.36 Part 10 para.73, varied: SI 2013/938 Reg.5
Sch.36 Part 10 para.74, varied: SI 2013/938 Reg.5
Sch.36 Part 10 para.75, varied: SI 2013/938 Reg.5
Sch.36 Part 10 para.76, varied: SI 2013/938 Reg.5
Sch.36 Part 10 para.77, varied: SI 2013/938 Reg.5
Sch.36 Part 10 para.78, varied: SI 2013/938 Reg.5
Sch.36 Part 10 para.79, varied: SI 2013/938 Reg.5
Sch.36 Part 10 para.80, varied: SI 2013/938 Reg.5
Sch.36 Part 10 para.81, varied: SI 2013/938 Reg.5
Sch.36 Part 10 para.82, varied: SI 2013/938 Reg.5
Sch.36 Part 10 para.83, varied: SI 2013/938 Reg.5
Sch.36 Part 10 para.84, varied: SI 2013/938 Reg.5
Sch.36 Part 10 para.85, varied: SI 2013/938 Reg.5
Sch.36 Part 10 para.86, varied: SI 2013/938 Reg.5
Sch.36 Part 10 para.87, varied: SI 2013/938 Reg.5
Sch.36 Part 10 para.88, varied: SI 2013/938 Reg.5
Sch.36 Part 10 para.89, varied: SI 2013/938 Reg.5
Sch.36 Part 10 para.90, varied: SI 2013/938 Reg.5
Sch.36 Part 10 para.91, varied: SI 2013/938 Reg.5
Sch.36 Part 10 para.92, varied: SI 2013/938 Reg.5
Sch.41 para.7, amended: 2013 c.29 Sch.51 para.6

13. Regulatory Enforcement and Sanctions Act 2008
Part 3, applied: SI 2013/755 Sch.7 para.12
s.4, enabling: SI 2013/2215
s.20, applied: SI 2013/2215
s.22, amended: 2013 c.24 s.67
s.24, amended: 2013 c.24 s.67
s.26, amended: 2013 c.24 s.67
s.28, enabling: SI 2013/2286
s.29, enabling: SI 2013/2286
s.30, amended: 2013 c.24 s.68
s.30, repealed (in part): 2013 c.24 s.68
s.37, amended: SI 2013/602 Sch.2 para.59
s.67, applied: SI 2013/755 Sch.7 para.12
Sch.3, amended: 2013 c.10 s.19, SI 2013/1575 Sch.1 para.13, SI 2013/2215 Art.2
Sch.5, amended: SI 2013/755 Sch.2 para.439
Sch.6, amended: 2013 c.32 Sch.12 para.94, SI 2013/1575 Sch.1 para.14

14. Health and Social Care Act 2008
Commencement Orders: SI 2013/159 Art.2
applied: SI 2013/376 Reg.35
Part 1, applied: SI 2013/2356 Reg.4
Part 1 c.2, applied: SI 2013/2677 Reg.7, SI 2013/2960 Sch.1 para.1
s.59, enabling: SI 2013/1413
s.120, enabling: SI 2013/391
s.161, enabling: SI 2013/1413
s.170, enabling: SI 2013/159
Sch.1 para.3, enabling: SI 2013/2157

17. Housing and Regeneration Act 2008
Commencement Orders: SI 2013/1469 Art.2, Art.3, Art.4, Art.5, Art.6, Art.7
s.1, applied: SI 2013/382 Sch.2 para.5
s.80, referred to: 2013 c.24 s.83, SI 2013/981 Reg.7
s.120, amended: SI 2013/496 Sch.11 para.8
s.153, amended: SI 2013/496 Sch.11 para.8
s.157, amended: SI 2013/496 Sch.11 para.8
s.163, amended: SI 2013/496 Sch.11 para.8
s.164, amended: SI 2013/496 Sch.11 para.8
s.165, amended: SI 2013/496 Sch.11 para.8
s.194, applied: SI 2013/382 Sch.2 para.5
s.212, amended: SI 2013/496 Sch.11 para.8
s.255, amended: SI 2013/496 Sch.11 para.8
s.318, applied: SI 2013/1722 Art.1
s.320, applied: SI 2013/1722
s.320, enabling: SI 2013/1722
s.321, enabling: SI 2013/1722
s.322, enabling: SI 2013/1469
s.325, enabling: SI 2013/1469

18. Crossrail Act 2008
Sch.11 para.5, repealed: 2013 c.2 Sch.1 Part 9

22. Human Fertilisation and Embryology Act 2008
see *G (Children) (Children: Sperm Donors: Leave to Apply for Children Act Orders), Re* [2013] EWHC 134 (Fam), [2013] 1 F.L.R. 1334 (Fam Div), Baker, J.
applied: SI 2013/422 Reg.8
s.35, amended: 2013 c.30 Sch.7 para.38
s.40, amended: 2013 c.30 Sch.7 para.39
s.42, amended: 2013 c.30 Sch.7 para.40
s.46, amended: 2013 c.30 Sch.7 para.41
s.54, see *D (Children) (Surrogacy: Parental Order), Re* [2012] EWHC 2631 (Fam), [2013] 1 W.L.R. 3135 (Fam Div), Baker, J.; see *G v G* [2012] EWHC 1979 (Fam), [2013] 1 F.L.R. 286 (Fam Div), Hedley, J.
s.54, amended: 2013 c.22 Sch.11 para.206
Sch.6 Part 1 para.20, repealed: 2013 c.22 Sch.10 para.99

23. Children and Young Persons Act 2008
Commencement Orders: SI 2013/2606 Art.2
s.1, applied: SI 2013/2668 Reg.1, Reg.25, Sch.3 para.12
s.2, applied: SI 2013/2668 Reg.7
s.44, enabling: SI 2013/2606

24. Employment Act 2008
s.5, repealed: 2013 c.24 Sch.1 para.12
s.8, repealed (in part): 2013 c.24 Sch.20 para.2
s.9, repealed (in part): 2013 c.24 Sch.20 para.2

25. Education and Skills Act 2008

Commencement Orders: SI 2013/1204 Art.2, Art.3
Part 1, disapplied: SI 2013/1205 Reg.6
s.1, amended: SI 2013/1204 Art.2
s.2, applied: SI 2013/1205 Reg.3
s.2, varied: SI 2013/1205 Reg.8
s.3, amended: SI 2013/1242 Art.2
s.3, applied: SI 2013/1205 Reg.2
s.3, repealed (in part): SI 2013/1242 Art.2
s.3, enabling: SI 2013/1205
s.4, applied: SI 2013/1205 Reg.3
s.4, enabling: SI 2013/1205
s.5, applied: SI 2013/1205 Reg.4, Reg.5, SI 2013/1243 Reg.2
s.5, enabling: SI 2013/1205, SI 2013/1243
s.6, amended: SI 2013/1242 Art.2
s.6, varied: SI 2013/1205 Reg.8
s.7, applied: SI 2013/1205 Reg.6
s.7, varied: SI 2013/1205 Reg.8
s.7, enabling: SI 2013/1205
s.8, amended: SI 2013/1242 Art.2
s.8, applied: SI 2013/1205 Reg.7
s.8, varied: SI 2013/1205 Reg.8
s.8, enabling: SI 2013/1205
s.39, amended: SI 2013/1204 Art.4
s.56, amended: 2013 c.22 s.26, Sch.9 para.52
s.57, amended: 2013 c.22 Sch.9 para.52
s.58, amended: 2013 c.22 Sch.9 para.52
s.59, amended: 2013 c.22 Sch.9 para.52
s.62, enabling: SI 2013/1205
s.65, amended: 2013 c.22 Sch.9 para.52
s.166, applied: SI 2013/1243
s.173, enabling: SI 2013/1204

26. Local Transport Act 2008
Commencement Orders: SI 2013/685 Art.2, Art.3; SI 2013/1644
Part 5, applied: SI 2013/2356 Sch.2 para.12
s.6, applied: SI 2013/1644
s.6, enabling: SI 2013/1644
s.134, enabling: SI 2013/685

27. Climate Change Act 2008
s.1, applied: 2013 c.32 s.2, s.5
s.4, applied: 2013 c.32 s.1, s.2, s.5
s.23, referred to: 2013 c.32 s.1
s.44, enabling: SI 2013/1119
s.46, enabling: SI 2013/1119
s.48, applied: SI 2013/1119
s.49, enabling: SI 2013/1119
s.50, disapplied: SI 2013/1119 Art.45
s.90, enabling: SI 2013/1119
Sch.2, enabling: SI 2013/1119
Sch.3 Part 3 para.9, enabling: SI 2013/1119
Sch.3 Part 3 para.10, applied: SI 2013/1119
Sch.3 Part 3 para.11, applied: SI 2013/1119
Sch.4 para.2, applied: SI 2013/1119 Art.45
Sch.4 para.4, applied: SI 2013/1119 Art.45
Sch.4 para.4, disapplied: SI 2013/1119 Art.45
Sch.4 para.5, disapplied: SI 2013/1119 Art.45

28. Counter-Terrorism Act 2008
see *Bank Mellat v HM Treasury* [2013] UKSC 38, [2013] 4 All E.R. 495 (SC), Lord Neuberger (President)
applied: SI 2013/1813 Art.7
s.7, amended: SI 2013/602 Sch.2 para.60
s.18, amended: 2013 c.22 Sch.8 para.188, SI 2013/602 Sch.2 para.60
s.18E, amended: 2013 c.22 Sch.8 para.186
s.42, applied: SI 2013/1554 r.63_1, r.68_1
s.51, amended: SI 2013/602 Sch.2 para.60
s.86, amended: SI 2013/602 Sch.2 para.60
s.88, amended: SI 2013/602 Sch.2 para.60
s.88, applied: SI 2013/602 Sch.3 para.19
Sch.4 para.5, amended: SI 2013/602 Sch.2 para.60
Sch.5 para.4, amended: SI 2013/602 Sch.2 para.60
Sch.5 para.9, amended: SI 2013/602 Sch.2 para.60
Sch.5 para.9, repealed (in part): SI 2013/602 Sch.2 para.60
Sch.7 Part 2 para.5, amended: SI 2013/3115 Sch.2 para.44
Sch.7 Part 2 para.7, amended: SI 2013/3115 Sch.2 para.44
Sch.7 Part 4 para.14, enabling: SI 2013/162
Sch.7 Part 4 para.16, enabling: SI 2013/162
Sch.7 Part 5 para.18, amended: SI 2013/1881 Sch.1 para.15
Sch.7 Part 5 para.18, repealed (in part): SI 2013/1881 Sch.1 para.15
Sch.7 Part 5 para.23, amended: SI 2013/1881 Sch.1 para.15
Sch.7 Part 5 para.24, amended: SI 2013/1881 Sch.1 para.15
Sch.7 Part 6 para.27, amended: SI 2013/1881 Sch.1 para.15
Sch.7 Part 6 para.28, amended: SI 2013/1881 Sch.1 para.15
Sch.7 Part 7 para.33, repealed (in part): SI 2013/1881 Sch.1 para.15
Sch.7 Part 8 para.39, amended: SI 2013/1881 Sch.1 para.15
Sch.7 Part 8 para.39, repealed (in part): SI 2013/1881 Sch.1 para.15
Sch.7 Part 8 para.45, amended: SI 2013/1881 Sch.1 para.15
Sch.7 Part 8 para.46, amended: SI 2013/1881 Sch.1 para.15, SI 2013/3115 Sch.2 para.44

29. Planning Act 2008
applied: SI 2013/1124 Art.6, Art.7, SI 2013/1883 Art.5, SI 2013/2086
Part 6 c.2, applied: SI 2013/1203

Part 6 c.3, applied: SI 2013/343, SI 2013/586, SI 2013/1752, SI 2013/1873, SI 2013/2809, SI 2013/3200
Part 6 c.4, applied: SI 2013/586, SI 2013/648, SI 2013/675, SI 2013/680, SI 2013/1203, SI 2013/1734, SI 2013/1752, SI 2013/1873, SI 2013/2808, SI 2013/2809, SI 2013/3200
s.4, enabling: SI 2013/498
s.7, enabling: SI 2013/522
s.8, applied: SI 2013/2809 Art.21
s.14, applied: SI 2013/343 Sch.1 para.1, SI 2013/586 Sch.1 Part 1
s.14, referred to: SI 2013/675 Sch.1, SI 2013/680 Sch.1 Part 1, SI 2013/1752 Sch.1, SI 2013/1873 Sch.1 para.1, SI 2013/2808 Sch.1, SI 2013/2809 Sch.1 Part 1, SI 2013/3200 Sch.1
s.14, enabling: SI 2013/1479, SI 2013/1883
s.15, applied: SI 2013/343 Sch.1 para.1, SI 2013/586 Sch.1 Part 1
s.15, referred to: SI 2013/680 Sch.1 Part 1, SI 2013/1873 Sch.1 para.1
s.16, amended: SI 2013/1479 Art.2
s.16, referred to: SI 2013/3200 Sch.1
s.22, referred to: SI 2013/675 Sch.1, SI 2013/2808 Sch.1
s.22, substituted: SI 2013/1883 Art.3
s.25, amended: SI 2013/1883 Art.4
s.25, referred to: SI 2013/2809 Sch.1 Part 1
s.30, referred to: SI 2013/1752 Sch.1
s.31, applied: SI 2013/1570 Reg.4
s.32, applied: SI 2013/648 Art.54
s.33, repealed (in part): 2013 c.27 s.1
s.35, applied: SI 2013/3221 Reg.2
s.35, substituted: 2013 c.27 s.26
s.35, enabling: SI 2013/3221
s.35A, amended: 2013 c.27 s
s.37, applied: SI 2013/520
2013/675, SI 2013/1203
2013/1873, SI 2013/2
s.42, enabling: SI 20
s.46, applied: SI 2
s.56, enabling:
s.74, applied:
2013/1734
s.83, appl
2013/6
2013
s.8

s.114, applied: SI 2013/648 A
s.114, enabling: SI 2013/343,
2013/586, SI 2013/648, SI 20
SI 2013/1203, SI 2013/1734
2013/1873, SI 2013/2808,
2013/3200
s.115, applied: SI 2013
2013/675 Sch.1, SI 2
2013/1203 Sch.1 p
2013/1734 Sch.1
2013/1873 Sch.
2013/2809 Sc
s.115, enabl
2013/648,
2013/120
2013/1
2013/
s.11
20

s.56, amended: 2013 c.24 Sch.2 para.41
s.58, amended: 2013 c.24 s.23, Sch.1 para.13
s.67, enabling: SI 2013/597
s.68, enabling: SI 2013/597
s.71, applied: SI 2013/597
s.75, applied: SI 2013/2734 Sch.2 para.9
s.99, enabling: SI 2013/2328, SI 2013/2556
s.108, enabling: SI 2013/627
s.119, enabling: SI 2013/627
s.143, applied: SI 2013/597, SI 2013/667, SI 2013/2328
s.144, enabling: SI 2013/597, SI 2013/627, SI 2013/667, SI 2013/2328, SI 2013/2556
Sch.5 Part 4 para.16A, enabling: SI 2013/627

31. Dormant Bank and Building Society Accounts Act 2008

s.5, referred to: SI 2013/598 Art.2

32. Energy Act 2008

s.41, amended: 2013 c.32 s.146
s.41, applied: SI 2013/1119 Sch.1 para.32
s.43, enabling: SI 2013/1099
s.45A, added: 2013 c.32 s.149
s.46, amended: 2013 c.32 s.149, Sch.12 para.96
s.48, applied: SI 2013/126 Reg.11
s.48, disapplied: SI 2013/126 Reg.14
s.49, amended: 2013 c.32 s.149
s.49, applied: SI 2013/126 Reg.13
s.49, disapplied: SI 2013/126 Reg.11, Reg.14
s.49, enabling: SI 2013/126
s.50, amended: 2013 c.32 Sch.12 para.97
s.50, enabling: SI 2013/126, SI 2013/1875
s.52, applied: SI 2013/126 Reg.6
s.53, applied: SI 2013/126 Reg.6
s.54, amended: 2013 c.32 Sch.12 para.98
s.54, enabling: SI 2013/126
s.55, enabling: SI 2013/126
s.59, amended: 2013 c.32 Sch.12 para.99
s.63, amended: 2013 c.32 Sch.12 para.100
s.65, repealed: 2013 c.32 Sch.12 para.30
s.66, amended: 2013 c.32 s.149
s.66, applied: SI 2013/126 Reg.11
s.100, applied: SI 2013/1033, SI 2013/2410, SI 2013/3179
s.100, enabling: SI 2013/1033, SI 2013/2410, SI 2013/3179
s.104, enabling: SI 2013/126, SI 2013/1033, SI 2013/1099, SI 2013/1875, SI 2013/2410, SI 2013/3179
s.105, applied: SI 2013/1033, SI 2013/2410, SI 2013/3179
s.112, amended: 2013 c.32 Sch.12 para.30

2009

1. Banking Act 2009

applied: SI 2013/614 Reg.12
Part 1, referred to: 2013 c.33 s.17
Part 3, applied: 2013 c.33 s.121
s.1, amended: 2013 c.33 Sch.2 para.12, SI 2013/504 Reg.25
s.2, amended: SI 2013/504 Reg.25
s.8A, added: 2013 c.33 Sch.2 para.3
s.12A, added: 2013 c.33 Sch.2 para.2
s.12A, applied: 2013 c.33 Sch.2 para.33
s.12B, added: 2013 c.33 Sch.2 para.2
s.13, amended: 2013 c.33 Sch.2 para.13
s.14, amended: SI 2013/3115 Sch.2 para.45
s.17, amended: 2013 c.33 Sch.2 para.14
s.18, amended: 2013 c.33 Sch.2 para.15
s.39A, amended: SI 2013/504 Reg.25
s.41A, added: 2013 c.33 Sch.2 para.5
s.42, amended: 2013 c.33 Sch.2 para.5
s.44, amended: 2013 c.33 Sch.2 para.16
s.44A, added: 2013 c.33 Sch.2 para.5
s.44B, added: 2013 c.33 Sch.2 para.5
s.44C, added: 2013 c.33 Sch.2 para.5
s.48A, amended: 2013 c.33 Sch.2 para.5
s.48B, added: 2013 c.33 Sch.2 para.4
s.48C, added: 2013 c.33 Sch.2 para.4
s.48D, added: 2013 c.33 Sch.2 para.4
s.48E, added: 2013 c.33 Sch.2 para.4
s.48F, added: 2013 c.33 Sch.2 para.4
s.48G, added: 2013 c.33 Sch.2 para.4
s.48H, added: 2013 c.33 Sch.2 para.4
s.48I, added: 2013 c.33 Sch.2 para.4
s.48J, added: 2013 c.33 Sch.2 para.4
s.48K, added: 2013 c.33 Sch.2 para.4
s.48L, added: 2013 c.33 Sch.2 para.4
s.48M, added: 2013 c.33 Sch.2 para.4
s.48N, added: 2013 c.33 Sch.2 para.4
s.48O, added: 2013 c.33 Sch.2 para.4
s.48P, added: 2013 c.33 Sch.2 para.4
s.48Q, added: 2013 c.33 Sch.2 para.4
s.48R, added: 2013 c.33 Sch.2 para.4
s.48S, added: 2013 c.33 Sch.2 para.4
s.48T, added: 2013 c.33 Sch.2 para.4
s.48U, added: 2013 c.33 Sch.2 para.4
s.48V, added: 2013 c.33 Sch.2 para.4
s.48W, added: 2013 c.33 Sch.2 para.4
s.49, amended: 2013 c.33 Sch.2 para.6
s.52, amended: 2013 c.33 Sch.2 para.6
s.52A, added: 2013 c.33 Sch.2 para.6
s.53, amended: 2013 c.33 Sch.2 para.6
s.54, amended: 2013 c.33 Sch.2 para.6
s.56, amended: 2013 c.33 Sch.2 para.6
s.57, amended: 2013 c.33 Sch.2 para.6
s.60A, added: 2013 c.33 Sch.2 para.6

s.60B, added: 2013 c.33 Sch.2 para.6
s.61, amended: 2013 c.33 Sch.2 para.6
s.62, amended: 2013 c.33 Sch.2 para.6
s.63, amended: 2013 c.33 Sch.2 para.17
s.66, amended: 2013 c.33 Sch.2 para.18
s.67, amended: 2013 c.33 Sch.2 para.19
s.68, amended: 2013 c.33 Sch.2 para.20
s.71, amended: 2013 c.33 Sch.2 para.21
s.72, amended: 2013 c.33 Sch.2 para.22
s.73, amended: 2013 c.33 Sch.2 para.23
s.74, amended: 2013 c.33 Sch.2 para.24
s.75, amended: SI 2013/504 Reg.25
s.80A, added: 2013 c.33 Sch.2 para.25
s.81A, amended: 2013 c.33 Sch.2 para.26
s.81BA, added: 2013 c.33 Sch.2 para.7
s.81CA, added: 2013 c.33 Sch.2 para.7
s.81D, amended: 2013 c.33 Sch.2 para.7
s.83A, amended: 2013 c.33 Sch.2 para.8
s.85, amended: 2013 c.33 Sch.2 para.27
s.89B, amended: 2013 c.33 Sch.2 para.9, Sch.10 para.7, SI 2013/504 Reg.25
s.89C, amended: SI 2013/504 Reg.25
s.89D, amended: SI 2013/504 Reg.25
s.89E, amended: SI 2013/504 Reg.25
s.89F, amended: SI 2013/504 Reg.25
s.89G, amended: SI 2013/504 Reg.25
s.120, amended: 2013 c.33 Sch.2 para.10
s.136, amended: 2013 c.33 Sch.2 para.28
s.152A, added: 2013 c.33 Sch.2 para.29
s.191, amended: 2013 c.33 Sch.10 para.8
s.191, applied: 2013 c.33 s.120
s.220, amended: 2013 c.33 Sch.2 para.30
s.232, amended: SI 2013/636 Sch.1 para.10
s.244, applied: 2013 c.33 s.109, s.110
s.246, amended: 2013 c.33 s.95
s.251, repealed (in part): 2013 c.33 Sch.9 para.4
s.256A, added: 2013 c.33 Sch.2 para.11
s.258A, amended: SI 2013/3115 Sch.2 para.45
s.259, amended: 2013 c.33 Sch.2 para.31, SI 2013/504 Reg.25
s.261, amended: 2013 c.33 Sch.2 para.32, SI 2013/504 Reg.25

01. Learning and Skills (Wales) Measure 2009
s.46, enabling: SI 2013/1793
s.48, enabling: SI 2013/1793

03. Healthy Eating in Schools (Wales) Measure 2009
Commencement Orders: SI 2013/1985 Art.2
s.4, applied: SI 2013/1984
s.4, enabling: SI 2013/1984, SI 2013/2750
s.10, enabling: SI 2013/2750
s.12, enabling: SI 2013/1985

3. Northern Ireland Act 2009
applied: 2013 c.12 Sch.1 para.1, 2013 c.28 Sch.1

4. Corporation Tax Act 2009
Part 3, applied: SI 2013/2819 Reg.17
Part 3 c.2, applied: SI 2013/2819 Reg.17
Part 4, applied: SI 2013/2242 Art.5, SI 2013/2819 Reg.17
Part 4 c.3, applied: SI 2013/2819 Reg.17
Part 5, applied: SI 2013/2242 Art.7, SI 2013/3209 Reg.3, Reg.11
Part 7, applied: SI 2013/1962 Reg.3
Part 10 c.5, applied: SI 2013/2819 Reg.31
Part 15A, applied: 2013 c.29 Sch.16 para.3
Part 15A, referred to: 2013 c.29 Sch.16 para.2
Part 15A c.1, added: 2013 c.29 Sch.16 para.1
Part 15B, referred to: 2013 c.29 Sch.17 para.2
s.2, amended: 2013 c.29 Sch.25 para.18
s.51, amended: 2013 c.29 s.78
s.57, applied: 2013 c.29 s.68
s.63, amended: 2013 c.29 Sch.28 para.6
s.104A, added: 2013 c.29 Sch.15 para.1
s.104B, added: 2013 c.29 Sch.15 para.1
s.104BA, added: 2013 c.29 Sch.15 para.1, Sch.18 para.8
s.104C, added: 2013 c.29 Sch.15 para.1
s.104D, added: 2013 c.29 Sch.15 para.1
s.104E, added: 2013 c.29 Sch.15 para.1
s.104F, added: 2013 c.29 Sch.15 para.1
s.104G, added: 2013 c.29 Sch.15 para.1
s.104H, added: 2013 c.29 Sch.15 para.1
s.104I, added: 2013 c.29 Sch.15 para.1
s.104J, added: 2013 c.29 Sch.15 para.1
s.104K, added: 2013 c.29 Sch.15 para.1
s.104L, added: 2013 c.29 Sch.15 para.1
s.104M, added: 2013 c.29 Sch.15 para.1
s.104N, added: 2013 c.29 Sch.15 para.1
s.104O, added: 2013 c.29 Sch.15 para.1
s.104P, added: 2013 c.29 Sch.15 para.1
s.104Q, added: 2013 c.29 Sch.15 para.1
s.104R, added: 2013 c.29 Sch.15 para.1
s.104S, added: 2013 c.29 Sch.15 para.1
s.104T, added: 2013 c.29 Sch.15 para.1
s.104U, added: 2013 c.29 Sch.15 para.1
s.104V, added: 2013 c.29 Sch.15 para.1
s.104W, added: 2013 c.29 Sch.15 para.1
s.104X, added: 2013 c.29 Sch.15 para.1
s.104Y, added: 2013 c.29 Sch.15 para.1
s.162, applied: 2013 c.29 s.229
s.214, amended: 2013 c.29 s.78
s.232, amended: 2013 c.29 Sch.28 para.7
s.317, applied: SI 2013/3209 Reg.3
s.328, enabling: SI 2013/1843, SI 2013/2781
s.333, applied: 2013 c.29 s.229
s.334, applied: 2013 c.29 s.229
s.413, amended: 2013 c.29 Sch.11 para.11
s.415, applied: SI 2013/3209 Reg.3
s.416, applied: SI 2013/3209 Reg.3

s.464, amended: 2013 c.29 s.87
s.464, referred to: 2013 c.29 s.212
s.476, disapplied: SI 2013/460 Reg.3
s.498, disapplied: SI 2013/460 Reg.3
s.502, amended: SI 2013/1881 Sch.1 para.16
s.539, repealed (in part): 2013 c.29 Sch.29 para.35
s.540, amended: 2013 c.29 Sch.29 para.36
s.550, amended: 2013 c.29 Sch.29 para.37
s.550, repealed (in part): 2013 c.29 Sch.29 para.37
s.582, amended: SI 2013/3218 Art.2
s.585, applied: SI 2013/3209 Reg.3
s.587, amended: SI 2013/1411 Reg.13
s.591, amended: SI 2013/636 Sch.1 para.11
s.606, enabling: SI 2013/1843, SI 2013/2781
s.609, applied: 2013 c.29 s.229
s.610, applied: 2013 c.29 s.229
s.643, amended: 2013 c.29 s.41
s.650, amended: 2013 c.29 s.41
s.659, amended: 2013 c.29 s.41
s.697, amended: SI 2013/504 Reg.26
s.699, referred to: 2013 c.29 s.212
s.701, enabling: SI 2013/3218
s.808A, added: 2013 c.29 Sch.18 para.9
s.808B, added: 2013 c.29 Sch.18 para.9
s.844, amended: 2013 c.29 s.61
s.845, amended: 2013 c.29 s.61
s.849A, added: 2013 c.29 s.61
s.849A, referred to: 2013 c.29 s.58
s.859, applied: 2013 c.29 s.229
s.862, applied: 2013 c.29 s.229
s.900, amended: 2013 c.29 Sch.46 para.138
s.906, referred to: 2013 c.29 s.212
s.932, repealed (in part): SI 2013/2819 Reg.38
s.936, amended: 2013 c.29 Sch.46 para.139
s.947, amended: 2013 c.29 Sch.46 para.140
s.971, repealed: SI 2013/2819 Reg.38
s.972, repealed: SI 2013/2819 Reg.38
s.973, repealed: SI 2013/2819 Reg.38
s.982, amended: SI 2013/2819 Reg.38
s.985, amended: 2013 c.29 Sch.18 para.21
s.999, amended: 2013 c.29 Sch.18 para.21
s.1000, amended: 2013 c.29 Sch.18 para.21
s.1005, amended: 2013 c.29 Sch.23 para.22
s.1009, amended: 2013 c.29 Sch.23 para.23, Sch.46 para.141
s.1010, amended: 2013 c.29 Sch.23 para.24
s.1011, amended: 2013 c.29 Sch.23 para.25
s.1013, amended: 2013 c.29 Sch.18 para.21
s.1017, amended: 2013 c.29 Sch.46 para.142
s.1018, amended: 2013 c.29 Sch.23 para.26
s.1019, amended: 2013 c.29 Sch.23 para.27
s.1021, amended: 2013 c.29 Sch.18 para.21
s.1022, amended: 2013 c.29 Sch.23 para.28
s.1025, amended: 2013 c.29 Sch.46 para.143
s.1026, amended: 2013 c.29 Sch.23 para.29
s.1027, amended: 2013 c.29 Sch.23 para.30
s.1032, amended: 2013 c.29 Sch.46 para.144
s.1033, amended: 2013 c.29 Sch.23 para.31
s.1034, amended: 2013 c.29 Sch.23 para.32
s.1037, amended: 2013 c.29 Sch.23 para.33
s.1038, amended: 2013 c.29 Sch.23 para.33
s.1038, substituted: 2013 c.29 s.40
s.1038A, added: 2013 c.29 s.40
s.1038A, amended: 2013 c.29 Sch.23 para.33
s.1038B, added: 2013 c.29 Sch.23 para.33
s.1038B, amended: 2013 c.29 Sch.23 para.33
s.1039, amended: 2013 c.29 Sch.15 para.13
s.1039, repealed (in part): 2013 c.29 Sch.15 para.13
s.1040A, added: 2013 c.29 Sch.15 para.2
s.1040ZA, added: 2013 c.29 Sch.18 para.10
s.1063, repealed: 2013 c.29 Sch.15 para.14
s.1064, repealed: 2013 c.29 Sch.15 para.14
s.1065, repealed: 2013 c.29 Sch.15 para.14
s.1066, repealed: 2013 c.29 Sch.15 para.14
s.1067, repealed: 2013 c.29 Sch.15 para.14
s.1068, repealed: 2013 c.29 Sch.15 para.15
s.1069, repealed: 2013 c.29 Sch.15 para.15
s.1070, repealed: 2013 c.29 Sch.15 para.15
s.1071, repealed: 2013 c.29 Sch.15 para.15
s.1072, repealed: 2013 c.29 Sch.15 para.15
s.1073, repealed: 2013 c.29 Sch.15 para.15
s.1074, repealed: 2013 c.29 Sch.15 para.16
s.1075, repealed: 2013 c.29 Sch.15 para.16
s.1076, repealed: 2013 c.29 Sch.15 para.16
s.1077, repealed: 2013 c.29 Sch.15 para.16
s.1078, repealed: 2013 c.29 Sch.15 para.16
s.1079, repealed: 2013 c.29 Sch.15 para.16
s.1080, repealed: 2013 c.29 Sch.15 para.16
s.1081, amended: 2013 c.29 Sch.15 para.17
s.1081, repealed (in part): 2013 c.29 Sch.15 para.17
s.1082, repealed: 2013 c.29 Sch.15 para.18
s.1083, repealed: 2013 c.29 Sch.15 para.19
s.1084, amended: 2013 c.29 Sch.15 para.20
s.1119, amended: 2013 c.29 Sch.15 para.21
s.1133, amended: 2013 c.29 Sch.15 para.22
s.1138, amended: 2013 c.29 Sch.15 para.2
s.1195, amended: 2013 c.29 Sch.18 para.12
s.1206, amended: 2013 c.29 Sch.18 para.13
s.1216A, added: 2013 c.29 Sch.16 para.1
s.1216AA, added: 2013 c.29 Sch.16 para.1
s.1216AA, applied: SI 2013/1831 Sch.2 para.12
s.1216AB, added: 2013 c.29 Sch.16 para.1
s.1216AB, applied: SI 2013/1831 Reg.5
s.1216AC, added: 2013 c.29 Sch.16 para.1
s.1216AD, added: 2013 c.29 Sch.16 para.1
s.1216AE, added: 2013 c.29 Sch.16 para.1

s.1216AF, added: 2013 c.29 Sch.16 para.1
s.1216AH, added: 2013 c.29 Sch.16 para.1
s.1216AI, added: 2013 c.29 Sch.16 para.1
s.1216AJ, added: 2013 c.29 Sch.16 para.1
s.1216B, added: 2013 c.29 Sch.16 para.1
s.1216BA, added: 2013 c.29 Sch.16 para.1
s.1216BB, added: 2013 c.29 Sch.16 para.1
s.1216BC, added: 2013 c.29 Sch.16 para.1
s.1216BD, added: 2013 c.29 Sch.16 para.1
s.1216BE, added: 2013 c.29 Sch.16 para.1
s.1216BF, added: 2013 c.29 Sch.16 para.1
s.1216C, added: 2013 c.29 Sch.16 para.1
s.1216CA, added: 2013 c.29 Sch.16 para.1
s.1216CB, added: 2013 c.29 Sch.16 para.1
s.1216CB, applied: SI 2013/1831, SI 2013/1831 Reg.3, Reg.4
s.1216CB, enabling: SI 2013/1831
s.1216CC, added: 2013 c.29 Sch.16 para.1
s.1216CC, applied: SI 2013/1831 Reg.6
s.1216CC, enabling: SI 2013/1831
s.1216CD, added: 2013 c.29 Sch.16 para.1
s.1216CE, added: 2013 c.29 Sch.16 para.1
s.1216CF, added: 2013 c.29 Sch.16 para.1
s.1216CG, added: 2013 c.29 Sch.16 para.1
s.1216CH, added: 2013 c.29 Sch.16 para.1
s.1216CI, added: 2013 c.29 Sch.16 para.1
s.1216CJ, added: 2013 c.29 Sch.16 para.1
s.1216CK, added: 2013 c.29 Sch.16 para.1
s.1216CL, added: 2013 c.29 Sch.16 para.1
s.1216CM, added: 2013 c.29 Sch.16 para.1
s.1216CN, added: 2013 c.29 Sch.16 para.1
s.1216D, added: 2013 c.29 Sch.16 para.1
s.1216DA, added: 2013 c.29 Sch.16 para.1
s.1216DB, added: 2013 c.29 Sch.16 para.1
s.1216DC, added: 2013 c.29 Sch.16 para.1
s.1216E, added: 2013 c.29 Sch.16 para.1
s.1216EA, added: 2013 c.29 Sch.16 para.1
s.1216EB, added: 2013 c.29 Sch.16 para.1
s.1216EC, added: 2013 c.29 Sch.16 para.1
s.1217, substituted: 2013 c.29 Sch.18 para.21
s.1217A, added: 2013 c.29 Sch.17 para.1
s.1217AA, added: 2013 c.29 Sch.17 para.1
s.1217AB, added: 2013 c.29 Sch.17 para.1
s.1217AC, added: 2013 c.29 Sch.17 para.1
s.1217AD, added: 2013 c.29 Sch.17 para.1
s.1217AE, added: 2013 c.29 Sch.17 para.1
s.1217AF, added: 2013 c.29 Sch.17 para.1
s.1217B, added: 2013 c.29 Sch.17 para.1
s.1217BA, added: 2013 c.29 Sch.17 para.1
s.1217BB, added: 2013 c.29 Sch.17 para.1
s.1217BC, added: 2013 c.29 Sch.17 para.1
s.1217BD, added: 2013 c.29 Sch.17 para.1
s.1217BE, added: 2013 c.29 Sch.17 para.1
s.1217C, added: 2013 c.29 Sch.17 para.1
s.1217CA, added: 2013 c.29 Sch.17 para.1
s.1217CB, added: 2013 c.29 Sch.17 para.1
s.1217CC, added: 2013 c.29 Sch.17 para.1
s.1217CD, added: 2013 c.29 Sch.17 para.1
s.1217CE, added: 2013 c.29 Sch.17 para.1
s.1217CF, added: 2013 c.29 Sch.17 para.1
s.1217CG, added: 2013 c.29 Sch.17 para.1
s.1217CH, added: 2013 c.29 Sch.17 para.1
s.1217CI, added: 2013 c.29 Sch.17 para.1
s.1217CJ, added: 2013 c.29 Sch.17 para.1
s.1217CK, added: 2013 c.29 Sch.17 para.1
s.1217CL, added: 2013 c.29 Sch.17 para.1
s.1217CM, added: 2013 c.29 Sch.17 para.1
s.1217CN, added: 2013 c.29 Sch.17 para.1
s.1217D, added: 2013 c.29 Sch.17 para.1
s.1217DA, added: 2013 c.29 Sch.17 para.1
s.1217DB, added: 2013 c.29 Sch.17 para.1
s.1217DC, added: 2013 c.29 Sch.17 para.1
s.1217E, added: 2013 c.29 Sch.17 para.1
s.1217EA, added: 2013 c.29 Sch.17 para.1
s.1217EB, added: 2013 c.29 Sch.17 para.1
s.1217EC, added: 2013 c.29 Sch.17 para.1
s.1218, substituted: 2013 c.29 Sch.18 para.21
s.1221, amended: 2013 c.29 Sch.29 para.38
s.1248, amended: 2013 c.29 Sch.29 para.39
s.1248, repealed (in part): 2013 c.29 Sch.29 para.39
s.1292, amended: 2013 c.29 Sch.23 para.34
s.1293, amended: 2013 c.29 Sch.23 para.35
s.1310, amended: 2013 c.29 Sch.18 para.14
Sch.1 Part 1 para.225, repealed: 2013 c.2 Sch.1 Part 10
Sch.1 Part 2 para.713, repealed: SI 2013/2819 Reg.41
Sch.4, amended: 2013 c.29 Sch.15 para.3, Sch.15 para.23, Sch.18 para.15, Sch.18 para.21, Sch.23 para.36, SI 2013/1411 Reg.13

10. Finance Act 2009

Commencement Orders: SI 2013/67 Art.2; SI 2013/280 Art.2; SI 2013/2472 Art.2
s.45, enabling: SI 2013/605
s.94, varied: SI 2013/938 Reg.16
s.96, enabling: SI 2013/1114
s.101, varied: SI 2013/938 Reg.14
s.103, varied: SI 2013/938 Reg.14
s.104, enabling: SI 2013/67, SI 2013/280, SI 2013/2472
Sch.19 para.4, repealed: 2013 c.29 Sch.29 para.40
Sch.19 para.13, repealed (in part): 2013 c.29 Sch.29 para.40, SI 2013/2819 Reg.41
Sch.53 Part 2 para.3, amended: 2013 c.29 Sch.51 para.7
Sch.53 Part 2 para.3, varied: SI 2013/938 Reg.14
Sch.53 Part 2 para.4, varied: SI 2013/938 Reg.14

Sch.54A para.2, amended: 2013 c.29 Sch.18 para.16
Sch.55, applied: 2013 c.29 s.233
Sch.55 para.1, amended: 2013 c.29 Sch.34 para.7, Sch.50 para.3, Sch.50 para.4
Sch.55 para.2, amended: 2013 c.29 Sch.50 para.5
Sch.55 para.6B, added: 2013 c.29 Sch.50 para.6
Sch.55 para.6C, added: 2013 c.29 Sch.50 para.6
Sch.55 para.6D, added: 2013 c.29 Sch.50 para.6
Sch.55 para.17A, added: 2013 c.29 Sch.51 para.8
Sch.55 para.17B, added: 2013 c.29 Sch.51 para.8
Sch.55 para.18, amended: 2013 c.29 Sch.50 para.7
Sch.55 para.19, amended: 2013 c.29 Sch.50 para.8
Sch.55 para.27, amended: 2013 c.29 Sch.50 para.9
Sch.56 para.1, amended: 2013 c.29 Sch.34 para.9, Sch.34 para.10, Sch.49 para.7, Sch.50 para.11
Sch.56 para.1, varied: 2013 c.29 Sch.34 para.10
Sch.56 para.2, varied: 2013 c.29 Sch.34 para.11
Sch.56 para.6, amended: 2013 c.29 Sch.50 para.12
Sch.56 para.9A, added: 2013 c.29 Sch.50 para.13
Sch.56 para.11, amended: 2013 c.29 Sch.50 para.14
Sch.56 para.11, repealed (in part): 2013 c.29 Sch.50 para.14

11. Borders, Citizenship and Immigration Act 2009

Part 1, applied: 2013 c.22 Sch.3 para.1
s.1, amended: 2013 c.32 Sch.12 para.101
s.1, applied: 2013 c.22 Sch.21 para.40
s.3, applied: 2013 c.22 Sch.21 para.40, SSI 2013/76 Reg.2
s.7, applied: 2013 c.22 Sch.21 para.40
s.11, applied: 2013 c.22 Sch.21 para.40, SSI 2013/76 Reg.2
s.22, amended: SI 2013/1542 Art.32
s.22, repealed (in part): SI 2013/1542 Art.32
s.23, enabling: SI 2013/1542
s.29, amended: SI 2013/602 Sch.2 para.61
s.37, applied: SI 2013/1542
s.37, enabling: SI 2013/1542
s.53, repealed: 2013 c.22 s.22

12. Political Parties and Elections Act 2009

Commencement Orders: 2013 c.6 s.23; SI 2013/99 Art.2, Art.3
s.23, repealed (in part): 2013 c.6 Sch.4 para.24
s.28, repealed: 2013 c.6 s.23
s.29, repealed: 2013 c.6 s.23
s.30, repealed (in part): 2013 c.6 Sch.4 para.24
s.31, repealed (in part): 2013 c.6 Sch.4 para.24
s.32, repealed (in part): 2013 c.6 Sch.4 para.24
s.33, repealed (in part): 2013 c.6 Sch.4 para.24
s.34, repealed (in part): 2013 c.6 Sch.4 para.24
s.35, repealed (in part): 2013 c.6 Sch.4 para.24
s.36, repealed (in part): 2013 c.6 Sch.4 para.24
s.37, repealed (in part): 2013 c.6 Sch.4 para.24
s.43, enabling: SI 2013/99

13. Parliamentary Standards Act 2009

Sch.4 Part 1 para.4, amended: 2013 c.22 Sch.9 para.117
Sch.4 Part 2 para.12, amended: 2013 c.22 Sch.9 para.117

20. Local Democracy, Economic Development and Construction Act 2009

applied: 2013 c.12 Sch.1 para.1, 2013 c.28 Sch.1
s.58, applied: SI 2013/66, SI 2013/68, SI 2013/69, SI 2013/70, SI 2013/1786, SI 2013/2794, SI 2013/2795, SI 2013/2797
s.59, enabling: SI 2013/66, SI 2013/68, SI 2013/69, SI 2013/70, SI 2013/1786, SI 2013/2794, SI 2013/2795, SI 2013/2797

21. Health Act 2009

s.2, applied: SI 2013/474 Reg.4
s.4, applied: SI 2013/317
s.4, enabling: SI 2013/317

22. Apprenticeships, Skills, Children and Learning Act 2009

Commencement Orders: SI 2013/975 Art.2, Art.3; SI 2013/1100 Art.2
Part 7, applied: SI 2013/2216 Sch.1 para.13
s.1, enabling: SI 2013/1968
s.2, enabling: SI 2013/1468
s.7, applied: SI 2013/1190 Reg.3
s.7, enabling: SI 2013/1190
s.8, applied: SI 2013/1190 Reg.3
s.8, enabling: SI 2013/1190
s.9, enabling: SI 2013/1190
s.10, applied: SI 2013/1191 Art.2
s.10, enabling: SI 2013/1191
s.19, applied: SI 2013/1202 Art.3
s.22, enabling: SI 2013/1202
s.25, applied: SI 2013/575
s.25, enabling: SI 2013/575
s.27, applied: SI 2013/575
s.28, applied: SI 2013/1192
s.28, enabling: SI 2013/1192, SI 2013/1238
s.31, applied: SI 2013/1192
s.83A, applied: SI 2013/560 Reg.2
s.83A, enabling: SI 2013/560
s.146, applied: SI 2013/975 Art.3
s.262, applied: SI 2013/1242, SI 2013/1468, SI 2013/1968
s.262, enabling: SI 2013/560, SI 2013/1191, SI 2013/1468, SI 2013/1968
s.265, enabling: SI 2013/1242
s.269, applied: SI 2013/975
s.269, enabling: SI 2013/975, SI 2013/1100

23. Marine and Coastal Access Act 2009

Commencement Orders: SI 2013/3055 Art.2

Part 4, applied: SI 2013/343 Art.12, SI 2013/414 Art.3, SI 2013/1873 Art.27
Part 4 c.1, applied: SI 2013/343 Art.12, SI 2013/1203 Art.10, SI 2013/1734 Art.8
s.12, applied: SI 2013/1570 Reg.6
s.16, amended: SI 2013/755 Sch.2 para.442
s.41, applied: SI 2013/3162 Art.2
s.41, enabling: SI 2013/3161
s.66, applied: SI 2013/343 Sch.2 para.2, SI 2013/1203 Sch.2 para.2, SI 2013/1734 Sch.2 para.2
s.72, applied: SI 2013/343 Sch.2 para.2
s.74, applied: SI 2013/526
s.74, enabling: SI 2013/526
s.98, applied: SI 2013/414, SI 2013/414 Art.2, Art.3
s.113, applied: SI 2013/414, SI 2013/414 Art.2, SI 2013/526, SI 2013/526 Art.1
s.147, amended: SI 2013/755 Sch.2 para.443
s.149, amended: SI 2013/755 Sch.2 para.444
s.152, amended: SI 2013/755 Sch.2 para.445
s.168, amended: SI 2013/755 Sch.2 para.446
s.232, amended: SI 2013/755 Sch.2 para.447
s.238, amended: SI 2013/755 Sch.2 para.448
s.313, repealed: SI 2013/755 Sch.2 para.449
s.316, enabling: SI 2013/414, SI 2013/526
s.324, enabling: SI 2013/3055
Sch.7, applied: SI 2013/414 Art.3
Sch.7 para.13, amended: SI 2013/602 Sch.2 para.62
Sch.8, applied: SI 2013/414 Art.3
Sch.9, applied: SI 2013/414 Art.3
Sch.10 para.9, amended: SI 2013/602 Sch.2 para.62
Sch.14 para.6, repealed: 2013 c.32 Sch.12 para.30

25. Coroners and Justice Act 2009

Commencement Orders: SI 2013/250 Art.2; SI 2013/705 Art.2; SI 2013/1104 Art.2; SI 2013/1628 Art.2; SI 2013/1869 Art.2, Art.3; SI 2013/2908 Art.2
applied: SI 2013/335 Reg.4, Reg.9, SI 2013/1554 r.6_1, SI 2013/1616 r.2, SI 2013/1629 Reg.14
referred to: SI 2013/1629 Reg.2
Part 1, applied: SI 2013/1629 Sch.1
Part 7, applied: 2013 c.22 s.1, SI 2013/1554 r.6_1
s.4, applied: SI 2013/1629 Sch.1
s.5, applied: SI 2013/1616 Sch.1
s.8, amended: 2013 c.22 Sch.9 para.73
s.34, enabling: SI 2013/1615
s.43, enabling: SI 2013/1629
s.45, enabling: SI 2013/1616
s.75, amended: 2013 c.22 Sch.8 para.186
s.76, applied: SI 2013/1554 r.6_1
s.77, amended: 2013 c.22 Sch.8 para.188
s.78, applied: SI 2013/1554 r.6_24
s.79, applied: SI 2013/1554 r.6_1
s.80, applied: SI 2013/1554 r.6_1
s.81, amended: 2013 c.22 Sch.8 para.187
s.86, applied: SI 2013/1554 r.16_6, r.29_1, r.29_26
s.88, applied: SI 2013/1554 r.29_19, r.29_22
s.89, applied: SI 2013/1554 r.29_22
s.91, applied: SI 2013/1554 r.29_1, r.29_21
s.92, applied: SI 2013/1554 r.29_1, r.29_21
s.93, applied: SI 2013/1554 r.29_1, r.29_21
s.120, applied: SI 2013/1554 r.37_10
s.122, applied: SI 2013/1554 r.9_10
s.125, see *R. v Healey (Robert)* [2012] EWCA Crim 1005, [2013] 1 Cr. App. R. (S.) 33 (CA (Crim Div)), Hughes, L.J.; see *R. v L* [2012] EWCA Crim 2291, [2013] 2 Cr. App. R. (S.) 1 (CA (Crim Div)), Aikens, L.J.
s.125, applied: SI 2013/1554 r.42_1
s.142, repealed (in part): SI 2013/2853 Art.2
s.143, referred to: SI 2013/817
s.161, amended: 2013 c.22 Sch.8 para.186
s.166, amended: 2013 c.22 Sch.8 para.186
s.170, repealed: 2013 c.22 Sch.8 para.189
s.176, applied: SI 2013/1874
s.176, enabling: SI 2013/250, SI 2013/1869
s.177, enabling: SI 2013/1874
s.182, enabling: SI 2013/250, SI 2013/705, SI 2013/1104, SI 2013/1628, SI 2013/1869, SI 2013/2908
Sch.2 para.1, applied: SI 2013/1625
Sch.2 para.1, enabling: SI 2013/1625
Sch.2 para.2, enabling: SI 2013/1626
Sch.3 Part 1 para.2, applied: SI 2013/1625
Sch.3 Part 1 para.2, enabling: SI 2013/1625
Sch.3 Part 4 para.14, applied: SI 2013/1674
Sch.7, enabling: SI 2013/1615
Sch.21 Part 1 para.51, amended: 2013 c.22 Sch.13 para.49
Sch.22 Part 1 para.1, enabling: SI 2013/1625

26. Policing and Crime Act 2009

s.43, amended: 2013 c.22 s.18
s.46B, amended: 2013 c.22 Sch.12 para.2
s.48, amended: 2013 c.22 s.18
s.48, repealed (in part): 2013 c.22 Sch.9 para.51
s.48, amended: 2013 c.22 Sch.12 para.3
s.49, amended: 2013 c.22 s.18
s.49, amended: 2013 c.22 Sch.12 para.4
Sch.5 para.1, amended: 2013 c.22 Sch.9 para.51, Sch.12 para.5
Sch.5A Part 1 para.1, amended: 2013 c.22 Sch.12 para.7
Sch.5A Part 1 para.1, repealed (in part): 2013 c.22 Sch.12 para.7

Sch.5A Part 2 para.4, amended: 2013 c.22 Sch.12 para.8
Sch.5A Part 2 para.5, amended: 2013 c.22 Sch.12 para.9
Sch.5A Part 2 para.6, amended: 2013 c.22 Sch.12 para.10
Sch.5A Part 2 para.8, amended: 2013 c.22 Sch.12 para.11
Sch.5A Part 2 para.9, amended: 2013 c.22 Sch.12 para.12
Sch.5A Part 2 para.10, amended: 2013 c.22 Sch.12 para.13
Sch.5A Part 2 para.12, amended: 2013 c.22 Sch.12 para.14
Sch.5A Part 2 para.12, repealed (in part): 2013 c.22 Sch.12 para.14
Sch.5A Part 3 para.15, amended: 2013 c.22 Sch.12 para.15
Sch.7 Part 8 para.116, repealed: 2013 c.29 Sch.48 para.24

2010

01. Children and Families (Wales) Measure 2010
Commencement Orders: SI 2013/18 Art.2; SI 2013/1830 Art.2, Art.3
Part 2, applied: SI 2013/3029 Sch.1 para.19, Sch.6 para.21, SI 2013/3035 Sch.1
s.6, amended: SI 2013/755 Sch.3 para.1
s.34, amended: 2013 c.22 Sch.11 para.208
s.43, amended: 2013 c.22 Sch.11 para.209
s.43, repealed (in part): 2013 c.22 Sch.11 para.209
s.74, enabling: SI 2013/18, SI 2013/1830
s.75, enabling: SI 2013/18, SI 2013/1830
Sch.1 para.1, repealed: 2013 c.22 Sch.10 para.99
Sch.1 para.2, repealed: 2013 c.22 Sch.10 para.99

4. Corporation Tax Act 2010
Part 3, applied: 2013 c.29 s.5
Part 3, disapplied: SI 2013/2819 Reg.25, Reg.29
Part 5, applied: SI 2013/2242 Art.5
Part 5 c.6, applied: 2013 asp 11 Sch.10 para.47, Sch.11 para.40
Part 8A, applied: SI 2013/420 Art.2
Part 13 c.9, applied: 2013 c.29 Sch.21 para.8, SI 2013/737 Sch.1 para.1
s.1, amended: 2013 c.29 Sch.14 para.2, Sch.20 para.2, Sch.29 para.42
s.1, repealed (in part): 2013 c.29 Sch.29 para.42, SI 2013/2819 Reg.39
s.3, applied: SI 2013/2819 Reg.25
s.5, amended: 2013 c.29 s.66
s.9C, added: 2013 c.29 s.66
s.32, amended: 2013 c.29 Sch.25 para.19
s.40, amended: 2013 c.29 s.92
s.43, amended: 2013 c.29 s.92
s.62, applied: SI 2013/2242 Art.5
s.105, amended: 2013 c.29 s.29
s.105, applied: 2013 c.29 s.29
s.105, referred to: 2013 c.29 s.29
s.107, amended: 2013 c.29 s.30
s.144, amended: SI 2013/463 Art.10
s.148, amended: SI 2013/463 Art.11
s.149, amended: SI 2013/463 Art.12
s.151, applied: 2013 asp 11 Sch.10 para.47, Sch.11 para.40
s.152, applied: SI 2013/2571 Sch.1 para.4
s.154, amended: 2013 c.29 s.31
s.155, amended: 2013 c.29 s.31
s.156, amended: 2013 c.29 s.31
s.158, applied: SI 2013/3209 Reg.4
s.159, applied: SI 2013/3209 Reg.4
s.160, applied: SI 2013/460 Reg.3
s.162, amended: 2013 c.29 s.43
s.162, repealed (in part): SI 2013/3209 Reg.12
s.164A, added: 2013 c.29 s.43
s.164A, repealed: SI 2013/3209 Reg.12
s.171, varied: 2013 asp 11 Sch.10 para.48, Sch.11 para.41
s.173, varied: 2013 asp 11 Sch.10 para.48, Sch.11 para.41
s.174, varied: 2013 asp 11 Sch.10 para.48, Sch.11 para.41
s.176, varied: 2013 asp 11 Sch.10 para.48, Sch.11 para.41
s.177, varied: 2013 asp 11 Sch.10 para.48, Sch.11 para.41
s.178, varied: 2013 asp 11 Sch.10 para.48, Sch.11 para.41
s.188, amended: 2013 c.29 s.31
s.220, amended: 2013 c.29 Sch.27 para.8
s.220A, added: 2013 c.29 Sch.27 para.9
s.220B, added: 2013 c.29 Sch.27 para.13
s.240, amended: 2013 c.29 Sch.27 para.10
s.244, amended: 2013 c.29 Sch.27 para.11
s.244, repealed (in part): 2013 c.29 Sch.27 para.11
s.287A, added: 2013 c.29 s.87
s.292, amended: 2013 c.29 Sch.31 para.2, Sch.31 para.18
s.292, repealed (in part): 2013 c.29 Sch.31 para.7, Sch.31 para.18
s.292, substituted: 2013 c.29 Sch.31 para.18
s.293, repealed: 2013 c.29 Sch.31 para.7
s.294, repealed: 2013 c.29 Sch.31 para.19
s.295, repealed: 2013 c.29 Sch.31 para.19
s.296, amended: 2013 c.29 Sch.31 para.2, Sch.31 para.20
s.296, substituted: 2013 c.29 Sch.31 para.20

s.298, repealed: 2013 c.29 Sch.31 para.10
s.298A, added: 2013 c.29 Sch.31 para.21
s.312, repealed (in part): 2013 c.29 Sch.15 para.24
s.330B, amended: 2013 c.29 s.88
s.330C, applied: SI 2013/2910 Art.2
s.337, amended: SI 2013/2910 Art.4
s.340, amended: SI 2013/2910 Art.5
s.341, amended: SI 2013/2910 Art.6
s.342, amended: SI 2013/2910 Art.7
s.344, amended: SI 2013/2910 Art.8
s.349, enabling: SI 2013/2910
s.349A, amended: SI 2013/2910 Art.9
s.349A, applied: SI 2013/2910 Art.2
s.349A, enabling: SI 2013/2910
s.356A, added: SI 2013/2910 Art.10
s.357, amended: SI 2013/2910 Art.11
s.357, substituted: SI 2013/2910 Art.11
s.357BB, applied: SI 2013/420 Art.2
s.357BB, enabling: SI 2013/420
s.357CG, amended: 2013 c.29 Sch.15 para.10, Sch.18 para.18
s.357CHA, added: 2013 c.29 Sch.18 para.19
s.357CK, amended: 2013 c.29 Sch.15 para.11, Sch.18 para.20
s.432, amended: 2013 c.29 Sch.14 para.2
s.438, amended: 2013 c.29 Sch.30 para.2
s.448, varied: 2013 c.29 s.172
s.453, applied: 2013 asp 11 Sch.10 para.29, Sch.10 para.38, Sch.11 para.21
s.455, amended: 2013 c.29 Sch.30 para.3
s.459, amended: 2013 c.29 Sch.30 para.4
s.464A, added: 2013 c.29 Sch.30 para.5
s.464B, added: 2013 c.29 Sch.30 para.5
s.464C, added: 2013 c.29 Sch.30 para.6
s.464D, added: 2013 c.29 Sch.30 para.6
s.465, amended: 2013 c.29 Sch.30 para.7
s.486, amended: SI 2013/2819 Reg.39
s.530, amended: 2013 c.29 Sch.19 para.2
s.530A, amended: 2013 c.29 Sch.19 para.3
s.531, amended: 2013 c.29 Sch.19 para.4
s.548, amended: 2013 c.29 Sch.19 para.5
s.549, amended: 2013 c.29 Sch.19 para.6
s.549A, added: 2013 c.29 Sch.19 para.7
s.549A, disapplied: 2013 c.29 Sch.19 para.13
s.550, amended: 2013 c.29 Sch.19 para.8
s.588, amended: 2013 c.29 Sch.19 para.9
s.589, amended: 2013 c.29 Sch.19 para.10
s.605, amended: 2013 c.29 Sch.19 para.11
s.614, disapplied: SI 2013/2819 Reg.25
s.618, disapplied: SI 2013/2819 Reg.25
s.620, varied: 2013 asp 11 s.45
s.621, repealed: SI 2013/2819 Reg.39
s.622, repealed: SI 2013/2819 Reg.39
s.658, amended: 2013 c.29 Sch.21 para.4
s.658, applied: 2013 c.29 Sch.21 para.8
s.659, amended: 2013 c.29 Sch.21 para.2
s.660, amended: 2013 c.29 Sch.21 para.3
s.660A, added: 2013 c.29 Sch.21 para.5
s.662, amended: 2013 c.29 Sch.21 para.6
s.663, amended: 2013 c.29 Sch.21 para.7
s.672, amended: 2013 c.29 Sch.13 para.1
s.676, substituted: 2013 c.29 s.32
s.705A, added: 2013 c.29 Sch.13 para.1
s.705B, added: 2013 c.29 Sch.13 para.1
s.705C, added: 2013 c.29 Sch.13 para.1
s.705D, added: 2013 c.29 Sch.13 para.1
s.705E, added: 2013 c.29 Sch.13 para.1
s.705F, added: 2013 c.29 Sch.13 para.1
s.705G, added: 2013 c.29 Sch.13 para.1
s.721, amended: 2013 c.29 Sch.13 para.1
s.725, amended: 2013 c.29 Sch.13 para.1
s.730, amended: 2013 c.29 Sch.13 para.1
s.730A, added: 2013 c.29 Sch.14 para.1
s.730B, added: 2013 c.29 Sch.14 para.1
s.730C, added: 2013 c.29 Sch.14 para.1
s.730C, varied: 2013 c.29 Sch.14 para.3
s.730D, added: 2013 c.29 Sch.14 para.1
s.778, amended: SI 2013/2819 Reg.39
s.780, repealed: 2013 c.29 Sch.29 para.43
s.781, repealed: 2013 c.29 Sch.29 para.43
s.782, repealed: 2013 c.29 Sch.29 para.43
s.783, repealed: 2013 c.29 Sch.29 para.43
s.784, repealed: 2013 c.29 Sch.29 para.43
s.785, repealed: 2013 c.29 Sch.29 para.43
s.786, repealed: 2013 c.29 Sch.29 para.43
s.787, repealed: 2013 c.29 Sch.29 para.43
s.788, repealed: 2013 c.29 Sch.29 para.43
s.789, repealed: 2013 c.29 Sch.29 para.43
s.790, repealed: 2013 c.29 Sch.29 para.43
s.791, repealed: 2013 c.29 Sch.29 para.43
s.792, repealed: 2013 c.29 Sch.29 para.43
s.793, repealed: 2013 c.29 Sch.29 para.43
s.794, repealed: 2013 c.29 Sch.29 para.43
s.795, repealed: 2013 c.29 Sch.29 para.43
s.796, repealed: 2013 c.29 Sch.29 para.43
s.797, repealed: 2013 c.29 Sch.29 para.43
s.798, repealed: 2013 c.29 Sch.29 para.43
s.799, repealed: 2013 c.29 Sch.29 para.43
s.800, repealed: 2013 c.29 Sch.29 para.43
s.801, repealed: 2013 c.29 Sch.29 para.43
s.802, repealed: 2013 c.29 Sch.29 para.43
s.803, repealed: 2013 c.29 Sch.29 para.43
s.804, repealed: 2013 c.29 Sch.29 para.43
s.805, repealed: 2013 c.29 Sch.29 para.43
s.806, repealed: 2013 c.29 Sch.29 para.43
s.807, repealed: 2013 c.29 Sch.29 para.43
s.808, repealed: 2013 c.29 Sch.29 para.43
s.809, repealed: 2013 c.29 Sch.29 para.43

s.810, repealed: 2013 c.29 Sch.29 para.43
s.811, repealed: 2013 c.29 Sch.29 para.43
s.812, amended: 2013 c.29 s.76
s.812, repealed: 2013 c.29 Sch.29 para.43
s.813, repealed: 2013 c.29 Sch.29 para.43
s.814, repealed: 2013 c.29 Sch.29 para.43
s.814A, added: 2013 c.29 Sch.29 para.2
s.814B, added: 2013 c.29 Sch.29 para.2
s.814C, added: 2013 c.29 Sch.29 para.2
s.814D, added: 2013 c.29 Sch.29 para.2
s.938O, added: 2013 c.29 Sch.20 para.3
s.938O, disapplied: 2013 c.29 Sch.20 para.6
s.938P, added: 2013 c.29 Sch.20 para.3
s.938Q, added: 2013 c.29 Sch.20 para.3
s.938R, added: 2013 c.29 Sch.20 para.3
s.938S, added: 2013 c.29 Sch.20 para.3
s.938T, added: 2013 c.29 Sch.20 para.3
s.938U, added: 2013 c.29 Sch.20 para.3
s.938V, added: 2013 c.29 Sch.20 para.3
s.986, amended: 2013 c.29 s.37
s.987A, added: 2013 c.29 s.38
s.987A, varied: 2013 c.29 s.38
s.1029, amended: 2013 c.29 s.43
s.1029, repealed (in part): SI 2013/3209 Reg.12
s.1032A, added: 2013 c.29 s.43
s.1032A, repealed: SI 2013/3209 Reg.12
s.1034, amended: 2013 c.29 Sch.46 para.145
s.1034, repealed (in part): 2013 c.29 Sch.46 para.145
s.1054, disapplied: SI 2013/460 Reg.3
s.1076, applied: 2013 c.1 s.2
s.1077, applied: 2013 c.1 s.2
s.1078, applied: 2013 c.1 s.2
s.1104, applied: SI 2013/2819 Reg.28
s.1107, applied: SI 2013/2819 Reg.28
s.1109, amended: 2013 c.29 Sch.29 para.44
s.1109, repealed (in part): 2013 c.29 Sch.29 para.44
s.1120, amended: SI 2013/636 Sch.1 para.12
s.1121, amended: SI 2013/1388 Reg.5
s.1122, applied: 2013 asp 11 s.23, s.58, Sch.17 para.24, 2013 c.29 s.172, SI 2013/2571 Sch.1 para.4
s.1122, varied: 2013 c.29 s.136
s.1123, referred to: 2013 c.29 s.172
s.1124, applied: 2013 asp 11 Sch.7 para.20
s.1155, applied: 2013 asp 11 Sch.10 para.45, Sch.11 para.38
s.1156, applied: 2013 asp 11 Sch.10 para.45, Sch.11 para.38
s.1157, applied: 2013 asp 11 Sch.10 para.45, Sch.11 para.38
s.1158, amended: 2013 c.29 s.45
s.1159, enabling: SI 2013/1406
s.1172, applied: 2013 c.29 s.30
s.1173, amended: 2013 c.29 Sch.15 para.24
s.1178, enabling: SI 2013/463
s.1179, enabling: SI 2013/463
Sch.1 Part 1 para.103, repealed: 2013 c.2 Sch.1 Part 10
Sch.1 Part 1 para.116, repealed: 2013 c.2 Sch.1 Part 10
Sch.1 Part 2 para.259, repealed: 2013 c.29 Sch.29 para.45
Sch.1 Part 2 para.537, repealed: 2013 c.29 Sch.29 para.45
Sch.1 Part 2 para.538, repealed: 2013 c.29 Sch.29 para.45
Sch.1 Part 2 para.539, repealed (in part): 2013 c.29 Sch.29 para.45
Sch.1 Part 2 para.540, repealed: 2013 c.29 Sch.12 para.16
Sch.1 Part 2 para.541, repealed: 2013 c.29 Sch.12 para.16
Sch.1 Part 2 para.542, repealed: 2013 c.29 Sch.12 para.16
Sch.1 Part 2 para.543, repealed: 2013 c.29 Sch.12 para.16
Sch.1 Part 2 para.544, repealed (in part): 2013 c.29 Sch.12 para.16
Sch.1 Part 2 para.635, repealed: 2013 c.29 Sch.29 para.45
Sch.1 Part 2 para.636, repealed: 2013 c.29 Sch.29 para.45
Sch.1 Part 2 para.663, repealed: SI 2013/2819 Reg.41
Sch.1 Part 2 para.671, repealed: 2013 c.29 Sch.15 para.24
Sch.1 Part 2 para.689, repealed (in part): 2013 c.29 Sch.29 para.45
Sch.2 Part 17 para.90, repealed: 2013 c.29 Sch.29 para.46
Sch.2 Part 17 para.91, repealed: 2013 c.29 Sch.29 para.46
Sch.2 Part 17 para.92, repealed: 2013 c.29 Sch.29 para.46
Sch.2 Part 17 para.93, repealed: 2013 c.29 Sch.29 para.46
Sch.2 Part 17 para.94, repealed: 2013 c.29 Sch.29 para.46
Sch.4, amended: 2013 c.29 Sch.13 para.2, Sch.14 para.2, Sch.20 para.4, Sch.29 para.47, SI 2013/2910 Art.12

7. Co-operative and Community Benefit Societies and Credit Unions Act 2010

Commencement Orders: SI 2013/2936 Art.2
s.4, amended: SI 2013/496 Sch.11 para.9
s.8, enabling: SI 2013/2936

9. Child Poverty Act 2010

s.8B, applied: SI 2013/411 Art.2, SI 2013/1980 Art.2, Art.3
s.8B, enabling: SI 2013/411, SI 2013/1980
s.28, enabling: SI 2013/411

13. Finance Act 2010

s.40, repealed: SI 2013/2819 Reg.41
s.64, amended: SI 2013/636 Sch.1 para.14
Sch.1 Part 3 para.44, amended: SI 2013/636 Sch.1 para.14
Sch.1 Part 3 para.45, amended: SI 2013/636 Sch.1 para.14
Sch.6 Part 1 para.7, amended: 2013 c.29 Sch.35 para.3
Sch.6 Part 2 para.21, repealed (in part): 2013 c.29 Sch.12 para.17
Sch.13 para.1, repealed: SI 2013/2819 Reg.41
Sch.13 para.2, repealed: SI 2013/2819 Reg.41
Sch.13 para.3, repealed: SI 2013/2819 Reg.41
Sch.13 para.4, repealed: SI 2013/2819 Reg.41

15. Equality Act 2010

see *Aderemi v London and South Eastern Railway Ltd* [2013] I.C.R. 591 (EAT), Langstaff, J. (President); see *Garrard v University of London* [2013] Eq. L.R. 746 (CC (Central London)), Judge Birtles; see *Nottingham City Transport Ltd v Harvey* [2013] Eq. L.R. 4 (EAT), Langstaff, J. (President); see *R. (on the application of Hodkin) v Registrar General of Births Deaths and Marriages* [2012] EWHC 3635 (Admin), [2013] P.T.S.R. 875 (QBD (Admin)), Ouseley, J.; see *Secretary of State for Work and Pensions v Higgins* [2013] Eq. L.R. 1180 (EAT), Judge David Richardson; see *Williams v Ministry of Defence* [2013] Eq. L.R. 27 (EAT), Judge McMullen Q.C.
applied: SI 2013/104 Reg.57, Reg.59, SI 2013/349 Sch.4 para.28, Sch.5 para.18, SI 2013/503 Reg.6, SI 2013/898 Sch.4 para.27, Sch.5 para.16, SI 2013/1893 Sch.2, SI 2013/3104 Sch.1 para.20
referred to: SI 2013/104 Reg.58
s.6, applied: SI 2013/560 Reg.2
s.9, amended: 2013 c.24 s.97
s.9, applied: SI 2013/2192 Reg.5, Reg.11, Reg.17, Reg.23, SI 2013/2193 Reg.5, Reg.11, Reg.17
s.9, referred to: 2013 c.24 s.97
s.23, amended: 2013 c.30 Sch.7 para.43
s.40, repealed (in part): 2013 c.24 s.65
s.42, amended: 2013 c.22 Sch.8 para.181, SI 2013/602 Sch.2 para.63
s.42, repealed (in part): SI 2013/602 Sch.2 para.63
s.43, amended: 2013 c.22 Sch.8 para.182, SI 2013/602 Sch.2 para.63
s.43, repealed (in part): SI 2013/602 Sch.2 para.63
s.50, amended: 2013 c.22 Sch.13 para.50
s.51, amended: 2013 c.22 Sch.13 para.51
s.65, applied: SI 2013/1237 Sch.3 para.3
s.69, applied: SI 2013/1237 Sch.3 para.3
s.85, see *P v Governing Body of A Primary School* [2013] UKUT 154 (AAC), [2013] Eq. L.R. 666 (UT (AAC)), David Williams; see *Parents of C v Stanbridge Earls School* [2013] Eq. L.R. 304 (FTT), Judge H Brayne
s.85, applied: SI 2013/1793 Reg.13
s.91, applied: SI 2013/1793 Reg.13
s.110, amended: 2013 c.30 s.2
s.114, amended: 2013 c.22 Sch.9 para.52
s.115, amended: 2013 c.18 Sch.2 para.12
s.118, amended: 2013 c.24 s.64
s.118, repealed (in part): 2013 c.24 s.64
s.119, amended: 2013 c.22 Sch.9 para.52
s.120, see *Uddin v General Medical Council* [2013] I.C.R. 793 (EAT), Slade, J.
s.120, amended: 2013 c.22 Sch.9 para.52
s.120, applied: SI 2013/1237 Sch.1
s.123, see *Richman v Knowsley MBC* [2013] Eq. L.R. 1164 (EAT), Judge McMullen Q.C.
s.123, amended: 2013 c.24 Sch.2 para.43
s.124, amended: 2013 c.22 Sch.9 para.52
s.127, amended: 2013 c.22 Sch.9 para.52
s.127, applied: SI 2013/1237 Sch.1
s.129, amended: 2013 c.24 Sch.2 para.44
s.131, applied: SI 2013/1237 Sch.3 para.3
s.138, amended: 2013 c.22 Sch.9 para.52
s.138, repealed: 2013 c.24 s.66
s.139, enabling: SI 2013/1669, SI 2013/1671
s.139A, added: 2013 c.24 s.98
s.140, amended: 2013 c.22 Sch.9 para.52
s.140B, added: 2013 c.24 Sch.2 para.45
s.143, amended: 2013 c.22 Sch.9 para.52
s.144, amended: 2013 c.24 s.23
s.146, applied: SI 2013/1237 Sch.1
s.147, amended: 2013 c.24 s.23
s.151, enabling: SSI 2013/170
s.152, applied: SSI 2013/170
s.183, applied: SI 2013/1931, SI 2013/3031
s.183, enabling: SI 2013/1931, SI 2013/3031
s.184, applied: SI 2013/1931, SI 2013/3031
s.207, amended: 2013 c.24 s.98
s.207, enabling: SI 2013/1669, SI 2013/1671, SI 2013/1931, SI 2013/3031
s.208, amended: 2013 c.24 s.98
Sch.3 Part 6A para.25A, added: 2013 c.30 s.2
Sch.3 Part 6 para.24, substituted: 2013 c.30 Sch.7 para.44
Sch.3 Part 6 para.25, substituted: 2013 c.30 Sch.7 para.44
Sch.3 Part 9 para.34, amended: SI 2013/1865 Reg.13

Sch.9 Part 1 para.2, amended: 2013 c.30 Sch.7 para.45
Sch.9 Part 3 para.18, amended: 2013 c.30 Sch.4 para.17
Sch.9 Part 3 para.18, applied: 2013 c.30 s.16
Sch.17 Part 2 para.4, amended: 2013 c.24 s.64
Sch.17 Part 2 para.4, repealed (in part): 2013 c.24 s.64
Sch.19 Part 1, amended: 2013 c.22 Sch.8 para.183, 2013 c.24 Sch.4 para.26, 2013 c.32 Sch.12 para.102, 2013 c.33 Sch.4 para.16
Sch.19 Part 2, amended: SI 2013/755 Sch.2 para.450
Sch.19 Part 3, amended: SI 2013/602 Sch.2 para.63, SSI 2013/170 Art.2
Sch.19 Part 3, substituted: SI 2013/602 Sch.2 para.63
Sch.19 Part 4, amended: SI 2013/755 Sch.2 para.450
Sch.21 para.4, amended: 2013 c.22 Sch.9 para.52
Sch.21 para.5, amended: 2013 c.22 Sch.9 para.52

17. Crime and Security Act 2010

s.26, applied: SI 2013/9 Reg.9
s.27, applied: SI 2013/9 Reg.9
s.29, applied: SI 2013/9 Reg.9
s.31, amended: 2013 c.22 Sch.8 para.179
s.31, repealed (in part): 2013 c.22 Sch.8 para.179

23. Bribery Act 2010

s.1, applied: 2013 c.22 Sch.17 para.26, SI 2013/175 Sch.9 para.1, SI 2013/435 Sch.1 Part 7
s.2, applied: 2013 c.22 Sch.17 para.26, SI 2013/175 Sch.9 para.1, SI 2013/435 Sch.1 Part 7
s.6, applied: 2013 c.22 Sch.17 para.26, SI 2013/175 Sch.9 para.1, SI 2013/435 Sch.1 Part 7
s.7, applied: 2013 c.22 Sch.17 para.26

24. Digital Economy Act 2010

s.43, amended: SI 2013/2352 Sch.1 para.14

25. Constitutional Reform and Governance Act 2010

Commencement Orders: SI 2013/2826 Art.2
s.10, disapplied: 2013 c.22 Sch.1 para.3
s.11, disapplied: 2013 c.22 Sch.1 para.3
s.12, disapplied: 2013 c.22 Sch.1 para.3
s.13, disapplied: 2013 c.22 Sch.1 para.3
s.14, disapplied: 2013 c.22 Sch.1 para.3
s.41, amended: 2013 c.29 Sch.46 para.147
s.52, enabling: SI 2013/2826
Sch.6 Part 1 para.12, repealed (in part): 2013 c.25 Sch.11 para.1
Sch.6 Part 1 para.16, amended: 2013 c.25 Sch.11 para.1
Sch.6 Part 1 para.16, repealed (in part): 2013 c.25 Sch.11 para.1
Sch.6 Part 2 para.29A, added: 2013 c.25 s.34
Sch.6 Part 3 para.36, repealed: 2013 c.25 Sch.11 para.7
Sch.6 Part 3 para.37, repealed: 2013 c.25 Sch.11 para.7

26. Children, Schools and Families Act 2010

Commencement Orders: 2013 c.22 s.17; SI 2013/668 Art.2; SI 2013/1573 Art.2
s.11, repealed: 2013 c.22 s.17
s.12, repealed: 2013 c.22 s.17
s.13, repealed: 2013 c.22 s.17
s.14, repealed: 2013 c.22 s.17
s.15, repealed: 2013 c.22 s.17
s.16, repealed: 2013 c.22 s.17
s.17, repealed: 2013 c.22 s.17
s.18, repealed: 2013 c.22 s.17
s.19, repealed: 2013 c.22 s.17
s.20, repealed: 2013 c.22 s.17
s.21, repealed: 2013 c.22 s.17
s.29, amended: 2013 c.22 s.17
s.29, repealed (in part): 2013 c.22 s.17
s.29, enabling: SI 2013/668, SI 2013/1573
Sch.3 Part 2 para.3, repealed: 2013 c.22 s.17
Sch.3 Part 2 para.4, repealed: 2013 c.22 s.17
Sch.3 Part 2 para.5, repealed: 2013 c.22 s.17
Sch.3 Part 2 para.6, repealed: 2013 c.22 s.17
Sch.3 Part 2 para.7, repealed: 2013 c.22 s.17
Sch.3 Part 2 para.8, repealed: 2013 c.22 s.17
Sch.3 Part 2 para.9, repealed: 2013 c.22 s.17
Sch.3 Part 2 para.10, repealed: 2013 c.22 s.17
Sch.3 Part 2 para.11, repealed: 2013 c.22 s.17
Sch.3 Part 2 para.12, repealed: 2013 c.22 s.17
Sch.3 Part 2 para.13, repealed: 2013 c.22 s.17
Sch.3 Part 2 para.14, repealed: 2013 c.22 s.17
Sch.4 Part 2, repealed: 2013 c.22 s.17

27. Energy Act 2010

s.5, referred to: 2013 c.32 s.1
s.11, enabling: SI 2013/519
s.31, enabling: SI 2013/519

29. Flood and Water Management Act 2010

Commencement Orders: SI 2013/1590 Art.3
s.6, amended: SI 2013/755 Sch.2 para.452
s.11, amended: SI 2013/755 Sch.2 para.453
s.12, amended: SI 2013/755 Sch.2 para.454
s.13, amended: SI 2013/755 Sch.2 para.455
s.14, amended: SI 2013/755 Sch.2 para.456
s.15, amended: SI 2013/755 Sch.2 para.457
s.17, amended: SI 2013/755 Sch.2 para.458
s.18, amended: SI 2013/755 Sch.2 para.459
s.18, substituted: SI 2013/755 Sch.2 para.459
s.22, amended: SI 2013/755 Sch.2 para.460
s.23, amended: SI 2013/755 Sch.2 para.461
s.25, amended: SI 2013/755 Sch.2 para.462
s.26A, added: SI 2013/755 Sch.2 para.463
s.38, amended: SI 2013/755 Sch.2 para.464

s.39, amended: SI 2013/755 Sch.2 para.465
s.48, enabling: SI 2013/1590
s.49, enabling: SI 2013/1590
Sch.1 para.1, amended: SI 2013/755 Sch.2 para.466
Sch.1 para.6, amended: SI 2013/755 Sch.2 para.466
Sch.3 para.11, amended: SI 2013/755 Sch.2 para.467
Sch.4 para.7, amended: SI 2013/755 Sch.2 para.468
Sch.4 para.12, amended: SI 2013/755 Sch.2 para.468
Sch.4 para.12, applied: SI 2013/1896 Reg.7
Sch.4 para.12, referred to: SI 2013/1896 Reg.7
Sch.4 para.16, disapplied: SI 2013/1590 Art.4
Sch.4 para.17, disapplied: SI 2013/1590 Art.4
Sch.4 para.18, disapplied: SI 2013/1590 Art.4
Sch.4 para.25, amended: SI 2013/755 Sch.2 para.468
Sch.4 para.33, amended: SI 2013/755 Sch.2 para.468
Sch.4 para.36, amended: SI 2013/755 Sch.2 para.468

32. Academies Act 2010

s.1, applied: SI 2013/488 Sch.1, SI 2013/2356 Sch.2 para.20, SI 2013/3109 Reg.16
s.4, applied: SI 2013/3037 Reg.1, Reg.3
s.7, applied: SI 2013/3037 Reg.6, Reg.7, Reg.8
s.7, enabling: SI 2013/3037
Sch.1 Part 1 para.2, applied: SI 2013/3109 Reg.16

33. Finance (No.3) Act 2010

s.13, repealed (in part): 2013 c.29 Sch.15 para.25
Sch.10 para.10, repealed: 2013 c.29 Sch.50 para.15

41. Loans to Ireland Act 2010

applied: 2013 c.12 Sch.1 para.1, 2013 c.28 Sch.1

2011

1. Parliamentary Voting System and Constituencies Act 2011

s.11, amended: 2013 c.6 s.6
s.14, amended: 2013 c.6 s.6

03. Domestic Fire Safety (Wales) Measure 2011

Commencement Orders: SI 2013/2727 Art.2
s.1, applied: SI 2013/2730 Reg.3
s.1, enabling: SI 2013/2730
s.6, amended: SI 2013/2723 Art.2
s.6, enabling: SI 2013/2723
s.8, applied: SI 2013/2730
s.8, enabling: SI 2013/2723, SI 2013/2727, SI 2013/2730
s.9, enabling: SI 2013/2727

04. Local Government (Wales) Measure 2011

s.8, applied: SI 2013/1050 Reg.4
s.9, enabling: SI 2013/2901
s.24, applied: SI 2013/2901 Reg.3
s.24, enabling: SI 2013/2901
s.25, applied: SI 2013/2901 Reg.9
s.25, enabling: SI 2013/2901
s.26, applied: SI 2013/2901 Reg.14
s.26, enabling: SI 2013/2901
s.27, applied: SI 2013/2901 Reg.20
s.27, enabling: SI 2013/2901
s.28, applied: SI 2013/2901 Reg.26
s.28, enabling: SI 2013/2901
s.29, enabling: SI 2013/2901
s.58, enabling: SI 2013/1050
s.172, enabling: SI 2013/1050, SI 2013/2901

5. Postal Services Act 2011

applied: SI 2013/3208 r.97, r.150
referred to: SI 2013/488 Sch.1
s.30, applied: SI 2013/3108
s.30, enabling: SI 2013/3108
s.51, amended: SI 2013/783 Art.6
s.59, amended: 2013 c.24 Sch.6 para.125
s.60, amended: 2013 c.24 Sch.6 para.126
s.65, applied: SSI 2013/50 Sch.3 para.6
s.70, applied: SI 2013/3208 r.8
s.70, referred to: SI 2013/3208 r.8, r.90
s.71, applied: SI 2013/3208 r.13
s.72, applied: SI 2013/3208 r.34
s.72, referred to: SI 2013/3208 r.6, r.20
s.73, enabling: SI 2013/3208
s.78, applied: SI 2013/3208 r.6, r.8, r.12
s.83, applied: SI 2013/3208 r.83
s.85, applied: SI 2013/3208 r.2
Sch.7 para.4, substituted: 2013 c.24 Sch.14 para.19

07. Education (Wales) Measure 2011

Commencement Orders: SI 2013/2090 Art.2
s.22, enabling: SI 2013/2124
s.23, enabling: SI 2013/2127
s.24, enabling: SI 2013/2127
s.32, enabling: SI 2013/2090, SI 2013/2124, SI 2013/2127

11. Finance Act 2011

s.11, repealed (in part): 2013 c.29 Sch.1 para.5
s.78, repealed: 2013 c.29 Sch.42 para.1
Sch.13 Part 2 para.22, repealed: 2013 c.29 Sch.29 para.49
Sch.13 Part 2 para.23, repealed: 2013 c.29 Sch.29 para.49
Sch.13 Part 2 para.24, repealed: 2013 c.29 Sch.29 para.49
Sch.16 Part 3 para.90, amended: 2013 c.29 s.50
Sch.16 Part 3 para.90, repealed (in part): 2013 c.29 s.50

Sch.16 Part 3 para.98, amended: 2013 c.29 s.50
Sch.16 Part 3 para.98, repealed (in part): 2013 c.29 s.50
Sch.18 Part 2 para.14, amended: 2013 c.29 s.47, SI 2013/1740 Reg.2
Sch.18 Part 2 para.14, applied: SSI 2013/174 Reg.2
Sch.18 Part 2 para.14, disapplied: 2013 c.29 Sch.22 para.1, SI 2013/1741 Reg.4
Sch.18 Part 2 para.14, repealed (in part): 2013 c.29 s.47
Sch.18 Part 2 para.15, added: 2013 c.29 s.47
Sch.18 Part 2 para.15, enabling: SI 2013/1740
Sch.18 Part 2 para.16, added: 2013 c.29 s.47
Sch.18 Part 2 para.16, enabling: SI 2013/1740
Sch.18 Part 2 para.17, added: 2013 c.29 s.47
Sch.18 Part 2 para.17, enabling: SI 2013/1740
Sch.19 Part 1 para.3, amended: 2013 c.29 s.204
Sch.19 Part 2 para.6, amended: 2013 c.29 s.202, s.203
Sch.19 Part 2 para.7, amended: 2013 c.29 s.202, s.203
Sch.19 Part 4 para.30, amended: SI 2013/636 Sch.1 para.15
Sch.19 Part 4 para.31, amended: SI 2013/636 Sch.1 para.15
Sch.19 Part 4 para.33, amended: SI 2013/636 Sch.1 para.15
Sch.19 Part 4 para.38, amended: SI 2013/636 Sch.1 para.15
Sch.19 Part 5 para.46, amended: 2013 c.29 s.204
Sch.19 Part 7 para.66, amended: 2013 c.29 s.204
Sch.19 Part 7 para.67, amended: 2013 c.29 s.204
Sch.19 Part 7 para.67A, amended: 2013 c.29 s.204
Sch.19 Part 7 para.68, amended: 2013 c.29 s.204
Sch.19 Part 7 para.69, amended: 2013 c.29 s.204
Sch.19 Part 7 para.69A, added: 2013 c.29 s.204
Sch.19 Part 7 para.69A, amended: 2013 c.29 s.204
Sch.19 Part 8 para.70, amended: 2013 c.29 s.205, SI 2013/636 Sch.1 para.15
Sch.19 Part 9 para.81, amended: SI 2013/636 Sch.1 para.15
Sch.20 para.1, repealed: 2013 c.29 Sch.42 para.1
Sch.20 para.2, repealed: 2013 c.29 Sch.42 para.1
Sch.20 para.3, repealed: 2013 c.29 Sch.42 para.1
Sch.20 para.4, repealed: 2013 c.29 Sch.42 para.1
Sch.20 para.5, repealed: 2013 c.29 Sch.42 para.1
Sch.20 para.6, repealed: 2013 c.29 Sch.42 para.1
Sch.20 para.7, repealed: 2013 c.29 Sch.42 para.1
Sch.20 para.8, amended: 2013 c.29 Sch.42 para.1
Sch.20 para.8, repealed: 2013 c.29 Sch.42 para.1
Sch.20 para.9, repealed: 2013 c.29 Sch.42 para.1
Sch.23 Part 1 para.1, enabling: SI 2013/1811
Sch.23 Part 2 para.13A, added: 2013 c.29 s.228

12. European Union Act 2011

s.2, applied: 2013 c.5 s.1, s.2
s.4, applied: 2013 c.5 s.1
s.7, applied: 2013 c.9 s.2
s.8, applied: 2013 c.9 s.1

13. Police Reform and Social Responsibility Act 2011

s.2, applied: SI 2013/2356 Sch.2 para.7
s.11, enabling: SI 2013/1816
s.65, repealed (in part): 2013 c.22 Sch.8 para.184
Sch.2 para.7A, varied: SI 2013/2319 Art.2
Sch.4 para.4A, varied: SI 2013/2319 Art.2
Sch.15 Part 4 para.24, enabling: SI 2013/2319

14. Fixed-term Parliaments Act 2011

s.3, amended: 2013 c.6 s.14

16. Energy Act 2011

Commencement Orders: SI 2013/125 Art.2, Art.3
applied: SI 2013/1047 r.102
referred to: SI 2013/1047 r.2
varied: SI 2013/1046 r.2
enabling: SI 2013/139
s.1, applied: SI 2013/380 Sch.6 para.8
s.3, enabling: SI 2013/139
s.4, enabling: SI 2013/139
s.6, enabling: SI 2013/139
s.9, enabling: SI 2013/10
s.10, enabling: SSI 2013/12
s.11, enabling: SI 2013/139
s.16, enabling: SI 2013/139
s.20, amended: SI 2013/1881 Sch.1 para.17
s.25, repealed: SI 2013/1881 Sch.1 para.17
s.26, repealed: SI 2013/1881 Sch.1 para.17
s.30, amended: SI 2013/1881 Sch.1 para.17
s.34, enabling: SI 2013/139
s.40, applied: SI 2013/10, SI 2013/139
s.40, enabling: SI 2013/10, SI 2013/139
s.74, enabling: SI 2013/10
s.75, enabling: SSI 2013/12
s.76, repealed: 2013 c.32 s.142
s.77, repealed: 2013 c.32 s.142
s.78, repealed: 2013 c.32 s.142
s.93, applied: SI 2013/1046 r.205
s.94, applied: SI 2013/1046 r.205
s.95, applied: SI 2013/1046 r.205
s.96, applied: SI 2013/1046, SI 2013/1046 r.205, SI 2013/2950
s.97, applied: SI 2013/1046 r.205
s.98, applied: SI 2013/1046 r.83, r.205
s.99, applied: SI 2013/1046 r.205, SI 2013/1047 r.59
s.100, applied: SI 2013/1046 r.205
s.101, applied: SI 2013/1046 r.205
s.102, applied: SI 2013/1046 r.2, r.205, SI 2013/1047 r.2
s.102, referred to: SI 2013/1046 r.207

s.121, enabling: SI 2013/125

18. Armed Forces Act 2011

Commencement Orders: SI 2013/784 Art.3; SI 2013/2501 Art.3
s.32, enabling: SI 2013/784, SI 2013/2501

19. Pensions Act 2011

Commencement Orders: SI 2013/585 Art.2
s.38, enabling: SI 2013/585

20. Localism Act 2011

Commencement Orders: SI 2013/722 Art.2; SI 2013/797 Art.2, Art.3; SI 2013/2931 Art.2
see *Arun DC v Secretary of State for Communities and Local Government* [2013] EWHC 190 (Admin), [2013] J.P.L. 1011 (QBD (Admin)), Judge Seys-Llewellyn Q.C.; see *R. (on the application of Daws Hill Neighbourhood Forum) v Wycombe DC* [2013] EWHC 513 (Admin), [2013] P.T.S.R. 970 (QBD (Admin)), Supperstone, J.; see *Tewkesbury BC v Secretary of State for Communities and Local Government* [2013] EWHC 286 (Admin), [2013] B.L.G.R. 399 (QBD (Admin)), Males, J.
applied: 2013 c.28 Sch.1
s.1, applied: SI 2013/2356 Reg.31
s.81, enabling: SI 2013/218
s.109, enabling: SI 2013/117, SI 2013/427, SI 2013/629, SI 2013/635, SI 2013/933, SI 2013/934, SI 2013/935
s.141, repealed (in part): 2013 c.27 s.24
s.159, amended: 2013 c.22 Sch.9 para.52
s.198, applied: SI 2013/2356 Sch.2 para.4
s.235, enabling: SI 2013/218
s.240, enabling: SI 2013/722, SI 2013/797, SI 2013/2931
Sch.22 para.60, repealed: 2013 c.27 s.24

24. Public Bodies Act 2011

s.1, enabling: SI 2013/64, SI 2013/252, SI 2013/686, SI 2013/687, SI 2013/2042, SI 2013/2314, SI 2013/2352, SI 2013/2853
s.2, applied: 2013 c.22 Sch.8 para.12
s.2, enabling: SI 2013/2329
s.4, applied: SI 2013/277
s.4, enabling: SI 2013/277
s.5, enabling: SI 2013/783
s.6, applied: SI 2013/783, SI 2013/2352
s.6, enabling: SI 2013/64, SI 2013/252, SI 2013/277, SI 2013/686, SI 2013/687, SI 2013/783, SI 2013/2042, SI 2013/2314, SI 2013/2329, SI 2013/2352, SI 2013/2853
s.8, applied: SI 2013/252(a), SI 2013/687(a), SI 2013/2042(a), SI 2013/64(a), SI 2013/64, SI 2013/252, SI 2013/277, SI 2013/686, SI 2013/687, SI 2013/783, SI 2013/2042, SI 2013/2314, SI 2013/2352, SI 2013/2853
s.8, referred to: SI 2013/277, SI 2013/686, SI 2013/783, SI 2013/2352, SI 2013/2853
s.9, applied: SI 2013/686, SI 2013/687, SI 2013/783, SI 2013/2042, SI 2013/2352
s.10, applied: SI 2013/64, SI 2013/252, SI 2013/277, SI 2013/783, SI 2013/2042, SI 2013/2314, SI 2013/2329, SI 2013/2352, SI 2013/2853
s.11, applied: SI 2013/64, SI 2013/252, SI 2013/277, SI 2013/686, SI 2013/687, SI 2013/783, SI 2013/2042, SI 2013/2314, SI 2013/2329, SI 2013/2352, SI 2013/2853
s.11, referred to: SI 2013/252, SI 2013/686, SI 2013/687, SI 2013/2329, SI 2013/2352, SI 2013/2853
s.13, enabling: SI 2013/755
s.14, enabling: SI 2013/755
s.15, enabling: SI 2013/755
s.16, applied: SI 2013/755
s.17, applied: SI 2013/755
s.18, applied: SI 2013/755
s.19, applied: SI 2013/755
s.19, referred to: SI 2013/755
s.21, applied: SI 2013/64, SI 2013/783, SI 2013/2352
s.23, applied: SI 2013/489 Art.2, SI 2013/2329 Art.2, SI 2013/2352, SI 2013/2352 Art.1
s.23, enabling: SI 2013/687, SI 2013/2329, SI 2013/2352
s.24, enabling: SI 2013/687, SI 2013/2329, SI 2013/2352
s.25, enabling: SI 2013/489, SI 2013/2242
s.26, amended: SI 2013/1821 Art.3
s.35, enabling: SI 2013/64, SI 2013/252, SI 2013/686, SI 2013/687, SI 2013/755, SI 2013/783, SI 2013/2042, SI 2013/2314, SI 2013/2329, SI 2013/2352, SI 2013/2853
s.36, amended: SI 2013/1821 Art.3
Sch.1, amended: SI 2013/64 Art.5, SI 2013/252 Art.6, SI 2013/686 Sch.1 para.10, SI 2013/687 Sch.1 para.15, SI 2013/2042 Sch.1 para.41, SI 2013/2314 Art.9, SI 2013/2352 Sch.1 para.15, SI 2013/2853 Art.2
Sch.2, amended: SI 2013/2329 Art.9
Sch.3, amended: SI 2013/2042 Sch.1 para.41
Sch.4, amended: SI 2013/2042 Sch.1 para.41
Sch.5, amended: SI 2013/2042 Sch.1 para.41

25. Charities Act 2011

Commencement Orders: SI 2013/1775 Sch.1 para.1
applied: SI 2013/641, SI 2013/3029 Sch.5 para.32, SI 2013/3035 Sch.1
s.25, enabling: SI 2013/1764
s.46, applied: SI 2013/1775 Sch.2 para.1

s.57, varied: SI 2013/1764 Reg.5
s.58, enabling: SI 2013/1764
s.73, applied: SI 2013/641
s.73, enabling: SI 2013/641
s.74, disapplied: SI 2013/1775 Sch.2 para.2
s.88, applied: SI 2013/641
s.97, amended: SI 2013/1773 Sch.1 para.44
s.101, amended: SI 2013/1773 Sch.1 para.44
s.104A, added: 2013 c.1 s.4
s.104B, added: 2013 c.1 s.4
s.149, applied: SI 2013/160 Sch.1 para.6
s.149, referred to: SI 2013/488 Sch.1
s.178, applied: SI 2013/1775 Sch.2 para.4
s.184, applied: SI 2013/1775 Sch.2 para.4
s.189, applied: SI 2013/641
s.230, amended: SI 2013/496 Sch.11 para.11
s.347, enabling: SI 2013/1764
s.353, enabling: SI 2013/641
Sch.9 para.29, enabling: SI 2013/1775

2012

6. Consumer Insurance (Disclosure and Representations) Act 2012

Commencement Orders: SI 2013/450 Art.2
s.12, enabling: SI 2013/450

7. Health and Social Care Act 2012

Commencement Orders: SI 2013/160 Art.2, Art.3, Art.4, Art.5, Art.6, Art.7, Art.8, Art.9, Sch.1 para.2, para.3, para.4, para.5, para.6; SI 2013/671 Art.2; SI 2013/2896 Art.2
applied: SI 2013/349 Sch.9 para.1, SI 2013/363 Sch.2 para.10
Part 3 c.3, applied: SI 2013/2677 Reg.2, SI 2013/2960 Art.2, Sch.1
s.32, varied: SI 2013/671 Art.3
s.33, applied: SI 2013/363 Sch.2 para.18
s.33, referred to: SI 2013/364 Sch.2 para.13
s.34, applied: SI 2013/363 Sch.1 para.19, Sch.2 para.18, SI 2013/364 Reg.54, Sch.1 para.13, SI 2013/365 Reg.24
s.34, referred to: SI 2013/364 Sch.2 para.13
s.56, disapplied: SI 2013/160 Art.8
s.58, amended: 2013 c.32 Sch.12 para.103
s.62, applied: SI 2013/257 Reg.3
s.72, amended: 2013 c.24 Sch.15 para.48
s.75, enabling: SI 2013/257, SI 2013/500, SI 2013/2891
s.76, applied: SI 2013/257 Reg.17, SI 2013/500 Reg.17
s.76, enabling: SI 2013/257, SI 2013/500
s.77, enabling: SI 2013/257, SI 2013/500
s.81, applied: SI 2013/2960 Sch.1 para.2
s.81, enabling: SI 2013/2677
s.83, applied: SI 2013/2677
s.83, enabling: SI 2013/2677
s.86, applied: SI 2013/2960 Art.2
s.86, enabling: SI 2013/2960
s.87, applied: SI 2013/2677 Reg.8, Reg.9
s.91, amended: SI 2013/671 Art.4
s.95, amended: SI 2013/671 Art.5
s.97, applied: SI 2013/2677 Reg.9
s.100, applied: SI 2013/2214 Reg.2
s.100, enabling: SI 2013/2214
s.101, amended: 2013 c.24 Sch.6 para.128
s.102, amended: 2013 c.24 Sch.6 para.129
s.103, amended: 2013 c.24 Sch.6 para.130
s.104, applied: SI 2013/2677 Reg.9
s.105, amended: 2013 c.24 Sch.14 para.21
s.105, applied: SI 2013/2214 Reg.3, Reg.4
s.105, enabling: SI 2013/2214
s.106, amended: 2013 c.24 Sch.14 para.22
s.116, applied: SI 2013/2214 Reg.5
s.118, applied: SI 2013/2214 Reg.6
s.118, enabling: SI 2013/2214
s.120, amended: 2013 c.24 Sch.6 para.131
s.120, applied: SI 2013/2214 Reg.5, Reg.6
s.120, enabling: SI 2013/2214
s.121, amended: 2013 c.24 Sch.6 para.132
s.121, applied: SI 2013/2214 Reg.6
s.122, amended: 2013 c.24 Sch.6 para.133
s.123, amended: 2013 c.24 Sch.6 para.134
s.128, applied: SI 2013/218 Reg.24, Reg.26, Reg.27
s.142, amended: 2013 c.24 Sch.6 para.135
s.149, amended: 2013 c.24 Sch.6 para.136
s.150, amended: 2013 c.24 Sch.6 para.137
s.150, enabling: SI 2013/2214, SI 2013/2677
s.194, applied: SI 2013/301 Reg.20
s.194, enabling: SI 2013/218
s.198, applied: SI 2013/301 Reg.20
s.234, applied: SI 2013/474 Reg.3
s.235, enabling: SI 2013/259
s.237, enabling: SI 2013/259
s.238, enabling: SI 2013/259
s.239, enabling: SI 2013/259
s.240, enabling: SI 2013/259
s.242, enabling: SI 2013/259
s.249, applied: SI 2013/160 Art.8
s.254, applied: SI 2013/160 Art.9
s.263, applied: SI 2013/160 Art.9
s.265, applied: SI 2013/160 Art.9
s.268, enabling: SI 2013/259
s.269, enabling: SI 2013/259
s.274, enabling: SI 2013/259
s.288, referred to: SI 2013/2960 Sch.1 para.1

s.300, applied: SI 2013/160 Art.7, Art.8, SI 2013/235 Sch.3 para.1, Sch.3 para.2, Sch.3 para.7, Sch.3 para.23, SI 2013/363 Sch.1 para.21, Sch.2 para.1, Sch.2 para.19, SI 2013/364 Sch.1 para.1, Sch.1 para.15, Sch.2 para.1, Sch.2 para.15, SI 2013/365 Reg.5, Reg.20
s.300, enabling: SI 2013/261
s.303, applied: SI 2013/160 Art.7, Art.8, SI 2013/2341
s.303, enabling: SI 2013/235, SI 2013/594, SI 2013/2341
s.304, applied: SI 2013/594, SI 2013/2214, SI 2013/2341, SI 2013/2677, SI 2013/2960
s.304, enabling: SI 2013/160, SI 2013/218, SI 2013/235, SI 2013/257, SI 2013/259, SI 2013/500, SI 2013/671, SI 2013/2214, SI 2013/2341, SI 2013/2677
s.306, enabling: SI 2013/160, SI 2013/671, SI 2013/2896
s.307, applied: SI 2013/160
Sch.4 Part 10 para.125, applied: SI 2013/160 Art.4
Sch.4 Part 10 para.125, disapplied: SI 2013/160 Art.4
Sch.8 para.11, amended: 2013 c.24 Sch.15 para.49
Sch.10 para.1, amended: 2013 c.24 Sch.6 para.138
Sch.10 para.2, amended: 2013 c.24 Sch.6 para.138
Sch.10 para.3, amended: 2013 c.24 Sch.6 para.138
Sch.10 para.4, amended: 2013 c.24 Sch.6 para.138
Sch.10 para.5, amended: 2013 c.24 Sch.6 para.138
Sch.10 para.6, amended: 2013 c.24 Sch.6 para.138
Sch.10 para.7, amended: 2013 c.24 Sch.6 para.138
Sch.10 para.8, amended: 2013 c.24 Sch.6 para.138
Sch.10 para.9, amended: 2013 c.24 Sch.6 para.138
Sch.10 para.10, amended: 2013 c.24 Sch.6 para.138
Sch.11 Part 1 para.1, applied: SI 2013/2214 Reg.3, Reg.4
Sch.12, applied: SI 2013/2214 Reg.6
Sch.12 para.2, amended: 2013 c.24 Sch.6 para.139
Sch.12 para.3, amended: 2013 c.24 Sch.6 para.139
Sch.12 para.3, repealed (in part): 2013 c.24 Sch.6 para.139
Sch.12 para.4, amended: 2013 c.24 Sch.6 para.139
Sch.12 para.5, amended: 2013 c.24 Sch.6 para.139
Sch.12 para.6, amended: 2013 c.24 Sch.6 para.139
Sch.12 para.7, amended: 2013 c.24 Sch.6 para.139
Sch.12 para.8, amended: 2013 c.24 Sch.6 para.139
Sch.12 para.9, amended: 2013 c.24 Sch.6 para.139
Sch.12 para.10, amended: 2013 c.24 Sch.6 para.139
Sch.12 para.11, amended: 2013 c.24 Sch.6 para.139
Sch.12 para.12, amended: 2013 c.24 Sch.6 para.139
Sch.16 para.8, enabling: SI 2013/259
Sch.21 para.4, referred to: SI 2013/160 Art.3
Sch.23, applied: SI 2013/261 Reg.15
Sch.23, enabling: SI 2013/261

9. Protection of Freedoms Act 2012

Commencement Orders: SI 2013/470 Art.2; SI 2013/1180 Art.2; SI 2013/1813 Art.2, Art.3, Art.4, Art.5, Art.6, Art.7, Art.8, Art.9; SI 2013/1814 Art.2, Art.3; SI 2013/1906 Art.2, Art.3; SI 2013/2104 Art.2, Art.3
s.1, referred to: SI 2013/1813 Art.2A
s.1, varied: SI 2013/1813 Art.2, Art.6
s.2, varied: SI 2013/1813 Art.2
s.3, varied: SI 2013/1813 Art.2, Art.4
s.4, varied: SI 2013/1813 Art.2
s.5, varied: SI 2013/1813 Art.2
s.6, varied: SI 2013/1813 Art.2
s.7, varied: SI 2013/1813 Art.2
s.8, varied: SI 2013/1813 Art.2
s.9, varied: SI 2013/1813 Art.2
s.10, varied: SI 2013/1813 Art.2
s.11, varied: SI 2013/1813 Art.2
s.12, varied: SI 2013/1813 Art.2
s.13, varied: SI 2013/1813 Art.2, Art.3
s.14, varied: SI 2013/1813 Art.2, Art.5
s.15, varied: SI 2013/1813 Art.2
s.16, varied: SI 2013/1813 Art.2
s.17, varied: SI 2013/1813 Art.2
s.18, varied: SI 2013/1813 Art.5A, Art.2
s.22, varied: SI 2013/1813 Art.2
s.25, enabling: SI 2013/1813, SI 2013/2580, SI 2013/2770
s.29, applied: SI 2013/1961
s.30, applied: SI 2013/1961
s.30, enabling: SI 2013/1961
s.33, applied: SI 2013/1961, SI 2013/1961 Art.3
s.33, enabling: SI 2013/1961
s.64, applied: SI 2013/2668 Sch.1 para.3, Sch.4 para.4, Sch.4 para.9, Sch.5 para.11
s.95, amended: 2013 c.22 Sch.8 para.185
s.109, disapplied: SI 2013/470 Art.3
s.110, disapplied: SI 2013/470 Art.3
s.110, referred to: SI 2013/470 Art.4, Art.6
s.115, enabling: SI 2013/862, SI 2013/1196, SI 2013/2343
s.116, enabling: SI 2013/470
s.120, enabling: SI 2013/470, SI 2013/1180, SI 2013/1566, SI 2013/1814, SI 2013/1906, SI 2013/2104
Sch.1 Part 1 para.1, applied: SI 2013/1813 Art.7
Sch.1 Part 2 para.2, applied: SI 2013/1813 Art.7
Sch.1 Part 3 para.3, applied: SI 2013/1813 Art.7
Sch.1 Part 3 para.4, applied: SI 2013/1813 Art.7
Sch.1 Part 4 para.5, applied: SI 2013/1813 Art.7

Sch.1 Part 5 para.6, varied: SI 2013/1813 Art.8
Sch.9 Part 10 para.136, disapplied: SI 2013/470 Art.3
Sch.9 Part 10 para.138, disapplied: SI 2013/470 Art.3
Sch.9 Part 10 para.140, disapplied: SI 2013/470 Art.3

10. Legal Aid, Sentencing and Punishment of Offenders Act 2012

Commencement Orders: SI 2013/77 Art.2, Art.3, Art.4; SI 2013/453 Art.2, Art.3, Art.4; SI 2013/534 Reg.6, Reg.7, Reg.8, Reg.9, Reg.10, Reg.11, Reg.12, Reg.13; SI 2013/773 Art.2; SI 2013/1127 Art.2
see *Simmons v Castle* [2012] EWCA Civ 1039, [2013] 1 W.L.R. 1239 (CA (Civ Div)), Lord Judge, L.C.J.
applied: 2013 c.28 Sch.1
Part 1, applied: SI 2013/772(a), SI 2013/104 Reg.11, Reg.12, Reg.20, Reg.29, Reg.32, Reg.33, SI 2013/104(a), SI 2013/104(b), SI 2013/457 Reg.3, SI 2013/480 Reg.4, SI 2013/609 Reg.5, SI 2013/772, SI 2013/1179 Sch.2 para.2, SI 2013/1407 Art.6, SI 2013/1410 Art.4, SI 2013/1893 Sch.3 para.1, Sch.3 para.18, SI 2013/3195
s.2, applied: SI 2013/9 Reg.8, Reg.17, SI 2013/104 Reg.10, SI 2013/480 Reg.5, SI 2013/534 Reg.8
s.2, enabling: SI 2013/422, SI 2013/435, SI 2013/503, SI 2013/2803, SI 2013/2877
s.5, enabling: SI 2013/9, SI 2013/104, SI 2013/422, SI 2013/435, SI 2013/471, SI 2013/480, SI 2013/483, SI 2013/503, SI 2013/511, SI 2013/512, SI 2013/611, SI 2013/614, SI 2013/1686
s.9, applied: SI 2013/422 Reg.11
s.9, enabling: SI 2013/748
s.10, see *A City Council v DC* [2013] EWHC 8 (Fam), [2013] 1 W.L.R. 3009 (Fam Div), Eleanor King, J.
s.10, applied: SI 2013/104 Reg.6, Reg.11, Reg.19, Reg.48, Reg.49, Reg.50, SI 2013/480 Reg.44, SI 2013/2877 Reg.5
s.10, referred to: SI 2013/480 Reg.2
s.11, applied: SI 2013/104(a), SI 2013/104, SI 2013/104 Reg.11, SI 2013/480 Reg.4, SI 2013/772, SI 2013/3195
s.11, enabling: SI 2013/104, SI 2013/772, SI 2013/3195
s.12, applied: SI 2013/104 Reg.9, SI 2013/611 Reg.21
s.13, applied: SI 2013/9 Reg.7, SI 2013/435 Reg.8, SI 2013/534 Reg.11
s.13, enabling: SI 2013/9
s.14, applied: SI 2013/9 Reg.9, SI 2013/435 Reg.8, Sch.4 para.7, Sch.4 para.10, Sch.4 para.12, SI 2013/471 Reg.17, SI 2013/614 Reg.6, SI 2013/1554 r.62_5
s.14, referred to: SI 2013/435 Reg.11, Sch.1 para.21, Sch.2 para.17, SI 2013/614 Reg.7, Reg.12
s.14, enabling: SI 2013/9
s.15, applied: SI 2013/9, SI 2013/9 Reg.11, Reg.13, Reg.15, Reg.16, SI 2013/435 Reg.7, Reg.8, Sch.4 para.8, SI 2013/471 Reg.7, Reg.8, Reg.10, Reg.14, SI 2013/534 Reg.11, SI 2013/1554 r.62_5, SI 2013/2790, SI 2013/2790 Reg.7, SI 2013/2791 Reg.16, SI 2013/2803 Reg.5
s.15, referred to: SI 2013/9 Reg.11, Reg.12
s.15, enabling: SI 2013/9, SI 2013/2790
s.16, applied: SI 2013/9 Reg.10, Reg.18, Reg.21, Reg.22, Reg.23, Reg.25, Reg.26, Reg.27, Reg.29, SI 2013/435 Reg.7, SI 2013/471 Reg.17, Reg.18, Reg.19, Reg.20, Reg.22, Reg.24, Reg.26, Reg.27, Reg.28, Reg.30, Reg.31, Reg.33, Reg.35, Reg.36, Reg.37, Reg.39, SI 2013/483 Reg.6, Reg.7, Reg.8, Reg.9, Reg.17, Reg.25, Reg.28, Reg.34, Reg.37, SI 2013/511 Reg.7, SI 2013/534 Reg.11, SI 2013/614 Reg.4, Reg.5, Reg.6, Reg.7, Reg.8, Reg.9, Reg.10, Reg.15, Reg.17, SI 2013/1554 r.62_5, SI 2013/2790 Reg.8, SI 2013/2791 Reg.15, SI 2013/2792 Reg.8
s.16, enabling: SI 2013/9
s.17, applied: SI 2013/104 Reg.11
s.17, enabling: SI 2013/9
s.18, enabling: SI 2013/9, SI 2013/2790
s.19, applied: SI 2013/9 Reg.18, SI 2013/435 Sch.3 para.2
s.19, enabling: SI 2013/614
s.21, applied: SI 2013/9 Reg.15, Reg.16, Reg.25, Reg.29, SI 2013/471 Reg.7, Reg.8, Reg.18, Reg.22, Reg.24, Reg.26, Reg.27, Reg.28, Reg.30, Reg.31, Reg.36, Reg.37, Reg.39, SI 2013/483 Reg.6, SI 2013/512 Reg.35
s.21, enabling: SI 2013/471, SI 2013/480, SI 2013/512, SI 2013/753, SI 2013/754, SI 2013/2790, SI 2013/2791
s.22, applied: SI 2013/628, SI 2013/628 Reg.4, Reg.4A, Reg.3, Reg.5, Reg.6, Reg.7
s.22, enabling: SI 2013/628, SI 2013/2726
s.23, applied: SI 2013/483 Reg.5, SI 2013/503 Reg.6, SI 2013/511 Reg.4
s.23, enabling: SI 2013/480, SI 2013/483, SI 2013/511, SI 2013/512, SI 2013/1686, SI 2013/2792
s.24, amended: 2013 c.22 Sch.9 para.52
s.24, enabling: SI 2013/483, SI 2013/511, SI 2013/1686

s.25, applied: SI 2013/503 Reg.22, SI 2013/534 Reg.10
s.25, varied: SI 2013/534 Reg.10
s.25, enabling: SI 2013/503, SI 2013/534
s.26, applied: SI 2013/611 Reg.13, Reg.15, Reg.16
s.26, enabling: SI 2013/611
s.27, applied: SI 2013/614 Reg.10, Reg.12, Reg.13, Reg.14, Reg.15, Reg.16, Reg.17, Reg.18, Reg.23
s.27, enabling: SI 2013/614, SI 2013/2814
s.28, applied: SI 2013/611 Reg.21
s.28, enabling: SI 2013/9, SI 2013/457
s.30, enabling: SI 2013/9, SI 2013/435, SI 2013/483, SI 2013/511, SI 2013/614, SI 2013/1686, SI 2013/2814
s.35, enabling: SI 2013/457
s.36, amended: 2013 c.22 Sch.9 para.52
s.38, disapplied: SI 2013/534 Reg.6
s.41, applied: SI 2013/104, SI 2013/611, SI 2013/614, SI 2013/628, SI 2013/748, SI 2013/772, SI 2013/2726, SI 2013/3195
s.41, enabling: SI 2013/9, SI 2013/104, SI 2013/422, SI 2013/435, SI 2013/471, SI 2013/480, SI 2013/483, SI 2013/503, SI 2013/511, SI 2013/512, SI 2013/614, SI 2013/628, SI 2013/748, SI 2013/753, SI 2013/754, SI 2013/772, SI 2013/1686, SI 2013/2790, SI 2013/2791, SI 2013/2792, SI 2013/2803, SI 2013/2814, SI 2013/2877, SI 2013/3195
s.44, see *Simmons v Castle* [2012] EWCA Civ 1288, [2013] 1 W.L.R. 1239 (CA (Civ Div)), Lord Judge, L.C.J.
s.46, see *Simmons v Castle* [2012] EWCA Civ 1288, [2013] 1 W.L.R. 1239 (CA (Civ Div)), Lord Judge, L.C.J.
s.55, applied: SI 2013/93 Art.2, SI 2013/262
s.55, enabling: SI 2013/93
s.56, applied: SI 2013/1635 Reg.3, Reg.5
s.56, referred to: SI 2013/1635 Reg.4, Reg.9, Reg.10
s.57, applied: SI 2013/1635 Reg.5
s.57, enabling: SI 2013/1635
s.58, enabling: SI 2013/1635
s.59, applied: SI 2013/1635 Reg.32
s.59, enabling: SI 2013/1635
s.60, enabling: SI 2013/1635
s.64, applied: SI 2013/1635
s.67, repealed (in part): 2013 c.22 Sch.16 para.22
s.72, repealed (in part): 2013 c.22 Sch.16 para.12, Sch.16 para.13
s.91, applied: SI 2013/507 Reg.3, SI 2013/1554 r.19_2, r.18_4
s.102, amended: 2013 c.22 s.19
s.102, applied: 2013 c.22 s.19, SI 2013/507 Reg.3
s.102, disapplied: 2013 c.22 s.19
s.103, enabling: SI 2013/507, SI 2013/2243
s.145, repealed: 2013 c.10 s.19
s.146, applied: SI 2013/2258 Sch.1 Part 1
s.146, repealed: 2013 c.10 s.19
s.147, repealed: 2013 c.10 s.19
s.149, enabling: SI 2013/534, SI 2013/621, SI 2013/903
s.151, enabling: SI 2013/77, SI 2013/453, SI 2013/773, SI 2013/1127
Sch.1 Part 1, applied: SI 2013/104 Reg.49
Sch.1 Part 1, referred to: SI 2013/104 Reg.47, Reg.50, Reg.51
Sch.1 Part 1 para.1, applied: SI 2013/480 Reg.5
Sch.1 Part 1 para.1, referred to: SI 2013/451 Reg.3
Sch.1 Part 1 para.2, referred to: SI 2013/451 Reg.3
Sch.1 Part 1 para.3, referred to: SI 2013/451 Reg.3
Sch.1 Part 1 para.4, referred to: SI 2013/451 Reg.3
Sch.1 Part 1 para.5, applied: SI 2013/480 Reg.5
Sch.1 Part 1 para.5, referred to: SI 2013/104 Reg.21, Reg.51, Reg.52, SI 2013/451 Reg.3, SI 2013/480 Reg.5
Sch.1 Part 1 para.6, referred to: SI 2013/451 Reg.3
Sch.1 Part 1 para.7, referred to: SI 2013/451 Reg.3
Sch.1 Part 1 para.8, referred to: SI 2013/265 Reg.2, SI 2013/451 Reg.3
Sch.1 Part 1 para.8A, added: SI 2013/748 Art.3
Sch.1 Part 1 para.8A, referred to: SI 2013/451 Reg.3
Sch.1 Part 1 para.9, referred to: SI 2013/451 Reg.3
Sch.1 Part 1 para.10, referred to: SI 2013/451 Reg.3
Sch.1 Part 1 para.11, referred to: SI 2013/451 Reg.3, SI 2013/480 Reg.12
Sch.1 Part 1 para.12, amended: SI 2013/748 Art.4
Sch.1 Part 1 para.12, referred to: SI 2013/104 Reg.25, Reg.27, Reg.69, SI 2013/451 Reg.3
Sch.1 Part 1 para.13, referred to: SI 2013/451 Reg.3
Sch.1 Part 1 para.14, referred to: SI 2013/104 Reg.24, SI 2013/451 Reg.3
Sch.1 Part 1 para.15, referred to: SI 2013/104 Reg.64, Reg.69, SI 2013/451 Reg.3
Sch.1 Part 1 para.16, referred to: SI 2013/451 Reg.3, SI 2013/480 Reg.12
Sch.1 Part 1 para.17, referred to: SI 2013/104 Reg.64, Reg.65, Reg.68, SI 2013/451 Reg.3, SI 2013/480 Reg.5, SI 2013/512 Reg.10
Sch.1 Part 1 para.18, amended: SI 2013/748 Art.5
Sch.1 Part 1 para.18, applied: SI 2013/104 Reg.65, Reg.71, SI 2013/480 Reg.5, SI 2013/512 Reg.10
Sch.1 Part 1 para.18, referred to: SI 2013/104 Reg.11, Reg.64, Reg.65, Reg.68, Reg.69, Reg.70,

SI 2013/451 Reg.3, SI 2013/480 Reg.5, SI 2013/512 Reg.10
Sch.1 Part 1 para.19, amended: SI 2013/748 Art.6
Sch.1 Part 1 para.19, referred to: SI 2013/451 Reg.3
Sch.1 Part 1 para.20, referred to: SI 2013/451 Reg.3
Sch.1 Part 1 para.21, applied: SI 2013/104 Reg.59
Sch.1 Part 1 para.21, referred to: SI 2013/104 Reg.57, Reg.58, SI 2013/451 Reg.3
Sch.1 Part 1 para.22, applied: SI 2013/104 Reg.59
Sch.1 Part 1 para.22, referred to: SI 2013/104 Reg.57, Reg.58, SI 2013/451 Reg.3
Sch.1 Part 1 para.23, referred to: SI 2013/451 Reg.3
Sch.1 Part 1 para.24, referred to: SI 2013/104 Reg.23, SI 2013/451 Reg.3, SI 2013/480 Reg.6
Sch.1 Part 1 para.25, referred to: SI 2013/104 Reg.22, Reg.60, SI 2013/451 Reg.3, SI 2013/480 Reg.6, Reg.8
Sch.1 Part 1 para.26, referred to: SI 2013/104 Reg.22, Reg.60, SI 2013/451 Reg.3, SI 2013/480 Reg.6, Reg.8
Sch.1 Part 1 para.27, referred to: SI 2013/104 Reg.22, Reg.60, SI 2013/451 Reg.3, SI 2013/480 Reg.6, Reg.8
Sch.1 Part 1 para.28, amended: SI 2013/748 Art.4
Sch.1 Part 1 para.28, referred to: SI 2013/104 Reg.22, Reg.60, SI 2013/451 Reg.3, SI 2013/480 Reg.6, Reg.8
Sch.1 Part 1 para.29, amended: SI 2013/748 Art.4
Sch.1 Part 1 para.29, referred to: SI 2013/104 Reg.22, Reg.60, SI 2013/451 Reg.3, SI 2013/480 Reg.6, Reg.8
Sch.1 Part 1 para.30, applied: SI 2013/480 Reg.44
Sch.1 Part 1 para.30, referred to: SI 2013/104 Reg.22, Reg.60, SI 2013/451 Reg.3, SI 2013/480 Reg.6
Sch.1 Part 1 para.31, referred to: SI 2013/104 Reg.23, SI 2013/451 Reg.3
Sch.1 Part 1 para.32, referred to: SI 2013/104 Reg.22, Reg.60, SI 2013/451 Reg.3, SI 2013/480 Reg.6, Reg.8
Sch.1 Part 1 para.33, applied: SI 2013/104 Reg.63, SI 2013/480 Reg.28
Sch.1 Part 1 para.33, referred to: SI 2013/104 Reg.61, Reg.62, SI 2013/451 Reg.3
Sch.1 Part 1 para.34, referred to: SI 2013/451 Reg.3
Sch.1 Part 1 para.35, applied: SI 2013/104 Reg.62
Sch.1 Part 1 para.35, referred to: SI 2013/104 Reg.62, SI 2013/451 Reg.3
Sch.1 Part 1 para.36, referred to: SI 2013/451 Reg.3
Sch.1 Part 1 para.37, referred to: SI 2013/104 Reg.62, SI 2013/451 Reg.3
Sch.1 Part 1 para.38, referred to: SI 2013/451 Reg.3
Sch.1 Part 1 para.39, referred to: SI 2013/451 Reg.3
Sch.1 Part 1 para.40, referred to: SI 2013/451 Reg.3
Sch.1 Part 1 para.41, referred to: SI 2013/104 Reg.30, SI 2013/451 Reg.3, SI 2013/480 Reg.10
Sch.1 Part 1 para.42, referred to: SI 2013/451 Reg.3
Sch.1 Part 1 para.43, referred to: SI 2013/451 Reg.3
Sch.1 Part 1 para.44, referred to: SI 2013/104 Reg.31, Reg.72, SI 2013/451 Reg.3, SI 2013/480 Reg.6, Reg.11, Reg.24
Sch.1 Part 1 para.45, referred to: SI 2013/104 Reg.22, SI 2013/451 Reg.3, SI 2013/480 Reg.5
Sch.1 Part 1 para.46, applied: SI 2013/451 Reg.3
Sch.1 Part 1 para.46, enabling: SI 2013/451
Sch.1 Part 2, disapplied: SI 2013/104 Reg.49
Sch.1 Part 2 para.11, applied: SI 2013/451 Reg.4
Sch.1 Part 2 para.13, applied: SI 2013/451 Reg.4
Sch.1 Part 2 para.14, applied: SI 2013/451 Reg.4
Sch.1 Part 2 para.18, added: SI 2013/748 Art.7
Sch.1 Part 3, disapplied: SI 2013/104 Reg.49
Sch.1 Part 3 para.5, amended: 2013 c.22 Sch.9 para.52
Sch.1 Part 4 para.5, applied: SI 2013/265 Reg.2
Sch.1 Part 4 para.5, enabling: SI 2013/265
Sch.2, enabling: SI 2013/1686
Sch.2 para.2, amended: 2013 c.22 Sch.9 para.52
Sch.3 para.3, applied: SI 2013/512 Reg.4, Reg.9, Reg.18
Sch.3 para.3, enabling: SI 2013/104
Sch.3 para.4, applied: SI 2013/9 Reg.33, Reg.34, SI 2013/512 Reg.4, Reg.33, Reg.35, Reg.37
Sch.3 para.4, enabling: SI 2013/9, SI 2013/512
Sch.3 para.5, applied: SI 2013/512 Reg.4, Reg.33, Reg.35, Reg.37
Sch.3 para.5, enabling: SI 2013/9
Sch.3 para.6, enabling: SI 2013/512, SI 2013/754
Sch.3 para.7, enabling: SI 2013/512
Sch.3 para.9, enabling: SI 2013/9, SI 2013/457, SI 2013/614
Sch.3 para.10, enabling: SI 2013/457
Sch.4 Part 1 para.4, amended: 2013 c.25 Sch.8 para.31
Sch.5, referred to: SI 2013/534 Reg.6
Sch.5 Part 1 para.1, referred to: SI 2013/534 Reg.6
Sch.5 Part 1 para.2, referred to: SI 2013/534 Reg.6
Sch.5 Part 1 para.10, referred to: SI 2013/534 Reg.6

Sch.5 Part 1 para.11, referred to: SI 2013/534 Reg.6
Sch.5 Part 1 para.55, referred to: SI 2013/534 Reg.6
Sch.5 Part 1 para.66, referred to: SI 2013/534 Reg.6
Sch.5 Part 1 para.70, referred to: SI 2013/534 Reg.6
Sch.5 Part 1 para.71, referred to: SI 2013/534 Reg.6
Sch.5 Part 2, referred to: SI 2013/534 Reg.6
Sch.26 para.19, repealed: 2013 c.22 Sch.16 para.23

14. Finance Act 2012

Commencement Orders: 2013 c.29 s.202; SI 2013/279 Art.2; SI 2013/587 Art.2
s.22, repealed: 2013 c.29 Sch.29 para.50
s.74, amended: SI 2013/2819 Reg.40
s.74, repealed (in part): SI 2013/2819 Reg.40
s.78, amended: 2013 c.29 Sch.15 para.26, Sch.29 para.50
s.139, amended: SI 2013/636 Sch.1 para.16
s.217, enabling: SI 2013/1401
s.221, applied: SI 2013/3209
s.221, enabling: SI 2013/460, SI 2013/3209
s.223, enabling: SI 2013/279
Sch.14 Part 6 para.36, enabling: SI 2013/587
Sch.16 Part 3 para.190, repealed: 2013 c.29 Sch.15 para.26
Sch.16 Part 3 para.220, repealed: 2013 c.29 Sch.29 para.50
Sch.16 Part 3 para.221, repealed: 2013 c.29 Sch.29 para.50
Sch.16 Part 3 para.222, repealed: 2013 c.29 Sch.29 para.50
Sch.16 Part 3 para.223, repealed: 2013 c.29 Sch.29 para.50
Sch.17 Part 2 para.22, amended: SI 2013/2244 Reg.2
Sch.17 Part 3 para.37, enabling: SI 2013/2244
Sch.22 para.21, enabling: SI 2013/744
Sch.22 para.22, enabling: SI 2013/2910
Sch.32 Part 1 para.1, repealed: 2013 c.29 Sch.42 para.1
Sch.32 Part 1 para.2, repealed: 2013 c.29 Sch.42 para.1
Sch.32 Part 1 para.3, repealed: 2013 c.29 Sch.42 para.1
Sch.32 Part 1 para.4, repealed: 2013 c.29 Sch.42 para.1
Sch.32 Part 1 para.5, repealed: 2013 c.29 Sch.42 para.1
Sch.32 Part 1 para.6, repealed: 2013 c.29 Sch.42 para.1
Sch.32 Part 1 para.7, repealed: 2013 c.29 Sch.42 para.1
Sch.32 Part 1 para.8, repealed: 2013 c.29 Sch.42 para.1
Sch.32 Part 1 para.9, repealed: 2013 c.29 Sch.42 para.1
Sch.32 Part 1 para.10, repealed: 2013 c.29 Sch.42 para.1
Sch.32 Part 1 para.11, repealed: 2013 c.29 Sch.42 para.1
Sch.32 Part 1 para.12, repealed: 2013 c.29 Sch.42 para.1
Sch.32 Part 1 para.13, repealed: 2013 c.29 Sch.42 para.1
Sch.32 Part 1 para.14, repealed: 2013 c.29 Sch.42 para.1
Sch.32 Part 1 para.15, repealed: 2013 c.29 Sch.42 para.1
Sch.32 Part 1 para.16, repealed: 2013 c.29 Sch.42 para.1
Sch.32 Part 1 para.17, repealed: 2013 c.29 Sch.42 para.1
Sch.32 Part 1 para.18, repealed: 2013 c.29 Sch.42 para.1
Sch.32 Part 1 para.19, repealed: 2013 c.29 Sch.42 para.1
Sch.32 Part 2 para.20, repealed: 2013 c.29 Sch.42 para.1
Sch.34 para.5, repealed: 2013 c.29 s.202
Sch.34 para.6, repealed (in part): 2013 c.29 s.203
Sch.34 para.7, amended: 2013 c.29 s.202
Sch.36 Part 5 para.26A, added: 2013 c.29 s.221
Sch.36 Part 5 para.26B, added: 2013 c.29 s.221
Sch.38 Part 1 para.1, varied: SI 2013/622 Reg.41, SI 2013/938 Reg.6
Sch.38 Part 1 para.2, varied: SI 2013/622 Reg.41, SI 2013/938 Reg.6
Sch.38 Part 1 para.3, varied: SI 2013/622 Reg.41, SI 2013/938 Reg.6
Sch.38 Part 2 para.4, varied: SI 2013/622 Reg.41, SI 2013/938 Reg.6
Sch.38 Part 2 para.5, varied: SI 2013/622 Reg.41, SI 2013/938 Reg.6
Sch.38 Part 2 para.6, varied: SI 2013/622 Reg.41, SI 2013/938 Reg.6
Sch.38 Part 3 para.7, varied: SI 2013/622 Reg.41, SI 2013/938 Reg.6
Sch.38 Part 3 para.8, varied: SI 2013/622 Reg.41, SI 2013/938 Reg.6
Sch.38 Part 3 para.9, varied: SI 2013/622 Reg.41, SI 2013/938 Reg.6
Sch.38 Part 3 para.10, varied: SI 2013/622 Reg.41, SI 2013/938 Reg.6

Sch.38 Part 3 para.11, varied: SI 2013/622 Reg.41, SI 2013/938 Reg.6
Sch.38 Part 3 para.12, varied: SI 2013/622 Reg.41, SI 2013/938 Reg.6
Sch.38 Part 3 para.13, varied: SI 2013/622 Reg.41, SI 2013/938 Reg.6
Sch.38 Part 3 para.14, varied: SI 2013/622 Reg.41, SI 2013/938 Reg.6
Sch.38 Part 3 para.15, varied: SI 2013/622 Reg.41, SI 2013/938 Reg.6
Sch.38 Part 3 para.16, varied: SI 2013/622 Reg.41, SI 2013/938 Reg.6
Sch.38 Part 3 para.17, varied: SI 2013/622 Reg.41, SI 2013/938 Reg.6
Sch.38 Part 3 para.18, varied: SI 2013/622 Reg.41, SI 2013/938 Reg.6
Sch.38 Part 3 para.19, varied: SI 2013/622 Reg.41, SI 2013/938 Reg.6
Sch.38 Part 3 para.20, varied: SI 2013/622 Reg.41, SI 2013/938 Reg.6
Sch.38 Part 3 para.21, varied: SI 2013/622 Reg.41, SI 2013/938 Reg.6
Sch.38 Part 3 para.22, varied: SI 2013/622 Reg.41, SI 2013/938 Reg.6
Sch.38 Part 3 para.23, varied: SI 2013/622 Reg.41, SI 2013/938 Reg.6
Sch.38 Part 3 para.24, varied: SI 2013/622 Reg.41, SI 2013/938 Reg.6
Sch.38 Part 3 para.25, varied: SI 2013/622 Reg.41, SI 2013/938 Reg.6
Sch.38 Part 4 para.26, varied: SI 2013/622 Reg.41, SI 2013/938 Reg.6
Sch.38 Part 4 para.27, varied: SI 2013/622 Reg.41, SI 2013/938 Reg.6
Sch.38 Part 4 para.28, varied: SI 2013/622 Reg.41, SI 2013/938 Reg.6
Sch.38 Part 5 para.29, varied: SI 2013/622 Reg.41, SI 2013/938 Reg.6
Sch.38 Part 5 para.30, varied: SI 2013/622 Reg.41, SI 2013/938 Reg.6
Sch.38 Part 5 para.31, varied: SI 2013/622 Reg.41, SI 2013/938 Reg.6
Sch.38 Part 5 para.32, varied: SI 2013/622 Reg.41, SI 2013/938 Reg.6
Sch.38 Part 5 para.33, varied: SI 2013/622 Reg.41, SI 2013/938 Reg.6
Sch.38 Part 5 para.34, varied: SI 2013/622 Reg.41, SI 2013/938 Reg.6
Sch.38 Part 5 para.35, varied: SI 2013/622 Reg.41, SI 2013/938 Reg.6
Sch.38 Part 6 para.36, varied: SI 2013/622 Reg.41, SI 2013/938 Reg.6
Sch.38 Part 6 para.37, varied: SI 2013/622 Reg.41, SI 2013/938 Reg.6
Sch.38 Part 6 para.38, varied: SI 2013/622 Reg.41, SI 2013/938 Reg.6
Sch.38 Part 6 para.39, varied: SI 2013/622 Reg.41, SI 2013/938 Reg.6
Sch.38 Part 6 para.40, varied: SI 2013/622 Reg.41, SI 2013/938 Reg.6
Sch.38 Part 6 para.41, varied: SI 2013/622 Reg.41, SI 2013/938 Reg.6
Sch.38 Part 6 para.42, varied: SI 2013/622 Reg.41, SI 2013/938 Reg.6
Sch.38 Part 6 para.43, varied: SI 2013/622 Reg.41, SI 2013/938 Reg.6
Sch.38 Part 7 para.44, varied: SI 2013/622 Reg.41
Sch.38 Part 7 para.45, varied: SI 2013/622 Reg.41
Sch.38 Part 7 para.46, varied: SI 2013/622 Reg.41
Sch.38 Part 7 para.47, varied: SI 2013/622 Reg.41
Sch.38 Part 7 para.48, varied: SI 2013/622 Reg.41
Sch.38 Part 7 para.49, varied: SI 2013/622 Reg.41
Sch.38 Part 7 para.50, varied: SI 2013/622 Reg.41
Sch.38 Part 7 para.51, varied: SI 2013/622 Reg.41
Sch.38 Part 7 para.52, varied: SI 2013/622 Reg.41
Sch.38 Part 7 para.53, varied: SI 2013/622 Reg.41
Sch.38 Part 7 para.54, varied: SI 2013/622 Reg.41
Sch.38 Part 7 para.55, varied: SI 2013/622 Reg.41
Sch.38 Part 7 para.56, varied: SI 2013/622 Reg.41
Sch.38 Part 7 para.57, varied: SI 2013/622 Reg.41
Sch.38 Part 7 para.58, varied: SI 2013/622 Reg.41

17. Local Government Finance Act 2012

s.20, applied: SI 2013/733
s.20, enabling: SI 2013/733

19. Civil Aviation Act 2012

Commencement Orders: SI 2013/589 Art.2, Art.5
s.24, amended: 2013 c.24 Sch.6 para.141
s.25, amended: 2013 c.24 Sch.6 para.142
s.26, amended: 2013 c.24 Sch.6 para.143
s.27, amended: 2013 c.24 Sch.6 para.144
s.28, amended: 2013 c.24 Sch.6 para.145
s.29, amended: 2013 c.24 Sch.6 para.146
s.30, amended: 2013 c.24 Sch.6 para.147
s.62, amended: 2013 c.24 Sch.15 para.51
s.63, amended: 2013 c.24 Sch.15 para.52
s.108, enabling: SI 2013/610
s.110, enabling: SI 2013/589
Sch.2, applied: 2013 c.24 Sch.4 para.48
Sch.2 Part 1 para.2, amended: 2013 c.24 Sch.6 para.148
Sch.2 Part 1 para.3, amended: 2013 c.24 Sch.6 para.148
Sch.2 Part 2 para.4, amended: 2013 c.24 Sch.6 para.148
Sch.2 Part 2 para.5, amended: 2013 c.24 Sch.6 para.148
Sch.2 Part 3 para.6, amended: 2013 c.24 Sch.6 para.148

Sch.2 Part 3 para.7, amended: 2013 c.24 Sch.6 para.148
Sch.2 Part 3 para.8, amended: 2013 c.24 Sch.6 para.148
Sch.2 Part 4 para.9, amended: 2013 c.24 Sch.6 para.148
Sch.2 Part 4 para.10, amended: 2013 c.24 Sch.6 para.148
Sch.2 Part 4 para.11, amended: 2013 c.24 Sch.6 para.148
Sch.2 Part 4 para.12, amended: 2013 c.24 Sch.6 para.148
Sch.2 Part 4 para.13, amended: 2013 c.24 Sch.6 para.148
Sch.2 Part 4 para.14, amended: 2013 c.24 Sch.6 para.148
Sch.2 Part 4 para.15, amended: 2013 c.24 Sch.6 para.148
Sch.2 Part 4 para.16, amended: 2013 c.24 Sch.6 para.148
Sch.2 Part 5 para.17, amended: 2013 c.24 Sch.6 para.148
Sch.2 Part 5 para.17, repealed (in part): 2013 c.24 Sch.6 para.148
Sch.2 Part 5 para.18, repealed: 2013 c.24 Sch.6 para.148
Sch.2 Part 5 para.19, amended: 2013 c.24 Sch.6 para.148
Sch.2 Part 5 para.20, amended: 2013 c.24 Sch.6 para.148
Sch.2 Part 5 para.21, amended: 2013 c.24 Sch.6 para.148
Sch.2 Part 5 para.22, amended: 2013 c.24 Sch.6 para.148
Sch.2 Part 6 para.23, amended: 2013 c.24 Sch.6 para.148
Sch.2 Part 6 para.24, amended: 2013 c.24 Sch.6 para.148
Sch.2 Part 6 para.25, amended: 2013 c.24 Sch.6 para.148
Sch.2 Part 6 para.26, amended: 2013 c.24 Sch.6 para.148
Sch.2 Part 6 para.27, amended: 2013 c.24 Sch.6 para.148
Sch.2 Part 6 para.28, amended: 2013 c.24 Sch.6 para.148
Sch.2 Part 6 para.30, amended: 2013 c.24 Sch.6 para.148
Sch.2 Part 6 para.31, amended: 2013 c.24 Sch.6 para.148
Sch.2 Part 6 para.32, amended: 2013 c.24 Sch.6 para.148
Sch.2 Part 6 para.34, amended: 2013 c.24 Sch.6 para.148
Sch.2 Part 6 para.35, amended: 2013 c.24 Sch.6 para.148
Sch.6 para.4, amended: SI 2013/1575 Sch.1 para.15

20. Prisons (Interference with Wireless Telegraphy) Act 2012

Commencement Orders: SI 2013/2460 Art.3
s.5, enabling: SI 2013/2460

21. Financial Services Act 2012

Commencement Orders: SI 2013/113 Art.2, Sch.1 Part 1, 2, 3, 4; SI 2013/423 Art.2, Art.3, Sch.1; SI 2013/651 Art.2
applied: SI 2013/161 Art.2, Art.6
varied: SI 2013/161 Art.6
Part 5, applied: SI 2013/161 Art.7
Part 6, applied: SI 2013/161 Art.7
Part 7, applied: SI 2013/418 Art.3
s.6, applied: SI 2013/472 Sch.2 para.156
s.14, repealed (in part): 2013 c.33 Sch.3 para.18
s.50, enabling: SI 2013/496
s.51, enabling: SI 2013/496
s.52, enabling: SI 2013/496
s.55, repealed: 2013 c.33 Sch.9 para.4
s.68, amended: 2013 c.33 s.105
s.68, applied: SI 2013/442 Art.7, SI 2013/1881 Art.65
s.73, amended: 2013 c.33 Sch.10 para.9
s.76A, added: 2013 c.33 s.106
s.77, amended: 2013 c.33 s.106
s.77, substituted: 2013 c.33 s.106
s.78, amended: 2013 c.33 s.106
s.79, amended: 2013 c.33 s.106
s.80, amended: 2013 c.33 s.106
s.81, amended: 2013 c.33 s.106
s.83, amended: 2013 c.33 s.105, s.106
s.84, applied: SI 2013/442 Art.61, Art.62
s.84, varied: SI 2013/442 Art.61
s.85, amended: 2013 c.33 Sch.3 para.19, Sch.10 para.10, SI 2013/1388 Reg.6
s.85, applied: SI 2013/161 Art.3
s.85, repealed (in part): 2013 c.33 Sch.3 para.19
s.85, varied: SI 2013/442 Art.61
s.87, applied: SI 2013/442 Art.61
s.93, applied: SI 2013/637 Art.2, Art.3, Art.4
s.93, enabling: SI 2013/637
s.94, applied: SI 2013/637
s.107, applied: SI 2013/1881 Art.66, SI 2013/1882
s.107, enabling: SI 2013/1882
s.109, applied: SI 2013/418 Art.2, Art.3
s.109, enabling: SI 2013/418
s.110, applied: SI 2013/418 Art.2, Art.3
s.110, enabling: SI 2013/418
s.115, enabling: SI 2013/161, SI 2013/418, SI 2013/440, SI 2013/441, SI 2013/442, SI 2013/472,

SI 2013/496, SI 2013/637, SI 2013/642, SI 2013/1765, SI 2013/1882, SI 2013/2984
s.116, applied: SI 2013/496, SI 2013/636, SI 2013/1882
s.118, enabling: SI 2013/472, SI 2013/496, SI 2013/555, SI 2013/636, SI 2013/642, SI 2013/1765, SI 2013/2984
s.119, applied: SI 2013/441 Art.18
s.119, enabling: SI 2013/161, SI 2013/440, SI 2013/441, SI 2013/442, SI 2013/472, SI 2013/642, SI 2013/1765
s.122, enabling: SI 2013/113, SI 2013/423, SI 2013/651
Sch.3, varied: SI 2013/161 Art.7
Sch.20 para.2, disapplied: SI 2013/161 Art.1
Sch.20 para.7, applied: SI 2013/161 Art.7

2013

3. Prevention of Social Housing Fraud Act 2013
Commencement Orders: SI 2013/2622 Art.2; SI 2013/2861 Art.2
Royal Assent, January 31, 2013
s.12, enabling: SI 2013/2622, SI 2013/2861

4. Disabled Persons Parking Badges Act 2013
Commencement Orders: SI 2013/2202 Art.2
Royal Assent, January 31, 2013
s.5, applied: SI 2013/2203 Reg.3
s.7, enabling: SI 2013/2202

5. European Union (Croatian Accession and Irish Protocol) Act 2013
Royal Assent, January 31, 2013
s.4, enabling: SI 2013/1460
s.5, applied: SI 2013/1460

6. Electoral Registration and Administration Act 2013
Commencement Orders: SI 2013/219 Art.2; SI 2013/702 Art.2, Art.3; SI 2013/969 Art.2
Royal Assent, January 31, 2013
s.11, applied: SI 2013/794, SI 2013/3197
s.11, enabling: SI 2013/794, SI 2013/3197
s.25, enabling: SI 2013/219, SI 2013/702, SI 2013/794, SI 2013/969
s.27, enabling: SI 2013/219, SI 2013/702, SI 2013/969
Sch.5 Part 1 para.4, applied: SI 2013/3197 Art.7
Sch.5 Part 1 para.4, disapplied: SI 2013/3197 Art.6
Sch.5 Part 1 para.4, enabling: SI 2013/3197
Sch.5 Part 3 para.8, applied: SI 2013/3197 Art.13, Art.17, Art.18
Sch.5 Part 3 para.8, enabling: SI 2013/3197
Sch.5 Part 3 para.9, enabling: SI 2013/794, SI 2013/3197
Sch.5 Part 3 para.11, applied: SI 2013/3197 Art.17, Art.18
Sch.5 Part 3 para.12, enabling: SI 2013/3197
Sch.5 Part 3 para.13, applied: SI 2013/3197 Art.17, Art.19, Art.20, Art.21
Sch.5 Part 3 para.13, enabling: SI 2013/3197
Sch.5 Part 4 para.17, applied: SI 2013/3197 Art.24
Sch.5 Part 4 para.17, enabling: SI 2013/3197
Sch.5 Part 7 para.29, enabling: SI 2013/3197

7. HGV Road User Levy Act 2013
Royal Assent, February 28, 2013
applied: SI 2013/3186 Reg.2, Reg.3
s.17, enabling: SI 2013/3186

8. Mental Health (Discrimination) Act 2013
Royal Assent, February 28, 2013
s.4, enabling: SI 2013/1694

9. European Union (Approvals) Act 2013
Royal Assent, February 28, 2013

11. Prisons (Property) Act 2013
Royal Assent, February 28, 2013

13. Presumption of Death Act 2013
Royal Assent, March 26, 2013

14. Mobile Homes Act 2013
Royal Assent, March 26, 2013
s.10, disapplied: SI 2013/1168 Art.2
s.15, enabling: SI 2013/1168

15. Antarctic Act 2013
Royal Assent, March 26, 2013

17. Jobseekers (Back to Work Schemes) Act 2013
Royal Assent, March 26, 2013

18. Justice and Security Act 2013
Commencement Orders: SI 2013/1482 Art.2, Art.3
Royal Assent, April 25, 2013
s.6, applied: SI 2013/1571
s.6, enabling: SSI 2013/238, SSI 2013/317
s.7, applied: SI 2013/1571
s.7, enabling: SSI 2013/238
s.8, applied: SI 2013/1571
s.8, enabling: SSI 2013/238
s.10, applied: SI 2013/1571
s.10, enabling: SSI 2013/238
s.11, applied: SI 2013/1571
s.11, enabling: SSI 2013/238, SSI 2013/317
s.18, applied: SI 2013/1571
s.19, enabling: SI 2013/1482
s.20, enabling: SI 2013/1482
Sch.3 Part 2 para.3, enabling: SI 2013/1571
Sch.3 Part 2 para.4, enabling: SI 2013/1482

19. Groceries Code Adjudicator Act 2013
Commencement Orders: SI 2013/1236 Art.2
Royal Assent, April 25, 2013
s.25, enabling: SI 2013/1236

21. Partnerships (Prosecution) (Scotland) Act 2013
Royal Assent, April 25, 2013

22. Crime and Courts Act 2013

Commencement Orders: SI 2013/1042 Art.2, Art.3, Art.4, Art.5; SI 2013/1682 Art.2, Art.3; SI 2013/1725 Art.2, Art.3; SI 2013/2200 Art.2, Art.3, Art.4, Art.5, Art.6; SI 2013/2349 Art.2; SI 2013/2981 Art.2, Art.3; SI 2013/3176 Art.2, Art.3

Royal Assent, April 25, 2013

s.10, applied: SI 2013/1958 Reg.3, Reg.4

s.14, enabling: SI 2013/1958

s.24, referred to: SI 2013/3176 Art.4

s.32, enabling: SI 2013/2786

s.58, applied: SI 2013/2786

s.58, enabling: SI 2013/1958, SI 2013/2384, SI 2013/3176

s.59, enabling: SI 2013/2318, SI 2013/2384, SI 2013/3176

s.60, enabling: SI 2013/1042, SI 2013/1682, SI 2013/2318, SI 2013/3176

s.61, enabling: SI 2013/1042, SI 2013/1682, SI 2013/1725, SI 2013/2200, SI 2013/2349, SI 2013/2981, SI 2013/3176

Sch.1 Part 2 para.13, applied: SI 2013/2325 Reg.2

Sch.8, applied: SI 2013/2326 Art.3

Sch.13 Part 1, applied: SI 2013/2193 Reg.23

Sch.13 Part 3, applied: SI 2013/2191 Reg.19

Sch.13 Part 3, referred to: SI 2013/2191 Reg.19

Sch.13 Part 4, disapplied: SI 2013/2192 Reg.48, Reg.49

Sch.14 Part 1 para.1, disapplied: SI 2013/2192 Reg.49

Sch.17, applied: SI 2013/1554 r.12_1

Sch.17 Part 1 para.2, applied: SI 2013/1554 r.12_1, r.12_4, r.12_7

Sch.17 Part 1 para.5, applied: SI 2013/1554 r.12_3

Sch.17 Part 1 para.6, applied: SI 2013/1554 r.12_2, r.12_3

Sch.17 Part 1 para.7, applied: SI 2013/1554 r.12_2, r.12_3

Sch.17 Part 1 para.8, applied: SI 2013/1554 r.12_2, r.12_4

Sch.17 Part 1 para.9, applied: SI 2013/1554 r.12_5

Sch.17 Part 1 para.10, applied: SI 2013/1554 r.12_2, r.12_6

Sch.17 Part 1 para.11, applied: SI 2013/1554 r.12_8

Sch.17 Part 1 para.12, applied: SI 2013/1554 r.12_9

Sch.17 Part 1 para.13, applied: SI 2013/1554 r.12_4

Sch.17 Part 2, applied: SI 2013/1554 r.12_3

Sch.24 para.1, enabling: SI 2013/2326

Sch.24 para.2, enabling: SI 2013/2326

Sch.24 para.3, enabling: SI 2013/2326

Sch.24 para.9, amended: SI 2013/2326 Art.3

23. Marine Navigation Act 2013

Commencement Orders: SI 2013/1489 Art.2, Art.3

Royal Assent, April 25, 2013

s.13, enabling: SI 2013/1489, SI 2013/2006, SSI 2013/254

24. Enterprise and Regulatory Reform Act 2013

Commencement Orders: SI 2013/1455 Art.2, Art.3, Sch.1 para.1, para.2, para.3, para.4, para.5, para.6, para.7, para.8, para.9, para.10, para.11, para.12, para.13, para.14, Sch.2 para.1, para.2, para.3, para.4, para.5, para.6, para.7, para.8, para.9; SI 2013/1648 Art.2; SI 2013/2227 Art.2, Art.3; SI 2013/2271 Art.2; SI 2013/2979 Art.2, Art.3, Sch.1 para.1, para.2, para.3, para.4, para.5, para.6, para.7, para.8, para.9

Royal Assent, April 25, 2013

s.2, applied: SI 2013/2880

s.2, enabling: SI 2013/2880

s.3, applied: SI 2013/2880 Art.2

s.4, applied: SI 2013/2880 Art.2

s.5, applied: SI 2013/2880 Art.2

s.6, applied: SI 2013/2880 Art.2

s.15, applied: SI 2013/1949

s.15, enabling: SI 2013/1949

s.19, see *Hurst v Kelly* [2013] I.C.R. 1225 (EAT), Judge Peter Clark

s.52, amended: 2013 c.33 s.67, Sch.8 para.11

s.60, applied: SI 2013/2148 Art.1

s.61, applied: SI 2013/2148 Art.1

s.63, applied: SI 2013/2148 Art.1, Art.5

s.63, disapplied: SI 2013/2146 Art.4

s.78, enabling: SI 2013/1782

s.83, applied: SI 2013/3192 Art.3

s.84, applied: SI 2013/3192 Art.3

s.87, enabling: SI 2013/3192

s.88, applied: SI 2013/3192

s.99, enabling: SI 2013/1666, SI 2013/1854, SI 2013/1956, SI 2013/2146, SI 2013/2268

s.100, enabling: SI 2013/1455, SI 2013/2146, SI 2013/2227, SI 2013/2271, SI 2013/2979

s.103, enabling: SI 2013/1455, SI 2013/1648, SI 2013/2227, SI 2013/2271, SI 2013/2979

Sch.4, applied: 2013 c.33 s.59, Sch.5 para.1, Sch.5 para.6

Sch.4 Part 1 para.16, amended: 2013 c.33 s.67, Sch.8 para.12

Sch.4 Part 3 para.35, amended: 2013 c.33 Sch.5 para.2

Sch.4 Part 3 para.38, amended: 2013 c.33 Sch.5 para.2

Sch.4 Part 3 para.48, amended: 2013 c.33 Sch.5 para.2

Sch.4 Part 4 para.61, enabling: SI 2013/2227

Sch.16, applied: SI 2013/2148 Art.1

Sch.17 para.1, applied: SI 2013/2148 Art.5
Sch.17 para.1, disapplied: SI 2013/2146 Art.4
Sch.17 para.2, applied: SI 2013/2148 Art.5
Sch.17 para.2, disapplied: SI 2013/2146 Art.4
Sch.17 para.3, applied: SI 2013/2148 Art.5
Sch.17 para.3, disapplied: SI 2013/2146 Art.4
Sch.17 para.4, applied: SI 2013/2148 Art.5
Sch.17 para.4, disapplied: SI 2013/2146 Art.4
Sch.17 para.5, applied: SI 2013/2148 Art.5
Sch.17 para.5, disapplied: SI 2013/2146 Art.4
Sch.17 para.6, applied: SI 2013/2148 Art.5
Sch.17 para.6, disapplied: SI 2013/2146 Art.4
Sch.17 para.7, applied: SI 2013/2148 Art.1
Sch.17 para.8, applied: SI 2013/2148 Art.1
Sch.17 para.9, applied: SI 2013/2148 Art.1
Sch.17 para.10, applied: SI 2013/2148 Art.1
Sch.17 para.11, applied: SI 2013/2148 Art.1
Sch.17 para.12, applied: SI 2013/2148 Art.5
Sch.17 para.12, disapplied: SI 2013/2146 Art.4
Sch.17 para.13, applied: SI 2013/2148 Art.5
Sch.17 para.13, disapplied: SI 2013/2146 Art.4
Sch.17 para.14, applied: SI 2013/2148 Art.1
Sch.17 para.15, applied: SI 2013/2148 Art.1
Sch.17 para.16, applied: SI 2013/2148 Art.1
Sch.17 para.17, applied: SI 2013/2148 Art.1
Sch.17 para.18, applied: SI 2013/2148 Art.1
Sch.17 para.19, applied: SI 2013/2148 Art.1
Sch.17 para.20, applied: SI 2013/2148 Art.1

25. Public Service Pensions Act 2013

Commencement Orders: SI 2013/1518 Art.2; SI 2013/2818 Art.2, Art.3, Art.4, Art.5
Royal Assent, April 25, 2013
s.11, applied: SI 2013/2356 Reg.63
s.14, applied: SI 2013/2356 Reg.89
s.36, applied: SI 2013/1518 Art.2
s.41, enabling: SI 2013/1518, SI 2013/2818

26. Defamation Act 2013

Commencement Orders: SI 2013/3027 Art.2
Royal Assent, April 25, 2013
s.5, applied: SI 2013/3028, SI 2013/3028 Reg.3, Reg.4, Reg.5
s.5, referred to: SI 2013/3028 Reg.2, Reg.4
s.5, enabling: SI 2013/3028
s.17, enabling: SI 2013/3027, SSI 2013/339

27. Growth and Infrastructure Act 2013

Commencement Orders: SI 2013/1124 Art.2, Art.3, Art.4, Art.9; SI 2013/1488 Art.2, Art.3, Art.4, Art.5, Art.6, Art.7; SI 2013/1766 Art.2, Art.3, Art.4; SI 2013/2143 Art.2; SI 2013/2878 Art.2
Royal Assent, April 25, 2013
s.23, applied: SI 2013/1124 Art.6
s.24, applied: SI 2013/1124 Art.7
s.25, applied: SI 2013/1124 Art.8s.27, applied: SI 2013/1124 Art.11
s.32, enabling: SI 2013/2879
s.33, enabling: SI 2013/2140, SI 2013/2879
s.35, enabling: SI 2013/1124, SI 2013/1488, SI 2013/1766, SI 2013/2143, SI 2013/2878, SSI 2013/303

29. Finance Act 2013

Commencement Orders: SI 2013/1755 Art.2; SI 2013/1817 Art.2
Royal Assent, July 17, 2013
s.43, repealed: SI 2013/3209 Reg.12
s.66, enabling: SI 2013/1815
s.94, applied: SI 2013/2571 Reg.3
s.99, applied: SI 2013/2571 Reg.4
s.102, applied: SI 2013/2571 Reg.4
s.124, applied: SI 2013/1844 Sch.1
s.125, applied: SI 2013/1844 Sch.1
s.217, applied: SI 2013/2819
s.217, enabling: SI 2013/2819
s.222, referred to: SI 2013/1962 Reg.22
s.222, enabling: SI 2013/1962
Sch.2 Part 2 para.31, enabling: SI 2013/2796
Sch.16 Part 2 para.2, enabling: SI 2013/1817
Sch.17 Part 2 para.2, enabling: SI 2013/1817
Sch.18 para.22, enabling: SI 2013/1817
Sch.22 Part 1 para.1, applied: SI 2013/1741 Reg.11
Sch.22 Part 1 para.3, enabling: SI 2013/1741
Sch.22 Part 1 para.4, enabling: SI 2013/1741
Sch.23 Part 5 para.38, enabling: SI 2013/1755
Sch.33 Part 1 para.1, enabling: SI 2013/1844
Sch.33 Part 1 para.3, applied: SI 2013/1844 Sch.1

30. Marriage (Same Sex Couples) Act 2013

Commencement Orders: SI 2013/2789 Art.2, Art.3
Royal Assent, July 17, 2013
s.21, enabling: SI 2013/2789

31. High Speed Rail (Preparation) Act 2013

Royal Assent, November 21, 2013

32. Energy Act 2013

Royal Assent, December 18, 2013

33. Financial Services (Banking Reform) Act 2013

Royal Assent, December 18, 2013
s.79, applied: 2013 c.24 Sch.4 para.

CURRENT LAW

STATUTORY INSTRUMENT CITATOR 2013

The Statute Citator covers the period 2013 and is up to date to February 24, 2014 (Orders and Acts received).It comprises in a single table:

(i) Statutory Instruments made between January 1, 2013 and February 24, 2014;
(ii) Amendments, modifications and repeals made to existing Statutory Instruments during this period;
(iii) Statutory Instruments judicially considered during this period;
(iv) Statutory Instruments made under the powers of any Statutory Instrument issued during this period.

The material is arranged in numerical order under the relevant year.

Definitions of legislative effects:

''added'' : new provisions are inserted by subsequent legislation

''amended'' : text of legislation is modified by subsequent legislation

''applied'' : brought to bear,or exercised by subsequent legislation

''consolidated'' : used where previous legislation in the same subject area is brought together in subsequent legislation, with or without amendments

''disapplied'' : an exception made to the application of an earlier enactment

''enabling'' : giving power for the relevant SI to be made

''referred to'' : direction from other legislation without specific effect or application

''repealed'' : rescinded by subsequent legislation

''restored'' : reinstated by subsequent legislation (where previously repealed/ revoked)

''substituted'' : text of provision is completely replaced by subsequent legislation

''varied'' : provisions modified in relation to their application to specified areas or circumstances, however the text itself remains unchanged

STATUTORY INSTRUMENTS ISSUED BY THE SCOTTISH PARLIAMENT

1999

1. Environmental Impact Assessment (Scotland) Regulations 1999
Reg.2, amended: SSI 2013/177 Sch.1 para.7

43. Environmental Impact Assessment (Forestry) (Scotland) Regulations 1999
Reg.2, amended: SSI 2013/177 Sch.1 para.8

202. Scottish Natural Heritage (Rum) Harbour Empowerment Order 1999
applied: SSI 2013/230 Art.4

2000

59. Disabled Persons (Badges for Motor Vehicles) (Scotland) Regulations 2000
Reg.4, amended: SSI 2013/65 Reg.5
Reg.6, amended: SSI 2013/65 Reg.5
Reg.6, revoked (in part): SSI 2013/65 Reg.5
Reg.9, amended: SSI 2013/65 Reg.5

62. Food Standards Act 1999 (Transitional and Consequential Provisions and Savings) (Scotland) Regulations 2000
Reg.6, revoked (in part): SSI 2013/307 Sch.3
Sch.4 Part V para.1, revoked: SSI 2013/307 Sch.3
Sch.4 Part V para.2, revoked: SSI 2013/307 Sch.3
Sch.4 Part V para.3, revoked: SSI 2013/307 Sch.3
Sch.4 Part V para.4, revoked: SSI 2013/307 Sch.3

110. Repayment of Student Loans (Scotland) Regulations 2000
Reg.2, amended: SSI 2013/65 Reg.6, SSI 2013/142 Reg.6
Reg.10, amended: SSI 2013/80 Reg.5
Reg.13A, amended: SSI 2013/80 Reg.6
Reg.13B, amended: SSI 2013/80 Reg.7
Reg.13B, revoked (in part): SSI 2013/80 Reg.7

121. European Communities (Lawyer's Practice) (Scotland) Regulations 2000
Reg.1, varied: SSI 2013/177 Reg.5
Reg.2, amended: SSI 2013/177 Reg.3
Reg.21, applied: SSI 2013/177 Reg.5
Reg.22, applied: SSI 2013/177 Reg.5

287. Protection of Wrecks (Designation) (Scotland) Order 2000
revoked: SSI 2013/276 Sch.1

320. Electricity Works (Environmental Impact Assessment) (Scotland) Regulations 2000
Reg.2, applied: SSI 2013/304 Reg.7
Reg.9, varied: SSI 2013/304 Reg.5
Reg.10, applied: SSI 2013/304 Reg.4
Sch.4 Part II para.1, varied: SSI 2013/304 Reg.5
Sch.4 Part II para.2, varied: SSI 2013/304 Reg.5
Sch.4 Part II para.3, varied: SSI 2013/304 Reg.5
Sch.4 Part II para.4, varied: SSI 2013/304 Reg.5
Sch.4 Part II para.5, varied: SSI 2013/304 Reg.5

365. Enzootic Bovine Leukosis (Scotland) Regulations 2000
Reg.2, amended: SSI 2013/173 Art.12
Reg.3, amended: SSI 2013/173 Art.12
Reg.4, amended: SSI 2013/173 Art.12
Reg.5, amended: SSI 2013/173 Art.12

2001

103. Miscellaneous Food Additives (Amendment) (Scotland) Regulations 2001
revoked: SSI 2013/266 Sch.5

151. Western Isles Salmon Fishery District Designation Order 2001
Sch.2 para.3, amended: SSI 2013/323 Reg.28

162. Milk and Milk Products (Pupils in Educational Establishments) (Scotland) Regulations 2001
amended: SI 2013/3235 Reg.15
Reg.2, amended: SI 2013/3235 Reg.15
Reg.3, amended: SI 2013/3235 Reg.15

207. Water Supply (Water Quality) (Scotland) Regulations 2001
Reg.27, amended: SI 2013/1387 Sch.5 para.4, SSI 2013/177 Sch.1 para.9
Reg.27, revoked (in part): SI 2013/1387 Sch.5 para.4

222. Education (Assisted Places) (Scotland) Regulations 2001
Reg.2, amended: SSI 2013/177 Sch.1 para.10

223. St Mary's Music School (Aided Places) (Scotland) Regulations 2001
Sch.1 Part I para.1, amended: SSI 2013/177 Sch.1 para.11

242. Protection of Wrecks (Designation) (Scotland) Order 2001
revoked: SSI 2013/276 Sch.1

302. Health Boards (Membership and Procedure) (Scotland) Regulations 2001
varied: SSI 2013/334 Reg.5

315. Parole Board (Scotland) Rules 2001
Part IV r.26, amended: SI 2013/2042 Sch.1 para.53
Part IV r.26, revoked (in part): SI 2013/2042 Sch.1 para.53

384. Protection of Wrecks (Designation) (No.2) (Scotland) Order 2001
revoked: SSI 2013/276 Sch.1

450. Miscellaneous Food Additives (Amendment) (No.2) (Scotland) Regulations 2001
revoked: SSI 2013/266 Sch.5

476. Panels of Persons to Safeguard the Interests of Children (Scotland) Regulations 2001
Reg.6, varied: SSI 2013/150 Art.26
477. Curators ad Litem and Reporting Officers (Panels) (Scotland) Regulations 2001
Reg.10, revoked (in part): SSI 2013/147 Sch.1 para.5

2002

34. Disease Control (Interim Measures) (Scotland) Order 2002
Art.2, amended: SSI 2013/173 Art.13
Art.7, amended: SSI 2013/173 Art.13
Sch.1 para.3, amended: SSI 2013/173 Art.13
Sch.3 para.7, amended: SSI 2013/173 Art.13
63. Children's Hearings (Legal Representation) (Scotland) Rules 2002
applied: SSI 2013/150 Art.25
132. Act of Sederunt (Summary Cause Rules) 2002
Sch.1 Appendix, amended: SSI 2013/91 Sch.3, SSI 2013/135 Sch.2, SSI 2013/171 r.5
Sch.1 Part 2A para.2A_1, added: SSI 2013/91 r.4
Sch.1 Part 2A para.2A_2, added: SSI 2013/91 r.4
133. Act of Sederunt (Small Claim Rules) 2002
Sch.1 Appendix1, amended: SSI 2013/91 Sch.4
Sch.1 Part 2A para.2A_1, added: SSI 2013/91 r.5
Sch.1 Part 2A para.2A_2, added: SSI 2013/91 r.5
138. Mull Salmon Fishery District Designation (Scotland) Order 2002
Sch.2 para.3, amended: SSI 2013/323 Reg.28
154. Aberdeen City Council and Aberdeenshire Council Boundaries (Blackburn) Amendment Order 2002
applied: SSI 2013/347 Sch.2
155. Argyll and Bute Council and West Dunbartonshire Council Boundaries (Ardoch Sewage Works) Amendment Order 2002
applied: SSI 2013/347 Sch.2
156. Glasgow City Council and Renfrewshire Council Boundaries (Braehead) Amendment Order 2002
applied: SSI 2013/347 Sch.2
157. City of Edinburgh Council and West Lothian Council Boundaries (West Farm, Broxburn) Amendment Order 2002
applied: SSI 2013/347 Sch.2
178. Forth Estuary Transport Authority Order 2002
revoked: 2013 asp 8 s.4
283. Animal By-Products (Identification) Amendment (Scotland) Regulations 2002
revoked: SSI 2013/307 Sch.3
292. Home Zones (Scotland) (No.2) Regulations 2002
Reg.2, amended: SSI 2013/119 Sch.3 para.4
Reg.5, amended: SSI 2013/119 Sch.3 para.4
Reg.14, amended: SSI 2013/119 Sch.3 para.4
303. Community Care (Personal Care and Nursing Care) (Scotland) Regulations 2002
Reg.2, amended: SSI 2013/108 Reg.2
494. Civil Legal Aid (Scotland) Regulations 2002
Reg.2, amended: SSI 2013/142 Reg.7
Reg.33, amended: SSI 2013/137 Reg.13, SSI 2013/142 Reg.7
Reg.44, amended: SI 2013/534 Sch.1 para.4
Sch.2 para.5, amended: SSI 2013/137 Reg.13
Sch.2 para.7, amended: SSI 2013/65 Reg.7, SSI 2013/142 Reg.7
Sch.3 para.7, amended: SSI 2013/137 Reg.13
Sch.3 para.8, amended: SSI 2013/142 Reg.7
523. Kava-kava in Food (Scotland) Regulations 2002
Reg.2, amended: SSI 2013/177 Sch.1 para.12
566. Act of Sederunt (Fees of Messengers-at-Arms) (No.2) 2002
Sch.1 para.15, amended: SSI 2013/346 Sch.1
567. Act of Sederunt (Fees of Sheriff Officers) (No.2) 2002
Sch.1 para.17, amended: SSI 2013/345 Sch.1

2003

1. Cairngorms National Park Designation, Transitional and Consequential Provisions (Scotland) Order 2003
Art.7, applied: SSI 2013/155 Reg.37
53. Animal By-Products (Identification) Amendment (Scotland) Regulations 2003
revoked: SSI 2013/307 Sch.3
85. Surface Waters (Fishlife) (Classification) (Scotland) Amendment Regulations 2003
revoked: SSI 2013/323 Reg.29
93. Proceeds of Crime Act 2002 (Disclosure of Information to and by Lord Advocate and Scottish Ministers) Order 2003
Art.3, amended: SI 2013/472 Sch.2 para.80
132. Miscellaneous Food Additives (Amendment) (Scotland) Regulations 2003
revoked: SSI 2013/266 Sch.5
176. Council Tax (Discounts) (Scotland) Consolidation and Amendment Order 2003
Art.4, amended: SSI 2013/65 Reg.8, SSI 2013/137 Reg.14, SSI 2013/142 Reg.8
179. Advice and Assistance (Assistance by Way of Representation) (Scotland) Regulations 2003
Reg.1, amended: SSI 2013/200 Reg.3
Reg.3A, added: SSI 2013/200 Reg.3
Reg.5A, amended: SI 2013/1389 Reg.47
Reg.13, amended: SSI 2013/200 Reg.3

Reg.14, added: SSI 2013/200 Reg.3

231. Rehabilitation of Offenders Act 1974 (Exclusions and Exceptions) (Scotland) Order 2003

revoked: SSI 2013/50 Sch.5

235. Landfill (Scotland) Regulations 2003

Reg.2, amended: SSI 2013/222 Reg.2
Reg.10, amended: SSI 2013/222 Reg.2
Reg.10A, added: SSI 2013/222 Reg.2
Reg.11, amended: SSI 2013/222 Reg.2
Sch.3 para.8, added: SSI 2013/222 Reg.2
Sch.4 para.7, added: SSI 2013/222 Reg.2

268. Litter (Fixed Penalty) (Scotland) Order 2003

revoked: SSI 2013/315 Art.4

290. Drugs Courts (Scotland) Order 2003

Sch.1 para.2, revoked: SSI 2013/302 Art.2

292. Road User Charging (Consultation and Publication) (Scotland) Regulations 2003

Reg.2, amended: SSI 2013/119 Sch.3 para.5
Reg.3, amended: SSI 2013/119 Sch.3 para.5
Reg.7, amended: SSI 2013/119 Sch.3 para.5

293. Fruit Juices and Fruit Nectars (Scotland) Regulations 2003

applied: SSI 2013/305 Reg.21
revoked: SSI 2013/305 Reg.19

354. Diseases of Poultry (Scotland) Order 2003

Art.3, amended: SSI 2013/173 Art.14
Art.4, amended: SSI 2013/173 Art.14

424. Children's Hearings (Provision of Information by Principal Reporter) (Prescribed Persons) (Scotland) Order 2003

Art.1, amended: SI 2013/472 Art.4

426. Classical Swine Fever (Scotland) Order 2003

Art.2, amended: SSI 2013/173 Art.15
Art.4, amended: SSI 2013/173 Art.15
Art.13, amended: SSI 2013/173 Art.15
Sch.1 Part I para.8, amended: SSI 2013/173 Art.15
Sch.1 Part II para.20, amended: SSI 2013/173 Art.15
Sch.2 Part I para.5, amended: SSI 2013/173 Art.15
Sch.2 Part II para.8, amended: SSI 2013/173 Art.15

453. Title Conditions (Scotland) Act 2003 (Conservation Bodies) Order 2003

Sch.1 Part II, amended: SSI 2013/289 Art.2

460. National Health Service (Travelling Expenses and Remission of Charges) (Scotland) (No.2) Regulations 2003

Reg.2, amended: SSI 2013/137 Reg.15, SSI 2013/142 Reg.9
Reg.3, applied: SI 2013/3029 Sch.9 para.46, Sch.10 para.43, SI 2013/3035 Sch.1
Reg.4, amended: SSI 2013/137 Reg.15, SSI 2013/142 Reg.9
Reg.5, applied: SI 2013/3029 Sch.9 para.46, Sch.10 para.43, SI 2013/3035 Sch.1
Reg.11, applied: SI 2013/3029 Sch.9 para.46, Sch.10 para.43, SI 2013/3035 Sch.1
Sch.1 Part I para.2, added: SSI 2013/327 Reg.2
Sch.1 Part I para.2, amended: SSI 2013/327 Reg.2
Sch.1 Part I para.2, substituted: SSI 2013/327 Reg.2
Sch.1 Part II para.4, added: SSI 2013/142 Reg.9
Sch.1 Part II para.4, amended: SSI 2013/142 Reg.9

531. Control of Pollution (Silage, Slurry and Agricultural Fuel Oil) (Scotland) Regulations 2003

Reg.1, amended: SSI 2013/177 Sch.1 para.13

586. African Swine Fever (Scotland) Order 2003

Art.2, amended: SSI 2013/173 Art.16
Art.4, amended: SSI 2013/173 Art.16
Art.12, amended: SI 2013/1506 Sch.5 para.5
Art.13, amended: SSI 2013/173 Art.16
Sch.1 Part I para.9, amended: SSI 2013/173 Art.16
Sch.1 Part II para.22, amended: SSI 2013/173 Art.16
Sch.2 Part I para.5, amended: SSI 2013/173 Art.16
Sch.2 Part II para.8, amended: SSI 2013/173 Art.16

599. Miscellaneous Food Additives Amendment (Scotland) (No.2) Regulations 2003

revoked: SSI 2013/266 Sch.5

608. Support and Assistance of Young People Leaving Care (Scotland) Regulations 2003

Reg.13, amended: SSI 2013/137 Reg.16, SSI 2013/147 Sch.1 para.6

615. Wester Ross Salmon Fishery District Designation Order 2003

Sch.2 para.3, amended: SSI 2013/323 Reg.28

2004

6. Meat Products (Scotland) Regulations 2004

Reg.2, amended: SSI 2013/177 Sch.1 para.14

38. National Health Service (Tribunal) (Scotland) Regulations 2004

Reg.33, revoked: SI 2013/2042 Sch.1 para.57

114. National Health Service (Primary Medical Services Performers Lists) (Scotland) Regulations 2004

Reg.2, amended: SI 2013/235 Sch.2 para.69, SSI 2013/177 Sch.1 para.15

115. National Health Service (General Medical Services Contracts) (Scotland) Regulations 2004

referred to: SI 2013/235 Sch.3 para.8
Reg.2, amended: SI 2013/235 Sch.2 para.70
Sch.5 Part 2 para.22, amended: SI 2013/235 Sch.2 para.70

Sch.5 Part 6 para.87, amended: SI 2013/235 Sch.2 para.70
Sch.5 Part 6 para.87, applied: SI 2013/235 Sch.3 para.10

116. National Health Service (Primary Medical Services Section 17C Agreements) (Scotland) Regulations 2004

referred to: SI 2013/235 Sch.3 para.8
Reg.2, amended: SI 2013/235 Sch.2 para.71
Sch.1 Part 6 para.52, amended: SI 2013/235 Sch.2 para.71
Sch.1 Part 6 para.52, applied: SI 2013/235 Sch.3 para.11
Sch.2 Part 2 para.15, amended: SI 2013/235 Sch.2 para.71

117. Housing (Scotland) Act 2001 (Assistance to Registered Social Landlords and Other Persons) (Grants) Regulations 2004

referred to: SSI 2013/7 Reg.3
Reg.2, amended: SSI 2013/7 Reg.2
Reg.3, amended: SSI 2013/7 Reg.2
Reg.4, amended: SSI 2013/7 Reg.2
Sch.1, applied: SSI 2013/7 Reg.4
Sch.1 Part 1 para.1, amended: SSI 2013/7 Reg.2
Sch.1 Part 3 para.4, amended: SSI 2013/7 Reg.2
Sch.1 Part 4 para.13, substituted: SSI 2013/7 Reg.2
Sch.2, applied: SSI 2013/7 Reg.3
Sch.2 Part 1 para.1, substituted: SSI 2013/7 Sch.1
Sch.2 Part 1 para.2, substituted: SSI 2013/7 Sch.1
Sch.2 Part 2 para.3, substituted: SSI 2013/7 Sch.1
Sch.2 Part 3 para.4, substituted: SSI 2013/7 Sch.1
Sch.2 Part 4 para.5, substituted: SSI 2013/7 Sch.1
Sch.2 Part 4 para.6, substituted: SSI 2013/7 Sch.1
Sch.2 Part 4 para.7, substituted: SSI 2013/7 Sch.1
Sch.2 Part 4 para.8, substituted: SSI 2013/7 Sch.1
Sch.2 Part 4 para.9, substituted: SSI 2013/7 Sch.1
Sch.5 Part 1 para.1, added: SSI 2013/7 Sch.2
Sch.5 Part 1 para.2, added: SSI 2013/7 Sch.2
Sch.5 Part 2 para.3, added: SSI 2013/7 Sch.2
Sch.5 Part 3 para.4, added: SSI 2013/7 Sch.2
Sch.5 Part 4 para.5, added: SSI 2013/7 Sch.2
Sch.5 Part 4 para.6, added: SSI 2013/7 Sch.2
Sch.5 Part 4 para.7, added: SSI 2013/7 Sch.2
Sch.5 Part 4 para.8, added: SSI 2013/7 Sch.2
Sch.5 Part 4 para.9, added: SSI 2013/7 Sch.2

133. Jam and Similar Products (Scotland) Regulations 2004

Reg.2, amended: SSI 2013/177 Sch.1 para.16, SSI 2013/266 Reg.18

144. Tobacco Advertising and Promotion (Point of Sale) (Scotland) Regulations 2004

revoked: SSI 2013/85 Reg.18

205. Sexual Offences Act 2003 (Travel Notification Requirements) (Scotland) Regulations 2004

Reg.5, amended: SSI 2013/216 Reg.3
Reg.5, applied: SSI 2013/216 Reg.4
Reg.6, amended: SSI 2013/216 Reg.3
Reg.7, amended: SSI 2013/216 Reg.3
Reg.10, amended: SSI 2013/119 Sch.1 para.26

211. Tobacco Advertising and Promotion (Specialist Tobacconist) (Scotland) Regulations 2004

Reg.2, amended: SSI 2013/85 Reg.19

219. Town and Country Planning (Fees for Applications and Deemed Applications) (Scotland) Regulations 2004

applied: SSI 2013/105 Reg.3
Reg.1, referred to: SSI 2013/105 Reg.3
Reg.12, amended: SSI 2013/105 Reg.2
Reg.13, amended: SSI 2013/105 Reg.2
Reg.14, amended: SSI 2013/105 Reg.2
Sch.1 Part II para.4, amended: SSI 2013/105 Reg.2
Sch.1 Part II para.5, amended: SSI 2013/105 Reg.2
Sch.1 Part II para.6, amended: SSI 2013/105 Reg.2
Sch.1 Part II para.7, amended: SSI 2013/105 Reg.2
Sch.1 Part III para.14, amended: SSI 2013/105 Reg.2, Sch.1

255. Potatoes Originating in Poland (Notification) (Scotland) Order 2004

revoked: SSI 2013/5 Art.5

257. Police (Scotland) Regulations 2004

applied: SSI 2013/35 Reg.26, Sch.1 para.2, Sch.2 para.2, Sch.3 para.7
referred to: SSI 2013/35 Sch.3 para.15, Sch.3 para.18
revoked: SSI 2013/35 Sch.3 para.20
varied: SSI 2013/35 Sch.3 para.6
Part 7, applied: SSI 2013/35 Sch.3 para.9
Reg.6, applied: SSI 2013/35 Sch.3 para.2
Reg.8, applied: SSI 2013/35 Sch.3 para.3
Reg.12, applied: SSI 2013/35 Sch.3 para.5
Reg.13, applied: SSI 2013/35 Sch.3 para.6
Reg.14, applied: SSI 2013/35 Sch.3 para.7
Reg.18, applied: SSI 2013/35 Sch.3 para.8
Reg.19, applied: SSI 2013/35 Sch.3 para.8
Reg.25, applied: SSI 2013/35 Sch.3 para.10
Reg.27, applied: SSI 2013/35 Sch.3 para.11, Sch.3 para.12
Reg.28, applied: SSI 2013/35 Sch.3 para.13
Reg.29, applied: SSI 2013/35 Sch.3 para.14
Reg.32, applied: SSI 2013/35 Sch.3 para.15
Reg.33, referred to: SSI 2013/35 Sch.3 para.16
Reg.45, referred to: SSI 2013/35 Sch.3 para.17
Reg.49, revoked: SSI 2013/39 Sch.1
Sch.3, applied: SSI 2013/35 Sch.3 para.18
Sch.3 para.1, varied: SSI 2013/35 Sch.3 para.19

358. Environmental Protection (Restriction on Use of Lead Shot) (Scotland) (No.2) Regulations 2004

Reg.4, amended: SSI 2013/349 Reg.2

Reg.4A, added: SSI 2013/349 Reg.2

386. Community Health Partnerships (Scotland) Regulations 2004

Reg.7, amended: SI 2013/235 Sch.2 para.72

406. Building (Scotland) Regulations 2004

Reg.5, applied: SSI 2013/143 Reg.5
Sch.3, applied: SSI 2013/143 Reg.5
Sch.5 Part 2 para.2_15, amended: SSI 2013/143 Reg.2
Sch.5 Part 3 para.3_25, amended: SSI 2013/143 Reg.2
Sch.5 Part 3 para.3_27, added: SSI 2013/143 Reg.2
Sch.5 Part 7 para.7_1, amended: SSI 2013/143 Reg.2
Sch.6 para.1, amended: SSI 2013/143 Reg.2

413. Miscellaneous Food Additives Amendment (Scotland) Regulations 2004

revoked: SSI 2013/266 Sch.5

428. Building (Procedure) (Scotland) Regulations 2004

Reg.2, amended: SSI 2013/143 Reg.3
Reg.2, revoked (in part): SSI 2013/119 Sch.2 para.20
Reg.41, amended: SSI 2013/143 Reg.3
Reg.57, amended: SSI 2013/143 Reg.3

477. Title Conditions (Scotland) Act 2003 (Rural Housing Bodies) Order 2004

Sch.1, amended: SSI 2013/100 Art.2

516. Water Environment (Register of Protected Areas) (Scotland) Regulations 2004

Sch.1 Part I paraA.1, added: SSI 2013/323 Reg.25
Sch.1 Part I para.2, revoked (in part): SSI 2013/323 Reg.25

519. Road User Charging (Exemption from Charges) (Scotland) Regulations 2004

Sch.1 para.1, amended: SSI 2013/119 Sch.3 para.6
Sch.1 para.2, amended: SSI 2013/119 Sch.3 para.6

520. Environmental Information (Scotland) Regulations 2004

Reg.19A, added: SSI 2013/127 Reg.2

2005

51. Council Tax (Discount for Unoccupied Dwellings) (Scotland) Regulations 2005

revoked: SSI 2013/45 Reg.7

125. Gender Recognition (Disclosure of Information) (Scotland) Order 2005

Art.6, amended: SI 2013/1881 Sch.1 para.28

127. Non-Domestic Rating (Valuation of Utilities) (Scotland) Order 2005

Art.2, amended: SSI 2013/36 Art.2
Art.3, amended: SSI 2013/36 Art.2

172. Building (Forms) (Scotland) Regulations 2005

Sch.1, amended: SSI 2013/143 Reg.4

214. Miscellaneous Food Additives Amendment (Scotland) Regulations 2005

revoked: SSI 2013/266 Sch.5

215. Smoke Flavourings (Scotland) Regulations 2005

revoked: SSI 2013/266 Sch.5

295. Electricity (Applications for Consent) Amendment (Scotland) Regulations 2005

Reg.2, revoked (in part): SSI 2013/58 Reg.3

298. Adam Smith College, Fife (Establishment) Order 2005

revoked: SSI 2013/179 Art.7

318. Regulation of Care (Social Service Workers) (Scotland) Order 2005

Art.1, amended: SSI 2013/141 Art.2

329. Fodder Plant Seed (Scotland) Regulations 2005

Reg.2, amended: SSI 2013/326 Reg.4
Sch.5 Part II para.23, amended: SSI 2013/326 Reg.5
Sch.5 Part II para.23A, added: SSI 2013/326 Reg.5
Sch.5 Part II para.24, substituted: SSI 2013/326 Reg.5
Sch.6 Part II para.8A, amended: SSI 2013/326 Reg.6
Sch.9, revoked: SSI 2013/326 Reg.7

342. Fire (Additional Function) (Scotland) Order 2005

Art.2, amended: SSI 2013/119 Sch.2 para.21
Art.3, amended: SSI 2013/119 Sch.2 para.21
Art.4, amended: SSI 2013/119 Sch.2 para.21
Art.5, amended: SSI 2013/119 Sch.2 para.21
Art.6, amended: SSI 2013/119 Sch.2 para.21
Art.7, revoked: SSI 2013/119 Sch.2 para.21

343. Fire (Charging) (Scotland) Order 2005

Art.2, amended: SSI 2013/119 Sch.2 para.22
Sch.1, amended: SSI 2013/119 Sch.2 para.22

393. Teachers Superannuation (Scotland) Regulations 2005

Part E regE.37, amended: SI 2013/472 Art.4
Part C regC.3, amended: SSI 2013/71 Reg.2

432. Regulation of Care (Prescribed Registers) (Scotland) Order 2005

Art.2, applied: SSI 2013/227 Reg.4

445. Mental Health (Care and Treatment) (Scotland) Act 2003 (Modification of Subordinate Legislation) Order 2005

Sch.1 para.44, revoked: SSI 2013/50 Sch.5

494. Civil Contingencies Act 2004 (Contingency Planning) (Scotland) Regulations 2005

Reg.2, amended: SSI 2013/119 Sch.1 para.27, SSI 2013/247 Reg.2

Reg.3, amended: SSI 2013/119 Sch.1 para.27, SSI 2013/247 Reg.2
Reg.6, amended: SSI 2013/119 Sch.1 para.27
Reg.7, amended: SSI 2013/119 Sch.1 para.27
Reg.8, amended: SSI 2013/119 Sch.1 para.27
Reg.12, amended: SSI 2013/119 Sch.1 para.27, SSI 2013/247 Reg.2
Reg.16, amended: SSI 2013/119 Sch.1 para.27
Reg.26, amended: SSI 2013/119 Sch.1 para.27
Reg.27, amended: SSI 2013/119 Sch.1 para.27
Reg.28, amended: SSI 2013/119 Sch.1 para.27
Reg.35, amended: SSI 2013/119 Sch.1 para.27

518. Additional Support for Learning (Co-ordinated Support Plan) (Scotland) Amendment Regulations 2005

Reg.10, amended: SSI 2013/147 Sch.1 para.7

519. Mental Health Tribunal for Scotland (Practice and Procedure) (No.2) Rules 2005

Part VII r.66, revoked (in part): SI 2013/2042 Sch.1 para.62

572. Civil Partnership Act 2004 (Modification of Subordinate Legislation) Order 2005

Art.51, revoked: SSI 2013/45 Reg.8
Art.52, revoked: SSI 2013/45 Reg.8

608. Feed (Hygiene and Enforcement) (Scotland) Regulations 2005

Reg.2, amended: SSI 2013/340 Reg.2
Reg.4, substituted: SSI 2013/340 Reg.2
Sch.2, substituted: SSI 2013/340 Sch.1

613. Plant Health (Scotland) Order 2005

Art.2, amended: SSI 2013/187 Art.3, SSI 2013/366 Art.3, Art.11
Art.4, amended: SSI 2013/366 Art.11
Art.8, amended: SSI 2013/366 Art.4
Art.19, amended: SSI 2013/187 Art.4
Art.19A, amended: SSI 2013/187 Art.4
Art.19A, substituted: SSI 2013/5 Art.3
Art.19B, added: SSI 2013/187 Art.4
Art.21, amended: SSI 2013/366 Art.5, Art.11
Art.22, amended: SSI 2013/187 Art.4, SSI 2013/366 Art.6
Art.24, amended: SSI 2013/366 Art.7
Art.31, amended: SSI 2013/187 Art.5
Art.40, amended: SSI 2013/187 Art.6
Art.45, amended: SSI 2013/187 Art.7
Sch.1 Part A, amended: SSI 2013/187 Art.8
Sch.1 Part B, amended: SSI 2013/187 Art.8
Sch.2 Part B, amended: SSI 2013/366 Art.8
Sch.4 Part A, amended: SSI 2013/187 Art.9, SSI 2013/366 Art.9
Sch.4 Part B, amended: SSI 2013/5 Art.4, SSI 2013/187 Art.9, SSI 2013/366 Art.9
Sch.5 Part A para.2A, added: SSI 2013/366 Art.10
Sch.5 Part A para.8, added: SSI 2013/187 Art.10
Sch.6 Part A para.3b, substituted: SSI 2013/187 Art.11
Sch.6 Part A para.10, added: SSI 2013/187 Art.11
Sch.6 Part A para.11, added: SSI 2013/187 Art.11
Sch.7 Part A para.3b, substituted: SSI 2013/187 Art.12
Sch.7 Part A para.10, added: SSI 2013/187 Art.12
Sch.7 Part A para.11, added: SSI 2013/187 Art.12
Sch.9 Part A para.7, amended: SSI 2013/366 Art.11
Sch.9 Part B para.2, amended: SSI 2013/366 Art.11
Sch.9 Part B para.3, amended: SSI 2013/366 Art.11
Sch.9 Part B para.4, amended: SSI 2013/366 Art.11
Sch.9 Part B para.5, amended: SSI 2013/366 Art.11
Sch.13 Part B, amended: SSI 2013/366 Art.11

2006

1. Public Contracts (Scotland) Regulations 2006

Reg.23, applied: SSI 2013/50 Sch.3 para.10
Reg.33, applied: SSI 2013/50 Sch.3 para.10

2. Utilities Contracts (Scotland) Regulations 2006

Reg.26, applied: SSI 2013/50 Sch.3 para.10
Reg.34, applied: SSI 2013/50 Sch.3 para.10

3. Food Hygiene (Scotland) Regulations 2006

Reg.2, amended: SSI 2013/336 Reg.2
Reg.13, amended: SSI 2013/84 Reg.11
Sch.1, amended: SSI 2013/333 Reg.3, SSI 2013/336 Reg.2
Sch.4 para.2, amended: SI 2013/3235 Reg.16
Sch.7 para.2, revoked: SSI 2013/307 Sch.3
Sch.7 para.3, revoked: SSI 2013/307 Sch.3
Sch.7 para.4, revoked: SSI 2013/307 Sch.3
Sch.7 para.5, revoked: SSI 2013/307 Sch.3
Sch.7 para.6, revoked: SSI 2013/307 Sch.3
Sch.7 para.7, revoked: SSI 2013/307 Sch.3
Sch.7 para.8, revoked: SSI 2013/307 Sch.3
Sch.7 para.9, revoked: SSI 2013/307 Sch.3
Sch.7 para.10, revoked: SSI 2013/307 Sch.3
Sch.7 para.11, revoked: SSI 2013/307 Sch.3

4. Older Cattle (Disposal) (Scotland) Regulations 2006

Reg.2, amended: SSI 2013/307 Sch.2 para.4

18. Electricity (Applications for Consent) Amendment (Scotland) Regulations 2006

revoked: SSI 2013/58 Reg.3

44. Foot-and-Mouth Disease (Scotland) Order 2006

Art.2, amended: SSI 2013/173 Art.17, SSI 2013/307 Sch.2 para.6

Art.8, amended: SSI 2013/173 Art.17
Art.26, amended: SSI 2013/307 Sch.2 para.7
Sch.2 para.1, amended: SSI 2013/173 Art.17
Sch.5 Part 1 para.2, amended: SSI 2013/307 Sch.2 para.8
Sch.7 para.1, amended: SSI 2013/173 Art.17

45. Foot-and-Mouth Disease (Slaughter and Vaccination) (Scotland) Regulations 2006
Reg.2, amended: SSI 2013/173 Art.18, SSI 2013/307 Sch.2 para.10
Reg.24, amended: SSI 2013/173 Art.18
Reg.26, amended: SSI 2013/173 Art.18

63. Management of Offenders etc (Scotland) Act 2005 (Designation of Partner Bodies) Order 2006
Art.2, amended: SSI 2013/119 Sch.1 para.28

88. Additional Support Needs Tribunals for Scotland (Practice and Procedure) Rules 2006
Part V r.27, revoked (in part): SI 2013/2042 Sch.1 para.64

107. National Bus Travel Concession Scheme for Older and Disabled Persons (Scotland) Order 2006
Art.12, amended: SSI 2013/114 Art.2

117. National Bus Travel Concession Scheme for Older and Disabled Persons (Eligible Persons and Eligible Services) (Scotland) Order 2006
Art.2, amended: SSI 2013/65 Reg.9
Art.3, amended: SSI 2013/65 Reg.9

135. National Health Service (General Ophthalmic Services) (Scotland) Regulations 2006
Reg.2, amended: SI 2013/235 Sch.2 para.102, SSI 2013/177 Sch.1 para.17, SSI 2013/355 Reg.3
Reg.6, amended: SSI 2013/355 Reg.4
Reg.7, amended: SSI 2013/355 Reg.5
Reg.14, amended: SSI 2013/355 Reg.6
Reg.21A, added: SSI 2013/355 Reg.7
Sch.1 para.6, amended: SSI 2013/355 Reg.8
Sch.1 para.13, amended: SSI 2013/355 Reg.8
Sch.1 para.13, revoked (in part): SSI 2013/355 Reg.8
Sch.1 para.14, amended: SSI 2013/355 Reg.8
Sch.2 Part A para.1, amended: SSI 2013/355 Reg.9
Sch.2 Part A para.4, revoked (in part): SSI 2013/355 Reg.9
Sch.2 Part B para.4, revoked (in part): SSI 2013/355 Reg.9
Sch.2 Part C para.2, revoked (in part): SSI 2013/355 Reg.9
Sch.3, amended: SSI 2013/355 Reg.10
Sch.4, revoked: SSI 2013/355 Reg.11
Sch.5 para.1, revoked: SSI 2013/355 Reg.11

170. Serious Organised Crime and Police Act 2005 (Specified Persons for Financial Reporting Orders) (Scotland) Order 2006
Art.1, amended: SSI 2013/119 Sch.1 para.29
Art.1, revoked (in part): SSI 2013/119 Sch.1 para.29
Art.2, amended: SSI 2013/119 Sch.1 para.29
Art.2, revoked (in part): SSI 2013/119 Sch.1 para.29

194. Rehabilitation of Offenders Act 1974 (Exclusions and Exceptions) (Amendment) (Scotland) Order 2006
revoked: SSI 2013/50 Sch.5

220. Protection of Charities Assets (Exemption) (Scotland) Order 2006
Sch.1 Part 1, amended: SSI 2013/169 Art.3

250. Public Transport Users Committee for Scotland Order 2006
Art.4, applied: SSI 2013/79 Art.2

330. National Health Service (Discipline Committees) (Scotland) Regulations 2006
Reg.16, revoked: SI 2013/2042 Sch.1 para.65

333. Education (Student Loans for Tuition Fees) (Scotland) Regulations 2006
Reg.2, amended: SSI 2013/80 Reg.9, SSI 2013/177 Sch.1 para.18
Reg.11, amended: SI 2013/1881 Sch.1 para.29
Sch.1 para.3, amended: SSI 2013/80 Reg.10

336. Avian Influenza and Influenza of Avian Origin in Mammals (Scotland) Order 2006
Art.2, amended: SSI 2013/173 Art.19
Art.9, amended: SSI 2013/173 Art.19
Art.63, amended: SSI 2013/173 Art.19
Art.68, amended: SSI 2013/173 Art.19

337. Avian Influenza (Slaughter and Vaccination) (Scotland) Regulations 2006
Reg.2, amended: SSI 2013/173 Art.20
Reg.17, amended: SSI 2013/173 Art.20

338. Firefighters Compensation Scheme (Scotland) Order 2006
Sch.1, amended: SSI 2013/177 Sch.1 para.19, SSI 2013/186 Art.3, Art.5, Art.6, Art.8
Sch.1, revoked: SSI 2013/186 Art.6, Art.7
Sch.1, substituted: SSI 2013/186 Art.4

456. Fire Safety (Scotland) Regulations 2006
Reg.23, amended: SSI 2013/119 Sch.2 para.23
Reg.24, amended: SSI 2013/119 Sch.2 para.23

484. National Health Service Central Register (Scotland) Regulations 2006
Sch.1, amended: SI 2013/235 Sch.2 para.103
Sch.2, amended: SI 2013/235 Sch.2 para.103, SSI 2013/119 Sch.1 para.30

511. Aberdeen City (Electoral Arrangements) Order 2006
Sch.1, amended: SSI 2013/115 Art.2

552. Police (Minimum Age for Appointment) (Scotland) Regulations 2006
revoked: SSI 2013/42 Sch.1 para.1
Reg.2, revoked: SSI 2013/35 Sch.3 para.20

582. Environmental Impact Assessment (Agriculture) (Scotland) Regulations 2006
Reg.2, amended: SSI 2013/177 Sch.1 para.20
588. Personal Injuries (NHS Charges) (Amounts) (Scotland) Regulations 2006
Reg.2E, amended: SSI 2013/53 Reg.2
Reg.2F, added: SSI 2013/53 Reg.2
Reg.3, amended: SSI 2013/53 Reg.2
Reg.6, amended: SSI 2013/53 Reg.2
593. Personal Injuries (NHS Charges) (Reviews and Appeals) (Scotland) Regulations 2006
Reg.8, applied: SI 2013/2380 Reg.8

2007

19. Tweed Regulation Order 2007
Art.14, revoked: SSI 2013/323 Reg.29
Art.15, revoked: SSI 2013/323 Reg.29
Art.16, revoked: SSI 2013/323 Reg.29
Art.17, revoked: SSI 2013/323 Reg.29
Art.18, revoked: SSI 2013/323 Reg.29
Art.19, revoked: SSI 2013/323 Reg.29
61. Avian Influenza (H5N1 in Wild Birds) (Scotland) Order 2007
Art.2, amended: SSI 2013/307 Sch.2 para.12
Art.13, amended: SSI 2013/307 Sch.2 para.13
Sch.1 Part 4 para.13, amended: SSI 2013/307 Sch.2 para.14
62. Avian Influenza (H5N1 in Poultry) (Scotland) Order 2007
Art.2, amended: SSI 2013/173 Art.21, SSI 2013/307 Sch.2 para.16
Art.3, amended: SSI 2013/307 Sch.2 para.17
Art.14, amended: SSI 2013/307 Sch.2 para.18
68. Police (Injury Benefit) (Scotland) Regulations 2007
Reg.3, revoked (in part): SI 2013/2318 Sch.1 para.82, SSI 2013/184 Reg.14
Reg.6, amended: SSI 2013/184 Reg.15
Reg.6, revoked (in part): SI 2013/2318 Sch.1 para.83
Reg.39, revoked (in part): SI 2013/2318 Sch.1 para.84
Reg.42, amended: SSI 2013/184 Reg.16
Sch.1 para.1, amended: SI 2013/2318 Sch.1 para.85, SSI 2013/184 Reg.17
Sch.1 para.1, revoked (in part): SI 2013/2318 Sch.1 para.85, SSI 2013/184 Reg.17
75. Rehabilitation of Offenders Act 1974 (Exclusions and Exceptions) (Scotland) Amendment Order 2007
revoked: SSI 2013/50 Sch.5
92. Management of Offenders etc (Scotland) Act 2005 (Specification of Persons) Order 2007
Sch.1, amended: SSI 2013/147 Sch.1 para.8
93. Sale of Alcohol to Children and Young Persons (Scotland) Regulations 2007
Reg.2, amended: SSI 2013/199 Reg.2
134. Police (Scotland) Amendment Regulations 2007
revoked: SSI 2013/35 Sch.3 para.20
147. Tuberculosis (Scotland) Order 2007
Art.2, amended: SSI 2013/173 Art.22
Art.4, amended: SSI 2013/173 Art.22
Art.5, amended: SSI 2013/173 Art.22
149. Education Authority Bursaries (Scotland) Regulations 2007
applied: SI 2013/3029 Sch.11 para.3, SI 2013/3035 Sch.1
Reg.2, amended: SSI 2013/80 Reg.12
Sch.1 para.3, amended: SSI 2013/80 Reg.13
Sch.1 para.9, amended: SSI 2013/80 Reg.13
151. Nursing and Midwifery Student Allowances (Scotland) Regulations 2007
Reg.2, amended: SSI 2013/80 Reg.15
Sch.1 para.3, amended: SSI 2013/80 Reg.16
Sch.1 para.9, amended: SSI 2013/80 Reg.16
152. Education (Fees and Awards) (Scotland) Regulations 2007
Reg.2, amended: SSI 2013/80 Reg.18
Sch.1 para.3, amended: SSI 2013/80 Reg.19
Sch.1 para.9, amended: SSI 2013/80 Reg.19
153. Students Allowances (Scotland) Regulations 2007
Reg.2, amended: SSI 2013/80 Reg.21
Reg.3, amended: SSI 2013/80 Reg.22
Reg.4, applied: SI 2013/3029 Sch.11 para.3, SI 2013/3035 Sch.1
Sch.1 para.3, amended: SSI 2013/80 Reg.23
Sch.1 para.9, amended: SSI 2013/80 Reg.23
154. Education (Student Loans) (Scotland) Regulations 2007
Reg.2, amended: SSI 2013/80 Reg.25
Reg.11, amended: SSI 2013/80 Reg.26
Reg.14, amended: SI 2013/1881 Sch.1 para.30
Sch.1 para.3, amended: SSI 2013/80 Reg.27
Sch.1 para.8A, amended: SSI 2013/80 Reg.27
156. Education Maintenance Allowances (Scotland) Regulations 2007
Reg.2, amended: SSI 2013/80 Reg.29
Sch.1 para.3, amended: SSI 2013/80 Reg.30
Sch.2 para.3, amended: SSI 2013/137 Reg.17
170. Representation of the People (Absent Voting at Local Government Elections) (Scotland) Regulations 2007
Reg.8, amended: SSI 2013/142 Reg.10
174. Cattle Identification (Scotland) Regulations 2007
applied: SSI 2013/3 Art.11, Art.14, Art.15, Art.17, Art.18

175. Town and Country Planning (Marine Fish Farming) (Scotland) Regulations 2007
revoked: SSI 2013/277 Reg.5

178. Surface Waters (Fishlife) (Classification) (Scotland) Amendment Regulations 2007
revoked: SSI 2013/323 Reg.29

183. Local Governance (Scotland) Act 2004 (Remuneration) Regulations 2007
Reg.2, amended: SSI 2013/119 Sch.3 para.7
Reg.3, amended: SSI 2013/119 Sch.3 para.7
Reg.6, amended: SSI 2013/351 Reg.2
Reg.7, amended: SSI 2013/351 Reg.2
Reg.10, amended: SSI 2013/351 Reg.2
Reg.11, revoked: SSI 2013/119 Sch.3 para.7
Reg.12, amended: SSI 2013/119 Sch.3 para.7, SSI 2013/351 Reg.2
Reg.12, revoked (in part): SSI 2013/119 Sch.3 para.7

199. Firefighters Pension Scheme (Scotland) Order 2007
Sch.1, amended: SSI 2013/129 Art.3, SSI 2013/186 Art.10, Art.12, Art.14, Art.15, Art.16, Art.17, Art.19
Sch.1, revoked: SSI 2013/186 Art.11, Art.12, Art.13, Art.16, Art.18, Art.20

201. Police Pensions (Scotland) Regulations 2007
Reg.3, amended: SI 2013/2318 Sch.1 para.87, SSI 2013/184 Reg.19
Reg.3, revoked (in part): SI 2013/2318 Sch.1 para.87, SSI 2013/184 Reg.19
Reg.4, amended: SI 2013/2318 Sch.1 para.88
Reg.5, amended: SI 2013/2318 Sch.1 para.89
Reg.5, revoked (in part): SI 2013/2318 Sch.1 para.89, SSI 2013/184 Reg.20
Reg.7, amended: SSI 2013/89 Reg.3
Reg.17, amended: SI 2013/2318 Sch.1 para.90, SSI 2013/184 Reg.21
Reg.17, revoked (in part): SI 2013/2318 Sch.1 para.90
Reg.18, amended: SI 2013/2318 Sch.1 para.91
Reg.18, revoked (in part): SI 2013/2318 Sch.1 para.91
Reg.19, amended: SI 2013/2318 Sch.1 para.92
Reg.20, amended: SI 2013/2318 Sch.1 para.93
Reg.23, amended: SI 2013/2318 Sch.1 para.94
Reg.51, amended: SI 2013/2318 Sch.1 para.95
Reg.52, revoked (in part): SI 2013/2318 Sch.1 para.96
Reg.87, revoked: SSI 2013/184 Reg.22
Reg.88, revoked: SSI 2013/184 Reg.22
Sch.1, amended: SI 2013/2318 Sch.1 para.97, SSI 2013/184 Reg.23

330. Bovine Semen (Scotland) Regulations 2007
applied: SSI 2013/151 Reg.7
Reg.4, applied: SSI 2013/151 Sch.3
Reg.7, applied: SSI 2013/151 Sch.3
Reg.10, applied: SSI 2013/151 Sch.3
Reg.40, applied: SSI 2013/151 Sch.3
Reg.41, revoked: SSI 2013/151 Sch.7
Reg.42, revoked: SSI 2013/151 Sch.7

363. Food (Suspension of the Use of E 128 Red 2G as Food Colour) (Scotland) Regulations 2007
revoked: SSI 2013/266 Sch.5

387. Disease Control (Interim Measures) (Scotland) Amendment Order 2007
Art.2, revoked (in part): SSI 2013/173 Art.23

400. Disease Control (Interim Measures) (Scotland) Amendment (No.2) Order 2007
Art.2, revoked (in part): SSI 2013/173 Art.24

421. Porcine Semen (Fees) (Scotland) Regulations 2007
revoked: SSI 2013/151 Sch.7

427. Surface Waters (Shellfish) (Classification) (Scotland) Amendment Regulations 2007
revoked: SSI 2013/323 Reg.29

436. Administrative Justice and Tribunals Council (Listed Tribunals) (Scotland) Order 2007
revoked: SI 2013/2042 Sch.1 para.68
Sch.1, amended: SSI 2013/119 Sch.1 para.31

483. Natural Mineral Water, Spring Water and Bottled Drinking Water (Scotland) (No.2) Regulations 2007
applied: SSI 2013/84 Sch.1

498. Plant Health (Scotland) Amendment (No.2) Order 2007
Art.6, revoked (in part): SSI 2013/187 Art.13

528. Police (Promotion) (Scotland) Amendment Regulations 2007
revoked: SSI 2013/39 Sch.1

529. Water Environment (Drinking Water Protected Areas) (Scotland) Order 2007
revoked: SSI 2013/29 Art.3

2008

16. Scottish Road Works Register (Prescribed Fees and Amounts) Regulations 2008
Reg.3, applied: SSI 2013/8 Reg.3

31. Justice of the Peace Courts (Sheriffdom of Lothian and Borders) etc Order 2008
Sch.1, amended: SSI 2013/153 Art.11, Art.12, Art.13

75. Intensive Support and Monitoring (Scotland) Regulations 2008
revoked: SSI 2013/210 Reg.1
Reg.2, amended: SSI 2013/6 Reg.6
Reg.9, revoked: SSI 2013/6 Reg.6

Sch.1, revoked: SSI 2013/6 Reg.6

81. Bankruptcy (Scotland) Act 1985 (Low Income, Low Asset Debtors etc.) Regulations 2008

Reg.2, amended: SSI 2013/137 Reg.18

93. Justice of the Peace Courts (Sheriffdom of Grampian, Highland and Islands) Order 2008

Sch.1, amended: SSI 2013/153 Art.4, Art.5, Art.6, Art.7, Art.8, Art.9

117. Police (Special Constables) (Scotland) Regulations 2008

applied: SSI 2013/43 Sch.3 para.3, Sch.3 para.4, Sch.3 para.6
referred to: SSI 2013/43 Sch.3 para.6
revoked: SSI 2013/43 Sch.3 para.9
Reg.2, amended: SSI 2013/43 Sch.3 para.7
Reg.5, applied: SSI 2013/43 Sch.3 para.2
Reg.8, applied: SSI 2013/43 Sch.3 para.3
Reg.9, applied: SSI 2013/43 Sch.3 para.4
Reg.12, applied: SSI 2013/43 Sch.3 para.5
Reg.13, applied: SSI 2013/43 Sch.3 para.5
Reg.17, applied: SSI 2013/43 Sch.3 para.6
Reg.18, amended: SSI 2013/43 Sch.3 para.7
Reg.18, revoked (in part): SSI 2013/43 Sch.3 para.7
Reg.19, amended: SSI 2013/43 Sch.3 para.7
Reg.19, revoked (in part): SSI 2013/43 Sch.3 para.7
Reg.21, amended: SSI 2013/43 Sch.3 para.7
Reg.21, revoked (in part): SSI 2013/43 Sch.3 para.7
Reg.22, amended: SSI 2013/43 Sch.3 para.7
Reg.22, applied: SSI 2013/43 Sch.3 para.6
Reg.23, amended: SSI 2013/43 Sch.3 para.7
Reg.23, applied: SSI 2013/43 Sch.3 para.6
Reg.28, applied: SSI 2013/43 Sch.3 para.8

128. Sexual Offences Act 2003 (Prescribed Police Stations) (Scotland) Regulations 2008

Sch.1, amended: SSI 2013/119 Sch.1 para.32

143. Protected Trust Deeds (Scotland) Regulations 2008

revoked: SSI 2013/318 Reg.30
Reg.19, referred to: SSI 2013/318 Reg.10
Sch.1, applied: SSI 2013/318 Reg.31

148. Specified Products from China (Restriction on First Placing on the Market) (Scotland) Regulations 2008

Reg.2, amended: SSI 2013/221 Reg.2
Reg.3, amended: SSI 2013/221 Reg.2
Reg.8, substituted: SSI 2013/221 Reg.2

159. Rural Development Contracts (Land Managers Options) (Scotland) Regulations 2008

Sch.2, amended: SSI 2013/309 Reg.3
Sch.2, revoked: SSI 2013/309 Reg.2, Reg.3
Sch.2, substituted: SSI 2013/309 Reg.3

202. National Scenic Areas (Scotland) Regulations 2008

Reg.8, revoked: SSI 2013/264 Sch.1

216. Spreadable Fats, Milk and Milk Products (Scotland) Regulations 2008

Reg.2, amended: SI 2013/3235 Reg.17
Reg.6, amended: SI 2013/3235 Reg.17

219. Diseases of Animals (Approved Disinfectants) (Scotland) Order 2008

Art.3, amended: SI 2013/1506 Sch.5 para.9
Art.6, amended: SI 2013/1506 Sch.5 para.9

224. National Health Service Pension Scheme (Scotland) Regulations 2008

applied: SSI 2013/174 Reg.1
revoked: SSI 2013/174 Sch.1
Reg.1, revoked (in part): SSI 2013/109 Reg.27
Reg.1, substituted: SSI 2013/109 Reg.27
Reg.1, amended: SSI 2013/109 Reg.29
Reg.1, revoked (in part): SSI 2013/109 Reg.40
Reg.1, amended: SSI 2013/109 Reg.49
Reg.1, revoked (in part): SSI 2013/109 Reg.58
Reg.2, revoked: SSI 2013/109 Reg.28
Reg.2, applied: SSI 2013/174 Reg.3
Reg.2, amended: SSI 2013/70 Reg.6, SSI 2013/109 Reg.33, SSI 2013/168 Reg.6
Reg.2, amended: SSI 2013/70 Reg.8, SSI 2013/109 Reg.54, SSI 2013/168 Reg.9
Reg.2A, added: SSI 2013/109 Reg.47
Reg.2A, added: SSI 2013/109 Reg.64
Reg.3, amended: SSI 2013/168 Reg.7
Reg.3, amended: SSI 2013/109 Reg.41
Reg.3, applied: SSI 2013/174 Reg.3
Reg.3, amended: SSI 2013/109 Reg.59
Reg.4, amended: SSI 2013/109 Reg.31
Reg.4, revoked (in part): SSI 2013/109 Reg.31
Reg.4, amended: SSI 2013/70 Reg.7, SSI 2013/109 Reg.34, SSI 2013/168 Reg.8
Reg.4, amended: SSI 2013/109 Reg.42
Reg.4, amended: SSI 2013/109 Reg.52
Reg.4, revoked (in part): SSI 2013/109 Reg.52
Reg.4, amended: SSI 2013/109 Reg.60
Reg.5, applied: SSI 2013/174 Reg.10
Reg.5, amended: SSI 2013/109 Reg.32
Reg.5, amended: SSI 2013/109 Reg.43
Reg.5, applied: SSI 2013/174 Reg.5
Reg.5, amended: SSI 2013/109 Reg.53
Reg.5, revoked (in part): SSI 2013/109 Reg.53
Reg.5, amended: SSI 2013/109 Reg.61
Reg.6, amended: SSI 2013/109 Reg.30
Reg.6, amended: SSI 2013/109 Reg.35
Reg.6, amended: SSI 2013/109 Reg.44
Reg.6, amended: SSI 2013/109 Reg.50
Reg.6, amended: SSI 2013/109 Reg.62
Reg.7, amended: SSI 2013/109 Reg.63

Reg.8, amended: SSI 2013/109 Reg.45
Reg.8, amended: SSI 2013/109 Reg.51
Reg.9, amended: SSI 2013/109 Reg.46
Reg.11, amended: SSI 2013/109 Reg.38
Reg.11, applied: SSI 2013/174 Reg.6
Reg.11, amended: SSI 2013/109 Reg.39
Reg.11, amended: SSI 2013/109 Reg.48
Reg.11, amended: SSI 2013/109 Reg.55
Reg.11, amended: SSI 2013/109 Reg.57
Reg.11, amended: SSI 2013/109 Reg.65
Reg.13, amended: SSI 2013/109 Reg.36
Reg.13, applied: SSI 2013/174 Reg.6
Reg.13, amended: SSI 2013/109 Reg.56
Reg.15, amended: SSI 2013/109 Reg.37

228. Local Government Pension Scheme (Administration) (Scotland) Regulations 2008

Reg.6, amended: SI 2013/472 Art.4
Sch.1, amended: SI 2013/472 Art.4
Sch.2, amended: SSI 2013/147 Sch.1 para.9

235. Graduate Endowment (Scotland) Regulations 2008

Reg.11, amended: SI 2013/1881 Sch.1 para.34

265. Nutritional Requirements for Food and Drink in Schools (Scotland) Regulations 2008

Reg.2, amended: SSI 2013/305 Sch.15 para.2

298. Action Programme for Nitrate Vulnerable Zones (Scotland) Regulations 2008

Reg.3, amended: SSI 2013/123 Reg.3
Reg.6, substituted: SSI 2013/123 Reg.4
Reg.10, amended: SSI 2013/123 Reg.5
Reg.12, amended: SSI 2013/123 Reg.6
Reg.15, amended: SSI 2013/123 Reg.7
Reg.20, amended: SSI 2013/123 Reg.8
Reg.25, amended: SSI 2013/123 Reg.9
Reg.26, amended: SSI 2013/123 Reg.10
Sch.3 Part C, amended: SSI 2013/123 Reg.11

299. Potatoes Originating in Poland (Notification) (Scotland) Amendment Order 2008

revoked: SSI 2013/5 Art.5

300. Plant Health (Scotland) Amendment Order 2008

Art.4, revoked (in part): SSI 2013/5 Art.5, SSI 2013/187 Art.13

309. Energy Performance of Buildings (Scotland) Regulations 2008

Reg.2, amended: SSI 2013/12 Reg.3
Reg.6, amended: SSI 2013/12 Reg.4
Reg.6A, amended: SSI 2013/12 Reg.5
Reg.10, amended: SSI 2013/12 Reg.6
Reg.11, amended: SSI 2013/12 Reg.7
Reg.12A, amended: SSI 2013/12 Reg.8
Reg.13, amended: SSI 2013/12 Reg.9
Reg.14A, added: SSI 2013/12 Reg.10
Sch.2 Part 1 para.1, added: SSI 2013/12 Sch.1
Sch.2 Part 1 para.2, added: SSI 2013/12 Sch.1
Sch.2 Part 1 para.3, added: SSI 2013/12 Sch.1
Sch.2 Part 1 para.4, added: SSI 2013/12 Sch.1
Sch.2 Part 1 para.5, added: SSI 2013/12 Sch.1
Sch.2 Part 1 para.6, added: SSI 2013/12 Sch.1
Sch.2 Part 1 para.7, added: SSI 2013/12 Sch.1
Sch.2 Part 1 para.8, added: SSI 2013/12 Sch.1
Sch.2 Part 1 para.9, added: SSI 2013/12 Sch.1
Sch.2 Part 1 para.10, added: SSI 2013/12 Sch.1
Sch.2 Part 1 para.11, added: SSI 2013/12 Sch.1
Sch.2 Part 1 para.12, added: SSI 2013/12 Sch.1
Sch.2 Part 1 para.13, added: SSI 2013/12 Sch.1
Sch.2 Part 1 para.14, added: SSI 2013/12 Sch.1
Sch.2 Part 1 para.15, added: SSI 2013/12 Sch.1
Sch.2 Part 1 para.16, added: SSI 2013/12 Sch.1
Sch.2 Part 1 para.17, added: SSI 2013/12 Sch.1
Sch.2 Part 1 para.18, added: SSI 2013/12 Sch.1
Sch.2 Part 1 para.19, added: SSI 2013/12 Sch.1
Sch.2 Part 1 para.20, added: SSI 2013/12 Sch.1
Sch.2 Part 1 para.21, added: SSI 2013/12 Sch.1
Sch.2 Part 1 para.22, added: SSI 2013/12 Sch.1
Sch.2 Part 1 para.23, added: SSI 2013/12 Sch.1
Sch.2 Part 2, added: SSI 2013/12 Sch.1

363. Justice of the Peace Courts (Sheriffdom of Tayside, Central and Fife) Order 2008

Sch.1, amended: SSI 2013/153 Art.15, Art.16

395. Eggs and Chicks (Scotland) (No.2) Regulations 2008

Reg.2, amended: SI 2013/3235 Reg.18
Reg.2, revoked (in part): SI 2013/3235 Reg.18
Reg.3, amended: SI 2013/3235 Reg.18
Reg.9, amended: SI 2013/3235 Reg.18
Sch.1 Part 1, amended: SI 2013/3235 Reg.18
Sch.2A, amended: SI 2013/3235 Reg.18
Sch.2 Part 1, substituted: SI 2013/3235 Reg.18
Sch.2 Part 2, amended: SI 2013/3235 Reg.18

396. Mental Health Tribunal for Scotland (Practice and Procedure) (No.2) Amendment Rules 2008

r.2, revoked (in part): SI 2013/2042 Sch.1 para.73

406. Housing (Scotland) Act 2006 (Scheme of Assistance) Regulations 2008

Reg.2, amended: SSI 2013/137 Reg.19
Reg.4, amended: SSI 2013/137 Reg.19

432. Town and Country Planning (Development Management Procedure) (Scotland) Regulations 2008

applied: SSI 2013/155 Reg.51
revoked: SSI 2013/155 Sch.9
Reg.9, applied: SSI 2013/155 Reg.49
Reg.10, applied: SSI 2013/155 Reg.49
Reg.11, applied: SSI 2013/155 Reg.49
Reg.12, applied: SSI 2013/155 Reg.49
Reg.47, applied: SSI 2013/155 Reg.51

433. Town and Country Planning (Schemes of Delegation and Local Review Procedure) (Scotland) Regulations 2008

revoked: SSI 2013/157 Reg.24
Sch.1, applied: SSI 2013/157 Reg.24
Sch.1 para.1, applied: SSI 2013/157 Reg.24

434. Town and Country Planning (Appeals) (Scotland) Regulations 2008

revoked: SSI 2013/156 Sch.5
Sch.1 para.1, applied: SSI 2013/156 Reg.34
Sch.1 para.1, varied: SSI 2013/156 Reg.34
Sch.1 para.2, varied: SSI 2013/156 Reg.34
Sch.1 para.3, varied: SSI 2013/156 Reg.34
Sch.1 para.4, varied: SSI 2013/156 Reg.34
Sch.1 para.5, varied: SSI 2013/156 Reg.34
Sch.2 para.1, applied: SSI 2013/156 Reg.34
Sch.2 para.1, varied: SSI 2013/156 Reg.34
Sch.2 para.2, varied: SSI 2013/156 Reg.34
Sch.2 para.3, varied: SSI 2013/156 Reg.34
Sch.2 para.4, varied: SSI 2013/156 Reg.34
Sch.2 para.5, varied: SSI 2013/156 Reg.34

2009

19. National Health Service (Superannuation Scheme, Pension Scheme and Injury Benefits) (Scotland) Amendment Regulations 2009

Reg.23, revoked: SSI 2013/174 Sch.1
Reg.24, revoked: SSI 2013/174 Sch.1
Reg.25, revoked: SSI 2013/174 Sch.1
Reg.26, revoked: SSI 2013/174 Sch.1
Reg.27, revoked: SSI 2013/174 Sch.1
Reg.28, revoked: SSI 2013/174 Sch.1
Reg.29, revoked: SSI 2013/174 Sch.1
Reg.30, revoked: SSI 2013/174 Sch.1
Reg.31, revoked: SSI 2013/174 Sch.1
Reg.32, revoked: SSI 2013/174 Sch.1
Reg.33, revoked: SSI 2013/174 Sch.1
Reg.34, revoked: SSI 2013/174 Sch.1
Reg.35, revoked: SSI 2013/174 Sch.1
Reg.36, revoked: SSI 2013/174 Sch.1
Reg.37, revoked: SSI 2013/174 Sch.1
Reg.38, revoked: SSI 2013/174 Sch.1
Reg.39, revoked: SSI 2013/174 Sch.1
Reg.40, revoked: SSI 2013/174 Sch.1
Reg.41, revoked: SSI 2013/174 Sch.1
Reg.42, revoked: SSI 2013/174 Sch.1
Reg.43, revoked: SSI 2013/174 Sch.1
Reg.44, revoked: SSI 2013/174 Sch.1
Reg.45, revoked: SSI 2013/174 Sch.1
Reg.46, revoked: SSI 2013/174 Sch.1
Reg.47, revoked: SSI 2013/174 Sch.1
Reg.48, revoked: SSI 2013/174 Sch.1
Reg.49, revoked: SSI 2013/174 Sch.1
Reg.50, revoked: SSI 2013/174 Sch.1
Reg.51, revoked: SSI 2013/174 Sch.1
Reg.52, revoked: SSI 2013/174 Sch.1
Reg.53, revoked: SSI 2013/174 Sch.1
Reg.54, revoked: SSI 2013/174 Sch.1
Reg.55, revoked: SSI 2013/174 Sch.1
Reg.56, revoked: SSI 2013/174 Sch.1
Reg.57, revoked: SSI 2013/174 Sch.1
Reg.58, revoked: SSI 2013/174 Sch.1
Reg.59, revoked: SSI 2013/174 Sch.1
Reg.60, revoked: SSI 2013/174 Sch.1
Reg.61, revoked: SSI 2013/174 Sch.1
Reg.62, revoked: SSI 2013/174 Sch.1
Reg.63, revoked: SSI 2013/174 Sch.1
Reg.64, revoked: SSI 2013/174 Sch.1
Reg.65, revoked: SSI 2013/174 Sch.1
Reg.66, revoked: SSI 2013/174 Sch.1
Reg.67, revoked: SSI 2013/174 Sch.1
Reg.68, revoked: SSI 2013/174 Sch.1
Reg.69, revoked: SSI 2013/174 Sch.1
Reg.70, revoked: SSI 2013/174 Sch.1
Reg.71, revoked: SSI 2013/174 Sch.1
Reg.72, revoked: SSI 2013/174 Sch.1
Reg.73, revoked: SSI 2013/174 Sch.1
Reg.74, revoked: SSI 2013/174 Sch.1
Reg.75, revoked: SSI 2013/174 Sch.1
Reg.76, revoked: SSI 2013/174 Sch.1
Reg.77, revoked: SSI 2013/174 Sch.1
Reg.78, revoked: SSI 2013/174 Sch.1
Reg.79, revoked: SSI 2013/174 Sch.1
Reg.80, revoked: SSI 2013/174 Sch.1
Reg.81, revoked: SSI 2013/174 Sch.1
Reg.82, revoked: SSI 2013/174 Sch.1
Reg.83, revoked: SSI 2013/174 Sch.1
Reg.84, revoked: SSI 2013/174 Sch.1
Reg.85, revoked: SSI 2013/174 Sch.1

27. Port Babcock Rosyth Harbour Empowerment Order 2009

applied: SSI 2013/288 Art.1, Art.2, Art.3, Art.24
Art.2, amended: SSI 2013/288 Art.2, Art.10
Art.3, applied: SSI 2013/288 Art.24
Art.7, applied: SSI 2013/288 Art.8
Art.10, disapplied: SSI 2013/288 Art.10
Sch.1, referred to: SSI 2013/288 Art.4

48. Home Energy Assistance Scheme (Scotland) Regulations 2009

applied: SSI 2013/148 Reg.4
revoked: SSI 2013/148 Reg.9
Reg.5, applied: SSI 2013/148 Reg.9

71. Victim Statements (Prescribed Offences) (No.2) (Scotland) Order 2009

Sch.1 para.8A, added: SSI 2013/119 Sch.1 para.33

85. Aquatic Animal Health (Scotland) Regulations 2009

Reg.6, applied: 2013 asp 7 s.15

118. Regulation of Care (Fitness of Employees in Relation to Care Services) (Scotland) (No.2) Regulations 2009
referred to: SSI 2013/227 Reg.8
revoked: SSI 2013/227 Reg.8
Reg.4, applied: SSI 2013/227 Reg.9
Reg.5, applied: SSI 2013/227 Reg.9
Reg.6, applied: SSI 2013/227 Reg.9

140. Renewables Obligation (Scotland) Order 2009
Art.2, amended: SSI 2013/116 Art.3
Art.4, amended: SSI 2013/116 Art.4
Art.13, amended: SSI 2013/116 Art.5
Art.13, revoked (in part): SSI 2013/116 Art.5
Art.22, amended: SSI 2013/116 Art.6
Art.22C, added: SSI 2013/116 Art.7
Art.24, amended: SSI 2013/116 Art.8
Art.25, amended: SSI 2013/116 Art.9
Art.25, revoked (in part): SSI 2013/116 Art.9
Art.26, amended: SSI 2013/116 Art.10
Art.26, revoked (in part): SSI 2013/116 Art.10
Art.27, amended: SSI 2013/116 Art.11
Art.28, substituted: SSI 2013/116 Art.12
Art.28A, added: SSI 2013/116 Art.13
Art.28B, added: SSI 2013/116 Art.13
Art.28C, added: SSI 2013/116 Art.13
Art.28D, added: SSI 2013/116 Art.13
Art.28E, added: SSI 2013/116 Art.13
Art.29, amended: SSI 2013/116 Art.14
Art.30, amended: SSI 2013/116 Art.15
Art.30, revoked (in part): SSI 2013/116 Art.15
Art.30A, amended: SSI 2013/116 Art.16
Art.30A, revoked (in part): SSI 2013/116 Art.16
Art.30A, substituted: SSI 2013/116 Art.16
Art.30B, added: SSI 2013/116 Art.17
Art.31, amended: SSI 2013/116 Art.18
Art.32, amended: SSI 2013/116 Art.19
Art.33, amended: SSI 2013/116 Art.20
Art.36, amended: SSI 2013/116 Art.21
Art.54, amended: SSI 2013/116 Art.22
Art.54, revoked (in part): SSI 2013/116 Art.22
Art.54A, amended: SSI 2013/116 Art.23
Art.58ZA, added: SSI 2013/116 Art.24
Art.60, amended: SSI 2013/116 Art.25
Sch.2 Part 1 para.1, amended: SSI 2013/116 Art.26
Sch.2 Part 2, substituted: SSI 2013/116 Art.27
Sch.2 Part 2A, added: SSI 2013/116 Art.28
Sch.2 Part 2B, added: SSI 2013/116 Art.28
Sch.2 Part 2C, added: SSI 2013/116 Art.28
Sch.2 Part 2D, added: SSI 2013/116 Art.28

152. Adoption Support Services and Allowances (Scotland) Regulations 2009
Reg.2, amended: SSI 2013/137 Reg.20
Reg.14, amended: SSI 2013/137 Reg.20

154. Adoption Agencies (Scotland) Regulations 2009
Reg.3, applied: SSI 2013/50 Sch.3 para.5
Reg.5, applied: SSI 2013/50 Sch.3 para.5
Reg.13, amended: SSI 2013/147 Sch.1 para.10
Reg.23, amended: SSI 2013/147 Sch.1 para.10

173. Swine Vesicular Disease (Scotland) Order 2009
Art.2, amended: SSI 2013/173 Art.25
Art.16, amended: SSI 2013/173 Art.25
Art.36, amended: SSI 2013/173 Art.25
Art.37, amended: SSI 2013/173 Art.25

178. Education (School Lunches) (Scotland) Regulations 2009
Reg.2, amended: SSI 2013/64 Reg.3
Reg.4A, added: SSI 2013/64 Reg.4

183. National Health Service (Pharmaceutical Services) (Scotland) Regulations 2009
Reg.2, amended: SI 2013/235 Sch.2 para.135
Sch.3 para.6, revoked (in part): SI 2013/2042 Sch.1 para.79
Sch.6 para.6, revoked: SI 2013/2042 Sch.1 para.79

208. National Health Service (Superannuation Scheme, Pension Scheme and Injury Benefits) (Scotland) Amendment (No.2) Regulations 2009
Reg.15, revoked: SSI 2013/174 Sch.1
Reg.16, revoked: SSI 2013/174 Sch.1
Reg.17, revoked: SSI 2013/174 Sch.1
Reg.18, revoked: SSI 2013/174 Sch.1
Reg.19, revoked: SSI 2013/174 Sch.1
Reg.20, revoked: SSI 2013/174 Sch.1
Reg.21, revoked: SSI 2013/174 Sch.1
Reg.22, revoked: SSI 2013/174 Sch.1
Reg.23, revoked: SSI 2013/174 Sch.1
Reg.24, revoked: SSI 2013/174 Sch.1
Reg.25, revoked: SSI 2013/174 Sch.1
Reg.26, revoked: SSI 2013/174 Sch.1
Reg.27, revoked: SSI 2013/174 Sch.1
Reg.28, revoked: SSI 2013/174 Sch.1
Reg.29, revoked: SSI 2013/174 Sch.1
Reg.30, revoked: SSI 2013/174 Sch.1
Reg.31, revoked: SSI 2013/174 Sch.1
Reg.32, revoked: SSI 2013/174 Sch.1
Reg.33, revoked: SSI 2013/174 Sch.1
Reg.34, revoked: SSI 2013/174 Sch.1
Reg.35, revoked: SSI 2013/174 Sch.1
Reg.36, revoked: SSI 2013/174 Sch.1
Reg.37, revoked: SSI 2013/174 Sch.1
Reg.38, revoked: SSI 2013/174 Sch.1
Reg.39, revoked: SSI 2013/174 Sch.1
Reg.40, revoked: SSI 2013/174 Sch.1
Reg.41, revoked: SSI 2013/174 Sch.1
Reg.42, revoked: SSI 2013/174 Sch.1
Reg.43, revoked: SSI 2013/174 Sch.1
Reg.44, revoked: SSI 2013/174 Sch.1
Reg.45, revoked: SSI 2013/174 Sch.1
Reg.46, revoked: SSI 2013/174 Sch.1

Reg.47, revoked: SSI 2013/174 Sch.1
Reg.48, revoked: SSI 2013/174 Sch.1
Reg.49, revoked: SSI 2013/174 Sch.1
Reg.50, revoked: SSI 2013/174 Sch.1
Reg.51, revoked: SSI 2013/174 Sch.1
Reg.52, revoked: SSI 2013/174 Sch.1
Reg.53, revoked: SSI 2013/174 Sch.1
Reg.54, revoked: SSI 2013/174 Sch.1
Reg.55, revoked: SSI 2013/174 Sch.1
Reg.56, revoked: SSI 2013/174 Sch.1
Reg.57, revoked: SSI 2013/174 Sch.1
Reg.58, revoked: SSI 2013/174 Sch.1
Reg.59, revoked: SSI 2013/174 Sch.1
Reg.60, revoked: SSI 2013/174 Sch.1
Reg.61, revoked: SSI 2013/174 Sch.1
Reg.62, revoked: SSI 2013/174 Sch.1
Reg.63, revoked: SSI 2013/174 Sch.1
Reg.64, revoked: SSI 2013/174 Sch.1
Reg.65, revoked: SSI 2013/174 Sch.1
Reg.66, revoked: SSI 2013/174 Sch.1
Reg.67, revoked: SSI 2013/174 Sch.1
Reg.68, revoked: SSI 2013/174 Sch.1
Reg.69, revoked: SSI 2013/174 Sch.1
Reg.70, revoked: SSI 2013/174 Sch.1
Reg.71, revoked: SSI 2013/174 Sch.1
Reg.72, revoked: SSI 2013/174 Sch.1
Reg.73, revoked: SSI 2013/174 Sch.1
Reg.74, revoked: SSI 2013/174 Sch.1
Reg.75, revoked: SSI 2013/174 Sch.1
Reg.76, revoked: SSI 2013/174 Sch.1
Reg.77, revoked: SSI 2013/174 Sch.1
Reg.78, revoked: SSI 2013/174 Sch.1
Reg.79, revoked: SSI 2013/174 Sch.1
Reg.80, revoked: SSI 2013/174 Sch.1
Reg.81, revoked: SSI 2013/174 Sch.1
Reg.82, revoked: SSI 2013/174 Sch.1
Reg.83, revoked: SSI 2013/174 Sch.1
Reg.84, revoked: SSI 2013/174 Sch.1
Reg.85, revoked: SSI 2013/174 Sch.1
Reg.86, revoked: SSI 2013/174 Sch.1

210. Looked After Children (Scotland) Regulations 2009

applied: SI 2013/3029 Sch.1 para.19, Sch.6 para.21, SI 2013/3035 Sch.1
Reg.2, amended: SSI 2013/147 Sch.1 para.11
Reg.3, applied: SSI 2013/194 r.80
Reg.4, applied: SSI 2013/194 r.80
Reg.5, amended: SSI 2013/147 Sch.1 para.11
Reg.6, amended: SSI 2013/14 Reg.2
Reg.7, amended: SSI 2013/147 Sch.1 para.11
Reg.8, amended: SSI 2013/147 Sch.1 para.11
Reg.10, amended: SSI 2013/147 Sch.1 para.11
Reg.11, amended: SSI 2013/147 Sch.1 para.11
Reg.13, amended: SSI 2013/147 Sch.1 para.11
Reg.17, applied: SSI 2013/50 Sch.3 para.5
Reg.19, applied: SSI 2013/50 Sch.3 para.5
Reg.21, amended: SSI 2013/147 Sch.1 para.11
Reg.27, amended: SSI 2013/147 Sch.1 para.11
Reg.29, amended: SSI 2013/147 Sch.1 para.11
Reg.33, amended: SSI 2013/147 Sch.1 para.11
Reg.33, applied: SI 2013/379 Reg.37, SI 2013/3029 Sch.9 para.31, SI 2013/3035 Sch.1
Reg.34, amended: SSI 2013/147 Sch.1 para.11
Reg.36, amended: SSI 2013/147 Sch.1 para.11
Reg.40, amended: SSI 2013/147 Sch.1 para.11
Reg.51, applied: SI 2013/379 Reg.37, SI 2013/3029 Sch.9 para.31, SI 2013/3035 Sch.1
Sch.4 para.1, amended: SSI 2013/147 Sch.1 para.11
Sch.4 para.6, amended: SSI 2013/147 Sch.1 para.11

217. Knife Dealers (Licence Conditions) Order 2009

revoked: SSI 2013/22 Art.5

220. Town and Country Planning (Miscellaneous Amendments) (Scotland) Regulations 2009

Reg.4, revoked: SSI 2013/156 Sch.5
Reg.5, revoked: SSI 2013/157 Reg.24
Reg.7, revoked: SSI 2013/155 Sch.9

225. Marketing of Horticultural Produce (Scotland) Regulations 2009

Reg.2, amended: SI 2013/3235 Reg.19

229. Control of Salmonella in Poultry (Breeding, Laying and Broiler Flocks) (Scotland) Order 2009

Art.2, amended: SSI 2013/151 Reg.5
Art.3, amended: SSI 2013/151 Reg.5
Art.8, amended: SSI 2013/151 Reg.5
Art.9, amended: SSI 2013/151 Reg.5
Art.12, amended: SSI 2013/151 Reg.5

230. Zoonoses and Animal By-Products (Fees) (Scotland) Regulations 2009

revoked: SSI 2013/151 Sch.7

241. A9 Trunk Road (Bankfoot) (Prohibition of Specified Turns) Order 2009

Art.4, amended: SSI 2013/119 Sch.2 para.25

242. Health Boards (Membership and Elections) (Scotland) Act 2009 (Commencement No 1) Order 2009

revoked: SSI 2013/364 Art.2

245. Proceeds of Crime Act 2002 (Investigations Code of Practice) (Scotland) Order 2009

applied: SI 2013/2605 Art.69

263. Feed (Hygiene and Enforcement) (Scotland) Amendment Regulations 2009

Reg.2, revoked (in part): SSI 2013/340 Reg.4

284. Act of Sederunt (Sheriff Court Rules Amendment) (Adoption and Children (Scotland) Act 2007) 2009

Sch.1, added: SSI 2013/139 r.3, r.4

Sch.1, amended: SSI 2013/139 r.3, r.4, r.5, Sch.1, SSI 2013/172 Art.6
Sch.1, revoked: SSI 2013/139 r.3, r.4
Sch.1, substituted: SSI 2013/139 r.3, r.4, SSI 2013/172 Art.6

292. Act of Sederunt (Commissary Business) (Amendment) 2009
revoked: SSI 2013/291 Sch.5

302. Health Boards (Membership) (Scotland) Regulations 2009
revoked: SSI 2013/334 Reg.4
Sch.1 para.1, varied: SSI 2013/334 Reg.5

312. Legal Aid (Supreme Court) (Scotland) Regulations 2009
Reg.7, revoked: SSI 2013/150 Art.27

331. Justice of the Peace Courts (Sheriffdom of North Strathclyde) etc Order 2009
Sch.1, amended: SSI 2013/153 Art.18

332. Justice of the Peace Courts (Sheriffdom of South Strathclyde, Dumfries and Galloway) etc Order 2009
Sch.1, amended: SSI 2013/153 Art.20, Art.21, Art.22, Art.23

334. Judiciary and Courts (Scotland) Act 2008 (Consequential Modifications) Order 2009
Art.4, revoked: SSI 2013/50 Sch.5

349. Regulation of Care (Fitness of Employees in Relation to Care Services) (Scotland) (No.2) Amendment Regulations 2009
revoked: SSI 2013/227 Reg.8

368. Glasgow City Council Area and North Lanarkshire Council Area (Cardowan by Stepps) Boundaries Amendment Order 2009
applied: SSI 2013/347 Sch.2

372. Police (Scotland) Amendment Regulations 2009
revoked: SSI 2013/43 Sch.3 para.9
Reg.2, revoked: SSI 2013/39 Sch.1
Reg.4, revoked: SSI 2013/35 Sch.3 para.20

388. Public Health etc (Scotland) Act 2008 (Sunbed) Regulations 2009
Reg.2, substituted: SSI 2013/201 Reg.2

392. Home Energy Assistance Scheme (Scotland) Amendment Regulations 2009
revoked: SSI 2013/148 Reg.9

416. Zoonoses and Animal By-Products (Fees) (Scotland) Amendment Regulations 2009
revoked: SSI 2013/151 Sch.7

429. Adoption and Children (Scotland) Act 2007 (Modification of Subordinate Legislation) Order 2009
Sch.1 para.5, revoked: SSI 2013/50 Sch.5

435. Food Enzymes (Scotland) Regulations 2009
Reg.3, revoked: SSI 2013/266 Sch.5
Reg.4, revoked: SSI 2013/266 Sch.5
Reg.5, revoked: SSI 2013/266 Sch.5
Reg.6, revoked: SSI 2013/266 Sch.5
Reg.9, revoked: SSI 2013/305 Reg.19

436. Food Additives (Scotland) Regulations 2009
Reg.3, revoked: SSI 2013/266 Sch.5
Reg.4, revoked: SSI 2013/266 Sch.5
Reg.5, revoked: SSI 2013/266 Sch.5
Reg.6, revoked: SSI 2013/266 Sch.5
Reg.7, revoked: SSI 2013/266 Sch.5
Reg.8, revoked: SSI 2013/266 Sch.5
Reg.9, revoked: SSI 2013/266 Sch.5
Reg.10, revoked: SSI 2013/266 Sch.5
Reg.11, revoked: SSI 2013/266 Sch.5
Reg.12, revoked: SSI 2013/266 Sch.5
Reg.13, revoked: SSI 2013/266 Sch.5
Reg.14, revoked: SSI 2013/266 Sch.5
Reg.15, revoked: SSI 2013/266 Sch.5
Reg.16, revoked: SSI 2013/266 Sch.5
Reg.17, revoked: SSI 2013/266 Sch.5
Reg.20, revoked: SSI 2013/266 Sch.5
Sch.1, revoked: SSI 2013/266 Sch.5

442. Angus Council Area and Dundee City Council Area (Fithiebank) Boundaries Amendment Order 2009
applied: SSI 2013/347 Sch.2

446. Official Feed and Food Controls (Scotland) Regulations 2009
Reg.2, amended: SSI 2013/333 Reg.4, SSI 2013/336 Reg.3
Reg.38, amended: SSI 2013/84 Reg.11
Reg.41, amended: SSI 2013/333 Reg.4
Sch.1, amended: SSI 2013/336 Reg.3

2010

21. Adoption and Children (Scotland) Act 2007 (Modification of Enactments) Order 2010
Sch.1 para.5, revoked: SSI 2013/147 Sch.1 para.12

22. National Health Service (Superannuation Scheme, Pension Scheme, Injury Benefits and Additional Voluntary Contributions) (Scotland) Amendment Regulations 2010
Reg.11, revoked: SSI 2013/174 Sch.1
Reg.12, revoked: SSI 2013/174 Sch.1
Reg.13, revoked: SSI 2013/174 Sch.1
Reg.14, revoked: SSI 2013/174 Sch.1
Reg.15, revoked: SSI 2013/174 Sch.1
Reg.16, revoked: SSI 2013/174 Sch.1
Reg.17, revoked: SSI 2013/174 Sch.1
Reg.18, revoked: SSI 2013/174 Sch.1
Reg.19, revoked: SSI 2013/174 Sch.1
Reg.20, revoked: SSI 2013/174 Sch.1
Reg.21, revoked: SSI 2013/174 Sch.1
Reg.22, revoked: SSI 2013/174 Sch.1
Reg.23, revoked: SSI 2013/174 Sch.1

Reg.24, revoked: SSI 2013/174 Sch.1
Reg.25, revoked: SSI 2013/174 Sch.1
Reg.26, revoked: SSI 2013/174 Sch.1
Reg.27, revoked: SSI 2013/174 Sch.1
Reg.28, revoked: SSI 2013/174 Sch.1
Reg.29, revoked: SSI 2013/174 Sch.1
Reg.30, revoked: SSI 2013/174 Sch.1
Reg.31, revoked: SSI 2013/174 Sch.1
Reg.32, revoked: SSI 2013/174 Sch.1
Reg.33, revoked: SSI 2013/174 Sch.1
Reg.34, revoked: SSI 2013/174 Sch.1
Reg.35, revoked: SSI 2013/174 Sch.1
Reg.36, revoked: SSI 2013/174 Sch.1
Reg.37, revoked: SSI 2013/174 Sch.1
Reg.38, revoked: SSI 2013/174 Sch.1
Reg.39, revoked: SSI 2013/174 Sch.1
Reg.40, revoked: SSI 2013/174 Sch.1
Reg.41, revoked: SSI 2013/174 Sch.1
Reg.42, revoked: SSI 2013/174 Sch.1
Reg.43, revoked: SSI 2013/174 Sch.1
Reg.44, revoked: SSI 2013/174 Sch.1
Reg.45, revoked: SSI 2013/174 Sch.1
Reg.46, revoked: SSI 2013/174 Sch.1
Reg.47, revoked: SSI 2013/174 Sch.1
Reg.48, revoked: SSI 2013/174 Sch.1
Reg.49, revoked: SSI 2013/174 Sch.1
Reg.50, revoked: SSI 2013/174 Sch.1
Reg.51, revoked: SSI 2013/174 Sch.1
Reg.52, revoked: SSI 2013/174 Sch.1
Reg.53, revoked: SSI 2013/174 Sch.1
Reg.54, revoked: SSI 2013/174 Sch.1
Reg.55, revoked: SSI 2013/174 Sch.1
Reg.56, revoked: SSI 2013/174 Sch.1
Reg.57, revoked: SSI 2013/174 Sch.1
Reg.58, revoked: SSI 2013/174 Sch.1
Reg.59, revoked: SSI 2013/174 Sch.1
Reg.60, revoked: SSI 2013/174 Sch.1
Reg.61, revoked: SSI 2013/174 Sch.1
Reg.62, revoked: SSI 2013/174 Sch.1
Reg.63, revoked: SSI 2013/174 Sch.1
Reg.64, revoked: SSI 2013/174 Sch.1
Reg.65, revoked: SSI 2013/174 Sch.1
Reg.66, revoked: SSI 2013/174 Sch.1
Reg.67, revoked: SSI 2013/174 Sch.1
Reg.68, revoked: SSI 2013/174 Sch.1
Reg.69, revoked: SSI 2013/174 Sch.1
Reg.70, revoked: SSI 2013/174 Sch.1
Reg.71, revoked: SSI 2013/174 Sch.1
Reg.72, revoked: SSI 2013/174 Sch.1
Reg.73, revoked: SSI 2013/174 Sch.1
Reg.74, revoked: SSI 2013/174 Sch.1
Reg.75, revoked: SSI 2013/174 Sch.1
Reg.76, revoked: SSI 2013/174 Sch.1
Reg.77, revoked: SSI 2013/174 Sch.1
Reg.78, revoked: SSI 2013/174 Sch.1
Reg.79, revoked: SSI 2013/174 Sch.1
Reg.80, revoked: SSI 2013/174 Sch.1
Reg.81, revoked: SSI 2013/174 Sch.1
Reg.82, revoked: SSI 2013/174 Sch.1
Reg.83, revoked: SSI 2013/174 Sch.1
Reg.84, revoked: SSI 2013/174 Sch.1
Reg.85, revoked: SSI 2013/174 Sch.1
Reg.86, revoked: SSI 2013/174 Sch.1
Reg.87, revoked: SSI 2013/174 Sch.1
Reg.88, revoked: SSI 2013/174 Sch.1
Reg.89, revoked: SSI 2013/174 Sch.1
Reg.90, revoked: SSI 2013/174 Sch.1
Reg.91, revoked: SSI 2013/174 Sch.1
Reg.92, revoked: SSI 2013/174 Sch.1
Reg.93, revoked: SSI 2013/174 Sch.1
Reg.94, revoked: SSI 2013/174 Sch.1
Reg.95, revoked: SSI 2013/174 Sch.1
Reg.96, revoked: SSI 2013/174 Sch.1
Reg.97, revoked: SSI 2013/174 Sch.1
Reg.98, revoked: SSI 2013/174 Sch.1
Reg.99, revoked: SSI 2013/174 Sch.1
Reg.100, revoked: SSI 2013/174 Sch.1
Reg.101, revoked: SSI 2013/174 Sch.1
Reg.102, revoked: SSI 2013/174 Sch.1
Reg.103, revoked: SSI 2013/174 Sch.1

60. Management of Extractive Waste (Scotland) Regulations 2010

Reg.3, revoked (in part): SSI 2013/155 Sch.9

77. Tobacco and Primary Medical Services (Scotland) Act 2010 (Ancillary Provisions) Order 2010

revoked: SSI 2013/106 Art.4

88. Zoonoses and Animal By-Products (Fees) (Scotland) Amendment Regulations 2010

revoked: SSI 2013/151 Sch.7

90. Fish Labelling (Scotland) Regulations 2010

revoked: SSI 2013/256 Reg.8

98. Road Traffic (Parking Adjudicators) (Renfrewshire Council) Regulations 2010

Reg.9, revoked (in part): SI 2013/2042 Sch.1 para.82

110. Home Energy Assistance Scheme (Scotland) Amendment Regulations 2010

revoked: SSI 2013/148 Reg.9

152. Additional Support Needs Tribunals for Scotland (Practice and Procedure) Amendment Rules 2010

r.15, revoked: SI 2013/2042 Sch.1 para.84

164. Parole Board (Scotland) Amendment Rules 2010

r.2, revoked (in part): SI 2013/2042 Sch.1 para.85

168. Police Act 1997 (Criminal Records) (Scotland) Regulations 2010

Reg.5, amended: SSI 2013/119 Sch.1 para.34
Reg.7, revoked (in part): SI 2013/2318 Sch.1 para.115, SSI 2013/119 Sch.1 para.34

Reg.8, amended: SI 2013/2318 Sch.1 para.116
Reg.8, revoked (in part): SI 2013/2318 Sch.1 para.116, SSI 2013/119 Sch.1 para.34
Reg.16, amended: SI 2013/2318 Sch.1 para.117
Reg.16, revoked (in part): SSI 2013/119 Sch.1 para.34

177. Transmissible Spongiform Encephalopathies (Scotland) Regulations 2010
Reg.2, amended: SSI 2013/307 Sch.2 para.20
Sch.1, amended: SSI 2013/307 Sch.2 para.21
Sch.6 Part 1 para.3, amended: SSI 2013/307 Sch.2 para.22
Sch.6 Part 2 para.18, amended: SSI 2013/307 Sch.2 para.22
Sch.9 para.1, revoked: SSI 2013/307 Sch.3
Sch.9 para.2, revoked: SSI 2013/307 Sch.3

199. Sports Grounds and Sporting Events (Designation) (Scotland) Order 2010
Sch.1 Part 1, amended: SSI 2013/4 Art.2
Sch.2 Part I para.1, substituted: SSI 2013/229 Art.2
Sch.2 Part I para.2, substituted: SSI 2013/229 Art.2
Sch.2 Part I para.7, revoked: SSI 2013/4 Art.2
Sch.2 Part II, amended: SSI 2013/229 Art.2

208. National Health Service (General Dental Services) (Scotland) Regulations 2010
Reg.2, amended: SI 2013/235 Sch.2 para.157

213. Parental Responsibility and Measures for the Protection of Children (International Obligations) (Scotland) Regulations 2010
Reg.2, amended: SSI 2013/147 Sch.1 para.13
Reg.5, amended: SSI 2013/147 Sch.1 para.13
Reg.10, amended: SSI 2013/147 Sch.1 para.13
Reg.12, amended: SSI 2013/147 Sch.1 para.13

214. Knives etc (Disposal of Forfeited Property) (Scotland) Order 2010
Art.2, amended: SSI 2013/119 Sch.1 para.35
Art.4, amended: SSI 2013/119 Sch.1 para.35

226. National Health Service (Discipline Committees) (Scotland) Amendment Regulations 2010
Reg.2, revoked (in part): SI 2013/2042 Sch.1 para.86

227. National Health Service (Tribunal) (Scotland) Amendment Regulations 2010
Reg.2, revoked (in part): SI 2013/2042 Sch.1 para.87

232. Police Pension Account (Scotland) Regulations 2010
revoked: SSI 2013/184 Reg.24

233. Local Government Pension Scheme (Management and Investment of Funds) (Scotland) Regulations 2010
Reg.3, amended: SI 2013/472 Art.4, Sch.2 para.183
Reg.6, amended: SI 2013/472 Art.4
Reg.7, amended: SI 2013/472 Art.4
Sch.1 Part 3 para.17, amended: SI 2013/472 Art.4

243. Rehabilitation of Offenders Act 1974 (Exclusions and Exceptions) (Scotland) Amendment Order 2010
revoked: SSI 2013/50 Sch.5

273. Less Favoured Area Support Scheme (Scotland) Regulations 2010
Reg.2, amended: SSI 2013/9 Reg.3
Reg.4, substituted: SSI 2013/9 Reg.4
Reg.15, amended: SSI 2013/9 Reg.5
Sch.7 para.5, amended: SSI 2013/9 Reg.6
Sch.7 para.6, amended: SSI 2013/9 Reg.6
Sch.7 para.8, amended: SSI 2013/9 Reg.6

280. Town and Country Planning (Fees for Applications and Deemed Applications) (Scotland) Amendment (No.2) Regulations 2010
Reg.3, applied: SSI 2013/105 Reg.3

329. Contaminants in Food (Scotland) Regulations 2010
applied: SSI 2013/84 Sch.1
revoked: SSI 2013/217 Sch.1
Reg.6, revoked: SSI 2013/84 Sch.4

330. Beef and Pig Carcase Classification (Scotland) Regulations 2010
Reg.2, amended: SI 2013/3235 Reg.20
Sch.1 Part 1, amended: SI 2013/3235 Reg.20
Sch.2, amended: SI 2013/3235 Reg.20

345. Tobacco and Primary Medical Services (Scotland) Act 2010 (Commencement No 1, Consequential and Saving Provisions) Order 2010
Art.3, revoked: SSI 2013/106 Art.4
Art.4, revoked: SSI 2013/106 Art.4

350. Regulation of Investigatory Powers (Prescription of Offices, etc and Specification of Public Authorities) (Scotland) Order 2010
Sch.1, amended: SSI 2013/119 Sch.1 para.36

353. East Dunbartonshire Council Area and Glasgow City Council Area (Princes Gate and Greenacres by Robroyston) Boundaries Alteration Order 2010
applied: SSI 2013/347 Sch.2

369. National Health Service (Superannuation Scheme, Pension Scheme, Injury Benefits and Additional Voluntary Contributions) (Scotland) Amendment (No.2) Regulations 2010
Reg.22, revoked: SSI 2013/174 Sch.1
Reg.23, revoked: SSI 2013/174 Sch.1
Reg.24, revoked: SSI 2013/174 Sch.1
Reg.25, revoked: SSI 2013/174 Sch.1
Reg.26, revoked: SSI 2013/174 Sch.1
Reg.27, revoked: SSI 2013/174 Sch.1
Reg.28, revoked: SSI 2013/174 Sch.1

Reg.29, revoked: SSI 2013/174 Sch.1
Reg.30, revoked: SSI 2013/174 Sch.1
Reg.31, revoked: SSI 2013/174 Sch.1
Reg.32, revoked: SSI 2013/174 Sch.1
Reg.33, revoked: SSI 2013/174 Sch.1
Reg.34, revoked: SSI 2013/174 Sch.1
Reg.35, revoked: SSI 2013/174 Sch.1
Reg.36, revoked: SSI 2013/174 Sch.1
Reg.37, revoked: SSI 2013/174 Sch.1
Reg.38, revoked: SSI 2013/174 Sch.1
Reg.39, revoked: SSI 2013/174 Sch.1
Reg.40, revoked: SSI 2013/174 Sch.1
Reg.41, revoked: SSI 2013/174 Sch.1
Reg.42, revoked: SSI 2013/174 Sch.1
Reg.43, revoked: SSI 2013/174 Sch.1
Reg.44, revoked: SSI 2013/174 Sch.1
Reg.45, revoked: SSI 2013/174 Sch.1
Reg.46, revoked: SSI 2013/174 Sch.1
Reg.47, revoked: SSI 2013/174 Sch.1
Reg.48, revoked: SSI 2013/174 Sch.1
Reg.49, revoked: SSI 2013/174 Sch.1
Reg.50, revoked: SSI 2013/174 Sch.1
Reg.51, revoked: SSI 2013/174 Sch.1
Reg.52, revoked: SSI 2013/174 Sch.1
Reg.53, revoked: SSI 2013/174 Sch.1
Reg.54, revoked: SSI 2013/174 Sch.1
Reg.55, revoked: SSI 2013/174 Sch.1
Reg.56, revoked: SSI 2013/174 Sch.1
Reg.57, revoked: SSI 2013/174 Sch.1
Reg.58, revoked: SSI 2013/174 Sch.1
Reg.59, revoked: SSI 2013/174 Sch.1
Reg.60, revoked: SSI 2013/174 Sch.1
Reg.61, revoked: SSI 2013/174 Sch.1
Reg.62, revoked: SSI 2013/174 Sch.1
Reg.63, revoked: SSI 2013/174 Sch.1
Reg.64, revoked: SSI 2013/174 Sch.1
Reg.65, revoked: SSI 2013/174 Sch.1
Reg.66, revoked: SSI 2013/174 Sch.1
Reg.67, revoked: SSI 2013/174 Sch.1
Reg.68, revoked: SSI 2013/174 Sch.1
Reg.69, revoked: SSI 2013/174 Sch.1
Reg.70, revoked: SSI 2013/174 Sch.1
Reg.71, revoked: SSI 2013/174 Sch.1
Reg.72, revoked: SSI 2013/174 Sch.1
Reg.73, revoked: SSI 2013/174 Sch.1
Reg.74, revoked: SSI 2013/174 Sch.1
Reg.75, revoked: SSI 2013/174 Sch.1
Reg.76, revoked: SSI 2013/174 Sch.1

373. Animal Feed (Scotland) Regulations 2010

Reg.2, amended: SSI 2013/340 Reg.3
Reg.4, amended: SSI 2013/340 Reg.3
Sch.1, substituted: SSI 2013/340 Sch.2

383. Police Act 1997 (Criminal Records) (Registration) (Scotland) Regulations 2010

Reg.7, revoked (in part): SSI 2013/119 Sch.1 para.37

398. Protected Trust Deeds (Scotland) Amendment Regulations 2010

revoked: SSI 2013/318 Reg.30

402. Beef and Veal Labelling (Scotland) Regulations 2010

Reg.2, amended: SI 2013/3235 Reg.21
Reg.3, amended: SI 2013/3235 Reg.21
Reg.4, amended: SI 2013/3235 Reg.21

406. Sale of Tobacco (Prescribed Document) Regulations 2010

revoked: SSI 2013/202 Reg.3

419. Sheep Scab (Scotland) Order 2010

Art.2, amended: SSI 2013/173 Art.26
Art.4, amended: SSI 2013/173 Art.26
Art.5, amended: SSI 2013/173 Art.26
Art.6, amended: SSI 2013/173 Art.26

432. Town and Country Planning (Modification and Discharge of Planning Obligations) (Scotland) Regulations 2010

Reg.5, applied: SSI 2013/156 Reg.29
Reg.7, referred to: SSI 2013/156 Reg.21
Reg.9, revoked: SSI 2013/156 Sch.5

433. Town and Country Planning (Modification and Discharge of Good Neighbour Agreement) (Scotland) Regulations 2010

Reg.5, applied: SSI 2013/156 Reg.29
Reg.7, applied: SSI 2013/156 Reg.22
Reg.9, revoked: SSI 2013/156 Sch.5

439. Flavourings in Food (Scotland) Regulations 2010

Reg.3, revoked: SSI 2013/266 Sch.5
Reg.4, revoked: SSI 2013/266 Sch.5
Reg.5, revoked: SSI 2013/266 Sch.5
Reg.6, revoked: SSI 2013/266 Sch.5
Reg.8, revoked: SSI 2013/266 Sch.5

443. Regulation of Care (Fitness of Employees in Relation to Care Services) (Scotland) (No.2) Amendment Regulations 2010

revoked: SSI 2013/227 Reg.8

446. Protection of Vulnerable Groups (Scotland) Act 2007 (Miscellaneous Provisions) Order 2010

Art.16, amended: SI 2013/2318 Sch.1 para.122
Art.16, revoked (in part): SI 2013/2318 Sch.1 para.122
Art.17, amended: SI 2013/2318 Sch.1 para.123
Art.17, revoked (in part): SI 2013/2318 Sch.1 para.123

460. National Scenic Areas (Consequential Modifications) (Scotland) Order 2010

Art.4, revoked: SSI 2013/264 Sch.1
Art.13, revoked: SSI 2013/155 Sch.9

2476. Scottish Parliament (Disqualification) Order 2010

Sch.1, amended: SSI 2013/119 Sch.1 para.38

2011

3. Restriction of Liberty Order and Restricted Movement Requirement (Scotland) Regulations 2011
revoked: SSI 2013/6 Reg.1

53. National Health Service (Superannuation Scheme and Pension Scheme) (Scotland) Amendment Regulations 2011
revoked: SSI 2013/174 Sch.1

55. National Health Service (Free Prescriptions and Charges for Drugs and Appliances) (Scotland) Regulations 2011
Reg.3, amended: SSI 2013/191 Reg.2

56. Home Energy Assistance Scheme (Scotland) Amendment Regulations 2011
revoked: SSI 2013/148 Reg.9

61. Scottish Crime and Drug Enforcement Agency (Scotland) Regulations 2011
Reg.11, revoked: SSI 2013/35 Sch.3 para.20
Reg.12, revoked (in part): SSI 2013/35 Sch.3 para.20
Reg.33, revoked: SSI 2013/35 Sch.3 para.20
Sch.2 para.4, revoked: SSI 2013/35 Sch.3 para.20

84. Drinking Milk (Scotland) Regulations 2011
Reg.2, amended: SI 2013/3235 Reg.22
Reg.4, revoked: SI 2013/3235 Reg.22
Reg.6, amended: SI 2013/3235 Reg.22

104. Additional Support Needs Tribunals for Scotland (Disability Claims Procedure) Rules 2011
Part 5 r.28, revoked (in part): SI 2013/2042 Sch.1 para.93

107. Individual Learning Account (Scotland) Regulations 2011
referred to: SSI 2013/75 Reg.3
Reg.3, amended: SSI 2013/75 Reg.2, SSI 2013/137 Reg.21
Reg.4, amended: SSI 2013/75 Reg.2
Reg.12, amended: SSI 2013/75 Reg.2

117. National Health Service Superannuation Scheme (Scotland) Regulations 2011
applied: SSI 2013/174 Reg.1, Reg.3, Reg.5
referred to: SSI 2013/174 Reg.1, Reg.2
Part A regA.2, amended: SSI 2013/109 Reg.3
Part B regB.1, amended: SSI 2013/109 Reg.4
Part B regB.2, amended: SSI 2013/109 Reg.5
Part B regB.2, applied: SSI 2013/174 Reg.1, Reg.3
Part B regB.2, referred to: SSI 2013/174 Reg.1
Part B regB.4, amended: SSI 2013/109 Reg.6
Part B regB.4, applied: SSI 2013/174 Reg.1
Part B regB.4, revoked (in part): SSI 2013/109 Reg.6
Part B regB.5, amended: SSI 2013/109 Reg.7
Part B regB.6, amended: SSI 2013/109 Reg.8
Part E, applied: SSI 2013/174 Reg.2
Part E regE.1, applied: SSI 2013/174 Reg.2
Part E regE.11, applied: SSI 2013/174 Reg.2, Reg.18, Reg.19
Part E regE.12, applied: SSI 2013/174 Reg.19
Part E regE.12, referred to: SSI 2013/174 Reg.9
Part E regE.2, applied: SSI 2013/174 Reg.1, Reg.2
Part E regE.3, applied: SSI 2013/174 Reg.2, Reg.3, Reg.11, Reg.12, Reg.14, Reg.16, Reg.17, Reg.18, Reg.19, Reg.21, Reg.22, Reg.23, Reg.24
Part E regE.3, referred to: SSI 2013/174 Reg.18, Reg.19
Part E regE.4, applied: SSI 2013/174 Reg.2, Reg.3, Reg.14, Reg.16, Reg.21, Reg.22
Part E regE.6, applied: SSI 2013/174 Reg.1, Reg.2
Part E regE.7, amended: SSI 2013/109 Reg.11
Part E regE.7, applied: SSI 2013/174 Reg.1, Reg.2
Part F regF.1, applied: SSI 2013/174 Reg.2, Reg.19, Reg.20
Part F regF.2, applied: SSI 2013/174 Reg.2, Reg.19, Reg.20
Part F regF.3, applied: SSI 2013/174 Reg.2, Reg.19, Reg.20
Part F regF.4, applied: SSI 2013/174 Reg.2, Reg.19, Reg.20
Part F regF.5, applied: SSI 2013/174 Reg.2, Reg.19, Reg.20
Part H regH.4, amended: SSI 2013/109 Reg.14
Part K regK.6, amended: SSI 2013/109 Reg.15
Part N regN.1, amended: SSI 2013/109 Reg.16
Part N regN.1, applied: SSI 2013/174 Reg.11, Reg.13
Part N regN.5, amended: SSI 2013/109 Reg.17
Part P regP.2, applied: SSI 2013/174 Reg.18, Reg.19
Part Q regQ.1, applied: SSI 2013/174 Reg.5, Reg.6, Reg.16, Reg.18
Part Q regQ.10, applied: SSI 2013/174 Reg.4
Part Q regQ.11, applied: SSI 2013/174 Reg.4
Part Q regQ.13, amended: SSI 2013/109 Reg.18
Part Q regQ.13, applied: SSI 2013/174 Reg.4
Part Q regQ.14, applied: SSI 2013/174 Reg.4
Part Q regQ.15, amended: SSI 2013/109 Reg.19
Part Q regQ.2, applied: SSI 2013/174 Reg.6
Part Q regQ.5, applied: SSI 2013/174 Reg.16, Reg.18
Part Q regQ.7, applied: SSI 2013/174 Reg.5, Reg.16, Reg.18
Part Q regQ.8, applied: SSI 2013/174 Reg.4
Part Q regQ.8, referred to: SSI 2013/174 Reg.4
Part r regR.3, applied: SSI 2013/174 Reg.3
Part r regR.4, applied: SSI 2013/174 Reg.1

Part r regR.8, referred to: SSI 2013/174 Reg.9
Part T regT.1A, added: SSI 2013/109 Reg.22
Part U regU.3, amended: SSI 2013/109 Reg.23
Part U regU.3, revoked (in part): SSI 2013/109 Reg.23
Part U regU.4, revoked: SSI 2013/109 Reg.24
Part L regL.1, applied: SSI 2013/174 Reg.7
Part C regC.1, applied: SSI 2013/174 Reg.7, Reg.9
Part C regC.2, applied: SSI 2013/174 Reg.3, Reg.5
Part C regC.3, applied: SSI 2013/174 Reg.2, Reg.5, Reg.6
Part C regC.4, applied: SSI 2013/174 Reg.3
Part D regD.1, amended: SSI 2013/70 Reg.3, SSI 2013/109 Reg.9, SSI 2013/168 Reg.3
Part D regD.1, applied: SSI 2013/174 Reg.1, Reg.2, Reg.6
Part D regD.2, amended: SSI 2013/109 Reg.10
Part M, applied: SSI 2013/174 Reg.1
Part M regM.2, applied: SSI 2013/174 Reg.1
Part M regM.7, applied: SSI 2013/174 Reg.17
Reg.G6, amended: SSI 2013/109 Reg.12
Reg.G14, amended: SSI 2013/109 Reg.13
Reg.G14, applied: SSI 2013/174 Reg.2, Reg.19, Reg.20
s.1, amended: SSI 2013/109 Reg.20
s.2, amended: SSI 2013/109 Reg.21
s.2, revoked (in part): SSI 2013/109 Reg.21
Sch.1 Part III para.11, applied: SSI 2013/174 Reg.7
Sch.1 Part IV para.14, amended: SSI 2013/70 Reg.4, SSI 2013/109 Reg.25, SSI 2013/168 Reg.4
Sch.1 Part XII para.31, applied: SSI 2013/174 Reg.3

124. National Assistance (Assessment of Resources) Amendment (Scotland) Regulations 2011
revoked: SSI 2013/41 Reg.5

131. Tobacco and Primary Medical Services (Scotland) Act 2010 (Commencement No 1, Consequential and Saving Provisions) Amendment Order 2011
revoked: SSI 2013/106 Art.4

138. Town and Country Planning (Miscellaneous Amendments) (Scotland) Regulations 2011
Reg.2, revoked: SSI 2013/155 Sch.9
Reg.3, revoked: SSI 2013/156 Sch.5
Reg.4, revoked: SSI 2013/157 Reg.24
Reg.6, revoked: SSI 2013/156 Sch.5
Reg.7, revoked: SSI 2013/156 Sch.5

139. Town and Country Planning (Environmental Impact Assessment) (Scotland) Regulations 2011
Reg.2, amended: SSI 2013/177 Sch.1 para.21
Reg.5, applied: SSI 2013/155 Sch.2 para.4
Reg.9, applied: SSI 2013/155 Sch.2 para.3
Reg.30, applied: SSI 2013/155 Sch.2 para.4
Reg.31, applied: SSI 2013/155 Sch.2 para.4
Reg.32, applied: SSI 2013/155 Sch.2 para.4
Reg.33, applied: SSI 2013/155 Sch.2 para.4
Reg.45, applied: SSI 2013/155 Sch.2 para.4
Reg.48, revoked: SSI 2013/155 Sch.9

141. Debt Arrangement Scheme (Scotland) Regulations 2011
Reg.2, amended: SSI 2013/225 Reg.6, Reg.16
Reg.3, amended: SSI 2013/225 Reg.6
Reg.4A, added: SSI 2013/225 Reg.5
Reg.9, amended: SSI 2013/225 Reg.7
Reg.12, amended: SSI 2013/225 Reg.6, Reg.16
Reg.16, amended: SSI 2013/225 Reg.8
Reg.17, amended: SSI 2013/225 Reg.8
Reg.18, amended: SSI 2013/225 Reg.19
Reg.19, amended: SSI 2013/225 Reg.9
Reg.20, applied: SSI 2013/225 Reg.20
Reg.22, amended: SSI 2013/225 Reg.10
Reg.23, amended: SSI 2013/225 Reg.11
Reg.23A, added: SSI 2013/225 Reg.11
Reg.27, amended: SSI 2013/225 Reg.12
Reg.30, amended: SSI 2013/225 Reg.16
Reg.36A, added: SSI 2013/225 Reg.13
Reg.37, amended: SSI 2013/225 Reg.13, Reg.18
Reg.39, amended: SSI 2013/225 Reg.13
Reg.40, amended: SSI 2013/225 Reg.14
Reg.40A, added: SSI 2013/225 Reg.14
Reg.42, amended: SSI 2013/225 Reg.14
Reg.44, amended: SSI 2013/225 Reg.14
Reg.44A, added: SSI 2013/225 Reg.14
Reg.46, amended: SSI 2013/225 Reg.19
Reg.46A, added: SSI 2013/225 Reg.15
Reg.46B, added: SSI 2013/225 Reg.15
Reg.46C, added: SSI 2013/225 Reg.15
Reg.46D, added: SSI 2013/225 Reg.15
Reg.47, substituted: SSI 2013/225 Reg.17
Reg.47A, substituted: SSI 2013/225 Reg.17
Reg.47B, substituted: SSI 2013/225 Reg.17
Sch.1, amended: SSI 2013/225 Sch.1
Sch.4 para.1, substituted: SI 2013/1881 Sch.1 para.43
Sch.4 para.5, substituted: SI 2013/1881 Sch.1 para.43

145. Town and Country Planning (Marine Fish Farming) (Scotland) Amendment Regulations 2011
revoked: SSI 2013/277 Reg.5

146. Disclosure (Persons engaged in the Investigation and Reporting of Crime or Sudden Deaths) (Scotland) Regulations 2011
Sch.1, amended: SI 2013/2318 Sch.1 para.124, SSI 2013/119 Sch.3 para.8

153. Fruit Juices and Fruit Nectars (Scotland) Amendment Regulations 2011
revoked: SSI 2013/305 Reg.19

161. Advice and Assistance and Legal Aid (Online Applications etc.) (Scotland) Regulations 2011
Reg.5, revoked: SSI 2013/150 Art.27
163. Criminal Legal Assistance (Duty Solicitors) (Scotland) Regulations 2011
Reg.3, amended: 2013 c.22 Sch.21 para.50
Reg.3, applied: 2013 c.22 Sch.21 para.50
Reg.3, disapplied: 2013 c.22 Sch.21 para.50
Reg.3, referred to: 2013 c.22 Sch.21 para.50
171. Animal By-Products (Enforcement) (Scotland) Regulations 2011
revoked: SSI 2013/307 Sch.3
Sch.2 para.48, revoked: SSI 2013/151 Sch.7
Sch.2 para.49, revoked: SSI 2013/151 Sch.7
Sch.2 para.50, revoked: SSI 2013/151 Sch.7
195. Scottish Statutory Instruments Regulations 2011
Reg.7, amended: SSI 2013/169 Art.4
Reg.11, amended: SSI 2013/169 Art.4
197. Retention of Samples etc (Children's Hearings) (Scotland) Order 2011
Art.3, amended: SSI 2013/147 Sch.1 para.14
209. Water Environment (Controlled Activities) (Scotland) Regulations 2011
applied: 2013 asp 5 s.7, s.21, s.38, s.50, Sch.1 para.2, Sch.1 para.3, Sch.1 para.7
referred to: 2013 asp 5 s.21, s.50
Reg.2, amended: SSI 2013/323 Reg.27
Reg.2, referred to: 2013 asp 5 s.21, s.50
Reg.3, amended: SSI 2013/176 Reg.2
Reg.9, revoked: SSI 2013/323 Reg.27
Reg.11, applied: 2013 asp 5 s.50
Reg.13, amended: SSI 2013/176 Reg.2
Reg.24, applied: 2013 asp 5 s.50
Sch.3 Part 1, amended: SSI 2013/176 Sch.1
Sch.3 Part 2, amended: SSI 2013/176 Reg.2
Sch.4 Part 1, amended: SSI 2013/323 Reg.27, SSI 2013/325 Reg.11
Sch.4 Part 2, amended: SSI 2013/323 Reg.27
Sch.8 para.1, amended: SSI 2013/323 Reg.27
Sch.8 para.1, revoked (in part): SSI 2013/323 Reg.27
210. Social Care and Social Work Improvement Scotland (Requirements for Care Services) Regulations 2011
Reg.6, amended: SSI 2013/110 Reg.2
Reg.6, revoked (in part): SSI 2013/110 Reg.2
Reg.6A, added: SSI 2013/110 Reg.2
Reg.6B, added: SSI 2013/110 Reg.2
Reg.6C, added: SSI 2013/110 Reg.2
211. Public Services Reform (Scotland) Act 2010 (Consequential Modifications) Order 2011
Sch.1 Part 2 para.29, revoked: SSI 2013/50 Sch.5
Sch.3 para.1, revoked: SSI 2013/50 Sch.5
215. Public Services Reform (General Teaching Council for Scotland) Order 2011
Sch.2 para.4, amended: SSI 2013/197 Sch.2 para.19
Sch.6 para.6, revoked: SSI 2013/50 Sch.5
217. Advice and Assistance and Civil Legal Aid (Financial Conditions and Contributions) (Scotland) Regulations 2011
Reg.8, amended: 2013 c.22 Sch.21 para.50
Reg.8, applied: 2013 c.22 Sch.21 para.50
228. Waste Management Licensing (Scotland) Regulations 2011
Sch.1 para.23, amended: SSI 2013/307 Sch.2 para.23
237. Scottish Charitable Incorporated Organisations (Removal from Register and Dissolution) Regulations 2011
Reg.2, amended: SSI 2013/362 Reg.2
Reg.8, amended: SSI 2013/362 Reg.2
238. Debt Arrangement Scheme (Interest, Fees, Penalties and Other Charges) (Scotland) Regulations 2011
Reg.2, amended: SSI 2013/225 Reg.3
Reg.4, amended: SSI 2013/225 Reg.3
Reg.5, amended: SSI 2013/225 Reg.3
Reg.5, substituted: SSI 2013/225 Reg.3
306. Extraction Solvents in Food Amendment (Scotland) Regulations 2011
revoked: SSI 2013/266 Sch.5
318. Poultrymeat (Scotland) Regulations 2011
applied: SSI 2013/84 Sch.1
Reg.1, amended: SI 2013/3235 Reg.23
Reg.2, amended: SI 2013/3235 Reg.23
Reg.11, amended: SI 2013/3235 Reg.23
Reg.22, revoked: SSI 2013/84 Sch.4
Sch.1 Part 1, amended: SI 2013/3235 Reg.23
Sch.1 Part 2, amended: SI 2013/3235 Reg.23
331. Prisons and Young Offenders Institutions (Scotland) Rules 2011
Part 8 r.68, amended: SSI 2013/119 Sch.1 para.39
350. Home Energy Assistance Scheme (Scotland) Amendment (No.2) Regulations 2011
revoked: SSI 2013/148 Reg.9
364. National Health Service Superannuation Scheme etc (Miscellaneous Amendments) (Scotland) Regulations 2011
Reg.15, revoked: SSI 2013/174 Sch.1
Reg.16, revoked: SSI 2013/174 Sch.1
Reg.17, revoked: SSI 2013/174 Sch.1
Reg.18, revoked: SSI 2013/174 Sch.1
Reg.19, revoked: SSI 2013/174 Sch.1
Reg.20, revoked: SSI 2013/174 Sch.1
Reg.21, revoked: SSI 2013/174 Sch.1
Reg.22, revoked: SSI 2013/174 Sch.1

Reg.23, revoked: SSI 2013/174 Sch.1
Reg.24, revoked: SSI 2013/174 Sch.1
Reg.25, revoked: SSI 2013/174 Sch.1
Reg.26, revoked: SSI 2013/174 Sch.1
Reg.27, revoked: SSI 2013/174 Sch.1
Reg.28, revoked: SSI 2013/174 Sch.1
Reg.29, revoked: SSI 2013/174 Sch.1
Reg.30, revoked: SSI 2013/174 Sch.1
Reg.31, revoked: SSI 2013/174 Sch.1
Reg.32, revoked: SSI 2013/174 Sch.1
Reg.33, revoked: SSI 2013/174 Sch.1
Reg.34, revoked: SSI 2013/174 Sch.1
Reg.35, revoked: SSI 2013/174 Sch.1
Reg.36, revoked: SSI 2013/174 Sch.1
Reg.37, revoked: SSI 2013/174 Sch.1
Reg.38, revoked: SSI 2013/174 Sch.1
Reg.39, revoked: SSI 2013/174 Sch.1
Reg.40, revoked: SSI 2013/174 Sch.1
Reg.41, revoked: SSI 2013/174 Sch.1
Reg.42, revoked: SSI 2013/174 Sch.1
Reg.43, revoked: SSI 2013/174 Sch.1
Reg.44, revoked: SSI 2013/174 Sch.1
Reg.45, revoked: SSI 2013/174 Sch.1
Reg.46, revoked: SSI 2013/174 Sch.1
Reg.47, revoked: SSI 2013/174 Sch.1
Reg.48, revoked: SSI 2013/174 Sch.1
Reg.49, revoked: SSI 2013/174 Sch.1
Reg.50, revoked: SSI 2013/174 Sch.1
Reg.51, revoked: SSI 2013/174 Sch.1
Reg.52, revoked: SSI 2013/174 Sch.1
Reg.53, revoked: SSI 2013/174 Sch.1
Reg.54, revoked: SSI 2013/174 Sch.1
Reg.55, revoked: SSI 2013/174 Sch.1
Reg.56, revoked: SSI 2013/174 Sch.1
Reg.57, revoked: SSI 2013/174 Sch.1
Reg.58, revoked: SSI 2013/174 Sch.1
Reg.59, revoked: SSI 2013/174 Sch.1
Reg.60, revoked: SSI 2013/174 Sch.1
Reg.61, revoked: SSI 2013/174 Sch.1
Reg.62, revoked: SSI 2013/174 Sch.1
Reg.63, revoked: SSI 2013/174 Sch.1
Reg.64, revoked: SSI 2013/174 Sch.1
Reg.65, revoked: SSI 2013/174 Sch.1
Reg.66, revoked: SSI 2013/174 Sch.1
Reg.67, revoked: SSI 2013/174 Sch.1
Reg.68, revoked: SSI 2013/174 Sch.1
Reg.69, revoked: SSI 2013/174 Sch.1
Reg.70, revoked: SSI 2013/174 Sch.1
Reg.71, revoked: SSI 2013/174 Sch.1
Reg.72, revoked: SSI 2013/174 Sch.1
Reg.73, revoked: SSI 2013/174 Sch.1
Reg.74, revoked: SSI 2013/174 Sch.1
Reg.75, revoked: SSI 2013/174 Sch.1
Reg.76, revoked: SSI 2013/174 Sch.1
Reg.77, revoked: SSI 2013/174 Sch.1
Reg.78, revoked: SSI 2013/174 Sch.1
Reg.79, revoked: SSI 2013/174 Sch.1
Reg.80, revoked: SSI 2013/174 Sch.1
Reg.81, revoked: SSI 2013/174 Sch.1
Reg.82, revoked: SSI 2013/174 Sch.1
Reg.83, revoked: SSI 2013/174 Sch.1
Reg.84, revoked: SSI 2013/174 Sch.1
Reg.85, revoked: SSI 2013/174 Sch.1
Reg.86, revoked: SSI 2013/174 Sch.1
Reg.87, revoked: SSI 2013/174 Sch.1
Reg.88, revoked: SSI 2013/174 Sch.1
Reg.89, revoked: SSI 2013/174 Sch.1
Reg.90, revoked: SSI 2013/174 Sch.1
Reg.91, revoked: SSI 2013/174 Sch.1
Reg.92, revoked: SSI 2013/174 Sch.1
Reg.93, revoked: SSI 2013/174 Sch.1
Reg.94, revoked: SSI 2013/174 Sch.1
Reg.95, revoked: SSI 2013/174 Sch.1
Reg.96, revoked: SSI 2013/174 Sch.1
Reg.97, revoked: SSI 2013/174 Sch.1
Reg.98, revoked: SSI 2013/174 Sch.1
Reg.99, revoked: SSI 2013/174 Sch.1
Reg.100, revoked: SSI 2013/174 Sch.1
Reg.101, revoked: SSI 2013/174 Sch.1
Reg.102, revoked: SSI 2013/174 Sch.1

377. Historic Environment (Amendment) (Scotland) Act 2011 (Saving, Transitional and Consequential Provisions) Order 2011

Art.9, revoked: SSI 2013/155 Sch.9

378. Town and Country Planning (Appeals) (Scotland) Amendment Regulations 2011

revoked: SSI 2013/156 Sch.5

389. Education (Fees) (Scotland) Regulations 2011

Reg.2, amended: SSI 2013/80 Reg.32
Sch.1 para.2, amended: SSI 2013/80 Reg.33
Sch.1 para.10, amended: SSI 2013/80 Reg.33

400. Act of Sederunt (Lands Valuation Appeal Court) 2011

revoked: SSI 2013/161 Art.2

405. Administrative Justice and Tribunals Council (Listed Tribunals) (Scotland) Amendment Order 2011

revoked: SI 2013/2042 Sch.1 para.94

416. Common Agricultural Policy Single Farm Payment and Support Schemes (Scotland) Regulations 2011

Reg.6, amended: SSI 2013/265 Reg.2
Reg.6A, added: SSI 2013/265 Reg.2

442. Bus Lane Contraventions (Charges, Adjudication and Enforcement) (Scotland) Regulations 2011

Reg.18, revoked (in part): SI 2013/2042 Sch.1 para.95

2012

11. Scottish Road Works Register (Prescribed Fees) Regulations 2012
revoked: SSI 2013/8 Reg.4
34. Home Energy Assistance Scheme (Scotland) Amendment Regulations 2012
revoked: SSI 2013/148 Reg.9
38. Housing (Scotland) Act 2010 (Consequential Modifications) Order 2012
Sch.1 Part 2 para.10, revoked: SSI 2013/148 Reg.9
41. Local Government Finance (Scotland) Order 2012
Art.2, revoked: SSI 2013/44 Art.5
Sch.1, amended: SSI 2013/44 Art.5
48. Non-Domestic Rates (Enterprise Areas) (Scotland) Regulations 2012
applied: SSI 2013/78 Reg.6
Reg.2, amended: SSI 2013/78 Reg.3
Reg.3, amended: SSI 2013/78 Reg.3
Sch.1 Part 1, amended: SSI 2013/78 Reg.4
Sch.1 Part 3, substituted: SSI 2013/78 Reg.5
67. National Assistance (Sums for Personal Requirements) (Scotland) Regulations 2012
revoked: SSI 2013/40 Reg.3
68. National Assistance (Assessment of Resources) Amendment (Scotland) Regulations 2012
revoked: SSI 2013/41 Reg.5
69. National Health Service (Superannuation Scheme and Pension Scheme) (Scotland) Amendment Regulations 2012
Reg.5, revoked: SSI 2013/174 Sch.1
Reg.6, revoked: SSI 2013/174 Sch.1
Reg.7, revoked: SSI 2013/174 Sch.1
Reg.8, revoked: SSI 2013/174 Sch.1
Reg.9, revoked: SSI 2013/174 Sch.1
78. Bovine Viral Diarrhoea (Scotland) Order 2012
referred to: SSI 2013/3 Sch.1 para.4
revoked: SSI 2013/3 Art.30
Art.4, applied: SSI 2013/3 Sch.1 para.5
Art.5, applied: SSI 2013/3 Sch.1 para.6
Art.6, applied: SSI 2013/3 Sch.1 para.5, Sch.1 para.6
Art.7, applied: SSI 2013/3 Sch.1 para.1, Sch.1 para.3, Sch.1 para.7
Art.8, applied: SSI 2013/3 Sch.1 para.3
Art.9, applied: SSI 2013/3 Sch.1 para.3
Art.12, applied: SSI 2013/3 Sch.1 para.10
Art.13, applied: SSI 2013/3 Sch.1 para.7
Art.14, applied: SSI 2013/3 Sch.1 para.8
Art.15, applied: SSI 2013/3 Sch.1 para.4, Sch.1 para.7
Art.16, applied: SSI 2013/3 Sch.1 para.7
Art.17, applied: SSI 2013/3 Sch.1 para.7, Sch.1 para.9
Art.18, applied: SSI 2013/3 Sch.1 para.7
88. Public Contracts (Scotland) Regulations 2012
Reg.3, amended: SSI 2013/119 Sch.3 para.9
Reg.3, revoked (in part): SSI 2013/119 Sch.3 para.9
Reg.23, applied: SSI 2013/50 Sch.3 para.10
Reg.23, referred to: SSI 2013/50 Sch.3 para.10
Reg.33, applied: SSI 2013/50 Sch.3 para.10
Reg.52, applied: SSI 2013/50 Sch.3 para.10
Sch.1, amended: 2013 c.24 Sch.20 para.2, SI 2013/252 Sch.1 Part 2, SSI 2013/119 Sch.3 para.9
Sch.6 para.1, amended: SSI 2013/282 Reg.2
Sch.6 para.2, amended: SSI 2013/282 Reg.2
Sch.6 para.3, amended: SSI 2013/282 Reg.2
Sch.7 Part B, amended: SSI 2013/50 Sch.5
89. Utilities Contracts (Scotland) Regulations 2012
Reg.26, applied: SSI 2013/50 Sch.3 para.10
Reg.34, applied: SSI 2013/50 Sch.3 para.10
Reg.49, applied: SSI 2013/50 Sch.3 para.10
Sch.5 Part B, amended: SSI 2013/50 Sch.5
109. Community Care (Personal Care and Nursing Care) (Scotland) Amendment Regulations 2012
revoked: SSI 2013/108 Reg.3
118. Bankruptcy Fees etc (Scotland) Regulations 2012
Reg.12, amended: SSI 2013/318 Reg.29
Sch.1, referred to: SSI 2013/318 Reg.23
Sch.1 Part 2, amended: SSI 2013/318 Reg.29
119. Food Additives (Scotland) Amendment Regulations 2012
Reg.2, revoked (in part): SSI 2013/266 Sch.5
139. Road Traffic (Parking Adjudicators) (East Ayrshire Council) Regulations 2012
Reg.9, revoked (in part): SI 2013/2042 Sch.1 para.96
142. Road Traffic (Parking Adjudicators) (South Ayrshire Council) Regulations 2012
Reg.9, revoked (in part): SI 2013/2042 Sch.1 para.97
146. Fire and Rescue Services (Framework) (Scotland) Order 2012
revoked: SSI 2013/97 Art.4
162. Equality Act 2010 (Specific Duties) (Scotland) Regulations 2012
Sch.1, amended: SSI 2013/119 Sch.3 para.10, SSI 2013/169 Art.5
163. National Health Service Superannuation Scheme etc (Miscellaneous Amendments) (Scotland) Regulations 2012
Reg.11, revoked: SSI 2013/174 Sch.1
Reg.12, revoked: SSI 2013/174 Sch.1
Reg.13, revoked: SSI 2013/174 Sch.1
Reg.14, revoked: SSI 2013/174 Sch.1

Reg.15, revoked: SSI 2013/174 Sch.1
Reg.16, revoked: SSI 2013/174 Sch.1
Reg.17, revoked: SSI 2013/174 Sch.1
Reg.18, revoked: SSI 2013/174 Sch.1
Reg.19, revoked: SSI 2013/174 Sch.1
Reg.20, revoked: SSI 2013/174 Sch.1
Reg.21, revoked: SSI 2013/174 Sch.1
Reg.22, revoked: SSI 2013/174 Sch.1
Reg.23, revoked: SSI 2013/174 Sch.1
Reg.24, revoked: SSI 2013/174 Sch.1
Reg.25, revoked: SSI 2013/174 Sch.1

165. Town and Country Planning (Development Management Procedure) (Scotland) Amendment Regulations 2012
revoked: SSI 2013/155 Sch.9

176. Poultry Health Scheme (Fees) (Scotland) Regulations 2012
revoked: SSI 2013/151 Sch.7

177. Trade in Animals and Related Products (Scotland) Regulations 2012
Reg.13, applied: SSI 2013/151 Reg.10, Sch.6

179. Animal By-Products (Miscellaneous Amendments) (Scotland) Regulations 2012
revoked: SSI 2013/307 Sch.3

245. Act of Sederunt (Registration Appeal Court) 2012
revoked: SSI 2013/236 Art.2

259. Town and Country Planning (Marine Fish Farming) (Scotland) Amendment Regulations 2012
revoked: SSI 2013/277 Reg.5

260. Town and Country Planning (Prescribed Date) (Scotland) Regulations 2012
revoked: SSI 2013/350 Reg.3

266. Plant Health (Scotland) Amendment Order 2012
Art.10, revoked (in part): SSI 2013/187 Art.13
Art.11, revoked (in part): SSI 2013/187 Art.13

273. Act of Sederunt (Actions for removing from heritable property) (Amendment) 2012
Art.2, amended: SSI 2013/135 r.7

282. Snares (Identification Numbers and Tags) (Scotland) Order 2012
Art.3, amended: SSI 2013/119 Sch.1 para.40
Art.4, amended: SSI 2013/119 Sch.1 para.40
Art.5, amended: SSI 2013/119 Sch.1 para.40
Art.5, revoked (in part): SSI 2013/119 Sch.1 para.40
Art.6, amended: SSI 2013/119 Sch.1 para.40

292. Justice of the Peace Court Fees (Scotland) Order 2012
Art.3, amended: SSI 2013/137 Reg.22

303. Council Tax Reduction (Scotland) Regulations 2012
Reg.2, amended: SSI 2013/48 Reg.3, SSI 2013/142 Reg.11, SSI 2013/287 Reg.3
Reg.2, revoked (in part): SSI 2013/48 Reg.3
Reg.4, amended: SSI 2013/287 Reg.4
Reg.4, revoked (in part): SSI 2013/48 Reg.4
Reg.12, amended: SSI 2013/287 Reg.5
Reg.14, amended: SSI 2013/218 Reg.3
Reg.20, amended: SSI 2013/48 Reg.5, SSI 2013/218 Reg.4
Reg.23, amended: SSI 2013/48 Reg.6, SSI 2013/287 Reg.6
Reg.23, revoked (in part): SSI 2013/287 Reg.6
Reg.26, amended: SSI 2013/287 Reg.7
Reg.26, revoked (in part): SSI 2013/287 Reg.7
Reg.28, amended: SSI 2013/142 Reg.11, SSI 2013/218 Reg.5, SSI 2013/287 Reg.8
Reg.32, amended: SSI 2013/287 Reg.9, Reg.10
Reg.40, amended: SSI 2013/48 Reg.7
Reg.41, amended: SSI 2013/48 Reg.8
Reg.48, amended: SSI 2013/48 Reg.9
Reg.51, amended: SSI 2013/218 Reg.6
Reg.64, amended: SSI 2013/48 Reg.10
Reg.67, amended: SSI 2013/48 Reg.11, SSI 2013/142 Reg.11
Reg.81, amended: SSI 2013/48 Reg.12, SSI 2013/142 Reg.11
Reg.90A, added: SSI 2013/218 Reg.7
Reg.90A, applied: SSI 2013/218 Reg.17
Reg.90B, added: SSI 2013/218 Reg.7
Reg.90C, added: SSI 2013/218 Reg.7
Reg.90D, added: SSI 2013/218 Reg.7
Reg.92, amended: SSI 2013/48 Reg.13
Sch.1 Part 1 para.1, amended: SSI 2013/48 Reg.14
Sch.1 Part 1 para.2, amended: SSI 2013/48 Reg.14
Sch.1 Part 1 para.3, amended: SSI 2013/48 Reg.14
Sch.1 Part 2 para.4, amended: SSI 2013/48 Reg.14
Sch.1 Part 3 para.8, amended: SSI 2013/142 Reg.11
Sch.1 Part 3 para.10, amended: SSI 2013/142 Reg.11
Sch.1 Part 3 para.11, amended: SSI 2013/142 Reg.11
Sch.1 Part 3 para.12, amended: SSI 2013/48 Reg.14, SSI 2013/142 Reg.11
Sch.1 Part 3 para.13, amended: SSI 2013/142 Reg.11
Sch.1 Part 4 para.17, amended: SSI 2013/48 Reg.14
Sch.1 Part 5 para.19, amended: SSI 2013/48 Reg.14
Sch.1 Part 5 para.23, amended: SSI 2013/48 Reg.14
Sch.1 Part 5 para.24, amended: SSI 2013/48 Reg.14
Sch.1 Part 6 para.25, amended: SSI 2013/48 Reg.14

Sch.1 Part 6 para.26, amended: SSI 2013/48 Reg.14
Sch.1 Part 6 para.26, revoked (in part): SSI 2013/48 Reg.14
Sch.1 Part 6 para.27, amended: SSI 2013/48 Reg.14
Sch.1 Part 6 para.28, amended: SSI 2013/48 Reg.14, SSI 2013/218 Reg.8
Sch.1 Part 6 para.30, added: SSI 2013/48 Reg.14
Sch.2 para.1, amended: SSI 2013/48 Reg.15, SSI 2013/287 Reg.11
Sch.2 para.2, amended: SSI 2013/142 Reg.11
Sch.4 para.10, amended: SSI 2013/142 Reg.11
Sch.4 para.31, amended: SSI 2013/48 Reg.16

318. Materials and Articles in Contact with Food (Scotland) Regulations 2012
applied: SSI 2013/84 Sch.1
Reg.20, substituted: SSI 2013/83 Reg.2
Reg.28, revoked: SSI 2013/84 Sch.4

319. Council Tax Reduction (State Pension Credit) (Scotland) Regulations 2012
Reg.2, amended: SSI 2013/49 Reg.3, SSI 2013/142 Reg.12, SSI 2013/287 Reg.13
Reg.2, revoked (in part): SSI 2013/49 Reg.3
Reg.4, amended: SSI 2013/287 Reg.14
Reg.4, revoked (in part): SSI 2013/49 Reg.4
Reg.12, amended: SSI 2013/287 Reg.15
Reg.14, amended: SSI 2013/218 Reg.10
Reg.27, amended: SSI 2013/49 Reg.5, SSI 2013/142 Reg.12
Reg.27, revoked (in part): SSI 2013/218 Reg.11
Reg.29, amended: SSI 2013/142 Reg.12, SSI 2013/218 Reg.12
Reg.30, amended: SSI 2013/287 Reg.16, Reg.17
Reg.35, amended: SSI 2013/49 Reg.6
Reg.48, amended: SSI 2013/49 Reg.7, SSI 2013/142 Reg.12
Reg.59, amended: SSI 2013/142 Reg.12
Reg.70A, added: SSI 2013/218 Reg.13
Reg.70A, applied: SSI 2013/218 Reg.18
Reg.70B, added: SSI 2013/218 Reg.13
Reg.70C, added: SSI 2013/218 Reg.13
Reg.72, added: SSI 2013/49 Reg.8
Sch.1 Part 1 para.2, amended: SSI 2013/49 Reg.9
Sch.1 Part 1 para.3, amended: SSI 2013/49 Reg.9
Sch.1 Part 3 para.6, amended: SSI 2013/142 Reg.12, SSI 2013/218 Reg.14
Sch.1 Part 3 para.7, amended: SSI 2013/142 Reg.12
Sch.1 Part 3 para.8, amended: SSI 2013/49 Reg.9, SSI 2013/142 Reg.12
Sch.1 Part 3 para.9, amended: SSI 2013/142 Reg.12
Sch.1 Part 4 para.13, amended: SSI 2013/49 Reg.9
Sch.2 para.5, amended: SSI 2013/142 Reg.12, SSI 2013/218 Reg.15
Sch.4 Part 1 para.21, amended: SSI 2013/142 Reg.12
Sch.5 para.1, amended: SSI 2013/49 Reg.10, SSI 2013/287 Reg.18
Sch.5 para.2, amended: SSI 2013/142 Reg.12
Sch.5 para.4, amended: SSI 2013/218 Reg.16

321. Welfare of Animals at the Time of Killing (Scotland) Regulations 2012
applied: SI 2013/2216 Sch.1 para.12

325. Town and Country Planning (Miscellaneous Amendments) (Scotland) Regulations 2012
revoked: SSI 2013/155 Sch.9

336. Children's Hearings (Scotland) Act 2011 (Safeguarders Further Provision) Regulations 2012
Reg.4, amended: SSI 2013/212 Reg.15

349. Marketing of Bananas (Scotland) Regulations 2012
Reg.2, amended: SI 2013/3235 Reg.24
Reg.3, amended: SI 2013/3235 Reg.24

353. Non-Domestic Rates (Levying) (Scotland) (No.3) Regulations 2012
Reg.6, amended: SSI 2013/34 Reg.2

2013

3. Bovine Viral Diarrhoea (Scotland) Order 2013
Art.2, amended: SSI 2013/337 Art.3, SSI 2013/363 Art.4
Art.3, amended: SSI 2013/337 Art.4
Art.9, amended: SSI 2013/21 Art.3
Art.11, amended: SSI 2013/21 Art.4, SSI 2013/337 Art.5
Art.12, amended: SSI 2013/21 Art.5, SSI 2013/337 Art.6
Art.14, amended: SSI 2013/21 Art.6, SSI 2013/337 Art.7
Art.16, revoked: SSI 2013/337 Art.8
Art.17, amended: SSI 2013/21 Art.7, SSI 2013/337 Art.9
Art.18, amended: SSI 2013/337 Art.10
Art.20, amended: SSI 2013/337 Art.11, SSI 2013/363 Art.5
Art.21, amended: SSI 2013/337 Art.12
Art.21, substituted: SSI 2013/363 Art.6
Art.22, substituted: SSI 2013/337 Art.13, SSI 2013/363 Art.6
Art.23, amended: SSI 2013/337 Art.14
Art.23, substituted: SSI 2013/363 Art.6
Art.23A, added: SSI 2013/337 Art.15
Art.23A, substituted: SSI 2013/363 Art.6
Art.23B, added: SSI 2013/337 Art.16

Art.23B, amended: SSI 2013/363 Art.7
Art.23C, added: SSI 2013/337 Art.16
Art.23C, amended: SSI 2013/363 Art.8
Art.23D, added: SSI 2013/337 Art.16
Art.23D, amended: SSI 2013/363 Art.9
Art.24, amended: SSI 2013/337 Art.17, SSI 2013/363 Art.10

6. Restriction of Liberty Order etc (Scotland) Regulations 2013

Reg.5, revoked (in part): SSI 2013/210 Reg.1
Sch.2, referred to: SSI 2013/210 Reg.8

20. Tenant Information Packs (Assured Tenancies) (Scotland) Order 2013

Sch.1, substituted: SSI 2013/90 Sch.1

35. Police Service of Scotland Regulations 2013

applied: SSI 2013/60 Reg.6
Reg.2, amended: SSI 2013/122 Reg.2, SSI 2013/125 Reg.2
Reg.5, applied: SSI 2013/60 Sch.1 para.8
Reg.6, amended: SSI 2013/122 Reg.2
Reg.7, amended: SSI 2013/125 Reg.2
Reg.16, applied: SSI 2013/60 Reg.25
Reg.24, amended: SSI 2013/125 Reg.2
Reg.32, amended: SSI 2013/125 Reg.2
Sch.3 para.20, amended: SSI 2013/125 Reg.2

39. Police Service of Scotland (Promotion) Regulations 2013

applied: SSI 2013/35 Reg.6, Reg.20

42. Police Service of Scotland (Police Cadets) Regulations 2013

Sch.1 Part 3 para.1, amended: SSI 2013/125 Reg.3

43. Police Service of Scotland (Special Constables) Regulations 2013

Reg.2, amended: SSI 2013/122 Reg.3
Reg.5, amended: SSI 2013/122 Reg.3
Reg.7, amended: SSI 2013/125 Reg.4
Reg.7, revoked (in part): SSI 2013/125 Reg.4

44. Local Government Finance (Scotland) Order 2013

Sch.1, substituted: SSI 2013/107 Sch.1
Sch.2, substituted: SSI 2013/107 Sch.2

50. Rehabilitation of Offenders Act 1974 (Exclusions and Exceptions) (Scotland) Order 2013

Art.2, amended: SI 2013/472 Sch.2 para.250, SI 2013/504 Reg.48, SI 2013/1388 Reg.15
Sch.1 para.3, substituted: SI 2013/2329 Sch.1 para.42
Sch.1 para.14, revoked: SI 2013/2329 Sch.1 para.42
Sch.1 para.29, added: SSI 2013/204 Art.3
Sch.2 Part 1 para.1, amended: SI 2013/472 Sch.2 para.250, SI 2013/504 Reg.48, SI 2013/1388 Reg.15
Sch.2 Part 1 para.3, amended: SI 2013/472 Sch.2 para.250
Sch.2 Part 1 para.4, amended: SI 2013/472 Sch.2 para.250
Sch.2 Part 1 para.6, amended: SI 2013/472 Sch.2 para.250
Sch.2 Part 1 para.7, amended: SI 2013/504 Reg.48
Sch.2 Part 2, amended: SI 2013/472 Sch.2 para.250, SI 2013/504 Reg.48, SI 2013/1388 Reg.15
Sch.3 para.6, amended: SI 2013/472 Sch.2 para.250
Sch.3 para.8, amended: SI 2013/2329 Sch.1 para.42
Sch.4 Part 2 para.19, revoked: SSI 2013/204 Art.4
Sch.4 Part 2 para.23, amended: SSI 2013/119 Sch.2 para.28

60. Police Service of Scotland (Conduct) Regulations 2013

applied: SSI 2013/63 r.5, r.6
Reg.11, applied: SSI 2013/63 r.6
Reg.19, applied: SSI 2013/63 r.6
Reg.28, applied: SSI 2013/63 r.6
Sch.2 para.10, amended: SSI 2013/125 Reg.5

61. Police Service of Scotland (Performance) Regulations 2013

applied: SSI 2013/35 Reg.11, SSI 2013/63 r.5, r.6
Reg.14, applied: SSI 2013/63 r.6
Reg.15, applied: SSI 2013/63 r.6
Reg.22, amended: SSI 2013/125 Reg.6
Reg.22, applied: SSI 2013/63 r.6
Reg.23, applied: SSI 2013/62 Reg.8, Reg.11, Reg.15, Reg.22, Reg.26, Reg.27
Sch.1 para.5, amended: SSI 2013/125 Reg.6
Sch.1 para.10, amended: SSI 2013/125 Reg.6

62. Police Service of Scotland (Senior Officers) (Conduct) Regulations 2013

applied: SSI 2013/63 r.6
Reg.19, applied: SSI 2013/63 r.6
Reg.24, applied: SSI 2013/63 r.6

67. Road Traffic (Permitted Parking Area and Special Parking Area) (East Renfrewshire Council) Designation Order 2013

referred to: SSI 2013/68 Reg.2

70. National Health Service (Superannuation Scheme and Pension Scheme) (Scotland) Amendment Regulations 2013

revoked: SSI 2013/174 Sch.1

84. Food Safety (Sampling and Qualifications) (Scotland) Regulations 2013

Sch.1, amended: SSI 2013/217 Reg.9

86. Police Federation (Scotland) Regulations 2013

referred to: SSI 2013/35 Reg.15

99. Children Hearings (Scotland) Act 2011 (Transfer of Children to Scotland Effect of Orders made in England and Wales or Northern Ireland) Regulations 2013

Reg.3, applied: SI 2013/1465 Art.15
Reg.4, applied: SI 2013/1465 Art.15
Reg.5, applied: SI 2013/1465 Art.15
Reg.6, applied: SI 2013/1465 Art.15

109. National Health Service Superannuation Scheme etc (Miscellaneous Amendments) (Scotland) Regulations 2013

Reg.21, revoked: SSI 2013/174 Sch.1
Reg.22, revoked: SSI 2013/174 Sch.1
Reg.23, revoked: SSI 2013/174 Sch.1
Reg.24, revoked: SSI 2013/174 Sch.1
Reg.25, revoked: SSI 2013/174 Sch.1
Reg.26, revoked: SSI 2013/174 Sch.1
Reg.27, revoked: SSI 2013/174 Sch.1
Reg.28, revoked: SSI 2013/174 Sch.1
Reg.29, revoked: SSI 2013/174 Sch.1
Reg.30, revoked: SSI 2013/174 Sch.1
Reg.31, revoked: SSI 2013/174 Sch.1
Reg.32, revoked: SSI 2013/174 Sch.1
Reg.33, revoked: SSI 2013/174 Sch.1
Reg.34, revoked: SSI 2013/174 Sch.1
Reg.35, revoked: SSI 2013/174 Sch.1
Reg.36, revoked: SSI 2013/174 Sch.1
Reg.37, revoked: SSI 2013/174 Sch.1
Reg.38, revoked: SSI 2013/174 Sch.1
Reg.39, revoked: SSI 2013/174 Sch.1
Reg.40, revoked: SSI 2013/174 Sch.1
Reg.41, revoked: SSI 2013/174 Sch.1
Reg.42, revoked: SSI 2013/174 Sch.1
Reg.43, revoked: SSI 2013/174 Sch.1
Reg.44, revoked: SSI 2013/174 Sch.1
Reg.45, revoked: SSI 2013/174 Sch.1
Reg.46, revoked: SSI 2013/174 Sch.1
Reg.47, revoked: SSI 2013/174 Sch.1
Reg.48, revoked: SSI 2013/174 Sch.1
Reg.49, revoked: SSI 2013/174 Sch.1
Reg.50, revoked: SSI 2013/174 Sch.1
Reg.51, revoked: SSI 2013/174 Sch.1
Reg.52, revoked: SSI 2013/174 Sch.1
Reg.53, revoked: SSI 2013/174 Sch.1
Reg.54, revoked: SSI 2013/174 Sch.1
Reg.55, revoked: SSI 2013/174 Sch.1
Reg.56, revoked: SSI 2013/174 Sch.1
Reg.57, revoked: SSI 2013/174 Sch.1
Reg.58, revoked: SSI 2013/174 Sch.1
Reg.59, revoked: SSI 2013/174 Sch.1

135. Act of Sederunt (Sheriff Court Rules) (Miscellaneous Amendments) 2013

r.1, amended: SSI 2013/171 r.4

148. Home Energy Assistance Scheme (Scotland) Regulations 2013

Reg.2, amended: SSI 2013/253 Reg.4
Reg.6, amended: SSI 2013/253 Reg.5

150. Children's Hearings (Scotland) Act 2011 (Transitional, Savings and Supplementary Provisions) Order 2013

applied: SSI 2013/172 Art.8

155. Town and Country Planning (Development Management Procedure) (Scotland) Regulations 2013

Reg.18, applied: SSI 2013/156 Reg.29, SSI 2013/157 Reg.20
Reg.19, applied: SSI 2013/156 Reg.29, SSI 2013/157 Reg.20
Reg.20, applied: SSI 2013/156 Reg.29, SSI 2013/157 Reg.20
Reg.25, applied: SSI 2013/156 Reg.29, SSI 2013/157 Reg.20

167. M898/A898 Trunk Road (Erskine Bridge) (Temporary Prohibition of Traffic and 40mph Speed Restriction) Order 2013

revoked: SSI 2013/248 Art.7

168. National Health Service (Superannuation Scheme and Pension Scheme) (Scotland) Amendment (No.2) Regulations 2013

Reg.5, revoked: SSI 2013/174 Sch.1
Reg.6, revoked: SSI 2013/174 Sch.1
Reg.7, revoked: SSI 2013/174 Sch.1
Reg.8, revoked: SSI 2013/174 Sch.1
Reg.9, revoked: SSI 2013/174 Sch.1

217. Contaminants in Food (Scotland) Regulations 2013

disapplied: SSI 2013/84 Sch.1

218. Council Tax Reduction (Scotland) Amendment (No.2) Regulations 2013

Reg.9, amended: SSI 2013/239 Reg.2

262. Scottish Civil Justice Council and Criminal Legal Assistance Act 2013 (Commencement No 2) Order 2013

Art.2, amended: SSI 2013/271 Art.2

310. Adoption (Recognition of Overseas Adoptions) (Scotland) Regulations 2013

Reg.3, amended: SSI 2013/335 Reg.2

311. Road Traffic (Permitted Parking Area and Special Parking Area) (East Dunbartonshire Council) Designation Order 2013

applied: SSI 2013/312 Reg.2

337. Bovine Viral Diarrhoea (Scotland) Amendment (No.2) Order 2013

Art.3, revoked: SSI 2013/363 Art.2
Art.12, revoked: SSI 2013/363 Art.2
Art.13, revoked: SSI 2013/363 Art.2
Art.14, revoked: SSI 2013/363 Art.2
Art.15, revoked: SSI 2013/363 Art.2

Art.17, revoked (in part): SSI 2013/363 Art.2

STATUTORY RULES ISSUED BY THE UK PARLIAMENT

1912

348. Public Trustee Rules 1912
r.30, amended: SI 2013/235 Sch.2 para.1

1929

952. Petroleum-spirit (Motor Vehicles etc.) Regulations 1929
Reg.15A, revoked (in part): SI 2013/448 Sch.1

1938

598. Gasholders (Record of Examination) Order 1938
revoked: SI 2013/448 Sch.1

1948

1275. National Insurance (Residence and Persons Abroad) Regulations 1948
Reg.5, see *Garland v Revenue and Customs Commissioners* [2013] S.T.C. 1608 (UT (Tax)), Judge Greg Sinfield

1949

1885. Agricultural Wages Committees Regulations 1949
Reg.3, revoked (in part): 2013 c.24 Sch.20 para.2
Reg.16, revoked (in part): 2013 c.24 Sch.20 para.2

1950

942. Town and Country Planning (General Development) (Scotland) Order, 1950
applied: SSI 2013/155 Reg.51

1977. Double Taxation Relief (Taxes on Income) (Brunei) Order 1950
Sch.1, added: SI 2013/3146 Sch.1 Part 1, Sch.1 Part 2
Sch.1, substituted: SI 2013/3146 Sch.1 Part 1

1954

448. Removal of Bodies Regulations 1954
Sch.2, amended: SI 2013/1869 Sch.1 para.1

1955

1125. Cinematograph (Safety) (Scotland) Regulations, 1955
Reg.5, amended: SSI 2013/119 Sch.2 para.1
Reg.21, amended: SSI 2013/119 Sch.2 para.1

1205. Double Taxation Relief (Taxes on Income) (Isle of Man) Order 1955
Sch.1, substituted: SI 2013/3148 Sch.1 Part 2

1956

1692. Coroners (Indictable Offences) Rules 1956
see *R. (on the application of Wilkinson) v HM Coroner for Greater Manchester South District* [2012] EWHC 2755 (Admin), [2013] C.P. Rep. 5 (QBD (Admin)), Foskett, J.

1768. Coal and Other Mines (Fire and Rescue) Order 1956
Sch.1, applied: SI 2013/1471 Sch.2 para.29

1957

358. Oil in Navigable Waters (Transfer Records) Regulations 1957
revoked: SI 2013/2944 Sch.1

1959

84. Reserve and Auxiliary Forces (Agricultural Tenants) Regulations 1959
Reg.3, amended: SI 2013/1036 Sch.2 para.51
Reg.5, amended: SI 2013/1036 Sch.2 para.52
Reg.6, amended: SI 2013/1036 Sch.2 para.53
Reg.8, added: SI 2013/1036 Sch.2 para.54

831. Arsenic in Food Regulations 1959
revoked (in part): SI 2013/466 Reg.3, SI 2013/545 Reg.3

928. Arsenic in Food (Scotland) Regulations, 1959
revoked: SSI 2013/83 Sch.1

1960

1932. Shipbuilding and Ship-repairing Regulations 1960
revoked: SI 2013/448 Sch.1

2261. Arsenic in Food (Amendment) Regulations 1960
revoked (in part): SI 2013/466 Reg.3, SI 2013/545 Reg.3

2344. Arsenic in Food (Scotland) Amendment Regulations, 1960
revoked: SSI 2013/83 Sch.1

1963

1172. Various Trunk Roads (Prohibition of Waiting)(Clearways) Order 1963
Sch.1, substituted: SI 2013/2808 Art.11

2126. Vehicles (Conditions of Use on Footpaths) Regulations 1963
revoked (in part): SI 2013/2987 Sch.3

1964

697. Continental Shelf (Designation of Areas) Order 1964
applied: SI 2013/3162 Art.1

1171. Artificial Insemination of Pigs (Scotland) Regulations 1964
applied: SSI 2013/151 Reg.8
Reg.2, applied: SSI 2013/151 Sch.4
Reg.4, applied: SSI 2013/151 Reg.8

1172. Artificial Insemination of Pigs (England and Wales) Regulations 1964
applied: SI 2013/1240 Reg.8, SI 2013/1241 Reg.8
Reg.2, applied: SI 2013/1240 Sch.5, SI 2013/1241 Sch.4

1755. Ecclesiastical Jurisdiction (Discipline) Rules 1964
r.49., applied: SI 2013/1918 Sch.2 para.4

1985. War Pensions (Naval Auxiliary Personnel) Scheme 1964
applied: SI 2013/380 Reg.61

2007. Pensions (Polish Forces) Scheme 1964
applied: SI 2013/380 Reg.61

2058. War Pensions (Mercantile Marine) Scheme 1964
applied: SI 2013/380 Reg.61

1965

1235. Burry Inlet Cockle Fishery Order 1965
Art.2, amended: SI 2013/755 Sch.4 para.2
Art.3, amended: SI 2013/755 Sch.4 para.3
Art.9, amended: SI 2013/755 Sch.4 para.3

1531. Continental Shelf (Designation of Additional Areas) Order 1965
applied: SI 2013/3162 Art.1

1776. Rules of the Supreme Court (Revision) 1965
Ord.45 r.7, see *Westminster City Council v Addbins Ltd* [2012] EWHC 3716 (QB), [2013] J.P.L. 654 (QBD), Males, J.
Ord.62 r.3, see *KS v ND (Schedule I: Appeal: Costs)* [2013] EWHC 464 (Fam), [2013] 2 F.L.R. 698 (Fam Div), Mostyn, J.
Sch.1 Part 6, revoked: SI 2013/294 Sch.1

1966

97. Police (Special Constables) (Scotland) Regulations 1966
revoked: SSI 2013/43 Sch.3 para.9

507. Export of Horses (Veterinary Examination) Order 1966
Art.2, amended: SSI 2013/173 Art.2
Art.3, amended: SSI 2013/173 Art.2

864. Vehicles (Conditions of Use on Footpaths) (Amendment) Regulations 1966
revoked (in part): SI 2013/2987 Sch.3

1073. Mineral Hydrocarbons in Food Regulations 1966
revoked (in part): SI 2013/2196 Reg.10, SI 2013/2493 Reg.10

1263. Mineral Hydrocarbons in Food (Scotland) Regulations 1966
revoked: SSI 2013/217 Sch.1

1967

149. Capital Gains Tax Regulations 1967
Reg.15, amended: SI 2013/557 Reg.2

450. Electricity (Compulsory Wayleaves) (Hearings Procedure) Rules 1967
revoked (in part): SI 2013/1987 r.20

1968

208. Police Cadets (Scotland) Regulations 1968
revoked: SSI 2013/42 Sch.1 Part 2
Reg.1, varied: SSI 2013/42 Reg.2
Reg.5, varied: SSI 2013/42 Reg.2
Sch.1, varied: SSI 2013/42 Reg.2
Sch.2, varied: SSI 2013/42 Reg.2

717. Police (Promotion) (Scotland) Regulations 1968
applied: SSI 2013/39 Sch.2 para.1
891. Continental Shelf (Designation of Additional Areas) Order 1968
applied: SI 2013/3162 Art.1

1969

414. Motor Vehicles (Competitions and Trials) Regulations 1969
applied: SI 2013/2496 Reg.2
Reg.6, amended: SI 2013/2496 Reg.4
Reg.7, amended: SI 2013/2496 Reg.4
Reg.8, substituted: SI 2013/2496 Reg.5
Reg.9, amended: SI 2013/2496 Reg.4
Reg.10, amended: SI 2013/2496 Reg.4
Reg.11, amended: SI 2013/2496 Reg.4
Reg.13, amended: SI 2013/2496 Reg.4
Sch.2, amended: SI 2013/2496 Reg.4, Reg.6
Sch.3, amended: SI 2013/2496 Reg.4
Sch.4, amended: SI 2013/2496 Reg.7
493. Police Cadets (Scotland) Amendment Regulations 1969
revoked: SSI 2013/42 Sch.1 Part 1
592. Civil Aviation Act 1949 (Overseas Territories) Order 1969
applied: SI 2013/2870
1787. Police Federation Regulations 1969
Reg.12, amended: SI 2013/3189 Reg.2
1820. Police Cadets (Scotland) Amendment (No.2) Regulations 1969
revoked: SSI 2013/42 Sch.1 Part 2

1970

424. Police Cadets (Scotland) Amendment Regulations 1970
revoked: SSI 2013/42 Sch.1 Part 2
1413. Police Cadets (Scotland) Amendment (No.2) Regulations 1970
revoked: SSI 2013/42 Sch.1 Part 1
1539. Foreign Marriage Order 1970
Art.3, amended: SI 2013/2875 Art.3
Art.7, revoked: SI 2013/2875 Art.4

1971

185. Police Cadets (Scotland) Amendment Regulations 1971
revoked: SSI 2013/42 Sch.1 Part 2
594. Continental Shelf (Designation of Additional Areas) Order 1971
applied: SI 2013/3162 Art.1
792. Motor Vehicles (International Motor Insurance Card) Regulations 1971
Reg.8, revoked: SI 2013/2904 Reg.3
795. Birmingham &mdash Great Yarmouth Trunk Road (Prohibition of Waiting) (Clearways) Order 1971
Sch.1, revoked: SI 2013/394 Sch.1 Part II
810. Police Cadets (Scotland) Amendment (No.2) Regulations 1971
revoked: SSI 2013/42 Sch.1 Part 1
844. Agricultural Wages Committees (Wages Structure) Regulations 1971
revoked (in part): 2013 c.24 Sch.20 para.2
1065. Rent Assessment Committees (England and Wales) Regulations 1971
Reg.1A, added: SI 2013/1036 Sch.2 para.1
1254. Transport Holding Company (Transfer of Assets) Order 1971
revoked (in part): SI 2013/2986 Sch.3
1267. Medicines (Surgical Materials) Order 1971
applied: SI 2013/532 Sch.4 para.6
2084. Indictments (Procedure) Rules 1971
r.6., applied: SI 2013/1554 r.14_1
r.7., applied: SI 2013/1554 r.14_1
r.8., applied: SI 2013/1554 r.14_1
r.9., applied: SI 2013/1554 r.14_1
r.10., applied: SI 2013/1554 r.14_1

1972

764. National Savings Bank Regulations 1972
Reg.2F, added: SI 2013/8 Reg.2
Reg.29L, amended: SI 2013/8 Reg.2
Reg.29P, amended: SI 2013/8 Reg.2
778. Police Cadets (Scotland) Amendment Regulations 1972
revoked: SSI 2013/42 Sch.1 Part 2
941. M67 Denton Relief Road Motorway and Connecting Roads Scheme 1972
Sch.1A, added: SI 2013/2173 Sch.1
1024. Transport Holding Company (Capital Debts) Order 1972
revoked: SI 2013/2844 Art.2
1217. Motor Vehicles (Third Party Risks) Regulations 1972
Reg.9, revoked: SI 2013/2904 Reg.2
1264. Electoral Law (Northern Ireland) Order 1972
Art.9, varied: SI 2013/3156 Art.5
1265. Health and Personal Social Services (Northern Ireland) Order 1972

applied: SI 2013/335 Reg.43
Art.15, see *JR 47's Application for Judicial Review, Re* [2013] NIQB 7, (2013) 16 C.C.L. Rep. 179 (QBD (NI)), McCloskey, J.
Art.15, applied: SI 2013/3029 Sch.5 para.28, SI 2013/3035 Sch.1
Art.15C, amended: SI 2013/235 Sch.2 para.2
Art.30, applied: SI 2013/3029 Sch.1 para.19, Sch.7 para.10, SI 2013/3035 Sch.1

1298. Pensions Increase (Annual Review) Order 1972
applied: SI 2013/604 Sch.1

1590. European Communities (Enforcement of Community Judgments) Order 1972
Art.2, amended: SI 2013/504 Reg.27

1929. Oil in Navigable Waters (Records) Regulations 1972
revoked: SI 2013/2944 Sch.1

1966. Salmon and Migratory Trout (Restrictions on Landing) Order 1972
Art.4, substituted: SI 2013/755 Sch.4 para.4

1973

19. Adoption (Designation of Overseas Adoptions) Order 1973
applied: SI 2013/1801 Art.4
revoked (in part): SI 2013/1801 Art.4, SSI 2013/310 Reg.5

69. Drainage (Northern Ireland) Order 1973
Sch.1, varied: SI 2013/3156 Art.7

290. Transport Holding Company (Capital Debts) Order 1973
revoked: SI 2013/2844 Art.2

338. Transport Holding Company (Dissolution) Order 1973
revoked (in part): SI 2013/2986 Sch.3
Art.2, applied: SI 2013/2986 Art.3
Art.3, applied: SI 2013/2986 Art.3

366. Transport Holding Company (Commencing Capital Debt) (Extinguishment) Order 1973
revoked: SI 2013/2844 Art.2

798. Misuse of Drugs (Safe Custody) Regulations 1973
applied: SI 2013/1294 Art.3

1039. Arsenic in Food (Scotland) Amendment Regulations 1973
revoked: SSI 2013/83 Sch.1

1052. Arsenic in Food (Amendment) Regulations 1973
revoked (in part): SI 2013/466 Reg.3, SI 2013/545 Reg.3

1138. Police Cadets (Scotland) Amendment Regulations 1973
revoked: SSI 2013/42 Sch.1 Part 1

1370. Pensions Increase (Annual Review) Order 1973
applied: SI 2013/604 Sch.1

2163. Northern Ireland (Modification of Enactments-;No 1) Order 1973
Art.14, applied: SI 2013/3150
Sch.5 para.16, applied: SI 2013/3150

1974

29. National Health Service (Venereal Diseases) Regulations 1974
Reg.2, amended: SI 2013/235 Sch.2 para.3

191. National Health Service (Family Practitioner Committees-Supply of Goods) Regulations 1974
Reg.2, amended: SI 2013/235 Sch.2 para.4
Reg.3, amended: SI 2013/235 Sch.2 para.4

266. National Health Service (Determination of Areas of Health Boards) (Scotland) Order 1974
revoked: SSI 2013/347 Art.4

284. National Health Service (Charges for Appliances) Regulations 1974
Reg.2, amended: SI 2013/365 Reg.27

495. National Health Service (Speech Therapists) Regulations 1974
Reg.4, revoked (in part): SI 2013/235 Sch.2 para.5

502. Motorways Traffic (Speed Limit) Regulations 1974
Reg.3, applied: SI 2013/3271 Art.9
Reg.3, varied: SI 2013/672 Art.10, SI 2013/2085 Art.12

515. Agricultural Wages Committees (Areas) Order 1974
Art.3, amended: 2013 c.24 Sch.20 para.2
Art.3, revoked (in part): 2013 c.24 Sch.20 para.2
Art.4, revoked: 2013 c.24 Sch.20 para.2
Sch.1 Part I, revoked: 2013 c.24 Sch.20 para.2
Sch.1 Part II, revoked: 2013 c.24 Sch.20 para.2

1079. Trunk Roads (40 m.p.h Speed Limit) (Dunbartonshire) (Consolidation) Order 1974
Sch.1, varied: SSI 2013/283 Art.3

1136. Plant Varieties and Seeds Tribunal Rules 1974
Part 1 r.2, amended: SI 2013/755 Sch.4 para.6
Sch.1, amended: SI 2013/755 Sch.4 para.7

1248. Police Cadets (Scotland) Amendment Regulations 1974
revoked: SSI 2013/42 Sch.1 Part 2

1373. Pensions Increase (Annual Review) Order 1974
applied: SI 2013/604 Sch.1

1489. Continental Shelf (Designation of Additional Areas) Order 1974
applied: SI 2013/3162 Art.1

1841. Celluloid and Cinematograph Film Act 1922 (Repeals and Modifications) Regulations 1974
revoked: SI 2013/448 Sch.1

2010. Social Security (Benefit) (Married Women and Widows Special Provisions) Regulations 1974
Reg.1, amended: SI 2013/630 Reg.20
Reg.3, amended: SI 2013/630 Reg.20

2056. Nuclear Installations Act 1965 etc (Repeals and Modifications) Regulations 1974
Sch.1, amended: 2013 c.32 Sch.12 para.30
Sch.2 para.1, revoked: 2013 c.32 Sch.12 para.30
Sch.2 para.2, revoked: 2013 c.32 Sch.12 para.30
Sch.2 para.3, revoked: 2013 c.32 Sch.12 para.30
Sch.2 para.6, revoked: 2013 c.32 Sch.12 para.30

2170. Clean Air Enactments (Repeals and Modifications) Regulations 1974
revoked: SI 2013/390 Reg.58

2212. Rabies (Control) Order 1974
Art.2, amended: SSI 2013/173 Art.3
Art.4, amended: SSI 2013/173 Art.3
Art.5, amended: SSI 2013/173 Art.3
Sch.2, amended: SSI 2013/173 Art.3

1975

467. Social Security (Employed Earners Employments for Industrial Injuries Purposes) Regulations 1975
Sch.1 Part I para.2, amended: SI 2013/602 Sch.2 para.66, SI 2013/2536 Reg.2
Sch.3, amended: SI 2013/602 Sch.2 para.66

493. Social Security (Benefit) (Members of the Forces) Regulations 1975
Reg.3, amended: SI 2013/630 Reg.21
Reg.5, amended: SI 2013/630 Reg.21

529. Social Security (Mariners Benefits) Regulations 1975
applied: SI 2013/379 Reg.83, SI 2013/3029 Sch.6 para.24, SI 2013/3035 Sch.1
Reg.1, amended: SI 2013/630 Reg.22
Reg.2, amended: SI 2013/630 Reg.22
Reg.6, amended: SI 2013/630 Reg.22

539. Act of Sederunt (Commissary Business) 1975
revoked: SSI 2013/291 Sch.5

556. Social Security (Credits) Regulations 1975
Reg.2, amended: SI 2013/630 Reg.70
Reg.7, amended: SI 2013/630 Reg.70
Reg.8A, amended: SI 2013/630 Reg.70
Reg.8A, revoked (in part): SI 2013/2536 Reg.3
Reg.8B, amended: SI 2013/630 Reg.70
Reg.8B, applied: SI 2013/3029 Sch.1 para.19, Sch.3 para.6, Sch.6 para.21, Sch.8 para.12, SI 2013/3035 Sch.1
Reg.8G, added: SI 2013/630 Reg.70
Reg.9D, applied: SI 2013/379 Reg.9
Reg.9E, applied: SI 2013/378 Reg.35, SI 2013/379 Reg.9

563. Social Security Benefit (Persons Abroad) Regulations 1975
Reg.1, amended: SI 2013/630 Reg.23
Reg.2, amended: SI 2013/388 Sch.1 para.8, SI 2013/591 Sch.1 para.1
Reg.5, applied: SI 2013/599 Reg.3, SI 2013/746 Reg.3
Reg.11, amended: SI 2013/630 Reg.23

629. Local Authorities etc (Miscellaneous Provision) (Scotland) Order 1975
see *Anton v South Ayrshire Council* 2013 S.L.T. 141 (OH), Lady Clark of Calton
Art.3, see *Anton v South Ayrshire Council* 2013 S.L.T. 141 (OH), Lady Clark of Calton

679. Town and Country Planning (General Development) (Scotland) Order 1975
applied: SSI 2013/155 Reg.51

1023. Rehabilitation of Offenders Act 1974 (Exceptions) Order 1975
see *R. (on the application of T) v Chief Constable of Greater Manchester* [2013] EWCA Civ 25, [2013] 1 W.L.R. 2515 (CA (Civ Div)), Lord Dyson (M.R.)
Art.2, amended: SI 2013/472 Sch.2 para.1, SI 2013/504 Reg.28, SI 2013/1198 Art.3, SI 2013/1388 Reg.7, SI 2013/1773 Sch.2 para.2
Art.2, revoked (in part): SI 2013/1198 Art.3
Art.2A, added: SI 2013/1198 Art.4
Art.3, amended: SI 2013/472 Sch.2 para.1, SI 2013/504 Reg.28, SI 2013/1198 Art.5, SI 2013/1388 Reg.7, SI 2013/2329 Sch.1 para.30
Art.3, revoked (in part): SI 2013/1198 Art.5
Art.3, substituted: SI 2013/1198 Art.5
Art.3A, amended: SI 2013/1198 Art.7
Art.3ZA, added: SI 2013/1198 Art.6
Art.4, amended: SI 2013/472 Sch.2 para.1, SI 2013/504 Reg.28, SI 2013/1198 Art.8, SI 2013/1388 Reg.7, SI 2013/1773 Sch.2 para.2
Art.4, revoked (in part): SI 2013/1198 Art.8
Art.4, substituted: SI 2013/1198 Art.8
Art.4ZA, added: SI 2013/1198 Art.9
Art.6, amended: SI 2013/1198 Art.10
Sch.1 Part I para.2, amended: SI 2013/1198 Art.11
Sch.1 Part I para.9, revoked (in part): SI 2013/1198 Art.11
Sch.1 Part II para.5, revoked (in part): SI 2013/1198 Art.11
Sch.1 Part II para.6, substituted: SI 2013/1198 Art.11
Sch.1 Part II para.7, amended: SI 2013/1198 Art.11
Sch.1 Part II para.8, amended: SI 2013/1198 Art.11

Sch.1 Part III para.6, amended: SI 2013/1198 Art.11
Sch.1 Part III para.6, revoked (in part): SI 2013/1198 Art.11
Sch.1 Part III para.7, revoked (in part): SI 2013/1198 Art.11
Sch.3 para.11, revoked (in part): SI 2013/1198 Art.12
Sch.3 para.11A, added: SI 2013/1198 Art.12
Sch.3 para.12, revoked (in part): SI 2013/1198 Art.12

1092. Colleges of Education (Compensation) Regulations 1975
applied: SI 2013/1893 Sch.2

1208. Motor Vehicles (International Circulation) Order 1975
Art.2, amended: SI 2013/3150 Art.2
Art.5, amended: SI 2013/3150 Art.2

1287. Land Compensation (Scotland) Development Order 1975
Art.4, see *Scottish Borders Council v Scottish Ministers* 2013 S.L.T. 41 (IH (Ex Div)), Lord Eassie

1379. Tribunals and Inquiries (Discretionary Inquiries) Order 1975
Sch.1 Part I para.19B, amended: SSI 2013/119 Sch.2 para.2

1384. Pensions Increase (Annual Review) Order 1975
applied: SI 2013/604 Sch.1

1452. Police Cadets (Scotland) Amendment Regulations 1975
revoked: SSI 2013/42 Sch.1 Part 1

1976

191. Consumer Credit Licensing (Representations) Order 1976
revoked (in part): SI 2013/1881 Art.21
Art.1, amended: SI 2013/472 Sch.2 para.2
Art.1, applied: SI 2013/1881 Art.22
Art.3, amended: SI 2013/472 Sch.2 para.2
Art.3, applied: SI 2013/1881 Art.22
Art.4, applied: SI 2013/1881 Art.22
Art.6, amended: SI 2013/472 Sch.2 para.2

409. Social Security (Invalid Care Allowance) Regulations 1976
Reg.9, amended: SI 2013/388 Sch.1 para.9, SI 2013/389 Reg.2, SI 2013/591 Sch.1 para.2
Reg.9A, added: SI 2013/389 Reg.2
Reg.9B, added: SI 2013/389 Reg.2

516. Sale of Goods for Mothers and Children (Designation and Charging) Regulations 1976
Reg.4, amended: SI 2013/294 Sch.1

615. Social Security (Medical Evidence) Regulations 1976
applied: SI 2013/376 Reg.8, Reg.28, SI 2013/379 Reg.16, SI 2013/380 Reg.18
Reg.1, amended: SI 2013/235 Sch.2 para.6, SI 2013/630 Reg.24
Sch.1 Part I, applied: SI 2013/376 Reg.99
Sch.1 Part I, referred to: SI 2013/378 Reg.16, SI 2013/386 Reg.6
Sch.2 Part II, amended: SI 2013/235 Sch.2 para.6

621. Police Cadets (Scotland) Amendment Regulations 1976
revoked: SSI 2013/42 Sch.1 Part 2

839. Trunk Road (Loggerheads) (Prohibition of Waiting) Order 1976
revoked: SI 2013/656 Art.5

1002. Consumer Credit (Termination of Licences) Regulations 1976
revoked (in part): SI 2013/1881 Art.21

1042. Sex Discrimination (Northern Ireland) Order 1976
applied: 2013 c.22 Sch.4 para.4
Part I, applied: 2013 c.22 Sch.4 para.4
Part II, applied: 2013 c.22 Sch.4 para.4
Part III, applied: 2013 c.22 Sch.4 para.4
Part IV, applied: 2013 c.22 Sch.4 para.4
Part V, applied: 2013 c.22 Sch.4 para.4
Part VI, applied: 2013 c.22 Sch.4 para.4
Part VII, applied: 2013 c.22 Sch.4 para.4
Part VIII, applied: 2013 c.22 Sch.4 para.4
Part IX, applied: 2013 c.22 Sch.4 para.4
Art.2, applied: 2013 c.22 Sch.4 para.4
Art.3, applied: 2013 c.22 Sch.4 para.4
Art.4, applied: 2013 c.22 Sch.4 para.4
Art.4A, applied: 2013 c.22 Sch.4 para.4
Art.5, applied: 2013 c.22 Sch.4 para.4
Art.5A, applied: 2013 c.22 Sch.4 para.4
Art.6, applied: 2013 c.22 Sch.4 para.4
Art.6A, applied: 2013 c.22 Sch.4 para.4
Art.7, applied: 2013 c.22 Sch.4 para.4
Art.8, applied: 2013 c.22 Sch.4 para.4
Art.8A, applied: 2013 c.22 Sch.4 para.4
Art.9, applied: 2013 c.22 Sch.4 para.4
Art.10, applied: 2013 c.22 Sch.4 para.4
Art.10A, applied: 2013 c.22 Sch.4 para.4
Art.10B, applied: 2013 c.22 Sch.4 para.4
Art.11, applied: 2013 c.22 Sch.4 para.4
Art.12, applied: 2013 c.22 Sch.4 para.4
Art.13, applied: 2013 c.22 Sch.4 para.4
Art.13A, applied: 2013 c.22 Sch.4 para.4
Art.13B, applied: 2013 c.22 Sch.4 para.4
Art.14, applied: 2013 c.22 Sch.4 para.4
Art.15, applied: 2013 c.22 Sch.4 para.4
Art.16, applied: 2013 c.22 Sch.4 para.4

Art.17, applied: 2013 c.22 Sch.4 para.4
Art.17(1A), applied: 2013 c.22 Sch.4 para.4
Art.17(1B), applied: 2013 c.22 Sch.4 para.4
Art.18, applied: 2013 c.22 Sch.4 para.4
Art.18(1A), applied: 2013 c.22 Sch.4 para.4
Art.21, applied: 2013 c.22 Sch.4 para.4
Art.22, applied: 2013 c.22 Sch.4 para.4
Art.22A, applied: 2013 c.22 Sch.4 para.4
Art.23, applied: 2013 c.22 Sch.4 para.4
Art.24, applied: 2013 c.22 Sch.4 para.4
Art.25, applied: 2013 c.22 Sch.4 para.4
Art.27, applied: 2013 c.22 Sch.4 para.4
Art.28, applied: 2013 c.22 Sch.4 para.4
Art.29, applied: 2013 c.22 Sch.4 para.4
Art.30, applied: 2013 c.22 Sch.4 para.4
Art.31, applied: 2013 c.22 Sch.4 para.4
Art.36, applied: 2013 c.22 Sch.4 para.4
Art.36A, applied: 2013 c.22 Sch.4 para.4
Art.38, applied: 2013 c.22 Sch.4 para.4
Art.39, applied: 2013 c.22 Sch.4 para.4
Art.40, applied: 2013 c.22 Sch.4 para.4
Art.41, applied: 2013 c.22 Sch.4 para.4
Art.42, applied: 2013 c.22 Sch.4 para.4
Art.46, applied: 2013 c.22 Sch.4 para.4
Art.53A, applied: 2013 c.22 Sch.4 para.4
Art.54, applied: 2013 c.22 Sch.4 para.4
Art.56, applied: 2013 c.22 Sch.4 para.4
Art.56A, applied: 2013 c.22 Sch.4 para.4
Art.58A, applied: 2013 c.22 Sch.4 para.4
Art.59, applied: 2013 c.22 Sch.4 para.4
Art.63, applied: 2013 c.22 Sch.4 para.4
Art.63A, applied: 2013 c.22 Sch.4 para.4
Art.64, applied: 2013 c.22 Sch.4 para.4
Art.65, applied: 2013 c.22 Sch.4 para.4
Art.66, applied: 2013 c.22 Sch.4 para.4
Art.66A, applied: 2013 c.22 Sch.4 para.4
Art.67, applied: 2013 c.22 Sch.4 para.4
Art.68, applied: 2013 c.22 Sch.4 para.4
Art.72, applied: 2013 c.22 Sch.4 para.4
Art.74, applied: 2013 c.22 Sch.4 para.4
Art.75, applied: 2013 c.22 Sch.4 para.4
Art.76, applied: 2013 c.22 Sch.4 para.4
Art.77, applied: 2013 c.22 Sch.4 para.4
Art.77A, applied: 2013 c.22 Sch.4 para.4
Art.78, applied: 2013 c.22 Sch.4 para.4
Art.80, applied: 2013 c.22 Sch.4 para.4
Art.81, applied: 2013 c.22 Sch.4 para.4
Art.82, applied: 2013 c.22 Sch.4 para.4
Art.83, applied: 2013 c.22 Sch.4 para.4
Art.84A, applied: 2013 c.22 Sch.4 para.4
Art.107, applied: 2013 c.22 Sch.4 para.4
Art.141, applied: 2013 c.22 Sch.4 para.4
Art.146, applied: 2013 c.22 Sch.4 para.4
para(.1)(a)., applied: 2013 c.22 Sch.4 para.4
para(.2)(b)., applied: 2013 c.22 Sch.4 para.4
para(.3A)., applied: 2013 c.22 Sch.4 para.4
Reg.2, applied: 2013 c.22 Sch.4 para.4
Reg.3, applied: 2013 c.22 Sch.4 para.4
Reg.4, applied: 2013 c.22 Sch.4 para.4
Reg.9, applied: 2013 c.22 Sch.4 para.4
Reg.17, applied: 2013 c.22 Sch.4 para.4
s.ub, applied: 2013 c.22 Sch.4 para.4
Sch.1, applied: 2013 c.22 Sch.4 para.4
Sch.2, applied: 2013 c.22 Sch.4 para.4
Sch.3, applied: 2013 c.22 Sch.4 para.4
Sch.4, applied: 2013 c.22 Sch.4 para.4
Sch.5, applied: 2013 c.22 Sch.4 para.4
Sch.6, applied: 2013 c.22 Sch.4 para.4
Sch.7, applied: 2013 c.22 Sch.4 para.4

1153. Continental Shelf (Designation of Additional Areas) Order 1976

applied: SI 2013/3162 Art.1

1213. Pharmacy (Northern Ireland) Order 1976

Sch.2A, amended: SI 2013/3036 Reg.8

1356. Pensions Increase (Annual Review) Order 1976

applied: SI 2013/604 Sch.1

2012. National Savings Stock Register Regulations 1976

Reg.2, amended: SI 2013/416 Reg.3
Reg.5, amended: SI 2013/416 Reg.4
Reg.10, amended: SI 2013/416 Reg.5
Reg.21, amended: SI 2013/416 Reg.6
Reg.21C, added: SI 2013/416 Reg.7
Reg.22, revoked (in part): SI 2013/416 Reg.8
Reg.25, amended: SI 2013/416 Reg.9
Reg.25, revoked (in part): SI 2013/416 Reg.9
Reg.30, amended: SI 2013/472 Art.4
Reg.30, revoked: SI 2013/416 Reg.10
Reg.30A, added: SI 2013/416 Reg.11
Reg.31, amended: SI 2013/416 Reg.12

2022. Town and Country Planning (General) (Scotland) Regulations 1976

Sch.1, see *Riva v Edinburgh Airport Ltd* 2013 S.L.T. (Lands Tr) 61 (Lands Tr (Scot)), J N Wright QC

1977

330. Consumer Credit (Conduct of Business) (Credit References) Regulations 1977

revoked (in part): SI 2013/1881 Art.21

343. Social Security Benefit (Dependency) Regulations 1977

Sch.2 Part I para.2B, amended: SI 2013/599 Reg.4

500. Safety Representatives and Safety Committees Regulations 1977

applied: SI 2013/1893 Sch.2, SI 2013/3104 Sch.2 para.30
Reg.6, amended: SI 2013/1471 Sch.4

539. Aircraft and Shipbuilding Industries (Aircraft Industry Vesting Date) Order 1977
revoked: SI 2013/687 Sch.2

540. Aircraft and Shipbuilding Industries (Shipbuilding Industry Vesting Date) Order 1977
revoked: SI 2013/687 Sch.2

626. British Shipbuilders Regulations 1977
revoked: SI 2013/687 Sch.2

691. Erucic Acid in Food Regulations 1977
revoked (in part): SI 2013/2196 Reg.10, SI 2013/2493 Reg.10

754. Aircraft and Shipbuilding Industries (Issue of Compensation Stock) Regulations 1977
revoked: SI 2013/687 Sch.2

944. Importation of Animals Order 1977
Art.2, amended: SSI 2013/173 Art.4
Art.4, amended: SSI 2013/173 Art.4
Art.5, amended: SSI 2013/173 Art.4

1020. Aircraft and Shipbuilding Industries Arbitration Tribunal (Scottish Proceedings) Rules 1977
revoked: SI 2013/686 Sch.2

1022. Aircraft and Shipbuilding Industries Arbitration Tribunal Rules 1977
revoked: SI 2013/686 Sch.2

1028. Erucic Acid in Food (Scotland) Regulations 1977
revoked: SSI 2013/217 Sch.1

1131. Police Cadets (Scotland) Amendment Regulations 1977
revoked: SSI 2013/42 Sch.1 Part 1

1210. National Savings Bank (Investment Deposits) (Limits) Order 1977
Art.3B, amended: SI 2013/8 Reg.3

1387. Pensions Increase (Annual Review) Order 1977
applied: SI 2013/604 Sch.1

1871. Continental Shelf (Designation of Additional Areas) Order 1977
applied: SI 2013/3162 Art.1

2009. Police Cadets (Scotland) Amendment (No.2) Regulations 1977
revoked: SSI 2013/42 Sch.1 Part 1

2157. Rates (Northern Ireland) Order 1977
applied: 2013 c.29 s.125, s.128
Art.25B, see *Moffett v Commissioner of Valuation for Northern Ireland* [2013] R.V.R. 103 (VT (NI)), JV Leonard (President)
Art.25B, referred to: 2013 c.29 s.125, s.128
Sch.8B, see *Moffett v Commissioner of Valuation for Northern Ireland* [2013] R.V.R. 103 (VT (NI)), JV Leonard (President)
Sch.12, see *Elias Altrincham Properties v Commissioner of Valuation* [2013] R.V.R. 223 (Lands Tr (NI)), M R Curry FRICS

1978

101. Trunk Road (Bethesda, Gwynedd) (Prohibition and Restriction of Waiting) Order 1978
revoked: SI 2013/791 Art.7

178. Continental Shelf (Designation of Additional Areas) Order 1978
applied: SI 2013/3162 Art.1

232. Shipbuilding Industry (Pension Schemes) Regulations 1978
revoked: SI 2013/687 Sch.2

393. Social Security (Graduated Retirement Benefit) (No.2) Regulations 1978
Sch.2 para.1, varied: SI 2013/574 Art.11
Sch.2 para.2, varied: SI 2013/574 Art.11
Sch.2 para.3, varied: SI 2013/574 Art.11
Sch.2 para.4, varied: SI 2013/574 Art.11

664. Protection of Wrecks (Designation No 3) 1978
revoked: SSI 2013/276 Sch.1

999. Police Cadets (Scotland) Amendment Regulations 1978
revoked: SSI 2013/42 Sch.1 Part 2

1029. Continental Shelf (Designation of Additional Areas) (No.2) Order 1978
applied: SI 2013/3162 Art.1

1039. Health and Safety at Work (Northern Ireland) Order 1978
amended: SI 2013/235 Sch.2 para.7
applied: SI 2013/1506 Reg.20, Reg.21, Reg.27, Reg.32, Reg.33
varied: SI 2013/1506 Reg.20
amended: SI 2013/235 Sch.2 para.7
applied: SI 2013/1506 Reg.20, Reg.21, Reg.27, Reg.32, Reg.33
varied: SI 2013/1506 Reg.20
amended: SI 2013/235 Sch.2 para.7
applied: SI 2013/1506 Reg.20, Reg.21, Reg.27, Reg.32, Reg.33
varied: SI 2013/1506 Reg.20
amended: SI 2013/235 Sch.2 para.7
applied: SI 2013/1506 Reg.20, Reg.21, Reg.27, Reg.32, Reg.33
varied: SI 2013/1506 Reg.20
amended: SI 2013/235 Sch.2 para.7
applied: SI 2013/1506 Reg.20, Reg.21, Reg.27, Reg.32, Reg.33
varied: SI 2013/1506 Reg.20
Part 1, amended: SI 2013/235 Sch.2 para.7

Part 1, applied: SI 2013/1506 Reg.20, Reg.21, Reg.27, Reg.32, Reg.33
Part 1, varied: SI 2013/1506 Reg.20
Part I, amended: SI 2013/235 Sch.2 para.7
Part I, applied: SI 2013/1506 Reg.20, Reg.21, Reg.27, Reg.32, Reg.33
Part I, varied: SI 2013/1506 Reg.20
Part 2, amended: SI 2013/235 Sch.2 para.7
Part 2, applied: SI 2013/1506 Reg.20, Reg.21, Reg.27, Reg.32, Reg.33
Part 2, varied: SI 2013/1506 Reg.20
Part II, amended: SI 2013/235 Sch.2 para.7
Part II, applied: SI 2013/1506 Reg.20, Reg.21, Reg.27, Reg.32, Reg.33
Part II, varied: SI 2013/1506 Reg.20
Part III, amended: SI 2013/235 Sch.2 para.7
Part III, applied: SI 2013/1506 Reg.20, Reg.21, Reg.27, Reg.32, Reg.33
Part III, varied: SI 2013/1506 Reg.20
Part IV, amended: SI 2013/235 Sch.2 para.7
Part IV, applied: SI 2013/1506 Reg.20, Reg.21, Reg.27, Reg.32, Reg.33
Part IV, varied: SI 2013/1506 Reg.20
Art., amended: SI 2013/235 Sch.2 para.7
Art., applied: SI 2013/1506 Reg.20, Reg.21, Reg.27, Reg.32, Reg.33
Art., varied: SI 2013/1506 Reg.20
Art.1, amended: SI 2013/235 Sch.2 para.7
Art.1, applied: SI 2013/1506 Reg.20, Reg.21, Reg.27, Reg.32, Reg.33
Art.1, varied: SI 2013/1506 Reg.20
Art.2, amended: SI 2013/235 Sch.2 para.7
Art.2, applied: SI 2013/1506 Reg.20, Reg.21, Reg.27, Reg.32, Reg.33
Art.2, varied: SI 2013/1506 Reg.20
Art.2, amended: SI 2013/235 Sch.2 para.7
Art.2, applied: SI 2013/1506 Reg.20, Reg.21, Reg.27, Reg.32, Reg.33
Art.2, varied: SI 2013/1506 Reg.20
Art.3, amended: SI 2013/235 Sch.2 para.7
Art.3, applied: SI 2013/1506 Reg.20, Reg.21, Reg.27, Reg.32, Reg.33
Art.3, varied: SI 2013/1506 Reg.20
Art.4, amended: SI 2013/235 Sch.2 para.7
Art.4, applied: SI 2013/1506 Reg.20, Reg.21, Reg.27, Reg.32, Reg.33
Art.4, varied: SI 2013/1506 Reg.20
Art.(5), amended: SI 2013/235 Sch.2 para.7
Art.(5), applied: SI 2013/1506 Reg.20, Reg.21, Reg.27, Reg.32, Reg.33
Art.(5), varied: SI 2013/1506 Reg.20
Art.5, amended: SI 2013/235 Sch.2 para.7
Art.5, applied: SI 2013/1506 Reg.20, Reg.21, Reg.27, Reg.32, Reg.33
Art.5, varied: SI 2013/1506 Reg.20
Art.6, amended: SI 2013/235 Sch.2 para.7
Art.6, applied: SI 2013/1506 Reg.20, Reg.21, Reg.27, Reg.32, Reg.33
Art.6, varied: SI 2013/1506 Reg.20
Art.6(b), amended: SI 2013/235 Sch.2 para.7
Art.6(b), applied: SI 2013/1506 Reg.20, Reg.21, Reg.27, Reg.32, Reg.33
Art.6(b), varied: SI 2013/1506 Reg.20
Art.6, amended: SI 2013/235 Sch.2 para.7
Art.6, applied: SI 2013/1506 Reg.20, Reg.21, Reg.27, Reg.32, Reg.33
Art.6, varied: SI 2013/1506 Reg.20
Art.7, amended: SI 2013/235 Sch.2 para.7
Art.7, applied: SI 2013/1506 Reg.20, Reg.21, Reg.27, Reg.32, Reg.33
Art.7, varied: SI 2013/1506 Reg.20
Art.8, amended: SI 2013/235 Sch.2 para.7
Art.8, applied: SI 2013/1506 Reg.20, Reg.21, Reg.27, Reg.32, Reg.33
Art.8, varied: SI 2013/1506 Reg.20
Art.9, amended: SI 2013/235 Sch.2 para.7
Art.9, applied: SI 2013/1506 Reg.20, Reg.21, Reg.27, Reg.32, Reg.33
Art.9, varied: SI 2013/1506 Reg.20
Art.12, amended: SI 2013/235 Sch.2 para.7
Art.12, applied: SI 2013/1506 Reg.20, Reg.21, Reg.27, Reg.32, Reg.33
Art.12, varied: SI 2013/1506 Reg.20
Art.13, amended: SI 2013/235 Sch.2 para.7
Art.13, applied: SI 2013/1506 Reg.20, Reg.21, Reg.27, Reg.32, Reg.33
Art.13, varied: SI 2013/1506 Reg.20
Art.15, amended: SI 2013/235 Sch.2 para.7
Art.15, applied: SI 2013/1506 Reg.20, Reg.21, Reg.27, Reg.32, Reg.33
Art.15, varied: SI 2013/1506 Reg.20
Art.16, amended: SI 2013/235 Sch.2 para.7
Art.16, applied: SI 2013/1506 Reg.20, Reg.21, Reg.27, Reg.32, Reg.33
Art.16, varied: SI 2013/1506 Reg.20
Art.17, amended: SI 2013/235 Sch.2 para.7
Art.17, applied: SI 2013/1506 Reg.20, Reg.21, Reg.27, Reg.32, Reg.33
Art.17, varied: SI 2013/1506 Reg.20
Art.17, amended: SI 2013/235 Sch.2 para.7
Art.17, applied: SI 2013/1506 Reg.20, Reg.21, Reg.27, Reg.32, Reg.33
Art.17, varied: SI 2013/1506 Reg.20
Art.17(4), amended: SI 2013/235 Sch.2 para.7
Art.17(4), applied: SI 2013/1506 Reg.20, Reg.21, Reg.27, Reg.32, Reg.33
Art.17(4), varied: SI 2013/1506 Reg.20
Art.17(5), amended: SI 2013/235 Sch.2 para.7

Art.17(5), applied: SI 2013/1506 Reg.20, Reg.21, Reg.27, Reg.32, Reg.33
Art.17(5), varied: SI 2013/1506 Reg.20
Art.17(6), amended: SI 2013/235 Sch.2 para.7
Art.17(6), applied: SI 2013/1506 Reg.20, Reg.21, Reg.27, Reg.32, Reg.33
Art.17(6), varied: SI 2013/1506 Reg.20
Art.18, amended: SI 2013/235 Sch.2 para.7
Art.18, applied: SI 2013/1506 Reg.20, Reg.21, Reg.27, Reg.32, Reg.33
Art.18, varied: SI 2013/1506 Reg.20
Art.20, amended: SI 2013/235 Sch.2 para.7
Art.20, applied: SI 2013/1506 Reg.20, Reg.21, Reg.27, Reg.32, Reg.33
Art.20, varied: SI 2013/1506 Reg.20
Art.21, amended: SI 2013/235 Sch.2 para.7
Art.21, applied: SI 2013/1506 Reg.20, Reg.21, Reg.27, Reg.32, Reg.33
Art.21, varied: SI 2013/1506 Reg.20
Art.22, amended: SI 2013/235 Sch.2 para.7
Art.22, applied: SI 2013/1506 Reg.20, Reg.21, Reg.27, Reg.32, Reg.33
Art.22, varied: SI 2013/1506 Reg.20
Art.23, amended: SI 2013/235 Sch.2 para.7
Art.23, applied: SI 2013/1506 Reg.20, Reg.21, Reg.27, Reg.32, Reg.33
Art.23, varied: SI 2013/1506 Reg.20
Art.24, amended: SI 2013/235 Sch.2 para.7
Art.24, applied: SI 2013/1506 Reg.20, Reg.21, Reg.27, Reg.32, Reg.33
Art.24, varied: SI 2013/1506 Reg.20
Art.25, amended: SI 2013/235 Sch.2 para.7
Art.25, applied: SI 2013/1506 Reg.20, Reg.21, Reg.27, Reg.32, Reg.33
Art.25, varied: SI 2013/1506 Reg.20
Art.26, amended: SI 2013/235 Sch.2 para.7
Art.26, applied: SI 2013/1506 Reg.20, Reg.21, Reg.27, Reg.32, Reg.33
Art.26, varied: SI 2013/1506 Reg.20
Art.27, amended: SI 2013/235 Sch.2 para.7
Art.27, applied: SI 2013/1506 Reg.20, Reg.21, Reg.27, Reg.32, Reg.33
Art.27, varied: SI 2013/1506 Reg.20
Art.27A, amended: SI 2013/235 Sch.2 para.7
Art.27A, applied: SI 2013/1506 Reg.20, Reg.21, Reg.27, Reg.32, Reg.33
Art.27A, varied: SI 2013/1506 Reg.20
Art.28, amended: SI 2013/235 Sch.2 para.7
Art.28, applied: SI 2013/1506 Reg.20, Reg.21, Reg.27, Reg.32, Reg.33
Art.28, varied: SI 2013/1506 Reg.20
Art.29, amended: SI 2013/235 Sch.2 para.7
Art.29, applied: SI 2013/1506 Reg.20, Reg.21, Reg.27, Reg.32, Reg.33
Art.29, varied: SI 2013/1506 Reg.20
Art.29A, amended: SI 2013/235 Sch.2 para.7
Art.29A, applied: SI 2013/1506 Reg.20, Reg.21, Reg.27, Reg.32, Reg.33
Art.29A, varied: SI 2013/1506 Reg.20
Art.30, amended: SI 2013/235 Sch.2 para.7
Art.30, applied: SI 2013/1506 Reg.20, Reg.21, Reg.27, Reg.32, Reg.33
Art.30, varied: SI 2013/1506 Reg.20
Art.31, amended: SI 2013/235 Sch.2 para.7
Art.31, applied: SI 2013/1506 Reg.20, Reg.21, Reg.27, Reg.32, Reg.33
Art.31, varied: SI 2013/1506 Reg.20
Art.32, amended: SI 2013/235 Sch.2 para.7
Art.32, applied: SI 2013/1506 Reg.20, Reg.21, Reg.27, Reg.32, Reg.33
Art.32, varied: SI 2013/1506 Reg.20
Art.33, amended: SI 2013/235 Sch.2 para.7
Art.33, applied: SI 2013/1506 Reg.20, Reg.21, Reg.27, Reg.32, Reg.33
Art.33, varied: SI 2013/1506 Reg.20
Art.34, amended: SI 2013/235 Sch.2 para.7
Art.34, applied: SI 2013/1506 Reg.20, Reg.21, Reg.27, Reg.32, Reg.33
Art.34, varied: SI 2013/1506 Reg.20
Art.34A, amended: SI 2013/235 Sch.2 para.7
Art.34A, applied: SI 2013/1506 Reg.20, Reg.21, Reg.27, Reg.32, Reg.33
Art.34A, varied: SI 2013/1506 Reg.20
Art.35, amended: SI 2013/235 Sch.2 para.7
Art.35, applied: SI 2013/1506 Reg.20, Reg.21, Reg.27, Reg.32, Reg.33
Art.35, varied: SI 2013/1506 Reg.20
Art.36, amended: SI 2013/235 Sch.2 para.7
Art.36, applied: SI 2013/1506 Reg.20, Reg.21, Reg.27, Reg.32, Reg.33
Art.36, varied: SI 2013/1506 Reg.20
Art.37, amended: SI 2013/235 Sch.2 para.7
Art.37, applied: SI 2013/1506 Reg.20, Reg.21, Reg.27, Reg.32, Reg.33
Art.37, varied: SI 2013/1506 Reg.20
Art.38, amended: SI 2013/235 Sch.2 para.7
Art.38, applied: SI 2013/1506 Reg.20, Reg.21, Reg.27, Reg.32, Reg.33
Art.38, varied: SI 2013/1506 Reg.20
Art.39, amended: SI 2013/235 Sch.2 para.7
Art.39, applied: SI 2013/1506 Reg.20, Reg.21, Reg.27, Reg.32, Reg.33
Art.39, varied: SI 2013/1506 Reg.20
Art.40, amended: SI 2013/235 Sch.2 para.7
Art.40, applied: SI 2013/1506 Reg.20, Reg.21, Reg.27, Reg.32, Reg.33
Art.40, varied: SI 2013/1506 Reg.20
Art.40, amended: SI 2013/235 Sch.2 para.7

Art.40, applied: SI 2013/1506 Reg.20, Reg.21, Reg.27, Reg.32, Reg.33
Art.40, varied: SI 2013/1506 Reg.20
Art.40(2), amended: SI 2013/235 Sch.2 para.7
Art.40(2), applied: SI 2013/1506 Reg.20, Reg.21, Reg.27, Reg.32, Reg.33
Art.40(2), varied: SI 2013/1506 Reg.20
Art.40(4), amended: SI 2013/235 Sch.2 para.7
Art.40(4), applied: SI 2013/1506 Reg.20, Reg.21, Reg.27, Reg.32, Reg.33
Art.40(4), varied: SI 2013/1506 Reg.20
Art.43, amended: SI 2013/235 Sch.2 para.7
Art.43, applied: SI 2013/1506 Reg.20, Reg.21, Reg.27, Reg.32, Reg.33
Art.43, varied: SI 2013/1506 Reg.20
Art.44, amended: SI 2013/235 Sch.2 para.7
Art.44, applied: SI 2013/1506 Reg.20, Reg.21, Reg.27, Reg.32, Reg.33
Art.44, varied: SI 2013/1506 Reg.20
Art.45, amended: SI 2013/235 Sch.2 para.7
Art.45, applied: SI 2013/1506 Reg.20, Reg.21, Reg.27, Reg.32, Reg.33
Art.45, varied: SI 2013/1506 Reg.20
Art.46, amended: SI 2013/235 Sch.2 para.7
Art.46, applied: SI 2013/1506 Reg.20, Reg.21, Reg.27, Reg.32, Reg.33
Art.46, varied: SI 2013/1506 Reg.20
Art.46, amended: SI 2013/235 Sch.2 para.7
Art.46, applied: SI 2013/1506 Reg.20, Reg.21, Reg.27, Reg.32, Reg.33
Art.46, varied: SI 2013/1506 Reg.20
Art.46(1), amended: SI 2013/235 Sch.2 para.7
Art.46(1), applied: SI 2013/1506 Reg.20, Reg.21, Reg.27, Reg.32, Reg.33
Art.46(1), varied: SI 2013/1506 Reg.20
Art.47A, amended: SI 2013/235 Sch.2 para.7
Art.47A, applied: SI 2013/1506 Reg.20, Reg.21, Reg.27, Reg.32, Reg.33
Art.47A, varied: SI 2013/1506 Reg.20
Art.48, amended: SI 2013/235 Sch.2 para.7
Art.48, applied: SI 2013/1506 Reg.20, Reg.21, Reg.27, Reg.32, Reg.33
Art.48, varied: SI 2013/1506 Reg.20
Art.49, amended: SI 2013/235 Sch.2 para.7
Art.49, applied: SI 2013/1506 Reg.20, Reg.21, Reg.27, Reg.32, Reg.33
Art.49, varied: SI 2013/1506 Reg.20
Art.51, amended: SI 2013/235 Sch.2 para.7
Art.51, applied: SI 2013/1506 Reg.20, Reg.21, Reg.27, Reg.32, Reg.33
Art.51, varied: SI 2013/1506 Reg.20
Art.53, amended: SI 2013/235 Sch.2 para.7
Art.53, applied: SI 2013/1506 Reg.20, Reg.21, Reg.27, Reg.32, Reg.33
Art.53, varied: SI 2013/1506 Reg.20
Art.(54, amended: SI 2013/235 Sch.2 para.7
Art.(54, applied: SI 2013/1506 Reg.20, Reg.21, Reg.27, Reg.32, Reg.33
Art.(54, varied: SI 2013/1506 Reg.20
Art.54, amended: SI 2013/235 Sch.2 para.7
Art.54, applied: SI 2013/1506 Reg.20, Reg.21, Reg.27, Reg.32, Reg.33
Art.54, varied: SI 2013/1506 Reg.20
Art.54, amended: SI 2013/235 Sch.2 para.7
Art.54, applied: SI 2013/1506 Reg.20, Reg.21, Reg.27, Reg.32, Reg.33
Art.54, varied: SI 2013/1506 Reg.20
Art.54(5), amended: SI 2013/235 Sch.2 para.7
Art.54(5), applied: SI 2013/1506 Reg.20, Reg.21, Reg.27, Reg.32, Reg.33
Art.54(5), varied: SI 2013/1506 Reg.20
Art.(55, amended: SI 2013/235 Sch.2 para.7
Art.(55, applied: SI 2013/1506 Reg.20, Reg.21, Reg.27, Reg.32, Reg.33
Art.(55, varied: SI 2013/1506 Reg.20
Art.55, amended: SI 2013/235 Sch.2 para.7
Art.55, applied: SI 2013/1506 Reg.20, Reg.21, Reg.27, Reg.32, Reg.33
Art.55, varied: SI 2013/1506 Reg.20
Art.55, amended: SI 2013/235 Sch.2 para.7
Art.55, applied: SI 2013/1506 Reg.20, Reg.21, Reg.27, Reg.32, Reg.33
Art.55, varied: SI 2013/1506 Reg.20
Art.55(2), amended: SI 2013/235 Sch.2 para.7
Art.55(2), applied: SI 2013/1506 Reg.20, Reg.21, Reg.27, Reg.32, Reg.33
Art.55(2), varied: SI 2013/1506 Reg.20
Art.56, amended: SI 2013/235 Sch.2 para.7
Art.56, applied: SI 2013/1506 Reg.20, Reg.21, Reg.27, Reg.32, Reg.33
Art.56, varied: SI 2013/1506 Reg.20
Art.71, amended: SI 2013/235 Sch.2 para.7
Art.71, applied: SI 2013/1506 Reg.20, Reg.21, Reg.27, Reg.32, Reg.33
Art.71, varied: SI 2013/1506 Reg.20
Art.105, amended: SI 2013/235 Sch.2 para.7
Art.105, applied: SI 2013/1506 Reg.20, Reg.21, Reg.27, Reg.32, Reg.33
Art.105, varied: SI 2013/1506 Reg.20
para., amended: SI 2013/235 Sch.2 para.7
para., applied: SI 2013/1506 Reg.20, Reg.21, Reg.27, Reg.32, Reg.33
para., varied: SI 2013/1506 Reg.20
para(.13)., amended: SI 2013/235 Sch.2 para.7
para(.13)., applied: SI 2013/1506 Reg.20, Reg.21, Reg.27, Reg.32, Reg.33
para(.13)., varied: SI 2013/1506 Reg.20
para(.15)., amended: SI 2013/235 Sch.2 para.7

para(.15)., applied: SI 2013/1506 Reg.20, Reg.21, Reg.27, Reg.32, Reg.33
para(.15)., varied: SI 2013/1506 Reg.20
para(.2)., amended: SI 2013/235 Sch.2 para.7
para(.2)., applied: SI 2013/1506 Reg.20, Reg.21, Reg.27, Reg.32, Reg.33
para(.2)., varied: SI 2013/1506 Reg.20
para(.6)., amended: SI 2013/235 Sch.2 para.7
para(.6)., applied: SI 2013/1506 Reg.20, Reg.21, Reg.27, Reg.32, Reg.33
para(.6)., varied: SI 2013/1506 Reg.20
para.1(1)., amended: SI 2013/235 Sch.2 para.7
para.1(1)., applied: SI 2013/1506 Reg.20, Reg.21, Reg.27, Reg.32, Reg.33
para.1(1)., varied: SI 2013/1506 Reg.20
r.5, amended: SI 2013/235 Sch.2 para.7
r.5, applied: SI 2013/1506 Reg.20, Reg.21, Reg.27, Reg.32, Reg.33
r.5, varied: SI 2013/1506 Reg.20
Reg.3, amended: SI 2013/235 Sch.2 para.7
Reg.3, applied: SI 2013/1506 Reg.20, Reg.21, Reg.27, Reg.32, Reg.33
Reg.3, varied: SI 2013/1506 Reg.20
Reg.35, amended: SI 2013/235 Sch.2 para.7
Reg.35, applied: SI 2013/1506 Reg.20, Reg.21, Reg.27, Reg.32, Reg.33
Reg.35, varied: SI 2013/1506 Reg.20
Reg.36, amended: SI 2013/235 Sch.2 para.7
Reg.36, applied: SI 2013/1506 Reg.20, Reg.21, Reg.27, Reg.32, Reg.33
Reg.36, varied: SI 2013/1506 Reg.20
Reg.37, amended: SI 2013/235 Sch.2 para.7
Reg.37, applied: SI 2013/1506 Reg.20, Reg.21, Reg.27, Reg.32, Reg.33
Reg.37, varied: SI 2013/1506 Reg.20
s.1, amended: SI 2013/235 Sch.2 para.7
s.1, applied: SI 2013/1506 Reg.20, Reg.21, Reg.27, Reg.32, Reg.33
s.1, varied: SI 2013/1506 Reg.20
s.2, amended: SI 2013/235 Sch.2 para.7
s.2, applied: SI 2013/1506 Reg.20, Reg.21, Reg.27, Reg.32, Reg.33
s.2, varied: SI 2013/1506 Reg.20
s.5, amended: SI 2013/235 Sch.2 para.7
s.5, applied: SI 2013/1506 Reg.20, Reg.21, Reg.27, Reg.32, Reg.33
s.5, varied: SI 2013/1506 Reg.20
s.27, amended: SI 2013/235 Sch.2 para.7
s.27, applied: SI 2013/1506 Reg.20, Reg.21, Reg.27, Reg.32, Reg.33
s.27, varied: SI 2013/1506 Reg.20
s.46, amended: SI 2013/235 Sch.2 para.7
s.46, applied: SI 2013/1506 Reg.20, Reg.21, Reg.27, Reg.32, Reg.33
s.46, varied: SI 2013/1506 Reg.20
s.55, amended: SI 2013/235 Sch.2 para.7
s.55, applied: SI 2013/1506 Reg.20, Reg.21, Reg.27, Reg.32, Reg.33
s.55, varied: SI 2013/1506 Reg.20
Sch.1, amended: SI 2013/235 Sch.2 para.7
Sch.1, applied: SI 2013/1506 Reg.20, Reg.21, Reg.27, Reg.32, Reg.33
Sch.1, varied: SI 2013/1506 Reg.20
Sch.2, amended: SI 2013/235 Sch.2 para.7
Sch.2, applied: SI 2013/1506 Reg.20, Reg.21, Reg.27, Reg.32, Reg.33
Sch.2, varied: SI 2013/1506 Reg.20
Sch.3, amended: SI 2013/235 Sch.2 para.7
Sch.3, applied: SI 2013/1506 Reg.20, Reg.21, Reg.27, Reg.32, Reg.33
Sch.3, varied: SI 2013/1506 Reg.20
Sch.3A, amended: SI 2013/235 Sch.2 para.7
Sch.3A, applied: SI 2013/1506 Reg.20, Reg.21, Reg.27, Reg.32, Reg.33
Sch.3A, varied: SI 2013/1506 Reg.20
Sch.4, amended: SI 2013/235 Sch.2 para.7
Sch.4, applied: SI 2013/1506 Reg.20, Reg.21, Reg.27, Reg.32, Reg.33
Sch.4, varied: SI 2013/1506 Reg.20
Sch.5, amended: SI 2013/235 Sch.2 para.7
Sch.5, applied: SI 2013/1506 Reg.20, Reg.21, Reg.27, Reg.32, Reg.33
Sch.5, varied: SI 2013/1506 Reg.20
Sch.6, amended: SI 2013/235 Sch.2 para.7
Sch.6, applied: SI 2013/1506 Reg.20, Reg.21, Reg.27, Reg.32, Reg.33
Sch.6, varied: SI 2013/1506 Reg.20
Sch.7, amended: SI 2013/235 Sch.2 para.7
Sch.7, applied: SI 2013/1506 Reg.20, Reg.21, Reg.27, Reg.32, Reg.33
Sch.7, varied: SI 2013/1506 Reg.20

1171. Police Cadets (Scotland) Amendment (No.2) Regulations 1978

revoked: SSI 2013/42 Sch.1 Part 1

1211. Pensions Increase (Annual Review) Order 1978

applied: SI 2013/604 Sch.1

1358. British Railways Board (Winding up of Closed Pension Funds) Order 1978

Art.1, amended: SI 2013/472 Art.4

1509. Act of Sederunt (Commissary Business) (Amendment) 1978

revoked: SSI 2013/291 Sch.5

1684. Public Service Vehicles (Lost Property) Regulations 1978

revoked (in part): SI 2013/2987 Sch.3
Reg.7, amended: SI 2013/1644 Sch.4

1689. Social Security (Categorisation of Earners) Regulations 1978

see *ITV Services Ltd v Revenue and Customs Commissioners* [2013] EWCA Civ 867, [2013] B.T.C. 633 (CA (Civ Div)), Sir James Munby (President, Fam)

1908. Rehabilitation of Offenders (Northern Ireland) Order 1978

applied: 2013 c.32 Sch.7 para.10

1910. European Communities (Services of Lawyers) Order 1978

Art.2, amended: SI 2013/1605 Reg.2, SSI 2013/177 Reg.2

Sch.1 Part 1, amended: SI 2013/1605 Reg.2

1979

427. Petroleum (Consolidation) Act 1928 (Enforcement) Regulations 1979

Reg.2, revoked (in part): SI 2013/448 Sch.1

432. Vaccine Damage Payments Regulations 1979

Reg.11, amended: SI 2013/2380 Reg.2

Reg.11A, added: SI 2013/2380 Reg.2

597. Social Security (Overlapping Benefits) Regulations 1979

applied: SI 2013/3029 Sch.1 para.10, Sch.2 para.5, Sch.7 para.8, SI 2013/3035 Sch.1

Reg.2, amended: SI 2013/388 Sch.1 para.10, SI 2013/591 Sch.1 para.3, SI 2013/630 Reg.25

Reg.6, amended: SI 2013/388 Sch.1 para.10, SI 2013/591 Sch.1 para.3

Reg.16, amended: SI 2013/388 Sch.1 para.10, SI 2013/591 Sch.1 para.3

Reg.17, amended: SI 2013/388 Sch.1 para.10

Sch.1, amended: SI 2013/388 Sch.1 para.10, SI 2013/591 Sch.1 para.3

642. Social Security (Widow's Benefit and Retirement Pensions) Regulations 1979

Reg.4, amended: SI 2013/630 Reg.26

791. Forestry (Felling of Trees) Regulations 1979

Reg.3, amended: SI 2013/755 Sch.4 para.9

Reg.4, amended: SI 2013/755 Sch.4 para.10

Reg.6, amended: SI 2013/755 Sch.4 para.11

Reg.7, amended: SI 2013/755 Sch.4 para.12

Reg.8A, amended: SI 2013/755 Sch.4 para.12

Reg.9, amended: SI 2013/755 Sch.4 para.12

Reg.10, amended: SI 2013/755 Sch.4 para.12

Reg.12, amended: SI 2013/755 Sch.4 para.12

Reg.13, amended: SI 2013/755 Sch.4 para.12

Reg.15, amended: SI 2013/755 Sch.4 para.12

Reg.16, amended: SI 2013/755 Sch.4 para.13

Sch.1, added: SI 2013/755 Sch.4 para.14

Sch.1, amended: SI 2013/755 Sch.4 para.14

792. Forestry (Exceptions from Restriction of Felling) Regulations 1979

Reg.4, amended: SI 2013/755 Sch.4 para.15

1047. Pensions Increase (Review) Order 1979

applied: SI 2013/604 Sch.1

1123. Local Authorities (Miscellaneous Provisions) Order 1979

Art.4, amended: SI 2013/3005 Art.11

1279. Trunk Roads (Route A9) (Golspie) (Restriction of Waiting) Order 1979

revoked: SSI 2013/88 Art.6

1405. Act of Sederunt (Commissary Business) (Amendment) 1979

revoked: SSI 2013/291 Sch.5

1447. Continental Shelf (Designation of Additional Areas) Order 1979

applied: SI 2013/3162 Art.1

1451. Ministry of Overseas Development (Dissolution) Order 1979

Sch.2 para.7, revoked: SI 2013/687 Sch.2

1573. Statutory Rules (Northern Ireland) Order 1979

applied: 2013 c.32 s.62

1698. Police Cadets (Scotland) Amendment Regulations 1979

revoked: SSI 2013/42 Sch.1 Part 1

1714. Perjury (Northern Ireland) Order 1979

Art.10, applied: 2013 c.33 s.87, SI 2013/971 Reg.26, SI 2013/2605 Art.19

1980

36. Chloroform in Food Regulations 1980

revoked (in part): SI 2013/466 Reg.3, SI 2013/545 Reg.3

51. Consumer Credit (Total Charge for Credit) Regulations 1980

revoked (in part): SI 2013/1881 Art.21

289. Chloroform in Food (Scotland) Regulations 1980

revoked: SSI 2013/83 Sch.1

346. Rules of the Court of Judicature (Northern Ireland) 1980

Ord.r62, see *Banks v Geddis (Costs)* [2013] P.N.L.R. 11 (QBD (NI)), Weatherup, J.

455. Act of Sederunt (Summary Cause Rules, Sheriff Court) (Amendment) 1980

r.22, see *South Lanarkshire Council v George* 2013 Hous. L.R. 49 (Sh Ct (South Strathclyde) (Hamilton)), Sheriff Principal B A Lockhart

568. Double Taxation Relief (Taxes on Income) (The United States of America) Order 1980

see *Anson v Revenue and Customs Commissioners* [2013] EWCA Civ 63, [2013] S.T.C. 557 (CA (Civ Div)), Laws, L.J.; see *FCE Bank Plc v Revenue and Customs Commissioners* [2012] EWCA Civ 1290, [2013] S.T.C. 14 (CA (Civ Div)), Pill, L.J.

765. Motorcycles (Sound Level Measurement Certificates) Regulations 1980
revoked: SI 2013/2987 Sch.2

1177. National Health Service (Superannuation)(Scotland) Regulations 1980
Reg.27, applied: SSI 2013/174 Reg.5
Reg.28, applied: SSI 2013/174 Reg.5

1302. Pensions Increase (Review) Order 1980
applied: SI 2013/604 Sch.1

1314. Celluloid and Cinematograph Film Act 1922 (Exemptions) Regulations 1980
revoked: SI 2013/448 Sch.1

1697. Rent Act 1977 (Forms etc.) Regulations 1980
Reg.8, amended: SI 2013/1036 Sch.2 para.3
Sch.1, amended: SI 2013/1036 Sch.2 para.4
Sch.4 para.1, amended: SI 2013/1036 Sch.2 para.4

1947. Friendly Societies (Life Assurance Premium Relief) (Change of Rate) Regulations 1980
Reg.2, amended: SI 2013/496 Sch.11 para.12
Reg.3, amended: SI 2013/496 Sch.11 para.12
Reg.5, amended: SI 2013/496 Sch.11 para.12
Reg.8, amended: SI 2013/496 Sch.11 para.12

1948. Industrial Assurance (Life Assurance Premium Relief) (Change of Rate) Regulations 1980
Reg.2, amended: SI 2013/496 Sch.11 para.13
Reg.3, amended: SI 2013/496 Sch.11 para.13
Reg.5, amended: SI 2013/496 Sch.11 para.13
Reg.8, amended: SI 2013/496 Sch.11 para.13

1981

15. Public Bodies Land (Appropriate Ministers) Order 1981
Art.2, amended: SI 2013/687 Sch.2

168. Trunk Road (Bethesda, Gwynedd) (Prohibition and Restriction of Waiting) (Variation) Order 1981
revoked: SI 2013/791 Art.7

179. Agricultural Wages Committees (New Combinations of Counties) Order 1981
revoked: 2013 c.24 Sch.20 para.2

231. Weights and Measures (Northern Ireland) Order 1981
Sch.6, amended: SI 2013/1478 Sch.5 para.2
Sch.6, revoked: SI 2013/1478 Sch.5 para.1
Sch.6, substituted: SI 2013/1478 Sch.5 para.2

257. Public Service Vehicles (Conditions of Fitness, Equipment, Use and Certification) Regulations 1981
Reg.3, amended: SI 2013/1644 Sch.2

476. Consular Fees Regulations 1981
Reg.3, amended: SI 2013/762 Reg.2

552. Magistrates Courts Rules 1981
r.12, see *Euro Foods Group v Cumbria CC* [2013] EWHC 2659 (Admin), (2013) 177 J.P. 614 (DC), Sir John Thomas (President)
r.65., amended: SI 2013/630 Reg.61

584. Merchant Shipping (Safety Convention) (Transitional Provisions) Regulations 1981
revoked: SI 2013/2944 Sch.1

614. Consumer Credit (Termination of Licences) (Amendment) Regulations 1981
revoked (in part): SI 2013/1881 Art.21

687. Gasholders and Steam Boilers Regulations (Metrication) Regulations 1981
revoked: SI 2013/448 Sch.1

830. Town and Country Planning (General Development) (Scotland) Order 1981
applied: SSI 2013/155 Reg.51

917. Health and Safety (First-Aid) Regulations 1981
Reg.3, amended: SI 2013/1512 Reg.4

1217. Pensions Increase (Review) Order 1981
applied: SI 2013/604 Sch.1

1327. Locomotives etc Regulations 1906 (Metrication) Regulations 1981
revoked: SI 2013/448 Sch.1

1499. Building (Procedure) (Scotland) Regulations 1981
Reg.20, amended: SSI 2013/119 Sch.2 para.3

1623. Public Service Vehicles (Lost Property) (Amendment) Regulations 1981
revoked (in part): SI 2013/2987 Sch.3

1675. Magistrates Courts (Northern Ireland) Order 1981
applied: SI 2013/233 Reg.9, Reg.13, SI 2013/2033 Reg.45
Art.19, disapplied: SI 2013/233 Reg.13
Art.95, applied: SSI 2013/189 Art.11
Art.146, applied: SI 2013/1387 Reg.8, Reg.19, Sch.2 para.9, SI 2013/1478 Reg.20
Sch.4, applied: 2013 c.15 s.11, 2013 c.32 Sch.10 para.8, SI 2013/233 Reg.6
Sch.6 Part I para.21, revoked: 2013 c.22 Sch.11 para.210
Sch.6 Part I para.25, revoked: 2013 c.22 Sch.11 para.210

1694. Motor Vehicles (Tests) Regulations 1981
Reg.20, amended: SI 2013/271 Reg.11
Reg.31, added: SI 2013/271 Reg.13
Sch.2 para.2, amended: SI 2013/271 Reg.12
Sch.2 para.3, amended: SI 2013/271 Reg.12
Sch.2 para.3A, amended: SI 2013/271 Reg.12
Sch.2 para.4, amended: SI 2013/271 Reg.12
Sch.2 para.5, amended: SI 2013/271 Reg.12
Sch.2 para.5A, amended: SI 2013/271 Reg.12

1794. Transfer of Undertakings (Protection of Employment) Regulations 1981

see *Foley v NHS Greater Glasgow and Clyde* [2013] I.C.R. 342 (EAT (SC)), Lady Smith

1828. Control of Noise (Code of Practice on Noise from Ice-Cream Van Chimes Etc.) Order 1981

revoked (in part): SI 2013/2036 Art.3

1982

18. Erucic Acid in Food (Scotland) Amendment Regulations 1982

revoked: SSI 2013/217 Sch.1

97. Agricultural Land Tribunals (Areas) Order 1982

revoked: SI 2013/1036 Sch.2 para.55

207. Warble Fly (Scotland) Order 1982

Art.2, amended: SSI 2013/173 Art.5
Art.4, amended: SSI 2013/173 Art.5
Art.11, amended: SSI 2013/173 Art.5
Art.12, amended: SSI 2013/173 Art.5
Art.14, amended: SSI 2013/173 Art.5
Art.15, amended: SSI 2013/173 Art.5
Sch.1, amended: SSI 2013/173 Art.5

264. Erucic Acid in Food (Amendment) Regulations 1982

revoked (in part): SI 2013/2196 Reg.10, SI 2013/2493 Reg.10

273. Police Cadets (Scotland) Amendment Regulations 1982

revoked: SSI 2013/42 Sch.1 Part 1

286. National Health Service (Notification of Births and Deaths) Regulations 1982

revoked (in part): SI 2013/261 Reg.12

630. Petroleum-Spirit (Plastic Containers) Regulations 1982

Reg.8, revoked (in part): SI 2013/448 Sch.1

648. Forestry Commission Byelaws 1982

Art.2, amended: SI 2013/755 Sch.4 para.17
Art.3, amended: SI 2013/755 Sch.4 para.18
Art.5, amended: SI 2013/755 Sch.4 para.18
Art.6, amended: SI 2013/755 Sch.4 para.18
Art.7, amended: SI 2013/755 Sch.4 para.18
Sch.1, amended: SI 2013/755 Sch.4 para.19

712. Land Compensation (Northern Ireland) Order 1982

Art.6, see *Kerr v Northern Ireland Housing Executive* [2013] R.V.R. 137 (Lands Tr (NI)), Coghlin, L.J.

719. Public Lending Right Scheme 1982 (Commencement) Order 1982

applied: SI 2013/3029 Sch.1 para.11, SI 2013/3035 Sch.1

894. Statutory Sick Pay (General) Regulations 1982

Reg.7, applied: SI 2013/380 Reg.17

1070. British Protectorates, Protected States and Protected Persons Order 1982

Art.11, applied: SI 2013/617 Sch.4 para.2

1072. Continental Shelf (Designation of Additional Areas) Order 1982

applied: SI 2013/3162 Art.1

1122. Valuation (Postponement of Revaluation) (Scotland) Order 1982

revoked: SSI 2013/113 Art.3

1163. Motorways Traffic (England and Wales) Regulations 1982

Reg.3, applied: SI 2013/800 Art.5
Reg.3, varied: SI 2013/1123 Reg.3, SI 2013/1201 Reg.3, SI 2013/2396 Reg.3, SI 2013/2397 Reg.3
Reg.4, varied: SI 2013/1123 Reg.3, SI 2013/1201 Reg.3
Reg.5, amended: SI 2013/2649 Art.6
Reg.5, disapplied: SI 2013/3100 Art.7, SI 2013/3124 Art.8, SI 2013/3132 Art.7
Reg.5, varied: SI 2013/19 Art.5, SI 2013/20 Art.6, SI 2013/26 Art.8, SI 2013/29 Art.4, SI 2013/57 Art.5, SI 2013/58 Art.7, SI 2013/119 Art.8, SI 2013/134 Art.5, SI 2013/150 Art.6, SI 2013/153 Art.3, SI 2013/168 Art.4, SI 2013/179 Art.4, SI 2013/184 Art.8, SI 2013/187 Art.5, SI 2013/196 Art.6, SI 2013/200 Art.7, SI 2013/231 Art.5, SI 2013/315 Art.7, SI 2013/327 Art.7, SI 2013/328 Art.7, SI 2013/354 Art.7, SI 2013/370 Art.7, SI 2013/403 Art.7, SI 2013/577 Art.7, SI 2013/681 Art.3, SI 2013/741 Art.4, SI 2013/743 Art.4, SI 2013/752 Art.5, SI 2013/800 Art.5, SI 2013/843 Art.7, SI 2013/853 Art.3, SI 2013/869 Art.6, SI 2013/872 Art.6, SI 2013/873 Art.5, SI 2013/902 Art.8, SI 2013/970 Art.8, SI 2013/972 Art.7, SI 2013/974 Art.5, SI 2013/978 Art.7, SI 2013/993 Art.5, SI 2013/994 Art.7, SI 2013/1002 Art.5, SI 2013/1004 Art.3, SI 2013/1006 Art.3, SI 2013/1015 Art.6, SI 2013/1071 Art.4, SI 2013/1078 Art.7, SI 2013/1079 Art.7, SI 2013/1093 Art.6, SI 2013/1094 Art.6, SI 2013/1154 Art.8, SI 2013/1176 Art.4, SI 2013/1207 Art.4, SI 2013/1234 Art.3, SI 2013/1258 Art.7, SI 2013/1259 Art.9, SI 2013/1275 Art.8, SI 2013/1276 Art.8, SI 2013/1288 Art.7, SI 2013/1292 Art.6, SI 2013/1311 Art.6, SI 2013/1313 Art.4, SI 2013/1332 Art.8, SI 2013/1335 Art.7, SI 2013/1336 Art.7, SI 2013/1339 Art.7, SI 2013/1341 Art.8, SI 2013/1346 Art.4, SI 2013/1347 Art.5, SI 2013/1351 Art.7, SI 2013/1359 Art.7, SI 2013/1369 Art.4, SI 2013/1372 Art.4, SI 2013/1374 Art.4, SI 2013/1383 Art.5, SI 2013/1438 Art.7, SI 2013/1449 Art.8, SI 2013/1499 Art.5, SI

2013/1515 Art.4, SI 2013/1524 Art.7, SI 2013/1527 Art.8, SI 2013/1557 Art.8, SI 2013/1622 Art.8, SI 2013/1630 Art.5, SI 2013/1647 Art.6, SI 2013/1681 Art.5, SI 2013/1684 Art.4, SI 2013/1732 Art.8, SI 2013/1789 Art.4, SI 2013/1850 Art.7, SI 2013/1886 Art.8, SI 2013/1891 Art.3, SI 2013/1903 Art.5, SI 2013/1912 Art.7, SI 2013/1914 Art.7, SI 2013/1957 Art.3, SI 2013/1989 Art.5, SI 2013/1997 Art.4, SI 2013/2003 Art.3, SI 2013/2004 Art.5, SI 2013/2018 Art.4, SI 2013/2035 Art.6, SI 2013/2041 Art.7, SI 2013/2085 Art.13, SI 2013/2151 Art.6, SI 2013/2165 Art.6, SI 2013/2166 Art.5, SI 2013/2167 Art.5, SI 2013/2168 Art.8, SI 2013/2176 Art.7, SI 2013/2208 Art.6, SI 2013/2211 Art.5, SI 2013/2229 Art.5, SI 2013/2239 Art.8, SI 2013/2255 Art.4, SI 2013/2267 Art.5, SI 2013/2279 Art.5, SI 2013/2284 Art.6, SI 2013/2303 Art.7, SI 2013/2310 Art.5, SI 2013/2320 Art.6, SI 2013/2358 Art.9, SI 2013/2362 Art.7, SI 2013/2363 Art.5, SI 2013/2371 Art.4, SI 2013/2372 Art.6, SI 2013/2383 Art.9, SI 2013/2390 Art.6, SI 2013/2414 Art.7, SI 2013/2433 Art.8, SI 2013/2443 Art.5, SI 2013/2455 Art.7, SI 2013/2469 Art.5, SI 2013/2479 Art.7, SI 2013/2483 Art.7, SI 2013/2486 Art.8, SI 2013/2495 Art.5, SI 2013/2516 Art.3, SI 2013/2568 Art.17, SI 2013/2573 Art.7, SI 2013/2608 Art.5, SI 2013/2631 Art.5, SI 2013/2634 Art.5, SI 2013/2639 Art.7, SI 2013/2673 Art.8, SI 2013/2680 Art.7, SI 2013/2681 Art.7, SI 2013/2686 Art.8, SI 2013/2690 Art.3, SI 2013/2707 Art.7, SI 2013/2718 Art.7, SI 2013/2749 Art.6, SI 2013/2762 Art.8, SI 2013/2771 Art.5, SI 2013/2777 Art.8, SI 2013/2811 Art.5, SI 2013/2835 Art.6, SI 2013/2840 Art.5, SI 2013/2863 Art.6, SI 2013/2868 Art.6, SI 2013/2885 Art.4, SI 2013/2886 Art.4, SI 2013/2924 Art.5, SI 2013/2956 Art.3, SI 2013/3002 Art.7, SI 2013/3003 Art.7, SI 2013/3058 Art.5, SI 2013/3061 Art.6, SI 2013/3063 Art.7, SI 2013/3067 Art.5, SI 2013/3082 Art.7, SI 2013/3201 Art.6, SI 2013/3252 Art.7, SI 2013/3255 Art.7, SI 2013/3258 Art.5, SI 2013/3264 Art.3, SI 2013/3274 Art.8, SI 2013/3276 Art.8, SI 2013/3277 Art.6, SI 2013/3284 Art.5, SI 2013/3285 Art.6, SI 2013/3287 Art.7, SI 2013/3291 Art.6, SI 2013/3310 Art.3, SI 2013/3314 Art.6

Reg.5A, varied: SI 2013/1123 Reg.3, SI 2013/1201 Reg.3

Reg.6, disapplied: SI 2013/3124 Art.8

Reg.6, varied: SI 2013/672 Art.9, SI 2013/1259 Art.9, SI 2013/2085 Art.11, SI 2013/2383 Art.9, SI 2013/3271 Art.8

Reg.7, varied: SI 2013/1123 Reg.3, SI 2013/1201 Reg.3, SI 2013/2396 Reg.3, SI 2013/2397 Reg.3

Reg.9, amended: SI 2013/2649 Art.6

Reg.9, disapplied: SI 2013/3100 Art.7, SI 2013/3124 Art.8, SI 2013/3132 Art.7

Reg.9, varied: SI 2013/19 Art.5, SI 2013/20 Art.6, SI 2013/26 Art.8, SI 2013/29 Art.4, SI 2013/57 Art.5, SI 2013/58 Art.7, SI 2013/119 Art.8, SI 2013/134 Art.5, SI 2013/150 Art.6, SI 2013/153 Art.3, SI 2013/168 Art.4, SI 2013/179 Art.4, SI 2013/184 Art.8, SI 2013/187 Art.5, SI 2013/196 Art.6, SI 2013/200 Art.7, SI 2013/231 Art.5, SI 2013/315 Art.7, SI 2013/327 Art.7, SI 2013/328 Art.7, SI 2013/354 Art.7, SI 2013/370 Art.7, SI 2013/403 Art.7, SI 2013/577 Art.7, SI 2013/681 Art.3, SI 2013/741 Art.4, SI 2013/743 Art.4, SI 2013/752 Art.5, SI 2013/800 Art.5, SI 2013/843 Art.7, SI 2013/853 Art.3, SI 2013/869 Art.6, SI 2013/872 Art.6, SI 2013/873 Art.5, SI 2013/902 Art.8, SI 2013/970 Art.8, SI 2013/972 Art.7, SI 2013/974 Art.5, SI 2013/978 Art.7, SI 2013/993 Art.5, SI 2013/994 Art.7, SI 2013/1002 Art.5, SI 2013/1004 Art.3, SI 2013/1006 Art.3, SI 2013/1015 Art.6, SI 2013/1071 Art.4, SI 2013/1078 Art.7, SI 2013/1079 Art.7, SI 2013/1093 Art.6, SI 2013/1094 Art.6, SI 2013/1123 Reg.3, SI 2013/1154 Art.8, SI 2013/1176 Art.4, SI 2013/1201 Reg.3, SI 2013/1207 Art.4, SI 2013/1234 Art.3, SI 2013/1275 Art.8, SI 2013/1276 Art.8, SI 2013/1288 Art.7, SI 2013/1292 Art.6, SI 2013/1311 Art.6, SI 2013/1313 Art.4, SI 2013/1332 Art.8, SI 2013/1335 Art.7, SI 2013/1336 Art.7, SI 2013/1339 Art.7, SI 2013/1341 Art.8, SI 2013/1346 Art.4, SI 2013/1347 Art.5, SI 2013/1351 Art.7, SI 2013/1359 Art.7, SI 2013/1369 Art.4, SI 2013/1372 Art.4, SI 2013/1374 Art.4, SI 2013/1383 Art.5, SI 2013/1438 Art.7, SI 2013/1449 Art.8, SI 2013/1499 Art.5, SI 2013/1515 Art.4, SI 2013/1524 Art.7, SI 2013/1527 Art.8, SI 2013/1557 Art.8, SI 2013/1622 Art.8, SI 2013/1630 Art.5, SI 2013/1647 Art.6, SI 2013/1681 Art.5, SI 2013/1684 Art.4, SI 2013/1732 Art.8, SI 2013/1789 Art.4, SI 2013/1850 Art.7, SI 2013/1886 Art.8, SI 2013/1891 Art.3, SI 2013/1903 Art.5, SI 2013/1912 Art.7, SI

2013/1914 Art.7, SI 2013/1957 Art.3, SI 2013/1989 Art.5, SI 2013/1997 Art.4, SI 2013/2003 Art.3, SI 2013/2004 Art.5, SI 2013/2018 Art.4, SI 2013/2035 Art.6, SI 2013/2041 Art.7, SI 2013/2085 Art.13, SI 2013/2151 Art.6, SI 2013/2165 Art.6, SI 2013/2166 Art.5, SI 2013/2167 Art.5, SI 2013/2168 Art.8, SI 2013/2176 Art.7, SI 2013/2208 Art.6, SI 2013/2211 Art.5, SI 2013/2229 Art.5, SI 2013/2239 Art.8, SI 2013/2255 Art.4, SI 2013/2267 Art.5, SI 2013/2279 Art.5, SI 2013/2284 Art.6, SI 2013/2303 Art.7, SI 2013/2310 Art.5, SI 2013/2320 Art.6, SI 2013/2358 Art.9, SI 2013/2362 Art.7, SI 2013/2363 Art.5, SI 2013/2371 Art.4, SI 2013/2372 Art.6, SI 2013/2383 Art.9, SI 2013/2390 Art.6, SI 2013/2396 Reg.3, SI 2013/2397 Reg.3, SI 2013/2414 Art.7, SI 2013/2433 Art.8, SI 2013/2443 Art.5, SI 2013/2455 Art.7, SI 2013/2469 Art.5, SI 2013/2479 Art.7, SI 2013/2483 Art.7, SI 2013/2486 Art.8, SI 2013/2495 Art.5, SI 2013/2516 Art.3, SI 2013/2568 Art.17, SI 2013/2573 Art.7, SI 2013/2608 Art.5, SI 2013/2631 Art.5, SI 2013/2634 Art.5, SI 2013/2639 Art.7, SI 2013/2673 Art.8, SI 2013/2680 Art.7, SI 2013/2681 Art.7, SI 2013/2686 Art.8, SI 2013/2690 Art.3, SI 2013/2707 Art.7, SI 2013/2718 Art.7, SI 2013/2749 Art.6, SI 2013/2762 Art.8, SI 2013/2771 Art.5, SI 2013/2777 Art.8, SI 2013/2811 Art.5, SI 2013/2835 Art.6, SI 2013/2840 Art.5, SI 2013/2863 Art.6, SI 2013/2868 Art.6, SI 2013/2885 Art.4, SI 2013/2886 Art.4, SI 2013/2924 Art.5, SI 2013/2956 Art.3, SI 2013/3002 Art.7, SI 2013/3003 Art.7, SI 2013/3058 Art.5, SI 2013/3061 Art.6, SI 2013/3063 Art.7, SI 2013/3067 Art.5, SI 2013/3082 Art.7, SI 2013/3201 Art.6, SI 2013/3252 Art.7, SI 2013/3255 Art.7, SI 2013/3258 Art.5, SI 2013/3264 Art.3, SI 2013/3274 Art.8, SI 2013/3276 Art.8, SI 2013/3277 Art.6, SI 2013/3284 Art.5, SI 2013/3285 Art.6, SI 2013/3287 Art.7, SI 2013/3291 Art.6, SI 2013/3310 Art.3, SI 2013/3314 Art.6

Reg.12, varied: SI 2013/1123 Reg.3, SI 2013/1201 Reg.3

Reg.14, varied: SI 2013/1123 Reg.3, SI 2013/2396 Reg.3, SI 2013/2397 Reg.3

Reg.16, enabled: SI 2013/19, SI 2013/20, SI 2013/26, SI 2013/29, SI 2013/57, SI 2013/58, SI 2013/119, SI 2013/150, SI 2013/153, SI 2013/168, SI 2013/179, SI 2013/196, SI 2013/200, SI 2013/231, SI 2013/315, SI 2013/327, SI 2013/328, SI 2013/354, SI 2013/370, SI 2013/403, SI 2013/577, SI 2013/681, SI 2013/741, SI 2013/743, SI 2013/800, SI 2013/843, SI 2013/853, SI 2013/869, SI 2013/872, SI 2013/873, SI 2013/899, SI 2013/900, SI 2013/902, SI 2013/970, SI 2013/974, SI 2013/993, SI 2013/994, SI 2013/1002, SI 2013/1004, SI 2013/1006, SI 2013/1015, SI 2013/1056, SI 2013/1071, SI 2013/1093, SI 2013/1094, SI 2013/1154, SI 2013/1176, SI 2013/1207, SI 2013/1234, SI 2013/1275, SI 2013/1276, SI 2013/1288, SI 2013/1311, SI 2013/1313, SI 2013/1332, SI 2013/1335, SI 2013/1336, SI 2013/1339, SI 2013/1341, SI 2013/1344, SI 2013/1346, SI 2013/1351, SI 2013/1359, SI 2013/1369, SI 2013/1372, SI 2013/1374, SI 2013/1438, SI 2013/1499, SI 2013/1515, SI 2013/1527, SI 2013/1557, SI 2013/1630, SI 2013/1647, SI 2013/1684, SI 2013/1732, SI 2013/1789, SI 2013/1850, SI 2013/1886, SI 2013/1891, SI 2013/1903, SI 2013/1904, SI 2013/1914, SI 2013/2003, SI 2013/2004, SI 2013/2018, SI 2013/2059, SI 2013/2151, SI 2013/2166, SI 2013/2167, SI 2013/2168, SI 2013/2176, SI 2013/2208, SI 2013/2211, SI 2013/2239, SI 2013/2255, SI 2013/2320, SI 2013/2358, SI 2013/2361, SI 2013/2362, SI 2013/2363, SI 2013/2371, SI 2013/2390, SI 2013/2433, SI 2013/2443, SI 2013/2469, SI 2013/2479, SI 2013/2483, SI 2013/2486, SI 2013/2568, SI 2013/2608, SI 2013/2634, SI 2013/2639, SI 2013/2649, SI 2013/2673, SI 2013/2680, SI 2013/2681, SI 2013/2690, SI 2013/2749, SI 2013/2771, SI 2013/2777, SI 2013/2811, SI 2013/2835, SI 2013/2863, SI 2013/2868, SI 2013/2885, SI 2013/2924, SI 2013/3002, SI 2013/3003, SI 2013/3058, SI 2013/3061, SI 2013/3063, SI 2013/3067, SI 2013/3082, SI 2013/3100, SI 2013/3216, SI 2013/3255, SI 2013/3258, SI 2013/3274, SI 2013/3276, SI 2013/3277, SI 2013/3284, SI 2013/3285, SI 2013/3287, SI 2013/3291, SI 2013/3314

1178. Pensions Increase (Review) Order 1982

applied: SI 2013/604 Sch.1

1357. Notification of Installations Handling Hazardous Substances Regulations 1982

revoked: SI 2013/448 Sch.1

1408. Social Security (General Benefit) Regulations 1982

Reg.9, amended: SI 2013/630 Reg.27

Reg.21, applied: SI 2013/376 Sch.4 para.15, Sch.4 para.16

1474. Rent Book (Forms of Notice) Regulations 1982
Sch.1 Part I, amended: SI 2013/630 Reg.68, SI 2013/1036 Sch.2 para.5
Sch.1 Part II, amended: SI 2013/630 Reg.68
Sch.1 Part III, amended: SI 2013/630 Reg.68
Sch.1 Part IV, amended: SI 2013/630 Reg.68

1768. Police Cadets (Scotland) Amendment (No.2) Regulations 1982
revoked: SSI 2013/42 Sch.1 Part 2

1983

270. Food and Drugs (Scotland) Act 1956 (Transfer of Enforcement Functions) Regulations 1983
Sch.2, amended: SSI 2013/83 Sch.2 para.1
Sch.3, amended: SSI 2013/83 Sch.2 para.1

318. Police Cadets (Scotland) Amendment Regulations 1983
revoked: SSI 2013/42 Sch.1 Part 2

344. Aujeszky's Disease Order 1983
Art.19, amended: SSI 2013/173 Art.6
Sch.1, amended: SSI 2013/173 Art.6

644. Docks, Shipbuilding etc (Metrication) Regulations 1983
revoked: SI 2013/448 Sch.1

686. Personal Injuries (Civilians) Scheme 1983
applied: SI 2013/380 Reg.61, SI 2013/471 Reg.20, Reg.33, SI 2013/480 Reg.24, SI 2013/483 Reg.10, SI 2013/628 Sch.1 para.3
Art.14, applied: SSI 2013/148 Reg.6
Art.15, applied: SSI 2013/148 Reg.6
Art.16, applied: SSI 2013/148 Reg.6
Art.25A, applied: SI 2013/3029 Sch.3 para.5, Sch.4 para.3, Sch.9 para.13, SI 2013/3035 Sch.1, SSI 2013/148 Reg.6
Art.25B, applied: SI 2013/388 Sch.1 para.1
Art.27, applied: SI 2013/3029 Sch.4 para.5, Sch.9 para.55, SI 2013/3035 Sch.1
Art.43, applied: SSI 2013/148 Reg.6
Art.44, applied: SSI 2013/148 Reg.6
Art.48A, applied: SSI 2013/148 Reg.6
Sch.3, substituted: SI 2013/707 Sch.1
Sch.4, referred to: SI 2013/3029 Sch.4 para.5, Sch.9 para.55
Sch.4, substituted: SI 2013/707 Sch.2

713. Civil Courts Order 1983
Sch.1, amended: SI 2013/415 Art.7
Sch.3, amended: SI 2013/415 Art.7
Sch.4, amended: SI 2013/415 Art.7

748. Mobile Homes (Commissions) Order 1983
applied: SI 2013/1168 Art.2
Art.2, amended: SI 2013/1723 Art.7

749. Mobile Homes (Written Statement) Regulations 1983
revoked (in part): SSI 2013/188 Reg.4

1264. Pensions Increase (Review) Order 1983
applied: SI 2013/604 Sch.1

1368. Police Cadets (Scotland) Amendment (No.2) Regulations 1983
revoked: SSI 2013/42 Sch.1 Part 1

1486. Passenger Car Fuel Consumption Order 1983
revoked (in part): SI 2013/2986 Sch.3

1553. Consumer Credit (Agreements) Regulations 1983
Reg.1, amended: SI 2013/1881 Art.23
Reg.8, amended: SI 2013/1881 Art.23
Sch.1, added: SI 2013/1881 Art.23
Sch.1, amended: SI 2013/1881 Art.23
Sch.7 para.1, amended: SI 2013/1881 Art.23
Sch.7 para.2, amended: SI 2013/1881 Art.23
Sch.7 para.3, amended: SI 2013/1881 Art.23
Sch.8 Part I, added: SI 2013/1881 Art.23
Sch.8 Part I, amended: SI 2013/1881 Art.23

1561. Consumer Credit (Enforcement, Default and Termination Notices) Regulations 1983
see *Citifinancial Europe Plc v Rice* 2013 Hous. L.R. 23 (Sh Ct (Glasgow)), Sheriff AF Deutsch
Sch.2, see *Citifinancial Europe Plc v Rice* 2013 Hous. L.R. 23 (Sh Ct (Glasgow)), Sheriff AF Deutsch

1565. Consumer Credit (Conduct of Business) (Pawn Records) Regulations 1983
revoked (in part): SI 2013/1881 Art.21

1590. Town and Country Planning (Structure and Local Plans) (Scotland) Regulations 1983
Reg.6, see *Uprichard v Scottish Ministers* [2013] UKSC 21, 2013 S.C. (U.K.S.C.) 219 (SC), Lord Hope, J.S.C. (Deputy President)

1984

252. High Court of Justiciary Fees Order 1984
Art.2A, amended: SSI 2013/137 Reg.8

467. Town and Country Planning (Control of Advertisements) (Scotland) Regulations 1984
disapplied: SSI 2013/290 Reg.15
varied: 2013 asp 14 Sch.4 para.28
Reg.3, applied: SSI 2013/290 Reg.15
Reg.3, referred to: SSI 2013/290 Reg.15
Reg.10, applied: SSI 2013/290 Reg.15
Reg.12, amended: SI 2013/602 Sch.2 para.67
Reg.13, referred to: SSI 2013/290 Reg.15
Reg.14, amended: SSI 2013/154 Reg.2
Reg.14, applied: SSI 2013/156 Reg.20
Reg.16, applied: SSI 2013/156 Reg.29

Reg.19, applied: SSI 2013/290 Reg.15
Reg.20, revoked (in part): SSI 2013/154 Reg.2
Reg.21, amended: SSI 2013/154 Reg.2
Reg.21, applied: SSI 2013/154 Reg.3, SSI 2013/156 Reg.1, Reg.19, Reg.20, Reg.29, Reg.33
Reg.21, revoked (in part): SSI 2013/154 Reg.2
Reg.24, amended: SSI 2013/154 Reg.2
Reg.24, applied: SSI 2013/156 Reg.14
Reg.25, applied: SSI 2013/154 Reg.3, SSI 2013/156 Reg.1, Reg.14
Reg.25, substituted: SSI 2013/154 Reg.2
Sch.1, referred to: SSI 2013/290 Reg.15
Sch.4, referred to: SSI 2013/290 Reg.15

552. Coroners Rules 1984
Part VI r.20, applied: SI 2013/335 Reg.4, Reg.9
Part VI r.24, applied: SI 2013/335 Reg.4, Reg.9
r.42, see *R. (on the application of Wilkinson) v HM Coroner for Greater Manchester South District* [2012] EWHC 2755 (Admin), [2013] C.P. Rep. 5 (QBD (Admin)), Foskett, J.
r.43, see *R. (on the application of Sreedharan) v HM Coroner for the County of Greater Manchester* [2013] EWCA Civ 181, [2013] Med. L.R. 89 (CA (Civ Div)), Lord Dyson (M.R.)
Sch.4, see *R. (on the application of Wilkinson) v HM Coroner for Greater Manchester South District* [2012] EWHC 2755 (Admin), [2013] C.P. Rep. 5 (QBD (Admin)), Foskett, J.

672. Driving Licences (Exchangeable Licences) Order 1984
revoked: SI 2013/22 Sch.2

969. Act of Sederunt (Commissary Business) (Amendment) 1984
revoked: SSI 2013/291 Sch.5

999. Drought Orders (Inquiries Procedure) Rules 1984
r.3, amended: SI 2013/755 Sch.4 para.20

1307. Pensions Increase (Review) Order 1984
applied: SI 2013/604 Sch.1

1406. Public Service Vehicles (Carrying Capacity) Regulations 1984
Reg.9, amended: SI 2013/1644 Sch.2

1684. Prevention of Oil Pollution Act 1971 (Application of section 1) Regulations 1984
revoked: SI 2013/2944 Sch.1

1719. Special Road (A55) (Llanddulas to Colwyn Bay) Regulations 1984
disapplied: SI 2013/729 Art.13
varied: SI 2013/729 Art.13, SI 2013/1911 Art.7
Reg.13, varied: SI 2013/332 Art.8, SI 2013/674 Art.9, SI 2013/2374 Art.7

2029. Police Cadets (Scotland) Amendment Regulations 1984
revoked: SSI 2013/42 Sch.1 Part 2

1985

65. Driving Licences (Exchangeable Licences) Order 1985
revoked: SI 2013/22 Sch.2

177. Reservoirs Act 1975 (Registers, Reports and Records) Regulations 1985
revoked (in part): SI 2013/1677 Reg.16

267. Local Authority Accounts (Scotland) Regulations 1985
applied: SSI 2013/121 Art.7
Reg.4, applied: SSI 2013/119 Art.3, SSI 2013/121 Art.10
Reg.6, applied: SSI 2013/121 Art.10
Sch.1, applied: SSI 2013/119 Art.3
Sch.1 para.1, amended: SSI 2013/119 Sch.1 para.22
Sch.1 para.4, amended: SSI 2013/119 Sch.1 para.22
Sch.1 para.7, amended: SSI 2013/119 Sch.1 para.22
Sch.1 para.8, amended: SSI 2013/119 Sch.1 para.22
Sch.1 para.10, amended: SSI 2013/119 Sch.1 para.22

454. Local Elections (Northern Ireland) Order 1985
Sch.2, amended: SI 2013/3021 Art.33
Sch.2, applied: SI 2013/3156 Art.10

548. Reservoirs Act 1975 (Registers, Reports and Records) (Amendment) Regulations 1985
revoked (in part): SI 2013/1677 Reg.16

621. Consumer Credit (Exempt Advertisements) Order 1985
revoked (in part): SI 2013/1881 Art.21

739. A47 Trunk Road (Birmingham &mdash Great Yarmouth) (24-Hour Main Carriageway Clearway) Order 1985
revoked: SI 2013/394 Sch.1 Part II

824. Special Road Order (Colwyn Bay to Glan Conwy) Regulations 1985
disapplied: SI 2013/729 Art.12
varied: SI 2013/1 Art.10, SI 2013/729 Art.12
Reg.3, varied: SI 2013/674 Art.12
Reg.13, varied: SI 2013/332 Art.9, SI 2013/674 Art.10, SI 2013/2374 Art.8, SI 2013/3238 Art.11

1000. Trunk Road (London-Great Yarmouth) (A12) (Prohibition of U-Turns) (B1068 Junction, Stratford St Mary) Order 1985
revoked: SI 2013/1076 Art.4

1068. Food (Revision of Penalties and Mode of Trial) (Scotland) Regulations 1985
Sch.1, amended: SSI 2013/83 Sch.2 para.2

Sch.2, amended: SSI 2013/83 Sch.2 para.2

1204. Betting, Gaming, Lotteries and Amusements (Northern Ireland) Order 1985

applied: SI 2013/3134 Reg.6

1205. Credit Unions (Northern Ireland) Order 1985

Art.2, amended: SI 2013/496 Sch.7 para.2
Art.2A, amended: SI 2013/496 Sch.7 para.3
Art.3, amended: SI 2013/496 Sch.7 para.4
Art.4, amended: SI 2013/496 Sch.7 para.5
Art.31, amended: SI 2013/496 Sch.7 para.6
Art.36, amended: SI 2013/496 Sch.7 para.7
Art.49, amended: SI 2013/496 Sch.7 para.8
Art.53, amended: SI 2013/496 Sch.7 para.9
Art.53, substituted: SI 2013/496 Sch.7 para.9
Art.60, amended: SI 2013/496 Sch.7 para.10
Art.61, amended: SI 2013/496 Sch.7 para.11
Art.62, amended: SI 2013/496 Sch.7 para.12
Art.63, amended: SI 2013/496 Sch.7 para.13
Art.65, amended: SI 2013/496 Sch.7 para.14
Art.66, amended: SI 2013/496 Sch.7 para.15
Sch.1, amended: SI 2013/496 Sch.7 para.16

1461. Driving Licences (Exchangeable Licences) (No.2) Order 1985

revoked: SI 2013/22 Sch.2

1531. Police Federation (Scotland) Regulations 1985

applied: SSI 2013/86 Sch.1 para.3
revoked: SSI 2013/86 Reg.19
Reg.7, applied: SSI 2013/86 Sch.1 para.7
Reg.10, applied: SSI 2013/86 Sch.1 para.6, Sch.1 para.7
Reg.12, applied: SSI 2013/86 Sch.1 para.5
Reg.17, applied: SSI 2013/86 Sch.1 para.3, Sch.1 para.6

1575. Pensions Increase (Review) Order 1985

applied: SI 2013/604 Sch.1

1884. Waste Regulation and Disposal (Authorities) Order 1985

applied: SI 2013/680 Art.7

1901. Public Transport Companies (Permitted Maximum and Required Minimum Numbers of Directors) Order 1985

revoked (in part): SI 2013/2986 Sch.3

1902. Transport Act 1985 (Exclusion of Bus Operating Powers and Exemption for Councils Running Small Bus Undertakings) Order 1985

Art.2, revoked (in part): SI 2013/2986 Sch.3
Art.3, revoked (in part): SI 2013/2986 Sch.3
Art.4, revoked (in part): SI 2013/2986 Sch.3
Sch.1 Part I, revoked (in part): SI 2013/2986 Sch.3
Sch.1 Part II, revoked (in part): SI 2013/2986 Sch.3
Sch.1 Part III, revoked (in part): SI 2013/2986 Sch.3

1903. Transport Act 1985 (Modifications in Schedule 4 to the Transport Act 1968) Order 1985

revoked (in part): SI 2013/2986 Sch.3

2042. Asbestos Products (Safety) Regulations 1985

revoked: SI 2013/2919 Reg.15

1986

17. Trunk Road (A55/A494) (Ewloe Interchange, Clwyd) (De-restriction) Order 1986

disapplied: SI 2013/729 Art.16
varied: SI 2013/729 Art.16

81. Public Passenger Transport Policies (Anticipatory Exercise of Powers) Order 1986

revoked: SI 2013/2986 Sch.2

121. Police Cadets (Scotland) Amendment Regulations 1986

revoked: SSI 2013/42 Sch.1 Part 1

183. Removal and Disposal of Vehicles Regulations 1986

Reg.5C, applied: SI 2013/361 Reg.3

267. Act of Sederunt (Commissary Business) (Amendment) 1986

revoked: SSI 2013/291 Sch.5

467. Reservoirs Act 1975 (Referees) (Appointment and Procedure) Rules 1986

revoked (in part): SI 2013/1676 r.5

468. Reservoirs Act 1975 (Certificates, Reports and Prescribed Information) Regulations 1986

revoked (in part): SI 2013/1677 Reg.16

524. National Health Service (Transfer of Officers) (No.2) Regulations 1986

Reg.1, amended: SI 2013/235 Sch.2 para.8

590. Value Added Tax Tribunals Rules 1986

r.29, see *Hewlett Packard Ltd v Revenue and Customs Commissioners* [2013] UKFTT 39 (TC), [2013] S.F.T.D. 409 (FTT (Tax)), Judge Barbara Mosedale; see *Usha Martin UK Ltd v Revenue and Customs Commissioners* [2013] UKFTT 793 (TC), [2013] S.F.T.D. 554 (FTT (Tax)), Judge Anne Scott

594. Education and Libraries (Northern Ireland) Order 1986

Art.2, applied: SI 2013/1119 Sch.2 para.9
Art.46, applied: SI 2013/1465 Art.14
Art.50, applied: SI 2013/3029 Sch.11 para.3

595. Mental Health (Northern Ireland) Order 1986

applied: SI 2013/3029 Reg.26
Art.4, applied: SI 2013/3035 Sch.1
Art.12, applied: SI 2013/3035 Sch.1

975. National Health Service (General Ophthalmic Services) Regulations 1986

Reg.2, amended: SI 2013/684 Reg.4

Reg.13, amended: SI 2013/684 Reg.4

1078. Road Vehicles (Construction and Use) Regulations 1986

Reg.10B, amended: SSI 2013/119 Sch.2 para.4
Reg.10C, amended: SSI 2013/119 Sch.2 para.4
Reg.18, amended: SI 2013/271 Reg.3
Reg.18A, added: SI 2013/271 Reg.4
Reg.36A, amended: SSI 2013/119 Sch.2 para.4
Reg.36B, amended: SSI 2013/119 Sch.2 para.4
Reg.37, amended: SSI 2013/119 Sch.2 para.4
Reg.82, amended: SSI 2013/119 Sch.2 para.4
Reg.101, amended: SSI 2013/119 Sch.2 para.4
Reg.107, amended: SSI 2013/119 Sch.2 para.4
Sch.12 Part I para.1, amended: SI 2013/602 Sch.2 para.68

1116. Pensions Increase (Review) Order 1986

applied: SI 2013/604 Sch.1

1335. Costs in Criminal Cases (General) Regulations 1986

Part II, applied: SI 2013/1554 r.76_1
Part IIA, applied: SI 2013/1554 r.76_1
Part IIB, applied: SI 2013/1554 r.76_1
Part III, applied: SI 2013/1554 r.76_4
Reg.3, applied: SI 2013/1554 r.76_1, r.76_8
Reg.3, see *R. (on the application of CPS) v Bolton Crown Court* [2012] EWHC 3570 (Admin), [2013] 1 W.L.R. 1880 (DC), Richards, L.J.; see *R. v Applied Language Solutions Ltd (now Capita Translation and Interpreting Ltd)* [2013] EWCA Crim 326, [2013] 1 W.L.R. 3820 (CA (Crim Div)), Sir John Thomas (President QBD)
Reg.3A, amended: SI 2013/534 Sch.1 para.1
Reg.3C, applied: SI 2013/1554 r.63_1, r.68_1
Reg.3D, amended: SI 2013/534 Sch.1 para.1
Reg.3D, applied: SI 2013/1554 r.76_1
Reg.3E, amended: SI 2013/534 Sch.1 para.1
Reg.3F, applied: SI 2013/1554 r.76_1
Reg.3H, applied: SI 2013/1554 r.63_1, r.68_1
Reg.3I, amended: SI 2013/534 Sch.1 para.1
Reg.3I, applied: SI 2013/1554 r.76_1
Reg.4, amended: SI 2013/2830 Reg.2
Reg.6, amended: SI 2013/534 Sch.1 para.1
Reg.7, amended: SI 2013/2830 Reg.2
Reg.14, amended: SI 2013/2526 Reg.2
Reg.15, amended: SI 2013/2526 Reg.2
Reg.16, amended: SI 2013/2526 Reg.2
Reg.26, amended: SI 2013/534 Sch.1 para.1

1510. Control of Pesticides Regulations 1986

disapplied: SI 2013/1506 Sch.2 para.2, Sch.2 para.3, Sch.2 para.4, Sch.2 para.5, Sch.2 para.6, Sch.2 para.7
Reg.3, amended: SI 2013/1478 Sch.5 para.5, SI 2013/1506 Sch.5 para.3
Sch.4 para.2, amended: SI 2013/755 Sch.4 para.21
Sch.4 para.6, amended: SI 2013/755 Sch.4 para.21

1544. Civil Aviation Authority (Economic Regulation of Airports) Regulations 1986

revoked: SI 2013/610 Reg.3

1628. Operation of Public Service Vehicles (Partnership) Regulations 1986

Sch.1 Part I, amended: SI 2013/1644 Sch.2
Sch.1 Part II, amended: SI 2013/1644 Sch.2

1629. Public Service Vehicles (Traffic Commissioners Publication and Inquiries) Regulations 1986

Reg.4, amended: SI 2013/1644 Sch.2
Reg.5, amended: SI 2013/1644 Sch.2

1671. Public Service Vehicles (Registration of Local Services) Regulations 1986

Reg.3, amended: SI 2013/1644 Sch.4
Reg.7, amended: SI 2013/1644 Sch.4
Reg.9, amended: SI 2013/1644 Sch.4
Reg.9A, amended: SI 2013/1644 Sch.4

1691. Public Service Vehicles (London Local Service Licences) Regulations 1986

revoked: SI 2013/2987 Sch.2

1711. Stamp Duty Reserve Tax Regulations 1986

Reg.2, amended: SI 2013/472 Art.4, Sch.2 para.4
Reg.4A, amended: SI 2013/472 Sch.2 para.4

1915. Insolvency (Scotland) Rules 1986

applied: SI 2013/1388 Sch.4 para.2
Part 001 r.0.2, applied: SI 2013/1388 Sch.4 para.1
Part 001 r.0.2, varied: SI 2013/1388 Sch.4 para.2
Part 4, applied: SI 2013/1388 Sch.4 para.1
Part 4 r.4.1, varied: SI 2013/1388 Sch.4 para.2, Sch.4 Part 2
Part 4 r.4.2, varied: SI 2013/1388 Sch.4 para.2
Part 4 r.4.3, varied: SI 2013/1388 Sch.4 para.2, Sch.4 Part 2
Part 4 r.4.4, varied: SI 2013/1388 Sch.4 para.2
Part 4 r.4.5, varied: SI 2013/1388 Sch.4 para.2
Part 4 r.4.6, varied: SI 2013/1388 Sch.4 para.2
Part 4 r.4.7, varied: SI 2013/1388 Sch.4 para.2
Part 4 r.4.8, varied: SI 2013/1388 Sch.4 para.2
Part 4 r.4.9, varied: SI 2013/1388 Sch.4 para.2
Part 4 r.4.10, varied: SI 2013/1388 Sch.4 para.2, Sch.4 Part 2
Part 4 r.4.11, varied: SI 2013/1388 Sch.4 para.2
Part 4 r.4.12, varied: SI 2013/1388 Sch.4 para.2, Sch.4 Part 2
Part 4 r.4.13, varied: SI 2013/1388 Sch.4 para.2
Part 4 r.4.14, varied: SI 2013/1388 Sch.4 para.2, Sch.4 Part 2
Part 4 r.4.14A, varied: SI 2013/1388 Sch.4 para.2
Part 4 r.4.15, varied: SI 2013/1388 Sch.4 para.2
Part 4 r.4.16, varied: SI 2013/1388 Sch.4 para.2, Sch.4 Part 2
Part 4 r.4.17, varied: SI 2013/1388 Sch.4 para.2, Sch.4 Part 2

Part 4 r.4.18, varied: SI 2013/1388 Sch.4 para.2, Sch.4 Part 2
Part 4 r.4.19, varied: SI 2013/1388 Sch.4 para.2, Sch.4 Part 2
Part 4 r.4.20, varied: SI 2013/1388 Sch.4 para.2
Part 4 r.4.21, varied: SI 2013/1388 Sch.4 para.2
Part 4 r.4.22, varied: SI 2013/1388 Sch.4 para.2, Sch.4 Part 2
Part 4 r.4.23, varied: SI 2013/1388 Sch.4 para.2
Part 4 r.4.24, varied: SI 2013/1388 Sch.4 para.2
Part 4 r.4.25, varied: SI 2013/1388 Sch.4 para.2
Part 4 r.4.26, varied: SI 2013/1388 Sch.4 para.2
Part 4 r.4.27, varied: SI 2013/1388 Sch.4 para.2
Part 4 r.4.28, varied: SI 2013/1388 Sch.4 para.2, Sch.4 Part 2
Part 4 r.4.28A, varied: SI 2013/1388 Sch.4 para.2
Part 4 r.4.29, varied: SI 2013/1388 Sch.4 para.2
Part 4 r.4.30, varied: SI 2013/1388 Sch.4 para.2
Part 4 r.4.31, varied: SI 2013/1388 Sch.4 para.2, Sch.4 Part 2
Part 4 r.4.32, varied: SI 2013/1388 Sch.4 para.2
Part 4 r.4.33, varied: SI 2013/1388 Sch.4 para.2
Part 4 r.4.34, varied: SI 2013/1388 Sch.4 para.2
Part 4 r.4.35, varied: SI 2013/1388 Sch.4 para.2
Part 4 r.4.36, varied: SI 2013/1388 Sch.4 para.2
Part 4 r.4.37, varied: SI 2013/1388 Sch.4 para.2
Part 4 r.4.37A, varied: SI 2013/1388 Sch.4 para.2
Part 4 r.4.38, varied: SI 2013/1388 Sch.4 para.2, Sch.4 Part 2
Part 4 r.4.39, varied: SI 2013/1388 Sch.4 para.2
Part 4 r.4.40, varied: SI 2013/1388 Sch.4 para.2
Part 4 r.4.41, varied: SI 2013/1388 Sch.4 para.2, Sch.4 Part 2
Part 4 r.4.42, varied: SI 2013/1388 Sch.4 para.2
Part 4 r.4.43, varied: SI 2013/1388 Sch.4 para.2
Part 4 r.4.44, varied: SI 2013/1388 Sch.4 para.2
Part 4 r.4.45, varied: SI 2013/1388 Sch.4 para.2
Part 4 r.4.46, varied: SI 2013/1388 Sch.4 para.2
Part 4 r.4.47, varied: SI 2013/1388 Sch.4 para.2
Part 4 r.4.48, varied: SI 2013/1388 Sch.4 para.2
Part 4 r.4.49, varied: SI 2013/1388 Sch.4 para.2
Part 4 r.4.50, varied: SI 2013/1388 Sch.4 para.2
Part 4 r.4.51, varied: SI 2013/1388 Sch.4 para.2
Part 4 r.4.52, varied: SI 2013/1388 Sch.4 para.2
Part 4 r.4.53, varied: SI 2013/1388 Sch.4 para.2
Part 4 r.4.54, varied: SI 2013/1388 Sch.4 para.2
Part 4 r.4.55, varied: SI 2013/1388 Sch.4 para.2
Part 4 r.4.56, varied: SI 2013/1388 Sch.4 para.2
Part 4 r.4.57, varied: SI 2013/1388 Sch.4 para.2
Part 4 r.4.58, varied: SI 2013/1388 Sch.4 para.2
Part 4 r.4.59, varied: SI 2013/1388 Sch.4 para.2, Sch.4 Part 2
Part 4 r.4.59A, varied: SI 2013/1388 Sch.4 para.2
Part 4 r.4.60, varied: SI 2013/1388 Sch.4 para.2
Part 4 r.4.61, varied: SI 2013/1388 Sch.4 para.2
Part 4 r.4.62, varied: SI 2013/1388 Sch.4 para.2
Part 4 r.4.63, varied: SI 2013/1388 Sch.4 para.2
Part 4 r.4.64, varied: SI 2013/1388 Sch.4 para.2
Part 4 r.4.65, varied: SI 2013/1388 Sch.4 para.2
Part 4 r.4.66, varied: SI 2013/1388 Sch.4 para.2, Sch.4 Part 2
Part 4 r.4.67, varied: SI 2013/1388 Sch.4 para.2, Sch.4 Part 2
Part 4 r.4.68, varied: SI 2013/1388 Sch.4 para.2, Sch.4 Part 2
Part 4 r.4.69, disapplied: SI 2013/1388 Sch.4 Part 2
Part 4 r.4.69, varied: SI 2013/1388 Sch.4 para.2
Part 4 r.4.70, disapplied: SI 2013/1388 Sch.4 Part 2
Part 4 r.4.70, varied: SI 2013/1388 Sch.4 para.2
Part 4 r.4.71, disapplied: SI 2013/1388 Sch.4 Part 2
Part 4 r.4.71, varied: SI 2013/1388 Sch.4 para.2
Part 4 r.4.72, disapplied: SI 2013/1388 Sch.4 Part 2
Part 4 r.4.72, varied: SI 2013/1388 Sch.4 para.2
Part 4 r.4.73, disapplied: SI 2013/1388 Sch.4 Part 2
Part 4 r.4.73, varied: SI 2013/1388 Sch.4 para.2
Part 4 r.4.74, varied: SI 2013/1388 Sch.4 para.2
Part 4 r.4.75, varied: SI 2013/1388 Sch.4 para.2, Sch.4 Part 2
Part 4 r.4.76, varied: SI 2013/1388 Sch.4 para.2
Part 4 r.4.77, varied: SI 2013/1388 Sch.4 para.2
Part 4 r.4.78, disapplied: SI 2013/1388 Sch.4 Part 2
Part 4 r.4.78, varied: SI 2013/1388 Sch.4 para.2
Part 4 r.4.79, disapplied: SI 2013/1388 Sch.4 Part 2
Part 4 r.4.79, varied: SI 2013/1388 Sch.4 para.2
Part 4 r.4.80, disapplied: SI 2013/1388 Sch.4 Part 2
Part 4 r.4.80, varied: SI 2013/1388 Sch.4 para.2
Part 4 r.4.81, disapplied: SI 2013/1388 Sch.4 Part 2
Part 4 r.4.81, varied: SI 2013/1388 Sch.4 para.2
Part 4 r.4.82, disapplied: SI 2013/1388 Sch.4 Part 2
Part 4 r.4.82, varied: SI 2013/1388 Sch.4 para.2
Part 4 r.4.83, disapplied: SI 2013/1388 Sch.4 Part 2
Part 4 r.4.83, varied: SI 2013/1388 Sch.4 para.2
Part 4 r.4.84, disapplied: SI 2013/1388 Sch.4 Part 2
Part 4 r.4.84, varied: SI 2013/1388 Sch.4 para.2
Part 4 r.4.85, varied: SI 2013/1388 Sch.4 para.2
Part 7, applied: SI 2013/1388 Sch.4 para.1

Part 7 r.7.1, varied: SI 2013/1388 Sch.4 para.2
Part 7 r.7.2, varied: SI 2013/1388 Sch.4 para.2
Part 7 r.7.3, varied: SI 2013/1388 Sch.4 para.2
Part 7 r.7.4, varied: SI 2013/1388 Sch.4 para.2
Part 7 r.7.5, varied: SI 2013/1388 Sch.4 para.2
Part 7 r.7.6, varied: SI 2013/1388 Sch.4 para.2
Part 7 r.7.7, varied: SI 2013/1388 Sch.4 para.2
Part 7 r.7.8, varied: SI 2013/1388 Sch.4 para.2
Part 7 r.7.9, varied: SI 2013/1388 Sch.4 para.2
Part 7 r.7.10, varied: SI 2013/1388 Sch.4 para.2
Part 7 r.7.11, varied: SI 2013/1388 Sch.4 para.2
Part 7 r.7.12, varied: SI 2013/1388 Sch.4 para.2
Part 7 r.7.13, varied: SI 2013/1388 Sch.4 para.2
Part 7 r.7.13A, varied: SI 2013/1388 Sch.4 para.2
Part 7 r.7.13B, varied: SI 2013/1388 Sch.4 para.2
Part 7 r.7.14, varied: SI 2013/1388 Sch.4 para.2
Part 7 r.7.15, varied: SI 2013/1388 Sch.4 para.2
Part 7 r.7.16, varied: SI 2013/1388 Sch.4 para.2
Part 7 r.7.17, varied: SI 2013/1388 Sch.4 para.2
Part 7 r.7.18, varied: SI 2013/1388 Sch.4 para.2, Sch.4 Part 2
Part 7 r.7.19, varied: SI 2013/1388 Sch.4 para.2
Part 7 r.7.20, varied: SI 2013/1388 Sch.4 para.2
Part 7 r.7.20A, varied: SI 2013/1388 Sch.4 para.2
Part 7 r.7.21, varied: SI 2013/1388 Sch.4 para.2
Part 7 r.7.21A, varied: SI 2013/1388 Sch.4 para.2, Sch.4 Part 2
Part 7 r.7.21B, varied: SI 2013/1388 Sch.4 para.2, Sch.4 Part 2
Part 7 r.7.21C, varied: SI 2013/1388 Sch.4 para.2
Part 7 r.7.21D, varied: SI 2013/1388 Sch.4 para.2
Part 7 r.7.22, varied: SI 2013/1388 Sch.4 para.2
Part 7 r.7.23, varied: SI 2013/1388 Sch.4 para.2
Part 7 r.7.24, varied: SI 2013/1388 Sch.4 para.2
Part 7 r.7.25, varied: SI 2013/1388 Sch.4 para.2
Part 7 r.7.26, varied: SI 2013/1388 Sch.4 para.2, Sch.4 Part 2
Part 7 r.7.27, varied: SI 2013/1388 Sch.4 para.2, Sch.4 Part 2
Part 7 r.7.28, varied: SI 2013/1388 Sch.4 para.2
Part 7 r.7.29, varied: SI 2013/1388 Sch.4 para.2
Part 7 r.7.30, varied: SI 2013/1388 Sch.4 para.2, Sch.4 Part 2
Part 7 r.7.30A, varied: SI 2013/1388 Sch.4 para.2
Part 7 r.7.30B, varied: SI 2013/1388 Sch.4 para.2
Part 7 r.7.31, varied: SI 2013/1388 Sch.4 para.2
Part 7 r.7.32, varied: SI 2013/1388 Sch.4 para.2, Sch.4 Part 2
Part 7 r.7.33, varied: SI 2013/1388 Sch.4 para.2, Sch.4 Part 2
Part 7 r.7.34, varied: SI 2013/1388 Sch.4 para.2, Sch.4 Part 2
Part 7 r.7.35, varied: SI 2013/1388 Sch.4 para.2
Part 7 r.7.36, varied: SI 2013/1388 Sch.4 para.2, Sch.4 Part 2
r.4.67, see *Joint Liquidators of the Scottish Coal Co Ltd, Petitioners* [2013] CSOH 124, 2013 S.L.T. 1055 (OH), Lord Hodge

1925. Insolvency Rules 1986

applied: SI 2013/1046 r.208
see *Appleyard v Wewelwala* [2012] EWHC 3302 (Ch), [2013] 1 W.L.R. 752 (Ch D), Briggs, J.; see *Davis v Price* [2013] EWHC 323 (Ch), [2013] B.P.I.R. 200 (Ch D), David Richards, J.; see *Smeaton v Equifax Plc* [2013] EWCA Civ 108, [2013] 2 All E.R. 959 (CA (Civ Div)), Tomlinson, L.J.
Part 0 r.0.2, amended: SI 2013/472 Sch.2 para.5
Part 4, applied: SI 2013/1388 Sch.3 para.1
Part 4 r.4.1, amended: SI 2013/472 Sch.2 para.5
Part 4 r.4.1, varied: SI 2013/1388 Sch.3 para.2
Part 4 r.4.2, varied: SI 2013/1388 Sch.3 para.2, Sch.3 Part 2
Part 4 r.4.3, varied: SI 2013/1388 Sch.3 para.2
Part 4 r.4.4, varied: SI 2013/1388 Sch.3 para.2, Sch.3 Part 2
Part 4 r.4.5, varied: SI 2013/1388 Sch.3 para.2, Sch.3 Part 2
Part 4 r.4.6, varied: SI 2013/1388 Sch.3 para.2, Sch.3 Part 2
Part 4 r.4.6A, varied: SI 2013/1388 Sch.3 para.2, Sch.3 Part 2
Part 4 r.4.7, amended: SI 2013/472 Sch.2 para.5
Part 4 r.4.7, varied: SI 2013/1388 Sch.3 para.2, Sch.3 Part 2
Part 4 r.4.8, varied: SI 2013/1388 Sch.3 para.2, Sch.3 Part 2
Part 4 r.4.9, varied: SI 2013/1388 Sch.3 para.2
Part 4 r.4.9A, varied: SI 2013/1388 Sch.3 para.2, Sch.3 Part 2
Part 4 r.4.10, amended: SI 2013/472 Sch.2 para.5
Part 4 r.4.10, varied: SI 2013/1388 Sch.3 para.2, Sch.3 Part 2
Part 4 r.4.11, varied: SI 2013/1388 Sch.3 para.2
Part 4 r.4.12, varied: SI 2013/1388 Sch.3 para.2, Sch.3 Part 2
Part 4 r.4.13, varied: SI 2013/1388 Sch.3 para.2, Sch.3 Part 2
Part 4 r.4.14, varied: SI 2013/1388 Sch.3 para.2
Part 4 r.4.15, varied: SI 2013/1388 Sch.3 para.2, Sch.3 Part 2
Part 4 r.4.16, varied: SI 2013/1388 Sch.3 para.2
Part 4 r.4.17, varied: SI 2013/1388 Sch.3 para.2
Part 4 r.4.18, varied: SI 2013/1388 Sch.3 para.2, Sch.3 Part 2
Part 4 r.4.18A, varied: SI 2013/1388 Sch.3 para.2
Part 4 r.4.19, varied: SI 2013/1388 Sch.3 para.2

Part 4 r.4.20, varied: SI 2013/1388 Sch.3 para.2
Part 4 r.4.21, varied: SI 2013/1388 Sch.3 para.2
Part 4 r.4.21A, varied: SI 2013/1388 Sch.3 para.2
Part 4 r.4.21B, varied: SI 2013/1388 Sch.3 para.2
Part 4 r.4.22, varied: SI 2013/1388 Sch.3 para.2
Part 4 r.4.23, varied: SI 2013/1388 Sch.3 para.2
Part 4 r.4.24, varied: SI 2013/1388 Sch.3 para.2
Part 4 r.4.25, varied: SI 2013/1388 Sch.3 para.2, Sch.3 Part 2
Part 4 r.4.25A, varied: SI 2013/1388 Sch.3 para.2
Part 4 r.4.26, varied: SI 2013/1388 Sch.3 para.2
Part 4 r.4.27, varied: SI 2013/1388 Sch.3 para.2
Part 4 r.4.28, varied: SI 2013/1388 Sch.3 para.2, Sch.3 Part 2
Part 4 r.4.29, varied: SI 2013/1388 Sch.3 para.2
Part 4 r.4.30, varied: SI 2013/1388 Sch.3 para.2
Part 4 r.4.31, varied: SI 2013/1388 Sch.3 para.2
Part 4 r.4.32, varied: SI 2013/1388 Sch.3 para.2
Part 4 r.4.33, varied: SI 2013/1388 Sch.3 para.2
Part 4 r.4.34, varied: SI 2013/1388 Sch.3 para.2
Part 4 r.4.34A, varied: SI 2013/1388 Sch.3 para.2
Part 4 r.4.35, varied: SI 2013/1388 Sch.3 para.2
Part 4 r.4.36, varied: SI 2013/1388 Sch.3 para.2
Part 4 r.4.37, varied: SI 2013/1388 Sch.3 para.2
Part 4 r.4.38, varied: SI 2013/1388 Sch.3 para.2
Part 4 r.4.39, varied: SI 2013/1388 Sch.3 para.2, Sch.3 Part 2
Part 4 r.4.40, varied: SI 2013/1388 Sch.3 para.2
Part 4 r.4.41, varied: SI 2013/1388 Sch.3 para.2
Part 4 r.4.42, varied: SI 2013/1388 Sch.3 para.2
Part 4 r.4.43, varied: SI 2013/1388 Sch.3 para.2, Sch.3 Part 2
Part 4 r.4.44, varied: SI 2013/1388 Sch.3 para.2
Part 4 r.4.45, varied: SI 2013/1388 Sch.3 para.2
Part 4 r.4.46, varied: SI 2013/1388 Sch.3 para.2
Part 4 r.4.47, varied: SI 2013/1388 Sch.3 para.2
Part 4 r.4.48, varied: SI 2013/1388 Sch.3 para.2, Sch.3 Part 2
Part 4 r.4.49, varied: SI 2013/1388 Sch.3 para.2
Part 4 r.4.49A, varied: SI 2013/1388 Sch.3 para.2
Part 4 r.4.49B, varied: SI 2013/1388 Sch.3 para.2, Sch.3 Part 2
Part 4 r.4.49C, varied: SI 2013/1388 Sch.3 para.2
Part 4 r.4.49D, varied: SI 2013/1388 Sch.3 para.2
Part 4 r.4.49E, varied: SI 2013/1388 Sch.3 para.2
Part 4 r.4.49F, varied: SI 2013/1388 Sch.3 para.2
Part 4 r.4.49G, varied: SI 2013/1388 Sch.3 para.2
Part 4 r.4.50, varied: SI 2013/1388 Sch.3 para.2
Part 4 r.4.51, varied: SI 2013/1388 Sch.3 para.2
Part 4 r.4.52, varied: SI 2013/1388 Sch.3 para.2
Part 4 r.4.53, varied: SI 2013/1388 Sch.3 para.2
Part 4 r.4.53A, varied: SI 2013/1388 Sch.3 para.2
Part 4 r.4.53B, varied: SI 2013/1388 Sch.3 para.2
Part 4 r.4.53C, varied: SI 2013/1388 Sch.3 para.2
Part 4 r.4.53D, varied: SI 2013/1388 Sch.3 para.2
Part 4 r.4.54, varied: SI 2013/1388 Sch.3 para.2
Part 4 r.4.55, varied: SI 2013/1388 Sch.3 para.2
Part 4 r.4.56, varied: SI 2013/1388 Sch.3 para.2
Part 4 r.4.57, varied: SI 2013/1388 Sch.3 para.2
Part 4 r.4.58, varied: SI 2013/1388 Sch.3 para.2, Sch.3 Part 2
Part 4 r.4.59, varied: SI 2013/1388 Sch.3 para.2
Part 4 r.4.60, varied: SI 2013/1388 Sch.3 para.2
Part 4 r.4.61, varied: SI 2013/1388 Sch.3 para.2
Part 4 r.4.62, varied: SI 2013/1388 Sch.3 para.2
Part 4 r.4.63, varied: SI 2013/1388 Sch.3 para.2
Part 4 r.4.63A, varied: SI 2013/1388 Sch.3 para.2
Part 4 r.4.64, varied: SI 2013/1388 Sch.3 para.2
Part 4 r.4.65, varied: SI 2013/1388 Sch.3 para.2
Part 4 r.4.66, varied: SI 2013/1388 Sch.3 para.2
Part 4 r.4.67, varied: SI 2013/1388 Sch.3 para.2
Part 4 r.4.68, varied: SI 2013/1388 Sch.3 para.2
Part 4 r.4.69, varied: SI 2013/1388 Sch.3 para.2
Part 4 r.4.70, varied: SI 2013/1388 Sch.3 para.2
Part 4 r.4.71, varied: SI 2013/1388 Sch.3 para.2
Part 4 r.4.72, amended: SI 2013/472 Sch.2 para.5
Part 4 r.4.72, varied: SI 2013/1388 Sch.3 para.2
Part 4 r.4.73, varied: SI 2013/1388 Sch.3 para.2
Part 4 r.4.74, varied: SI 2013/1388 Sch.3 para.2
Part 4 r.4.75, varied: SI 2013/1388 Sch.3 para.2
Part 4 r.4.76, varied: SI 2013/1388 Sch.3 para.2
Part 4 r.4.77, varied: SI 2013/1388 Sch.3 para.2
Part 4 r.4.78, varied: SI 2013/1388 Sch.3 para.2
Part 4 r.4.79, varied: SI 2013/1388 Sch.3 para.2, Sch.3 Part 2
Part 4 r.4.80, varied: SI 2013/1388 Sch.3 para.2
Part 4 r.4.81, varied: SI 2013/1388 Sch.3 para.2
Part 4 r.4.82, varied: SI 2013/1388 Sch.3 para.2
Part 4 r.4.83, varied: SI 2013/1388 Sch.3 para.2, Sch.3 Part 2
Part 4 r.4.84, varied: SI 2013/1388 Sch.3 para.2
Part 4 r.4.85, varied: SI 2013/1388 Sch.3 para.2
Part 4 r.4.86, varied: SI 2013/1388 Sch.3 para.2
Part 4 r.4.87, varied: SI 2013/1388 Sch.3 para.2
Part 4 r.4.88, varied: SI 2013/1388 Sch.3 para.2
Part 4 r.4.89, varied: SI 2013/1388 Sch.3 para.2
Part 4 r.4.90, varied: SI 2013/1388 Sch.3 para.2, Sch.3 Part 2
Part 4 r.4.91, varied: SI 2013/1388 Sch.3 para.2
Part 4 r.4.92, varied: SI 2013/1388 Sch.3 para.2
Part 4 r.4.93, varied: SI 2013/1388 Sch.3 para.2
Part 4 r.4.94, varied: SI 2013/1388 Sch.3 para.2
Part 4 r.4.95, varied: SI 2013/1388 Sch.3 para.2
Part 4 r.4.96, varied: SI 2013/1388 Sch.3 para.2
Part 4 r.4.97, varied: SI 2013/1388 Sch.3 para.2
Part 4 r.4.98, varied: SI 2013/1388 Sch.3 para.2, Sch.3 Part 2
Part 4 r.4.99, varied: SI 2013/1388 Sch.3 para.2

Part 4 r.4.100, varied: SI 2013/1388 Sch.3 para.2
Part 4 r.4.101, varied: SI 2013/1388 Sch.3 para.2
Part 4 r.4.101A, varied: SI 2013/1388 Sch.3 para.2
Part 4 r.4.101B, varied: SI 2013/1388 Sch.3 para.2
Part 4 r.4.102, varied: SI 2013/1388 Sch.3 para.2
Part 4 r.4.103, varied: SI 2013/1388 Sch.3 para.2
Part 4 r.4.104, varied: SI 2013/1388 Sch.3 para.2
Part 4 r.4.105, varied: SI 2013/1388 Sch.3 para.2
Part 4 r.4.106, varied: SI 2013/1388 Sch.3 para.2
Part 4 r.4.106A, varied: SI 2013/1388 Sch.3 para.2
Part 4 r.4.107, varied: SI 2013/1388 Sch.3 para.2
Part 4 r.4.108, varied: SI 2013/1388 Sch.3 para.2
Part 4 r.4.108A, varied: SI 2013/1388 Sch.3 para.2
Part 4 r.4.109, varied: SI 2013/1388 Sch.3 para.2
Part 4 r.4.110, varied: SI 2013/1388 Sch.3 para.2
Part 4 r.4.111, varied: SI 2013/1388 Sch.3 para.2
Part 4 r.4.112, varied: SI 2013/1388 Sch.3 para.2
Part 4 r.4.113, varied: SI 2013/1388 Sch.3 para.2
Part 4 r.4.114, varied: SI 2013/1388 Sch.3 para.2
Part 4 r.4.115, varied: SI 2013/1388 Sch.3 para.2
Part 4 r.4.116, varied: SI 2013/1388 Sch.3 para.2
Part 4 r.4.117, varied: SI 2013/1388 Sch.3 para.2
Part 4 r.4.118, varied: SI 2013/1388 Sch.3 para.2
Part 4 r.4.119, varied: SI 2013/1388 Sch.3 para.2
Part 4 r.4.120, varied: SI 2013/1388 Sch.3 para.2
Part 4 r.4.121, varied: SI 2013/1388 Sch.3 para.2
Part 4 r.4.122, varied: SI 2013/1388 Sch.3 para.2
Part 4 r.4.123, varied: SI 2013/1388 Sch.3 para.2
Part 4 r.4.124, varied: SI 2013/1388 Sch.3 para.2, Sch.3 Part 2
Part 4 r.4.125, varied: SI 2013/1388 Sch.3 para.2, Sch.3 Part 2
Part 4 r.4.125A, varied: SI 2013/1388 Sch.3 para.2
Part 4 r.4.126, varied: SI 2013/1388 Sch.3 para.2
Part 4 r.4.126A, varied: SI 2013/1388 Sch.3 para.2
Part 4 r.4.127, varied: SI 2013/1388 Sch.3 para.2
Part 4 r.4.127A, varied: SI 2013/1388 Sch.3 para.2
Part 4 r.4.127B, varied: SI 2013/1388 Sch.3 para.2
Part 4 r.4.128, varied: SI 2013/1388 Sch.3 para.2, Sch.3 Part 2
Part 4 r.4.129, varied: SI 2013/1388 Sch.3 para.2
Part 4 r.4.129A, varied: SI 2013/1388 Sch.3 para.2
Part 4 r.4.130, varied: SI 2013/1388 Sch.3 para.2
Part 4 r.4.131, varied: SI 2013/1388 Sch.3 para.2, Sch.3 Part 2
Part 4 r.4.131A, varied: SI 2013/1388 Sch.3 para.2
Part 4 r.4.131B, varied: SI 2013/1388 Sch.3 para.2
Part 4 r.4.131C, varied: SI 2013/1388 Sch.3 para.2
Part 4 r.4.132, varied: SI 2013/1388 Sch.3 para.2
Part 4 r.4.133, varied: SI 2013/1388 Sch.3 para.2
Part 4 r.4.134, varied: SI 2013/1388 Sch.3 para.2
Part 4 r.4.135, varied: SI 2013/1388 Sch.3 para.2
Part 4 r.4.136, varied: SI 2013/1388 Sch.3 para.2
Part 4 r.4.137, varied: SI 2013/1388 Sch.3 para.2
Part 4 r.4.138, varied: SI 2013/1388 Sch.3 para.2, Sch.3 Part 2
Part 4 r.4.139, varied: SI 2013/1388 Sch.3 para.2
Part 4 r.4.140, varied: SI 2013/1388 Sch.3 para.2
Part 4 r.4.141, varied: SI 2013/1388 Sch.3 para.2
Part 4 r.4.142, varied: SI 2013/1388 Sch.3 para.2
Part 4 r.4.143, varied: SI 2013/1388 Sch.3 para.2
Part 4 r.4.144, varied: SI 2013/1388 Sch.3 para.2
Part 4 r.4.145, varied: SI 2013/1388 Sch.3 para.2
Part 4 r.4.146, varied: SI 2013/1388 Sch.3 para.2
Part 4 r.4.147, varied: SI 2013/1388 Sch.3 para.2
Part 4 r.4.148, varied: SI 2013/1388 Sch.3 para.2
Part 4 r.4.148A, varied: SI 2013/1388 Sch.3 para.2
Part 4 r.4.148B, varied: SI 2013/1388 Sch.3 para.2
Part 4 r.4.148C, varied: SI 2013/1388 Sch.3 para.2
Part 4 r.4.148D, varied: SI 2013/1388 Sch.3 para.2
Part 4 r.4.148E, varied: SI 2013/1388 Sch.3 para.2
Part 4 r.4.149, varied: SI 2013/1388 Sch.3 para.2, Sch.3 Part 2
Part 4 r.4.150, varied: SI 2013/1388 Sch.3 para.2
Part 4 r.4.151, varied: SI 2013/1388 Sch.3 para.2
Part 4 r.4.152, amended: SI 2013/472 Sch.2 para.5
Part 4 r.4.152, varied: SI 2013/1388 Sch.3 para.2, Sch.3 Part 2
Part 4 r.4.153, varied: SI 2013/1388 Sch.3 para.2
Part 4 r.4.154, varied: SI 2013/1388 Sch.3 para.2
Part 4 r.4.155, varied: SI 2013/1388 Sch.3 para.2
Part 4 r.4.156, varied: SI 2013/1388 Sch.3 para.2
Part 4 r.4.157, varied: SI 2013/1388 Sch.3 para.2
Part 4 r.4.158, varied: SI 2013/1388 Sch.3 para.2
Part 4 r.4.159, varied: SI 2013/1388 Sch.3 para.2
Part 4 r.4.160, varied: SI 2013/1388 Sch.3 para.2
Part 4 r.4.161, varied: SI 2013/1388 Sch.3 para.2
Part 4 r.4.162, varied: SI 2013/1388 Sch.3 para.2
Part 4 r.4.163, varied: SI 2013/1388 Sch.3 para.2
Part 4 r.4.164, varied: SI 2013/1388 Sch.3 para.2
Part 4 r.4.165, varied: SI 2013/1388 Sch.3 para.2
Part 4 r.4.166, varied: SI 2013/1388 Sch.3 para.2
Part 4 r.4.167, varied: SI 2013/1388 Sch.3 para.2
Part 4 r.4.168, varied: SI 2013/1388 Sch.3 para.2
Part 4 r.4.169, varied: SI 2013/1388 Sch.3 para.2
Part 4 r.4.170, varied: SI 2013/1388 Sch.3 para.2
Part 4 r.4.171, varied: SI 2013/1388 Sch.3 para.2
Part 4 r.4.171A, varied: SI 2013/1388 Sch.3 para.2, Sch.3 Part 2
Part 4 r.4.172, varied: SI 2013/1388 Sch.3 para.2
Part 4 r.4.172A, varied: SI 2013/1388 Sch.3 para.2
Part 4 r.4.173, varied: SI 2013/1388 Sch.3 para.2
Part 4 r.4.174, varied: SI 2013/1388 Sch.3 para.2
Part 4 r.4.174A, varied: SI 2013/1388 Sch.3 para.2
Part 4 r.4.175, varied: SI 2013/1388 Sch.3 para.2
Part 4 r.4.176, varied: SI 2013/1388 Sch.3 para.2
Part 4 r.4.177, varied: SI 2013/1388 Sch.3 para.2
Part 4 r.4.178, varied: SI 2013/1388 Sch.3 para.2

Part 4 r.4.179, varied: SI 2013/1388 Sch.3 para.2
Part 4 r.4.180, varied: SI 2013/1388 Sch.3 para.2
Part 4 r.4.181, varied: SI 2013/1388 Sch.3 para.2
Part 4 r.4.182, varied: SI 2013/1388 Sch.3 para.2
Part 4 r.4.182A, varied: SI 2013/1388 Sch.3 para.2
Part 4 r.4.183, varied: SI 2013/1388 Sch.3 para.2
Part 4 r.4.184, varied: SI 2013/1388 Sch.3 para.2
Part 4 r.4.185, varied: SI 2013/1388 Sch.3 para.2
Part 4 r.4.186, varied: SI 2013/1388 Sch.3 para.2
Part 4 r.4.187, varied: SI 2013/1388 Sch.3 para.2
Part 4 r.4.188, varied: SI 2013/1388 Sch.3 para.2, Sch.3 Part 2
Part 4 r.4.189, varied: SI 2013/1388 Sch.3 para.2
Part 4 r.4.190, varied: SI 2013/1388 Sch.3 para.2
Part 4 r.4.190A, varied: SI 2013/1388 Sch.3 para.2
Part 4 r.4.191, varied: SI 2013/1388 Sch.3 para.2
Part 4 r.4.191A, varied: SI 2013/1388 Sch.3 para.2
Part 4 r.4.192, varied: SI 2013/1388 Sch.3 para.2
Part 4 r.4.193, varied: SI 2013/1388 Sch.3 para.2
Part 4 r.4.194, varied: SI 2013/1388 Sch.3 para.2
Part 4 r.4.195, varied: SI 2013/1388 Sch.3 para.2
Part 4 r.4.196, varied: SI 2013/1388 Sch.3 para.2
Part 4 r.4.197, varied: SI 2013/1388 Sch.3 para.2
Part 4 r.4.198, varied: SI 2013/1388 Sch.3 para.2
Part 4 r.4.199, varied: SI 2013/1388 Sch.3 para.2
Part 4 r.4.200, varied: SI 2013/1388 Sch.3 para.2
Part 4 r.4.201, varied: SI 2013/1388 Sch.3 para.2
Part 4 r.4.202, varied: SI 2013/1388 Sch.3 para.2
Part 4 r.4.203, varied: SI 2013/1388 Sch.3 para.2
Part 4 r.4.204, varied: SI 2013/1388 Sch.3 para.2
Part 4 r.4.205, varied: SI 2013/1388 Sch.3 para.2
Part 4 r.4.206, varied: SI 2013/1388 Sch.3 para.2
Part 4 r.4.207, varied: SI 2013/1388 Sch.3 para.2
Part 4 r.4.208, varied: SI 2013/1388 Sch.3 para.2
Part 4 r.4.209, varied: SI 2013/1388 Sch.3 para.2
Part 4 r.4.210, varied: SI 2013/1388 Sch.3 para.2
Part 4 r.4.211, varied: SI 2013/1388 Sch.3 para.2
Part 4 r.4.212, varied: SI 2013/1388 Sch.3 para.2
Part 4 r.4.213, varied: SI 2013/1388 Sch.3 para.2, Sch.3 Part 2
Part 4 r.4.214, varied: SI 2013/1388 Sch.3 para.2
Part 4 r.4.215, varied: SI 2013/1388 Sch.3 para.2
Part 4 r.4.216, varied: SI 2013/1388 Sch.3 para.2
Part 4 r.4.217, varied: SI 2013/1388 Sch.3 para.2
Part 4 r.4.218, varied: SI 2013/1388 Sch.3 para.2, Sch.3 Part 2
Part 4 r.4.218A, varied: SI 2013/1388 Sch.3 para.2
Part 4 r.4.218B, varied: SI 2013/1388 Sch.3 para.2
Part 4 r.4.218C, varied: SI 2013/1388 Sch.3 para.2
Part 4 r.4.218D, varied: SI 2013/1388 Sch.3 para.2
Part 4 r.4.218E, varied: SI 2013/1388 Sch.3 para.2
Part 4 r.4.219, varied: SI 2013/1388 Sch.3 para.2
Part 4 r.4.220, varied: SI 2013/1388 Sch.3 para.2, Sch.3 Part 2
Part 4 r.4.221, varied: SI 2013/1388 Sch.3 para.2
Part 4 r.4.222, varied: SI 2013/1388 Sch.3 para.2
Part 4 r.4.223, varied: SI 2013/1388 Sch.3 para.2
Part 4 r.4.224, varied: SI 2013/1388 Sch.3 para.2
Part 4 r.4.225, varied: SI 2013/1388 Sch.3 para.2
Part 4 r.4.226, varied: SI 2013/1388 Sch.3 para.2
Part 4 r.4.227, varied: SI 2013/1388 Sch.3 para.2
Part 4 r.4.227A, varied: SI 2013/1388 Sch.3 para.2
Part 4 r.4.228, varied: SI 2013/1388 Sch.3 para.2
Part 4 r.4.229, varied: SI 2013/1388 Sch.3 para.2
Part 4 r.4.230, varied: SI 2013/1388 Sch.3 para.2
Part 4 r.4.231, varied: SI 2013/1388 Sch.3 para.2
Part 6, revoked: SI 2013/2135 r.3
Part 6A r.6A.4, amended: SI 2013/2135 r.3
Part 7, applied: SI 2013/1388 Sch.3 para.1
Part 7 r.7.1, varied: SI 2013/1388 Sch.3 para.2, Sch.3 Part 2
Part 7 r.7.2, varied: SI 2013/1388 Sch.3 para.2
Part 7 r.7.3, varied: SI 2013/1388 Sch.3 para.2
Part 7 r.7.3A, varied: SI 2013/1388 Sch.3 para.2
Part 7 r.7.4, varied: SI 2013/1388 Sch.3 para.2
Part 7 r.7.4A, varied: SI 2013/1388 Sch.3 para.2
Part 7 r.7.5, varied: SI 2013/1388 Sch.3 para.2
Part 7 r.7.5A, varied: SI 2013/1388 Sch.3 para.2
Part 7 r.7.6, varied: SI 2013/1388 Sch.3 para.2
Part 7 r.7.6A, varied: SI 2013/1388 Sch.3 para.2
Part 7 r.7.7, varied: SI 2013/1388 Sch.3 para.2
Part 7 r.7.7A, varied: SI 2013/1388 Sch.3 para.2
Part 7 r.7.8, varied: SI 2013/1388 Sch.3 para.2
Part 7 r.7.9, varied: SI 2013/1388 Sch.3 para.2
Part 7 r.7.10, varied: SI 2013/1388 Sch.3 para.2
Part 7 r.7.10A, varied: SI 2013/1388 Sch.3 para.2
Part 7 r.7.10B, varied: SI 2013/1388 Sch.3 para.2
Part 7 r.7.10C, varied: SI 2013/1388 Sch.3 para.2
Part 7 r.7.10D, varied: SI 2013/1388 Sch.3 para.2
Part 7 r.7.10ZA, varied: SI 2013/1388 Sch.3 para.2
Part 7 r.7.11, varied: SI 2013/1388 Sch.3 para.2
Part 7 r.7.12, varied: SI 2013/1388 Sch.3 para.2
Part 7 r.7.13, varied: SI 2013/1388 Sch.3 para.2
Part 7 r.7.14, varied: SI 2013/1388 Sch.3 para.2
Part 7 r.7.15, varied: SI 2013/1388 Sch.3 para.2
Part 7 r.7.16, varied: SI 2013/1388 Sch.3 para.2
Part 7 r.7.17, varied: SI 2013/1388 Sch.3 para.2
Part 7 r.7.18, varied: SI 2013/1388 Sch.3 para.2
Part 7 r.7.19, varied: SI 2013/1388 Sch.3 para.2
Part 7 r.7.20, varied: SI 2013/1388 Sch.3 para.2
Part 7 r.7.21, varied: SI 2013/1388 Sch.3 para.2
Part 7 r.7.22, varied: SI 2013/1388 Sch.3 para.2
Part 7 r.7.23, varied: SI 2013/1388 Sch.3 para.2
Part 7 r.7.24, varied: SI 2013/1388 Sch.3 para.2
Part 7 r.7.25, varied: SI 2013/1388 Sch.3 para.2
Part 7 r.7.26, varied: SI 2013/1388 Sch.3 para.2
Part 7 r.7.27, varied: SI 2013/1388 Sch.3 para.2
Part 7 r.7.28, varied: SI 2013/1388 Sch.3 para.2

Part 7 r.7.29, varied: SI 2013/1388 Sch.3 para.2
Part 7 r.7.30, varied: SI 2013/1388 Sch.3 para.2
Part 7 r.7.31, varied: SI 2013/1388 Sch.3 para.2
Part 7 r.7.31A, varied: SI 2013/1388 Sch.3 para.2, Sch.3 Part 2
Part 7 r.7.32, varied: SI 2013/1388 Sch.3 para.2
Part 7 r.7.33, varied: SI 2013/1388 Sch.3 para.2
Part 7 r.7.33A, varied: SI 2013/1388 Sch.3 para.2
Part 7 r.7.34, varied: SI 2013/1388 Sch.3 para.2
Part 7 r.7.34A, varied: SI 2013/1388 Sch.3 para.2
Part 7 r.7.35, varied: SI 2013/1388 Sch.3 para.2
Part 7 r.7.36, varied: SI 2013/1388 Sch.3 para.2
Part 7 r.7.37, varied: SI 2013/1388 Sch.3 para.2
Part 7 r.7.37A, varied: SI 2013/1388 Sch.3 para.2
Part 7 r.7.38, varied: SI 2013/1388 Sch.3 para.2
Part 7 r.7.39, varied: SI 2013/1388 Sch.3 para.2
Part 7 r.7.40, varied: SI 2013/1388 Sch.3 para.2
Part 7 r.7.41, varied: SI 2013/1388 Sch.3 para.2, Sch.3 Part 2
Part 7 r.7.42, varied: SI 2013/1388 Sch.3 para.2
Part 7 r.7.43, varied: SI 2013/1388 Sch.3 para.2
Part 7 r.7.44, varied: SI 2013/1388 Sch.3 para.2
Part 7 r.7.45, varied: SI 2013/1388 Sch.3 para.2
Part 7 r.7.45A, varied: SI 2013/1388 Sch.3 para.2
Part 7 r.7.46, varied: SI 2013/1388 Sch.3 para.2
Part 7 r.7.47, varied: SI 2013/1388 Sch.3 para.2
Part 7 r.7.48, varied: SI 2013/1388 Sch.3 para.2
Part 7 r.7.49, varied: SI 2013/1388 Sch.3 para.2
Part 7 r.7.49A, varied: SI 2013/1388 Sch.3 para.2
Part 7 r.7.50, varied: SI 2013/1388 Sch.3 para.2
Part 7 r.7.51, varied: SI 2013/1388 Sch.3 para.2
Part 7 r.7.51A, varied: SI 2013/1388 Sch.3 para.2
Part 7 r.7.52, varied: SI 2013/1388 Sch.3 para.2
Part 7 r.7.53, varied: SI 2013/1388 Sch.3 para.2
Part 7 r.7.54, varied: SI 2013/1388 Sch.3 para.2
Part 7 r.7.55, varied: SI 2013/1388 Sch.3 para.2
Part 7 r.7.56, varied: SI 2013/1388 Sch.3 para.2, Sch.3 Part 2
Part 7 r.7.57, varied: SI 2013/1388 Sch.3 para.2
Part 7 r.7.58, varied: SI 2013/1388 Sch.3 para.2
Part 7 r.7.59, varied: SI 2013/1388 Sch.3 para.2
Part 7 r.7.60, varied: SI 2013/1388 Sch.3 para.2
Part 7 r.7.61, varied: SI 2013/1388 Sch.3 para.2
Part 7 r.7.62, varied: SI 2013/1388 Sch.3 para.2
Part 7 r.7.63, varied: SI 2013/1388 Sch.3 para.2
Part 7 r.7.64, varied: SI 2013/1388 Sch.3 para.2
Part 8 r.8.1, varied: SI 2013/1388 Sch.3 para.2
Part 8 r.8.2, varied: SI 2013/1388 Sch.3 para.2
Part 8 r.8.3, varied: SI 2013/1388 Sch.3 para.2
Part 8 r.8.4, varied: SI 2013/1388 Sch.3 para.2
Part 8 r.8.5, varied: SI 2013/1388 Sch.3 para.2, Sch.3 Part 2
Part 8 r.8.6, varied: SI 2013/1388 Sch.3 para.2
Part 8 r.8.7, varied: SI 2013/1388 Sch.3 para.2
Part 8 r.8.8, varied: SI 2013/1388 Sch.3 para.2
Part 9 r.9.1, varied: SI 2013/1388 Sch.3 para.2
Part 9 r.9.2, varied: SI 2013/1388 Sch.3 para.2
Part 9 r.9.3, varied: SI 2013/1388 Sch.3 para.2
Part 9 r.9.4, varied: SI 2013/1388 Sch.3 para.2
Part 9 r.9.5, varied: SI 2013/1388 Sch.3 para.2
Part 9 r.9.6, varied: SI 2013/1388 Sch.3 para.2
Part 10 r.10.1, varied: SI 2013/1388 Sch.3 para.2
Part 10 r.10.2, varied: SI 2013/1388 Sch.3 para.2
Part 10 r.10.3, varied: SI 2013/1388 Sch.3 para.2
Part 10 r.10.4, varied: SI 2013/1388 Sch.3 para.2
Part 11 r.11.1, varied: SI 2013/1388 Sch.3 para.2
Part 11 r.11.2, varied: SI 2013/1388 Sch.3 para.2
Part 11 r.11.3, varied: SI 2013/1388 Sch.3 para.2
Part 11 r.11.4, varied: SI 2013/1388 Sch.3 para.2
Part 11 r.11.5, varied: SI 2013/1388 Sch.3 para.2
Part 11 r.11.6, varied: SI 2013/1388 Sch.3 para.2, Sch.3 Part 2
Part 11 r.11.7, varied: SI 2013/1388 Sch.3 para.2
Part 11 r.11.8, varied: SI 2013/1388 Sch.3 para.2
Part 11 r.11.9, varied: SI 2013/1388 Sch.3 para.2
Part 11 r.11.10, varied: SI 2013/1388 Sch.3 para.2
Part 11 r.11.11, varied: SI 2013/1388 Sch.3 para.2
Part 11 r.11.12, varied: SI 2013/1388 Sch.3 para.2
Part 11 r.11.13, varied: SI 2013/1388 Sch.3 para.2
Part 12 r.12.1, varied: SI 2013/1388 Sch.3 para.2
Part 12 r.12.2, varied: SI 2013/1388 Sch.3 para.2
Part 12 r.12.3, varied: SI 2013/1388 Sch.3 para.2
Part 12 r.12.4, varied: SI 2013/1388 Sch.3 para.2
Part 12 r.12.4A, varied: SI 2013/1388 Sch.3 para.2
Part 12 r.12.5, varied: SI 2013/1388 Sch.3 para.2
Part 12 r.12.6, varied: SI 2013/1388 Sch.3 para.2
Part 12 r.12.7, varied: SI 2013/1388 Sch.3 para.2
Part 12 r.12.8, varied: SI 2013/1388 Sch.3 para.2
Part 12 r.12.9, varied: SI 2013/1388 Sch.3 para.2
Part 12 r.12.10, varied: SI 2013/1388 Sch.3 para.2
Part 12 r.12.11, varied: SI 2013/1388 Sch.3 para.2
Part 12 r.12.12, varied: SI 2013/1388 Sch.3 para.2
Part 12 r.12.13, varied: SI 2013/1388 Sch.3 para.2
Part 12 r.12.14, varied: SI 2013/1388 Sch.3 para.2
Part 12 r.12.15, varied: SI 2013/1388 Sch.3 para.2
Part 12 r.12.15A, varied: SI 2013/1388 Sch.3 para.2
Part 12 r.12.16, varied: SI 2013/1388 Sch.3 para.2
Part 12 r.12.17, varied: SI 2013/1388 Sch.3 para.2
Part 12 r.12.18, varied: SI 2013/1388 Sch.3 para.2, Sch.3 Part 2
Part 12 r.12.19, varied: SI 2013/1388 Sch.3 para.2
Part 12 r.12.20, varied: SI 2013/1388 Sch.3 para.2
Part 12 r.12.21, varied: SI 2013/1388 Sch.3 para.2
Part 12 r.12.22, varied: SI 2013/1388 Sch.3 para.2
Part 12A r.12A.1, varied: SI 2013/1388 Sch.3 para.2

Part 12A r.12A.2, varied: SI 2013/1388 Sch.3 para.2
Part 12A r.12A.3, varied: SI 2013/1388 Sch.3 para.2
Part 12A r.12A.4, varied: SI 2013/1388 Sch.3 para.2
Part 12A r.12A.5, varied: SI 2013/1388 Sch.3 para.2
Part 12A r.12A.6, varied: SI 2013/1388 Sch.3 para.2
Part 12A r.12A.7, varied: SI 2013/1388 Sch.3 para.2
Part 12A r.12A.8, varied: SI 2013/1388 Sch.3 para.2
Part 12A r.12A.9, varied: SI 2013/1388 Sch.3 para.2
Part 12A r.12A.10, varied: SI 2013/1388 Sch.3 para.2
Part 12A r.12A.11, varied: SI 2013/1388 Sch.3 para.2
Part 12A r.12A.12, varied: SI 2013/1388 Sch.3 para.2
Part 12A r.12A.13, varied: SI 2013/1388 Sch.3 para.2
Part 12A r.12A.14, varied: SI 2013/1388 Sch.3 para.2
Part 12A r.12A.15, varied: SI 2013/1388 Sch.3 para.2
Part 12A r.12A.16, varied: SI 2013/1388 Sch.3 para.2
Part 12A r.12A.17, varied: SI 2013/1388 Sch.3 para.2
Part 12A r.12A.18, varied: SI 2013/1388 Sch.3 para.2, Sch.3 Part 2
Part 12A r.12A.19, varied: SI 2013/1388 Sch.3 para.2
Part 12A r.12A.20, varied: SI 2013/1388 Sch.3 para.2
Part 12A r.12A.21, varied: SI 2013/1388 Sch.3 para.2
Part 12A r.12A.22, varied: SI 2013/1388 Sch.3 para.2
Part 12A r.12A.23, varied: SI 2013/1388 Sch.3 para.2
Part 12A r.12A.24, varied: SI 2013/1388 Sch.3 para.2
Part 12A r.12A.25, varied: SI 2013/1388 Sch.3 para.2
Part 12A r.12A.26, varied: SI 2013/1388 Sch.3 para.2
Part 12A r.12A.27, varied: SI 2013/1388 Sch.3 para.2
Part 12A r.12A.28, varied: SI 2013/1388 Sch.3 para.2
Part 12A r.12A.29, varied: SI 2013/1388 Sch.3 para.2
Part 12A r.12A.30, varied: SI 2013/1388 Sch.3 para.2, Sch.3 Part 2
Part 12A r.12A.31, varied: SI 2013/1388 Sch.3 para.2
Part 12A r.12A.32, varied: SI 2013/1388 Sch.3 para.2
Part 12A r.12A.33, varied: SI 2013/1388 Sch.3 para.2
Part 12A r.12A.34, varied: SI 2013/1388 Sch.3 para.2, Sch.3 Part 2
Part 12A r.12A.35, varied: SI 2013/1388 Sch.3 para.2
Part 12A r.12A.36, varied: SI 2013/1388 Sch.3 para.2
Part 12A r.12A.37, varied: SI 2013/1388 Sch.3 para.2
Part 12A r.12A.38, varied: SI 2013/1388 Sch.3 para.2
Part 12A r.12A.39, varied: SI 2013/1388 Sch.3 para.2, Sch.3 Part 2
Part 12A r.12A.40, varied: SI 2013/1388 Sch.3 para.2
Part 12A r.12A.41, varied: SI 2013/1388 Sch.3 para.2
Part 12A r.12A.42, varied: SI 2013/1388 Sch.3 para.2
Part 12A r.12A.43, varied: SI 2013/1388 Sch.3 para.2, Sch.3 Part 2
Part 12A r.12A.44, varied: SI 2013/1388 Sch.3 para.2
Part 12A r.12A.45, varied: SI 2013/1388 Sch.3 para.2
Part 12A r.12A.46, varied: SI 2013/1388 Sch.3 para.2
Part 12A r.12A.47, varied: SI 2013/1388 Sch.3 para.2
Part 12A r.12A.48, varied: SI 2013/1388 Sch.3 para.2
Part 12A r.12A.49, varied: SI 2013/1388 Sch.3 para.2
Part 12A r.12A.50, varied: SI 2013/1388 Sch.3 para.2
Part 12A r.12A.51, varied: SI 2013/1388 Sch.3 para.2
Part 12A r.12A.52, varied: SI 2013/1388 Sch.3 para.2
Part 12A r.12A.53, varied: SI 2013/1388 Sch.3 para.2, Sch.3 Part 2
Part 12A r.12A.54, varied: SI 2013/1388 Sch.3 para.2
Part 12A r.12A.55, varied: SI 2013/1388 Sch.3 para.2

Part 12A r.12A.56, varied: SI 2013/1388 Sch.3 para.2
Part 12A r.12A.57, varied: SI 2013/1388 Sch.3 para.2
Part 13, applied: SI 2013/1388 Sch.3 para.1
Part 13 r.13.1, varied: SI 2013/1388 Sch.3 para.2
Part 13 r.13.2, varied: SI 2013/1388 Sch.3 para.2
Part 13 r.13.3, varied: SI 2013/1388 Sch.3 para.2
Part 13 r.13.4, varied: SI 2013/1388 Sch.3 para.2
Part 13 r.13.5, varied: SI 2013/1388 Sch.3 para.2
Part 13 r.13.6, varied: SI 2013/1388 Sch.3 para.2
Part 13 r.13.7, varied: SI 2013/1388 Sch.3 para.2
Part 13 r.13.8, varied: SI 2013/1388 Sch.3 para.2
Part 13 r.13.9, varied: SI 2013/1388 Sch.3 para.2
Part 13 r.13.9A, varied: SI 2013/1388 Sch.3 para.2
Part 13 r.13.10, varied: SI 2013/1388 Sch.3 para.2
Part 13 r.13.11, varied: SI 2013/1388 Sch.3 para.2
Part 13 r.13.12, varied: SI 2013/1388 Sch.3 para.2
Part 13 r.13.12A, amended: SI 2013/472 Art.4
Part 13 r.13.12A, varied: SI 2013/1388 Sch.3 para.2
Part 13 r.13.13, varied: SI 2013/1388 Sch.3 para.2
Part 13 r.13.14, varied: SI 2013/1388 Sch.3 para.2
Part 13 r.13.15, varied: SI 2013/1388 Sch.3 para.2
Pt 5 r.5.21, see *Davis v Price* [2013] EWHC 323 (Ch), [2013] B.P.I.R. 200 (Ch D), David Richards, J.
Pt 5 r.5.22, see *McNally, Re* [2013] EWHC 1685 (Ch), [2013] B.P.I.R. 604 (Ch D), Judge Purle Q.C.
Pt 5 r.5.24, see *Bonney v Mirpuri* [2013] B.P.I.R. 412 (Ch D), Registrar Jones
r.1.23, see *Portsmouth City Football Club Ltd (In Liquidation), Re* [2012] EWHC 3088 (Ch), [2013] 1 All E.R. 975 (Ch D (Companies Ct)), Morgan, J.
r.2.67, see *Bickland Ltd, Re* [2012] EWHC 706 (Ch), [2013] Bus. L.R. 361 (Ch D), Mann, J.; see *Bloom v Pensions Regulator* [2013] UKSC 52, [2013] 3 W.L.R. 504 (SC), Lord Neuberger, J.S.C.; see *Portsmouth City Football Club Ltd (In Liquidation), Re* [2012] EWHC 3088 (Ch), [2013] 1 All E.R. 975 (Ch D (Companies Ct)), Morgan, J.; see *UK Housing Alliance (North West) Ltd (In Administration), Re* [2013] EWHC 2553 (Ch), [2013] B.C.C. 752 (Ch D (Companies Ct)), Martin Mann Q.C.
r.2.78, see *BESTrustees Plc v Kaupthing Singer & Friedlander (In Administration)* [2013] EWHC 2407 (Ch), [2013] Pens. L.R. 339 (Ch D (Companies Ct)), Sir Terence Etherton (Chancellor)
r.4.79, see *MG Rover Dealer Properties Ltd v Hunt* [2013] B.C.C. 698 (Ch D (Companies Ct)), Registrar Baister
r.4.84, see *Danka Business Systems Plc (In Liquidation), Re* [2013] EWCA Civ 92, [2013] Ch. 506 (CA (Civ Div)), Mummery, L.J.
r.4.86, see *Danka Business Systems Plc (In Liquidation), Re* [2013] EWCA Civ 92, [2013] Ch. 506 (CA (Civ Div)), Mummery, L.J.
r.4.182A, see *Danka Business Systems Plc (In Liquidation), Re* [2013] EWCA Civ 92, [2013] Ch. 506 (CA (Civ Div)), Mummery, L.J.
r.4.218, see *Bickland Ltd, Re* [2012] EWHC 706 (Ch), [2013] Bus. L.R. 361 (Ch D), Mann, J.; see *Portsmouth City Football Club Ltd (In Liquidation), Re* [2012] EWHC 3088 (Ch), [2013] 1 All E.R. 975 (Ch D (Companies Ct)), Morgan, J.
r.6.5, see *Darbyshire v Turpin* [2013] EWHC 954 (Ch), [2013] B.P.I.R. 558 (Ch D), Arnold, J.
r.6.26, see *Kasumu v Arrow Global (Guernsey) Ltd* [2013] EWHC 789 (Ch), [2013] B.P.I.R. 1047 (Ch D), Asplin, J.
r.6.185, see *Hunt v Conwy CBC* [2013] EWHC 1154 (Ch), [2013] B.P.I.R. 790 (Ch D), Sir William Blackburne
r.6.215, see *Kapoor (In Bankruptcy), Re* [2013] EWHC 2204 (Ch), [2013] B.P.I.R. 745 (Ch D), Penelope Reed QC
r.7.31A, see *Times Newspapers Ltd v McNamara* [2013] B.P.I.R. 1092 (Ch D (Bankruptcy Ct)), Registrar Baister
r.7.55, see *Care People Ltd (In Administration), Re* [2013] EWHC 1734 (Ch), [2013] B.C.C. 466 (Ch D (Birmingham)), Judge Purle Q.C.; see *Euromaster Ltd, Re* [2012] EWHC 2356 (Ch), [2013] Bus. L.R. 466 (Ch D), Norris, J.; see *Kasumu v Arrow Global (Guernsey) Ltd* [2013] EWHC 789 (Ch), [2013] B.P.I.R. 1047 (Ch D), Asplin, J.
r.8.1, see *Horler v Rubin* [2012] EWCA Civ 4, [2013] 1 B.C.L.C. 1 (CA (Civ Div)), Mummery, L.J.
r.8.3, see *Horler v Rubin* [2012] EWCA Civ 4, [2013] 1 B.C.L.C. 1 (CA (Civ Div)), Mummery, L.J.
r.12.2, see *Bloom v Pensions Regulator* [2013] UKSC 52, [2013] 3 W.L.R. 504 (SC), Lord Neuberger, J.S.C.
r.12.3, see *Bloom v Pensions Regulator* [2013] UKSC 52, [2013] 3 W.L.R. 504 (SC), Lord Neuberger, J.S.C.; see *Consolidated Finance Ltd v Collins* [2013] EWCA Civ 475, [2013] E.C.C. 21 (CA (Civ Div)), Arden, L.J.
r.13.12, see *Bloom v Pensions Regulator* [2013] UKSC 52, [2013] 3 W.L.R. 504 (SC), Lord Neuberger, J.S.C.

1960. Statutory Maternity Pay (General) Regulations 1986

Reg.6, amended: SI 2013/574 Art.9

2097. Companies (Forms) (Amendment) Regulations 1986

revoked: SI 2013/1947 Sch.2 Part 1

2211. Charitable Deductions (Approved Schemes) Regulations 1986

Reg.16, revoked: 2013 c.2 Sch.1 Part 10

2297. Act of Sederunt (Sheriff Court Company Insolvency Rules) 1986

Part II r.10, amended: SSI 2013/171 r.3
Part II r.11, amended: SSI 2013/171 r.3
Part II r.12, amended: SSI 2013/171 r.3
Part II r.14A, amended: SSI 2013/171 r.3
r.3, amended: SSI 2013/171 r.3
r.3A, amended: SSI 2013/171 r.3

2327. A47 Trunk Road (Birmingham-Great Yarmouth) (24 Hour Main Carriageway Clearway) Order 1986

Sch.1, revoked: SI 2013/394 Sch.1 Part II

1987

37. Dangerous Substances in Harbour Areas Regulations 1987

Reg.3, amended: SI 2013/1478 Sch.5 para.7
Reg.30, amended: SSI 2013/119 Sch.2 para.5

130. Pensions Increase (Review) Order 1987

applied: SI 2013/604 Sch.1

148. Trunk Road (A5) (Bethesda, Gwynedd) (Prohibition of Waiting) Order 1987

revoked: SI 2013/791 Art.7

180. Control of Industrial Air Pollution (Transfer of Powers of Enforcement) Regulations 1987

revoked: SI 2013/390 Reg.58

235. Statutory Maternity Pay (Medical Evidence) Regulations 1987

Reg.1, amended: SI 2013/235 Sch.2 para.9
Sch.1 Part II, amended: SI 2013/235 Sch.2 para.9

257. Police Pensions Regulations 1987

Reg.1, amended: SI 2013/2318 Sch.1 para.8, SSI 2013/184 Reg.7
Reg.1, amended: SI 2013/2318 Sch.1 para.11
Reg.1, amended: SI 2013/2318 Sch.1 para.12
Reg.2, amended: SSI 2013/184 Reg.8
Reg.2, amended: SI 2013/487 Reg.2, SSI 2013/89 Reg.2
Reg.2A, amended: SI 2013/2318 Sch.1 para.9
Reg.2A, revoked (in part): SI 2013/2318 Sch.1 para.9
Reg.3, amended: SSI 2013/184 Reg.10
Reg.4, revoked (in part): SI 2013/2318 Sch.1 para.13
Reg.5A, amended: SI 2013/487 Reg.4
Reg.5A, applied: SI 2013/487 Reg.5
Reg.5A, revoked (in part): SI 2013/487 Reg.4
Reg.6, amended: SI 2013/2318 Sch.1 para.2
Reg.6, revoked (in part): SI 2013/2318 Sch.1 para.2, SSI 2013/184 Reg.3
Reg.6, amended: SSI 2013/184 Reg.11
Reg.8, amended: SI 2013/2318 Sch.1 para.10, SSI 2013/184 Reg.9
Reg.12, amended: SI 2013/2318 Sch.1 para.3
Reg.15, revoked (in part): SSI 2013/184 Reg.4
Reg.16, amended: SI 2013/2318 Sch.1 para.4
Reg.16, revoked (in part): SI 2013/2318 Sch.1 para.4, SSI 2013/184 Reg.5
Reg.17, amended: SI 2013/2318 Sch.1 para.5, SSI 2013/184 Reg.6
Reg.17, revoked (in part): SI 2013/2318 Sch.1 para.5
Reg.18, amended: SI 2013/2318 Sch.1 para.6
Reg.19, amended: SI 2013/2318 Sch.1 para.7
Sch.A, amended: SI 2013/2318 Sch.1 para.14, SSI 2013/184 Reg.12
Sch.A, revoked (in part): SI 2013/2318 Sch.1 para.14, SSI 2013/184 Reg.12

299. Prosecution of Offences (Custody Time Limits) Regulations 1987

Reg.4, applied: SI 2013/1554 r.19_16
Reg.5, applied: SI 2013/1554 r.19_16

337. Transport Act 1985 (Modifications in Schedule 4 to the Transport Act 1968) (Amendment) Order 1987

revoked: SI 2013/2986 Sch.3

390. Artificial Insemination (Cattle and Pigs) (Fees) Regulations 1987

revoked (in part): SI 2013/1241 Reg.11

427. Act of Sederunt (Legal Aid Rules) (Children) 1987

revoked: SSI 2013/172 Art.7

492. Act of Sederunt (Civil Legal Aid Rules) 1987

r.6, see *H v B* [2013] CSOH 53, 2013 S.L.T. 681 (OH), Lord Bannatyne

530. Income Tax (Entertainers and Sportsmen) Regulations 1987

Reg.3, amended: SI 2013/605 Reg.3

764. Town and Country Planning (Use Classes) Order 1987

see *Telford and Wrekin Council v Secretary of State for Communities and Local Government* [2013] EWHC 79 (Admin), [2013] 1 E.G.L.R. 87 (QBD (Admin)), Beatson, L.J.

790. Infectious Diseases of Horses Order 1987

Art.3, amended: SSI 2013/173 Art.7
Art.4, amended: SSI 2013/173 Art.7

Art.7, amended: SSI 2013/173 Art.7
Art.9, amended: SSI 2013/173 Art.7
Sch.1, amended: SSI 2013/173 Art.7

1110. Personal Pension Schemes (Disclosure of Information) Regulations 1987
revoked: SI 2013/2734 Reg.1
Reg.6, amended: SI 2013/472 Sch.2 para.6
Sch.1 para.10, amended: SI 2013/472 Art.5
Sch.3 para.4, amended: SI 2013/472 Sch.2 para.6

1112. Personal Pension Schemes (Transfer Values) Regulations 1987
Reg.3, applied: SI 2013/2734 Sch.6 para.5, Sch.8 para.12
Reg.4, applied: SI 2013/2734 Sch.6 para.5, Sch.8 para.12

1229. Section 19 Minibus (Designated Bodies) Order 1987
Art.4, amended: SI 2013/1644 Sch.2

1501. London-Great Yarmouth Trunk Road (A12) (Prohibition of U-Turns Opposite The Junction With Squirrels Hall Lane) Order 1987
revoked: SI 2013/1076 Art.4

1529. Town and Country Planning (Listed Buildings and Buildings in Conservation Areas) (Scotland) Regulations 1987
Reg.5, applied: SSI 2013/156 Reg.29

1806. Value Added Tax (Tour Operators) Order 1987
see *Secret Hotels2 Ltd (formerly Med Hotels Ltd) v Revenue and Customs Commissioners* [2012] EWCA Civ 1571, [2013] S.T.C. 452 (CA (Civ Div)), Ward, L.J.
Art.3, see *Secret Hotels2 Ltd (formerly Med Hotels Ltd) v Revenue and Customs Commissioners* [2012] EWCA Civ 1571, [2013] S.T.C. 452 (CA (Civ Div)), Ward, L.J.

1850. Local Government Superannuation (Scotland) Regulations 1987
Part E regE.2A, amended: SSI 2013/147 Sch.1 para.1
Part T regT.1, amended: SSI 2013/147 Sch.1 para.1
Sch.3 Part I para.4, amended: SSI 2013/147 Sch.1 para.1

1878. Police Cadets (Scotland) Amendment (No.2) Regulations 1987
revoked: SSI 2013/42 Sch.1 Part 2

1967. Income Support (General) Regulations 1987
see *Yarce (Adequate Maintenance: Benefits), Re* [2013] Imm. A.R. 177 (UT (IAC)), Judge Storey
Reg.2, amended: SI 2013/235 Sch.2 para.10, SI 2013/276 Reg.13, SI 2013/388 Sch.1 para.11, SI 2013/443 Reg.2, SI 2013/591 Sch.1 para.4, SI 2013/630 Reg.28, SI 2013/2536 Reg.4
Reg.2, applied: SI 2013/3029 Sch.6 para.31
Reg.4, amended: SI 2013/388 Sch.1 para.11, SI 2013/591 Sch.1 para.4
Reg.4ZA, applied: SI 2013/3029 Sch.1 para.19, Sch.6 para.21, SI 2013/3035 Sch.1
Reg.4ZA, revoked (in part): SI 2013/2536 Reg.4
Reg.6, applied: SI 2013/3029 Sch.6 para.34, SI 2013/3035 Sch.1
Reg.13, amended: SI 2013/1465 Sch.1 para.12
Reg.13, revoked (in part): SI 2013/2536 Reg.4
Reg.14, amended: SI 2013/630 Reg.28
Reg.17, referred to: SI 2013/574 Art.16
Reg.18, referred to: SI 2013/574 Art.16
Reg.21, referred to: SI 2013/574 Art.16
Reg.21AA, amended: SI 2013/1474 Reg.2, SI 2013/2536 Reg.4
Reg.21AA, revoked (in part): SI 2013/2536 Reg.4
Reg.21AA, see *Secretary of State for Work and Pensions v Czop (C-147/11)* [2013] P.T.S.R. 334 (ECJ (3rd Chamber)), Judge Lenaerts (President); see *St Prix v Secretary of State for Work and Pensions* [2013] 1 All E.R. 752 (SC), Lord Neuberger (President)
Reg.22A, referred to: SI 2013/574 Sch.4
Reg.22B, revoked: SI 2013/2536 Reg.4
Reg.31, amended: SI 2013/630 Reg.28
Reg.40, amended: SI 2013/630 Reg.28
Reg.42, amended: SI 2013/276 Reg.13
Reg.51, amended: SI 2013/276 Reg.13
Reg.51, applied: SI 2013/3029 Sch.6 para.31, SI 2013/3035 Sch.1
Reg.51A, amended: SI 2013/458 Sch.2 para.1
Reg.54, amended: SI 2013/443 Reg.2
Reg.75, amended: SI 2013/630 Reg.28
Sch.1B para.2, substituted: SI 2013/1465 Sch.1 para.12
Sch.1B para.4, amended: SI 2013/388 Sch.1 para.11, SI 2013/591 Sch.1 para.4
Sch.1B para.7, applied: SI 2013/3029 Sch.1 para.19, Sch.6 para.21, SI 2013/3035 Sch.1
Sch.1B para.14, applied: SI 2013/3029 Sch.1 para.19, Sch.6 para.21, SI 2013/3035 Sch.1
Sch.2 Part I para.1, referred to: 2013 c.16 Sch.1 para.1, SI 2013/471 Reg.12, SI 2013/480 Reg.25, SSI 2013/200 Sch.1 para.10
Sch.2 Part I para.1, substituted: SI 2013/574 Sch.2
Sch.2 Part I para.2, referred to: SI 2013/471 Reg.12, SI 2013/480 Reg.25, SSI 2013/200 Sch.1 para.10
Sch.2 Part I para.2, substituted: SI 2013/574 Sch.2
Sch.2 Part II para.3, referred to: SI 2013/574 Art.16
Sch.2 Part III para.7, amended: SI 2013/388 Sch.1 para.11, SI 2013/591 Sch.1 para.4
Sch.2 Part III para.11, applied: SI 2013/379 Reg.7

Sch.2 Part III para.12, amended: SI 2013/388 Sch.1 para.11, SI 2013/591 Sch.1 para.4
Sch.2 Part III para.12, applied: SI 2013/379 Reg.7
Sch.2 Part III para.13, amended: SI 2013/388 Sch.1 para.11, SI 2013/591 Sch.1 para.4
Sch.2 Part III para.13A, amended: SI 2013/388 Sch.1 para.11, SI 2013/591 Sch.1 para.4
Sch.2 Part III para.13A, referred to: SI 2013/574 Art.16
Sch.2 Part III para.14, amended: SI 2013/388 Sch.1 para.11, SI 2013/591 Sch.1 para.4
Sch.2 Part III para.14, referred to: SI 2013/574 Art.16
Sch.2 Part IV para.15, substituted: SI 2013/574 Sch.3
Sch.3 para.1, amended: SI 2013/630 Reg.28
Sch.3 para.3, amended: SI 2013/443 Reg.2
Sch.3 para.5, referred to: SI 2013/574 Sch.4
Sch.3 para.6, applied: SI 2013/386 Reg.29
Sch.3 para.6, referred to: SI 2013/574 Sch.4
Sch.3 para.7, referred to: SI 2013/574 Sch.4
Sch.3 para.8, applied: SI 2013/386 Reg.29
Sch.3 para.8, referred to: SI 2013/574 Sch.4
Sch.3 para.10, referred to: SI 2013/574 Sch.4
Sch.3 para.11, referred to: SI 2013/574 Sch.4
Sch.3 para.12, applied: SI 2013/376 Sch.5 para.12
Sch.3 para.12, referred to: SI 2013/574 Sch.4
Sch.3 para.14, applied: SI 2013/386 Reg.29
Sch.3 para.15, applied: SI 2013/386 Reg.29
Sch.3 para.16, applied: SI 2013/386 Reg.29
Sch.3 para.17, applied: SI 2013/386 Reg.29
Sch.3 para.18, amended: SI 2013/388 Sch.1 para.11, SI 2013/443 Reg.2, SI 2013/574 Art.16, SI 2013/591 Sch.1 para.4, SI 2013/630 Reg.28
Sch.7, referred to: SI 2013/574 Sch.4
Sch.8 para.7, amended: SI 2013/602 Sch.2 para.69, SI 2013/2536 Reg.4
Sch.8 para.7, revoked (in part): SI 2013/2536 Reg.4
Sch.9, see *Yarce (Adequate Maintenance: Benefits), Re* [2013] Imm. A.R. 177 (UT (IAC)), Judge Storey
Sch.9 para.1A, amended: SI 2013/276 Reg.13
Sch.9 para.6, amended: SI 2013/388 Sch.1 para.11
Sch.9 para.7, amended: SI 2013/630 Reg.28
Sch.9 para.9, amended: SI 2013/388 Sch.1 para.11
Sch.9 para.27, amended: SI 2013/235 Sch.2 para.10
Sch.9 para.27, revoked (in part): SI 2013/235 Sch.2 para.10
Sch.9 para.31A, added: SI 2013/443 Reg.2
Sch.9 para.46, amended: SI 2013/443 Reg.2
Sch.9 para.52, revoked: SI 2013/458 Sch.1
Sch.9 para.76A, added: SI 2013/591 Sch.1 para.4
Sch.10 para.1A, amended: SI 2013/276 Reg.13
Sch.10 para.7, amended: SI 2013/630 Reg.28
Sch.10 para.7, applied: SI 2013/3029 Sch.5 para.22, SI 2013/3035 Sch.1
Sch.10 para.18A, added: SI 2013/443 Reg.2
Sch.10 para.36, amended: SI 2013/443 Reg.2

1968. Social Security (Claims and Payments) Regulations 1987

applied: SI 2013/386 Reg.13, Reg.15, SI 2013/983 Art.5, SI 2013/3029 Sch.13 para.3, SI 2013/3035 Sch.1
Reg.1, amended: SI 2013/380 Sch.3 para.1
Reg.1, substituted: SI 2013/380 Sch.3 para.1
Reg.2, amended: SI 2013/380 Sch.3 para.1, SI 2013/630 Reg.29, SI 2013/1508 Reg.2
Reg.3, applied: SI 2013/383 Reg.5
Reg.4, amended: SI 2013/458 Sch.1
Reg.4B, amended: SI 2013/458 Sch.1
Reg.4D, amended: SI 2013/458 Sch.1
Reg.4H, amended: SI 2013/458 Sch.1
Reg.5, amended: SI 2013/2536 Reg.5
Reg.5, applied: SI 2013/387 Reg.6
Reg.6, referred to: SI 2013/386 Reg.15
Reg.16A, amended: SI 2013/630 Reg.29
Reg.19, applied: SI 2013/983 Art.5
Reg.32B, amended: SI 2013/458 Sch.1
Reg.32ZZA, amended: SI 2013/458 Sch.1
Reg.33, amended: SI 2013/458 Sch.2 para.2
Reg.33, applied: SI 2013/387 Reg.28, Reg.30, SI 2013/3029 Sch.13 para.1, SI 2013/3035 Sch.1
Reg.35, applied: SI 2013/386 Reg.22
Reg.43, revoked (in part): SI 2013/235 Sch.2 para.11
Sch.4, applied: SI 2013/983 Art.5
Sch.9, applied: SI 2013/386 Reg.22
Sch.9 para.4, amended: SI 2013/599 Reg.5, SI 2013/2536 Reg.5
Sch.9 para.6, amended: SI 2013/443 Reg.3
Sch.9 para.7C, amended: SI 2013/1508 Reg.2
Sch.9A para.7, amended: SI 2013/456 Reg.2
Sch.9B para.2, amended: SI 2013/1508 Reg.2
Sch.9B para.5, amended: SI 2013/1654 Reg.3
Sch.9B para.6, amended: SI 2013/1654 Reg.3

1969. Income Support (Transitional) Regulations 1987

Reg.15, varied: SI 2013/574 Art.17

1979. Asbestos Products (Safety) (Amendment) Regulations 1987

revoked: SI 2013/2919 Reg.15

2088. Registration of Births and Deaths Regulations 1987

Reg.2, amended: SI 2013/1869 Sch.1 para.2
Reg.43, amended: SI 2013/1869 Sch.1 para.2
Reg.70, revoked (in part): SI 2013/1869 Sch.1 para.2

2117. Consumer Protection (Cancellation of Contracts Concluded away from Business Premises) Regulations 1987

see *Robertson v Swift* [2012] EWCA Civ 1794, [2013] Bus. L.R. 479 (CA (Civ Div)), Mummery, L.J.

2203. Adoption (Northern Ireland) Order 1987

applied: SI 2013/3029 Reg.8, SI 2013/3035 Sch.1

2244. Secretary of State's Traffic Orders (Procedure) (Scotland) Regulations 1987

Part II, applied: SSI 2013/207
Part III, applied: SSI 2013/207

1988

35. Social Fund (Recovery by Deductions from Benefits) Regulations 1988

Reg.3, amended: SI 2013/384 Reg.32

93. Department of Trade and Industry (Fees) Order 1988

enabled: SI 2013/2236, SI 2013/2237

159. Gas (Register) Order 1988

revoked: SI 2013/1420 Art.2

166. London Traffic Control System (Transfer) Order 1988

revoked: SI 2013/2986 Sch.2

217. Pensions Increase (Review) Order 1988

applied: SI 2013/604 Sch.1

332. Local Authorities (Publicity Account) (Exemption) (Scotland) Order 1988

Sch.1 para.5, amended: SSI 2013/119 Sch.1 para.23

408. Public Service Vehicles (London Local Service Licences) (Amendment) Regulations 1988

revoked: SI 2013/2987 Sch.2

664. Social Security (Payments on account, Overpayments and Recovery) Regulations 1988

applied: SI 2013/381 Sch.3 para.13
Part II, referred to: SI 2013/383 Reg.19
Reg.1, amended: SI 2013/384 Reg.31
Reg.2, revoked: SI 2013/383 Reg.19
Reg.3, revoked: SI 2013/383 Reg.19
Reg.4, revoked: SI 2013/383 Reg.19
Reg.5, amended: SI 2013/384 Reg.31
Reg.5, applied: SI 2013/381 Sch.3 para.13
Reg.8, amended: SI 2013/384 Reg.31
Reg.10, amended: SI 2013/472 Art.4
Reg.11, amended: SI 2013/384 Reg.31
Reg.11, applied: SI 2013/381 Sch.3 para.13
Reg.13, amended: SI 2013/384 Reg.31
Reg.13, applied: SI 2013/381 Sch.3 para.13
Reg.15, amended: SI 2013/384 Reg.31
Reg.16, amended: SI 2013/380 Sch.3 para.2, SI 2013/384 Reg.31
Reg.29A, added: SI 2013/384 Reg.31

668. Pneumoconiosis etc (Workers Compensation) (Payment of Claims) Regulations 1988

Reg.2, revoked (in part): SI 2013/690 Reg.2
Reg.3, amended: SI 2013/690 Reg.2
Reg.3, revoked (in part): SI 2013/690 Reg.2
Reg.4, amended: SI 2013/690 Reg.2
Reg.5, amended: SI 2013/690 Reg.2
Reg.6, amended: SI 2013/690 Reg.2
Reg.7, revoked (in part): SI 2013/690 Reg.2
Reg.8, amended: SI 2013/690 Reg.2
Sch.1 Part 1, substituted: SI 2013/690 Sch.1
Sch.1 Part 2, substituted: SI 2013/690 Sch.1

865. National Health Service (Payment of Remuneration Special Arrangement) Order 1988

revoked (in part): SI 2013/235 Sch.2 para.12
Art.2, amended: SI 2013/235 Sch.2 para.12

900. Urban Development Corporations (Appropriate Ministers) Order 1988

Art.2, amended: SI 2013/687 Sch.2

1155. Trunk Road (Great Yarmouth Western Bypass) (Prohibition of Right Turns) Order 1988

varied: SI 2013/1352 Art.5

1284. Service Charge Contributions (Authorised Investments) Order 1988

Art.2, amended: SI 2013/472 Art.4

1291. Farm Woodland Scheme 1988

Art.6, amended: SI 2013/1036 Sch.2 para.56

1352. Set-Aside Regulations 1988

Reg.12, amended: SI 2013/1036 Sch.2 para.57

1359. Companies (Forms) (Amendment) Regulations 1988

revoked: SI 2013/1947 Sch.2 Part 1

1401. British Shipbuilders Borrowing Powers (Increase of Limit) Order 1988

revoked: SI 2013/687 Sch.2

1478. Goods Vehicles (Plating and Testing) Regulations 1988

Reg.16, amended: SI 2013/271 Reg.6
Reg.42B, added: SI 2013/271 Reg.9
Sch.3 Part I para.3A, added: SI 2013/271 Reg.7
Sch.3 Part I para.3B, added: SI 2013/271 Reg.7
Sch.3 Part II para.4, amended: SI 2013/271 Reg.8

1585. A500 (Barthomley Link to M6)/A500 East of Crewe to North of Newcastle-Under-Lyme Trunk Road (De-restriction) Order 1988

varied: SI 2013/2702 Art.6

1640. Motorcycles (Sound Level Measurement Certificates) (Amendment) Regulations 1988

revoked: SI 2013/2987 Sch.2

1655. Docks Regulations 1988

revoked: SI 2013/1512 Sch.1

1724. Social Fund Cold Weather Payments (General) Regulations 1988
Reg.1, amended: SI 2013/248 Reg.2
Reg.1A, amended: SI 2013/248 Reg.2
Sch.1, substituted: SI 2013/2538 Sch.1
Sch.2, substituted: SI 2013/2538 Sch.2
Sch.2 para.1, substituted: SI 2013/2538 Sch.2
Sch.2 para.2, substituted: SI 2013/2538 Sch.2

1729. Mines (Safety of Exit) Regulations 1988
Reg.3, amended: SI 2013/1471 Sch.4
Reg.4, applied: SI 2013/1471 Sch.2 para.40
Reg.7, amended: SI 2013/1471 Sch.4

1760. Spirits (Rectifying, Compounding and Drawback) Regulations 1988
revoked: SI 2013/1229 Reg.2

2039. Weights and Measures (Intoxicating Liquor) Order 1988
Sch.A1, amended: SI 2013/3235 Reg.12

2153. London Regional Transport Levy (General Rate Act 1967) (Modification) Order 1988
revoked: SI 2013/2986 Sch.3

2199. Assured Tenancies and Agricultural Occupancies (Rent Information) Order 1988
Art.3, substituted: SI 2013/1036 Sch.2 para.7
Art.4, amended: SI 2013/1036 Sch.2 para.8
Sch.1 para.11, amended: SI 2013/1036 Sch.2 para.9

1989

90. Edinburgh &mdash Thurso Trunk Road (A9) (Golspie) (Prohibition of Waiting) Order 1989
revoked: SSI 2013/88 Art.6

338. Civil Legal Aid (Assessment of Resources) Regulations 1989
applied: SI 2013/534 Reg.9
Reg.4, applied: SI 2013/534 Reg.9
Sch.3 para.10, applied: SI 2013/534 Reg.9

339. Civil Legal Aid (General) Regulations 1989
Reg.143, amended: SI 2013/294 Sch.1
Reg.151, revoked: SI 2013/294 Sch.1

364. National Health Service (Charges to Overseas Visitors) (Scotland) Regulations 1989
Reg.1, amended: SSI 2013/177 Sch.1 para.6
Reg.4, amended: SSI 2013/177 Sch.1 para.6
Reg.4A, amended: SSI 2013/177 Sch.1 para.6
Reg.5, amended: SSI 2013/177 Sch.1 para.6

433. Grant-aided Colleges (Scotland) Grant Regulations 1989
applied: SSI 2013/179 Art.4, SSI 2013/180 Art.4, SSI 2013/181 Art.4, SSI 2013/182 Art.4, SSI 2013/183 Art.4, SSI 2013/267 Art.4, SSI 2013/268 Art.4, SSI 2013/269 Art.4, SSI 2013/270 Art.4, SSI 2013/354 Art.17

477. Pensions Increase (Review) Order 1989
applied: SI 2013/604 Sch.1

482. Territorial Sea (Limits) Order 1989
Art.4, amended: SI 2013/3164 Art.2
Sch.1, substituted: SI 2013/3164 Sch.1

507. Community Charges (Deductions from Income Support) (Scotland) Regulations 1989
applied: SI 2013/381 Sch.3 para.11
Reg.1, amended: SI 2013/612 Reg.19
Reg.2, amended: SI 2013/612 Reg.20
Reg.3, amended: SI 2013/612 Reg.21
Reg.3, applied: SI 2013/380 Sch.6 para.3, Sch.6 para.5
Reg.4, amended: SI 2013/612 Reg.22

596. Consumer Credit (Total Charge for Credit and Rebate on Early Settlement) (Amendment) Regulations 1989
revoked (in part): SI 2013/1881 Art.21

713. Motorcycles (Sound Level Measurement Certificates) (Amendment) Regulations 1989
revoked: SI 2013/2987 Sch.2

869. Consumer Credit (Exempt Agreements) Order 1989
revoked (in part): SI 2013/1881 Art.21

878. Tuberculosis (Deer) Order 1989
Art.2, amended: SSI 2013/173 Art.8
Art.4, amended: SSI 2013/173 Art.8
Art.5, amended: SSI 2013/173 Art.8
Art.7, amended: SSI 2013/173 Art.8

971. Offshore Installations (Safety Representatives and Safety Committees) Regulations 1989
Reg.17, amended: SI 2013/1471 Sch.4

1058. Non-Domestic Rating (Collection and Enforcement) (Local Lists) Regulations 1989
Reg.13, see *Chowdhury v Westminster City Council* [2013] EWHC 1921 (Admin), [2013] R.V.R. 271 (DC), Aikens, L.J.

1173. Agricultural Wages Committees (Cleveland, Durham, Northumberland and Tyne and Wear) Order 1989
revoked: 2013 c.24 Sch.20 para.2

1202. Patents (Licences of Right) (Exception of Pesticidal Use) Order 1989
Art.2, amended: SI 2013/1478 Sch.5 para.9

1263. Sludge (Use in Agriculture) Regulations 1989
Reg.7, amended: SI 2013/755 Sch.4 para.23
Reg.8, amended: SI 2013/755 Sch.4 para.23
Reg.11, amended: SI 2013/755 Sch.4 para.24
Sch.2 para.2, amended: SI 2013/755 Sch.4 para.25

1274. Trunk Road (A500 Hanford &mdash North of Hanchurch) (50 MPH Speed Limit) Order 1989
revoked: SI 2013/1485 Art.7

1339. Limitation (Northern Ireland) Order 1989
Art.4, applied: 2013 c.15 s.2, s.3
Art.72A, amended: 2013 c.22 Sch.8 para.37
Art.72AB, added: SI 2013/2604 Art.5
Art.72B, amended: SI 2013/2604 Art.5

1341. Police and Criminal Evidence (Northern Ireland) Order 1989
Art.17, applied: 2013 c.33 s.88, SI 2013/504 Reg.17
Art.18, applied: 2013 c.33 s.88, SI 2013/504 Reg.17
Art.61, see *Public Prosecution Service v McKee* [2013] UKSC 32, [2013] 1 W.L.R. 1611 (SC), Lord Neuberger, J.S.C.
Art.63A, amended: SI 2013/602 Sch.2 para.70

1401. Fire Precautions (Sub-surface Railway Stations) Regulations 1989
Reg.2, amended: SSI 2013/119 Sch.2 para.6
Reg.5, amended: SSI 2013/119 Sch.2 para.6
Reg.9, amended: SSI 2013/119 Sch.2 para.6
Reg.12, amended: SSI 2013/119 Sch.2 para.6

1461. Companies Act 1985 (Modifications for Statutory Water Companies) Regulations 1989
revoked: SI 2013/1947 Sch.2 Part 1

1490. Civil Legal Aid (Scotland) (Fees) Regulations 1989
Reg.2, amended: SSI 2013/144 Reg.3
Reg.3, see *Smith v Scottish Legal Aid Board* 2013 S.C. 45 (IH (1 Div)), The Lord President (Hamilton)
Reg.3, amended: SSI 2013/144 Reg.3
Reg.5, see *Scottish Ministers v Stirton* 2013 S.C.L.R. 209 (OH), Lady Stacey
Reg.11, see *Smith v Scottish Legal Aid Board* 2013 S.C. 45 (IH (1 Div)), The Lord President (Hamilton)
Sch.4 Part 003, amended: SSI 2013/144 Reg.3
Sch.4 Part 004, added: SSI 2013/144 Reg.3
Sch.4 Part 004, amended: SSI 2013/144 Reg.3
Sch.5, amended: SSI 2013/250 Reg.4
Sch.7, amended: SSI 2013/144 Reg.3

1491. Criminal Legal Aid (Scotland) (Fees) Regulations 1989
varied: SSI 2013/320 Reg.1
see *HM Advocate v McCrossan (Darryl)* [2013] HCJAC 95, 2013 S.L.T. 1026 (HCJ), Lady Paton
Reg.7A, added: SSI 2013/320 Reg.3
Reg.11, see *Scottish Legal Aid Board v Dalling* 2013 S.L.T. (Sh Ct) 27 (Sh Ct (Tayside) (Stirling)), Sheriff Principal R A Dunlop, QC
Sch.1, amended: SI 2013/7 Art.15, SSI 2013/250 Reg.5, SSI 2013/320 Reg.5, Reg.6
Sch.1 para.1, amended: SSI 2013/320 Reg.4
Sch.1 para.3, amended: SSI 2013/320 Reg.4
Sch.1 para.3A, added: SSI 2013/320 Reg.4
Sch.1 para.3B, added: SSI 2013/320 Reg.4
Sch.2 Part 001, amended: SI 2013/7 Art.15
Sch.2 para.3, amended: SI 2013/7 Art.15

1591. Motorcycles (Sound Level Measurement Certificates) (Amendment) (No.2) Regulations 1989
revoked: SI 2013/2987 Sch.2

1796. Road Vehicles Lighting Regulations 1989
Reg.3, amended: SI 2013/755 Sch.4 para.26, SSI 2013/119 Sch.2 para.7
Reg.11, amended: SSI 2013/119 Sch.2 para.7
Sch.17 Part II, amended: SSI 2013/119 Sch.2 para.7
Sch.18 Part II, amended: SSI 2013/119 Sch.2 para.7

1841. Consumer Credit (Exempt Agreements) (Amendment) Order 1989
revoked (in part): SI 2013/1881 Art.21

1958. A55 Trunk Road (Penmaenmawr, Gwynedd) (Derestriction) Order 1989
disapplied: SI 2013/729 Art.10
varied: SI 2013/195 Art.13, SI 2013/333 Art.16, SI 2013/692 Art.12, SI 2013/729 Art.10, SI 2013/3257 Art.13

2068. A500 Trunk Road (Longbridge Hayes) (De-Restriction) Order 1989
revoked: SI 2013/2702 Art.3

2158. Trunk Road (A55) (Llanfairfechan, Gwynedd) (Derestriction) Order 1989
disapplied: SI 2013/729 Art.6
varied: SI 2013/333 Art.15, SI 2013/692 Art.11, SI 2013/729 Art.6

2209. Construction (Head Protection) Regulations 1989
revoked: SI 2013/448 Sch.1

2261. Non-Domestic Rating (Unoccupied Property) Regulations 1989
Reg.2, see *Pall Mall Investments Ltd v Leeds City Council* [2013] EWHC 3307 (Admin), [2013] R.V.R. 330 (QBD (Admin)), Judge Roger Kaye Q.C.

2337. Consumer Credit (Exempt Agreements) (Amendment) (No.2) Order 1989
revoked (in part): SI 2013/1881 Art.21

2405. Insolvency (Northern Ireland) Order 1989
applied: 2013 c.33 s.128, SI 2013/1388 Reg.17, Reg.18, Sch.5 para.1
Part VI, applied: SI 2013/1388 Reg.17, Reg.18
Part VIIA, applied: 2013 c.32 Sch.7 para.10
Art.2, varied: SI 2013/1388 Sch.2 para.4
Art.3, varied: SI 2013/1388 Sch.2 para.4
Art.4, varied: SI 2013/1388 Sch.2 para.4
Art.5, varied: SI 2013/1388 Sch.2 para.4
Art.6, varied: SI 2013/1388 Sch.2 para.4

Art.17A, amended: SI 2013/472 Sch.2 para.7, SI 2013/642 Art.2
Art.104A, applied: SI 2013/1388 Reg.17
Art.104A, varied: SI 2013/1388 Sch.2 para.4
Art.105, varied: SI 2013/1388 Sch.2 para.4
Art.106, varied: SI 2013/1388 Sch.2 para.4
Art.107, varied: SI 2013/1388 Sch.2 para.4
Art.108, varied: SI 2013/1388 Sch.2 para.4
Art.109, varied: SI 2013/1388 Sch.2 para.4
Art.110, varied: SI 2013/1388 Sch.2 para.4
Art.111, varied: SI 2013/1388 Sch.2 para.4
Art.112, varied: SI 2013/1388 Sch.2 para.4
Art.113, varied: SI 2013/1388 Sch.2 para.4
Art.114, varied: SI 2013/1388 Sch.2 para.4
Art.115, varied: SI 2013/1388 Sch.2 para.4
Art.116, varied: SI 2013/1388 Sch.2 para.4
Art.117, varied: SI 2013/1388 Sch.2 para.4
Art.118, varied: SI 2013/1388 Sch.2 para.4
Art.120, varied: SI 2013/1388 Sch.2 para.4
Art.121, varied: SI 2013/1388 Sch.2 para.4
Art.122, varied: SI 2013/1388 Sch.2 para.4
Art.123, varied: SI 2013/1388 Sch.2 para.4
Art.124, varied: SI 2013/1388 Sch.2 para.4
Art.125, varied: SI 2013/1388 Sch.2 para.4
Art.131, varied: SI 2013/1388 Sch.2 para.4
Art.133, varied: SI 2013/1388 Sch.2 para.4
Art.134, varied: SI 2013/1388 Sch.2 para.4
Art.136, varied: SI 2013/1388 Sch.2 para.4
Art.137, varied: SI 2013/1388 Sch.2 para.4
Art.138, varied: SI 2013/1388 Sch.2 para.4
Art.139, varied: SI 2013/1388 Sch.2 para.4
Art.142, varied: SI 2013/1388 Sch.2 para.4
Art.143, varied: SI 2013/1388 Sch.2 para.4
Art.144, varied: SI 2013/1388 Sch.2 para.4
Art.146, varied: SI 2013/1388 Sch.2 para.4
Art.148, varied: SI 2013/1388 Sch.2 para.4
Art.152, varied: SI 2013/1388 Sch.2 para.4
Art.153, varied: SI 2013/1388 Sch.2 para.4
Art.154, varied: SI 2013/1388 Sch.2 para.4
Art.155, varied: SI 2013/1388 Sch.2 para.4
Art.156, varied: SI 2013/1388 Sch.2 para.4
Art.157, varied: SI 2013/1388 Sch.2 para.4
Art.159, varied: SI 2013/1388 Sch.2 para.4
Art.160, varied: SI 2013/1388 Sch.2 para.4
Art.162, varied: SI 2013/1388 Sch.2 para.4
Art.163, varied: SI 2013/1388 Sch.2 para.4
Art.164, varied: SI 2013/1388 Sch.2 para.4
Art.165, varied: SI 2013/1388 Sch.2 para.4
Art.170, varied: SI 2013/1388 Sch.2 para.4
Art.171, varied: SI 2013/1388 Sch.2 para.4
Art.172, varied: SI 2013/1388 Sch.2 para.4
Art.173, varied: SI 2013/1388 Sch.2 para.4
Art.174, varied: SI 2013/1388 Sch.2 para.4
Art.175, varied: SI 2013/1388 Sch.2 para.4
Art.176, applied: SI 2013/1388 Reg.18
Art.176, varied: SI 2013/1388 Sch.2 para.4
Art.177, applied: SI 2013/1388 Reg.18
Art.177, varied: SI 2013/1388 Sch.2 para.4
Art.178, applied: SI 2013/1388 Reg.18
Art.178, varied: SI 2013/1388 Sch.2 para.4
Art.179, applied: SI 2013/1388 Reg.18
Art.179, varied: SI 2013/1388 Sch.2 para.4
Art.182, varied: SI 2013/1388 Sch.2 para.4
Art.183, varied: SI 2013/1388 Sch.2 para.4
Art.188, varied: SI 2013/1388 Sch.2 para.4
Art.193, varied: SI 2013/1388 Sch.2 para.4
Art.194, varied: SI 2013/1388 Sch.2 para.4
Art.195, varied: SI 2013/1388 Sch.2 para.4
Art.196, varied: SI 2013/1388 Sch.2 para.4
Art.198, varied: SI 2013/1388 Sch.2 para.4
Art.199, varied: SI 2013/1388 Sch.2 para.4
Art.200, varied: SI 2013/1388 Sch.2 para.4
Art.201, varied: SI 2013/1388 Sch.2 para.4
Art.202, varied: SI 2013/1388 Sch.2 para.4
Art.203, varied: SI 2013/1388 Sch.2 para.4
Art.204, varied: SI 2013/1388 Sch.2 para.4
Art.205, varied: SI 2013/1388 Sch.2 para.4
Art.208, varied: SI 2013/1388 Sch.2 para.4
Art.271, see *Official Receiver v Sinnamon* [2013] NICh 11, [2013] B.P.I.R. 900 (Ch D (NI)), Deeny, J.
Art.272, see *Official Receiver v Sinnamon* [2013] NICh 11, [2013] B.P.I.R. 900 (Ch D (NI)), Deeny, J.
Art.273, see *Official Receiver v Sinnamon* [2013] NICh 11, [2013] B.P.I.R. 900 (Ch D (NI)), Deeny, J.
Art.277, see *Official Receiver v Sinnamon* [2013] NICh 11, [2013] B.P.I.R. 900 (Ch D (NI)), Deeny, J.
Art.279B, applied: SI 2013/1554 r.60_4
Art.288, see *Liggett v Northern Bank Ltd* [2013] B.P.I.R. 595 (Ch D (NI)), Master Kelly
Art.293, see *Liggett v Northern Bank Ltd* [2013] B.P.I.R. 595 (Ch D (NI)), Master Kelly
Art.312, see *Official Receiver for Northern Ireland v Mallon* [2013] B.P.I.R. 621 (Ch D (NI)), Master Kelly
Art.314, see *Official Receiver for Northern Ireland v Mallon* [2013] B.P.I.R. 621 (Ch D (NI)), Master Kelly
Art.315, see *Official Receiver for Northern Ireland v Mallon* [2013] B.P.I.R. 621 (Ch D (NI)), Master Kelly
Art.348, varied: SI 2013/1388 Sch.2 para.4
Art.366, amended: SI 2013/472 Sch.2 para.7
Art.373, varied: SI 2013/1388 Sch.2 para.4
Art.374, varied: SI 2013/1388 Sch.2 para.4

Art.385, varied: SI 2013/1388 Sch.2 para.4
Sch.A1 para.54, amended: SI 2013/472 Sch.2 para.7
Sch.B1 para.41, amended: SI 2013/472 Sch.2 para.7
Sch.B1 para.43, amended: SI 2013/472 Sch.2 para.7
Sch.B1 para.83, amended: SI 2013/472 Sch.2 para.7
Sch.2A, applied: SI 2013/349 Reg.105, Sch.7 para.29
Sch.2 Part I para.1, varied: SI 2013/1388 Sch.2 para.4
Sch.2 Part I para.2, varied: SI 2013/1388 Sch.2 para.4
Sch.2 Part I para.3, varied: SI 2013/1388 Sch.2 para.4
Sch.2 Part I para.3A, varied: SI 2013/1388 Sch.2 para.4
Sch.2 Part II para.4, varied: SI 2013/1388 Sch.2 para.4
Sch.2 Part II para.5, varied: SI 2013/1388 Sch.2 para.4
Sch.2 Part III para.6, varied: SI 2013/1388 Sch.2 para.4
Sch.2 Part III para.7, varied: SI 2013/1388 Sch.2 para.4
Sch.2 Part III para.8, varied: SI 2013/1388 Sch.2 para.4
Sch.2 Part III para.8A, varied: SI 2013/1388 Sch.2 para.4
Sch.2 Part III para.9, varied: SI 2013/1388 Sch.2 para.4
Sch.2 Part III para.10, varied: SI 2013/1388 Sch.2 para.4
Sch.2 Part III para.11, varied: SI 2013/1388 Sch.2 para.4
Sch.2 Part III para.12, varied: SI 2013/1388 Sch.2 para.4
Sch.2 Part III para.13, varied: SI 2013/1388 Sch.2 para.4
Sch.2 Part III para.14, varied: SI 2013/1388 Sch.2 para.4
Sch.2 Part III para.16, varied: SI 2013/1388 Sch.2 para.4
Sch.2 Part III para.21, varied: SI 2013/1388 Sch.2 para.4
Sch.7, varied: SI 2013/1388 Sch.2 para.4
Sch.7 para.3, varied: SI 2013/1388 Sch.2 para.4
Sch.7 para.6, varied: SI 2013/1388 Sch.2 para.4

1990

194. Electricity (Register) Order 1990
revoked: SI 2013/1420 Art.3

200. Official Secrets Act 1989 (Prescription) Order 1990
Sch.1, amended: SI 2013/602 Sch.2 para.71
Sch.2, amended: SI 2013/602 Sch.2 para.71

266. Fossil Fuel Levy Regulations 1990
Reg.30, amended: SI 2013/472 Art.4

304. Dangerous Substances (Notification and Marking of Sites) Regulations 1990
Reg.2, amended: SI 2013/448 Reg.3, SSI 2013/119 Sch.2 para.8
Reg.4, amended: SI 2013/448 Reg.3, SSI 2013/119 Sch.2 para.8
Reg.8, amended: SI 2013/448 Reg.3, SSI 2013/119 Sch.2 para.8
Reg.10, amended: SI 2013/448 Reg.3
Sch.1 para.2, revoked (in part): SI 2013/448 Sch.1
Sch.2 Part I para.1, amended: SI 2013/448 Reg.3
Sch.2 Part I para.2, amended: SI 2013/448 Reg.3
Sch.2 Part I para.3, amended: SI 2013/448 Reg.3
Sch.2 Part I para.4, amended: SI 2013/448 Reg.3
Sch.2 Part I para.4A, added: SI 2013/448 Reg.3
Sch.2 Part I para.4A, amended: SI 2013/448 Reg.3
Sch.2 Part I para.5, amended: SI 2013/448 Reg.3
Sch.2 Part I para.6, added: SI 2013/448 Reg.3
Sch.2 Part I para.6, amended: SI 2013/448 Reg.3
Sch.2 Part II para.1, amended: SI 2013/448 Reg.3
Sch.2 Part II para.2, amended: SI 2013/448 Reg.3
Sch.2 Part II para.2, substituted: SI 2013/448 Reg.3
Sch.2 Part II para.3, amended: SI 2013/448 Reg.3

328. Trunk Road (A55) (Penmaenbach-Dwygyfylchi, Gwynedd) (One-Way Traffic) Order 1990
varied: SI 2013/195 Art.9, SI 2013/3257 Art.9

455. Electricity (Applications for Consent) Regulations 1990
Reg.3, amended: SI 2013/495 Reg.2
Reg.11, amended: SI 2013/495 Reg.2, SSI 2013/58 Reg.2
Reg.11A, added: SI 2013/495 Reg.2

479. Employment Tribunals (Interest) Order 1990
Art.2, amended: SI 2013/1671 Art.2
Art.3, amended: SI 2013/1671 Art.3

483. Pensions Increase (Review) Order 1990
applied: SI 2013/604 Sch.1

545. Community Charges (Deductions from Income Support) (No.2) Regulations 1990
applied: SI 2013/381 Sch.3 para.11
Reg.1, amended: SI 2013/612 Reg.14
Reg.2, amended: SI 2013/612 Reg.15
Reg.3, amended: SI 2013/612 Reg.16
Reg.3, applied: SI 2013/380 Sch.6 para.3, Sch.6 para.5

Reg.4, amended: SI 2013/612 Reg.17

556. Control of Asbestos in the Air Regulations 1990
revoked: SI 2013/390 Reg.58

564. General Drainage Charges (Forms) Regulations 1990
Reg.2, amended: SI 2013/755 Sch.4 para.28
Reg.3, amended: SI 2013/755 Sch.4 para.28
Sch.1, amended: SI 2013/755 Sch.4 para.29

572. Companies (Forms) (Amendment) Regulations 1990
revoked: SI 2013/1947 Sch.2 Part 1

1020. Public Service Vehicles (Conduct of Drivers, Inspectors, Conductors and Passengers) Regulations 1990
Reg.14, amended: SI 2013/1865 Reg.13

1095. Trunk Road (A55) (Travellers Inn, Clwyd) (Derestriction) Order 1990
disapplied: SI 2013/729 Art.15
varied: SI 2013/729 Art.15

1137. Trunk Road (A48) (Foelgastell, Dyfed) (De–Restriction) Order 1990
varied: SI 2013/1620 Art.6

1159. Insurance Companies (Legal Expenses Insurance) Regulations 1990
Reg.2, amended: SI 2013/472 Art.4
Reg.6, see *Brown-Quinn v Equity Syndicate Management Ltd* [2012] EWCA Civ 1633, [2013] 1 W.L.R. 1740 (CA (Civ Div)), Longmore, L.J.

1323. Ungraded Eggs (Hygiene) Regulations 1990
revoked (in part): SI 2013/466 Reg.3, SI 2013/545 Reg.3

1395. Definition of Subsidiary (Consequential Amendments) Regulations 1990
revoked: SI 2013/1947 Sch.2 Part 1

1504. Companies (No.2) (Northern Ireland) Order 1990
Art.98, amended: SI 2013/1773 Sch.2 para.3

1519. Planning (Listed Buildings and Conservation Areas) Regulations 1990
Reg.3, amended: SI 2013/2146 Sch.1 para.1
Reg.3A, amended: SI 2013/1239 Reg.2
Reg.3A, revoked (in part): SI 2013/1239 Reg.2
Reg.4, amended: SI 2013/2146 Sch.1 para.1
Reg.8, amended: SI 2013/2115 Reg.2, SI 2013/2146 Sch.1 para.1
Reg.8A, amended: SI 2013/2146 Sch.1 para.1
Reg.12, substituted: SI 2013/2146 Sch.1 para.1
Reg.13, amended: SI 2013/2146 Sch.1 para.1
Reg.15, amended: SI 2013/2146 Sch.1 para.1
Sch.1 Part II, amended: SI 2013/2115 Reg.2, SI 2013/2146 Sch.1 para.1
Sch.1 Part III, amended: SI 2013/2146 Sch.1 para.1
Sch.2 Part II, amended: SI 2013/2146 Sch.1 para.1
Sch.3, substituted: SI 2013/2146 Sch.1 para.1

1534. Education (Access Funds) (Scotland) Regulations 1990
Reg.2, amended: SSI 2013/80 Reg.3

1560. Further Education Student Records (Scotland) Regulations 1990
Reg.2, amended: SSI 2013/147 Sch.1 para.2
Reg.8, amended: SSI 2013/147 Sch.1 para.2

1586. Special Road (Glan Conwy to Conwy Morfa) Regulations 1990
disapplied: SI 2013/729 Art.11
varied: SI 2013/1 Art.9, SI 2013/195 Art.12, SI 2013/729 Art.11, SI 2013/3238 Art.10, SI 2013/3257 Art.12
Reg.13, varied: SI 2013/693 Art.4

1766. Companies (Forms Amendment No 2 and Company's Type and Principal Business Activities) Regulations 1990
revoked: SI 2013/1947 Sch.2 Part 1

1904. Non-Domestic Rating (Payment of Interest) Regulations 1990
Reg.4, amended: SI 2013/472 Art.4

1918. Nuclear Installations Act 1965 (Repeal and Modifications) Regulations 1990
Sch.1 para.1, revoked: 2013 c.32 Sch.12 para.30

2024. National Health Service Trusts (Membership and Procedure) Regulations 1990
Reg.1, amended: SI 2013/235 Sch.2 para.13
Reg.11, revoked (in part): SI 2013/235 Sch.1 para.1, Sch.2 para.13

2035. Overhead Lines (Exemption) Regulations 1990
applied: SSI 2013/264 Reg.6
revoked: SSI 2013/264 Sch.1

2237. Planning (Listed Buildings and Conservation Areas) (Isles of Scilly) Order 1990
revoked: SI 2013/2148 Art.5

2360. Public Lending Right Scheme 1982 (Commencement of Variations) Order 1990
Part I para.2, amended: SI 2013/2352 Sch.2 para.1
Part I para.3, amended: SI 2013/2352 Sch.2 para.1
Part III para.10, amended: SI 2013/2352 Sch.2 para.1
Part III para.12, amended: SI 2013/2352 Sch.2 para.1
Part III para.14, amended: SI 2013/2352 Sch.2 para.1
Part III para.14A, amended: SI 2013/2352 Sch.2 para.1
Part III para.16, amended: SI 2013/2352 Sch.2 para.1
Part III para.17, amended: SI 2013/2352 Sch.2 para.1
Part III para.17A, amended: SI 2013/2352 Sch.2 para.1

Part III para.18, amended: SI 2013/2352 Sch.2 para.1
Part III para.21, amended: SI 2013/2352 Sch.2 para.1
Part III para.23, amended: SI 2013/2352 Sch.2 para.1
Part III para.24, amended: SI 2013/2352 Sch.2 para.1
Part III para.25, amended: SI 2013/2352 Sch.2 para.1
Part III para.26, amended: SI 2013/2352 Sch.2 para.1
Part III para.28, amended: SI 2013/2352 Sch.2 para.1
Part III para.29, amended: SI 2013/2352 Sch.2 para.1
Part III para.30, amended: SI 2013/2352 Sch.2 para.1
Part III para.32, amended: SI 2013/2352 Sch.2 para.1
Part III para.33, amended: SI 2013/2352 Sch.2 para.1
Part III para.34, amended: SI 2013/2352 Sch.2 para.1
Part III para.35, amended: SI 2013/2352 Sch.2 para.1
Part III para.7, amended: SI 2013/2352 Sch.2 para.1
Part III para.8, amended: SI 2013/2352 Sch.2 para.1
Part III para.9A, amended: SI 2013/2352 Sch.2 para.1
Part IV para.36, amended: SI 2013/2352 Sch.2 para.1
Part IV para.38, amended: SI 2013/2352 Sch.2 para.1
Part IV para.39, amended: SI 2013/2352 Sch.2 para.1
Part IV para.40, amended: SI 2013/2352 Sch.2 para.1
Part IV para.41, amended: SI 2013/2352 Sch.2 para.1
Part IV para.42, amended: SI 2013/2352 Sch.2 para.1
Part IV para.43, amended: SI 2013/2352 Sch.2 para.1
Part IV para.44, amended: SI 2013/2352 Sch.2 para.1
Part V para.48, amended: SI 2013/2352 Sch.2 para.1
Part V para.49, amended: SI 2013/2352 Sch.2 para.1
Part V para.50, amended: SI 2013/2352 Sch.2 para.1

2435. Royal Free Hampstead National Health Service Trust (Establishment) Order 1990
Art.1, amended: SI 2013/593 Art.2

2446. St Helens and Knowsley Hospital Services National Health Service Trust (Establishment) Order 1990
Art.1, amended: SI 2013/593 Art.2

2451. Walsall Hospitals National Health Service Trust (Establishment) Order 1990
Art.1, amended: SI 2013/593 Art.2
Art.4, amended: SI 2013/59 Art.2

2455. Weston Area National Health Service Trust (Establishment) Order 1990
Art.1, amended: SI 2013/593 Art.2

2463. Food Safety (Sampling and Qualifications) Regulations 1990
revoked (in part): SI 2013/264 Reg.12, SI 2013/479 Reg.12, SSI 2013/84 Sch.4
Reg.4, applied: SI 2013/264 Reg.5, SI 2013/479 Reg.5, SSI 2013/84 Reg.5

2507. Milk and Dairies (Scotland) Regulations 1990
Reg.2, amended: SI 2013/3235 Reg.14

2573. Protection of Wrecks (Designation No 3) Order 1990
revoked: SSI 2013/276 Sch.1

2625. Food Safety Act 1990 (Consequential Modifications) (Scotland) Order 1990
Sch.1 Part I, amended: SSI 2013/83 Sch.2 para.3
Sch.1 Part II, amended: SSI 2013/83 Sch.2 para.3
Sch.2, amended: SSI 2013/83 Sch.2 para.3
Sch.3 Part I, amended: SSI 2013/83 Sch.2 para.3
Sch.3 Part II, amended: SSI 2013/83 Sch.2 para.3
Sch.4, amended: SSI 2013/83 Sch.2 para.3
Sch.6, amended: SSI 2013/83 Sch.2 para.3
Sch.8, amended: SSI 2013/83 Sch.2 para.3

1991

109. Northern Devon Healthcare National Health Service Trust (Establishment) Order 1991
Art.1, amended: SI 2013/593 Art.2

167. Occupational Pension Schemes (Preservation of Benefit) Regulations 1991
Reg.1, amended: SI 2013/459 Reg.2, SI 2013/2734 Sch.9 para.1
Reg.9, amended: SI 2013/2734 Sch.9 para.1
Reg.11B, added: SI 2013/459 Reg.2
Reg.12, amended: SI 2013/459 Reg.2

288. Traffic Areas (Reorganisation) Order 1991
Art.5, amended: SI 2013/1644 Sch.2

481. National Health Service (Remuneration and Conditions of Service) Regulations 1991
Reg.1, amended: SI 2013/235 Sch.2 para.14

510. National Bus Company (Dissolution) Order 1991
revoked (in part): SI 2013/2986 Sch.3
Art.3, applied: SI 2013/2986 Art.4
Art.5, applied: SI 2013/2986 Art.4

589. Statutory Sick Pay (National Health Service Employees) Regulations 1991
Reg.1, revoked (in part): SI 2013/235 Sch.2 para.15
Reg.2, amended: SI 2013/235 Sch.2 para.15
Reg.2, applied: SI 2013/235 Sch.3 para.1
Reg.5, amended: SI 2013/235 Sch.2 para.15
Reg.5, revoked (in part): SI 2013/235 Sch.2 para.15

590. Statutory Maternity Pay (National Health Service Employees) Regulations 1991
Reg.1, revoked (in part): SI 2013/235 Sch.2 para.16
Reg.2, amended: SI 2013/235 Sch.2 para.16
Reg.2, applied: SI 2013/235 Sch.3 para.2
Reg.5, amended: SI 2013/235 Sch.2 para.16
Reg.5, revoked (in part): SI 2013/235 Sch.2 para.16

684. Pensions Increase (Review) Order 1991
applied: SI 2013/604 Sch.1

701. Building Societies (Deferred Shares) Order 1991
Sch.1, amended: SI 2013/496 Sch.10 para.1

879. Companies (Forms) Regulations 1991
revoked: SI 2013/1947 Sch.2 Part 1

880. Financial Markets and Insolvency Regulations 1991
Reg.7, amended: SI 2013/504 Reg.30
Reg.11, amended: SI 2013/504 Reg.30
Reg.16, amended: SI 2013/472 Sch.2 para.9

892. Definition of Independent Visitors (Children) Regulations 1991
Reg.2, amended: SI 2013/3005 Art.3

1091. Estate Agents (Specified Offences) (No.2) Order 1991
Sch.1, amended: SI 2013/1575 Sch.1 para.17, SI 2013/1881 Sch.1 para.18

1092. Trunk Road (A477) (Kilgetty, Dyfed) (De-Restriction) Order 1991
varied: SI 2013/2955 Art.8

1184. County Courts (Interest on Judgment Debts) Order 1991
varied: SI 2013/1169 r.13

1220. Planning(Northern Ireland) Order 1991
Art.111, applied: SI 2013/1119 Sch.7 para.11
Art.127, varied: SI 2013/1119 Sch.7 para.13

1259. Companies (Forms) (No.2) Regulations 1991
revoked: SI 2013/1947 Sch.2 Part 1

1304. Police Pensions (Additional Voluntary Contributions) Regulations 1991
Reg.2, amended: SI 2013/472 Art.4

1393. Consumer Credit (Exempt Agreements) (Amendment) Order 1991
revoked (in part): SI 2013/1881 Art.21

1397. Act of Sederunt (Messengers-at-Arms and Sheriff Officers Rules) 1991
Part II r.5A, added: SSI 2013/23 r.2
Part II r.6, amended: SSI 2013/23 r.2
Part VI r.14, amended: SSI 2013/23 r.2
Part VI r.15, amended: SSI 2013/23 r.2
Part VII r.18A, added: SSI 2013/23 r.2

1408. Broadcasting (Independent Productions) Order 1991
Art.3, amended: SI 2013/2217 Reg.5

1505. Children (Secure Accommodation) Regulations 1991
Reg.6, amended: SI 2013/663 Reg.2
Reg.6, revoked (in part): SI 2013/663 Reg.2
Reg.7, amended: SI 2013/235 Sch.2 para.17

1507. Refuges (Children's Homes and Foster Placements) Regulations 1991
Reg.2, amended: SI 2013/706 Reg.9

1531. Control of Explosives Regulations 1991
applied: SSI 2013/50 Sch.1 para.10
Reg.4, applied: SSI 2013/50 Sch.1 para.10, Sch.3 para.3, Sch.4 para.4
Reg.5, applied: SSI 2013/50 Sch.1 para.10
Reg.6, applied: SSI 2013/50 Sch.1 para.10

1560. British Shipbuilders Regulations 1991
revoked: SI 2013/687 Sch.2

1597. Bathing Waters (Classification) Regulations 1991
revoked: SI 2013/1675 Reg.19
Reg.2, amended: SI 2013/1675 Reg.18

1620. Construction Products Regulations 1991
applied: SI 2013/1387 Reg.29
revoked: SI 2013/1387 Reg.28
Part II, applied: SI 2013/1387 Reg.29
Reg.5, applied: SI 2013/1387 Reg.29
Reg.6, applied: SI 2013/1387 Reg.29
Reg.7, applied: SI 2013/1387 Reg.29
Reg.8, applied: SI 2013/1387 Reg.29
Reg.17, applied: SI 2013/1387 Reg.29
Reg.21, applied: SI 2013/1387 Reg.29

1624. Controlled Waste (Registration of Carriers and Seizure of Vehicles) Regulations 1991
Reg.2, amended: SI 2013/2952 Sch.2 para.1, SSI 2013/307 Sch.2 para.2

1707. Access to Personal Files and Medical Reports (Northern Ireland) Order 1991
Art.6, amended: SI 2013/472 Art.4

1744. Dangerous Dogs Compensation and Exemption Schemes Order 1991
Art.9, applied: SI 2013/1302 Art.2

1746. Disability Living Allowance Advisory Board Regulations 1991
revoked: SI 2013/252 Sch.1 Part 2

1949. Consumer Credit (Exempt Agreements) (Amendment) (No.2) Order 1991
revoked (in part): SI 2013/1881 Art.21

1997. Companies Act 1989 (Eligibility for Appointment as Company Auditor) (Consequential Amendments) Regulations 1991
Sch.1 para.29, revoked: SI 2013/687 Sch.2

2034. Children (Secure Accommodation) (No.2) Regulations 1991
Reg.2, amended: SI 2013/235 Sch.2 para.18
Reg.2, applied: SI 2013/235 Sch.3 para.3

2328. Bath Mental Health Care National Health Service Trust (Establishment) Order 1991
Art.1, amended: SI 2013/593 Art.2

2340. Ealing Hospital National Health Service Trust (Establishment) Order 1991
Art.1, amended: SI 2013/593 Art.2

2370. Mid Essex Hospital Services National Health Service Trust (Establishment) Order 1991
Art.1, amended: SI 2013/593 Art.2

2392. Royal United Hospital, Bath, National Health Service Trust (Establishment) Order 1991
Art.1, amended: SI 2013/593 Art.2

2401. South Downs Health National Health Service Trust (Establishment) Order 1991
Art.1, amended: SI 2013/593 Art.2

2509. Coal Mining Subsidence (Notices and Claims) Regulations 1991
Sch.1, see *Newbold v Coal Authority* [2013] EWCA Civ 584, [2013] R.V.R. 247 (CA (Civ Div)), Longmore, L.J.

2564. Spirits Regulations 1991
Reg.2, revoked: SI 2013/1229 Reg.3
Reg.3, amended: SI 2013/1229 Reg.3
Reg.7, added: SI 2013/1229 Reg.3
Reg.18, amended: SI 2013/1229 Reg.3
Reg.19, amended: SI 2013/1229 Reg.3
Reg.26, amended: SI 2013/1229 Reg.3

2684. Solicitors Recognised Bodies Order 1991
Sch.1, amended: SI 2013/294 Sch.1

2740. Social Security (Attendance Allowance) Regulations 1991
Reg.1, amended: SI 2013/389 Reg.3
Reg.2, amended: SI 2013/389 Reg.3
Reg.2, revoked (in part): SI 2013/389 Reg.3
Reg.2A, added: SI 2013/389 Reg.3
Reg.2B, added: SI 2013/389 Reg.3
Reg.5, amended: SI 2013/389 Reg.3
Reg.6, amended: SI 2013/389 Reg.3
Reg.6, applied: SI 2013/376 Reg.83, Sch.4 para.15, Sch.4 para.16
Reg.7, amended: SI 2013/389 Reg.3, SI 2013/2270 Reg.5
Reg.7, applied: SI 2013/376 Reg.83
Reg.7, revoked (in part): SI 2013/389 Reg.3
Reg.8, amended: SI 2013/389 Reg.3
Reg.8, revoked (in part): SI 2013/389 Reg.3
Reg.8A, amended: SI 2013/389 Reg.3

2814. Anthrax Order 1991
Art.2, amended: SSI 2013/173 Art.9
Art.4, amended: SSI 2013/173 Art.9
Art.7, amended: SSI 2013/173 Art.9
Art.9, amended: SSI 2013/173 Art.9

2844. Consumer Credit (Exempt Agreements) (Amendment) (No.3) Order 1991
revoked (in part): SI 2013/1881 Art.21

2848. A483 Trunk Road (Ruabon and Newbridge by-pass, Ruabon, Clwyd) (Derestriction) Order 1991
varied: SI 2013/771 Art.9

2890. Social Security (Disability Living Allowance) Regulations 1991
Reg.1, amended: SI 2013/389 Reg.4
Reg.2, amended: SI 2013/389 Reg.4
Reg.2, applied: SI 2013/387 Reg.26
Reg.2, revoked (in part): SI 2013/389 Reg.4
Reg.2A, added: SI 2013/389 Reg.4
Reg.2B, added: SI 2013/389 Reg.4
Reg.4, amended: SI 2013/574 Art.12
Reg.7, amended: SI 2013/389 Reg.4
Reg.8, amended: SI 2013/389 Reg.4
Reg.8, applied: SI 2013/376 Reg.83, Sch.4 para.15, Sch.4 para.16
Reg.8, referred to: SI 2013/387 Reg.25
Reg.9, amended: SI 2013/389 Reg.4, SI 2013/2270 Reg.6
Reg.9, applied: SI 2013/376 Reg.83, SI 2013/387 Reg.25
Reg.9, revoked (in part): SI 2013/389 Reg.4
Reg.10, amended: SI 2013/389 Reg.4
Reg.10, referred to: SI 2013/387 Reg.25
Reg.10, revoked (in part): SI 2013/389 Reg.4
Reg.10A, amended: SI 2013/389 Reg.4
Reg.12A, amended: SI 2013/389 Reg.4
Reg.12A, referred to: SI 2013/387 Reg.25
Reg.12B, amended: SI 2013/389 Reg.4
Reg.12B, referred to: SI 2013/387 Reg.25
Reg.12B, revoked (in part): SI 2013/389 Reg.4
Sch.1 para.4, amended: SI 2013/389 Reg.4

2891. Social Security (Introduction of Disability Living Allowance) Regulations 1991
Reg.24, amended: SI 2013/252 Sch.1 Part 2

1992

46. Opencast Coal (Rate of Interest on Compensation) Order 1992

Art.2, amended: SI 2013/472 Art.4

129. Firemen's Pension Scheme Order 1992

applied: SI 2013/1392 Art.3

Part AI para.3, amended: SI 2013/703 Art.3, SI 2013/736 Art.3

Part I, amended: SI 2013/1392 Sch.1 para.15, SSI 2013/185 Art.8

Part I para.1, amended: SI 2013/1392 Sch.1 para.17

Part I para.1, amended: SI 2013/1392 Sch.1 para.18

Part I para.1, revoked (in part): SI 2013/1392 Sch.1 para.21

Part I para.1, amended: SI 2013/1392 Sch.1 para.22

Part I para.1, revoked (in part): SI 2013/1392 Sch.1 para.22

Part I para.1, amended: SI 2013/1392 Sch.1 para.23

Part I para.2, revoked (in part): SI 2013/1392 Sch.1 para.21

Part I para.2, amended: SI 2013/1392 Sch.1 para.22

Part I para.2, substituted: SI 2013/1392 Sch.1 para.23

Part I para.2B, added: SI 2013/1392 Sch.1 para.23

Part I para.3, amended: SI 2013/1392 Sch.1 para.22

Part I para.3, revoked (in part): SI 2013/1392 Sch.1 para.22

Part I para.3, amended: SI 2013/1392 Sch.1 para.23

Part I para.4, amended: SI 2013/1392 Sch.1 para.22

Part I para.4, amended: SI 2013/1392 Sch.1 para.23

Part I para.6A, added: SI 2013/1392 Sch.1 para.23

Part I para.8, amended: SI 2013/1392 Sch.1 para.23

Part 1A para.3, amended: SSI 2013/128 Art.3

Part II para.1, revoked (in part): SI 2013/1392 Sch.1 para.21

Part II para.1, revoked (in part): SI 2013/1392 Sch.1 para.23

Part II para.2, amended: SI 2013/1392 Sch.1 para.20

Part II para.2, revoked (in part): SI 2013/1392 Sch.1 para.21

Part II para.2, revoked (in part): SI 2013/1392 Sch.1 para.23

Part II para.3, revoked (in part): SI 2013/1392 Sch.1 para.21

Part II para.3, amended: SI 2013/1392 Sch.1 para.22

Part II para.3, revoked (in part): SI 2013/1392 Sch.1 para.23

Part II para.4, revoked (in part): SI 2013/1392 Sch.1 para.21

Part II para.4, revoked (in part): SI 2013/1392 Sch.1 para.23

Part III para.1, revoked (in part): SI 2013/1392 Sch.1 para.17

Part III para.1, revoked (in part): SI 2013/1392 Sch.1 para.21

Part III para.1, revoked (in part): SI 2013/1392 Sch.1 para.24

Part III para.2, amended: SI 2013/1392 Sch.1 para.19

Part III para.2, revoked (in part): SI 2013/1392 Sch.1 para.21

Part III para.2, revoked (in part): SI 2013/1392 Sch.1 para.24

Part III para.3, revoked (in part): SI 2013/1392 Sch.1 para.21

Part III para.3, revoked (in part): SI 2013/1392 Sch.1 para.24

Part III para.5, amended: SI 2013/1392 Sch.1 para.20

Part III para.6A, amended: SI 2013/1392 Sch.1 para.20

Part IV para.1, revoked (in part): SI 2013/1392 Sch.1 para.18

Part IV para.1, revoked (in part): SI 2013/1392 Sch.1 para.21

Part IV para.1, revoked (in part): SI 2013/1392 Sch.1 para.24

Part IV para.10, revoked (in part): SI 2013/1392 Sch.1 para.24

Part IV para.11, revoked (in part): SI 2013/1392 Sch.1 para.24

Part IV para.12, revoked (in part): SI 2013/1392 Sch.1 para.24

Part IV para.13, revoked (in part): SI 2013/1392 Sch.1 para.24

Part IV para.14, revoked (in part): SI 2013/1392 Sch.1 para.24

Part IV para.15, revoked (in part): SI 2013/1392 Sch.1 para.24

Part IV para.16, revoked (in part): SI 2013/1392 Sch.1 para.24

Part IV para.17, revoked (in part): SI 2013/1392 Sch.1 para.24

Part IV para.18, revoked (in part): SI 2013/1392 Sch.1 para.24

Part IV para.19, revoked (in part): SI 2013/1392 Sch.1 para.24

Part IV para.2, revoked (in part): SI 2013/1392 Sch.1 para.18
Part IV para.2, revoked (in part): SI 2013/1392 Sch.1 para.21
Part IV para.2, revoked (in part): SI 2013/1392 Sch.1 para.24
Part IV para.20, revoked (in part): SI 2013/1392 Sch.1 para.24
Part IV para.21, revoked (in part): SI 2013/1392 Sch.1 para.24
Part IV para.22, revoked (in part): SI 2013/1392 Sch.1 para.24
Part IV para.3, revoked (in part): SI 2013/1392 Sch.1 para.18
Part IV para.3, revoked (in part): SI 2013/1392 Sch.1 para.21
Part IV para.3, revoked (in part): SI 2013/1392 Sch.1 para.24
Part IV para.4, revoked (in part): SI 2013/1392 Sch.1 para.24
Part IV para.5, revoked (in part): SI 2013/1392 Sch.1 para.24
Part IV para.6, amended: SI 2013/1392 Sch.1 para.20
Part IV para.6, revoked (in part): SI 2013/1392 Sch.1 para.24
Part IV para.7, revoked (in part): SI 2013/1392 Sch.1 para.24
Part IV para.8, revoked (in part): SI 2013/1392 Sch.1 para.24
Part IV para.9, revoked (in part): SI 2013/1392 Sch.1 para.24
Part V para.1, revoked (in part): SI 2013/1392 Sch.1 para.21
Part V para.1, amended: SI 2013/1392 Sch.1 para.24
Part V para.10, revoked (in part): SI 2013/1392 Sch.1 para.21
Part V para.2, revoked (in part): SI 2013/1392 Sch.1 para.21
Part V para.2, revoked (in part): SI 2013/1392 Sch.1 para.24
Part V para.3, revoked (in part): SI 2013/1392 Sch.1 para.21
Part V para.3, amended: SI 2013/1392 Sch.1 para.24
Part V para.4, revoked (in part): SI 2013/1392 Sch.1 para.21
Part V para.4, revoked (in part): SI 2013/1392 Sch.1 para.24
Part V para.5, revoked (in part): SI 2013/1392 Sch.1 para.21
Part V para.6, revoked (in part): SI 2013/1392 Sch.1 para.21
Part V para.7, revoked (in part): SI 2013/1392 Sch.1 para.21
Part V para.8, revoked (in part): SI 2013/1392 Sch.1 para.21
Part V para.9, revoked (in part): SI 2013/1392 Sch.1 para.21
Part VI para.1, revoked (in part): SI 2013/1392 Sch.1 para.21
Part VI para.2, revoked (in part): SI 2013/1392 Sch.1 para.21
Part VI para.3, revoked (in part): SI 2013/1392 Sch.1 para.21
Part VIA para.2, amended: SI 2013/1392 Sch.1 para.16
Sch.2 Part A paraA.3, amended: SI 2013/1392 Sch.1 para.1
Sch.2 Part A paraA.3, revoked (in part): SI 2013/1392 Sch.1 para.1
Sch.2 Part A paraA.4, amended: SSI 2013/185 Art.3
Sch.2 Part A paraA.4, revoked (in part): SI 2013/1392 Sch.1 para.1
Sch.2 Part A paraA.5, revoked (in part): SI 2013/1392 Sch.1 para.1
Sch.2 Part A paraA.6, revoked (in part): SI 2013/1392 Sch.1 para.1
Sch.2 Part A paraA.7, revoked (in part): SI 2013/1392 Sch.1 para.1
Sch.2 Part A paraA.8, revoked (in part): SI 2013/1392 Sch.1 para.1
Sch.2 Part A paraA.12, revoked (in part): SI 2013/1392 Sch.1 para.1
Sch.2 Part A paraA.14, revoked (in part): SI 2013/1392 Sch.1 para.1
Sch.2 Part A paraA.15, revoked (in part): SI 2013/1392 Sch.1 para.1
Sch.2 Part B paraB.1, amended: SI 2013/1392 Sch.1 para.2, SSI 2013/185 Art.4
Sch.2 Part B paraB.2, amended: SI 2013/1392 Sch.1 para.2
Sch.2 Part B paraB.3, amended: SI 2013/1392 Sch.1 para.2
Sch.2 Part B paraB.5, amended: SI 2013/1392 Sch.1 para.2
Sch.2 Part B paraB.5, revoked (in part): SI 2013/1392 Sch.1 para.2
Sch.2 Part B paraB.5A, amended: SI 2013/1392 Sch.1 para.2
Sch.2 Part B paraB.5B, amended: SI 2013/1392 Sch.1 para.2
Sch.2 Part B paraB.5C, substituted: SI 2013/1392 Sch.1 para.2
Sch.2 Part B paraB.5D, amended: SI 2013/1392 Sch.1 para.2

Sch.2 Part B paraB.7, amended: SI 2013/1392 Sch.1 para.2
Sch.2 Part B paraB.8, amended: SI 2013/1392 Sch.1 para.2
Sch.2 Part B paraB.9, amended: SI 2013/1392 Sch.1 para.2
Sch.2 Part B paraB.12, amended: SI 2013/1392 Sch.1 para.2
Sch.2 Part E paraE.1, amended: SI 2013/1392 Sch.1 para.5
Sch.2 Part E paraE.3, amended: SI 2013/1392 Sch.1 para.5
Sch.2 Part E paraE.4, amended: SI 2013/1392 Sch.1 para.5
Sch.2 Part E paraE.5, amended: SI 2013/1392 Sch.1 para.5
Sch.2 Part E paraE.6, amended: SI 2013/1392 Sch.1 para.5
Sch.2 Part E paraE.7, amended: SI 2013/1392 Sch.1 para.5
Sch.2 Part E paraE.8, substituted: SI 2013/1392 Sch.1 para.5
Sch.2 Part E paraE.8A, added: SI 2013/1392 Sch.1 para.5
Sch.2 Part F paraF.1, amended: SI 2013/1392 Sch.1 para.6
Sch.2 Part F paraF.1A, added: SI 2013/1392 Sch.1 para.6
Sch.2 Part F paraF.2, amended: SI 2013/1392 Sch.1 para.6, SSI 2013/185 Art.5
Sch.2 Part F paraF.4, revoked (in part): SI 2013/1392 Sch.1 para.6
Sch.2 Part F paraF.6, revoked (in part): SI 2013/1392 Sch.1 para.6
Sch.2 Part F paraF.6A, amended: SI 2013/1392 Sch.1 para.6
Sch.2 Part F paraF.6B, amended: SI 2013/1392 Sch.1 para.6
Sch.2 Part F paraF.8, amended: SI 2013/1392 Sch.1 para.6
Sch.2 Part F paraF.8A, revoked (in part): SSI 2013/185 Art.6
Sch.2 Part F paraF.9, amended: SI 2013/1392 Sch.1 para.6
Sch.2 Part G, added: SI 2013/1392 Sch.1 para.7
Sch.2 Part G, amended: SI 2013/1392 Sch.1 para.7, SI 2013/2125 Art.2
Sch.2 Part G, revoked (in part): SI 2013/1392 Sch.1 para.7
Sch.2 Part H paraH.1A, added: SI 2013/1392 Sch.1 para.8
Sch.2 Part H paraH.2, substituted: SI 2013/1392 Sch.1 para.8
Sch.2 Part H paraH.3, substituted: SI 2013/1392 Sch.1 para.8
Sch.2 Part J paraJ.1, amended: SI 2013/1392 Sch.1 para.11
Sch.2 Part K paraK.1, amended: SI 2013/1392 Sch.1 para.12
Sch.2 Part K paraK.1A, amended: SI 2013/1392 Sch.1 para.12
Sch.2 Part K paraK.4, substituted: SI 2013/1392 Sch.1 para.12
Sch.2 Part I paraI.1, amended: SI 2013/1392 Sch.1 para.9
Sch.2 Part I paraI.2, amended: SI 2013/1392 Sch.1 para.9
Sch.2 Part I paraI.2, substituted: SI 2013/1392 Sch.1 para.9
Sch.2 Part I paraI.3, amended: SI 2013/1392 Sch.1 para.9
Sch.2 Part I paraI.3, revoked (in part): SI 2013/1392 Sch.1 para.9
Sch.2 Part I paraI.4, amended: SI 2013/1392 Sch.1 para.9
Sch.2 Part I paraI.5, amended: SI 2013/1392 Sch.1 para.9
Sch.2 Part I paraI.5, revoked (in part): SI 2013/1392 Sch.1 para.9
Sch.2 Part I paraI.6, amended: SI 2013/1392 Sch.1 para.9
Sch.2 Part I paraI.7, amended: SI 2013/1392 Sch.1 para.9
Sch.2 Part I paraI.8, added: SI 2013/1392 Sch.1 para.9
Sch.2 Part I paraI.8, amended: SI 2013/1392 Sch.1 para.9
Sch.2 Part IA paraIA.1, amended: SI 2013/1392 Sch.1 para.10
Sch.2 Part IA paraIA.2, amended: SI 2013/1392 Sch.1 para.10
Sch.2 Part IA paraIA.3, amended: SI 2013/1392 Sch.1 para.10
Sch.2 Part L paraL.3, amended: SI 2013/1392 Sch.1 para.13
Sch.2 Part L paraL.4, amended: SI 2013/1392 Sch.1 para.13
Sch.2 Part LA paraLA.1, revoked (in part): SSI 2013/185 Art.7
Sch.2 Part LA paraLA.2, amended: SI 2013/1392 Sch.1 para.14, SI 2013/2125 Art.2
Sch.2 Part LA paraLA.2, referred to: SI 2013/1392 Art.3
Sch.2 Part LA paraLA.2, revoked (in part): SSI 2013/185 Art.7
Sch.2 Part LA paraLA.3, amended: SI 2013/1392 Sch.1 para.14

Sch.2 Part LA paraLA.3, revoked (in part): SSI 2013/185 Art.7
Sch.2 Part LA paraLA.4, revoked (in part): SSI 2013/185 Art.7
Sch.2 Part LA paraLA.5, revoked (in part): SSI 2013/185 Art.7
Sch.2 Part LA paraLA.6, revoked (in part): SSI 2013/185 Art.7
Sch.2 Part LA paraLA.7, revoked (in part): SSI 2013/185 Art.7
Sch.2 Part LA paraLA.8, revoked (in part): SSI 2013/185 Art.7
Sch.2 Part LA paraLA.9, revoked (in part): SSI 2013/185 Art.7
Sch.2 Part LA paraLA.10, revoked (in part): SSI 2013/185 Art.7
Sch.2 Part C paraC.1, amended: SI 2013/1392 Sch.1 para.3
Sch.2 Part C paraC.10, amended: SI 2013/1392 Sch.1 para.3
Sch.2 Part D paraD.5, substituted: SI 2013/1392 Sch.1 para.4

198. Pensions Increase (Review) Order 1992
applied: SI 2013/604 Sch.1

223. Town and Country Planning (General Permitted Development) (Scotland) Order 1992
Art.3, applied: SSI 2013/288 Sch.2 para.1
Art.3, varied: SSI 2013/288 Sch.2 para.1
Sch.1 Part 11 para.29, varied: SSI 2013/288 Sch.2 para.1
Sch.1 Part 13 para.35, varied: SSI 2013/288 Sch.2 para.1

224. Town and Country Planning (General Development Procedure) (Scotland) Order 1992
applied: SSI 2013/155 Reg.51
Part 1, applied: SSI 2013/155 Reg.51
Part 2, applied: SSI 2013/155 Reg.51
Art.3, applied: SSI 2013/155 Reg.49
Art.4, applied: SSI 2013/155 Reg.49
Art.5, applied: SSI 2013/155 Reg.49
Art.6, applied: SSI 2013/155 Reg.49
Sch.2, applied: SSI 2013/155 Reg.51
Sch.4, applied: SSI 2013/155 Reg.51

231. Electricity (Northern Ireland) Order 1992
Art.2, amended: 2013 c.24 Sch.6 para.150
Art.10, applied: 2013 c.32 s.22, s.24, s.26, Sch.2 para.12, Sch.2 para.13, SI 2013/1119 Sch.1 para.4
Art.15, amended: 2013 c.24 Sch.6 para.151
Art.15, applied: 2013 c.24 Sch.4 para.35
Art.15A, amended: 2013 c.24 Sch.6 para.152
Art.16, amended: 2013 c.24 Sch.6 para.153
Art.17, amended: 2013 c.24 Sch.6 para.154
Art.17A, amended: 2013 c.24 Sch.6 para.155
Art.18, amended: 2013 c.24 Sch.6 para.156
Art.39, referred to: 2013 c.32 Sch.4 para.1
Art.46, amended: 2013 c.24 Sch.14 para.23, Sch.15 para.53
Art.53, amended: 2013 c.24 Sch.6 para.157
Art.53, revoked (in part): 2013 c.24 Sch.6 para.157

434. National Health Service (Service Committees and Tribunal) (Scotland) Regulations 1992
applied: SSI 2013/174 Reg.12

548. Council Tax (Discount Disregards) Order 1992
Art.3, amended: SI 2013/388 Sch.1 para.12, SI 2013/591 Sch.1 para.5, SI 2013/630 Reg.55, SI 2013/638 Art.2, SI 2013/1048 Art.2

549. Council Tax (Chargeable Dwellings) Order 1992
see *Listing Officer v Callear* [2012] EWHC 3697 (Admin), [2013] R.V.R. 34 (QBD (Admin)), Judge Shaun Spencer Q.C.
Art.2, see *Patel v Simpson (Listing Officer)* [2013] R.V.R. 100 (VT), R Bennett
Art.3, see *Patel v Simpson (Listing Officer)* [2013] R.V.R. 100 (VT), R Bennett

551. Council Tax (Liability for Owners) Regulations 1992
see *Naz v Redbridge LBC* [2013] EWHC 1268 (Admin), [2013] R.V.R. 226 (QBD (Admin)), David Holgate QC

552. Council Tax (Additional Provisions for Discount Disregards) Regulations 1992
Sch.1 Part II para.3, amended: SI 2013/388 Sch.1 para.3, SI 2013/591 Sch.1 para.6, SI 2013/639 Reg.2, SI 2013/725 Reg.2, SI 2013/1049 Reg.2

554. Council Tax (Reductions for Disabilities) Regulations 1992
see *Arca v Carlisle City Council* [2013] R.A. 248 (VT), Graham Zellick Q.C. (President)
Reg.3, see *Arca v Carlisle City Council* [2013] R.A. 248 (VT), Graham Zellick Q.C. (President)

558. Council Tax (Exempt Dwellings) Order 1992
Art.3, see *Harrow LBC v Ayiku* [2012] EWHC 1200 (Admin), [2013] P.T.S.R. 365 (QBD (Admin)), Sales, J.

613. Council Tax (Administration and Enforcement) Regulations 1992
Reg.1, amended: SI 2013/62 Reg.2, SI 2013/570 Reg.3, SI 2013/590 Reg.2, SI 2013/630 Reg.56, SI 2013/2977 Reg.5
Reg.2, amended: SI 2013/62 Reg.2
Reg.4, amended: SI 2013/62 Reg.2
Reg.5A, added: SI 2013/570 Reg.4, SI 2013/590 Reg.2
Reg.5B, added: SI 2013/570 Reg.4, SI 2013/590 Reg.2
Reg.5C, added: SI 2013/570 Reg.4, SI 2013/590 Reg.2
Reg.9, amended: SI 2013/62 Reg.2

Reg.10, amended: SI 2013/62 Reg.2
Reg.11, amended: SI 2013/62 Reg.2
Reg.14, see *Smith v Nottingham City Council* [2013] R.A. 404 (VT), Graham Zellick Q.C. (President)
Reg.15, amended: SI 2013/62 Reg.2
Reg.16, amended: SI 2013/62 Reg.2
Reg.20, amended: SI 2013/62 Reg.2
Reg.20, applied: SI 2013/3035 Sch.1
Reg.20, referred to: SI 2013/3029 Sch.13 para.10
Reg.21, amended: SI 2013/62 Reg.2
Reg.27, amended: SI 2013/570 Reg.5, SI 2013/590 Reg.2
Reg.29, amended: SI 2013/570 Reg.6, SI 2013/590 Reg.2
Reg.32, amended: SI 2013/570 Reg.7, SI 2013/630 Reg.56
Reg.52, amended: SI 2013/570 Reg.8, SI 2013/630 Reg.56
Reg.54, amended: SI 2013/570 Reg.9, SI 2013/630 Reg.56
Reg.58, amended: SI 2013/570 Reg.10, SI 2013/590 Reg.2
Sch.1 Part I para.2, amended: SI 2013/62 Reg.2, SI 2013/590 Reg.2
Sch.1 Part III para.10, amended: SI 2013/62 Reg.2
Sch.3 Part 1 para.32, amended: SI 2013/570 Reg.11, SI 2013/630 Reg.56

640. Fire Service College Trading Fund Order 1992
revoked: SI 2013/490 Art.2

656. Planning (Hazardous Substances) Regulations 1992
Reg.10, amended: SI 2013/755 Sch.4 para.30

662. National Health Service (Pharmaceutical Services) Regulations 1992
applied: SI 2013/349 Sch.4 para.25, Sch.4 para.26, Sch.5 para.15, Sch.5 para.16, SI 2013/898 Reg.6, Reg.20, Reg.49, Sch.5 para.15
revoked: SI 2013/898 Sch.8 para.1
Reg.9, applied: SI 2013/898 Reg.5, Reg.49
Reg.11ZA, applied: SI 2013/898 Reg.11
Reg.13, applied: SI 2013/898 Reg.11
Reg.14, applied: SI 2013/898 Reg.49
Reg.15, applied: SI 2013/898 Reg.49
Sch.2A, applied: SI 2013/898 Sch.5 para.12, Sch.5 para.14

664. National Health Service (Service Committees and Tribunal) Regulations 1992
applied: SI 2013/349 Sch.9 para.1, Sch.9 para.13, Sch.9 para.14
Part II, applied: SI 2013/898 Sch.4 para.2, Sch.6 para.2
Part II, referred to: SI 2013/898 Sch.5 para.1
Reg.2, amended: SI 2013/898 Sch.7 para.1
Reg.9, applied: SI 2013/898 Reg.43
Reg.10, amended: SI 2013/2042 Sch.1 para.44
Reg.33, revoked: SI 2013/2042 Sch.1 para.45
Sch.4 para.5, amended: SI 2013/2042 Sch.1 para.46

666. Town and Country Planning (Control of Advertisements) Regulations 1992
Reg.2, amended: SI 2013/755 Sch.4 para.31

709. Transfer of Functions (Magistrates Courts and Family Law) Order 1992
Sch.2, amended: 2013 c.22 Sch.10 para.99

905. Farm Woodland Premium Scheme 1992
Art.6, amended: SI 2013/1036 Sch.2 para.58

1151. Protection of Wrecks (Designation No.3) Order 1992
revoked: SSI 2013/276 Sch.1

1213. Road Traffic (Carriage of Dangerous Goods and Substances) (Amendment) Regulations 1992
revoked (in part): SI 2013/2987 Sch.3

1215. Road Traffic (Temporary Restrictions) Procedure Regulations 1992
Reg.2, amended: SSI 2013/119 Sch.2 para.9
Reg.3, amended: SSI 2013/119 Sch.2 para.9
Reg.6, amended: SSI 2013/119 Sch.2 para.9
Reg.10, amended: SSI 2013/119 Sch.2 para.9
Reg.13, amended: SSI 2013/119 Sch.2 para.9

1228. Legal Aid in Contempt of Court Proceedings (Scotland) (Fees) Regulations 1992
Sch.1 para.5, substituted: SSI 2013/250 Reg.3

1229. Protection of Wrecks (Designation No 2) Order 1992
revoked: SSI 2013/276 Sch.1

1332. Council Tax (Administration and Enforcement) (Scotland) Regulations 1992
Reg.3, revoked (in part): SSI 2013/119 Sch.1 para.24

1409. Council Tax (Discounts) (Scotland) Regulations 1992
Reg.2, amended: SSI 2013/65 Reg.2, SSI 2013/142 Reg.2

1492. Town and Country Planning General Regulations 1992
Reg.3, amended: SI 2013/2145 Reg.2
Reg.4A, added: SI 2013/2145 Reg.2

1620. Town and Country Planning (Isles of Scilly) Order 1992
applied: SI 2013/2148 Art.5

1691. Street Works (Maintenance) Regulations 1992
applied: SI 2013/2389 Sch.1, SI 2013/2399 Sch.1

1703. Housing (Right to Buy) (Prescribed Persons) Order 1992
Sch.1, amended: SI 2013/755 Sch.4 para.32

1813. Child Support (Maintenance Assessment Procedure) Regulations 1992

Reg.1, amended: SI 2013/630 Reg.40
Reg.10, amended: SI 2013/2380 Reg.3
Reg.17, amended: SI 2013/2380 Reg.3
Reg.17A, added: SI 2013/2380 Reg.3
Reg.18, amended: SI 2013/2380 Reg.3
Reg.23, amended: SI 2013/630 Reg.40
Sch.1 para.1, substituted: SI 2013/1517 Reg.2
Sch.1 para.8, added: SI 2013/1517 Reg.2
Sch.2 para.3, amended: SI 2013/1517 Reg.2

1815. Child Support (Maintenance Assessments and Special Cases) Regulations 1992

Reg.1, amended: SI 2013/235 Sch.2 para.20, SI 2013/458 Sch.1, SI 2013/630 Reg.41, SI 2013/1517 Reg.3
Reg.10C, added: SI 2013/630 Reg.41
Reg.11, amended: SI 2013/458 Sch.1
Reg.28, applied: SI 2013/380 Sch.6 para.10
Sch.1 Part I para.1, amended: SI 2013/602 Sch.2 para.72
Sch.1 Pt I para.2A, see *Gray v Secretary of State for Work and Pensions* [2012] EWCA Civ 1412, [2013] P.T.S.R. 520 (CA (Civ Div)), Ward, L.J.
Sch.2 para.7, amended: SI 2013/458 Sch.1
Sch.2 para.7A, added: SI 2013/630 Reg.41
Sch.2 para.8, amended: SI 2013/591 Sch.1 para.7
Sch.2 para.8, substituted: SI 2013/388 Sch.1 para.13
Sch.2 para.15, amended: SI 2013/388 Sch.1 para.13, SI 2013/591 Sch.1 para.7
Sch.2 para.30, amended: SI 2013/235 Sch.2 para.20
Sch.4, amended: SI 2013/388 Sch.1 para.13, SI 2013/591 Sch.1 para.7

1816. Child Support (Arrears, Interest and Adjustment of Maintenance Assessments) Regulations 1992

Reg.8, referred to: SI 2013/380 Sch.7 para.3

1878. Act of Sederunt (Fees of Witnesses and Shorthand Writers in the Sheriff Court) 1992

Sch.2 para.1, amended: SSI 2013/112 Art.2
Sch.2 para.4, amended: SSI 2013/112 Art.2
Sch.2 para.5, amended: SSI 2013/112 Art.2

1989. Child Support (Collection and Enforcement) Regulations 1992

Reg.25A, amended: SI 2013/1517 Reg.4
Reg.25A, revoked (in part): SI 2013/1517 Reg.4
Reg.25C, amended: SI 2013/1517 Reg.4
Reg.25G, amended: SI 2013/1517 Reg.4

1991. Local Government Superannuation (National Rivers Authority) Regulations 1992

Reg.5, amended: SI 2013/472 Art.4

2182. Fines (Deductions from Income Support) Regulations 1992

applied: SI 2013/381 Sch.3 para.10
Reg.1, amended: SI 2013/612 Reg.3
Reg.2, amended: SI 2013/612 Reg.4
Reg.4, amended: SI 2013/612 Reg.5
Reg.4, applied: SI 2013/380 Sch.6 para.3, Sch.6 para.5
Reg.4, revoked (in part): SI 2013/612 Reg.5
Reg.7, amended: SI 2013/612 Reg.6

2184. Non-Domestic Rating (Payment of Interest) (Scotland) Regulations 1992

Reg.4, amended: SI 2013/472 Art.4

2257. Education (London Residuary Body) (Transfer of Functions and Property) (No.2) Order 1992

Art.1, amended: SI 2013/472 Art.4

2428. Local Authorities (Funds) (England) Regulations 1992

Reg.2, amended: SI 2013/2974 Reg.2
Reg.8, amended: SI 2013/472 Art.4
Reg.10A, added: SI 2013/2974 Reg.2
Sch.2 Part I para.2, amended: SI 2013/2974 Reg.2
Sch.2 Part II para.6, amended: SI 2013/2974 Reg.2
Sch.3, amended: SI 2013/472 Art.4

2461. East Cheshire National Health Service Trust (Establishment) Order 1992

Art.1, amended: SI 2013/593 Art.2

2473. Southern Derbyshire Mental Health National Health Service Trust (Establishment) Order 1992

Art.1, amended: SI 2013/593 Art.2

2510. Whittington Hospital National Health Service Trust (Establishment) Order 1992

Art.1, amended: SI 2013/593 Art.2

2559. North Staffordshire Hospital Centre National Health Service Trust (Establishment) Order 1992

Art.1, amended: SI 2013/593 Art.2

2645. Child Support (Maintenance Arrangements and Jurisdiction) Regulations 1992

Reg.7A, amended: SI 2013/235 Sch.2 para.21
Reg.7A, revoked (in part): SI 2013/235 Sch.2 para.21

2790. Statistics of Trade (Customs and Excise) Regulations 1992

Reg.3, amended: SI 2013/3043 Reg.2
Reg.4, amended: SI 2013/3043 Reg.2

2793. Manual Handling Operations Regulations 1992

Reg.4, see *Kennedy v Chivas Brothers Ltd* [2013] CSIH 57, 2013 S.L.T. 981 (IH (2 Div)), The Lord Justice Clerk (Carloway)

2832. Town and Country Planning (Modification and Discharge of Planning Obligations) Regulations 1992

Reg.2A, added: SI 2013/147 Reg.3

2884. Faculty Jurisdiction (Injunctions and Restoration Orders) Rules 1992

revoked: SI 2013/1916 r.20_2

2903. Levying Bodies (General) Regulations 1992

Reg.10, amended: SI 2013/472 Art.4

2929. Local Authorities (Funds) (Wales) Regulations 1992

Reg.8, amended: SI 2013/472 Art.4
Sch.3, amended: SI 2013/472 Art.4

2957. River Roach Oyster Fishery Order 1992

revoked: SI 2013/1979 Art.8

2966. Personal Protective Equipment at Work Regulations 1992

see *Chief Constable of Hampshire v Taylor* [2013] EWCA Civ 496, [2013] I.C.R. 1150 (CA (Civ Div)), Elias, L.J.; see *Kennedy v Cordia (Services) LLP* [2013] CSOH 130, 2013 Rep. L.R. 126 (OH), Lord McEwan
Reg.3, revoked (in part): SI 2013/448 Sch.1
Reg.4, see *French v Strathclyde Fire Board* [2013] CSOH 3, 2013 S.L.T. 247 (OH), Lord Drummond Young; see *McKeown v Inverclyde Council* [2013] CSOH 141, 2013 S.L.T. 937 (OH), Lord Burns
Sch.2 Part III para.5, revoked: SI 2013/448 Sch.1
Sch.2 Part X para.23, revoked: SI 2013/448 Sch.1
Sch.2 Part X para.24, revoked: SI 2013/448 Sch.1
Sch.2 Part X para.25, revoked: SI 2013/448 Sch.1

2977. National Assistance (Assessment of Resources) Regulations 1992

Reg.2, amended: SI 2013/388 Sch.1 para.14, SI 2013/458 Sch.1, SI 2013/591 Sch.1 para.8, SI 2013/633 Reg.2, SI 2013/634 Reg.2, SSI 2013/65 Reg.3, SSI 2013/142 Reg.3
Reg.6, amended: SI 2013/518 Reg.3, SI 2013/631 Reg.4
Reg.9A, added: SI 2013/518 Reg.4, SI 2013/631 Reg.4
Reg.10, revoked (in part): SI 2013/518 Reg.5, SI 2013/631 Reg.4
Reg.11, revoked (in part): SI 2013/518 Reg.5, SI 2013/631 Reg.4
Reg.12, revoked (in part): SI 2013/518 Reg.5, SI 2013/631 Reg.4
Reg.13, revoked (in part): SI 2013/518 Reg.5, SI 2013/631 Reg.4
Reg.14, revoked (in part): SI 2013/518 Reg.5, SI 2013/631 Reg.4
Reg.15, amended: SI 2013/518 Reg.6, SI 2013/631 Reg.4
Reg.18, amended: SI 2013/518 Reg.7, SI 2013/631 Reg.4
Reg.20, amended: SSI 2013/41 Reg.2
Reg.20A, amended: SI 2013/631 Reg.4
Reg.28, amended: SSI 2013/41 Reg.3
Sch.2 para.1, revoked (in part): SI 2013/518 Reg.8, SI 2013/631 Reg.4
Sch.2 para.2, revoked (in part): SI 2013/518 Reg.8, SI 2013/631 Reg.4
Sch.2 para.3, revoked (in part): SI 2013/518 Reg.8, SI 2013/631 Reg.4
Sch.2 para.4, revoked (in part): SI 2013/518 Reg.8, SI 2013/631 Reg.4
Sch.2 para.5, revoked (in part): SI 2013/518 Reg.8, SI 2013/631 Reg.4
Sch.2 para.6, revoked (in part): SI 2013/518 Reg.8, SI 2013/631 Reg.4
Sch.3 Part I para.4, amended: SI 2013/388 Sch.1 para.14, SI 2013/634 Reg.2, SSI 2013/65 Reg.3
Sch.3 Part I para.4A, added: SI 2013/591 Sch.1 para.8, SI 2013/633 Reg.3, SSI 2013/142 Reg.3
Sch.3 Part I para.6, amended: SI 2013/388 Sch.1 para.14, SI 2013/634 Reg.2, SSI 2013/65 Reg.3
Sch.3 Part I para.11, amended: SI 2013/633 Reg.3
Sch.3 Part I para.11A, added: SI 2013/633 Reg.3
Sch.3 Part I para.11B, added: SI 2013/633 Reg.3
Sch.3 Part I para.28, revoked (in part): SI 2013/458 Sch.1
Sch.3 Part I para.28, substituted: SI 2013/634 Reg.2
Sch.3 Part I para.28G, amended: SSI 2013/41 Reg.4
Sch.3 Part II para.31, amended: SI 2013/633 Reg.3

3004. Workplace (Health, Safety and Welfare) Regulations 1992

see *Brown v East Lothian Council* [2013] CSOH 62, 2013 S.L.T. 721 (OH), Lord Jones
Reg.2, see *Brown v East Lothian Council* [2013] CSOH 62, 2013 S.L.T. 721 (OH), Lord Jones
Reg.3, amended: SI 2013/448 Reg.4
Reg.5, see *Brown v East Lothian Council* [2013] CSOH 62, 2013 S.L.T. 721 (OH), Lord Jones; see *McKeown v Inverclyde Council* [2013] CSOH 141, 2013 S.L.T. 937 (OH), Lord Burns
Reg.12, see *Brown v East Lothian Council* [2013] CSOH 62, 2013 S.L.T. 721 (OH), Lord Jones; see *Gillie v Scottish Borders Council* [2013] CSOH 76, 2013 Rep. L.R. 86 (OH), Lord Boyd of Duncansby; see *McKeown v Inverclyde Council* [2013] CSOH 141, 2013 S.L.T. 937 (OH), Lord Burns

3006. Companies (Forms) (Amendment) Regulations 1992

revoked: SI 2013/1947 Sch.2 Part 1

3122. Value Added Tax (Cars) Order 1992

see *Pendragon Plc v Revenue and Customs Commissioners* [2013] EWCA Civ 868, [2013] B.V.C. 414 (CA (Civ Div)), Lloyd, L.J.

3159. Specified Diseases (Notification and Slaughter) Order 1992

Art.2, amended: SI 2013/1662 Reg.40

3161. Artificial Insemination of Pigs (EEC) Regulations 1992

applied: SI 2013/1241 Reg.8, SSI 2013/151 Reg.8
Reg.2, applied: SSI 2013/151 Reg.8

3182. Residential Accommodation (Determination of District Health Authority) Regulations 1992
Reg.2, amended: SI 2013/235 Sch.2 para.22

3238. Non-Domestic Rating Contributions (Wales) Regulations 1992
Sch.4, substituted: SI 2013/3046 Sch.1

1993

10. Town and Country Planning (Public Path Orders) Regulations 1993
Sch.1, amended: SI 2013/2201 Reg.2

11. Public Path Orders Regulations 1993
Sch.1, amended: SI 2013/755 Sch.4 para.33

12. Wildlife and Countryside (Definitive Maps and Statements) Regulations 1993
Reg.2, see *R. (on the application of Trail Riders' Fellowship) v Dorset CC* [2013] EWCA Civ 553, [2013] P.T.S.R. 987 (CA (Civ Div)), Maurice Kay, L.J. (VP, CA Civ)

27. Mayday Healthcare National Health Service Trust (Establishment) Order 1993
Art.1, amended: SI 2013/593 Art.2

165. General Drainage Charges (Relevant Quotient) Regulations 1993
Reg.3, amended: SI 2013/755 Sch.4 para.34

176. Motor Vehicles (Wearing of Seat Belts) Regulations 1993
Reg.6, amended: SSI 2013/119 Sch.2 para.10

223. Drainage Rates (Forms) Regulations 1993
Sch.1, amended: SI 2013/755 Sch.4 para.35

255. Council Tax (Demand Notices) (Wales) Regulations 1993
Sch.1 para.7, amended: SI 2013/63 Reg.2
Sch.1 para.7, revoked (in part): SI 2013/63 Reg.2
Sch.1 para.8, amended: SI 2013/63 Reg.2
Sch.1 para.8A, added: SI 2013/63 Reg.2

323. Town and Country Planning (Hazardous Substances) (Scotland) Regulations 1993
Reg.11, amended: SSI 2013/119 Sch.2 para.11
Reg.11, revoked (in part): SSI 2013/119 Sch.2 para.11

346. Consumer Credit (Exempt Agreements) (Amendment) Order 1993
revoked (in part): SI 2013/1881 Art.21

494. Council Tax (Deductions from Income Support) Regulations 1993
applied: SI 2013/381 Sch.3 para.11
Reg.1, amended: SI 2013/612 Reg.8
Reg.2, amended: SI 2013/612 Reg.9
Reg.3, amended: SI 2013/612 Reg.10
Reg.5, amended: SI 2013/612 Reg.11
Reg.5, applied: SI 2013/380 Sch.6 para.3, Sch.6 para.5
Reg.5, revoked (in part): SI 2013/612 Reg.11
Reg.8, amended: SI 2013/612 Reg.12

623. Maintenance Orders (Backdating) Order 1993
Art.3, revoked: 2013 c.22 Sch.10 para.99
Sch.2, revoked: 2013 c.22 Sch.10 para.99
Sch.2 para.2, revoked: 2013 c.22 Sch.10 para.99

690. Adoption (Designation of Overseas Adoptions) (Variation) Order 1993
revoked: SI 2013/1801 Art.4

694. Lewisham Hospital National Health Service Trust (Establishment) Order 1993
Art.1, amended: SI 2013/593 Art.2, SI 2013/2376 Art.2
Art.2, amended: SI 2013/2376 Art.2
Art.4, amended: SI 2013/2376 Art.3
Art.5, substituted: SI 2013/2376 Art.4
Art.6, revoked: SI 2013/2376 Art.5

779. Pensions Increase (Review) Order 1993
applied: SI 2013/604 Sch.1

811. Walsgrave Hospitals National Health Service Trust (Establishment) Order 1993
Art.1, amended: SI 2013/593 Art.2

823. Hinchingbrooke Health Care National Health Service Trust (Establishment) Order 1993
Art.1, amended: SI 2013/593 Art.2

1019. Aberdeen-Fraserburgh Trunk Road (A92/A952) (Crimond Village) (40mph Speed Limit) Order 1993
revoked: SSI 2013/11 Art.3

1122. Road Traffic (Training of Drivers of Vehicles Carrying Dangerous Goods) (Amendment) Regulations 1993
revoked (in part): SI 2013/2987 Sch.3

1188. Serbia and Montenegro (United Nations Sanctions) Order 1993
Art.5, amended: SI 2013/1644 Sch.2

1450. Parking Attendants (Wearing of Uniforms) (London) Regulations 1993
revoked (in part): SI 2013/2987 Sch.3

1629. A61 Trunk Road (Hallwood Road to A6135 Birdwell) and the A616 Trunk Road (Stockbridge Bypass) (Derestriction) Order 1993
revoked: SI 2013/1680 Art.4

1658. Extraction Solvents in Food Regulations 1993
revoked (in part): SI 2013/2210 Sch.5, SI 2013/2591 Sch.5, SSI 2013/266 Sch.5

1801. Double Taxation Relief (Taxes on Income) (India) Order 1993
Sch.1 Part I, added: SI 2013/3147 Sch.1
Sch.1 Part I, revoked: SI 2013/3147 Sch.1
Sch.1 Part I, substituted: SI 2013/3147 Sch.1

1813. Channel Tunnel (International Arrangements) Order 1993
Sch.4 para.5, amended: SI 2013/3032 Sch.2 para.1
1857. A47 Trunk Road (Castor Ailsworth Bypass) (24 Hour Clearway) Order 1993
revoked: SI 2013/394 Sch.1 Part II
1956. Act of Sederunt (Sheriff Court Ordinary Cause Rules) 1993
see *Weddell v Anderson* [2013] CSIH 34, 2013 S.C. 405 (IH (Ex Div)), Lord Clarke
Sch.1, applied: SI 2013/3029 Sch.10 para.49, SI 2013/3035 Sch.1
Sch.1, see *Gray v Westlake-Tritton* 2013 Rep. L.R. 10 (Sh Ct (Grampian) (Aberdeen)), Sheriff M Garden; see *Simpson v Downie* 2013 S.L.T. 178 (IH (Ex Div)), Lord Emslie; see *Weddell v Anderson* [2013] CSIH 34, 2013 S.C. 405 (IH (Ex Div)), Lord Clarke; see *Yazdanparast v Yazdanparast* [2013] CSIH 27, 2013 Fam. L.R. 44 (IH (Ex Div)), Lady Paton
2004. Income Tax (Manufactured Overseas Dividends) Regulations 1993
Reg.2B, see *Chappell v Revenue and Customs Commissioners* [2013] UKFTT 98 (TC), [2013] S.F.T.D. 733 (FTT (Tax)), Judge John Walters Q.C.
Reg.5B, amended: SI 2013/504 Reg.31
2008. Vegetable Seeds Regulations 1993
Sch.1, amended: SSI 2013/326 Reg.2
2073. Enforcement of Road Traffic Debts Order 1993
referred to: SI 2013/1783 Reg.20
varied: SI 2013/1783 Reg.20
Art.2, referred to: SI 2013/1783 Reg.20
Art.3, referred to: SI 2013/1783 Reg.20
Art.3, varied: SI 2013/1783 Reg.20
2152. A55 Trunk Road (Bodelwyddan &mdash St Asaph, Clwyd) (Derestriction) Order 1993
disapplied: SI 2013/729 Art.14
varied: SI 2013/729 Art.14
2164. Housing (Preservation of Right to Buy) (Scotland) Regulations 1993
Sch.2, amended: SSI 2013/119 Sch.3 para.2
2407. Leasehold Reform (Collective Enfranchisement and Lease Renewal) Regulations 1993
Sch.1 para.3, amended: SI 2013/1036 Sch.2 para.11
Sch.1 para.6, amended: SI 2013/1036 Sch.2 para.11
Sch.1 para.7, amended: SI 2013/1036 Sch.2 para.11
Sch.2 para.7, amended: SI 2013/1036 Sch.2 para.12
2451. National Health Service (Pharmaceutical Services) Amendment Regulations 1993
revoked: SI 2013/898 Sch.8 para.2
2544. Churchill John Radcliffe National Health Service Trust (Establishment) Order 1993
Art.1, amended: SI 2013/593 Art.2
2551. George Eliot Hospital National Health Service Trust (Establishment) Order 1993
Art.1, amended: SI 2013/593 Art.2
2552. Hereford Hospitals National Health Service Trust (Establishment) Order 1993
Art.1, amended: SI 2013/593 Art.2
2561. Northampton General Hospital National Health Service Trust (Establishment) Order 1993
Art.1, amended: SI 2013/593 Art.2
2568. Plymouth Hospitals National Health Service Trust (Establishment) Order 1993
Art.1, amended: SI 2013/593 Art.2
2574. Royal Wolverhampton Hospitals National Health Service Trust (Establishment) Order 1993
Art.1, amended: SI 2013/593 Art.2
2635. North Staffordshire Combined Healthcare National Health Service Trust (Establishment) Order 1993
Art.1, amended: SI 2013/593 Art.2
2642. Dartford and Gravesham National Health Service Trust (Establishment) Order 1993
Art.1, amended: SI 2013/2375 Art.2
Art.3, substituted: SI 2013/2375 Art.3
Art.5, substituted: SI 2013/2375 Art.4
Art.6, revoked: SI 2013/2375 Art.5
Art.7, revoked: SI 2013/2375 Art.5
2661. European Communities (Designation) (No.3) Order 1993
Sch.1, amended: SI 2013/1445 Art.5
Sch.1, applied: SI 2013/1445 Art.5
2797. Transport Act 1985 (Modifications in Schedule 4 to the Transport Act 1968) (Further Modification) Order 1993
revoked (in part): SI 2013/2986 Sch.3
2854. Employment Appeal Tribunal Rules 1993
r.2, amended: SI 2013/1693 r.2
r.3, amended: SI 2013/1693 r.3
r.3, revoked (in part): SI 2013/1693 r.3
r.6, amended: SI 2013/1693 r.4
r.6, revoked (in part): SI 2013/1693 r.4
r.17A, added: SI 2013/1693 r.5
r.26, substituted: SI 2013/1693 r.6
r.34A, amended: SI 2013/1693 r.7
r.34C, amended: SI 2013/1693 r.8
Sch.1, amended: SI 2013/1693 r.9
2909. Transport Act 1985 (Modifications in Schedule 4 to the Transport Act 1968) (Further Modification) (Amendment) Order 1993
revoked (in part): SI 2013/2986 Sch.3

2922. Consumer Credit (Exempt Agreements) (Amendment) (No.2) Order 1993
revoked (in part): SI 2013/1881 Art.21
3053. Commercial Agents (Council Directive) Regulations 1993
see *Rossetti Marketing Ltd v Diamond Sofa Co Ltd* [2012] EWCA Civ 1021, [2013] 1 All E.R. (Comm) 308 (CA (Civ Div)), Lord Neuberger (M.R.)
Reg.2, see *Invicta UK v International Brands Ltd* [2013] EWHC 1564 (QB), [2013] E.C.C. 30 (QBD), Judge Ralls, Q.C.
Reg.3, see *Crocs Europe BV v Anderson (t/a Spectrum Agencies (A Partnership))* [2012] EWCA Civ 1400, [2013] 1 Lloyd's Rep. 1 (CA (Civ Div)), Mummery, L.J.
Reg.5, see *Crocs Europe BV v Anderson (t/a Spectrum Agencies (A Partnership))* [2012] EWCA Civ 1400, [2013] 1 Lloyd's Rep. 1 (CA (Civ Div)), Mummery, L.J.
Reg.17, see *Invicta UK v International Brands Ltd* [2013] EWHC 1564 (QB), [2013] E.C.C. 30 (QBD), Judge Ralls, Q.C.
Reg.18, see *Rossetti Marketing Ltd v Diamond Sofa Co Ltd* [2012] EWCA Civ 1021, [2013] 1 All E.R. (Comm) 308 (CA (Civ Div)), Lord Neuberger (M.R.)
3080. Act of Sederunt (Fees of Solicitors in the Sheriff Court) (Amendment and Further Provisions) 1993
applied: SI 2013/1237 Sch.1
3088. A47 Trunk Road (East Winch to Little Fransham) (24 Hour Clearway) Order 1993
revoked: SI 2013/394 Sch.1 Part II
3160. Roads (Northern Ireland) Order 1993
Art.65A, amended: 2013 c.7 s.16
3167. Redundancy Payments (National Health Service) (Modification) Order 1993
Sch.1 para.2B, added: SI 2013/235 Sch.2 para.24
Sch.1 para.2C, added: SI 2013/235 Sch.2 para.24
Sch.1 para.2D, added: SI 2013/235 Sch.2 para.24
Sch.1 para.2E, added: SI 2013/235 Sch.2 para.24
3252. Parliamentary Pensions (Additional Voluntary Contributions Scheme) Regulations 1993
Reg.6, amended: SI 2013/472 Art.4
Reg.9, amended: SI 2013/472 Art.4

1994

117. Companies (Welsh Language Forms and Documents) Regulations 1994
revoked: SI 2013/1947 Sch.2 Part 1
166. Royal West Sussex National Health Service Trust (Establishment) Order 1994
Art.1, amended: SI 2013/593 Art.2
192. Trunk Road (A55) (Pen-y-clip Section, Gwynedd) (One Way Traffic) Order 1994
varied: SI 2013/692 Art.8
340. Financial Services (Disclosure of Information) (Designated Authorities) (No.8) Order 1994
Art.3, revoked: SI 2013/2329 Sch.1 para.32
515. A282 Trunk Road (Dartford Tunnels and Approaches) (One Way Traffic and Weight Restriction) Order 1994
disapplied: SI 2013/3125 Art.7
varied: SI 2013/976 Art.6
606. Railways (Class and Miscellaneous Exemptions) Order 1994
Art.3, applied: SI 2013/339 Art.11
Art.5, applied: SI 2013/339 Art.11
Art.6, applied: SI 2013/339 Art.11
Art.7, applied: SI 2013/339 Art.12, Art.13, Art.14
607. Railways (Alternative Closure Procedure) Order 1994
Art.2, applied: SI 2013/339 Art.15
731. Child Support Act 1991 (Consequential Amendments) Order 1994
Art.3, revoked: 2013 c.22 Sch.10 para.99
Art.4, revoked: 2013 c.22 Sch.11 para.210
776. Pensions Increase (Review) Order 1994
applied: SI 2013/604 Sch.1
790. A55 Trunk Road (Pen-y-clip Section, Gwynedd) (Derestriction) Order 1994
disapplied: SI 2013/729 Art.8
varied: SI 2013/333 Art.13, SI 2013/692 Art.9, SI 2013/729 Art.8
1057. Surface Waters (River Ecosystem) (Classification) Regulations 1994
Reg.3, amended: SI 2013/755 Sch.4 para.36
1137. Transfrontier Shipment of Waste Regulations 1994
applied: SI 2013/2258 Sch.1 Part 2
1226. Cycle Racing on Highways (Tour de France 1994) Regulations 1994
revoked: SI 2013/2987 Sch.2
1443. Act of Sederunt (Rules of the Court of Session 1994) 1994
see *MBR (Iran) v Secretary of State for the Home Department* [2013] CSIH 66, 2013 S.L.T. 1108 (IH (2 Div)), The Lord Justice Clerk (Carloway)
Sch.2, see *Grant v Fife Council* [2013] CSOH 11, 2013 Rep. L.R. 73 (OH), Lord Stewart; see *Logan v Johnston* [2013] CSOH 109, 2013 S.L.T. 971 (OH), Lord Glennie; see *M v S* [2013] CSOH 79, 2013 Fam. L.R. 52 (OH), Lord Brailsford
Sch.2 Part 3, applied: SSI 2013/162 r.7
Sch.2 Part 3 para.24_6, added: SSI 2013/162 r.2
Sch.2 Part 3 para.24_6, amended: SSI 2013/317 r.2

Sch.2 Part 3 para.38_11A, added: SSI 2013/294 r.2
Sch.2 Part 3 para.40_9A, added: SSI 2013/294 r.2
Sch.2 Part 3 para.41_27, substituted: SSI 2013/162 r.3
Sch.2 Part 3 para.41_35, amended: SSI 2013/162 r.3
Sch.2 Part 3 para.41_35, substituted: SSI 2013/162 r.3
Sch.2 Part 3 para.41_36, substituted: SSI 2013/162 r.3
Sch.2 Part 3 para.41_37, amended: SSI 2013/162 r.3
Sch.2 Part 3 para.41_37, substituted: SSI 2013/162 r.3
Sch.2 Part 3 para.41_38, substituted: SSI 2013/162 r.3
Sch.2 Part 3 para.41_39, substituted: SSI 2013/162 r.3
Sch.2 Part 3 para.41_40, substituted: SSI 2013/162 r.3
Sch.2 Part 3 para.41_46, added: SSI 2013/238 r.2
Sch.2 Part 3 para.41_46A, added: SSI 2013/238 r.2
Sch.2 Part 3 para.41_47, added: SSI 2013/238 r.2
Sch.2 Part 3 para.41_48, added: SSI 2013/238 r.2
Sch.2 Part 3 para.41_49, added: SSI 2013/238 r.2
Sch.2 Part 3 para.41_50, added: SSI 2013/238 r.2
Sch.2 Part 3 para.41_51, added: SSI 2013/238 r.2
Sch.2 Part 3 para.41_52, revoked (in part): SSI 2013/162 r.4
Sch.2 Part 3 para.41_52, added: SSI 2013/238 r.2
Sch.2 Part 3 para.41_52A, added: SSI 2013/238 r.2
Sch.2 Part 3 para.41_52B, added: SSI 2013/238 r.2
Sch.2 Part 3 para.41_52C, added: SSI 2013/238 r.2
Sch.2 Part 3 para.41_53, added: SSI 2013/238 r.2
Sch.2 Part 3 para.41_54, added: SSI 2013/238 r.2
Sch.2 Part 3 para.41_55, added: SSI 2013/238 r.2
Sch.2 Part 3 para.41_57, added: SSI 2013/238 r.2
Sch.2 Part 3 para.41_57, amended: SSI 2013/294 r.3
Sch.2 Part 3 para.42_16, amended: SSI 2013/111 r.2
Sch.2 Part 4, added: SSI 2013/120 r.2
Sch.2 Part 4, added: SSI 2013/81 r.2
Sch.2 Part 4 para.55_2D, amended: SSI 2013/120 r.3
Sch.2 Part 4 para.55_5B, substituted: SSI 2013/120 r.3
Sch.2 Part 4 para.55_5C, substituted: SSI 2013/120 r.3
Sch.2 Part 4 para.58A_1, amended: SSI 2013/120 r.4
Sch.2 Part 5, added: SSI 2013/238 r.3
Sch.2 Part 5 para.62_90, amended: SI 2013/472 Sch.2 para.10
Sch.2 Part 5 para.62_91, amended: SI 2013/472 Sch.2 para.10
Sch.2 Part 5 para.74_1, amended: SSI 2013/162 r.5
Sch.2 Part 5 para.74_3, amended: SSI 2013/162 r.5
Sch.2 Part 5 para.74_11, amended: SSI 2013/162 r.5
Sch.2 Part 5 para.74_36, amended: SI 2013/472 Sch.2 para.10
Sch.2 Part 5 para.74_45, amended: SI 2013/472 Sch.2 para.10
Sch.2 Part 5 para.74_46, amended: SI 2013/472 Sch.2 para.10
Sch.2 Part 5 para.74_54, amended: SI 2013/472 Sch.2 para.10
Sch.2 Part 5 para.76_36, amended: SSI 2013/294 r.4
Sch.2 Part 5 para.76_37, amended: SSI 2013/294 r.5, SSI 2013/317 r.3
Sch.2 Part 5 para.76_37A, added: SSI 2013/162 r.6
Sch.2 Part 5 para.76_37A, amended: SSI 2013/294 r.5
Sch.2 Part 5 para.104_5, amended: SSI 2013/317 r.4
Sch.2 para.7.7, see *Farstad Supply AS v Enviroco Ltd* [2013] CSIH 9, 2013 S.C. 302 (IH (Ex Div)), Lord Eassie
Sch.2 para.36.1, see *Shehadeh v Advocate General for Scotland* 2013 S.L.T. 205 (OH), Lord Doherty
Sch.2 para.41.3, see *MBR (Iran) v Secretary of State for the Home Department* [2013] CSIH 66, 2013 S.L.T. 1108 (IH (2 Div)), The Lord Justice Clerk (Carloway)
Sch.2 para.42A_5, see *Logan v Johnston* [2013] CSOH 109, 2013 S.L.T. 971 (OH), Lord Glennie
Sch.2 para.42.14, see *Scottish Ministers v Stirton* 2013 S.C.L.R. 209 (OH), Lady Stacey
Sch.2 para.58.3, see *NJ v Lord Advocate* [2013] CSOH 27, 2013 S.L.T. 347 (OH), Lord Brailsford
Sch.2 para.58.9, see *SA (Nigeria) v Secretary of State for the Home Department* [2013] CSIH 62, 2013 S.L.T. 1132 (IH (2 Div)), The Lord Justice Clerk (Carloway)
Sch.2 para.58.12, see *G v Watson* [2013] CSOH 88, 2013 S.L.T. 934 (OH), Lord McEwan; see *Shehadeh v Advocate General for Scotland* 2013 S.L.T. 205 (OH), Lord Doherty
Sch.2 para.74.15, see *Joint Administrators of Prestonpans (Trading) Ltd, Petitioners* 2013 S.L.T. 138 (OH), Lord Malcolm
Sch.2 para.100.5, see *SGL Carbon Fibres Ltd, Petitioners* [2013] CSOH 21, 2013 S.L.T. 307 (OH), Lord Hodge

Sch.2 para.100.6, see *SGL Carbon Fibres Ltd, Petitioners* [2013] CSOH 21, 2013 S.L.T. 307 (OH), Lord Hodge
Sch.2 para.102.1, see *BBC, Applicants* 2013 S.L.T. 324 (OH), Lord Glennie

1623. Employment Tribunals Extension of Jurisdiction (England and Wales) Order 1994
applied: SI 2013/1893 Sch.2

1624. Employment Tribunals Extension of Jurisdiction (Scotland) Order 1994
applied: SI 2013/1893 Sch.2

1662. European Parliamentary (United Kingdom Representatives) Pensions (Consolidation and Amendment) Order 1994
referred to: SI 2013/481 Art.6
varied: SI 2013/2826 Art.3
Art.2, amended: SI 2013/481 Art.4
Art.5, amended: SI 2013/481 Art.5
Art.5, applied: SI 2013/481 Art.6

1738. Air Passenger Duty Regulations 1994
see *Ryanair Ltd v Revenue and Customs Commissioners* [2013] UKUT 176 (TCC), [2013] S.T.C. 1360 (UT (Tax)), Warren, J.
Reg.2, amended: SI 2013/493 Reg.3
Reg.4, amended: SI 2013/493 Reg.4
Reg.9, amended: SI 2013/493 Reg.5
Reg.10, amended: SI 2013/493 Reg.5
Reg.10A, added: SI 2013/493 Reg.6
Reg.10B, added: SI 2013/493 Reg.6
Reg.10C, added: SI 2013/493 Reg.6
Reg.10D, added: SI 2013/493 Reg.6
Reg.10E, added: SI 2013/493 Reg.6
Reg.10F, added: SI 2013/493 Reg.6

1774. Insurance Premium Tax Regulations 1994
Reg.20, amended: SI 2013/472 Art.5

1821. Air Passenger Duty (Connected Flights) Order 1994
see *Ryanair Ltd v Revenue and Customs Commissioners* [2013] UKUT 176 (TCC), [2013] S.T.C. 1360 (UT (Tax)), Warren, J.
Sch.1 para.1, see *Ryanair Ltd v Revenue and Customs Commissioners* [2013] UKUT 176 (TCC), [2013] S.T.C. 1360 (UT (Tax)), Warren, J.

1983. Friendly Societies (Accounts and Related Provisions) Regulations 1994
Sch.3 para.12, amended: SI 2013/496 Sch.10 para.6

2402. National Health Service (Pharmaceutical Services and Charges for Drugs and Appliances) Amendment Regulations 1994
revoked: SI 2013/898 Sch.8 para.3

2420. Consumer Credit (Exempt Agreements) (Amendment) Order 1994
revoked (in part): SI 2013/1881 Art.21

2421. Insolvent Partnerships Order 1994
Sch.1 Part I, amended: SI 2013/472 Sch.2 para.11
Sch.2 para.17, amended: SI 2013/472 Sch.2 para.11
Sch.7 para.2, amended: SI 2013/472 Art.4

2488. Roads (Traffic Calming) (Scotland) Regulations 1994
Reg.4, amended: SSI 2013/119 Sch.2 para.12

2507. Insolvency Regulations 1994
Reg.3, amended: SI 2013/472 Art.4

2524. Salmon (Fish Passes and Screens) (Scotland) Regulations 1994
revoked: SSI 2013/323 Reg.29

2716. Conservation (Natural Habitats, &c.) Regulations 1994
applied: SSI 2013/155 Sch.2 para.4

2716. Conservation (Natural Habitats, &c.) Regulations 1994
Reg.44, see *William Grant & Sons Distillers Ltd v Scottish Ministers* 2013 S.C.L.R. 19 (OH), Lord Malcolm

2745. A500 Trunk Road (M6 Junction 16 to A34 at Talke) (De-restriction) Order 1994
revoked: SI 2013/2702 Art.5

2841. Urban Waste Water Treatment (England and Wales) Regulations 1994
Reg.2, amended: SI 2013/755 Sch.4 para.38
Reg.3, amended: SI 2013/755 Sch.4 para.39
Reg.4, amended: SI 2013/755 Sch.4 para.40
Reg.4, applied: SI 2013/1582 Reg.1
Reg.5, amended: SI 2013/755 Sch.4 para.41
Reg.6, amended: SI 2013/755 Sch.4 para.42
Reg.8, amended: SI 2013/755 Sch.4 para.43
Reg.10, amended: SI 2013/755 Sch.4 para.44
Reg.11, amended: SI 2013/755 Sch.4 para.45
Reg.12, amended: SI 2013/755 Sch.4 para.46
Sch.3 Part II para.1, amended: SI 2013/755 Sch.4 para.47

2924. Teachers Superannuation (Additional Voluntary Contributions) Regulations 1994
Reg.2, amended: SI 2013/472 Art.4

2946. Social Security (Incapacity Benefit) Regulations 1994
Reg.10, amended: SI 2013/574 Art.13
Reg.26, amended: SI 2013/388 Sch.1 para.15, SI 2013/591 Sch.1 para.9

2973. Industry-Wide Coal Staff Superannuation Scheme Regulations 1994
see *Industry-Wide Coal Staff Superannuation Scheme Co-ordinator Ltd v Industry-Wide Coal Staff Superannuation Scheme Trustees Ltd* [2012] EWHC 3712 (Ch), [2013] Pens. L.R. 55 (Ch D), Morgan, J.
Appendix 19 para.1., amended: SI 2013/472 Art.4

2974. Industry-Wide Mineworkers Pension Scheme Regulations 1994
Sch.1, amended: SI 2013/472 Art.4
3024. Charitable Institutions (Fund-Raising) Regulations 1994
Reg.1, amended: SI 2013/472 Art.4
3051. Construction Products (Amendment) Regulations 1994
revoked: SI 2013/1387 Reg.28
3087. A55 Trunk Road (Abergwyngregyn, Gwynedd) (Derestriction) Order 1994
disapplied: SI 2013/729 Art.5
varied: SI 2013/333 Art.17, SI 2013/692 Art.13
3088. A55 Trunk Road (Penmaenbach Tunnel, Gwynedd) (Closure of Central Reservation Crossings) Order 1994
varied: SI 2013/195 Art.10, SI 2013/3257 Art.10
3178. Pathfinder National Health Service Trust (Establishment) Order 1994
Art.1, amended: SI 2013/593 Art.2
3200. Non-Domestic Rating (Unoccupied Property) (Scotland) Regulations 1994
Reg.1, amended: SSI 2013/37 Reg.3
Reg.2, substituted: SSI 2013/37 Reg.4
Reg.3, amended: SSI 2013/37 Reg.5
Reg.4, added: SSI 2013/37 Reg.6
Sch.1 Part 1A, added: SSI 2013/37 Reg.7
3251. Education (Inter-authority Recoupment) Regulations 1994
Reg.1A, added: SI 2013/492 Reg.2
Reg.1B, added: SI 2013/492 Reg.2

1995

185. Public Service Vehicles (Lost Property) (Amendment) Regulations 1995
revoked (in part): SI 2013/2987 Sch.3
300. National Health Service Pension Scheme Regulations 1995
Reg.1, amended: SI 2013/413 Reg.5
Reg.1, amended: SI 2013/413 Reg.7, SI 2013/1414 Reg.3
Reg.1, applied: SI 2013/469 Sch.1
Reg.1, amended: SI 2013/413 Reg.16
Reg.1, applied: SI 2013/469 Sch.1
Reg.1A, added: SI 2013/413 Reg.18
Reg.2, amended: SI 2013/413 Reg.3
Reg.2, revoked (in part): SI 2013/413 Reg.3
Reg.2, amended: SI 2013/413 Reg.8
Reg.2, applied: SI 2013/469 Sch.1
Reg.3, amended: SI 2013/413 Reg.4
Reg.3, applied: SI 2013/469 Sch.1
Reg.3, revoked (in part): SI 2013/413 Reg.19
Reg.3A, amended: SI 2013/413 Reg.9
Reg.4, amended: SI 2013/413 Reg.6
Reg.4, revoked (in part): SI 2013/413 Reg.6
Reg.4, amended: SI 2013/413 Reg.12
Reg.4, revoked: SI 2013/413 Reg.20
Reg.6, amended: SI 2013/413 Reg.10
Reg.6, amended: SI 2013/413 Reg.13
Reg.13, amended: SI 2013/413 Reg.14
Reg.14, amended: SI 2013/413 Reg.11
Reg.15, amended: SI 2013/413 Reg.15
s.art S Reg.2, amended: SI 2013/413 Reg.17
Sch.2, referred to: SI 2013/469 Sch.1
Sch.2 para.1, amended: SI 2013/413 Reg.21
Sch.2 para.2, amended: SI 2013/413 Reg.21
Sch.2 para.3, amended: SI 2013/413 Reg.21
Sch.2 para.4, amended: SI 2013/413 Reg.21
Sch.2 para.5, amended: SI 2013/413 Reg.21
Sch.2 para.6, amended: SI 2013/413 Reg.21
Sch.2 para.8, amended: SI 2013/413 Reg.21
Sch.2 para.10, amended: SI 2013/413 Reg.21, SI 2013/1414 Reg.4
Sch.2 para.17A, applied: SI 2013/469 Sch.1
Sch.2 para.19, amended: SI 2013/413 Reg.21
Sch.2 para.23, amended: SI 2013/413 Reg.21
Sch.2 para.23, applied: SI 2013/469 Sch.1
Sch.2 para.23, referred to: SI 2013/469 Sch.1
310. Social Security (Incapacity Benefit) (Transitional) Regulations 1995
Reg.18, amended: SI 2013/574 Art.14
311. Social Security (Incapacity for Work) (General) Regulations 1995
Reg.2, amended: SI 2013/252 Sch.1 Part 2
Reg.13A, applied: SI 2013/3029 Sch.1 para.20, Sch.7 para.10, SI 2013/3035 Sch.1
Reg.17, applied: SI 2013/3035 Sch.1
Reg.17, revoked (in part): SI 2013/252 Sch.1 Part 2
401. Local Government Residuary Body (England) Order 1995
Art.24, amended: SI 2013/472 Art.4
402. Local Government Changes For England (Property Transfer and Transitional Payments) Regulations 1995
Reg.18, amended: SI 2013/472 Art.4
418. Town and Country Planning (General Permitted Development) Order 1995
applied: SI 2013/648 Art.80, Sch.2 para.3, Sch.2 para.4
disapplied: SI 2013/680 Art.3
Art.1, amended: SI 2013/755 Sch.4 para.49, SI 2013/1101 Art.3
Art.3, applied: SI 2013/648 Art.68, Art.82
Art.3, disapplied: SI 2013/648 Art.80
Art.3, varied: SI 2013/648 Art.80

Art.4, amended: SI 2013/1776 Art.2
Art.4, applied: SI 2013/1102 Reg.3
Art.5, applied: SI 2013/1102 Reg.3, Reg.4, Reg.7
Art.6, applied: SI 2013/1102 Reg.3
Sch.1 Part 4 para.1, added: SI 2013/1101 Art.3
Sch.1 Part 4 para.2, added: SI 2013/1101 Art.3
Sch.2 Part 1, applied: SI 2013/1102 Reg.2
Sch.2 Part 1 paraA, substituted: SI 2013/1776 Sch.1
Sch.2 Part 1 paraB, substituted: SI 2013/1776 Sch.1
Sch.2 Part 1 paraC, substituted: SI 2013/1776 Sch.1
Sch.2 Part 1 paraD, substituted: SI 2013/1776 Sch.1
Sch.2 Part 1 paraE, substituted: SI 2013/1776 Sch.1
Sch.2 Part 1 paraF, substituted: SI 2013/1776 Sch.1
Sch.2 Part 1, substituted: SI 2013/1776 Sch.1
Sch.2 Part 1 paraH, substituted: SI 2013/1776 Sch.1
Sch.2 Part 1 paraI, substituted: SI 2013/1776 Sch.1
Sch.2 Part 1 paraA.1, amended: SI 2013/1101 Art.4
Sch.2 Part 1 paraA.1, substituted: SI 2013/1776 Sch.1
Sch.2 Part 1 paraB.1, substituted: SI 2013/1776 Sch.1
Sch.2 Part 1 paraC.1, substituted: SI 2013/1776 Sch.1
Sch.2 Part 1 paraD.1, substituted: SI 2013/1776 Sch.1
Sch.2 Part 1 paraE.1, substituted: SI 2013/1776 Sch.1
Sch.2 Part 1 paraF.1, substituted: SI 2013/1776 Sch.1
Sch.2 Part 1 paraH.1, substituted: SI 2013/1776 Sch.1
Sch.2 Part 1 paraI.1, substituted: SI 2013/1776 Sch.1
Sch.2 Part 1 paraA.2, substituted: SI 2013/1776 Sch.1
Sch.2 Part 1 paraB.2, substituted: SI 2013/1776 Sch.1
Sch.2 Part 1 paraC.2, substituted: SI 2013/1776 Sch.1
Sch.2 Part 1 paraE.2, substituted: SI 2013/1776 Sch.1
Sch.2 Part 1 paraF.2, substituted: SI 2013/1776 Sch.1
Sch.2 Part 1 paraH.2, substituted: SI 2013/1776 Sch.1
Sch.2 Part 1 paraI.2, substituted: SI 2013/1776 Sch.1
Sch.2 Part 1 paraA.3, substituted: SI 2013/1776 Sch.1
Sch.2 Part 1 paraB.3, substituted: SI 2013/1776 Sch.1
Sch.2 Part 1 paraC.3, substituted: SI 2013/1776 Sch.1
Sch.2 Part 1 paraE.3, substituted: SI 2013/1776 Sch.1
Sch.2 Part 1 paraF.3, substituted: SI 2013/1776 Sch.1
Sch.2 Part 1 paraH.3, substituted: SI 2013/1776 Sch.1
Sch.2 Part 1 paraA.4, added: SI 2013/1101 Art.4
Sch.2 Part 1 paraA.4, substituted: SI 2013/1776 Sch.1
Sch.2 Part 1 paraB.4, substituted: SI 2013/1776 Sch.1
Sch.2 Part 1 paraE.4, substituted: SI 2013/1776 Sch.1
Sch.2 Part 1 paraH.4, substituted: SI 2013/1776 Sch.1
Sch.2 Part 1 paraA.5, substituted: SI 2013/1776 Sch.1
Sch.2 Part 1 paraB.5, substituted: SI 2013/1776 Sch.1
Sch.2 Part 1 paraE.5, substituted: SI 2013/1776 Sch.1
Sch.2 Part 1 paraH.5, substituted: SI 2013/1776 Sch.1
Sch.2 Part 1 paraA.6, substituted: SI 2013/1776 Sch.1
Sch.2 Part 1 paraB.6, substituted: SI 2013/1776 Sch.1
Sch.2 Part 1 paraH.6, substituted: SI 2013/1776 Sch.1
Sch.2 Part 1 paraA.7, substituted: SI 2013/1776 Sch.1
Sch.2 Part 1 paraA.8, substituted: SI 2013/1776 Sch.1
Sch.2 Part 2, applied: SI 2013/1102 Reg.2
Sch.2 Part 2 paraA.1, amended: SI 2013/1101 Art.5
Sch.2 Part 2 paraA.2, added: SI 2013/1101 Art.5
Sch.2 Part 3, applied: SI 2013/1102 Reg.2
Sch.2 Part 3, added: SI 2013/1101 Art.6
Sch.2 Part 3, applied: SI 2013/1102 Reg.2
Sch.2 Part 3, added: SI 2013/1101 Art.6
Sch.2 Part 3, applied: SI 2013/1102 Reg.2
Sch.2 Part 3, added: SI 2013/1101 Art.6
Sch.2 Part 3, applied: SI 2013/1102 Reg.2
Sch.2 Part 3, added: SI 2013/1101 Art.6
Sch.2 Part 3, applied: SI 2013/1102 Reg.2

Sch.2 Part 3, added: SI 2013/1101 Art.6
Sch.2 Part 3 paraB.1, amended: SI 2013/1101 Art.6
Sch.2 Part 4, applied: SI 2013/648 Sch.2 para.3
Sch.2 Part 4, added: SI 2013/1101 Art.7
Sch.2 Part 4, applied: SI 2013/1102 Reg.2
Sch.2 Part 4, added: SI 2013/1101 Art.7
Sch.2 Part 4, applied: SI 2013/1102 Reg.2
Sch.2 Part 4, added: SI 2013/1101 Art.7
Sch.2 Part 5, applied: SI 2013/648 Sch.2 para.3
Sch.2 Part 8, applied: SI 2013/1102 Reg.2
Sch.2 Part 8 paraA.1, amended: SI 2013/1101 Art.8
Sch.2 Part 8 paraA.2A, added: SI 2013/1101 Art.8
Sch.2 Part 14 paraA.1, amended: SI 2013/755 Sch.4 para.50
Sch.2 Part 15 paraA, amended: SI 2013/755 Sch.4 para.50
Sch.2 Part 15 paraA, substituted: SI 2013/755 Sch.4 para.50
Sch.2 Part 15 paraA.1, substituted: SI 2013/755 Sch.4 para.50
Sch.2 Part 15 paraA.2, substituted: SI 2013/755 Sch.4 para.50
Sch.2 Part 17, applied: SI 2013/648 Art.68, Art.82
Sch.2 Part 17 paraA, varied: SI 2013/648 Art.80
Sch.2 Part 17, disapplied: SI 2013/648 Art.80
Sch.2 Part 17 paraB, varied: SI 2013/648 Art.80
Sch.2 Part 17 paraC, varied: SI 2013/648 Art.80
Sch.2 Part 17, referred to: SI 2013/648 Art.80
Sch.2 Part 17 paraD, varied: SI 2013/648 Art.80
Sch.2 Part 17 paraE, varied: SI 2013/648 Art.80
Sch.2 Part 17 paraF, varied: SI 2013/648 Art.80
Sch.2 Part 17, varied: SI 2013/648 Art.80
Sch.2 Part 17 paraH, varied: SI 2013/648 Art.80
Sch.2 Part 17 paraI, varied: SI 2013/648 Art.80
Sch.2 Part 17 paraJ, varied: SI 2013/648 Art.80
Sch.2 Part 17 paraK, varied: SI 2013/648 Art.80
Sch.2 Part 17 paraA.1, varied: SI 2013/648 Art.80
Sch.2 Part 17 paraB.1, referred to: SI 2013/648 Art.80
Sch.2 Part 17 paraB.1, varied: SI 2013/648 Art.80
Sch.2 Part 17 paraE.1, varied: SI 2013/648 Art.80
Sch.2 Part 17 paraF.1, varied: SI 2013/648 Art.80
Sch.2 Part 17 paraH.1, varied: SI 2013/648 Art.80
Sch.2 Part 17 paraI.1, varied: SI 2013/648 Art.80
Sch.2 Part 17 paraJ.1, varied: SI 2013/648 Art.80
Sch.2 Part 17 paraA.2, varied: SI 2013/648 Art.80
Sch.2 Part 17 paraB.2, varied: SI 2013/648 Art.80
Sch.2 Part 17 paraE.2, varied: SI 2013/648 Art.80
Sch.2 Part 17 paraF.2, varied: SI 2013/648 Art.80
Sch.2 Part 24, applied: SI 2013/1102 Reg.2
Sch.2 Part 24 paraA.1, amended: SI 2013/1868 Art.2
Sch.2 Part 24 paraA.2, amended: SI 2013/1101 Art.9, SI 2013/1868 Art.2
Sch.2 Part 24 paraA.2, disapplied: SI 2013/1102 Reg.2
Sch.2 Part 24 paraA.3, amended: SI 2013/1101 Art.9, SI 2013/1868 Art.2
Sch.2 Part 24 paraA.3, applied: SI 2013/1102 Reg.2
Sch.2 Part 24 paraA.4, amended: SI 2013/1101 Art.9, SI 2013/1868 Art.2
Sch.2 Part 24 paraA.4A, added: SI 2013/1868 Art.2
Sch.2 Part 24 paraA.4B, added: SI 2013/1868 Art.2
Sch.2 Part 31 paraA.1, substituted: SI 2013/2147 Art.2
Sch.2 Part 31 paraB.1, added: SI 2013/2435 Art.2
Sch.2 Part 31 paraA.3, amended: SI 2013/2147 Art.2
Sch.2 Part 32, applied: SI 2013/1102 Reg.2
Sch.2 Part 32, added: SI 2013/1101 Art.10
Sch.2 Part 40, applied: SI 2013/1102 Reg.2
Sch.2 Part 41, applied: SI 2013/1102 Reg.2
Sch.2 Part 41 paraA.1, amended: SI 2013/1101 Art.11
Sch.2 Part 41 paraA.2A, added: SI 2013/1101 Art.11
Sch.2 Part 42, applied: SI 2013/1102 Reg.2
Sch.2 Part 42 paraA.1, amended: SI 2013/1101 Art.12
Sch.2 Part 42 paraA.2A, added: SI 2013/1101 Art.12
Sch.2 Part 43, applied: SI 2013/1102 Reg.2

539. Fresh Meat (Hygiene and Inspection) Regulations 1995

applied: SI 2013/2996 Sch.7 para.1

540. Poultry Meat, Farmed Game Bird Meat and Rabbit Meat (Hygiene and Inspection) Regulations 1995

applied: SI 2013/2996 Sch.7 para.1

572. Valuation Appeal Committee (Procedure in Appeals under the Valuation Acts) (Scotland) Regulations 1995

Reg.4, see *JD Wetherspoon v Assessor for Scottish Borders Council* [2013] R.V.R. 122 (Lands Tr (Scot)), J N Wright, QC
Reg.5, see *Coal Pension Properties Ltd v Assessor for Lanarkshire* [2013] R.V.R. 9 (Lands Tr (Scot)), J N Wright, QC
Reg.6, see *IKEA v Assessor for Lothian Valuation Joint Board* 2013 S.L.T. (Lands Tr) 53 (Lands Tr (Scot)), Lord McGhie

614. Animal By-Products (Identification) Regulations 1995

revoked (in part): SI 2013/2952 Reg.28, SSI 2013/307 Sch.3

644. National Health Service (Pharmaceutical Services) Amendment Regulations 1995
revoked: SI 2013/898 Sch.8 para.4

708. Pensions Increase (Review) Order 1995
applied: SI 2013/604 Sch.1

731. Welfare of Animals (Slaughter or Killing) Regulations 1995
applied: SI 2013/2216 Sch.1 para.12

734. Companies (Welsh Language Forms and Documents) (Amendment) Regulations 1995
revoked: SI 2013/1947 Sch.2 Part 1

736. Companies (Forms) (Amendment) Regulations 1995
revoked: SI 2013/1947 Sch.2 Part 1

738. Offshore Installations and Pipeline Works (Management and Administration) Regulations 1995
applied: SI 2013/1471 Reg.3

739. European Parliamentary (United Kingdom Representatives) Pensions (Additional Voluntary Contributions Scheme) (No.2) Order 1995
varied: SI 2013/2826 Art.3
Art.6, amended: SI 2013/472 Art.4
Art.9, amended: SI 2013/472 Art.4

755. Children (Northern Ireland) Order 1995
applied: SI 2013/1465 Art.14
Art.2, applied: SI 2013/3029 Sch.9 para.30
Art.2, referred to: SI 2013/3035 Sch.1
Art.12, applied: SSI 2013/193 Art.3
Art.15, applied: SI 2013/3029 Sch.9 para.30, SI 2013/3035 Sch.1
Art.33, applied: SSI 2013/99 Reg.5
Art.49, referred to: SI 2013/1465 Art.14
Art.50, applied: SSI 2013/99 Reg.5, Reg.6
Art.55, applied: SSI 2013/99 Reg.6
Art.70, amended: SI 2013/1465 Sch.1 para.13
Art.70, applied: SI 2013/1465 Art.10
Sch.1 para.17, applied: SI 2013/3029 Sch.9 para.30, SI 2013/3035 Sch.1

866. National Health Service (Injury Benefits) Regulations 1995
Reg.2, amended: SI 2013/413 Reg.82
Reg.2, revoked (in part): SI 2013/413 Reg.82
Reg.3, amended: SI 2013/413 Reg.83
Reg.4, amended: SI 2013/413 Reg.84
Reg.4A, amended: SI 2013/413 Reg.85
Reg.18A, amended: SI 2013/413 Reg.86
Reg.18B, added: SI 2013/413 Reg.87
Reg.21A, amended: SI 2013/413 Reg.88
Reg.21B, amended: SI 2013/413 Reg.89

1019. Local Government Pension Scheme Regulations 1995
Sch.A1, amended: SI 2013/472 Art.4
Sch.C4 para.23, amended: SI 2013/472 Art.4

1053. Personal and Occupational Pension Schemes (Pensions Ombudsman) (Procedure) Rules 1995
r.5, see *Pensions Ombudsman v EMC Europe Ltd* [2012] EWHC 3508 (Ch), [2013] I.C.R. 567 (Ch D), Briggs, J.

1268. Value Added Tax (Special Provisions) Order 1995
see *Pendragon Plc v Revenue and Customs Commissioners* [2013] EWCA Civ 868, [2013] B.V.C. 414 (CA (Civ Div)), Lloyd, L.J.

1371. Motor Vehicles (Off Road Events) Regulations 1995
applied: SI 2013/2494 Reg.2
Reg.3, amended: SI 2013/2494 Reg.4
Reg.4, applied: SI 2013/2494 Reg.3
Reg.5, amended: SI 2013/2494 Reg.5
Reg.5, applied: SI 2013/2494 Reg.3

1440. Extraction Solvents in Food (Amendment) Regulations 1995
revoked (in part): SI 2013/2210 Sch.5, SI 2013/2591 Sch.5, SSI 2013/266 Sch.5

1442. Credit Institutions (Protection of Depositors) Regulations 1995
Reg.2, amended: SI 2013/472 Art.4, Sch.2 para.12, SI 2013/3115 Sch.2 para.46
Reg.46, amended: SI 2013/472 Sch.2 para.12
Reg.49, amended: SI 2013/472 Sch.2 para.12

1479. Companies (Forms) (No.2) Regulations 1995
revoked: SI 2013/1947 Sch.2 Part 1

1480. Companies (Welsh Language Forms and Documents) (No.2) Regulations 1995
revoked: SI 2013/1947 Sch.2 Part 1

1508. Companies (Welsh Language Forms and Documents) (No.3) Regulations 1995
revoked: SI 2013/1947 Sch.2 Part 1

1614. Adoption (Designation of Overseas Adoptions) (Variation) (Scotland) Order 1995
revoked: SSI 2013/310 Reg.5

1755. Equine Viral Arteritis Order 1995
Art.3, amended: SSI 2013/173 Art.10
Art.4, amended: SSI 2013/173 Art.10
Art.6, amended: SSI 2013/173 Art.10
Sch.1 Part 1 para.3, amended: SSI 2013/173 Art.10
Sch.1 Part 1 para.5, amended: SSI 2013/173 Art.10
Sch.1 Part II para.7, amended: SSI 2013/173 Art.10

1945. Fees in the Registers of Scotland Order 1995
Art.2, amended: SSI 2013/147 Sch.1 para.3
Art.2, revoked (in part): SSI 2013/119 Sch.3 para.3
Sch.1 Part I paraA, amended: SSI 2013/119 Sch.3 para.3
Sch.1 Part II paraA, amended: SSI 2013/119 Sch.3 para.3

Sch.1 Part XI, revoked: SSI 2013/59 Art.2

1955. Bovine Offal (Prohibition) (England, Wales and Scotland) (Revocation) Regulations 1995

Reg.3, revoked (in part): SSI 2013/307 Sch.3
Sch.1, amended: SSI 2013/307 Sch.3

2262. Acquisition of Land (Rate of Interest after Entry) Regulations 1995

Reg.2, amended: SI 2013/472 Art.4

2294. Civil Aviation Authority (Economic Regulation of Airports) (Northern Ireland) Regulations 1995

revoked: SI 2013/610 Reg.2

2478. Bovine Embryo (Collection, Production and Transfer) Regulations 1995

applied: SI 2013/1240 Reg.9, SI 2013/1241 Reg.9, SSI 2013/151 Reg.9
Reg.13, applied: SI 2013/1240 Sch.6, SSI 2013/151 Sch.5
Reg.16, applied: SI 2013/1240 Sch.6, SI 2013/1241 Sch.5, SSI 2013/151 Sch.5
Reg.19, applied: SI 2013/1240 Sch.6, SI 2013/1241 Sch.5, SSI 2013/151 Sch.5

2479. Bovine Embryo (Collection, Production and Transfer) (Fees) Regulations 1995

revoked (in part): SI 2013/1240 Reg.11, SI 2013/1241 Reg.11, SSI 2013/151 Sch.7

2507. Motorways Traffic (Scotland) Regulations 1995

Reg.14, amended: SSI 2013/119 Sch.2 para.13

2518. Value Added Tax Regulations 1995

see *McAndrew Utilities Ltd v Revenue and Customs Commissioners* [2013] S.F.T.D. 608 (FTT (Tax)), Judge Jonathan Cannan; see *Systems Aluminium Ltd v Revenue and Customs Commissioners* [2013] UKFTT 201 (TC), [2013] S.F.T.D. 929 (FTT (Tax)), Judge J Gordon Reid Q.C.
Part XVII, amended: SI 2013/701 Reg.6
Reg.4B, amended: SI 2013/701 Reg.4
Reg.14, see *McAndrew Utilities Ltd v Revenue and Customs Commissioners* [2013] S.F.T.D. 608 (FTT (Tax)), Judge Jonathan Cannan
Reg.29, see *Our Communications Ltd v Revenue and Customs Commissioners* [2013] S.F.T.D. 55 (FTT (Tax)), Judge Greg Sinfield
Reg.35, see *R. (on the application of Capital Accommodation (London) Ltd (In Liquidation)) v Revenue and Customs Commissioners* [2013] S.T.C. 303 (UT (Tax)), Sales, J.
Reg.37, see *Taylor Clark Leisure Plc v Revenue and Customs Commissioners* [2013] UKFTT 792 (TC), [2013] S.F.T.D. 381 (FTT (Tax)), Judge J Gordon Reid Q.C.
Reg.43C, see *Systems Aluminium Ltd v Revenue and Customs Commissioners* [2013] UKFTT 201 (TC), [2013] S.F.T.D. 929 (FTT (Tax)), Judge J Gordon Reid Q.C.
Reg.103, see *South African Tourist Board v Revenue and Customs Commissioners* [2013] UKFTT 780 (TC), [2013] S.F.T.D. 508 (FTT (Tax)), Judge Barbara Mosedale
Reg.111, see *Cambrian Hydro Power Ltd v Revenue and Customs Commissioners* [2013] S.F.T.D. 302 (FTT (Tax)), Sir Stephen Oliver Q.C.; see *Noor v Revenue and Customs Commissioners* [2013] UKUT 71 (TCC), [2013] S.T.C. 998 (UT (Tax)), Warren, J (President)
Reg.129, amended: SI 2013/2241 Reg.3
Reg.135, amended: SI 2013/2241 Reg.4
Reg.137, amended: SI 2013/3211 Reg.3
Reg.146, substituted: SI 2013/701 Reg.5
Reg.147, substituted: SI 2013/701 Reg.5
Reg.148, amended: SI 2013/701 Reg.6
Reg.148, substituted: SI 2013/701 Reg.5
Reg.148A, added: SI 2013/701 Reg.7
Reg.148A, substituted: SI 2013/701 Reg.5
Reg.149, substituted: SI 2013/701 Reg.5
Reg.150, substituted: SI 2013/701 Reg.5
Reg.151, substituted: SI 2013/701 Reg.5
Reg.152, substituted: SI 2013/701 Reg.5
Reg.153, substituted: SI 2013/701 Reg.5
Reg.154, substituted: SI 2013/701 Reg.5
Reg.155, substituted: SI 2013/701 Reg.5
Reg.198, see *Our Communications Ltd v Revenue and Customs Commissioners* [2013] S.F.T.D. 55 (FTT (Tax)), Judge Greg Sinfield
Reg.199, see *Our Communications Ltd v Revenue and Customs Commissioners* [2013] S.F.T.D. 55 (FTT (Tax)), Judge Greg Sinfield

2562. Local Authorities (Precepts) (Wales) Regulations 1995

Reg.8, amended: SI 2013/472 Art.4

2705. Jobseekers (Northern Ireland) Order 1995

Part II, applied: SI 2013/480 Reg.6, SI 2013/628 Sch.1 para.22

2791. Acquisition of Land (Rate of Interest after Entry) (Scotland) Regulations 1995

Reg.2, amended: SI 2013/472 Art.4

2800. National Health Service Litigation Authority (Establishment and Constitution) Order 1995

Art.1, amended: SI 2013/295 Art.2
Art.3, amended: SI 2013/295 Art.3
Art.4, substituted: SI 2013/295 Art.4
Art.5, revoked: SI 2013/295 Art.6
Art.6, added: SI 2013/295 Art.5
Art.7, added: SI 2013/295 Art.5

2801. National Health Service Litigation Authority Regulations 1995

Reg.1, amended: SI 2013/235 Sch.2 para.26

Reg.7, amended: SI 2013/235 Sch.2 para.26

2803. National Park Authorities (Wales) Order 1995

Art.9, amended: SI 2013/755 Sch.4 para.52
Art.13, amended: SI 2013/755 Sch.4 para.52
Sch.3 para.6, amended: SI 2013/755 Sch.4 para.52
Sch.3 para.9, amended: SI 2013/755 Sch.4 para.52

2814. Teachers Superannuation (Additional Voluntary Contributions) (Scotland) Regulations 1995

Reg.9, amended: SI 2013/472 Art.4

2869. Goods Vehicles (Licensing of Operators) Regulations 1995

Reg.4, amended: SI 2013/1644 Sch.2
Reg.5, amended: SI 2013/1644 Sch.2
Reg.6, amended: SI 2013/1644 Sch.2
Reg.7, amended: SI 2013/1644 Sch.2
Reg.8, amended: SI 2013/1644 Sch.2
Reg.9, amended: SI 2013/1644 Sch.2
Reg.11, amended: SI 2013/1644 Sch.2
Reg.13, amended: SI 2013/1644 Sch.2
Reg.14, amended: SI 2013/1644 Sch.2
Reg.15, amended: SI 2013/1644 Sch.2
Reg.18, amended: SI 2013/1644 Sch.2
Reg.19, amended: SI 2013/1644 Sch.2
Reg.21, amended: SI 2013/1644 Sch.2
Reg.22, amended: SI 2013/1644 Sch.2
Reg.23, amended: SI 2013/1644 Sch.2
Reg.24, amended: SI 2013/1644 Sch.2
Reg.25, amended: SI 2013/1644 Sch.2
Reg.27, amended: SI 2013/1644 Sch.2
Reg.28, amended: SI 2013/1644 Sch.2
Reg.29, amended: SI 2013/1644 Sch.2
Reg.30, amended: SI 2013/1644 Sch.2
Reg.31, amended: SI 2013/1644 Sch.2
Reg.35, amended: SI 2013/1644 Sch.2
Sch.1 para.2, amended: SI 2013/1644 Sch.2
Sch.2 para.2, amended: SI 2013/1644 Sch.2
Sch.3 Part I para.6, amended: SI 2013/602 Sch.2 para.73
Sch.3 Part I para.23A, added: SI 2013/1750 Reg.2
Sch.3 Part I para.30, added: SI 2013/1753 Reg.4
Sch.4 para.1, amended: SI 2013/1644 Sch.2
Sch.4 para.5, amended: SI 2013/1644 Sch.2
Sch.4 para.6, amended: SI 2013/1644 Sch.2
Sch.4 para.8, amended: SI 2013/1644 Sch.2

2880. Sale of Registration Marks Regulations 1995

see *Tanjoukian v Revenue and Customs Commissioners* [2013] S.T.C. 825 (UT (Tax)), Henderson, J.

2908. Public Service Vehicles (Operators Licences) Regulations 1995

Reg.3, amended: SI 2013/1865 Reg.13
Reg.4, amended: SI 2013/1644 Sch.2
Reg.5, amended: SI 2013/1644 Sch.2
Reg.7, amended: SI 2013/1865 Reg.13
Reg.8, substituted: SI 2013/1644 Sch.2
Reg.9, amended: SI 2013/1644 Sch.2
Reg.13, amended: SI 2013/1644 Sch.2
Reg.14, amended: SI 2013/1644 Sch.2
Reg.15, amended: SI 2013/1644 Sch.2
Reg.16, amended: SI 2013/1644 Sch.2
Reg.17, amended: SI 2013/1644 Sch.2
Reg.19, amended: SI 2013/1644 Sch.2
Reg.20, amended: SI 2013/1644 Sch.2

2914. Consumer Credit (Exempt Agreements) (Amendment) (No.2) Order 1995

revoked (in part): SI 2013/1881 Art.21

2922. Animal Health Orders (Divisional Veterinary Manager Amendment) Order 1995

revoked (in part): SSI 2013/173 Art.27

2994. Road Traffic (Northern Ireland) Order 1995

Art.25, amended: SI 2013/3021 Art.2

3000. Goods Vehicles (Licensing of Operators) (Fees) Regulations 1995

Reg.3, amended: SI 2013/1644 Sch.2

3019. National Park Authorities (Levies) (Wales) Regulations 1995

Reg.9, amended: SI 2013/472 Art.4

3163. Reporting of Injuries, Diseases and Dangerous Occurrences Regulations 1995

revoked: SI 2013/1471 Sch.4

3186. Agricultural Wages Committees (Areas) (England) Order 1995

revoked: 2013 c.24 Sch.20 para.2

3213. Pensions (Northern Ireland) Order 1995

Art.49, amended: SI 2013/472 Art.4
Art.75, see *Pensions Regulator v Desmond* [2013] NICA 62 (CA (NI)), Morgan, L.C.J

1996

90. London Ambulance Service National Health Service Trust (Establishment) Order 1996

Art.1, amended: SI 2013/593 Art.2

207. Jobseeker's Allowance Regulations 1996

applied: SI 2013/276 Reg.6
Reg.1, amended: SI 2013/235 Sch.2 para.27, SI 2013/276 Reg.8, SI 2013/388 Sch.1 para.16, SI 2013/443 Reg.4, SI 2013/591 Sch.1 para.10, SI 2013/630 Reg.30, SI 2013/2536 Reg.6
Reg.1, applied: SI 2013/3029 Sch.6 para.31
Reg.1, revoked (in part): SI 2013/2536 Reg.6
Reg.1, substituted: SI 2013/630 Reg.30
Reg.4, amended: SI 2013/602 Sch.2 para.74, SI 2013/2536 Reg.6
Reg.14, amended: SI 2013/276 Reg.14
Reg.14A, amended: SI 2013/2722 Reg.2

Reg.17A, referred to: SI 2013/3029 Sch.6 para.19, Sch.6 para.30, SI 2013/3035 Sch.1
Reg.19, applied: SI 2013/3029 Sch.6 para.19, SI 2013/3035 Sch.1
Reg.19, referred to: SI 2013/3029 Sch.6 para.19, SI 2013/3035 Sch.1
Reg.24A, amended: SI 2013/458 Sch.1
Reg.25, amended: SI 2013/276 Reg.14, SI 2013/443 Reg.4
Reg.26, amended: SI 2013/443 Reg.4
Reg.45B, amended: SI 2013/2536 Reg.6
Reg.47, varied: SI 2013/983 Art.13
Reg.51, see *Saunderson v Secretary of State for Work and Pensions* 2013 S.L.T. 115 (IH (Ex Div)), Lord Eassie
Reg.51, amended: SI 2013/388 Sch.1 para.16, SI 2013/591 Sch.1 para.10
Reg.53, amended: SI 2013/276 Reg.14, SI 2013/602 Sch.2 para.74, SI 2013/2536 Reg.6
Reg.53, revoked (in part): SI 2013/2536 Reg.6
Reg.55, amended: SI 2013/2536 Reg.6
Reg.67, amended: SI 2013/443 Reg.4
Reg.69, applied: SI 2013/386 Reg.32, Reg.33, SI 2013/983 Art.17, Art.18, Art.19
Reg.69A, applied: SI 2013/386 Reg.32, Reg.33, SI 2013/983 Art.17, Art.18, Art.19
Reg.69B, amended: SI 2013/443 Reg.4
Reg.69B, applied: SI 2013/386 Reg.32, Reg.33, SI 2013/983 Art.17, Art.18, Art.19
Reg.70A, amended: SI 2013/443 Reg.4
Reg.74B, applied: SI 2013/386 Reg.32
Reg.75, amended: SI 2013/443 Reg.4
Reg.75, referred to: SI 2013/3029 Sch.6 para.19, Sch.6 para.30, SI 2013/3035 Sch.1
Reg.76, amended: SI 2013/630 Reg.30
Reg.79, amended: SI 2013/574 Art.21, SI 2013/2536 Reg.6
Reg.83, referred to: SI 2013/574 Art.22
Reg.84, referred to: SI 2013/574 Art.22
Reg.85, referred to: SI 2013/574 Art.22
Reg.85A, amended: SI 2013/1474 Reg.3, SI 2013/2536 Reg.6, SI 2013/3196 Reg.2
Reg.85A, revoked (in part): SI 2013/2536 Reg.6
Reg.94, amended: SI 2013/2536 Reg.6
Reg.96, amended: SI 2013/630 Reg.30
Reg.98, amended: SI 2013/2536 Reg.6
Reg.101, amended: SI 2013/2536 Reg.6
Reg.102, substituted: SI 2013/2536 Reg.6
Reg.103, amended: SI 2013/630 Reg.30
Reg.105, amended: SI 2013/276 Reg.9
Reg.113, amended: SI 2013/276 Reg.10
Reg.113, applied: SI 2013/3029 Sch.1 para.29, Sch.6 para.31, SI 2013/3035 Sch.1
Reg.114, amended: SI 2013/458 Sch.2 para.3
Reg.117, amended: SI 2013/443 Reg.4
Reg.140, amended: SI 2013/388 Sch.1 para.16, SI 2013/443 Reg.4, SI 2013/591 Sch.1 para.10
Reg.145, referred to: SI 2013/574 Sch.12
Reg.146A, amended: SI 2013/388 Sch.1 para.16, SI 2013/591 Sch.1 para.10
Reg.146G, referred to: SI 2013/574 Sch.12
Reg.153, amended: SI 2013/630 Reg.30
Reg.163, amended: SI 2013/2536 Reg.6
Reg.172, amended: SI 2013/574 Art.23
Sch.A1 para.3, amended: SI 2013/388 Sch.1 para.16, SI 2013/591 Sch.1 para.10
Sch.1 Part I para.1, referred to: 2013 c.16 Sch.1 para.1
Sch.1 Part I para.1, substituted: SI 2013/574 Sch.9
Sch.1 Part I para.2, substituted: SI 2013/574 Sch.9
Sch.1 Part II para.4, referred to: SI 2013/574 Art.22
Sch.1 Part III para.8, amended: SI 2013/388 Sch.1 para.16, SI 2013/591 Sch.1 para.10
Sch.1 Part III para.14, amended: SI 2013/388 Sch.1 para.16, SI 2013/591 Sch.1 para.10
Sch.1 Part III para.15, amended: SI 2013/388 Sch.1 para.16, SI 2013/591 Sch.1 para.10
Sch.1 Part III para.15A, amended: SI 2013/388 Sch.1 para.16, SI 2013/591 Sch.1 para.10
Sch.1 Part III para.15A, referred to: SI 2013/574 Art.22
Sch.1 Part III para.16, amended: SI 2013/388 Sch.1 para.16, SI 2013/591 Sch.1 para.10
Sch.1 Part III para.16, referred to: SI 2013/574 Art.22
Sch.1 Part IV, substituted: SI 2013/574 Sch.10
Sch.1 Part IVA para.20D, amended: SI 2013/388 Sch.1 para.16, SI 2013/591 Sch.1 para.10
Sch.1 Part IVA para.20H, amended: SI 2013/388 Sch.1 para.16, SI 2013/591 Sch.1 para.10
Sch.1 Part IVA para.20I, amended: SI 2013/388 Sch.1 para.16, SI 2013/591 Sch.1 para.10
Sch.1 Part IVA para.20IA, amended: SI 2013/388 Sch.1 para.16, SI 2013/591 Sch.1 para.10
Sch.1 Part IVB para.20M, substituted: SI 2013/574 Sch.11
Sch.2 para.1, amended: SI 2013/630 Reg.30
Sch.2 para.3, amended: SI 2013/443 Reg.4
Sch.2 para.5, referred to: SI 2013/574 Sch.12
Sch.2 para.6, applied: SI 2013/386 Reg.29
Sch.2 para.6, referred to: SI 2013/574 Sch.12
Sch.2 para.7, applied: SI 2013/386 Reg.29
Sch.2 para.7, referred to: SI 2013/574 Sch.12
Sch.2 para.9, referred to: SI 2013/574 Sch.12
Sch.2 para.10, referred to: SI 2013/574 Sch.12
Sch.2 para.11, referred to: SI 2013/574 Sch.12
Sch.2 para.13, applied: SI 2013/386 Reg.29

Sch.2 para.14, applied: SI 2013/386 Reg.29
Sch.2 para.15, applied: SI 2013/386 Reg.29
Sch.2 para.16, applied: SI 2013/386 Reg.29
Sch.2 para.17, amended: SI 2013/388 Sch.1 para.16, SI 2013/443 Reg.4, SI 2013/574 Art.22, SI 2013/591 Sch.1 para.10, SI 2013/630 Reg.30
Sch.5 para.4, referred to: SI 2013/574 Sch.12
Sch.5 para.14, referred to: SI 2013/574 Sch.12
Sch.5A para.3, referred to: SI 2013/574 Sch.12
Sch.6 para.9, amended: SI 2013/602 Sch.2 para.74, SI 2013/2536 Reg.6
Sch.6 para.9, revoked (in part): SI 2013/2536 Reg.6
Sch.7 paraA.3, added: SI 2013/276 Reg.11
Sch.7 para.7, amended: SI 2013/388 Sch.1 para.16
Sch.7 para.8, amended: SI 2013/630 Reg.30
Sch.7 para.10, amended: SI 2013/388 Sch.1 para.16
Sch.7 para.28, amended: SI 2013/235 Sch.2 para.27
Sch.7 para.28, revoked (in part): SI 2013/235 Sch.2 para.27
Sch.7 para.33A, added: SI 2013/443 Reg.4
Sch.7 para.45, amended: SI 2013/443 Reg.4
Sch.7 para.51, revoked: SI 2013/458 Sch.1
Sch.7 para.72A, added: SI 2013/591 Sch.1 para.10
Sch.8 paraA.3, added: SI 2013/276 Reg.12
Sch.8 para.12, amended: SI 2013/630 Reg.30
Sch.8 para.12, applied: SI 2013/3029 Sch.5 para.22, SI 2013/3035 Sch.1
Sch.8 para.23A, added: SI 2013/443 Reg.4
Sch.8 para.35, amended: SI 2013/443 Reg.4

221. Police (Promotion) (Scotland) Regulations 1996
applied: SSI 2013/39 Sch.2 para.1, Sch.2 para.2, Sch.2 para.3
revoked: SSI 2013/39 Sch.1
Reg.2, applied: SSI 2013/39 Sch.2 para.4
Reg.4, applied: SSI 2013/39 Sch.2 para.4

240. Drivers Hours (Passenger and Goods Vehicles) (Exemption) Regulations 1996
revoked (in part): SI 2013/2987 Sch.3

251. National Health Service (Clinical Negligence Scheme) Regulations 1996
Reg.1, amended: SI 2013/497 Reg.2
Reg.3, amended: SI 2013/497 Reg.3
Reg.3, revoked (in part): SI 2013/497 Reg.3
Reg.4, amended: SI 2013/497 Reg.4
Reg.7, amended: SI 2013/497 Reg.5
Reg.8, amended: SI 2013/497 Reg.6
Reg.9, amended: SI 2013/497 Reg.7

266. European Communities (Designation) Order 1996
Sch.1, amended: SI 2013/755 Sch.4 para.53

275. Gas (Northern Ireland) Order 1996
Art.2, amended: 2013 c.24 Sch.6 para.159
Art.15, amended: 2013 c.24 Sch.6 para.160
Art.15A, amended: 2013 c.24 Sch.6 para.161
Art.16, amended: 2013 c.24 Sch.6 para.162
Art.17, amended: 2013 c.24 Sch.6 para.163, Sch.6 para.164
Art.17A, amended: 2013 c.24 Sch.6 para.164
Art.18, amended: 2013 c.24 Sch.6 para.165
Art.23, amended: 2013 c.24 Sch.15 para.54
Art.32, amended: 2013 c.24 Sch.6 para.166
Art.32, revoked (in part): 2013 c.24 Sch.6 para.166

282. Merchant Shipping (Prevention of Pollution) (Law of the Sea Convention) Order 1996
Art.2, enabled: SI 2013/3042

293. Fossil Fuel Levy (Scotland) Regulations 1996
Reg.25, amended: SI 2013/472 Art.4

301. A282 Trunk Road (Dartford East Tunnel) (Weight Restriction) Order 1996
disapplied: SI 2013/3125 Art.7
varied: SI 2013/976 Art.6

417. A33 and A34 Trunk Roads (Winnall to Kings Worthy) (50 and 60 Miles Per Hour speed Limits) Order 1996
revoked: SI 2013/2636 Art.4

508. Environmental Licences (Suspension and Revocation) Regulations 1996
Reg.3, amended: SI 2013/755 Sch.4 para.54

513. Act of Adjournal (Criminal Procedure Rules) 1996
Sch.2 Appendix, amended: SSI 2013/72 Sch.1 Part 1, Sch.1 Part 2, Sch.1 Part 3, SSI 2013/196 r.2, r.3, SSI 2013/198 r.2, r.4, r.5
Sch.2 Appendix, substituted: SSI 2013/198 r.5
Sch.2 Part V para.20_19, amended: SSI 2013/198 r.2
Sch.2 Part VI, amended: SSI 2013/72 r.3
Sch.2 Part VI para.23A_1, amended: SSI 2013/72 r.3
Sch.2 Part VII, substituted: SSI 2013/72 r.4
Sch.2 Part VII para.40_12, amended: SSI 2013/198 r.3
Sch.2 Part VII para.40_13, amended: SSI 2013/198 r.3
Sch.2 para.15.15, see *Singh (Sukhdev) v HM Advocate* [2013] HCJAC 69, 2013 S.C.C.R. 337 (HCJ), The Lord Justice Clerk (Carloway)

551. Gas Safety (Management) Regulations 1996
Reg.7, amended: SI 2013/1471 Sch.4

594. Companies (Forms) (Amendment) Regulations 1996
revoked: SI 2013/1947 Sch.2 Part 1

595. Companies (Welsh Language Forms and Documents) Regulations 1996
revoked: SI 2013/1947 Sch.2 Part 1

686. National Health Service (Existing Liabilities Scheme) Regulations 1996

Reg.3, revoked (in part): SI 2013/235 Sch.2 para.28

698. National Health Service (Pharmaceutical Services) Amendment Regulations 1996

revoked: SI 2013/898 Sch.8 para.5

701. National Health Service (Appointment of Consultants) Regulations 1996

Reg.2, amended: SI 2013/235 Sch.2 para.29
Reg.5, amended: SI 2013/235 Sch.2 para.29
Sch.1 para.2, revoked (in part): SI 2013/235 Sch.2 para.29

705. National Health Service (General Ophthalmic Services) Amendment Regulations 1996

revoked (in part): SI 2013/365 Reg.28

729. Trade Marks Act 1994 (Isle of Man) Order 1996

revoked: SI 2013/2601 Art.3

752. Gas (Extent of Domestic Supply Licences) Order 1996

revoked: SI 2013/2174 Art.2

800. Pensions Increase (Review) Order 1996

applied: SI 2013/604 Sch.1

825. Pipelines Safety Regulations 1996

Reg.13A, applied: SI 2013/805 Sch.1, SI 2013/806 Sch.1, SI 2013/807 Sch.1, SI 2013/808 Sch.1, SI 2013/809 Sch.1, SI 2013/810 Sch.1, SI 2013/811 Sch.1, SI 2013/812 Sch.1, SI 2013/813 Sch.1, SI 2013/814 Sch.1
Sch.6 Part II para.1, revoked: SI 2013/448 Sch.1
Sch.6 Part II para.2, revoked: SI 2013/448 Sch.1
Sch.6 Part II para.3, revoked: SI 2013/448 Sch.1
Sch.6 Part II para.4, revoked: SI 2013/448 Sch.1
Sch.6 Part II para.5, revoked: SI 2013/448 Sch.1

913. Offshore Installations and Wells (Design and Construction, etc.) Regulations 1996

Reg.9, amended: SI 2013/1471 Sch.4

1005. Sheriff Court Districts (Alteration of Boundaries) Order 1996

Sch.1, amended: SSI 2013/152 Art.4, Art.5, Art.6, Art.7, Art.8, Art.9, Art.10, Art.11, Art.12, Art.13

1023. Employment Protection (Continuity of Employment of National Health Service Employees) (Modification) Order 1996

Art.1, amended: SI 2013/235 Sch.2 para.30

1076. Statutory Nuisance (Appeals) (Scotland) Regulations 1996

Reg.2, see *Safdar and A&N Brothers (A Partnership) v Falkirk Council* 2013 S.L.T. (Sh Ct) 127 (Sh Ct (Tayside) (Falkirk)), Sheriff J K Mundy

1105. Companies (Principal Business Activities) (Amendment) Regulations 1996

revoked: SI 2013/1947 Sch.2 Part 1

1132. Passenger Car Fuel Consumption (Amendment) Order 1996

revoked (in part): SI 2013/2986 Sch.3

1172. Occupational Pension Schemes (Contracting-out) Regulations 1996

applied: SI 2013/1893 Sch.2
Reg.1, referred to: SI 2013/2356 Reg.97
Reg.3, amended: SI 2013/2734 Sch.9 para.2
Reg.42, amended: SI 2013/459 Reg.3
Reg.60, applied: SSI 2013/174 Reg.17, Reg.21

1299. Proceeds of Crime (Northern Ireland) Order 1996

Art.49, amended: 2013 c.22 Sch.8 para.53
Sch.2 para.3A, amended: 2013 c.22 Sch.8 para.54

1313. National Health Service (Appointment of Consultants) (Wales) Regulations 1996

Reg.5, amended: SI 2013/235 Sch.2 para.31

1445. Consumer Credit (Exempt Agreements) (Amendment) Order 1996

revoked (in part): SI 2013/1881 Art.21

1462. Contracting-out (Transfer and Transfer Payment) Regulations 1996

Reg.1, amended: SI 2013/459 Reg.4
Reg.4, amended: SI 2013/459 Reg.4
Reg.7, amended: SI 2013/459 Reg.4
Reg.9, amended: SI 2013/459 Reg.4

1499. Food Labelling Regulations 1996

Reg.2, amended: SI 2013/2210 Reg.20, SI 2013/2591 Reg.20, SI 2013/3235 Reg.6, SSI 2013/266 Reg.18
Reg.4, amended: SI 2013/3235 Reg.6
Reg.17A, added: SI 2013/2750 Sch.15 para.1, SI 2013/2775 Sch.15 para.1, SSI 2013/305 Sch.15 para.1
Reg.35, applied: SI 2013/2750 Reg.15, SI 2013/2775 Reg.15, SSI 2013/305 Reg.15
Reg.36, applied: SI 2013/2750 Reg.15, SI 2013/2775 Reg.15, SSI 2013/305 Reg.15
Reg.38, applied: SI 2013/2750 Reg.15, SI 2013/2775 Reg.15, SSI 2013/305 Reg.15
Reg.43, amended: SI 2013/3235 Reg.6
Reg.44, see *Torfaen CBC v Douglas Willis Ltd* [2013] UKSC 59, [2013] 4 All E.R. 1 (SC), Lady Hale (Deputy President)
Reg.45, amended: SI 2013/3235 Reg.6
Reg.50, amended: SI 2013/466 Reg.2, SI 2013/545 Reg.2
Sch.3 Part I, amended: SI 2013/3235 Reg.6

1513. Health and Safety (Consultation with Employees) Regulations 1996

applied: SI 2013/1893 Sch.2, SI 2013/3104 Sch.2 para.30
Reg.5, amended: SI 2013/1471 Sch.4

1527. Landfill Tax Regulations 1996

Reg.21, amended: SI 2013/755 Sch.4 para.55
Reg.31, amended: SI 2013/658 Reg.3
Reg.33, amended: SI 2013/658 Reg.4

1642. Police (Conduct) (Scotland) Regulations 1996
applied: SSI 2013/35 Reg.11, SSI 2013/60 Sch.2 para.3, Sch.2 para.4
referred to: SSI 2013/60 Sch.2 para.5, Sch.2 para.6, Sch.2 para.7
see *C v Chief Constable of Strathclyde* [2013] CSOH 65, 2013 S.L.T. 699 (OH), Lord Drummond Young
Reg.1, revoked: SSI 2013/60 Sch.2 para.2
Reg.2, revoked: SSI 2013/60 Sch.2 para.2
Reg.3, revoked: SSI 2013/60 Sch.2 para.2
Reg.3, varied: SSI 2013/60 Sch.2 para.10
Reg.4, revoked: SSI 2013/60 Sch.2 para.2
Reg.4, varied: SSI 2013/60 Sch.2 para.10
Reg.5, applied: SSI 2013/60 Sch.2 para.3, Sch.2 para.6
Reg.5, revoked: SSI 2013/60 Sch.2 para.2
Reg.5, varied: SSI 2013/60 Sch.2 para.10
Reg.6, applied: SSI 2013/60 Sch.2 para.3
Reg.6, revoked: SSI 2013/60 Sch.2 para.2
Reg.6, varied: SSI 2013/60 Sch.2 para.10
Reg.6, see *C v Chief Constable of Strathclyde* [2013] CSOH 65, 2013 S.L.T. 699 (OH), Lord Drummond Young
Reg.7, revoked: SSI 2013/60 Sch.2 para.2
Reg.7, varied: SSI 2013/60 Sch.2 para.10
Reg.7A, applied: SSI 2013/60 Sch.2 para.3
Reg.7A, revoked: SSI 2013/60 Sch.2 para.2
Reg.7A, varied: SSI 2013/60 Sch.2 para.10
Reg.8, revoked: SSI 2013/60 Sch.2 para.2
Reg.8, varied: SSI 2013/60 Sch.2 para.10
Reg.9, revoked: SSI 2013/60 Sch.2 para.2
Reg.9, varied: SSI 2013/60 Sch.2 para.10
Reg.10, revoked: SSI 2013/60 Sch.2 para.2
Reg.10, varied: SSI 2013/60 Sch.2 para.10
Reg.11, revoked: SSI 2013/60 Sch.2 para.2
Reg.11, varied: SSI 2013/60 Sch.2 para.10
Reg.12, revoked: SSI 2013/60 Sch.2 para.2
Reg.12, varied: SSI 2013/60 Sch.2 para.10
Reg.13, applied: SSI 2013/60 Sch.2 para.3
Reg.13, revoked: SSI 2013/60 Sch.2 para.2
Reg.13, varied: SSI 2013/60 Sch.2 para.10
Reg.14, revoked: SSI 2013/60 Sch.2 para.2
Reg.14, varied: SSI 2013/60 Sch.2 para.10
Reg.15, revoked: SSI 2013/60 Sch.2 para.2
Reg.16, revoked: SSI 2013/60 Sch.2 para.2
Reg.17, applied: SSI 2013/60 Sch.2 para.3
Reg.17, revoked: SSI 2013/60 Sch.2 para.2
Reg.17, varied: SSI 2013/60 Sch.2 para.10
Reg.18, applied: SSI 2013/60 Sch.2 para.8
Reg.18, revoked: SSI 2013/60 Sch.2 para.2
Reg.18, varied: SSI 2013/60 Sch.2 para.10
Reg.19, revoked: SSI 2013/60 Sch.2 para.2
Reg.19, varied: SSI 2013/60 Sch.2 para.10
Reg.20, applied: SSI 2013/60 Sch.2 para.3
Reg.20, referred to: SSI 2013/60 Sch.2 para.3
Reg.20, revoked: SSI 2013/60 Sch.2 para.2
Reg.20, varied: SSI 2013/60 Sch.2 para.10
Reg.21, applied: SSI 2013/60 Sch.2 para.3
Reg.21, revoked: SSI 2013/60 Sch.2 para.2
Reg.21, varied: SSI 2013/60 Sch.2 para.10
Reg.22, applied: SSI 2013/60 Sch.2 para.9
Reg.22, revoked: SSI 2013/60 Sch.2 para.2
Reg.22, varied: SSI 2013/60 Sch.2 para.10
Reg.23, applied: SSI 2013/60 Sch.2 para.5
Reg.23, revoked: SSI 2013/60 Sch.2 para.2
Reg.24, applied: SSI 2013/60 Reg.7
Reg.24, revoked: SSI 2013/60 Sch.2 para.2
Reg.24, varied: SSI 2013/60 Sch.2 para.10
Reg.25, amended: SSI 2013/60 Sch.2 para.2
Reg.25, referred to: SSI 2013/60 Sch.2 para.2
Sch.1 para.1, revoked: SSI 2013/60 Sch.2 para.2
Sch.1 para.2, revoked: SSI 2013/60 Sch.2 para.2
Sch.1 para.3, revoked: SSI 2013/60 Sch.2 para.2
Sch.1 para.4, revoked: SSI 2013/60 Sch.2 para.2
Sch.1 para.5, revoked: SSI 2013/60 Sch.2 para.2
Sch.1 para.6, revoked: SSI 2013/60 Sch.2 para.2
Sch.1 para.7, revoked: SSI 2013/60 Sch.2 para.2
Sch.1 para.8, revoked: SSI 2013/60 Sch.2 para.2
Sch.1 para.9, revoked: SSI 2013/60 Sch.2 para.2
Sch.2, referred to: SSI 2013/60 Sch.2 para.2

1643. Police (Efficiency) (Scotland) Regulations 1996
applied: SSI 2013/35 Reg.11
referred to: SSI 2013/61 Sch.1 para.4, Sch.1 para.5, Sch.1 para.6, Sch.1 para.7
revoked: SSI 2013/61 Sch.1 para.2
Reg.2, applied: SSI 2013/61 Sch.1 para.5
Reg.2, varied: SSI 2013/61 Sch.1 para.10
Reg.3, applied: SSI 2013/61 Sch.1 para.3
Reg.3, varied: SSI 2013/61 Sch.1 para.10
Reg.4, varied: SSI 2013/61 Sch.1 para.10
Reg.5, varied: SSI 2013/61 Sch.1 para.10
Reg.6, applied: SSI 2013/61 Sch.1 para.3
Reg.8, varied: SSI 2013/61 Sch.1 para.10
Reg.9, varied: SSI 2013/61 Sch.1 para.10
Reg.10, applied: SSI 2013/61 Sch.1 para.3
Reg.10, varied: SSI 2013/61 Sch.1 para.10
Reg.12, applied: SSI 2013/61 Sch.1 para.3
Reg.12, varied: SSI 2013/61 Sch.1 para.10
Reg.13, varied: SSI 2013/61 Sch.1 para.10
Reg.14, applied: SSI 2013/61 Sch.1 para.7
Reg.14, varied: SSI 2013/61 Sch.1 para.10
Reg.15, varied: SSI 2013/61 Sch.1 para.10
Reg.16, applied: SSI 2013/61 Sch.1 para.3
Reg.16, varied: SSI 2013/61 Sch.1 para.10

Reg.17, applied: SSI 2013/61 Sch.1 para.8, Sch.1 para.9
Reg.17, referred to: SSI 2013/61 Sch.1 para.3
Reg.17, varied: SSI 2013/61 Sch.1 para.10
Reg.18, applied: SSI 2013/61 Sch.1 para.3, Sch.1 para.8
Reg.18, varied: SSI 2013/61 Sch.1 para.10
Reg.19, applied: SSI 2013/61 Sch.1 para.3
Reg.19, varied: SSI 2013/61 Sch.1 para.10
Reg.20, varied: SSI 2013/61 Sch.1 para.10
Reg.21, applied: SSI 2013/61 Sch.1 para.3

1644. Police Appeals Tribunals (Scotland) Rules 1996
applied: SSI 2013/63 Sch.1 para.3, SSI 2013/119 Art.2, SSI 2013/121 Art.12
disapplied: SSI 2013/63 Sch.1 para.2
revoked: SSI 2013/63 Sch.1 para.5
r.1, applied: SSI 2013/119 Art.2
r.1, varied: SSI 2013/63 Sch.1 para.3
r.2, varied: SSI 2013/63 Sch.1 para.3
r.3, varied: SSI 2013/63 Sch.1 para.3
r.5, varied: SSI 2013/63 Sch.1 para.3
r.16, varied: SSI 2013/63 Sch.1 para.3
r.19, varied: SSI 2013/63 Sch.1 para.3

1655. Occupational Pension Schemes (Disclosure of Information) Regulations 1996
applied: SI 2013/1893 Sch.2
revoked: SI 2013/2734 Reg.1
Reg.5, applied: SI 2013/2356 Reg.17

1678. Deregulation (Model Appeal Provisions) Order 1996
Sch.1 Part I para.6, revoked (in part): SI 2013/2042 Sch.1 para.47
Sch.1 Part I para.37, revoked: SI 2013/2042 Sch.1 para.47

1685. Police (Promotion) Regulations 1996
Sch.1 para.5, amended: SI 2013/1780 Reg.2

1715. Occupational Pension Schemes (Scheme Administration) Regulations 1996
Reg.1, amended: SI 2013/472 Art.4
Reg.15, amended: SI 2013/472 Art.4
Reg.16, amended: SI 2013/2556 Reg.2

1847. Occupational Pension Schemes (Transfer Values) Regulations 1996
applied: SSI 2013/174 Reg.6
Reg.2, amended: SI 2013/459 Reg.6
Reg.11, amended: SI 2013/2734 Sch.9 para.3
Sch.1 para.3, amended: SI 2013/472 Sch.2 para.14

1880. Local Authorities (Contracting Out of Tax Billing, Collection and Enforcement Functions) Order 1996
applied: SI 2013/501 Reg.3, SI 2013/588 Reg.3
Art.2, amended: SI 2013/502 Art.2, SI 2013/695 Art.2
Art.3, amended: SI 2013/502 Art.2, SI 2013/695 Art.2
Art.12, amended: SI 2013/502 Art.2, SI 2013/695 Art.2
Art.13A, added: SI 2013/502 Art.2, SI 2013/695 Art.2
Art.13B, added: SI 2013/502 Art.2, SI 2013/695 Art.2
Art.19, amended: SI 2013/502 Art.2, SI 2013/695 Art.2

1898. Welsh Language Schemes (Public Bodies) Order 1996
Sch.1, amended: SI 2013/755 Sch.4 para.56

1921. Industrial Tribunals (Northern Ireland) Order 1996
Art.3, applied: SI 2013/1506 Reg.27

1975. Occupational Pension Schemes (Requirement to obtain Audited Accounts and a Statement from the Auditor) Regulations 1996
Reg.2, amended: SI 2013/2734 Sch.9 para.4
Sch.1 para.5, amended: SI 2013/2734 Sch.9 para.4
Sch.1 para.5A, added: SI 2013/2734 Sch.9 para.4

2128. Merchant Shipping (Prevention of Pollution) (Limits) Regulations 1996
revoked: SI 2013/3042 Reg.2

2186. Goods Vehicles (Licensing of Operators) (Temporary Use in Great Britain) Regulations 1996
Sch.6 Part I, amended: SI 2013/1644 Sch.2

2256. Social Landlords (Permissible Additional Purposes or Objects) Order 1996
Art.2, amended: SI 2013/472 Art.4

2282. Teachers Superannuation (Provision of Information and Administrative Expenses etc.) Regulations 1996
Reg.3, amended: SI 2013/472 Sch.2 para.15

2320. National Health Service (General Ophthalmic Services) Amendment (No.2) Regulations 1996
revoked (in part): SI 2013/365 Reg.28

2349. Employment Protection (Recoupment of Benefits) Regulations 1996
amended: SI 2013/630 Reg.50
Reg.1, amended: SI 2013/630 Reg.50
Reg.2, amended: SI 2013/630 Reg.50
Reg.4, amended: SI 2013/630 Reg.50
Reg.8, amended: SI 2013/630 Reg.50
Reg.10, amended: SI 2013/630 Reg.50

2424. National Health Service Pension Scheme (Provision of Information and Administrative Expenses etc.) Regulations 1996
Reg.3, amended: SI 2013/472 Sch.2 para.16
Reg.5, amended: SI 2013/472 Sch.2 para.16

2447. Advice and Assistance (Scotland) Regulations 1996

see *Donaldson v Scottish Legal Aid Board* 2013 S.L.T. 35 (OH), Lord Drummond Young
Reg.2, amended: SSI 2013/142 Reg.4, SSI 2013/200 Reg 4
Reg.4, amended: SSI 2013/137 Reg.9
Reg.6, amended: SSI 2013/200 Reg.4
Reg.8B, see *Donaldson v Scottish Legal Aid Board* 2013 S.L.T. 35 (OH), Lord Drummond Young
Reg.16, amended: SSI 2013/65 Reg.4, SSI 2013/137 Reg.9, SSI 2013/142 Reg.4, SSI 2013/250 Reg.2
Sch.2 para.4A, amended: SSI 2013/200 Reg.4
Sch.2 para.5, amended: SSI 2013/137 Reg.9, SSI 2013/142 Reg.4
Sch.3 Part I para.1, amended: SSI 2013/144 Reg.2, SSI 2013/250 Reg.2
Sch.3 Part II para.1, amended: SSI 2013/144 Reg.2, SSI 2013/250 Reg.2

2459. A47 Trunk Road (Walpole Highway/Tilney High End Bypass, Norfolk) (24 Hours Clearway) Order 1996
revoked: SI 2013/394 Sch.1 Part II

2475. Personal and Occupational Pension Schemes (Pensions Ombudsman) Regulations 1996
Reg.4, amended: SI 2013/627 Reg.7
Reg.4, revoked (in part): SI 2013/627 Reg.7
Reg.6, amended: SI 2013/472 Art.4

2555. Criminal Legal Aid (Scotland) Regulations 1996
Reg.4, amended: SI 2013/7 Art.16

2628. Specified Diseases (Notification) Order 1996
Art.2, amended: SSI 2013/173 Art.11
Art.5, amended: SSI 2013/173 Art.11
Sch.1 Part I, amended: SI 2013/1662 Reg.40

2714. Greater Manchester (Light Rapid Transit System) (Eccles Extension) Order 1996
Art.20, applied: SI 2013/2587 Art.39
Art.35, applied: SI 2013/2587 Art.39
Art.37, applied: SI 2013/2587 Art.39
Art.40, applied: SI 2013/2587 Art.39
Art.41, applied: SI 2013/2587 Art.39
Art.42, applied: SI 2013/2587 Art.39
Art.43, applied: SI 2013/2587 Art.39
Art.44, applied: SI 2013/2587 Art.39
Art.45, applied: SI 2013/2587 Art.39
Art.46, applied: SI 2013/2587 Art.39
Art.47, applied: SI 2013/2587 Art.39

2745. Social Security Benefit (Computation of Earnings) Regulations 1996
Reg.2, amended: SI 2013/235 Sch.2 para.32
Reg.7, applied: SI 2013/574 Art.6
Sch.1 para.7, amended: SI 2013/235 Sch.2 para.32
Sch.1 para.9, amended: SI 2013/602 Sch.2 para.75, SI 2013/2536 Reg.7
Sch.1 para.9, revoked (in part): SI 2013/2536 Reg.7
Sch.2 para.8, amended: SI 2013/388 Sch.1 para.17, SI 2013/458 Sch.1, SI 2013/591 Sch.1 para.12
Sch.2 para.8, revoked (in part): SI 2013/458 Sch.1

2794. National Park Authorities (Levies) (England) Regulations 1996
Reg.8, amended: SI 2013/472 Art.4

2798. Civil Aviation (Investigation of Air Accidents and Incidents) Regulations 1996
applied: SI 2013/1471 Reg.14

2803. Employment Tribunals (Interest on Awards in Discrimination Cases) Regulations 1996
Reg.3, amended: SI 2013/1669 Reg.2
Reg.8, revoked: SI 2013/1669 Reg.3

2890. Housing Renewal Grants Regulations 1996
Reg.2, amended: SI 2013/235 Sch.2 para.33, SI 2013/276 Reg.8, SI 2013/388 Sch.1 para.18, SI 2013/458 Sch.1, SI 2013/552 Reg.2, SI 2013/591 Sch.1 para.11, SI 2013/630 Reg.57, SI 2013/1788 Reg.5, SI 2013/3138 Reg.2
Reg.10, amended: SI 2013/552 Reg.2, SI 2013/630 Reg.57, SI 2013/1788 Reg.5
Reg.10, revoked (in part): SI 2013/458 Sch.1, SI 2013/552 Reg.2
Reg.11, amended: SI 2013/630 Reg.57, SI 2013/1788 Reg.5
Reg.19, amended: SI 2013/388 Sch.1 para.18, SI 2013/552 Reg.2, SI 2013/591 Sch.1 para.11, SI 2013/630 Reg.57, SI 2013/1788 Reg.5, SI 2013/3138 Reg.2
Reg.26, amended: SI 2013/235 Sch.2 para.33
Reg.31, amended: SI 2013/276 Reg.9, SI 2013/630 Reg.57, SI 2013/1788 Reg.5
Reg.38, amended: SI 2013/276 Reg.10
Sch.1 Part III para.12, amended: SI 2013/388 Sch.1 para.18, SI 2013/552 Reg.2, SI 2013/591 Sch.1 para.11, SI 2013/3138 Reg.2
Sch.1 Part III para.13, amended: SI 2013/388 Sch.1 para.18, SI 2013/552 Reg.2, SI 2013/591 Sch.1 para.11, SI 2013/3138 Reg.2
Sch.1 Part III para.13A, amended: SI 2013/388 Sch.1 para.18, SI 2013/552 Reg.2, SI 2013/591 Sch.1 para.11, SI 2013/3138 Reg.2
Sch.1 Part III para.14, amended: SI 2013/388 Sch.1 para.18, SI 2013/552 Reg.2, SI 2013/591 Sch.1 para.11, SI 2013/3138 Reg.2
Sch.1 Part III para.15, amended: SI 2013/388 Sch.1 para.18, SI 2013/552 Reg.2, SI 2013/591 Sch.1 para.11, SI 2013/3138 Reg.2
Sch.1A Part III para.7, amended: SI 2013/388 Sch.1 para.18, SI 2013/552 Reg.2, SI 2013/591 Sch.1 para.11, SI 2013/3138 Reg.2

Sch.1A Part III para.8, amended: SI 2013/591 Sch.1 para.11, SI 2013/3138 Reg.2
Sch.1A Part III para.8, substituted: SI 2013/388 Sch.1 para.18, SI 2013/552 Reg.2
Sch.1A Part III para.9, amended: SI 2013/388 Sch.1 para.18, SI 2013/552 Reg.2, SI 2013/591 Sch.1 para.11, SI 2013/3138 Reg.2
Sch.2 para.12, amended: SI 2013/458 Sch.1, SI 2013/552 Reg.2
Sch.3 paraA.3, added: SI 2013/276 Reg.11
Sch.3 para.4, amended: SI 2013/458 Sch.1, SI 2013/552 Reg.2
Sch.3 para.5, amended: SI 2013/388 Sch.1 para.18, SI 2013/552 Reg.2, SI 2013/591 Sch.1 para.11, SI 2013/3138 Reg.2
Sch.3 para.24, amended: SI 2013/235 Sch.2 para.33
Sch.3 para.24, revoked (in part): SI 2013/235 Sch.2 para.33
Sch.3 para.49, revoked (in part): SI 2013/458 Sch.1, SI 2013/552 Reg.2
Sch.4 paraA.3, added: SI 2013/276 Reg.12
Sch.4 para.6, amended: SI 2013/458 Sch.1, SI 2013/552 Reg.2
Sch.4 para.45, revoked (in part): SI 2013/458 Sch.1, SI 2013/552 Reg.2

2907. Child Support Departure Direction and Consequential Amendments Regulations 1996
Reg.1, amended: SI 2013/630 Reg.42
Reg.9, amended: SI 2013/630 Reg.42
Reg.12, amended: SI 2013/458 Sch.2 para.4, SI 2013/630 Reg.42
Reg.15, amended: SI 2013/388 Sch.1 para.19, SI 2013/591 Sch.1 para.13
Reg.18, amended: SI 2013/1517 Reg.5

2971. Control of Pollution (Applications, Appeals and Registers) Regulations 1996
Reg.1, amended: SI 2013/755 Sch.4 para.58
Reg.8, amended: SI 2013/755 Sch.4 para.58
Reg.11, amended: SI 2013/755 Sch.4 para.58
Reg.12, amended: SI 2013/755 Sch.4 para.59
Reg.13, amended: SI 2013/755 Sch.4 para.60
Reg.15, amended: SI 2013/755 Sch.4 para.60
Reg.16, amended: SI 2013/755 Sch.4 para.60
Reg.17, amended: SI 2013/755 Sch.4 para.60

2991. Insurance Companies (Reserves) (Tax) Regulations 1996
Reg.2, amended: SI 2013/472 Sch.2 para.17
Reg.8A, amended: SI 2013/472 Sch.2 para.17
Reg.8A, revoked (in part): SI 2013/472 Sch.2 para.17

3001. Surface Waters (Abstraction for Drinking Water) (Classification) Regulations 1996
Reg.4, amended: SI 2013/755 Sch.4 para.62
Reg.5, amended: SI 2013/755 Sch.4 para.62
Reg.6, amended: SI 2013/755 Sch.4 para.62
Reg.7, amended: SI 2013/755 Sch.4 para.62

3030. Chemical Weapons (Licence Appeal Provisions) Order 1996
revoked: SI 2013/1129 Art.2

3061. Code of Practice on Environmental Procedures for Flood Defence Operating Authorities (Environment Agency and Natural Resources Body for Wales) Approval Order 1996
amended: SI 2013/755 Sch.4 para.64
Art.1, amended: SI 2013/755 Sch.4 para.64
Art.2, amended: SI 2013/755 Sch.4 para.65

3081. Consumer Credit (Exempt Agreements) (Amendment) (No.2) Order 1996
revoked (in part): SI 2013/1881 Art.21

3126. Occupational Pension Schemes (Winding Up) Regulations 1996
Reg.2, applied: SI 2013/2734 Reg.24
Reg.6, amended: SI 2013/459 Reg.5
Reg.7, amended: SI 2013/2734 Sch.9 para.5
Reg.11, amended: SI 2013/2734 Sch.9 para.5

3147. Employment Protection (Continuity of Employment) Regulations 1996
Reg.2, amended: SI 2013/1956 Sch.1 para.1

3195. Social Security (Child Maintenance Bonus) Regulations 1996
Reg.14, revoked (in part): SI 2013/458 Sch.1

3255. Secure Accommodation (Scotland) Regulations 1996
applied: SSI 2013/205 Reg.14, Reg.15
revoked: SSI 2013/205 Reg.16
Reg.5, applied: SSI 2013/205 Reg.5
Reg.6, applied: SSI 2013/150 Art.28
Reg.7, applied: SSI 2013/150 Art.29
Reg.9, applied: SSI 2013/150 Art.30
Reg.13, applied: SSI 2013/205 Reg.14
Reg.14, applied: SSI 2013/205 Reg.14
Reg.15, applied: SSI 2013/205 Reg.14

3256. Residential Establishments Child Care (Scotland) Regulations 1996
Reg.2, amended: SSI 2013/147 Sch.1 para.4
Reg.9, amended: SSI 2013/119 Sch.2 para.14

3260. Children's Hearing (Transmission of Information etc.) (Scotland) Regulations 1996
applied: SI 2013/1465 Art.4
revoked: SI 2013/1465 Sch.2 Part 2, SSI 2013/149 Reg.10

3261. Children's Hearings (Scotland) Rules 1996
Part II r.3, applied: SSI 2013/121 Art.15
Part IV, applied: SSI 2013/121 Art.15

3267. Children (Reciprocal Enforcement of Prescribed Orders etc (England and Wales and Northern Ireland)) (Scotland) Regulations 1996

Reg.1, amended: SI 2013/1465 Sch.1 para.14
Reg.2, revoked: SI 2013/1465 Sch.1 para.14
Reg.3, revoked: SI 2013/1465 Sch.1 para.14
Reg.4, amended: SI 2013/1465 Sch.1 para.14
Reg.4, revoked (in part): SI 2013/1465 Sch.1 para.14
Reg.4, substituted: SI 2013/1465 Sch.1 para.14
Reg.5, amended: SI 2013/1465 Sch.1 para.14
Reg.5, revoked (in part): SI 2013/1465 Sch.1 para.14
Reg.5, substituted: SI 2013/1465 Sch.1 para.14
Sch.1, revoked: SI 2013/1465 Sch.1 para.14
Sch.2, revoked: SI 2013/1465 Sch.1 para.14
Sch.3, revoked: SI 2013/1465 Sch.1 para.14
Sch.4, amended: SI 2013/1465 Sch.1 para.14
Sch.5, amended: SI 2013/1465 Sch.1 para.14

3275. Gas (Extent of Domestic Supply Licences) (Amendment) Order 1996
revoked: SI 2013/2174 Art.2

1997

194. Assured Tenancies and Agricultural Occupancies (Forms) Regulations 1997
Reg.3, amended: SI 2013/1036 Sch.2 para.14
Sch.1, amended: SI 2013/630 Reg.69, SI 2013/1036 Sch.2 para.15, Sch.2 para.16, Sch.2 para.17

211. Consumer Credit (Quotations) (Revocation) Regulations 1997
revoked (in part): SI 2013/1881 Art.21

265. Life Assurance and Other Policies (Keeping of Information and Duties of Insurers) Regulations 1997
Reg.2, amended: SI 2013/1820 Reg.6
Reg.3, amended: SI 2013/1820 Reg.6
Reg.9, amended: SI 2013/1820 Reg.6

291. Act of Sederunt (Child Care and Maintenance Rules) 1997
Part 1 r.1.2, amended: SSI 2013/172 Art.2
Part 3, revoked: SSI 2013/172 Art.3
Part 3, substituted: SSI 2013/172 Art.3
Part 3, added: SSI 2013/172 Art.3
Part 3, substituted: SSI 2013/172 Art.3
Part 3, added: SSI 2013/172 Art.3
Part 3, substituted: SSI 2013/172 Art.3
Part 3 r.3.1, amended: SSI 2013/172 Art.3
Part 3 r.3.1, substituted: SSI 2013/172 Art.3
Part 3 r.3.2, substituted: SSI 2013/172 Art.3
Part 3 r.3.3, substituted: SSI 2013/172 Art.3
Part 3 r.3.3A, substituted: SSI 2013/172 Art.3
Part 3 r.3.4, amended: SSI 2013/172 Art.3
Part 3 r.3.4, revoked (in part): SSI 2013/172 Art.3
Part 3 r.3.4, substituted: SSI 2013/172 Art.3
Part 3 r.3.5, amended: SSI 2013/172 Art.3
Part 3 r.3.5, substituted: SSI 2013/172 Art.3
Part 3 r.3.5A, added: SSI 2013/172 Art.3
Part 3 r.3.5A, substituted: SSI 2013/172 Art.3
Part 3 r.3.6, amended: SSI 2013/172 Art.3
Part 3 r.3.6, substituted: SSI 2013/172 Art.3
Part 3 r.3.7, amended: SSI 2013/172 Art.3
Part 3 r.3.7, substituted: SSI 2013/172 Art.3
Part 3 r.3.8, amended: SSI 2013/172 Art.3
Part 3 r.3.8, substituted: SSI 2013/172 Art.3
Part 3 r.3.9, substituted: SSI 2013/172 Art.3
Part 3 r.3.10, revoked: SSI 2013/172 Art.3
Part 3 r.3.10, substituted: SSI 2013/172 Art.3
Part 3 r.3.11, amended: SSI 2013/172 Art.3
Part 3 r.3.11, substituted: SSI 2013/172 Art.3
Part 3 r.3.12, amended: SSI 2013/172 Art.3
Part 3 r.3.12, revoked (in part): SSI 2013/172 Art.3
Part 3 r.3.12, substituted: SSI 2013/172 Art.3
Part 3 r.3.13, amended: SSI 2013/172 Art.3
Part 3 r.3.13, substituted: SSI 2013/172 Art.3
Part 3 r.3.14, amended: SSI 2013/172 Art.3
Part 3 r.3.14, substituted: SSI 2013/172 Art.3
Part 3 r.3.15, substituted: SSI 2013/172 Art.3
Part 3 r.3.16, amended: SSI 2013/172 Art.3
Part 3 r.3.16, substituted: SSI 2013/172 Art.3
Part 3 r.3.17, amended: SSI 2013/172 Art.3
Part 3 r.3.17, substituted: SSI 2013/172 Art.3
Part 3 r.3.18, substituted: SSI 2013/172 Art.3
Part 3 r.3.19, substituted: SSI 2013/172 Art.3
Part 3 r.3.20, substituted: SSI 2013/172 Art.3
Part 3 r.3.21, substituted: SSI 2013/172 Art.3
Part 3 r.3.22, substituted: SSI 2013/172 Art.3
Part 3 r.3.23, substituted: SSI 2013/172 Art.3
Part 3 r.3.24, substituted: SSI 2013/172 Art.3
Part 3 r.3.25, amended: SSI 2013/172 Art.3
Part 3 r.3.25, substituted: SSI 2013/172 Art.3
Part 3 r.3.26, substituted: SSI 2013/172 Art.3
Part 3 r.3.27, amended: SSI 2013/172 Art.3
Part 3 r.3.27, substituted: SSI 2013/172 Art.3
Part 3 r.3.28, substituted: SSI 2013/172 Art.3
Part 3 r.3.29, amended: SSI 2013/172 Art.3
Part 3 r.3.29, substituted: SSI 2013/172 Art.3
Part 3 r.3.30, substituted: SSI 2013/172 Art.3
Part 3 r.3.31, amended: SSI 2013/172 Art.3
Part 3 r.3.31, substituted: SSI 2013/172 Art.3
Part 3 r.3.32, amended: SSI 2013/172 Art.3
Part 3 r.3.32, substituted: SSI 2013/172 Art.3
Part 3 r.3.33, amended: SSI 2013/172 Art.3
Part 3 r.3.33, substituted: SSI 2013/172 Art.3
Part 3 r.3.34, amended: SSI 2013/172 Art.3
Part 3 r.3.34, substituted: SSI 2013/172 Art.3
Part 3 r.3.35, substituted: SSI 2013/172 Art.3
Part 3 r.3.36, amended: SSI 2013/172 Art.3
Part 3 r.3.36, substituted: SSI 2013/172 Art.3

Part 3 r.3.37, substituted: SSI 2013/172 Art.3
Part 3 r.3.38, amended: SSI 2013/172 Art.3
Part 3 r.3.38, substituted: SSI 2013/172 Art.3
Part 3 r.3.39, substituted: SSI 2013/172 Art.3
Part 3 r.3.40, amended: SSI 2013/172 Art.3
Part 3 r.3.40, substituted: SSI 2013/172 Art.3
Part 3 r.3.41, substituted: SSI 2013/172 Art.3
Part 3 r.3.42, substituted: SSI 2013/172 Art.3
Part 3 r.3.43, substituted: SSI 2013/172 Art.3
Part 3 r.3.44, amended: SSI 2013/172 Art.3
Part 3 r.3.44, substituted: SSI 2013/172 Art.3
Part 3 r.3.45, amended: SSI 2013/172 Art.3
Part 3 r.3.45, substituted: SSI 2013/172 Art.3
Part 3 r.3.46, amended: SSI 2013/172 Art.3
Part 3 r.3.46, substituted: SSI 2013/172 Art.3
Part 3 r.3.46A, added: SSI 2013/172 Art.3
Part 3 r.3.46A, substituted: SSI 2013/172 Art.3
Part 3 r.3.47, amended: SSI 2013/172 Art.3
Part 3 r.3.47, substituted: SSI 2013/172 Art.3
Part 3 r.3.48, amended: SSI 2013/172 Art.3
Part 3 r.3.48, substituted: SSI 2013/172 Art.3
Part 3 r.3.49, amended: SSI 2013/172 Art.3
Part 3 r.3.49, substituted: SSI 2013/172 Art.3
Part 3 r.3.50, amended: SSI 2013/172 Art.3
Part 3 r.3.50, substituted: SSI 2013/172 Art.3
Part 3 r.3.51, amended: SSI 2013/172 Art.3
Part 3 r.3.51, substituted: SSI 2013/172 Art.3
Part 3 r.3.52, substituted: SSI 2013/172 Art.3
Part 3 r.3.53, amended: SSI 2013/172 Art.3
Part 3 r.3.53, substituted: SSI 2013/172 Art.3
Part 3 r.3.54, amended: SSI 2013/172 Art.3
Part 3 r.3.54, substituted: SSI 2013/172 Art.3
Part 3 r.3.55, amended: SSI 2013/172 Art.3
Part 3 r.3.55, substituted: SSI 2013/172 Art.3
Part 3 r.3.56, amended: SSI 2013/172 Art.3
Part 3 r.3.56, substituted: SSI 2013/172 Art.3
Part 3 r.3.57, amended: SSI 2013/172 Art.3
Part 3 r.3.57, substituted: SSI 2013/172 Art.3
Part 3 r.3.58, amended: SSI 2013/172 Art.3
Part 3 r.3.58, substituted: SSI 2013/172 Art.3
Part 3 r.3.58A, substituted: SSI 2013/172 Art.3
Part 3 r.3.58B, substituted: SSI 2013/172 Art.3
Part 3 r.3.59, amended: SSI 2013/172 Art.3
Part 3 r.3.59, substituted: SSI 2013/172 Art.3
Part 3 r.3.60, amended: SSI 2013/172 Art.3
Part 3 r.3.60, substituted: SSI 2013/172 Art.3
Part 3 r.3.61, substituted: SSI 2013/172 Art.3
Part 3 r.3.61A, added: SSI 2013/172 Art.3
Part 3 r.3.61A, substituted: SSI 2013/172 Art.3
Part 3 r.3.62, substituted: SSI 2013/172 Art.3
Part 3 r.3.63, amended: SSI 2013/172 Art.3
Part 3 r.3.63, substituted: SSI 2013/172 Art.3
Part 3 r.3.64, revoked: SSI 2013/172 Art.3
Part 3 r.3.64, substituted: SSI 2013/172 Art.3
Part 3 r.3.64A, substituted: SSI 2013/172 Art.3
Part 3 r.3.64B, substituted: SSI 2013/172 Art.3
Part 3 r.3.64C, substituted: SSI 2013/172 Art.3
Part 3 r.3.65, amended: SSI 2013/172 Art.3
Part 3 r.3.65, substituted: SSI 2013/172 Art.3
Part 3 r.3.66, amended: SSI 2013/172 Art.3
Part 3 r.3.66, substituted: SSI 2013/172 Art.3
Part 3 r.3.67, substituted: SSI 2013/172 Art.3
Part 3 r.3.68, amended: SSI 2013/172 Art.3
Part 3 r.3.68, substituted: SSI 2013/172 Art.3
Part 3 r.3.69, substituted: SSI 2013/172 Art.3
Part 3 r.3.69A, substituted: SSI 2013/172 Art.3
Part 3 r.3.69B, amended: SSI 2013/172 Art.3
Part 3 r.3.69B, substituted: SSI 2013/172 Art.3
Part 3 r.3.69C, substituted: SSI 2013/172 Art.3
Part 3 r.3.70, substituted: SSI 2013/172 Art.3
Part 3 r.3.71, amended: SSI 2013/172 Art.3
Part 3 r.3.71, substituted: SSI 2013/172 Art.3
Part 3 r.3.72, substituted: SSI 2013/172 Art.3
Part 3 r.3.73, substituted: SSI 2013/172 Art.3
Part 3 r.3.74, substituted: SSI 2013/172 Art.3
Part 3 r.3.75, amended: SSI 2013/172 Art.3
Part 3 r.3.75, substituted: SSI 2013/172 Art.3
Part 3 r.3.76, amended: SSI 2013/172 Art.3
Part 3 r.3.76, substituted: SSI 2013/172 Art.3
Part 3 r.3.76A, substituted: SSI 2013/172 Art.3
Part 3 r.3.77, substituted: SSI 2013/172 Art.3
Part 3 r.3.78, substituted: SSI 2013/172 Art.3
Part 3 r.3.78, amended: SSI 2013/172 Art.3
Part 3 r.3.78, substituted: SSI 2013/172 Art.3
Part 3 r.3.79, substituted: SSI 2013/172 Art.3
Part 3 r.3.79, amended: SSI 2013/172 Art.3
Part 3 r.3.79, substituted: SSI 2013/172 Art.3
Part 3 r.3.80, substituted: SSI 2013/172 Art.3
Part 3 r.3.81, substituted: SSI 2013/172 Art.3
Part 3 r.3.81A, added: SSI 2013/172 Art.3
Part 3 r.3.81A, substituted: SSI 2013/172 Art.3
Sch.1, added: SSI 2013/172 Art.4
Sch.1, amended: SSI 2013/135 r.5, SSI 2013/172 Art.4, Sch.1
Sch.1, substituted: SSI 2013/172 Art.4

316. Independent Qualified Conveyancers (Scotland) Regulations 1997

Reg.2, amended: SI 2013/472 Art.4

317. Executry Practitioners (Scotland) Regulations 1997

Reg.2, amended: SI 2013/472 Art.4

319. Local Authorities (Capital Finance) Regulations 1997

Reg.16, applied: SI 2013/3104 Reg.8

420. Town and Country Planning (Determination of Appeals by Appointed Persons) (Prescribed Classes) Regulations 1997

Reg.3, amended: SI 2013/2146 Sch.1 para.2

506. Merchant Shipping (Prevention of Pollution) (Limits) Regulations 1997
revoked: SI 2013/3042 Reg.2

540. Residuary Body for Wales (Dyffryn House and Gardens) Order 1997
Art.2, amended: SI 2013/472 Art.4

553. Railway Safety (Miscellaneous Provisions) Regulations 1997
Reg.3, revoked (in part): SI 2013/1666 Art.2

634. Pensions Increase (Review) Order 1997
applied: SI 2013/604 Sch.1

639. Animals (Third Country Imports) (Charges) Regulations 1997
revoked (in part): SI 2013/1240 Reg.11, SI 2013/1241 Reg.11, SSI 2013/151 Sch.7

640. Leasehold Reform (Notices) Regulations 1997
Sch.1, amended: SI 2013/1036 Sch.2 para.18

687. Sheriff Court Fees Order 1997
Art.7, amended: SSI 2013/137 Reg.10

688. Court of Session etc Fees Order 1997
Art.5, amended: SSI 2013/137 Reg.11

690. Legal Aid (Scotland) (Children) Regulations 1997
applied: SSI 2013/150 Art.2
revoked: SSI 2013/150 Art.27

729. Reporters (Appeals against Dismissal) (Scotland) Regulations 1997
referred to: SSI 2013/150 Art.22

784. Occupational Pension Schemes (Discharge of Liability) Regulations 1997
Reg.2, amended: SI 2013/472 Art.4
Reg.6, amended: SI 2013/2734 Sch.9 para.6

785. Occupational Pension Schemes (Assignment, Forfeiture, Bankruptcy etc.) Regulations 1997
Reg.2, applied: SSI 2013/174 Reg.6

818. National Health Service (Optical Charges and Payments) Regulations 1997
applied: SI 2013/461 Reg.28
referred to: SI 2013/461 Reg.28
revoked (in part): SI 2013/461 Sch.4
Reg.1, amended: SI 2013/543 Reg.2, SI 2013/684 Reg.6
Reg.6, applied: SI 2013/461 Reg.28
Reg.8, amended: SI 2013/684 Reg.6
Reg.9, applied: SI 2013/461 Reg.28
Reg.10, applied: SI 2013/461 Reg.28
Reg.11, applied: SI 2013/461 Reg.28
Reg.12, applied: SI 2013/543 Reg.5
Reg.16, applied: SI 2013/461 Reg.28
Reg.17, applied: SI 2013/543 Reg.5
Reg.19, amended: SI 2013/543 Reg.3
Reg.20, applied: SI 2013/461 Reg.28
Sch.1, amended: SI 2013/543 Reg.4
Sch.2 para.1, amended: SI 2013/543 Reg.4
Sch.2 para.2, amended: SI 2013/543 Reg.4
Sch.3, substituted: SI 2013/543 Sch.1

826. Gas (Extent of Domestic Supply Licences) Order 1997
revoked: SI 2013/2174 Art.2

829. Farm Woodland Premium Scheme 1997
Art.6, amended: SI 2013/1036 Sch.2 para.59

869. Race Relations (Northern Ireland) Order 1997
Part II, applied: 2013 c.22 Sch.4 para.4
Art.32, applied: 2013 c.22 Sch.4 para.4
Art.54A, amended: 2013 c.18 Sch.2 para.10

980. National Health Service (Indicative Amounts) Regulations 1997
Reg.1, amended: SI 2013/898 Sch.7 para.2

1152. Dangerous Dogs (Fees) Order 1997
revoked (in part): SI 2013/1302 Art.3, SSI 2013/178 Art.2

1160. Hedgerows Regulations 1997
applied: SI 2013/586 Art.15
Sch.1 Part II para.6, amended: SI 2013/755 Sch.4 para.66

1183. Social Security (Recovery of Benefits) (Northern Ireland) Order 1997
Sch.1 Part I para.5, amended: SI 2013/472 Art.4

1331. Surface Waters (Fishlife) (Classification) Regulations 1997
Reg.4, amended: SI 2013/755 Sch.4 para.68
Reg.5, amended: SI 2013/755 Sch.4 para.69
Reg.6, amended: SI 2013/755 Sch.4 para.70
Sch.1 Part I, amended: SI 2013/755 Sch.4 para.71

1332. Surface Waters (Shellfish) (Classification) Regulations 1997
Reg.4, amended: SI 2013/755 Sch.4 para.73
Reg.5, amended: SI 2013/755 Sch.4 para.74
Reg.6, amended: SI 2013/755 Sch.4 para.75

1413. Miscellaneous Food Additives (Amendment) Regulations 1997
revoked (in part): SSI 2013/266 Sch.5

1612. Local Government Pension Scheme Regulations 1997
Sch.5A para.1, amended: SI 2013/472 Sch.2 para.18

1682. Satellite Television Service Regulations 1997
Reg.3, amended: SI 2013/2217 Reg.9
Sch.1 para.14, revoked: SI 2013/2217 Reg.9

1729. Animals and Animal Products (Examination for Residues and Maximum Residue Limits) Regulations 1997
applied: SSI 2013/84 Sch.1
disapplied: SI 2013/264 Sch.1
referred to: SI 2013/479 Sch.1
Reg.2, amended: SI 2013/804 Reg.2
Reg.2, revoked (in part): SI 2013/804 Reg.2
Reg.7, substituted: SI 2013/804 Reg.2

Reg.9, amended: SI 2013/804 Reg.2
Reg.15, amended: SI 2013/804 Reg.2
Reg.16, amended: SI 2013/804 Reg.2
Reg.20, amended: SI 2013/804 Reg.2
Reg.22, amended: SI 2013/804 Reg.2
Reg.34, amended: SI 2013/804 Reg.2
Reg.35, revoked (in part): SSI 2013/84 Sch.4
Reg.37, added: SI 2013/804 Reg.2

1750. Fishery Limits Order 1997
revoked: SI 2013/3163 Art.2

1829. Firemen's Pensions (Provision of Information) Regulations 1997
Reg.3, amended: SI 2013/472 Sch.2 para.19

1854. Rent Assessment Committee (England and Wales) (Leasehold Valuation Tribunal) (Amendment) Regulations 1997
Reg.1A, added: SI 2013/1036 Sch.2 para.19

1898. Family Law Act 1996 (Modifications of Enactments) Order 1997
Art.2, revoked: 2013 c.22 Sch.10 para.99

1908. Police (Property) Regulations 1997
Reg.3, amended: SI 2013/2318 Sch.1 para.31
Reg.6, amended: SI 2013/2318 Sch.1 para.32
Reg.8, amended: SI 2013/2318 Sch.1 para.33

1912. Police Pensions (Provision of Information) Regulations 1997
Reg.3, amended: SI 2013/472 Sch.2 para.20

1984. Rent Officers (Housing Benefit Functions) Order 1997
see *R. (on the application of Zacchaeus 2000 Trust) v Secretary of State for Work and Pensions* [2013] EWCA Civ 1202, [2013] P.T.S.R. 1427 (CA (Civ Div)), Sullivan, L.J.; see *R. (on the application of Zacchaeus 2000 Trust) v Secretary of State for Work and Pensions* [2013] EWHC 233 (Admin), [2013] P.T.S.R. 785 (QBD (Admin)), Underhill, J.
Art.2, amended: SI 2013/1544 Art.2
Art.4B, amended: SI 2013/1544 Art.2
Art.4B, applied: SI 2013/382 Art.3, Art.4
Sch.2 para.1, amended: SI 2013/2827 Art.2
Sch.2 para.1A, substituted: SI 2013/666 Art.2
Sch.2 para.3, added: SI 2013/666 Art.2
Sch.2 para.3, substituted: SI 2013/2827 Art.2
Sch.3B, applied: SI 2013/382 Art.3
Sch.3B para.2, amended: SI 2013/1544 Art.2
Sch.3B para.2, revoked (in part): SI 2013/1544 Art.2
Sch.3B para.2, substituted: SI 2013/2978 Art.2
Sch.3B para.6, added: SI 2013/2978 Art.2

1995. Rent Officers (Housing Benefit Functions) (Scotland) Order 1997
applied: SI 2013/382 Art.3, Art.4
Art.2, amended: SI 2013/1544 Art.3
Art.4B, amended: SI 2013/1544 Art.3
Sch.2 para.1, amended: SI 2013/2827 Art.3
Sch.2 para.1A, substituted: SI 2013/666 Art.3
Sch.2 para.3, added: SI 2013/666 Art.3
Sch.2 para.3, substituted: SI 2013/2827 Art.3
Sch.3B para.2, amended: SI 2013/1544 Art.3
Sch.3B para.2, revoked (in part): SI 2013/1544 Art.3
Sch.3B para.2, substituted: SI 2013/2978 Art.3
Sch.3B para.6, added: SI 2013/2978 Art.3

2020. Roads (Queensway to Normacot Road) (50 Miles Per Hour Speed Limit) Order 1997
revoked: SI 2013/2703 Art.4
varied: SI 2013/1485 Art.8

2073. Animal By-Products (Identification) (Amendment) Regulations 1997
revoked (in part): SI 2013/2952 Reg.28, SSI 2013/307 Sch.3

2196. Gaming Duty Regulations 1997
Reg.5, amended: SI 2013/1819 Reg.4

2389. Airports (Groundhandling) Regulations 1997
Reg.27, amended: SI 2013/610 Sch.1 para.2, Sch.2 para.2

2400. Zebra, Pelican and Puffin Pedestrian Crossings Regulations and General Directions 1997
Reg.12, amended: SSI 2013/119 Sch.2 para.15
Reg.13, amended: SSI 2013/119 Sch.2 para.15
Reg.21, amended: SSI 2013/119 Sch.2 para.15

2470. Surface Waters (Shellfish) (Classification) (Scotland) Regulations 1997
revoked: SSI 2013/323 Reg.29

2471. Surface Waters (Fishlife) (Classification) (Scotland) Regulations 1997
revoked: SSI 2013/323 Reg.29

2488. National Health Service (Optical Charges and Payments) Amendment Regulations 1997
revoked (in part): SI 2013/461 Sch.4

2560. Surface Waters (Dangerous Substances) (Classification) Regulations 1997
Reg.4, amended: SI 2013/755 Sch.4 para.76

2776. Diving at Work Regulations 1997
Sch.2 para.5, revoked: SI 2013/1471 Sch.4

2791. Police Cadets (Scotland) Amendment Regulations 1997
revoked: SSI 2013/42 Sch.1 Part 1

2862. Local Authorities (Contracts) Regulations 1997
Reg.2, amended: SI 2013/1466 Sch.1 para.1

2962. Merchant Shipping and Fishing Vessels (Health and Safety at Work) Regulations 1997
see *Cairns v Northern Lighthouse Board* [2013] CSOH 22, 2013 S.L.T. 645 (OH), Lord Drummond Young

Reg.2, see *Cairns v Northern Lighthouse Board* [2013] CSOH 22, 2013 S.L.T. 645 (OH), Lord Drummond Young
Reg.5, see *Cairns v Northern Lighthouse Board* [2013] CSOH 22, 2013 S.L.T. 645 (OH), Lord Drummond Young

3001. Teachers Pensions Regulations 1997
Reg.4, applied: SI 2013/275 Reg.7

3008. Long Residential Tenancies (Principal Forms) Regulations 1997
Reg.3, amended: SI 2013/1036 Sch.2 para.21
Sch.1, added: SI 2013/1036 Sch.2 para.22, Sch.2 para.23, Sch.2 para.24, Sch.2 para.25
Sch.1, amended: SI 2013/1036 Sch.2 para.22, Sch.2 para.23, Sch.2 para.24, Sch.2 para.25

1998

192. Local Government (Discretionary Payments and Injury Benefits) (Scotland) Regulations 1998
Reg.38, amended: SSI 2013/119 Sch.1 para.25

211. Education (Student Loans) Regulations 1998
Sch.2 Part I para.1, amended: SI 2013/388 Sch.1 para.20, SI 2013/591 Sch.1 para.14, SI 2013/630 Reg.51, SI 2013/1881 Sch.1 para.20, SSI 2013/142 Reg.5

212. Building Societies (Transfer of Business) Regulations 1998
Reg.2, amended: SI 2013/496 Sch.10 para.4
Sch.1 Part I para.28, amended: SI 2013/496 Sch.10 para.4
Sch.1 Part II para.10, amended: SI 2013/496 Sch.10 para.4
Sch.3 para.1, amended: SI 2013/496 Sch.10 para.4
Sch.3 para.2, amended: SI 2013/496 Sch.10 para.4

366. Local Government Pension Scheme (Scotland) Regulations 1998
see *City of Edinburgh Council v Scottish Council for Research in Education* [2013] CSIH 15, 2013 S.C. 357 (IH (Ex Div)), Lord Clarke
Reg.77, see *City of Edinburgh Council v Scottish Council for Research in Education* [2013] CSIH 15, 2013 S.C. 357 (IH (Ex Div)), Lord Clarke

389. Surface Waters (Dangerous Substances) (Classification) Regulations 1998
Reg.4, amended: SI 2013/755 Sch.4 para.77

494. Health and Safety (Enforcing Authority) Regulations 1998
applied: SI 2013/1506 Reg.9
disapplied: SI 2013/1506 Reg.9, Reg.18
Reg.4, amended: SI 2013/602 Sch.2 para.76

499. National Health Service (Optical Charges and Payments) Amendment Regulations 1998
revoked (in part): SI 2013/461 Sch.4

503. Pensions Increase (Review) Order 1998
applied: SI 2013/604 Sch.1

504. Building Societies (Accounts and Related Provisions) Regulations 1998
Sch.4 para.13, amended: SI 2013/496 Sch.10 para.2
Sch.11 para.5, amended: SI 2013/472 Sch.2 para.21

562. Income-related Benefits (Subsidy to Authorities) Order 1998
Art.4, amended: SI 2013/266 Art.3
Art.14, amended: SI 2013/2989 Art.3
Art.18, amended: SI 2013/2989 Art.2
Sch.1, substituted: SI 2013/266 Sch.1, SI 2013/2989 Sch.1
Sch.4A Part I para.1, amended: SI 2013/266 Art.4
Sch.4A Part II para.2, amended: SI 2013/266 Art.4
Sch.4A Part III, substituted: SI 2013/266 Sch.2, SI 2013/2989 Sch.2
Sch.4A Part V, substituted: SI 2013/266 Sch.3, SI 2013/2989 Sch.3

574. Medicines for Human Use and Medical Devices (Fees and Miscellaneous Amendments) Regulations 1998
revoked: SI 2013/532 Sch.9

642. National Health Service (Optical Charges and Payments) (Scotland) Regulations 1998
Reg.1, amended: SSI 2013/137 Reg.12
Reg.8, amended: SSI 2013/137 Reg.12
Reg.12, applied: SSI 2013/96 Reg.3
Reg.17, applied: SSI 2013/96 Reg.3
Reg.19, amended: SSI 2013/96 Reg.2
Sch.1, amended: SSI 2013/96 Reg.2
Sch.2, substituted: SSI 2013/96 Sch.1
Sch.3 para.1, amended: SSI 2013/96 Reg.2
Sch.3 para.2, amended: SSI 2013/96 Reg.2

648. Construction Contracts (England and Wales) Exclusion Order 1998
Art.4, amended: SI 2013/1466 Sch.1 para.2

649. Scheme for Construction Contracts (England and Wales) Regulations 1998
see *KNN Colburn LLP v GD City Holdings Ltd* [2013] EWHC 2879 (TCC), [2013] T.C.L.R. 10 (QBD (TCC)), Stuart-Smith, J.; see *Systech International Ltd v PC Harrington Contractors Ltd* [2012] EWCA Civ 1371, [2013] 2 All E.R. 69 (CA (Civ Div)), Lord Dyson (M.R.)
Sch.1 Pt I para.7, see *KNN Colburn LLP v GD City Holdings Ltd* [2013] EWHC 2879 (TCC), [2013] T.C.L.R. 10 (QBD (TCC)), Stuart-Smith, J.
Sch.1 Pt I para.8, see *Systech International Ltd v PC Harrington Contractors Ltd* [2012] EWCA

Civ 1371, [2013] 2 All E.R. 69 (CA (Civ Div)), Lord Dyson (M.R.)
Sch.1 Pt I para.9, see *Systech International Ltd v PC Harrington Contractors Ltd* [2012] EWCA Civ 1371, [2013] 2 All E.R. 69 (CA (Civ Div)), Lord Dyson (M.R.)
Sch.1 Pt I para.11, see *Systech International Ltd v PC Harrington Contractors Ltd* [2012] EWCA Civ 1371, [2013] 2 All E.R. 69 (CA (Civ Div)), Lord Dyson (M.R.)
Sch.1 para.19, see *KNN Colburn LLP v GD City Holdings Ltd* [2013] EWHC 2879 (TCC), [2013] T.C.L.R. 10 (QBD (TCC)), Stuart-Smith, J.

651. Surrey and Sussex Healthcare National Health Service Trust (Establishment) Order 1998
Art.1, amended: SI 2013/593 Art.2

654. London Traffic Control System (Transfer) (Amendment) Order 1998
revoked: SI 2013/2986 Sch.2

678. Welsh Ambulance Services National Health Service Trust (Establishment) Order 1998
Art.1, amended: SI 2013/2729 Art.2
Art.3, amended: SI 2013/2729 Art.3

681. National Health Service (Pharmaceutical Services) Amendment Regulations 1998
revoked: SI 2013/898 Sch.8 para.6

722. Wireless Telegraphy (Control of Interference from Videosenders) Order 1998
Art.3, amended: SI 2013/1854 Art.3

811. European Primary and Specialist Dental Qualifications Regulations 1998
Reg.10, amended: SI 2013/3036 Reg.5

880. Education (Publication of Local Authority Inspection Reports) Regulations 1998
Reg.4, amended: SI 2013/235 Sch.2 para.34

892. Mines (Notice of Abandonment) Regulations 1998
Reg.2, amended: SI 2013/755 Sch.4 para.78

1130. Cash Ratio Deposits (Eligible Liabilities) Order 1998
Art.2, amended: SI 2013/3115 Sch.2 para.47

1277. Food (Cheese) (Emergency Control) Order 1998
revoked (in part): SI 2013/2996 Sch.9

1284. Food (Cheese) (Emergency Control) (Amendment) Order 1998
revoked (in part): SI 2013/2996 Sch.9

1448. Road Humps (Scotland) Regulations 1998
Reg.3, amended: SSI 2013/119 Sch.2 para.16

1451. National Health Service Superannuation Scheme (Scotland) (Additional Voluntary Contributions) Regulations 1998
applied: SSI 2013/174 Reg.4, Reg.7
Reg.2, amended: SI 2013/472 Art.4

1594. National Health Service (Scotland) (Injury Benefits) Regulations 1998
Reg.2, amended: SSI 2013/109 Reg.67
Reg.3, amended: SSI 2013/52 Reg.3
Reg.4, amended: SSI 2013/52 Reg.4, SSI 2013/109 Reg.68
Reg.4, revoked (in part): SSI 2013/109 Reg.68
Reg.4A, amended: SSI 2013/52 Reg.5
Reg.18A, amended: SSI 2013/109 Reg.69
Reg.18A, substituted: SSI 2013/52 Reg.6
Reg.18B, added: SSI 2013/52 Reg.7
Reg.18B, amended: SSI 2013/109 Reg.70
Reg.21A, added: SSI 2013/52 Reg.8

1609. Merchant Shipping (Small Workboats and Pilot Boats) Regulations 1998
Sch.1, amended: SI 2013/1785 Reg.3

1673. Food (Cheese) (Emergency Control) (Amendment No 2) Order 1998
revoked (in part): SI 2013/2996 Sch.9

1702. Companies (Forms) (Amendment) Regulations 1998
revoked: SI 2013/1947 Sch.2 Part 1

1713. Faculty Jurisdiction (Appeals) Rules 1998
referred to: SI 2013/1922 Sch.1 Part TABLEa

1760. Education (Student Support) (Northern Ireland) Order 1998
Art.3, amended: SI 2013/1881 Sch.1 para.21
Art.3, applied: SI 2013/3029 Sch.11 para.4, Sch.11 para.10, SI 2013/3035 Sch.1

1782. A500 Trunk Road (Talke Porthill, Staffordshire) (Derestriction) Order 1998
revoked: SI 2013/2702 Art.4

1833. Working Time Regulations 1998
applied: SI 2013/1893 Sch.2
see *Benkharbouche v Embassy of Sudan* [2013] I.R.L.R. 918 (EAT), Langstaff, J. (President); see *R. (on the application of United Road Transport Union) v Secretary of State for Transport* [2013] EWCA Civ 962, [2013] I.R.L.R. 890 (CA (Civ Div)), Jackson, L.J.
Reg.13, amended: SI 2013/2228 Reg.2
Reg.13, see *Sood Enterprises Ltd v Healy* [2013] I.C.R. 1361 (EAT (SC)), Lady Stacey
Reg.13A, see *Sood Enterprises Ltd v Healy* [2013] I.C.R. 1361 (EAT (SC)), Lady Stacey
Reg.15, amended: SI 2013/2228 Reg.2
Reg.16, see *Dhunna v Creditsights Ltd* [2013] I.C.R. 909 (EAT), Slade, J.
Reg.35, amended: SI 2013/1956 Sch.1 para.2
Reg.43, amended: SI 2013/2228 Reg.2
Reg.43, substituted: SI 2013/2228 Reg.2
Sch.2 para.1, amended: SI 2013/2228 Reg.2
Sch.2 para.2, amended: SI 2013/2228 Reg.2
Sch.2 para.3, amended: SI 2013/2228 Reg.2

1870. Individual Savings Account Regulations 1998
Reg.2, amended: SI 2013/472 Sch.2 para.22, SI 2013/605 Reg.4, SI 2013/1743 Reg.3, SI 2013/1773 Sch.2 para.4
Reg.2F, amended: SI 2013/1743 Reg.4
Reg.4, amended: SI 2013/472 Sch.2 para.22
Reg.4ZA, amended: SI 2013/267 Reg.2
Reg.4ZB, amended: SI 2013/267 Reg.2
Reg.5E, added: SI 2013/623 Reg.2
Reg.6, amended: SI 2013/472 Sch.2 para.22
Reg.7, amended: SI 2013/1743 Reg.5
Reg.9, amended: SI 2013/472 Art.4
Reg.10, amended: SI 2013/605 Reg.4
Reg.12, amended: SI 2013/605 Reg.4
Reg.12A, amended: SI 2013/605 Reg.4
Reg.14, amended: SI 2013/472 Sch.2 para.22, SI 2013/1765 Art.3
Reg.21, amended: SI 2013/1743 Reg.6
Reg.21B, amended: SI 2013/1743 Reg.7
Reg.30, revoked (in part): SI 2013/623 Reg.2

1941. Firearms Rules 1998
r.3, amended: SI 2013/1945 r.3, SI 2013/2970 r.3
r.4, revoked (in part): SI 2013/1945 r.4, SI 2013/2970 r.4
r.5, amended: SI 2013/1945 r.5, SI 2013/2970 r.5
r.6, amended: SI 2013/2970 r.6
r.7, substituted: SI 2013/1945 r.6
r.9, amended: SI 2013/2970 r.7
Sch.1 Part I, amended: SI 2013/1945 Sch.1
Sch.1 Part I, substituted: SI 2013/1945 r.7
Sch.1 Part II, amended: SI 2013/2970 Sch.1
Sch.1 Part II, substituted: SI 2013/1945 r.7
Sch.1 Part III, revoked: SI 2013/2970 Sch.1
Sch.1 Part III, substituted: SI 2013/1945 r.7
Sch.1 Part IV, added: SI 2013/1945 Sch.2
Sch.1 Part IV, substituted: SI 2013/1945 r.7
Sch.2 Part I, revoked: SI 2013/1945 r.8
Sch.2 Part I, substituted: SI 2013/1945 r.8
Sch.2 Part II, amended: SI 2013/2970 Sch.2
Sch.2 Part II, substituted: SI 2013/1945 r.8
Sch.4 Part III, amended: SI 2013/2970 Sch.3
Sch.4 Part IV, revoked: SI 2013/2970 Sch.3

1943. Education (Infant Class Sizes) (Wales) Regulations 1998
revoked: SI 2013/1141 Reg.3

1944. Consumer Credit (Exempt Agreements) (Amendment) Order 1998
revoked (in part): SI 2013/1881 Art.21

1967. Assured and Protected Tenancies (Lettings to Students) Regulations 1998
Sch.2, amended: SI 2013/38 Reg.2, SI 2013/1461 Reg.2

2257. Extraction Solvents in Food (Amendment) Regulations 1998
revoked (in part): SI 2013/2210 Sch.5, SI 2013/2591 Sch.5, SSI 2013/266 Sch.5

2306. Provision and Use of Work Equipment Regulations 1998
see *Hill v Norside Ltd* 2013 Rep. L.R. 22 (OH), Lady Dorrian; see *Willock v Corus UK Ltd* [2013] EWCA Civ 519, [2013] P.I.Q.R. P21 (CA (Civ Div)), Lord Hughes of Ombersley
Reg.3, see *French v Strathclyde Fire Board* [2013] CSOH 3, 2013 S.L.T. 247 (OH), Lord Drummond Young
Reg.4, see *French v Strathclyde Fire Board* [2013] CSOH 3, 2013 S.L.T. 247 (OH), Lord Drummond Young; see *Hide v Steeplechase Co (Cheltenham) Ltd* [2013] EWCA Civ 545, [2013] P.I.Q.R. P22 (CA (Civ Div)), Longmore, L.J.; see *Kennedy v Chivas Brothers Ltd* [2013] CSIH 57, 2013 S.L.T. 981 (IH (2 Div)), The Lord Justice Clerk (Carloway); see *Smith v James Strang Ltd* 2013 Rep. L.R. 19 (OH), Temporary Judge M Wise, QC
Reg.5, see *Brumder v Motornet Service and Repairs Ltd* [2013] EWCA Civ 195, [2013] 1 W.L.R. 2783 (CA (Civ Div)), Ward, L.J.; see *Kennedy v Chivas Brothers Ltd* [2013] CSIH 57, 2013 S.L.T. 981 (IH (2 Div)), The Lord Justice Clerk (Carloway)
Reg.11, see *Smith v James Strang Ltd* 2013 Rep. L.R. 19 (OH), Temporary Judge M Wise, QC
Reg.12, revoked (in part): SI 2013/448 Sch.1
Reg.12, see *Whitehead v Trustees of the Chatsworth Settlement* [2012] EWCA Civ 263, [2013] 1 W.L.R. 251 (CA (Civ Div)), Sir Andrew Morritt (Chancellor)
Reg.17, see *Smith v James Strang Ltd* 2013 Rep. L.R. 19 (OH), Temporary Judge M Wise, QC, see *Willock v Corus UK Ltd* [2013] EWCA Civ 519, [2013] P.I.Q.R. P21 (CA (Civ Div)), Lord Hughes of Ombersley
Reg.20, see *Hill v Norside Ltd* 2013 Rep. L.R. 22 (OH), Lady Dorrian
Sch.1, amended: SI 2013/1387 Sch.5 para.1

2307. Lifting Operations and Lifting Equipment Regulations 1998
Reg.9, revoked (in part): SI 2013/448 Sch.1
Reg.13, revoked: SI 2013/448 Sch.1
Sch.2, amended: SI 2013/448 Sch.1

2451. Gas Safety (Installation and Use) Regulations 1998
Reg.16, applied: SI 2013/805 Sch.1, SI 2013/806 Sch.1, SI 2013/807 Sch.1, SI 2013/808 Sch.1, SI 2013/809 Sch.1, SI 2013/810 Sch.1, SI 2013/811 Sch.1, SI 2013/812 Sch.1, SI 2013/813 Sch.1, SI 2013/814 Sch.1
Reg.36, applied: SSI 2013/20 Art.2

2535. Religious Character of Schools (Designation Procedure) Regulations 1998
referred to: SI 2013/2029
Reg.3, applied: SI 2013/1624 Reg.18
2573. Employers Liability (Compulsory Insurance) Regulations 1998
Sch.2 para.16, amended: SI 2013/1466 Sch.1 para.3
2771. Merchant Shipping (Vessels in Commercial Use for Sport or Pleasure) Regulations 1998
Sch.2, amended: SI 2013/1785 Reg.3
2859. Residuary Body for Wales (Winding Up) Order 1998
Art.2, amended: SI 2013/472 Art.4
3069. Leicestershire and Rutland Healthcare National Health Service Trust (Establishment) Order 1998
Art.1, amended: SI 2013/593 Art.2
3090. M4 Motorway (London Borough of Hounslow) (Bus Lane) Order 1998
revoked: SI 2013/2306 Art.2
3132. Civil Procedure Rules 1998
applied: SI 2013/1046 r.126, SI 2013/1169 r.12, r.13, SI 2013/1916 r.19_5, SI 2013/3208 r.130
referred to: SI 2013/534 Reg.14
varied: SI 2013/1169 r.13
see *Appleyard v Wewelwala* [2012] EWHC 3302 (Ch), [2013] 1 W.L.R. 752 (Ch D), Briggs, J.; see *Cosmotrade SA v Kairos Shipping Ltd* [2013] EWHC 1904 (Comm), [2013] 2 Lloyd's Rep. 535 (QBD (Comm)), Simon, J.; see *Durham CC v D* [2012] EWCA Civ 1654, [2013] 1 W.L.R. 2305 (CA (Civ Div)), Maurice Kay, L.J. (VP, CA Civ); see *Fons HF v Corporal Ltd* [2013] EWHC 1278 (Ch), [2013] 4 Costs L.O. 646 (Ch D (Manchester)), Judge Pelling Q.C.; see *Murray v Neil Dowlman Architecture Ltd* [2013] EWHC 872 (TCC), [2013] T.C.L.R. 5 (QBD (TCC)), Coulson, J.; see *R. (on the application of HS) v Upper Tribunal (Immigration and Asylum Chamber)* [2012] EWHC 3126 (Admin), [2013] Imm. A.R. 579 (QBD (Admin)), Charles, J.; see *Venulum Property Investments Ltd v Space Architecture Ltd* [2013] EWHC 1242 (TCC), [2013] 4 Costs L.R. 596 (QBD (TCC)), Edwards-Stuart, J.
Part 00 r.0, amended: SI 2013/262 r.21
Part 1 r.1.1, amended: SI 2013/262 r.4
Part 1 r.1.2, amended: SI 2013/1571 r.3
Part 2 r.2.8, applied: SI 2013/1046 r.198, SI 2013/3208 r.199
Part 3, amended: SI 2013/262 r.5
Part 3 r.3.1, amended: SI 2013/262 r.5
Part 3 r.3.1, amended: SI 2013/262 r.5, SI 2013/1974 r.4
Part 3 r.3.1, applied: SI 2013/1046 r.198, SI 2013/3208 r.199
Part 3 r.3.2, amended: SI 2013/262 r.5
Part 3 r.3.3, amended: SI 2013/262 r.5
Part 3 r.3.4, amended: SI 2013/262 r.5
Part 3 r.3.5, amended: SI 2013/262 r.5
Part 3 r.3.5A, amended: SI 2013/262 r.5
Part 3 r.3.6, amended: SI 2013/262 r.5
Part 3 r.3.6A, amended: SI 2013/262 r.5
Part 3 r.3.7, amended: SI 2013/262 r.5
Part 3 r.3.7, amended: SI 2013/262 r.5, SI 2013/1974 r.4
Part 3 r.3.7A, amended: SI 2013/262 r.5
Part 3 r.3.7B, amended: SI 2013/262 r.5
Part 3 r.3.7B, amended: SI 2013/262 r.5, SI 2013/1974 r.4
Part 3 r.3.8, amended: SI 2013/262 r.5
Part 3 r.3.9, amended: SI 2013/262 r.5
Part 3 r.3.10, amended: SI 2013/262 r.5
Part 3 r.3.11, amended: SI 2013/262 r.5
Part 3 r.3.12, added: SI 2013/262 r.5
Part 3 r.3.12, amended: SI 2013/262 r.5, SI 2013/515 r.4
Part 3 r.3.13, added: SI 2013/262 r.5
Part 3 r.3.13, amended: SI 2013/262 r.5
Part 3 r.3.14, added: SI 2013/262 r.5
Part 3 r.3.14, amended: SI 2013/262 r.5
Part 3 r.3.15, added: SI 2013/262 r.5
Part 3 r.3.15, amended: SI 2013/262 r.5
Part 3 r.3.16, added: SI 2013/262 r.5
Part 3 r.3.16, amended: SI 2013/262 r.5
Part 3 r.3.17, added: SI 2013/262 r.5
Part 3 r.3.17, amended: SI 2013/262 r.5
Part 3 r.3.18, added: SI 2013/262 r.5
Part 3 r.3.18, amended: SI 2013/262 r.5
Part 3 r.3.19, added: SI 2013/262 r.5
Part 3 r.3.19, amended: SI 2013/262 r.5
Part 3 r.3.20, added: SI 2013/262 r.5
Part 3 r.3.20, amended: SI 2013/262 r.5
Part 3 r.3.21, added: SI 2013/262 r.5
Part 3 r.3.21, amended: SI 2013/262 r.5
Part 5, applied: SI 2013/362 Reg.22
Part 6, applied: SI 2013/1046 r.153, r.167, r.168, SI 2013/3208 r.157, r.170, r.172
Part 7 r.7.2, amended: SI 2013/1974 r.5
Part 8 r.8.2, amended: SI 2013/1974 r.6
Part 8 r.8.3, amended: SI 2013/1974 r.6
Part 12 r.12.3, amended: SI 2013/1571 r.4
Part 14 r.14.1B, amended: SI 2013/1695 r.4
Part 15 r.15.6, amended: SI 2013/1974 r.7
Part 15 r.15.8, substituted: SI 2013/1974 r.7
Part 16 r.16.2, amended: SI 2013/1974 r.8
Part 16 r.16.3, amended: SI 2013/262 r.6

Part 18, applied: SI 2013/1046 r.131, r.141, SI 2013/3208 r.135, r.145
Part 21 r.21.1, amended: SI 2013/1974 r.9
Part 21 r.21.10, amended: SI 2013/262 r.7
Part 21 r.21.11, applied: SI 2013/3029 Sch.5 para.17, Sch.10 para.48, SI 2013/3035 Sch.1
Part 21 r.21.12, amended: SI 2013/262 r.7, SI 2013/1974 r.9
Part 22, applied: SI 2013/3208 r.130
Part 25, applied: 2013 c.29 s.234
Part 25 r.25.6, applied: SI 2013/503 Reg.16
Part 25 r.25.14, amended: SI 2013/1974 r.10
Part 26 r.26.2A, amended: SI 2013/262 r.8
Part 26 r.26.3, amended: SI 2013/262 r.8
Part 26 r.26.3, revoked (in part): SI 2013/262 r.8
Part 26 r.26.4, amended: SI 2013/262 r.8
Part 26 r.26.5, amended: SI 2013/262 r.8
Part 26 r.26.5, revoked (in part): SI 2013/262 r.8
Part 26 r.26.6, amended: SI 2013/262 r.8
Part 26 r.26.7, revoked (in part): SI 2013/262 r.8
Part 26 r.26.9, amended: SI 2013/262 r.8
Part 26 r.26.9, revoked (in part): SI 2013/262 r.8
Part 26 r.26.11, substituted: SI 2013/3112 r.2
Part 27 r.27.1, amended: SI 2013/262 r.9
Part 27 r.27.5, amended: SI 2013/262 r.9
Part 27 r.27.14, amended: SI 2013/262 r.9, SI 2013/1695 r.5
Part 27 r.27.14, revoked (in part): SI 2013/262 r.9
Part 28 r.28.2, amended: SI 2013/1974 r.11
Part 29, applied: SI 2013/3208 r.130
Part 29, disapplied: SI 2013/1046 r.126
Part 29 r.29.1, amended: SI 2013/262 r.10
Part 29 r.29.2, amended: SI 2013/262 r.10
Part 29 r.29.4, substituted: SI 2013/262 r.10
Part 29 r.29.8, amended: SI 2013/262 r.10, SI 2013/1974 r.12
Part 30 r.30.3, amended: SI 2013/1571 r.5
Part 31, applied: SI 2013/1046 r.17, r.131, SI 2013/3208 r.135
Part 31, disapplied: SI 2013/1046 r.21, SI 2013/3208 r.17, r.21
Part 31 r.31.1, varied: SI 2013/1554 r.61_9
Part 31 r.31.2, varied: SI 2013/1554 r.61_9
Part 31 r.31.3, varied: SI 2013/1554 r.61_9
Part 31 r.31.4, varied: SI 2013/1554 r.61_9
Part 31 r.31.5, amended: SI 2013/1974 r.13
Part 31 r.31.5, substituted: SI 2013/262 r.11
Part 31 r.31.5, varied: SI 2013/1554 r.61_9
Part 31 r.31.6, varied: SI 2013/1554 r.61_9
Part 31 r.31.7, varied: SI 2013/1554 r.61_9
Part 31 r.31.8, varied: SI 2013/1554 r.61_9
Part 31 r.31.9, varied: SI 2013/1554 r.61_9
Part 31 r.31.10, varied: SI 2013/1554 r.61_9
Part 31 r.31.11, varied: SI 2013/1554 r.61_9
Part 31 r.31.12, varied: SI 2013/1554 r.61_9
Part 31 r.31.13, varied: SI 2013/1554 r.61_9
Part 31 r.31.14, varied: SI 2013/1554 r.61_9
Part 31 r.31.15, varied: SI 2013/1554 r.61_9
Part 31 r.31.16, varied: SI 2013/1554 r.61_9
Part 31 r.31.17, varied: SI 2013/1554 r.61_9
Part 31 r.31.18, varied: SI 2013/1554 r.61_9
Part 31 r.31.19, varied: SI 2013/1554 r.61_9
Part 31 r.31.20, varied: SI 2013/1554 r.61_9
Part 31 r.31.21, varied: SI 2013/1554 r.61_9
Part 31 r.31.22, varied: SI 2013/1554 r.61_9
Part 31 r.31.23, varied: SI 2013/1554 r.61_9
Part 32, applied: SI 2013/3208 r.130
Part 32 r.32.2, amended: SI 2013/262 r.12
Part 35 r.35.4, amended: SI 2013/262 r.13
Part 36, amended: SI 2013/1695 r.6
Part 36 r.36.A1, amended: SI 2013/1695 r.6
Part 36 r.36.1, amended: SI 2013/1974 r.14
Part 36 r.36.10, amended: SI 2013/1695 r.6, SI 2013/1974 r.14
Part 36 r.36.10A, added: SI 2013/1695 r.6
Part 36 r.36.14, amended: SI 2013/262 r.14, SI 2013/1695 r.6, SI 2013/1974 r.14
Part 36 r.36.14A, added: SI 2013/1695 r.6
Part 36 r.36.16, amended: SI 2013/1695 r.6
Part 36 r.36.17, amended: SI 2013/1695 r.6
Part 36 r.36.18, amended: SI 2013/1695 r.6
Part 36 r.36.19, amended: SI 2013/1695 r.6
Part 36 r.36.20, amended: SI 2013/1695 r.6
Part 36 r.36.21, amended: SI 2013/1695 r.6
Part 36 r.36.22, amended: SI 2013/1695 r.6
Part 37, applied: SI 2013/1046 r.130, SI 2013/3208 r.134
Part 38 r.38.6, amended: SI 2013/1974 r.15
Part 38 r.38.8, amended: SI 2013/1974 r.15
Part 39 r.39.4, amended: SI 2013/1974 r.16
Part 40 r.40.18, amended: SI 2013/1974 r.17
Part 42 r.42.2, amended: SI 2013/534 Sch.1 para.13, SI 2013/1974 r.18
Part 43 r.43.1, revoked: SI 2013/262 r.15
Part 43 r.43.2, referred to: SI 2013/534 Reg.14
Part 43 r.43.2, revoked: SI 2013/262 r.15
Part 43 r.43.3, revoked: SI 2013/262 r.15
Part 43 r.43.4, revoked: SI 2013/262 r.15
Part 44 r.44.1, substituted: SI 2013/262 Sch.1
Part 44 r.44.2, substituted: SI 2013/262 Sch.1
Part 44 r.44.3, substituted: SI 2013/262 Sch.1
Part 44 r.44.3, amended: SI 2013/515 r.5
Part 44 r.44.3, applied: SI 2013/480 Reg.47, SI 2013/512 Reg.32
Part 44 r.44.3, substituted: SI 2013/262 Sch.1
Part 44 r.44.3A, substituted: SI 2013/262 Sch.1
Part 44 r.44.3B, substituted: SI 2013/262 Sch.1
Part 44 r.44.3C, substituted: SI 2013/262 Sch.1

Part 44 r.44.4, substituted: SI 2013/262 Sch.1
Part 44 r.44.5, substituted: SI 2013/262 Sch.1
Part 44 r.44.6, substituted: SI 2013/262 Sch.1
Part 44 r.44.7, substituted: SI 2013/262 Sch.1
Part 44 r.44.8, substituted: SI 2013/262 Sch.1
Part 44 r.44.9, substituted: SI 2013/262 Sch.1
Part 44 r.44.9, amended: SI 2013/1974 r.19
Part 44 r.44.9, substituted: SI 2013/262 Sch.1
Part 44 r.44.10, substituted: SI 2013/262 Sch.1
Part 44 r.44.11, substituted: SI 2013/262 Sch.1
Part 44 r.44.12, substituted: SI 2013/262 Sch.1
Part 44 r.44.12A, substituted: SI 2013/262 Sch.1
Part 44 r.44.12B, substituted: SI 2013/262 Sch.1
Part 44 r.44.12C, substituted: SI 2013/262 Sch.1
Part 44 r.44.13, substituted: SI 2013/262 Sch.1
Part 44 r.44.14, substituted: SI 2013/262 Sch.1
Part 44 r.44.15, substituted: SI 2013/262 Sch.1
Part 44 r.44.16, substituted: SI 2013/262 Sch.1
Part 44 r.44.17, substituted: SI 2013/262 Sch.1
Part 44 r.44.18, substituted: SI 2013/262 Sch.1
Part 44 r.44.19, substituted: SI 2013/262 Sch.1
Part 44 r.44.20, substituted: SI 2013/262 Sch.1
Part 45, applied: SI 2013/609 Reg.4
Part 45, substituted: SI 2013/1695 r.7
Part 45, added: SI 2013/1695 Sch.1
Part 45, amended: SI 2013/1974 r.20
Part 45 r.45.1, substituted: SI 2013/262 Sch.1
Part 45 r.45.2, substituted: SI 2013/262 Sch.1
Part 45 r.45.2A, substituted: SI 2013/262 Sch.1
Part 45 r.45.3, substituted: SI 2013/262 Sch.1
Part 45 r.45.4, substituted: SI 2013/262 Sch.1
Part 45 r.45.4A, substituted: SI 2013/262 Sch.1
Part 45 r.45.5, substituted: SI 2013/262 Sch.1
Part 45 r.45.6, substituted: SI 2013/262 Sch.1
Part 45 r.45.7, substituted: SI 2013/262 Sch.1
Part 45 r.45.8, substituted: SI 2013/262 Sch.1
Part 45 r.45.9, amended: SI 2013/1695 r.7
Part 45 r.45.9, substituted: SI 2013/262 Sch.1
Part 45 r.45.10, substituted: SI 2013/262 Sch.1
Part 45 r.45.11, substituted: SI 2013/262 Sch.1
Part 45 r.45.12, substituted: SI 2013/262 Sch.1
Part 45 r.45.13, substituted: SI 2013/262 Sch.1
Part 45 r.45.14, substituted: SI 2013/262 Sch.1
Part 45 r.45.15, substituted: SI 2013/262 Sch.1
Part 45 r.45.16, amended: SI 2013/1695 r.7
Part 45 r.45.16, substituted: SI 2013/262 Sch.1
Part 45 r.45.17, amended: SI 2013/1695 r.7
Part 45 r.45.17, substituted: SI 2013/262 Sch.1
Part 45 r.45.18, amended: SI 2013/789 r.3, SI 2013/1695 r.7, SI 2013/1974 r.20
Part 45 r.45.18, substituted: SI 2013/262 Sch.1
Part 45 r.45.19, amended: SI 2013/1695 r.7
Part 45 r.45.19, revoked (in part): SI 2013/1695 r.7
Part 45 r.45.19, substituted: SI 2013/262 Sch.1
Part 45 r.45.20, amended: SI 2013/1695 r.7
Part 45 r.45.20, substituted: SI 2013/262 Sch.1
Part 45 r.45.21, amended: SI 2013/1695 r.7
Part 45 r.45.21, substituted: SI 2013/262 Sch.1
Part 45 r.45.22, amended: SI 2013/1695 r.7
Part 45 r.45.22, substituted: SI 2013/262 Sch.1
Part 45 r.45.23, substituted: SI 2013/262 Sch.1
Part 45 r.45.23A, added: SI 2013/1695 r.7
Part 45 r.45.23A, substituted: SI 2013/262 Sch.1
Part 45 r.45.23B, added: SI 2013/1695 r.7
Part 45 r.45.23B, substituted: SI 2013/262 Sch.1
Part 45 r.45.24, amended: SI 2013/1695 r.7
Part 45 r.45.24, substituted: SI 2013/262 Sch.1
Part 45 r.45.25, amended: SI 2013/1695 r.7
Part 45 r.45.25, substituted: SI 2013/262 Sch.1
Part 45 r.45.26, amended: SI 2013/1695 r.7
Part 45 r.45.26, substituted: SI 2013/262 Sch.1
Part 45 r.45.27, substituted: SI 2013/262 Sch.1
Part 45 r.45.28, amended: SI 2013/1695 r.7
Part 45 r.45.28, substituted: SI 2013/262 Sch.1
Part 45 r.45.29, substituted: SI 2013/262 Sch.1
Part 45 r.45.29A, substituted: SI 2013/262 Sch.1
Part 45 r.45.29B, substituted: SI 2013/262 Sch.1
Part 45 r.45.29C, substituted: SI 2013/262 Sch.1
Part 45 r.45.29D, substituted: SI 2013/262 Sch.1
Part 45 r.45.29E, amended: SI 2013/1974 r.20
Part 45 r.45.29E, substituted: SI 2013/262 Sch.1
Part 45 r.45.29F, substituted: SI 2013/262 Sch.1
Part 45 r.45.29G, substituted: SI 2013/262 Sch.1
Part 45 r.45.29H, amended: SI 2013/1974 r.20
Part 45 r.45.29H, substituted: SI 2013/262 Sch.1
Part 45 r.45.29I, substituted: SI 2013/262 Sch.1
Part 45 r.45.29J, substituted: SI 2013/262 Sch.1
Part 45 r.45.29K, substituted: SI 2013/262 Sch.1
Part 45 r.45.29L, substituted: SI 2013/262 Sch.1
Part 45 r.45.30, amended: SI 2013/1974 r.20
Part 45 r.45.30, substituted: SI 2013/262 Sch.1
Part 45 r.45.31, amended: SI 2013/1974 r.20
Part 45 r.45.31, substituted: SI 2013/262 Sch.1
Part 45 r.45.32, substituted: SI 2013/262 Sch.1
Part 45 r.45.33, substituted: SI 2013/262 Sch.1
Part 45 r.45.34, substituted: SI 2013/262 Sch.1
Part 45 r.45.35, substituted: SI 2013/262 Sch.1
Part 45 r.45.36, substituted: SI 2013/262 Sch.1
Part 45 r.45.37, substituted: SI 2013/262 Sch.1
Part 45 r.45.38, amended: SI 2013/1974 r.20
Part 45 r.45.38, substituted: SI 2013/262 Sch.1
Part 45 r.45.39, substituted: SI 2013/262 Sch.1
Part 45 r.45.40, substituted: SI 2013/262 Sch.1
Part 45 r.45.41, substituted: SI 2013/262 Sch.1
Part 45 r.45.42, substituted: SI 2013/262 Sch.1
Part 45 r.45.43, substituted: SI 2013/262 Sch.1
Part 45 r.45.44, substituted: SI 2013/262 Sch.1
Part 45 r.45.45, substituted: SI 2013/262 Sch.1

Part 45 r.45.46, substituted: SI 2013/262 Sch.1
Part 45 r.45.47, substituted: SI 2013/262 Sch.1
Part 46 r.46.1, substituted: SI 2013/262 Sch.1
Part 46 r.46.2, substituted: SI 2013/262 Sch.1
Part 46 r.46.2, referred to: SI 2013/534 Reg.14
Part 46 r.46.2, substituted: SI 2013/262 Sch.1
Part 46 r.46.3, substituted: SI 2013/262 Sch.1
Part 46 r.46.4, substituted: SI 2013/262 Sch.1
Part 46 r.46.5, substituted: SI 2013/262 Sch.1
Part 46 r.46.6, amended: SI 2013/1974 r.21
Part 46 r.46.6, substituted: SI 2013/262 Sch.1
Part 46 r.46.7, amended: SI 2013/1974 r.21
Part 46 r.46.7, substituted: SI 2013/262 Sch.1
Part 46 r.46.8, substituted: SI 2013/262 Sch.1
Part 46 r.46.9, amended: SI 2013/534 Sch.1 para.2
Part 46 r.46.9, substituted: SI 2013/262 Sch.1
Part 46 r.46.10, substituted: SI 2013/262 Sch.1
Part 46 r.46.11, substituted: SI 2013/262 Sch.1
Part 46 r.46.12, substituted: SI 2013/262 Sch.1
Part 46 r.46.13, substituted: SI 2013/262 Sch.1
Part 46 r.46.14, substituted: SI 2013/262 Sch.1
Part 47, applied: SI 2013/480 Reg.46, SI 2013/503 Reg.6, SI 2013/512 Reg.31, SI 2013/3208 r.117, r.118
Part 47, amended: SI 2013/534 Sch.1 para.2
Part 47 r.47.1, substituted: SI 2013/262 Sch.1
Part 47 r.47.2, substituted: SI 2013/262 Sch.1
Part 47 r.47.3, substituted: SI 2013/262 Sch.1
Part 47 r.47.4, substituted: SI 2013/262 Sch.1
Part 47 r.47.5, substituted: SI 2013/262 Sch.1
Part 47 r.47.6, amended: SI 2013/1695 r.8
Part 47 r.47.6, substituted: SI 2013/262 Sch.1
Part 47 r.47.7, substituted: SI 2013/262 Sch.1
Part 47 r.47.8, amended: SI 2013/534 Sch.1 para.2
Part 47 r.47.8, substituted: SI 2013/262 Sch.1
Part 47 r.47.9, substituted: SI 2013/262 Sch.1
Part 47 r.47.10, substituted: SI 2013/262 Sch.1
Part 47 r.47.11, substituted: SI 2013/262 Sch.1
Part 47 r.47.12, substituted: SI 2013/262 Sch.1
Part 47 r.47.13, substituted: SI 2013/262 Sch.1
Part 47 r.47.14, substituted: SI 2013/262 Sch.1
Part 47 r.47.15, amended: SI 2013/1974 r.22
Part 47 r.47.15, substituted: SI 2013/262 Sch.1
Part 47 r.47.16, substituted: SI 2013/262 Sch.1
Part 47 r.47.17, substituted: SI 2013/262 Sch.1
Part 47 r.47.17A, substituted: SI 2013/262 Sch.1
Part 47 r.47.18, amended: SI 2013/534 Sch.1 para.2
Part 47 r.47.18, substituted: SI 2013/262 Sch.1
Part 47 r.47.19, substituted: SI 2013/262 Sch.1
Part 47 r.47.20, substituted: SI 2013/262 Sch.1
Part 47 r.47.21, substituted: SI 2013/262 Sch.1
Part 47 r.47.22, substituted: SI 2013/262 Sch.1
Part 47 r.47.23, substituted: SI 2013/262 Sch.1
Part 47 r.47.24, substituted: SI 2013/262 Sch.1
Part 47 r.47.25, substituted: SI 2013/262 Sch.1
Part 47 r.47.26, substituted: SI 2013/262 Sch.1
Part 47 r.47.27, substituted: SI 2013/262 Sch.1
Part 48 r.48.1, substituted: SI 2013/262 Sch.1
Part 48 r.48.2, substituted: SI 2013/262 Sch.1
Part 48 r.48.3, substituted: SI 2013/262 Sch.1
Part 48 r.48.4, substituted: SI 2013/262 Sch.1
Part 48 r.48.5, substituted: SI 2013/262 Sch.1
Part 48 r.48.6, substituted: SI 2013/262 Sch.1
Part 48 r.48.6A, substituted: SI 2013/262 Sch.1
Part 48 r.48.7, substituted: SI 2013/262 Sch.1
Part 48 r.48.8, substituted: SI 2013/262 Sch.1
Part 48 r.48.9, substituted: SI 2013/262 Sch.1
Part 48 r.48.10, substituted: SI 2013/262 Sch.1
Part 51, applied: SI 2013/262 r.22
Part 52, applied: SI 2013/1046 r.125, SI 2013/1554 r.76_13, SI 2013/3208 r.129
Part 52, referred to: SI 2013/435 Reg.30, SI 2013/1046 r.125, SI 2013/3208 r.129
Part 52 r.52.1, amended: SI 2013/1974 r.23
Part 52 r.52.9A, added: SI 2013/262 r.17
Part 52 r.52.15, amended: SI 2013/1412 r.3
Part 54 r.54.5, amended: SI 2013/1412 r.4
Part 54 r.54.6, amended: SI 2013/262 r.18
Part 54 r.54.12, amended: SI 2013/1412 r.4
Part 55 r.55.9, amended: SI 2013/1974 r.24
Part 62 r.62.7, amended: SI 2013/1974 r.25
Part 63, substituted: SI 2013/1974 r.26
Part 63 r.63.1, amended: SI 2013/1974 r.26
Part 63 r.63.2, amended: SI 2013/1974 r.26
Part 63 r.63.3, amended: SI 2013/1974 r.26
Part 63 r.63.8, amended: SI 2013/1974 r.26
Part 63 r.63.13, amended: SI 2013/1974 r.26
Part 63 r.63.17, amended: SI 2013/1974 r.26
Part 63 r.63.17A, added: SI 2013/1974 r.26
Part 63 r.63.18, substituted: SI 2013/1974 r.26
Part 63 r.63.19, amended: SI 2013/1974 r.26
Part 63 r.63.19, substituted: SI 2013/1974 r.26
Part 63 r.63.22, amended: SI 2013/1974 r.26
Part 63 r.63.23, amended: SI 2013/1974 r.26
Part 63 r.63.25, amended: SI 2013/1974 r.26
Part 63 r.63.26, amended: SI 2013/1974 r.26
Part 63 r.63.27, amended: SI 2013/262 r.19, SI 2013/1974 r.26
Part 63 r.63.27, revoked (in part): SI 2013/1974 r.26
Part 63 r.63.28, amended: SI 2013/1974 r.26
Part 67 r.67.1, amended: SI 2013/1974 r.27
Part 67 r.67.3, amended: SI 2013/1974 r.27
Part 68 r.68.1, substituted: SI 2013/1974 Sch.1
Part 68 r.68.2, substituted: SI 2013/1974 Sch.1
Part 68 r.68.2A, substituted: SI 2013/1974 Sch.1
Part 68 r.68.3, substituted: SI 2013/1974 Sch.1

Part 68 r.68.4, substituted: SI 2013/1974 Sch.1
Part 68 r.68.5, substituted: SI 2013/1974 Sch.1
Part 74 r.74.13, amended: SI 2013/534 Sch.1 para.13
Part 82 r.82.1, added: SI 2013/1571 Sch.1
Part 82 r.82.2, added: SI 2013/1571 Sch.1
Part 82 r.82.3, added: SI 2013/1571 Sch.1
Part 82 r.82.4, added: SI 2013/1571 Sch.1
Part 82 r.82.5, added: SI 2013/1571 Sch.1
Part 82 r.82.6, added: SI 2013/1571 Sch.1
Part 82 r.82.7, added: SI 2013/1571 Sch.1
Part 82 r.82.8, added: SI 2013/1571 Sch.1
Part 82 r.82.9, added: SI 2013/1571 Sch.1
Part 82 r.82.10, added: SI 2013/1571 Sch.1
Part 82 r.82.11, added: SI 2013/1571 Sch.1
Part 82 r.82.12, added: SI 2013/1571 Sch.1
Part 82 r.82.13, added: SI 2013/1571 Sch.1
Part 82 r.82.14, added: SI 2013/1571 Sch.1
Part 82 r.82.15, added: SI 2013/1571 Sch.1
Part 82 r.82.16, added: SI 2013/1571 Sch.1
Part 82 r.82.17, added: SI 2013/1571 Sch.1
Part 82 r.82.18, added: SI 2013/1571 Sch.1
Part 82 r.82.19, added: SI 2013/1571 Sch.1
Part 82 r.82.20, added: SI 2013/1571 Sch.1
Part 82 r.82.21, added: SI 2013/1571 Sch.1
Part 82 r.82.22, added: SI 2013/1571 Sch.1
Part 82 r.82.23, added: SI 2013/1571 Sch.1
Part 82 r.82.24, added: SI 2013/1571 Sch.1
Part 82 r.82.25, added: SI 2013/1571 Sch.1
Part 82 r.82.26, added: SI 2013/1571 Sch.1
Part 82 r.82.27, added: SI 2013/1571 Sch.1
Part 82 r.82.28, added: SI 2013/1571 Sch.1
Part 82 r.82.29, added: SI 2013/1571 Sch.1
Part 82 r.82.30, added: SI 2013/1571 Sch.1
Part 82 r.82.31, added: SI 2013/1571 Sch.1
Part 82 r.82.32, added: SI 2013/1571 Sch.1
Pt 1., see *JD Wetherspoon Plc v Harris* [2013] EWHC 1088 (Ch), [2013] 1 W.L.R. 3296 (Ch D), Sir Terence Etherton (Chancellor)
Pt 19., see *Fort Gilkicker Ltd, Re* [2013] EWHC 348 (Ch), [2013] Ch. 551 (Ch D (Companies Ct)), Briggs, J.
Pt 20., see *Harrison v Technical Sign Co Ltd* [2012] EWHC 2887 (TCC), [2013] B.L.R. 244 (QBD (TCC)), Judge David Grant
Pt 21., see *Baker Tilly v Makar* [2013] EWHC 759 (QB), [2013] 3 Costs L.R. 444 (QBD), Sir Raymond Jack
Pt 23., see *Thames Chambers Solicitors v Miah* [2013] EWHC 1245 (QB), [2013] 4 Costs L.R. 582 (QBD), Tugendhat, J.
Pt 24., see *Standard Bank Plc v Via Mat International Ltd* [2013] EWCA Civ 490, [2013] 2 All E.R. (Comm) 1222 (CA (Civ Div)), Moore-Bick, L.J.
Pt 3., see *Syngenta Ltd v Chemsource Ltd* [2012] EWHC 1507 (Pat), [2013] F.S.R. 11 (Ch D (Patents Ct)), Daniel Alexander Q.C.
Pt 31., see *Durham CC v D* [2012] EWCA Civ 1654, [2013] 1 W.L.R. 2305 (CA (Civ Div)), Maurice Kay, L.J. (VP, CA Civ)
Pt 32., see *Fenty v Arcadia Group Brands Ltd (t/a Topshop)* [2013] EWHC 1945 (Ch), [2013] Bus. L.R. 1165 (Ch D), Birss, J.
Pt 35., see *Fenty v Arcadia Group Brands Ltd (t/a Topshop)* [2013] EWHC 1945 (Ch), [2013] Bus. L.R. 1165 (Ch D), Birss, J.; see *Wall v Mutuelle De Poitiers Assurances* [2013] EWHC 53 (QB), [2013] 1 W.L.R. 3890 (QBD), Tugendhat, J.
Pt 36., see *Bellway Homes Ltd v Seymour (Civil Engineering Contractors) Ltd* [2013] EWHC 1890 (TCC), [2013] T.C.L.R. 8 (QBD (TCC)), Akenhead, J.; see *F&C Alternative Investments (Holdings) Ltd v Barthelemy (Costs)* [2012] EWCA Civ 843, [2013] 1 W.L.R. 548 (CA (Civ Div)), Arden, L.J.; see *KC v MGN Ltd (Costs)* [2013] EWCA Civ 3, [2013] 2 Costs L.R. 269 (CA (Civ Div)), Lord Judge, L.C.J.; see *Langsam v Beachcroft LLP* [2012] EWCA Civ 1230, [2013] 1 Costs L.O. 112 (CA (Civ Div)), Arden, L.J.; see *Procter & Gamble Co v Svenska Cellulosa Aktiebolaget SCA* [2012] EWHC 2839 (Ch), [2013] 1 W.L.R. 1464 (Ch D), Hildyard, J; see *SG (A Child) v Hewitt (Costs)* [2012] EWCA Civ 1053, [2013] 1 All E.R. 1118 (CA (Civ Div)), Pill, L.J.; see *Wilson v Ministry of Defence* [2013] C.P. Rep. 33 (CC (Winchester)), Judge Iain Hughes QC
Pt 44., see *Nutting v Khaliq* [2012] EWCA Civ 1726, [2013] B.P.I.R. 340 (CA (Civ Div)), Mummery, L.J.; see *Sycamore Bidco Ltd v Breslin* [2013] EWHC 583 (Ch), [2013] 4 Costs L.O. 572 (Ch D), Mann, J.
Pt 45., see *Patterson v Ministry of Defence* [2012] EWHC 2767 (QB), [2013] 2 Costs L.R. 197 (QBD), Males, J.; see *Wilson v Ministry of Defence* [2013] C.P. Rep. 33 (CC (Winchester)), Judge Iain Hughes QC
Pt 48., see *Brown-Quinn v Equity Syndicate Management Ltd* [2012] EWCA Civ 1633, [2013] 1 W.L.R. 1740 (CA (Civ Div)), Longmore, L.J.
Pt 54., see *R. (on the application of Lyon) v Cambridge City Council* [2012] EWHC 2684 (Admin), [2013] Env. L.R. 11 (QBD (Admin)), Judge Birtles
Pt 6., see *Weston v Bates* [2012] EWHC 590 (QB), [2013] 1 W.L.R. 189 (QBD), Tugendhat, J.

Pt 61., see *Cosmotrade SA v Kairos Shipping Ltd* [2013] EWHC 1904 (Comm), [2013] 2 Lloyd's Rep. 535 (QBD (Comm)), Simon, J.
Pt 63., see *Ningbo Wentai Sports Equipment Co Ltd v Wang* [2013] F.S.R. 40 (PCC), Judge Birss Q.C.
Pt 64., see *Green v Astor* [2013] EWHC 1857 (Ch), [2013] W.T.L.R. 1489 (Ch D), Roth, J.
Pt 69., see *Glatt v Sinclair* [2013] EWCA Civ 241, [2013] 1 W.L.R. 3602 (CA (Civ Div)), Maurice Kay, L.J.
Pt 7., see *Bamford v Harvey* [2012] EWHC 2858 (Ch), [2013] Bus. L.R. 589 (Ch D), Roth, J.; see *Eaton v Natural England* [2012] EWHC 2401 (Admin), [2013] 1 C.M.L.R. 10 (QBD (Admin)), Judge Waksman Q.C.; see *Sykes & Sons Ltd, Re* [2012] EWHC 1005 (Ch), [2013] Bus. L.R. 106 (Ch D), Richard Snowden QC
Pt 79., see *Bank Mellat v HM Treasury* [2013] UKSC 38, [2013] 4 All E.R. 495 (SC), Lord Neuberger (President); see *Mastafa v HM Treasury* [2012] EWHC 3578 (Admin), [2013] 1 W.L.R. 1621 (QBD (Admin)), Collins, J.
Pt 8., see *Manolete Partners Plc v Hastings BC* [2013] EWHC 842 (TCC), [2013] B.L.R. 361 (QBD (TCC)), Ramsey, J.; see *TSG Building Services Plc v South Anglia Housing Ltd* [2013] EWHC 1151 (TCC), [2013] B.L.R. 484 (QBD (TCC)), Akenhead, J.; see *Vimercati v BV Trustco Ltd* [2012] EWHC 1410 (Ch), [2013] W.T.L.R. 157 (Ch D), Charles Hollander Q.C.; see *West Country Renovations Ltd v McDowell* [2012] EWHC 307 (TCC), [2013] 1 W.L.R. 416 (QBD (TCC)), Akenhead, J.
r.1.1, see *Atrium Training Services Ltd (In Liquidation), Re* [2013] EWHC 1562 (Ch), [2013] 5 Costs L.O. 707 (Ch D), Henderson, J.; see *Fons HF v Corporal Ltd* [2013] EWHC 1278 (Ch), [2013] 4 Costs L.O. 646 (Ch D (Manchester)), Judge Pelling Q.C.; see *Tinkler v Elliott* [2012] EWCA Civ 1289, [2013] C.P. Rep. 4 (CA (Civ Div)), Sir Maurice Kay (VP CA Civ); see *Venulum Property Investments Ltd v Space Architecture Ltd* [2013] EWHC 1242 (TCC), [2013] 4 Costs L.R. 596 (QBD (TCC)), Edwards-Stuart, J.
r.1.3, see *JSC BTA Bank v Ablyazov* [2012] EWCA Civ 1551, [2013] 1 W.L.R. 1845 (CA (Civ Div)), Sir Maurice Kay (VP CA Civ)
r.1.4, see *Interflora Inc v Marks & Spencer Plc* [2012] EWCA Civ 1501, [2013] 2 All E.R. 663 (CA (Civ Div)), Hughes, L.J.; see *Lazari v London and Newcastle (Camden) Ltd* [2013] EWHC 97 (TCC), [2013] C.P. Rep. 26 (QBD (TCC)), Akenhead, J.
r.2.5, see *Engel v Joint Committee for Parking and Traffic Regulation outside London (PATROL)* [2013] I.C.R. 1086 (EAT), Mitting, J.
r.3.1, see *Ali v Ali* [2013] EWHC 1233 (QB), [2013] 5 Costs L.O. 676 (QBD), Swift, J.; see *Atrium Training Services Ltd (In Liquidation), Re* [2013] EWHC 1562 (Ch), [2013] 5 Costs L.O. 707 (Ch D), Henderson, J.; see *Kesabo v African Barrick Gold Plc* [2013] EWHC 3198 (QB), [2013] 6 Costs L.R. 954 (QBD), Simon, J.; see *Lazari v London and Newcastle (Camden) Ltd* [2013] EWHC 97 (TCC), [2013] C.P. Rep. 26 (QBD (TCC)), Akenhead, J.; see *UK Highways A55 Ltd v Hyder Consulting (UK) Ltd* [2012] EWHC 3505 (TCC), [2013] B.L.R. 95 (QBD (TCC)), Edwards-Stuart, J.; see *Wilson v Ministry of Defence* [2013] C.P. Rep. 33 (CC (Winchester)), Judge Iain Hughes QC
r.3.4, see *Barclay Pharmaceuticals Ltd v Waypharm LP* [2013] EWHC 503 (Comm), [2013] 2 B.C.L.C. 551 (QBD (Comm)), Gloster, J.; see *Mears Ltd v Shoreline Housing Partnership Ltd* [2013] EWCA Civ 639, [2013] C.P. Rep. 39 (CA (Civ Div)), McCombe, L.J.; see *Peaktone Ltd v Joddrell* [2012] EWCA Civ 1035, [2013] 1 W.L.R. 784 (CA (Civ Div)), Etherton, L.J.; see *Vince v Wyatt* [2013] EWCA Civ 495, [2013] 1 W.L.R. 3525 (CA (Civ Div)), Thorpe, L.J.
r.3.9, see *Giggs v News Group Newspapers Ltd* [2012] EWHC 431 (QB), [2013] E.M.L.R. 5 (QBD), Tugendhat, J.; see *Kesabo v African Barrick Gold Plc* [2013] EWHC 3198 (QB), [2013] 6 Costs L.R. 954 (QBD), Simon, J.; see *Light on Line Ltd v Zumtobel Lighting Ltd* [2012] EWHC 3376 (QB), [2013] 1 Costs L.R. 129 (QBD), Slade, J.; see *Murray v Neil Dowlman Architecture Ltd* [2013] EWHC 872 (TCC), [2013] T.C.L.R. 5 (QBD (TCC)), Coulson, J.; see *O'Flaherty v Revenue and Customs Commissioners* [2013] UKUT 161 (TCC), [2013] S.T.C. 1946 (UT (Tax)), Judge Roger Berner; see *Raayan Al Iraq Co Ltd v Trans Victory Marine Inc* [2013] EWHC 2696 (Comm), [2013] 6 Costs L.R. 911 (QBD (Comm)), Andrew Smith, J.; see *Ryder Plc v Beever* [2012] EWCA Civ 1737, [2013] 2 Costs L.O. 364 (CA (Civ Div)), Etherton, L.J.; see *Travel & Holidays LLC v Hajj Charter Ltd* [2013] EWHC 1212 (QB), [2013] 5 Costs L.O. 657 (QBD), Leggatt, J.; see *UK Highways A55 Ltd v Hyder Consulting (UK) Ltd* [2012] EWHC 3505 (TCC), [2013] B.L.R. 95 (QBD (TCC)), Edwards-Stuart, J.; see *Venulum Property Investments Ltd v*

Space Architecture Ltd [2013] EWHC 1242 (TCC), [2013] 4 Costs L.R. 596 (QBD (TCC)), Edwards-Stuart, J.
r.3.12, see *Murray v Neil Dowlman Architecture Ltd* [2013] EWHC 872 (TCC), [2013] T.C.L.R. 5 (QBD (TCC)), Coulson, J.
r.3.15, see *Elvanite Full Circle Ltd v AMEC Earth & Environmental (UK) Ltd* [2013] EWHC 1643 (TCC), [2013] 4 All E.R. 765 (QBD (TCC)), Coulson, J.
r.3.18, see *Elvanite Full Circle Ltd v AMEC Earth & Environmental (UK) Ltd* [2013] EWHC 1643 (TCC), [2013] 4 All E.R. 765 (QBD (TCC)), Coulson, J.; see *Murray v Neil Dowlman Architecture Ltd* [2013] EWHC 872 (TCC), [2013] T.C.L.R. 5 (QBD (TCC)), Coulson, J.
r.6.9, see *Actavis Group hf v Eli Lilly & Co* [2013] EWCA Civ 517, [2013] R.P.C. 37 (CA (Civ Div)), Longmore, L.J.
r.6.14, see *Kesabo v African Barrick Gold Plc* [2013] EWHC 3198 (QB), [2013] 6 Costs L.R. 954 (QBD), Simon, J.
r.6.15, see *Abela v Baadarani* [2013] UKSC 44, [2013] 1 W.L.R. 2043 (SC), Lord Neuberger (President)
r.6.20, see *Greene Wood & McClean LLP v Templeton Insurance Ltd* [2009] EWCA Civ 65, [2009] 1 W.L.R. 2013 (CA (Civ Div)), Sir Anthony Clarke, M.R.
r.6.21, see *Greene Wood & McClean LLP v Templeton Insurance Ltd* [2009] EWCA Civ 65, [2009] 1 W.L.R. 2013 (CA (Civ Div)), Sir Anthony Clarke, M.R.
r.6.36, see *Aeroflot - Russian Airlines v Berezovsky* [2013] EWCA Civ 784, [2013] 2 Lloyd's Rep. 242 (CA (Civ Div)), Laws, L.J.
r.6.37, see *Abela v Baadarani* [2013] UKSC 44, [2013] 1 W.L.R. 2043 (SC), Lord Neuberger (President)
r.6.40, see *Weston v Bates* [2012] EWHC 590 (QB), [2013] 1 W.L.R. 189 (QBD), Tugendhat, J.
r.7.4, see *Kesabo v African Barrick Gold Plc* [2013] EWHC 3198 (QB), [2013] 6 Costs L.R. 954 (QBD), Simon, J.
r.7.5, see *Kesabo v African Barrick Gold Plc* [2013] EWHC 3198 (QB), [2013] 6 Costs L.R. 954 (QBD), Simon, J.; see *Venulum Property Investments Ltd v Space Architecture Ltd* [2013] EWHC 1242 (TCC), [2013] 4 Costs L.R. 596 (QBD (TCC)), Edwards-Stuart, J.; see *Weston v Bates* [2012] EWHC 590 (QB), [2013] 1 W.L.R. 189 (QBD), Tugendhat, J.
r.8.1, see *Green v Astor* [2013] EWHC 1857 (Ch), [2013] W.T.L.R. 1489 (Ch D), Roth, J.
r.13.1, see *Latmar Holdings Corp v Media Focus Ltd* [2013] EWCA Civ 4, [2013] I.L.Pr. 19 (CA (Civ Div)), Pill, L.J.
r.14.1, see *Berg v Blackburn Rovers Football Club & Athletic Plc* [2013] EWHC 1070 (Ch), [2013] I.R.L.R. 537 (Ch D (Manchester)), Judge Pelling Q.C.; see *Tchenguiz v Director of the Serious Fraud Office* [2013] EWHC 1578 (QB), [2013] Lloyd's Rep. F.C. 535 (QBD), Eder, J.
r.15.5, see *Giggs v News Group Newspapers Ltd* [2012] EWHC 431 (QB), [2013] E.M.L.R. 5 (QBD), Tugendhat, J.
r.16.4, see *Kesabo v African Barrick Gold Plc* [2013] EWHC 3198 (QB), [2013] 6 Costs L.R. 954 (QBD), Simon, J.
r.17.1, see *San Vicente v Secretary of State for Communities and Local Government* [2012] EWHC 3585 (Admin), [2013] J.P.L. 642 (QBD (Admin)), Philip Mott Q.C.; see *San Vicente v Secretary of State for Communities and Local Government* [2013] EWCA Civ 817, [2013] J.P.L. 1516 (CA (Civ Div)), Lloyd, L.J.
r.17.4, see *San Vicente v Secretary of State for Communities and Local Government* [2012] EWHC 3585 (Admin), [2013] J.P.L. 642 (QBD (Admin)), Philip Mott Q.C.; see *San Vicente v Secretary of State for Communities and Local Government* [2013] EWCA Civ 817, [2013] J.P.L. 1516 (CA (Civ Div)), Lloyd, L.J.
r.19.2, see *Hounslow LBC v Cumar* [2012] EWCA Civ 1426, [2013] H.L.R. 17 (CA (Civ Div)), Lord Dyson (M.R.); see *Owners of the Theresa Libra v Owners of the MSC Pamela* [2013] EWHC 2792 (Admlty), [2013] 2 Lloyd's Rep. 596 (QBD (Admlty)), Teare, J.
r.19.5, see *Insight Group Ltd v Kingston Smith (A Firm)* [2012] EWHC 3644 (QB), [2013] 3 All E.R. 518 (QBD), Leggatt, J.; see *Owners of the Theresa Libra v Owners of the MSC Pamela* [2013] EWHC 2792 (Admlty), [2013] 2 Lloyd's Rep. 596 (QBD (Admlty)), Teare, J.
r.21.3, see *Baker Tilly v Makar* [2013] EWHC 759 (QB), [2013] 3 Costs L.R. 444 (QBD), Sir Raymond Jack
r.21.10, see *RH v University Hospitals Bristol NHS Foundation Trust (formerly United Bristol Healthcare NHS Trust)* [2013] EWHC 299 (QB), [2013] P.I.Q.R. P12 (QBD), Swift, J.
r.23.8, see *Church v MGN Ltd* [2012] EWHC 693 (QB), [2013] 1 W.L.R. 284 (QBD), Tugendhat, J.
r.23.10, see *Mackay v Ashwood Enterprises Ltd* [2013] EWCA Civ 959, [2013] 5 Costs L.R. 816 (CA (Civ Div)), Lloyd, L.J.

r.24.2, see *Vince v Wyatt* [2013] EWCA Civ 495, [2013] 1 W.L.R. 3525 (CA (Civ Div)), Thorpe, L.J.
r.25.1, see *Cosmotrade SA v Kairos Shipping Ltd* [2013] EWHC 1904 (Comm), [2013] 2 Lloyd's Rep. 535 (QBD (Comm)), Simon, J.
r.25.3, see *O'Farrell v O'Farrell* [2012] EWHC 123 (QB), [2013] 1 F.L.R. 77 (QBD), Tugendhat, J.
r.25.6, see *Lazari v London and Newcastle (Camden) Ltd* [2013] EWHC 97 (TCC), [2013] C.P. Rep. 26 (QBD (TCC)), Akenhead, J.
r.25.7, see *GKN Holdings Plc v Revenue and Customs Commissioners* [2013] EWHC 108 (Ch), [2013] B.T.C. 113 (Ch D), Henderson, J.; see *Lazari v London and Newcastle (Camden) Ltd* [2013] EWHC 97 (TCC), [2013] C.P. Rep. 26 (QBD (TCC)), Akenhead, J.
r.25.13, see *Moondance Maritime Enterprises SA v Carbofer Maritime Trading APS* [2012] EWHC 3618 (Comm), [2013] 1 Lloyd's Rep. 269 (QBD (Comm)), Field, J.
r.25.14, see *Chilab v King's College London* [2012] EWCA Civ 1178, [2013] 2 Costs L.R. 191 (CA (Civ Div)), Hughes, L.J.
r.30.3, see *Crocuer Enterprises Ltd v Giordano Poultry-Plast SpA* [2013] EWHC 2491 (Ch), [2013] F.S.R. 44 (Ch D (Patents Ct)), Mann, J.
r.31.8, see *Mueller Europe Ltd v Central Roofing (South Wales) Ltd* [2012] EWHC 3417 (TCC), [2013] T.C.L.R. 2 (QBD (TCC)), Coulson, J.
r.32.1, see *Interflora Inc v Marks & Spencer Plc* [2012] EWCA Civ 1501, [2013] 2 All E.R. 663 (CA (Civ Div)), Hughes, L.J.
r.32.2, see *Fenty v Arcadia Group Brands Ltd (t/a Topshop)* [2013] EWHC 1945 (Ch), [2013] Bus. L.R. 1165 (Ch D), Birss, J.
r.32.4, see *JD Wetherspoon Plc v Harris* [2013] EWHC 1088 (Ch), [2013] 1 W.L.R. 3296 (Ch D), Sir Terence Etherton (Chancellor)
r.32.14, see *Berry Piling Systems Ltd v Sheer Projects Ltd* [2013] EWHC 347 (TCC), [2013] B.L.R. 232 (QBD (TCC)), Akenhead, J.
r.33.4, see *Boyd v Incommunities Ltd* [2013] EWCA Civ 756, [2013] H.L.R. 44 (CA (Civ Div)), Longmore, L.J.
r.35.1, see *Speak v Myerson* [2012] EWCA Civ 1723, [2013] R.V.R. 78 (CA (Civ Div)), Richards, L.J.; see *Turner v Walsall Hospital NHS Trust* [2013] EWHC 1221 (QB), [2013] Med. L.R. 379 (QBD), Globe, J.
r.35.4, see *Fenty v Arcadia Group Brands Ltd (t/a Topshop)* [2013] EWHC 1945 (Ch), [2013] Bus. L.R. 1165 (Ch D), Birss, J.
r.35.12, see *Mueller Europe Ltd v Central Roofing (South Wales) Ltd* [2012] EWHC 3417 (TCC), [2013] T.C.L.R. 2 (QBD (TCC)), Coulson, J.
r.36.2, see *Jolly v Harsco Infrastructure Services Ltd* [2012] EWHC 3086 (QB), [2013] 1 Costs L.R. 115 (QBD), Cranston, J.; see *Mehjoo v Harben Barker (A Firm)* [2013] EWHC 1669 (QB), [2013] 5 Costs L.R. 645 (QBD), Silber, J.; see *Procter & Gamble Co v Svenska Cellulosa Aktiebolaget SCA* [2012] EWHC 2839 (Ch), [2013] 1 W.L.R. 1464 (Ch D), Hildyard, J
r.36.3, see *Jolly v Harsco Infrastructure Services Ltd* [2012] EWHC 3086 (QB), [2013] 1 Costs L.R. 115 (QBD), Cranston, J.
r.36.8, see *Mehjoo v Harben Barker (A Firm)* [2013] EWHC 1669 (QB), [2013] 5 Costs L.R. 645 (QBD), Silber, J.
r.36.9, see *Wilson v Ministry of Defence* [2013] C.P. Rep. 33 (CC (Winchester)), Judge Iain Hughes QC
r.36.10, see *Bellway Homes Ltd v Seymour (Civil Engineering Contractors) Ltd* [2013] EWHC 1890 (TCC), [2013] T.C.L.R. 8 (QBD (TCC)), Akenhead, J.; see *Jolly v Harsco Infrastructure Services Ltd* [2012] EWHC 3086 (QB), [2013] 1 Costs L.R. 115 (QBD), Cranston, J.; see *Mehjoo v Harben Barker (A Firm)* [2013] EWHC 1669 (QB), [2013] 5 Costs L.R. 645 (QBD), Silber, J.; see *SG (A Child) v Hewitt (Costs)* [2012] EWCA Civ 1053, [2013] 1 All E.R. 1118 (CA (Civ Div)), Pill, L.J.
r.36.11, see *Jolly v Harsco Infrastructure Services Ltd* [2012] EWHC 3086 (QB), [2013] 1 Costs L.R. 115 (QBD), Cranston, J.
r.36.13, see *Beasley v Alexander* [2012] EWHC 2715 (QB), [2013] 1 W.L.R. 762 (QBD), Sir Raymond Jack
r.36.14, see *F&C Alternative Investments (Holdings) Ltd v Barthelemy (Costs)* [2012] EWCA Civ 843, [2013] 1 W.L.R. 548 (CA (Civ Div)), Arden, L.J.; see *Jolly v Harsco Infrastructure Services Ltd* [2012] EWHC 3086 (QB), [2013] 1 Costs L.R. 115 (QBD), Cranston, J.; see *Mehjoo v Harben Barker (A Firm)* [2013] EWHC 1669 (QB), [2013] 5 Costs L.R. 645 (QBD), Silber, J.; see *Procter & Gamble Co v Svenska Cellulosa Aktiebolaget SCA* [2012] EWHC 2839 (Ch), [2013] 1 W.L.R. 1464 (Ch D), Hildyard, J; see *R. (on the application of Hemming (t/a Simply Pleasure Ltd)) v Westminster City Council* [2013] EWCA Civ 591, [2013] P.T.S.R. 1377 (CA (Civ Div)), Lord Dyson (M.R.); see *Virgin Atlantic Airways Ltd v Jet Airways (India) Ltd* [2012] EWHC 3318 (Pat),

[2013] 1 W.L.R. 1005 (Ch D (Patents Ct)), Floyd, J.
r.38.6, see *Fortress Value Recovery Fund I LLC v Blue Skye Special Opportunities Fund LP* [2013] EWHC 14 (Comm), [2013] 1 All E.R. (Comm) 973 (QBD (Comm)), Flaux, J.; see *Nelson's Yard Management Co v Eziefula* [2013] EWCA Civ 235, [2013] C.P. Rep. 29 (CA (Civ Div)), Arden, L.J.
r.39.2, see *Deripaska v Cherney* [2012] EWCA Civ 1235, [2013] C.P. Rep. 1 (CA (Civ Div)), Maurice Kay, L.J.; see *FI Call Ltd, Re* [2013] EWCA Civ 819, [2013] 1 W.L.R. 2993 (CA (Civ Div)), Maurice Kay, L.J.; see *MXB v East Sussex Hospitals NHS Trust* [2012] EWHC 3279 (QB), (2013) 177 J.P. 31 (QBD), Tugendhat, J.; see *Times Newspapers Ltd v McNamara* [2013] B.P.I.R. 1092 (Ch D (Bankruptcy Ct)), Registrar Baister
r.39.3, see *Tinkler v Elliott* [2012] EWCA Civ 1289, [2013] C.P. Rep. 4 (CA (Civ Div)), Sir Maurice Kay (VP CA Civ)
r.40.11, see *AB v CD Ltd* [2013] EWHC 1376 (TCC), [2013] B.L.R. 435 (QBD (TCC)), Edwards-Stuart, J.
r.40.12, see *Joshi v Mahida* [2013] EWHC 486 (Ch), [2013] W.T.L.R. 859 (Ch D), Jonathan Gaunt, Q.C.
r.40.20, see *McManus v European Risk Insurance Co hf* [2013] EWHC 18 (Ch), [2013] Lloyd's Rep. I.R. 533 (Ch D), Vivien Rose
r.43.2, see *Henderson v All Around The World Recordings Ltd (Costs)* [2013] EWPCC 19, [2013] F.S.R. 42 (PCC), Judge Birss Q.C.
r.44.2, see *Hammersmatch Properties (Welwyn) Ltd v Saint-Gobain Ceramics & Plastics Ltd* [2013] EWHC 2227 (TCC), [2013] B.L.R. 554 (QBD (TCC)), Ramsey, J.
r.44.3, see *Churchill Insurance Co Ltd v Fitzgerald* [2012] EWCA Civ 1465, [2013] 3 Costs L.O. 424 (CA (Civ Div)), Sir Maurice Kay (VP CA Civ); see *F&C Alternative Investments (Holdings) Ltd v Barthelemy (Costs)* [2012] EWCA Civ 843, [2013] 1 W.L.R. 548 (CA (Civ Div)), Arden, L.J.; see *Henderson v All Around The World Recordings Ltd (Costs)* [2013] EWPCC 19, [2013] F.S.R. 42 (PCC), Judge Birss Q.C.; see *Jolly v Harsco Infrastructure Services Ltd* [2012] EWHC 3086 (QB), [2013] 1 Costs L.R. 115 (QBD), Cranston, J.; see *Jones v Secretary of State for Energy and Climate Change* [2012] EWHC 3647 (QB), [2013] 2 Costs L.R. 230 (QBD), Swift, J.; see *KS v ND (Schedule I: Appeal: Costs)* [2013] EWHC 464 (Fam), [2013] 2 F.L.R. 698 (Fam Div), Mostyn, J.; see *Magical Marking Ltd v Ware and Kay LLP* [2013] EWHC 636 (Ch), [2013] 4 Costs L.R. 535 (Ch D (Leeds)), Briggs, J.; see *Procter & Gamble Co v Svenska Cellulosa Aktiebolaget SCA* [2012] EWHC 2839 (Ch), [2013] 1 W.L.R. 1464 (Ch D), Hildyard, J; see *R. (on the application of Naureen) v Salford City Council* [2012] EWCA Civ 1795, [2013] 2 Costs L.R. 257 (CA (Civ Div)), Moore-Bick, L.J.; see *Vava v Anglo American South Africa Ltd* [2013] EWHC 2326 (QB), [2013] 5 Costs L.R. 805 (QBD), Andrew Smith, J.
r.44.3B, see *Light on Line Ltd v Zumtobel Lighting Ltd* [2012] EWHC 3376 (QB), [2013] 1 Costs L.R. 129 (QBD), Slade, J.
r.44.5, see *A (Children) v Lancashire CC* [2013] EWHC 851 (Fam), [2013] 2 F.L.R. 1221 (Fam Div), Peter Jackson, J.; see *Connell v Mutch (t/a Southey Building Services)* [2012] EWCA Civ 1589, [2013] C.P. Rep. 11 (CA (Civ Div)), Mummery, L.J.; see *North Oxford Golf Club v A2 Dominion Homes Ltd* [2013] EWHC 852 (QB), [2013] 3 Costs L.R. 509 (QBD), Royce, J.
r.44.10, see *Mackay v Ashwood Enterprises Ltd* [2013] EWCA Civ 959, [2013] 5 Costs L.R. 816 (CA (Civ Div)), Lloyd, L.J.
r.44.12, see *Vava v Anglo American South Africa Ltd* [2013] EWHC 2326 (QB), [2013] 5 Costs L.R. 805 (QBD), Andrew Smith, J.
r.44.14, see *R. (on the application of Gassama) v Secretary of State for the Home Department* [2012] EWHC 3049 (Admin), [2013] P.N.L.R. 10 (QBD (Admin)), Haddon-Cave, J.
r.44.18, see *Syngenta Ltd v Chemsource Ltd* [2012] EWHC 1507 (Pat), [2013] F.S.R. 11 (Ch D (Patents Ct)), Daniel Alexander Q.C.
r.45.13, see *Costin v Merron* [2013] EWCA Civ 380, [2013] 3 Costs L.R. 391 (CA (Civ Div)), Leveson, L.J.
r.45.15, see *Wilson v Ministry of Defence* [2013] C.P. Rep. 33 (CC (Winchester)), Judge Iain Hughes QC
r.45.30, see *Henderson v All Around The World Recordings Ltd (Costs)* [2013] EWPCC 19, [2013] F.S.R. 42 (PCC), Judge Birss Q.C.
r.47.6, see *Light on Line Ltd v Zumtobel Lighting Ltd* [2012] EWHC 3376 (QB), [2013] 1 Costs L.R. 129 (QBD), Slade, J.
r.48.2, see *Bank of Scotland v Qutb (Costs)* [2012] EWCA Civ 1661, [2013] C.P. Rep. 14 (CA (Civ Div)), Mummery, L.J.
r.48.4, see *Davies v Watkins* [2012] EWCA Civ 1570, [2013] C.P. Rep. 10 (CA (Civ Div)), Thorpe, L.J.

r.48.6, see *Sinclair v Dhillon* [2012] EWHC 3517 (Admin), [2013] Lloyd's Rep. F.C. 224 (QBD (Admin)), Haddon-Cave, J.
r.48.6A, see *Jones v Secretary of State for Energy and Climate Change* [2012] EWHC 3647 (QB), [2013] 2 Costs L.R. 230 (QBD), Swift, J.
r.48.7, see *Thames Chambers Solicitors v Miah* [2013] EWHC 1245 (QB), [2013] 4 Costs L.R. 582 (QBD), Tugendhat, J.
r.52.3, see *Manchester College v Hazel* [2013] EWCA Civ 281, [2013] C.P. Rep. 28 (CA (Civ Div)), Jackson, L.J.; see *R. (on the application of Parekh) v Upper Tribunal (Immigration and Asylum Chamber)* [2013] EWCA Civ 679, [2013] C.P. Rep. 38 (CA (Civ Div)), Hallett, L.J.; see *Thursfield v Thursfield* [2013] EWCA Civ 840, [2013] C.P. Rep. 44 (CA (Civ Div)), Lloyd, L.J.
r.52.9, see *Manchester College v Hazel* [2013] EWCA Civ 281, [2013] C.P. Rep. 28 (CA (Civ Div)), Jackson, L.J.
r.52.9A, see *Manchester College v Hazel* [2013] EWCA Civ 281, [2013] C.P. Rep. 28 (CA (Civ Div)), Jackson, L.J.
r.52.10, see *Johnson v Westminster City Council* [2013] EWCA Civ 773, [2013] H.L.R. 45 (CA (Civ Div)), Aikens, L.J.
r.52.11, see *A (A Child) (Intractable Contact Dispute: Human Rights Violations), Re* [2013] EWCA Civ 1104, [2013] 3 F.C.R. 257 (CA (Civ Div)), Aikens L.J.; see *Oraki v Dean & Dean* [2012] EWHC 2885 (Ch), [2013] B.P.I.R. 88 (Ch D (Bankruptcy Ct)), Robert Ham, Q.C.; see *Turner v Walsall Hospital NHS Trust* [2013] EWHC 1221 (QB), [2013] Med. L.R. 379 (QBD), Globe, J.
r.52.13, see *R. (on the application of NB (Algeria)) v Secretary of State for the Home Department* [2012] EWCA Civ 1050, [2013] 1 W.L.R. 31 (CA (Civ Div)), Lord Neuberger (M.R.)
r.52.15, see *R. (on the application of Parekh) v Upper Tribunal (Immigration and Asylum Chamber)* [2013] EWCA Civ 679, [2013] C.P. Rep. 38 (CA (Civ Div)), Hallett, L.J.
r.52.17, see *R. (on the application of Tajik) v City of Westminster Magistrates' Court* [2012] EWHC 3347 (Admin), [2013] 1 W.L.R. 2283 (DC), Moses, L.J.; see *Serious Organised Crime Agency v O'Docherty* [2013] EWCA Civ 518, [2013] C.P. Rep. 35 (CA (Civ Div)), Mummery, L.J.
r.54.5, see *R. (on the application of Anand) v Revenue and Customs Commissioners* [2012] EWHC 2989 (Admin), [2013] C.P. Rep. 2 (DC), Pitchford, L.J.; see *R. (on the application of Lyon) v Cambridge City Council* [2012] EWHC 2684 (Admin), [2013] Env. L.R. 11 (QBD (Admin)), Judge Birtles; see *R. (on the application of Nash) v Barnet LBC* [2013] EWHC 1067 (Admin), [2013] B.L.G.R. 515 (QBD (Admin)), Underhill, L.J.
r.54.7A, see *R. (on the application of HS) v Upper Tribunal (Immigration and Asylum Chamber)* [2012] EWHC 3126 (Admin), [2013] Imm. A.R. 579 (QBD (Admin)), Charles, J.; see *R. (on the application of Parekh) v Upper Tribunal (Immigration and Asylum Chamber)* [2013] EWCA Civ 679, [2013] C.P. Rep. 38 (CA (Civ Div)), Hallett, L.J.
r.58.5, see *Raayan Al Iraq Co Ltd v Trans Victory Marine Inc* [2013] EWHC 2696 (Comm), [2013] 6 Costs L.R. 911 (QBD (Comm)), Andrew Smith, J.
r.62.2, see *AES Ust-Kamenogorsk Hydropower Plant LLP v Ust-Kamenogorsk Hydropower Plant JSC* [2013] UKSC 35, [2013] 1 W.L.R. 1889 (SC), Lord Neuberger, J.S.C.; see *Cruz City 1 Mauritius Holdings v Unitech Ltd* [2013] EWHC 1323 (Comm), [2013] 2 All E.R. (Comm) 1137 (QBD (Comm)), Field, J.
r.62.5, see *AES Ust-Kamenogorsk Hydropower Plant LLP v Ust-Kamenogorsk Hydropower Plant JSC* [2013] UKSC 35, [2013] 1 W.L.R. 1889 (SC), Lord Neuberger, J.S.C.
r.63.14, see *Actavis Group hf v Eli Lilly & Co* [2013] EWCA Civ 517, [2013] R.P.C. 37 (CA (Civ Div)), Longmore, L.J.
r.66.7, see *O'Farrell v O'Farrell* [2012] EWHC 123 (QB), [2013] 1 F.L.R. 77 (QBD), Tugendhat, J.
r.69.7, see *Glatt v Sinclair* [2013] EWCA Civ 241, [2013] 1 W.L.R. 3602 (CA (Civ Div)), Maurice Kay, L.J.; see *Sinclair v Dhillon* [2012] EWHC 3517 (Admin), [2013] Lloyd's Rep. F.C. 224 (QBD (Admin)), Haddon-Cave, J.
r.69.11, see *Glatt v Sinclair* [2013] EWCA Civ 241, [2013] 1 W.L.R. 3602 (CA (Civ Div)), Maurice Kay, L.J.
r.72.8, see *JGD Construction Ltd v Mills* [2013] EWHC 572 (Ch), [2013] B.P.I.R. 811 (Ch D (Bristol)), Judge McCahill Q.C.
r.81.18, see *Utopia Tableware Ltd v BBP Marketing Ltd* [2013] EWPCC 28, [2013] F.S.R. 43 (PCC), Birss, J.
Sch.1 Part 17 para.8, amended: SI 2013/1974 r.29
Sch.1 Part 79 para.9, amended: SI 2013/1695 r.9
Sch.1 Part 115, applied: SI 2013/9 Reg.19
Sch.2 Part 27 para.7A, revoked (in part): SI 2013/262 r.20

3162. Fair Employment and Treatment (Northern Ireland) Order 1998

Part I, applied: 2013 c.22 Sch.4 para.4
Part II, applied: 2013 c.22 Sch.4 para.4
Part III, applied: 2013 c.22 Sch.4 para.4
Part IV, applied: 2013 c.22 Sch.4 para.4
Part V, applied: 2013 c.22 Sch.4 para.4
Part VI, applied: 2013 c.22 Sch.4 para.4
Part VIII, applied: 2013 c.22 Sch.4 para.4
Part IX, applied: 2013 c.22 Sch.4 para.4
Part X, applied: 2013 c.22 Sch.4 para.4
Part XI, applied: 2013 c.22 Sch.4 para.4
Part XII, applied: 2013 c.22 Sch.4 para.4
Art.36, applied: 2013 c.22 Sch.4 para.4
Sch.1, applied: 2013 c.22 Sch.4 para.4
Sch.2, applied: 2013 c.22 Sch.4 para.4
Sch.2A, applied: 2013 c.22 Sch.4 para.4
Sch.3, applied: 2013 c.22 Sch.4 para.4
Sch.4, applied: 2013 c.22 Sch.4 para.4
Sch.5, applied: 2013 c.22 Sch.4 para.4

3175. Corporation Tax (Instalment Payments) Regulations 1998

Reg.6, varied: 2013 c.29 s.202
Reg.7, varied: 2013 c.29 s.202
Reg.8, varied: 2013 c.29 s.202
Reg.9, varied: 2013 c.29 s.202
Reg.10, varied: 2013 c.29 s.202
Reg.11, varied: 2013 c.29 s.202
Reg.13, varied: 2013 c.29 s.202

3186. Building Societies (Business Names) Regulations 1998

Reg.3, amended: SI 2013/496 Sch.10 para.3

3316. Carmarthenshire National Health Service Trust (Establishment) Order 1998

Art.1, amended: SI 2013/593 Art.2

1999

71. Allocation of Housing and Homelessness (Review Procedures) Regulations 1999

Reg.8, see *Ibrahim v Wandsworth LBC* [2013] EWCA Civ 20, [2013] P.T.S.R. 898 (CA (Civ Div)), Mummery, L.J.; see *Obiorah v Lewisham LBC* [2013] EWCA Civ 325, [2013] H.L.R. 35 (CA (Civ Div)), Kitchin, L.J.

137. National Lottery (Imposition of Penalties and Revocation of Licences) Procedure Regulations 1999

Reg.3, amended: SI 2013/2329 Sch.1 para.33
Reg.4, amended: SI 2013/2329 Sch.1 para.33
Reg.5, amended: SI 2013/2329 Sch.1 para.33
Reg.6, amended: SI 2013/2329 Sch.1 para.33
Reg.7, amended: SI 2013/2329 Sch.1 para.33
Reg.8, amended: SI 2013/2329 Sch.1 para.33
Reg.9, amended: SI 2013/2329 Sch.1 para.33
Reg.10, amended: SI 2013/2329 Sch.1 para.33
Reg.11, amended: SI 2013/2329 Sch.1 para.33
Reg.12, amended: SI 2013/2329 Sch.1 para.33
Reg.13, amended: SI 2013/2329 Sch.1 para.33
Reg.14, amended: SI 2013/2329 Sch.1 para.33
Reg.15, amended: SI 2013/2329 Sch.1 para.33
Reg.16, amended: SI 2013/2329 Sch.1 para.33
Reg.17, amended: SI 2013/2329 Sch.1 para.33
Reg.18, amended: SI 2013/2329 Sch.1 para.33

186. Protection of Wrecks (Designation) Order 1999

revoked: SSI 2013/276 Sch.1

220. National Institute for Clinical Excellence (Establishment and Constitution) Order 1999

revoked: SI 2013/235 Sch.2 para.179

260. National Institute for Clinical Excellence Regulations 1999

revoked: SI 2013/235 Sch.2 para.180

293. Town and Country Planning (Environmental Impact Assessment) (England and Wales) Regulations 1999

see *R. (on the application of Burridge) v Breckland DC* [2013] EWCA Civ 228, [2013] J.P.L. 1308 (CA (Civ Div)), Pill, L.J.; see *R. (on the application of Evans) v Secretary of State for Communities and Local Government* [2013] EWCA Civ 114, [2013] J.P.L. 1027 (CA (Civ Div)), Patten, L.J.; see *R. (on the application of Loader) v Secretary of State for Communities and Local Government* [2012] EWCA Civ 869, [2013] P.T.S.R. 406 (CA (Civ Div)), Pill, L.J.; see *R. (on the application of Save Woolley Valley Action Group Ltd) v Bath and North East Somerset Council* [2012] EWHC 2161 (Admin), [2013] Env. L.R. 8 (QBD (Admin)), Lang, J.
Reg.2, amended: SI 2013/755 Sch.4 para.79
Reg.2, revoked (in part): SI 2013/755 Sch.4 para.79
Reg.2, see *R. (on the application of Loader) v Secretary of State for Communities and Local Government* [2012] EWCA Civ 869, [2013] P.T.S.R. 406 (CA (Civ Div)), Pill, L.J.; see *R. (on the application of TWS) v Manchester City Council* [2013] EWHC 55 (Admin), [2013] J.P.L. 972 (QBD (Admin)), Lindblom, J.
Reg.4, see *Gregory v Welsh Ministers* [2013] EWHC 63 (Admin), [2013] Env. L.R. 19 (QBD (Admin)), Judge Keyser Q.C.; see *R. (on the application of TWS) v Manchester City Council* [2013] EWHC 55 (Admin), [2013] J.P.L. 972 (QBD (Admin)), Lindblom, J.; see *Threadneedle Property Investments Ltd v Southwark LBC* [2012] EWHC 855 (Admin), [2013] Env. L.R. 1 (QBD (Admin)), Lindblom, J.

Reg.7, see *R. (on the application of Burridge) v Breckland DC* [2013] EWCA Civ 228, [2013] J.P.L. 1308 (CA (Civ Div)), Pill, L.J.
Reg.9, see *Gregory v Welsh Ministers* [2013] EWHC 63 (Admin), [2013] Env. L.R. 19 (QBD (Admin)), Judge Keyser Q.C.
Sch.2, see *Gregory v Welsh Ministers* [2013] EWHC 63 (Admin), [2013] Env. L.R. 19 (QBD (Admin)), Judge Keyser Q.C.; see *R. (on the application of Burridge) v Breckland DC* [2013] EWCA Civ 228, [2013] J.P.L. 1308 (CA (Civ Div)), Pill, L.J.; see *R. (on the application of TWS) v Manchester City Council* [2013] EWHC 55 (Admin), [2013] J.P.L. 972 (QBD (Admin)), Lindblom, J.; see *Thomas v Carmarthenshire Council* [2013] EWHC 783 (Admin), [2013] J.P.L. 1266 (QBD (Admin)), Burton, J.
Sch.2 para.3, see *R. (on the application of Burridge) v Breckland DC* [2013] EWCA Civ 228, [2013] J.P.L. 1308 (CA (Civ Div)), Pill, L.J.
Sch.3, see *R. (on the application of TWS) v Manchester City Council* [2013] EWHC 55 (Admin), [2013] J.P.L. 972 (QBD (Admin)), Lindblom, J.
Sch.4 Pt II para.4, see *R. (on the application of Gray) v Southwark LBC* [2012] EWCA Civ 1738, [2013] Env. L.R. 22 (CA (Civ Div)), Pill, L.J.

358. Corporation Tax (Treatment of Unrelieved Surplus Advance Corporation Tax) Regulations 1999
Reg.6, amended: SI 2013/157 Reg.2

367. Environmental Impact Assessment (Fish Farming in Marine Waters) Regulations 1999
Reg.2, amended: SI 2013/755 Sch.4 para.81
Sch.3 para.2, amended: SI 2013/755 Sch.4 para.82

491. Criminal Legal Aid (Fixed Payments) (Scotland) Regulations 1999
Reg.2, amended: SI 2013/7 Art.17
Reg.4A, amended: SSI 2013/92 Reg.2

522. Pensions Increase (Review) Order 1999
applied: SI 2013/604 Sch.1

566. Medicines for Human Use and Medical Devices (Fees and Miscellaneous Amendments) Regulations 1999
revoked: SI 2013/532 Sch.9

584. National Minimum Wage Regulations 1999
applied: SI 2013/378 Reg.25, SI 2013/379 Reg.57
Reg.2, see *Nambalat v Taher* [2012] EWCA Civ 1249, [2013] I.C.R. 1024 (CA (Civ Div)), Pill, L.J.; see *Onu v Akwiwu* [2013] I.C.R. 1039 (EAT), Langstaff, J. (President)
Reg.11, amended: SI 2013/1975 Reg.2
Reg.11, referred to: SI 2013/376 Reg.41, Reg.90
Reg.12, amended: SI 2013/630 Reg.52
Reg.13, amended: SI 2013/1975 Reg.2
Reg.13, applied: SI 2013/376 Reg.90
Reg.13, referred to: SI 2013/376 Reg.90
Reg.19, applied: SI 2013/376 Reg.90
Reg.36, amended: SI 2013/1975 Reg.2
Reg.38, revoked (in part): 2013 c.24 Sch.20 para.2

609. National Health Service (Optical Charges and Payments) Amendment Regulations 1999
revoked (in part): SI 2013/461 Sch.4

614. Local Authorities Traffic Orders (Procedure) (Scotland) Regulations 1999
Reg.2, amended: SSI 2013/119 Sch.2 para.17
Reg.4, amended: SSI 2013/119 Sch.2 para.17

625. North Bristol National Health Service Trust (Establishment) Order 1999
Art.1, amended: SI 2013/593 Art.2

672. National Assembly for Wales (Transfer of Functions) Order 1999
Art.2, see *Attorney General v National Assembly for Wales Commission* [2013] 1 A.C. 792 (SC), Lord Neuberger (President)
Sch.1, amended: SI 2013/755 Sch.4 para.83, SI 2013/1821 Art.29
Sch.1, see *Attorney General v National Assembly for Wales Commission* [2013] 1 A.C. 792 (SC), Lord Neuberger (President)
Sch.2, amended: SI 2013/1821 Art.29

678. Transfer of Functions (Lord Advocate and Secretary of State) Order 1999
Sch.1, amended: SI 2013/686 Sch.2

681. Magistrates Courts (Hearsay Evidence in Civil Proceedings) Rules 1999
r.3, applied: SI 2013/1554 r.50_6
r.4, applied: SI 2013/1554 r.50_6
r.5, applied: SI 2013/1554 r.50_6

693. National Health Service (General Ophthalmic Services) (Amendment) Regulations 1999
revoked (in part): SI 2013/365 Reg.28

696. National Health Service (Pharmaceutical Services) Amendment Regulations 1999
revoked: SI 2013/898 Sch.8 para.7

728. Prison Rules 1999
Part I r.2, amended: SI 2013/235 Sch.2 para.35
Part II r.55AB, added: SI 2013/2462 Sch.1 para.1
Part II r.55B, amended: SI 2013/2462 Sch.1 para.2
Part II r.61, amended: SI 2013/2462 Sch.1 para.3
Part II r.61A, added: SI 2013/2462 Sch.1 para.4
Part VI r.82, amended: SI 2013/2462 Sch.1 para.5

743. Control of Major Accident Hazards Regulations 1999
applied: SI 2013/1893 Sch.2
Reg.2, amended: SI 2013/235 Sch.2 para.36, SI 2013/755 Sch.4 para.85
Reg.3, amended: SI 2013/766 Reg.3
Reg.7, amended: SI 2013/755 Sch.4 para.86

Reg.7, applied: SI 2013/755 Sch.7 para.9
Reg.9, amended: SI 2013/235 Sch.2 para.36, SI 2013/755 Sch.4 para.86
Reg.10, amended: SI 2013/235 Sch.2 para.36, SI 2013/755 Sch.4 para.86
Reg.15, amended: SI 2013/1471 Sch.4
Reg.20, amended: SI 2013/755 Sch.4 para.86
Reg.22, amended: SI 2013/755 Sch.4 para.86

786. Road Traffic (NHS Charges) (Reviews and Appeals) Regulations 1999
Reg.1, amended: SI 2013/2586 Reg.2
Reg.3, amended: SI 2013/2586 Reg.2
Reg.3, applied: SI 2013/2586 Reg.4
Reg.3, revoked (in part): SI 2013/2586 Reg.2

848. Epsom and St Helier National Health Service Trust (Establishment) Order 1999
Art.1, amended: SI 2013/593 Art.2

873. National Health Service (Liabilities to Third Parties Scheme) Regulations 1999
Reg.3, amended: SI 2013/235 Sch.2 para.37
Reg.3, revoked (in part): SI 2013/235 Sch.2 para.37

874. National Health Service (Property Expenses Scheme) Regulations 1999
Reg.3, amended: SI 2013/235 Sch.2 para.38
Reg.3, revoked (in part): SI 2013/235 Sch.2 para.38

915. Water Protection Zone (River Dee Catchment) Designation Order 1999
Art.2, amended: SI 2013/1478 Sch.5 para.10
Art.3, amended: SI 2013/755 Sch.4 para.87

916. Water Protection Zone (River Dee Catchment) (Procedural and Other Provisions) Regulations 1999
Reg.2, amended: SI 2013/755 Sch.4 para.89
Reg.4, amended: SI 2013/755 Sch.4 para.89
Reg.5, amended: SI 2013/755 Sch.4 para.89
Reg.6, amended: SI 2013/755 Sch.4 para.89
Reg.7, amended: SI 2013/755 Sch.4 para.89, Sch.4 para.90
Reg.8, amended: SI 2013/755 Sch.4 para.89
Reg.9, amended: SI 2013/755 Sch.4 para.89
Reg.10, amended: SI 2013/755 Sch.4 para.89
Reg.11, amended: SI 2013/755 Sch.4 para.89
Reg.12, amended: SI 2013/755 Sch.4 para.89
Reg.13, amended: SI 2013/755 Sch.4 para.89
Reg.14, amended: SI 2013/755 Sch.4 para.89

929. Act of Sederunt (Summary Applications, Statutory Applications and Appeals etc Rules) 1999
see *Freddie Williams Bookmakers v East Ayrshire Licensing Board* 2013 S.C. 62 (IH (Ex Div)), Lady Paton
Part I r.1.4, amended: SSI 2013/91 r.3
Part 1A r.1A.1, added: SSI 2013/91 r.3
Part 1A r.1A.2, added: SSI 2013/91 r.3
Part 2 r.2.7, amended: SSI 2013/135 r.2
Part 3, added: SSI 2013/293 r.3
Part 3 r.3.4.8, amended: SSI 2013/135 r.2
Part 3 r.3.16.1, amended: SSI 2013/293 r.2
Part 3 r.3.16.4, amended: SSI 2013/171 r.2, SSI 2013/293 r.2
Part 3 r.3.16.4, substituted: SSI 2013/171 r.2
Part 3 r.3.16.8, amended: SSI 2013/293 r.2
Part 3 r.3.16.8, revoked (in part): SSI 2013/171 r.2
Part 3 r.3.19.20A, added: SSI 2013/241 r.2
Part 3 r.3.19.20B, added: SSI 2013/241 r.2
Sch.1, added: SSI 2013/135 r.6
Sch.1, amended: SSI 2013/91 Sch.2, SSI 2013/135 r.2, r.6, Sch.1, SSI 2013/293 r.2

985. Social Landlords (Additional Purposes or Objects) Order 1999
Art.3, amended: SI 2013/472 Art.4

991. Social Security and Child Support (Decisions and Appeals) Regulations 1999
applied: SI 2013/379 Reg.7, Reg.85
see *JK v Secretary of State for Work and Pensions* [2013] UKUT 218 (AAC), [2013] 3 C.M.L.R. 32 (UT (AAC)), Judge Mesher
Reg.1, amended: SI 2013/381 Reg.55
Reg.1, see *JK v Secretary of State for Work and Pensions* [2013] UKUT 218 (AAC), [2013] 3 C.M.L.R. 32 (UT (AAC)), Judge Mesher
Reg.3, amended: SI 2013/2380 Reg.4
Reg.3B, added: SI 2013/2380 Reg.4
Reg.3ZA, added: SI 2013/2380 Reg.4
Reg.4, amended: SI 2013/2380 Reg.4
Reg.9ZA, amended: SI 2013/2380 Reg.4
Reg.9ZB, added: SI 2013/2380 Reg.4
Reg.25, amended: SI 2013/2380 Reg.4
Reg.26, amended: SI 2013/2380 Reg.4
Reg.29, amended: SI 2013/2380 Reg.4
Reg.29, revoked (in part): SI 2013/2380 Reg.4
Reg.32, applied: SI 2013/983 Art.21
Reg.32, revoked: SI 2013/2380 Reg.4
Reg.33, applied: SI 2013/983 Art.21
Reg.33, revoked: SI 2013/2380 Reg.4
Reg.34, applied: SI 2013/983 Art.21
Reg.34, revoked: SI 2013/2380 Reg.4
Sch.2 para.20, referred to: SI 2013/383 Reg.20
Sch.2 para.20, revoked (in part): SI 2013/383 Reg.20
Sch.2 para.20A, added: SI 2013/383 Reg.20
Sch.3A para.3, amended: SI 2013/388 Sch.1 para.21
Sch.3B para.2, amended: SI 2013/443 Reg.5, SI 2013/591 Sch.1 para.15
Sch.3B para.2, substituted: SI 2013/443 Reg.5
Sch.3B para.2A, added: SI 2013/443 Reg.5
Sch.3C para.3, amended: SI 2013/2536 Reg.8

1006. Anti-Pollution Works Regulations 1999
Reg.1, amended: SI 2013/755 Sch.4 para.92
Reg.2, amended: SI 2013/755 Sch.4 para.92
Reg.3, amended: SI 2013/755 Sch.4 para.92
Reg.4, amended: SI 2013/755 Sch.4 para.92
Reg.6, amended: SI 2013/755 Sch.4 para.92

1026. Highways (Traffic Calming) Regulations 1999
applied: SI 2013/2587 Art.10
referred to: SI 2013/3244 Art.7
Reg.3, applied: SI 2013/1933 Art.7

1029. Personal Portfolio Bonds (Tax) Regulations 1999
Reg.2, amended: SI 2013/472 Sch.2 para.24

1053. Non-Road Mobile Machinery (Emission of Gaseous and Particulate Pollutants) Regulations 1999
Reg.2, amended: SI 2013/1687 Reg.3
Reg.3C, amended: SI 2013/1687 Reg.4
Reg.7A, amended: SI 2013/1687 Reg.5
Sch.9 Part 2 para.6, amended: SI 2013/1687 Reg.6
Sch.9 Part 2 para.7, amended: SI 2013/1687 Reg.6
Sch.9 Part 2 para.7, substituted: SI 2013/1687 Reg.6
Sch.9 Part 2 para.7A, added: SI 2013/1687 Reg.6
Sch.9 Part 2 para.7A, amended: SI 2013/1687 Reg.6
Sch.9 Part 2 para.8, amended: SI 2013/1687 Reg.6
Sch.9 Part 2 para.9, amended: SI 2013/1687 Reg.6
Sch.9 Part 2 para.9, substituted: SI 2013/1687 Reg.6
Sch.9 Part 2 para.10, amended: SI 2013/1687 Reg.6
Sch.9 Part 2 para.10, substituted: SI 2013/1687 Reg.6
Sch.9 Part 2 para.10, amended: SI 2013/1687 Reg.6
Sch.9 Part 2 para.11, amended: SI 2013/1687 Reg.6
Sch.9 Part 2 para.11, substituted: SI 2013/1687 Reg.6
Sch.9 Part 2 para.11, amended: SI 2013/1687 Reg.6
Sch.9 Part 2 para.12, amended: SI 2013/1687 Reg.6
Sch.9 Part 2 para.12, substituted: SI 2013/1687 Reg.6
Sch.9 Part 2 para.12, amended: SI 2013/1687 Reg.6
Sch.9 Part 2 para.12A, amended: SI 2013/1687 Reg.6
Sch.9 Part 2 para.12B, amended: SI 2013/1687 Reg.6
Sch.9 Part 2 para.12C, amended: SI 2013/1687 Reg.6
Sch.9 Part 2 para.12D, amended: SI 2013/1687 Reg.6
Sch.9 Part 2 para.13, amended: SI 2013/1687 Reg.6

1072. Police (Conduct) (Scotland) Amendment Regulations 1999
revoked: SSI 2013/60 Sch.2 para.11

1074. Police (Conduct)(Senior Officers)(Scotland) Regulations 1999
applied: SSI 2013/62 Sch.2 para.4, Sch.2 para.5
referred to: SSI 2013/62 Sch.2 para.3, Sch.2 para.6
revoked: SSI 2013/62 Sch.2 para.2
Reg.2, applied: SSI 2013/62 Sch.2 para.3
Reg.2, varied: SSI 2013/62 Sch.2 para.9
Reg.3, varied: SSI 2013/62 Sch.2 para.9
Reg.5, applied: SSI 2013/62 Sch.2 para.3, Sch.2 para.6
Reg.5, varied: SSI 2013/62 Sch.2 para.9
Reg.6, applied: SSI 2013/62 Sch.2 para.3
Reg.6, varied: SSI 2013/62 Sch.2 para.9
Reg.7, varied: SSI 2013/62 Sch.2 para.9
Reg.8, applied: SSI 2013/62 Sch.2 para.3
Reg.8, varied: SSI 2013/62 Sch.2 para.9
Reg.9, varied: SSI 2013/62 Sch.2 para.9
Reg.10, applied: SSI 2013/62 Sch.2 para.3
Reg.10, varied: SSI 2013/62 Sch.2 para.9
Reg.12, varied: SSI 2013/62 Sch.2 para.9
Reg.13, applied: SSI 2013/62 Sch.2 para.3
Reg.13, disapplied: SSI 2013/62 Sch.2 para.3
Reg.13, varied: SSI 2013/62 Sch.2 para.9
Reg.14, varied: SSI 2013/62 Sch.2 para.9
Reg.15, varied: SSI 2013/62 Sch.2 para.9
Reg.16, varied: SSI 2013/62 Sch.2 para.9
Reg.21, varied: SSI 2013/62 Sch.2 para.9
Reg.22, applied: SSI 2013/62 Sch.2 para.3
Reg.22, varied: SSI 2013/62 Sch.2 para.9
Reg.23, applied: SSI 2013/62 Sch.2 para.3, Sch.2 para.7
Reg.23, varied: SSI 2013/62 Sch.2 para.9
Reg.24, varied: SSI 2013/62 Sch.2 para.9
Reg.25, applied: SSI 2013/62 Sch.2 para.8
Reg.25, referred to: SSI 2013/62 Sch.2 para.8
Reg.25, varied: SSI 2013/62 Sch.2 para.8, Sch.2 para.9
Reg.26, varied: SSI 2013/62 Sch.2 para.9
Reg.27, varied: SSI 2013/62 Sch.2 para.9
Reg.28, varied: SSI 2013/62 Sch.2 para.9
Reg.29, varied: SSI 2013/62 Sch.2 para.9
Reg.30, varied: SSI 2013/62 Sch.2 para.9

1082. Scotland Act 1998 (Transitory and Transitional Provisions) (Scottish Parliamentary Pension Scheme) Order 1999
Sch.6 para.5, amended: SI 2013/472 Art.4
Sch.6 para.8, amended: SI 2013/472 Art.4

1136. Miscellaneous Food Additives (Amendment) Regulations 1999

revoked (in part): SSI 2013/266 Sch.5

1148. Water Supply (Water Fittings) Regulations 1999

Reg.1, amended: SI 2013/1387 Sch.5 para.2
Reg.4, amended: SI 2013/1387 Sch.5 para.2
Reg.4, revoked (in part): SI 2013/1387 Sch.5 para.2

1204. Traffic Areas (Reorganisation) (Wales) Order 1999

Art.4, amended: SI 2013/1644 Sch.2

1215. Building Societies (Merger Notification Statement) Regulations 1999

Reg.2, amended: SI 2013/496 Sch.10 para.5
Sch.1 para.1, amended: SI 2013/496 Sch.10 para.5
Sch.1 para.2, amended: SI 2013/496 Sch.10 para.5

1319. Scotland Act 1998 (Cross-Border Public Authorities) (Specification) Order 1999

Sch.1, amended: SI 2013/235 Sch.2 para.39, SI 2013/1644 Sch.2, SI 2013/2042 Sch.1 para.49

1347. Act of Sederunt (Proceedings for Determination of Devolution Issues Rules) 1999

Art.10, see *South Lanarkshire Council v McKenna* 2013 S.C. 212 (IH (Ex Div)), Lord Clarke

1380. North and West Salmon Fishery District Designation Order 1999

Sch.2 para.2, amended: SSI 2013/323 Reg.28

1381. Conon Salmon Fishery District Designation Order 1999

Sch.2 para.2, amended: SSI 2013/323 Reg.28

1382. Lochaber Salmon Fishery District Designation Order 1999

Sch.2 para.2, amended: SSI 2013/323 Reg.28

1549. Public Interest Disclosure (Prescribed Persons) Order 1999

Sch.1, amended: SI 2013/472 Sch.2 para.25, SI 2013/2213 Art.3, Art.4, Art.5, Art.8, Sch.1
Sch.1, referred to: SI 2013/1237 Sch.1

1592. Scotland Act 1998 (Concurrent Functions) Order 1999

Sch.2 para.2, amended: SI 2013/602 Sch.2 para.77

1641. Driving Licences (Exchangeable Licences) Order 1999

Art.2, amended: SI 2013/22 Art.4
Art.2, revoked (in part): SI 2013/22 Art.4
Art.3, amended: SI 2013/22 Art.4
Art.4, amended: SI 2013/22 Art.4
Sch.1, amended: SI 2013/22 Art.4

1672. Public Gas Transporter Pipe-line Works (Environmental Impact Assessment) Regulations 1999

Reg.2, amended: SI 2013/755 Sch.4 para.93

1741. Fishery Limits Order 1999

revoked: SI 2013/3163 Art.2

1747. Scotland Act 1998 (Cross-Border Public Authorities) (Adaptation of Functions etc.) Order 1999

Sch.1, amended: SI 2013/2042 Sch.1 para.51

1750. Scotland Act 1998 (Transfer of Functions to the Scottish Ministers etc.) Order 1999

Sch.1, amended: 2013 c.32 Sch.12 para.30, SI 2013/686 Sch.2
Sch.2, amended: SI 2013/602 Sch.2 para.78
Sch.3, amended: 2013 c.32 Sch.12 para.30
Sch.4 para.1, amended: SI 2013/602 Sch.2 para.78

1783. Environmental Impact Assessment (Land Drainage Improvement Works) Regulations 1999

Reg.2, amended: SI 2013/755 Sch.4 para.94

1820. Scotland Act 1998 (Consequential Modifications) (No.2) Order 1999

Sch.2 Part I para.13, revoked: SSI 2013/169 Art.2

1892. Town and Country Planning (Trees) Regulations 1999

Reg.10, amended: SI 2013/755 Sch.4 para.96
Sch.1, amended: SI 2013/755 Sch.4 para.97

1956. Consumer Credit (Exempt Agreements) (Amendment) Order 1999

revoked (in part): SI 2013/1881 Art.21

2024. Quarries Regulations 1999

applied: SI 2013/1471 Sch.2 para.51, SI 2013/1896 Reg.3
Reg.2, referred to: SI 2013/1471 Sch.2 para.50
Reg.40, amended: SI 2013/1471 Sch.4
Sch.5 Part II, amended: SI 2013/1471 Sch.4

2083. Unfair Terms in Consumer Contracts Regulations 1999

see *Clipper Ventures Ltd v Boyde* 2013 S.C.L.R. 313 (Sh Ct (Lothian) (Edinburgh)), Sheriff Principal M M Stephen; see *Parker v National Farmers Union Mutual Insurance Society Ltd* [2012] EWHC 2156 (Comm), [2013] Lloyd's Rep. I.R. 253 (QBD (Comm)), Teare, J.
Reg.3, amended: SI 2013/783 Art.10
Reg.5, amended: SI 2013/472 Sch.2 para.26
Reg.5, see *Clipper Ventures Ltd v Boyde* 2013 S.C.L.R. 313 (Sh Ct (Lothian) (Edinburgh)), Sheriff Principal M M Stephen
Reg.7, see *AJ Building and Plastering Ltd v Turner* [2013] EWHC 484 (QB), [2013] Lloyd's Rep. I.R. 629 (QBD (Merc) (Cardiff)), Judge Keyser Q.C.
Reg.8, amended: SI 2013/1865 Reg.13
Reg.10, substituted: SI 2013/783 Art.10
Reg.11, revoked: SI 2013/783 Art.10
Reg.13, amended: SI 2013/783 Art.10
Reg.16, amended: SI 2013/472 Sch.2 para.26
Sch.1 Part I para.10, amended: SI 2013/472 Sch.2 para.26

2164. Education (Transfer of Functions Concerning School Lunches etc.) (England) (No.2) Order 1999

Art.2, amended: SI 2013/3111 Art.2

2218. National Institute for Clinical Excellence (Amendment) Regulations 1999
revoked: SI 2013/235 Sch.2 para.181

2219. National Institute for Clinical Excellence Establishment and Constitution Amendment Order 1999
revoked: SI 2013/235 Sch.2 para.182

2228. Environmental Impact Assessment (Forestry) (England and Wales) Regulations 1999
Reg.2, amended: SI 2013/755 Sch.4 para.99, Sch.4 para.100
Reg.4, amended: SI 2013/755 Sch.4 para.101
Reg.5, amended: SI 2013/755 Sch.4 para.102
Reg.6, amended: SI 2013/755 Sch.4 para.102
Reg.6, substituted: SI 2013/755 Sch.4 para.102
Reg.7, amended: SI 2013/755 Sch.4 para.103
Reg.9, amended: SI 2013/755 Sch.4 para.103
Reg.10, amended: SI 2013/755 Sch.4 para.103
Reg.11, amended: SI 2013/755 Sch.4 para.103
Reg.12, amended: SI 2013/755 Sch.4 para.103
Reg.13, amended: SI 2013/755 Sch.4 para.103
Reg.14, amended: SI 2013/755 Sch.4 para.103
Reg.15, amended: SI 2013/755 Sch.4 para.103
Reg.16, amended: SI 2013/755 Sch.4 para.104
Reg.17, amended: SI 2013/755 Sch.4 para.105
Reg.17, substituted: SI 2013/755 Sch.4 para.105
Reg.20, amended: SI 2013/755 Sch.4 para.106
Reg.21, amended: SI 2013/755 Sch.4 para.107
Reg.23, amended: SI 2013/755 Sch.4 para.107, Sch.4 para.108
Reg.24, amended: SI 2013/755 Sch.4 para.109
Reg.25, amended: SI 2013/755 Sch.4 para.110
Sch.2 para.1, amended: SI 2013/755 Sch.4 para.111
Sch.2 para.4, amended: SI 2013/755 Sch.4 para.111

2244. Railway Safety Regulations 1999
Reg.7, revoked: SI 2013/1471 Sch.4

2245. Licensing of Air Carriers Regulations 1999
revoked: SI 2013/486 Reg.38

2277. Redundancy Payments (Continuity of Employment in Local Government, etc.) (Modification) Order 1999
Sch.1 para.20, amended: SI 2013/1465 Sch.1 para.15
Sch.2 Part II para.1A, added: SI 2013/1784 Art.2
Sch.2 Part II para.1B, added: SI 2013/1784 Art.2

2356. Companies (Forms) (Amendment) Regulations 1999
revoked: SI 2013/1947 Sch.2 Part 1

2357. Companies (Welsh Language Forms) (Amendment) Regulations 1999
revoked: SI 2013/1947 Sch.2 Part 1

2506. Education (Special Educational Needs) (Information) (England) Regulations 1999
Reg.2, amended: SI 2013/235 Sch.2 para.40
Reg.4, amended: SI 2013/235 Sch.2 para.40

2562. National Health Service (Optical Charges and Payments) and (General Ophthalmic Services) (Amendment) Regulations 1999
revoked: SI 2013/461 Sch.4

2622. A50 Trunk Road (Blythe Bridge Bypass to Normacot, Stoke on Trent) (40 Miles Per Hour and 50 Miles Per Hour Speed Limit) Order 1999
Sch.1, varied: SI 2013/2703 Art.5

2678. Companies (Forms) (Amendment) (No.2) Regulations 1999
revoked: SI 2013/1947 Sch.2 Part 1

2679. Companies (Welsh Language Forms) (Amendment) (No.2) Regulations 1999
revoked: SI 2013/1947 Sch.2 Part 1

2725. Consumer Credit (Content of Quotations) and Consumer Credit (Advertisements) (Amendment) Regulations 1999
revoked (in part): SI 2013/1881 Art.21

2734. Housing Benefit (General) Amendment (No.3) Regulations 1999
Reg.13, applied: SI 2013/3029 Sch.4 para.24, Sch.9 para.10, SI 2013/3035 Sch.1

2864. Motor Vehicles (Driving Licences) Regulations 1999
Reg.3, amended: SI 2013/1644 Sch.2, SI 2013/1753 Reg.2
Reg.9, amended: SI 2013/2184 Reg.2
Reg.23, amended: SI 2013/602 Sch.2 para.79, SSI 2013/119 Sch.2 para.18
Reg.24, amended: SSI 2013/119 Sch.2 para.18
Reg.37, amended: SI 2013/1753 Reg.2
Reg.56, amended: SI 2013/1644 Sch.2
Reg.57, amended: SI 2013/1644 Sch.2
Reg.71, revoked (in part): SI 2013/258 Reg.2
Reg.72, amended: SI 2013/258 Reg.3
Reg.73, amended: SI 2013/258 Reg.4
Reg.74, amended: SI 2013/1013 Reg.2
Reg.75, amended: SI 2013/258 Reg.5
Reg.81, amended: SI 2013/1644 Sch.2
Reg.82, amended: SI 2013/1644 Sch.2
Reg.82, revoked (in part): SI 2013/1644 Sch.2

2892. Nuclear Reactors (Environmental Impact Assessment for Decommissioning) Regulations 1999
Reg.2, amended: SI 2013/755 Sch.4 para.112

2921. University Hospitals of Leicester National Health Service Trust (Establishment) Order 1999
Art.1, amended: SI 2013/593 Art.2

2979. Financial Markets and Insolvency (Settlement Finality) Regulations 1999
applied: SI 2013/504 Reg.55

Reg.2, amended: SI 2013/472 Sch.2 para.27, SI 2013/504 Reg.32, SI 2013/3115 Sch.2 para.48
Reg.2, revoked (in part): SI 2013/504 Reg.32
Reg.4, amended: SI 2013/472 Sch.2 para.27
Reg.6, amended: SI 2013/504 Reg.32
Reg.7, amended: SI 2013/472 Sch.2 para.27
Reg.7, applied: SI 2013/472 Sch.2 para.28
Reg.7, revoked (in part): SI 2013/472 Sch.2 para.27
Reg.10, amended: SI 2013/472 Sch.2 para.27, SI 2013/504 Reg.32
Reg.13, amended: SI 2013/504 Reg.32
Reg.13, revoked (in part): SI 2013/504 Reg.32
Reg.20, amended: SI 2013/504 Reg.32
Sch.1 para.4, amended: SI 2013/472 Sch.2 para.27

3107. Motor Fuel (Composition and Content) Regulations 1999
Reg.3, amended: SI 2013/2897 Reg.3

3110. Tax Credit (New Category of Child Care Provider) Regulations 1999
applied: SI 2013/3029 Sch.1 para.19, Sch.6 para.21, SI 2013/3035 Sch.1

3177. Consumer Credit (Total Charge for Credit, Agreements and Advertisements) (Amendment) Regulations 1999
Reg.3, revoked (in part): SI 2013/1881 Art.21
Reg.5, revoked (in part): SI 2013/1881 Art.21

3181. Education (School Day and School Year) (England) Regulations 1999
Reg.3, amended: SI 2013/473 Art.2

3232. Ionising Radiations Regulations 1999
applied: SI 2013/1471 Reg.14
Sch.1 para.1, amended: SI 2013/755 Sch.4 para.113
Sch.1 para.1A, added: SI 2013/755 Sch.4 para.113
Sch.9 para.6, revoked: SI 2013/1471 Sch.4

3242. Management of Health and Safety at Work Regulations 1999
applied: SI 2013/805 Sch.1, SI 2013/806 Sch.1, SI 2013/807 Sch.1, SI 2013/808 Sch.1, SI 2013/809 Sch.1, SI 2013/810 Sch.1, SI 2013/811 Sch.1, SI 2013/812 Sch.1, SI 2013/813 Sch.1, SI 2013/814 Sch.1
see *Kennedy v Cordia (Services) LLP* [2013] CSOH 130, 2013 Rep. L.R. 126 (OH), Lord McEwan
Reg.3, applied: SI 2013/645 Reg.5
Reg.3, see *Grant v Fife Council* [2013] CSOH 11, 2013 Rep. L.R. 73 (OH), Lord Stewart
Reg.4, see *Grant v Fife Council* [2013] CSOH 11, 2013 Rep. L.R. 73 (OH), Lord Stewart
Reg.5, see *Grant v Fife Council* [2013] CSOH 11, 2013 Rep. L.R. 73 (OH), Lord Stewart; see *R. v Merlin Attractions Operations Ltd* [2012] EWCA Crim 2670, [2013] 2 Cr. App. R. (S.) 36 (CA (Crim Div)), Gross, L.J.
Reg.10, see *Grant v Fife Council* [2013] CSOH 11, 2013 Rep. L.R. 73 (OH), Lord Stewart
Reg.22, substituted: SI 2013/1667 Reg.3

3312. Maternity and Parental Leave etc Regulations 1999
see *Hair Division Ltd v MacMillan* [2013] Eq. L.R. 18 (EAT (SC)), Lady Smith
Reg.2, amended: SI 2013/388 Sch.1 para.22, SI 2013/591 Sch.1 para.16
Reg.14, amended: SI 2013/283 Reg.3, SI 2013/388 Sch.1 para.22, SI 2013/591 Sch.1 para.16
Reg.14, revoked (in part): SI 2013/283 Reg.3
Reg.15, amended: SI 2013/388 Sch.1 para.22, SI 2013/591 Sch.1 para.16
Reg.16A, added: SI 2013/283 Reg.3
Sch.2 para.2, amended: SI 2013/388 Sch.1 para.22, SI 2013/591 Sch.1 para.16
Sch.2 para.7, amended: SI 2013/388 Sch.1 para.22, SI 2013/591 Sch.1 para.16

3323. Transnational Information and Consultation of Employees Regulations 1999
Reg.41, amended: SI 2013/1956 Sch.1 para.3

3441. Water Industry (Charges) (Vulnerable Groups) Regulations 1999
Reg.2, amended: SI 2013/630 Reg.86

3442. Water Industry (Prescribed Conditions) Regulations 1999
Reg.3, amended: SI 2013/755 Sch.4 para.115
Reg.4, amended: SI 2013/755 Sch.4 para.116

2000

128. Pressure Systems Safety Regulations 2000
Reg.2, referred to: SI 2013/1471 Sch.2 para.2

212. National Health Service Trusts (Trust Funds Appointment of Trustees) Order 2000
Art.4, amended: SI 2013/679 Art.2
Sch.1, amended: SI 2013/679 Art.2

237. Maidstone and Tunbridge Wells National Health Service Trust (Establishment) Order 2000
Art.1, amended: SI 2013/593 Art.2

262. Competition Act 1998 (Small Agreements and Conduct of Minor Significance) Regulations 2000
Sch.1 para.1, amended: SI 2013/3115 Sch.2 para.49

291. Consumer Credit (Conduct of Business) (Credit References) (Amendment) Regulations 2000
revoked (in part): SI 2013/1881 Art.21

309. Competition Act 1998 (Determination of Turnover for Penalties) Order 2000

Sch.1 para.1, amended: SI 2013/3115 Sch.2 para.50

414. Data Protection (Subject Access Modification) (Education) Order 2000

Art.2, amended: SI 2013/1465 Sch.1 para.16

415. Data Protection (Subject Access Modification) (Social Work) Order 2000

Art.2, amended: SI 2013/1465 Sch.1 para.17
Sch.1 para.1, amended: SI 2013/235 Sch.2 para.41, SI 2013/1465 Sch.1 para.17
Sch.1 para.1, revoked (in part): SI 2013/235 Sch.2 para.41

441. Community Legal Service (Costs) Regulations 2000

Reg.24, amended: SI 2013/472 Art.4

516. Community Legal Service (Financial) Regulations 2000

applied: SI 2013/534 Reg.9
Reg.4, amended: SI 2013/630 Reg.62
Reg.5, applied: SI 2013/534 Reg.9
Reg.5A, applied: SI 2013/534 Reg.9
Reg.19, amended: SI 2013/591 Sch.1 para.18, SI 2013/626 Reg.2
Reg.23, applied: SI 2013/534 Reg.9
Reg.24, applied: SI 2013/534 Reg.9
Reg.32, applied: SI 2013/534 Reg.9
Reg.32A, applied: SI 2013/534 Reg.9
Reg.32B, applied: SI 2013/534 Reg.9
Reg.35, applied: SI 2013/534 Reg.9
Reg.38, applied: SI 2013/534 Reg.9

535. East and North Hertfordshire National Health Service Trust (Establishment) Order 2000

Art.1, amended: SI 2013/593 Art.2

540. Valuation for Rating (Plant and Machinery) (England) Regulations 2000

Sch.1, see *Iceland Foods Ltd v Berry (Valuation Officer)* [2013] R.A. 95 (VT), X Holt

592. Medicines for Human Use and Medical Devices (Fees and Miscellaneous Amendments) Regulations 2000

revoked: SI 2013/532 Sch.9

594. National Health Service (Optical Charges and Payments) Amendment Regulations 2000

revoked: SI 2013/461 Sch.4

617. NHS Bodies and Local Authorities Partnership Arrangements Regulations 2000

Reg.5, amended: SI 2013/235 Sch.2 para.42, SI 2013/1617 Reg.18
Reg.6, amended: SI 2013/235 Sch.2 para.42

619. National Health Service Pension Scheme (Additional Voluntary Contributions) Regulations 2000

Reg.2, amended: SI 2013/413 Reg.78, SI 2013/472 Art.4
Reg.4, amended: SI 2013/413 Reg.79
Reg.4, applied: SI 2013/469 Sch.1
Reg.15, amended: SI 2013/413 Reg.80

620. National Health Service (Charges for Drugs and Appliances) Regulations 2000

applied: SI 2013/349 Reg.96
Reg.2, amended: SI 2013/349 Sch.10 para.1, SI 2013/475 Reg.4
Reg.2, revoked (in part): SI 2013/475 Reg.4
Reg.3, amended: SI 2013/475 Reg.2, Reg.5
Reg.3, referred to: SI 2013/349 Sch.4 para.7, Sch.5 para.6, Sch.7 para.5, SI 2013/461 Reg.8
Reg.4, amended: SI 2013/475 Reg.2, Reg.6
Reg.4, referred to: SI 2013/349 Sch.6 para.4
Reg.4A, amended: SI 2013/475 Reg.2, Reg.7
Reg.5, amended: SI 2013/475 Reg.2, Reg.8
Reg.5, substituted: SI 2013/475 Reg.8
Reg.6, amended: SI 2013/475 Reg.2, Reg.9
Reg.6A, amended: SI 2013/475 Reg.2, Reg.10
Reg.6B, added: SI 2013/475 Reg.11
Reg.7, amended: SI 2013/475 Reg.12
Reg.7, applied: SI 2013/349 Sch.4 para.7, Sch.5 para.6, Sch.6 para.4, Sch.7 para.5
Reg.7, referred to: SI 2013/349 Sch.4 para.7, Sch.5 para.6, Sch.6 para.4, Sch.7 para.5
Reg.7A, amended: SI 2013/475 Reg.13
Reg.10, amended: SI 2013/475 Reg.14
Reg.10, applied: SI 2013/349 Reg.96, Sch.7 para.18
Reg.11, amended: SI 2013/475 Reg.15
Sch.1, amended: SI 2013/475 Reg.2
Sch.1, referred to: SI 2013/475 Reg.3

636. Social Security (Immigration and Asylum) Consequential Amendments Regulations 2000

Reg.1, amended: SI 2013/388 Sch.1 para.23, SI 2013/630 Reg.31
Reg.2, amended: SI 2013/388 Sch.1 para.23, SI 2013/458 Sch.1, SI 2013/630 Reg.31
Reg.2, applied: SI 2013/377 Reg.16
Reg.2, revoked (in part): SI 2013/2536 Reg.9
Sch.1 Part I para.1, amended: SI 2013/630 Reg.31
Sch.1 Part I para.1, revoked: SI 2013/2536 Reg.9
Sch.1 Part I para.2, amended: SI 2013/630 Reg.31
Sch.1 Part I para.3, amended: SI 2013/630 Reg.31
Sch.1 Part I para.4, amended: SI 2013/630 Reg.31
Sch.1 Part II para.1, amended: SI 2013/388 Sch.1 para.23, SI 2013/1474 Reg.8
Sch.1 Part II para.2, amended: SI 2013/388 Sch.1 para.23
Sch.1 Part II para.3, amended: SI 2013/388 Sch.1 para.23
Sch.1 Part II para.4, amended: SI 2013/388 Sch.1 para.23

672. Pensions Increase (Review) Order 2000

applied: SI 2013/604 Sch.1

682. Disabled Persons (Badges for Motor Vehicles) (England) Regulations 2000

applied: SI 2013/387 Reg.31
Reg.2, amended: SI 2013/2203 Reg.2
Reg.4, amended: SI 2013/388 Sch.1 para.4
Reg.4, applied: SI 2013/387 Reg.31
Reg.4, referred to: SI 2013/387 Reg.31
Reg.6, amended: SI 2013/388 Sch.1 para.4
Reg.7, applied: SI 2013/387 Reg.31
Reg.8, amended: SI 2013/2203 Reg.2
Reg.9, amended: SI 2013/2203 Reg.2
Reg.9, disapplied: SI 2013/387 Reg.31
Reg.9, revoked (in part): SI 2013/2203 Reg.2
Reg.10, substituted: SI 2013/2203 Reg.2
Reg.11, amended: SI 2013/2203 Reg.2
Reg.11, revoked: SI 2013/2203 Reg.2
Reg.12, amended: SI 2013/2203 Reg.2
Reg.13, amended: SI 2013/2203 Reg.2
Reg.14, amended: SI 2013/2203 Reg.2
Reg.15, amended: SI 2013/2203 Reg.2
Reg.16, amended: SI 2013/2203 Reg.2
Sch.1, substituted: SI 2013/2203 Sch.1
Sch.1 Part I, substituted: SI 2013/2203 Sch.1
Sch.1 Part IA, substituted: SI 2013/2203 Sch.1
Sch.1 Part II, substituted: SI 2013/2203 Sch.1
Sch.1 Part IIA, substituted: SI 2013/2203 Sch.1
Sch.1 Part III, substituted: SI 2013/2203 Sch.1
Sch.1 Part IIIA para.1, substituted: SI 2013/2203 Sch.1
Sch.1 Part IIIA para.2, substituted: SI 2013/2203 Sch.1
Sch.1 Part IIIA para.3, substituted: SI 2013/2203 Sch.1

704. Asylum Support Regulations 2000

Reg.4, amended: SI 2013/630 Reg.59

729. Social Fund Winter Fuel Payment Regulations 2000

Reg.2, amended: SI 2013/1509 Reg.2
Reg.3, amended: SI 2013/1509 Reg.2

823. Conditional Fee Agreements Order 2000

revoked: SI 2013/689 Art.7

1038. General Osteopathic Council (Application for Registration and Fees) Rules Order of Council 2000

Sch.1, amended: SI 2013/1026 Sch.1

1043. Environmental Protection (Disposal of Polychlorinated Biphenyls and other Dangerous Substances) (England and Wales) Regulations 2000

Reg.2, amended: SI 2013/755 Sch.4 para.118
Reg.3, amended: SI 2013/755 Sch.4 para.119
Reg.6, amended: SI 2013/755 Sch.4 para.120
Reg.7, amended: SI 2013/755 Sch.4 para.121
Reg.8, amended: SI 2013/755 Sch.4 para.122
Reg.9, amended: SI 2013/755 Sch.4 para.123
Reg.10, amended: SI 2013/755 Sch.4 para.124
Reg.11, amended: SI 2013/755 Sch.4 para.125
Reg.12, amended: SI 2013/755 Sch.4 para.126
Reg.13B, amended: SI 2013/755 Sch.4 para.127

1048. Pensions on Divorce etc (Provision of Information) Regulations 2000

Reg.11, added: SI 2013/2734 Sch.9 para.7

1053. Pension Sharing (Implementation and Discharge of Liability) Regulations 2000

Reg.1, amended: SI 2013/472 Art.4
Reg.11, amended: SI 2013/472 Art.4

1054. Pension Sharing (Pension Credit Benefit) Regulations 2000

Reg.1, amended: SI 2013/472 Art.4
Reg.5, amended: SI 2013/472 Art.4
Reg.8, amended: SI 2013/2734 Sch.9 para.8
Reg.10, amended: SI 2013/2734 Sch.9 para.8
Reg.15, amended: SI 2013/2734 Sch.9 para.8
Reg.32, substituted: SI 2013/459 Reg.7

1119. European Communities (Lawyer's Practice) Regulations 2000

Reg.1, varied: SI 2013/1605 Reg.4
Reg.2, amended: SI 2013/1605 Reg.3
Sch.1, amended: SI 2013/3176 Art.4
Sch.3 Part 1, amended: SI 2013/534 Sch.1 para.3

1161. Immigration (Leave to Enter and Remain) Order 2000

Art.1, amended: SI 2013/1749 Art.3
Art.8, substituted: SI 2013/1749 Art.4
Art.10, amended: SI 2013/1749 Art.5
Art.11, amended: SI 2013/1749 Art.6

1386. A30 and A303 Trunk Road (Exeter to Marsh) (24 Hours Clearway) Order 2000

Art.3, varied: SI 2013/1649 Art.2
Art.4, varied: SI 2013/1649 Art.2
Sch.1, varied: SI 2013/1649 Art.2

1403. Stakeholder Pension Schemes Regulations 2000

Reg.1, amended: SI 2013/459 Reg.8, SI 2013/472 Art.4, Sch.2 para.31, SI 2013/2734 Sch.9 para.9
Reg.1, revoked (in part): SI 2013/2734 Sch.9 para.9
Reg.2, amended: SI 2013/459 Reg.8
Reg.8, amended: SI 2013/472 Art.4
Reg.14, amended: SI 2013/459 Reg.8
Reg.14, revoked (in part): SI 2013/459 Reg.8
Reg.15, amended: SI 2013/472 Sch.2 para.31
Reg.18, amended: SI 2013/2734 Sch.9 para.9
Reg.18, revoked (in part): SI 2013/2734 Sch.9 para.9
Reg.18A, amended: SI 2013/2734 Sch.9 para.9
Reg.18A, revoked (in part): SI 2013/2734 Sch.9 para.9
Reg.18B, amended: SI 2013/2734 Sch.9 para.9

Reg.18B, revoked (in part): SI 2013/2734 Sch.9 para.9
Reg.18C, amended: SI 2013/2734 Sch.9 para.9
Reg.18E, amended: SI 2013/2734 Sch.9 para.9
Reg.18E, revoked (in part): SI 2013/2734 Sch.9 para.9
Reg.18F, added: SI 2013/2734 Sch.9 para.9
Reg.22, revoked: SI 2013/459 Reg.8
Reg.23, revoked: SI 2013/459 Reg.8
Reg.24, amended: SI 2013/459 Reg.8
Reg.24, revoked (in part): SI 2013/459 Reg.8
Sch.3 para.2, revoked (in part): SI 2013/459 Reg.8
Sch.3 para.6, amended: SI 2013/2734 Sch.9 para.9

1462. Regulation of Bus Services in Greater London (Transitional Provisions) Order 2000
revoked: SI 2013/2986 Sch.2

1551. Part-time Workers (Prevention of Less Favourable Treatment) Regulations 2000
see *Department of Constitutional Affairs v O'Brien* [2013] UKSC 6, [2013] 1 W.L.R. 522 (SC), Lord Hope, J.S.C.

1597. Education (National Curriculum) (Attainment Targets and Programmes of Study in Music) (England) Order 2000
revoked: SI 2013/2232 Sch.1

1598. Education (National Curriculum) (Attainment Targets and Programmes of Study in Mathematics) (England) Order 2000
applied: SI 2013/2232 Art.6
revoked: SI 2013/2232 Sch.1

1601. Education (National Curriculum) (Attainment Targets and Programmes of Study in Information and Communication Technology) (England) Order 2000
revoked: SI 2013/2232 Sch.1

1602. Education (National Curriculum) (Attainment Targets and Programmes of Study in Art and Design) (England) Order 2000
revoked: SI 2013/2232 Sch.1

1604. Education (National Curriculum) (Attainment Targets and Programmes of Study in English) (England) Order 2000
applied: SI 2013/2232 Art.6
revoked: SI 2013/2232 Sch.1

1605. Education (National Curriculum) (Attainment Targets and Programmes of Study in Geography) (England) Order 2000
revoked: SI 2013/2232 Sch.1

1606. Education (National Curriculum) (Attainment Targets and Programmes of Study in History) (England) Order 2000
revoked: SI 2013/2232 Sch.1

1607. Education (National Curriculum) (Attainment Targets and Programmes of Study in Physical Education) (England) Order 2000
revoked: SI 2013/2232 Sch.1

1624. Town and Country Planning (Inquiries Procedure) (England) Rules 2000
r.2, amended: SI 2013/2146 Sch.1 para.3
r.3, revoked (in part): SI 2013/2146 Sch.1 para.3
r.23B, added: SI 2013/2137 r.3

1625. Town and Country Planning Appeals (Determination by Inspectors) (Inquiries Procedure) (England) Rules 2000
see *Wainhomes (South West) Holdings Ltd v Secretary of State for Communities and Local Government* [2013] EWHC 597 (Admin), [2013] J.P.L. 1145 (QBD (Admin)), Stuart-Smith, J.
r.2, amended: SI 2013/2137 r.4, SI 2013/2146 Sch.1 para.4
r.3, amended: SI 2013/2146 Sch.1 para.4
r.4, amended: SI 2013/2137 r.4
r.6, amended: SI 2013/2137 r.4
r.6, revoked (in part): SI 2013/2137 r.4
r.7, amended: SI 2013/2137 r.4
r.10, amended: SI 2013/2137 r.4
r.11, amended: SI 2013/2137 r.4
r.15, amended: SI 2013/2137 r.4
r.16, amended: SI 2013/2137 r.4
r.19, see *East Northamptonshire DC v Secretary of State for Communities and Local Government* [2013] EWHC 473 (Admin), [2013] 2 P. & C.R. 5 (QBD (Admin)), Lang, J.
r.22, amended: SI 2013/2137 r.4
r.24, amended: SI 2013/2137 r.4
r.24, revoked (in part): SI 2013/2137 r.4

1626. Town and Country Planning (Hearings Procedure) (England) Rules 2000
see *San Vicente v Secretary of State for Communities and Local Government* [2012] EWHC 3585 (Admin), [2013] J.P.L. 642 (QBD (Admin)), Philip Mott Q.C.; see *San Vicente v Secretary of State for Communities and Local Government* [2013] EWCA Civ 817, [2013] J.P.L. 1516 (CA (Civ Div)), Lloyd, L.J.
r.2, amended: SI 2013/2137 r.5
r.3, revoked (in part): SI 2013/2146 Sch.1 para.5
r.4, amended: SI 2013/2137 r.5
r.6, amended: SI 2013/2137 r.5
r.6A, added: SI 2013/2137 r.5
r.7, amended: SI 2013/2137 r.5
r.11, amended: SI 2013/2137 r.5
r.18, amended: SI 2013/2137 r.5
r.20, amended: SI 2013/2137 r.5

1786. Disabled Persons (Badges for Motor Vehicles) (Wales) Regulations 2000
Reg.2, amended: SI 2013/438 Reg.2
Reg.4, amended: SI 2013/438 Reg.2
Reg.6, amended: SI 2013/438 Reg.2

Reg.9A, added: SI 2013/438 Reg.2
Sch.1 Part IIIA para.2, amended: SI 2013/438 Reg.2

1797. Consumer Credit (Advertisements and Content of Quotations) (Amendment) Regulations 2000
revoked (in part): SI 2013/1881 Art.21

1822. Sierra Leone (United Nations Sanctions) (Overseas Territories) Order 2000
revoked: SI 2013/237 Sch.2

1927. Electricity Works (Environmental Impact Assessment) (England and Wales) Regulations 2000
varied: SI 2013/1570 Reg.7
Reg.2, amended: SI 2013/755 Sch.4 para.129
Reg.9, applied: SI 2013/1570 Reg.5
Reg.9, varied: SI 2013/1570 Reg.7
Reg.11, varied: SI 2013/1570 Reg.7
Sch.2, added: SI 2013/755 Sch.4 para.130
Sch.2, amended: SI 2013/755 Sch.4 para.130
Sch.4 Part II para.1, varied: SI 2013/1570 Reg.7
Sch.4 Part II para.2, varied: SI 2013/1570 Reg.7
Sch.4 Part II para.3, varied: SI 2013/1570 Reg.7
Sch.4 Part II para.4, varied: SI 2013/1570 Reg.7
Sch.4 Part II para.5, varied: SI 2013/1570 Reg.7

1928. Pipe-line Works (Environmental Impact Assessment) Regulations 2000
Reg.2, amended: SI 2013/755 Sch.4 para.131

1973. Pollution Prevention and Control (England and Wales) Regulations 2000
applied: SI 2013/2258 Sch.1 Part 2

2047. Faculty Jurisdiction Rules 2000
referred to: SI 2013/1922 Sch.1 Part TABLE
revoked: SI 2013/1916 r.20_2

2048. Faculty Jurisdiction (Care of Places of Worship) Rules 2000
applied: SI 2013/1922 Sch.1 Part TABLE
revoked: SI 2013/1916 r.20_2

2062. A30 Trunk Road (Sowton Lane to Junction 29, M5) (40 mph Speed Limit and Derestriction) Order 2000
revoked: SI 2013/1650 Art.3

2083. Charitable Deductions (Approved Schemes) (Amendment No 2) Regulations 2000
Reg.8, revoked: 2013 c.2 Sch.1 Part 10

2122. Education (School Government) (Terms of Reference) (England) Regulations 2000
revoked: SI 2013/1624 Reg.3

2129. Tonnage Tax (Training Requirement) Regulations 2000
Reg.2, amended: SI 2013/2245 Reg.3
Reg.15, amended: SI 2013/5 Reg.3, SI 2013/2245 Reg.3
Reg.21, amended: SI 2013/5 Reg.3, SI 2013/2245 Reg.3

2152. Burry Port Harbour Revision Order 2000
Art.19, amended: SI 2013/755 Sch.4 para.133
Art.46, amended: SI 2013/755 Sch.4 para.134
Sch.2 para.1, amended: SI 2013/755 Sch.4 para.135
Sch.2 para.2, amended: SI 2013/755 Sch.4 para.135
Sch.2 para.3, amended: SI 2013/755 Sch.4 para.135
Sch.2 para.4, amended: SI 2013/755 Sch.4 para.135
Sch.2 para.5, amended: SI 2013/755 Sch.4 para.135
Sch.2 para.6, amended: SI 2013/755 Sch.4 para.135
Sch.2 para.7, amended: SI 2013/755 Sch.4 para.135
Sch.2 para.8, amended: SI 2013/755 Sch.4 para.135
Sch.2 para.9, amended: SI 2013/755 Sch.4 para.135
Sch.2 para.10, amended: SI 2013/755 Sch.4 para.135
Sch.2 para.11, amended: SI 2013/755 Sch.4 para.135
Sch.2 para.12, amended: SI 2013/755 Sch.4 para.135
Sch.2 para.13, amended: SI 2013/755 Sch.4 para.135

2334. Consumer Protection (Distance Selling) Regulations 2000
disapplied: SI 2013/3134 Reg.2
Reg.3, amended: SI 2013/783 Art.11
Reg.26, amended: SI 2013/783 Art.11
Reg.26A, added: SI 2013/783 Art.11
Reg.27, amended: SI 2013/783 Art.11
Reg.28, amended: SI 2013/783 Art.11
Reg.29, amended: SI 2013/783 Art.11

2413. Companies (Welsh Language Forms) (Amendment) Regulations 2000
revoked: SI 2013/1947 Sch.2 Part 1

2562. West London Mental Health National Health Service Trust (Establishment) Order 2000
Art.1, amended: SI 2013/593 Art.2

2692. Personal Pension Schemes (Payments by Employers) Regulations 2000
Reg.5, amended: SI 2013/2556 Reg.3
Reg.5A, amended: SI 2013/2734 Sch.9 para.10

2724. Immigration (Designation of Travel Bans) Order 2000
Sch.1 Part 1, amended: SI 2013/1745 Art.2
Sch.1 Part 2, amended: SI 2013/678 Art.2, SI 2013/1745 Art.3

2792. Fixed Penalty Order 2000
Sch.1, amended: SI 2013/1569 Art.2

Sch.2 para.1, amended: SI 2013/1569 Art.3
Sch.2 para.2, amended: SI 2013/1569 Art.3
Sch.2 para.3, amended: SI 2013/1569 Art.3
Sch.2 para.4, amended: SI 2013/1569 Art.3
Sch.2 para.5, amended: SI 2013/1569 Art.3
Sch.2 para.6, amended: SI 2013/1569 Art.3

2831. Genetically Modified Organisms (Contained Use) Regulations 2000
Reg.26, amended: SI 2013/1666 Art.3

2853. Local Authorities (Functions and Responsibilities) (England) Regulations 2000
see *R. (on the application of Buck) v Doncaster MBC* [2012] EWHC 2293 (Admin), [2013] P.T.S.R. 316 (QBD (Admin)), Hickinbottom, J.; see *R. (on the application of Champion) v North Norfolk DC* [2013] EWHC 1065 (Admin), [2013] Env. L.R. 38 (QBD (Admin)), James Dingemans Q.C.
Sch.1, amended: SI 2013/2146 Sch.1 para.6, SI 2013/2190 Reg.3
Sch.4, see *R. (on the application of Buck) v Doncaster MBC* [2013] EWCA Civ 1190, [2013] B.L.G.R. 847 (CA (Civ Div)), Master of the Rolls

2908. Nottinghamshire Healthcare National Health Service Trust (Establishment) Order 2000
Art.1, amended: SI 2013/593 Art.2

2993. National Health Service Bodies and Local Authorities Partnership Arrangements (Wales) Regulations 2000
Reg.10, amended: SI 2013/3005 Art.4

3029. National Health Service (Optical Charges and Payments) Amendment (No.2) Regulations 2000
revoked: SI 2013/461 Sch.4

3062. Continental Shelf (Designation of Areas) (Consolidation) Order 2000
revoked: SI 2013/3162 Art.1

3184. Water Supply (Water Quality) Regulations 2000
applied: SI 2013/277 Sch.1
Reg.2, amended: SI 2013/235 Sch.2 para.43
Reg.20, amended: SI 2013/235 Sch.2 para.43
Reg.24, amended: SI 2013/235 Sch.2 para.43
Reg.31, amended: SI 2013/1387 Sch.5 para.3
Reg.31, revoked (in part): SI 2013/1387 Sch.5 para.3
Reg.35, amended: SI 2013/235 Sch.2 para.43

3226. Transport Tribunal Rules 2000
Part II r.5, amended: SI 2013/1644 Sch.2
Part II r.6, amended: SI 2013/1644 Sch.2
Part II r.8, amended: SI 2013/1644 Sch.2
Part II r.10, amended: SI 2013/1644 Sch.2
Part III r.12, amended: SI 2013/1644 Sch.2
Part III r.13, amended: SI 2013/1644 Sch.2
Part III r.14, amended: SI 2013/1644 Sch.2
Part III r.15, amended: SI 2013/1644 Sch.2
Part V r.23, amended: SI 2013/1644 Sch.2
Part V r.25, amended: SI 2013/1644 Sch.2
Part V r.28, amended: SI 2013/1644 Sch.2
Part V r.29, amended: SI 2013/1644 Sch.2
Part V r.32, amended: SI 2013/1644 Sch.2
Part V r.35, amended: SI 2013/1644 Sch.2

3371. Young Offender Institution Rules 2000
Part I r.2, amended: SI 2013/235 Sch.2 para.44
Part II r.60AB, added: SI 2013/2462 Sch.2 para.1
Part II r.60B, amended: SI 2013/2462 Sch.2 para.2
Part II r.64, amended: SI 2013/2462 Sch.2 para.3
Part II r.64A, added: SI 2013/2462 Sch.2 para.4
Part VI r.86, amended: SI 2013/2462 Sch.2 para.5

2001

104. Stakeholder Pension Schemes (Amendment) Regulations 2001
Reg.2, revoked: SI 2013/459 Reg.10

155. Child Support (Maintenance Calculations and Special Cases) Regulations 2001
Reg.1, amended: SI 2013/630 Reg.43, SI 2013/1517 Reg.6
Reg.4, amended: SI 2013/630 Reg.43
Reg.4, referred to: SI 2013/380 Sch.7 para.5
Reg.5, amended: SI 2013/630 Reg.43
Reg.8, amended: SI 2013/1517 Reg.6
Sch.Part II para.4, amended: SI 2013/602 Sch.2 para.80

156. Child Support (Variations) Regulations (2000) 2001
Reg.11, amended: SI 2013/388 Sch.1 para.24, SI 2013/591 Sch.1 para.17
Reg.32, amended: SI 2013/458 Sch.2 para.5

157. Child Support (Maintenance Calculation Procedure) Regulations 2001
Sch.1 para.1, substituted: SI 2013/1517 Reg.7
Sch.1 para.8, added: SI 2013/1517 Reg.7
Sch.2 para.3, amended: SI 2013/1517 Reg.7
Sch.3 para.3, amended: SI 2013/1517 Reg.7

192. Terrorism Act 2000 (Crown Servants and Regulators) Regulations 2001
Reg.4, amended: SI 2013/472 Sch.2 para.32

251. Pig Industry Restructuring (Capital Grant) Scheme 2001
Art.2, amended: SI 2013/472 Art.4

252. Pig Industry Restructuring (Non-Capital Grant) Scheme 2001
Art.2, amended: SI 2013/472 Art.4

341. Representation of the People (England and Wales) Regulations 2001
Reg.3, amended: SI 2013/3198 Reg.3
Reg.4, amended: SI 2013/3198 Reg.4

Reg.5, amended: SI 2013/3198 Reg.5
Reg.6, amended: SI 2013/3198 Reg.6
Reg.7, amended: SI 2013/3198 Reg.42
Reg.20, revoked: SI 2013/3198 Sch.2
Reg.23, amended: SI 2013/3198 Reg.7
Reg.24, amended: SI 2013/3198 Reg.8
Reg.25A, amended: SI 2013/3198 Reg.9
Reg.26, applied: SI 2013/3197 Art.17, Art.19, Art.24, SI 2013/3198 Reg.45
Reg.26, substituted: SI 2013/3198 Reg.10
Reg.26A, added: SI 2013/3198 Reg.11
Reg.26B, added: SI 2013/3198 Reg.11
Reg.27, amended: SI 2013/3198 Reg.12
Reg.28, amended: SI 2013/3198 Reg.13
Reg.29, amended: SI 2013/3198 Reg.15
Reg.29ZA, added: SI 2013/3198 Reg.14
Reg.29ZA, varied: SI 2013/3198 Reg.14
Reg.29ZB, added: SI 2013/3198 Reg.14
Reg.31A, amended: SI 2013/3198 Reg.42
Reg.31B, amended: SI 2013/3198 Reg.16
Reg.31C, substituted: SI 2013/3198 Reg.17
Reg.31D, amended: SI 2013/3198 Reg.18
Reg.31F, amended: SI 2013/3198 Reg.19
Reg.31FA, added: SI 2013/3198 Reg.20
Reg.31I, amended: SI 2013/3198 Reg.21
Reg.31J, amended: SI 2013/3198 Reg.21
Reg.32ZA, added: SI 2013/3198 Reg.22
Reg.32ZA, applied: SI 2013/3198 Reg.45
Reg.32ZB, added: SI 2013/3198 Reg.22
Reg.32ZC, added: SI 2013/3198 Reg.22
Reg.32ZD, added: SI 2013/3198 Reg.22
Reg.32ZE, added: SI 2013/3198 Reg.22
Reg.32ZF, added: SI 2013/3198 Reg.22
Reg.32ZG, added: SI 2013/3198 Reg.22
Reg.32ZH, added: SI 2013/3198 Reg.22
Reg.32ZI, added: SI 2013/3198 Reg.22
Reg.35, applied: SI 2013/3197 Art.7
Reg.36, amended: SI 2013/3198 Reg.42
Reg.53, amended: SI 2013/388 Sch.1 para.25, SI 2013/591 Sch.1 para.20
Reg.55, amended: SI 2013/3198 Reg.23
Reg.55A, added: SI 2013/3198 Reg.24
Reg.56, amended: SI 2013/3198 Reg.25
Reg.60A, varied: SI 2013/1599 Reg.2
Reg.60B, added: SI 2013/3198 Reg.26
Reg.61, amended: SI 2013/3198 Reg.27
Reg.61C, added: SI 2013/3198 Reg.28
Reg.71, substituted: SI 2013/3198 Reg.29
Reg.78A, added: SI 2013/3198 Reg.30
Reg.81, revoked (in part): SI 2013/3198 Sch.2
Reg.84, amended: SI 2013/3198 Reg.31
Reg.84, revoked (in part): SI 2013/3198 Reg.31
Reg.85, revoked: SI 2013/3198 Sch.2
Reg.85A, amended: SI 2013/3198 Reg.32
Reg.85B, revoked: SI 2013/3198 Sch.2
Reg.86A, amended: SI 2013/3198 Reg.33
Reg.87, amended: SI 2013/3198 Reg.34
Reg.89, amended: SI 2013/3198 Reg.35
Reg.89, revoked (in part): SI 2013/3198 Reg.35
Reg.91, amended: SI 2013/3198 Reg.36
Reg.92, amended: SI 2013/3198 Reg.37, Reg.42
Reg.93, amended: SI 2013/3198 Reg.38, Reg.39
Reg.93A, added: SI 2013/3198 Reg.40
Reg.98, amended: SI 2013/3198 Reg.41, Reg.42
Reg.99, amended: SI 2013/3198 Reg.42
Reg.100, amended: SI 2013/3198 Reg.42, Reg.43
Reg.101, amended: SI 2013/3198 Reg.42
Reg.102, amended: SI 2013/3198 Reg.42
Reg.109A, amended: SI 2013/3198 Reg.42
Reg.111, amended: SI 2013/3198 Reg.42
Reg.112, amended: SI 2013/3198 Reg.42
Reg.113, amended: SI 2013/472 Sch.2 para.33
Reg.114, amended: SI 2013/472 Sch.2 para.33, SI 2013/1881 Sch.1 para.22
Reg.118, amended: SI 2013/3198 Reg.44
Sch.3, amended: SI 2013/3198 Reg.49, Sch.4
Sch.4, amended: SI 2013/3198 Reg.50

414. National Health Service (Optical Charges and Payments) and (General Ophthalmic Services) Amendment Regulations 2001

revoked: SI 2013/461 Sch.4

497. Representation of the People (Scotland) Regulations 2001

Reg.3, amended: SI 2013/3206 Reg.3
Reg.3, varied: 2013 asp 13 Sch.1 Part 3
Reg.4, amended: SI 2013/3206 Reg.4
Reg.4, varied: 2013 asp 13 Sch.1 Part 3
Reg.5, amended: SI 2013/3206 Reg.5
Reg.5, varied: 2013 asp 13 Sch.1 Part 3
Reg.6, amended: SI 2013/3206 Reg.6
Reg.6, varied: 2013 asp 13 Sch.1 Part 3
Reg.7, amended: SI 2013/3206 Reg.44
Reg.8, varied: 2013 asp 13 Sch.1 Part 3
Reg.11, varied: 2013 asp 13 Sch.1 Part 3
Reg.14, varied: 2013 asp 13 Sch.1 Part 3
Reg.15, varied: 2013 asp 13 s.7A, Sch.1 Part 3
Reg.17, varied: 2013 asp 13 Sch.1 Part 3
Reg.20, revoked: SI 2013/3206 Sch.2
Reg.23, amended: SI 2013/3206 Reg.7
Reg.23, varied: 2013 asp 13 Sch.1 Part 3
Reg.24, amended: SI 2013/3206 Reg.8
Reg.24, varied: 2013 asp 13 Sch.1 Part 3
Reg.25A, amended: SI 2013/3206 Reg.9
Reg.26, applied: SI 2013/3197 Art.17, Art.19, Art.24
Reg.26, referred to: SI 2013/3206 Reg.47
Reg.26, substituted: SI 2013/3206 Reg.10
Reg.26, varied: 2013 asp 13 Sch.1 Part 3

Reg.26A, added: SI 2013/3206 Reg.11
Reg.26B, added: SI 2013/3206 Reg.11
Reg.27, amended: SI 2013/3206 Reg.12
Reg.27, varied: 2013 asp 13 Sch.1 Part 3
Reg.28, amended: SI 2013/3206 Reg.13
Reg.29, amended: SI 2013/3206 Reg.15
Reg.29, disapplied: SI 2013/3197 Art.5
Reg.29, varied: 2013 asp 13 Sch.1 Part 3
Reg.29ZA, added: SI 2013/3206 Reg.14
Reg.29ZB, added: SI 2013/3206 Reg.14
Reg.30, varied: 2013 asp 13 Sch.1 Part 3
Reg.31, varied: 2013 asp 13 Sch.1 Part 3
Reg.31A, amended: SI 2013/3206 Reg.44
Reg.31A, varied: 2013 asp 13 Sch.1 Part 3
Reg.31B, amended: SI 2013/3206 Reg.16
Reg.31B, varied: 2013 asp 13 Sch.1 Part 3
Reg.31C, substituted: SI 2013/3206 Reg.17
Reg.31C, varied: 2013 asp 13 Sch.1 Part 3
Reg.31D, amended: SI 2013/3206 Reg.18
Reg.31D, varied: 2013 asp 13 Sch.1 Part 3
Reg.31E, varied: 2013 asp 13 Sch.1 Part 3
Reg.31F, amended: SI 2013/3206 Reg.19
Reg.31F, varied: 2013 asp 13 Sch.1 Part 3
Reg.31FA, added: SI 2013/3206 Reg.20
Reg.31G, applied: SSI 2013/357 Art.3, Art.4
Reg.31G, varied: 2013 asp 13 Sch.1 Part 3
Reg.31H, applied: SSI 2013/357 Art.3, Art.4
Reg.31H, varied: 2013 asp 13 Sch.1 Part 3
Reg.31I, amended: SI 2013/3206 Reg.21
Reg.31I, applied: SSI 2013/357 Art.3
Reg.31I, varied: 2013 asp 13 Sch.1 Part 3
Reg.31J, amended: SI 2013/602 Sch.2 para.81, SI 2013/3206 Reg.21
Reg.31J, applied: SSI 2013/357 Art.4
Reg.31J, varied: 2013 asp 13 Sch.1 Part 3
Reg.32, varied: 2013 asp 13 Sch.1 Part 3
Reg.32A, varied: 2013 asp 13 Sch.1 Part 3
Reg.32ZA, added: SI 2013/3206 Reg.22
Reg.32ZA, referred to: SI 2013/3206 Reg.47
Reg.32ZB, added: SI 2013/3206 Reg.22
Reg.32ZC, added: SI 2013/3206 Reg.22
Reg.32ZD, added: SI 2013/3206 Reg.22
Reg.32ZE, added: SI 2013/3206 Reg.22
Reg.32ZF, added: SI 2013/3206 Reg.22
Reg.32ZG, added: SI 2013/3206 Reg.22
Reg.32ZH, added: SI 2013/3206 Reg.22
Reg.32ZI, added: SI 2013/3206 Reg.22
Reg.35, applied: SI 2013/3197 Art.7
Reg.35, varied: 2013 asp 13 Sch.1 Part 3
Reg.36, amended: SI 2013/3206 Reg.44
Reg.36, varied: 2013 asp 13 Sch.1 Part 3
Reg.36A, varied: 2013 asp 13 Sch.1 Part 3
Reg.37, varied: 2013 asp 13 Sch.1 Part 3
Reg.40, varied: 2013 asp 13 Sch.1 Part 3
Reg.41, varied: 2013 asp 13 Sch.1 Part 3
Reg.41A, varied: 2013 asp 13 Sch.1 Part 3
Reg.45A, varied: 2013 asp 13 Sch.1 Part 3
Reg.45B, varied: 2013 asp 13 Sch.1 Part 3
Reg.45C, varied: 2013 asp 13 Sch.1 Part 3
Reg.45F, varied: 2013 asp 13 Sch.1 Part 3
Reg.53, amended: SI 2013/388 Sch.1 para.26, SI 2013/591 Sch.1 para.21
Reg.55, amended: SI 2013/3206 Reg.23
Reg.55A, added: SI 2013/3206 Reg.24
Reg.56, amended: SI 2013/3206 Reg.25
Reg.60A, varied: SI 2013/1599 Reg.3
Reg.60B, added: SI 2013/3206 Reg.26
Reg.61, amended: SI 2013/3206 Reg.27
Reg.61C, added: SI 2013/3206 Reg.28
Reg.71, substituted: SI 2013/3206 Reg.29
Reg.78, amended: SI 2013/3206 Reg.30
Reg.78A, added: SI 2013/3206 Reg.31
Reg.81, revoked (in part): SI 2013/3206 Sch.2
Reg.84, amended: SI 2013/3206 Reg.32
Reg.84, revoked (in part): SI 2013/3206 Reg.32
Reg.85, revoked: SI 2013/3206 Sch.2
Reg.85A, amended: SI 2013/3206 Reg.33
Reg.85B, revoked: SI 2013/3206 Sch.2
Reg.86A, amended: SI 2013/3206 Reg.34
Reg.87, amended: SI 2013/3206 Reg.35
Reg.89, amended: SI 2013/3206 Reg.36
Reg.89, revoked (in part): SI 2013/3206 Reg.36
Reg.91, amended: SI 2013/3206 Reg.37
Reg.91A, added: SI 2013/3206 Reg.38
Reg.92, amended: SI 2013/3206 Reg.39, Reg.44
Reg.93, amended: SI 2013/3206 Reg.40, Reg.41
Reg.93A, added: SI 2013/3206 Reg.42
Reg.97, amended: SI 2013/3206 Reg.43, Reg.44
Reg.97A, amended: SI 2013/3206 Reg.44
Reg.98, amended: SI 2013/3206 Reg.44
Reg.99, amended: SI 2013/3206 Reg.44, Reg.45
Reg.100, amended: SI 2013/3206 Reg.44
Reg.101, amended: SI 2013/3206 Reg.44
Reg.108A, amended: SI 2013/3206 Reg.44
Reg.110, amended: SI 2013/3206 Reg.44
Reg.111, amended: SI 2013/3206 Reg.44
Reg.112, amended: SI 2013/472 Sch.2 para.34
Reg.113, amended: SI 2013/472 Sch.2 para.34, SI 2013/1881 Sch.1 para.23
Reg.115, varied: 2013 asp 13 Sch.1 Part 3
Reg.118, amended: SI 2013/3206 Reg.46
Sch.1, amended: SI 2013/3206 Reg.44
Sch.3, amended: SI 2013/3206 Reg.51, Sch.4
Sch.4, amended: SI 2013/3206 Reg.52

544. Financial Services and Markets Act 2000 (Regulated Activities) Order 2001

applied: SI 2013/1773 Reg.78, SI 2013/1881 Art.59, Art.63, Art.64

see *Digital Satellite Warranty Cover Ltd, Re* [2013] UKSC 7, [2013] 1 W.L.R. 605 (SC), Lord Neuberger (President)
Part II, added: SI 2013/1881 Art.4
Part II, added: SI 2013/1881 Art.5
Part II, amended: SI 2013/1773 Sch.2 para.1
Part II, added: SI 2013/1881 Art.6
Part II, added: SI 2013/655 Art.5
Art.3, amended: SI 2013/504 Reg.33, SI 2013/1773 Sch.2 para.1, SI 2013/1881 Art.3, SI 2013/3115 Sch.2 para.51
Art.4, amended: SI 2013/1773 Sch.2 para.1, SI 2013/1881 Art.3
Art.5, applied: SI 2013/598 Art.2
Art.5, referred to: SI 2013/556 Art.2
Art.6, applied: SI 2013/598 Art.2
Art.8, amended: SI 2013/1773 Sch.2 para.1
Art.9AA, amended: SI 2013/1773 Sch.2 para.1
Art.9C, amended: SI 2013/472 Sch.2 para.35, SI 2013/3115 Sch.2 para.51
Art.9D, amended: SI 2013/472 Art.4, Sch.2 para.35
Art.9E, amended: SI 2013/472 Art.4, Sch.2 para.35
Art.9F, amended: SI 2013/472 Art.4, Sch.2 para.35
Art.9G, amended: SI 2013/472 Sch.2 para.35
Art.9G, revoked (in part): SI 2013/472 Sch.2 para.35
Art.9H, amended: SI 2013/472 Sch.2 para.35
Art.9K, amended: SI 2013/472 Sch.2 para.35
Art.10, referred to: SI 2013/556 Art.2, SI 2013/1635 Sch.1 para.3
Art.12A, amended: SI 2013/1773 Sch.2 para.1
Art.14, referred to: SI 2013/637 Art.2
Art.15, amended: SI 2013/1773 Sch.2 para.1
Art.16, amended: SI 2013/1773 Sch.2 para.1
Art.20, amended: SI 2013/1773 Sch.2 para.1
Art.21, referred to: SI 2013/637 Art.2, SI 2013/1635 Sch.1 para.3
Art.24, amended: SI 2013/1773 Sch.2 para.1
Art.25, referred to: SI 2013/637 Art.2, SI 2013/1635 Sch.1 para.3
Art.33, amended: SI 2013/1773 Sch.2 para.1
Art.35, amended: SI 2013/472 Sch.2 para.35, SI 2013/504 Reg.33
Art.35A, added: SI 2013/504 Reg.33
Art.36, amended: SI 2013/1773 Sch.2 para.1
Art.36A, applied: SI 2013/1881 Art.59A
Art.36A, referred to: SI 2013/1881 Art.12, Art.31, Art.56
Art.36B, applied: SI 2013/1881 Art.56
Art.36H, applied: SI 2013/1881 Art.59A
Art.36H, referred to: SI 2013/1881 Art.31, Art.56
Art.39, amended: SI 2013/1773 Sch.2 para.1
Art.39A, referred to: SI 2013/637 Art.2, SI 2013/1635 Sch.1 para.3
Art.39C, amended: SI 2013/1773 Sch.2 para.1
Art.39D, applied: SI 2013/1881 Art.59A, Art.60
Art.39E, applied: SI 2013/1881 Art.59A, Art.60
Art.39F, applied: SI 2013/1881 Art.59A
Art.39G, applied: SI 2013/1881 Art.59A
Art.39G, referred to: SI 2013/1881 Art.56
Art.40, referred to: SI 2013/1773 Reg.76
Art.42A, added: SI 2013/1773 Sch.2 para.1
Art.42A, applied: SI 2013/1773 Reg.76
Art.44, amended: SI 2013/1773 Sch.2 para.1
Art.45, referred to: SI 2013/637 Art.2
Art.50, amended: SI 2013/1773 Sch.2 para.1
Art.51, amended: SI 2013/1388 Reg.9
Art.51, referred to: SI 2013/637 Art.2
Art.51, substituted: SI 2013/1773 Sch.2 para.1
Art.51A, amended: SI 2013/1773 Sch.2 para.1
Art.51ZA, applied: SI 2013/637 Art.2
Art.51ZB, applied: SI 2013/637 Art.2
Art.51ZC, applied: SI 2013/637 Art.2
Art.51ZD, applied: SI 2013/637 Art.2
Art.51ZE, applied: SI 2013/637 Art.2
Art.52, referred to: SI 2013/637 Art.2
Art.52A, amended: SI 2013/1773 Sch.2 para.1
Art.53, referred to: SI 2013/637 Art.2, SI 2013/1635 Sch.1 para.3
Art.54, amended: SI 2013/472 Sch.2 para.35
Art.55, amended: SI 2013/1773 Sch.2 para.1
Art.57, referred to: SI 2013/556 Art.2, SI 2013/598 Art.2, SI 2013/637 Art.2, SI 2013/1635 Sch.1 para.3
Art.58, applied: SI 2013/556 Art.2
Art.58, referred to: SI 2013/598 Art.2, SI 2013/1635 Sch.1 para.3
Art.58A, amended: SI 2013/1773 Sch.2 para.1
Art.60A, amended: SI 2013/1773 Sch.2 para.1
Art.60B, applied: SI 2013/1881 Art.59A, Art.48, SI 2013/3128 Art.4
Art.60B, referred to: SI 2013/1881 Art.56
Art.60L, applied: SI 2013/1881 Art.56
Art.60N, applied: SI 2013/1881 Art.59A, Art.56
Art.63A, amended: SI 2013/1773 Sch.2 para.1
Art.63E, amended: SI 2013/1773 Sch.2 para.1
Art.63I, amended: SI 2013/1773 Sch.2 para.1
Art.64, amended: SI 2013/1773 Sch.2 para.1, SI 2013/1881 Art.8
Art.64, applied: SI 2013/1881 Art.59A, Art.60
Art.64, referred to: SI 2013/637 Art.2, SI 2013/1635 Sch.1 para.3, SI 2013/1881 Art.56
Art.68, amended: SI 2013/1773 Sch.2 para.1
Art.69, amended: SI 2013/1773 Sch.2 para.1
Art.72, amended: SI 2013/504 Reg.33
Art.72AA, added: SI 2013/1773 Sch.2 para.1

Art.72B, amended: SI 2013/1881 Art.9
Art.72B, referred to: SI 2013/1881 Art.59A
Art.72E, amended: SI 2013/1773 Sch.2 para.1
Art.75, referred to: SI 2013/1635 Sch.1 para.3, SI 2013/1773 Reg.10
Art.76, referred to: SI 2013/1773 Reg.10
Art.88D, added: SI 2013/1881 Art.7
Art.88E, added: SI 2013/1881 Art.7
Art.89A, added: SI 2013/1881 Art.8
Art.89A, applied: SI 2013/1881 Art.59A, Art.60
Art.89B, added: SI 2013/1881 Art.8
Art.89B, applied: SI 2013/1881 Art.59A, SI 2013/3128 Art.4
Art.89C, added: SI 2013/1881 Art.8
Art.89D, added: SI 2013/1881 Art.8
Art.89E, added: SI 2013/1881 Art.8
Art.90, revoked: SI 2013/1881 Art.9
Art.91, revoked: SI 2013/1881 Art.9
Art.92, amended: SI 2013/472 Sch.2 para.35
Art.93, amended: SI 2013/472 Art.4, Sch.2 para.35
Art.94, amended: SI 2013/472 Sch.2 para.35
Art.95, amended: SI 2013/472 Sch.2 para.35
Art.96, amended: SI 2013/472 Sch.2 para.35
Art.97, amended: SI 2013/472 Art.4
Sch.1 para.16, see *Digital Satellite Warranty Cover Ltd, Re* [2013] UKSC 7, [2013] 1 W.L.R. 605 (SC), Lord Neuberger (President)
Sch.5, added: SI 2013/655 Art.6
Sch.6 para.1, added: SI 2013/1773 Sch.2 para.1
Sch.6 para.2, added: SI 2013/1773 Sch.2 para.1
Sch.6 para.3, added: SI 2013/1773 Sch.2 para.1
Sch.7, added: SI 2013/1773 Sch.2 para.1
Sch.8 para.1, added: SI 2013/1773 Sch.2 para.1
Sch.8 para.2, added: SI 2013/1773 Sch.2 para.1
Sch.8 para.3, added: SI 2013/1773 Sch.2 para.1
Sch.8 para.4, added: SI 2013/1773 Sch.2 para.1
Sch.8 para.5, added: SI 2013/1773 Sch.2 para.1
Sch.8 para.6, added: SI 2013/1773 Sch.2 para.1
Sch.8 para.7, added: SI 2013/1773 Sch.2 para.1
Sch.8 para.8, added: SI 2013/1773 Sch.2 para.1
Sch.8 para.9, added: SI 2013/1773 Sch.2 para.1
Sch.8 para.10, added: SI 2013/1773 Sch.2 para.1
Sch.8 para.11, added: SI 2013/1773 Sch.2 para.1
Sch.8 para.11, amended: SI 2013/1773 Reg.81
Sch.8 para.11, revoked: SI 2013/1797 Sch.2 para.2

643. Pig Industry Restructuring Grant (Wales) Scheme 2001

Art.2, amended: SI 2013/472 Art.4

664. Pensions Increase (Review) Order 2001

applied: SI 2013/604 Sch.1

713. National Treatment Agency (Establishment and Constitution) Order 2001

revoked: SI 2013/235 Sch.1 para.3

715. National Treatment Agency Regulations 2001

revoked: SI 2013/235 Sch.1 para.4

749. National Health Service (Optical Charges and Payments) Amendment Regulations 2001

revoked: SI 2013/461 Sch.4

769. Social Security (Crediting and Treatment of Contributions, and National Insurance Numbers) Regulations 2001

Reg.1, amended: SI 2013/630 Reg.71
Reg.4, amended: SI 2013/3165 Reg.2
Reg.5, applied: SI 2013/381 Reg.17, Reg.29
Reg.6, applied: SI 2013/381 Reg.17, Reg.29
Reg.6C, applied: SI 2013/381 Reg.17

838. Climate Change Levy (General) Regulations 2001

Reg.11, amended: SI 2013/713 Reg.3
Reg.40A, added: SI 2013/713 Reg.4
Reg.51A, amended: SI 2013/713 Reg.5
Reg.51G, amended: SI 2013/713 Reg.6
Reg.51G, revoked (in part): SI 2013/713 Reg.6
Reg.51H, amended: SI 2013/713 Reg.7
Reg.51H, revoked (in part): SI 2013/713 Reg.7
Reg.51N, added: SI 2013/713 Reg.8
Reg.52, amended: SI 2013/713 Reg.9
Reg.60, amended: SI 2013/713 Reg.10
Sch.1 para.2, amended: SI 2013/713 Reg.11
Sch.1 para.2, substituted: SI 2013/713 Reg.11
Sch.2 para.2, amended: SI 2013/713 Reg.12
Sch.2 para.2, revoked (in part): SI 2013/713 Reg.12
Sch.3 para.1, added: SI 2013/713 Reg.13
Sch.3 para.1, amended: SI 2013/1716 Reg.3
Sch.3 para.2, added: SI 2013/713 Reg.13
Sch.3 para.2, amended: SI 2013/1716 Reg.3
Sch.3 para.3, added: SI 2013/713 Reg.13
Sch.3 para.4, added: SI 2013/713 Reg.13
Sch.3 para.4, amended: SI 2013/1716 Reg.3
Sch.3 para.5, added: SI 2013/713 Reg.13
Sch.3 para.5, amended: SI 2013/1716 Reg.3
Sch.3 para.6, added: SI 2013/713 Reg.13
Sch.3 para.7, added: SI 2013/713 Reg.13

856. Criminal Defence Service (Recovery of Defence Costs Orders) Regulations 2001

Reg.4, amended: SI 2013/630 Reg.63

880. Biocidal Products Regulations 2001

applied: SI 2013/1506 Reg.15, SI 2013/1507 Reg.7
Reg.1, revoked: SI 2013/1506 Reg.34
Reg.2, applied: SI 2013/1506 Sch.2 para.10
Reg.2, revoked: SI 2013/1506 Reg.34
Reg.3, applied: SI 2013/1506 Sch.2 para.10
Reg.3, revoked: SI 2013/1506 Reg.34
Reg.3A, revoked: SI 2013/1506 Reg.34
Reg.4, revoked: SI 2013/1506 Reg.34
Reg.5, revoked: SI 2013/1506 Reg.34
Reg.6, revoked: SI 2013/1506 Reg.34

Reg.7, revoked: SI 2013/1506 Reg.34
Reg.8, revoked: SI 2013/1506 Reg.34
Reg.9, applied: SI 2013/1506 Sch.2 para.10
Reg.9, revoked: SI 2013/1506 Reg.34
Reg.10, applied: SI 2013/1506 Sch.2 para.10
Reg.10, revoked: SI 2013/1506 Reg.34
Reg.11, applied: SI 2013/1506 Sch.2 para.10
Reg.11, revoked: SI 2013/1506 Reg.34
Reg.12, applied: SI 2013/1506 Sch.2 para.10
Reg.12, revoked: SI 2013/1506 Reg.34
Reg.13, applied: SI 2013/1506 Sch.2 para.10
Reg.13, revoked: SI 2013/1506 Reg.34
Reg.14, applied: SI 2013/1506 Sch.2 para.10
Reg.14, revoked: SI 2013/1506 Reg.34
Reg.15, applied: SI 2013/1506 Sch.2 para.10
Reg.15, revoked: SI 2013/1506 Reg.34
Reg.15A, revoked: SI 2013/1506 Reg.34
Reg.16, revoked: SI 2013/1506 Reg.34
Reg.17, applied: SI 2013/1506 Sch.2 para.10
Reg.17, revoked: SI 2013/1506 Reg.34
Reg.18, applied: SI 2013/1506 Sch.2 para.10
Reg.18, revoked: SI 2013/1506 Reg.34
Reg.19, revoked: SI 2013/1506 Reg.34
Reg.20, revoked: SI 2013/1506 Reg.34
Reg.21, revoked: SI 2013/1506 Reg.34
Reg.22, revoked: SI 2013/1506 Reg.34
Reg.23, revoked: SI 2013/1506 Reg.34
Reg.24, revoked: SI 2013/1506 Reg.34
Reg.25, applied: SI 2013/1506 Sch.2 para.10
Reg.25, revoked: SI 2013/1506 Reg.34
Reg.26, revoked: SI 2013/1506 Reg.34
Reg.27, revoked: SI 2013/1506 Reg.34
Reg.28, revoked: SI 2013/1506 Reg.34
Reg.29, revoked: SI 2013/1506 Reg.34
Reg.30, revoked: SI 2013/1506 Reg.34
Reg.31, revoked: SI 2013/1506 Reg.34
Reg.32, applied: SI 2013/1506 Sch.2 para.10
Reg.32, revoked: SI 2013/1506 Reg.34
Reg.33, revoked: SI 2013/1506 Reg.34
Reg.34, applied: SI 2013/1506 Sch.2 para.10
Reg.34, revoked: SI 2013/1506 Reg.34
Reg.35, applied: SI 2013/1506 Sch.2 para.10
Reg.35, revoked: SI 2013/1506 Reg.34
Reg.36, revoked: SI 2013/1506 Reg.34
Reg.37, applied: SI 2013/1506 Sch.2 para.10
Reg.37, revoked: SI 2013/1506 Reg.34
Reg.38, revoked: SI 2013/1506 Reg.34
Reg.39, revoked: SI 2013/1507 Reg.8
Reg.39A, revoked: SI 2013/1507 Reg.8
Reg.40, revoked: SI 2013/1506 Reg.34
Reg.41, revoked: SI 2013/1506 Reg.34
Reg.42, revoked: SI 2013/1506 Reg.34
Sch.1, revoked: SI 2013/1506 Reg.34
Sch.2, amended: SI 2013/1478 Sch.5 para.12
Sch.2, revoked: SI 2013/1506 Reg.34
Sch.3, applied: SI 2013/1506 Sch.2 para.10
Sch.3 para.1, revoked: SI 2013/1506 Reg.34
Sch.3 para.2, revoked: SI 2013/1506 Reg.34
Sch.3 para.3, revoked: SI 2013/1506 Reg.34
Sch.3 para.4, revoked: SI 2013/1506 Reg.34
Sch.4, applied: SI 2013/1506 Sch.2 para.10
Sch.4 para.1, revoked: SI 2013/1506 Reg.34
Sch.4 para.2, revoked: SI 2013/1506 Reg.34
Sch.4 para.3, revoked: SI 2013/1506 Reg.34
Sch.4 para.4, revoked: SI 2013/1506 Reg.34
Sch.4 para.5, revoked: SI 2013/1506 Reg.34
Sch.4 para.6, revoked: SI 2013/1506 Reg.34
Sch.4 para.7, revoked: SI 2013/1506 Reg.34
Sch.4 para.8, revoked: SI 2013/1506 Reg.34
Sch.4 para.9, revoked: SI 2013/1506 Reg.34
Sch.4 para.10, revoked: SI 2013/1506 Reg.34
Sch.4 para.11, revoked: SI 2013/1506 Reg.34
Sch.4 para.12, revoked: SI 2013/1506 Reg.34
Sch.4 para.13, revoked: SI 2013/1506 Reg.34
Sch.5, applied: SI 2013/1506 Sch.2 para.10
Sch.5A, revoked: SI 2013/1506 Reg.34
Sch.5 para.1, revoked: SI 2013/1506 Reg.34
Sch.5 para.2, revoked: SI 2013/1506 Reg.34
Sch.5 para.3, revoked: SI 2013/1506 Reg.34
Sch.5 para.4, revoked: SI 2013/1506 Reg.34
Sch.5 para.5, revoked: SI 2013/1506 Reg.34
Sch.5 para.6, revoked: SI 2013/1506 Reg.34
Sch.5 para.7, revoked: SI 2013/1506 Reg.34
Sch.5 para.8, revoked: SI 2013/1506 Reg.34
Sch.6 para.1, revoked: SI 2013/1506 Reg.34
Sch.6 para.2, revoked: SI 2013/1506 Reg.34
Sch.6 para.3, revoked: SI 2013/1506 Reg.34
Sch.6 para.4, revoked: SI 2013/1506 Reg.34
Sch.6 para.5, revoked: SI 2013/1506 Reg.34
Sch.6 para.6, revoked: SI 2013/1506 Reg.34
Sch.6 para.7, revoked: SI 2013/1506 Reg.34
Sch.6 para.8, revoked: SI 2013/1506 Reg.34
Sch.6 para.9, revoked: SI 2013/1506 Reg.34
Sch.6 para.10, revoked: SI 2013/1506 Reg.34
Sch.6 para.11, revoked: SI 2013/1506 Reg.34
Sch.6 para.12, revoked: SI 2013/1506 Reg.34
Sch.6 para.13, revoked: SI 2013/1506 Reg.34
Sch.6 para.14, revoked: SI 2013/1506 Reg.34
Sch.6 para.15, revoked: SI 2013/1506 Reg.34
Sch.7 para.1, revoked: SI 2013/1506 Reg.34
Sch.7 para.2, revoked: SI 2013/1506 Reg.34
Sch.7 para.3, revoked: SI 2013/1506 Reg.34
Sch.7 para.4, revoked: SI 2013/1506 Reg.34
Sch.7 para.5, revoked: SI 2013/1506 Reg.34
Sch.7 para.6, revoked: SI 2013/1506 Reg.34
Sch.7 para.7, revoked: SI 2013/1506 Reg.34
Sch.7 para.8, revoked: SI 2013/1506 Reg.34
Sch.7 para.9, revoked: SI 2013/1506 Reg.34

Sch.7 para.10, revoked: SI 2013/1506 Reg.34
Sch.8 para.1, revoked: SI 2013/1506 Reg.34
Sch.8 para.2, revoked: SI 2013/1506 Reg.34
Sch.8 para.3, revoked: SI 2013/1506 Reg.34
Sch.8 para.4, revoked: SI 2013/1506 Reg.34
Sch.8 para.5, revoked: SI 2013/1506 Reg.34
Sch.8 para.6, revoked: SI 2013/1506 Reg.34
Sch.8 para.7, revoked: SI 2013/1506 Reg.34
Sch.8 para.8, revoked: SI 2013/1506 Reg.34
Sch.8 para.9, revoked: SI 2013/1506 Reg.34
Sch.8 para.10, revoked: SI 2013/1506 Reg.34
Sch.9 para.1, revoked: SI 2013/1506 Reg.34
Sch.9 para.2, revoked: SI 2013/1506 Reg.34
Sch.9 para.3, revoked: SI 2013/1506 Reg.34
Sch.9 para.4, revoked: SI 2013/1506 Reg.34
Sch.9 para.5, revoked: SI 2013/1506 Reg.34
Sch.9 para.6, revoked: SI 2013/1506 Reg.34
Sch.9 para.7, revoked: SI 2013/1506 Reg.34
Sch.9 para.8, revoked: SI 2013/1506 Reg.34
Sch.9 para.9, revoked: SI 2013/1506 Reg.34
Sch.9 para.10, revoked: SI 2013/1506 Reg.34
Sch.9 para.11, revoked: SI 2013/1506 Reg.34
Sch.9 para.12, revoked: SI 2013/1506 Reg.34
Sch.9 para.13, revoked: SI 2013/1506 Reg.34
Sch.9 para.14, revoked: SI 2013/1506 Reg.34
Sch.10 Part I para.1, revoked: SI 2013/1506 Reg.34
Sch.10 Part I para.2, revoked: SI 2013/1506 Reg.34
Sch.10 Part I para.3, revoked: SI 2013/1506 Reg.34
Sch.10 Part I para.4, revoked: SI 2013/1506 Reg.34
Sch.10 Part I para.5, revoked: SI 2013/1506 Reg.34
Sch.10 Part II para.6, revoked: SI 2013/1506 Reg.34
Sch.10 Part II para.7, revoked: SI 2013/1506 Reg.34
Sch.10 Part II para.8, revoked: SI 2013/1506 Reg.34
Sch.10 Part II para.9, revoked: SI 2013/1506 Reg.34
Sch.10 Part II para.10, revoked: SI 2013/1506 Reg.34
Sch.10 Part II para.11, revoked: SI 2013/1506 Reg.34
Sch.10 Part II para.12, revoked: SI 2013/1506 Reg.34
Sch.10 Part II para.13, revoked: SI 2013/1506 Reg.34
Sch.11 para.1, revoked: SI 2013/1506 Reg.34
Sch.11 para.2, revoked: SI 2013/1506 Reg.34
Sch.11 para.3, revoked: SI 2013/1506 Reg.34
Sch.11 para.4, revoked: SI 2013/1506 Reg.34
Sch.11 para.5, revoked: SI 2013/1506 Reg.34
Sch.12 para.1, revoked: SI 2013/1507 Reg.8
Sch.12 para.2, revoked: SI 2013/1507 Reg.8
Sch.12 para.3, revoked: SI 2013/1507 Reg.8
Sch.12 para.4, revoked: SI 2013/1507 Reg.8
Sch.12 para.5, revoked: SI 2013/1507 Reg.8
Sch.12 para.6, revoked: SI 2013/1507 Reg.8
Sch.12 para.7, revoked: SI 2013/1507 Reg.8
Sch.12 para.8, revoked: SI 2013/1507 Reg.8
Sch.12 para.9, revoked: SI 2013/1507 Reg.8
Sch.12 para.10, revoked: SI 2013/1507 Reg.8
Sch.12 para.11, revoked: SI 2013/1507 Reg.8
Sch.12 para.12, revoked: SI 2013/1507 Reg.8
Sch.12A para.1, revoked: SI 2013/1507 Reg.8
Sch.12A para.2, revoked: SI 2013/1507 Reg.8
Sch.12A para.3, revoked: SI 2013/1507 Reg.8
Sch.12A para.4, revoked: SI 2013/1507 Reg.8
Sch.12A para.5, revoked: SI 2013/1507 Reg.8
Sch.12A para.6, revoked: SI 2013/1507 Reg.8
Sch.12A para.7, revoked: SI 2013/1507 Reg.8
Sch.12A para.8, revoked: SI 2013/1507 Reg.8
Sch.12A para.9, revoked: SI 2013/1507 Reg.8
Sch.12A para.10, revoked: SI 2013/1507 Reg.8
Sch.12A para.11, revoked: SI 2013/1507 Reg.8
Sch.12A para.12, revoked: SI 2013/1507 Reg.8
Sch.12A para.13, revoked: SI 2013/1507 Reg.8
Sch.12A para.14, revoked: SI 2013/1507 Reg.8
Sch.12A para.15, applied: SI 2013/1507 Reg.7
Sch.12A para.15, revoked: SI 2013/1507 Reg.8
Sch.12A para.16, revoked: SI 2013/1507 Reg.8
Sch.12A para.17, revoked: SI 2013/1507 Reg.8
Sch.12A para.18, revoked: SI 2013/1507 Reg.8
Sch.12A para.19, revoked: SI 2013/1507 Reg.8
Sch.13 para.1, revoked: SI 2013/1506 Reg.34
Sch.13 para.1A, revoked: SI 2013/1506 Reg.34
Sch.13 para.2, revoked: SI 2013/1506 Reg.34
Sch.13 para.2A, revoked: SI 2013/1506 Reg.34
Sch.13 para.3, revoked: SI 2013/1506 Reg.34
Sch.13 para.4, revoked: SI 2013/1506 Reg.34
Sch.13 para.5, revoked: SI 2013/1506 Reg.34
Sch.13 para.6, applied: SI 2013/1506 Sch.2 para.8
Sch.13 para.6, revoked: SI 2013/1506 Reg.34
Sch.13 para.7, applied: SI 2013/1506 Sch.2 para.8
Sch.13 para.7, revoked: SI 2013/1506 Reg.34
Sch.13 para.8, applied: SI 2013/1506 Sch.2 para.8
Sch.13 para.8, revoked: SI 2013/1506 Reg.34
Sch.13 para.9, applied: SI 2013/1506 Sch.2 para.8
Sch.13 para.9, revoked: SI 2013/1506 Reg.34
Sch.13 para.10, applied: SI 2013/1506 Sch.2 para.8
Sch.13 para.10, revoked: SI 2013/1506 Reg.34
Sch.13 para.11, applied: SI 2013/1506 Sch.2 para.8

Sch.13 para.11, revoked: SI 2013/1506 Reg.34
Sch.13 para.12, applied: SI 2013/1506 Sch.2 para.8
Sch.13 para.12, revoked: SI 2013/1506 Reg.34
Sch.13 para.13, applied: SI 2013/1506 Sch.2 para.7
Sch.13 para.13, revoked: SI 2013/1506 Reg.34
Sch.13 para.14, revoked: SI 2013/1506 Reg.34
Sch.13 para.15, revoked: SI 2013/1506 Reg.34
Sch.13 para.16, revoked: SI 2013/1506 Reg.34

934. Stakeholder Pension Schemes (Amendment) (No.2) Regulations 2001

Reg.14, revoked: SI 2013/459 Reg.10
Reg.15, revoked: SI 2013/459 Reg.10

946. Liberia (United Nations Sanctions) (Overseas Territories) Order 2001

revoked: SI 2013/237 Sch.2

995. Financial Services and Markets Act 2000 (Recognition Requirements for Investment Exchanges and Clearing Houses) Regulations 2001

applied: SI 2013/1908 Reg.6
disapplied: SI 2013/504 Reg.52
Reg.3, amended: SI 2013/472 Sch.2 para.36, SI 2013/504 Reg.5, SI 2013/1908 Reg.3, SI 2013/3115 Sch.2 para.52
Reg.5, amended: SI 2013/504 Reg.5
Reg.5A, added: SI 2013/504 Reg.5
Reg.6, amended: SI 2013/472 Sch.2 para.36
Reg.7, amended: SI 2013/472 Sch.2 para.36
Sch.Part I para.1, amended: SI 2013/472 Sch.2 para.36
Sch.Part I para.2, amended: SI 2013/472 Sch.2 para.36
Sch.Part I para.4A, amended: SI 2013/472 Sch.2 para.36
Sch.Part I para.4B, amended: SI 2013/472 Sch.2 para.36
Sch.Part I para.6, amended: SI 2013/472 Sch.2 para.36
Sch.Part I para.7B, amended: SI 2013/472 Sch.2 para.36, SI 2013/3115 Sch.2 para.52
Sch.Part II para.15, revoked: SI 2013/472 Sch.2 para.36
Sch.Part III para.16, amended: SI 2013/472 Sch.2 para.36
Sch.Part III para.17, amended: SI 2013/472 Sch.2 para.36
Sch.Part III para.20, amended: SI 2013/472 Sch.2 para.36
Sch.Part III para.21A, amended: SI 2013/504 Reg.5
Sch.Part III para.23A, added: SI 2013/1908 Reg.3
Sch.Part III para.23A, applied: SI 2013/1908 Reg.6
Sch.Part III para.23B, varied: SI 2013/1908 Reg.6
Sch.Part IV para.28, amended: SI 2013/472 Sch.2 para.36
Sch.Part IV para.28A, varied: SI 2013/1908 Reg.6
Sch.Part V para.29, added: SI 2013/504 Reg.5
Sch.Part V para.29A, added: SI 2013/504 Reg.5, SI 2013/1908 Reg.3
Sch.Part V para.29B, added: SI 2013/504 Reg.5, SI 2013/1908 Reg.3
Sch.Part V para.30, added: SI 2013/504 Reg.5
Sch.Part V para.31, added: SI 2013/504 Reg.5
Sch.Part VI para.32, added: SI 2013/504 Reg.5
Sch.Part VI para.33, added: SI 2013/504 Reg.5
Sch.Part VI para.34, added: SI 2013/504 Reg.5
Sch.Part VI para.35, added: SI 2013/504 Reg.5
Sch.Part VI para.36, added: SI 2013/504 Reg.5, SI 2013/1908 Reg.3

1002. Housing Benefit and Council Tax Benefit (Decisions and Appeals) Regulations 2001

Reg.1, referred to: SI 2013/3029 Sch.10 para.12, SI 2013/3035 Sch.1
Reg.4, referred to: SI 2013/111 Reg.3
Reg.5, referred to: SI 2013/111 Reg.3
Reg.11, applied: SI 2013/111 Reg.3, SI 2013/215 Reg.2
Reg.13, applied: SI 2013/215 Reg.2

1004. Social Security (Contributions) Regulations 2001

referred to: SI 2013/622 Reg.32
Reg.1, amended: SI 2013/630 Reg.72
Reg.10, amended: SI 2013/558 Reg.3
Reg.11, amended: SI 2013/558 Reg.4
Reg.22, amended: SI 2013/1907 Reg.3
Reg.22A, see *Cheshire Employer and Skills Development Ltd v Revenue and Customs Commissioners* [2012] EWCA Civ 1429, [2013] S.T.C. 2121 (CA (Civ Div)), Mummery, L.J.
Reg.40, revoked (in part): SI 2013/622 Reg.33
Reg.48, amended: SI 2013/622 Reg.34
Reg.50C, added: SI 2013/622 Reg.35
Reg.50C, amended: SI 2013/718 Reg.2
Reg.50C, varied: SI 2013/718 Reg.3
Reg.52A, amended: SI 2013/622 Reg.36
Reg.60, applied: SI 2013/381 Reg.17, Reg.29
Reg.61B, added: SI 2013/622 Reg.37
Reg.61B, amended: SI 2013/718 Reg.2
Reg.61B, varied: SI 2013/718 Reg.3
Reg.63A, added: SI 2013/622 Reg.38
Reg.71, see *Marcia Willetts Ltd v Revenue and Customs Commissioners* [2013] S.F.T.D. 65 (FTT (Tax)), Judge Rachel Short
Reg.90NA, revoked (in part): SI 2013/622 Reg.3
Reg.125, amended: SI 2013/619 Reg.2
Sch.2 para.14, amended: SI 2013/622 Reg.39
Sch.3 Part V, applied: SI 2013/3029 Sch.1 para.12, Sch.6 para.14, SI 2013/3035 Sch.1

Sch.3 Pt X para.5, see *Knowledgepoint 360 Group Ltd v Revenue and Customs Commissioners* [2013] UKUT 7 (TCC), [2013] S.T.C. 1690 (UT (Tax)), Judge Timothy Herrington
Sch.3 Part V para.6A, revoked: SI 2013/622 Reg.40
Sch.3 Part V para.7A, amended: SI 2013/622 Reg.40
Sch.3 Part VI para.10A, added: SI 2013/622 Reg.40
Sch.3 Pt VIII para.7A, see *Cheshire Employer and Skills Development Ltd v Revenue and Customs Commissioners* [2012] EWCA Civ 1429, [2013] S.T.C. 2121 (CA (Civ Div)), Mummery, L.J.
Sch.3 Part VIII para.16, amended: SI 2013/1907 Reg.4
Sch.3 Part X para.23, added: SI 2013/1142 Reg.2
Sch.3 Part X para.24, added: SI 2013/1907 Reg.4
Sch.4 Part I para.1, amended: SI 2013/622 Reg.4
Sch.4 Part I para.1, revoked (in part): SI 2013/622 Reg.6
Sch.4 Part II para.6, amended: SI 2013/622 Reg.4
Sch.4 Part IIIB para.29N, amended: SI 2013/622 Reg.19
Sch.4 Part IIIB para.29O, revoked (in part): SI 2013/622 Reg.4
Sch.4 Part III para.10, amended: SI 2013/622 Reg.7
Sch.4 Part III para.11, amended: SI 2013/622 Reg.8
Sch.4 Part III para.11ZA, amended: SI 2013/622 Reg.9
Sch.4 Part III para.21A, amended: SI 2013/622 Reg.10, SI 2013/2301 Reg.3
Sch.4 Part III para.21A, applied: SI 2013/622 Reg.30, Reg.31
Sch.4 Part III para.21A, revoked (in part): SI 2013/622 Reg.10
Sch.4 Part III para.21AA, added: SI 2013/622 Reg.11
Sch.4 Part III para.21AB, added: SI 2013/622 Reg.11
Sch.4 Part III para.21AC, added: SI 2013/622 Reg.11
Sch.4 Part III para.21AD, added: SI 2013/622 Reg.11
Sch.4 Part III para.21B, amended: SI 2013/622 Reg.12
Sch.4 Part III para.21B, revoked (in part): SI 2013/622 Reg.12
Sch.4 Part III para.21CA, added: SI 2013/622 Reg.13
Sch.4 Part III para.21D, amended: SI 2013/622 Reg.14
Sch.4 Part III para.21D, applied: SI 2013/622 Reg.30, Reg.31
Sch.4 Part III para.21D, revoked (in part): SI 2013/622 Reg.14
Sch.4 Part III para.21E, amended: SI 2013/622 Reg.15
Sch.4 Part III para.21E, revoked (in part): SI 2013/622 Reg.15
Sch.4 Part III para.21EA, added: SI 2013/622 Reg.16
Sch.4 Part III para.21EA, amended: SI 2013/2301 Reg.4
Sch.4 Part III para.21F, amended: SI 2013/622 Reg.17
Sch.4 Part III para.21F, revoked (in part): SI 2013/622 Reg.17
Sch.4 Part III para.22, amended: SI 2013/622 Reg.18
Sch.4 Part III para.26, amended: SI 2013/622 Reg.4
Sch.4 Part IV para.30A, added: SI 2013/622 Reg.20
Sch.4 Part IV para.31, amended: SI 2013/622 Reg.21
Sch.4 Part IV para.31A, added: SI 2013/622 Reg.22
Sch.4A para.2, amended: SI 2013/622 Reg.24
Sch.4A para.2A, added: SI 2013/622 Reg.25
Sch.4A para.3A, added: SI 2013/622 Reg.26
Sch.4A para.3A, referred to: SI 2013/622 Reg.30
Sch.4A para.6, referred to: SI 2013/622 Reg.30
Sch.4A para.7, referred to: SI 2013/622 Reg.30
Sch.4A para.8, referred to: SI 2013/622 Reg.30
Sch.4A para.9, referred to: SI 2013/622 Reg.30
Sch.4A para.10, referred to: SI 2013/622 Reg.30
Sch.4A para.12, referred to: SI 2013/622 Reg.30
Sch.4A para.12, substituted: SI 2013/622 Reg.27
Sch.4A para.12A, added: SI 2013/622 Reg.28
Sch.4A para.12B, added: SI 2013/622 Reg.28
Sch.4A para.12C, added: SI 2013/622 Reg.28
Sch.4A para.12D, added: SI 2013/622 Reg.28
Sch.6 Part 1, applied: SI 2013/378 Reg.41, Reg.44, Reg.54, Sch.1 para.6, Sch.1 para.12, SI 2013/3029 Sch.3 para.3, Sch.8 para.9, SI 2013/3035 Sch.1

1060. Financial Services and Markets Act 2000 (Promotion of Collective Investment Schemes) (Exemptions) Order 2001

Art.2, amended: SI 2013/1388 Reg.10, SI 2013/1773 Sch.2 para.5
Art.16, substituted: SI 2013/1773 Sch.2 para.5
Art.30, amended: SI 2013/472 Sch.2 para.37
Sch.1 Part I para.1, amended: SI 2013/472 Sch.2 para.37

Sch.1 Part II para.2, amended: SI 2013/472 Sch.2 para.37

1062. Financial Services and Markets Act 2000 (Collective Investment Schemes) Order 2001

Art.2, amended: SI 2013/1388 Reg.11
Sch.para.1, amended: SI 2013/1388 Reg.11
Sch.para.5, amended: SI 2013/1773 Sch.2 para.6

1077. Community Legal Service (Funding) (Counsel in Family Proceedings) Order 2001

applied: SI 2013/422 Reg.8

1091. Offshore Combustion Installations (Prevention and Control of Pollution) Regulations 2001

revoked: SI 2013/971 Reg.38
Reg.13, applied: SI 2013/971 Reg.24

1136. Climate Change Levy (Electricity and Gas) Regulations 2001

Reg.5, amended: 2013 c.29 Sch.42 para.20

1167. Discretionary Financial Assistance Regulations 2001

Reg.1, amended: SI 2013/1139 Reg.2
Reg.2, amended: SI 2013/458 Sch.1, SI 2013/1139 Reg.2
Reg.2, applied: SI 2013/3029 Sch.9 para.64, Sch.10 para.12, SI 2013/3035 Sch.1
Reg.2, revoked (in part): SI 2013/458 Sch.1
Reg.3, amended: SI 2013/458 Sch.1, SI 2013/1139 Reg.2
Reg.3, revoked (in part): SI 2013/458 Sch.1
Reg.4, amended: SI 2013/458 Sch.1
Reg.4, revoked (in part): SI 2013/458 Sch.1
Reg.4, substituted: SI 2013/1139 Reg.2
Reg.5, amended: SI 2013/458 Sch.1, SI 2013/1139 Reg.2
Reg.6, amended: SI 2013/458 Sch.1, SI 2013/1139 Reg.2

1177. Financial Services and Markets Act 2000 (Carrying on Regulated Activities by Way of Business) Order 2001

Art.3, amended: SI 2013/1773 Sch.2 para.7
Art.3E, added: SI 2013/1881 Art.13

1184. European Parliamentary Elections (Franchise of Relevant Citizens of the Union) Regulations 2001

Reg.8, amended: SI 2013/2876 Reg.4
Sch., amended: SI 2013/2876 Reg.5

1201. Financial Services and Markets Act 2000 (Exemption) Order 2001

Art.5, amended: SI 2013/1773 Sch.2 para.8
Sch.Part III para.37, amended: SI 2013/504 Reg.34
Sch.Part IV para.40, amended: SI 2013/1881 Art.14
Sch.Part IV para.44, amended: SI 2013/1773 Sch.2 para.8
Sch.Part IV para.45, amended: SI 2013/1773 Sch.2 para.8
Sch.Part IV para.47, amended: SI 2013/1881 Art.14
Sch.Part IV para.51, amended: SI 2013/472 Sch.2 para.38
Sch.Part IV para.52, added: SI 2013/1881 Art.14
Sch.Part IV para.53, added: SI 2013/1881 Art.14
Sch.Part IV para.54, added: SI 2013/1881 Art.14

1217. Financial Services and Markets Act 2000 (Appointed Representatives) Regulations 2001

Reg.1, amended: SI 2013/3115 Sch.2 para.53
Reg.2, amended: SI 2013/1881 Art.15
Reg.3, amended: SI 2013/472 Sch.2 para.39, SI 2013/1881 Art.15

1227. Financial Services and Markets Act 2000 (Professions) (Non-Exempt Activities) Order 2001

Art.2, amended: SI 2013/472 Sch.2 para.40
Art.4, amended: SI 2013/1773 Sch.2 para.9

1228. Open-Ended Investment Companies Regulations 2001

Reg.2, amended: SI 2013/472 Sch.2 para.41
Reg.3, amended: SI 2013/472 Sch.2 para.41
Reg.5, amended: SI 2013/472 Sch.2 para.41
Reg.6, amended: SI 2013/472 Sch.2 para.41
Reg.7, amended: SI 2013/472 Sch.2 para.41
Reg.10, amended: SI 2013/472 Sch.2 para.41
Reg.11B, amended: SI 2013/472 Sch.2 para.41
Reg.12, applied: SI 2013/1773 Reg.54
Reg.14, amended: SI 2013/472 Sch.2 para.41
Reg.14, applied: SSI 2013/50 Sch.2 para.1
Reg.15, amended: SI 2013/472 Art.4, Sch.2 para.41, SI 2013/1773 Sch.2 para.10
Reg.21, amended: SI 2013/472 Sch.2 para.41
Reg.21, applied: SSI 2013/50 Sch.2 para.1
Reg.22A, amended: SI 2013/472 Sch.2 para.41
Reg.25, amended: SI 2013/472 Sch.2 para.41
Reg.25, applied: SSI 2013/50 Sch.2 para.1
Reg.27, amended: SI 2013/472 Sch.2 para.41
Reg.33, amended: SI 2013/472 Sch.2 para.41
Reg.34, amended: SI 2013/472 Sch.2 para.41
Reg.38, amended: SI 2013/472 Sch.2 para.41
Reg.39, amended: SI 2013/472 Sch.2 para.41
Reg.40, amended: SI 2013/472 Sch.2 para.41
Reg.42, amended: SI 2013/472 Sch.2 para.41
Reg.44, amended: SI 2013/472 Sch.2 para.41
Reg.62, amended: SI 2013/1773 Sch.2 para.10
Reg.65, amended: SI 2013/472 Sch.2 para.41
Reg.66, amended: SI 2013/472 Sch.2 para.41
Reg.68, amended: SI 2013/472 Sch.2 para.41
Reg.77, amended: SI 2013/472 Sch.2 para.41
Reg.80, amended: SI 2013/472 Sch.2 para.41
Sch.1 para.5, amended: SI 2013/472 Sch.2 para.41
Sch.2 para.2, amended: SI 2013/472 Sch.2 para.41
Sch.2 para.3, amended: SI 2013/472 Sch.2 para.41
Sch.2 para.4, amended: SI 2013/472 Sch.2 para.41

Sch.2 para.5, amended: SI 2013/472 Sch.2 para.41
Sch.3 para.11, amended: SI 2013/472 Sch.2 para.41
Sch.4 para.1, amended: SI 2013/472 Sch.2 para.41
Sch.5 para.13, amended: SI 2013/472 Sch.2 para.41
Sch.5 para.16, amended: SI 2013/472 Sch.2 para.41
Sch.5 para.18, amended: SI 2013/472 Sch.2 para.41
Sch.5 para.20, amended: SI 2013/472 Sch.2 para.41
Sch.6 para.6, amended: SI 2013/472 Sch.2 para.41

1230. North and East Devon Partnership National Health Service Trust (Establishment) Order 2001
Art.1, amended: SI 2013/593 Art.2

1323. Additional Pension and Social Security Pensions (Home Responsibilities) (Amendment) Regulations 2001
Reg.5B, added: SI 2013/630 Reg.73

1330. Barnet, Enfield and Haringey Mental Health National Health Service Trust (Establishment) Order 2001
Art.1, amended: SI 2013/593 Art.2

1367. Greater Manchester (Light Rapid Transit System) (Trafford Park) Order 2001
Art.5, amended: SI 2013/1030 Art.7

1368. Greater Manchester (Light Rapid Transit System) (Mumps Surface Crossing) Order 2001
Art.5, amended: SI 2013/1030 Art.7

1403. Immigration and Asylum Act 1999 (Part V Exemption Educational Institutions and Health Sector Bodies) Order 2001
Sch.3 para.1, amended: SI 2013/235 Sch.2 para.45
Sch.3 para.1, revoked (in part): SI 2013/235 Sch.2 para.45

1420. Financial Services and Markets Act 2000 (Service of Notices) Regulations 2001
Reg.1, amended: SI 2013/472 Sch.2 para.42
Reg.4, amended: SI 2013/472 Sch.2 para.42
Reg.5, amended: SI 2013/472 Sch.2 para.42
Reg.6, amended: SI 2013/472 Sch.2 para.42
Reg.8, amended: SI 2013/472 Sch.2 para.42
Reg.9, amended: SI 2013/472 Sch.2 para.42
Reg.10, amended: SI 2013/472 Sch.2 para.42

1437. Criminal Defence Service (General) (No.2) Regulations 2001
Reg.3, amended: SI 2013/472 Sch.2 para.43
Reg.5, amended: SI 2013/630 Reg.64
Reg.13, amended: SI 2013/472 Sch.2 para.43
Sch.1 para.8, amended: SI 2013/591 Sch.1 para.19, SI 2013/626 Reg.3

1534. Financial Services and Markets Act 2000 (Transitional Provisions and Savings) (Rules) Order 2001
Art.7, amended: SI 2013/472 Sch.2 para.44
Art.8, amended: SI 2013/472 Sch.2 para.44

1543. National Health Service (Payments by Local Authorities to Health Authorities) (Prescribed Functions) (Wales) Regulations 2001
Reg.2, amended: SI 2013/898 Sch.7 para.3

1712. Tobacco Products Regulations 2001
Reg.23, amended: SI 2013/2720 Reg.3

1742. National Patient Safety Agency Regulations 2001
revoked: SI 2013/235 Sch.2 para.183

1783. Financial Services and Markets Act 2000 (Compensation Scheme Electing Participants) Regulations 2001
Reg.1, amended: SI 2013/1773 Sch.2 para.11, SI 2013/3115 Sch.2 para.54
Reg.2, amended: SI 2013/1773 Sch.2 para.11
Reg.3, amended: SI 2013/1773 Sch.2 para.11
Reg.4, amended: SI 2013/1773 Sch.2 para.11

1784. Education (Nutritional Standards for School Lunches) (Wales) Regulations 2001
revoked: SI 2013/1984 Reg.3

1820. Financial Services and Markets Act 2000 (Commencement No 3) Order 2001
Sch.1, amended: SI 2013/472 Art.4

1821. Financial Services and Markets Act 2000 (Consequential and Transitional Provisions) (Miscellaneous) Order 2001
Art.3, revoked: SI 2013/472 Sch.2 para.45

1857. Financial Services and Markets Act 2000 (Disclosure of Information by Prescribed Persons) Regulations 2001
Reg.3, amended: SI 2013/472 Sch.2 para.46
Sch.1, amended: SI 2013/472 Sch.2 para.46

1867. Liberia (United Nations Sanctions) (Overseas Territories) (No.2) Order 2001
revoked: SI 2013/237 Sch.2

1888. Mersey Care National Health Service Trust (Establishment) Order 2001
Art.1, amended: SI 2013/593 Art.2

2127. Health and Safety at Work etc Act 1974 (Application outside Great Britain) Order 2001
revoked: SI 2013/240 Art.1

2188. Financial Services and Markets Act 2000 (Disclosure of Confidential Information) Regulations 2001
Reg.2, amended: SI 2013/472 Sch.2 para.47, SI 2013/504 Reg.35, SI 2013/1162 Reg.13, SI 2013/1773 Sch.2 para.12, SI 2013/3115 Sch.2 para.55
Reg.3, amended: SI 2013/472 Sch.2 para.47
Reg.5, amended: SI 2013/472 Sch.2 para.47

Reg.5, varied: SI 2013/1635 Reg.12
Reg.7, amended: SI 2013/472 Sch.2 para.47
Reg.8, amended: SI 2013/504 Reg.35
Reg.8, varied: SI 2013/1635 Reg.12
Reg.9, amended: SI 2013/472 Sch.2 para.47, SI 2013/504 Reg.35, SI 2013/1773 Sch.2 para.12, SI 2013/3115 Sch.2 para.55
Reg.9, varied: SI 2013/1635 Reg.12
Reg.10, varied: SI 2013/1635 Reg.12
Reg.11, amended: SI 2013/504 Reg.35
Reg.12A, amended: SI 2013/2329 Sch.1 para.34
Reg.12A, varied: SI 2013/1635 Reg.12
Reg.12B, amended: SI 2013/472 Sch.2 para.47
Reg.13, amended: SI 2013/472 Sch.2 para.47
Sch.1 Part 1, amended: SI 2013/472 Sch.2 para.47, SI 2013/3115 Sch.2 para.55
Sch.1 Part 4, amended: SI 2013/472 Sch.2 para.47, SI 2013/504 Reg.35
Sch.2, amended: SI 2013/504 Reg.35, SI 2013/2329 Sch.1 para.34
Sch.3, amended: SI 2013/472 Sch.2 para.47, SI 2013/2329 Sch.1 para.34

2218. Special Educational Needs (Provision of Information by Local Authorities) (England) Regulations 2001
Reg.1, amended: SI 2013/235 Sch.2 para.46
Reg.3, amended: SI 2013/235 Sch.2 para.46

2256. Financial Services and Markets Act 2000 (Rights of Action) Regulations 2001
Reg.2, amended: SI 2013/472 Art.4
Reg.3, amended: SI 2013/1881 Art.16
Reg.4, amended: SI 2013/472 Art.4, Sch.2 para.48
Reg.6, amended: SI 2013/472 Art.4, Sch.2 para.48
Reg.7, amended: SI 2013/472 Sch.2 para.48

2283. Standards Committees (Wales) Regulations 2001
Reg.2, amended: SI 2013/3005 Art.5
Reg.8, revoked (in part): SI 2013/3005 Art.5
Reg.9, revoked (in part): SI 2013/3005 Art.5

2292. Local Authorities (Referendums) (Petitions and Directions) (Wales) Regulations 2001
Reg.3, amended: SI 2013/3005 Art.6
Reg.17, amended: SI 2013/3005 Art.6
Reg.20, amended: SI 2013/3005 Art.6
Reg.24, amended: SI 2013/3005 Art.6
Reg.24, revoked (in part): SI 2013/3005 Art.6

2303. Trunk Road Charging Schemes (Bridges and Tunnels) (England) Procedure Regulations 2001
Reg.4, applied: SI 2013/2249

2326. Financial Services and Markets Act 2000 (Transitional Provisions) (Ombudsman Scheme and Complaints Scheme) Order 2001
Art.15, amended: SI 2013/472 Sch.2 para.49
Art.18, amended: SI 2013/472 Sch.2 para.49
Art.18, revoked (in part): SI 2013/472 Sch.2 para.49

2383. Financial Services and Markets Act 2000 (Collective Investment Schemes Constituted in Other EEA States) Regulations 2001
Reg.4, amended: SI 2013/472 Sch.2 para.59
Reg.5, amended: SI 2013/472 Sch.2 para.59

2412. Social Security (Contributions) (Amendment No 5) Regulations 2001
Reg.3, revoked (in part): SI 2013/622 Reg.42
Reg.4, revoked: SI 2013/622 Reg.42
Reg.5, revoked (in part): SI 2013/622 Reg.42

2507. Financial Services and Markets Act 2000 (Variation of Threshold Conditions) Order 2001
Art.1, amended: SI 2013/472 Sch.2 para.50
Art.2, substituted: SI 2013/472 Sch.2 para.50
Art.3, amended: SI 2013/472 Sch.2 para.50
Art.4, amended: SI 2013/472 Sch.2 para.50

2509. Financial Services and Markets Act 2000 (Consultation with Competent Authorities) Regulations 2001
revoked: SI 2013/3115 Sch.3
Reg.2, amended: SI 2013/472 Sch.2 para.60
Reg.3, amended: SI 2013/472 Sch.2 para.60
Reg.4, amended: SI 2013/472 Sch.2 para.60
Reg.5, amended: SI 2013/1773 Sch.2 para.13
Reg.6, amended: SI 2013/472 Sch.2 para.60
Reg.7, amended: SI 2013/472 Sch.2 para.60
Reg.8, amended: SI 2013/472 Sch.2 para.60

2511. Financial Services and Markets Act 2000 (EEA Passport Rights) Regulations 2001
applied: SI 2013/642 Art.4
Reg.1, amended: SI 2013/642 Art.3
Reg.2, amended: SI 2013/642 Art.3, SI 2013/1773 Sch.2 para.14, SI 2013/1797 Reg.5, SI 2013/3115 Sch.2 para.56
Reg.2A, added: SI 2013/439 Reg.2
Reg.2A, amended: SI 2013/3115 Sch.2 para.56
Reg.3, amended: SI 2013/642 Art.3, SI 2013/1773 Sch.2 para.14
Reg.3A, added: SI 2013/439 Reg.2
Reg.4, amended: SI 2013/642 Art.3
Reg.5, amended: SI 2013/642 Art.3
Reg.6, amended: SI 2013/642 Art.3
Reg.7, amended: SI 2013/642 Art.3
Reg.7A, added: SI 2013/1773 Sch.2 para.14
Reg.8, amended: SI 2013/642 Art.3
Reg.9, amended: SI 2013/642 Art.3
Reg.10, amended: SI 2013/642 Art.3
Reg.10A, added: SI 2013/642 Art.3
Reg.11, amended: SI 2013/642 Art.3, SI 2013/3115 Sch.2 para.56
Reg.11A, amended: SI 2013/642 Art.3
Reg.12, amended: SI 2013/642 Art.3

Reg.12A, amended: SI 2013/642 Art.3
Reg.13, amended: SI 2013/642 Art.3
Reg.15, amended: SI 2013/642 Art.3
Reg.16, amended: SI 2013/642 Art.3
Reg.17A, added: SI 2013/1773 Sch.2 para.14
Reg.17A, amended: SI 2013/1797 Reg.5
Reg.19A, added: SI 2013/439 Reg.2
Reg.20, amended: SI 2013/642 Art.3
Reg.21, amended: SI 2013/642 Art.3

2541. Capital Allowances (Energy-saving Plant and Machinery) Order 2001

Art.2, amended: SI 2013/1763 Art.3

2564. Life Sentences (Northern Ireland) Order 2001

Art.3, see *Corey's Application for Judicial Review, Re* [2013] UKSC 76, [2013] 3 W.L.R. 1612 (SC), Lord Mance, J.S.C.
Art.6, see *Corey's Application for Judicial Review, Re* [2013] UKSC 76, [2013] 3 W.L.R. 1612 (SC), Lord Mance, J.S.C.
Art.9, see *Corey's Application for Judicial Review, Re* [2013] UKSC 76, [2013] 3 W.L.R. 1612 (SC), Lord Mance, J.S.C.

2587. Financial Services and Markets Act 2000 (Communications by Auditors) Regulations 2001

applied: SI 2013/472 Sch.2 para.52
Reg.1, amended: SI 2013/472 Art.4, Sch.2 para.51
Reg.2, amended: SI 2013/472 Sch.2 para.51
Reg.2, applied: SI 2013/472 Sch.2 para.52

2599. Northern Ireland Assembly (Elections) Order 2001

Appendix 1., amended: 2013 c.6 s.14

2617. Financial Services and Markets Act 2000 (Mutual Societies) Order 2001

Art.1, revoked: SI 2013/1765 Art.4
Art.2, revoked: SI 2013/1765 Art.4
Art.4, revoked (in part): SI 2013/1765 Art.4
Art.5, revoked: SI 2013/1765 Art.4
Art.6, revoked: SI 2013/1765 Art.4
Art.7, amended: SI 2013/1765 Art.4
Art.8, revoked: SI 2013/1765 Art.4
Art.9, revoked: SI 2013/1765 Art.4
Art.10, revoked: SI 2013/1765 Art.4
Art.11, revoked: SI 2013/1765 Art.4
Art.12, revoked: SI 2013/1765 Art.4
Art.13, revoked: SI 2013/1765 Art.4
Sch.1 Part I, revoked: SI 2013/1765 Art.4
Sch.1 Part II, revoked: SI 2013/1765 Art.4
Sch.1 Part III, revoked: SI 2013/1765 Art.4
Sch.2 para.1, revoked: SI 2013/1765 Art.4
Sch.2 para.2, revoked: SI 2013/1765 Art.4
Sch.2 para.3, revoked: SI 2013/1765 Art.4
Sch.2 para.4, revoked: SI 2013/1765 Art.4
Sch.2 para.5, revoked: SI 2013/1765 Art.4
Sch.2 para.6, revoked: SI 2013/1765 Art.4
Sch.2 para.7, revoked: SI 2013/1765 Art.4
Sch.2 para.8, revoked: SI 2013/1765 Art.4
Sch.2 para.9, revoked: SI 2013/1765 Art.4
Sch.2 para.10, revoked: SI 2013/1765 Art.4
Sch.2 para.11, revoked: SI 2013/1765 Art.4
Sch.2 para.12, revoked: SI 2013/1765 Art.4
Sch.2 para.13, revoked: SI 2013/1765 Art.4
Sch.2 para.14, revoked: SI 2013/1765 Art.4
Sch.2 para.15, revoked: SI 2013/1765 Art.4
Sch.2 para.16, revoked: SI 2013/1765 Art.4
Sch.2 para.17, revoked: SI 2013/1765 Art.4
Sch.3 Part I, revoked: SI 2013/1765 Art.4
Sch.3 Part II, revoked: SI 2013/1765 Art.4
Sch.3 Part III, revoked: SI 2013/1765 Art.4
Sch.3 Part IV, revoked: SI 2013/1765 Art.4
Sch.5 para.1, revoked: SI 2013/1765 Art.4
Sch.5 para.2, revoked: SI 2013/1765 Art.4
Sch.5 para.3, revoked: SI 2013/1765 Art.4
Sch.5 para.4, revoked: SI 2013/1765 Art.4
Sch.5 para.6, revoked: SI 2013/1765 Art.4
Sch.5 para.8, revoked: SI 2013/1765 Art.4
Sch.5 para.9, revoked: SI 2013/1765 Art.4
Sch.5 para.10, revoked: SI 2013/1765 Art.4
Sch.5 para.20, revoked: SI 2013/1765 Art.4
Sch.5 para.23, amended: SI 2013/472 Art.4
Sch.5 para.23, revoked: SI 2013/1765 Art.4
Sch.5 para.24, revoked: SI 2013/1765 Art.4
Sch.5 para.25, revoked (in part): SI 2013/1765 Art.4
Sch.5 para.26, revoked: SI 2013/1765 Art.4
Sch.5 para.27, revoked: SI 2013/1765 Art.4
Sch.5 para.28, amended: SI 2013/472 Art.4
Sch.5 para.28, revoked: SI 2013/1765 Art.4
Sch.5 para.29, revoked: SI 2013/1765 Art.4

2632. Financial Services and Markets Act 2000 (Commencement No 5) Order 2001

Sch.1 Part 2, amended: SI 2013/472 Art.4

2636. Financial Services and Markets Act 2000 (Transitional Provisions) (Authorised Persons etc.) Order 2001

Art.8, amended: SI 2013/472 Art.4

2637. Financial Services and Markets Act 2000 (Transitional Provisions) (Controllers) Order 2001

Art.2, amended: SI 2013/472 Sch.2 para.53
Art.12, amended: SI 2013/472 Sch.2 para.53
Art.13, amended: SI 2013/472 Sch.2 para.53
Art.14, amended: SI 2013/472 Sch.2 para.53

2639. Financial Services and Markets Act 2000 (Own-initiative Power) (Overseas Regulators) Regulations 2001

Reg.2, amended: SI 2013/472 Sch.2 para.54
Reg.3, amended: SI 2013/472 Sch.2 para.54

2659. Financial Services and Markets Act 2000 (Consequential and Transitional Provisions) (Miscellaneous) (No.2) Order 2001
Art.1, amended: SI 2013/472 Art.4
Art.3, amended: SI 2013/472 Art.4

2793. Road User Charging And Workplace Parking Levy (Classes Of Motor Vehicles) (England) Regulations 2001
Reg.2, referred to: SI 2013/2249 Art.4
Sch.1, referred to: SI 2013/2249 Art.4

2917. Limited Liability Partnerships (Welsh Language Forms) Regulations 2001
revoked: SI 2013/1947 Sch.2 Part 1

2956. Financial Services and Markets Act 2000 (Official Listing of Securities) Regulations 2001
Reg.2, amended: SI 2013/472 Sch.2 para.55
Reg.6, amended: SI 2013/472 Sch.2 para.55
Reg.7, amended: SI 2013/472 Sch.2 para.55

2960. Tyne Tunnel (Revision of Tolls and Traffic Classification) Order 2001
referred to: SI 2013/3087 Art.2

2967. Financial Services and Markets Act 2000 (Transitional Provisions, Repeals and Savings) (Financial Services Compensation Scheme) Order 2001
Art.6, amended: SI 2013/472 Sch.2 para.56
Art.8, amended: SI 2013/472 Sch.2 para.56
Art.9, amended: SI 2013/472 Sch.2 para.56
Art.9A, amended: SI 2013/472 Sch.2 para.56
Art.10, amended: SI 2013/472 Sch.2 para.56
Art.12, amended: SI 2013/472 Sch.2 para.56
Art.23, amended: SI 2013/472 Sch.2 para.56
Sch.1 Part 1 para.2, amended: SI 2013/472 Sch.2 para.56

2975. Radiation (Emergency Preparedness and Public Information) Regulations 2001
Reg.2, amended: SI 2013/235 Sch.2 para.47
Reg.7, amended: SI 2013/235 Sch.2 para.47
Reg.8, amended: SI 2013/235 Sch.2 para.47
Reg.9, amended: SI 2013/235 Sch.2 para.47
Reg.13, amended: SI 2013/235 Sch.2 para.47
Sch.11 para.10, revoked: SI 2013/1471 Sch.4

3022. Excise Duty Points (Duty Suspended Movements of Excise Goods) Regulations 2001
Reg.3, see *SDM European Transport Ltd v Revenue and Customs Commissioners* [2013] UKUT 251 (TCC), [2013] S.T.C. 2052 (UT (Tax)), Judge Greg Sinfield
Reg.4, see *SDM European Transport Ltd v Revenue and Customs Commissioners* [2013] UKUT 251 (TCC), [2013] S.T.C. 2052 (UT (Tax)), Judge Greg Sinfield
Reg.7, see *SDM European Transport Ltd v Revenue and Customs Commissioners* [2013] UKUT 251 (TCC), [2013] S.T.C. 2052 (UT (Tax)), Judge Greg Sinfield

3066. National Health Service (Optical Charges and Payments) and (General Ophthalmic Services) Amendment (No.2) Regulations 2001
revoked: SI 2013/461 Sch.4

3083. Financial Services and Markets Act 2000 (Transitional Provisions and Savings) (Civil Remedies, Discipline, Criminal Offences etc.) (No.2) Order 2001
Art.2, amended: SI 2013/472 Sch.2 para.57
Art.3, amended: SI 2013/472 Sch.2 para.57
Art.4, amended: SI 2013/472 Sch.2 para.57
Art.6, amended: SI 2013/472 Sch.2 para.57
Art.7, amended: SI 2013/472 Sch.2 para.57
Art.8, amended: SI 2013/472 Sch.2 para.57
Art.9, amended: SI 2013/472 Sch.2 para.57
Art.10, amended: SI 2013/472 Sch.2 para.57
Art.11, amended: SI 2013/472 Sch.2 para.57
Art.15, amended: SI 2013/472 Sch.2 para.57
Art.16, amended: SI 2013/472 Sch.2 para.57
Art.17, amended: SI 2013/472 Sch.2 para.57
Art.18, amended: SI 2013/472 Sch.2 para.57
Art.21, amended: SI 2013/472 Sch.2 para.57

3084. Financial Services and Markets Act 2000 (Gibraltar) Order 2001
Art.2, amended: SI 2013/472 Sch.2 para.58, SI 2013/3115 Sch.2 para.57
Art.4, amended: SI 2013/3115 Sch.2 para.57

3301. Access to the Countryside (Maps in Draft Form) (England) Regulations 2001
revoked: SI 2013/1798 Reg.6

3352. Railway Administration Order Rules 2001
Part 2 r.2.8, amended: SI 2013/472 Art.4

3367. Civil Aviation Act 1982 (Overseas Territories) (No.2) Order 2001
applied: SI 2013/2870

3374. Financial Services and Markets Act 2000 (Interim Permissions) Order 2001
Art.2, amended: SI 2013/472 Art.4
Art.3, amended: SI 2013/472 Art.4
Art.4, amended: SI 2013/472 Art.4
Art.6, amended: SI 2013/472 Art.4
Art.7, amended: SI 2013/472 Art.4
Art.8, amended: SI 2013/472 Art.4
Art.11, amended: SI 2013/472 Art.4
Sch.1 para.2, amended: SI 2013/472 Art.4

3455. Education (Special Educational Needs) (England) (Consolidation) Regulations 2001
Reg.2, amended: SI 2013/235 Sch.2 para.48
Reg.6, amended: SI 2013/235 Sch.2 para.48
Reg.7, amended: SI 2013/235 Sch.2 para.48
Reg.7, applied: SI 2013/235 Sch.3 para.4
Reg.9, amended: SI 2013/235 Sch.2 para.48
Reg.12, amended: SI 2013/235 Sch.2 para.48

Reg.18, amended: SI 2013/235 Sch.2 para.48
Sch.2, amended: SI 2013/235 Sch.2 para.48

3510. Seeds (National Lists of Varieties) Regulations 2001
Reg.16, revoked (in part): SI 2013/2042 Sch.1 para.52

3523. Passenger Car (Fuel Consumption and CO2 Emissions Information) Regulations 2001
Reg.3, amended: SI 2013/65 Reg.3
Reg.4, amended: SI 2013/65 Reg.4
Reg.4, revoked (in part): SI 2013/65 Reg.4
Reg.12, added: SI 2013/65 Reg.5
Sch.2 para.1, amended: SI 2013/65 Reg.6

3591. Bankruptcy (Financial Services and Markets Act 2000) (Scotland) Rules 2001
r.2, amended: SI 2013/472 Sch.2 para.61
r.3, amended: SI 2013/472 Sch.2 para.61
r.5, amended: SI 2013/472 Sch.2 para.61

3592. Financial Services and Markets Act 2000 (Transitional Provisions) (Partly Completed Procedures) Order 2001
Art.2, amended: SI 2013/472 Art.4
Art.3, amended: SI 2013/472 Art.4
Art.8, amended: SI 2013/472 Art.4
Art.18, amended: SI 2013/472 Art.4
Art.26, amended: SI 2013/472 Art.4
Art.28, amended: SI 2013/472 Art.4
Art.29, amended: SI 2013/472 Art.4
Art.30, amended: SI 2013/472 Art.4
Art.31, amended: SI 2013/472 Art.4
Art.64, amended: SI 2013/472 Art.4
Art.71, amended: SI 2013/472 Art.4
Art.72, amended: SI 2013/472 Art.4
Art.98, amended: SI 2013/472 Art.4
Art.107, amended: SI 2013/472 Art.4
Art.114, amended: SI 2013/472 Art.4
Art.121, amended: SI 2013/472 Art.4
Art.128, amended: SI 2013/472 Art.4

3625. Financial Services and Markets Act 2000 (Control of Business Transfers) (Requirements on Applicants) Regulations 2001
applied: SI 2013/472 Sch.2 para.63
Reg.3, amended: SI 2013/472 Sch.2 para.62
Reg.3, applied: SI 2013/472 Sch.2 para.63
Reg.4, amended: SI 2013/472 Sch.2 para.62
Reg.5, amended: SI 2013/472 Sch.2 para.62
Reg.5, applied: SI 2013/472 Sch.2 para.63
Reg.6, amended: SI 2013/472 Sch.2 para.62

3626. Financial Services and Markets Act 2000 (Control of Transfers of Business Done at Lloyd's) Order 2001
Art.3, amended: SI 2013/1765 Art.5
Art.4, amended: SI 2013/472 Sch.2 para.64, SI 2013/1765 Art.5
Art.4, applied: SI 2013/472 Sch.2 para.65
Art.5, amended: SI 2013/1765 Art.5

3632. Financial Services and Markets Tribunal (Legal Assistance) Regulations 2001
Reg.2, amended: SI 2013/472 Sch.2 para.66

3633. Financial Services and Markets Tribunal (Legal Assistance Scheme-Costs) Regulations 2001
Reg.2, amended: SI 2013/472 Sch.2 para.67

3634. Bankruptcy (Financial Services and Markets Act 2000) Rules 2001
r.2, amended: SI 2013/472 Sch.2 para.68

3635. Insurers (Winding Up) Rules 2001
r.2, amended: SI 2013/472 Sch.2 para.69
r.5, amended: SI 2013/472 Art.5
r.16, amended: SI 2013/472 Art.5
Sch.2 para.3, amended: SI 2013/472 Art.5

3645. Financial Services and Markets Act 2000 (Misleading Statements and Practices) Order 2001
revoked: SI 2013/472 Sch.1

3648. Financial Services and Markets Act 2000 (Confidential Information) (Bank of England) (Consequential Provisions) Order 2001
Art.2, amended: SI 2013/3115 Sch.2 para.58
Art.4, amended: SI 2013/3115 Sch.2 para.58
Art.6, amended: SI 2013/3115 Sch.2 para.58

3650. Financial Services and Markets Act 2000 (Miscellaneous Provisions) Order 2001
Art.18, amended: SI 2013/472 Sch.2 para.70
Art.22, amended: SI 2013/472 Sch.2 para.70
Art.24, amended: SI 2013/472 Sch.2 para.70
Art.25, substituted: SI 2013/472 Sch.2 para.70
Art.27, amended: SI 2013/472 Art.4
Art.28, amended: SI 2013/472 Sch.2 para.70
Art.28, revoked (in part): SI 2013/472 Sch.2 para.70
Art.30, amended: SI 2013/472 Art.4

3670. Continental Shelf (Designation of Areas) Order 2001
revoked: SI 2013/3162 Art.1

3678. Registered Designs (Isle of Man) Order 2001
revoked: SI 2013/2533 Art.4

3711. Parent Governor Representatives and Church Representatives (Wales) Regulations 2001
Reg.2, amended: SI 2013/3005 Art.7
Reg.2, revoked (in part): SI 2013/3005 Art.7
Reg.3, revoked: SI 2013/3005 Art.7
Reg.11, revoked: SI 2013/3005 Art.7

3729. Friendly Societies Act 1974 (Seal of the Financial Conduct Authority) Regulations 2001
applied: SI 2013/472 Sch.2 para.72
amended: SI 2013/472 Sch.2 para.71
Reg.1, amended: SI 2013/472 Sch.2 para.71
Reg.2, amended: SI 2013/472 Sch.2 para.71

3755. Uncertificated Securities Regulations 2001

Reg.3, amended: SI 2013/472 Sch.2 para.73, SI 2013/632 Reg.2
Reg.4, amended: SI 2013/632 Reg.2
Reg.4, applied: SI 2013/632 Reg.3
Reg.5, amended: SI 2013/632 Reg.2
Reg.6, amended: SI 2013/632 Reg.2
Reg.6, revoked (in part): SI 2013/632 Reg.2
Reg.7, amended: SI 2013/632 Reg.2
Reg.8, amended: SI 2013/632 Reg.2
Reg.8, applied: SI 2013/418 Art.2
Reg.9, amended: SI 2013/472 Sch.2 para.73, SI 2013/632 Reg.2, SI 2013/1773 Sch.2 para.15
Reg.9, applied: SI 2013/418 Art.2
Reg.10, amended: SI 2013/632 Reg.2
Reg.11, substituted: SI 2013/632 Reg.2
Reg.12, amended: SI 2013/632 Reg.2
Reg.13, amended: SI 2013/632 Reg.2
Reg.13, substituted: SI 2013/632 Reg.2
Sch.1 para.3, amended: SI 2013/632 Reg.2
Sch.1 para.5, amended: SI 2013/504 Reg.36
Sch.1 para.28, amended: SI 2013/472 Sch.2 para.73, SI 2013/3115 Sch.2 para.59
Sch.2 para.1, substituted: SI 2013/632 Sch.1
Sch.2 para.2, substituted: SI 2013/632 Sch.1
Sch.2 para.3, substituted: SI 2013/632 Sch.1
Sch.2 para.4, substituted: SI 2013/632 Sch.1
Sch.2 para.4A, substituted: SI 2013/632 Sch.1
Sch.2 para.4B, substituted: SI 2013/632 Sch.1
Sch.2 para.5, substituted: SI 2013/632 Sch.1
Sch.2 para.6, substituted: SI 2013/632 Sch.1
Sch.2 para.7, substituted: SI 2013/632 Sch.1
Sch.2 para.8, substituted: SI 2013/632 Sch.1
Sch.3 para.1, substituted: SI 2013/632 Reg.2
Sch.3 para.2, amended: SI 2013/632 Reg.2
Sch.3 para.3, substituted: SI 2013/632 Reg.2
Sch.3 para.4, substituted: SI 2013/632 Reg.2
Sch.3 para.5, amended: SI 2013/632 Reg.2
Sch.3 para.6, substituted: SI 2013/632 Reg.2
Sch.3 para.7, amended: SI 2013/632 Reg.2
Sch.3 para.8, substituted: SI 2013/632 Reg.2

3929. Civil Jurisdiction and Judgments Order 2001

Sch.3 para.5, revoked: 2013 c.22 Sch.10 para.99
Sch.3 para.11, revoked: 2013 c.22 Sch.10 para.99
Sch.3 para.12, revoked (in part): 2013 c.22 Sch.10 para.99

3967. Children's Homes Regulations 2001

Reg.2, amended: SI 2013/235 Sch.2 para.49, SI 2013/3239 Reg.3
Reg.3, amended: SI 2013/1394 Reg.36
Reg.4, amended: SI 2013/3239 Reg.4
Reg.8, amended: SI 2013/3239 Reg.5
Reg.11, amended: SI 2013/3239 Reg.6
Reg.12A, amended: SI 2013/706 Reg.10
Reg.12B, added: SI 2013/3239 Reg.7
Reg.16, amended: SI 2013/3239 Reg.8
Reg.26, amended: SI 2013/3239 Reg.9
Reg.31, amended: SI 2013/3239 Reg.10
Reg.33, substituted: SI 2013/3239 Reg.11
Reg.34, amended: SI 2013/3239 Reg.12
Sch.1, substituted: SI 2013/3239 Reg.13
Sch.3, amended: SI 2013/3239 Reg.14
Sch.5, amended: SI 2013/235 Sch.2 para.49, SI 2013/3239 Reg.15
Sch.6, substituted: SI 2013/3239 Reg.16

3981. Goods Vehicles (Enforcement Powers) Regulations 2001

Reg.9, amended: SI 2013/1644 Sch.2
Reg.10, amended: SI 2013/1644 Sch.2
Reg.11, amended: SI 2013/1644 Sch.2
Reg.12, amended: SI 2013/1644 Sch.2
Reg.13, amended: SI 2013/1644 Sch.2
Reg.14, amended: SI 2013/1644 Sch.2
Reg.15, amended: SI 2013/1644 Sch.2

3997. Misuse of Drugs (Designation) Order 2001

Sch.1 Part I para.1, amended: SI 2013/177 Art.3, Art.4, Art.5, Art.6, SI 2013/624 Art.2
Sch.1 Part I para.3, substituted: SI 2013/177 Art.7
Sch.1 Part II para.4, added: SI 2013/624 Art.3

3998. Misuse of Drugs Regulations 2001

applied: SI 2013/1294 Art.3
Reg.2, amended: SI 2013/235 Sch.2 para.50
Reg.15, amended: SI 2013/235 Sch.2 para.50
Reg.15, applied: SI 2013/235 Sch.3 para.5
Reg.16, amended: SI 2013/235 Sch.2 para.50
Reg.16, applied: SI 2013/235 Sch.3 para.5
Reg.22, amended: SI 2013/625 Reg.3, Reg.4
Reg.27, amended: SI 2013/625 Reg.5
Sch.1 para.1, amended: SI 2013/176 Reg.3, Reg.4, Reg.5, Reg.6, SI 2013/625 Reg.6
Sch.1 para.3, substituted: SI 2013/176 Reg.7
Sch.2, referred to: SI 2013/2033 Sch.3 para.6
Sch.3, referred to: SI 2013/2033 Sch.3 para.6
Sch.4, applied: SI 2013/349 Sch.7 para.3
Sch.4, referred to: SI 2013/349 Sch.4 para.5, Sch.4 para.6, Sch.4 para.8, Sch.6 para.2, Sch.7 para.3, Sch.7 para.4, Sch.7 para.6, SI 2013/898 Sch.4 para.5, Sch.4 para.6, Sch.4 para.8, Sch.6 para.4, SI 2013/2033 Sch.3 para.6
Sch.4 Part I para.5, added: SI 2013/625 Reg.7
Sch.5, applied: SI 2013/349 Sch.7 para.3
Sch.5, referred to: SI 2013/349 Sch.4 para.5, Sch.4 para.6, Sch.4 para.8, Sch.6 para.2, Sch.7 para.3, Sch.7 para.4, Sch.7 para.6, SI 2013/898 Sch.4 para.5, Sch.4 para.6, Sch.4 para.8, Sch.6 para.4

4001. Countryside Access (Draft Maps) (Wales) Regulations 2001

Reg.2, amended: SI 2013/755 Sch.5 para.2
Reg.3, amended: SI 2013/755 Sch.5 para.3

Reg.4, amended: SI 2013/755 Sch.5 para.3
Reg.5, amended: SI 2013/755 Sch.5 para.3
Reg.6, amended: SI 2013/755 Sch.5 para.3
Reg.7, amended: SI 2013/755 Sch.5 para.3
Sch.1, amended: SI 2013/755 Sch.5 para.4

4002. Countryside Access (Local Access Forums) (Wales) Regulations 2001
Reg.10, amended: SI 2013/755 Sch.5 para.6
Reg.15, amended: SI 2013/755 Sch.5 para.6
Reg.17, amended: SI 2013/755 Sch.5 para.7

4022. Social Security (Loss of Benefit) Regulations 2001
applied: SI 2013/386 Reg.35
Reg.1, amended: SI 2013/385 Reg.3, SI 2013/591 Sch.1 para.22
Reg.1A, amended: SI 2013/385 Reg.4
Reg.2, amended: SI 2013/385 Reg.5
Reg.2A, added: SI 2013/385 Reg.6
Reg.3, amended: SI 2013/385 Reg.7
Reg.3A, amended: SI 2013/385 Reg.10
Reg.3ZA, added: SI 2013/385 Reg.8
Reg.3ZB, added: SI 2013/385 Reg.9
Reg.5, amended: SI 2013/385 Reg.11, SI 2013/591 Sch.1 para.22
Reg.11, amended: SI 2013/385 Reg.12, SI 2013/591 Sch.1 para.22
Reg.16A, added: SI 2013/385 Reg.13
Reg.16B, added: SI 2013/385 Reg.13
Reg.16C, added: SI 2013/385 Reg.13
Reg.16D, added: SI 2013/385 Reg.14
Reg.16E, added: SI 2013/385 Reg.14
Reg.16F, added: SI 2013/385 Reg.14
Reg.16G, added: SI 2013/385 Reg.14
Reg.16H, added: SI 2013/385 Reg.14
Reg.19, amended: SI 2013/385 Reg.15

4040. Insurers (Winding Up) (Scotland) Rules 2001
r.2, amended: SI 2013/472 Sch.2 para.74
r.5, amended: SI 2013/472 Art.5
r.15, amended: SI 2013/472 Art.5
Sch.2 para.3, amended: SI 2013/472 Art.5

4044. National Treatment Agency (Amendment) Regulations 2001
revoked: SI 2013/235 Sch.1 para.5

2002

35. National Health Service (Optical Charges and Payments) Amendment (England) Regulations 2002
revoked: SI 2013/461 Sch.4

233. Police Act 1997 (Criminal Records) Regulations 2002
Reg.2, amended: SI 2013/1194 Reg.2
Reg.5, referred to: SI 2013/2668 Sch.1 para.4, Sch.4 para.4, Sch.4 para.9, Sch.5 para.11
Reg.5A, amended: SI 2013/1194 Reg.2, SI 2013/2669 Reg.2
Reg.5A, applied: SI 2013/1394 Sch.2 para.2
Reg.5A, revoked (in part): SI 2013/1194 Reg.2, SI 2013/2669 Reg.2
Reg.5B, added: SI 2013/1194 Sch.1
Reg.5C, added: SI 2013/2669 Sch.1
Reg.6, added: SI 2013/1194 Sch.1
Reg.7, added: SI 2013/1194 Sch.1

253. Nursing and Midwifery Order (2001) 2002
Art.29, see *Adesina v Nursing and Midwifery Council* [2013] EWCA Civ 818, [2013] 1 W.L.R. 3156 (CA (Civ Div)), Maurice Kay, L.J.
Art.43, applied: SI 2013/235 Sch.3 para.6
Sch.1 Part I para.1A, revoked (in part): SI 2013/235 Sch.2 para.51
Sch.4, amended: SI 2013/235 Sch.2 para.51

254. Health and Social Work Professions Order 2002
applied: SSI 2013/50 Sch.4 para.11
Art.3, enabled: SI 2013/3004
Sch.1 Part I para.1A, revoked (in part): SI 2013/235 Sch.2 para.52
Sch.1 Part I para.1B, enabled: SI 2013/3004

438. Education Standards Grants (Wales) Regulations 2002
Reg.6, amended: SI 2013/1466 Sch.1 para.4

459. Occupational Pension Schemes (Winding Up Notices and Reports etc.) Regulations 2002
Reg.8, amended: SI 2013/2734 Sch.9 para.11

547. National Health Service (Optical Charges and Payments) Amendment (No.2) Regulations 2002
revoked: SI 2013/461 Sch.4

618. Medical Devices Regulations 2002
Reg.2, amended: SI 2013/2327 Reg.2
Reg.8, amended: SI 2013/2327 Reg.3
Reg.13, amended: SI 2013/2327 Reg.4
Reg.13, revoked (in part): SI 2013/2327 Reg.4
Reg.15, amended: SI 2013/2327 Reg.5
Reg.16, amended: SI 2013/2327 Reg.6
Reg.17, revoked (in part): SI 2013/2327 Reg.7
Reg.18, amended: SI 2013/2327 Reg.8
Reg.19A, revoked: SI 2013/2327 Reg.9
Reg.22, amended: SI 2013/2327 Reg.10
Reg.27, amended: SI 2013/2327 Reg.11
Reg.28, amended: SI 2013/2327 Reg.12
Reg.29, amended: SI 2013/2327 Reg.13
Reg.45, amended: SI 2013/2327 Reg.14
Reg.47, revoked (in part): SI 2013/2327 Reg.15
Reg.54, amended: SI 2013/2327 Reg.16
Reg.56, amended: SI 2013/525 Reg.2
Reg.61, amended: SI 2013/2327 Reg.17
Reg.67, added: SI 2013/2327 Reg.18

Sch.1 para.1, substituted: SI 2013/2327 Reg.19
Sch.2 para.5, added: SI 2013/2327 Reg.20

635. Disqualification from Caring for Children (England) Regulations 2002
Reg.2, amended: SI 2013/1465 Sch.1 para.18
Sch.1 para.2, amended: SI 2013/1465 Sch.1 para.18
Sch.1 para.4, amended: SI 2013/1465 Sch.1 para.18

679. Education (Capital Grants) (Wales) Regulations 2002
Reg.5, amended: SI 2013/1466 Sch.1 para.5

682. Financial Services and Markets Act 2000 (Regulated Activities) (Amendment) Order 2002
Art.9, amended: SI 2013/472 Art.4

690. Limited Liability Partnerships (Forms) Regulations 2002
revoked: SI 2013/1947 Sch.2 Part 1

691. Companies (Forms) (Amendment) Regulations 2002
revoked: SI 2013/1947 Sch.2 Part 1

699. Pensions Increase (Review) Order 2002
applied: SI 2013/604 Sch.1

704. Financial Services and Markets Act 2000 (Permission and Applications) (Credit Unions etc.) Order 2002
Art.2, amended: SI 2013/472 Art.4
Art.3, amended: SI 2013/472 Art.4
Art.5, amended: SI 2013/472 Art.5
Art.7, amended: SI 2013/472 Art.4
Art.9, amended: SI 2013/472 Art.4

791. Adjacent Waters Boundaries (Northern Ireland) Order 2002
Art.3, applied: SI 2013/1570 Reg.5

802. Local Authorities (Executive Arrangements) (Discharge of Functions) (Wales) Regulations 2002
Reg.2, revoked (in part): SI 2013/3005 Art.8
Reg.5, revoked: SI 2013/3005 Art.8
Reg.12, amended: SI 2013/3005 Art.8
Reg.12, revoked (in part): SI 2013/3005 Art.8

836. Occupational and Personal Pension Schemes (Bankruptcy) (No.2) Regulations 2002
Reg.5, amended: SI 2013/630 Reg.32
Reg.14, amended: SI 2013/630 Reg.32

888. National Health Service (Local Pharmaceutical Services and Pharmaceutical Services) Regulations 2002
revoked: SI 2013/349 Sch.10 para.2

919. Registration of Social Care and Independent Health Care (Wales) Regulations 2002
Sch.1 Part I para.1, amended: SI 2013/225 Reg.4
Sch.1 Part I para.2, amended: SI 2013/225 Reg.4
Sch.3 Part I para.2C, added: SI 2013/225 Reg.4

1015. Bus Service Operators Grant (England) Regulations 2002
Reg.2, amended: SI 2013/2100 Reg.2
Reg.3, amended: SI 2013/630 Reg.85, SI 2013/2100 Reg.2

1322. Bradford District Care Trust (Establishment) and the Bradford Community Health National Health Service Trust (Dissolution) Order 2002
Art.1, amended: SI 2013/593 Art.2

1341. Mid Yorkshire Hospitals National Health Service Trust (Establishment) and the Pinderfields and Pontefract Hospitals National Health Service Trust and the Dewsbury Health Care National Health Service Trust (Dissolution) Order 2002
Art.1, amended: SI 2013/593 Art.2

1355. Offshore Chemicals Regulations 2002
applied: SI 2013/343 Sch.2 para.5, SI 2013/1203 Sch.2 para.8, SI 2013/1734 Sch.2 para.7, SI 2013/1873 Sch.4 para.2

1364. Sandwell and West Birmingham Hospitals National Health Service Trust (Establishment) and the City Hospital National Health Service Trust and Sandwell Healthcare National Health Service Trust (Dissolution) Order 2002
Art.1, amended: SI 2013/593 Art.2

1441. Welsh Language Schemes (Public Bodies) Order 2002
Sch.1, amended: SI 2013/472 Sch.2 para.75

1501. Financial Services and Markets Act 2000 (Consequential Amendments and Transitional Provisions) (Credit Unions) Order 2002
Art.1, amended: SI 2013/472 Sch.2 para.76
Art.4, revoked: SI 2013/472 Sch.2 para.76
Art.5, amended: SI 2013/472 Art.4
Art.6, amended: SI 2013/472 Art.4
Art.12, amended: SI 2013/472 Sch.2 para.76
Art.14, amended: SI 2013/472 Sch.2 para.76
Art.16, amended: SI 2013/472 Sch.2 para.76

1559. Landfill (England and Wales) Regulations 2002
Reg.17, applied: SI 2013/2258 Sch.1 Part 2

1593. Driving Licences (Exchangeable Licences) (Amendment) Order 2002
revoked: SI 2013/22 Sch.2

1619. Animal By-Products (Identification) (Amendment) (England) Regulations 2002
revoked: SI 2013/2952 Reg.28

1710. Access to the Countryside (Provisional and Conclusive Maps) (England) Regulations 2002
revoked: SI 2013/1798 Reg.6

1759. National Institute for Clinical Excellence (Amendment) Regulations 2002
revoked: SI 2013/235 Sch.2 para.184

1760. National Institute for Clinical Excellence (Establishment and Constitution) Amendment Order 2002

revoked: SI 2013/235 Sch.2 para.185

1772. Wildlife and Countryside (Sites of Special Scientific Interest, Appeals) (Wales) Regulations 2002

Reg.2, amended: SI 2013/755 Sch.5 para.9
Reg.3, amended: SI 2013/755 Sch.5 para.10
Reg.6, amended: SI 2013/755 Sch.5 para.10
Reg.7, amended: SI 2013/755 Sch.5 para.10
Reg.8, amended: SI 2013/755 Sch.5 para.10
Reg.9, amended: SI 2013/755 Sch.5 para.10
Reg.10, amended: SI 2013/755 Sch.5 para.10
Reg.12, amended: SI 2013/755 Sch.5 para.10
Reg.13, amended: SI 2013/755 Sch.5 para.10
Reg.14, amended: SI 2013/755 Sch.5 para.10
Reg.16, amended: SI 2013/755 Sch.5 para.10
Reg.19, amended: SI 2013/755 Sch.5 para.10

1775. Electronic Commerce Directive (Financial Services and Markets) Regulations 2002

Reg.2, amended: SI 2013/472 Sch.2 para.77
Reg.3, amended: SI 2013/472 Sch.2 para.77
Reg.3, revoked (in part): SI 2013/472 Sch.2 para.77
Reg.4, amended: SI 2013/472 Sch.2 para.77
Reg.5, amended: SI 2013/472 Sch.2 para.77
Reg.5, revoked: SI 2013/472 Sch.1
Reg.6, amended: SI 2013/472 Sch.2 para.77
Reg.7, amended: SI 2013/472 Sch.2 para.77
Reg.12, amended: SI 2013/472 Sch.2 para.77

1792. State Pension Credit Regulations 2002

Reg.1, amended: SI 2013/235 Sch.2 para.54, SI 2013/388 Sch.1 para.27, SI 2013/443 Reg.6, SI 2013/591 Sch.1 para.23, SI 2013/630 Reg.33, SI 2013/2536 Reg.10
Reg.1, revoked (in part): SI 2013/2536 Reg.10
Reg.2, amended: SI 2013/1474 Reg.4, SI 2013/2536 Reg.10
Reg.2, revoked (in part): SI 2013/2536 Reg.10
Reg.6, amended: SI 2013/574 Art.24
Reg.6, referred to: SI 2013/574 Sch.13
Reg.7, amended: SI 2013/574 Art.24
Reg.7, referred to: SI 2013/574 Art.24, Sch.13
Reg.9, amended: SI 2013/630 Reg.33
Reg.13, applied: SI 2013/3029 Reg.2
Reg.13, referred to: SI 2013/3035 Sch.1
Reg.13A, amended: SI 2013/630 Reg.33
Reg.13B, amended: SI 2013/630 Reg.33
Reg.15, amended: SI 2013/388 Sch.1 para.27, SI 2013/591 Sch.1 para.23
Reg.15, revoked (in part): SI 2013/458 Sch.1
Reg.17B, amended: SI 2013/235 Sch.2 para.54
Reg.18, referred to: SI 2013/376 Reg.74
Reg.21, applied: SI 2013/3029 Sch.1 para.29, SI 2013/3035 Sch.1
Reg.22, amended: SI 2013/458 Sch.2 para.6
Sch.1 Part I para.1, amended: SI 2013/388 Sch.1 para.27, SI 2013/591 Sch.1 para.23
Sch.1 Part I para.2, amended: SI 2013/388 Sch.1 para.27, SI 2013/591 Sch.1 para.23
Sch.2, referred to: SI 2013/3029 Sch.4 para.12, SI 2013/3035 Sch.1
Sch.2 para.1, amended: SI 2013/388 Sch.1 para.27, SI 2013/591 Sch.1 para.23, SI 2013/630 Reg.33
Sch.2 para.4, amended: SI 2013/443 Reg.6
Sch.2 para.6, referred to: SI 2013/574 Sch.13
Sch.2 para.7, referred to: SI 2013/574 Sch.13
Sch.2 para.8, referred to: SI 2013/574 Sch.13
Sch.2 para.9, referred to: SI 2013/574 Sch.13
Sch.2 para.14, amended: SI 2013/388 Sch.1 para.27, SI 2013/443 Reg.6, SI 2013/574 Art.24, SI 2013/591 Sch.1 para.23, SI 2013/630 Reg.33
Sch.3 para.1, amended: SI 2013/388 Sch.1 para.27, SI 2013/574 Art.24, SI 2013/591 Sch.1 para.23
Sch.3 para.2, referred to: SI 2013/574 Sch.13
Sch.5 Part I para.13, applied: SI 2013/376 Reg.76
Sch.5 Part I para.15, applied: SI 2013/376 Reg.76
Sch.5 Part I para.20, amended: SI 2013/388 Sch.1 para.27, SI 2013/443 Reg.6, SI 2013/591 Sch.1 para.23, SI 2013/630 Reg.33
Sch.5 Part I para.20A, amended: SI 2013/458 Sch.1, SI 2013/630 Reg.33, SI 2013/2536 Reg.10
Sch.5 Part I para.20A, applied: SI 2013/3029 Sch.5 para.22, SI 2013/3035 Sch.1
Sch.6 para.2, amended: SI 2013/602 Sch.2 para.82, SI 2013/2536 Reg.10
Sch.6 para.2, revoked (in part): SI 2013/2536 Reg.10
Sch.6 para.4, amended: SI 2013/388 Sch.1 para.27, SI 2013/591 Sch.1 para.23

1794. Countryside Access (Appeals Procedures) (Wales) Regulations 2002

Reg.2, amended: SI 2013/755 Sch.5 para.11

1796. Countryside Access (Provisional and Conclusive Maps) (Wales) Regulations 2002

Reg.2, amended: SI 2013/755 Sch.5 para.13
Reg.3, amended: SI 2013/755 Sch.5 para.14
Reg.4, amended: SI 2013/755 Sch.5 para.14
Reg.5, amended: SI 2013/755 Sch.5 para.14
Reg.6, amended: SI 2013/755 Sch.5 para.14
Reg.7, amended: SI 2013/755 Sch.5 para.14
Reg.8, amended: SI 2013/755 Sch.5 para.14
Reg.9, amended: SI 2013/755 Sch.5 para.14
Reg.10, amended: SI 2013/755 Sch.5 para.14
Sch.1, amended: SI 2013/755 Sch.5 para.15

1837. Penalties for Disorderly Behaviour (Amount of Penalty) Order 2002

Art.2, amended: SI 2013/903 Reg.2, SI 2013/1165 Art.2, SI 2013/1579 Art.3
Art.3, revoked: SI 2013/903 Reg.2
Sch.1 Part I, amended: SI 2013/903 Reg.2, SI 2013/1165 Art.2, SI 2013/1579 Art.3
Sch.1 Part II, amended: SI 2013/903 Reg.2, SI 2013/1165 Art.2, SI 2013/1579 Art.3

1857. Education (Assembly Learning Grant Scheme) (Wales) Regulations 2002
Reg.6, amended: SI 2013/1466 Sch.1 para.6

1871. Representation of the People (England and Wales) (Amendment) Regulations 2002
Reg.14, revoked: SI 2013/3198 Sch.2

1872. Representation of the People (Scotland) (Amendment) Regulations 2002
Reg.13, revoked: SI 2013/3206 Sch.2

1889. Companies (Disclosure of Information) (Designated Authorities) (No.2) Order 2002
Art.2, amended: SI 2013/2329 Sch.1 para.35
Art.3, amended: SI 2013/2329 Sch.1 para.35

1891. Agricultural or Forestry Tractors (Emission of Gaseous and Particulate Pollutants) Regulations 2002
Reg.2, amended: SI 2013/3171 Reg.3
Reg.4, amended: SI 2013/3171 Reg.4
Reg.7, added: SI 2013/3171 Reg.5
Sch.1, amended: SI 2013/3171 Reg.6
Sch.3 para.5, amended: SI 2013/3171 Reg.7

1970. Exchange Gains and Losses (Bringing into Account Gains or Losses) Regulations 2002
Reg.5, amended: SI 2013/1843 Reg.2
Reg.8, amended: SI 2013/1843 Reg.2

1998. Wye Navigation Order 2002
Art.3, amended: SI 2013/755 Sch.4 para.136
Art.17, amended: SI 2013/472 Art.4

2005. Working Tax Credit (Entitlement and Maximum Rate) Regulations 2002
Reg.2, amended: SI 2013/388 Sch.1 para.28, SI 2013/591 Sch.1 para.24, SI 2013/630 Reg.77
Reg.4, amended: SI 2013/1736 Reg.2
Reg.9, amended: SI 2013/388 Sch.1 para.28, SI 2013/591 Sch.1 para.24, SI 2013/630 Reg.77
Reg.13, amended: SI 2013/388 Sch.1 para.28, SI 2013/591 Sch.1 para.24, SI 2013/630 Reg.77, SI 2013/1736 Reg.3
Reg.14, amended: SI 2013/388 Sch.1 para.28, SI 2013/591 Sch.1 para.24
Reg.17, amended: SI 2013/388 Sch.1 para.28, SI 2013/591 Sch.1 para.24
Reg.20, applied: SI 2013/3029 Sch.3 para.10, Sch.8 para.18, SI 2013/3035 Sch.1
Reg.20, referred to: SI 2013/379 Reg.9, SI 2013/3029 Sch.1 para.20, Sch.7 para.10, SI 2013/3035 Sch.1
Sch.2, amended: SI 2013/750 Reg.3
Sch.2, applied: SI 2013/3029 Sch.3 para.5, SI 2013/3035 Sch.1

2006. Tax Credits (Definition and Calculation of Income) Regulations 2002
Reg.2, varied: SI 2013/386 Sch.1 para.16
Reg.3, varied: SI 2013/386 Sch.1 para.17
Reg.4, varied: SI 2013/386 Sch.1 para.18
Reg.5, varied: SI 2013/386 Sch.1 para.19
Reg.6, varied: SI 2013/386 Sch.1 para.20
Reg.6A, varied: SI 2013/386 Sch.1 para.21
Reg.6B, varied: SI 2013/386 Sch.1 para.21
Reg.7, amended: SI 2013/388 Sch.1 para.29, SI 2013/630 Reg.78
Reg.7, varied: SI 2013/386 Sch.1 para.22
Reg.8, varied: SI 2013/386 Sch.1 para.23
Reg.10, varied: SI 2013/386 Sch.1 para.24
Reg.11, varied: SI 2013/386 Sch.1 para.25
Reg.12, varied: SI 2013/386 Sch.1 para.26
Reg.13, varied: SI 2013/386 Sch.1 para.27
Reg.17, amended: SI 2013/630 Reg.78
Reg.18, varied: SI 2013/386 Sch.1 para.28
Reg.19, amended: SI 2013/235 Sch.2 para.55, SI 2013/591 Sch.1 para.25

2007. Child Tax Credit Regulations 2002
Reg.2, amended: SI 2013/388 Sch.1 para.30, SI 2013/591 Sch.1 para.26, SI 2013/1465 Sch.1 para.19
Reg.3, amended: SI 2013/1465 Sch.1 para.19
Reg.5, amended: SI 2013/630 Reg.79
Reg.7, amended: SI 2013/750 Reg.2
Reg.8, amended: SI 2013/388 Sch.1 para.30, SI 2013/591 Sch.1 para.26

2008. Tax Credits (Income Thresholds and Determination of Rates) Regulations 2002
Reg.2, varied: SI 2013/386 Sch.1 para.30
Reg.3, amended: SI 2013/750 Reg.4
Reg.5, amended: SI 2013/750 Reg.4
Reg.7, varied: SI 2013/386 Sch.1 para.31
Reg.8, amended: SI 2013/750 Reg.4
Reg.8, applied: SSI 2013/148 Reg.6
Reg.8, varied: SI 2013/386 Sch.1 para.32

2013. Electronic Commerce (EC Directive) Regulations 2002
Reg.2, see *Football Association Premier League Ltd v British Sky Broadcasting Ltd* [2013] EWHC 2058 (Ch), [2013] E.C.D.R. 14 (Ch D), Arnold, J.
Reg.2, amended: SI 2013/2217 Reg.8

2014. Tax Credits (Claims and Notifications) Regulations 2002
applied: SI 2013/386 Reg.13, Reg.15
disapplied: SI 2013/386 Reg.13
Reg.2, amended: SI 2013/388 Sch.1 para.31, SI 2013/591 Sch.1 para.27
Reg.4, varied: SI 2013/386 Sch.1 para.34

Reg.7, referred to: SI 2013/386 Reg.15
Reg.8, referred to: SI 2013/386 Reg.15
Reg.10, varied: SI 2013/386 Sch.1 para.35
Reg.11, referred to: SI 2013/386 Reg.15
Reg.11, varied: SI 2013/386 Sch.1 para.36
Reg.12, referred to: SI 2013/386 Reg.15
Reg.12, varied: SI 2013/386 Sch.1 para.37
Reg.13, varied: SI 2013/386 Sch.1 para.38
Reg.15, varied: SI 2013/386 Sch.1 para.39
Reg.21, varied: SI 2013/386 Sch.1 para.40
Reg.26A, amended: SI 2013/388 Sch.1 para.31, SI 2013/591 Sch.1 para.27
Reg.27, varied: SI 2013/386 Sch.1 para.41
Reg.33, varied: SI 2013/386 Sch.1 para.42

2016. National Health Service (Local Pharmaceutical Services and Pharmaceutical Services) (No.2) Regulations 2002
revoked: SI 2013/349 Sch.10 para.3
Reg.4, applied: SI 2013/349 Reg.28

2022. Bus Service Operators Grant (Wales) Regulations 2002
Reg.3, amended: SI 2013/1788 Reg.6

2034. Fixed-term Employees (Prevention of Less Favourable Treatment) Regulations 2002
Pt 5., see *Hudson v Department for Work and Pensions* [2012] EWCA Civ 1416, [2013] 1 All E.R. 1370 (CA (Civ Div)), Sir Maurice Kay (VP CA Civ)
Reg.8, see *Hudson v Department for Work and Pensions* [2012] EWCA Civ 1416, [2013] 1 All E.R. 1370 (CA (Civ Div)), Sir Maurice Kay (VP CA Civ)
Reg.9, see *Hudson v Department for Work and Pensions* [2012] EWCA Civ 1416, [2013] 1 All E.R. 1370 (CA (Civ Div)), Sir Maurice Kay (VP CA Civ)
Reg.18, see *Hudson v Department for Work and Pensions* [2012] EWCA Civ 1416, [2013] 1 All E.R. 1370 (CA (Civ Div)), Sir Maurice Kay (VP CA Civ)
Reg.19, see *Hudson v Department for Work and Pensions* [2012] EWCA Civ 1416, [2013] 1 All E.R. 1370 (CA (Civ Div)), Sir Maurice Kay (VP CA Civ)

2051. Homelessness (Priority Need for Accommodation) (England) Order 2002
Art.5, see *Johnson v Solihull MBC* [2013] EWCA Civ 752, [2013] H.L.R. 39 (CA (Civ Div)), Arden, L.J.

2073. East Lancashire Hospitals National Health Service Trust (Establishment) and the Blackburn, Hyndburn and Ribble Valley Health Care National Health Service Trust and Burnley Health Care National Health Service Trust (Dissolution) Order 2002
Art.1, amended: SI 2013/593 Art.2

2173. Tax Credits (Payments by the Commissioners) Regulations 2002
Reg.7, varied: SI 2013/386 Sch.1 para.44

2186. Road Traffic (Permitted Parking Area and Special Parking Area) (County of Essex) (Borough of Colchester) Order 2002
revoked: SI 2013/992 Art.2

2359. A52 Trunk Road (Derby Road, Nottingham) (Bus/Cycle Lane) Order 2002
varied: SI 2013/1158 Art.6

2375. National Health Service (Functions of Strategic Health Authorities and Primary Care Trusts and Administration Arrangements) (England) Regulations 2002
revoked: SI 2013/235 Sch.2 para.186

2379. Driving Licences (Exchangeable Licences) Order 2002
Art.2, amended: SI 2013/22 Art.4
Art.3, amended: SI 2013/22 Art.4
Art.4, amended: SI 2013/22 Art.4
Sch.1, amended: SI 2013/22 Art.4

2419. Buckinghamshire Hospitals National Health Service Trust (Establishment) and the South Buckinghamshire National Health Service Trust and Stoke Mandeville Hospital National Health Service Trust (Dissolution) Order 2002
Art.1, amended: SI 2013/593 Art.2

2549. A4042 Trunk Road (Llanellen, Abergavenny, Monmouthshire) (40 MPH Speed Limit) Order 2002
varied: SI 2013/11 Art.7

2665. Electricity Safety, Quality and Continuity Regulations 2002
applied: SI 2013/1471 Reg.14
Sch.3 Part II para.7, amended: SI 2013/1869 Sch.1 para.3

2677. Control of Substances Hazardous to Health Regulations 2002
see *Chief Constable of Hampshire v Taylor* [2013] EWCA Civ 496, [2013] I.C.R. 1150 (CA (Civ Div)), Elias, L.J.
Sch.2, amended: SI 2013/1478 Sch.5 para.13

2682. Town and Country Planning (Enforcement Notices and Appeals) (England) Regulations 2002
Reg.9, amended: SI 2013/2146 Sch.1 para.7

2683. Town and Country Planning (Enforcement) (Written Representations Procedure) (England) Regulations 2002
Reg.7, amended: SI 2013/2146 Sch.1 para.8

2684. Town and Country Planning (Enforcement) (Hearings Procedure) (England) Rules 2002
r.3, amended: SI 2013/2146 Sch.1 para.9

r.4, amended: SI 2013/2146 Sch.1 para.9

2685. Town and Country Planning (Enforcement) (Determination by Inspectors) (Inquiries Procedure) (England) Rules 2002

r.3, amended: SI 2013/2146 Sch.1 para.10
r.4, amended: SI 2013/2146 Sch.1 para.10

2686. Town and Country Planning (Enforcement) (Inquiries Procedure) (England) Rules 2002

r.3, amended: SI 2013/2146 Sch.1 para.11
r.4, amended: SI 2013/2146 Sch.1 para.11

2706. Financial Services and Markets Act 2000 (Fourth Motor Insurance Directive) Regulations 2002

Reg.2, amended: SI 2013/472 Art.4, Sch.2 para.78
Reg.2, substituted: SI 2013/472 Sch.2 para.78

2707. Financial Services and Markets Act 2000 (Variation of Threshold Conditions) Order 2002

revoked: SI 2013/472 Sch.1

2742. Road Vehicles (Registration and Licensing) Regulations 2002

Reg.6, amended: 2013 c.29 s.188
Reg.6, revoked (in part): 2013 c.29 s.188
Reg.22, applied: SI 2013/1783 Reg.6
Reg.23, applied: SI 2013/1783 Reg.6
Reg.24, applied: SI 2013/1783 Reg.6
Reg.33, amended: SI 2013/2909 Reg.3
Sch.4 Part II para.5, revoked: SI 2013/2909 Reg.4
Sch.4 Part III para.9, revoked: SI 2013/2909 Reg.4

2818. Statutory Paternity Pay and Statutory Adoption Pay (Weekly Rates) Regulations 2002

Reg.2, amended: SI 2013/574 Art.10
Reg.3, amended: SI 2013/574 Art.10

2819. Statutory Paternity Pay and Statutory Adoption Pay (National Health Service Employees) Regulations 2002

Reg.1, amended: SI 2013/235 Sch.2 para.56
Reg.2, amended: SI 2013/235 Sch.2 para.56
Reg.2, applied: SI 2013/235 Sch.3 para.7
Reg.5, amended: SI 2013/235 Sch.2 para.56
Reg.5, revoked (in part): SI 2013/235 Sch.2 para.56

2832. Freedom of Information (Excluded Welsh Authorities) Order 2002

Sch.1 Part II, amended: SI 2013/1644 Sch.2

2848. Double Taxation Relief (Taxes on Income) (The United States of America) Order 2002

see *Anson v Revenue and Customs Commissioners* [2013] EWCA Civ 63, [2013] S.T.C. 557 (CA (Civ Div)), Laws, L.J.

2979. Notification of Installations Handling Hazardous Substances (Amendment) Regulations 2002

revoked: SI 2013/448 Sch.1

2998. Magistrates Courts (Detention and Forfeiture of Cash) Rules 2002

r.6, amended: SI 2013/2318 Sch.1 para.35
r.8, amended: SI 2013/2318 Sch.1 para.36

3026. Forest Reproductive Material (Great Britain) Regulations 2002

applied: SI 2013/755 Sch.7 para.10
Reg.2, amended: SI 2013/755 Sch.4 para.138
Reg.5, amended: SI 2013/755 Sch.4 para.139
Reg.6, amended: SI 2013/755 Sch.4 para.140
Reg.7, amended: SI 2013/755 Sch.4 para.141
Reg.8, amended: SI 2013/755 Sch.4 para.142
Reg.9, amended: SI 2013/755 Sch.4 para.143
Reg.11, amended: SI 2013/755 Sch.4 para.144
Reg.13, amended: SI 2013/755 Sch.4 para.145
Reg.14, amended: SI 2013/755 Sch.4 para.146
Reg.16, amended: SI 2013/755 Sch.4 para.147
Reg.17, amended: SI 2013/755 Sch.4 para.148
Reg.18, amended: SI 2013/755 Sch.4 para.149
Reg.20, amended: SI 2013/755 Sch.4 para.150
Reg.21, amended: SI 2013/755 Sch.4 para.151
Reg.22, amended: SI 2013/755 Sch.4 para.152
Reg.23, amended: SI 2013/755 Sch.4 para.153
Reg.24, amended: SI 2013/755 Sch.4 para.154
Reg.25, amended: SI 2013/755 Sch.4 para.155
Reg.26, amended: SI 2013/755 Sch.4 para.156
Reg.27, amended: SI 2013/755 Sch.4 para.157
Reg.32, amended: SI 2013/755 Sch.4 para.158
Sch.2 para.2, amended: SI 2013/755 Sch.4 para.159
Sch.3, amended: SI 2013/755 Sch.4 para.160
Sch.3 para.1, amended: SI 2013/755 Sch.4 para.160
Sch.3 para.2, amended: SI 2013/755 Sch.4 para.160
Sch.3 para.3, amended: SI 2013/755 Sch.4 para.160
Sch.3 para.4, amended: SI 2013/755 Sch.4 para.160
Sch.3 para.5, amended: SI 2013/755 Sch.4 para.160
Sch.3 para.6, amended: SI 2013/755 Sch.4 para.160
Sch.3 para.8, amended: SI 2013/755 Sch.4 para.160
Sch.3 para.9, amended: SI 2013/755 Sch.4 para.160
Sch.3 para.10, amended: SI 2013/755 Sch.4 para.160
Sch.4 para.1, amended: SI 2013/755 Sch.4 para.161
Sch.4 para.2, amended: SI 2013/755 Sch.4 para.161
Sch.4 para.3, amended: SI 2013/755 Sch.4 para.161
Sch.4 para.4, amended: SI 2013/755 Sch.4 para.161

Sch.5 para.1, amended: SI 2013/755 Sch.4 para.162
Sch.5 para.2, amended: SI 2013/755 Sch.4 para.162
Sch.5 para.3, amended: SI 2013/755 Sch.4 para.162
Sch.5 para.4, amended: SI 2013/755 Sch.4 para.162
Sch.5 para.5, amended: SI 2013/755 Sch.4 para.162

3036. Tax Credits (Administrative Arrangements) Regulations 2002
Reg.5, amended: SI 2013/630 Reg.80

3048. Local Authority (Overview and Scrutiny Committees Health Scrutiny Functions) Regulations 2002
revoked: SI 2013/218 Reg.33
Reg.2, applied: SI 2013/218 Reg.34
Reg.3, applied: SI 2013/218 Reg.34
Reg.4, applied: SI 2013/218 Reg.34
Reg.4A, applied: SI 2013/218 Reg.34

3081. Companies (Principal Business Activities) (Amendment) Regulations 2002
revoked: SI 2013/1947 Sch.2 Part 1

3113. Traffic Signs Regulations and General Directions 2002
applied: SI 2013/1030 Art.6, SI 2013/2389 Sch.1, SI 2013/2587 Art.44, SSI 2013/15 Art.3, Art.4, Art.5, SSI 2013/16 Art.3, Art.4, Art.5, SSI 2013/17 Art.3, Art.4, Art.5, SSI 2013/18 Art.3, Art.4, Art.5, SSI 2013/27 Art.3, SSI 2013/28 Art.2, Art.3, Art.4, SSI 2013/30 Art.2, SSI 2013/54 Art.3, Art.4, Art.5, SSI 2013/55 Art.3, Art.4, Art.5, SSI 2013/56 Art.3, Art.4, Art.5, SSI 2013/57 Art.3, Art.4, Art.5, SSI 2013/66 Art.2, SSI 2013/101 Art.3, Art.4, Art.5, SSI 2013/102 Art.3, Art.4, Art.5, SSI 2013/103 Art.3, Art.4, Art.5, SSI 2013/104 Art.3, Art.4, Art.5, SSI 2013/130 Art.3, Art.4, Art.5, SSI 2013/132 Art.3, Art.4, Art.5, SSI 2013/133 Art.3, Art.4, Art.5, SSI 2013/134 Art.3, Art.4, Art.5, SSI 2013/138 Art.2, Art.3, Art.4, SSI 2013/140 Art.2, SSI 2013/145 Art.2, SSI 2013/158 Art.3, Art.4, Art.5, SSI 2013/164 Art.3, Art.4, Art.5, SSI 2013/165 Art.3, Art.4, Art.5, SSI 2013/166 Art.3, Art.4, Art.5, SSI 2013/167 Art.2, Art.3, SSI 2013/206 Art.3, Art.4, Art.5, SSI 2013/208 Art.3, Art.4, Art.5, SSI 2013/209 Art.3, Art.4, Art.5, SSI 2013/213 Art.3, Art.4, Art.5, SSI 2013/223 Art.2, SSI 2013/224 Art.2, Art.3, SSI 2013/231 Art.2, Art.3, SSI 2013/232 Art.3, Art.4, Art.5, SSI 2013/233 Art.5, SSI 2013/234 Art.3, Art.4, Art.5, SSI 2013/235 Art.3, Art.4, Art.5, SSI 2013/237 Art.2, SSI 2013/240 Art.2, SSI 2013/242 Art.2, SSI 2013/243 Art.3, Art.4, Art.5, SSI 2013/244 Art.3, Art.4, Art.5, SSI 2013/245 Art.3, Art.4, Art.5, SSI 2013/246 Art.3, Art.4, Art.5, SSI 2013/248, SSI 2013/248 Art.3, Art.4, SSI 2013/251 Art.2, SSI 2013/255 Art.2, SSI 2013/257 Art.2, SSI 2013/263 Art.2, SSI 2013/272 Art.3, Art.4, Art.5, SSI 2013/273 Art.3, Art.4, Art.5, SSI 2013/274 Art.3, Art.4, Art.5, SSI 2013/275 Art.3, Art.4, Art.5, SSI 2013/284 Art.2, SSI 2013/285 Art.2, SSI 2013/297 Art.2, SSI 2013/298 Art.3, Art.4, Art.5, SSI 2013/299 Art.3, Art.4, Art.5, SSI 2013/300 Art.3, Art.4, Art.5, SSI 2013/301 Art.3, Art.4, Art.5, SSI 2013/306 Art.2, SSI 2013/316 Art.2, SSI 2013/329 Art.3, Art.4, Art.5, SSI 2013/330 Art.3, Art.4, Art.5, SSI 2013/331 Art.3, Art.4, Art.5, SSI 2013/332 Art.3, Art.4, Art.5, SSI 2013/338 Art.2, SSI 2013/343 Art.2, SSI 2013/352 Art.2, SSI 2013/353 Art.2, SSI 2013/358 Art.3, Art.4, Art.5, SSI 2013/359 Art.3, Art.4, Art.5, SSI 2013/360 Art.3, Art.4, Art.5, SSI 2013/361 Art.3, Art.4, Art.5
see *Wilson v Watson* 2013 S.C.C.R. 5 (HCJ), The Lord Justice Clerk (Carloway)
Part I, applied: SSI 2013/233 Art.3, Art.4
Pt I reg.11, see *Wilson v Watson* 2013 S.C.C.R. 5 (HCJ), The Lord Justice Clerk (Carloway)
Reg.4, amended: SSI 2013/119 Sch.2 para.19
Reg.15, amended: SSI 2013/119 Sch.2 para.19
Reg.26, amended: SSI 2013/119 Sch.2 para.19
Reg.27, amended: SSI 2013/119 Sch.2 para.19
Reg.36, amended: SSI 2013/119 Sch.2 para.19

3133. Proceeds of Crime Act 2002 (Enforcement in different parts of the United Kingdom) Order 2002
applied: SI 2013/1554 r.57_14
Art.6, applied: SI 2013/1554 r.57_4, r.57_5, r.57_6

3138. Double Taxation Relief (Taxes on Income) (South Africa) Order 2002
see *Revenue and Customs Commissioners v Ben Nevis (Holdings) Ltd* [2013] EWCA Civ 578, [2013] S.T.C. 1579 (CA (Civ Div)), Jackson, L.J.

3148. Trade Marks Act 1994 (Isle of Man) (Amendment) Order 2002
revoked: SI 2013/2601 Art.3

3150. Company Directors Disqualification (Northern Ireland) Order 2002
applied: SI 2013/349 Reg.105, Sch.7 para.29

3152. Insolvency (Northern Ireland) Order 2002
Art.2, amended: SI 2013/472 Sch.2 para.79

3153. Environment (Northern Ireland) Order 2002
Sch.1 Part I para.9B, amended: SI 2013/3135 Reg.15
Sch.1 Part II para.26, amended: SI 2013/3135 Reg.16

3188. Genetically Modified Organisms (Deliberate Release) (Wales) Regulations 2002

Reg.13, amended: SI 2013/755 Sch.5 para.16
Reg.13, revoked (in part): SI 2013/755 Sch.5 para.16

3189. National Health Service (Pharmaceutical Services) and (General Medical Services) (Amendment) (Wales) Regulations 2002

revoked: SI 2013/898 Sch.8 para.8

3213. Residential Family Centres Regulations 2002

Reg.2, amended: SI 2013/499 Reg.3
Reg.3, amended: SI 2013/499 Reg.4
Reg.3, revoked (in part): SI 2013/499 Reg.4
Reg.4, amended: SI 2013/499 Reg.5
Reg.10, amended: SI 2013/499 Reg.6
Reg.13, amended: SI 2013/499 Reg.7
Reg.13A, added: SI 2013/499 Reg.8
Reg.14, amended: SI 2013/499 Reg.9
Reg.14, revoked (in part): SI 2013/499 Reg.9
Reg.19, amended: SI 2013/499 Reg.10
Reg.20, amended: SI 2013/499 Reg.11
Reg.21, revoked (in part): SI 2013/499 Reg.12
Reg.21A, added: SI 2013/499 Reg.13
Reg.22, revoked (in part): SI 2013/499 Reg.14
Reg.23, amended: SI 2013/499 Reg.15
Reg.25, amended: SI 2013/499 Reg.16
Reg.31, revoked: SI 2013/499 Reg.17
Sch.1 para.2, substituted: SI 2013/499 Reg.18
Sch.1 para.10, revoked: SI 2013/499 Reg.18
Sch.1 para.19, added: SI 2013/499 Reg.18
Sch.3 para.5, amended: SI 2013/499 Reg.3
Sch.3 para.13A, added: SI 2013/499 Reg.19
Sch.4 para.2, amended: SI 2013/499 Reg.3
Sch.4 para.6, revoked: SI 2013/499 Reg.20
Sch.5, amended: SI 2013/235 Sch.2 para.57

3231. Animal By-Products (Identification) (Amendment) (England) (No.2) Regulations 2002

revoked: SI 2013/2952 Reg.28

3236. Flexible Working (Eligibility, Complaints and Remedies) Regulations 2002

Reg.2, amended: SI 2013/388 Sch.1 para.32, SI 2013/591 Sch.1 para.28

2003

32. Access to the Countryside (Provisional and Conclusive Maps) (England) (Amendment) Regulations 2003

revoked: SI 2013/1798 Reg.6

61. Limited Liability Partnerships (Welsh Language Forms) Regulations 2003

revoked: SI 2013/1947 Sch.2 Part 1

62. Companies (Welsh Language Forms) Regulations 2003

revoked: SI 2013/1947 Sch.2 Part 1

74. Wireless Telegraphy (Exemption) Regulations 2003

Sch.3 Part III para.3, amended: SI 2013/1254 Reg.2
Sch.3 Part IV, amended: SI 2013/1254 Reg.2
Sch.5 Part III, amended: SI 2013/1254 Reg.2

82. Proceeds of Crime Act 2002 (Appeals under Part 2) Order 2003

applied: SI 2013/1554 r.71_1, r.71_5, r.71_8
Art.2, amended: SI 2013/24 Art.3
Art.3, amended: SI 2013/24 Art.4, Art.5
Art.6, amended: SI 2013/24 Art.7
Art.6, applied: SI 2013/1554 r.71_2, r.72_1
Art.6, substituted: SI 2013/24 Art.6
Art.7, applied: SI 2013/1554 r.71_2, r.71_3
Art.7, substituted: SI 2013/24 Art.8
Art.8, amended: SI 2013/24 Art.9
Art.8, referred to: SI 2013/1554 r.71_6, r.71_7
Art.9, amended: SI 2013/24 Art.10
Art.10, revoked (in part): SI 2013/24 Art.11
Art.10A, added: SI 2013/24 Art.12
Art.10B, added: SI 2013/24 Art.12
Art.10C, added: SI 2013/24 Art.12
Art.12, applied: SI 2013/1554 r.71_10
Art.14, amended: SI 2013/24 Art.14
Art.14, substituted: SI 2013/24 Art.13
Art.15, referred to: SI 2013/1554 r.71_10

96. Community Investment Tax Relief (Accreditation of Community Development Finance Institutions) Regulations 2003

Reg.2, amended: SI 2013/417 Reg.5
Reg.7, amended: SI 2013/417 Reg.12
Reg.8, amended: SI 2013/417 Reg.6
Reg.12, amended: SI 2013/417 Reg.12
Reg.12A, added: SI 2013/417 Reg.7
Reg.13, amended: SI 2013/417 Reg.8, Reg.12
Reg.15, amended: SI 2013/417 Reg.12
Reg.15A, amended: SI 2013/417 Reg.9
Reg.15B, amended: SI 2013/417 Reg.10
Reg.16, amended: SI 2013/417 Reg.12
Sch.1 para.2, amended: SI 2013/417 Reg.12
Sch.1 para.4, amended: SI 2013/417 Reg.11, Reg.12
Sch.1 para.9, amended: SI 2013/417 Reg.11
Sch.1 para.11, amended: SI 2013/417 Reg.11

135. Countryside Access (Dedication of Land as Access Land) (Wales) Regulations 2003

Reg.2, amended: SI 2013/755 Sch.5 para.18
Reg.4, amended: SI 2013/755 Sch.5 para.19
Reg.4, revoked (in part): SI 2013/755 Sch.5 para.19

139. National Health Service (General Medical Services) and (Pharmaceutical Services) (Amendment) (Wales) Regulations 2003

revoked: SI 2013/898 Sch.8 para.9

142. Countryside Access (Exclusion or Restriction of Access) (Wales) Regulations 2003

Reg.2, amended: SI 2013/755 Sch.5 para.21
Reg.12, amended: SI 2013/755 Sch.5 para.22
Reg.14, amended: SI 2013/755 Sch.5 para.22

154. Health, Social Care and Well-being Strategies (Wales) Regulations 2003

Reg.2, amended: SI 2013/235 Sch.2 para.59

164. Water Resources (Environmental Impact Assessment) (England and Wales) Regulations 2003

Reg.2, amended: SI 2013/755 Sch.4 para.164
Reg.4, amended: SI 2013/755 Sch.4 para.165
Reg.6, amended: SI 2013/755 Sch.4 para.166
Reg.7, amended: SI 2013/755 Sch.4 para.167
Reg.8, amended: SI 2013/755 Sch.4 para.167
Reg.9, amended: SI 2013/755 Sch.4 para.167
Reg.10, amended: SI 2013/755 Sch.4 para.167
Reg.11, amended: SI 2013/755 Sch.4 para.167
Reg.12, amended: SI 2013/755 Sch.4 para.167
Reg.13, amended: SI 2013/755 Sch.4 para.167
Reg.14, amended: SI 2013/755 Sch.4 para.167
Reg.15, amended: SI 2013/755 Sch.4 para.167
Reg.16, amended: SI 2013/755 Sch.4 para.167

216. East Sussex Hospitals National Health Service Trust (Establishment) and the Eastbourne Hospitals National Health Service Trust and Hastings and Rother National Health Service Trust (Dissolution) Order 2003

Art.1, amended: SI 2013/593 Art.2

237. Fostering Services (Wales) Regulations 2003

applied: SI 2013/3029 Sch.1 para.19, Sch.6 para.21, SI 2013/3035 Sch.1

282. Income and Corporation Taxes (Electronic Communications) Regulations 2003

Reg.2, amended: 2013 c.2 Sch.1 Part 10

367. Voluntary Adoption Agencies and the Adoption Agencies (Miscellaneous Amendments) Regulations 2003

Reg.19, amended: SI 2013/235 Sch.2 para.60
Reg.24K, amended: SI 2013/235 Sch.2 para.60
Sch.4, amended: SI 2013/235 Sch.2 para.60

403. Nuclear Industries Security Regulations 2003

Reg.2, amended: SI 2013/190 Reg.3
Reg.4, amended: SI 2013/190 Reg.4
Reg.8, amended: SI 2013/190 Reg.5

419. Energy (Northern Ireland) Order 2003

Art.6, amended: 2013 c.24 Sch.6 para.168
Art.6, revoked (in part): 2013 c.24 Sch.6 para.168
Art.38, amended: 2013 c.24 Sch.6 para.169
Art.41A, applied: 2013 c.32 s.22, Sch.2 para.12
Art.42, amended: 2013 c.24 Sch.14 para.25
Art.42, revoked (in part): 2013 c.24 Sch.14 para.25
Art.45, amended: 2013 c.24 Sch.14 para.26
Art.56, varied: 2013 c.32 s.55
Art.63, amended: SI 2013/472 Sch.2 para.81
Art.63, applied: 2013 c.32 Sch.2 para.10
Art.63, disapplied: 2013 c.32 s.19
Sch.1 para.9, amended: 2013 c.24 Sch.15 para.55
Sch.2, amended: 2013 c.24 Sch.6 para.170
Sch.2 para.1, amended: 2013 c.24 Sch.6 para.170
Sch.2 para.2, amended: 2013 c.24 Sch.6 para.170
Sch.2 para.3, amended: 2013 c.24 Sch.6 para.170
Sch.2 para.4, amended: 2013 c.24 Sch.6 para.170
Sch.2 para.5, amended: 2013 c.24 Sch.6 para.170
Sch.2 para.6, amended: 2013 c.24 Sch.6 para.170

429. Biocidal Products (Amendment) Regulations 2003

Reg.1, revoked (in part): SI 2013/1506 Reg.34
Reg.2, revoked (in part): SI 2013/1506 Reg.34
Reg.3, revoked (in part): SI 2013/1506 Reg.34, SI 2013/1507 Reg.8
Reg.4, revoked (in part): SI 2013/1506 Reg.34
Sch.1, revoked: SI 2013/1507 Reg.8
Sch.2, revoked (in part): SI 2013/1506 Reg.34

492. Child Benefit and Guardian's Allowance (Administration) Regulations 2003

Reg.19, amended: SI 2013/630 Reg.81

494. Child Benefit and Guardian's Allowance (Administrative Arrangements) Regulations 2003

Reg.5, amended: SI 2013/630 Reg.82

507. School Organisation Proposals by the Learning and Skills Council for England Regulations 2003

Reg.4, amended: SI 2013/235 Sch.2 para.61
Reg.16, amended: SI 2013/235 Sch.2 para.61

523. Education (Governors Allowances) (England) Regulations 2003

revoked: SI 2013/1624 Reg.3

527. Police Regulations 2003

Reg.3, amended: SI 2013/2318 Sch.1 para.44
Reg.10, amended: SI 2013/2793 Reg.3
Reg.10B, added: SI 2013/2793 Reg.4
Reg.13A, added: SI 2013/2793 Reg.5
Reg.44A, amended: SI 2013/2318 Sch.1 para.45
Sch.3 para.1, amended: SI 2013/2318 Sch.1 para.46

548. British Nationality (General) Regulations 2003

Reg.5A, substituted: SI 2013/2541 Reg.3
Sch.2A para.1, added: SI 2013/2541 Reg.4
Sch.2A para.2, added: SI 2013/2541 Reg.4

609. A483 Trunk Road (Gresford Interchange, Wrexham) (Derestriction) Order 2003

varied: SI 2013/771 Art.7

625. Medicines for Human Use and Medical Devices (Fees Amendments) Regulations 2003

revoked: SI 2013/532 Sch.9

628. National Assistance (Sums for Personal Requirements) (England) Regulations 2003

Reg.2, amended: SI 2013/518 Reg.2

654. Tax Credits (Residence) Regulations 2003

Reg.3, varied: SI 2013/386 Sch.1 para.46

657. National Health Service (Optical Charges and Payments) and (General Ophthalmic Services) Amendment Regulations 2003

revoked: SI 2013/461 Sch.4

658. Immigration (Notices) Regulations 2003

Reg.4, see *Syed (Curtailment of Leave: Notice), Re* [2013] UKUT 144 (IAC), [2013] Imm. A.R. 685 (UT (IAC)), Judge Spencer

Reg.7, see *Syed (Curtailment of Leave: Notice), Re* [2013] UKUT 144 (IAC), [2013] Imm. A.R. 685 (UT (IAC)), Judge Spencer

Reg.7, amended: SI 2013/793 Reg.2

681. Pensions Increase (Review) Order 2003

applied: SI 2013/604 Sch.1

783. National Health Service (Pharmaceutical Services) (Amendment) (Wales) Regulations 2003

revoked: SI 2013/898 Sch.8 para.10

839. Public Lending Right (Increase of Limit) Order 2003

Art.2, amended: SI 2013/2352 Sch.2 para.2

860. Education (Remission of Charges Relating to Residential Trips) (Wales) Regulations 2003

Reg.2, amended: SI 2013/2731 Reg.2

Reg.6, added: SI 2013/2731 Reg.3

1034. Special Immigration Appeals Commission (Procedure) Rules 2003

Part 1 r.2, amended: SI 2013/2995 r.2

Part 1 r.3, amended: SI 2013/2995 r.3

Part 1 r.5, amended: SI 2013/2995 r.4

Part 2 r.6, substituted: SI 2013/2995 r.5, r.6

Part 2 r.7, amended: SI 2013/2995 r.7, r.8

Part 2 r.7, substituted: SI 2013/2995 r.5

Part 2 r.8, amended: SI 2013/2995 r.9, r.10

Part 2 r.8, substituted: SI 2013/2995 r.5

Part 2 r.9, amended: SI 2013/2995 r.11, r.12

Part 2 r.9, substituted: SI 2013/2995 r.5

Part 2 r.9A, amended: SI 2013/2995 r.13

Part 2 r.9A, substituted: SI 2013/2995 r.5

Part 2 r.10, amended: SI 2013/2995 r.14, r.15

Part 2 r.10, substituted: SI 2013/2995 r.5

Part 2 r.10A, amended: SI 2013/2995 r.16, r.17

Part 2 r.10A, substituted: SI 2013/2995 r.5

Part 2 r.10B, added: SI 2013/2995 r.18

Part 2 r.10B, substituted: SI 2013/2995 r.5

Part 2 r.11, amended: SI 2013/2995 r.19, r.20

Part 2 r.11, substituted: SI 2013/2995 r.5

Part 2 r.11A, amended: SI 2013/2995 r.21, r.22

Part 2 r.11A, substituted: SI 2013/2995 r.5

Part 2 r.11B, substituted: SI 2013/2995 r.5, r.23

Part 2 r.12, amended: SI 2013/2995 r.24, r.25

Part 2 r.12, substituted: SI 2013/2995 r.5

Part 5 r.26, substituted: SI 2013/2995 r.26

Part 7 r.34, amended: SI 2013/2995 r.27

Part 7 r.37, amended: SI 2013/2995 r.28

Part 7 r.40, amended: SI 2013/2995 r.29

Part 7 r.43A, amended: SI 2013/2995 r.30

1038. Education (National Curriculum) (Key Stage 2 Assessment Arrangements) (England) Order 2003

Art.3, amended: SI 2013/1513 Art.2

Art.3, revoked (in part): SI 2013/1513 Art.2

Art.4, amended: SI 2013/1513 Art.2

Art.5, amended: SI 2013/1513 Art.2

Art.5, revoked (in part): SI 2013/1513 Art.2

Art.5A, revoked: SI 2013/1513 Art.2

Art.5B, added: SI 2013/1513 Art.2

Art.6, amended: SI 2013/1513 Art.2

Art.6, revoked (in part): SI 2013/1513 Art.2

Art.6A, revoked: SI 2013/1513 Art.2

Art.6B, added: SI 2013/1513 Art.2

Art.7, amended: SI 2013/1513 Art.2

Art.7, revoked (in part): SI 2013/1513 Art.2

Art.11, revoked (in part): SI 2013/1513 Art.2

1073. Superannuation (Admission to Schedule 1 to the Superannuation Act 1972) Order 2003

Art.2, amended: SI 2013/2352 Sch.2 para.3

Art.2, revoked (in part): SI 2013/2352 Sch.2 para.3

Art.3, amended: SI 2013/2352 Sch.2 para.3

Art.3, revoked (in part): SI 2013/2352 Sch.2 para.3

1181. Financial Services and Markets Act 2000 (Collective Investment Schemes) (Designated Countries and Territories) Order 2003

revoked: SI 2013/1773 Sch.2 para.16

1238. Bathing Waters (Classification) (England) Regulations 2003

revoked: SI 2013/1675 Reg.19

1248. Merchant Shipping (Categorisation of Registries of Relevant British Possessions) Order 2003

Art.6, amended: SI 2013/1115 Art.2

1249. Patents Act 1977 (Isle of Man) Order 2003

revoked: SI 2013/2602 Art.3

1294. Financial Services and Markets Act 2000 (Communications by Actuaries) Regulations 2003

applied: SI 2013/472 Sch.2 para.83

Reg.1, amended: SI 2013/472 Sch.2 para.82

Reg.2, amended: SI 2013/472 Sch.2 para.82

Reg.2, applied: SI 2013/472 Sch.2 para.83

1325. Government Resources and Accounts Act 2000 (Rights of Access of Comptroller and Auditor General) Order 2003

Art.2, amended: SI 2013/388 Sch.1 para.33, SI 2013/591 Sch.1 para.29

1368. Enterprise Act 2002 (Super-complaints to Regulators) Order 2003

Sch.1, amended: SI 2013/610 Sch.1 para.3

1370. Enterprise Act 2002 (Merger Fees and Determination of Turnover) Order 2003

Sch.1 para.1, amended: SI 2013/3115 Sch.2 para.60

1372. Competition Appeal Tribunal Rules 2003

r.8, see *John Lewis Plc v Office of Fair Trading* [2013] CAT 7, [2013] Comp. A.R. 301 (CAT), Vivien Rose (Chairman); see *Somerfield Stores Ltd v Office of Fair Trading* [2013] CAT 12, [2013] Comp. A.R. 321 (CAT), Marcus Smith Q.C.; see *Somerfield Stores Ltd v Office of Fair Trading* [2013] CAT 5, [2013] Comp. A.R. 165 (CAT), Marcus Smith Q.C.

r.40, see *Deutsche Bahn AG v Morgan Crucible Co Plc* [2012] EWCA Civ 1055, [2013] Bus. L.R. 125 (CA (Civ Div)), Mummery, L.J.

1374. Enterprise Act 2002 (Part 8 Community Infringements Specified UK Laws) Order 2003

Sch.1, amended: SI 2013/472 Sch.2 para.84

1376. Enterprise Act 2002 (Part 8 Notice to OFT of Intended Prosecution Specified Enactments, Revocation and Transitional Provision) Order 2003

Sch.1, amended: SI 2013/1575 Sch.1 para.18

1377. School Governance (Procedures) (England) Regulations 2003

revoked: SI 2013/1624 Reg.3

Reg.14, see *R. (on the application of McCormack) v St Edmund Campion Catholic School Governing Body* [2012] EWHC 3928 (Admin), [2013] E.L.R. 169 (QBD (Admin)), Beatson, J.

1417. Land Registration Rules 2003

Part 8 r.93, amended: SI 2013/534 Sch.1 para.5

Part 9 r.111, amended: SI 2013/600 Sch.2 para.5

Sch.1, amended: SI 2013/2318 Sch.1 para.41

Sch.2, applied: SI 2013/1627 Art.2

Sch.4, amended: SI 2013/534 Sch.1 para.5

Sch.5, amended: SI 2013/472 Sch.2 para.85, SI 2013/2318 Sch.1 para.42

1471. Tobacco Products (Descriptions of Products) Order 2003

Art.4, amended: SI 2013/2721 Art.3

Art.7, amended: SI 2013/2721 Art.3

1474. Financial Services and Markets Act 2000 (Misleading Statements and Practices) (Amendment) Order 2003

revoked: SI 2013/472 Sch.1

1475. Financial Services and Markets Act 2000 (Regulated Activities) (Amendment) (No.1) Order 2003

Art.27, amended: SI 2013/472 Art.4

Art.29, amended: SI 2013/472 Art.4

1476. Financial Services and Markets Act 2000 (Regulated Activities) (Amendment) (No.2) Order 2003

Art.20, amended: SI 2013/472 Art.4

Art.23, amended: SI 2013/472 Art.4

Art.25, amended: SI 2013/472 Art.4

Art.27, amended: SI 2013/472 Art.4

1484. Animal By-Products (Identification) (Amendment) (England) Regulations 2003

revoked: SI 2013/2952 Reg.28

1497. National Health Service (Functions of Strategic Health Authorities and Primary Care Trusts and Administration Arrangements) (England) (Amendment) Regulations 2003

revoked: SI 2013/235 Sch.2 para.187

1564. Fruit Juices and Fruit Nectars (England) Regulations 2003

applied: SI 2013/2775 Reg.22

revoked: SI 2013/2775 Reg.20

1590. Health Professions Order 2001 (Consequential Amendments) Order 2003

Sch.1 Part 2 para.7, revoked (in part): SSI 2013/50 Sch.5

1591. Access to the Countryside (Correction of Provisional and Conclusive Maps) (England) Regulations 2003

revoked: SI 2013/1798 Reg.6

1592. Enterprise Act 2002 (Protection of Legitimate Interests) Order 2003

Sch.4 para.5, revoked: SI 2013/610 Sch.2 para.3

Sch.4 para.13, revoked: SI 2013/610 Sch.1 para.4

1593. Enterprise Act 2002 (Part 8 Domestic Infringements) Order 2003

Sch.1 Part I, amended: SI 2013/1575 Sch.1 para.19

1633. Uncertificated Securities (Amendment) (Eligible Debt Securities) Regulations 2003

Sch.2 para.13, revoked (in part): SI 2013/687 Sch.2

1660. Employment Equality (Religion or Belief) Regulations 2003

see *CVS Solicitors LLP v Van der Borgh* [2013] Eq. L.R. 934 (EAT), Slade, J.

Reg.3, see *Pasab Ltd (t/a Jhoots Pharmacy) v Woods* [2012] EWCA Civ 1578, [2013] I.R.L.R. 305 (CA (Civ Div)), Hallett, L.J.

Reg.5, see *Heafield v Times Newspaper Ltd* [2013] Eq. L.R. 345 (EAT), Underhill, J.

1661. Employment Equality (Sexual Orientation) Regulations 2003

Reg.5, see *Smith v Ideal Shopping Direct Ltd* [2013] Eq. L.R. 943 (EAT), Recorder Luba Q.C.

1697. Medical Devices (Amendment) Regulations 2003

Reg.2, amended: SI 2013/2327 Reg.21

Reg.2, revoked (in part): SI 2013/2327 Reg.21

Reg.6, revoked: SI 2013/2327 Reg.21

Reg.7, revoked: SI 2013/2327 Reg.21

Reg.9, revoked: SI 2013/2327 Reg.21

Reg.13, revoked: SI 2013/2327 Reg.21
Reg.14, revoked: SI 2013/2327 Reg.21
Reg.16, revoked: SI 2013/2327 Reg.21

1730. Insolvency (Amendment) Rules 2003
Sch.1 Part 6 para.46, revoked: SI 2013/2135 r.4
Sch.1 Part 7 para.53, amended: SI 2013/2135 r.4

1745. Charitable Deductions (Approved Schemes) (Amendment) Regulations 2003
Reg.7, revoked: 2013 c.2 Sch.1 Part 10

1788. Urban Waste Water Treatment (England and Wales) (Amendment) Regulations 2003
Reg.2, amended: SI 2013/755 Sch.4 para.168
Reg.3, amended: SI 2013/755 Sch.4 para.168

1827. National Treatment Agency (Establishment and Constitution) Amendment Order 2003
revoked: SI 2013/235 Sch.1 para.6

1847. Coast Protection (Notices) (Wales) Regulations 2003
Reg.4, amended: SI 2013/755 Sch.5 para.23

1876. Liberia (United Nations Sanctions) (Overseas Territories) (Amendment) Order 2003
revoked: SI 2013/237 Sch.2

1882. Freedom of Information (Additional Public Authorities) Order 2003
Sch.1, amended: SI 2013/472 Sch.2 para.86

1917. Education (Teacher Student Loans) (Repayment etc.) Regulations 2003
Reg.11, applied: SI 2013/3029 Sch.9 para.17, SI 2013/3035 Sch.1

1941. Packaging (Essential Requirements) Regulations 2003
Reg.2, amended: SI 2013/2212 Reg.2
Sch.2 para.2, amended: SI 2013/755 Sch.4 para.169
Sch.5, substituted: SI 2013/2212 Reg.2

1962. School Governance (Collaboration) (England) Regulations 2003
Reg.2, amended: SI 2013/1624 Sch.2 para.1
Reg.3, substituted: SI 2013/1624 Sch.2 para.1
Reg.6, amended: SI 2013/1624 Sch.2 para.1
Reg.7, amended: SI 2013/1624 Sch.2 para.1

1982. A487 Trunk Road (Aberarth, Ceredigion) (30mph and 40 mph Speed limits) Order 2003
varied: SI 2013/1470 Art.7

1987. Service Charges (Consultation Requirements) (England) Regulations 2003
see *BDW Trading Ltd v South Anglia Housing Ltd* [2013] EWHC 2169 (Ch), [2013] L. & T.R. 25 (Ch D), Nicholas Strauss Q.C.; see *City & County Properties Ltd v Yeats* [2013] R.V.R. 47 (UT (Lands)), Judge Huskinson; see *Peverel Properties Ltd v Hughes* [2013] L. & T.R. 6 (UT (Lands)), Judge Huskinson; see *Phillips v Francis* [2012] EWHC 3650 (Ch), [2013] 1 W.L.R. 2343 (Ch D), Sir Andrew Morritt (Chancellor)
Reg.3, see *BDW Trading Ltd v South Anglia Housing Ltd* [2013] EWHC 2169 (Ch), [2013] L. & T.R. 25 (Ch D), Nicholas Strauss Q.C.
Sch.4 Pt 2, see *Daejan Investments Ltd v Benson* [2013] UKSC 14, [2013] 1 W.L.R. 854 (SC), Lord Neuberger (President); see *Peverel Properties Ltd v Hughes* [2013] L. & T.R. 6 (UT (Lands)), Judge Huskinson
Sch.4 Pt 2 para.4, see *Peverel Properties Ltd v Hughes* [2013] L. & T.R. 6 (UT (Lands)), Judge Huskinson

1993. Public Interest Disclosure (Prescribed Persons) (Amendment) Order 2003
Sch.1, amended: SI 2013/472 Art.4

1994. Education (Mandatory Awards) Regulations 2003
Sch.2 Part 2 para.7, referred to: SI 2013/3029 Sch.11 para.5, SI 2013/3035 Sch.1
Sch.2 Part 2 para.9, applied: SI 2013/3029 Sch.11 para.3, SI 2013/3035 Sch.1
Sch.2 Part 3, applied: SI 2013/3029 Sch.11 para.4, SI 2013/3035 Sch.1

2002. Merchant Shipping (Safe Loading and Unloading of Bulk Carriers) Regulations 2003
Reg.12, revoked (in part): SI 2013/1512 Sch.1

2066. Collective Investment Schemes (Miscellaneous Amendments) Regulations 2003
Reg.6, revoked: SI 2013/3115 Sch.3

2076. Capital Allowances (Environmentally Beneficial Plant and Machinery) Order 2003
Art.2, amended: SI 2013/1762 Art.3
Art.3, amended: SI 2013/1762 Art.4

2098. Leasehold Valuation Tribunals (Fees)(England) Regulations 2003
revoked: SI 2013/1036 Sch.2 para.26

2099. Leasehold Valuation Tribunals (Procedure) (England) Regulations 2003
revoked: SI 2013/1036 Sch.2 para.27
Reg.21, revoked: SI 2013/2042 Sch.1 para.54

2114. Land Registration (Referral to the Adjudicator to HM Land Registry) Rules 2003
r.3, amended: SI 2013/1036 Sch.2 para.64
r.5, amended: SI 2013/1036 Sch.2 para.65

2155. Communications Act 2003 (Consequential Amendments) Order 2003
Sch.1 Part 5 para.29, revoked (in part): SSI 2013/264 Sch.1

2171. Adjudicator to Her Majesty's Land Registry (Practice and Procedure) Rules 2003
revoked: SI 2013/1036 Sch.2 para.66
Part 4 r.30, amended: SI 2013/2042 Sch.1 para.55

Part 4 r.30, revoked (in part): SI 2013/2042 Sch.1 para.55

2277. Delayed Discharges (England) Regulations 2003

Reg.2, revoked (in part): SI 2013/235 Sch.2 para.62
Reg.12, revoked: SI 2013/235 Sch.2 para.62
Reg.13, revoked: SI 2013/235 Sch.2 para.62
Reg.14, revoked: SI 2013/235 Sch.2 para.62
Reg.15, revoked: SI 2013/235 Sch.2 para.62
Reg.16, revoked: SI 2013/235 Sch.2 para.62
Reg.17, revoked: SI 2013/235 Sch.2 para.62

2314. Religious Character of Schools (Designation Procedure) (Independent Schools) (England) Regulations 2003

applied: SI 2013/2867
referred to: SI 2013/2162, SI 2013/3268

2342. Land Registration (Acting Adjudicator) Regulations 2003

revoked: SI 2013/1036 Sch.2 para.67

2346. Shrewsbury and Telford Hospital National Health Service Trust (Establishment) and the Princess Royal Hospital National Health Service Trust and the Royal Shrewsbury Hospitals National Health Service Trust (Dissolution) Order 2003

Art.1, amended: SI 2013/593 Art.2

2381. National Health Service (Optical Charges and Payments) and (General Ophthalmic Services) Amendment (No.2) Regulations 2003

revoked: SI 2013/461 Sch.4

2382. National Health Service (Travel Expenses and Remission of Charges) Regulations 2003

Part IV, applied: SI 2013/461 Reg.3, Reg.8
Reg.2, amended: SI 2013/475 Reg.17
Reg.3, amended: SI 2013/475 Reg.18
Reg.3, revoked (in part): SI 2013/475 Reg.18
Reg.5, amended: SI 2013/475 Reg.19, SI 2013/1600 Reg.4
Reg.5, applied: SI 2013/349 Sch.4 para.7, Sch.5 para.6, Sch.6 para.4, Sch.7 para.5, SI 2013/3029 Sch.9 para.46, Sch.10 para.43, SI 2013/3035 Sch.1
Reg.5, referred to: SI 2013/349 Sch.5 para.6
Reg.6, applied: SI 2013/3029 Sch.9 para.46, Sch.10 para.43, SI 2013/3035 Sch.1
Reg.10, amended: SI 2013/475 Reg.20
Reg.12, amended: SI 2013/475 Reg.21
Reg.12, applied: SI 2013/3029 Sch.9 para.46, Sch.10 para.43, SI 2013/3035 Sch.1
Reg.13, amended: SI 2013/475 Reg.22
Reg.14, amended: SI 2013/475 Reg.23
Reg.17, amended: SI 2013/458 Sch.2 para.7
Reg.18A, added: SI 2013/1600 Reg.3
Sch.1, amended: SI 2013/475 Reg.24, SI 2013/1600 Reg.2, Reg.3
Sch.1, applied: SI 2013/461 Reg.3, Reg.8
Sch.1, substituted: SI 2013/475 Reg.24

2553. Electronic Communications Code (Conditions and Restrictions) Regulations 2003

applied: SI 2013/1403 Reg.3
Reg.2, amended: SI 2013/755 Sch.4 para.171, SI 2013/1403 Sch.1 para.1
Reg.4, amended: SI 2013/1403 Sch.1 para.2
Reg.4, revoked (in part): SI 2013/1403 Sch.1 para.2
Reg.5, amended: SI 2013/1403 Sch.1 para.3
Reg.5, revoked (in part): SI 2013/1403 Sch.1 para.3
Reg.6, amended: SI 2013/1403 Sch.1 para.4
Reg.6A, added: SI 2013/1403 Sch.1 para.5
Reg.6A, revoked: SI 2013/1403 Sch.1 para.5
Reg.7, amended: SI 2013/1403 Sch.1 para.6
Reg.7A, added: SI 2013/1403 Sch.1 para.7
Reg.7A, revoked: SI 2013/1403 Sch.1 para.7
Reg.8, amended: SI 2013/755 Sch.4 para.172, SI 2013/1403 Sch.1 para.8
Reg.8, revoked (in part): SI 2013/1403 Sch.1 para.8
Reg.8A, added: SI 2013/1403 Sch.1 para.9
Reg.8A, revoked: SI 2013/1403 Sch.1 para.9

2603. Freedom of Information Act 2000 (Commencement No 3) Order 2003

Sch.1 Part 1, amended: SI 2013/687 Sch.2

2613. Council Tax and Non-Domestic Rating (Demand Notices) (England) Regulations 2003

Sch.2 Part 1 para.7, substituted: SI 2013/694 Reg.3
Sch.2 Part 2, amended: SI 2013/694 Reg.4
Sch.2 Part 3 para.3, substituted: SI 2013/694 Reg.5

2617. Scotland Act 1998 (Transfer of Functions to the Scottish Ministers etc.) (No.2) Order 2003

Sch.1 para.1, amended: SI 2013/602 Sch.2 para.83

2624. National Health Service (Amendments concerning Supplementary and Independent Nurse Prescribing) (Wales) Regulations 2003

revoked: SI 2013/898 Sch.8 para.11

2682. Income Tax (Pay As You Earn) Regulations 2003

applied: SI 2013/376 Reg.55, Reg.61
see *Telfer v Sakellarios* [2013] EWHC 1556 (Comm), [2013] S.T.C. 2413 (QBD (Comm)), Judge Mackie, Q.C.
Reg.2, amended: SI 2013/521 Reg.6
Reg.2A, amended: SI 2013/521 Reg.14
Reg.2A, revoked (in part): SI 2013/521 Reg.14
Reg.2B, revoked (in part): SI 2013/521 Reg.15
Reg.10, amended: SI 2013/521 Reg.7
Reg.11, amended: SI 2013/521 Reg.7
Reg.12, amended: SI 2013/521 Reg.7
Reg.14B, added: SI 2013/521 Reg.3

Reg.21, see *Telfer v Sakellarios* [2013] EWHC 1556 (Comm), [2013] S.T.C. 2413 (QBD (Comm)), Judge Mackie, Q.C.
Reg.34, amended: SI 2013/521 Reg.4
Reg.34, revoked: SI 2013/521 Reg.5
Reg.35, revoked: SI 2013/521 Reg.5
Reg.36, amended: SI 2013/521 Reg.16
Reg.46, amended: SI 2013/521 Reg.17
Reg.58, amended: SI 2013/521 Reg.12
Reg.58A, added: SI 2013/521 Reg.13
Reg.62, amended: SI 2013/521 Reg.8
Reg.67B, amended: SI 2013/2300 Reg.2
Reg.67B, revoked (in part): SI 2013/521 Reg.18
Reg.67BA, added: SI 2013/521 Reg.19
Reg.67BB, added: SI 2013/521 Reg.19
Reg.67BC, added: SI 2013/521 Reg.19
Reg.67C, amended: SI 2013/521 Reg.20
Reg.67D, amended: SI 2013/521 Reg.21
Reg.67D, revoked (in part): SI 2013/521 Reg.21
Reg.67E, amended: SI 2013/521 Reg.22
Reg.67E, revoked (in part): SI 2013/521 Reg.22
Reg.67EA, added: SI 2013/521 Reg.23
Reg.67F, amended: SI 2013/521 Reg.24
Reg.67G, amended: SI 2013/521 Reg.25
Reg.67H, amended: SI 2013/521 Reg.26
Reg.69, amended: SI 2013/521 Reg.27
Reg.70, amended: SI 2013/521 Reg.28
Reg.71, amended: SI 2013/521 Reg.29
Reg.75A, amended: SI 2013/521 Reg.30
Reg.75B, amended: SI 2013/521 Reg.31
Reg.80, amended: SI 2013/521 Reg.32
Reg.82, amended: SI 2013/521 Reg.33
Reg.97N, amended: SI 2013/521 Reg.34
Reg.97O, revoked (in part): SI 2013/521 Reg.9
Reg.104, amended: SI 2013/521 Reg.35
Reg.148, amended: SI 2013/630 Reg.83
Reg.199, amended: SI 2013/521 Reg.36
Reg.206, revoked (in part): SI 2013/521 Reg.10
Reg.211, amended: SI 2013/521 Reg.11
Sch.A1 para.2, referred to: SI 2013/622 Reg.29, Reg.30
Sch.A1 para.3, referred to: SI 2013/622 Reg.29, Reg.30
Sch.A1 para.4, referred to: SI 2013/622 Reg.29, Reg.30
Sch.A1 para.5, amended: SI 2013/521 Reg.37
Sch.A1 para.7, amended: SI 2013/521 Reg.37
Sch.A1 para.13, amended: SI 2013/521 Reg.37
Sch.A1 para.14A, added: SI 2013/521 Reg.37
Sch.A1 para.14B, added: SI 2013/521 Reg.37
Sch.A1 para.22A, added: SI 2013/521 Reg.37
Sch.A1 para.26A, added: SI 2013/521 Reg.37
Sch.A1 para.27, amended: SI 2013/521 Reg.37
Sch.A1 para.28, amended: SI 2013/521 Reg.37
Sch.A1 para.30A, added: SI 2013/521 Reg.37
Sch.A1 para.31A, added: SI 2013/521 Reg.37
Sch.A1 para.34A, added: SI 2013/521 Reg.37
Sch.A1 para.41, amended: SI 2013/521 Reg.37
Sch.A1 para.43, amended: SI 2013/521 Reg.37
Sch.A1 para.44, revoked: SI 2013/521 Reg.37

2818. Nationality, Immigration and Asylum Act 2002 (Juxtaposed Controls) Order 2003
Sch.2 para.5, amended: SI 2013/3032 Sch.2 para.2

2913. African Swine Fever (England) Order 2003
Art.12, amended: SI 2013/1506 Sch.5 para.4

2982. Companies (Forms) (Amendment) Regulations 2003
revoked: SI 2013/1947 Sch.2 Part 1

3041. Fruit Juices and Fruit Nectars (Wales) Regulations 2003
applied: SI 2013/2750 Reg.22
revoked: SI 2013/2750 Reg.20

3049. Merchant Shipping (Working Time Inland Waterways) Regulations 2003
applied: SI 2013/1893 Sch.2
Reg.19, amended: SI 2013/1956 Sch.1 para.4

3100. Registration of Establishments (Laying Hens) (England) Regulations 2003
Reg.4, amended: SI 2013/235 Sch.2 para.63

3138. A40 Trunk Road (Narberth Road and Fishguard Road, Haverfordwest, Pembrokeshire) (40 MPH Speed Limit) Order 2003
revoked: SI 2013/2507 Art.3

3146. Local Authorities (Capital Finance and Accounting) (England) Regulations 2003
Reg.1, amended: SI 2013/1751 Reg.3
Reg.13, amended: SI 2013/472 Art.4
Reg.14, amended: SI 2013/476 Reg.3
Reg.14, revoked (in part): SI 2013/476 Reg.3
Reg.15, revoked: SI 2013/476 Reg.3
Reg.16, revoked: SI 2013/476 Reg.3
Reg.16A, revoked: SI 2013/476 Reg.3
Reg.16B, revoked: SI 2013/476 Reg.3
Reg.17, revoked: SI 2013/476 Reg.3
Reg.18, revoked: SI 2013/476 Reg.3
Reg.19, revoked: SI 2013/476 Reg.3
Reg.23, amended: SI 2013/476 Reg.5
Reg.30A, amended: SI 2013/476 Reg.6
Sch.1, substituted: SI 2013/476 Sch.1
Sch.1 para.1, substituted: SI 2013/476 Sch.1
Sch.1 para.2, substituted: SI 2013/476 Sch.1
Sch.1 para.3, substituted: SI 2013/476 Sch.1
Sch.1 para.4, amended: SI 2013/1751 Reg.4
Sch.1 para.4, substituted: SI 2013/476 Sch.1
Sch.1 para.5, substituted: SI 2013/476 Sch.1
Sch.1 para.6, substituted: SI 2013/476 Sch.1
Sch.1 para.7, substituted: SI 2013/476 Sch.1
Sch.1 para.8, substituted: SI 2013/476 Sch.1

Sch.1 para.9, substituted: SI 2013/476 Sch.1
Sch.1 para.10, substituted: SI 2013/476 Sch.1
Sch.1 para.11, substituted: SI 2013/476 Sch.1
Sch.1 para.12, substituted: SI 2013/476 Sch.1
Sch.1 para.13, substituted: SI 2013/476 Sch.1

3226. Financial Collateral Arrangements (No.2) Regulations 2003

Reg.3, amended: SI 2013/3115 Sch.2 para.61
Reg.4, amended: SI 2013/600 Sch.2 para.4
Reg.5, revoked: SI 2013/600 Sch.2 para.4

3236. National Health Service (Pharmaceutical Services) (Amendment) (No.2) (Wales) Regulations 2003

revoked: SI 2013/898 Sch.8 para.12

3242. Water Environment (Water Framework Directive) (England and Wales) Regulations 2003

applied: SI 2013/1675 Reg.7
Reg.2, amended: SI 2013/755 Sch.4 para.174
Reg.3, amended: SI 2013/755 Sch.4 para.175
Reg.4, amended: SI 2013/755 Sch.4 para.176
Reg.5, amended: SI 2013/755 Sch.4 para.177
Reg.7, amended: SI 2013/755 Sch.4 para.178
Reg.8, amended: SI 2013/755 Sch.4 para.178
Reg.9, amended: SI 2013/755 Sch.4 para.178
Reg.10, amended: SI 2013/755 Sch.4 para.179
Reg.11, amended: SI 2013/755 Sch.4 para.180
Reg.12, amended: SI 2013/755 Sch.4 para.181
Reg.12, revoked (in part): SI 2013/755 Sch.4 para.181
Reg.13, amended: SI 2013/755 Sch.4 para.182
Reg.14, amended: SI 2013/755 Sch.4 para.182
Reg.15, amended: SI 2013/755 Sch.4 para.182
Reg.16, amended: SI 2013/755 Sch.4 para.183
Reg.17, amended: SI 2013/755 Sch.4 para.184
Reg.18, amended: SI 2013/755 Sch.4 para.185
Reg.19, amended: SI 2013/755 Sch.4 para.186
Reg.20, amended: SI 2013/755 Sch.4 para.187
Sch.2 Part 2 para.11, revoked: SI 2013/1675 Reg.19
Sch.2 Part 2 para.26, revoked: SI 2013/1675 Reg.19
Sch.2 Part 2 para.29, revoked: SI 2013/1675 Reg.19
Sch.2 Part 2 para.30, added: SI 2013/755 Sch.4 para.188
Sch.2 Part 2 para.31, added: SI 2013/755 Sch.4 para.188
Sch.2 Part 2 para.32, added: SI 2013/755 Sch.4 para.188
Sch.2 Part 2 para.33, added: SI 2013/1675 Reg.19

3245. Water Environment (Water Framework Directive) (Northumbria River Basin District) Regulations 2003

applied: SI 2013/1675 Reg.7

3273. African Swine Fever (Wales) Order 2003

Art.12, amended: SI 2013/1506 Sch.5 para.6

3284. Designation of Schools Having a Religious Character (Independent Schools) (England) (No.2) Order 2003

Sch.1, amended: SI 2013/2867 Sch.2

3319. Conduct of Employment Agencies and Employment Businesses Regulations 2003

Reg.25, amended: SI 2013/3115 Sch.2 para.62

3333. Extradition Act 2003 (Designation of Part 1 Territories) Order 2003

Art.2, amended: SI 2013/1583 Art.2

3334. Extradition Act 2003 (Designation of Part 2 Territories) Order 2003

Art.2, amended: SI 2013/1583 Art.3
Art.3, amended: SI 2013/1583 Art.3
Art.4, amended: SI 2013/1583 Art.3

3372. A483 Trunk Road (Newbridge By Pass, Wrexham County Borough) (Derestriction) Order 2003

varied: SI 2013/771 Art.8

2004

99. Water Environment (Water Framework Directive) (Solway Tweed River Basin District) Regulations 2004

applied: SI 2013/1675 Reg.7
Sch.2 Part 2 para.11, revoked: SI 2013/1675 Reg.19
Sch.2 Part 2 para.26, revoked: SI 2013/1675 Reg.19
Sch.2 Part 2 para.28, substituted: SI 2013/1675 Reg.19

121. Borough of Doncaster (Electoral Changes) Order 2004

revoked: SI 2013/2969 Art.4

219. Domiciliary Care Agencies (Wales) Regulations 2004

applied: SI 2013/3029 Sch.1 para.19, Sch.6 para.21, SI 2013/3035 Sch.1
Reg.2, amended: SI 2013/225 Reg.3
Reg.8, amended: SI 2013/225 Reg.3
Reg.9, amended: SI 2013/225 Reg.3
Reg.10, amended: SI 2013/225 Reg.3
Sch.2 para.6A, added: SI 2013/225 Reg.3
Sch.2 para.6B, added: SI 2013/225 Reg.3

291. National Health Service (General Medical Services Contracts) Regulations 2004

applied: SI 2013/363 Sch.1 para.3, Sch.1 para.21
Reg.2, amended: SI 2013/363 Reg.3
Reg.3, substituted: SI 2013/363 Reg.4
Reg.4, amended: SI 2013/363 Reg.5

Reg.5, amended: SI 2013/363 Reg.6
Reg.6, amended: SI 2013/363 Reg.7
Reg.6, applied: SI 2013/363 Sch.1 para.5, Sch.1 para.6
Reg.7, amended: SI 2013/363 Reg.8
Reg.9, amended: SI 2013/363 Reg.9
Reg.10, amended: SI 2013/363 Reg.10
Reg.14, amended: SI 2013/363 Reg.11
Reg.15, amended: SI 2013/363 Reg.12
Reg.17, amended: SI 2013/363 Reg.13
Reg.17, applied: SI 2013/363 Sch.1 para.8
Reg.17, revoked (in part): SI 2013/363 Reg.13
Reg.18, amended: SI 2013/363 Reg.14
Reg.20A, added: SI 2013/363 Reg.15
Reg.22, amended: SI 2013/363 Reg.16
Reg.22, applied: SI 2013/363 Sch.1 para.7
Reg.23, substituted: SI 2013/363 Reg.17
Reg.24, amended: SI 2013/363 Reg.18
Reg.26, amended: SI 2013/363 Reg.19
Reg.26A, revoked: SI 2013/363 Reg.20
Reg.26B, added: SI 2013/363 Reg.20
Reg.27, amended: SI 2013/363 Reg.21
Reg.31, amended: SI 2013/363 Reg.22
Reg.31, applied: SI 2013/363 Sch.1 para.8
Reg.32, revoked: SI 2013/363 Reg.23
Sch.2 para.2, amended: SI 2013/363 Reg.24
Sch.2 para.6, amended: SI 2013/363 Reg.24
Sch.3 para.1, amended: SI 2013/363 Reg.25
Sch.3 para.1, revoked (in part): SI 2013/363 Reg.25
Sch.3 para.2, amended: SI 2013/363 Reg.25
Sch.3 para.2, revoked (in part): SI 2013/363 Reg.25
Sch.3 para.3, amended: SI 2013/363 Reg.25
Sch.3 para.3, revoked (in part): SI 2013/363 Reg.25
Sch.3 para.4, amended: SI 2013/363 Reg.25
Sch.3 para.4, applied: SI 2013/363 Sch.1 para.8
Sch.3 para.5, revoked: SI 2013/363 Reg.25
Sch.3 para.6, amended: SI 2013/363 Reg.25
Sch.5 para.1, amended: SI 2013/363 Reg.26
Sch.6 Part 1 para.3, amended: SI 2013/363 Reg.27
Sch.6 Part 1 para.4, amended: SI 2013/363 Reg.27
Sch.6 Part 1 para.7, amended: SI 2013/363 Reg.27
Sch.6 Part 1 para.11, applied: SI 2013/363 Sch.1 para.9
Sch.6 Part 1 para.11A, amended: SI 2013/363 Reg.27
Sch.6 Part 1 para.12, amended: SI 2013/363 Reg.27
Sch.6 Part 1 para.13, amended: SI 2013/363 Reg.27
Sch.6 Part 2, applied: SI 2013/257 Reg.11, SI 2013/500 Reg.11
Sch.6 Part 2, amended: SI 2013/363 Reg.27
Sch.6 Part 2 para.14, amended: SI 2013/363 Reg.27
Sch.6 Part 2 para.15, amended: SI 2013/363 Reg.27
Sch.6 Part 2 para.16, amended: SI 2013/363 Reg.27
Sch.6 Part 2 para.16, applied: SI 2013/350 Reg.2
Sch.6 Part 2 para.17, amended: SI 2013/363 Reg.27
Sch.6 Part 2 para.19, amended: SI 2013/363 Reg.27
Sch.6 Part 2 para.20, amended: SI 2013/363 Reg.27
Sch.6 Part 2 para.21, amended: SI 2013/363 Reg.27
Sch.6 Part 2 para.22, amended: SI 2013/363 Reg.27
Sch.6 Part 2 para.23, amended: SI 2013/363 Reg.27
Sch.6 Part 2 para.24, amended: SI 2013/363 Reg.27
Sch.6 Part 2 para.25, amended: SI 2013/363 Reg.27
Sch.6 Part 2 para.26, amended: SI 2013/363 Reg.27
Sch.6 Part 2 para.27, amended: SI 2013/363 Reg.27
Sch.6 Part 2 para.28, amended: SI 2013/363 Reg.27
Sch.6 Part 2 para.29A, amended: SI 2013/363 Reg.27
Sch.6 Part 2 para.29B, amended: SI 2013/363 Reg.27
Sch.6 Part 2 para.29C, amended: SI 2013/363 Reg.27
Sch.6 Part 2 para.29D, amended: SI 2013/363 Reg.27
Sch.6 Part 2 para.29E, amended: SI 2013/363 Reg.27
Sch.6 Part 2 para.32, amended: SI 2013/363 Reg.27
Sch.6 Part 2 para.33, amended: SI 2013/363 Reg.27
Sch.6 Part 2 para.34, substituted: SI 2013/363 Reg.27
Sch.6 Part 2 para.35, substituted: SI 2013/363 Reg.27
Sch.6 Part 2 para.36, amended: SI 2013/363 Reg.27
Sch.6 Part 2 para.37, amended: SI 2013/363 Reg.27
Sch.6 Part 3 para.39, amended: SI 2013/363 Reg.27

Sch.6 Part 3 para.39, applied: SI 2013/349 Sch.6 para.3
Sch.6 Part 3 para.39A, amended: SI 2013/363 Reg.27
Sch.6 Part 3 para.39A, applied: SI 2013/349 Sch.6 para.3
Sch.6 Part 3 para.39B, amended: SI 2013/363 Reg.27
Sch.6 Part 3 para.40, amended: SI 2013/363 Reg.27
Sch.6 Part 3 para.41, amended: SI 2013/363 Reg.27
Sch.6 Part 3 para.42, amended: SI 2013/363 Reg.27
Sch.6 Part 3 para.42, referred to: SI 2013/349 Sch.6 para.3
Sch.6 Part 3 para.43, amended: SI 2013/363 Reg.27
Sch.6 Part 3 para.46, amended: SI 2013/363 Reg.27
Sch.6 Part 4, amended: SI 2013/363 Reg.27
Sch.6 Part 4 para.53, amended: SI 2013/363 Reg.27
Sch.6 Part 4 para.53, revoked (in part): SI 2013/363 Reg.27
Sch.6 Part 4 para.57, amended: SI 2013/363 Reg.27
Sch.6 Part 4 para.64, amended: SI 2013/363 Reg.27
Sch.6 Part 4 para.64, applied: SI 2013/363 Sch.1 para.10
Sch.6 Part 4 para.65, amended: SI 2013/363 Reg.27
Sch.6 Part 4 para.68, amended: SI 2013/363 Reg.27
Sch.6 Part 4 para.69, amended: SI 2013/363 Reg.27
Sch.6 Part 4 para.69, applied: SI 2013/363 Sch.1 para.11
Sch.6 Part 4 para.70, amended: SI 2013/363 Reg.27
Sch.6 Part 4 para.70, applied: SI 2013/363 Sch.1 para.12, Sch.1 para.13
Sch.6 Part 4 para.71, amended: SI 2013/363 Reg.27
Sch.6 Part 4 para.71, applied: SI 2013/363 Sch.1 para.13
Sch.6 Part 4 para.72, amended: SI 2013/363 Reg.27
Sch.6 Part 4 para.72, applied: SI 2013/363 Sch.1 para.13
Sch.6 Part 5, applied: SI 2013/363 Sch.1 para.14
Sch.6 Part 5, amended: SI 2013/363 Reg.27
Sch.6 Part 5 para.73, amended: SI 2013/363 Reg.27
Sch.6 Part 5 para.76, applied: SI 2013/363 Sch.1 para.15
Sch.6 Part 5 para.77, amended: SI 2013/363 Reg.27
Sch.6 Part 5 para.79, amended: SI 2013/363 Reg.27
Sch.6 Part 5 para.79, applied: SI 2013/363 Sch.1 para.14
Sch.6 Part 5 para.81, amended: SI 2013/363 Reg.27
Sch.6 Part 5 para.82, amended: SI 2013/363 Reg.27
Sch.6 Part 5 para.83, revoked: SI 2013/363 Reg.27
Sch.6 Part 5 para.84, amended: SI 2013/363 Reg.27
Sch.6 Part 5 para.85, amended: SI 2013/363 Reg.27
Sch.6 Part 5 para.86, amended: SI 2013/363 Reg.27
Sch.6 Part 5 para.87, amended: SI 2013/363 Reg.27
Sch.6 Part 5 para.87, revoked (in part): SI 2013/363 Reg.27
Sch.6 Part 5 para.88, amended: SI 2013/363 Reg.27
Sch.6 Part 5 para.89, amended: SI 2013/363 Reg.27
Sch.6 Part 5 para.91A, revoked: SI 2013/363 Reg.27
Sch.6 Part 5 para.91B, added: SI 2013/363 Reg.27
Sch.6 Part 6 para.92, referred to: SI 2013/363 Sch.1 para.16
Sch.6 Part 6 para.92, revoked (in part): SI 2013/363 Reg.27
Sch.6 Part 6 para.97, amended: SI 2013/363 Reg.27
Sch.6 Part 6 para.97, applied: SI 2013/363 Sch.1 para.17
Sch.6 Part 7, applied: SI 2013/363 Sch.1 para.18
Sch.6 Part 7 para.99, amended: SI 2013/363 Reg.27
Sch.6 Part 7 para.100, amended: SI 2013/363 Reg.27
Sch.6 Part 8, applied: SI 2013/363 Sch.1 para.19
Sch.6 Part 8, amended: SI 2013/363 Reg.27
Sch.6 Part 8 para.104, amended: SI 2013/363 Reg.27
Sch.6 Part 8 para.105, amended: SI 2013/363 Reg.27
Sch.6 Part 8 para.106, amended: SI 2013/363 Reg.27

Sch.6 Part 8 para.107, amended: SI 2013/363 Reg.27
Sch.6 Part 8 para.107A, amended: SI 2013/363 Reg.27
Sch.6 Part 8 para.108, amended: SI 2013/363 Reg.27
Sch.6 Part 8 para.109, amended: SI 2013/363 Reg.27
Sch.6 Part 8 para.110, amended: SI 2013/363 Reg.27
Sch.6 Part 8 para.111, amended: SI 2013/363 Reg.27
Sch.6 Part 8 para.112, amended: SI 2013/363 Reg.27
Sch.6 Part 8 para.113, amended: SI 2013/363 Reg.27
Sch.6 Part 8 para.114, amended: SI 2013/363 Reg.27
Sch.6 Part 8 para.114A, amended: SI 2013/363 Reg.27
Sch.6 Part 8 para.115, amended: SI 2013/363 Reg.27
Sch.6 Part 8 para.116, amended: SI 2013/363 Reg.27
Sch.6 Part 8 para.117, amended: SI 2013/363 Reg.27
Sch.6 Part 8 para.118, amended: SI 2013/363 Reg.27
Sch.6 Part 8 para.119, amended: SI 2013/363 Reg.27
Sch.6 Part 8 para.120, amended: SI 2013/363 Reg.27
Sch.6 Part 8 para.120, applied: SI 2013/363 Sch.1 para.20
Sch.6 Part 9, added: SI 2013/363 Reg.27
Sch.6 Part 9 para.121A, amended: SI 2013/363 Reg.27
Sch.6 Part 9 para.124, amended: SI 2013/363 Reg.27
Sch.6 Part 9 para.124, applied: SI 2013/335 Reg.26
Sch.6 Part 9 para.125, amended: SI 2013/363 Reg.27
Sch.6 Part 9 para.125, applied: SI 2013/363 Sch.1 para.9
Sch.7 para.1, revoked: SI 2013/363 Reg.23
Sch.7 para.2, revoked: SI 2013/363 Reg.23
Sch.7 para.3, revoked: SI 2013/363 Reg.23
Sch.7 para.4, revoked: SI 2013/363 Reg.23
Sch.7 para.5, revoked: SI 2013/363 Reg.23
Sch.7 para.6, revoked: SI 2013/363 Reg.23
Sch.7 para.7, revoked: SI 2013/363 Reg.23
Sch.10, referred to: SI 2013/363 Sch.1 para.15
Sch.10 para.18, amended: SI 2013/363 Reg.28
Sch.10 para.19, substituted: SI 2013/363 Reg.28
Sch.10 para.20, substituted: SI 2013/363 Reg.28
Sch.10 para.28, substituted: SI 2013/363 Reg.28

293. European Parliamentary Elections Regulations 2004

Appendix 3., added: SI 2013/2876 Sch.4
Reg.2, amended: SI 2013/2876 Reg.6
Reg.2, revoked (in part): SI 2013/2876 Reg.6
Reg.5, amended: SI 2013/2876 Reg.7
Reg.6, amended: SI 2013/2876 Reg.8
Reg.15, amended: SI 2013/2876 Reg.9
Reg.15A, added: SI 2013/2876 Reg.10
Reg.25, revoked (in part): SI 2013/2876 Reg.11
Reg.28, amended: SI 2013/2876 Reg.12
Reg.68, amended: SI 2013/2876 Reg.13
Reg.69, amended: SI 2013/2876 Reg.14
Reg.70, amended: SI 2013/2876 Reg.15
Reg.114, amended: SI 2013/2876 Reg.16
Reg.125A, added: SI 2013/2876 Reg.17
Sch.A1, revoked: SI 2013/2876 Reg.18
Sch.1 Part 2 para.9, substituted: SI 2013/2876 Reg.19
Sch.1 Part 2 para.9A, added: SI 2013/2876 Reg.20
Sch.1 Part 2 para.13, amended: SI 2013/2876 Reg.21
Sch.1 Part 3 para.32, amended: SI 2013/2876 Reg.22
Sch.1 Part 3 para.34, added: SI 2013/2876 Reg.23
Sch.1 Part 3 para.36, amended: SI 2013/2876 Reg.24
Sch.1 Part 3 para.41, amended: SI 2013/2876 Reg.25
Sch.1 Part 3 para.51, amended: SI 2013/2876 Reg.26
Sch.1 Part 3 para.59, amended: SI 2013/2876 Reg.27
Sch.1 Part 3 para.60A, added: SI 2013/2876 Reg.28
Sch.1 Part 4 para.61, amended: SI 2013/2876 Reg.29
Sch.1 Part 6 para.69, amended: SI 2013/2876 Reg.30
Sch.1 Part 7, amended: SI 2013/2876 Reg.31, Sch.1, Sch.2
Sch.2 Part 1 para.1, amended: SI 2013/2876 Reg.32
Sch.2 Part 1 para.2, amended: SI 2013/2876 Reg.33
Sch.2 Part 1 para.5, amended: SI 2013/2876 Reg.34
Sch.2 Part 2 para.23, amended: SI 2013/388 Sch.1 para.34, SI 2013/591 Sch.1 para.30
Sch.2 Part 2 para.25, amended: SI 2013/2876 Reg.35

Sch.2 Part 2 para.25A, added: SI 2013/2876 Reg.36
Sch.2 Part 2 para.26, amended: SI 2013/2876 Reg.37
Sch.2 Part 2 para.27, amended: SI 2013/2876 Reg.38
Sch.2 Part 2 para.31, varied: SI 2013/1599 Reg.4
Sch.2 Part 2 para.31A, added: SI 2013/2876 Reg.39
Sch.2 Part 2 para.31B, added: SI 2013/2876 Reg.39
Sch.2 Part 2 para.32, amended: SI 2013/2876 Reg.40
Sch.2 Part 3 para.26, revoked: SI 2013/2876 Reg.41
Sch.2 Part 3 para.27, revoked: SI 2013/2876 Reg.41
Sch.2 Part 3 para.28, revoked: SI 2013/2876 Reg.41
Sch.2 Part 3 para.29, revoked: SI 2013/2876 Reg.41
Sch.2 Part 3 para.30, revoked: SI 2013/2876 Reg.41
Sch.2 Part 3 para.31, revoked: SI 2013/2876 Reg.41
Sch.2 Part 3 para.32, revoked: SI 2013/2876 Reg.41
Sch.2 Part 3 para.33, revoked: SI 2013/2876 Reg.41
Sch.2 Part 3 para.34, revoked: SI 2013/2876 Reg.41
Sch.2 Part 3 para.35, revoked: SI 2013/2876 Reg.41
Sch.2 Part 3 para.36, revoked: SI 2013/2876 Reg.41
Sch.2 Part 3 para.37, revoked: SI 2013/2876 Reg.41
Sch.2 Part 3 para.38, revoked: SI 2013/2876 Reg.41
Sch.2 Part 3 para.39, revoked: SI 2013/2876 Reg.41
Sch.2 Part 3 para.40, revoked: SI 2013/2876 Reg.41
Sch.2 Part 3 para.41, revoked: SI 2013/2876 Reg.41
Sch.2 Part 3 para.42, revoked: SI 2013/2876 Reg.41
Sch.2 Part 3 para.43, revoked: SI 2013/2876 Reg.41
Sch.2 Part 3 para.44, revoked: SI 2013/2876 Reg.41
Sch.2 Part 3 para.45, revoked: SI 2013/2876 Reg.41
Sch.2 Part 3 para.46, revoked: SI 2013/2876 Reg.41
Sch.2 Part 3 para.47, revoked: SI 2013/2876 Reg.41
Sch.2 Part 3 para.48, revoked: SI 2013/2876 Reg.41
Sch.2 Part 3 para.49, revoked: SI 2013/2876 Reg.41
Sch.2 Part 3 para.50, revoked: SI 2013/2876 Reg.41
Sch.2 Part 3 para.51, revoked: SI 2013/2876 Reg.41
Sch.2 Part 3 para.52, revoked: SI 2013/2876 Reg.41
Sch.2 Part 4 para.47, substituted: SI 2013/2876 Reg.42
Sch.2 Part 4 para.54A, added: SI 2013/2876 Reg.43
Sch.2 Part 4 para.57, revoked (in part): SI 2013/2876 Reg.44
Sch.2 Part 4 para.60, amended: SI 2013/2876 Reg.45
Sch.2 Part 4 para.60, revoked (in part): SI 2013/2876 Reg.45
Sch.2 Part 4 para.62, revoked: SI 2013/2876 Reg.46
Sch.2 Part 4 para.63, amended: SI 2013/2876 Reg.47
Sch.2 Part 4 para.64, revoked: SI 2013/2876 Reg.48
Sch.2 Part 4 para.66, amended: SI 2013/2876 Reg.49
Sch.2 Part 4 para.67, amended: SI 2013/2876 Reg.50
Sch.2 Part 4 para.69, amended: SI 2013/2876 Reg.51
Sch.2 Part 4 para.69, revoked (in part): SI 2013/2876 Reg.51
Sch.2 Part 4 para.70, amended: SI 2013/2876 Reg.52
Sch.2 Part 4 para.71, added: SI 2013/2876 Reg.53
Sch.2 Part 5, amended: SI 2013/2876 Reg.54, Sch.3
Sch.2 Part 5, substituted: SI 2013/2876 Reg.54
Sch.3 Part 1 para.8, substituted: SI 2013/2876 Reg.56
Sch.3 Part 1 para.11, amended: SI 2013/2876 Reg.57
Sch.3 Part 1 para.24, substituted: SI 2013/2876 Reg.58
Sch.3 Part 1 para.28, substituted: SI 2013/2876 Reg.59
Sch.3 Part 1 para.29, substituted: SI 2013/2876 Reg.59

Sch.3 Part 2 para.7, substituted: SI 2013/2876 Reg.60
Sch.3 Part 2 para.10, amended: SI 2013/2876 Reg.61
Sch.3 Part 2 para.23, substituted: SI 2013/2876 Reg.62
Sch.3 Part 2 para.27, substituted: SI 2013/2876 Reg.63
Sch.3 Part 2 para.28, substituted: SI 2013/2876 Reg.63
Sch.4 Part 2 para.4, amended: SI 2013/2876 Reg.65

301. Driving Licences (Exchangeable Licences) Order 2004

Art.2, amended: SI 2013/22 Art.4
Art.3, amended: SI 2013/22 Art.4
Sch.1, amended: SI 2013/22 Art.4

353. Insurers (Reorganisation and Winding Up) Regulations 2004

Reg.2, amended: SI 2013/472 Art.4, Sch.2 para.88
Reg.9, amended: SI 2013/472 Sch.2 para.88
Reg.10, amended: SI 2013/472 Sch.2 para.88
Reg.12, amended: SI 2013/472 Sch.2 para.88
Reg.16, amended: SI 2013/472 Sch.2 para.88
Reg.50, amended: SI 2013/472 Sch.2 para.88

354. Designation of Schools Having a Religious Character (Independent Schools) (England) (No.2) Order 2004

Sch.1, amended: SI 2013/2162 Sch.2

400. High Court Enforcement Officers Regulations 2004

Reg.5, amended: SI 2013/1881 Sch.1 para.25

454. Financial Services and Markets Act 2000 (Transitional Provisions) (Complaints Relating to General Insurance and Mortgages) Order 2004

Art.3, amended: SI 2013/472 Sch.2 para.89
Art.9, amended: SI 2013/472 Sch.2 para.89
Art.12, amended: SI 2013/472 Sch.2 para.89

478. National Health Service (General Medical Services Contracts) (Wales) Regulations 2004

referred to: SI 2013/235 Sch.3 para.8
Reg.2, amended: SI 2013/235 Sch.2 para.64, SI 2013/898 Sch.7 para.4
Reg.4, amended: SI 2013/235 Sch.2 para.64
Reg.5, amended: SI 2013/235 Sch.2 para.64
Reg.24, applied: SI 2013/898 Sch.6 para.9
Sch.5, applied: SI 2013/898 Sch.6 para.9
Sch.6 Part 2 para.22, amended: SI 2013/235 Sch.2 para.64
Sch.6 Part 3 para.39, applied: SI 2013/898 Sch.6 para.5
Sch.6 Part 3 para.42, applied: SI 2013/898 Sch.6 para.5
Sch.6 Part 3 para.47, amended: SI 2013/898 Sch.7 para.4
Sch.6 Part 3 para.48, amended: SI 2013/898 Sch.7 para.4
Sch.6 Part 3 para.49, amended: SI 2013/898 Sch.7 para.4
Sch.6 Part 4 para.67, amended: SI 2013/235 Sch.2 para.64
Sch.6 Part 5A para.89A, applied: SI 2013/898 Sch.6 para.10
Sch.6 Part 6, applied: SI 2013/898 Sch.6 para.10
Sch.6 Part 6 para.95, amended: SI 2013/235 Sch.2 para.64
Sch.6 Part 6 para.95, applied: SI 2013/235 Sch.3 para.9, SI 2013/898 Sch.6 para.10
Sch.6 Part 8 para.111, amended: SI 2013/235 Sch.2 para.64

572. Street Works (Inspection Fees) (England) (Amendment) Regulations 2004

applied: SI 2013/2398 Sch.1

574. Housing Benefit and Council Tax Benefit (Supply of Information) Amendment Regulations 2004

applied: SI 2013/1781 Sch.1

585. National Health Service (Performers Lists) Regulations 2004

revoked: SI 2013/335 Reg.46
Reg.18A, applied: SI 2013/335 Sch.2 para.10
Reg.19, applied: SI 2013/335 Sch.2 para.10

627. National Health Service (Personal Medical Services Agreements) Regulations 2004

applied: SI 2013/363 Sch.2 para.3, Sch.2 para.19
Reg.2, amended: SI 2013/363 Reg.31
Reg.3, substituted: SI 2013/363 Reg.32
Reg.5, amended: SI 2013/363 Reg.33
Reg.6, amended: SI 2013/363 Reg.34
Reg.6, applied: SI 2013/363 Sch.2 para.5, Sch.2 para.6
Reg.7, amended: SI 2013/363 Reg.35
Reg.8, amended: SI 2013/363 Reg.36
Reg.9, amended: SI 2013/363 Reg.37
Reg.11, revoked (in part): SI 2013/363 Reg.38
Reg.11A, added: SI 2013/363 Reg.39
Reg.13, amended: SI 2013/363 Reg.40
Reg.13, applied: SI 2013/363 Sch.2 para.7
Reg.14, substituted: SI 2013/363 Reg.41
Reg.15, amended: SI 2013/363 Reg.42
Reg.16, amended: SI 2013/363 Reg.43
Reg.16, applied: SI 2013/363 Sch.2 para.8
Reg.16, revoked (in part): SI 2013/363 Reg.43
Reg.18, substituted: SI 2013/363 Reg.44
Reg.18A, revoked: SI 2013/363 Reg.45
Reg.18B, added: SI 2013/363 Reg.45
Reg.19, amended: SI 2013/363 Reg.46
Reg.19, applied: SI 2013/363 Sch.2 para.9

Reg.21, revoked: SI 2013/363 Reg.47
Sch.3, amended: SI 2013/363 Reg.48
Sch.4 para.1, amended: SI 2013/363 Reg.49
Sch.4 para.1, applied: SI 2013/363 Sch.2 para.8
Sch.4 para.1, revoked (in part): SI 2013/363 Reg.49
Sch.4 para.2, revoked: SI 2013/363 Reg.49
Sch.4 para.3, amended: SI 2013/363 Reg.49
Sch.5 Part 1 para.4, amended: SI 2013/363 Reg.50
Sch.5 Part 1 para.5, amended: SI 2013/363 Reg.50
Sch.5 Part 1 para.9, applied: SI 2013/363 Sch.2 para.11
Sch.5 Part 1 para.9A, amended: SI 2013/363 Reg.50
Sch.5 Part 1 para.10, amended: SI 2013/363 Reg.50
Sch.5 Part 1 para.11, amended: SI 2013/363 Reg.50
Sch.5 Part 2, applied: SI 2013/257 Reg.11, SI 2013/500 Reg.11
Sch.5 Part 2 para.12, revoked (in part): SI 2013/363 Reg.50
Sch.5 Part 2 para.13, amended: SI 2013/363 Reg.50
Sch.5 Part 2 para.14, amended: SI 2013/363 Reg.50
Sch.5 Part 2 para.15, amended: SI 2013/363 Reg.50
Sch.5 Part 2 para.15, applied: SI 2013/350 Reg.2
Sch.5 Part 2 para.16, amended: SI 2013/363 Reg.50
Sch.5 Part 2 para.18, amended: SI 2013/363 Reg.50
Sch.5 Part 2 para.19, amended: SI 2013/363 Reg.50
Sch.5 Part 2 para.20, amended: SI 2013/363 Reg.50
Sch.5 Part 2 para.21, amended: SI 2013/363 Reg.50
Sch.5 Part 2 para.22, amended: SI 2013/363 Reg.50
Sch.5 Part 2 para.23, amended: SI 2013/363 Reg.50
Sch.5 Part 2 para.24, amended: SI 2013/363 Reg.50
Sch.5 Part 2 para.25, amended: SI 2013/363 Reg.50
Sch.5 Part 2 para.26, amended: SI 2013/363 Reg.50
Sch.5 Part 2 para.27, amended: SI 2013/363 Reg.50
Sch.5 Part 2 para.28A, amended: SI 2013/363 Reg.50
Sch.5 Part 2 para.28B, amended: SI 2013/363 Reg.50
Sch.5 Part 2 para.28C, amended: SI 2013/363 Reg.50
Sch.5 Part 2 para.28D, amended: SI 2013/363 Reg.50
Sch.5 Part 2 para.28E, amended: SI 2013/363 Reg.50
Sch.5 Part 2 para.31, amended: SI 2013/363 Reg.50
Sch.5 Part 2 para.32, amended: SI 2013/363 Reg.50
Sch.5 Part 2 para.33, substituted: SI 2013/363 Reg.50
Sch.5 Part 2 para.34, substituted: SI 2013/363 Reg.50
Sch.5 Part 2 para.35, amended: SI 2013/363 Reg.50
Sch.5 Part 2 para.36, amended: SI 2013/363 Reg.50
Sch.5 Part 3 para.38, amended: SI 2013/363 Reg.50
Sch.5 Part 3 para.38A, amended: SI 2013/363 Reg.50
Sch.5 Part 3 para.38B, amended: SI 2013/363 Reg.50
Sch.5 Part 3 para.39, amended: SI 2013/363 Reg.50
Sch.5 Part 3 para.40, amended: SI 2013/363 Reg.50
Sch.5 Part 3 para.41, amended: SI 2013/363 Reg.50
Sch.5 Part 3 para.42, amended: SI 2013/363 Reg.50
Sch.5 Part 3 para.44, amended: SI 2013/363 Reg.50
Sch.5 Part 4, amended: SI 2013/363 Reg.50
Sch.5 Part 4 para.53, amended: SI 2013/363 Reg.50
Sch.5 Part 4 para.53, revoked (in part): SI 2013/363 Reg.50
Sch.5 Part 4 para.57, amended: SI 2013/363 Reg.50
Sch.5 Part 4 para.63, amended: SI 2013/363 Reg.50
Sch.5 Part 4 para.63, applied: SI 2013/363 Sch.2 para.10
Sch.5 Part 4 para.65, amended: SI 2013/363 Reg.50
Sch.5 Part 4 para.68, amended: SI 2013/363 Reg.50
Sch.5 Part 4 para.69, amended: SI 2013/363 Reg.50

Sch.5 Part 4 para.69, applied: SI 2013/363 Sch.2 para.12
Sch.5 Part 5, applied: SI 2013/363 Sch.2 para.13
Sch.5 Part 5, amended: SI 2013/363 Reg.50
Sch.5 Part 5 para.70, amended: SI 2013/363 Reg.50
Sch.5 Part 5 para.72, applied: SI 2013/363 Sch.2 para.14
Sch.5 Part 5 para.73, amended: SI 2013/363 Reg.50
Sch.5 Part 5 para.75, amended: SI 2013/363 Reg.50
Sch.5 Part 5 para.75, applied: SI 2013/363 Sch.2 para.13
Sch.5 Part 5 para.77, amended: SI 2013/363 Reg.50
Sch.5 Part 5 para.78, amended: SI 2013/363 Reg.50
Sch.5 Part 5 para.79, revoked: SI 2013/363 Reg.50
Sch.5 Part 5 para.80, amended: SI 2013/363 Reg.50
Sch.5 Part 5 para.81, amended: SI 2013/363 Reg.50
Sch.5 Part 5 para.81, revoked (in part): SI 2013/363 Reg.50
Sch.5 Part 5 para.82, amended: SI 2013/363 Reg.50
Sch.5 Part 5 para.83, amended: SI 2013/363 Reg.50
Sch.5 Part 5 para.85, amended: SI 2013/363 Reg.50
Sch.5 Part 5 para.85A, revoked: SI 2013/363 Reg.50
Sch.5 Part 5 para.85B, added: SI 2013/363 Reg.50
Sch.5 Part 6 para.86, applied: SI 2013/363 Sch.2 para.15
Sch.5 Part 6 para.86, revoked (in part): SI 2013/363 Reg.50
Sch.5 Part 6 para.91, amended: SI 2013/363 Reg.50
Sch.5 Part 6 para.91, applied: SI 2013/363 Sch.2 para.16
Sch.5 Part 7, applied: SI 2013/363 Sch.2 para.17
Sch.5 Part 7 para.93, amended: SI 2013/363 Reg.50
Sch.5 Part 7 para.94, amended: SI 2013/363 Reg.50
Sch.5 Part 8, applied: SI 2013/363 Sch.2 para.18
Sch.5 Part 8 para.98, amended: SI 2013/363 Reg.50
Sch.5 Part 8 para.99, amended: SI 2013/363 Reg.50
Sch.5 Part 8 para.99A, amended: SI 2013/363 Reg.50
Sch.5 Part 8 para.100, amended: SI 2013/363 Reg.50
Sch.5 Part 8 para.101, amended: SI 2013/363 Reg.50
Sch.5 Part 8 para.104, amended: SI 2013/363 Reg.50
Sch.5 Part 8 para.105, amended: SI 2013/363 Reg.50
Sch.5 Part 8 para.106, amended: SI 2013/363 Reg.50
Sch.5 Part 8 para.106A, amended: SI 2013/363 Reg.50
Sch.5 Part 8 para.107, amended: SI 2013/363 Reg.50
Sch.5 Part 8 para.108, amended: SI 2013/363 Reg.50
Sch.5 Part 8 para.109, amended: SI 2013/363 Reg.50
Sch.5 Part 8 para.110, amended: SI 2013/363 Reg.50
Sch.5 Part 8 para.111, amended: SI 2013/363 Reg.50
Sch.5 Part 9 para.112A, substituted: SI 2013/363 Reg.50
Sch.5 Part 9 para.112B, added: SI 2013/363 Reg.50
Sch.5 Part 9 para.115, amended: SI 2013/363 Reg.50
Sch.5 Part 9 para.115, applied: SI 2013/363 Sch.2 para.11
Sch.5 Part 9 para.117, amended: SI 2013/363 Reg.50
Sch.6 para.1, revoked: SI 2013/363 Reg.47
Sch.6 para.2, revoked: SI 2013/363 Reg.47
Sch.6 para.3, revoked: SI 2013/363 Reg.47
Sch.6 para.4, revoked: SI 2013/363 Reg.47
Sch.6 para.5, revoked: SI 2013/363 Reg.47
Sch.6 para.6, revoked: SI 2013/363 Reg.47
Sch.7 para.1, revoked: SI 2013/363 Reg.51
Sch.7 para.2, revoked: SI 2013/363 Reg.51
Sch.7 para.3, revoked: SI 2013/363 Reg.51
Sch.7 para.4, revoked: SI 2013/363 Reg.51
Sch.7 para.5, revoked: SI 2013/363 Reg.51
Sch.7 para.6, revoked: SI 2013/363 Reg.51
Sch.7 para.7, revoked: SI 2013/363 Reg.51
Sch.7 para.8, revoked: SI 2013/363 Reg.51
Sch.7 para.9, revoked: SI 2013/363 Reg.51
Sch.7 para.10, revoked: SI 2013/363 Reg.51
Sch.7 para.11, revoked: SI 2013/363 Reg.51
Sch.7 para.12, revoked: SI 2013/363 Reg.51
Sch.7 para.13, revoked: SI 2013/363 Reg.51
Sch.7 para.14, revoked: SI 2013/363 Reg.51
Sch.10, applied: SI 2013/363 Sch.2 para.14
Sch.10 para.16, substituted: SI 2013/363 Reg.52

Sch.10 para.17, revoked: SI 2013/363 Reg.52
Sch.10 para.18, revoked: SI 2013/363 Reg.52
Sch.10 para.26, substituted: SI 2013/363 Reg.52
Sch.10 para.27, revoked: SI 2013/363 Reg.52

629. National Health Service (General Medical Services Contracts) (Prescription of Drugs etc.) Regulations 2004
Sch.2, added: SI 2013/2194 Reg.2
Sch.2, amended: SI 2013/363 Reg.54, SI 2013/2194 Reg.2
Sch.2, referred to: SI 2013/349 Sch.4 para.5, Sch.4 para.8, Sch.6 para.2, Sch.6 para.3, Sch.6 para.5, Sch.7 para.3, Sch.7 para.6

672. Independent Police Complaints Commission (Forces Maintained Otherwise than by Police Authorities) Order 2004
applied: SI 2013/1779 Art.2
revoked: SI 2013/1779 Art.2

692. Communications (Television Licensing) Regulations 2004
Reg.10, revoked: SI 2013/1854 Art.2
Reg.11, revoked: SI 2013/1854 Art.2

693. Enterprise Act 2002 (Part 9 Restrictions on Disclosure of Information) (Specification) Order 2004
Sch.1, amended: SI 2013/1478 Sch.5 para.16

701. Water Industry (Prescribed Conditions) (Undertakers Wholly or Mainly in Wales) Regulations 2004
Reg.3, amended: SI 2013/755 Sch.5 para.24

747. Children (Leaving Care) Social Security Benefits (Scotland) Regulations 2004
Reg.2, amended: SI 2013/1465 Sch.1 para.20

752. Employment Act 2002 (Dispute Resolution) Regulations 2004
Reg.9, see *Abercrombie v Aga Rangemaster Ltd* [2013] I.C.R. 213 (EAT), Silber, J.

753. ACAS Arbitration Scheme (Great Britain) Order 2004
Sch.1 Part VII para.26, amended: SI 2013/1956 Sch.1 para.5

754. Settlement Agreements (Description of Person) Order 2004
amended: SI 2013/1956 Sch.1 para.10
Art.1, amended: SI 2013/1956 Sch.1 para.10

756. Civil Aviation (Working Time) Regulations 2004
Reg.4, see *British Airways Plc v Williams* [2013] 1 All E.R. 443 (SC), Lord Hope, J.S.C. (Deputy President)
Reg.7, see *British Airways Plc v Williams* [2013] 1 All E.R. 443 (SC), Lord Hope, J.S.C. (Deputy President)

758. Pensions Increase (Review) Order 2004
applied: SI 2013/604 Sch.1

906. Primary Medical Services (Sale of Goodwill and Restrictions on Sub-contracting) Regulations 2004
Reg.2, amended: SI 2013/363 Reg.55
Reg.2A, added: SI 2013/363 Reg.55

915. Railway Safety Accreditation Scheme Regulations 2004
Sch.1 para.1, amended: SI 2013/903 Reg.3
Sch.1 para.11, amended: SI 2013/903 Reg.3

935. Enterprise Act 2002 (Part 8) (Designation of the Financial Services Authority as a Designated Enforcer) Order 2004
revoked: SI 2013/478 Art.4

994. Good Laboratory Practice (Codification Amendments Etc.) Regulations 2004
Reg.4, revoked: SI 2013/1478 Sch.5 para.15

1007. Police Act 1997 (Criminal Records) (Fees) Order 2004
Art.2, amended: SI 2013/1196 Art.2

1018. National Health Service (Pharmaceutical Services etc.), (Repeatable Prescriptions) (Amendment) (Wales) Regulations 2004
revoked: SI 2013/898 Sch.8 para.13

1020. National Health Service (Performers Lists) (Wales) Regulations 2004
Reg.2, amended: SI 2013/235 Sch.2 para.65
Reg.4, amended: SI 2013/235 Sch.2 para.65
Reg.11, amended: SI 2013/235 Sch.2 para.65
Reg.16, amended: SI 2013/235 Sch.2 para.65
Reg.20, amended: SI 2013/235 Sch.2 para.65

1021. National Health Service (Pharmaceutical Services) (Amendment) (Wales) Regulations 2004
revoked: SI 2013/898 Sch.8 para.14

1022. National Health Service (General Medical Services Contracts) (Prescription of Drugs Etc.) (Wales) Regulations 2004
Sch.2, amended: SI 2013/683 Reg.2
Sch.2, referred to: SI 2013/898 Sch.4 para.5, Sch.6 para.4

1031. Medicines for Human Use (Clinical Trials) Regulations 2004
Reg.2, amended: SI 2013/235 Sch.2 para.66
Reg.17, amended: SI 2013/532 Reg.58
Reg.24, amended: SI 2013/532 Reg.58
Reg.24, applied: SI 2013/532 Reg.19
Reg.27, applied: SI 2013/532 Sch.1 para.2
Reg.28, applied: SI 2013/532 Reg.33
Reg.31, applied: SI 2013/532 Sch.1 para.2
Reg.38, amended: SI 2013/532 Reg.58
Reg.44, amended: SI 2013/532 Reg.58
Reg.44, applied: SI 2013/532 Reg.18
Sch.1, applied: SI 2013/235 Sch.3 para.15
Sch.2 para.3, amended: SI 2013/235 Sch.2 para.66
Sch.3 Part 2 para.10, applied: SI 2013/532 Reg.19

Sch.3 Part 2 para.11, applied: SI 2013/532 Reg.19, Sch.7 para.10
Sch.5 para.3, referred to: SI 2013/532 Reg.40
Sch.5 para.4, referred to: SI 2013/532 Reg.40

1034. Crime (International Co-operation) Act 2003 (Designation of Prosecuting Authorities) Order 2004
Art.2, amended: SI 2013/472 Sch.2 para.90

1045. Credit Institutions (Reorganisation and Winding up) Regulations 2004
applied: SI 2013/472 Sch.2 para.92
Pt 3., see *Joint Administrators of Heritable Bank Plc v Winding Up Board of Landsbanki Islands HF* [2013] UKSC 13, [2013] 1 W.L.R. 725 (SC), Lord Hope, J.S.C. (Deputy President)
Pt 4., see *Joint Administrators of Heritable Bank Plc v Winding Up Board of Landsbanki Islands HF* [2013] UKSC 13, [2013] 1 W.L.R. 725 (SC), Lord Hope, J.S.C. (Deputy President)
Reg.2, amended: SI 2013/472 Art.4, Sch.2 para.91, SI 2013/3115 Sch.2 para.63
Reg.5, see *Joint Administrators of Heritable Bank Plc v Winding Up Board of Landsbanki Islands HF* [2013] UKSC 13, [2013] 1 W.L.R. 725 (SC), Lord Hope, J.S.C. (Deputy President)
Reg.5, amended: SI 2013/3115 Sch.2 para.63
Reg.8, amended: SI 2013/472 Sch.2 para.91
Reg.8, applied: SI 2013/472 Sch.2 para.92
Reg.9, amended: SI 2013/472 Sch.2 para.91
Reg.9, applied: SI 2013/472 Sch.2 para.92
Reg.10, amended: SI 2013/472 Sch.2 para.91
Reg.11, amended: SI 2013/472 Art.4, Sch.2 para.91
Reg.11, applied: SI 2013/472 Sch.2 para.92
Reg.14, amended: SI 2013/472 Sch.2 para.91
Reg.14, applied: SI 2013/472 Sch.2 para.92
Reg.18, amended: SI 2013/472 Sch.2 para.91
Reg.28, see *Joint Administrators of Heritable Bank Plc v Winding Up Board of Landsbanki Islands HF* [2013] UKSC 13, [2013] 1 W.L.R. 725 (SC), Lord Hope, J.S.C. (Deputy President)
Reg.38, amended: SI 2013/472 Sch.2 para.91

1215. A40 Trunk Road (Meidrim Junction, Carmarthenshire) (De-Restriction) Order 2004
varied: SI 2013/1620 Art.6

1239. Crime Prevention (Designated Areas) Order 2004
revoked: SI 2013/1760 Sch.1

1267. European Parliamentary Elections (Northern Ireland) Regulations 2004
Reg.2, amended: SI 2013/2893 Reg.2
Reg.5, amended: SI 2013/2893 Reg.3
Reg.29, amended: SI 2013/2893 Reg.4
Reg.76H, amended: SI 2013/2893 Reg.5
Reg.76I, substituted: SI 2013/2893 Reg.6
Reg.115A, added: SI 2013/2893 Reg.7
Sch.1 Part II para.7, substituted: SI 2013/2893 Reg.8
Sch.1 Part II para.7A, added: SI 2013/2893 Reg.9
Sch.1 Part II para.11, amended: SI 2013/2893 Reg.10
Sch.1 Part III para.31, amended: SI 2013/3114 Reg.2
Sch.1 Part III para.39, amended: SI 2013/2893 Reg.11
Sch.1 Part III para.52, amended: SI 2013/2893 Reg.12
Sch.1 Part III para.54, amended: SI 2013/2893 Reg.13
Sch.1 Part III para.55, amended: SI 2013/2893 Reg.14
Sch.1 Part III para.59, amended: SI 2013/2893 Reg.15
Sch.1 Part III para.63, amended: SI 2013/2893 Reg.16
Sch.1 Part IV para.64, amended: SI 2013/2893 Reg.17
Sch.1 Part IV para.65, amended: SI 2013/2893 Reg.18
Sch.1 Part VI para.72, amended: SI 2013/2893 Reg.19
Sch.2 Part I para.2A, added: SI 2013/2893 Reg.20
Sch.2 Part I para.2B, added: SI 2013/2893 Reg.20
Sch.2 Part I para.4, amended: SI 2013/2893 Reg.21, SI 2013/3021 Art.34
Sch.2 Part I para.6, amended: SI 2013/2893 Reg.22
Sch.6 para.14A, added: SI 2013/3114 Reg.3
Sch.6 para.14B, added: SI 2013/3114 Reg.3
Sch.6 para.17A, added: SI 2013/3114 Reg.3

1396. Meat Products (Wales) Regulations 2004
Reg.6, referred to: SI 2013/1984 Sch.3 para.8
Sch.2, referred to: SI 2013/1984 Sch.3 para.8

1404. Plant Health (Export Certification) (England) Order 2004
Sch.3, substituted: SI 2013/572 Art.2
Sch.4, substituted: SI 2013/572 Art.2

1411. A40 Trunk Road (Banc-y-felin Junction, Carmarthenshire) (De&ndash Restriction) Order 2004
varied: SI 2013/1620 Art.6

1412. Isles of Scilly (Functions) (Review and Scrutiny of Health Services) Order 2004
revoked: SI 2013/643 Art.3

1427. Local Authority (Overview and Scrutiny Committees Health Scrutiny Functions) Amendment Regulations 2004
revoked: SI 2013/218 Reg.33

1432. Registration of Establishments (Laying Hens) (Wales) Regulations 2004

Reg.5, amended: SI 2013/235 Sch.2 para.67

1450. Child Trust Funds Regulations 2004

Reg.1, revoked (in part): SI 2013/263 Reg.2
Reg.2, amended: SI 2013/263 Reg.2, SI 2013/472 Sch.2 para.93, SI 2013/1744 Reg.3, Reg.4, SI 2013/1773 Sch.2 para.18
Reg.9, amended: SI 2013/263 Reg.2
Reg.11, amended: SI 2013/472 Sch.2 para.93
Reg.12, amended: SI 2013/472 Art.4, SI 2013/1744 Reg.5
Reg.14, amended: SI 2013/472 Sch.2 para.93, SI 2013/1765 Art.8
Reg.14, revoked (in part): SI 2013/263 Reg.2
Reg.19, substituted: SI 2013/1744 Reg.6
Reg.20, amended: SI 2013/1744 Reg.7
Reg.21, amended: SI 2013/263 Reg.2, SI 2013/1744 Reg.8
Reg.30, revoked: SI 2013/263 Reg.2
Reg.31, amended: SI 2013/1744 Reg.9
Reg.33A, amended: SI 2013/1465 Sch.1 para.21
Sch.1 para.2, amended: SI 2013/472 Art.4, SI 2013/1744 Reg.10

1483. Consumer Credit (Early Settlement) Regulations 2004

Reg.1, amended: SI 2013/1881 Art.24

1484. Consumer Credit (Advertisements) Regulations 2004

revoked (in part): SI 2013/1881 Art.21
Reg.1, amended: SI 2013/472 Art.4
Reg.4, see *Motor Depot Ltd v Kingston upon Hull City Council* [2012] EWHC 3257 (Admin), (2013) 177 J.P. 41 (DC), Elias, L.J.
Sch.2, see *Motor Depot Ltd v Kingston upon Hull City Council* [2012] EWHC 3257 (Admin), (2013) 177 J.P. 41 (DC), Elias, L.J.

1490. Landfill Allowances Scheme (Wales) Regulations 2004

Reg.5, amended: SI 2013/755 Sch.5 para.25

1497. Trade Marks Act 1994 (Isle of Man) (Amendment) Order 2004

revoked: SI 2013/2601 Art.3

1633. Environmental Assessment of Plans and Programmes Regulations 2004

see *Cogent Land LLP v Rochford DC* [2012] EWHC 2542 (Admin), [2013] 1 P. & C.R. 2 (QBD (Admin)), Singh, J.; see *R. (on the application of Wakil (t/a Orya Textiles)) v Hammersmith and Fulham LBC* [2012] EWHC 1411 (QB), [2013] Env. L.R. 3 (QBD (Admin)), Wilkie, J.
Reg.4, amended: SI 2013/755 Sch.4 para.189
Reg.9, see *R. (on the application of Wakil (t/a Orya Textiles)) v Hammersmith and Fulham LBC* [2012] EWHC 1411 (QB), [2013] Env. L.R. 3 (QBD (Admin)), Wilkie, J.

1652. Broadcasting (Original Productions) Order 2004

Art.5, amended: SI 2013/2217 Reg.6
Sch.1, revoked: SI 2013/2217 Reg.6

1656. Environmental Assessment of Plans and Programmes (Wales) Regulations 2004

Reg.4, amended: SI 2013/755 Sch.5 para.26

1684. Plant Health (Export Certification) (Forestry) (Great Britain) Order 2004

Art.2, amended: SI 2013/755 Sch.4 para.191
Art.3, amended: SI 2013/755 Sch.4 para.192
Art.4, amended: SI 2013/755 Sch.4 para.192

1713. Fishing Vessels (Working Time Sea-fishermen) Regulations 2004

applied: SI 2013/1893 Sch.2
Reg.20, amended: SI 2013/1956 Sch.1 para.6

1746. Offshore Installations (Safety Zones) (No.3) Order 2004

Sch.1, amended: SI 2013/1758 Art.3

1761. Nursing and Midwifery Council (Fitness to Practise) Rules Order of Council 2004

see *Perry v Nursing and Midwifery Council* [2013] EWCA Civ 145, [2013] 1 W.L.R. 3423 (CA (Civ Div)), Hughes, L.J.

1764. Nursing and Midwifery Council (Midwives) Rules Order of Council 2004

applied: SI 2013/235 Sch.3 para.6

1766. European Nursing and Midwifery Qualifications Designation Order of Council 2004

Art.5, amended: SI 2013/3036 Reg.6
Art.10, amended: SI 2013/3036 Reg.6

1769. Justification of Practices Involving Ionising Radiation Regulations 2004

Reg.18, amended: SI 2013/235 Sch.2 para.68, SI 2013/1821 Art.32
Reg.22, amended: SI 2013/235 Sch.2 para.68, SI 2013/1821 Art.32

1771. Health Act 1999 (Consequential Amendments) (Nursing and Midwifery) Order 2004

Sch.1 Part 2 para.17, revoked (in part): SSI 2013/50 Sch.5

1794. Education (National Curriculum) (Attainment Targets and Programmes of Study in Design and Technology in respect of the First, Second and Third Key Stages) (England) (No.2) Order 2004

revoked: SI 2013/2232 Sch.1

1800. Education (National Curriculum) (Attainment Targets and Programmes of Study in Science in respect of the First, Second Third and Fourth Key Stages) (England) (No.2) Order 2004

applied: SI 2013/2232 Art.6
revoked: SI 2013/2232 Sch.1

1822. Water Industry (Scotland) Act 2002 (Consequential Modifications) Order 2004

Sch.1 Part 1 para.5, revoked: 2013 c.32 Sch.12 para.30

1861. Employment Tribunals (Constitution and Rules of Procedure) Regulations 2004

applied: SI 2013/1237 Reg.15
revoked: SI 2013/1237 Reg.2
see *Duffy v George* [2013] EWCA Civ 908, [2013] I.C.R. 1229 (CA (Civ Div)), Mummery, L.J.
Appendix 1., amended: SI 2013/472 Art.4, Sch.2 para.94
Reg.2, amended: SI 2013/1956 Sch.1 para.7
Reg.4, applied: SI 2013/2191 Reg.5, SI 2013/2192 Reg.17
Reg.6, applied: SI 2013/2191 Reg.4
Reg.8, applied: SI 2013/2191 Reg.4, Reg.6, Reg.8, SI 2013/2192 Reg.4
Sch.1 para.7, applied: SI 2013/1237 Reg.15
Sch.1 para.8, amended: SI 2013/1956 Sch.1 para.7
Sch.1 para.25, see *Fox v Bassetlaw DC* [2013] Eq. L.R. 219 (EAT), Judge Peter Clark
Sch.1 para.40, see *Sud v Ealing LBC* [2013] EWCA Civ 949, [2013] 5 Costs L.R. 777 (CA (Civ Div)), Maurice Kay, L.J. (VP, CA Civ)
Sch.2 para.9, revoked (in part): SI 2013/2042 Sch.1 para.56
Sch.3, applied: SI 2013/1237 Reg.15
Sch.4, applied: SI 2013/1237 Reg.15, SI 2013/1506 Reg.27
Sch.5, applied: SI 2013/1237 Reg.15

1862. Financial Conglomerates and Other Financial Groups Regulations 2004

referred to: SI 2013/472 Sch.2 para.96
Reg.1, amended: SI 2013/472 Sch.2 para.95, SI 2013/1162 Reg.3, SI 2013/1773 Sch.2 para.17, SI 2013/3115 Sch.2 para.64
Reg.2, amended: SI 2013/472 Sch.2 para.95
Reg.3, amended: SI 2013/472 Art.4, Sch.2 para.95
Reg.4, amended: SI 2013/472 Sch.2 para.95
Reg.5, amended: SI 2013/472 Art.4, Sch.2 para.95
Reg.6, amended: SI 2013/472 Sch.2 para.95
Reg.7, amended: SI 2013/1773 Sch.2 para.17, SI 2013/3115 Sch.2 para.64
Reg.8, amended: SI 2013/472 Sch.2 para.95, SI 2013/1162 Reg.4
Reg.9, amended: SI 2013/472 Art.4, Sch.2 para.95, SI 2013/1162 Reg.5, SI 2013/1773 Sch.2 para.17, SI 2013/3115 Sch.2 para.64
Reg.10, amended: SI 2013/472 Sch.2 para.95, SI 2013/1162 Reg.6, SI 2013/1773 Sch.2 para.17, SI 2013/3115 Sch.2 para.64
Reg.12, amended: SI 2013/472 Sch.2 para.95
Reg.13, revoked: SI 2013/3115 Sch.3
Reg.15, amended: SI 2013/472 Art.4, Sch.2 para.95, SI 2013/3115 Sch.2 para.64

1958. Single European Sky (National Supervisory Authority) Regulations 2004

revoked: SI 2013/2620 Reg.1

2095. Financial Services (Distance Marketing) Regulations 2004

Reg.2, amended: SI 2013/472 Sch.2 para.97, SI 2013/1881 Sch.1 para.26
Reg.11, amended: SI 2013/1881 Sch.1 para.26, SI 2013/3134 Sch.4 para.4

2204. Town and Country Planning (Local Development) (England) Regulations 2004

see *R. (on the application of Wakil (t/a Orya Textiles)) v Hammersmith and Fulham LBC* [2012] EWHC 1411 (QB), [2013] Env. L.R. 3 (QBD (Admin)), Wilkie, J.
Reg.6, see *R. (on the application of Wakil (t/a Orya Textiles)) v Hammersmith and Fulham LBC* [2012] EWHC 1411 (QB), [2013] Env. L.R. 3 (QBD (Admin)), Wilkie, J.
Reg.7, see *R. (on the application of Wakil (t/a Orya Textiles)) v Hammersmith and Fulham LBC* [2012] EWHC 1411 (QB), [2013] Env. L.R. 3 (QBD (Admin)), Wilkie, J.

2333. ACAS (Flexible Working) Arbitration Scheme (Great Britain) Order 2004

Sch.1 Part VII para.26, amended: SI 2013/1956 Sch.1 para.8

2409. Football Spectators (Prescription) Order 2004

Art.3, amended: SI 2013/1709 Art.2
Art.4, amended: SI 2013/1709 Art.2
Art.4, revoked (in part): SI 2013/1709 Art.2

2443. Business Improvement Districts (England) Regulations 2004

Reg.1, amended: SI 2013/2265 Reg.3, Reg.4, Reg.5
Reg.1A, added: SI 2013/2265 Reg.3
Reg.3, amended: SI 2013/2265 Reg.5
Reg.4, amended: SI 2013/2265 Reg.5
Reg.5, amended: SI 2013/2265 Reg.5
Sch.1 para.1, amended: SI 2013/2265 Reg.5
Sch.2 Part 002 para.3, amended: SI 2013/2265 Reg.5
Sch.3 Part 1 para.1, amended: SI 2013/2265 Reg.6
Sch.4 para.9, amended: SI 2013/2265 Reg.7
Sch.4 para.13, amended: SI 2013/2265 Reg.7
Sch.4 para.14, amended: SI 2013/2265 Reg.7
Sch.5 Part 001 para.1, added: SI 2013/2265 Sch.1
Sch.5 Part 002 para.2, added: SI 2013/2265 Sch.1
Sch.5 Part 002 para.3, added: SI 2013/2265 Sch.1
Sch.5 Part 002 para.4, added: SI 2013/2265 Sch.1
Sch.5 Part 002 para.5, added: SI 2013/2265 Sch.1
Sch.5 Part 002 para.6, added: SI 2013/2265 Sch.1
Sch.5 Part 002 para.7, added: SI 2013/2265 Sch.1
Sch.5 Part 002 para.8, added: SI 2013/2265 Sch.1

Sch.5 Part 002 para.9, added: SI 2013/2265 Sch.1
Sch.5 Part 002 para.10, added: SI 2013/2265 Sch.1
Sch.5 Part 002 para.11, added: SI 2013/2265 Sch.1
Sch.5 Part 002 para.12, added: SI 2013/2265 Sch.1
Sch.5 Part 002 para.13, added: SI 2013/2265 Sch.1
Sch.5 Part 002 para.14, added: SI 2013/2265 Sch.1
Sch.5 Part 002 para.15, added: SI 2013/2265 Sch.1
Sch.5 Part 002 para.16, added: SI 2013/2265 Sch.1
Sch.5 Part 002 para.17, added: SI 2013/2265 Sch.1
Sch.5 Part 002 para.18, added: SI 2013/2265 Sch.1
Sch.5 Part 002 para.19, added: SI 2013/2265 Sch.1
Sch.5 Part 002 para.20, added: SI 2013/2265 Sch.1
Sch.5 Part 002 para.21, added: SI 2013/2265 Sch.1
Sch.5 Part 002 para.22, added: SI 2013/2265 Sch.1
Sch.5 Part 002 para.23, added: SI 2013/2265 Sch.1
Sch.5 Part 002 para.24, added: SI 2013/2265 Sch.1

2608. General Medical Council (Fitness to Practise) Rules Order of Council 2004

Sch.1, added: SI 2013/815 Sch.1
Sch.1, amended: SI 2013/815 Sch.1
Sch.1, revoked: SI 2013/815 Sch.1
Sch.1, substituted: SI 2013/815 Sch.1
Sch.1, see *R. (on the application of D) v General Medical Council* [2013] EWHC 2839 (Admin), (2013) 134 B.M.L.R. 118 (QBD (Admin)), Haddon-Cave, J.

2611. General Medical Council (Constitution of Panels and Investigation Committee) Rules Order of Council 2004

Sch.1, amended: SI 2013/815 Sch.1
Sch.1, substituted: SI 2013/815 Sch.1

2615. Financial Services and Markets Act 2000 (TransitionalProvisions) (Mortgages) Order 2004

Art.1, amended: SI 2013/472 Art.4
Art.2, amended: SI 2013/472 Art.4
Sch.1 para.2, amended: SI 2013/472 Art.4

2668. Renewable Energy Zone (Designation of Area) Order 2004

revoked: SI 2013/3161 Art.1

2682. Public Service Vehicles (Traffic Regulation Conditions) (England and Wales) Regulations 2004

Reg.6, amended: SI 2013/1644 Sch.4
Reg.7, amended: SI 2013/1644 Sch.4
Reg.8, amended: SI 2013/1644 Sch.4
Reg.9, amended: SI 2013/1644 Sch.4

2695. Disqualification from Caring for Children (Wales) Regulations 2004

Sch.1 Part I para.10, amended: SI 2013/1465 Sch.1 para.22
Sch.1 Part I para.20A, added: SI 2013/1465 Sch.1 para.22
Sch.1 Part II para.22, amended: SI 2013/1465 Sch.1 para.22
Sch.1 Part II para.23A, added: SI 2013/1465 Sch.1 para.22

2737. Financial Services and Markets Act 2000 (Regulated Activities)(Amendment)(No.2) Order 2004

Art.4, amended: SI 2013/472 Art.4

2738. Financial Services and Markets Act 2000 (Stakeholder Products) Regulations 2004

Reg.2, amended: SI 2013/472 Art.4, Sch.2 para.98, SI 2013/1388 Reg.12
Reg.9, amended: SI 2013/1388 Reg.12

2783. Education (National Curriculum) (Key Stage 1 Assessment Arrangements) (England) Order 2004

Art.1, amended: SI 2013/1513 Art.3
Art.3, amended: SI 2013/1513 Art.3
Art.4, amended: SI 2013/1513 Art.3
Art.5A, amended: SI 2013/1513 Art.3
Art.6B, added: SI 2013/1513 Art.3

2876. A55 Trunk Road (Penmaenmawr &mdash Conwy Morfa, Conwy) (Derestriction) Order 2004

disapplied: SI 2013/729 Art.9
varied: SI 2013/195 Art.11, SI 2013/333 Art.14, SI 2013/692 Art.10, SI 2013/729 Art.9, SI 2013/3257 Art.11

3096. Landlord and Tenant (Notice of Rent) (England) Regulations 2004

Sch.1, amended: SI 2013/1036 Sch.2 para.29

3098. Leasehold Valuation Tribunals (Procedure) (Amendment) (England) Regulations 2004

revoked: SI 2013/1036 Sch.2 para.28

3120. Non-Contentious Probate Fees Order 2004

Art.5, revoked: SI 2013/2302 Art.3
Sch.1, amended: SI 2013/1408 Art.3
Sch.1A para.1, amended: SI 2013/388 Sch.1 para.35, SI 2013/534 Sch.1 para.14, SI 2013/591 Sch.1 para.31
Sch.1A para.1, substituted: SI 2013/2302 Sch.1
Sch.1A para.2, substituted: SI 2013/2302 Sch.1
Sch.1A para.3, substituted: SI 2013/2302 Sch.1
Sch.1A para.4, substituted: SI 2013/2302 Sch.1
Sch.1A para.5, substituted: SI 2013/2302 Sch.1
Sch.1A para.6, substituted: SI 2013/2302 Sch.1
Sch.1A para.7, substituted: SI 2013/2302 Sch.1
Sch.1A para.8, substituted: SI 2013/2302 Sch.1
Sch.1A para.9, substituted: SI 2013/2302 Sch.1
Sch.1A para.10, substituted: SI 2013/2302 Sch.1
Sch.1A para.11, substituted: SI 2013/2302 Sch.1
Sch.1A para.12, substituted: SI 2013/2302 Sch.1
Sch.1A para.13, substituted: SI 2013/2302 Sch.1
Sch.1A para.14, substituted: SI 2013/2302 Sch.1
Sch.1A para.15, substituted: SI 2013/2302 Sch.1
Sch.1A para.16, substituted: SI 2013/2302 Sch.1
Sch.1A para.17, substituted: SI 2013/2302 Sch.1
Sch.1A para.18, substituted: SI 2013/2302 Sch.1
Sch.1A para.19, substituted: SI 2013/2302 Sch.1

Sch.1A para.20, substituted: SI 2013/2302 Sch.1

3200. Building Societies Act 1986 (Modification of the Lending Limit and Funding Limit Calculations) Order 2004

Art.2, amended: SI 2013/3115 Sch.2 para.65

3212. Landfill Allowances and Trading Scheme (England) Regulations 2004

referred to: SI 2013/141 Reg.8
revoked: SI 2013/141 Reg.7

3213. Plant Health (Forestry) (Phytophthora ramorum) (Great Britain) Order 2004

Art.2, amended: SI 2013/755 Sch.4 para.194
Art.3, amended: SI 2013/755 Sch.4 para.195
Art.4, amended: SI 2013/755 Sch.4 para.195
Art.5, amended: SI 2013/755 Sch.4 para.196
Art.6, amended: SI 2013/755 Sch.4 para.197
Art.8, amended: SI 2013/755 Sch.4 para.198
Art.10, amended: SI 2013/755 Sch.4 para.199
Art.13, amended: SI 2013/755 Sch.4 para.200

3256. Loan Relationships and Derivative Contracts (Disregard and Bringing into Account of Profits and Losses) Regulations 2004

Reg.2, amended: SI 2013/2781 Reg.2, SI 2013/3209 Reg.10
Reg.3, amended: SI 2013/2781 Reg.2, SI 2013/3209 Reg.10
Reg.4, amended: SI 2013/2781 Reg.2, SI 2013/3209 Reg.10
Reg.6, amended: SI 2013/3209 Reg.10

3279. General Food Regulations 2004

Reg.2, amended: SI 2013/3007 Reg.2, SSI 2013/333 Reg.2
Reg.3, revoked (in part): SI 2013/2996 Sch.9
Reg.4, revoked (in part): SI 2013/2996 Sch.9
Reg.5, revoked (in part): SI 2013/2996 Sch.9
Reg.6, revoked (in part): SI 2013/2996 Sch.9
Reg.6A, revoked (in part): SI 2013/2996 Sch.9
Reg.7, revoked (in part): SI 2013/2996 Sch.9

3351. Financial Services and Markets Act 2000 (Transitional Provisions) (General Insurance Intermediaries) Order 2004

Art.1, amended: SI 2013/472 Art.4
Art.2, amended: SI 2013/472 Art.4
Sch.1 para.2, amended: SI 2013/472 Art.4

3391. Environmental Information Regulations 2004

applied: SI 2013/971 Reg.39
see *R. (on the application of Evans) v Attorney General* [2013] EWHC 1960 (Admin), [2013] 3 W.L.R. 1631 (DC), Lord Judge, L.C.J.
Reg.18, see *R. (on the application of Evans) v Attorney General* [2013] EWHC 1960 (Admin), [2013] 3 W.L.R. 1631 (DC), Lord Judge, L.C.J.

3426. Information and Consultation of Employees Regulations 2004

applied: SI 2013/1893 Sch.2
Reg.25, applied: SI 2013/1773 Reg.37
Reg.40, amended: SI 2013/1956 Sch.1 para.9

2005

7. Asylum Seekers (Reception Conditions) Regulations 2005

Reg.6, see *EU (Afghanistan) v Secretary of State for the Home Department* [2013] EWCA Civ 32, [2013] Imm. A.R. 496 (CA (Civ Div)), Maurice Kay, L.J. (VP, CA Civ); see *KA (Afghanistan) v Secretary of State for the Home Department* [2012] EWCA Civ 1014, [2013] 1 W.L.R. 615 (CA (Civ Div)), Maurice Kay, L.J.; see *SHL (Tracing Obligation/Trafficking: Afghanistan), Re* [2013] UKUT 312 (IAC), [2013] Imm. A.R. 875 (UT (IAC)), McCloskey, J.

37. Supply of Extended Warranties on Domestic Electrical Goods Order 2005

Art.2, amended: SI 2013/3134 Sch.4 para.5

42. Licensing Act 2003 (Premises licences and club premises certificates) Regulations 2005

Sch.4, amended: SI 2013/432 Sch.1
Sch.4B, amended: SI 2013/432 Sch.2
Sch.10, amended: SI 2013/432 Sch.3

50. Blood Safety and Quality Regulations 2005

Reg.1, amended: SI 2013/235 Sch.2 para.77

52. Education (Student Support) Regulations 2005

Reg.13, applied: SI 2013/3029 Sch.11 para.3, SI 2013/3035 Sch.1

67. Trunk Road (A48/A40) (Carmarthen, Dyfed) (De-restriction) Order 1983 (Variation) Order 2005

varied: SI 2013/1620 Art.6

205. Town and Country Planning (Timetable for Decisions) (England) Order 2005

Art.2, amended: SI 2013/2146 Sch.1 para.12

206. Town and Country Planning (Temporary Stop Notice)(England) Regulations 2005

revoked: SI 2013/830 Reg.2

230. Asylum and Immigration Tribunal (Procedure) Rules 2005

r.17, see *EG (UT Rule 17: Withdrawal: Rule 24: Scope: Ethiopia), Re* [2013] UKUT 143 (IAC), [2013] Imm. A.R. 670 (UT (IAC)), Judge Eshun

232. Export Control (Iraq and Ivory Coast) Order 2005

revoked: SI 2013/3182 Sch.1

251. Health Service Commissioner for England (Special Health Authorities) Order 2005

Sch.1, amended: SI 2013/235 Sch.1 para.2, Sch.2 para.78

253. Ivory Coast (United Nations Sanctions) Order 2005

Art.2, amended: SI 2013/472 Art.4

255. Pensions (Northern Ireland) Order 2005

Art.34, see *Pensions Regulator v Desmond* [2013] NICA 62 (CA (NI)), Morgan, L.C.J

Art.91, see *Pensions Regulator v Desmond* [2013] NICA 62 (CA (NI)), Morgan, L.C.J

Art.97, see *Pensions Regulator v Desmond* [2013] NICA 62 (CA (NI)), Morgan, L.C.J

Sch.3, amended: SI 2013/472 Sch.2 para.101

Sch.7, amended: SI 2013/472 Sch.2 para.101

263. End-of-Life Vehicles (Producer Responsibility) Regulations 2005

Reg.24, amended: SI 2013/755 Sch.4 para.201

265. European Communities (Jurisdiction and Judgments in Matrimonial and Parental Responsibility Matters) Regulations 2005

Reg.4, revoked: 2013 c.22 Sch.10 para.99

277. Pension Protection Fund (Partially Guaranteed Schemes) (Modification) Regulations 2005

Reg.3, amended: SI 2013/627 Reg.8

Reg.8, amended: SI 2013/627 Reg.8

Reg.10, amended: SI 2013/627 Reg.8

368. Accounts and Audit (Wales) Regulations 2005

Reg.7, amended: SI 2013/217 Reg.2

Reg.9, amended: SI 2013/1466 Sch.1 para.7

Reg.10, amended: SI 2013/1466 Sch.1 para.7

Reg.11, amended: SI 2013/1466 Sch.1 para.7

Reg.12, amended: SI 2013/1466 Sch.1 para.7

Reg.13, amended: SI 2013/1466 Sch.1 para.7

Reg.14, amended: SI 2013/1466 Sch.1 para.7

Reg.15, amended: SI 2013/1466 Sch.1 para.7

Reg.16, amended: SI 2013/1466 Sch.1 para.7

Reg.17, amended: SI 2013/1466 Sch.1 para.7

Reg.18, amended: SI 2013/1466 Sch.1 para.7

Reg.19, amended: SI 2013/1466 Sch.1 para.7

Reg.20, amended: SI 2013/1466 Sch.1 para.7

382. Investment Recommendation (Media) Regulations 2005

Reg.9, amended: SI 2013/472 Sch.2 para.102

384. Criminal Procedure Rules 2005

r.67.2, see *R. v Mian (Yousaf)* [2012] EWCA Crim 792, [2013] 1 W.L.R. 772 (CA (Crim Div)), Rix, L.J.

389. Adoption Agencies Regulations 2005

Part 4, applied: SI 2013/985 Reg.11

Reg.2, amended: SI 2013/985 Reg.3

Reg.19A, added: SI 2013/985 Reg.4

Reg.21, substituted: SI 2013/985 Reg.5

Reg.22, substituted: SI 2013/985 Reg.5

Reg.23, substituted: SI 2013/985 Reg.5

Reg.24, substituted: SI 2013/985 Reg.5

Reg.25, substituted: SI 2013/985 Reg.5

Reg.26, substituted: SI 2013/985 Reg.5

Reg.27, substituted: SI 2013/985 Reg.5

Reg.28, substituted: SI 2013/985 Reg.5

Reg.29, substituted: SI 2013/985 Reg.5

Reg.30, substituted: SI 2013/985 Reg.5

Reg.30A, substituted: SI 2013/985 Reg.5

Reg.30B, substituted: SI 2013/985 Reg.5

Reg.30C, substituted: SI 2013/985 Reg.5

Reg.30D, substituted: SI 2013/985 Reg.5

Reg.30E, substituted: SI 2013/985 Reg.5

Reg.30F, substituted: SI 2013/985 Reg.5

Reg.30G, substituted: SI 2013/985 Reg.5

Reg.30H, substituted: SI 2013/985 Reg.5

Reg.32, amended: SI 2013/985 Reg.6

Reg.35, amended: SI 2013/235 Sch.2 para.79

Reg.42, amended: SI 2013/985 Reg.7

Sch.3 Part 1 para.1, amended: SI 2013/985 Reg.8

Sch.3 Part 1 para.2, amended: SI 2013/985 Reg.8

Sch.3 Part 1 para.2, substituted: SI 2013/985 Reg.8

Sch.3 Part 1 para.3, amended: SI 2013/985 Reg.8

Sch.3 Part 1 para.3, substituted: SI 2013/985 Reg.8

Sch.3 Part 1 para.4, amended: SI 2013/985 Reg.8

Sch.3 Part 1 para.5, amended: SI 2013/985 Reg.8

Sch.3 Part 1 para.6, amended: SI 2013/985 Reg.8

Sch.3 Part 1 para.7, amended: SI 2013/985 Reg.8

Sch.3 Part 1 para.7, substituted: SI 2013/985 Reg.8

Sch.3 Part 1 para.8, amended: SI 2013/985 Reg.8

Sch.3 Part 1 para.8, substituted: SI 2013/985 Reg.8

Sch.3 Part 1 para.9, amended: SI 2013/985 Reg.8

Sch.3 Part 1 para.10, amended: SI 2013/985 Reg.8

Sch.3 Part 1 para.10, revoked: SI 2013/985 Reg.8

Sch.3 Part 1 para.11, amended: SI 2013/985 Reg.8

Sch.4 Part 1 para.1, substituted: SI 2013/985 Reg.9

Sch.4 Part 1 para.2, substituted: SI 2013/985 Reg.9

Sch.4 Part 1 para.3, substituted: SI 2013/985 Reg.9

Sch.4 Part 1 para.4, substituted: SI 2013/985 Reg.9

Sch.4 Part 1 para.5, substituted: SI 2013/985 Reg.9

Sch.4 Part 1 para.6, substituted: SI 2013/985 Reg.9

Sch.4 Part 1 para.7, substituted: SI 2013/985 Reg.9

Sch.4 Part 1 para.8, substituted: SI 2013/985 Reg.9

Sch.4 Part 1 para.9, substituted: SI 2013/985 Reg.9

Sch.4 Part 1 para.10, substituted: SI 2013/985 Reg.9

Sch.4 Part 1 para.11, substituted: SI 2013/985 Reg.9

Sch.4 Part 1 para.12, substituted: SI 2013/985 Reg.9

Sch.4 Part 1 para.13, substituted: SI 2013/985 Reg.9

Sch.4 Part 1 para.14, substituted: SI 2013/985 Reg.9

Sch.4 Part 1 para.15, substituted: SI 2013/985 Reg.9

Sch.4 Part 1 para.16, substituted: SI 2013/985 Reg.9
Sch.4 Part 1 para.17, substituted: SI 2013/985 Reg.9
Sch.4 Part 1 para.18, substituted: SI 2013/985 Reg.9
Sch.4 Part 1 para.19, substituted: SI 2013/985 Reg.9
Sch.4 Part 1 para.20, substituted: SI 2013/985 Reg.9
Sch.4 Part 1 para.21, substituted: SI 2013/985 Reg.9
Sch.4 Part 1 para.22, substituted: SI 2013/985 Reg.9
Sch.4 Part 1 para.23, substituted: SI 2013/985 Reg.9
Sch.4 Part 1 para.24, substituted: SI 2013/985 Reg.9
Sch.4 Part 1 para.25, substituted: SI 2013/985 Reg.9
Sch.4 Part 1 para.26, substituted: SI 2013/985 Reg.9
Sch.4 Part 1 para.27, substituted: SI 2013/985 Reg.9
Sch.4 Part 1 para.28, substituted: SI 2013/985 Reg.9
Sch.4 Part 1 para.29, substituted: SI 2013/985 Reg.9
Sch.4 Part 1 para.30, substituted: SI 2013/985 Reg.9
Sch.4 Part 2 para.1, substituted: SI 2013/985 Reg.9
Sch.4 Part 2 para.2, substituted: SI 2013/985 Reg.9
Sch.4 Part 2 para.3, substituted: SI 2013/985 Reg.9
Sch.4 Part 2 para.4, substituted: SI 2013/985 Reg.9
Sch.4 Part 2 para.5, substituted: SI 2013/985 Reg.9
Sch.4 Part 2 para.6, substituted: SI 2013/985 Reg.9
Sch.4 Part 2 para.7, substituted: SI 2013/985 Reg.9
Sch.4 Part 2 para.8, substituted: SI 2013/985 Reg.9
Sch.4 Part 3 para.1, substituted: SI 2013/985 Reg.9
Sch.4 Part 3 para.2, substituted: SI 2013/985 Reg.9
Sch.4 Part 3 para.3, substituted: SI 2013/985 Reg.9
Sch.4 Part 3 para.4, substituted: SI 2013/985 Reg.9
Sch.4 Part 3 para.5, substituted: SI 2013/985 Reg.9
Sch.4 Part 3 para.6, substituted: SI 2013/985 Reg.9
Sch.4 Part 3 para.7, substituted: SI 2013/985 Reg.9
Sch.4 Part 3 para.8, substituted: SI 2013/985 Reg.9
Sch.4 Part 3 para.9, substituted: SI 2013/985 Reg.9
Sch.4 Part 3 para.10, substituted: SI 2013/985 Reg.9
Sch.4 Part 3 para.11, substituted: SI 2013/985 Reg.9
Sch.4 Part 3 para.12, substituted: SI 2013/985 Reg.9
Sch.4 Part 3 para.13, substituted: SI 2013/985 Reg.9
Sch.4 Part 3 para.14, substituted: SI 2013/985 Reg.9
Sch.4 Part 3 para.15, substituted: SI 2013/985 Reg.9
Sch.4 Part 3 para.16, substituted: SI 2013/985 Reg.9
Sch.4 Part 3 para.17, substituted: SI 2013/985 Reg.9
Sch.4 Part 3 para.18, substituted: SI 2013/985 Reg.9
Sch.4 Part 3 para.19, substituted: SI 2013/985 Reg.9
Sch.4 Part 3 para.20, substituted: SI 2013/985 Reg.9
Sch.4 Part 3 para.21, substituted: SI 2013/985 Reg.9

390. Tractor etc (EC Type-Approval) Regulations 2005

Reg.2, amended: SI 2013/3171 Reg.8

392. Adoptions with a Foreign Element Regulations 2005

Reg.2, amended: SI 2013/985 Sch.1 para.2
Reg.4, amended: SI 2013/985 Sch.1 para.2
Reg.5, amended: SI 2013/235 Sch.2 para.80
Reg.13, amended: SI 2013/985 Sch.1 para.2
Reg.14, amended: SI 2013/985 Sch.1 para.2
Reg.15, amended: SI 2013/985 Sch.1 para.2
Reg.15, applied: SI 2013/985 Reg.10
Reg.16, amended: SI 2013/985 Sch.1 para.2
Reg.17, amended: SI 2013/985 Sch.1 para.2
Reg.18, amended: SI 2013/985 Sch.1 para.2
Reg.19, amended: SI 2013/985 Sch.1 para.2
Reg.20, amended: SI 2013/985 Sch.1 para.2
Reg.22, amended: SI 2013/235 Sch.2 para.80

425. Crime (International Co-operation) Act 2003 (Exercise of Functions) Order 2005

revoked: SI 2013/2733 Art.12

437. Armed Forces Early Departure Payments Scheme Order 2005

Art.4, amended: SI 2013/2914 Art.3
Art.14, amended: SI 2013/2914 Art.4

453. Social Security (Deferral of Retirement Pensions) Regulations 2005

Reg.3, amended: SI 2013/630 Reg.34

454. Social Security (Graduated Retirement Benefit) Regulations 2005

Sch.1, applied: SI 2013/3029 Sch.1 para.16, Sch.5 para.27, SI 2013/3035 Sch.1
Sch.1 Part 1 para.1, varied: SI 2013/574 Art.11
Sch.1 Part 1 para.2, varied: SI 2013/574 Art.11
Sch.1 Part 1 para.3, varied: SI 2013/574 Art.11
Sch.1 Part 1 para.4, varied: SI 2013/574 Art.11

Sch.1 Part 1 para.5, varied: SI 2013/574 Art.11
Sch.1 Part 1 para.6, varied: SI 2013/574 Art.11
Sch.1 Part 1 para.7, varied: SI 2013/574 Art.11
Sch.1 Part 1 para.8, varied: SI 2013/574 Art.11
Sch.1 Part 1 para.9, varied: SI 2013/574 Art.11
Sch.1 Part 1 para.10, varied: SI 2013/574 Art.11
Sch.1 Part 2A para.20A, varied: SI 2013/574 Art.11
Sch.1 Part 2A para.20B, varied: SI 2013/574 Art.11
Sch.1 Part 2A para.20C, varied: SI 2013/574 Art.11
Sch.1 Part 2A para.20D, varied: SI 2013/574 Art.11
Sch.1 Part 2 para.11, varied: SI 2013/574 Art.11
Sch.1 Part 2 para.12, varied: SI 2013/574 Art.11
Sch.1 Part 2 para.13, varied: SI 2013/574 Art.11
Sch.1 Part 2 para.14, varied: SI 2013/574 Art.11
Sch.1 Part 2 para.15, varied: SI 2013/574 Art.11
Sch.1 Part 2 para.16, varied: SI 2013/574 Art.11
Sch.1 Part 2 para.17, varied: SI 2013/574 Art.11
Sch.1 Part 2 para.18, varied: SI 2013/574 Art.11
Sch.1 Part 2 para.19, varied: SI 2013/574 Art.11
Sch.1 Part 2 para.20, varied: SI 2013/574 Art.11
Sch.1 Part 2 para.20ZA, varied: SI 2013/574 Art.11
Sch.1 Part 2 para.20ZB, varied: SI 2013/574 Art.11
Sch.1 Part 3 para.21, varied: SI 2013/574 Art.11

464. Smoke Flavourings (England) Regulations 2005
revoked: SI 2013/2210 Sch.5

497. National Institute for Clinical Excellence (Establishment and Constitution) Amendment Order 2005
revoked: SI 2013/235 Sch.2 para.188

498. National Institute for Clinical Excellence (Amendment) Regulations 2005
revoked: SI 2013/235 Sch.2 para.189

499. Health and Social Care Information Centre (Establishment and Constitution) Order 2005
revoked: SI 2013/235 Sch.2 para.190

500. Health and Social Care Information Centre Regulations 2005
revoked: SI 2013/235 Sch.2 para.191

551. Central Rating List (England) Regulations 2005
Sch.1 Part 8, amended: SI 2013/408 Reg.2
Sch.1 Part 9, amended: SI 2013/408 Reg.2
Sch.1 Part 12, amended: SI 2013/2887 Reg.2

553. Justices of the Peace (Size and Chairmanship of Bench) Rules 2005
applied: SI 2013/1554 r.37_1, SI 2013/1878 Sch.1 para.1

554. Local Justice Areas Order 2005
Sch.1, amended: SI 2013/1777 Art.4, SI 2013/1878 Art.4

590. Pension Protection Fund (Entry Rules) Regulations 2005
Reg.1, amended: SI 2013/472 Art.4
Reg.5, amended: SI 2013/472 Art.4
Reg.18, amended: SI 2013/472 Art.4

598. Local Government (Best Value) Performance Indicators and Performance Standards (England) Order 2005
Art.1, amended: SI 2013/2146 Sch.1 para.13

639. Road Transport (Working Time) Regulations 2005
applied: SI 2013/1893 Sch.2
see *R. (on the application of United Road Transport Union) v Secretary of State for Transport* [2013] EWCA Civ 962, [2013] I.R.L.R. 890 (CA (Civ Div)), Jackson, L.J.

641. National Health Service (Pharmaceutical Services) Regulations 2005
applied: SI 2013/349 Reg.2, Reg.7, Reg.36, Reg.40, Reg.42, Reg.66, Reg.115, Reg.117, Sch.4 para.25, Sch.4 para.26, Sch.5 para.13, Sch.5 para.15, Sch.5 para.16, Sch.9 para.1, Sch.9 para.2, Sch.9 para.4, Sch.9 para.7, Sch.9 para.8, Sch.9 para.9, Sch.9 para.10, Sch.9 para.11, Sch.9 para.13, Sch.9 para.14
Part 5, applied: SI 2013/349 Sch.9 para.4
Reg.5, applied: SI 2013/349 Sch.9 para.2, Sch.9 para.13
Reg.6, applied: SI 2013/349 Reg.24
Reg.7, applied: SI 2013/349 Reg.24
Reg.12, applied: SI 2013/349 Sch.9 para.8
Reg.13, applied: SI 2013/349 Reg.24, Reg.64, Reg.65, Reg.66, Sch.9 para.2, Sch.9 para.8
Reg.14, applied: SI 2013/349 Reg.66
Reg.15, applied: SI 2013/349 Reg.24, Sch.9 para.2
Reg.16, applied: SI 2013/349 Reg.24
Reg.18, applied: SI 2013/349 Reg.51
Reg.18ZA, applied: SI 2013/349 Reg.41
Reg.20, applied: SI 2013/349 Reg.47, Sch.9 para.9, Sch.9 para.10
Reg.22, applied: SI 2013/349 Reg.40
Reg.35, applied: SI 2013/349 Sch.9 para.9
Reg.40, applied: SI 2013/349 Sch.9 para.2, Sch.9 para.13
Reg.40, referred to: SI 2013/349 Sch.9 para.2
Reg.41, applied: SI 2013/349 Sch.9 para.2
Reg.54, applied: SI 2013/349 Sch.9 para.2, Sch.9 para.13
Reg.58, applied: SI 2013/349 Sch.9 para.13
Reg.60, applied: SI 2013/349 Sch.9 para.4
Reg.65, applied: SI 2013/349 Reg.55

669. Pension Protection Fund (Review and Reconsideration of Reviewable Matters) Regulations 2005

Reg.3, amended: SI 2013/627 Reg.2
Reg.27, revoked: SI 2013/2042 Sch.1 para.58

670. Pension Protection Fund (Compensation) Regulations 2005

Reg.1, amended: SI 2013/627 Reg.3
Reg.2, revoked (in part): SI 2013/627 Reg.3
Reg.2A, added: SI 2013/627 Reg.3
Reg.2B, added: SI 2013/627 Reg.3
Reg.2C, added: SI 2013/627 Reg.3
Reg.2C, amended: SI 2013/1754 Reg.2
Reg.2D, added: SI 2013/627 Reg.3
Reg.4, amended: SI 2013/627 Reg.3
Reg.7, amended: SI 2013/627 Reg.3
Reg.10, amended: SI 2013/627 Reg.3
Reg.19, amended: SI 2013/627 Reg.3
Reg.20, revoked (in part): SI 2013/627 Reg.3
Reg.22, amended: SI 2013/627 Reg.3

672. Pension Protection Fund (Valuation) Regulations 2005

Reg.1, amended: SI 2013/627 Reg.4
Reg.6, amended: SI 2013/627 Reg.4
Reg.7, amended: SI 2013/627 Reg.4
Reg.7A, amended: SI 2013/627 Reg.4

674. Pension Protection Fund (Provision of Information) Regulations 2005

Sch.1 para.1, amended: SI 2013/627 Reg.10

678. Occupational Pension Schemes (Employer Debt) Regulations 2005

see *BESTrustees Plc v Kaupthing Singer & Friedlander (In Administration)* [2013] EWHC 2407 (Ch), [2013] Pens. L.R. 339 (Ch D (Companies Ct)), Sir Terence Etherton (Chancellor)
Sch.1A para.4, amended: SI 2013/627 Reg.9

691. Adoption Support Services Regulations 2005

Reg.2, amended: SI 2013/235 Sch.2 para.81, SI 2013/630 Reg.45
Reg.5, amended: SI 2013/235 Sch.2 para.81
Reg.11, amended: SI 2013/630 Reg.45, SI 2013/985 Sch.1 para.1
Reg.14, amended: SI 2013/235 Sch.2 para.81
Reg.16, amended: SI 2013/235 Sch.2 para.81

703. Occupational Pension Schemes (Independent Trustee) Regulations 2005

Reg.13, amended: SI 2013/2734 Sch.9 para.12

704. Personal and Occupational Pension Schemes (Indexation and Disclosure of Information) (Miscellaneous Amendments) Regulations 2005

Reg.15, revoked: SI 2013/459 Reg.10

706. Occupational Pension Schemes (Winding up etc.) Regulations 2005

Reg.6, amended: SI 2013/2734 Sch.9 para.13
Reg.7, amended: SI 2013/2734 Sch.9 para.13

712. Charities (National Trust) Order 2005

Appendix 1., amended: SI 2013/755 Sch.4 para.202

735. Work at Height Regulations 2005

see *Grant v Fife Council* [2013] CSOH 11, 2013 Rep. L.R. 73 (OH), Lord Stewart; see *Hill v Norside Ltd* 2013 Rep. L.R. 22 (OH), Lady Dorrian
Reg.3, revoked (in part): SI 2013/1512 Sch.1
Reg.4, see *Hill v Norside Ltd* 2013 Rep. L.R. 22 (OH), Lady Dorrian
Reg.6, see *Hill v Norside Ltd* 2013 Rep. L.R. 22 (OH), Lady Dorrian
Reg.7, see *Grant v Fife Council* [2013] CSOH 11, 2013 Rep. L.R. 73 (OH), Lord Stewart; see *Hill v Norside Ltd* 2013 Rep. L.R. 22 (OH), Lady Dorrian
Reg.8, see *Hill v Norside Ltd* 2013 Rep. L.R. 22 (OH), Lady Dorrian
Reg.8A, added: SI 2013/1512 Reg.5
Sch.6 para.1, see *Hill v Norside Ltd* 2013 Rep. L.R. 22 (OH), Lady Dorrian
Sch.6 para.3, see *Hill v Norside Ltd* 2013 Rep. L.R. 22 (OH), Lady Dorrian
Sch.6 para.5, see *Hill v Norside Ltd* 2013 Rep. L.R. 22 (OH), Lady Dorrian
Sch.9 para.1, added: SI 2013/1512 Reg.5
Sch.9 para.2, added: SI 2013/1512 Reg.5

758. Non-Domestic Rating (Alteration of Lists and Appeals) (Wales) Regulations 2005

Reg.14, see *Roberts (Valuation Officer) v West Coast Marine (Pwllheli) Ltd* [2013] UKUT 413 (LC) (UT (Lands)), Martin Rodger Q.C.

824. Pension Protection Fund (PPF Ombudsman) Order 2005

Art.7, amended: SI 2013/472 Sch.2 para.105, SI 2013/504 Reg.38
Art.7, revoked (in part): SI 2013/2042 Sch.1 para.59

829. Crime Prevention (Designated Areas) Order 2005

revoked: SI 2013/1760 Sch.1

858. Pensions Increase (Review) Order 2005

applied: SI 2013/604 Sch.1

880. Landfill Allowances and Trading Scheme (England)(Amendment) Regulations 2005

revoked: SI 2013/141 Reg.7

886. Courts Act 2003 (Consequential Provisions) Order 2005

Sch.1 para.57, revoked: 2013 c.22 Sch.11 para.210

894. Hazardous Waste (England and Wales) Regulations 2005

applied: SI 2013/2258 Sch.1 Part 2
Reg.11, amended: SI 2013/755 Sch.4 para.204
Sch.7 para.4, amended: SI 2013/755 Sch.4 para.205
Sch.7 para.5, amended: SI 2013/755 Sch.4 para.205
Sch.7 para.6, amended: SI 2013/755 Sch.4 para.205

895. List of Wastes (England) Regulations 2005
referred to: SI 2013/141 Reg.4
Sch.2 para.5, revoked: SI 2013/141 Reg.7
Sch.2 para.6, revoked: SI 2013/141 Reg.7
Sch.2 para.7, revoked: SI 2013/141 Reg.7
Sch.2 para.8, revoked: SI 2013/141 Reg.7

902. Crime and Disorder Act 1998 (Service of Prosecution Evidence) Regulations 2005
applied: SI 2013/435 Sch.1 para.22, Sch.2 para.21

914. Crime Prevention (Designated Areas) (No.2) Order 2005
revoked: SI 2013/1760 Sch.1

916. Gender Recognition (Disclosure of Information) (England, Wales and Northern Ireland) (No.2) Order 2005
Art.6, amended: SI 2013/1881 Sch.1 para.27

921. Water Fluoridation (Consultation) (England) Regulations 2005
revoked: SI 2013/301 Reg.25

930. Immigration and Asylum (Provision of Accommodation to Failed Asylum-Seekers) Regulations 2005
Reg.3, see *YMCA Glasgow v Hamad* 2013 Hous. L.R. 81 (Sh Ct (Glasgow)), Sheriff McCormick

1013. National Health Service (Pharmaceutical Services) (Amendment) (Wales) Regulations 2005
revoked: SI 2013/898 Sch.8 para.15

1015. National Health Service (Pharmaceutical Services) Amendment Regulations 2005
revoked: SI 2013/349 Sch.10 para.4

1082. Manufacture and Storage of Explosives Regulations 2005
Reg.9, applied: SI 2013/1471 Sch.2 para.5
Reg.10, applied: SI 2013/1471 Sch.2 para.5
Reg.11, applied: SI 2013/449 Reg.8, SI 2013/1471 Sch.2 para.5
Reg.13, applied: SI 2013/449 Reg.8
Sch.5 Part 2 para.40, revoked: SI 2013/1471 Sch.4

1109. Special Guardianship Regulations 2005
Reg.2, amended: SI 2013/630 Reg.46
Reg.4, amended: SI 2013/235 Sch.2 para.82
Reg.5, see *Suffolk CC v Nottinghamshire CC* [2012] EWCA Civ 1640, [2013] P.T.S.R. 619 (CA (Civ Div)), Thorpe, L.J.
Reg.9, amended: SI 2013/630 Reg.46
Reg.12, amended: SI 2013/235 Sch.2 para.82
Reg.14, amended: SI 2013/235 Sch.2 para.82

1118. A48 Trunk Road (Porthyrhyd Junction, Carmarthenshire) (De-Restriction) Order 2005
varied: SI 2013/1620 Art.6

1133. Revenue and Customs (Inspections) Regulations 2005
Reg.10, amended: SI 2013/602 Sch.2 para.84

1313. Adoption Agencies (Wales) Regulations 2005
Reg.36, amended: SI 2013/235 Sch.2 para.83

1350. Smoke Flavourings (Wales) Regulations 2005
revoked: SI 2013/2591 Sch.5

1379. Displaced Persons (Temporary Protection) Regulations 2005
Reg.3, applied: SI 2013/376 Reg.9, SI 2013/3029 Reg.28, SI 2013/3035 Sch.1
Reg.14, amended: SI 2013/630 Reg.60

1398. Education (Admission Appeals Arrangements) (Wales) Regulations 2005
Reg.2, amended: SI 2013/2535 Reg.2
Reg.6, substituted: SI 2013/2535 Reg.2
Reg.7, substituted: SI 2013/2535 Reg.2

1437. Education (Pupil Information) (England) Regulations 2005
Sch.1 para.2, amended: SI 2013/3212 Reg.3
Sch.1 para.2, revoked (in part): SI 2013/3212 Reg.3
Sch.1 para.3, amended: SI 2013/3212 Reg.3
Sch.2 para.6, amended: SI 2013/3212 Reg.4

1447. NHS Institute for Innovation and Improvement Regulations 2005
revoked: SI 2013/235 Sch.2 para.192

1475. General Optical Council (Fitness to Practise Rules) Order of Council 2005
revoked: SI 2013/2537 Sch.1

1477. General Optical Council (Registration Appeals Rules) Order of Council 2005
Sch.1, amended: SI 2013/472 Sch.2 para.106

1478. General Optical Council (Registration Rules) Order of Council 2005
Sch.1, amended: SI 2013/472 Sch.2 para.107

1512. Adoption Support Services (Local Authorities) (Wales) Regulations 2005
Reg.2, amended: SI 2013/2091 Reg.2
Reg.2, revoked (in part): SI 2013/2091 Reg.2
Reg.5, amended: SI 2013/235 Sch.2 para.84
Reg.5, revoked (in part): SI 2013/235 Sch.2 para.84
Reg.8, amended: SI 2013/235 Sch.2 para.84
Reg.10, amended: SI 2013/235 Sch.2 para.84
Reg.12, amended: SI 2013/2091 Reg.2
Reg.13, amended: SI 2013/235 Sch.2 para.84
Reg.17, amended: SI 2013/2091 Reg.2

1513. Special Guardianship (Wales) Regulations 2005
Reg.1, amended: SI 2013/2091 Reg.3

Reg.3, amended: SI 2013/235 Sch.2 para.85
Reg.6, amended: SI 2013/235 Sch.2 para.85
Reg.11, amended: SI 2013/235 Sch.2 para.85
Reg.12, amended: SI 2013/2091 Reg.3

1514. Adoption Support Agencies (Wales) Regulations 2005
Reg.27, amended: SI 2013/235 Sch.2 para.86
Sch.4, amended: SI 2013/235 Sch.2 para.86

1524. Denatured Alcohol Regulations 2005
Reg.13, amended: SI 2013/1195 Reg.3
Reg.14, substituted: SI 2013/1195 Reg.4
Sch.1 para.1, substituted: SI 2013/1195 Reg.5
Sch.1 para.4, amended: SI 2013/1195 Reg.5
Sch.1 para.5, amended: SI 2013/1195 Reg.5
Sch.1 para.6, amended: SI 2013/1195 Reg.5
Sch.1 para.8, revoked: SI 2013/1195 Reg.5
Sch.1 para.9, revoked: SI 2013/1195 Reg.5
Sch.1 para.10, revoked: SI 2013/1195 Reg.5
Sch.1 para.11, revoked: SI 2013/1195 Reg.5

1529. Financial Services and Markets Act 2000 (Financial Promotion) Order 2005
Art.16, amended: SI 2013/472 Sch.2 para.108, SI 2013/1765 Art.6
Art.28B, amended: SI 2013/1765 Art.6, SI 2013/1881 Art.17
Art.29, amended: SI 2013/1773 Sch.2 para.19
Art.30, amended: SI 2013/1881 Art.17
Art.36, amended: SI 2013/472 Sch.2 para.108
Art.40, amended: SI 2013/1773 Sch.2 para.19
Art.46, amended: SI 2013/1881 Art.17
Art.46A, added: SI 2013/1881 Art.17
Art.70, amended: SI 2013/472 Sch.2 para.108
Sch.1 Part I para.4B, added: SI 2013/1881 Art.17
Sch.1 Part I para.4C, added: SI 2013/1881 Art.17
Sch.1 Part I para.5A, added: SI 2013/1881 Art.17
Sch.1 Part I para.5B, added: SI 2013/1881 Art.17
Sch.1 Part I para.10BA, added: SI 2013/1881 Art.17
Sch.1 Part I para.10BB, added: SI 2013/1881 Art.17
Sch.1 Part II para.26D, added: SI 2013/1881 Art.17
Sch.1 Part II para.26E, added: SI 2013/1881 Art.17
Sch.1 Part II para.28, amended: SI 2013/1881 Art.17
Sch.5 Part I para.1, amended: SI 2013/472 Sch.2 para.108
Sch.5 Part II para.2, amended: SI 2013/472 Sch.2 para.108

1541. Regulatory Reform (Fire Safety) Order 2005
applied: SI 2013/1394 Reg.28
see *R. v Adeyeme (Lookman)* [2012] EWCA Crim 1391, [2013] 1 Cr. App. R. (S.) 24 (CA (Crim Div)), Sir John Thomas (President)
Art.17, applied: SI 2013/1959 Reg.13
Art.23, disapplied: SI 2013/1394 Reg.28
Art.25, amended: 2013 c.32 Sch.12 para.88
Art.25, revoked (in part): 2013 c.32 Sch.12 para.88
Art.25, substituted: 2013 c.32 Sch.12 para.88
Art.26, amended: 2013 c.32 Sch.12 para.89
Art.26, applied: 2013 c.32 s.89

1585. Wireless Telegraphy (Automotive Short Range Radar) (Exemption) (No.2) Regulations 2005
revoked: SI 2013/1437 Reg.3

1711. Restriction on the Preparation of Adoption Reports Regulations 2005
Reg.4, amended: SI 2013/985 Sch.1 para.3

1712. Suitability of Adopters Regulations 2005
Reg.3, amended: SI 2013/985 Sch.1 para.4
Reg.3, revoked (in part): SI 2013/985 Sch.1 para.4
Reg.4, amended: SI 2013/985 Sch.1 para.4
Reg.5, amended: SI 2013/985 Sch.1 para.4

1714. Climate Change Levy (Combined Heat and Power Stations) Regulations 2005
Reg.4, substituted: SI 2013/232 Reg.3
Reg.7, revoked: SI 2013/232 Reg.4

1788. Community Interest Company Regulations 2005
Reg.2, amended: SI 2013/496 Sch.11 para.14

1806. Hazardous Waste (Wales) Regulations 2005
applied: SI 2013/2258 Sch.1 Part 2
Reg.5, amended: SI 2013/755 Sch.5 para.28
Reg.11, amended: SI 2013/755 Sch.5 para.29
Reg.21, amended: SI 2013/755 Sch.5 para.30
Reg.23, amended: SI 2013/755 Sch.5 para.30
Reg.24, amended: SI 2013/755 Sch.5 para.30
Reg.25, amended: SI 2013/755 Sch.5 para.30
Reg.26, amended: SI 2013/755 Sch.5 para.30
Reg.27, amended: SI 2013/755 Sch.5 para.30
Reg.28, amended: SI 2013/755 Sch.5 para.30
Reg.33, amended: SI 2013/755 Sch.5 para.30
Reg.42, amended: SI 2013/755 Sch.5 para.30
Reg.47, amended: SI 2013/755 Sch.5 para.30
Reg.49, amended: SI 2013/755 Sch.5 para.30
Reg.51, amended: SI 2013/755 Sch.5 para.30
Reg.53, amended: SI 2013/755 Sch.5 para.30
Reg.55, amended: SI 2013/755 Sch.5 para.30
Reg.56, amended: SI 2013/755 Sch.5 para.31, Sch.5 para.32
Reg.57, amended: SI 2013/755 Sch.5 para.31
Reg.58, amended: SI 2013/755 Sch.5 para.31, Sch.5 para.32
Reg.59, amended: SI 2013/755 Sch.5 para.31
Reg.60, amended: SI 2013/755 Sch.5 para.31, Sch.5 para.32
Reg.62, amended: SI 2013/755 Sch.5 para.32
Reg.63, amended: SI 2013/755 Sch.5 para.32
Reg.64, amended: SI 2013/755 Sch.5 para.32
Reg.65A, amended: SI 2013/755 Sch.5 para.33

Reg.70, amended: SI 2013/755 Sch.5 para.34
Reg.71, amended: SI 2013/755 Sch.5 para.34
Sch.7 para.4, amended: SI 2013/755 Sch.5 para.35
Sch.7 para.5, amended: SI 2013/755 Sch.5 para.35
Sch.10, amended: SI 2013/755 Sch.5 para.36

1905. Drought Plan Regulations 2005
Reg.2, amended: SI 2013/755 Sch.4 para.206

1970. Air Navigation Order 2005
Art.75, applied: SI 2013/435 Sch.1 Part 7

1972. Children Act 2004 (Children's Services) Regulations 2005
Reg.2, amended: SI 2013/523 Reg.7

1986. Financial Assistance Scheme Regulations 2005
Reg.2, amended: SI 2013/472 Art.4
Reg.13, amended: SI 2013/472 Art.4

1987. Partnerships and Unlimited Companies (Accounts) (Amendment) Regulations 2005
revoked: SI 2013/2005 Reg.7

1998. Insurers (Reorganisation and Winding Up) (Lloyd's) Regulations 2005
Reg.2, amended: SI 2013/472 Sch.2 para.109
Reg.6, amended: SI 2013/472 Sch.2 para.109
Reg.7, amended: SI 2013/472 Sch.2 para.109
Reg.8, amended: SI 2013/472 Sch.2 para.109
Reg.10, amended: SI 2013/472 Sch.2 para.109
Reg.11, amended: SI 2013/472 Sch.2 para.109
Reg.14, amended: SI 2013/472 Sch.2 para.109
Reg.31, amended: SI 2013/472 Sch.2 para.109
Reg.33, amended: SI 2013/472 Sch.2 para.109
Reg.48, amended: SI 2013/472 Sch.2 para.109

2011. Dentists Act 1984 (Amendment) Order 2005
Sch.6 Part 2 para.14, revoked (in part): SSI 2013/50 Sch.5

2022. Clergy Discipline Rules 2005
Part II r.4, amended: SI 2013/1917 r.2
Part II r.6, amended: SI 2013/1917 r.3
Part II r.8, amended: SI 2013/1917 r.4
Part III r.9, amended: SI 2013/1917 r.5
Part III r.10, amended: SI 2013/1917 r.6
Part III r.10, revoked (in part): SI 2013/1917 r.6
Part IV r.17, amended: SI 2013/1917 r.7
Part IV r.27, amended: SI 2013/1917 r.8
Part IV r.28, amended: SI 2013/1917 r.9
Part VI r.31, amended: SI 2013/1917 r.10
Part VIII r.37, amended: SI 2013/1917 r.11
Part VIII r.42, amended: SI 2013/1917 r.12
Part VIII r.50, amended: SI 2013/1917 r.13
Part VIII r.52, amended: SI 2013/1917 r.14
Part X r.60, amended: SI 2013/1917 r.15
Part X r.61A, added: SI 2013/1917 r.16
Part X r.61B, added: SI 2013/1917 r.16
Part X r.62, amended: SI 2013/1917 r.17
Part X r.63, substituted: SI 2013/1917 r.18
Part X r.64, amended: SI 2013/1917 r.19
Part X r.65, amended: SI 2013/1917 r.20
Part X r.66, amended: SI 2013/1917 r.21
Part XI r.67, amended: SI 2013/1917 r.22
Part XI r.67A, added: SI 2013/1917 r.23
Part XI r.68, amended: SI 2013/1917 r.24
Part XII r.75, amended: SI 2013/1917 r.25
Part XII r.77, amended: SI 2013/1917 r.26
Part XIII r.86A, added: SI 2013/1917 r.27
Part XIII r.86B, added: SI 2013/1917 r.27
Part XVI r.102A, added: SI 2013/1917 r.28
Part XVI r.106, amended: SI 2013/1917 r.29
Sch.1, added: SI 2013/1917 r.33, Sch.1
Sch.1, amended: SI 2013/1917 r.30, r.31, r.32, r.34, r.35
Sch.1, substituted: SI 2013/1917 r.30

2024. Pension Protection Fund (Reference of Reviewable Matters to the PPF Ombudsman) Regulations 2005
Reg.14, revoked: SI 2013/2042 Sch.1 para.60

2027. Access to the Countryside (Correction of Provisional and Conclusive Maps) (England) (Amendment) Regulations 2005
revoked: SI 2013/1798 Reg.6

2045. Income Tax (Construction Industry Scheme) Regulations 2005
Reg.32, amended: SI 2013/620 Reg.3
Reg.56, amended: SI 2013/620 Reg.4

2055. Offshore Petroleum Activities (Oil Pollution Prevention and Control) Regulations 2005
Reg.19, revoked: SI 2013/971 Reg.38
Sch.1 para.1, revoked: SI 2013/971 Reg.38
Sch.1 para.2, revoked: SI 2013/971 Reg.38
Sch.1 para.3, revoked: SI 2013/971 Reg.38
Sch.1 para.4, revoked: SI 2013/971 Reg.38
Sch.1 para.5, revoked: SI 2013/971 Reg.38
Sch.1 para.6, revoked: SI 2013/971 Reg.38
Sch.1 para.7, revoked: SI 2013/971 Reg.38

2085. Town and Country Planning (Isles of Scilly) Order 2005
revoked: SI 2013/2148 Art.5
Art.5, applied: SI 2013/2148 Art.5

2189. Financial Assistance Scheme (Provision of Information and Administration of Payments) Regulations 2005
Reg.2, amended: SI 2013/472 Art.4

2222. River Tyne (Tunnels) Order 2005
applied: SI 2013/3087 Art.2
Sch.14, enabled: SI 2013/3087

2414. NHS Business Services Authority (Awdurdod Gwasanaethau Busnes y GIG) (Establishment and Constitution) Order 2005
Art.1, amended: SI 2013/235 Sch.2 para.87
Art.3, amended: SI 2013/235 Sch.2 para.87

2415. NHS Business Services Authority (Awdurdod Gwasanaethau Busnes y GIG) Regulations 2005
Reg.1, amended: SI 2013/235 Sch.2 para.88
Reg.3, amended: SI 2013/235 Sch.2 para.88
Reg.3, revoked (in part): SI 2013/235 Sch.2 para.88
2451. Biocidal Products (Amendment) Regulations 2005
revoked (in part): SI 2013/1506 Reg.34
2463. Crime Prevention (Designated Areas) (No.3) Order 2005
revoked: SI 2013/1760 Sch.1
2483. Energy Administration Rules 2005
Part 15 r.185, amended: SI 2013/472 Art.4
2517. Plant Health (Forestry) Order 2005
applied: SI 2013/755 Sch.7 para.11
Art.2, amended: SI 2013/755 Sch.4 para.208, SI 2013/2691 Art.3
Art.2A, added: SI 2013/755 Sch.4 para.209
Art.3, amended: SI 2013/755 Sch.4 para.210
Art.4, amended: SI 2013/755 Sch.4 para.211
Art.6, amended: SI 2013/755 Sch.4 para.212
Art.7, amended: SI 2013/755 Sch.4 para.213
Art.8, amended: SI 2013/755 Sch.4 para.214, SI 2013/2691 Art.4
Art.8, revoked (in part): SI 2013/2691 Art.4
Art.9, amended: SI 2013/755 Sch.4 para.215
Art.10, amended: SI 2013/755 Sch.4 para.216
Art.11, amended: SI 2013/755 Sch.4 para.217
Art.12, amended: SI 2013/755 Sch.4 para.218
Art.16, amended: SI 2013/755 Sch.4 para.219
Art.17, amended: SI 2013/755 Sch.4 para.220
Art.18, amended: SI 2013/755 Sch.4 para.221
Art.19, amended: SI 2013/755 Sch.4 para.222
Art.20, amended: SI 2013/755 Sch.4 para.223, SI 2013/2691 Art.5
Art.21, substituted: SI 2013/2691 Art.6
Art.22, amended: SI 2013/755 Sch.4 para.224
Art.24, substituted: SI 2013/755 Sch.4 para.225
Art.25, amended: SI 2013/755 Sch.4 para.226
Art.26, amended: SI 2013/755 Sch.4 para.227
Art.27, amended: SI 2013/755 Sch.4 para.228
Art.28, amended: SI 2013/755 Sch.4 para.229
Art.29, amended: SI 2013/755 Sch.4 para.230
Art.30, amended: SI 2013/755 Sch.4 para.231
Art.31, amended: SI 2013/755 Sch.4 para.232
Art.32, amended: SI 2013/755 Sch.4 para.233
Art.33, amended: SI 2013/755 Sch.4 para.234
Art.34, amended: SI 2013/755 Sch.4 para.235
Art.36, amended: SI 2013/755 Sch.4 para.236
Art.38, amended: SI 2013/755 Sch.4 para.237
Art.39, amended: SI 2013/755 Sch.4 para.238
Art.40, amended: SI 2013/755 Sch.4 para.239
Art.41, amended: SI 2013/755 Sch.4 para.240
Art.42, amended: SI 2013/755 Sch.4 para.241
Art.43, amended: SI 2013/755 Sch.4 para.242
Sch.2 Part A, amended: SI 2013/2691 Art.7
Sch.4 Part A, amended: SI 2013/2691 Art.8
Sch.4 Part B, amended: SI 2013/2691 Art.8
Sch.5 Part A para.2A, added: SI 2013/2691 Art.9
Sch.5 Part A para.4, amended: SI 2013/2691 Art.9
Sch.6 Part A para.4a, substituted: SI 2013/2691 Art.10
Sch.7 Part A para.2, amended: SI 2013/755 Sch.4 para.243
Sch.7 Part A para.4a, substituted: SI 2013/2691 Art.11
Sch.9 para.3, amended: SI 2013/755 Sch.4 para.244
Sch.9 para.7, amended: SI 2013/755 Sch.4 para.244
Sch.13 Part A para.2, amended: SI 2013/755 Sch.4 para.245
2530. Plant Health (England) Order 2005
Art.2, amended: SI 2013/1477 Art.3, SI 2013/2687 Art.3
Art.6, amended: SI 2013/1477 Art.4
Art.8, amended: SI 2013/2687 Art.4
Art.12, amended: SI 2013/1477 Art.5
Art.12, applied: SI 2013/494 Reg.2
Art.19, amended: SI 2013/23 Art.2, SI 2013/2687 Art.5
Art.21, amended: SI 2013/2687 Art.6
Art.22, amended: SI 2013/23 Art.2, SI 2013/1477 Art.6, SI 2013/2687 Art.7
Art.24, amended: SI 2013/2687 Art.8
Art.40, referred to: SI 2013/494 Reg.4
Art.41, referred to: SI 2013/494 Reg.4
Sch.1 Part A, amended: SI 2013/1477 Art.7
Sch.2 Part B, amended: SI 2013/2687 Art.9
Sch.3, amended: SI 2013/1477 Art.8
Sch.4 Part A, amended: SI 2013/1477 Art.9, SI 2013/2687 Art.10
Sch.4 Part B, amended: SI 2013/1477 Art.9, SI 2013/2687 Art.10
Sch.5 Part A para.2A, added: SI 2013/2687 Art.11
Sch.5 Part A para.8, added: SI 2013/1477 Art.10
Sch.6 Part A para.3B, added: SI 2013/1477 Art.11
Sch.6 Part A para.8, substituted: SI 2013/1477 Art.11
Sch.6 Part A para.10, added: SI 2013/1477 Art.11
Sch.6 Part A para.11, added: SI 2013/1477 Art.11
Sch.7 Part A para.3B, added: SI 2013/1477 Art.12
Sch.7 Part A para.8, substituted: SI 2013/1477 Art.12
Sch.7 Part A para.10, added: SI 2013/1477 Art.12
Sch.7 Part A para.11, added: SI 2013/1477 Art.12

2531. NHS Blood and Transplant (Gwaed a Thrawsblaniadau'r GIG) Regulations 2005
Reg.1, amended: SI 2013/235 Sch.2 para.89
2628. Railways (Provision etc of Railway Facilities) (Exemptions) Order 2005
Art.3, applied: SI 2013/339 Art.16
2693. Civil Aviation (Investigation of Military Air Accidents at Civil Aerodromes) Regulations 2005
applied: SI 2013/1471 Reg.14
2720. Adoption Support Agencies (England) and Adoption Agencies (Miscellaneous Amendments) Regulations 2005
Reg.24, amended: SI 2013/235 Sch.2 para.90
Sch.4, amended: SI 2013/235 Sch.2 para.90
2746. Companies (Welsh Language Forms) (Amendment) Regulations 2005
revoked: SI 2013/1947 Sch.2 Part 1
2747. Companies (Forms) (Amendment) Regulations 2005
revoked: SI 2013/1947 Sch.2 Part 1
2755. Bus Lane Contraventions (Approved Local Authorities) (England) Order 2005
Sch.2, amended: SI 2013/992 Art.5, SI 2013/2594 Art.6
2761. Civil Partnership (Registration Abroad and Certificates) Order 2005
Art.15, revoked: SI 2013/2872 Art.2
2798. Criminal Justice Act 2003 (Mandatory Life Sentences Appeals in Transitional Cases) Order 2005
Art.12, applied: SI 2013/1554 r.74_1, r.74_2
Art.13, applied: SI 2013/1554 r.74_2
2839. Town and Country Planning (Local Development Plan) (Wales) Regulations 2005
Reg.2, amended: SI 2013/755 Sch.5 para.37
Reg.2, revoked (in part): SI 2013/755 Sch.5 para.37
2903. Greenhouse Gas Emissions Trading Scheme (Amendment) and National Emissions Inventory Regulations 2005
Reg.1A, added: SI 2013/3135 Reg.8
Reg.3, amended: SI 2013/3135 Reg.9
Reg.11, revoked: SI 2013/3135 Reg.10
Reg.12, amended: SI 2013/3135 Reg.10
Reg.13, revoked (in part): SI 2013/3135 Reg.11
Reg.14, added: SI 2013/3135 Reg.12
Reg.15, added: SI 2013/3135 Reg.12
Reg.16, added: SI 2013/3135 Reg.12
Reg.17, added: SI 2013/3135 Reg.12
Reg.18, added: SI 2013/3135 Reg.12
2905. Railway Heritage Scheme Order 2005
revoked: SI 2013/64 Art.6
2914. Government of Maintained Schools (Wales) Regulations 2005
Reg.24, applied: SI 2013/2124 Reg.4, Reg.5
Reg.30, applied: SI 2013/2124 Reg.4, Reg.5
Reg.42, applied: SI 2013/2127 Reg.3, Reg.4
Reg.43, referred to: SI 2013/2127 Reg.3, Reg.4
Reg.55, applied: SI 2013/2127 Reg.4
Reg.56, applied: SI 2013/2127 Reg.4
Reg.57, applied: SI 2013/2127 Reg.4
Reg.58, applied: SI 2013/2127 Reg.4
Reg.58, referred to: SI 2013/2127 Reg.4
Sch.5, applied: SI 2013/2124 Reg.4, Reg.5
Sch.5 para.5, applied: SI 2013/2124 Reg.4, Reg.5
Sch.5 para.11A, added: SI 2013/2124 Reg.6
Sch.5 para.13, amended: SI 2013/2124 Reg.6
2993. Designation of Schools Having a Religious Character (Independent Schools) (England) (No.2) Order 2005
Sch.1, amended: SI 2013/2162 Sch.2
3061. Social Fund Maternity and Funeral Expenses (General) Regulations 2005
Reg.3, amended: SI 2013/247 Reg.2
Reg.5, amended: SI 2013/247 Reg.2
Reg.7, amended: SI 2013/247 Reg.2
Reg.7, revoked (in part): SI 2013/247 Reg.2
Reg.8, amended: SI 2013/247 Reg.2
Reg.10, amended: SI 2013/247 Reg.2, SI 2013/591 Sch.1 para.32
3117. Offshore Installations (Safety Case) Regulations 2005
Sch.9 para.4, revoked: SI 2013/1471 Sch.4
3168. Marriages and Civil Partnerships (Approved Premises) Regulations 2005
Reg.4, amended: SI 2013/2294 Reg.2
Sch.A1, amended: SI 2013/2294 Reg.2
3172. Water Services etc (Scotland) Act 2005 (Consequential Provisions and Modifications) Order 2005
Art.2, amended: 2013 c.24 Sch.6 para.172
Art.3, amended: 2013 c.24 Sch.6 para.173
Art.4, amended: 2013 c.24 Sch.6 para.174
Art.5, amended: 2013 c.24 Sch.6 para.175
Art.6, amended: 2013 c.24 Sch.6 para.176
Art.7, amended: 2013 c.24 Sch.6 para.177
Art.8, amended: 2013 c.24 Sch.6 para.178
Art.9, amended: 2013 c.24 Sch.6 para.179
Art.10, amended: 2013 c.24 Sch.6 para.180
3181. Proceeds of Crime Act 2002 (External Requests and Orders) Order 2005
applied: SI 2013/2605 Art.5, Art.39
Part 2, applied: SI 2013/2605 Art.19, Art.26, Art.31
Part 3, applied: SI 2013/2605 Art.53, Art.60, Art.65
Part 4, applied: SI 2013/2605 Art.19, Art.26, Art.31
Art.141A, added: SI 2013/2604 Art.3

Art.141B, added: SI 2013/2604 Art.3
Art.141C, added: SI 2013/2604 Art.3
Art.141D, added: SI 2013/2604 Art.3
Art.141E, added: SI 2013/2604 Art.3
Art.141F, added: SI 2013/2604 Art.3
Art.141G, added: SI 2013/2604 Art.3
Art.141H, added: SI 2013/2604 Art.3
Art.141I, added: SI 2013/2604 Art.3
Art.141J, added: SI 2013/2604 Art.3
Art.141K, added: SI 2013/2604 Art.3
Art.141L, added: SI 2013/2604 Art.3
Art.141M, added: SI 2013/2604 Art.3
Art.141N, added: SI 2013/2604 Art.3
Art.141O, added: SI 2013/2604 Art.3
Art.141P, added: SI 2013/2604 Art.3
Art.141Q, added: SI 2013/2604 Art.3
Art.141R, added: SI 2013/2604 Art.3
Art.141ZA, added: SI 2013/2604 Art.3
Art.141ZB, added: SI 2013/2604 Art.3
Art.141ZC, added: SI 2013/2604 Art.3
Art.141ZD, added: SI 2013/2604 Art.3
Art.141ZE, added: SI 2013/2604 Art.3
Art.141ZF, added: SI 2013/2604 Art.3
Art.141ZG, added: SI 2013/2604 Art.3
Art.141ZH, added: SI 2013/2604 Art.3
Art.141ZI, added: SI 2013/2604 Art.3
Art.141ZJ, added: SI 2013/2604 Art.3
Art.141ZK, added: SI 2013/2604 Art.3
Art.141ZL, added: SI 2013/2604 Art.3
Art.141ZM, added: SI 2013/2604 Art.3
Art.141ZN, added: SI 2013/2604 Art.3
Art.149, amended: SI 2013/534 Sch.1 para.15
Art.157, amended: SI 2013/534 Sch.1 para.15
Art.193, amended: SI 2013/472 Sch.2 para.110
Art.205, amended: SI 2013/472 Sch.2 para.110
Pt 2., see *Serious Organised Crime Agency v Perry* [2013] 1 A.C. 182 (SC), Lord Phillips, J.S.C.

3201. Clergy Discipline Appeal Rules 2005

r.3, amended: SI 2013/1921 r.2
r.4A, added: SI 2013/1921 r.3
r.4B, added: SI 2013/1921 r.3
r.4C, added: SI 2013/1921 r.3
r.4D, added: SI 2013/1921 r.3
r.5, amended: SI 2013/1921 r.4
r.6, amended: SI 2013/1921 r.5
r.8, amended: SI 2013/1921 r.6
r.9, amended: SI 2013/1921 r.7
r.10, amended: SI 2013/1921 r.8
r.11, amended: SI 2013/1921 r.9
r.12A, added: SI 2013/1921 r.10
r.15, amended: SI 2013/1921 r.11
r.21, amended: SI 2013/1921 r.12
r.23, amended: SI 2013/1921 r.13
r.24, amended: SI 2013/1921 r.14
r.25, amended: SI 2013/1921 r.15
r.43, amended: SI 2013/1921 r.16
Sch.1, amended: SI 2013/1921 r.17, r.18, Sch.1

3204. Sports Grounds and Sporting Events (Designation) Order 2005

Sch.2 Part I para.1, amended: SI 2013/1710 Art.2
Sch.2 Part 2, amended: SI 2013/1710 Art.2

3262. Healthy Start Scheme and Welfare Food (Amendment) Regulations 2005

Reg.2, amended: SI 2013/235 Sch.2 para.91
Reg.8A, amended: SI 2013/235 Sch.2 para.91

3273. Financial Assistance Scheme (Appeals) Regulations 2005

Reg.21, revoked: SI 2013/2042 Sch.1 para.61
Reg.28, amended: SI 2013/472 Sch.2 para.111, SI 2013/504 Reg.39
Reg.28, revoked (in part): SI 2013/2042 Sch.1 para.61

3280. Feed (Hygiene and Enforcement) (England) Regulations 2005

Reg.2, amended: SI 2013/3133 Reg.2
Reg.4, substituted: SI 2013/3133 Reg.2
Sch.2, substituted: SI 2013/3133 Sch.1

3320. Hydrocarbon Oil Duties (Reliefs for Electricity Generation) Regulations 2005

Reg.2, amended: SI 2013/657 Reg.3
Reg.3, amended: SI 2013/657 Reg.4
Reg.6, amended: SI 2013/657 Reg.5
Reg.7, amended: SI 2013/657 Reg.6
Reg.9, substituted: SI 2013/657 Reg.7
Reg.10, amended: SI 2013/657 Reg.1
Reg.10, revoked (in part): SI 2013/657 Reg.1
Reg.10, substituted: SI 2013/657 Reg.7
Reg.11, amended: SI 2013/657 Reg.6
Reg.13, amended: SI 2013/657 Reg.8
Sch.1, amended: SI 2013/657 Reg.8
Sch.1, substituted: SI 2013/657 Reg.9

3336. Civil Partnership (Family Proceedings and Housing Consequential Amendments) Order 2005

Art.3, revoked: 2013 c.22 Sch.11 para.210

3360. Social Security (Hospital In-Patients) Regulations 2005

applied: SI 2013/3029 Sch.1 para.10, SI 2013/3035 Sch.1
Reg.2, applied: SI 2013/3029 Sch.1 para.19, Sch.6 para.21

3361. National Health Service (General Dental Services Contracts) Regulations 2005

applied: SI 2013/364 Sch.1 para.3, Sch.1 para.15
Reg.2, amended: SI 2013/364 Reg.3
Reg.3, substituted: SI 2013/364 Reg.4
Reg.4, amended: SI 2013/364 Reg.5
Reg.5, amended: SI 2013/364 Reg.6
Reg.6, amended: SI 2013/364 Reg.7

Reg.6, applied: SI 2013/364 Sch.1 para.5, Sch.1 para.6
Reg.7, amended: SI 2013/364 Reg.8
Reg.8, amended: SI 2013/364 Reg.9
Reg.9, amended: SI 2013/364 Reg.10
Reg.13, amended: SI 2013/364 Reg.11
Reg.17, amended: SI 2013/364 Reg.12
Reg.19, amended: SI 2013/364 Reg.13
Reg.21, amended: SI 2013/364 Reg.14
Reg.21, applied: SI 2013/364 Sch.1 para.7, SI 2013/469 Sch.1
Reg.24, amended: SI 2013/364 Reg.15
Reg.24, applied: SI 2013/469 Sch.1
Reg.24A, revoked: SI 2013/364 Reg.16
Reg.24B, added: SI 2013/364 Reg.17
Sch.1 Part 1 para.2, amended: SI 2013/364 Reg.18
Sch.1 Part 2 para.5, amended: SI 2013/364 Reg.18
Sch.1 Part 2 para.6, amended: SI 2013/364 Reg.18
Sch.1 Part 2 para.8, amended: SI 2013/364 Reg.18
Sch.1 Part 2 para.8, applied: SI 2013/469 Sch.1
Sch.3 Part 1 para.3, amended: SI 2013/364 Reg.19
Sch.3 Part 1 para.5, amended: SI 2013/364 Reg.19
Sch.3 Part 2 para.6, amended: SI 2013/364 Reg.19
Sch.3 Part 2 para.7, amended: SI 2013/364 Reg.19
Sch.3 Part 2 para.8, amended: SI 2013/364 Reg.19
Sch.3 Part 2 para.8, applied: SI 2013/469 Sch.1
Sch.3 Part 2 para.9, amended: SI 2013/364 Reg.19
Sch.3 Part 3 para.19, amended: SI 2013/364 Reg.19
Sch.3 Part 4 para.21, substituted: SI 2013/364 Reg.19
Sch.3 Part 4 para.23, amended: SI 2013/364 Reg.19
Sch.3 Part 4 para.24, amended: SI 2013/364 Reg.19
Sch.3 Part 4 para.30, substituted: SI 2013/364 Reg.19
Sch.3 Part 4 para.31, amended: SI 2013/364 Reg.19
Sch.3 Part 5, applied: SI 2013/364 Sch.1 para.8
Sch.3 Part 5 para.32, amended: SI 2013/364 Reg.19
Sch.3 Part 5 para.34, amended: SI 2013/364 Reg.19
Sch.3 Part 5 para.34, applied: SI 2013/364 Sch.1 para.9
Sch.3 Part 5 para.35, amended: SI 2013/364 Reg.19
Sch.3 Part 5 para.35, applied: SI 2013/469 Reg.2, Sch.1
Sch.3 Part 5 para.35, referred to: SI 2013/469 Sch.1
Sch.3 Part 5 para.37, amended: SI 2013/364 Reg.19
Sch.3 Part 5 para.37, applied: SI 2013/364 Sch.1 para.8, SI 2013/469 Reg.2, Sch.1
Sch.3 Part 5 para.38, amended: SI 2013/364 Reg.19
Sch.3 Part 5 para.38, applied: SI 2013/469 Sch.1
Sch.3 Part 5 para.39, amended: SI 2013/364 Reg.19
Sch.3 Part 5 para.39, applied: SI 2013/469 Sch.1
Sch.3 Part 5 para.40, amended: SI 2013/364 Reg.19
Sch.3 Part 5 para.41, amended: SI 2013/364 Reg.19
Sch.3 Part 5 para.42, amended: SI 2013/364 Reg.19
Sch.3 Part 5 para.42B, added: SI 2013/364 Reg.19
Sch.3 Part 5 para.44, amended: SI 2013/364 Reg.19
Sch.3 Part 5 para.44, applied: SI 2013/469 Reg.2, Sch.1
Sch.3 Part 5 para.46A, applied: SI 2013/364 Sch.1 para.10
Sch.3 Part 5 para.46A, substituted: SI 2013/364 Reg.19
Sch.3 Part 6 para.47, revoked: SI 2013/364 Reg.19
Sch.3 Part 6 para.48, revoked: SI 2013/364 Reg.19
Sch.3 Part 6 para.49, revoked: SI 2013/364 Reg.19
Sch.3 Part 6 para.50, revoked: SI 2013/364 Reg.19
Sch.3 Part 6 para.51, amended: SI 2013/364 Reg.19
Sch.3 Part 6 para.51, applied: SI 2013/364 Sch.1 para.11
Sch.3 Part 6 para.52, amended: SI 2013/364 Reg.19
Sch.3 Part 7, applied: SI 2013/364 Sch.1 para.12
Sch.3 Part 7 para.53, amended: SI 2013/364 Reg.19
Sch.3 Part 7 para.54, amended: SI 2013/364 Reg.19
Sch.3 Part 8 para.58, amended: SI 2013/364 Reg.19
Sch.3 Part 8 para.58, applied: SI 2013/469 Sch.1
Sch.3 Part 8 para.59, amended: SI 2013/364 Reg.19
Sch.3 Part 8 para.59, applied: SI 2013/469 Sch.1
Sch.3 Part 9, applied: SI 2013/364 Sch.1 para.13
Sch.3 Part 9 para.60, amended: SI 2013/364 Reg.19
Sch.3 Part 9 para.61, amended: SI 2013/364 Reg.19
Sch.3 Part 9 para.62, amended: SI 2013/364 Reg.19
Sch.3 Part 9 para.63, amended: SI 2013/364 Reg.19

Sch.3 Part 9 para.64, amended: SI 2013/364 Reg.19
Sch.3 Part 9 para.65, amended: SI 2013/364 Reg.19
Sch.3 Part 9 para.66, amended: SI 2013/364 Reg.19
Sch.3 Part 9 para.67, amended: SI 2013/364 Reg.19
Sch.3 Part 9 para.68, amended: SI 2013/364 Reg.19
Sch.3 Part 9 para.69, amended: SI 2013/364 Reg.19
Sch.3 Part 9 para.70, amended: SI 2013/364 Reg.19
Sch.3 Part 9 para.71, amended: SI 2013/364 Reg.19
Sch.3 Part 9 para.72, amended: SI 2013/364 Reg.19
Sch.3 Part 9 para.73, amended: SI 2013/364 Reg.19
Sch.3 Part 9 para.74, amended: SI 2013/364 Reg.19
Sch.3 Part 9 para.75, amended: SI 2013/364 Reg.19
Sch.3 Part 9 para.76, amended: SI 2013/364 Reg.19
Sch.3 Part 9 para.77, amended: SI 2013/364 Reg.19
Sch.3 Part 10 para.79, amended: SI 2013/364 Reg.19
Sch.3 Part 10 para.79A, added: SI 2013/364 Reg.19
Sch.3 Part 10 para.83, amended: SI 2013/364 Reg.19
Sch.3 Part 10 para.83, applied: SI 2013/335 Reg.33
Sch.3 Part 10 para.84, amended: SI 2013/364 Reg.19
Sch.3 Part 10 para.84, applied: SI 2013/364 Sch.1 para.14
Sch.4 para.2A, added: SI 2013/364 Reg.20
Sch.4 para.15, amended: SI 2013/364 Reg.20
Sch.4 para.21, amended: SI 2013/364 Reg.20
Sch.4 para.21, substituted: SI 2013/364 Reg.20

3368. Feed (Hygiene and Enforcement) (Wales) Regulations 2005

Reg.2, amended: SI 2013/3207 Reg.2
Reg.4, substituted: SI 2013/3207 Reg.2
Sch.3, amended: SI 2013/3207 Sch.1

3369. A40 Trunk Road (Redstone Cross, Pembrokeshire) (De-Restriction) Order 2005

revoked: SI 2013/2197 Art.6

3373. National Health Service (Personal Dental Services Agreements) Regulations 2005

applied: SI 2013/364 Sch.2 para.3
disapplied: SI 2013/364 Sch.2 para.3
Reg.2, amended: SI 2013/364 Reg.23
Reg.3, substituted: SI 2013/364 Reg.24
Reg.4, amended: SI 2013/364 Reg.25
Reg.5, amended: SI 2013/364 Reg.26
Reg.6, amended: SI 2013/364 Reg.27
Reg.6, applied: SI 2013/364 Sch.2 para.6
Reg.7, amended: SI 2013/364 Reg.28
Reg.8, amended: SI 2013/364 Reg.29
Reg.9, amended: SI 2013/364 Reg.30
Reg.13, amended: SI 2013/364 Reg.31
Reg.15, amended: SI 2013/364 Reg.32
Reg.17, amended: SI 2013/364 Reg.33
Reg.17, applied: SI 2013/364 Sch.2 para.7, SI 2013/469 Sch.1
Reg.20, amended: SI 2013/364 Reg.34
Reg.20, applied: SI 2013/469 Sch.1
Reg.20A, revoked: SI 2013/364 Reg.35
Reg.20B, added: SI 2013/364 Reg.36
Reg.21, amended: SI 2013/364 Reg.37
Sch.1 Part 1 para.2, amended: SI 2013/364 Reg.38
Sch.1 Part 2 para.5, amended: SI 2013/364 Reg.38
Sch.1 Part 2 para.8, amended: SI 2013/364 Reg.38
Sch.1 Part 2 para.8, applied: SI 2013/469 Sch.1
Sch.3 Part 1 para.3, amended: SI 2013/364 Reg.39
Sch.3 Part 1 para.5, amended: SI 2013/364 Reg.39
Sch.3 Part 2 para.6, amended: SI 2013/364 Reg.39
Sch.3 Part 2 para.7, amended: SI 2013/364 Reg.39
Sch.3 Part 2 para.8, amended: SI 2013/364 Reg.39
Sch.3 Part 2 para.9, amended: SI 2013/364 Reg.39
Sch.3 Part 2 para.9, applied: SI 2013/469 Sch.1
Sch.3 Part 2 para.10, amended: SI 2013/364 Reg.39
Sch.3 Part 2 para.17, amended: SI 2013/364 Reg.39
Sch.3 Part 3 para.20, amended: SI 2013/364 Reg.39
Sch.3 Part 4 para.22, substituted: SI 2013/364 Reg.39
Sch.3 Part 4 para.24, amended: SI 2013/364 Reg.39
Sch.3 Part 4 para.25, amended: SI 2013/364 Reg.39
Sch.3 Part 4 para.31, substituted: SI 2013/364 Reg.39
Sch.3 Part 4 para.32, amended: SI 2013/364 Reg.39
Sch.3 Part 5, referred to: SI 2013/364 Sch.2 para.8
Sch.3 Part 5A para.46B, referred to: SI 2013/364 Sch.2 para.10
Sch.3 Part 5 para.33, amended: SI 2013/364 Reg.39

Sch.3 Part 5 para.35, amended: SI 2013/364 Reg.39
Sch.3 Part 5 para.35, applied: SI 2013/364 Sch.2 para.9
Sch.3 Part 5 para.35, disapplied: SI 2013/364 Sch.2 para.9
Sch.3 Part 5 para.36, amended: SI 2013/364 Reg.39
Sch.3 Part 5 para.36, applied: SI 2013/469 Reg.2, Sch.1
Sch.3 Part 5 para.38, amended: SI 2013/364 Reg.39
Sch.3 Part 5 para.38, applied: SI 2013/469 Reg.2, Sch.1
Sch.3 Part 5 para.38, referred to: SI 2013/364 Sch.2 para.8
Sch.3 Part 5 para.39, amended: SI 2013/364 Reg.39
Sch.3 Part 5 para.39, applied: SI 2013/469 Sch.1
Sch.3 Part 5 para.39, revoked (in part): SI 2013/364 Reg.39
Sch.3 Part 5 para.40, amended: SI 2013/364 Reg.39
Sch.3 Part 5 para.40, applied: SI 2013/469 Sch.1
Sch.3 Part 5 para.41, amended: SI 2013/364 Reg.39
Sch.3 Part 5 para.42, substituted: SI 2013/364 Reg.39
Sch.3 Part 5 para.42A, added: SI 2013/364 Reg.39
Sch.3 Part 5 para.42B, added: SI 2013/364 Reg.39
Sch.3 Part 5 para.44, amended: SI 2013/364 Reg.39
Sch.3 Part 5 para.44, applied: SI 2013/469 Reg.2, Sch.1
Sch.3 Part 5 para.46A, substituted: SI 2013/364 Reg.39
Sch.3 Part 6 para.47, revoked: SI 2013/364 Reg.39
Sch.3 Part 6 para.48, revoked: SI 2013/364 Reg.39
Sch.3 Part 6 para.49, revoked: SI 2013/364 Reg.39
Sch.3 Part 6 para.50, revoked: SI 2013/364 Reg.39
Sch.3 Part 6 para.51, amended: SI 2013/364 Reg.39
Sch.3 Part 6 para.51, applied: SI 2013/364 Sch.2 para.11
Sch.3 Part 6 para.52, amended: SI 2013/364 Reg.39
Sch.3 Part 7, referred to: SI 2013/364 Sch.2 para.12
Sch.3 Part 7 para.53, amended: SI 2013/364 Reg.39
Sch.3 Part 7 para.54, amended: SI 2013/364 Reg.39
Sch.3 Part 8 para.58, amended: SI 2013/364 Reg.39
Sch.3 Part 8 para.58, applied: SI 2013/469 Sch.1
Sch.3 Part 8 para.59, amended: SI 2013/364 Reg.39
Sch.3 Part 8 para.59, applied: SI 2013/469 Sch.1
Sch.3 Part 9, applied: SI 2013/364 Sch.2 para.13
Sch.3 Part 9, referred to: SI 2013/364 Sch.2 para.13
Sch.3 Part 9 para.60, amended: SI 2013/364 Reg.39
Sch.3 Part 9 para.61, amended: SI 2013/364 Reg.39
Sch.3 Part 9 para.62, amended: SI 2013/364 Reg.39
Sch.3 Part 9 para.63, amended: SI 2013/364 Reg.39
Sch.3 Part 9 para.64, amended: SI 2013/364 Reg.39
Sch.3 Part 9 para.65, amended: SI 2013/364 Reg.39
Sch.3 Part 9 para.66, amended: SI 2013/364 Reg.39
Sch.3 Part 9 para.67, amended: SI 2013/364 Reg.39
Sch.3 Part 9 para.68, amended: SI 2013/364 Reg.39
Sch.3 Part 9 para.69, amended: SI 2013/364 Reg.39
Sch.3 Part 9 para.70, amended: SI 2013/364 Reg.39
Sch.3 Part 9 para.71, amended: SI 2013/364 Reg.39
Sch.3 Part 9 para.72, amended: SI 2013/364 Reg.39
Sch.3 Part 9 para.72, substituted: SI 2013/364 Reg.39
Sch.3 Part 9 para.73, amended: SI 2013/364 Reg.39
Sch.3 Part 9 para.74, amended: SI 2013/364 Reg.39
Sch.3 Part 9 para.75, amended: SI 2013/364 Reg.39
Sch.3 Part 10 para.77, amended: SI 2013/364 Reg.39
Sch.3 Part 10 para.77, revoked (in part): SI 2013/364 Reg.39
Sch.3 Part 10 para.77A, added: SI 2013/364 Reg.39
Sch.3 Part 10 para.81, amended: SI 2013/364 Reg.39
Sch.3 Part 10 para.82, amended: SI 2013/364 Reg.39
Sch.3 Part 10 para.82, applied: SI 2013/364 Sch.2 para.14
Sch.4 para.2A, added: SI 2013/364 Reg.40

Sch.4 para.2B, added: SI 2013/364 Reg.40
Sch.4 para.14, amended: SI 2013/364 Reg.40
Sch.4 para.20, amended: SI 2013/364 Reg.40
Sch.4 para.21, substituted: SI 2013/364 Reg.40
Sch.5 para.1, revoked: SI 2013/364 Reg.41
Sch.5 para.2, revoked: SI 2013/364 Reg.41
Sch.5 para.3, revoked: SI 2013/364 Reg.41

3377. Occupational Pension Schemes (Scheme Funding) Regulations 2005
Sch.2 para.1, applied: SI 2013/2734 Reg.24
Sch.3 para.2, revoked: SI 2013/2734 Sch.9 para.14
Sch.3 para.3, revoked: SI 2013/2734 Sch.9 para.14

3378. Occupational Pension Schemes (Investment) Regulations 2005
Reg.1, amended: SI 2013/472 Art.4
Reg.13, applied: SI 2013/2734 Sch.3 para.32
Reg.15A, amended: SI 2013/472 Art.4

3390. Local Authority (Adoption) (Miscellaneous Provisions) Regulations 2005
Reg.5, amended: SI 2013/985 Sch.1 para.5

3428. Health Service Commissioner for England (Special Health Authorities) (No.2) Order 2005
Sch.1, amended: SI 2013/235 Sch.2 para.92

3454. Registered Pension Schemes (Accounting and Assessment) Regulations 2005
Reg.3, amended: SI 2013/1111 Reg.2

3477. National Health Service (Dental Charges) Regulations 2005
applied: SI 2013/364 Reg.54
Reg.2, amended: SI 2013/364 Reg.44
Reg.3, amended: SI 2013/364 Reg.45
Reg.4, amended: SI 2013/364 Reg.46, SI 2013/475 Reg.16, SI 2013/711 Reg.4
Reg.5, amended: SI 2013/364 Reg.47
Reg.6, amended: SI 2013/711 Reg.4
Reg.7, amended: SI 2013/364 Reg.48
Reg.7, applied: SI 2013/469 Sch.1
Reg.8, amended: SI 2013/364 Reg.49
Reg.12, substituted: SI 2013/364 Reg.50
Reg.13A, added: SI 2013/364 Reg.51, SI 2013/711 Reg.4
Reg.13A, amended: SI 2013/475 Reg.16
Reg.13B, added: SI 2013/364 Reg.51, SI 2013/711 Reg.4
Sch.1A, added: SI 2013/364 Sch.3

3491. National Health Service (Performers Lists) Amendment Regulations 2005
Sch.1, applied: SI 2013/335 Reg.9

2006

5. Public Contracts Regulations 2006
applied: SI 2013/257 Reg.13, Reg.17, SI 2013/500 Reg.13, Reg.17, SI 2013/1582 Reg.6, Reg.8
see *R. (on the application of Nash) v Barnet LBC* [2013] EWHC 1067 (Admin), [2013] B.L.G.R. 515 (QBD (Admin)), Underhill, L.J.
Reg.4, see *AJ v Calderdale BC* [2012] EWHC 3552 (Admin), (2013) 16 C.C.L. Rep. 50 (QBD (Admin)), Judge Pelling Q.C.
Reg.5, applied: SI 2013/1582 Reg.6
Reg.14, applied: SI 2013/1582 Reg.6
Sch.1, amended: 2013 c.24 Sch.20 para.2, SI 2013/252 Sch.1 Part 2
Sch.6 para.1, amended: SI 2013/1431 Reg.2
Sch.6 para.2, amended: SI 2013/1431 Reg.2
Sch.6 para.3, amended: SI 2013/1431 Reg.2

6. Utilities Contracts Regulations 2006
applied: SI 2013/1582 Reg.6, Reg.8
referred to: SI 2013/1582 Reg.6
Reg.2, varied: SI 2013/1582 Reg.6
Reg.4, varied: SI 2013/1582 Reg.6
Reg.5, applied: SI 2013/1582 Reg.6
Reg.12, varied: SI 2013/1582 Reg.6
Reg.13, varied: SI 2013/1582 Reg.6
Reg.14, varied: SI 2013/1582 Reg.6
Reg.16, varied: SI 2013/1582 Reg.6
Reg.17, applied: SI 2013/1582 Reg.6
Reg.17, varied: SI 2013/1582 Reg.6
Reg.18, varied: SI 2013/1582 Reg.6
Reg.21, varied: SI 2013/1582 Reg.6
Reg.22, varied: SI 2013/1582 Reg.6
Reg.23, varied: SI 2013/1582 Reg.6
Reg.24, varied: SI 2013/1582 Reg.6
Reg.25, varied: SI 2013/1582 Reg.6
Reg.26, varied: SI 2013/1582 Reg.6
Reg.27, varied: SI 2013/1582 Reg.6
Reg.28, varied: SI 2013/1582 Reg.6
Reg.29, varied: SI 2013/1582 Reg.6
Reg.29A, varied: SI 2013/1582 Reg.6
Reg.30, varied: SI 2013/1582 Reg.6
Reg.33, varied: SI 2013/1582 Reg.6
Reg.33A, varied: SI 2013/1582 Reg.6
Reg.35, varied: SI 2013/1582 Reg.6
Reg.36, varied: SI 2013/1582 Reg.6
Reg.37, varied: SI 2013/1582 Reg.6
Reg.40, varied: SI 2013/1582 Reg.6
Reg.41, varied: SI 2013/1582 Reg.6
Reg.42, varied: SI 2013/1582 Reg.6
Reg.43, varied: SI 2013/1582 Reg.6
Reg.45, varied: SI 2013/1582 Reg.6
Reg.45A, varied: SI 2013/1582 Reg.6
Reg.45B, varied: SI 2013/1582 Reg.6
Reg.45C, varied: SI 2013/1582 Reg.6
Reg.45D, varied: SI 2013/1582 Reg.6
Reg.45E, varied: SI 2013/1582 Reg.6

Reg.45F, varied: SI 2013/1582 Reg.6
Reg.45G, varied: SI 2013/1582 Reg.6
Reg.45H, varied: SI 2013/1582 Reg.6
Reg.45I, varied: SI 2013/1582 Reg.6
Reg.45J, varied: SI 2013/1582 Reg.6
Reg.45K, varied: SI 2013/1582 Reg.6
Reg.45L, varied: SI 2013/1582 Reg.6
Reg.45M, varied: SI 2013/1582 Reg.6
Reg.45N, varied: SI 2013/1582 Reg.6
Reg.45O, varied: SI 2013/1582 Reg.6
Reg.45P, varied: SI 2013/1582 Reg.6
Reg.45Q, varied: SI 2013/1582 Reg.6
Reg.45R, varied: SI 2013/1582 Reg.6
Reg.46, varied: SI 2013/1582 Reg.6
s.Art.9 Reg.45S, varied: SI 2013/1582 Reg.6
Sch.1, amended: SI 2013/610 Sch.1 para.5
Sch.2, varied: SI 2013/1582 Reg.6
Sch.4, varied: SI 2013/1582 Reg.6

14. Food Hygiene (England) Regulations 2006
revoked: SI 2013/2996 Sch.9
see *R. v Crestdane Ltd* [2012] EWCA Crim 958, [2013] 1 Cr. App. R. (S.) 19 (CA (Crim Div)), Lord Judge, L.C.J.
Reg.7, see *R. v Crestdane Ltd* [2012] EWCA Crim 958, [2013] 1 Cr. App. R. (S.) 19 (CA (Crim Div)), Lord Judge, L.C.J.
Reg.13, amended: SI 2013/264 Reg.11
Reg.17, see *R. v Crestdane Ltd* [2012] EWCA Crim 958, [2013] 1 Cr. App. R. (S.) 19 (CA (Crim Div)), Lord Judge, L.C.J.

31. Food Hygiene (Wales) Regulations 2006
Reg.2, amended: SI 2013/3049 Reg.2
Reg.13, amended: SI 2013/479 Reg.11
Sch.1, amended: SI 2013/3007 Reg.3, SI 2013/3049 Reg.2

131. Registered Pension Schemes (Enhanced Lifetime Allowance) Regulations 2006
applied: SSI 2013/174 Reg.2

136. Pension Benefits (Insurance Company Liable as Scheme Administrator) Regulations 2006
Reg.2, amended: SI 2013/1114 Art.6

138. Pension Schemes (Reduction in Pension Rates) Regulations 2006
Reg.3, amended: SI 2013/1111 Reg.3
Reg.4, amended: SI 2013/1111 Reg.3
Reg.4A, added: SI 2013/1111 Reg.3

177. Education (Variation of Admission Arrangements) (Wales) Regulations 2006
revoked: SI 2013/1140 Reg.1

182. Foot-and-Mouth Disease (England) Order 2006
Art.2, amended: SI 2013/2952 Sch.2 para.2
Art.26, amended: SI 2013/2952 Sch.2 para.2
Art.27, amended: SI 2013/2952 Sch.2 para.2
Sch.5 Part 2 para.20, amended: SI 2013/2952 Sch.2 para.2
Sch.5 Part 3 para.33, amended: SI 2013/2952 Sch.2 para.2
Sch.6 Part 1 para.2, amended: SI 2013/2952 Sch.2 para.2
Sch.6 Part 1 para.3, amended: SI 2013/2952 Sch.2 para.2
Sch.6 Part 1 para.5, amended: SI 2013/2952 Sch.2 para.2
Sch.6 Part 1 para.6, amended: SI 2013/2952 Sch.2 para.2
Sch.6 Part 1 para.7, amended: SI 2013/2952 Sch.2 para.2
Sch.6 Part 1 para.8, amended: SI 2013/2952 Sch.2 para.2

183. Foot-and-Mouth Disease (Control of Vaccination) (England) Regulations 2006
Sch.1 Part 3 para.18, amended: SI 2013/2952 Sch.2 para.3

202. Duty Stamps Regulations 2006
Reg.19, amended: SI 2013/1229 Reg.4
Reg.31, amended: SI 2013/1229 Reg.4

206. Pension Schemes (Categories of Country and Requirements for Overseas Pension Schemes and Recognised Overseas Pension Schemes) Regulations 2006
Reg.3, amended: SI 2013/2259 Reg.8

208. Pension Schemes (Information Requirements Qualifying Overseas Pension Schemes, Qualifying Recognised Overseas Pensions Schemes and Corresponding Relief) Regulations 2006
Reg.1, amended: SI 2013/2259 Reg.10
Reg.3, amended: SI 2013/2259 Reg.11, Reg.12, Reg.13, Reg.14
Reg.3, applied: SI 2013/2259 Reg.3
Reg.3, substituted: SI 2013/2259 Reg.11
Reg.3A, amended: SI 2013/2259 Reg.15, Reg.16, Reg.17
Reg.3B, amended: SI 2013/2259 Reg.18, Reg.19
Reg.3C, substituted: SI 2013/2259 Reg.20
Reg.5, added: SI 2013/2259 Reg.21

213. Housing Benefit Regulations 2006
applied: SI 2013/386 Reg.13, Reg.15
see *Burnip v Birmingham City Council* [2012] EWCA Civ 629, [2013] P.T.S.R. 117 (CA (Civ Div)), Maurice Kay, L.J.; see *R. (on the application of MA) v Secretary of State for Work and Pensions* [2013] EWHC 2213 (QB), [2013] P.T.S.R. 1521 (DC), Laws, L.J.; see *R. (on the application of Zacchaeus 2000 Trust) v Secretary of State for Work and Pensions* [2013] EWCA Civ 1202, [2013] P.T.S.R. 1427 (CA (Civ Div)), Sullivan, L.J.

Part 3 regB.13, amended: SI 2013/665 Reg.2, SI 2013/2828 Reg.2
Reg.2, amended: SI 2013/235 Sch.2 para.93, SI 2013/276 Reg.8, SI 2013/388 Sch.1 para.36, SI 2013/443 Reg.7, SI 2013/591 Sch.1 para.34, SI 2013/630 Reg.35, SI 2013/665 Reg.2, SI 2013/1465 Sch.1 para.23, SI 2013/2070 Reg.7, SI 2013/2536 Reg.11, SI 2013/2828 Reg.2
Reg.2, revoked (in part): SI 2013/2536 Reg.11
Reg.5, amended: SI 2013/2070 Reg.7
Reg.7, amended: SI 2013/443 Reg.7, SI 2013/2070 Reg.7
Reg.10, amended: SI 2013/1474 Reg.5, SI 2013/2536 Reg.11
Reg.10, revoked (in part): SI 2013/2536 Reg.11
Reg.13D, amended: SI 2013/665 Reg.2, SI 2013/1465 Sch.1 para.23, SI 2013/2828 Reg.2
Reg.13D, see *Burnip v Birmingham City Council* [2012] EWCA Civ 629, [2013] P.T.S.R. 117 (CA (Civ Div)), Maurice Kay, L.J.
Reg.14, amended: SI 2013/665 Reg.2, SI 2013/2828 Reg.2
Reg.19, amended: SI 2013/630 Reg.35
Reg.21, amended: SI 2013/1465 Sch.1 para.23
Reg.27, referred to: SI 2013/574 Art.19
Reg.28, amended: SI 2013/388 Sch.1 para.36, SI 2013/591 Sch.1 para.34, SI 2013/630 Reg.35
Reg.40, amended: SI 2013/630 Reg.35
Reg.42, amended: SI 2013/276 Reg.9
Reg.47, applied: SI 2013/3029 Sch.1 para.29
Reg.49, amended: SI 2013/276 Reg.10
Reg.49, applied: SI 2013/3029 Sch.6 para.31
Reg.56, amended: SI 2013/630 Reg.35, SI 2013/2070 Reg.7
Reg.74, amended: SI 2013/388 Sch.1 para.36, SI 2013/574 Art.19, SI 2013/591 Sch.1 para.34, SI 2013/630 Reg.35, SI 2013/665 Reg.2
Reg.79, amended: SI 2013/388 Sch.1 para.36, SI 2013/591 Sch.1 para.34
Reg.81, referred to: SI 2013/3029 Sch.7 para.4, SI 2013/3035 Sch.1
Reg.82, amended: SI 2013/380 Sch.3 para.3
Reg.82, applied: SI 2013/380 Reg.57
Reg.83, amended: SI 2013/2070 Reg.7
Reg.83, referred to: SI 2013/386 Reg.15
Reg.87, amended: SI 2013/2536 Reg.11
Reg.87, revoked (in part): SI 2013/2536 Reg.11
Reg.102, amended: SI 2013/630 Reg.35
Reg.105, amended: SI 2013/384 Reg.33
Reg.106A, added: SI 2013/384 Reg.33
Reg.109, amended: SI 2013/458 Sch.1
Sch.1 Part 1 para.2, amended: SI 2013/574 Art.19
Sch.1 Part 2 para.6, amended: SI 2013/574 Art.19
Sch.1 Part 2 para.6, referred to: SI 2013/574 Art.19
Sch.2 para.2, amended: SI 2013/665 Reg.2, SI 2013/2828 Reg.2
Sch.3 Part 1 para.1, referred to: 2013 c.16 Sch.1 para.1
Sch.3 Part 1 para.1, substituted: SI 2013/574 Sch.5
Sch.3 Part 1 para.2, substituted: SI 2013/574 Sch.5
Sch.3 Part 2 para.3, applied: SI 2013/3029 Sch.7 para.4, SI 2013/3035 Sch.1
Sch.3 Part 2 para.3, referred to: SI 2013/574 Art.19
Sch.3 Part 3 para.7, amended: SI 2013/388 Sch.1 para.36, SI 2013/591 Sch.1 para.34
Sch.3 Part 3 para.13, amended: SI 2013/388 Sch.1 para.36, SI 2013/591 Sch.1 para.34
Sch.3 Part 3 para.14, amended: SI 2013/388 Sch.1 para.36, SI 2013/591 Sch.1 para.34
Sch.3 Part 3 para.15, amended: SI 2013/388 Sch.1 para.36, SI 2013/591 Sch.1 para.34
Sch.3 Part 3 para.16, amended: SI 2013/388 Sch.1 para.36, SI 2013/591 Sch.1 para.34
Sch.3 Part 4, substituted: SI 2013/574 Sch.6
Sch.3 Part 5 para.21, amended: SI 2013/630 Reg.35
Sch.3 Part 5 para.21, substituted: SI 2013/443 Reg.7
Sch.3 Part 6 para.25, amended: SI 2013/574 Art.19
Sch.3 Part 6 para.26, amended: SI 2013/574 Art.19
Sch.3 Part 7 para.27, amended: SI 2013/630 Reg.35
Sch.3 Part 7 para.28, amended: SI 2013/443 Reg.7
Sch.3 Part 7 para.29, amended: SI 2013/630 Reg.35
Sch.4 para.8, amended: SI 2013/602 Sch.2 para.85, SI 2013/2536 Reg.11
Sch.4 para.10A, amended: SI 2013/630 Reg.35
Sch.4 para.12, amended: SI 2013/2070 Reg.7
Sch.4 para.17, referred to: SI 2013/574 Art.19
Sch.5 paraA.3, added: SI 2013/276 Reg.11
Sch.5 para.4, amended: SI 2013/2070 Reg.7
Sch.5 para.6, amended: SI 2013/388 Sch.1 para.36, SI 2013/591 Sch.1 para.34
Sch.5 para.7, amended: SI 2013/630 Reg.35
Sch.5 para.14, see *Lloyd v Lewisham LBC* [2013] EWCA Civ 923, [2013] P.T.S.R. 1442 (CA (Civ Div)), Arden, L.J.
Sch.5 para.27, amended: SI 2013/235 Sch.2 para.93
Sch.5 para.27, revoked (in part): SI 2013/235 Sch.2 para.93
Sch.5 para.31A, added: SI 2013/443 Reg.7
Sch.5 para.41, amended: SI 2013/443 Reg.7
Sch.5 para.51, revoked: SI 2013/458 Sch.1
Sch.5 para.56, referred to: SI 2013/574 Art.19
Sch.6 paraA.3, added: SI 2013/276 Reg.12
Sch.6 para.5, amended: SI 2013/2070 Reg.7

Sch.6 para.9, amended: SI 2013/630 Reg.35
Sch.6 para.20A, added: SI 2013/443 Reg.7
Sch.6 para.37, amended: SI 2013/443 Reg.7

214. Housing Benefit (Persons who have attained the qualifying age for state pension credit) Regulations 2006

applied: SI 2013/386 Reg.13, Reg.15
Reg.2, amended: SI 2013/235 Sch.2 para.94, SI 2013/388 Sch.1 para.37, SI 2013/443 Reg.8, SI 2013/591 Sch.1 para.35, SI 2013/630 Reg.36, SI 2013/665 Reg.3, SI 2013/2536 Reg.12, SI 2013/2828 Reg.3
Reg.2, revoked (in part): SI 2013/2536 Reg.12
Reg.5, amended: SI 2013/2070 Reg.8
Reg.7, amended: SI 2013/443 Reg.8
Reg.10, amended: SI 2013/1474 Reg.6, SI 2013/2536 Reg.12
Reg.10, revoked (in part): SI 2013/2536 Reg.12
Reg.12B, referred to: SI 2013/3035 Sch.1
Reg.13D, amended: SI 2013/665 Reg.3, SI 2013/1465 Sch.1 para.24, SI 2013/2828 Reg.3
Reg.14, amended: SI 2013/665 Reg.3, SI 2013/2828 Reg.3
Reg.19, amended: SI 2013/630 Reg.36
Reg.21, amended: SI 2013/1465 Sch.1 para.24
Reg.29, amended: SI 2013/388 Sch.1 para.37, SI 2013/591 Sch.1 para.35
Reg.29, revoked (in part): SI 2013/458 Sch.1
Reg.30, referred to: SI 2013/574 Art.20
Reg.31, amended: SI 2013/388 Sch.1 para.37, SI 2013/591 Sch.1 para.35, SI 2013/630 Reg.36
Reg.38, amended: SI 2013/235 Sch.2 para.94
Reg.38, revoked (in part): SI 2013/235 Sch.2 para.94
Reg.47, applied: SI 2013/3029 Sch.1 para.29, SI 2013/3035 Sch.1
Reg.49, applied: SI 2013/3035 Sch.1
Reg.55, amended: SI 2013/388 Sch.1 para.37, SI 2013/574 Art.20, SI 2013/591 Sch.1 para.35, SI 2013/630 Reg.36, SI 2013/665 Reg.3
Reg.59, amended: SI 2013/388 Sch.1 para.37, SI 2013/591 Sch.1 para.35
Reg.64, referred to: SI 2013/386 Reg.15
Reg.68, amended: SI 2013/2536 Reg.12
Reg.68, revoked (in part): SI 2013/2536 Reg.12
Reg.83, amended: SI 2013/630 Reg.36
Reg.86, amended: SI 2013/384 Reg.34
Reg.87A, added: SI 2013/384 Reg.34
Reg.90, amended: SI 2013/458 Sch.1
Sch.1 Part 1 para.2, amended: SI 2013/574 Art.20
Sch.1 Part 2 para.6, amended: SI 2013/574 Art.20
Sch.1 Part 2 para.6, referred to: SI 2013/574 Art.20
Sch.2 para.2, amended: SI 2013/665 Reg.3, SI 2013/2828 Reg.3
Sch.3 Part 1 para.1, substituted: SI 2013/574 Sch.7
Sch.3 Part 1 para.2, amended: SI 2013/574 Sch.7
Sch.3 Part 2 para.3, referred to: SI 2013/574 Art.20
Sch.3 Part 3 para.5, amended: SI 2013/388 Sch.1 para.37, SI 2013/591 Sch.1 para.35
Sch.3 Part 3 para.6, amended: SI 2013/388 Sch.1 para.37, SI 2013/591 Sch.1 para.35
Sch.3 Part 3 para.7, amended: SI 2013/388 Sch.1 para.37, SI 2013/591 Sch.1 para.35
Sch.3 Part 3 para.8, amended: SI 2013/388 Sch.1 para.37, SI 2013/591 Sch.1 para.35
Sch.3 Part 4, substituted: SI 2013/574 Sch.8
Sch.4 para.3, amended: SI 2013/602 Sch.2 para.86, SI 2013/2536 Reg.12
Sch.4 para.5, amended: SI 2013/388 Sch.1 para.37, SI 2013/458 Sch.1, SI 2013/591 Sch.1 para.35, SI 2013/630 Reg.36
Sch.4 para.5A, amended: SI 2013/630 Reg.36
Sch.4 para.9, referred to: SI 2013/574 Art.20
Sch.5 para.21, referred to: SI 2013/574 Art.20
Sch.6 Part 1 para.21, amended: SI 2013/388 Sch.1 para.37, SI 2013/443 Reg.8, SI 2013/591 Sch.1 para.35, SI 2013/630 Reg.36
Sch.6 Part 1 para.22, amended: SI 2013/458 Sch.1, SI 2013/2536 Reg.12
Sch.6 Part 1 para.26E, added: SI 2013/443 Reg.8

215. Council Tax Benefit Regulations 2006

applied: SI 2013/358 Art.10
Reg.2, amended: SI 2013/276 Reg.8
Reg.32, amended: SI 2013/276 Reg.9
Reg.39, amended: SI 2013/276 Reg.10
Reg.69, varied: SI 2013/358 Sch.5 para.2
Reg.69, see *Arca v Carlisle City Council* [2013] R.A. 248 (VT), Graham Zellick Q.C. (President)
Reg.72, varied: SI 2013/358 Sch.5 para.3
Reg.73, varied: SI 2013/358 Sch.5 para.4
Reg.74, varied: SI 2013/358 Sch.5 para.5
Sch.4 paraA.3, added: SI 2013/276 Reg.11
Sch.5 paraA.3, added: SI 2013/276 Reg.12
Sch.5 para.9, applied: SI 2013/3029 Sch.5 para.22, SI 2013/3035 Sch.1

216. Council Tax Benefit (Persons who have attained the qualifying age for state pension credit) Regulations 2006

applied: SI 2013/358 Art.10
Reg.50, applied: SI 2013/111 Reg.5, SI 2013/215 Reg.3
Reg.53, varied: SI 2013/358 Sch.5 para.2
Reg.57, varied: SI 2013/358 Sch.5 para.3
Reg.58, varied: SI 2013/358 Sch.5 para.4
Reg.59, varied: SI 2013/358 Sch.5 para.5
Sch.1 Part 2 para.3, applied: SI 2013/3029 Sch.7 para.4, SI 2013/3035 Sch.1

223. Child Benefit (General) Regulations 2006

Reg.8, amended: SI 2013/630 Reg.84
Reg.18, amended: SI 2013/1465 Sch.1 para.25

225. Hill Farm Allowance Regulations 2006
revoked: SI 2013/109 Reg.9

246. Transfer of Undertakings (Protection of Employment) Regulations 2006
applied: 2013 asp 8 s.3, SI 2013/278 Reg.5, SI 2013/1893 Sch.2
disapplied: 2013 c.32 Sch.13 para.2
referred to: 2013 c.24 s.27, 2013 c.32 Sch.11 para.4
see *Ceva Freight (UK) Ltd v Seawell Ltd* [2013] CSIH 59, 2013 S.L.T. 922 (IH (Ex Div)), Lord Eassie; see *Liddell's Coaches v Cook* [2013] I.C.R. 547 (EAT (SC)), Lady Smith; see *Manchester College v Hazel* [2013] EWCA Civ 281, [2013] C.P. Rep. 28 (CA (Civ Div)), Jackson, L.J.; see *Optimum Group Services Plc v Muir* [2013] I.R.L.R. 339 (EAT (SC)), Lady Smith
Reg.2, see *Ceva Freight (UK) Ltd v Seawell Ltd* [2013] CSIH 59, 2013 S.L.T. 922 (IH (Ex Div)), Lord Eassie
Reg.3, see *Ceva Freight (UK) Ltd v Seawell Ltd* [2013] CSIH 59, 2013 S.L.T. 922 (IH (Ex Div)), Lord Eassie; see *Hunter v McCarrick* [2012] EWCA Civ 1399, [2013] I.C.R. 235 (CA (Civ Div)), Sir Maurice Kay (VP CA Civ); see *Liddell's Coaches v Cook* [2013] I.C.R. 547 (EAT (SC)), Lady Smith; see *SNR Denton UK LLP v Kirwan* [2013] I.C.R. 101 (EAT), Langstaff, J. (President)
Reg.4, see *Ceva Freight (UK) Ltd v Seawell Ltd* [2013] CSIH 59, 2013 S.L.T. 922 (IH (Ex Div)), Lord Eassie; see *Fox Cross Claimants v Glasgow City Council* [2013] I.C.R. 954 (EAT (SC)), Langstaff, J. (President)
Reg.7, see *Kavanagh v Crystal Palace FC 2000 Ltd* [2013] I.R.L.R. 291 (EAT), Wilkie, J.; see *Manchester College v Hazel* [2013] EWCA Civ 281, [2013] C.P. Rep. 28 (CA (Civ Div)), Jackson, L.J.
Reg.10, varied: SI 2013/278 Reg.4
Reg.11, applied: SI 2013/278 Reg.5
Reg.12, applied: SI 2013/278 Reg.5
Reg.13, applied: SI 2013/278 Reg.5, SI 2013/3104 Sch.2 para.30
Reg.13, see *I Lab Facilities Ltd v Metcalfe* [2013] I.R.L.R. 605 (EAT), Underhill, J.
Reg.13A, applied: SI 2013/278 Reg.5
Reg.14, applied: SI 2013/278 Reg.5
Reg.15, applied: SI 2013/278 Reg.5
Reg.15, see *I Lab Facilities Ltd v Metcalfe* [2013] I.R.L.R. 605 (EAT), Underhill, J.
Reg.16, applied: SI 2013/278 Reg.5

264. Community Benefit Societies (Restriction on Use of Assets) Regulations 2006
Reg.2, amended: SI 2013/472 Sch.2 para.113
Reg.8, substituted: SI 2013/472 Sch.2 para.113

302. Crime Prevention (Designated Areas) Order 2006
revoked: SI 2013/1760 Sch.1

349. Occupational and Personal Pension Schemes (Consultation by Employers and Miscellaneous Amendment) Regulations 2006
applied: SI 2013/1893 Sch.2
Reg.11, amended: SI 2013/2734 Sch.9 para.15
Sch.1 para.12, amended: SI 2013/1956 Sch.1 para.11
Sch.1 para.13, amended: SI 2013/1956 Sch.1 para.11

359. National Health Service (Functions of Strategic Health Authorities and Primary Care Trusts and Administration Arrangements) (England) (Amendment) Regulations 2006
revoked: SI 2013/235 Sch.2 para.193

367. Housing (Empty Dwelling Management Orders) (Prescribed Exceptions and Requirements) (England) Order 2006
see *Braithwaite v Secretary of State for Communities and Local Government* [2012] EWHC 2835 (Admin), [2013] J.P.L. 312 (QBD (Admin)), Kenneth Parker, J.
Art.4, amended: SI 2013/1036 Sch.2 para.30

371. Licensing of Houses in Multiple Occupation (Prescribed Descriptions) (England) Order 2006
Art.3, see *Islington LBC v Unite Group Plc* [2013] EWHC 508 (Admin), [2013] P.T.S.R. 1078 (QBD (Admin)), Blake, J.

373. Licensing and Management of Houses in Multiple Occupation and Other Houses (Miscellaneous Provisions) (England) Regulations 2006
Reg.11, amended: SI 2013/1036 Sch.2 para.32
Reg.12, amended: SI 2013/1036 Sch.2 para.32
Reg.13, amended: SI 2013/1036 Sch.2 para.32, Sch.2 para.33

405. Greater Manchester (Light Rapid Transit System) Order 2006
Art.4, amended: SI 2013/2587 Art.39
Art.5, amended: SI 2013/2587 Art.39

438. Management of Health and Safety at Work (Amendment) Regulations 2006
revoked: SI 2013/1667 Reg.4

489. National Health Service (Personal Dental Services Agreements) (Wales) Regulations 2006
Reg.2, amended: SI 2013/235 Sch.2 para.95
Reg.4, amended: SI 2013/235 Sch.2 para.95

Sch.3 Part 2 para.15, amended: SI 2013/235 Sch.2 para.95
Sch.3 Part 2 para.15, applied: SI 2013/235 Sch.3 para.16
Sch.3 Part 4 para.31, amended: SI 2013/235 Sch.2 para.95
Sch.3 Part 6 para.51, amended: SI 2013/235 Sch.2 para.95
Sch.3 Part 6 para.51, applied: SI 2013/235 Sch.3 para.13
Sch.3 Part 9 para.69, amended: SI 2013/235 Sch.2 para.95

490. National Health Service (General Dental Services Contracts) (Wales) Regulations 2006
Reg.2, amended: SI 2013/235 Sch.2 para.96
Reg.4, amended: SI 2013/235 Sch.2 para.96
Sch.3 Part 2 para.14, amended: SI 2013/235 Sch.2 para.96
Sch.3 Part 2 para.14, applied: SI 2013/235 Sch.3 para.17
Sch.3 Part 4 para.30, amended: SI 2013/235 Sch.2 para.96
Sch.3 Part 6 para.51, amended: SI 2013/235 Sch.2 para.96
Sch.3 Part 6 para.51, applied: SI 2013/235 Sch.3 para.14
Sch.3 Part 9 para.71, amended: SI 2013/235 Sch.2 para.96

491. National Health Service (Dental Charges) (Wales) Regulations 2006
Reg.2, amended: SI 2013/235 Sch.2 para.97
Reg.4, amended: SI 2013/544 Reg.2
Reg.12, amended: SI 2013/235 Sch.2 para.97

501. Fines Collection Regulations 2006
Reg.30, amended: SI 2013/534 Sch.1 para.16

518. Hill Farm Allowance (Amendment) Regulations 2006
revoked: SI 2013/109 Reg.9

537. Highways Act 1980 (Gating Orders) (England) Regulations 2006
Reg.2, amended: SI 2013/235 Sch.2 para.98

552. National Health Service (Local Pharmaceutical Services etc.) Regulations 2006
applied: SI 2013/349 Reg.2, Sch.9 para.1, Sch.9 para.2, Sch.9 para.15
referred to: SI 2013/349 Sch.9 para.1
revoked: SI 2013/349 Sch.10 para.5
Part 2, applied: SI 2013/349 Sch.9 para.16
Reg.4, applied: SI 2013/349 Reg.32, Reg.99, Reg.100, Reg.101
Reg.6, applied: SI 2013/349 Reg.101
Reg.12, applied: SI 2013/349 Sch.7 para.29
Reg.15, applied: SI 2013/349 Reg.28, Reg.108
Reg.17, applied: SI 2013/349 Sch.7 para.29
Sch.2 para.16, applied: SI 2013/349 Sch.7 para.29

557. Health and Safety (Enforcing Authority for Railways and Other Guided Transport Systems) Regulations 2006
applied: SI 2013/1506 Reg.9, Reg.18
Reg.2, amended: SI 2013/950 Reg.2
Reg.3, referred to: SI 2013/1471 Reg.17
Reg.4, amended: SI 2013/950 Reg.2
Reg.8, added: SI 2013/950 Reg.2

567. Registered Pension Schemes (Provision of Information) Regulations 2006
Reg.2, amended: SI 2013/1742 Reg.3
Reg.3, amended: SI 2013/1742 Reg.4
Reg.3, disapplied: SI 2013/2259 Reg.6
Reg.11, amended: SI 2013/1742 Reg.5
Reg.11BA, amended: SI 2013/1742 Reg.6
Reg.11BA, disapplied: SI 2013/2259 Reg.6
Reg.11BA, referred to: SI 2013/2259 Reg.6
Reg.15A, applied: SSI 2013/174 Reg.2

569. Registered Pension Schemes (Splitting of Schemes) Regulations 2006
Sch.3 Part 1, amended: SI 2013/1114 Art.7
Sch.3 Part 1A, amended: SI 2013/1114 Art.7

570. Registered Pension Schemes and Overseas Pension Schemes (Electronic Communication of Returns and Information) Regulations 2006
Sch.2, added: SI 2013/1114 Art.8
Sch.2, amended: SI 2013/2259 Reg.23
Sch.2, revoked: SI 2013/1114 Art.8

575. Pension Protection Fund (Tax) Regulations 2006
Reg.2, amended: SI 2013/1117 Reg.3
Reg.5, amended: SI 2013/1117 Reg.4
Reg.6, amended: SI 2013/1117 Reg.5, Reg.6
Reg.8, amended: SI 2013/1117 Reg.7
Reg.14, amended: SI 2013/1117 Reg.8
Reg.23A, added: SI 2013/1117 Reg.9
Reg.28A, added: SI 2013/1117 Reg.10
Reg.42, substituted: SI 2013/1117 Reg.11

580. Pension Protection Fund (General and Miscellaneous Amendments) Regulations 2006
Reg.1, amended: SI 2013/472 Art.4, SI 2013/627 Reg.5
Reg.7, amended: SI 2013/627 Reg.5
Reg.8, amended: SI 2013/627 Reg.5
Reg.9A, added: SI 2013/627 Reg.5

596. Functions of Primary Care Trusts and Strategic Health Authorities and the NHS Business Services Authority (Awdurdod Gwasanaethau Busnes y GIG) (Primary Dental Services) (England) Regulations 2006
applied: SI 2013/469 Reg.4
revoked: SI 2013/469 Reg.5

599. Railways and Other Guided Transport Systems (Safety) Regulations 2006
Reg.2, amended: SI 2013/950 Reg.3

Reg.2A, added: SI 2013/950 Reg.3
Reg.3, amended: SI 2013/950 Reg.3
Reg.5, amended: SI 2013/950 Reg.3
Reg.5, revoked (in part): SI 2013/950 Reg.3
Reg.17, amended: SI 2013/950 Reg.3
Reg.17, revoked (in part): SI 2013/950 Reg.3
Reg.18A, amended: SI 2013/950 Reg.3
Reg.20, amended: SI 2013/950 Reg.3
Reg.21, amended: SI 2013/950 Reg.3
Reg.24, amended: SI 2013/950 Reg.3
Reg.27, amended: SI 2013/950 Reg.3
Reg.27, revoked (in part): SI 2013/2042 Sch.1 para.63
Reg.29, revoked (in part): SI 2013/950 Reg.3
Sch.2 Part 1 para.1, amended: SI 2013/950 Reg.3
Sch.3 Part 1 para.2, amended: SI 2013/950 Reg.3
Sch.3 Part 1 para.6, amended: SI 2013/950 Reg.3
Sch.3 Part 2 para.1, amended: SI 2013/950 Reg.3
Sch.3 Part 2 para.1, revoked (in part): SI 2013/950 Reg.3
Sch.4 para.1, amended: SI 2013/950 Reg.3
Sch.5 para.1, revoked: SI 2013/950 Reg.3
Sch.5 para.2, revoked: SI 2013/950 Reg.3
Sch.5 para.3, revoked: SI 2013/950 Reg.3
Sch.5 para.4, revoked: SI 2013/950 Reg.3
Sch.5 para.5, revoked: SI 2013/950 Reg.3
Sch.5 para.6, revoked: SI 2013/950 Reg.3
Sch.5 para.7, revoked: SI 2013/950 Reg.3
Sch.5 para.8, revoked: SI 2013/950 Reg.3
Sch.5 para.9, revoked: SI 2013/950 Reg.3
Sch.5 para.10, revoked: SI 2013/950 Reg.3
Sch.5 para.11, revoked: SI 2013/950 Reg.3
Sch.5 para.12, revoked: SI 2013/950 Reg.3
Sch.5 para.13, revoked: SI 2013/950 Reg.3
Sch.5 para.14, revoked: SI 2013/950 Reg.3
Sch.6 para.1, revoked: SI 2013/1471 Sch.4

606. Naval, Military and Air Forces Etc (Disablement and Death) Service Pensions Order 2006

applied: SI 2013/241, SI 2013/380 Reg.61, SI 2013/471 Reg.20, Reg.33, SI 2013/480 Reg.24, SI 2013/483 Reg.10, SI 2013/628 Sch.1 para.25, SI 2013/3029 Sch.9 para.53
Part II, applied: SI 2013/3029 Sch.4 para.13, Sch.9 para.53, SI 2013/3035 Sch.1
Part III, applied: SI 2013/3029 Sch.4 para.13, Sch.9 para.53, SI 2013/3035 Sch.1
Art.8, referred to: SSI 2013/148 Reg.6
Art.10, amended: SI 2013/630 Reg.49
Art.15, amended: SI 2013/630 Reg.49
Art.20, amended: SI 2013/388 Sch.1 para.38
Art.20, applied: SI 2013/3029 Sch.3 para.5, Sch.4 para.3, Sch.9 para.13, SI 2013/3035 Sch.1, SSI 2013/148 Reg.6
Art.23, applied: SI 2013/3029 Sch.4 para.4, Sch.9 para.54, SI 2013/3035 Sch.1
Art.23, referred to: SI 2013/3029 Sch.4 para.6, Sch.9 para.56
Art.33, amended: SI 2013/241 Art.3
Art.42, amended: SI 2013/241 Art.4
Art.50, amended: SI 2013/630 Reg.49
Art.53, applied: SI 2013/376 Reg.83
Art.56, amended: SI 2013/388 Sch.1 para.38, SI 2013/630 Reg.49
Sch.1 Part II, substituted: SI 2013/241 Sch.1
Sch.1 Part III, substituted: SI 2013/241 Sch.2
Sch.1 Part IV, substituted: SI 2013/241 Sch.3
Sch.2 Part II, substituted: SI 2013/241 Sch.4
Sch.2 Part III, substituted: SI 2013/241 Sch.5

641. Water Resources (Abstraction and Impounding) Regulations 2006

Reg.2, amended: SI 2013/755 Sch.4 para.247
Reg.3, amended: SI 2013/755 Sch.4 para.247
Reg.4, amended: SI 2013/755 Sch.4 para.247
Reg.5, amended: SI 2013/755 Sch.4 para.247
Reg.6, amended: SI 2013/755 Sch.4 para.247
Reg.7, amended: SI 2013/755 Sch.4 para.247
Reg.8, amended: SI 2013/755 Sch.4 para.247
Reg.9, amended: SI 2013/755 Sch.4 para.247
Reg.10, amended: SI 2013/755 Sch.4 para.247
Reg.11, amended: SI 2013/755 Sch.4 para.247
Reg.12, amended: SI 2013/755 Sch.4 para.247
Reg.13, amended: SI 2013/755 Sch.4 para.247
Reg.14, amended: SI 2013/755 Sch.4 para.247
Reg.15, amended: SI 2013/755 Sch.4 para.247
Reg.16, amended: SI 2013/755 Sch.4 para.247
Reg.17, amended: SI 2013/755 Sch.4 para.247
Reg.18, amended: SI 2013/755 Sch.4 para.247
Reg.19, amended: SI 2013/755 Sch.4 para.247
Reg.20, amended: SI 2013/755 Sch.4 para.247
Reg.21, amended: SI 2013/755 Sch.4 para.247
Reg.22, amended: SI 2013/755 Sch.4 para.247
Reg.23, amended: SI 2013/755 Sch.4 para.247
Reg.24, amended: SI 2013/755 Sch.4 para.247
Reg.25, amended: SI 2013/755 Sch.4 para.247
Reg.26, amended: SI 2013/755 Sch.4 para.247
Reg.27, amended: SI 2013/755 Sch.4 para.247
Reg.29, amended: SI 2013/755 Sch.4 para.247
Reg.30, amended: SI 2013/755 Sch.4 para.247
Reg.31, amended: SI 2013/755 Sch.4 para.247
Reg.32, amended: SI 2013/755 Sch.4 para.247
Reg.34, amended: SI 2013/755 Sch.4 para.247
Sch.2 para.1, amended: SI 2013/755 Sch.4 para.247
Sch.2 para.2, amended: SI 2013/755 Sch.4 para.247
Sch.2 para.3, amended: SI 2013/755 Sch.4 para.247

Sch.2 para.4, amended: SI 2013/755 Sch.4 para.247
Sch.2 para.5, amended: SI 2013/755 Sch.4 para.247
Sch.2 para.6, amended: SI 2013/755 Sch.4 para.247
Sch.2 para.7, amended: SI 2013/755 Sch.4 para.247
Sch.2 para.8, amended: SI 2013/755 Sch.4 para.247

655. Olympic Lotteries (Payments out of Fund) Regulations 2006
Reg.3, amended: SI 2013/2329 Sch.1 para.36

659. Weights and Measures (Packaged Goods) Regulations 2006
Reg.2, amended: SI 2013/1478 Sch.5 para.17
Reg.5, amended: SI 2013/1478 Sch.5 para.17
Reg.6, amended: SI 2013/1478 Sch.5 para.17

676. Judicial Discipline (Prescribed Procedures) Regulations 2006
revoked: SI 2013/1674 Reg.25
Reg.27, applied: SI 2013/1674 Reg.24

679. Permitted Persons (Designation) Order 2006
Art.2, amended: SI 2013/472 Sch.2 para.114

714. Occupational Pension Schemes (Member-nominated Trustees and Directors) Regulations 2006
Reg.1, amended: SI 2013/472 Art.4

741. Pensions Increase (Review) Order 2006
applied: SI 2013/604 Sch.1

758. Gender Recognition (Application Fees) Order 2006
Art.1, revoked (in part): SI 2013/2302 Art.4
Art.2, substituted: SI 2013/2302 Art.4
Art.3, substituted: SI 2013/2302 Art.4
Art.3A, added: SI 2013/2302 Art.4
Art.4, revoked: SI 2013/2302 Art.4
Art.5, revoked: SI 2013/2302 Art.4
Sch.1 para.1, added: SI 2013/2302 Sch.1
Sch.1 para.2, added: SI 2013/2302 Sch.1
Sch.1 para.3, added: SI 2013/2302 Sch.1
Sch.1 para.4, added: SI 2013/2302 Sch.1
Sch.1 para.5, added: SI 2013/2302 Sch.1
Sch.1 para.6, added: SI 2013/2302 Sch.1
Sch.1 para.7, added: SI 2013/2302 Sch.1
Sch.1 para.8, added: SI 2013/2302 Sch.1
Sch.1 para.9, added: SI 2013/2302 Sch.1
Sch.1 para.10, added: SI 2013/2302 Sch.1
Sch.1 para.11, added: SI 2013/2302 Sch.1
Sch.1 para.12, added: SI 2013/2302 Sch.1
Sch.1 para.13, added: SI 2013/2302 Sch.1
Sch.1 para.14, added: SI 2013/2302 Sch.1
Sch.1 para.15, added: SI 2013/2302 Sch.1
Sch.1 para.16, added: SI 2013/2302 Sch.1
Sch.1 para.17, added: SI 2013/2302 Sch.1
Sch.1 para.18, added: SI 2013/2302 Sch.1
Sch.1 para.19, added: SI 2013/2302 Sch.1
Sch.1 para.20, added: SI 2013/2302 Sch.1

759. Occupational Pension Schemes (Modification of Schemes) Regulations 2006
Reg.3, amended: SI 2013/459 Reg.9
Reg.8A, added: SI 2013/1754 Reg.3

782. Nottingham University Hospitals National Health Service Trust (Establishment) and the Nottingham City Hospital National Health Service Trust and the Queen's Medical Centre... 2006
Art.1, amended: SI 2013/593 Art.2

788. Great Western Ambulance Service National Health Service Trust (Establishment) and the Avon Ambulance Service National Health Service Trust, the Gloucestershire Ambulance Service National... 2006
revoked: SI 2013/4 Art.2

802. Occupational Pension Schemes (Payments to Employer) Regulations 2006
Reg.10, amended: SI 2013/2734 Sch.9 para.16
Reg.15, amended: SI 2013/2734 Sch.9 para.16

913. National Health Service (Miscellaneous Amendments Relating to Independent Prescribing) Regulations 2006
Reg.4, revoked: SI 2013/349 Sch.10 para.5

932. Police (Injury Benefit) Regulations 2006
see *R. (on the application of Commissioner of Police of the Metropolis) v Police Medical Appeal Board* [2013] EWHC 1203 (Admin), [2013] I.C.R. 1245 (QBD (Admin)), Collins, J.
Reg.3, revoked (in part): SI 2013/2318 Sch.1 para.54
Reg.6, revoked (in part): SI 2013/2318 Sch.1 para.55
Reg.7, see *R. (on the application of Commissioner of Police of the Metropolis) v Police Medical Appeal Board* [2013] EWHC 1203 (Admin), [2013] I.C.R. 1245 (QBD (Admin)), Collins, J.
Reg.30, see *R. (on the application of Commissioner of Police of the Metropolis) v Police Medical Appeal Board* [2013] EWHC 1203 (Admin), [2013] I.C.R. 1245 (QBD (Admin)), Collins, J.
Reg.37, see *R. (on the application of Commissioner of Police of the Metropolis) v Police Medical Appeal Board* [2013] EWHC 1203 (Admin), [2013] I.C.R. 1245 (QBD (Admin)), Collins, J.
Reg.39, revoked (in part): SI 2013/2318 Sch.1 para.56
Sch.1, amended: SI 2013/2318 Sch.1 para.57
Sch.1, revoked (in part): SI 2013/2318 Sch.1 para.57
Sch.4 para.1, amended: SI 2013/630 Reg.75

946. General Dental Services and Personal Dental Services Transitional and Consequential Provisions (Wales) Order 2006

Sch.1 para.6, revoked: SI 2013/898 Sch.8 para.16

964. Authorised Investment Funds (Tax) Regulations 2006

Reg.8, amended: SI 2013/472 Sch.2 para.115
Reg.14B, amended: SI 2013/472 Sch.2 para.115
Reg.17, amended: SI 2013/2819 Reg.42
Reg.23, amended: SI 2013/472 Sch.2 para.115
Reg.26, amended: SI 2013/2994 Reg.3
Reg.27, amended: SI 2013/2994 Reg.7
Reg.29, amended: SI 2013/2994 Reg.8
Reg.30, amended: SI 2013/2994 Reg.9
Reg.31, amended: SI 2013/2994 Reg.10
Reg.33, amended: SI 2013/2994 Reg.11
Reg.33A, added: SI 2013/2994 Reg.4
Reg.46A, added: SI 2013/1772 Reg.2
Reg.46A, amended: SI 2013/2994 Reg.5
Reg.46B, added: SI 2013/1772 Reg.2
Reg.46B, amended: SI 2013/2994 Reg.6
Reg.52D, amended: SI 2013/1411 Reg.14
Reg.69Q, amended: SI 2013/472 Sch.2 para.115
Reg.69Z39, amended: SI 2013/472 Sch.2 para.115
Reg.69Z51, amended: SI 2013/472 Sch.2 para.115
Reg.69Z53, amended: SI 2013/472 Sch.2 para.115
Reg.100, revoked (in part): SI 2013/1400 Reg.14
Reg.102, revoked (in part): SI 2013/1400 Reg.14
Reg.104, revoked (in part): SI 2013/1400 Reg.14
Reg.106, revoked: SI 2013/1400 Reg.14
Reg.109, revoked (in part): SI 2013/1400 Reg.14

965. Child Benefit (Rates) Regulations 2006

Reg.2, applied: SI 2013/716 Art.3

987. Serious Organised Crime and Police Act 2005 (Application and Modification of Certain Enactments to Designated Staff of SOCA) Order 2006

referred to: 2013 c.22 Sch.8 para.7
Art.2, varied: 2013 c.22 Sch.8 para.7
Art.3, varied: 2013 c.22 Sch.8 para.7
Art.4, varied: 2013 c.22 Sch.8 para.7
Art.5, varied: 2013 c.22 Sch.8 para.7
Art.6, varied: 2013 c.22 Sch.8 para.7
Art.7, varied: 2013 c.22 Sch.8 para.7
Sch.1 para.1, varied: 2013 c.22 Sch.8 para.7
Sch.1 para.2, varied: 2013 c.22 Sch.8 para.7
Sch.1 para.3, varied: 2013 c.22 Sch.8 para.7
Sch.1 para.4, varied: 2013 c.22 Sch.8 para.7
Sch.1 para.5, varied: 2013 c.22 Sch.8 para.7
Sch.1 para.6, varied: 2013 c.22 Sch.8 para.7
Sch.1 para.7, varied: 2013 c.22 Sch.8 para.7
Sch.1 para.8, varied: 2013 c.22 Sch.8 para.7
Sch.1 para.9, varied: 2013 c.22 Sch.8 para.7
Sch.1 para.10, varied: 2013 c.22 Sch.8 para.7
Sch.1 para.11, varied: 2013 c.22 Sch.8 para.7
Sch.1 para.12, varied: 2013 c.22 Sch.8 para.7
Sch.1 para.13, varied: 2013 c.22 Sch.8 para.7
Sch.1 para.14, varied: 2013 c.22 Sch.8 para.7
Sch.1 para.15, varied: 2013 c.22 Sch.8 para.7
Sch.1 para.16, varied: 2013 c.22 Sch.8 para.7
Sch.1 para.17, varied: 2013 c.22 Sch.8 para.7
Sch.1 para.18, varied: 2013 c.22 Sch.8 para.7
Sch.1 para.19, varied: 2013 c.22 Sch.8 para.7
Sch.1 para.20, varied: 2013 c.22 Sch.8 para.7
Sch.1 para.21, varied: 2013 c.22 Sch.8 para.7
Sch.2 para.6, varied: 2013 c.22 Sch.8 para.7

1003. Immigration (European Economic Area) Regulations 2006

applied: SI 2013/617 Sch.3 para.2, SI 2013/3032 Sch.3 para.2
referred to: SI 2013/617 Reg.5
see *Ahmed (Amos: Zambrano: Reg. 15A(3)(c) 2006 EEA Regs), Re* [2013] UKUT 89 (IAC), [2013] Imm. A.R. 540 (UT (IAC)), Lang, J.; see *Pryce v Southwark LBC* [2012] EWCA Civ 1572, [2013] 1 W.L.R. 996 (CA (Civ Div)), Pill, L.J.; see *RM (Zimbabwe) v Secretary of State for the Home Department* [2013] EWCA Civ 775, [2013] 3 C.M.L.R. 44 (CA (Civ Div)), Longmore, L.J.; see *Shabani (EEA: Jobseekers: Nursery Education), Re* [2013] UKUT 315 (IAC), [2013] Imm. A.R. 934 (UT (IAC)), Judge Storey; see *Zubair (EEA Regs: Self-employed Persons), Re* [2013] UKUT 196 (IAC), [2013] Imm. A.R. 740 (UT (IAC)), Blake, J. (President)
Reg.2, amended: SI 2013/3032 Sch.1 para.1
Reg.4, see *Seye (Chen Children: Employment), Re* [2013] UKUT 178 (IAC), [2013] Imm. A.R. 704 (UT (IAC)), Judge Storey
Reg.5, amended: SI 2013/3032 Sch.1 para.2
Reg.5, see *Zubair (EEA Regs: Self-employed Persons), Re* [2013] UKUT 196 (IAC), [2013] Imm. A.R. 740 (UT (IAC)), Blake, J. (President)
Reg.6, amended: SI 2013/3032 Sch.1 para.3
Reg.6, applied: SI 2013/376 Reg.9, Reg.92, SI 2013/1460 Reg.7, SI 2013/3029 Reg.28, SI 2013/3032 Sch.3 para.1, SI 2013/3035 Sch.1
Reg.6, disapplied: SI 2013/1460 Reg.5
Reg.6, referred to: SI 2013/376 Reg.92, SI 2013/3035 Sch.1
Reg.6, varied: SI 2013/1460 Reg.7
Reg.6, see *Konodyba v Kensington and Chelsea RLBC* [2012] EWCA Civ 982, [2013] P.T.S.R. 13 (CA (Civ Div)), Lord Neuberger (M.R.); see *Samin v Westminster City Council* [2012] EWCA Civ 1468, [2013] 2 C.M.L.R. 6 (CA (Civ Div)), Hughes, L.J.; see *Seye (Chen Children: Employment), Re* [2013] UKUT 178 (IAC), [2013] Imm. A.R. 704 (UT (IAC)), Judge Storey; see

Shabani (EEA: Jobseekers: Nursery Education), Re [2013] UKUT 315 (IAC), [2013] Imm. A.R. 934 (UT (IAC)), Judge Storey; see *Zubair (EEA Regs: Self-employed Persons), Re* [2013] UKUT 196 (IAC), [2013] Imm. A.R. 740 (UT (IAC)), Blake, J. (President)
Reg.7, applied: SI 2013/376 Reg.9, SI 2013/3029 Reg.28, SI 2013/3035 Sch.1
Reg.7B, added: SI 2013/3032 Sch.1 para.4
Reg.8, see *Aladeselu v Secretary of State for the Home Department* [2013] EWCA Civ 144, [2013] Imm. A.R. 780 (CA (Civ Div)), Pill, L.J.; see *Soares v Secretary of State for the Home Department* [2013] EWCA Civ 575, [2013] 3 C.M.L.R. 31 (CA (Civ Div)), Longmore, L.J.
Reg.9, referred to: SI 2013/3032 Sch.3 para.2
Reg.9, substituted: SI 2013/3032 Sch.1 para.5
Reg.10, applied: SI 2013/3032 Sch.3 para.2
Reg.11, amended: SI 2013/3032 Sch.1 para.6
Reg.12, amended: SI 2013/3032 Sch.1 para.7
Reg.13, amended: SI 2013/3032 Sch.1 para.8
Reg.13, applied: SI 2013/376 Reg.9, SI 2013/3029 Reg.28, SI 2013/3035 Sch.1
Reg.14, amended: SI 2013/3032 Sch.1 para.9
Reg.14, applied: SI 2013/3029 Reg.28, SI 2013/3035 Sch.1
Reg.14, see *Seye (Chen Children: Employment), Re* [2013] UKUT 178 (IAC), [2013] Imm. A.R. 704 (UT (IAC)), Judge Storey
Reg.15, amended: SI 2013/3032 Sch.1 para.10
Reg.15, applied: SI 2013/376 Reg.9, SI 2013/1460 Reg.2, SI 2013/3029 Reg.28, SI 2013/3032 Sch.3 para.2, SI 2013/3035 Sch.1
Reg.15A, amended: SI 2013/3032 Sch.1 para.11
Reg.15A, applied: SI 2013/376 Reg.9, SI 2013/3029 Reg.28, SI 2013/3035 Sch.1
Reg.15A, see *Seye (Chen Children: Employment), Re* [2013] UKUT 178 (IAC), [2013] Imm. A.R. 704 (UT (IAC)), Judge Storey; see *Shabani (EEA: Jobseekers: Nursery Education), Re* [2013] UKUT 315 (IAC), [2013] Imm. A.R. 934 (UT (IAC)), Judge Storey
Reg.15B, amended: SI 2013/3032 Sch.1 para.12
Reg.16, amended: SI 2013/1391 Reg.2
Reg.16, applied: SI 2013/1460 Reg.7
Reg.17, revoked (in part): SI 2013/1391 Reg.2
Reg.17, see *Aladeselu v Secretary of State for the Home Department* [2013] EWCA Civ 144, [2013] Imm. A.R. 780 (CA (Civ Div)), Pill, L.J.
Reg.18, revoked (in part): SI 2013/1391 Reg.2
Reg.18A, amended: SI 2013/1391 Reg.2
Reg.19, amended: SI 2013/3032 Sch.1 para.13
Reg.19, applied: SI 2013/1460 Reg.6, SI 2013/3032 Sch.3 para.3
Reg.19, see *R. (on the application of Nouazli) v Secretary of State for the Home Department* [2013] EWHC 567 (Admin), [2013] 2 C.M.L.R. 54 (QBD (Admin)), Eder, J.
Reg.20, amended: SI 2013/3032 Sch.1 para.14
Reg.20A, amended: SI 2013/3032 Sch.1 para.15
Reg.20B, added: SI 2013/3032 Sch.1 para.16
Reg.21, see *MG (EU deportation â€" Article 28(3) â€" imprisonment) (Portugal), Re* [2013] 1 C.M.L.R. 20 (UT (IAC)), Judge Storey; see *R. (on the application of Essa) v Upper Tribunal (Immigration and Asylum Chamber)* [2012] EWCA Civ 1718, [2013] Imm. A.R. 644 (CA (Civ Div)), Maurice Kay, L.J.; see *R. (on the application of Nouazli) v Secretary of State for the Home Department* [2013] EWHC 567 (Admin), [2013] 2 C.M.L.R. 54 (QBD (Admin)), Eder, J.; see *Secretary of State for the Home Department v FV (Italy)* [2012] EWCA Civ 1199, [2013] 1 W.L.R. 3339 (CA (Civ Div)), Pill, L.J.
Reg.21A, revoked (in part): SI 2013/3032 Sch.1 para.17
Reg.21B, added: SI 2013/3032 Sch.1 para.18
Reg.21B, referred to: SI 2013/3032 Sch.3 para.3
Reg.22, amended: SI 2013/3032 Sch.1 para.19
Reg.23, amended: SI 2013/3032 Sch.1 para.20
Reg.24, amended: SI 2013/3032 Sch.1 para.21
Reg.24, see *R. (on the application of Nouazli) v Secretary of State for the Home Department* [2013] EWHC 567 (Admin), [2013] 2 C.M.L.R. 54 (QBD (Admin)), Eder, J.
Reg.25, applied: SI 2013/3032 Sch.3 para.2
Reg.26, amended: SI 2013/3032 Sch.1 para.22
Reg.26, applied: SI 2013/1460 Reg.6, SI 2013/3032 Sch.3 para.2
Reg.27, amended: SI 2013/3032 Sch.1 para.23
Reg.28A, added: SI 2013/3032 Sch.1 para.24
Sch.2 para.1, amended: SI 2013/1460 Sch.1 para.2
Sch.2 para.3, amended: SI 2013/3032 Sch.1 para.25
Sch.2 para.4, amended: SI 2013/1460 Sch.1 para.3, SI 2013/3032 Sch.1 para.25
Sch.2 para.4, applied: SI 2013/617 Sch.3 para.2

1004. Renewables Obligation Order 2006

Art.6, see *R. (on the application of Infinis Plc) v Gas and Electricity Markets Authority* [2013] EWCA Civ 70, [2013] J.P.L. 1037 (CA (Civ Div)), Sir James Munby (President, Fam)

1016. Lord Chancellor (Transfer of Functions and Supplementary Provisions) (No.2) Order 2006

Sch.1 para.6, revoked: 2013 c.22 Sch.11 para.210
Sch.1 para.7, revoked: 2013 c.22 Sch.11 para.210

1028. Intellectual Property (Enforcement, etc.) Regulations 2006

see *Hollister Inc v Medik Ostomy Supplies Ltd* [2012] EWCA Civ 1419, [2013] Bus. L.R. 428 (CA (Civ Div)), Jackson, L.J.

1030. Cross-Border Insolvency Regulations 2006

see *Rubin v Eurofinance SA* [2013] 1 A.C. 236 (SC), Lord Walker, J.S.C.; see *Schmitt v Deichmann* [2012] EWHC 62 (Ch), [2013] Ch. 61 (Ch D), Proudman, J.

Sch.2 Part 1 para.1, amended: SI 2013/472 Sch.2 para.116

Sch.2 Part 6 para.21, amended: SI 2013/472 Sch.2 para.116

Sch.2 Part 6 para.25, amended: SI 2013/472 Sch.2 para.116

Sch.2 Part 6 para.26, amended: SI 2013/472 Sch.2 para.116

Sch.3 Part 1 para.1, amended: SI 2013/472 Sch.2 para.116

Sch.3 Part 3 para.6, amended: SI 2013/472 Sch.2 para.116

Sch.3 Part 3 para.7, amended: SI 2013/472 Sch.2 para.116

Sch.5, amended: SI 2013/472 Sch.2 para.116

1031. Employment Equality (Age) Regulations 2006

see *CVS Solicitors LLP v Van der Borgh* [2013] Eq. L.R. 934 (EAT), Slade, J.; see *King v Health Professions Council* [2013] I.C.R. 39 (EAT), Langstaff, J. (President)

Reg.3, see *Lockwood v Department of Work and Pensions* [2013] EWCA Civ 1195, [2013] I.R.L.R. 941 (CA (Civ Div)), Rimer, L.J.

1056. Smoking, Health and Social Care (Scotland) Act 2005 (Consequential Modifications) (England, Wales and Northern Ireland) Order 2006

Sch.1 Part 1 para.7, revoked (in part): 2013 c.24 s.20

1058. Beer, Cider and Perry, Spirits, and Wine and Made-wine (Amendment) Regulations 2006

Reg.6, revoked: SI 2013/1229 Reg.5

1116. Criminal Justice Act 1988 (Reviews of Sentencing) Order 2006

Sch.1 para.3, amended: SI 2013/862 Sch.1 para.1

1159. A470 Trunk Road (Abercynon Roundabout, Rhondda Cynon Taf) (50 mph Speed Limit) Order 2006

revoked: SI 2013/1018 Art.3

1161. Seed Potatoes (England) Regulations 2006

Reg.8, applied: SI 2013/494 Reg.3

Reg.9, applied: SI 2013/494 Reg.3

1254. Fire and Rescue Services (Northern Ireland) Order 2006

Art.18, applied: SI 2013/602 Art.18

Art.18, referred to: SI 2013/602 Art.22

Art.19, applied: SI 2013/602 Art.18

Art.19, referred to: SI 2013/602 Art.18, Art.22

Art.20, applied: SI 2013/602 Art.18

Art.20, varied: SI 2013/602 Art.18

Art.21, applied: SI 2013/602 Art.18

Art.22, applied: SI 2013/602 Art.18

1273. Consumer Credit (Exempt Agreements) (Amendment) Order 2006

revoked (in part): SI 2013/1881 Art.21

1276. Credit Unions (Maximum Interest Rate on Loans) Order 2006

revoked: SI 2013/2589 Art.3

1294. Allocation of Housing and Homelessness (Eligibility) (England) Regulations 2006

Reg.2, amended: SI 2013/1467 Reg.2

Reg.4, amended: SI 2013/1467 Reg.2

Reg.6, amended: SI 2013/1467 Reg.2

1466. Transport and Works (Applications and Objections Procedure) (England and Wales) Rules 2006

applied: SI 2013/198, SI 2013/533, SI 2013/767, SI 2013/1888, SI 2013/1933, SI 2013/1967, SI 2013/3244

r.4, amended: SI 2013/755 Sch.4 para.249

r.7, amended: SI 2013/755 Sch.4 para.250

r.8, amended: SI 2013/755 Sch.4 para.251

r.12, amended: SI 2013/755 Sch.4 para.252

r.24, applied: SI 2013/1888

Sch.5, amended: SI 2013/755 Sch.4 para.253

Sch.6, amended: SI 2013/755 Sch.4 para.254

1543. Tax Avoidance Schemes (Prescribed Descriptions of Arrangements) Regulations 2006

Reg.5, amended: SI 2013/2595 Reg.9

Reg.6, amended: SI 2013/2595 Reg.3, Reg.4, Reg.5

Reg.7, amended: SI 2013/2595 Reg.7, Reg.8

Reg.7, substituted: SI 2013/2595 Reg.6

Reg.17A, substituted: SI 2013/2595 Reg.10

Reg.18, revoked: SI 2013/2595 Reg.10

1619. East of England Ambulance Service National Health Service Trust (Establishment) Order 2006

Art.1, amended: SI 2013/593 Art.2

1620. East Midlands Ambulance Service National Health Service Trust (Establishment) Order 2006

Art.1, amended: SI 2013/593 Art.2

1622. North West Ambulance Service National Health Service Trust (Establishment) Order 2006

Art.1, amended: SI 2013/593 Art.2

1626. West Midlands Ambulance Service National Health Service Trust (Establishment) Order 2006

Art.1, amended: SI 2013/593 Art.2

1627. Yorkshire Ambulance Service National Health Service Trust (Establishment) Order 2006

Art.1, amended: SI 2013/593 Art.2

1643. Plant Health (Wales) Order 2006

Art.2, amended: SI 2013/888 Art.2
Art.8, amended: SI 2013/888 Art.2
Art.12, applied: SI 2013/1700 Reg.2
Art.19, amended: SI 2013/2939 Art.2
Art.22, amended: SI 2013/888 Art.2, SI 2013/2939 Art.2
Art.40, applied: SI 2013/1700 Reg.4
Art.40, substituted: SI 2013/888 Art.2
Art.41, amended: SI 2013/888 Art.2
Art.41, applied: SI 2013/1700 Reg.4
Sch.1 Part B para.1, substituted: SI 2013/888 Art.2
Sch.1 Part B para.2, substituted: SI 2013/888 Art.2
Sch.2 Part B, amended: SI 2013/888 Art.2
Sch.4 Part A, amended: SI 2013/888 Art.2
Sch.4 Part B, amended: SI 2013/888 Art.2
Sch.5 Part A para.1, amended: SI 2013/888 Art.2
Sch.5 Part A para.2, amended: SI 2013/888 Art.2
Sch.6 Part A para.9, added: SI 2013/888 Art.2
Sch.7 Part A para.9, added: SI 2013/888 Art.2

1644. Companies (Disclosure of Information) (Designated Authorities) Order 2006
Art.2, revoked: SI 2013/2329 Sch.1 para.37

1694. Representation of the People (Form of Canvass) (England and Wales) Regulations 2006
revoked: SI 2013/3198 Sch.2
Sch.1 Part 1, varied: SI 2013/794 Art.4
Sch.1 Part 2, varied: SI 2013/794 Art.4

1701. Plant Health (Export Certification) (Wales) Order 2006
Sch.3, substituted: SI 2013/1658 Art.2
Sch.4, substituted: SI 2013/1658 Art.2

1705. Local Safeguarding Children Boards (Wales) Regulations 2006
see *X (Children) (Serious Case Review: Publication), Re* [2012] EWCA Civ 1500, [2013] 2 F.L.R. 628 (CA (Civ Div)), Pill, L.J.

1722. Enterprise Act 2002 (Disqualification from Office General) Order 2006
Sch.2 Part 1 para.2, revoked: SI 2013/686 Sch.2

1738. Children Act 1989 Representations Procedure (England) Regulations 2006
applied: SI 2013/1394 Reg.20
Reg.4, amended: SI 2013/985 Sch.1 para.6

1751. Education (Pupil Registration) (England) Regulations 2006
Reg.7, amended: SI 2013/756 Reg.2
Reg.7, revoked (in part): SI 2013/756 Reg.2
Reg.8, amended: SI 2013/756 Reg.2

1832. Mental Capacity Act 2005 (Independent Mental Capacity Advocates) (General) Regulations 2006
Reg.3, amended: SI 2013/235 Sch.2 para.99
Reg.3, revoked (in part): SI 2013/235 Sch.2 para.99

1836. Representation of the People (Form of Canvass) (Scotland) Regulations 2006
revoked: SI 2013/3206 Sch.2
Sch.1 Part 1, varied: SI 2013/794 Art.4
Sch.1 Part 2, varied: SI 2013/794 Art.4

1944. Recovery of Health Services Charges (Northern Ireland) Order 2006
Sch.1 para.4, amended: SI 2013/472 Art.4

1958. Pensions Schemes (Taxable Property Provisions) Regulations 2006
Reg.10, amended: SI 2013/605 Reg.5, SI 2013/1810 Reg.3
Reg.10, revoked (in part): SI 2013/1810 Reg.3

1969. Financial Services and Markets Act 2000 (Regulated Activities) (Amendment) Order 2006
Art.5, amended: SI 2013/472 Art.4
Sch.1 para.2, amended: SI 2013/472 Art.4

1975. Registered Designs Rules 2006
Part 2 r.7, amended: SI 2013/444 r.7
Part 2 r.8, amended: SI 2013/444 r.7
Part 2 r.9, amended: SI 2013/444 r.7
Part 2 r.10, amended: SI 2013/444 r.7
Part 3 r.12, amended: SI 2013/444 r.7
Part 3 r.13, amended: SI 2013/444 r.7
Part 4 r.23, amended: SI 2013/444 r.6
Part 5 r.29, amended: SI 2013/444 r.7
Part 5 r.30, amended: SI 2013/444 r.7
Part 6 r.43, amended: SI 2013/444 r.7

2059. European Cooperative Society (Involvement of Employees) Regulations 2006
applied: SI 2013/1893 Sch.2
Reg.41, amended: SI 2013/1956 Sch.1 para.12

2078. European Cooperative Society Regulations 2006
Reg.3, amended: SI 2013/496 Sch.11 para.15
Reg.8, amended: SI 2013/496 Sch.11 para.15
Reg.13, amended: SI 2013/496 Sch.11 para.15

2125. Medicines for Human Use (Fees Amendments) Regulations 2006
revoked: SI 2013/532 Sch.9

2135. Serious Organised Crime and Police Act 2005 (Appeals under Section 74) Order 2006
Art.15, applied: SI 2013/1554 r.74_1, r.74_2
Art.16, applied: SI 2013/1554 r.74_2

2138. Crime and Disorder Act 1998 (Intervention Orders) Order 2006
Art.2, amended: SI 2013/235 Sch.2 para.100
Art.2, revoked (in part): SI 2013/235 Sch.2 para.100

2170. Immigration (Continuation of Leave) (Notices) Regulations 2006
Reg.2, see *Ahmadi (S.47 Decision: Validity: Sapkota: Afghanistan), Re* [2013] EWCA Civ 512, [2013] 4 All E.R. 442 (CA (Civ Div)), Sullivan, L.J.

2183. Merchant Shipping and Fishing Vessels (Provision and Use of Work Equipment) Regulations 2006
Sch.1, amended: SI 2013/1387 Sch.5 para.5

2383. Financial Services and Markets Act 2000 (Regulated Activities) (Amendment) (No.2) Order 2006
Art.1, amended: SI 2013/472 Art.4
Art.37, amended: SI 2013/472 Art.4
Sch.1 para.2, amended: SI 2013/472 Art.4

2492. Criminal Defence Service (Financial Eligibility) Regulations 2006
Reg.2, amended: SI 2013/591 Sch.1 para.33, SI 2013/626 Reg.4
Reg.5, amended: SI 2013/630 Reg.65

2601. Education (Information About Individual Pupils) (England) Regulations 2006
revoked: SI 2013/2094 Sch.2

2646. Homelessness (Wales) Regulations 2006
Reg.2, amended: SI 2013/1788 Reg.7
Reg.3, amended: SI 2013/1788 Reg.7

2657. Terrorism (United Nations Measures) Order 2006
see *R. (on the application of Irfan) v Secretary of State for the Home Department* [2012] EWCA Civ 1471, [2013] Q.B. 885 (CA (Civ Div)), Sir Maurice Kay (VP CA Civ)

2695. Plant Health (Wood Packaging Material Marking) (Forestry) Order 2006
Art.2, amended: SI 2013/755 Sch.4 para.256
Art.3, amended: SI 2013/755 Sch.4 para.257
Art.4, amended: SI 2013/755 Sch.4 para.257
Art.5, amended: SI 2013/755 Sch.4 para.257
Art.6, amended: SI 2013/755 Sch.4 para.257
Art.7, amended: SI 2013/755 Sch.4 para.257
Art.8, amended: SI 2013/755 Sch.4 para.257
Art.9, amended: SI 2013/755 Sch.4 para.257
Art.10, amended: SI 2013/755 Sch.4 para.257
Art.11, amended: SI 2013/755 Sch.4 para.257
Sch.2, amended: SI 2013/755 Sch.4 para.258

2697. Plant Health (Fees) (Forestry) Regulations 2006
Reg.2, amended: SI 2013/755 Sch.4 para.260
Reg.3, amended: SI 2013/755 Sch.4 para.261

2883. Mental Capacity Act 2005 (Independent Mental Capacity Advocates) (Expansion of Role) Regulations 2006
Reg.1, amended: SI 2013/235 Sch.2 para.101
Reg.1, revoked (in part): SI 2013/235 Sch.2 para.101

2910. Representation of the People (England and Wales) (Amendment) (No.2) Regulations 2006
Reg.38, revoked: SI 2013/3198 Sch.2
Reg.39, amended: SI 2013/3198 Sch.2
Reg.47, revoked (in part): SI 2013/3198 Sch.2
Reg.65, revoked (in part): SI 2013/3198 Sch.2
Sch.2, amended: SI 2013/3198 Sch.2

2929. Seed Potatoes (Wales) Regulations 2006
applied: SI 2013/1700 Reg.3
Reg.8, applied: SI 2013/1700 Reg.3
Reg.9, applied: SI 2013/1700 Reg.3

2958. North Korea (United Nations Measures) Order 2006
Art.2, amended: SI 2013/472 Art.4

2968. Housing Benefit and Council Tax Benefit (Electronic Communications) Order 2006
Art.4, revoked: SI 2013/458 Sch.1
Art.5, revoked: SI 2013/458 Sch.1

2985. National Health Service (Pharmaceutical Services) (Amendment) (Wales) Regulations 2006
revoked: SI 2013/898 Sch.8 para.17

2988. Radioactive Contaminated Land (Modification of Enactments) (Wales) Regulations 2006
Reg.18, amended: SI 2013/755 Sch.5 para.38

2989. Contaminated Land (Wales) Regulations 2006
Reg.5, amended: SI 2013/755 Sch.5 para.40
Reg.7, amended: SI 2013/755 Sch.5 para.40
Reg.13, amended: SI 2013/755 Sch.5 para.40
Sch.3 para.10, amended: SI 2013/755 Sch.5 para.40
Sch.3 para.13, amended: SI 2013/755 Sch.5 para.40

3104. Single European Sky (Functions of the National Supervisory Authority) Regulations 2006
revoked: SI 2013/2620 Reg.1

3107. Banks (Former Authorised Institutions) (Insolvency) Order 2006
Sch.1 para.4, substituted: SI 2013/472 Sch.2 para.117
Sch.1 para.5, amended: SI 2013/472 Sch.2 para.117
Sch.1 para.6, amended: SI 2013/472 Sch.2 para.117
Sch.1 para.7, substituted: SI 2013/472 Sch.2 para.117

3148. Controlled Drugs (Supervision of Management and Use) Regulations 2006
revoked: SI 2013/373 Reg.21

3221. Capital Requirements Regulations 2006
revoked: SI 2013/3115 Reg.3, Sch.3
Part 2, amended: SI 2013/472 Sch.2 para.118
Part 3, amended: SI 2013/472 Sch.2 para.118
Reg.1, amended: SI 2013/472 Sch.2 para.118, SI 2013/1162 Reg.8
Reg.2, amended: SI 2013/472 Sch.2 para.118, SI 2013/1162 Reg.9
Reg.3, amended: SI 2013/472 Sch.2 para.118
Reg.4, amended: SI 2013/472 Sch.2 para.118
Reg.5, amended: SI 2013/472 Sch.2 para.118

Reg.6, amended: SI 2013/472 Sch.2 para.118
Reg.7, amended: SI 2013/472 Sch.2 para.118
Reg.8, amended: SI 2013/472 Sch.2 para.118
Reg.9, amended: SI 2013/472 Sch.2 para.118
Reg.10, amended: SI 2013/472 Sch.2 para.118
Reg.10A, amended: SI 2013/472 Sch.2 para.118
Reg.10B, amended: SI 2013/472 Sch.2 para.118
Reg.11, amended: SI 2013/472 Sch.2 para.118, SI 2013/1162 Reg.10
Reg.12, amended: SI 2013/472 Sch.2 para.118
Reg.12A, amended: SI 2013/472 Sch.2 para.118, SI 2013/1162 Reg.11
Reg.13, amended: SI 2013/472 Sch.2 para.118
Reg.14, amended: SI 2013/472 Sch.2 para.118
Reg.15, amended: SI 2013/472 Sch.2 para.118
Reg.16, amended: SI 2013/472 Sch.2 para.118
Reg.16A, amended: SI 2013/472 Sch.2 para.118
Reg.16B, amended: SI 2013/472 Sch.2 para.118
Reg.16C, amended: SI 2013/472 Sch.2 para.118
Reg.16D, amended: SI 2013/472 Sch.2 para.118
Reg.16E, amended: SI 2013/472 Sch.2 para.118
Reg.16E, substituted: SI 2013/472 Sch.2 para.118
Reg.16G, amended: SI 2013/472 Sch.2 para.118
Reg.17, amended: SI 2013/472 Sch.2 para.118
Reg.22, amended: SI 2013/472 Sch.2 para.118
Reg.23, amended: SI 2013/472 Sch.2 para.118
Reg.24, amended: SI 2013/472 Sch.2 para.118
Reg.25, amended: SI 2013/472 Sch.2 para.118
Reg.26, amended: SI 2013/472 Sch.2 para.118
Reg.27, amended: SI 2013/472 Sch.2 para.118
Sch.1 Part 1 para.1, amended: SI 2013/472 Sch.2 para.118
Sch.1 Part 1 para.2, amended: SI 2013/472 Sch.2 para.118
Sch.1 Part 1 para.3, amended: SI 2013/472 Sch.2 para.118
Sch.1 Part 1 para.4, amended: SI 2013/472 Sch.2 para.118
Sch.1 Part 1 para.5, amended: SI 2013/472 Sch.2 para.118
Sch.1 Part 1 para.6, amended: SI 2013/472 Sch.2 para.118
Sch.1 Part 1 para.7, amended: SI 2013/472 Sch.2 para.118
Sch.1 Part 1 para.7A, amended: SI 2013/472 Sch.2 para.118
Sch.1 Part 2 para.8, amended: SI 2013/472 Sch.2 para.118
Sch.1 Part 2 para.9, amended: SI 2013/472 Sch.2 para.118
Sch.1 Part 2 para.10, amended: SI 2013/472 Sch.2 para.118
Sch.2 para.1, amended: SI 2013/472 Sch.2 para.118
Sch.2 para.2, amended: SI 2013/472 Sch.2 para.118
Sch.2 para.3, amended: SI 2013/472 Sch.2 para.118
Sch.2 para.4, amended: SI 2013/472 Sch.2 para.118
Sch.2 para.5, amended: SI 2013/472 Sch.2 para.118

3247. Avian Influenza (H5N1 in Poultry) (England) Order 2006

Art.2, amended: SI 2013/2952 Sch.2 para.4
Art.3, amended: SI 2013/2952 Sch.2 para.4
Art.14, amended: SI 2013/2952 Sch.2 para.4

3249. Avian Influenza (H5N1 in Wild Birds) (England) Order 2006

Art.2, amended: SI 2013/2952 Sch.2 para.5
Art.13, amended: SI 2013/2952 Sch.2 para.5
Sch.1 Part 4 para.13, amended: SI 2013/2952 Sch.2 para.5
Sch.1 Part 5 para.14, amended: SI 2013/2952 Sch.2 para.5
Sch.1 Part 5 para.15, amended: SI 2013/2952 Sch.2 para.5

3259. Compensation Act 2006 (Contribution for Mesothelioma Claims) Regulations 2006

Reg.2, amended: SI 2013/472 Sch.2 para.120
Reg.3, amended: SI 2013/472 Sch.2 para.120
Reg.4, amended: SI 2013/472 Sch.2 para.120

3284. Gambling (Operating Licence and Single-Machine Permit Fees) Regulations 2006

Reg.23, amended: SI 2013/472 Sch.2 para.121, SI 2013/3115 Sch.2 para.66

3289. Waste Electrical and Electronic Equipment Regulations 2006

applied: SI 2013/2258 Sch.1 Part 2
Reg.1, revoked: SI 2013/3113 Reg.96
Reg.2, amended: SI 2013/755 Sch.4 para.263, SI 2013/3134 Sch.4 para.7
Reg.2, revoked: SI 2013/3113 Reg.96
Reg.3, revoked: SI 2013/3113 Reg.96
Reg.5, revoked: SI 2013/3113 Reg.96
Reg.6, revoked: SI 2013/3113 Reg.96
Reg.7, revoked: SI 2013/3113 Reg.96
Reg.8, revoked: SI 2013/3113 Reg.96
Reg.9, revoked: SI 2013/3113 Reg.96
Reg.10, revoked: SI 2013/3113 Reg.96
Reg.11, revoked: SI 2013/3113 Reg.96
Reg.12, revoked: SI 2013/3113 Reg.96
Reg.13, revoked: SI 2013/3113 Reg.96
Reg.14, revoked: SI 2013/3113 Reg.96
Reg.15, revoked: SI 2013/3113 Reg.96
Reg.16, revoked: SI 2013/3113 Reg.96
Reg.17, revoked: SI 2013/3113 Reg.96
Reg.18, revoked: SI 2013/3113 Reg.96

Reg.19, revoked: SI 2013/3113 Reg.96
Reg.20, revoked: SI 2013/3113 Reg.96
Reg.21, revoked: SI 2013/3113 Reg.96
Reg.22, revoked: SI 2013/3113 Reg.96
Reg.23, revoked: SI 2013/3113 Reg.96
Reg.24, revoked: SI 2013/3113 Reg.96
Reg.25, revoked: SI 2013/3113 Reg.96
Reg.26, revoked: SI 2013/3113 Reg.96
Reg.27, revoked: SI 2013/3113 Reg.96
Reg.28, revoked: SI 2013/3113 Reg.96
Reg.28A, revoked: SI 2013/3113 Reg.96
Reg.29, revoked: SI 2013/3113 Reg.96
Reg.30, revoked: SI 2013/3113 Reg.96
Reg.31, revoked: SI 2013/3113 Reg.96
Reg.32, revoked: SI 2013/3113 Reg.96
Reg.33, revoked: SI 2013/3113 Reg.96
Reg.34, revoked: SI 2013/3113 Reg.96
Reg.35, revoked: SI 2013/3113 Reg.96
Reg.36, revoked: SI 2013/3113 Reg.96
Reg.37, revoked: SI 2013/3113 Reg.96
Reg.38, revoked: SI 2013/3113 Reg.96
Reg.39, revoked: SI 2013/3113 Reg.96
Reg.40, revoked: SI 2013/3113 Reg.96
Reg.40A, revoked: SI 2013/3113 Reg.96
Reg.41, amended: SI 2013/755 Sch.4 para.264
Reg.41, revoked: SI 2013/3113 Reg.96
Reg.42, revoked: SI 2013/3113 Reg.96
Reg.43, amended: SI 2013/755 Sch.4 para.265
Reg.43, revoked: SI 2013/3113 Reg.96
Reg.44, revoked: SI 2013/3113 Reg.96
Reg.45, amended: SI 2013/755 Sch.4 para.266
Reg.45, revoked: SI 2013/3113 Reg.96
Reg.46, revoked: SI 2013/3113 Reg.96
Reg.47, amended: SI 2013/755 Sch.4 para.267
Reg.47, revoked: SI 2013/3113 Reg.96
Reg.48, amended: SI 2013/755 Sch.4 para.268
Reg.48, revoked: SI 2013/3113 Reg.96
Reg.49, revoked: SI 2013/3113 Reg.96
Reg.50, revoked: SI 2013/3113 Reg.96
Reg.51, amended: SI 2013/755 Sch.4 para.269
Reg.51, revoked: SI 2013/3113 Reg.96
Reg.52, revoked: SI 2013/3113 Reg.96
Reg.53, revoked: SI 2013/3113 Reg.96
Reg.54, revoked: SI 2013/3113 Reg.96
Reg.55, revoked: SI 2013/3113 Reg.96
Reg.56, revoked: SI 2013/3113 Reg.96
Reg.57, revoked: SI 2013/3113 Reg.96
Reg.58, revoked: SI 2013/3113 Reg.96
Reg.59, revoked: SI 2013/3113 Reg.96
Reg.59A, revoked: SI 2013/3113 Reg.96
Reg.60, revoked: SI 2013/3113 Reg.96
Reg.61, revoked: SI 2013/3113 Reg.96
Reg.62, revoked: SI 2013/3113 Reg.96
Reg.63, revoked: SI 2013/3113 Reg.96
Reg.64, revoked: SI 2013/3113 Reg.96
Reg.65, revoked: SI 2013/3113 Reg.96
Reg.66, amended: SI 2013/755 Sch.4 para.270, SI 2013/1821 Art.22
Reg.66, revoked: SI 2013/3113 Reg.96
Reg.67, revoked: SI 2013/3113 Reg.96
Reg.68, revoked: SI 2013/3113 Reg.96
Reg.69, revoked: SI 2013/3113 Reg.96
Reg.70, amended: SI 2013/755 Sch.4 para.271
Reg.70, revoked: SI 2013/3113 Reg.96
Reg.71, revoked: SI 2013/3113 Reg.96
Reg.72, revoked: SI 2013/3113 Reg.96
Reg.73, revoked: SI 2013/3113 Reg.96
Reg.74, revoked: SI 2013/3113 Reg.96
Reg.75, revoked: SI 2013/3113 Reg.96
Sch.3 para.2, revoked: SI 2013/3113 Reg.96
Sch.3 para.3, revoked: SI 2013/3113 Reg.96
Sch.3 para.4, revoked: SI 2013/3113 Reg.96
Sch.3 para.5, revoked: SI 2013/3113 Reg.96
Sch.3 para.6, revoked: SI 2013/3113 Reg.96
Sch.3 para.7, revoked: SI 2013/3113 Reg.96
Sch.3 para.8, revoked: SI 2013/3113 Reg.96
Sch.3 para.9, revoked: SI 2013/3113 Reg.96
Sch.3 para.10, revoked: SI 2013/3113 Reg.96
Sch.3 para.11, revoked: SI 2013/3113 Reg.96
Sch.5 Part 1 para.1, revoked: SI 2013/3113 Reg.96
Sch.5 Part 1 para.2, revoked: SI 2013/3113 Reg.96
Sch.5 Part 1 para.3, revoked: SI 2013/3113 Reg.96
Sch.5 Part 1 para.4, revoked: SI 2013/3113 Reg.96
Sch.5 Part 1 para.5, revoked: SI 2013/3113 Reg.96
Sch.5 Part 1 para.6, revoked: SI 2013/3113 Reg.96
Sch.5 Part 2 para.1, revoked: SI 2013/3113 Reg.96
Sch.5 Part 2 para.2, revoked: SI 2013/3113 Reg.96
Sch.5 Part 2 para.3, revoked: SI 2013/3113 Reg.96
Sch.5 Part 2 para.4, revoked: SI 2013/3113 Reg.96
Sch.5 Part 2 para.5, revoked: SI 2013/3113 Reg.96
Sch.5 Part 2 para.6, revoked: SI 2013/3113 Reg.96
Sch.7 Part 1 para.1, revoked: SI 2013/3113 Reg.96
Sch.7 Part 1 para.2, revoked: SI 2013/3113 Reg.96
Sch.7 Part 1 para.3, revoked: SI 2013/3113 Reg.96
Sch.7 Part 1 para.4, revoked: SI 2013/3113 Reg.96
Sch.7 Part 1 para.5, revoked: SI 2013/3113 Reg.96
Sch.7 Part 1 para.6, revoked: SI 2013/3113 Reg.96
Sch.7 Part 2 para.1, revoked: SI 2013/3113 Reg.96
Sch.7 Part 2 para.2, revoked: SI 2013/3113 Reg.96
Sch.7 Part 2 para.3, revoked: SI 2013/3113 Reg.96
Sch.7 Part 2 para.4, revoked: SI 2013/3113 Reg.96
Sch.7 Part 2 para.5, revoked: SI 2013/3113 Reg.96
Sch.7 Part 2 para.6, revoked: SI 2013/3113 Reg.96
Sch.7 Part 2 para.7, revoked: SI 2013/3113 Reg.96
Sch.7 Part 2 para.8, revoked: SI 2013/3113 Reg.96
Sch.7 Part 2 para.9, revoked: SI 2013/3113 Reg.96
Sch.7 Part 2 para.10, revoked: SI 2013/3113 Reg.96

Sch.7 Part 3, revoked: SI 2013/3113 Reg.96
Sch.7 Part 4 para.1, revoked: SI 2013/3113 Reg.96
Sch.7 Part 4 para.2, revoked: SI 2013/3113 Reg.96
Sch.7 Part 4 para.3, revoked: SI 2013/3113 Reg.96
Sch.7 Part 4 para.4, revoked: SI 2013/3113 Reg.96
Sch.7 Part 4 para.5, revoked: SI 2013/3113 Reg.96
Sch.7 Part 4 para.6, revoked: SI 2013/3113 Reg.96
Sch.7 Part 4 para.7, revoked: SI 2013/3113 Reg.96
Sch.8 Part 1 para.1, revoked: SI 2013/3113 Reg.96
Sch.8 Part 1 para.2, revoked: SI 2013/3113 Reg.96
Sch.8 Part 1 para.3, revoked: SI 2013/3113 Reg.96
Sch.8 Part 1 para.4, revoked: SI 2013/3113 Reg.96
Sch.8 Part 1 para.5, revoked: SI 2013/3113 Reg.96
Sch.8 Part 1 para.6, revoked: SI 2013/3113 Reg.96
Sch.8 Part 1 para.7, revoked: SI 2013/3113 Reg.96
Sch.8 Part 1 para.8, revoked: SI 2013/3113 Reg.96
Sch.8 Part 2 para.1, revoked: SI 2013/3113 Reg.96
Sch.8 Part 2 para.2, revoked: SI 2013/3113 Reg.96
Sch.8 Part 2 para.2A, revoked: SI 2013/3113 Reg.96
Sch.8 Part 2 para.3, revoked: SI 2013/3113 Reg.96
Sch.8 Part 2 para.4, revoked: SI 2013/3113 Reg.96
Sch.8 Part 2 para.4A, revoked: SI 2013/3113 Reg.96
Sch.8 Part 2 para.5, revoked: SI 2013/3113 Reg.96
Sch.8 Part 2 para.6, revoked: SI 2013/3113 Reg.96
Sch.8 Part 2 para.7, revoked: SI 2013/3113 Reg.96
Sch.8 Part 2 para.8, revoked: SI 2013/3113 Reg.96
Sch.8 Part 2 para.8A, revoked: SI 2013/3113 Reg.96
Sch.8 Part 2 para.8B, revoked: SI 2013/3113 Reg.96
Sch.8 Part 2 para.9, revoked: SI 2013/3113 Reg.96
Sch.8 Part 2 para.10, revoked: SI 2013/3113 Reg.96
Sch.8 Part 2 para.11, revoked: SI 2013/3113 Reg.96
Sch.8 Part 2 para.12, revoked: SI 2013/3113 Reg.96
Sch.8 Part 2 para.13, revoked: SI 2013/3113 Reg.96
Sch.8 Part 2 para.14, revoked: SI 2013/3113 Reg.96
Sch.8 Part 2 para.15, revoked: SI 2013/3113 Reg.96
Sch.8 Part 3 para.1, revoked: SI 2013/3113 Reg.96
Sch.8 Part 3 para.2, revoked: SI 2013/3113 Reg.96
Sch.8 Part 3 para.2A, revoked: SI 2013/3113 Reg.96
Sch.8 Part 3 para.3, revoked: SI 2013/3113 Reg.96
Sch.8 Part 3 para.4, revoked: SI 2013/3113 Reg.96
Sch.8 Part 3 para.5, revoked: SI 2013/3113 Reg.96
Sch.8 Part 3 para.5A, revoked: SI 2013/3113 Reg.96
Sch.8 Part 3 para.6, revoked: SI 2013/3113 Reg.96
Sch.8 Part 3 para.7, revoked: SI 2013/3113 Reg.96
Sch.8 Part 3 para.8, revoked: SI 2013/3113 Reg.96
Sch.8 Part 3 para.9, revoked: SI 2013/3113 Reg.96

3305. Local Elections (Parishes and Communities) (England and Wales) Rules 2006

r.5, varied: SI 2013/2277 Art.4

3317. Accession (Immigration and Worker Authorisation) Regulations 2006

Reg.2, applied: SI 2013/1460 Reg.2
Reg.7, amended: SI 2013/3032 Sch.2 para.3
Reg.11, amended: SI 2013/3032 Sch.2 para.3

3336. Water and Sewerage Services (Northern Ireland) Order 2006

Art.2, amended: 2013 c.24 Sch.6 para.182
Art.2, revoked (in part): 2013 c.24 Sch.6 para.182
Art.19, amended: 2013 c.24 Sch.6 para.183
Art.21, amended: 2013 c.24 Sch.6 para.184
Art.22, amended: 2013 c.24 Sch.6 para.185
Art.24, amended: 2013 c.24 Sch.6 para.186
Art.25, amended: 2013 c.24 Sch.6 para.187
Art.26, amended: 2013 c.24 Sch.6 para.188
Art.27, amended: 2013 c.24 Sch.6 para.189
Art.28, amended: 2013 c.24 Sch.6 para.190
Art.31, amended: 2013 c.24 Sch.14 para.28
Art.31, revoked (in part): 2013 c.24 Sch.14 para.28
Art.35, amended: 2013 c.24 Sch.14 para.29
Art.57, amended: 2013 c.24 Sch.6 para.191
Art.265, amended: SI 2013/472 Sch.2 para.122

3363. Enterprise Act 2002 (Amendment) Regulations 2006

amended: SI 2013/472 Sch.2 para.123
Reg.23, amended: SI 2013/472 Sch.2 para.123

3373. National Health Service (Pharmaceutical Services) (Amendment) Regulations 2006

revoked: SI 2013/349 Sch.10 para.6

3374. Superannuation (Admission to Schedule 1 to the Superannuation Act 1972) Order 2006

Art.2, amended: SI 2013/1036 Sch.2 para.68
Art.2, revoked (in part): SI 2013/1036 Sch.2 para.68

3384. Financial Services and Markets Act 2000 (Regulated Activities) (Amendment No 3) Order 2006

Art.1, amended: SI 2013/472 Art.4
Art.38, revoked: SI 2013/3115 Sch.3

3398. Personal Injuries (NHS Charges) (Reviews and Appeals) and Road Traffic (NHS Charges) (Reviews and Appeals) (Amendment) Regulations 2006

Reg.1, amended: SI 2013/2586 Reg.3
Reg.4, amended: SI 2013/2586 Reg.3
Reg.4, applied: SI 2013/2586 Reg.4
Reg.5, amended: SI 2013/2586 Reg.3
Reg.5, applied: SI 2013/2586 Reg.4
Reg.6, applied: SI 2013/2586 Reg.4

Reg.6, revoked: SI 2013/2586 Reg.3
Reg.7, applied: SI 2013/2586 Reg.4
Reg.7, revoked: SI 2013/2586 Reg.3

3415. Police Pensions Regulations 2006
Reg.3, amended: SI 2013/2318 Sch.1 para.59
Reg.3, revoked (in part): SI 2013/2318 Sch.1 para.59
Reg.4, amended: SI 2013/2318 Sch.1 para.60
Reg.5, amended: SI 2013/2318 Sch.1 para.61
Reg.5, revoked (in part): SI 2013/2318 Sch.1 para.61
Reg.7, amended: SI 2013/487 Reg.3
Reg.17, amended: SI 2013/2318 Sch.1 para.62
Reg.17, revoked (in part): SI 2013/2318 Sch.1 para.62
Reg.18, amended: SI 2013/2318 Sch.1 para.63
Reg.18, revoked (in part): SI 2013/2318 Sch.1 para.63
Reg.19, amended: SI 2013/2318 Sch.1 para.64
Reg.20, amended: SI 2013/2318 Sch.1 para.65
Reg.23, substituted: SI 2013/2318 Sch.1 para.66
Reg.42, amended: SI 2013/630 Reg.76
Reg.51, amended: SI 2013/2318 Sch.1 para.67
Reg.52, revoked (in part): SI 2013/2318 Sch.1 para.68
Sch.1, amended: SI 2013/2318 Sch.1 para.69

3432. Firefighters Pension Scheme (England) Order 2006
Sch.1, added: SI 2013/1393 Sch.1 para.2, Sch.1 para.6
Sch.1, amended: SI 2013/704 Art.3, Art.4, SI 2013/1393 Sch.1 para.1, Sch.1 para.2, Sch.1 para.4, Sch.1 para.5, Sch.1 para.6, Sch.1 para.7, Sch.1 para.8
Sch.1, substituted: SI 2013/1393 Sch.1 para.3

2007

63. Joint Municipal Waste Management Strategies (Disapplication of Duties) (England) Regulations 2007
Reg.2, revoked (in part): SI 2013/141 Reg.7

86. A47 Trunk Road (Little Fransham to Acle Road Roundabout, Great Yarmouth) (24 Hours Clearway) Order 2007
revoked: SI 2013/394 Sch.1 Part II

95. Driving Licences (Exchangeable Licences) Order 2007
Art.2, amended: SI 2013/22 Art.4
Art.3, amended: SI 2013/22 Art.4
Sch.1, amended: SI 2013/22 Art.4

115. Personal Injuries (NHS Charges) (Amounts) Regulations 2007
Reg.2, amended: SI 2013/282 Reg.2

121. National Health Service (Free Prescriptions and Charges for Drugs and Appliances) (Wales) Regulations 2007
Reg.2, amended: SI 2013/235 Sch.2 para.104, SI 2013/898 Sch.7 para.5
Reg.3, applied: SI 2013/898 Sch.5 para.6
Reg.3, referred to: SI 2013/898 Sch.4 para.7
Reg.4, applied: SI 2013/898 Sch.6 para.6
Reg.8, applied: SI 2013/898 Sch.4 para.7, Sch.5 para.6, Sch.6 para.6
Reg.11, amended: SI 2013/235 Sch.2 para.104
Sch.2 para.1, revoked: SI 2013/898 Sch.8 para.18

126. Financial Services and Markets Act 2000 (Markets in Financial Instruments) Regulations 2007
Reg.2, amended: SI 2013/472 Sch.2 para.125
Reg.4, amended: SI 2013/472 Art.4, Sch.2 para.125
Reg.4A, amended: SI 2013/472 Art.4, Sch.2 para.125
Reg.4B, amended: SI 2013/472 Art.4
Reg.4C, amended: SI 2013/472 Art.4, Sch.2 para.125, SI 2013/3115 Sch.2 para.67
Reg.7, amended: SI 2013/472 Art.4
Sch.6 Part 2 para.16, revoked: SI 2013/3115 Sch.3
Sch.8, amended: SI 2013/472 Art.4

205. National Health Service (Miscellaneous Amendments concerning Independent Nurse Prescribers, Supplementary Prescribers, Nurse Independent Prescribers and Pharmacist Independent... 2007
Reg.3, revoked: SI 2013/898 Sch.8 para.19

226. Tax Credits (Approval of Child Care Providers) (Wales) Scheme 2007
Art.9, substituted: SI 2013/2273 Art.2

236. National Assembly for Wales (Representation of the People) Order 2007
Sch.1 para.4, amended: SI 2013/388 Sch.1 para.39, SI 2013/591 Sch.1 para.36
Sch.1 para.12, varied: SI 2013/1514 Art.2

266. Copyright (Certification of Licensing Scheme for Educational Recording of Broadcasts) (Educational Recording Agency Limited) Order 2007
referred to: SI 2013/158, SI 2013/1924
Sch.1, amended: SI 2013/158 Art.2, SI 2013/1924 Art.2
Sch.1, substituted: SI 2013/158 Art.2

276. Patents (Convention Countries) Order 2007
Sch.1, amended: SI 2013/538 Art.2

277. Designs (Convention Countries) Order 2007
Sch.1, amended: SI 2013/539 Art.2

281. Iran (Financial Sanctions) Order 2007
Art.2, amended: SI 2013/472 Art.4
Sch.1 para.6, amended: SI 2013/472 Sch.2 para.126

293. Biocidal Products (Amendment) Regulations 2007

revoked: SI 2013/1506 Reg.34
Reg.2, applied: SI 2013/1506 Sch.2 para.10
Reg.3, applied: SI 2013/1506 Sch.2 para.10
Reg.4, applied: SI 2013/1506 Sch.2 para.10
Reg.8, applied: SI 2013/1506 Sch.2 para.10
Reg.9, applied: SI 2013/1506 Sch.2 para.10
Reg.10, applied: SI 2013/1506 Sch.2 para.10
Reg.11, applied: SI 2013/1506 Sch.2 para.10
Reg.21, applied: SI 2013/1506 Sch.2 para.10

310. Placement of Children (Wales) Regulations 2007

Reg.2, amended: SI 2013/235 Sch.2 para.105
Reg.6, amended: SI 2013/235 Sch.2 para.105

320. Construction (Design and Management) Regulations 2007

applied: SI 2013/805 Sch.1, SI 2013/806 Sch.1, SI 2013/807 Sch.1, SI 2013/808 Sch.1, SI 2013/809 Sch.1, SI 2013/810 Sch.1, SI 2013/811 Sch.1, SI 2013/812 Sch.1, SI 2013/813 Sch.1, SI 2013/814 Sch.1
Reg.19, amended: SI 2013/1471 Sch.4
Reg.45, revoked: SI 2013/1666 Art.4

339. Traffic Management (Guidance on Intervention Criteria) (England) Order 2007

Sch.1 para.40, amended: SI 2013/1644 Sch.5

383. Financial Services and Markets Act 2000 (Ombudsman Scheme) (Consumer Credit Jurisdiction) Order 2007

revoked: SI 2013/1881 Art.18

399. Local Authorities (Executive Arrangements) (Functions and Responsibilities) (Wales) Regulations 2007

Sch.1, amended: SI 2013/2902 Reg.3, SI 2013/3005 Art.10
Sch.2 para.25, added: SI 2013/2438 Reg.2

415. Environmental Noise (Identification of Noise Sources) (England) Regulations 2007

revoked: SI 2013/2854 Reg.2

448. Diseases of Animals (Approved Disinfectants) (England) Order 2007

Art.3, amended: SI 2013/1506 Sch.5 para.7
Art.6, amended: SI 2013/1506 Sch.5 para.7

478. NHS Direct National Health Service Trust (Establishment) Order 2007

Art.1, amended: SI 2013/235 Sch.2 para.106

529. Cattle Identification Regulations 2007

Reg.18, added: SI 2013/517 Reg.3
Sch.2, applied: SI 2013/109 Sch.1 para.1
Sch.2 para.2, amended: SI 2013/517 Reg.4
Sch.3 Part 1 para.3, amended: SI 2013/2952 Sch.2 para.6
Sch.3 Part 2 para.11, amended: SI 2013/517 Reg.5
Sch.4 para.1, amended: SI 2013/517 Reg.6
Sch.4 para.2, amended: SI 2013/517 Reg.6
Sch.4 para.2, revoked (in part): SI 2013/517 Reg.6

559. National Health Service (Functions of Strategic Health Authorities and Primary Care Trusts and Administration Arrangements) (England) (Amendment) Regulations 2007

revoked: SI 2013/235 Sch.2 para.194

572. Rent Repayment Orders (Supplementary Provisions) (England) Regulations 2007

Reg.1, amended: SI 2013/630 Reg.58
Reg.2, amended: SI 2013/630 Reg.58, SI 2013/1036 Sch.2 para.35
Reg.3, amended: SI 2013/1036 Sch.2 para.36

605. Vehicle Drivers (Certificates of Professional Competence) Regulations 2007

Reg.2, amended: SI 2013/602 Sch.2 para.87
Reg.3, amended: SI 2013/2667 Reg.2
Reg.5A, amended: SI 2013/1753 Reg.3

619. Hill Farm Allowance Regulations 2007

revoked: SI 2013/109 Reg.9

674. National Health Service (Pharmaceutical Services) (Remuneration for Persons providing Pharmaceutical Services) (Amendment) Regulations 2007

Reg.8, revoked: SI 2013/349 Sch.10 para.5

694. Her Majesty's Chief Inspector of Education, Children's Services and Skills (Fees and Frequency of Inspections) (Children's Homes etc.) Regulations 2007

Reg.2, amended: SI 2013/1394 Sch.8 para.1, SI 2013/2668 Sch.2 para.1
Reg.7A, added: SI 2013/1394 Sch.8 para.2
Reg.7B, added: SI 2013/2668 Sch.2 para.2
Reg.13A, added: SI 2013/2668 Sch.2 para.3
Reg.14, amended: SI 2013/523 Reg.2
Reg.15, amended: SI 2013/523 Reg.3
Reg.17, amended: SI 2013/523 Reg.4
Reg.17A, added: SI 2013/1394 Sch.8 para.3
Reg.18, amended: SI 2013/523 Reg.5
Reg.19, amended: SI 2013/1394 Sch.8 para.4
Reg.19, revoked (in part): SI 2013/523 Reg.6

701. Controls on Dogs (Non-application to Designated Land) (Wales) Order 2007

Sch.1, amended: SI 2013/755 Sch.5 para.41

722. Childcare (Supply and Disclosure of Information) (England) Regulations 2007

Reg.4, amended: SI 2013/630 Reg.47

727. Water Resources Management Plan Regulations 2007

Reg.2, amended: SI 2013/755 Sch.4 para.272

783. Town and Country Planning (Control of Advertisements) (England) Regulations 2007

applied: SI 2013/648 Sch.2 para.4, Sch.2 para.7, Sch.2 para.8, Sch.2 para.9, Sch.2 para.11, Sch.2

para.12, Sch.2 para.13, Sch.2 para.14, Sch.2 para.15
Part 3, applied: SI 2013/2114 Reg.5
Reg.8, applied: SI 2013/2114 Reg.5
Sch.3, see *Winfield v Secretary of State for Communities and Local Government* [2012] EWCA Civ 1415, [2013] 1 W.L.R. 948 (CA (Civ Div)), Sir Maurice Kay (VP CA Civ)
Sch.4 Part 3 para.1, amended: SI 2013/2114 Reg.3
Sch.4 Part 3 para.2, amended: SI 2013/2114 Reg.3
Sch.4 Part 4, amended: SI 2013/2114 Reg.3
Sch.4 Part 4, revoked: SI 2013/2114 Reg.3
Sch.4 Part 4, substituted: SI 2013/2114 Reg.3
Sch.4 Part 5 para.1, amended: SI 2013/2114 Reg.3
Sch.4 Part 5 para.1, revoked: SI 2013/2114 Reg.3
Sch.4 Part 5 para.1, substituted: SI 2013/2114 Reg.3
Sch.4 Part 5 para.2, amended: SI 2013/2114 Reg.3

797. Housing (Tenancy Deposits) (Prescribed Information) Order 2007
Art.2, see *Ayannuga v Swindells* [2012] EWCA Civ 1789, [2013] H.L.R. 9 (CA (Civ Div)), Etherton, L.J.

801. Pensions Increase (Review) Order 2007
applied: SI 2013/604 Sch.1

827. Consumer Credit (Advertisements) (Amendment) Regulations 2007
revoked (in part): SI 2013/1881 Art.21

841. Electricity Generating Stations and Overhead Lines (Inquiries Procedure) (England and Wales) Rules 2007
applied: SI 2013/1570 Reg.8

842. Cattle Identification (Wales) Regulations 2007
Reg.2, amended: SI 2013/821 Reg.3
Reg.10, amended: SI 2013/821 Reg.4
Reg.12, amended: SI 2013/821 Reg.5
Sch.2 para.2, amended: SI 2013/821 Reg.6
Sch.3 Part 2 para.11, amended: SI 2013/821 Reg.7
Sch.4 para.1, amended: SI 2013/821 Reg.8
Sch.4 para.2, amended: SI 2013/821 Reg.8
Sch.4 para.2, revoked (in part): SI 2013/821 Reg.8

846. Financial Services and Markets Act 2000 (Administration Orders Relating to Insurers)(Northern Ireland) Order 2007
Art.3, amended: SI 2013/472 Sch.2 para.127
Sch.1 para.1, amended: SI 2013/472 Sch.2 para.127
Sch.1 para.2, amended: SI 2013/472 Sch.2 para.127
Sch.1 para.3, amended: SI 2013/472 Sch.2 para.127
Sch.1 para.6, amended: SI 2013/472 Sch.2 para.127
Sch.1 para.7, amended: SI 2013/472 Sch.2 para.127

854. Further Education Corporations (Publication of Draft Orders) (Wales) Regulations 2007
applied: SI 2013/374

860. Building Societies Act 1986 (Substitution of Specified Amounts and Modification of the Funding Limit Calculation) Order 2007
Art.3, amended: 2013 c.33 Sch.9 para.3

871. Producer Responsibility Obligations (Packaging Waste) Regulations 2007
applied: SI 2013/2258 Sch.1 Part 2
Reg.2, amended: SI 2013/755 Sch.4 para.274, SI 2013/1821 Art.23
Reg.40B, amended: SI 2013/755 Sch.4 para.275
Sch.2 para.3, amended: SI 2013/1857 Reg.2

925. Representation of the People (Scotland) (Amendment) Regulations 2007
Reg.35, revoked (in part): SI 2013/3206 Sch.2
Reg.54, revoked (in part): SI 2013/3206 Sch.2
Reg.55, revoked: SI 2013/3206 Sch.2
Sch.2, amended: SI 2013/3206 Sch.2

930. Serious Organised Crime and Police Act 2005 (Designated Sites under Section 128) Order 2007
Art.2, amended: SI 2013/1562 Art.3, Art.4
Art.2, revoked (in part): SI 2013/1562 Art.3
Sch.12, added: SI 2013/1562 Art.3
Sch.13, added: SI 2013/1562 Art.4

934. Regulation of Investigatory Powers (Authorisations Extending to Scotland) Order 2007
Sch.1, amended: SI 2013/472 Sch.2 para.128

938. Offshore Combustion Installations (Prevention and Control of Pollution) (Amendment) Regulations 2007
revoked: SI 2013/971 Reg.38

957. School Governance (Constitution) (England) Regulations 2007
applied: SI 2013/1624 Reg.19
Sch.3 para.2, amended: SI 2013/235 Sch.2 para.107
Sch.5 para.2, applied: SI 2013/1624 Sch.1 para.2
Sch.6, applied: SI 2013/1624 Reg.17
Sch.6 para.5, applied: SI 2013/1624 Reg.17

958. School Governance (New Schools) (England) Regulations 2007
Sch.1 para.2, amended: SI 2013/235 Sch.2 para.108

960. School Governance (Federations) (England) Regulations 2007
Sch.4 para.2, amended: SI 2013/235 Sch.2 para.109

1025. Representation of the People (England and Wales) and the Representation of the People

(Combination of Polls) (England and Wales) (Amendment) Regulations 2007

Reg.2, amended: SI 2013/3198 Sch.2
Sch.1, amended: SI 2013/3198 Sch.2

1072. Firefighters Pension Scheme (Wales) Order 2007

Sch.1, added: SI 2013/1577 Sch.1 para.2, Sch.1 para.3
Sch.1, amended: SI 2013/735 Art.3, Art.4, SI 2013/1577 Sch.1 para.1, Sch.1 para.2
Sch.1, revoked: SI 2013/1577 Sch.1 para.2
Sch.1, substituted: SI 2013/1577 Sch.1 para.2

1098. Police, Public Order and Criminal Justice (Scotland) Act 2006 (Consequential Provisions and Modifications) Order 2007

applied: 2013 c.22 Sch.6 para.18
Art.2, amended: 2013 c.22 Sch.6 para.18, SI 2013/602 Sch.2 para.88
Art.2, revoked (in part): SI 2013/602 Sch.2 para.88
Art.3, amended: SI 2013/602 Sch.2 para.88
Art.3, revoked (in part): SI 2013/602 Sch.2 para.88
Art.4, amended: 2013 c.22 s.11, Sch.6 para.18
Art.4, applied: SI 2013/602 Sch.3 para.4
Art.4, revoked (in part): 2013 c.22 Sch.6 para.18
Sch.1 Part 1 para.4, revoked (in part): SI 2013/602 Sch.2 para.88

1104. National Health Service (Travelling Expenses and Remission of Charges) (Wales) Regulations 2007

Reg.2, amended: SI 2013/684 Reg.8
Reg.4, applied: SI 2013/898 Sch.4 para.7
Reg.5, amended: SI 2013/684 Reg.8
Reg.5, applied: SI 2013/898 Sch.5 para.6, Sch.6 para.6, SI 2013/3029 Sch.9 para.46, Sch.10 para.43, SI 2013/3035 Sch.1
Reg.6, applied: SI 2013/3029 Sch.9 para.46, Sch.10 para.43, SI 2013/3035 Sch.1
Reg.11, applied: SI 2013/3029 Sch.9 para.46, Sch.10 para.43, SI 2013/3035 Sch.1
Reg.16, amended: SI 2013/684 Reg.8
Sch.1, amended: SI 2013/684 Reg.8
Sch.1, substituted: SI 2013/684 Reg.8

1112. National Health Service (Pharmaceutical Services) (Remuneration for Persons providing Pharmaceutical Services) (Amendment) (Wales) Regulations 2007

Reg.3, revoked: SI 2013/898 Sch.8 para.20
Reg.4, revoked: SI 2013/898 Sch.8 para.20
Reg.5, revoked: SI 2013/898 Sch.8 para.20
Reg.6, revoked: SI 2013/898 Sch.8 para.20
Reg.7, revoked: SI 2013/898 Sch.8 para.20
Reg.8, revoked: SI 2013/898 Sch.8 para.20

1167. Consumer Credit (Information Requirements and Duration of Licences and Charges) Regulations 2007

Reg.42, revoked: SI 2013/1881 Art.25
Reg.43, revoked: SI 2013/1881 Art.25

1168. Consumer Credit (Exempt Agreements) Order 2007

revoked (in part): SI 2013/1881 Art.21
Art.5, amended: SI 2013/472 Art.4

1170. Her Majesty's Inspectors of Constabulary (Specified Organisations) Order 2007

Art.2, revoked (in part): SI 2013/2318 Sch.1 para.79

1174. Criminal Defence Service (Funding) Order 2007

applied: SI 2013/534 Reg.12
see *R. v Muoka (Costs)* [2013] 3 Costs L.R. 523 (Sen Cts Costs Office), Costs Judge Simons; see *R. v Noon (Costs)* [2013] 4 Costs L.R. 633 (Sen Cts Costs Office), Costs Judge Gordon-Saker
Art.2, applied: SI 2013/534 Reg.7
Art.5, see *R. v Ajufo (Costs)* [2013] 2 Costs L.R. 369 (Sen Cts Costs Office), Costs Judge Simons
Art.6, see *R. v Hart-Badger (Costs)* [2013] 1 Costs L.R. 181 (Sen Cts Costs Office), Senior Costs Judge Hurst; see *R. v Taylor (Costs)* [2013] 2 Costs L.R. 374 (Sen Cts Costs Office), Costs Judge Gordon-Saker
Art.32, see *R. v Taylor (Costs)* [2013] 2 Costs L.R. 374 (Sen Cts Costs Office), Costs Judge Gordon-Saker
Sch.1 Pt 1 para.1, see *Lord Chancellor v Woodhall* [2013] EWHC 764 (QB), [2013] 4 Costs L.R. 527 (QBD), Leggatt, J.; see *R. v Ajufo (Costs)* [2013] 2 Costs L.R. 369 (Sen Cts Costs Office), Costs Judge Simons
Sch.1 Pt 1 para.2, see *Lord Chancellor v Woodhall* [2013] EWHC 764 (QB), [2013] 4 Costs L.R. 527 (QBD), Leggatt, J.; see *R. v Nettleton (Costs)* [2013] 1 Costs L.R. 186 (Sen Cts Costs Office), Costs Judge Gordon-Saker
Sch.1 Pt 4 para.9, see *R. v Muoka (Costs)* [2013] 3 Costs L.R. 523 (Sen Cts Costs Office), Costs Judge Simons
Sch.2 Pt 3 para.15, see *R. v Noon (Costs)* [2013] 4 Costs L.R. 633 (Sen Cts Costs Office), Costs Judge Gordon-Saker
Sch.2 Part 4 para.25, amended: SI 2013/2804 Art.3

1253. Lasting Powers of Attorney, Enduring Powers of Attorney and Public Guardian Regulations 2007

Reg.12, amended: SI 2013/506 Reg.3
Reg.14, amended: SI 2013/506 Reg.4
Reg.14, applied: SI 2013/506 Reg.10
Reg.14A, amended: SI 2013/506 Reg.5
Reg.15, amended: SI 2013/506 Reg.6
Reg.15, applied: SI 2013/506 Reg.10
Reg.34, amended: SI 2013/472 Art.4
Reg.35, amended: SI 2013/506 Reg.7
Reg.37, amended: SI 2013/506 Reg.8

Sch.1 Part 1, amended: SI 2013/506 Reg.9
Sch.1 Part 2, amended: SI 2013/506 Reg.9
Sch.2, amended: SI 2013/506 Reg.10
Sch.4 Part 1, amended: SI 2013/506 Reg.11
Sch.4 Part 2, amended: SI 2013/506 Reg.12
Sch.4 Part 2, revoked: SI 2013/506 Reg.12

1257. Service Charges (Summary of Rights and Obligations, and Transitional Provision) (England) Regulations 2007

Reg.3, amended: SI 2013/1036 Sch.2 para.40

1258. Administration Charges (Summary of Rights and Obligations) (England) Regulations 2007

Reg.2, amended: SI 2013/1036 Sch.2 para.38

1263. Equality Act (Sexual Orientation) Regulations 2007

see *Black v Wilkinson* [2013] EWCA Civ 820, [2013] 1 W.L.R. 2490 (CA (Civ Div)), Lord Dyson (M.R.)
Reg.3, see *Black v Wilkinson* [2013] EWCA Civ 820, [2013] 1 W.L.R. 2490 (CA (Civ Div)), Lord Dyson (M.R.); see *Hall v Bull* [2013] UKSC 73, [2013] 1 W.L.R. 3741 (SC), Lord Neuberger (President)
Reg.4, see *Black v Wilkinson* [2013] EWCA Civ 820, [2013] 1 W.L.R. 2490 (CA (Civ Div)), Lord Dyson (M.R.)
Reg.6, see *Black v Wilkinson* [2013] EWCA Civ 820, [2013] 1 W.L.R. 2490 (CA (Civ Div)), Lord Dyson (M.R.)

1288. School Organisation (Establishment and Discontinuance of Schools) (England) Regulations 2007

applied: SI 2013/3109 Reg.3
revoked: SI 2013/3109 Reg.3
Reg.2, amended: SI 2013/235 Sch.2 para.110
Reg.5, amended: SI 2013/235 Sch.2 para.110
Reg.10, amended: SI 2013/235 Sch.2 para.110
Reg.13, amended: SI 2013/235 Sch.2 para.110
Reg.15, amended: SI 2013/235 Sch.2 para.110
Reg.25, amended: SI 2013/235 Sch.2 para.110

1289. School Organisation (Prescribed Alterations to Maintained Schools) (England) Regulations 2007

applied: SI 2013/3110 Reg.8
revoked: SI 2013/3110 Reg.8
Reg.2, amended: SI 2013/235 Sch.2 para.111
Sch.1 Part 2 para.5, amended: SI 2013/235 Sch.2 para.111
Sch.1 Part 2 para.7, amended: SI 2013/235 Sch.2 para.111
Sch.3 Part 2 para.27, amended: SI 2013/235 Sch.2 para.111
Sch.3 Part 2 para.28, amended: SI 2013/235 Sch.2 para.111
Sch.3 Part 2 para.34, amended: SI 2013/235 Sch.2 para.111
Sch.5 Part 2 para.27, amended: SI 2013/235 Sch.2 para.111
Sch.5 Part 2 para.28, amended: SI 2013/235 Sch.2 para.111
Sch.5 Part 2 para.34, amended: SI 2013/235 Sch.2 para.111

1319. Bovine Semen (England) Regulations 2007

Reg.4, applied: SI 2013/1240 Sch.4
Reg.7, applied: SI 2013/1240 Sch.4
Reg.10, applied: SI 2013/1240 Sch.4
Reg.40, applied: SI 2013/1240 Sch.4
Reg.41, substituted: SI 2013/1240 Reg.7
Reg.42, revoked: SI 2013/1240 Reg.7

1320. Health Service Medicines (Information Relating to Sales of Branded Medicines etc.) Regulations 2007

Reg.1A, added: SI 2013/2881 Reg.2
Reg.2, amended: SI 2013/235 Sch.2 para.112, SI 2013/2881 Reg.2
Reg.3, amended: SI 2013/2881 Reg.2
Reg.4, substituted: SI 2013/2881 Reg.2
Reg.8, added: SI 2013/2881 Reg.2
Sch.1 para.1, amended: SI 2013/2881 Reg.2
Sch.1 para.2, amended: SI 2013/2881 Reg.2

1333. A40 Trunk Road (Monmouth, Monmouthshire) (50 MPH Speed Limit) Order 2007

varied: SI 2013/214 Art.6, SI 2013/550 Art.8

1334. Export Control (North Korea) Order 2007

revoked: SI 2013/3182 Sch.1

1355. School Organisation (Transitional Provisions) (England) Regulations 2007

revoked: SI 2013/3109 Reg.3
Reg.2, amended: SI 2013/235 Sch.2 para.113
Reg.17, amended: SI 2013/235 Sch.2 para.113
Reg.18, amended: SI 2013/235 Sch.2 para.113
Reg.28, amended: SI 2013/235 Sch.2 para.113

1388. Government of Wales Act 2006 (Consequential Modifications and Transitional Provisions) Order 2007

Sch.1 para.110, revoked (in part): 2013 c.22 Sch.13 para.8

1398. Transfer of State Pensions and Benefits Regulations 2007

Reg.1, amended: SI 2013/630 Reg.74

1492. Whole of Government Accounts (Designation of Bodies) Order 2007

Sch.1, amended: SI 2013/687 Sch.2

1518. Marine Works (Environmental Impact Assessment) Regulations 2007

applied: SSI 2013/46 Art.5
Reg.2, amended: SI 2013/755 Sch.4 para.276

1598. Integration Loans for Refugees and Others Regulations 2007

Reg.9, amended: SI 2013/380 Sch.3 para.4

1609. Justices of the Peace (Training and Development Committee) Rules 2007

applied: SI 2013/1878 Sch.1 para.1

1610. Family Proceedings Courts (Constitution of Committees and Right to Preside) Rules 2007

applied: SI 2013/1878 Sch.1 para.1

1611. Youth Courts (Constitution of Committees and Right to Preside) Rules 2007

applied: SI 2013/1554 r.37_1, SI 2013/1878 Sch.1 para.1

1655. Civil Jurisdiction and Judgments Regulations 2007

Sch.1 Part 1 para.9, revoked: 2013 c.22 Sch.10 para.99

1711. Transfrontier Shipment of Waste Regulations 2007

applied: SI 2013/2258 Sch.1 Part 2

Reg.23, see *R. v Ezeemo (Godwin Chukwnaenya)* [2012] EWCA Crim 2064, [2013] 4 All E.R. 1016 (CA (Crim Div)), Pitchford, L.J.

Reg.57, see *R. v Ezeemo (Godwin Chukwnaenya)* [2012] EWCA Crim 2064, [2013] 4 All E.R. 1016 (CA (Crim Div)), Pitchford, L.J.

1712. Traffic Management (Guidance on Intervention Criteria) (Wales) Order 2007

Sch.1 para.37, amended: SI 2013/1644 Sch.6

1744. Court of Protection Rules 2007

see *A Local Authority v K* [2013] EWHC 242 (COP), (2013) 130 B.M.L.R. 195 (CP), Cobb, J.; see *J Council v GU* [2012] EWHC 3531 (COP), (2013) 16 C.C.L. Rep. 31 (CP), Mostyn, J.; see *SK, Re* [2012] EWHC 1990 (COP), [2013] P.I.Q.R. P4 (CP), Bodey, J.

Part 3 r.6, amended: SI 2013/534 Sch.1 para.17

Part 18 r.151, amended: SI 2013/534 Sch.1 para.17

Part 18 r.151, substituted: SI 2013/534 Sch.1 para.17

r.73, see *SK, Re* [2012] EWHC 1990 (COP), [2013] P.I.Q.R. P4 (CP), Bodey, J.

r.75, see *SK, Re* [2012] EWHC 1990 (COP), [2013] P.I.Q.R. P4 (CP), Bodey, J.

r.90, see *J Council v GU* [2012] EWHC 3531 (COP), (2013) 16 C.C.L. Rep. 31 (CP), Mostyn, J.

r.91, see *J Council v GU* [2012] EWHC 3531 (COP), (2013) 16 C.C.L. Rep. 31 (CP), Mostyn, J.

r.92, see *A Local Authority v K* [2013] EWHC 242 (COP), (2013) 130 B.M.L.R. 195 (CP), Cobb, J.

r.156, see *Clarke, Re (Costs)* [2012] EWHC 2947 (COP), [2013] W.T.L.R. 59 (CP), Peter Jackson, J.; see *MA v Halifax Bank* [2013] W.T.L.R. 271 (CP), Senior Judge Denzil Lush

r.159, see *MA v Halifax Bank* [2013] W.T.L.R. 271 (CP), Senior Judge Denzil Lush

1745. Court of Protection Fees Order 2007

Art.3, amended: SI 2013/2302 Art.5

Art.8, substituted: SI 2013/2302 Art.5

Art.9, revoked: SI 2013/2302 Art.5

Sch.1, substituted: SI 2013/2302 Art.5

Sch.2 para.1, added: SI 2013/2302 Sch.1

Sch.2 para.2, added: SI 2013/2302 Sch.1

Sch.2 para.3, added: SI 2013/2302 Sch.1

Sch.2 para.4, added: SI 2013/2302 Sch.1

Sch.2 para.5, added: SI 2013/2302 Sch.1

Sch.2 para.6, added: SI 2013/2302 Sch.1

Sch.2 para.7, added: SI 2013/2302 Sch.1

Sch.2 para.8, added: SI 2013/2302 Sch.1

Sch.2 para.9, added: SI 2013/2302 Sch.1

Sch.2 para.10, added: SI 2013/2302 Sch.1

Sch.2 para.11, added: SI 2013/2302 Sch.1

Sch.2 para.12, added: SI 2013/2302 Sch.1

Sch.2 para.13, added: SI 2013/2302 Sch.1

Sch.2 para.14, added: SI 2013/2302 Sch.1

Sch.2 para.14, substituted: SI 2013/2302 Art.5

Sch.2 para.15, added: SI 2013/2302 Sch.1

Sch.2 para.16, added: SI 2013/2302 Sch.1

Sch.2 para.16, amended: SI 2013/2302 Art.5

Sch.2 para.17, added: SI 2013/2302 Sch.1

Sch.2 para.18, added: SI 2013/2302 Sch.1

Sch.2 para.19, added: SI 2013/2302 Sch.1

Sch.2 para.20, added: SI 2013/2302 Sch.1

1797. Childcare Providers (Information, Advice and Training) Regulations 2007

Reg.4, amended: SI 2013/630 Reg.48

1818. National Health Service (Functions of Strategic Health Authorities and Primary Care Trusts and Administration Arrangements) (England) (Amendment No.2) Regulations 2007

revoked: SI 2013/235 Sch.2 para.195

1819. Community Drivers Hours and Recording Equipment Regulations 2007

Sch.1 Part 1 para.1, amended: SI 2013/235 Sch.2 para.114

1829. Crime Prevention (Designated Areas) Order 2007

revoked: SI 2013/1760 Sch.1

1831. Crime and Disorder (Prescribed Information) Regulations 2007

Reg.1, amended: SI 2013/235 Sch.2 para.115

Sch.1 para.9, amended: SI 2013/235 Sch.2 para.115

Sch.1 para.10, amended: SI 2013/235 Sch.2 para.115

Sch.1 para.11, amended: SI 2013/235 Sch.2 para.115

Sch.1 para.12, amended: SI 2013/235 Sch.2 para.115

1842. Offshore Marine Conservation (Natural Habitats, &c.) Regulations 2007
Reg.25, amended: SI 2013/755 Sch.4 para.278
Reg.71, amended: SI 2013/755 Sch.4 para.279

1867. Education (Penalty Notices) (England) Regulations 2007
Reg.3, amended: SI 2013/757 Reg.2
Reg.4, amended: SI 2013/757 Reg.2
Reg.5, amended: SI 2013/757 Reg.2
Reg.7, amended: SI 2013/757 Reg.2

1887. Nursing and Midwifery Council (Midwives) (Amendment) Rules Order of Council 2007
applied: SI 2013/235 Sch.3 para.6

1932. Police Pension Fund Regulations 2007
Reg.2, amended: SI 2013/2318 Sch.1 para.76
Reg.2, revoked (in part): SI 2013/2318 Sch.1 para.76
Reg.12A, amended: SI 2013/2318 Sch.1 para.77
Reg.12B, revoked: SI 2013/2318 Sch.1 para.78

1933. Mobile Roaming (European Communities) Regulations 2007
varied: SI 2013/822 Reg.11
Reg.1, amended: SI 2013/822 Reg.2
Reg.2A, added: SI 2013/822 Reg.3
Reg.2B, added: SI 2013/822 Reg.3
Reg.3, amended: SI 2013/822 Reg.4
Reg.4, amended: SI 2013/822 Reg.5
Reg.4, revoked (in part): SI 2013/822 Reg.5
Reg.4, varied: SI 2013/822 Reg.11
Reg.4A, added: SI 2013/822 Reg.6
Reg.5, amended: SI 2013/822 Reg.7
Reg.5, revoked (in part): SI 2013/822 Reg.7
Reg.5, varied: SI 2013/822 Reg.11
Reg.6A, added: SI 2013/822 Reg.8
Reg.7, varied: SI 2013/822 Reg.11
Reg.8, varied: SI 2013/822 Reg.11
Reg.9, varied: SI 2013/822 Reg.11
Reg.10, varied: SI 2013/822 Reg.11
Reg.11, amended: SI 2013/822 Reg.9
Reg.11, varied: SI 2013/822 Reg.11
Reg.12, varied: SI 2013/822 Reg.11
Reg.13, varied: SI 2013/822 Reg.11
Reg.14, varied: SI 2013/822 Reg.11
Reg.17, added: SI 2013/822 Reg.10
Reg.18, added: SI 2013/822 Reg.10
Reg.19, added: SI 2013/822 Reg.10

1951. Street Works (Registers, Notices, Directions and Designations) (England) Regulations 2007
applied: SI 2013/2389 Sch.1
referred to: SI 2013/805 Sch.1, SI 2013/806 Sch.1, SI 2013/807 Sch.1, SI 2013/808 Sch.1, SI 2013/810 Sch.1, SI 2013/811 Sch.1, SI 2013/812 Sch.1, SI 2013/813 Sch.1, SI 2013/814 Sch.1, SI 2013/2399 Sch.1
varied: SI 2013/1781 Sch.1

2051. Public Guardian (Fees, etc) Regulations 2007
applied: SI 2013/1748 Reg.2
Reg.10, amended: SI 2013/1748 Reg.4
Sch.1, amended: SI 2013/1748 Reg.5

2128. Secretary of State for Justice Order 2007
Sch.1 Part 1 para.10, amended: SI 2013/2853 Art.2

2157. Money Laundering Regulations 2007
applied: SI 2013/1881 Sch.1 para.32
Part 5, applied: SI 2013/1881 Sch.1 para.32
Reg.2, amended: SI 2013/472 Sch.2 para.129, SI 2013/1881 Sch.1 para.31, SI 2013/3115 Sch.2 para.68
Reg.3, amended: SI 2013/3115 Sch.2 para.68
Reg.17, revoked (in part): SI 2013/1881 Sch.1 para.31
Reg.22, amended: SI 2013/1881 Sch.1 para.31
Reg.22, revoked (in part): SI 2013/1881 Sch.1 para.31
Reg.23, amended: SI 2013/1881 Sch.1 para.31
Reg.23, revoked (in part): SI 2013/1881 Sch.1 para.31
Reg.24, amended: SI 2013/472 Sch.2 para.129
Reg.24A, amended: SI 2013/472 Sch.2 para.129
Reg.27, applied: SI 2013/1881 Sch.1 para.32
Reg.31, amended: SI 2013/472 Sch.2 para.129
Reg.32, revoked (in part): SI 2013/1881 Sch.1 para.31
Reg.34, amended: SI 2013/1881 Sch.1 para.31
Reg.35, amended: SI 2013/429 Reg.2, SI 2013/1881 Sch.1 para.31
Reg.35, applied: SI 2013/1881 Sch.1 para.32
Reg.36, amended: SI 2013/1881 Sch.1 para.31
Reg.36, revoked (in part): SI 2013/1881 Sch.1 para.31
Reg.40, amended: SI 2013/1881 Sch.1 para.31
Reg.41, amended: SI 2013/1881 Sch.1 para.31
Reg.42, amended: SI 2013/472 Sch.2 para.129, SI 2013/1881 Sch.1 para.31
Reg.42, applied: SI 2013/418 Art.2
Reg.44, amended: SI 2013/1881 Sch.1 para.31
Reg.44, revoked (in part): SI 2013/1881 Sch.1 para.31
Reg.45, applied: 2013 c.22 Sch.17 para.27
Reg.46, amended: SI 2013/1881 Sch.1 para.31
Reg.46, revoked (in part): SI 2013/1881 Sch.1 para.31
Reg.49, amended: SI 2013/472 Sch.2 para.129
Reg.49, revoked (in part): SI 2013/1881 Sch.1 para.31
Sch.1, amended: SI 2013/3115 Sch.2 para.68
Sch.5 Part 1 para.2, amended: SI 2013/472 Sch.2 para.129

2264. Further Education Teachers Qualifications (England) Regulations 2007
revoked: SI 2013/1976 Sch.1

2266. Food (Suspension of the Use of E 128 Red 2G as Food Colour) (England) Regulations 2007
revoked: SI 2013/2210 Sch.5

2310. Education (Fees and Awards) (Wales) Regulations 2007
Reg.2, amended: SI 2013/1792 Reg.4
Sch.1 para.9, amended: SI 2013/1792 Reg.5

2315. Food (Suspension of the use of E 128 Red 2G as Food Colour) (Wales) (No.2) Regulations 2007
revoked: SI 2013/2591 Sch.5

2324. Education (School Performance Information) (England) Regulations 2007
Reg.2, amended: SI 2013/1759 Reg.2
Reg.5, amended: SI 2013/1759 Reg.2
Reg.12ZA, added: SI 2013/1759 Reg.2
Reg.12ZA, amended: SI 2013/3212 Reg.6
Reg.12ZA, revoked (in part): SI 2013/3212 Reg.6
Reg.13, revoked: SI 2013/1759 Reg.2
Reg.14, revoked: SI 2013/1759 Reg.2
Sch.1 para.2, amended: SI 2013/1759 Reg.2
Sch.8 Part 1 para.1, amended: SI 2013/1759 Reg.2
Sch.8 Part 2 para.1, amended: SI 2013/1759 Reg.2
Sch.8 Part 2 para.1, revoked: SI 2013/3212 Reg.7
Sch.8 Part 3 para.1, revoked: SI 2013/1759 Reg.2
Sch.8 Part 3 para.2, revoked: SI 2013/1759 Reg.2

2325. Large Combustion Plants (National Emission Reduction Plan) Regulations 2007
Reg.2, amended: SI 2013/755 Sch.4 para.281
Reg.6, amended: SI 2013/755 Sch.4 para.282
Reg.7, amended: SI 2013/755 Sch.4 para.283
Reg.9, amended: SI 2013/755 Sch.4 para.284
Reg.12, amended: SI 2013/755 Sch.4 para.285
Sch.1 Part 1 para.1, amended: SI 2013/755 Sch.4 para.286

2334. Dedicated Highways (Registers under Section 31A of the Highways Act 1980 (England) Regulations 2007
Reg.2, amended: SI 2013/1774 Reg.8
Reg.3, amended: SI 2013/1774 Reg.8
Reg.4, amended: SI 2013/1774 Reg.8
Reg.5, amended: SI 2013/1774 Reg.8

2359. Education (Nutritional Standards and Requirements for School Food) (England) Regulations 2007
Reg.2, amended: SI 2013/2775 Sch.15 para.2

2458. Environmental Noise (Identification of Noise Sources) (England) (Amendment) Regulations 2007
revoked: SI 2013/2854 Reg.2

2459. Zoonoses (Monitoring) (Wales) Regulations 2007
Reg.7, amended: SI 2013/755 Sch.5 para.42

2501. Political Parties, Elections and Referendums Act 2000 (Northern Ireland Political Parties) Order 2007
Art.11, amended: SI 2013/472 Sch.2 para.130

2538. Independent Living Fund (2006) Order 2007
Art.10, revoked: SI 2013/458 Sch.1
Art.11, revoked: SI 2013/458 Sch.1

2586. Porcine Semen (Fees) (England) Regulations 2007
revoked: SI 2013/1240 Reg.11

2734. Water Supply (Water Quality) Regulations 2000 (Amendment) Regulations 2007
Reg.2, revoked (in part): SI 2013/1387 Sch.5 para.6

2755. Imperial College Healthcare National Health Service Trust (Establishment) and the Hammersmith Hospitals National Health Service Trust and the St Mary's National Health Service Trust... 2007
Art.1, amended: SI 2013/593 Art.2

2781. European Communities (Recognition of Professional Qualifications) Regulations 2007
Reg.26, amended: SI 2013/732 Reg.2
Sch.5, amended: SI 2013/3176 Art.4

2785. Natural Mineral Water, Spring Water and Bottled Drinking Water (England) Regulations 2007
disapplied: SI 2013/264 Sch.1

2803. Diseases of Animals (Approved Disinfectants) (Wales) Order 2007
Art.3, amended: SI 2013/1506 Sch.5 para.8
Art.6, amended: SI 2013/1506 Sch.5 para.8

2876. Administrative Justice and Tribunals Council (Listed Tribunals) (Wales) Order 2007
revoked: SI 2013/2042 Sch.1 para.66

2915. Scotland Act 1998 (Transfer of Functions to the Scottish Ministers etc.) Order 2007
Sch.1 para.1, revoked (in part): SI 2013/602 Sch.2 para.89

2933. Environmental Impact Assessment (Agriculture) (Wales) Regulations 2007
Reg.2, amended: SI 2013/755 Sch.5 para.44
Reg.2, revoked (in part): SI 2013/755 Sch.5 para.44
Reg.5, amended: SI 2013/755 Sch.5 para.45

2951. Administrative Justice and Tribunals Council (Listed Tribunals) Order 2007
revoked: SI 2013/2042 Sch.1 para.67
Art.2, amended: SI 2013/686 Sch.2, SI 2013/1036 Sch.2 para.69, SI 2013/1644 Sch.2, SI 2013/1881 Sch.1 para.33

2974. Companies (Cross-Border Mergers) Regulations 2007
applied: SI 2013/1893 Sch.2
see *Diamond Resorts (Europe) Ltd, Re* [2012] EWHC 3576 (Ch), [2013] B.C.C. 275 (Ch D (Companies Ct)), Sales, J.; see *Itau BBA*

International Ltd, Re [2012] EWHC 1783 (Ch), [2013] Bus. L.R. 490 (Ch D), Henderson, J
Reg.2, see *House-Clean Ltd, Re* [2013] EWHC 2337 (Ch), [2013] Bus. L.R. 1145 (Ch D (Companies Ct)), Roth, J.
Reg.3, see *Itau BBA International Ltd, Re* [2012] EWHC 1783 (Ch), [2013] Bus. L.R. 490 (Ch D), Henderson, J
Reg.6, see *House-Clean Ltd, Re* [2013] EWHC 2337 (Ch), [2013] Bus. L.R. 1145 (Ch D (Companies Ct)), Roth, J.
Reg.7, see *House-Clean Ltd, Re* [2013] EWHC 2337 (Ch), [2013] Bus. L.R. 1145 (Ch D (Companies Ct)), Roth, J.
Reg.8, see *House-Clean Ltd, Re* [2013] EWHC 2337 (Ch), [2013] Bus. L.R. 1145 (Ch D (Companies Ct)), Roth, J.
Reg.10, see *House-Clean Ltd, Re* [2013] EWHC 2337 (Ch), [2013] Bus. L.R. 1145 (Ch D (Companies Ct)), Roth, J.
Reg.11, see *Honda Motor Europe Ltd, Re* [2013] EWHC 2842 (Ch), [2013] B.C.C. 767 (Ch D), Norris, J.
Reg.12, see *House-Clean Ltd, Re* [2013] EWHC 2337 (Ch), [2013] Bus. L.R. 1145 (Ch D (Companies Ct)), Roth, J.
Reg.16, see *Diamond Resorts (Europe) Ltd, Re* [2012] EWHC 3576 (Ch), [2013] B.C.C. 275 (Ch D (Companies Ct)), Sales, J.; see *House-Clean Ltd, Re* [2013] EWHC 2337 (Ch), [2013] Bus. L.R. 1145 (Ch D (Companies Ct)), Roth, J.
Reg.62, amended: SI 2013/1956 Sch.1 para.13

2978. Education (Pupil Referral Units) (Management Committees etc.) (England) Regulations 2007
Reg.21, substituted: SI 2013/1624 Sch.3 para.1
Sch.3 para.1, substituted: SI 2013/1624 Sch.3 para.1
Sch.3 para.2, substituted: SI 2013/1624 Sch.3 para.1
Sch.3 para.3, substituted: SI 2013/1624 Sch.3 para.1
Sch.3 para.4, substituted: SI 2013/1624 Sch.3 para.1
Sch.3 para.5, substituted: SI 2013/1624 Sch.3 para.1
Sch.3 para.6, substituted: SI 2013/1624 Sch.3 para.1
Sch.3 para.7, substituted: SI 2013/1624 Sch.3 para.1
Sch.3 para.8, substituted: SI 2013/1624 Sch.3 para.1
Sch.3 para.9, substituted: SI 2013/1624 Sch.3 para.1
Sch.3 para.10, substituted: SI 2013/1624 Sch.3 para.1
Sch.3 para.11, substituted: SI 2013/1624 Sch.3 para.1
Sch.3 para.12, substituted: SI 2013/1624 Sch.3 para.1
Sch.3 para.13, substituted: SI 2013/1624 Sch.3 para.1
Sch.3 para.14, substituted: SI 2013/1624 Sch.3 para.1
Sch.3 para.15, substituted: SI 2013/1624 Sch.3 para.1
Sch.3 para.16, substituted: SI 2013/1624 Sch.3 para.1

2979. Education (Pupil Referral Units) (Application of Enactments) (England) Regulations 2007
Sch.1 Part 2 para.29, substituted: SI 2013/3037 Reg.4

3072. Renewable Transport Fuel Obligations Order 2007
Art.2, amended: SI 2013/816 Art.3
Art.3, amended: SI 2013/816 Art.4, Art.5, Art.6
Art.4, amended: SI 2013/816 Art.7, Art.8
Art.5, amended: SI 2013/816 Art.9, Art.10
Art.17, amended: SI 2013/816 Art.11
Art.23, amended: SI 2013/816 Art.12

3105. Agricultural Land Tribunals (Rules) Order 2007
Art.2, amended: SI 2013/1036 Sch.2 para.61
Sch.1, amended: SI 2013/1036 Sch.2 para.62
Sch.1, revoked: SI 2013/1036 Sch.2 para.62

3106. Persistent Organic Pollutants Regulations 2007
Reg.3, amended: SI 2013/755 Sch.4 para.287

3141. PPP Administration Order Rules 2007
Part 2 r.10, amended: SI 2013/472 Art.4

3165. Natural Mineral Water, Spring Water and Bottled Drinking Water (Wales) Regulations 2007
referred to: SI 2013/479 Sch.1

3255. Financial Services and Markets Act 2000 (Reinsurance Directive) Regulations 2007
Reg.4, revoked: SI 2013/3115 Sch.3

3291. Patents Rules 2007
r.50, see *Virgin Atlantic Airways Ltd v Jet Airways (India) Ltd* [2012] EWHC 2153 (Pat), [2013] R.P.C. 10 (Ch D (Patents Ct)), Floyd, J.
r.107, see *Tulane Education Fund, Re* [2012] EWHC 932 (Pat), [2013] Bus. L.R. 53 (Ch D), Roger Wyand Q.C.; see *Tulane Education Fund, Re* [2013] EWCA Civ 890, [2013] Bus. L.R. 1225 (CA (Civ Div)), Sir Terence Etherton
r.116, see *Tulane Education Fund, Re* [2013] EWCA Civ 890, [2013] Bus. L.R. 1225 (CA (Civ Div)), Sir Terence Etherton

3292. Patents (Fees) Rules 2007

r.6, see *Tulane Education Fund, Re* [2013] EWCA Civ 890, [2013] Bus. L.R. 1225 (CA (Civ Div)), Sir Terence Etherton

3298. Transfer of Funds (Information on the Payer) Regulations 2007

Reg.1, amended: SI 2013/472 Sch.2 para.131
Reg.2, amended: SI 2013/472 Sch.2 para.131
Reg.4, amended: SI 2013/472 Sch.2 para.131
Reg.5, amended: SI 2013/429 Reg.2
Reg.11, applied: SI 2013/418 Art.2
Sch.2 para.1, amended: SI 2013/472 Sch.2 para.131

3353. Armed Forces (Redress of Individual Grievances) Regulations 2007

see *Williams v Ministry of Defence* [2013] Eq. L.R. 27 (EAT), Judge McMullen Q.C.

3372. Traffic Management Permit Scheme (England) Regulations 2007

applied: SI 2013/805 Sch.1, SI 2013/806 Sch.1, SI 2013/807 Sch.1, SI 2013/808 Sch.1, SI 2013/809 Sch.1, SI 2013/810 Sch.1, SI 2013/811 Sch.1, SI 2013/812 Sch.1, SI 2013/813 Sch.1, SI 2013/814 Sch.1, SI 2013/1781 Sch.1, SI 2013/2389 Sch.1, SI 2013/2398 Sch.1, SI 2013/2399 Sch.1
referred to: SI 2013/805 Sch.1, SI 2013/806 Sch.1, SI 2013/807 Sch.1, SI 2013/808 Sch.1, SI 2013/809 Sch.1, SI 2013/810 Sch.1, SI 2013/811 Sch.1, SI 2013/812 Sch.1, SI 2013/813 Sch.1, SI 2013/814 Sch.1, SI 2013/2389 Sch.1, SI 2013/2399 Sch.1
see *Thames Water Utilities Ltd v Transport for London* [2013] EWHC 187 (Admin), [2013] P.T.S.R. 627 (DC), Laws, L.J.
Part 3, applied: SI 2013/805 Sch.1, SI 2013/806 Sch.1, SI 2013/807 Sch.1, SI 2013/808 Sch.1, SI 2013/809 Sch.1, SI 2013/810 Sch.1, SI 2013/812 Sch.1, SI 2013/813 Sch.1, SI 2013/814 Sch.1
Part 5, applied: SI 2013/805 Sch.1, SI 2013/806 Sch.1, SI 2013/807 Sch.1, SI 2013/808 Sch.1, SI 2013/809 Sch.1, SI 2013/810 Sch.1, SI 2013/811 Sch.1, SI 2013/812 Sch.1, SI 2013/813 Sch.1, SI 2013/814 Sch.1
Part 7, applied: SI 2013/1781 Sch.1, SI 2013/2398 Sch.1
Part 8, applied: SI 2013/805 Art.4, SI 2013/806 Art.4, SI 2013/807 Art.4, SI 2013/808 Art.4, SI 2013/809 Art.4, SI 2013/810 Art.4, SI 2013/811 Art.4, SI 2013/812 Art.4, SI 2013/813 Art.4, SI 2013/814 Art.4, SI 2013/1781 Art.4, SI 2013/2389 Art.4, SI 2013/2398 Art.4, SI 2013/2399 Art.4
Part 8, disapplied: SI 2013/805 Sch.1, SI 2013/806 Sch.1, SI 2013/807 Sch.1, SI 2013/808 Sch.1, SI 2013/809 Sch.1, SI 2013/810 Sch.1, SI 2013/811 Sch.1, SI 2013/812 Sch.1, SI 2013/813 Sch.1, SI 2013/814 Sch.1
Reg.10, applied: SI 2013/805 Sch.1, SI 2013/806 Sch.1, SI 2013/807 Sch.1, SI 2013/808 Sch.1, SI 2013/809 Sch.1, SI 2013/810 Sch.1, SI 2013/811 Sch.1, SI 2013/812 Sch.1, SI 2013/813 Sch.1, SI 2013/814 Sch.1, SI 2013/2389 Sch.1, SI 2013/2398 Sch.1, SI 2013/2399 Sch.1
Reg.10, referred to: SI 2013/2399 Sch.1
Reg.14, applied: SI 2013/805 Sch.1, SI 2013/806 Sch.1, SI 2013/807 Sch.1, SI 2013/808 Sch.1, SI 2013/809 Sch.1, SI 2013/810 Sch.1, SI 2013/811 Sch.1, SI 2013/812 Sch.1, SI 2013/813 Sch.1, SI 2013/814 Sch.1
Reg.15, applied: SI 2013/1781 Sch.1, SI 2013/2398 Sch.1, SI 2013/2399 Sch.1
Reg.16, applied: SI 2013/805 Sch.1, SI 2013/806 Sch.1, SI 2013/807 Sch.1, SI 2013/808 Sch.1, SI 2013/809 Sch.1, SI 2013/810 Sch.1, SI 2013/811 Sch.1, SI 2013/812 Sch.1, SI 2013/813 Sch.1, SI 2013/814 Sch.1
Reg.18, applied: SI 2013/805 Sch.1, SI 2013/806 Sch.1, SI 2013/807 Sch.1, SI 2013/808 Sch.1, SI 2013/809 Sch.1, SI 2013/810 Sch.1, SI 2013/811 Sch.1, SI 2013/812 Sch.1, SI 2013/813 Sch.1, SI 2013/814 Sch.1, SI 2013/2389 Sch.1
Reg.18, referred to: SI 2013/2399 Sch.1
Reg.19, applied: SI 2013/805 Sch.1, SI 2013/806 Sch.1, SI 2013/807 Sch.1, SI 2013/808 Sch.1, SI 2013/809 Sch.1, SI 2013/810 Sch.1, SI 2013/811 Sch.1, SI 2013/812 Sch.1, SI 2013/813 Sch.1, SI 2013/814 Sch.1, SI 2013/2389 Sch.1
Reg.19, referred to: SI 2013/2399 Sch.1
Reg.19, see *Thames Water Utilities Ltd v Transport for London* [2013] EWHC 187 (Admin), [2013] P.T.S.R. 627 (DC), Laws, L.J.
Reg.20, applied: SI 2013/805 Sch.1, SI 2013/806 Sch.1, SI 2013/807 Sch.1, SI 2013/808 Sch.1, SI 2013/809 Sch.1, SI 2013/810 Sch.1, SI 2013/811 Sch.1, SI 2013/812 Sch.1, SI 2013/813 Sch.1, SI 2013/814 Sch.1, SI 2013/2389 Sch.1, SI 2013/2398 Sch.1
Reg.20, referred to: SI 2013/2399 Sch.1
Reg.21, applied: SI 2013/805 Sch.1, SI 2013/807 Sch.1, SI 2013/808 Sch.1, SI 2013/809 Sch.1, SI 2013/810 Sch.1, SI 2013/811 Sch.1, SI 2013/812 Sch.1, SI 2013/813 Sch.1, SI 2013/814 Sch.1
Reg.24, applied: SI 2013/805 Sch.1, SI 2013/806 Sch.1, SI 2013/807 Sch.1, SI 2013/808 Sch.1, SI 2013/809 Sch.1, SI 2013/810 Sch.1, SI 2013/811 Sch.1, SI 2013/812 Sch.1, SI 2013/813 Sch.1, SI 2013/814 Sch.1
Reg.30, applied: SI 2013/2398 Sch.1

Reg.33, applied: SI 2013/1781 Sch.1, SI 2013/2398 Sch.1
Reg.34, applied: SI 2013/1781 Sch.1, SI 2013/2398 Sch.1
Reg.39, applied: SI 2013/805 Sch.1, SI 2013/806 Sch.1, SI 2013/807 Sch.1, SI 2013/808 Sch.1, SI 2013/809 Sch.1, SI 2013/810 Sch.1, SI 2013/811 Sch.1, SI 2013/812 Sch.1, SI 2013/813 Sch.1, SI 2013/814 Sch.1
Reg.39, referred to: SI 2013/805 Sch.1, SI 2013/806 Sch.1, SI 2013/807 Sch.1, SI 2013/808 Sch.1, SI 2013/809 Sch.1, SI 2013/810 Sch.1, SI 2013/811 Sch.1, SI 2013/812 Sch.1, SI 2013/813 Sch.1, SI 2013/814 Sch.1

3373. Education (Information About Individual Pupils) (England) (Amendment) Regulations 2007
revoked: SI 2013/2094 Sch.2

3454. Waste Electrical and Electronic Equipment (Amendment) Regulations 2007
revoked: SI 2013/3113 Reg.96

3464. School Organisation and Governance (Amendment) (England) Regulations 2007
Reg.2, revoked: SI 2013/3109 Reg.3
Reg.3, revoked: SI 2013/3109 Reg.3
Reg.4, revoked: SI 2013/3109 Reg.3
Reg.5, revoked: SI 2013/3109 Reg.3
Reg.6, revoked: SI 2013/3109 Reg.3
Reg.7, revoked: SI 2013/3109 Reg.3
Reg.8, revoked: SI 2013/3109 Reg.3
Reg.9, revoked: SI 2013/3109 Reg.3
Reg.10, revoked: SI 2013/3109 Reg.3
Reg.11, revoked: SI 2013/3109 Reg.3
Reg.12, revoked: SI 2013/3109 Reg.3
Reg.13, revoked: SI 2013/3109 Reg.3
Reg.14, revoked: SI 2013/3109 Reg.3
Reg.15, revoked: SI 2013/3109 Reg.3
Reg.16, revoked: SI 2013/3109 Reg.3
Reg.17, revoked: SI 2013/3110 Reg.8
Reg.18, revoked: SI 2013/3110 Reg.8
Reg.19, revoked: SI 2013/3110 Reg.8
Reg.20, revoked: SI 2013/3110 Reg.8
Reg.21, revoked: SI 2013/3110 Reg.8
Reg.22, revoked: SI 2013/3110 Reg.8
Reg.23, revoked: SI 2013/3110 Reg.8
Reg.24, revoked: SI 2013/3110 Reg.8
Reg.25, revoked: SI 2013/3110 Reg.8

3468. Air Navigation (Overseas Territories) Order 2007
revoked: SI 2013/2870 Sch.1

3474. Fire and Rescue Services (Appointment of Inspector) Order 2007
revoked: SI 2013/1120 Art.3

3482. Civil Enforcement of Parking Contraventions (England) Representations and Appeals Regulations 2007
Reg.3, see *R. (on the application of Hackney Drivers Association Ltd) v Parking Adjudicator* [2012] EWHC 3394 (Admin), [2013] R.T.R. 34 (QBD (Admin)), Judge Raynor

3483. Civil Enforcement of Parking Contraventions (England) General Regulations 2007
Reg.17, applied: SI 2013/1783 Reg.12

3494. Statutory Auditors and Third Country Auditors Regulations 2007
Reg.29, revoked: SI 2013/1672 Sch.1
Reg.34, revoked: SI 2013/1672 Sch.1
Reg.35, revoked: SI 2013/1672 Sch.1
Reg.36, revoked: SI 2013/1672 Sch.1
Reg.37, revoked: SI 2013/1672 Sch.1
Reg.38, revoked: SI 2013/1672 Sch.1
Reg.39, revoked: SI 2013/1672 Sch.1
Reg.40, revoked: SI 2013/1672 Sch.1

3510. Financial Services and Markets Act 2000 (Regulated Activities) (Amendment) (No.2) Order 2007
Art.4, amended: SI 2013/472 Art.4
Art.7, amended: SI 2013/472 Art.4

3521. Infant Formula and Follow-on Formula (England) Regulations 2007
Reg.2, amended: SI 2013/3243 Reg.2
Reg.8, amended: SI 2013/3243 Reg.2
Reg.9, substituted: SI 2013/3243 Reg.2
Reg.15, amended: SI 2013/3243 Reg.2
Reg.16, amended: SI 2013/3243 Reg.2

3531. Channel Tunnel (Safety) Order 2007
Art.1, amended: SI 2013/407 Art.2
Art.1, revoked (in part): SI 2013/407 Art.2
Art.4, amended: SI 2013/407 Art.2
Art.6, amended: SI 2013/407 Art.2
Art.9, revoked: SI 2013/407 Art.2
Art.11, added: SI 2013/407 Art.2
Sch.1, substituted: SI 2013/407 Sch.1

3532. Registered Pension Schemes (Authorised Member Payments) Regulations 2007
Reg.2, amended: SI 2013/472 Sch.2 para.132

3538. Environmental Permitting (England and Wales) Regulations 2007
see *R. v Hinchcliffe (Roy)* [2012] EWCA Crim 1691, [2013] 1 Cr. App. R. (S.) 79 (CA (Crim Div)), Griffith Williams, J.
Reg.12, see *R. v Hinchcliffe (Roy)* [2012] EWCA Crim 1691, [2013] 1 Cr. App. R. (S.) 79 (CA (Crim Div)), Griffith Williams, J.
Reg.38, applied: SI 2013/2258 Sch.1 Part 2

Reg.38, see *R. v Hinchcliffe (Roy)* [2012] EWCA Crim 1691, [2013] 1 Cr. App. R. (S.) 79 (CA (Crim Div)), Griffith Williams, J.

3544. Legislative and Regulatory Reform (Regulatory Functions) Order 2007

Sch.1 Part 1, amended: SI 2013/472 Sch.2 para.133, SI 2013/610 Sch.1 para.6, Sch.2 para.4, SI 2013/755 Sch.4 para.288, SI 2013/2318 Sch.1 para.80, SI 2013/2329 Sch.1 para.38

Sch.1 Part 2, amended: SI 2013/2952 Sch.2 para.7, SI 2013/3235 Reg.7

Sch.1 Part 3, amended: SI 2013/1478 Sch.5 para.19, SI 2013/1575 Sch.1 para.21, SI 2013/3134 Sch.4 para.8

Sch.1 Part 6, amended: SI 2013/1575 Sch.1 para.22, SI 2013/3134 Sch.4 para.8

Sch.1 Part 8, amended: SI 2013/1478 Sch.5 para.20

Sch.1 Part 13, amended: SI 2013/1478 Sch.5 para.21

3562. Education (Information About Individual Pupils) (Wales) Regulations 2007

Reg.3, amended: SI 2013/3137 Reg.2

Sch.2 Part 3 para.1, substituted: SI 2013/3137 Reg.2

2008

4. Information as to Provision of Education (England) Regulations 2008

Reg.3, amended: SI 2013/2149 Reg.3

Reg.5, amended: SI 2013/2149 Reg.4

Sch.1 para.6B, added: SI 2013/1255 Reg.2

Sch.1 para.6C, added: SI 2013/1255 Reg.2

Sch.1 para.6ZA, added: SI 2013/1255 Reg.2

Sch.1 para.6ZB, added: SI 2013/1255 Reg.2

Sch.2 para.1, substituted: SI 2013/2149 Reg.5

Sch.2 para.2, substituted: SI 2013/2149 Reg.5

Sch.2 para.3, substituted: SI 2013/2149 Reg.5

Sch.2 para.4, substituted: SI 2013/2149 Reg.5

Sch.2 para.5, substituted: SI 2013/2149 Reg.5

Sch.2 para.6, substituted: SI 2013/2149 Reg.5

Sch.2 para.7, substituted: SI 2013/2149 Reg.5

Sch.2 para.8, substituted: SI 2013/2149 Reg.5

Sch.2 para.9, substituted: SI 2013/2149 Reg.5

Sch.2 para.10, substituted: SI 2013/2149 Reg.5

Sch.2 para.11, substituted: SI 2013/2149 Reg.5

Sch.2 para.12, substituted: SI 2013/2149 Reg.5

Sch.2 para.13, substituted: SI 2013/2149 Reg.5

51. Hill Farm Allowance Regulations 2008

revoked: SI 2013/109 Reg.9

169. Childcare Act 2006 (Local Authority Assessment) (Wales) Regulations 2008

revoked: SI 2013/2274 Reg.12

224. National Health Service (Functions of Strategic Health Authorities and Primary Care Trusts and Administration Arrangements) (England) (Amendment) Regulations 2008

revoked: SI 2013/235 Sch.2 para.196

237. Wireless Telegraphy (Automotive Short Range Radar) (Exemption) (No.2) (Amendment) Regulations 2008

revoked: SI 2013/1437 Reg.3

238. Local Government Pension Scheme (Transitional Provisions) Regulations 2008

Reg.15, amended: SI 2013/755 Sch.4 para.289

239. Local Government Pension Scheme (Administration) Regulations 2008

Reg.7, amended: SI 2013/472 Art.4

Reg.8A, applied: SI 2013/2356 Sch.2 Part 4

Reg.8C, added: SI 2013/755 Sch.4 para.290

Sch.1, amended: SI 2013/472 Art.4

Sch.2 Part 2 para.7, amended: SI 2013/2318 Sch.1 para.98

254. Rent Repayment Orders (Supplementary Provisions) (Wales) Regulations 2008

Reg.1, amended: SI 2013/1788 Reg.8

Reg.2, amended: SI 2013/1788 Reg.8

295. Controlled Drugs (Drug Precursors)(Intra-Community Trade) Regulations 2008

Reg.5, amended: SI 2013/602 Sch.2 para.90

Reg.5, revoked (in part): SI 2013/602 Sch.2 para.90

305. Representation of the People (Scotland) (Amendment) Regulations 2008

Reg.9, revoked: SI 2013/3206 Sch.2

Reg.10, amended: SI 2013/3206 Sch.2

Reg.12, revoked (in part): SI 2013/3206 Sch.2

Sch.1, amended: SI 2013/3206 Sch.2

314. Site Waste Management Plans Regulations 2008

revoked: SI 2013/2854 Reg.2

346. Regulated Covered Bonds Regulations 2008

applied: SI 2013/161 Art.6

referred to: SI 2013/161 Art.6

Reg.1, amended: SI 2013/472 Sch.2 para.134, SI 2013/3115 Sch.2 para.69

Reg.2, amended: SI 2013/3115 Sch.2 para.69

Reg.5, amended: SI 2013/472 Art.4

Reg.9, amended: SI 2013/472 Art.4

Reg.30, applied: SI 2013/418 Art.2

Reg.31, applied: SI 2013/418 Art.2

Reg.33, applied: SI 2013/418 Art.2

Reg.34, applied: SI 2013/418 Art.2

Reg.36A, added: SI 2013/429 Reg.2

Reg.37, substituted: SI 2013/472 Sch.2 para.134

Reg.38, amended: SI 2013/472 Sch.2 para.134

Reg.42, amended: SI 2013/472 Sch.2 para.134

Reg.43, amended: SI 2013/472 Sch.2 para.134
Reg.45, amended: SI 2013/472 Sch.2 para.134
Sch.1 Part 1 para.3, amended: SI 2013/472 Sch.2 para.134
Sch.1 Part 1 para.4A, added: SI 2013/472 Sch.2 para.134
Sch.1 Part 1 para.5, substituted: SI 2013/472 Sch.2 para.134

373. Companies (Revision of Defective Accounts and Reports) Regulations 2008

Reg.2, amended: SI 2013/1971 Reg.3, SI 2013/2224 Reg.4
Reg.3, amended: SI 2013/1971 Reg.4, SI 2013/2224 Reg.5
Reg.4A, added: SI 2013/1971 Reg.5, SI 2013/2224 Reg.6
Reg.6A, added: SI 2013/1971 Reg.6, SI 2013/2224 Reg.7
Reg.7, amended: SI 2013/1971 Reg.7, SI 2013/2224 Reg.8
Reg.9, amended: SI 2013/1971 Reg.8, SI 2013/2224 Reg.9
Reg.11, amended: SI 2013/1971 Reg.9, SI 2013/2224 Reg.10
Reg.12, amended: SI 2013/1971 Reg.10, SI 2013/2224 Reg.11
Reg.17, revoked: SI 2013/1971 Reg.11, SI 2013/2224 Reg.12
Reg.19, amended: SI 2013/1971 Reg.12, SI 2013/2224 Reg.13
Reg.19, revoked (in part): SI 2013/1971 Reg.12, SI 2013/2224 Reg.13

374. Companies (Summary Financial Statement) Regulations 2008

revoked: SI 2013/1973 Reg.3
Reg.5, applied: SI 2013/1973 Reg.3

386. Non-Domestic Rating (Unoccupied Property) (England) Regulations 2008

Reg.4, see *Sunderland City Council v Stirling Investment Properties LLP* [2013] EWHC 1413 (Admin), [2013] R.A. 411 (QBD (Admin)), Wilkie, J.

409. Small Companies and Groups (Accounts and Directors Report) Regulations 2008

applied: SI 2013/3008 Reg.3
disapplied: SI 2013/3008 Reg.3
Reg.3, amended: SI 2013/3008 Reg.9
Reg.4, amended: SI 2013/3008 Reg.9
Reg.5, amended: SI 2013/3008 Reg.9
Reg.5A, added: SI 2013/3008 Reg.9
Reg.6, amended: SI 2013/3008 Reg.9
Sch.1 Part 1, added: SI 2013/3008 Reg.10
Sch.1 Part 1, substituted: SI 2013/3008 Reg.10
Sch.1 Part 1 para.1, amended: SI 2013/3008 Reg.10
Sch.1 Part 1 para.2, amended: SI 2013/3008 Reg.10
Sch.1 Part 1 para.2A, added: SI 2013/3008 Reg.10
Sch.1 Part 1 para.6, amended: SI 2013/3008 Reg.10
Sch.1 Part 2 para.19, amended: SI 2013/3008 Reg.11
Sch.1 Part 2 para.21, amended: SI 2013/3008 Reg.11
Sch.1 Part 2 para.26, amended: SI 2013/3008 Reg.11
Sch.1 Part 2 para.28, amended: SI 2013/3008 Reg.11
Sch.2 Part 1 para.8, amended: SI 2013/2005 Reg.5
Sch.5 para.4, revoked: SI 2013/1970 Reg.8
Sch.5 para.6, revoked: SI 2013/1970 Reg.8
Sch.6 Part 1 para.1, amended: SI 2013/3008 Reg.12
Sch.6 Part 1 para.17, amended: SI 2013/3008 Reg.12
Sch.6 Part 2 para.34, amended: SI 2013/2005 Reg.5
Sch.8 para.8, amended: SI 2013/3008 Reg.13
Sch.8 para.11, amended: SI 2013/3008 Reg.13

410. Large and Medium-sized Companies and Groups (Accounts and Reports) Regulations 2008

applied: SI 2013/1981 Reg.4
Reg.10, amended: SI 2013/1970 Reg.7
Reg.11, amended: SI 2013/1981 Reg.2
Reg.11, revoked (in part): SI 2013/1981 Reg.2
Sch.3 Part 1 para.10, amended: SI 2013/472 Art.5, Sch.2 para.135
Sch.3 Part 2 para.56, amended: SI 2013/472 Art.5, Sch.2 para.135
Sch.3 Part 4 para.91, amended: SI 2013/472 Art.5, Sch.2 para.135
Sch.4 Part 1 para.7, amended: SI 2013/2005 Reg.6
Sch.7 Part 1 para.1A, added: SI 2013/1970 Reg.7
Sch.7 Part 1 para.2, revoked: SI 2013/1970 Reg.7
Sch.7 Part 1 para.5, revoked: SI 2013/1970 Reg.7
Sch.7 Part 2 para.8, amended: SI 2013/1970 Reg.7
Sch.7 Part 5 para.12, revoked: SI 2013/1970 Reg.7
Sch.7 Part 7 para.15, added: SI 2013/1970 Reg.7
Sch.7 Part 7 para.16, added: SI 2013/1970 Reg.7
Sch.7 Part 7 para.17, added: SI 2013/1970 Reg.7
Sch.7 Part 7 para.18, added: SI 2013/1970 Reg.7
Sch.7 Part 7 para.19, added: SI 2013/1970 Reg.7
Sch.7 Part 7 para.20, added: SI 2013/1970 Reg.7
Sch.8 Part 1 para.1, substituted: SI 2013/1981 Sch.1
Sch.8 Part 1 para.2, substituted: SI 2013/1981 Sch.1

Sch.8 Part 2 para.2, substituted: SI 2013/1981 Sch.1
Sch.8 Part 2 para.3, substituted: SI 2013/1981 Sch.1
Sch.8 Part 2 para.4, substituted: SI 2013/1981 Sch.1
Sch.8 Part 2 para.5, substituted: SI 2013/1981 Sch.1
Sch.8 Part 2 para.6, substituted: SI 2013/1981 Sch.1
Sch.8 Part 3 para.4, substituted: SI 2013/1981 Sch.1
Sch.8 Part 3 para.5, substituted: SI 2013/1981 Sch.1
Sch.8 Part 3 para.6, substituted: SI 2013/1981 Sch.1
Sch.8 Part 3 para.7, substituted: SI 2013/1981 Sch.1
Sch.8 Part 3 para.8, substituted: SI 2013/1981 Sch.1
Sch.8 Part 3 para.9, substituted: SI 2013/1981 Sch.1
Sch.8 Part 3 para.10, substituted: SI 2013/1981 Sch.1
Sch.8 Part 3 para.11, substituted: SI 2013/1981 Sch.1
Sch.8 Part 3 para.12, substituted: SI 2013/1981 Sch.1
Sch.8 Part 3 para.13, substituted: SI 2013/1981 Sch.1
Sch.8 Part 3 para.14, substituted: SI 2013/1981 Sch.1
Sch.8 Part 3 para.15, substituted: SI 2013/1981 Sch.1
Sch.8 Part 3 para.16, substituted: SI 2013/1981 Sch.1
Sch.8 Part 3 para.17, substituted: SI 2013/1981 Sch.1
Sch.8 Part 3 para.18, substituted: SI 2013/1981 Sch.1
Sch.8 Part 3 para.19, substituted: SI 2013/1981 Sch.1
Sch.8 Part 3 para.20, substituted: SI 2013/1981 Sch.1
Sch.8 Part 3 para.21, substituted: SI 2013/1981 Sch.1
Sch.8 Part 3 para.22, substituted: SI 2013/1981 Sch.1
Sch.8 Part 3 para.23, substituted: SI 2013/1981 Sch.1
Sch.8 Part 4 para.17, substituted: SI 2013/1981 Sch.1
Sch.8 Part 4 para.18, substituted: SI 2013/1981 Sch.1
Sch.8 Part 4 para.19, substituted: SI 2013/1981 Sch.1
Sch.8 Part 4 para.20, substituted: SI 2013/1981 Sch.1
Sch.8 Part 4 para.21, substituted: SI 2013/1981 Sch.1
Sch.8 Part 4 para.22, substituted: SI 2013/1981 Sch.1
Sch.8 Part 4 para.24, substituted: SI 2013/1981 Sch.1
Sch.8 Part 4 para.25, substituted: SI 2013/1981 Sch.1
Sch.8 Part 4 para.26, substituted: SI 2013/1981 Sch.1
Sch.8 Part 4 para.27, substituted: SI 2013/1981 Sch.1
Sch.8 Part 4 para.28, substituted: SI 2013/1981 Sch.1
Sch.8 Part 4 para.29, substituted: SI 2013/1981 Sch.1
Sch.8 Part 4 para.30, substituted: SI 2013/1981 Sch.1
Sch.8 Part 4 para.31, substituted: SI 2013/1981 Sch.1
Sch.8 Part 4 para.32, substituted: SI 2013/1981 Sch.1
Sch.8 Part 4 para.33, substituted: SI 2013/1981 Sch.1
Sch.8 Part 4 para.34, substituted: SI 2013/1981 Sch.1
Sch.8 Part 4 para.35, substituted: SI 2013/1981 Sch.1
Sch.8 Part 4 para.36, substituted: SI 2013/1981 Sch.1
Sch.8 Part 4 para.37, substituted: SI 2013/1981 Sch.1
Sch.8 Part 4 para.38, substituted: SI 2013/1981 Sch.1
Sch.8 Part 4 para.39, substituted: SI 2013/1981 Sch.1
Sch.8 Part 4 para.40, substituted: SI 2013/1981 Sch.1
Sch.8 Part 5 para.41, substituted: SI 2013/1981 Sch.1
Sch.8 Part 6, applied: SI 2013/1981 Reg.4
Sch.8 Part 6 para.42, substituted: SI 2013/1981 Sch.1
Sch.8 Part 6 para.43, substituted: SI 2013/1981 Sch.1
Sch.8 Part 7 para.44, substituted: SI 2013/1981 Sch.1
Sch.8 Part 7 para.45, substituted: SI 2013/1981 Sch.1

Sch.8 Part 7 para.46, substituted: SI 2013/1981 Sch.1
Sch.8 Part 7 para.47, substituted: SI 2013/1981 Sch.1
Sch.8 Part 7 para.48, substituted: SI 2013/1981 Sch.1
Sch.8 Part 7 para.49, substituted: SI 2013/1981 Sch.1

432. Northern Rock plc Transfer Order 2008
Art.5, amended: SI 2013/472 Sch.2 para.136
Art.14, amended: SI 2013/472 Sch.2 para.136
Art.15, amended: SI 2013/472 Sch.2 para.136
Art.16, amended: SI 2013/472 Sch.2 para.136

499. Statutory Auditors and Third Country Auditors (Amendment) Regulations 2008
revoked: SI 2013/1672 Sch.1

519. Health and Social Care Information Centre (Transfer of Staff, Property and Liabilities) Order 2008
revoked: SI 2013/235 Sch.2 para.197

524. Control of Salmonella in Poultry (Wales) Order 2008
Art.2, amended: SI 2013/1241 Reg.4
Art.3, amended: SI 2013/1241 Reg.4
Sch.1 para.8, amended: SI 2013/1241 Reg.4
Sch.1 para.12, amended: SI 2013/1241 Reg.4

553. National Health Service (Optical Charges and Payments) Amendment Regulations 2008
revoked: SI 2013/461 Sch.4

565. Insurance Accounts Directive (Miscellaneous Insurance Undertakings) Regulations 2008
Reg.2, amended: SI 2013/472 Art.4, Sch.2 para.137
Reg.8, amended: SI 2013/472 Sch.2 para.137
Reg.9, amended: SI 2013/472 Sch.2 para.137
Reg.14, amended: SI 2013/472 Sch.2 para.137
Sch.1 para.3, amended: SI 2013/472 Sch.2 para.137

567. Bank Accounts Directive (Miscellaneous Banks) Regulations 2008
Reg.2, amended: SI 2013/472 Sch.2 para.138
Reg.3, amended: SI 2013/472 Art.4
Reg.10, amended: SI 2013/472 Sch.2 para.138
Sch.1 para.10, amended: SI 2013/472 Sch.2 para.138

569. Partnerships (Accounts) Regulations 2008
Reg.2, amended: SI 2013/2005 Reg.4
Reg.2, revoked (in part): SI 2013/2005 Reg.4
Reg.3, substituted: SI 2013/2005 Reg.4
Reg.4, amended: SI 2013/2005 Reg.4
Reg.4, referred to: SI 2013/3008 Reg.3
Reg.6, amended: SI 2013/2005 Reg.4
Reg.9, referred to: SI 2013/3008 Reg.3
Sch.1 Part 1, referred to: SI 2013/3008 Reg.3

570. Supply of Information (Register of Deaths) (England and Wales) Order 2008
Art.1, amended: SI 2013/472 Art.4
Sch.1 para.11, substituted: SI 2013/1881 Sch.1 para.35

580. Town and Country Planning (Mayor of London) Order 2008
Sch.1 Part 1, applied: SI 2013/2140 Art.26
Sch.1 Part 1, referred to: SI 2013/2140 Art.26
Sch.1 Part 2, referred to: SI 2013/2140 Art.26

608. Civil Enforcement of Parking Contraventions (Representations and Appeals) (Wales) Regulations 2008
revoked: SI 2013/359 Reg.13

609. Civil Enforcement of Parking Contraventions (Penalty Charge Notices, Enforcement and Adjudication) (Wales) Regulations 2008
revoked: SI 2013/362 Reg.27

613. Civil Enforcement of Parking Contraventions (Guidelines on Levels of Charges) (Wales) Order 2008
revoked: SI 2013/1969 Art.3

615. Civil Enforcement of Parking Contraventions (Representations and Appeals) Removed Vehicles (Wales) Regulations 2008
revoked: SI 2013/361 Reg.7

629. Charities (Accounts and Reports) Regulations 2008
Sch.1 Part 3 para.11, amended: SI 2013/472 Art.4

645. Consumer Credit (Exempt Agreements) (Amendment) Order 2008
revoked (in part): SI 2013/1881 Art.21

653. National Health Service Pension Scheme Regulations 2008
Part 3, applied: SI 2013/469 Sch.1
Reg.1, revoked (in part): SI 2013/413 Reg.23
Reg.1, amended: SI 2013/413 Reg.25
Reg.1, revoked (in part): SI 2013/413 Reg.25
Reg.1, amended: SI 2013/413 Reg.31
Reg.1, revoked (in part): SI 2013/413 Reg.41
Reg.1, amended: SI 2013/413 Reg.51
Reg.1, revoked (in part): SI 2013/413 Reg.51
Reg.1, revoked (in part): SI 2013/413 Reg.68
Reg.2, revoked: SI 2013/413 Reg.24
Reg.2, amended: SI 2013/413 Reg.32, SI 2013/1414 Reg.6
Reg.2, amended: SI 2013/413 Reg.62, SI 2013/1414 Reg.9
Reg.2A, added: SI 2013/413 Reg.48
Reg.2A, added: SI 2013/413 Reg.74
Reg.3, amended: SI 2013/1414 Reg.7
Reg.3, amended: SI 2013/413 Reg.42
Reg.3, amended: SI 2013/413 Reg.69
Reg.3, amended: SI 2013/413 Reg.76
Reg.4, amended: SI 2013/413 Reg.29

Reg.4, revoked (in part): SI 2013/413 Reg.29
Reg.4, amended: SI 2013/413 Reg.33, SI 2013/1414 Reg.8
Reg.4, amended: SI 2013/413 Reg.43
Reg.4, amended: SI 2013/413 Reg.60
Reg.4, revoked (in part): SI 2013/413 Reg.60
Reg.4, amended: SI 2013/413 Reg.70
Reg.5, amended: SI 2013/413 Reg.30
Reg.5, amended: SI 2013/413 Reg.34
Reg.5, amended: SI 2013/413 Reg.44
Reg.5, amended: SI 2013/413 Reg.61
Reg.5, revoked (in part): SI 2013/413 Reg.61
Reg.5, amended: SI 2013/413 Reg.63
Reg.5, applied: SI 2013/469 Sch.1
Reg.5, amended: SI 2013/413 Reg.66
Reg.5, amended: SI 2013/413 Reg.71
Reg.6, amended: SI 2013/413 Reg.26
Reg.6, amended: SI 2013/413 Reg.35
Reg.6, amended: SI 2013/413 Reg.45
Reg.6, amended: SI 2013/413 Reg.52
Reg.6, amended: SI 2013/413 Reg.72
Reg.7, amended: SI 2013/413 Reg.53
Reg.7, amended: SI 2013/413 Reg.73
Reg.8, amended: SI 2013/413 Reg.27
Reg.8, amended: SI 2013/413 Reg.46
Reg.8, amended: SI 2013/413 Reg.54
Reg.9, amended: SI 2013/413 Reg.47
Reg.9, amended: SI 2013/413 Reg.55
Reg.10, amended: SI 2013/413 Reg.40
Reg.10, amended: SI 2013/413 Reg.56
Reg.11, amended: SI 2013/413 Reg.38
Reg.11, amended: SI 2013/413 Reg.39
Reg.11, amended: SI 2013/413 Reg.64
Reg.11, amended: SI 2013/413 Reg.67
Reg.12, amended: SI 2013/413 Reg.49
Reg.13, amended: SI 2013/413 Reg.36
Reg.13, amended: SI 2013/413 Reg.57
Reg.13, amended: SI 2013/413 Reg.65
Reg.14, amended: SI 2013/413 Reg.50
Reg.14, amended: SI 2013/413 Reg.75
Reg.14, applied: SI 2013/469 Sch.1
Reg.14, referred to: SI 2013/469 Sch.1
Reg.15, amended: SI 2013/413 Reg.28
Reg.15, amended: SI 2013/413 Reg.37
Reg.15, amended: SI 2013/413 Reg.58
Reg.16, amended: SI 2013/413 Reg.59

700. Supply of Information (Register of Deaths) (Northern Ireland) Order 2008

Art.1, amended: SI 2013/472 Art.4
Sch.1 para.12, substituted: SI 2013/1881 Sch.1 para.36

711. Pensions Increase (Review) Order 2008

applied: SI 2013/604 Sch.1

718. Northern Rock plc Compensation Scheme Order 2008

Sch.1, amended: SI 2013/472 Sch.2 para.139

729. Companies (Authorised Minimum) Regulations 2008

Reg.4, amended: SI 2013/472 Art.4

794. Employment and Support Allowance Regulations 2008

applied: SI 2013/386 Reg.31, SI 2013/983 Art.16, SI 2013/3029 Sch.1 para.19, Sch.6 para.21, Sch.11 para.3, SI 2013/3035 Sch.1
Reg.1, substituted: SI 2013/630 Reg.37
Reg.2, amended: SI 2013/235 Sch.2 para.116, SI 2013/276 Reg.15, SI 2013/388 Sch.1 para.40, SI 2013/443 Reg.9, SI 2013/591 Sch.1 para.37, SI 2013/630 Reg.37, SI 2013/2536 Reg.13
Reg.2, applied: SI 2013/3029 Sch.6 para.31
Reg.2, revoked (in part): SI 2013/2536 Reg.13
Reg.2, varied: SI 2013/983 Art.11
Reg.4, amended: SI 2013/2536 Reg.13
Reg.5, amended: SI 2013/2536 Reg.13
Reg.5, varied: SI 2013/983 Art.11
Reg.7, applied: SI 2013/3029 Sch.7 para.18, SI 2013/3035 Sch.1
Reg.7, referred to: SI 2013/3029 Sch.3 para.5
Reg.7, varied: SI 2013/983 Art.11
Reg.9, amended: SI 2013/2536 Reg.13
Reg.10, varied: SI 2013/983 Art.11
Reg.18, amended: SI 2013/388 Sch.1 para.40, SI 2013/591 Sch.1 para.37
Reg.19, amended: SI 2013/2536 Reg.13
Reg.19, varied: SI 2013/983 Art.11
Reg.20, amended: SI 2013/2536 Reg.13
Reg.20, substituted: SI 2013/2536 Reg.13
Reg.21, amended: SI 2013/2536 Reg.13
Reg.22, amended: SI 2013/2536 Reg.13
Reg.23, amended: SI 2013/2536 Reg.13
Reg.26, amended: SI 2013/2536 Reg.13
Reg.29, amended: SI 2013/2536 Reg.13
Reg.30, amended: SI 2013/2536 Reg.13
Reg.30, applied: SI 2013/3029 Sch.7 para.25, Sch.7 para.28, SI 2013/3035 Sch.1
Reg.30, revoked (in part): SI 2013/2536 Reg.13
Reg.30, varied: SI 2013/983 Art.11
Reg.32, amended: SI 2013/2536 Reg.13
Reg.32A, amended: SI 2013/2536 Reg.13
Reg.34, amended: SI 2013/2536 Reg.13
Reg.34, revoked (in part): SI 2013/2536 Reg.13
Reg.34, varied: SI 2013/983 Art.11
Reg.36, amended: SI 2013/2536 Reg.13
Reg.37, amended: SI 2013/2536 Reg.13
Reg.38, amended: SI 2013/2536 Reg.13
Reg.40, amended: SI 2013/2536 Reg.13

Reg.40, revoked (in part): SI 2013/252 Sch.1 Part 2
Reg.43, amended: SI 2013/602 Sch.2 para.91, SI 2013/2536 Reg.13
Reg.45, amended: SI 2013/2536 Reg.13
Reg.45, applied: SI 2013/3035 Sch.1
Reg.63, amended: SI 2013/630 Reg.37
Reg.63, applied: SI 2013/386 Reg.30, Reg.31, SI 2013/983 Art.14, Art.15, Art.16, SI 2013/3029 Sch.6 para.17, SI 2013/3035 Sch.1
Reg.70, amended: SI 2013/1474 Reg.7, SI 2013/2536 Reg.13
Reg.70, revoked (in part): SI 2013/2536 Reg.13
Reg.76, amended: SI 2013/2536 Reg.13
Reg.93, amended: SI 2013/630 Reg.37
Reg.95, amended: SI 2013/2536 Reg.13
Reg.104, amended: SI 2013/2536 Reg.13
Reg.106, amended: SI 2013/2536 Reg.13
Reg.107, amended: SI 2013/276 Reg.15, SI 2013/2536 Reg.13
Reg.108, amended: SI 2013/2536 Reg.13
Reg.115, amended: SI 2013/276 Reg.15
Reg.115, applied: SI 2013/3029 Sch.1 para.29, Sch.6 para.31, SI 2013/3035 Sch.1
Reg.116, amended: SI 2013/458 Sch.2 para.8
Reg.119, amended: SI 2013/443 Reg.9
Reg.145, applied: SI 2013/3029 Sch.7 para.27, SI 2013/3035 Sch.1
Reg.147A, amended: SI 2013/2380 Reg.7
Reg.147A, revoked (in part): SI 2013/2380 Reg.7
Reg.147A, varied: SI 2013/983 Art.11
Reg.158, amended: SI 2013/388 Sch.1 para.40, SI 2013/591 Sch.1 para.37
Reg.167, amended: SI 2013/630 Reg.37
Reg.168, substituted: SI 2013/2536 Reg.13
Sch.2 Part 1, amended: SI 2013/2536 Reg.13
Sch.2 Part 2, amended: SI 2013/2536 Reg.13
Sch.3, amended: SI 2013/2536 Reg.13
Sch.4 Part 1 para.1, applied: 2013 c.16 Sch.1 para.1
Sch.4 Part 1 para.1, substituted: SI 2013/574 Sch.14
Sch.4 Part 2 para.4, amended: SI 2013/388 Sch.1 para.40, SI 2013/591 Sch.1 para.37
Sch.4 Part 2 para.6, amended: SI 2013/388 Sch.1 para.40, SI 2013/591 Sch.1 para.37
Sch.4 Part 2 para.7, amended: SI 2013/388 Sch.1 para.40, SI 2013/591 Sch.1 para.37
Sch.4 Part 3 para.11, substituted: SI 2013/574 Sch.15
Sch.4 Part 4 para.12, amended: SI 2013/574 Art.25
Sch.4 Part 4 para.13, amended: SI 2013/574 Art.25
Sch.5 Part 2, amended: SI 2013/2536 Reg.13
Sch.6 para.1, amended: SI 2013/630 Reg.37
Sch.6 para.5, amended: SI 2013/443 Reg.9
Sch.6 para.7, referred to: SI 2013/574 Sch.16
Sch.6 para.8, applied: SI 2013/386 Reg.29
Sch.6 para.8, referred to: SI 2013/574 Sch.16
Sch.6 para.9, applied: SI 2013/386 Reg.29
Sch.6 para.9, referred to: SI 2013/574 Sch.16
Sch.6 para.11, referred to: SI 2013/574 Sch.16
Sch.6 para.12, referred to: SI 2013/574 Sch.16
Sch.6 para.13, referred to: SI 2013/574 Sch.16
Sch.6 para.15, amended: SI 2013/388 Sch.1 para.40, SI 2013/591 Sch.1 para.37
Sch.6 para.15, applied: SI 2013/386 Reg.29
Sch.6 para.16, applied: SI 2013/386 Reg.29
Sch.6 para.17, applied: SI 2013/386 Reg.29
Sch.6 para.18, applied: SI 2013/386 Reg.29
Sch.6 para.19, amended: SI 2013/388 Sch.1 para.40, SI 2013/574 Art.25, SI 2013/591 Sch.1 para.37, SI 2013/630 Reg.37, SI 2013/2536 Reg.13
Sch.8 para.1A, amended: SI 2013/276 Reg.15
Sch.8 para.2A, amended: SI 2013/2536 Reg.13
Sch.8 para.8, amended: SI 2013/388 Sch.1 para.40
Sch.8 para.9, amended: SI 2013/630 Reg.37
Sch.8 para.11, amended: SI 2013/388 Sch.1 para.40
Sch.8 para.29, amended: SI 2013/235 Sch.2 para.116
Sch.8 para.29, revoked (in part): SI 2013/235 Sch.2 para.116
Sch.8 para.35A, added: SI 2013/443 Reg.9
Sch.8 para.44, amended: SI 2013/443 Reg.9
Sch.8 para.65, revoked: SI 2013/458 Sch.1
Sch.8 para.66, added: SI 2013/591 Sch.1 para.37
Sch.9 para.1A, amended: SI 2013/276 Reg.15
Sch.9 para.11, amended: SI 2013/630 Reg.37
Sch.9 para.11, applied: SI 2013/3029 Sch.5 para.22, SI 2013/3035 Sch.1
Sch.9 para.23A, added: SI 2013/443 Reg.9
Sch.9 para.35, amended: SI 2013/443 Reg.9

831. Consumer Credit Act 2006 (Commencement No 4 and Transitional Provisions) Order 2008

Art.4, see *Santander UK Plc v Harrison* [2013] EWHC 199 (QB), [2013] Bus. L.R. 501 (QBD), Males, J.

915. Local Involvement Networks (Duty of Services-Providers to Allow Entry) Regulations 2008

revoked: SI 2013/351 Reg.15

946. Proceeds of Crime Act 2002 (Investigations in England, Wales and Northern Ireland Code of Practice) Order 2008

applied: SI 2013/2605 Art.35

948. Companies Act 2006 (Consequential Amendments etc) Order 2008

Sch.1 Part 1 para.1, revoked (in part): SI 2013/687 Sch.2

Sch.1 Part 2 para.45, revoked: SI 2013/687 Sch.2

1035. Scotland Act 1998 (Agency Arrangements) (Specification) Order 2008

revoked: SI 2013/3157 Art.3

1040. Bovine Semen (Wales) Regulations 2008

applied: SI 2013/1241 Reg.7
Reg.2, amended: SI 2013/398 Reg.3
Reg.4, applied: SI 2013/1241 Sch.3
Reg.7, applied: SI 2013/1241 Sch.3
Reg.10, amended: SI 2013/398 Reg.4
Reg.10, applied: SI 2013/1241 Sch.3
Reg.16, amended: SI 2013/398 Reg.5
Reg.21, substituted: SI 2013/398 Reg.6
Reg.24, amended: SI 2013/398 Reg.7
Reg.28, amended: SI 2013/398 Reg.8
Reg.40, applied: SI 2013/1241 Sch.3
Reg.41, substituted: SI 2013/1241 Reg.7
Reg.42, revoked: SI 2013/1241 Reg.7
Sch.3 Part 1 para.2, amended: SI 2013/398 Reg.9
Sch.5 Part 1 para.2, amended: SI 2013/398 Reg.10
Sch.7 para.1, amended: SI 2013/398 Reg.11
Sch.7 para.2, amended: SI 2013/398 Reg.11

1052. Magistrates Courts Fees Order 2008

Sch.1, substituted: SI 2013/1409 Sch.1
Sch.2 para.1, amended: SI 2013/388 Sch.1 para.41, SI 2013/534 Sch.1 para.20, SI 2013/591 Sch.1 para.38
Sch.2 para.1, substituted: SI 2013/2302 Sch.1
Sch.2 para.2, substituted: SI 2013/2302 Sch.1
Sch.2 para.3, substituted: SI 2013/2302 Sch.1
Sch.2 para.4, substituted: SI 2013/2302 Sch.1
Sch.2 para.5, substituted: SI 2013/2302 Sch.1
Sch.2 para.6, substituted: SI 2013/2302 Sch.1
Sch.2 para.7, substituted: SI 2013/2302 Sch.1
Sch.2 para.8, substituted: SI 2013/2302 Sch.1
Sch.2 para.9, substituted: SI 2013/2302 Sch.1
Sch.2 para.10, substituted: SI 2013/2302 Sch.1
Sch.2 para.11, substituted: SI 2013/2302 Sch.1
Sch.2 para.12, substituted: SI 2013/2302 Sch.1
Sch.2 para.13, substituted: SI 2013/2302 Sch.1
Sch.2 para.14, substituted: SI 2013/2302 Sch.1
Sch.2 para.15, substituted: SI 2013/2302 Sch.1
Sch.2 para.16, substituted: SI 2013/2302 Sch.1
Sch.2 para.17, substituted: SI 2013/2302 Sch.1
Sch.2 para.18, substituted: SI 2013/2302 Sch.1
Sch.2 para.19, substituted: SI 2013/2302 Sch.1
Sch.2 para.20, substituted: SI 2013/2302 Sch.1

1053. Civil Proceedings Fees Order 2008

Art.5, substituted: SI 2013/2302 Art.6
Sch.1, amended: SI 2013/534 Sch.1 para.7, SI 2013/734 Art.3, SI 2013/2302 Art.6
Sch.1, applied: SI 2013/1410 Art.4
Sch.1, substituted: SI 2013/1410 Sch.1
Sch.2 para.1, amended: SI 2013/388 Sch.1 para.42, SI 2013/534 Sch.1 para.18, SI 2013/591 Sch.1 para.39
Sch.2 para.1, substituted: SI 2013/2302 Sch.1
Sch.2 para.2, substituted: SI 2013/2302 Sch.1
Sch.2 para.3, substituted: SI 2013/2302 Sch.1
Sch.2 para.4, substituted: SI 2013/2302 Sch.1
Sch.2 para.5, substituted: SI 2013/2302 Sch.1
Sch.2 para.6, substituted: SI 2013/2302 Sch.1
Sch.2 para.7, substituted: SI 2013/2302 Sch.1
Sch.2 para.8, substituted: SI 2013/2302 Sch.1
Sch.2 para.9, substituted: SI 2013/2302 Sch.1
Sch.2 para.10, substituted: SI 2013/2302 Sch.1
Sch.2 para.11, substituted: SI 2013/2302 Sch.1
Sch.2 para.12, substituted: SI 2013/2302 Sch.1
Sch.2 para.13, substituted: SI 2013/2302 Sch.1
Sch.2 para.14, substituted: SI 2013/2302 Sch.1
Sch.2 para.15, substituted: SI 2013/2302 Sch.1
Sch.2 para.16, substituted: SI 2013/2302 Sch.1
Sch.2 para.17, substituted: SI 2013/2302 Sch.1
Sch.2 para.18, substituted: SI 2013/2302 Sch.1
Sch.2 para.19, substituted: SI 2013/2302 Sch.1
Sch.2 para.20, substituted: SI 2013/2302 Sch.1

1054. Family Proceedings Fees Order 2008

Sch.1, amended: SI 2013/534 Sch.1 para.8
Sch.1, substituted: SI 2013/1407 Sch.1
Sch.2 para.1, amended: SI 2013/388 Sch.1 para.43, SI 2013/534 Sch.1 para.19, SI 2013/591 Sch.1 para.40
Sch.2 para.1, substituted: SI 2013/2302 Sch.1
Sch.2 para.2, substituted: SI 2013/2302 Sch.1
Sch.2 para.3, substituted: SI 2013/2302 Sch.1
Sch.2 para.4, substituted: SI 2013/2302 Sch.1
Sch.2 para.5, substituted: SI 2013/2302 Sch.1
Sch.2 para.6, substituted: SI 2013/2302 Sch.1
Sch.2 para.7, substituted: SI 2013/2302 Sch.1
Sch.2 para.8, substituted: SI 2013/2302 Sch.1
Sch.2 para.9, substituted: SI 2013/2302 Sch.1
Sch.2 para.10, substituted: SI 2013/2302 Sch.1
Sch.2 para.11, substituted: SI 2013/2302 Sch.1
Sch.2 para.12, substituted: SI 2013/2302 Sch.1
Sch.2 para.13, substituted: SI 2013/2302 Sch.1
Sch.2 para.14, substituted: SI 2013/2302 Sch.1
Sch.2 para.15, substituted: SI 2013/2302 Sch.1
Sch.2 para.16, substituted: SI 2013/2302 Sch.1
Sch.2 para.17, substituted: SI 2013/2302 Sch.1
Sch.2 para.18, substituted: SI 2013/2302 Sch.1
Sch.2 para.19, substituted: SI 2013/2302 Sch.1
Sch.2 para.20, substituted: SI 2013/2302 Sch.1

1079. Specified Products from China (Restriction on First Placing on the Market) (England) Regulations 2008

applied: SI 2013/1683 Reg.3
Reg.2, amended: SI 2013/1683 Reg.2

Reg.3, amended: SI 2013/1683 Reg.2
Reg.8, substituted: SI 2013/1683 Reg.2

1080. Specified Products from China (Restriction on First Placing on the Market) (Wales) Regulations 2008

Reg.2, amended: SI 2013/1653 Reg.2
Reg.3, amended: SI 2013/1653 Reg.2
Reg.8, substituted: SI 2013/1653 Reg.2

1097. Bathing Water Regulations 2008

Reg.1, revoked: SI 2013/1675 Reg.19
Reg.2, amended: SI 2013/755 Sch.4 para.292
Reg.2, revoked: SI 2013/1675 Reg.19
Reg.3, amended: SI 2013/755 Sch.4 para.293
Reg.3, revoked: SI 2013/1675 Reg.19
Reg.4, revoked: SI 2013/1675 Reg.19
Reg.5, amended: SI 2013/755 Sch.4 para.294
Reg.5, revoked: SI 2013/1675 Reg.19
Reg.6, amended: SI 2013/755 Sch.4 para.295
Reg.6, revoked: SI 2013/1675 Reg.19
Reg.7, amended: SI 2013/755 Sch.4 para.295
Reg.7, revoked: SI 2013/1675 Reg.19
Reg.8, amended: SI 2013/755 Sch.4 para.295
Reg.8, revoked: SI 2013/1675 Reg.19
Reg.9, amended: SI 2013/755 Sch.4 para.295
Reg.9, revoked: SI 2013/1675 Reg.19
Reg.10, amended: SI 2013/755 Sch.4 para.295
Reg.10, revoked: SI 2013/1675 Reg.19
Reg.11, amended: SI 2013/755 Sch.4 para.295
Reg.11, revoked: SI 2013/1675 Reg.19
Reg.12, amended: SI 2013/755 Sch.4 para.295
Reg.12, revoked: SI 2013/1675 Reg.19
Reg.13, amended: SI 2013/755 Sch.4 para.295
Reg.13, revoked: SI 2013/1675 Reg.19
Reg.14, amended: SI 2013/755 Sch.4 para.295
Reg.14, revoked: SI 2013/1675 Reg.19
Reg.15, amended: SI 2013/755 Sch.4 para.295
Reg.15, revoked: SI 2013/1675 Reg.19
Reg.16, amended: SI 2013/755 Sch.4 para.296
Reg.16, revoked: SI 2013/1675 Reg.19
Reg.17, amended: SI 2013/755 Sch.4 para.297
Reg.17, revoked: SI 2013/1675 Reg.19
Reg.18, amended: SI 2013/755 Sch.4 para.297
Reg.18, revoked: SI 2013/1675 Reg.19
Reg.19, revoked: SI 2013/1675 Reg.19
Sch.1, revoked: SI 2013/1675 Reg.19
Sch.2 para.1, revoked: SI 2013/1675 Reg.19
Sch.2 para.2, amended: SI 2013/755 Sch.4 para.298
Sch.2 para.2, revoked: SI 2013/1675 Reg.19
Sch.3 Part 1 para.1, amended: SI 2013/755 Sch.4 para.298
Sch.3 Part 1 para.1, revoked: SI 2013/1675 Reg.19
Sch.3 Part 1 para.2, amended: SI 2013/755 Sch.4 para.298
Sch.3 Part 1 para.2, revoked: SI 2013/1675 Reg.19
Sch.3 Part 1 para.3, amended: SI 2013/755 Sch.4 para.298
Sch.3 Part 1 para.3, revoked: SI 2013/1675 Reg.19
Sch.3 Part 1 para.4, amended: SI 2013/755 Sch.4 para.298
Sch.3 Part 1 para.4, revoked: SI 2013/1675 Reg.19
Sch.3 Part 1 para.5, amended: SI 2013/755 Sch.4 para.298
Sch.3 Part 1 para.5, revoked: SI 2013/1675 Reg.19
Sch.3 Part 1 para.6, amended: SI 2013/755 Sch.4 para.298
Sch.3 Part 1 para.6, revoked: SI 2013/1675 Reg.19
Sch.3 Part 1 para.7, amended: SI 2013/755 Sch.4 para.298
Sch.3 Part 1 para.7, revoked: SI 2013/1675 Reg.19
Sch.3 Part 2 para.8, amended: SI 2013/755 Sch.4 para.298
Sch.3 Part 2 para.8, revoked: SI 2013/1675 Reg.19
Sch.3 Part 3 para.9, amended: SI 2013/755 Sch.4 para.298
Sch.3 Part 3 para.9, revoked: SI 2013/1675 Reg.19
Sch.3 Part 4 para.10, amended: SI 2013/755 Sch.4 para.298
Sch.3 Part 4 para.10, revoked: SI 2013/1675 Reg.19
Sch.4 para.1, amended: SI 2013/755 Sch.4 para.298
Sch.4 para.1, revoked: SI 2013/1675 Reg.19
Sch.4 para.2, amended: SI 2013/755 Sch.4 para.298
Sch.4 para.2, revoked: SI 2013/1675 Reg.19
Sch.4 para.3, amended: SI 2013/755 Sch.4 para.298
Sch.4 para.3, revoked: SI 2013/1675 Reg.19

1098. Export Control (Burma) Order 2008

revoked: SI 2013/1964 Sch.1

1184. Mental Health (Hospital, Guardianship and Treatment) (England) Regulations 2008

Reg.7, amended: SI 2013/235 Sch.2 para.117
Reg.9, amended: SI 2013/235 Sch.2 para.117
Reg.17, amended: SI 2013/235 Sch.2 para.117
Reg.31, amended: SI 2013/235 Sch.2 para.117

1185. General Ophthalmic Services Contracts Regulations 2008

applied: SI 2013/365 Reg.6
Reg.2, amended: SI 2013/365 Reg.4, Sch.1 para.1, Sch.1 para.2
Reg.3, amended: SI 2013/365 Sch.1 para.3
Reg.4, amended: SI 2013/365 Sch.1 para.4
Reg.5, amended: SI 2013/365 Sch.1 para.5
Reg.5, applied: SI 2013/365 Reg.8, Reg.9
Reg.6, amended: SI 2013/365 Sch.1 para.6
Reg.6, applied: SI 2013/365 Reg.9
Reg.7, amended: SI 2013/365 Sch.1 para.7

Reg.8, amended: SI 2013/365 Sch.1 para.8
Reg.12, amended: SI 2013/365 Sch.1 para.9
Reg.13, applied: SI 2013/461 Reg.9
Reg.13, revoked (in part): SI 2013/365 Reg.4
Reg.15, amended: SI 2013/365 Sch.1 para.10
Reg.15, referred to: SI 2013/365 Reg.10
Reg.16, amended: SI 2013/365 Sch.1 para.11
Reg.16, applied: SI 2013/365 Reg.11
Sch.1 Part 3 para.8, amended: SI 2013/365 Sch.1 para.12
Sch.1 Part 4, applied: SI 2013/365 Reg.13
Sch.1 Part 4A, referred to: SI 2013/365 Reg.16
Sch.1 Part 4 para.13, amended: SI 2013/365 Sch.1 para.12
Sch.1 Part 4 para.14, amended: SI 2013/365 Sch.1 para.12
Sch.1 Part 4 para.14, applied: SI 2013/365 Reg.12, Reg.14
Sch.1 Part 4 para.16, amended: SI 2013/365 Sch.1 para.12
Sch.1 Part 4 para.17, amended: SI 2013/365 Sch.1 para.12
Sch.1 Part 4 para.18, amended: SI 2013/365 Sch.1 para.12
Sch.1 Part 4 para.19, amended: SI 2013/365 Sch.1 para.12
Sch.1 Part 4 para.19, applied: SI 2013/365 Reg.14
Sch.1 Part 4 para.20, substituted: SI 2013/365 Sch.1 para.12
Sch.1 Part 5, referred to: SI 2013/365 Reg.16
Sch.1 Part 5 para.22, revoked: SI 2013/365 Reg.4
Sch.1 Part 5 para.23, revoked: SI 2013/365 Reg.4
Sch.1 Part 5 para.24, revoked: SI 2013/365 Reg.4
Sch.1 Part 5 para.25, revoked: SI 2013/365 Reg.4
Sch.1 Part 5 para.26, amended: SI 2013/365 Sch.1 para.12
Sch.1 Part 5 para.26, applied: SI 2013/365 Reg.17
Sch.1 Part 5 para.27, amended: SI 2013/365 Sch.1 para.12
Sch.1 Part 6, applied: SI 2013/365 Reg.18
Sch.1 Part 6 para.28, amended: SI 2013/365 Sch.1 para.12
Sch.1 Part 6 para.29, amended: SI 2013/365 Sch.1 para.12
Sch.1 Part 7, referred to: SI 2013/365 Reg.19
Sch.1 Part 7 para.33, amended: SI 2013/365 Sch.1 para.12
Sch.1 Part 7 para.34, amended: SI 2013/365 Sch.1 para.12
Sch.1 Part 7 para.35, amended: SI 2013/365 Sch.1 para.12
Sch.1 Part 7 para.36, amended: SI 2013/365 Sch.1 para.12
Sch.1 Part 7 para.37, amended: SI 2013/365 Sch.1 para.12
Sch.1 Part 7 para.38, amended: SI 2013/365 Sch.1 para.12
Sch.1 Part 7 para.39, amended: SI 2013/365 Sch.1 para.12
Sch.1 Part 7 para.40, amended: SI 2013/365 Sch.1 para.12
Sch.1 Part 7 para.41, amended: SI 2013/365 Sch.1 para.12
Sch.1 Part 7 para.42, amended: SI 2013/365 Sch.1 para.12
Sch.1 Part 7 para.43, amended: SI 2013/365 Sch.1 para.12
Sch.1 Part 7 para.44, amended: SI 2013/365 Sch.1 para.12
Sch.1 Part 7 para.45, amended: SI 2013/365 Sch.1 para.12
Sch.1 Part 7 para.46, amended: SI 2013/365 Sch.1 para.12
Sch.1 Part 7 para.47, amended: SI 2013/365 Sch.1 para.12
Sch.1 Part 7 para.48, amended: SI 2013/365 Sch.1 para.12
Sch.1 Part 7 para.49, amended: SI 2013/365 Sch.1 para.12
Sch.1 Part 7 para.50, amended: SI 2013/365 Sch.1 para.12
Sch.1 Part 8 para.52, amended: SI 2013/365 Sch.1 para.12
Sch.1 Part 8 para.52, applied: SI 2013/335 Reg.39
Sch.1 Part 8 para.53, amended: SI 2013/365 Sch.1 para.12
Sch.1 Part 8 para.56, added: SI 2013/365 Sch.1 para.12
Sch.2 para.3, applied: SI 2013/365 Reg.15
Sch.2 para.5, amended: SI 2013/365 Sch.1 para.13
Sch.2 para.5, applied: SI 2013/365 Reg.14
Sch.2 para.6, amended: SI 2013/365 Sch.1 para.13
Sch.2 para.6, applied: SI 2013/365 Reg.13
Sch.3 para.1, amended: SI 2013/365 Sch.1 para.14
Sch.3 para.3, substituted: SI 2013/365 Reg.4
Sch.3 para.4, amended: SI 2013/365 Sch.1 para.14
Sch.3 para.5, amended: SI 2013/365 Sch.1 para.14
Sch.3 para.8, amended: SI 2013/365 Sch.1 para.14
Sch.3 para.9, revoked: SI 2013/365 Sch.1 para.14
Sch.4, referred to: SI 2013/365 Reg.15
Sch.4 para.10, amended: SI 2013/365 Sch.1 para.15

1186. Primary Ophthalmic Services Regulations 2008

Reg.2, amended: SI 2013/365 Reg.23, Sch.2 para.1
Reg.3, amended: SI 2013/365 Reg.23, SI 2013/2555 Reg.2
Reg.4, amended: SI 2013/365 Sch.2 para.2

Reg.5, amended: SI 2013/365 Sch.2 para.3
Reg.5, applied: SI 2013/365 Reg.26
Reg.8, amended: SI 2013/365 Sch.2 para.4

1187. National Health Service (Performers Lists) Amendment and Transitional Provisions Regulations 2008

Sch.1, applied: SI 2013/335 Reg.9

1214. Civil Enforcement of Parking Contraventions (General Provisions) (Wales) (No.2) Regulations 2008

revoked: SI 2013/362 Reg.27

1215. Civil Enforcement of Parking Contraventions (Approved Devices) (Wales) (No.2) Order 2008

revoked: SI 2013/360 Art.3

1270. Specified Animal Pathogens (Wales) Order 2008

applied: SI 2013/1662 Reg.4

1276. Business Protection from Misleading Marketing Regulations 2008

see *R. (on the application of Ahmed) v York Magistrates' Court* [2012] EWHC 3636 (Admin), (2013) 177 J.P. 233 (QBD (Admin)), Hickinbottom, J.
Reg.2, amended: SI 2013/783 Art.12, SI 2013/2701 Reg.3
Reg.13, amended: SI 2013/783 Art.12, SI 2013/2701 Reg.4
Reg.13, substituted: SI 2013/783 Art.12
Reg.15, amended: SI 2013/2701 Reg.5
Reg.17, amended: SI 2013/2701 Reg.6
Reg.20, amended: SI 2013/783 Art.12
Reg.22, amended: SI 2013/2701 Reg.7
Reg.23, amended: SI 2013/2701 Reg.8
Reg.23, see *R. (on the application of Ahmed) v York Magistrates' Court* [2012] EWHC 3636 (Admin), (2013) 177 J.P. 233 (QBD (Admin)), Hickinbottom, J.
Reg.24, amended: SI 2013/2701 Reg.9
Reg.24, see *R. (on the application of Ahmed) v York Magistrates' Court* [2012] EWHC 3636 (Admin), (2013) 177 J.P. 233 (QBD (Admin)), Hickinbottom, J.

1277. Consumer Protection from Unfair Trading Regulations 2008

see *R. v X Ltd* [2013] EWCA Crim 818, [2013] 3 All E.R. 995 (CA (Crim Div)), Leveson, L.J.
Reg.2, amended: SI 2013/783 Art.13
Reg.3, see *R. v X Ltd* [2013] EWCA Crim 818, [2013] 3 All E.R. 995 (CA (Crim Div)), Leveson, L.J.
Reg.5, referred to: SI 2013/3134 Sch.2
Reg.5, see *R. v X Ltd* [2013] EWCA Crim 818, [2013] 3 All E.R. 995 (CA (Crim Div)), Leveson, L.J.
Reg.8, see *R. v X Ltd* [2013] EWCA Crim 818, [2013] 3 All E.R. 995 (CA (Crim Div)), Leveson, L.J.
Reg.9, see *Motor Depot Ltd v Kingston upon Hull City Council* [2012] EWHC 3257 (Admin), (2013) 177 J.P. 41 (DC), Elias, L.J.; see *Price v Cheshire East BC* [2012] EWHC 2927 (Admin), [2013] 1 W.L.R. 1232 (QBD (Admin)), Collins, J.; see *R. v X Ltd* [2013] EWCA Crim 818, [2013] 3 All E.R. 995 (CA (Crim Div)), Leveson, L.J.
Reg.11, see *Price v Cheshire East BC* [2012] EWHC 2927 (Admin), [2013] 1 W.L.R. 1232 (QBD (Admin)), Collins, J.
Reg.12, see *R. v X Ltd* [2013] EWCA Crim 818, [2013] 3 All E.R. 995 (CA (Crim Div)), Leveson, L.J.
Reg.15, see *Motor Depot Ltd v Kingston upon Hull City Council* [2012] EWHC 3257 (Admin), (2013) 177 J.P. 41 (DC), Elias, L.J.
Reg.19, amended: SI 2013/783 Art.13
Reg.19, substituted: SI 2013/783 Art.13
Reg.27A, added: SI 2013/3134 Reg.39
Sch.1 para.12, see *R. v X Ltd* [2013] EWCA Crim 818, [2013] 3 All E.R. 995 (CA (Crim Div)), Leveson, L.J.
Sch.1 para.29, revoked: SI 2013/3134 Sch.4 para.9

1284. Cosmetic Products (Safety) Regulations 2008

applied: SI 2013/1478 Reg.3
revoked: SI 2013/1478 Sch.1

1287. Spreadable Fats (Marketing Standards) and the Milk and Milk Products (Protection of Designations) (England) Regulations 2008

Reg.2, amended: SI 2013/2854 Reg.3, SI 2013/3235 Reg.11
Reg.3, amended: SI 2013/2854 Reg.3
Reg.3, revoked (in part): SI 2013/2854 Reg.3
Reg.4, revoked: SI 2013/2854 Reg.3
Reg.6, amended: SI 2013/3235 Reg.11
Reg.6, revoked (in part): SI 2013/2854 Reg.3

1317. Drinking Milk (England) Regulations 2008

Reg.2, amended: SI 2013/3235 Reg.4
Reg.2, revoked (in part): SI 2013/3235 Reg.4
Reg.3, amended: SI 2013/3235 Reg.4
Reg.4, revoked: SI 2013/3235 Reg.4
Reg.5, amended: SI 2013/3235 Reg.4
Reg.6, amended: SI 2013/3235 Reg.4

1319. Electoral Administration Act 2006 (Regulation of Loans etc Northern Ireland) Order 2008

Art.5, amended: SI 2013/320 Art.3
Art.5, applied: SI 2013/320
Art.5, enabled: SI 2013/320

1341. Spreadable Fats (Marketing Standards) and the Milk and Milk Products (Protection of Designations) (Wales) Regulations 2008

Reg.2, amended: SI 2013/3270 Reg.9
Reg.6, amended: SI 2013/3270 Reg.9

1344. Cash Ratio Deposits (Value Bands and Ratios) Order 2008
revoked: SI 2013/1189 Art.2

1472. Dee Estuary Cockle Fishery Order 2008
Art.2, amended: SI 2013/755 Sch.4 para.300
Art.5, amended: SI 2013/755 Sch.4 para.301

1586. Criminal Justice and Immigration Act 2008 (Commencement No 2 and Transitional and Saving Provisions) Order 2008
see *R. (on the application of Modhej) v Secretary of State for Justice* [2012] EWCA Civ 957, [2013] 1 W.L.R. 801 (CA (Civ Div)), Lord Judge, L.C.J.

1595. Mesothelioma Lump Sum Payments (Claims and Reconsiderations) Regulations 2008
Reg.4, amended: SI 2013/2380 Reg.5
Reg.4A, added: SI 2013/2380 Reg.5
Reg.4B, added: SI 2013/2380 Reg.5
Reg.5, revoked (in part): SI 2013/2380 Reg.5
Reg.6, revoked: SI 2013/2380 Reg.5

1657. National Health Service (Optical Charges and Payments) Amendment (No.2) Regulations 2008
revoked: SI 2013/461 Sch.4

1659. Companies Act 1985 (Annual Return) and Companies (Principal Business Activities) (Amendment) Regulations 2008
Reg.5, revoked: SI 2013/1947 Sch.2 Part 2

1660. Cross-border Railway Services (Working Time) Regulations 2008
Reg.18, amended: SI 2013/1956 Sch.1 para.14

1730. Network Access Appeal Rules 2008
revoked: SI 2013/1036 Sch.2 para.70

1731. Adjudicator to Her Majesty's Land Registry (Practice and Procedure) (Amendment) Rules 2008
revoked: SI 2013/1036 Sch.2 para.71
r.19, revoked: SI 2013/2042 Sch.1 para.69

1737. Political Parties, Elections and Referendums Act 2000 (Northern Ireland Political Parties) Order 2008
Art.11, amended: SI 2013/472 Sch.2 para.140

1738. Company Names Adjudicator Rules 2008
r.8, revoked (in part): SI 2013/2042 Sch.1 para.70

1741. Representation of the People (Northern Ireland) Regulations 2008
Reg.42, amended: SI 2013/1846 Reg.2
Reg.46A, added: SI 2013/1846 Reg.3
Reg.46B, added: SI 2013/1846 Reg.3
Reg.57, amended: SI 2013/3021 Art.32
Reg.112, amended: SI 2013/1881 Sch.1 para.37
Reg.112A, added: SI 2013/1846 Reg.4
Reg.114, amended: SI 2013/1846 Reg.4
Sch.3, amended: SI 2013/1846 Reg.5, Sch.1

1748. Land Registration (Network Access) Rules 2008
Part 5 r.8, amended: SI 2013/1036 Sch.2 para.73
Part 5 r.10, amended: SI 2013/1036 Sch.2 para.74

1752. Education (National Curriculum) (Attainment Targets and Programme of Study in Art and Design in respect of the Third Key Stage) (England) Order 2008
revoked: SI 2013/2232 Sch.1

1753. Education (National Curriculum) (Attainment Targets and Programmes of Study in Citizenship in respect of the Third and Fourth Key Stages) (England) Order 2008
revoked: SI 2013/2232 Sch.1

1754. Education (National Curriculum) (Attainment Targets and Programme of Study in Design and Technology in respect of the Third Key Stage) (England) Order 2008
revoked: SI 2013/2232 Sch.1

1755. Education (National Curriculum) (Attainment Targets and Programmes of Study in English in respect of the Third and Fourth Key Stages) (England) Order 2008
applied: SI 2013/2232 Art.6
revoked: SI 2013/2232 Sch.1

1756. Education (National Curriculum) (Attainment Targets and Programme of Study in Geography in respect of the Third Key Stage) (England) Order 2008
revoked: SI 2013/2232 Sch.1

1757. Education (National Curriculum) (Attainment Targets and Programme of Study in History in respect of the Third Key Stage) (England) Order 2008
revoked: SI 2013/2232 Sch.1

1758. Education (National Curriculum) (Attainment Targets and Programmes of Study in Information and Communication Technology in respect of the Third and Fourth Key Stages) (England) Order 2008
revoked: SI 2013/2232 Sch.1

1759. Education (National Curriculum) (Attainment Targets and Programmes of Study in Mathematics in respect of the Third and Fourth Key Stages) (England) Order 2008
applied: SI 2013/2232 Art.6
revoked: SI 2013/2232 Sch.1

1760. Education (National Curriculum) (Attainment Targets and Programme of Study in Modern Foreign Languages in respect of the Third Key Stage) (England) Order 2008
revoked: SI 2013/2232 Sch.1

1761. Education (National Curriculum) (Attainment Targets and Programme of Study in Music in respect of the Third Key Stage) (England) Order 2008
revoked: SI 2013/2232 Sch.1

1762. Education (National Curriculum) (Attainment Targets and Programmes of Study in Physical Education in respect of the Third and Fourth Key Stages) (England) Order 2008
revoked: SI 2013/2232 Sch.1

1763. Education (National Curriculum) (Attainment Targets and Programme of Study in Science in respect of the Third Key Stage) (England) Order 2008
revoked: SI 2013/2232 Sch.1
1766. Education (National Curriculum) (Modern Foreign Languages) (England) Order 2008
revoked: SI 2013/2230 Art.4
1797. Trade Marks Rules 2008
r.2, amended: SI 2013/2235 r.2
r.12, amended: SI 2013/444 r.4
r.17, amended: SI 2013/444 r.4, SI 2013/2235 r.2
r.17A, added: SI 2013/2235 r.2
r.18, amended: SI 2013/444 r.3
r.18, applied: SI 2013/444 r.8
r.19, amended: SI 2013/2235 r.2
r.20, amended: SI 2013/2235 r.2
r.25, amended: SI 2013/444 r.4
r.30, amended: SI 2013/444 r.4
r.32, amended: SI 2013/444 r.4
r.43, amended: SI 2013/444 r.4
r.62, amended: SI 2013/2235 r.2
r.63, amended: SI 2013/2235 r.2
r.71, amended: SI 2013/444 r.4, SI 2013/2235 r.2
r.77, amended: SI 2013/444 r.4
1816. Cancellation of Contracts made in a Consumer's Home or Place of Work etc Regulations 2008
disapplied: SI 2013/3134 Reg.2
see *Robertson v Swift* [2012] EWCA Civ 1794, [2013] Bus. L.R. 479 (CA (Civ Div)), Mummery, L.J.
Reg.2, amended: SI 2013/1881 Sch.1 para.38
Reg.2, see *Robertson v Swift* [2012] EWCA Civ 1794, [2013] Bus. L.R. 479 (CA (Civ Div)), Mummery, L.J.
Reg.5, see *Robertson v Swift* [2012] EWCA Civ 1794, [2013] Bus. L.R. 479 (CA (Civ Div)), Mummery, L.J.
Reg.6, amended: SI 2013/1881 Sch.1 para.38
Reg.6, see *Robertson v Swift* [2012] EWCA Civ 1794, [2013] Bus. L.R. 479 (CA (Civ Div)), Mummery, L.J.
Reg.7, see *Robertson v Swift* [2012] EWCA Civ 1794, [2013] Bus. L.R. 479 (CA (Civ Div)), Mummery, L.J.
Reg.10, see *Robertson v Swift* [2012] EWCA Civ 1794, [2013] Bus. L.R. 479 (CA (Civ Div)), Mummery, L.J.
Sch.3, see *Robertson v Swift* [2012] EWCA Civ 1794, [2013] Bus. L.R. 479 (CA (Civ Div)), Mummery, L.J.
1858. Mental Capacity (Deprivation of Liberty Standard Authorisations, Assessments and Ordinary Residence) Regulations 2008
Reg.17, amended: SI 2013/235 Sch.2 para.118
Reg.17, substituted: SI 2013/235 Sch.2 para.118
Reg.18, substituted: SI 2013/235 Sch.2 para.118
Reg.19, substituted: SI 2013/235 Sch.2 para.118
1860. Companies (Welsh Language Forms) (Amendment) Regulations 2008
revoked: SI 2013/1947 Sch.2 Part 1
1861. Companies (Forms) (Amendment) Regulations 2008
revoked: SI 2013/1947 Sch.2 Part 1
1863. Serious Crime Act 2007 (Appeals under Section 24) Order 2008
Part 3, applied: SI 2013/1554 r.76_1, r.76_4
Art.13, amended: SI 2013/534 Sch.1 para.6
Art.14, applied: SI 2013/1554 r.76_1
Art.15, applied: SI 2013/1554 r.76_1
Art.16, applied: SI 2013/1554 r.76_1
Art.17, amended: SI 2013/534 Sch.1 para.6
Art.17, applied: SI 2013/1554 r.76_1
Art.18, applied: SI 2013/1554 r.76_1
Art.31, amended: SI 2013/534 Sch.1 para.6
Art.31, applied: SI 2013/1554 r.76_1
1890. Welsh Language Schemes (Public Bodies) Order 2008
Sch.1, amended: SI 2013/2318 Sch.1 para.99, SI 2013/2329 Sch.1 para.39
1907. Whole of Government Accounts (Designation of Bodies) (No.2) Order 2008
Sch.1, amended: SI 2013/687 Sch.2
1908. Serious Organised Crime and Police Act 2005 (Disclosure of Information by SOCA) Order 2008
Art.2, amended: SI 2013/472 Sch.2 para.141
1909. Proceeds of Crime Act 2002 (Disclosure of Information) Order 2008
Art.3, amended: SI 2013/472 Sch.2 para.142
1911. Limited Liability Partnerships (Accounts and Audit) (Application of Companies Act 2006) Regulations 2008
referred to: SI 2013/3008 Reg.3
Reg.5, amended: SI 2013/2005 Reg.3
Reg.5, substituted: SI 2013/2005 Reg.3
Reg.24, amended: SI 2013/472 Sch.2 para.143
Reg.26, amended: SI 2013/2005 Reg.3
Reg.26, substituted: SI 2013/2005 Reg.3
Reg.32, amended: SI 2013/472 Sch.2 para.143
Reg.47, amended: SI 2013/472 Sch.2 para.143
1912. Small Limited Liability Partnerships (Accounts) Regulations 2008
referred to: SI 2013/3008 Reg.3
1914. European Parliamentary Elections (Returning Officers) Order 2008
revoked: SI 2013/2064 Art.2
1950. Insurance Accounts Directive (Lloyd's Syndicate and Aggregate Accounts) Regulations 2008
referred to: SI 2013/472 Sch.2 para.145

Reg.2, amended: SI 2013/472 Sch.2 para.144

1958. Trade Marks (Fees) Rules 2008
Sch.1, amended: SI 2013/2236 r.2

1963. Mesothelioma Lump Sum Payments (Conditions and Amounts) Regulations 2008
Sch.1, amended: SI 2013/670 Reg.2

1976. Private Dentistry (Wales) Regulations 2008
Reg.2, amended: SI 2013/235 Sch.2 para.119
Reg.5, amended: SI 2013/235 Sch.2 para.119

1977. Crown Office Fees Order 2008
revoked: SI 2013/986 Art.3

1978. Proceeds of Crime Act 2002 (Investigative Powers of Prosecutors in England, Wales and Northern Ireland Code of Practice) Order 2008
applied: SI 2013/2605 Art.35

2072. Milk and Milk Products (Pupils in Educational Establishments) (England) Regulations 2008
Reg.2, amended: SI 2013/3235 Reg.9
Reg.3, amended: SI 2013/3235 Reg.9

2098. Judicial Discipline (Prescribed Procedures) (Amendment) Regulations 2008
revoked: SI 2013/1674 Reg.25

2102. Dartmouth-Kingswear Floating Bridge (Vehicle Classifications & Revision of Charges) Order 2008
revoked: SI 2013/2916 Art.4

2108. Export and Import of Dangerous Chemicals Regulations 2008
revoked: SI 2013/1506 Reg.34

2141. School Milk (Wales) Regulations 2008
Reg.2, amended: SI 2013/3270 Reg.7

2173. Cosmetic Products (Safety) (Amendment) Regulations 2008
revoked: SI 2013/1478 Sch.1

2206. Trade Marks (International Registration) Order 2008
Sch.2 para.6, amended: SI 2013/445 Art.3
Sch.3 para.2, amended: SI 2013/445 Art.4
Sch.3 para.3, amended: SI 2013/445 Art.4
Sch.4 para.1, amended: SI 2013/445 Art.5
Sch.6, amended: SI 2013/2237 Art.2

2252. Care Quality Commission (Membership) Regulations 2008
Reg.2, amended: SI 2013/2157 Reg.2

2349. Nitrate Pollution Prevention Regulations 2008
referred to: SI 2013/1001
Reg.4, substituted: SI 2013/1001 Reg.4
Reg.6, amended: SI 2013/1001 Reg.5
Reg.7, amended: SI 2013/1001 Reg.3, SI 2013/2619 Reg.3
Reg.7, revoked (in part): SI 2013/2619 Reg.3
Reg.13, substituted: SI 2013/1001 Reg.6
Reg.13A, amended: SI 2013/1001 Reg.7, SI 2013/2619 Reg.4
Reg.13B, revoked: SI 2013/1001 Reg.8
Reg.16, amended: SI 2013/1001 Reg.9, SI 2013/2619 Reg.5
Reg.16A, added: SI 2013/1001 Reg.10
Reg.17, substituted: SI 2013/1001 Reg.11
Reg.17A, added: SI 2013/1001 Reg.12
Reg.21, amended: SI 2013/1001 Reg.13
Reg.22, amended: SI 2013/1001 Reg.14, SI 2013/2619 Reg.6
Reg.23, amended: SI 2013/1001 Reg.15
Reg.25, amended: SI 2013/1001 Reg.16
Reg.27, amended: SI 2013/1001 Reg.17
Reg.28, amended: SI 2013/1001 Reg.18
Reg.29, amended: SI 2013/1001 Reg.17
Reg.31, amended: SI 2013/1001 Reg.19
Reg.32, amended: SI 2013/1001 Reg.20
Reg.47A, amended: SI 2013/1001 Reg.21
Sch.A1 Part 1 para.1, added: SI 2013/1001 Reg.22
Sch.A1 Part 1 para.2, added: SI 2013/1001 Reg.22
Sch.A1 Part 1 para.3, added: SI 2013/1001 Reg.22
Sch.A1 Part 1 para.4, added: SI 2013/1001 Reg.22
Sch.A1 Part 1 para.5, added: SI 2013/1001 Reg.22
Sch.A1 Part 1 para.6, added: SI 2013/1001 Reg.22
Sch.A1 Part 2 para.7, added: SI 2013/1001 Reg.22
Sch.A1 Part 2 para.8, added: SI 2013/1001 Reg.22
Sch.A1 Part 2 para.9, added: SI 2013/1001 Reg.22
Sch.A1 Part 2 para.10, added: SI 2013/1001 Reg.22
Sch.A1 Part 2 para.11, added: SI 2013/1001 Reg.22
Sch.A1 Part 2 para.12, added: SI 2013/1001 Reg.22
Sch.1, amended: SI 2013/1001 Reg.23, SI 2013/2619 Reg.7
Sch.2 Part 2 para.1, substituted: SI 2013/1001 Reg.24
Sch.4 para.1, amended: SI 2013/1001 Reg.25
Sch.4 para.3A, added: SI 2013/1001 Reg.25
Sch.4 para.3A, amended: SI 2013/2619 Reg.7
Sch.4 para.5, amended: SI 2013/1001 Reg.25
Sch.4 para.7, amended: SI 2013/1001 Reg.25
Sch.4 para.12, amended: SI 2013/1001 Reg.25
Sch.4 para.13, amended: SI 2013/1001 Reg.25
Sch.4 para.14, amended: SI 2013/1001 Reg.25
Sch.4 para.15, amended: SI 2013/1001 Reg.25
Sch.4 para.19, amended: SI 2013/1001 Reg.25

2431. Dudley and Walsall Mental Health Partnership National Health Service Trust (Establishment) Order 2008
Art.1, amended: SI 2013/593 Art.2

2439. Mental Health (Hospital, Guardianship, Community Treatment and Consent to Treatment) (Wales) Regulations 2008
Reg.23, amended: SI 2013/235 Sch.2 para.120

Reg.25, amended: SI 2013/235 Sch.2 para.120
Reg.26, amended: SI 2013/235 Sch.2 para.120

2449. Primary Ophthalmic Services and National Health Service (Optical Charges and Payments) Amendment Regulations 2008
Reg.3, revoked: SI 2013/461 Sch.4

2546. Bradford & Bingley plc Transfer of Securities and Property etc Order 2008
Art.2, amended: SI 2013/472 Sch.2 para.146
Art.15, amended: SI 2013/472 Sch.2 para.146
Art.37, amended: SI 2013/472 Sch.2 para.146
Art.38, amended: SI 2013/472 Sch.2 para.146

2551. Child Support Information Regulations 2008
Reg.9A, amended: SI 2013/1654 Reg.4
Reg.13, revoked (in part): SI 2013/2380 Reg.7

2566. Cosmetic Products (Safety) (Amendment No 2) Regulations 2008
revoked: SI 2013/1478 Sch.1

2567. Civil Enforcement of Parking Contraventions (The County Council of Durham) (Durham District) Designation Order 2008
revoked: SI 2013/992 Art.2

2639. Statutory Auditors and Third Country Auditors (Amendment) (No.2) Regulations 2008
revoked: SI 2013/1672 Sch.1

2644. Heritable Bank plc Transfer of Certain Rights and Liabilities Order 2008
Art.2, amended: SI 2013/472 Sch.2 para.147
Art.27, amended: SI 2013/472 Sch.2 para.147
Art.28, amended: SI 2013/472 Sch.2 para.147

2666. Transfer of Rights and Liabilities to ING Order 2008
Art.2, amended: SI 2013/472 Sch.2 para.148
Art.18, amended: SI 2013/472 Sch.2 para.148
Art.19, amended: SI 2013/472 Sch.2 para.148

2674. Kaupthing Singer & Friedlander Limited Transfer of Certain Rights and Liabilities Order 2008
Art.2, amended: SI 2013/472 Sch.2 para.149
Art.29, amended: SI 2013/472 Sch.2 para.149
Art.30, amended: SI 2013/472 Sch.2 para.149

2677. National Health Service (Directions by Strategic Health Authorities to Primary Care Trusts Regarding Arrangements for Involvement) (No.2) Regulations 2008
revoked: SI 2013/235 Sch.2 para.198

2682. Income Tax (Deposit-takers and Building Societies) (Interest Payments) Regulations 2008
Reg.6, amended: SI 2013/380 Sch.3 para.5

2683. Tribunals, Courts and Enforcement Act 2007 (Transitional and Consequential Provisions) Order 2008
Sch.1 para.52, revoked: SI 2013/2042 Sch.1 para.71
Sch.1 para.53, revoked: SI 2013/2042 Sch.1 para.71
Sch.1 para.54, revoked: SI 2013/2042 Sch.1 para.71
Sch.1 para.72, revoked (in part): SI 2013/2042 Sch.1 para.71
Sch.1 para.129, revoked: SI 2013/2042 Sch.1 para.71
Sch.1 para.137, revoked: SI 2013/2042 Sch.1 para.71
Sch.1 para.176, revoked: SI 2013/2042 Sch.1 para.71
Sch.1 para.238, revoked: SI 2013/2042 Sch.1 para.71
Sch.1 para.256, revoked (in part): SI 2013/2042 Sch.1 para.71
Sch.1 para.288, revoked: SI 2013/2042 Sch.1 para.71
Sch.1 para.289, revoked: SI 2013/2042 Sch.1 para.71
Sch.1 para.299, revoked: SI 2013/2042 Sch.1 para.71
Sch.1 para.301, revoked: SI 2013/2042 Sch.1 para.71
Sch.1 para.302, revoked: SI 2013/2042 Sch.1 para.71
Sch.1 para.303, revoked: SI 2013/2042 Sch.1 para.71
Sch.1 para.331, revoked: SI 2013/2042 Sch.1 para.71

2685. Tribunal Procedure (First-tier Tribunal) (Social Entitlement Chamber) Rules 2008
Part 1 r.1, amended: SI 2013/477 r.23
Part 2 r.5, amended: SI 2013/2067 r.23
Part 2 r.17, amended: SI 2013/477 r.24
Part 2 r.19, amended: SI 2013/2067 r.24
Part 3 r.22, amended: SI 2013/477 r.25, SI 2013/2067 r.25
Part 3 r.22, revoked (in part): SI 2013/477 r.25
Part 3 r.23, amended: SI 2013/477 r.26, SI 2013/2067 r.26
Part 3 r.24, amended: SI 2013/477 r.27
Part 3 r.33, amended: SI 2013/477 r.28
Part 3 r.34, amended: SI 2013/477 r.29
Part 4 r.38, amended: SI 2013/477 r.30
Sch.1, amended: SI 2013/477 r.31
Sch.1, substituted: SI 2013/477 r.31
Sch.2, added: SI 2013/477 r.32
Sch.2, amended: SI 2013/477 r.32

2686. Tribunal Procedure (First-tier Tribunal) (War Pensions and Armed Forces Compensation Chamber) Rules 2008
Part 2 r.17, amended: SI 2013/477 r.45
Part 3 r.31, amended: SI 2013/477 r.46

Part 3 r.32, amended: SI 2013/477 r.47
Part 4 r.36, amended: SI 2013/477 r.48, SI 2013/2067 r.28

2692. Qualifications for Appointment of Members to the First-tier Tribunal and Upper Tribunal Order 2008

Art.2, amended: SI 2013/1185 Art.3
Art.2, applied: SI 2013/379 Reg.37

2698. Tribunal Procedure (Upper Tribunal) Rules 2008

applied: SI 2013/442 Art.12
see *Azimi-Moayed (Decisions Affecting Children: Onward Appeals), Re* [2013] UKUT 197 (IAC), [2013] Imm. A.R. 696 (UT (IAC)), Blake, J. (President); see *R. (on the application of NB (Algeria)) v Secretary of State for the Home Department* [2012] EWCA Civ 1050, [2013] 1 W.L.R. 31 (CA (Civ Div)), Lord Neuberger (M.R.)
Part 1 r.1, amended: SI 2013/606 r.2, SI 2013/2067 r.4
Part 1 r.1, referred to: SI 2013/2067 r.29
Part 2 r.5, amended: SI 2013/606 r.2
Part 2 r.8, amended: SI 2013/2067 r.5
Part 2 r.10, amended: SI 2013/477 r.50, r.51, r.52, r.53, SI 2013/2067 r.6
Part 2 r.11, amended: SI 2013/2067 r.7
Part 2 r.13, amended: SI 2013/2067 r.8
Part 2 r.17, amended: SI 2013/477 r.54
Part 2 r.17A, amended: SI 2013/2067 r.9
Part 2 r.18, amended: SI 2013/477 r.55
Part 2 r.18, referred to: SI 2013/534 Reg.14
Part 4 r.28, amended: SI 2013/2067 r.10
Part 4 r.28A, amended: SI 2013/2067 r.11
Part 4 r.29, amended: SI 2013/2067 r.12
Part 4 r.30, amended: SI 2013/2067 r.13
Part 4 r.30, referred to: SI 2013/2067 r.29
Part 5 r.34, amended: SI 2013/2067 r.14
Part 6 r.39, amended: SI 2013/2067 r.15
Part 6 r.40, amended: SI 2013/477 r.56, SI 2013/2067 r.16
Part 7 r.43, amended: SI 2013/2067 r.17
Part 7 r.44, amended: SI 2013/2067 r.18
Part 7 r.45, amended: SI 2013/2067 r.19
Part 7 r.48, amended: SI 2013/2067 r.20
r.15, see *IY (Turkey) v Secretary of State for the Home Department* [2012] EWCA Civ 1560, [2013] Imm. A.R. 391 (CA (Civ Div)), Longmore, L.J.
r.17, see *EG (UT Rule 17: Withdrawal: Rule 24: Scope: Ethiopia), Re* [2013] UKUT 143 (IAC), [2013] Imm. A.R. 670 (UT (IAC)), Judge Eshun
r.24, see *EG (UT Rule 17: Withdrawal: Rule 24: Scope: Ethiopia), Re* [2013] UKUT 143 (IAC), [2013] Imm. A.R. 670 (UT (IAC)), Judge Eshun
r.25, see *Azimi-Moayed (Decisions Affecting Children: Onward Appeals), Re* [2013] UKUT 197 (IAC), [2013] Imm. A.R. 696 (UT (IAC)), Blake, J. (President)
r.44, see *R. (on the application of NB (Algeria)) v Secretary of State for the Home Department* [2012] EWCA Civ 1050, [2013] 1 W.L.R. 31 (CA (Civ Div)), Lord Neuberger (M.R.)
Sch.1 para.4, amended: SI 2013/477 r.57
Sch.1 para.7, amended: SI 2013/477 r.57
Sch.1 para.8, revoked: SI 2013/477 r.57
Sch.2 para.10, amended: SI 2013/2067 r.21
Sch.2 para.11, amended: SI 2013/2067 r.21
Sch.3 para.1, amended: SI 2013/606 r.2
Sch.3 para.2, amended: SI 2013/606 r.2
Sch.3 para.3, amended: SI 2013/606 r.2
Sch.3 para.4, amended: SI 2013/606 r.2
Sch.3 para.4A, added: SI 2013/606 r.2
Sch.3 para.5, amended: SI 2013/606 r.2
Sch.3 para.6, amended: SI 2013/606 r.2
Sch.3 para.7, amended: SI 2013/606 r.2
Sch.3 para.8, amended: SI 2013/606 r.2
Sch.3 para.9, amended: SI 2013/606 r.2

2699. Tribunal Procedure (First-tier Tribunal) (Health, Education and Social Care Chamber) Rules 2008

applied: SI 2013/349 Reg.35, Reg.79, Reg.82, Reg.84, SI 2013/898 Reg.32, Reg.34, Reg.35, Reg.38, Reg.39, Reg.40
Part 1 r.1, amended: SI 2013/477 r.11
Part 1 r.1, revoked (in part): SI 2013/477 r.11
Part 2 r.10, amended: SI 2013/477 r.12, r.13, r.14, r.15
Part 2 r.11, amended: SI 2013/477 r.16
Part 2 r.17, amended: SI 2013/477 r.17
Part 3 r.30, amended: SI 2013/477 r.18
Part 4 r.33, revoked (in part): SI 2013/477 r.19
Part 4 r.41, amended: SI 2013/477 r.20
Part 5 r.46, amended: SI 2013/477 r.21
r.10, see *Buckinghamshire CC v ST* [2013] UKUT 468 (AAC), [2013] E.L.R. 528 (UT (AAC)), Judge Edward Jacobs
r.15, see *MM v Nottinghamshire Healthcare NHS Trust* [2013] UKUT 107 (AAC), [2013] M.H.L.R. 161 (UT (AAC)), Judge Jacobs

2705. Mental Health Review Tribunal for Wales Rules 2008

Part 1 r.2, revoked (in part): SI 2013/235 Sch.2 para.121
Part 3 r.16, revoked (in part): SI 2013/235 Sch.2 para.121
r.3, see *RC v NHS Islington* [2013] UKUT 167 (AAC), [2013] M.H.L.R. 167 (UT (AAC)), Judge EAL Bano

r.21, see *RC v NHS Islington* [2013] UKUT 167 (AAC), [2013] M.H.L.R. 167 (UT (AAC)), Judge EAL Bano
Sch.1 Part A para.16, revoked: SI 2013/235 Sch.2 para.121

2716. Zoonoses and Animal By-Products (Fees) (Wales) Regulations 2008
revoked: SI 2013/1241 Reg.11

2770. Non-Domestic Rating (Small Business Relief) (Wales) Order 2008
Art.7, amended: SI 2013/371 Art.2
Art.11, amended: SI 2013/371 Art.2
Art.11A, amended: SI 2013/371 Art.2
Sch.1 para.6, amended: SI 2013/472 Sch.2 para.150

2833. Transfer of Tribunal Functions Order 2008
Sch.3 para.104, revoked (in part): SI 2013/2042 Sch.1 para.72

2836. Allocation and Transfer of Proceedings Order 2008
Sch.1, amended: SI 2013/421 Art.4

2841. Cremation (England and Wales) Regulations 2008
Reg.2, amended: SI 2013/1869 Sch.1 para.4
Reg.18, amended: SI 2013/1869 Sch.1 para.4
Sch.1, amended: SI 2013/1869 Sch.1 para.4

2852. REACH Enforcement Regulations 2008
applied: SI 2013/1893 Sch.2
Reg.2, amended: SI 2013/755 Sch.4 para.303, SI 2013/2919 Reg.3
Reg.6, amended: SI 2013/2919 Reg.4
Reg.6, revoked (in part): SI 2013/2919 Reg.4
Reg.8A, added: SI 2013/2919 Reg.5
Reg.21, amended: SI 2013/755 Sch.4 para.304
Reg.24, added: SI 2013/2919 Reg.6
Sch.1, amended: SI 2013/755 Sch.4 para.305, SI 2013/2919 Reg.7
Sch.2 para.1, amended: SI 2013/755 Sch.4 para.306
Sch.2 para.6, added: SI 2013/2919 Reg.8
Sch.3 Part 1 para.1, revoked (in part): SI 2013/2919 Reg.9
Sch.3 Part 3 para.5, amended: SSI 2013/119 Sch.2 para.24
Sch.3 Part 5 para.1, added: SI 2013/2919 Reg.9
Sch.5 Part 1 para.8, amended: SI 2013/2919 Reg.10
Sch.5A para.1, added: SI 2013/2919 Sch.1
Sch.5A para.2, added: SI 2013/2919 Sch.1
Sch.5A para.3, added: SI 2013/2919 Sch.1
Sch.5A para.4, added: SI 2013/2919 Sch.1
Sch.6 Part 1 para.1, amended: SI 2013/755 Sch.4 para.307
Sch.6 Part 1 para.2, amended: SI 2013/755 Sch.4 para.307
Sch.6 Part 1 para.3, amended: SI 2013/755 Sch.4 para.307
Sch.6 Part 1 para.4, amended: SI 2013/755 Sch.4 para.307
Sch.6 Part 1 para.5, amended: SI 2013/755 Sch.4 para.307
Sch.6 Part 1 para.6, amended: SI 2013/755 Sch.4 para.307
Sch.6 Part 1 para.7, amended: SI 2013/755 Sch.4 para.307
Sch.6 Part 1 para.8, amended: SI 2013/755 Sch.4 para.307
Sch.6 Part 1 para.9, amended: SI 2013/755 Sch.4 para.307
Sch.6 Part 1 para.10, amended: SI 2013/755 Sch.4 para.307
Sch.6 Part 1 para.11, amended: SI 2013/755 Sch.4 para.307
Sch.6 Part 1 para.12, amended: SI 2013/755 Sch.4 para.307
Sch.6 Part 1 para.13, amended: SI 2013/755 Sch.4 para.307
Sch.6 Part 1 para.14, amended: SI 2013/755 Sch.4 para.307
Sch.6 Part 1 para.15, amended: SI 2013/755 Sch.4 para.307
Sch.6 Part 1 para.16, amended: SI 2013/755 Sch.4 para.307
Sch.6 Part 1 para.17, amended: SI 2013/755 Sch.4 para.307
Sch.6 Part 1 para.18, amended: SI 2013/755 Sch.4 para.307
Sch.6 Part 1 para.19, amended: SI 2013/755 Sch.4 para.307
Sch.6 Part 1 para.20, amended: SI 2013/755 Sch.4 para.307
Sch.6 Part 1 para.21, amended: SI 2013/755 Sch.4 para.307
Sch.6 Part 1 para.22, amended: SI 2013/755 Sch.4 para.307
Sch.6 Part 1 para.23, amended: SI 2013/755 Sch.4 para.307
Sch.6 Part 1 para.24, amended: SI 2013/755 Sch.4 para.307
Sch.6 Part 1 para.25, amended: SI 2013/755 Sch.4 para.307
Sch.6 Part 1 para.26, amended: SI 2013/755 Sch.4 para.307
Sch.6 Part 1 para.27, amended: SI 2013/755 Sch.4 para.307
Sch.6 Part 1 para.28, amended: SI 2013/755 Sch.4 para.307

Sch.6 Part 1 para.29, amended: SI 2013/755 Sch.4 para.307
Sch.6 Part 1 para.30, amended: SI 2013/755 Sch.4 para.307
Sch.6 Part 1 para.31, amended: SI 2013/755 Sch.4 para.307
Sch.6 Part 1 para.32, amended: SI 2013/755 Sch.4 para.307
Sch.6 Part 1 para.33, amended: SI 2013/755 Sch.4 para.307
Sch.6 Part 1 para.34, amended: SI 2013/755 Sch.4 para.307
Sch.6 Part 1 para.35, amended: SI 2013/755 Sch.4 para.307
Sch.6 Part 2 para.1, amended: SI 2013/2919 Reg.12
Sch.6 Part 2 para.2, amended: SI 2013/2919 Reg.12
Sch.6 Part 2 para.3, amended: SI 2013/2919 Reg.12
Sch.6 Part 2 para.4, amended: SI 2013/2919 Reg.12
Sch.6 Part 2 para.5, amended: SI 2013/2919 Reg.12
Sch.6 Part 2 para.6, amended: SI 2013/2919 Reg.12
Sch.6 Part 2 para.7, amended: SI 2013/2919 Reg.12
Sch.6 Part 2 para.8, amended: SI 2013/2919 Reg.12
Sch.6 Part 2 para.9, amended: SI 2013/2919 Reg.12
Sch.6 Part 2 para.9A, added: SI 2013/2919 Reg.12
Sch.6 Part 2 para.9A, amended: SI 2013/2919 Reg.12
Sch.6 Part 2 para.10, amended: SI 2013/2919 Reg.12
Sch.6 Part 2 para.10, revoked: SI 2013/2919 Reg.12
Sch.6 Part 2 para.11, amended: SI 2013/2919 Reg.12
Sch.6 Part 2 para.12, amended: SI 2013/2919 Reg.12
Sch.6 Part 2 para.13, amended: SI 2013/2919 Reg.12
Sch.6 Part 2 para.14, amended: SI 2013/2919 Reg.12
Sch.6 Part 2 para.15, amended: SI 2013/2919 Reg.12
Sch.6 Part 2 para.16, amended: SI 2013/2919 Reg.12
Sch.6 Part 2 para.17, amended: SI 2013/2919 Reg.12
Sch.6 Part 2 para.18, amended: SI 2013/2919 Reg.12
Sch.6 Part 2 para.19, amended: SI 2013/2919 Reg.12
Sch.6 Part 2 para.20, added: SI 2013/2919 Reg.12
Sch.6 Part 2 para.20, amended: SI 2013/2919 Reg.12
Sch.7 Part 1 para.1, amended: SI 2013/755 Sch.4 para.308
Sch.7 Part 3 para.3, amended: SI 2013/2919 Reg.13
Sch.8 Part 1 para.1, amended: SI 2013/755 Sch.4 para.309
Sch.8 Part 1 para.2, amended: SI 2013/755 Sch.4 para.309
Sch.8 Part 1 para.3, amended: SI 2013/755 Sch.4 para.309
Sch.8 Part 1 para.4, amended: SI 2013/755 Sch.4 para.309
Sch.8 Part 1 para.5, amended: SI 2013/755 Sch.4 para.309
Sch.8 Part 1 para.6, amended: SI 2013/755 Sch.4 para.309
Sch.8 Part 1 para.7, added: SI 2013/2919 Reg.14
Sch.8 Part 1 para.7, amended: SI 2013/755 Sch.4 para.309
Sch.8 Part 2 para.2, amended: SI 2013/1948 Reg.7
Sch.8 Part 2 para.3, amended: SI 2013/1948 Reg.7

2860. Companies Act 2006 (Commencement No 8, Transitional Provisions and Savings) Order 2008
Sch.2 para.97, substituted: SI 2013/1947 Reg.2

2969. Rail Vehicle Accessibility (London Underground Victoria Line 09TS Vehicles) Exemption Order 2008
revoked: SI 2013/3031 Art.5

2975. Rail Vehicle Accessibility Exemption Orders (Parliamentary Procedures) Regulations 2008
Reg.5, applied: SI 2013/1931, SI 2013/3031

2995. Judicial Appointments Order 2008
Sch.1 Part 1, amended: SI 2013/1948 Reg.6
Sch.1 Part 2, amended: SI 2013/3022 Art.3

2996. Companies (Particulars of Company Charges) Regulations 2008
revoked: SI 2013/600 Reg.4

2998. Pre-release Access to Official Statistics Order 2008
Sch.1 Part 2 para.12, amended: SI 2013/472 Sch.2 para.151

3048. Immigration (Biometric Registration) Regulations 2008
Reg.3, applied: SI 2013/617 Sch.3 para.2
Reg.13, applied: SI 2013/617 Sch.3 para.2
Reg.17, applied: SI 2013/617 Sch.3 para.2
Reg.19, applied: SI 2013/617 Sch.3 para.2

3051. Social Security (Lone Parents and Miscellaneous Amendments) Regulations 2008
applied: SI 2013/379 Reg.7
3072. Education (Information About Individual Pupils) (England) (Amendment) Regulations 2008
revoked: SI 2013/2094 Sch.2
3080. National Child Measurement Programme Regulations 2008
revoked: SI 2013/218 Reg.18
3087. Transfrontier Shipment of Radioactive Waste and Spent Fuel Regulations 2008
Reg.2, amended: SI 2013/755 Sch.4 para.311
Reg.16, amended: SI 2013/755 Sch.4 para.312
3093. School Information (England) Regulations 2008
Sch.4 para.4, amended: SI 2013/2912 Reg.2
Sch.4 para.13, added: SI 2013/758 Reg.2
3100. Smoke Control Areas (Authorised Fuels) (Wales) Regulations 2008
Sch.1 para.11A, added: SI 2013/562 Reg.2
Sch.1 para.17A, added: SI 2013/562 Reg.2
Sch.1 para.18B, added: SI 2013/562 Reg.2
Sch.1 para.23A, added: SI 2013/562 Reg.2
Sch.1 para.29A, added: SI 2013/562 Reg.2
Sch.1 para.30B, added: SI 2013/562 Reg.2
Sch.1 para.43A, added: SI 2013/562 Reg.2
Sch.1 para.43B, added: SI 2013/562 Reg.2
3117. European Communities (Designation) (No.4) Order 2008
Art.3, revoked: SI 2013/1445 Art.5
3125. Air Navigation (Overseas Territories) (Amendment) Order 2008
revoked: SI 2013/2870 Sch.1
3143. Nitrate Pollution Prevention (Wales) Regulations 2008
applied: SI 2013/2506 Reg.4
revoked: SI 2013/2506 Reg.51
Reg.6, amended: SI 2013/755 Sch.5 para.47
Reg.7, amended: SI 2013/755 Sch.5 para.48
Reg.8, amended: SI 2013/755 Sch.5 para.48
Reg.13A, amended: SI 2013/755 Sch.5 para.48
Reg.13B, amended: SI 2013/755 Sch.5 para.48
Reg.13C, amended: SI 2013/755 Sch.5 para.48
Reg.13D, amended: SI 2013/755 Sch.5 para.48
Reg.49, amended: SI 2013/755 Sch.5 para.49
Sch.4 para.19, amended: SI 2013/755 Sch.5 para.50
3166. Mental Health Act 1983 (Independent Mental Health Advocates) (England) Regulations 2008
Reg.2, amended: SI 2013/261 Reg.16
Reg.3, substituted: SI 2013/261 Reg.16
Reg.4, revoked: SI 2013/261 Reg.16
Reg.5, revoked: SI 2013/261 Reg.16
3198. Civil Enforcement of Parking Contraventions (County of Cheshire) (City of Chester and Borough of Ellesmere Port & Neston) Designation Order 2008
revoked: SI 2013/2594 Art.2
3229. Companies (Model Articles) Regulations 2008
Sch.1, revoked: 2013 c.8 s.3
Sch.2, revoked: 2013 c.8 s.3
Sch.3, revoked: 2013 c.8 s.3
3231. Export Control Order 2008
Sch.2, substituted: SI 2013/428 Sch.1
Sch.2 Part 1, substituted: SI 2013/428 Sch.1
Sch.2 Part 2, substituted: SI 2013/428 Sch.1
Sch.4 Part 4, amended: SI 2013/3182 Art.14
3232. Employment Act 2008 (Commencement No 1, Transitional Provisions and Savings) Order 2008
see *Abercrombie v Aga Rangemaster Ltd* [2013] I.C.R. 213 (EAT), Silber, J.
3242. Fines Collection (Disclosure of Information) (Prescribed Benefits) Regulations 2008
Reg.1, amended: SI 2013/630 Reg.66
Reg.2, amended: SI 2013/630 Reg.66
3249. Bradford & Bingley plc Compensation Scheme Order 2008
Sch.1, amended: SI 2013/472 Sch.2 para.152
3258. Health Service Branded Medicines (Control of Prices and Supply of Information) (No.2) Regulations 2008
Reg.1, amended: SI 2013/2881 Reg.3
Reg.1A, added: SI 2013/2881 Reg.3
Reg.2, substituted: SI 2013/2881 Reg.3
Reg.3, amended: SI 2013/2881 Reg.3
Reg.4, substituted: SI 2013/2881 Reg.3
Reg.11, added: SI 2013/2881 Reg.3

2009

38. Health Protection (Vaccination) Regulations 2009
Reg.1, amended: SI 2013/235 Sch.2 para.122
41. Operation of Air Services in the Community Regulations 2009
Reg.1A, added: SI 2013/486 Reg.37
Reg.15, substituted: SI 2013/486 Reg.37
Reg.16, substituted: SI 2013/486 Reg.37
Sch.3 para.1, added: SI 2013/486 Reg.37
Sch.3 para.2, added: SI 2013/486 Reg.37
Sch.3 para.3, added: SI 2013/486 Reg.37
Sch.3 para.4, added: SI 2013/486 Reg.37
Sch.3 para.5, added: SI 2013/486 Reg.37
Sch.4 para.1, added: SI 2013/486 Reg.37
Sch.4 para.2, added: SI 2013/486 Reg.37
Sch.4 para.3, added: SI 2013/486 Reg.37
Sch.4 para.4, added: SI 2013/486 Reg.37
Sch.4 para.5, added: SI 2013/486 Reg.37

Sch.4 para.6, added: SI 2013/486 Reg.37
Sch.4 para.7, added: SI 2013/486 Reg.37
Sch.4 para.8, added: SI 2013/486 Reg.37
Sch.4 para.9, added: SI 2013/486 Reg.37
Sch.4 para.10, added: SI 2013/486 Reg.37
Sch.4 para.11, added: SI 2013/486 Reg.37
Sch.4 para.12, added: SI 2013/486 Reg.37
Sch.4 para.13, added: SI 2013/486 Reg.37
Sch.4 para.14, added: SI 2013/486 Reg.37
Sch.4 para.15, added: SI 2013/486 Reg.37
Sch.4 para.16, added: SI 2013/486 Reg.37
Sch.4 para.17, added: SI 2013/486 Reg.37

56. Transfer of Tribunal Functions and Revenue and Customs Appeals Order 2009

see *Noor v Revenue and Customs Commissioners* [2013] UKUT 71 (TCC), [2013] S.T.C. 998 (UT (Tax)), Warren, J (President)
Sch.1 para.188, amended: SI 2013/2042 Sch.1 para.74
Sch.1 para.221, see *R. (on the application of ToTel Ltd) v First-tier Tribunal (Tax Chamber)* [2012] EWCA Civ 1401, [2013] Q.B. 860 (CA (Civ Div)), Lord Neuberger (M.R.)
Sch.3 para.6, see *Hewlett Packard Ltd v Revenue and Customs Commissioners* [2013] UKFTT 39 (TC), [2013] S.F.T.D. 409 (FTT (Tax)), Judge Barbara Mosedale
Sch.3 para.7, see *Hewlett Packard Ltd v Revenue and Customs Commissioners* [2013] UKFTT 39 (TC), [2013] S.F.T.D. 409 (FTT (Tax)), Judge Barbara Mosedale; see *Usha Martin UK Ltd v Revenue and Customs Commissioners* [2013] UKFTT 793 (TC), [2013] S.F.T.D. 554 (FTT (Tax)), Judge Anne Scott

105. Joint Waste Authorities (Proposals) Regulations 2009

Sch.2 para.8, revoked: SI 2013/141 Reg.7

112. National Health Service (Functions of Strategic Health Authorities and Primary Care Trusts and Administration Arrangements) (England) (Amendment) Regulations 2009

revoked: SI 2013/235 Sch.2 para.199

153. Environmental Damage (Prevention and Remediation) Regulations 2009

Reg.10, amended: SI 2013/755 Sch.4 para.313

154. Adoption Agencies (Scotland) Regulations 2009

applied: SI 2013/3029 Reg.8, SI 2013/3035 Sch.1

209. Payment Services Regulations 2009

applied: SI 2013/161 Art.6, SSI 2013/50 Sch.2 para.1
referred to: SI 2013/161 Art.6
Part 8, disapplied: 2013 c.33 s.108
Reg.2, amended: SI 2013/472 Sch.2 para.155, SI 2013/3115 Sch.2 para.70
Reg.7, applied: SSI 2013/50 Sch.2 para.1
Reg.18, amended: SI 2013/3115 Sch.2 para.70
Reg.19, amended: SI 2013/3115 Sch.2 para.70
Reg.26, revoked: SI 2013/1881 Sch.1 para.40
Reg.42, disapplied: SI 2013/472 Sch.2 para.156
Reg.52, revoked (in part): SI 2013/1881 Sch.1 para.40
Reg.62, amended: SI 2013/3134 Sch.4 para.10
Reg.84, applied: SI 2013/418 Art.2
Reg.85, applied: SI 2013/418 Art.2
Reg.87, applied: SI 2013/418 Art.2
Reg.88, applied: SI 2013/418 Art.2
Reg.90, applied: SI 2013/418 Art.2
Reg.92, amended: SI 2013/429 Reg.2, SI 2013/472 Sch.2 para.155
Reg.94, amended: SI 2013/472 Sch.2 para.155
Reg.97, applied: 2013 c.33 s.108
Reg.121, amended: SI 2013/3115 Sch.2 para.70
Reg.125B, added: SI 2013/472 Sch.2 para.155
Sch.3 Part 2 para.5, amended: SI 2013/3115 Sch.2 para.70
Sch.5 Part 1 para.1, amended: SI 2013/472 Sch.2 para.155
Sch.5 Part 1 para.2, amended: SI 2013/472 Sch.2 para.155
Sch.5 Part 1 para.2, revoked (in part): SI 2013/472 Sch.2 para.155
Sch.5 Part 1 para.3, amended: SI 2013/472 Sch.2 para.155
Sch.5 Part 1 para.3, revoked (in part): SI 2013/472 Sch.2 para.155
Sch.5 Part 1 para.4, substituted: SI 2013/472 Sch.2 para.155
Sch.5 Part 1 para.5, amended: SI 2013/472 Sch.2 para.155
Sch.5 Part 1 para.6, amended: SI 2013/472 Sch.2 para.155
Sch.5 Part 1 para.7, amended: SI 2013/472 Sch.2 para.155

214. Companies (Disclosure of Address) Regulations 2009

Sch.1, amended: SI 2013/472 Sch.2 para.157
Sch.2 Part 2 para.7, amended: SI 2013/472 Sch.2 para.157

216. Ozone-Depleting Substances (Qualifications) Regulations 2009

Reg.7, amended: SI 2013/755 Sch.4 para.314

223. Gas Importation and Storage Zone (Designation of Area) Order 2009

revoked: SI 2013/3161 Art.1

224. Judicial Committee (Appellate Jurisdiction) Rules Order 2009

Sch.1, added: SI 2013/246 Sch.1 para.1, Sch.1 para.3, Sch.1 para.9, Sch.1 para.12, Sch.1 para.14

Sch.1, amended: SI 2013/246 Sch.1 para.1, Sch.1 para.2, Sch.1 para.4, Sch.1 para.6
Sch.1, revoked: SI 2013/246 Sch.1 para.13
Sch.1, substituted: SI 2013/246 Sch.1 para.5, Sch.1 para.7, Sch.1 para.8, Sch.1 para.10, Sch.1 para.11, Sch.1 para.15

227. Double Taxation Relief and International Tax Enforcement (Taxes on Income and Capital) (Netherlands) Order 2009
Sch.1, substituted: SI 2013/3143 Sch.1

261. Fluorinated Greenhouse Gases Regulations 2009
Reg.3, amended: SI 2013/755 Sch.4 para.316
Reg.56, amended: SI 2013/755 Sch.4 para.317

273. Tribunal Procedure (First-tier Tribunal) (Tax Chamber) Rules 2009
see *Foulser v Revenue and Customs Commissioners* [2013] UKUT 38 (TCC), [2013] S.T.C. 917 (UT (Tax)), Morgan, J.; see *Hewlett Packard Ltd v Revenue and Customs Commissioners* [2013] UKFTT 39 (TC), [2013] S.F.T.D. 409 (FTT (Tax)), Judge Barbara Mosedale
Part 1 r.1, amended: SI 2013/477 r.34
Part 2 r.10, amended: SI 2013/477 r.35, r.36, r.37, r.38
Part 2 r.17, amended: SI 2013/477 r.39
Part 3 r.21, amended: SI 2013/477 r.40
Part 3 r.23, amended: SI 2013/477 r.41
Part 3 r.35, amended: SI 2013/477 r.42
Part 4 r.39, amended: SI 2013/477 r.43
r.2, see *Eclipse Film Partners No.35 LLP v Revenue and Customs Commissioners* [2013] UKUT 141 (TCC), [2013] S.T.C. 1618 (UT (Tax)), Judge Roger Berner
r.5, see *Eclipse Film Partners No.35 LLP v Revenue and Customs Commissioners* [2013] UKUT 141 (TCC), [2013] S.T.C. 1618 (UT (Tax)), Judge Roger Berner; see *Foulser v Revenue and Customs Commissioners* [2013] UKUT 38 (TCC), [2013] S.T.C. 917 (UT (Tax)), Morgan, J.
r.7, see *Foulser v Revenue and Customs Commissioners* [2013] UKUT 38 (TCC), [2013] S.T.C. 917 (UT (Tax)), Morgan, J.
r.8, see *Foulser v Revenue and Customs Commissioners* [2013] UKUT 38 (TCC), [2013] S.T.C. 917 (UT (Tax)), Morgan, J.; see *Spring Capital Ltd v Revenue and Customs Commissioners* [2013] UKFTT 41 (TC), [2013] S.F.T.D. 570 (FTT (Tax)), Judge Barbara Mosedale
r.10, see *Eclipse Film Partners No.35 LLP v Revenue and Customs Commissioners* [2013] UKUT 141 (TCC), [2013] S.T.C. 1618 (UT (Tax)), Judge Roger Berner; see *Hewlett Packard Ltd v Revenue and Customs Commissioners* [2013] UKFTT 39 (TC), [2013] S.F.T.D. 409 (FTT (Tax)), Judge Barbara Mosedale; see *Usha Martin UK Ltd v Revenue and Customs Commissioners* [2013] UKFTT 793 (TC), [2013] S.F.T.D. 554 (FTT (Tax)), Judge Anne Scott
r.23, see *Dreams Plc v Revenue and Customs Commissioners* [2013] S.F.T.D. 111 (FTT (Tax)), Judge Colin Bishopp; see *Eclipse Film Partners No.35 LLP v Revenue and Customs Commissioners* [2013] UKUT 141 (TCC), [2013] S.T.C. 1618 (UT (Tax)), Judge Roger Berner

309. Local Authority Social Services and National Health Service Complaints (England) Regulations 2009
applied: SI 2013/235 Art.7, Sch.3 para.19, Sch.3 para.20, SI 2013/349 Sch.4 para.34, Sch.5 para.24, Sch.7 para.25, SI 2013/363 Sch.1 para.16, Sch.2 para.15, SI 2013/364 Sch.1 para.10, Sch.2 para.10
Reg.2, amended: SI 2013/235 Sch.2 para.123, SI 2013/349 Sch.10 para.7
Reg.2, revoked (in part): SI 2013/235 Sch.2 para.123
Reg.6, amended: SI 2013/235 Sch.2 para.123
Reg.7, amended: SI 2013/235 Sch.2 para.123
Reg.7, applied: SI 2013/235 Sch.3 para.18
Reg.13, amended: SI 2013/235 Sch.2 para.123
Reg.18, amended: SI 2013/235 Sch.2 para.123
Reg.18, revoked (in part): SI 2013/235 Sch.2 para.123
Reg.23, applied: SI 2013/364 Sch.1 para.10
Reg.23, referred to: SI 2013/364 Sch.2 para.10
Sch.1 para.2, revoked: SI 2013/349 Sch.10 para.7

312. Banking Act 2009 (Bank Administration) (Modification for Application to Banks in Temporary Public Ownership) Regulations 2009
Sch.1, amended: SI 2013/472 Sch.2 para.158
Sch.1, substituted: SI 2013/472 Sch.2 para.158

314. Bank Administration (Sharing Information) Regulations 2009
Reg.9, amended: SI 2013/472 Sch.2 para.159

322. Banking Act 2009 (Restriction of Partial Property Transfers) Order 2009
Art.1, amended: SI 2013/472 Sch.2 para.160, SI 2013/3115 Sch.2 para.71
Art.5, amended: SI 2013/472 Art.4, Sch.2 para.160

350. Bank Administration (Scotland) Rules 2009
Part 1 r.4, revoked (in part): SI 2013/472 Sch.2 para.161
Part 1 r.5, amended: SI 2013/472 Sch.2 para.161
Part 2 r.13, amended: SI 2013/472 Sch.2 para.161
Part 2 r.15, amended: SI 2013/472 Sch.2 para.161
Part 2 r.16, amended: SI 2013/472 Sch.2 para.161

Part 2 r.17, amended: SI 2013/472 Sch.2 para.161
Part 3 r.22A, amended: SI 2013/472 Sch.2 para.161
Part 3 r.29, amended: SI 2013/472 Sch.2 para.161
Part 3 r.33, amended: SI 2013/472 Sch.2 para.161
Part 3 r.35A, amended: SI 2013/472 Sch.2 para.161
Part 3 r.36, amended: SI 2013/472 Sch.2 para.161
Part 4 r.42, amended: SI 2013/472 Sch.2 para.161

351. Bank Insolvency (Scotland) Rules 2009
Part 1 r.3, amended: SI 2013/472 Sch.2 para.162
Part 2 r.8, amended: SI 2013/472 Sch.2 para.162
Part 3 r.11, amended: SI 2013/472 Sch.2 para.162
Part 3 r.12, amended: SI 2013/472 Sch.2 para.162
Part 6 r.24, amended: SI 2013/472 Sch.2 para.162
Part 7 r.30, amended: SI 2013/472 Sch.2 para.162
Part 8 r.31, amended: SI 2013/472 Sch.2 para.162
Part 8 r.36, amended: SI 2013/472 Sch.2 para.162
Part 8 r.39, amended: SI 2013/472 Sch.2 para.162
Part 8 r.41, amended: SI 2013/472 Sch.2 para.162
Part 8 r.44, amended: SI 2013/472 Sch.2 para.162
Part 14 r.101, amended: SI 2013/472 Sch.2 para.162

356. Bank Insolvency (England and Wales) Rules 2009
Part 1 r.3, amended: SI 2013/472 Sch.2 para.163
Part 2 r.10, amended: SI 2013/472 Sch.2 para.163
Part 2 r.16, amended: SI 2013/472 Sch.2 para.163
Part 3 r.20, amended: SI 2013/472 Sch.2 para.163
Part 3 r.22, amended: SI 2013/472 Sch.2 para.163
Part 6 r.41, amended: SI 2013/472 Sch.2 para.163
Part 6 r.42, amended: SI 2013/472 Sch.2 para.163
Part 6 r.45, amended: SI 2013/472 Sch.2 para.163
Part 7 r.73, amended: SI 2013/472 Sch.2 para.163
Part 9 r.84, amended: SI 2013/472 Sch.2 para.163
Part 9 r.87, amended: SI 2013/472 Sch.2 para.163
Part 9 r.88, amended: SI 2013/472 Sch.2 para.163
Part 9 r.90, amended: SI 2013/472 Sch.2 para.163
Part 9 r.94, amended: SI 2013/472 Sch.2 para.163
Part 9 r.96, amended: SI 2013/472 Sch.2 para.163
Part 9 r.106, amended: SI 2013/472 Sch.2 para.163
Part 9 r.107, amended: SI 2013/472 Sch.2 para.163
Part 18 r.209, amended: SI 2013/472 Sch.2 para.163

357. Bank Administration (England and Wales) Rules 2009
Part 1 r.4, revoked (in part): SI 2013/472 Sch.2 para.164
Part 1 r.5, amended: SI 2013/472 Sch.2 para.164
Part 2 r.12, amended: SI 2013/472 Sch.2 para.164
Part 2 r.15, amended: SI 2013/472 Sch.2 para.164
Part 2 r.20, amended: SI 2013/472 Sch.2 para.164
Part 2 r.22, amended: SI 2013/472 Sch.2 para.164
Part 2 r.24, amended: SI 2013/472 Sch.2 para.164
Part 2 r.25, amended: SI 2013/472 Sch.2 para.164
Part 3 r.30A, amended: SI 2013/472 Sch.2 para.164
Part 3 r.37, amended: SI 2013/472 Sch.2 para.164
Part 3 r.45, amended: SI 2013/472 Sch.2 para.164
Part 3 r.47A, amended: SI 2013/472 Sch.2 para.164
Part 3 r.48, amended: SI 2013/472 Sch.2 para.164
Part 4 r.52, amended: SI 2013/472 Sch.2 para.164
Part 5 r.61, amended: SI 2013/472 Sch.2 para.164

365. Section 19 Permit Regulations 2009
Reg.2, amended: SI 2013/1644 Sch.2
Reg.10, amended: SI 2013/1644 Sch.2
Reg.11, amended: SI 2013/1644 Sch.2
Reg.12, amended: SI 2013/1644 Sch.2
Reg.13, amended: SI 2013/1644 Sch.2

366. Community Bus Regulations 2009
Reg.6, amended: SI 2013/1644 Sch.2
Reg.7, amended: SI 2013/1644 Sch.2
Reg.11, amended: SI 2013/1644 Sch.2
Reg.12, amended: SI 2013/1644 Sch.2
Reg.13, amended: SI 2013/1644 Sch.2

395. Independent Review of Determinations (Adoption and Fostering) Regulations 2009
Reg.2, amended: SI 2013/985 Sch.1 para.7
Reg.3, amended: SI 2013/985 Sch.1 para.7
Reg.5, amended: SI 2013/985 Sch.1 para.7
Reg.10, amended: SI 2013/985 Sch.1 para.7
Reg.11, amended: SI 2013/985 Sch.1 para.7
Reg.12, amended: SI 2013/985 Sch.1 para.7
Reg.13, amended: SI 2013/985 Sch.1 para.7
Reg.18, amended: SI 2013/985 Sch.1 para.7

409. National Health Service (Amendments Relating to Optical Charges and Payments) Regulations 2009
revoked: SI 2013/461 Sch.4

443. Public Service Vehicles (Registration Restrictions) (England and Wales) Regulations 2009
Reg.2, amended: SI 2013/1644 Sch.4
Reg.3, amended: SI 2013/1644 Sch.4
Reg.4, amended: SI 2013/1644 Sch.4
Reg.5, amended: SI 2013/1644 Sch.4
Reg.6, amended: SI 2013/1644 Sch.4

445. Quality Partnership Schemes (England) Regulations 2009
Reg.2, amended: SI 2013/1644 Sch.5
Reg.5, amended: SI 2013/1644 Sch.5
Reg.7, amended: SI 2013/1644 Sch.5
Reg.8, amended: SI 2013/1644 Sch.5
Reg.10, amended: SI 2013/1644 Sch.5
Reg.11, amended: SI 2013/1644 Sch.5
Reg.12, amended: SI 2013/1644 Sch.5
Reg.13, amended: SI 2013/1644 Sch.5
Reg.14, amended: SI 2013/1644 Sch.5
Reg.15, amended: SI 2013/1644 Sch.5

Reg.16, amended: SI 2013/1644 Sch.5
Reg.18, amended: SI 2013/1644 Sch.5

452. Town and Country Planning (Appeals) (Written Representations Procedure) (England) Regulations 2009

Part 1, applied: SI 2013/2114 Reg.4, SI 2013/2137 r.6
Reg.2, amended: SI 2013/2114 Reg.2
Reg.3, amended: SI 2013/2114 Reg.2
Reg.4, amended: SI 2013/2114 Reg.2
Reg.5, amended: SI 2013/2114 Reg.2
Reg.6, amended: SI 2013/2114 Reg.2
Reg.7, amended: SI 2013/2114 Reg.2
Reg.8, amended: SI 2013/2114 Reg.2
Reg.9, amended: SI 2013/2114 Reg.2
Reg.9, applied: SI 2013/2114 Reg.4, SI 2013/2137 r.6
Reg.10, amended: SI 2013/2114 Reg.2
Reg.12, amended: SI 2013/2114 Reg.2
Reg.13, amended: SI 2013/2114 Reg.2
Reg.14, amended: SI 2013/2114 Reg.2
Reg.14, revoked (in part): SI 2013/2114 Reg.2
Reg.15, amended: SI 2013/2114 Reg.2
Reg.18, amended: SI 2013/2114 Reg.2
Sch.1 para.1, added: SI 2013/2114 Reg.2
Sch.1 para.2, added: SI 2013/2114 Reg.2
Sch.1 para.3, added: SI 2013/2114 Reg.2
Sch.1 para.4, added: SI 2013/2114 Reg.2
Sch.1 para.5, added: SI 2013/2114 Reg.2

460. Police Act 1997 (Criminal Records) Regulations 2009

Reg.2, revoked (in part): SI 2013/602 Sch.2 para.92

462. Health and Social Care Act 2008 (Commencement No.9, Consequential Amendments and Transitory, Transitional and Saving Provisions) Order 2009

Art.13, revoked: SI 2013/235 Sch.2 para.124
Sch.3 para.2, revoked (in part): SI 2013/235 Sch.2 para.124

468. General Osteopathic Council (Constitution of the Statutory Committees) Rules Order of Council 2009

Sch.1, amended: SI 2013/235 Sch.2 para.125

470. Education (Student Loans) (Repayment) Regulations 2009

Part 3, applied: SI 2013/607 Reg.1
Part 4, applied: SI 2013/607 Reg.1
Reg.3, amended: SI 2013/607 Reg.3
Reg.9, amended: SI 2013/388 Sch.1 para.44, SI 2013/591 Sch.1 para.42
Reg.13, amended: SI 2013/607 Reg.4
Reg.19, amended: SI 2013/607 Reg.5
Reg.20, amended: SI 2013/607 Reg.6
Reg.21, amended: SI 2013/1881 Sch.1 para.41
Reg.21A, amended: SI 2013/607 Reg.7, SI 2013/1881 Sch.1 para.41
Reg.29, amended: SI 2013/607 Reg.8
Reg.33, amended: SI 2013/607 Reg.9
Reg.41A, revoked (in part): SI 2013/607 Reg.10
Reg.43, amended: SI 2013/607 Reg.11
Reg.43A, amended: SI 2013/607 Reg.12
Reg.44, amended: SI 2013/607 Reg.13
Reg.59B, revoked (in part): SI 2013/607 Reg.14
Reg.59BA, added: SI 2013/607 Reg.15
Reg.59BB, added: SI 2013/607 Reg.15
Reg.59E, amended: SI 2013/607 Reg.16
Reg.59E, revoked (in part): SI 2013/607 Reg.16
Reg.59F, amended: SI 2013/607 Reg.17
Reg.59F, revoked (in part): SI 2013/607 Reg.17
Reg.59G, added: SI 2013/607 Reg.18

471. Social Security (National Insurance Number Information Exemption) Regulations 2009

Reg.11, revoked: SI 2013/458 Sch.1
Reg.12, revoked: SI 2013/458 Sch.1

492. Road Safety (Financial Penalty Deposit) (Appropriate Amount) Order 2009

Art.2, amended: SI 2013/2025 Art.2
Sch.1 Part 1, amended: SI 2013/2025 Art.3
Sch.1 Part 2, amended: SI 2013/2025 Art.3
Sch.2, amended: SI 2013/2025 Art.4

496. Control of Trade in Endangered Species (Fees) Regulations 2009

Reg.3, amended: SI 2013/1240 Reg.4
Reg.4, substituted: SI 2013/1240 Reg.4
Reg.5, amended: SI 2013/1240 Reg.4
Reg.6, amended: SI 2013/1240 Reg.4
Sch.1, substituted: SI 2013/1240 Sch.1

509. Mutual Societies (Transfers) Order 2009

Art.7, amended: SI 2013/496 Sch.10 para.7
Art.18, amended: SI 2013/496 Sch.10 para.7

510. Designation of Schools Having a Religious Character (Independent Schools) (England) Order 2009

Sch.1, amended: SI 2013/2162 Sch.2

555. Unit Trusts (Electronic Communications) Order 2009

Art.2, amended: SI 2013/472 Sch.2 para.165

590. Discipline of Judges (Designation) Order 2009

Art.3, amended: SI 2013/1948 Reg.5

596. Civil Enforcement of Parking Contraventions (City of Newcastle upon Tyne) Designation Order 2009

Sch.1, revoked (in part): SI 2013/2594 Art.3

599. National Health Service (Pharmaceutical Services and Local Pharmaceutical Services) Amendment Regulations 2009

revoked: SI 2013/349 Sch.10 para.8

605. Factories Act 1961 and Offices, Shops and Railway Premises Act 1963 (Repeals and Modifications) Regulations 2009
Reg.4, revoked (in part): SI 2013/448 Sch.1

665. Co-ordination of Regulatory Enforcement (Enforcement Action) Order 2009
Art.2, amended: SI 2013/2286 Art.2
Art.3, amended: SI 2013/2286 Art.2

669. Co-ordination of Regulatory Enforcement (Regulatory Functions in Scotland and Northern Ireland) Order 2009
Sch.1 Part 2, amended: SI 2013/1575 Sch.1 para.23, SI 2013/3134 Sch.4 para.11
Sch.1 Part 4, amended: SI 2013/1478 Sch.5 para.25
Sch.2 Part 2, amended: SI 2013/1478 Sch.5 para.26

692. Pensions Increase (Review) Order 2009
applied: SI 2013/604 Sch.1

711. Department for Transport (Fees) Order 2009
Sch.1 Part 2 para.7, amended: SI 2013/1644 Sch.2
Sch.1 Part 2 para.8, amended: SI 2013/1644 Sch.2
Sch.1 Part 2 para.9, amended: SI 2013/1644 Sch.2
Sch.1 Part 2 para.10, amended: SI 2013/1644 Sch.2
Sch.1 Part 2 para.11, amended: SI 2013/1644 Sch.2
Sch.1 Part 2 para.14, amended: SI 2013/1644 Sch.2
Sch.1 Part 2 para.15, amended: SI 2013/1644 Sch.2
Sch.1 Part 2 para.16, amended: SI 2013/1644 Sch.2
Sch.1 Part 2 para.18, amended: SI 2013/1644 Sch.2
Sch.1 Part 2 para.19, amended: SI 2013/1644 Sch.2
Sch.1 Part 2 para.20, amended: SI 2013/1644 Sch.2
Sch.1 Part 5 para.44, amended: SI 2013/1644 Sch.2
Sch.1 Part 5 para.45, amended: SI 2013/1644 Sch.2
Sch.1 Part 5 para.46, amended: SI 2013/1644 Sch.2
Sch.1 Part 5 para.47, amended: SI 2013/1644 Sch.2

716. Chemicals (Hazard Information and Packaging for Supply) Regulations 2009
amended: SI 2013/1506 Sch.4 para.1
Reg.1, revoked: SI 2013/1506 Reg.36
Reg.2, revoked: SI 2013/1506 Reg.36
Reg.3, amended: SI 2013/1478 Sch.5 para.27, SI 2013/1506 Sch.4 para.2
Reg.3, revoked: SI 2013/1506 Reg.36
Reg.4, revoked: SI 2013/1506 Reg.36
Reg.5, revoked: SI 2013/1506 Reg.36
Reg.5A, added: SI 2013/1506 Sch.4 para.3
Reg.6, revoked: SI 2013/1506 Reg.36
Reg.7, revoked: SI 2013/1506 Reg.36
Reg.8, revoked: SI 2013/1506 Reg.36
Reg.9, revoked: SI 2013/1506 Reg.36
Reg.10, revoked: SI 2013/1506 Reg.36
Reg.11, revoked: SI 2013/1506 Reg.36
Reg.12, revoked: SI 2013/1506 Reg.36
Reg.13, revoked: SI 2013/1506 Reg.36
Reg.14, amended: SI 2013/1506 Sch.4 para.4, SI 2013/1666 Art.5
Reg.14, revoked (in part): SI 2013/1506 Reg.36, SI 2013/1666 Art.5
Reg.15, revoked: SI 2013/1506 Reg.36
Reg.16, revoked: SI 2013/1506 Reg.36
Reg.17, revoked: SI 2013/1506 Reg.36
Reg.18, revoked: SI 2013/1506 Reg.36

717. Road Vehicles (Approval) Regulations 2009
Reg.5, amended: SI 2013/602 Sch.2 para.93
Reg.5, revoked (in part): SI 2013/602 Sch.2 para.93

750. Western Sussex Hospitals and the Royal West Sussex National Health Service Trust and the Worthing and Southlands Hospitals National Health Service Trust (Dissolution) Order 2009
Art.1, amended: SI 2013/593 Art.2

772. South London Healthcare (Establishment) and the Bromley Hospitals, the Queen Elizabeth Hospital and the Queen Mary's Sidcup National Health Service Trust (Dissolution) Order 2009
revoked: SI 2013/2378 Art.2
Art.1, amended: SI 2013/593 Art.2

774. Financial Services and Markets Act 2000 (Controllers) (Exemption) Order 2009
Art.2, amended: SI 2013/3115 Sch.2 para.72
Art.4, amended: SI 2013/472 Sch.2 para.166
Art.6A, added: SI 2013/1881 Art.19

778. Local Health Boards (Establishment and Dissolution) (Wales) Order 2009
Sch.1, amended: SI 2013/2918 Art.2

779. Local Health Boards (Constitution, Membership and Procedures) (Wales) Regulations 2009
Reg.2, amended: SI 2013/235 Sch.2 para.126
Sch.2 Part 1 para.1, amended: SI 2013/235 Sch.2 para.126

785. Renewables Obligation Order 2009
applied: SI 2013/768 Art.27
Art.2, amended: SI 2013/768 Art.2
Art.4, amended: SI 2013/768 Art.3
Art.13, amended: SI 2013/768 Art.4
Art.13, revoked (in part): SI 2013/768 Art.4

Art.21, see *R. (on the application of Infinis Plc) v Gas and Electricity Markets Authority* [2013] EWCA Civ 70, [2013] J.P.L. 1037 (CA (Civ Div)), Sir James Munby (President, Fam)
Art.22, amended: SI 2013/768 Art.5
Art.24, amended: SI 2013/768 Art.6
Art.25, amended: SI 2013/768 Art.7
Art.25, revoked (in part): SI 2013/768 Art.7
Art.26, amended: SI 2013/768 Art.8
Art.26, revoked (in part): SI 2013/768 Art.8
Art.27, amended: SI 2013/768 Art.9
Art.28, substituted: SI 2013/768 Art.10
Art.28A, added: SI 2013/768 Art.11
Art.28B, added: SI 2013/768 Art.11
Art.28C, added: SI 2013/768 Art.11
Art.28D, added: SI 2013/768 Art.11
Art.28E, added: SI 2013/768 Art.11
Art.29, amended: SI 2013/768 Art.12
Art.30, amended: SI 2013/768 Art.13
Art.30, revoked (in part): SI 2013/768 Art.13
Art.30A, amended: SI 2013/768 Art.14
Art.30A, revoked (in part): SI 2013/768 Art.14
Art.30B, added: SI 2013/768 Art.15
Art.31, amended: SI 2013/768 Art.16
Art.32, amended: SI 2013/768 Art.17
Art.33, amended: SI 2013/768 Art.18
Art.36, amended: SI 2013/768 Art.19
Art.54, amended: SI 2013/768 Art.20
Art.54, revoked (in part): SI 2013/768 Art.20
Art.54A, amended: SI 2013/768 Art.21
Art.54A, referred to: SI 2013/768
Art.58ZA, added: SI 2013/768 Art.22
Art.60, amended: SI 2013/768 Art.23
Sch.2 Part 1 para.1, amended: SI 2013/768 Art.24
Sch.2 Part 2, substituted: SI 2013/768 Art.25
Sch.2 Part 2A, added: SI 2013/768 Art.26
Sch.2 Part 2B, added: SI 2013/768 Art.26
Sch.2 Part 2C, added: SI 2013/768 Art.26
Sch.2 Part 2D, added: SI 2013/768 Art.26

796. Cosmetic Products (Safety) (Amendment) Regulations 2009

revoked: SI 2013/1478 Sch.1

805. Building Societies (Insolvency and Special Administration) Order 2009

Sch.1 Part 1 para.3, amended: SI 2013/496 Sch.11 para.16
Sch.1 Part 2 para.13, amended: SI 2013/496 Sch.11 para.16
Sch.1 Part 2 para.16, amended: SI 2013/496 Sch.11 para.16
Sch.1 Part 2 para.17, amended: SI 2013/496 Sch.11 para.16
Sch.1 Part 2 para.21, amended: SI 2013/496 Sch.11 para.16
Sch.1 Part 3 para.30, amended: SI 2013/472 Sch.2 para.169, SI 2013/496 Sch.11 para.16
Sch.1 Part 3 para.32A, amended: SI 2013/496 Sch.11 para.16
Sch.1 Part 3 para.35, amended: SI 2013/472 Sch.2 para.169

806. Building Society Special Administration (Scotland) Rules 2009

Part 1 r.4, amended: SI 2013/472 Sch.2 para.170
Part 1 r.4, revoked (in part): SI 2013/472 Sch.2 para.170
Part 2 r.13, amended: SI 2013/472 Sch.2 para.170
Part 2 r.15, amended: SI 2013/472 Sch.2 para.170
Part 2 r.16, amended: SI 2013/472 Sch.2 para.170
Part 3 r.28, amended: SI 2013/472 Sch.2 para.170
Part 3 r.32, amended: SI 2013/472 Sch.2 para.170
Part 3 r.35, amended: SI 2013/472 Sch.2 para.170
Part 3 r.36, amended: SI 2013/472 Sch.2 para.170
Part 4 r.40, amended: SI 2013/472 Sch.2 para.170
Part 4 r.41, amended: SI 2013/472 Sch.2 para.170

814. Amendments to Law (Resolution of Dunfermline Building Society) Order 2009

Art.6, amended: SI 2013/472 Sch.2 para.167
Art.9, amended: SI 2013/472 Sch.2 para.167
Art.10, amended: SI 2013/472 Sch.2 para.167

828. Education (Infant Class Sizes) (Wales) (Amendment) Regulations 2009

revoked: SI 2013/1141 Reg.3

847. Zimbabwe (Financial Sanctions) Regulations 2009

Reg.2, amended: SI 2013/472 Art.4
Reg.6, disapplied: SI 2013/795 Reg.2
Reg.7, disapplied: SI 2013/795 Reg.2
Reg.8, disapplied: SI 2013/795 Reg.2
Reg.9, disapplied: SI 2013/795 Reg.2
Reg.10, disapplied: SI 2013/795 Reg.2
Sch.1 para.6, amended: SI 2013/472 Sch.2 para.171

871. Access to Justice Act 1999 (Destination of Appeals) (Family Proceedings) Order 2009

Art.3, revoked (in part): 2013 c.22 Sch.11 para.210
Art.5, revoked: 2013 c.22 Sch.11 para.210
Art.6, revoked: 2013 c.22 Sch.11 para.210
Art.7, revoked: 2013 c.22 Sch.11 para.210
Art.8, revoked: 2013 c.22 Sch.11 para.210
Art.9, revoked (in part): 2013 c.22 Sch.9 para.141, Sch.11 para.210

890. Waste Batteries and Accumulators Regulations 2009

Reg.2, amended: SI 2013/755 Sch.4 para.319, SI 2013/3134 Sch.4 para.12
Reg.3, amended: SI 2013/755 Sch.4 para.320
Reg.13, amended: SI 2013/755 Sch.4 para.321
Reg.83, amended: SI 2013/755 Sch.4 para.322

Reg.83, revoked (in part): SI 2013/755 Sch.4 para.322
Reg.86, amended: SI 2013/755 Sch.4 para.323

975. Proceeds of Crime Act 2002 (References to Financial Investigators) Order 2009
Art.1, amended: SI 2013/2318 Sch.1 para.112
Sch.1, added: SI 2013/472 Sch.2 para.168
Sch.1, amended: SI 2013/472 Sch.2 para.168, SI 2013/755 Sch.4 para.324, SI 2013/2318 Sch.1 para.113

992. Court Martial Appeal Court (Bail) Order 2009
applied: SI 2013/1852 Art.24

995. Environmental Damage (Prevention and Remediation) (Wales) Regulations 2009
Reg.10, amended: SI 2013/755 Sch.5 para.52
Reg.11, amended: SI 2013/755 Sch.5 para.53
Reg.31, amended: SI 2013/755 Sch.5 para.54

1059. Armed Forces Act 2006 (Transitional Provisions etc) Order 2009
Art.25, applied: SI 2013/1852 Art.3

1098. Armed Forces (Custody Proceedings) Rules 2009
Part 3 r.20, substituted: SI 2013/2527 r.3
Part 3 r.22, amended: SI 2013/2527 r.4

1114. Upper Tribunal (Lands Chamber) Fees Order 2009
Art.4, amended: SI 2013/2302 Art.8
Art.4, substituted: SI 2013/1199 Art.4
Art.5, revoked: SI 2013/1199 Art.5
Art.7, revoked: SI 2013/2302 Art.8
Art.7A, added: SI 2013/2302 Art.8
Art.8, revoked: SI 2013/2302 Art.8
Sch.1, substituted: SI 2013/2302 Art.8
Sch.2 para.1, added: SI 2013/2302 Sch.1
Sch.2 para.2, added: SI 2013/2302 Sch.1
Sch.2 para.3, added: SI 2013/2302 Sch.1
Sch.2 para.4, added: SI 2013/2302 Sch.1
Sch.2 para.5, added: SI 2013/2302 Sch.1
Sch.2 para.6, added: SI 2013/2302 Sch.1
Sch.2 para.7, added: SI 2013/2302 Sch.1
Sch.2 para.8, added: SI 2013/2302 Sch.1
Sch.2 para.9, added: SI 2013/2302 Sch.1
Sch.2 para.10, added: SI 2013/2302 Sch.1
Sch.2 para.11, added: SI 2013/2302 Sch.1
Sch.2 para.12, added: SI 2013/2302 Sch.1
Sch.2 para.13, added: SI 2013/2302 Sch.1
Sch.2 para.14, added: SI 2013/2302 Sch.1
Sch.2 para.15, added: SI 2013/2302 Sch.1
Sch.2 para.16, added: SI 2013/2302 Sch.1
Sch.2 para.17, added: SI 2013/2302 Sch.1
Sch.2 para.18, added: SI 2013/2302 Sch.1
Sch.2 para.19, added: SI 2013/2302 Sch.1
Sch.2 para.20, added: SI 2013/2302 Sch.1

1168. Armed Forces (Review of Court Martial Sentence) Order 2009
Sch.1 para.1, amended: SI 2013/862 Sch.1 para.2

1171. Registered Pension Schemes (Authorised Payments) Regulations 2009
Reg.6, applied: SI 2013/2356 Reg.34
Reg.7, revoked (in part): SI 2013/1818 Reg.2
Reg.11, applied: SI 2013/2356 Reg.34
Reg.12, applied: SI 2013/2356 Reg.34, SSI 2013/174 Reg.6
Reg.20, amended: SI 2013/1818 Reg.2

1182. Health Care and Associated Professions (Miscellaneous Amendments and Practitioner Psychologists) Order 2009
Sch.4 Part 1 para.9, revoked (in part): SSI 2013/50 Sch.5
Sch.4 Part 3 para.28, revoked (in part): SSI 2013/50 Sch.5

1209. Armed Forces (Service Civilian Court) Rules 2009
Part 3 r.21, substituted: SI 2013/2527 r.20
Part 3 r.22, amended: SI 2013/2527 r.21
Part 12 r.84A, added: SI 2013/2527 r.22
Part 12 r.84B, added: SI 2013/2527 r.22
Part 12 r.84C, added: SI 2013/2527 r.22

1211. Armed Forces (Summary Appeal Court) Rules 2009
Part 4 r.29, substituted: SI 2013/2527 r.6
Part 4 r.30, amended: SI 2013/2527 r.7
Part 11 r.74A, added: SI 2013/2527 r.8
Part 11 r.74B, added: SI 2013/2527 r.8
Part 11 r.74C, added: SI 2013/2527 r.8

1212. Armed Forces (Financial Penalty Enforcement Orders) Regulations 2009
Reg.3, amended: SI 2013/1761 Reg.2
Reg.3A, added: SI 2013/1761 Reg.2
Reg.3B, added: SI 2013/1761 Reg.2

1216. Armed Forces (Summary Hearing and Activation of Suspended Sentences of Service Detention) Rules 2009
Part 2 r.11A, added: SI 2013/2527 r.10
Part 2 r.15A, added: SI 2013/2527 r.11
Part 2 r.15B, added: SI 2013/2527 r.11
Part 2 r.27, amended: SI 2013/2527 r.12
Part 3 r.33A, added: SI 2013/2527 r.13
Part 3 r.36, amended: SI 2013/2527 r.14

1302. Infrastructure Planning (National Policy Statement Consultation) Regulations 2009
Reg.2, amended: SI 2013/522 Reg.2
Reg.3, amended: SI 2013/522 Reg.2, SI 2013/755 Sch.4 para.325
Reg.3, revoked (in part): SI 2013/522 Reg.2

1307. Transfer of Tribunal Functions (Lands Tribunal and Miscellaneous Amendments) Order 2009
Sch.2 para.121, revoked: SI 2013/2042 Sch.1 para.75

1342. Financial Services and Markets Act 2000 (Regulated Activities) (Amendment) Order 2009
Art.1, amended: SI 2013/472 Art.4
Art.32, amended: SI 2013/472 Art.4
Sch.1 para.2, amended: SI 2013/472 Art.4
Sch.1 para.3, amended: SI 2013/472 Art.4

1345. Health and Care Professions Council (Constitution) Order 2009
amended: SI 2013/3004 Art.2
Art.1, amended: SI 2013/3004 Art.2
Art.2, amended: SI 2013/3004 Art.2
Art.10, amended: SI 2013/3004 Art.2

1346. Cosmetic Products (Safety) (Amendment No.2) Regulations 2009
revoked: SI 2013/1478 Sch.1

1348. Carriage of Dangerous Goods and Use of Transportable Pressure Equipment Regulations 2009
applied: SI 2013/1471 Sch.2 para.64
Reg.2, amended: SSI 2013/119 Sch.2 para.26
Sch.1 Part 1 para.4, amended: SSI 2013/119 Sch.2 para.26
Sch.2 para.4, amended: SI 2013/235 Sch.2 para.127
Sch.2 para.5, amended: SSI 2013/119 Sch.2 para.26

1361. Marketing of Fresh Horticultural Produce Regulations 2009
Reg.2, amended: SI 2013/3235 Reg.8

1385. Public Health Wales National Health Service Trust (Membership and Procedure) Regulations 2009
Reg.1, amended: SI 2013/235 Sch.2 para.128
Reg.15, amended: SI 2013/235 Sch.2 para.128

1491. National Health Service (Pharmaceutical Services) (Amendment) (Wales) Regulation 2009
revoked: SI 2013/898 Sch.8 para.21

1495. Burma/Myanmar (Financial Restrictions) Regulations 2009
revoked: SI 2013/1096 Reg.2
Reg.2, amended: SI 2013/472 Art.4
Sch.1 para.6, amended: SI 2013/472 Sch.2 para.172

1511. Local Health Boards (Directed Functions) (Wales) Regulations 2009
Reg.3, amended: SI 2013/235 Sch.2 para.129

1547. Childcare (Disqualification) Regulations 2009
Sch.1 para.10, amended: SI 2013/1465 Sch.1 para.26
Sch.1 para.13A, added: SI 2013/1465 Sch.1 para.26
Sch.3 para.2, amended: SI 2013/1465 Sch.1 para.26
Sch.3 para.7, amended: SI 2013/1465 Sch.1 para.26

1551. Marketing of Fresh Horticultural Produce (Wales) Regulations 2009
Reg.2, amended: SI 2013/3270 Reg.6

1555. Education (Student Support) Regulations 2009
Sch.1 Pt 2 para.5, see *R. (on the application of Arogundade) v Secretary of State for Business, Innovation and Skills* [2013] EWCA Civ 823, [2013] E.L.R. 466 (CA (Civ Div)), Longmore, L.J.

1556. School Organisation and Governance (Amendment) (England) Regulations 2009
Reg.5, revoked: SI 2013/3109 Reg.3
Reg.6, revoked: SI 2013/3110 Reg.8

1563. Education (Individual Pupil Information) (Prescribed Persons) (England) Regulations 2009
Reg.3, amended: SI 2013/235 Sch.2 para.130, SI 2013/1193 Reg.2
Reg.3, revoked (in part): SI 2013/235 Sch.2 para.130, SI 2013/1193 Reg.2

1574. Meat (Official Controls Charges) (England) Regulations 2009
see *R. (on the application of Jaspers (Treburley) Ltd) v Food Standards Agency* [2013] EWHC 1788 (Admin), [2013] P.T.S.R. 1271 (QBD (Admin)), Singh, J.
Sch.2, see *R. (on the application of Jaspers (Treburley) Ltd) v Food Standards Agency* [2013] EWHC 1788 (Admin), [2013] P.T.S.R. 1271 (QBD (Admin)), Singh, J.

1603. Supreme Court Rules 2009
see *Bank Mellat v HM Treasury* [2013] UKSC 38, [2013] 4 All E.R. 495 (SC), Lord Neuberger (President)
Part 7, applied: SI 2013/480 Reg.46, SI 2013/503 Reg.6, SI 2013/512 Reg.31
r.27, see *Bank Mellat v HM Treasury* [2013] UKSC 38, [2013] 4 All E.R. 495 (SC), Lord Neuberger (President)
r.29, see *Bank Mellat v HM Treasury* [2013] UKSC 38, [2013] 4 All E.R. 495 (SC), Lord Neuberger (President)

1735. Air Navigation (Single European Sky) (Penalties) Order 2009
Art.2, amended: SI 2013/2874 Art.3
Art.8, amended: SI 2013/2874 Art.4
Art.9, amended: SI 2013/2874 Art.5
Art.11, amended: SI 2013/2874 Art.6
Art.12, amended: SI 2013/2874 Art.7
Art.14, added: SI 2013/2874 Art.8

1798. Police Act 1997 (Criminal Records) (Disclosure) (Amendment) Regulations (Northern Ireland) 2009
Reg.2, revoked (in part): SI 2013/602 Sch.2 para.94

1801. Overseas Companies Regulations 2009
Part 5, referred to: SI 2013/3008 Reg.3

Part 6, referred to: SI 2013/3008 Reg.3
Sch.1, amended: SI 2013/472 Sch.2 para.173
Sch.2 Part 2 para.7, amended: SI 2013/472 Sch.2 para.173

1803. Registrar of Companies and Applications for Striking Off Regulations 2009

Reg.8, amended: SI 2013/600 Sch.2 para.6

1804. Limited Liability Partnerships (Application of Companies Act 2006) Regulations 2009

Part 9, applied: SI 2013/618 Reg.8
Reg.32, substituted: SI 2013/618 Sch.1
Reg.33, substituted: SI 2013/618 Sch.1
Reg.34, substituted: SI 2013/618 Sch.1
Reg.35, substituted: SI 2013/618 Sch.1
Reg.36, substituted: SI 2013/618 Sch.1
Reg.37, substituted: SI 2013/618 Sch.1
Reg.38, substituted: SI 2013/618 Sch.1
Reg.39, substituted: SI 2013/618 Sch.1
Reg.40, substituted: SI 2013/618 Sch.1
Reg.41, substituted: SI 2013/618 Sch.1
Reg.42, substituted: SI 2013/618 Sch.1
Reg.43, substituted: SI 2013/618 Sch.1
Reg.44, substituted: SI 2013/618 Sch.1
Reg.48, amended: SI 2013/472 Sch.2 para.174
Reg.64, amended: SI 2013/618 Reg.3
Reg.66, amended: SI 2013/618 Reg.4
Reg.67, amended: SI 2013/618 Reg.5
Reg.68, amended: SI 2013/618 Reg.6
Reg.74, amended: SI 2013/618 Reg.7

1810. Dunfermline Building Society Independent Valuer Order 2009

Art.17, amended: SI 2013/472 Sch.2 para.175

1828. Stamp Duty and Stamp Duty Reserve Tax (Investment Exchanges and Clearing Houses) Regulations (No.9) 2009

Reg.4, amended: SI 2013/504 Reg.40
Reg.4A, added: SI 2013/504 Reg.40

1834. Transfer of Functions of the Charity Tribunal Order 2009

Art.4, revoked (in part): SI 2013/2042 Sch.1 para.76
Sch.2 para.1, revoked: SI 2013/2042 Sch.1 para.76

1835. Transfer of Functions of the Consumer Credit Appeals Tribunal Order 2009

Sch.2 para.2, revoked: SI 2013/2042 Sch.1 para.77

1843. Criminal Defence Service (Funding) (Amendment) Order 2009

see *R. v Noon (Costs)* [2013] 4 Costs L.R. 633 (Sen Cts Costs Office), Costs Judge Gordon-Saker

1882. Police Act 1997 (Criminal Records) (No.2) Regulations 2009

Reg.5, amended: SI 2013/2669 Reg.3

1887. Community Care, Services for Carers and Children's Services (Direct Payments) (England) Regulations 2009

applied: SI 2013/1617 Reg.7
Reg.13, amended: SI 2013/2270 Reg.3
Sch.2A, added: SI 2013/2270 Reg.4

1922. Police and Criminal Evidence Act 1984 (Armed Forces) Order 2009

Art.2, amended: SI 2013/2554 Art.2
Art.15, substituted: SI 2013/2554 Art.2
Sch.2 para.5A, added: SI 2013/2554 Art.2
Sch.2 para.17, amended: SI 2013/2554 Art.2

1926. General Insurers Technical Provisions (Appropriate Amount) (Tax) Regulations 2009

Reg.8, amended: SI 2013/472 Sch.2 para.176

1927. Major Accident Off-Site Emergency Plan (Management of Waste from Extractive Industries) (England and Wales) Regulations 2009

Reg.2, amended: SI 2013/235 Sch.2 para.131, SI 2013/755 Sch.4 para.327
Reg.4, amended: SI 2013/755 Sch.4 para.328
Reg.9, amended: SI 2013/755 Sch.4 para.329
Reg.10, amended: SI 2013/755 Sch.4 para.329

1931. Solicitors (Non-Contentious Business) Remuneration Order 2009

applied: SI 2013/1918 Sch.1 Part TABLEa, Sch.2 para.4, SI 2013/1922 Sch.1 para.3

1941. Companies Act 2006 (Consequential Amendments, Transitional Provisions and Savings) Order 2009

Sch.1 para.36, revoked (in part): SI 2013/687 Sch.2

1964. Public Service Vehicles (Enforcement Powers) Regulations 2009

Reg.9, amended: SI 2013/1644 Sch.2
Reg.11, amended: SI 2013/1644 Sch.2
Reg.12, amended: SI 2013/1644 Sch.2
Reg.13, amended: SI 2013/1644 Sch.2
Reg.14, amended: SI 2013/1644 Sch.2
Reg.15, amended: SI 2013/1644 Sch.2
Reg.16, amended: SI 2013/1644 Sch.2

1973. Whole of Government Accounts (Designation of Bodies) Order 2009

Sch.1, amended: SI 2013/687 Sch.2

1976. Tribunal Procedure (First-tier Tribunal) (General Regulatory Chamber) Rules 2009

Part 2 r.10, amended: SI 2013/477 r.3, r.4, r.5, r.6
Part 2 r.17, amended: SI 2013/477 r.7
Part 3 r.38, amended: SI 2013/477 r.8
Part 4 r.42, amended: SI 2013/477 r.9

2033. Tax Avoidance Schemes (Prescribed Descriptions of Arrangements) (Amendment) Regulations 2009

revoked: SI 2013/2595 Reg.11

2034. Investment Trusts (Dividends) (Optional Treatment as Interest Distributions) Regulations 2009
Reg.14, amended: SI 2013/605 Reg.6
Reg.16, amended: SI 2013/605 Reg.6
Reg.17, amended: SI 2013/605 Reg.6
Reg.18, amended: SI 2013/605 Reg.6
Reg.20, amended: SI 2013/605 Reg.6

2041. Armed Forces (Court Martial) Rules 2009
Part 3 r.22, substituted: SI 2013/2527 r.16
Part 3 r.23, amended: SI 2013/2527 r.17
Part 4 r.29, amended: SI 2013/1851 r.3
Part 4 r.29A, added: SI 2013/1851 r.4
Part 12 r.100A, added: SI 2013/2527 r.18
Part 12 r.100B, added: SI 2013/2527 r.18
Part 12 r.100C, added: SI 2013/2527 r.18
Part 18 r.151A, added: SI 2013/1851 r.5
Sch.2 Part 8 para.25, revoked: SI 2013/1851 r.6
Sch.2 Part 8 para.26, revoked: SI 2013/1851 r.6
Sch.2 Part 8 para.27, revoked: SI 2013/1851 r.6
Sch.2 Part 8 para.28, revoked: SI 2013/1851 r.6
Sch.2 Part 8 para.29, revoked: SI 2013/1851 r.6
Sch.2 Part 8 para.30, revoked: SI 2013/1851 r.6
Sch.2 Part 8 para.31, revoked: SI 2013/1851 r.6
Sch.2 Part 8 para.32, revoked: SI 2013/1851 r.6
Sch.2 Part 8 para.33, revoked: SI 2013/1851 r.6

2048. Port Security Regulations 2009
applied: SI 2013/516 Art.3, Art.4, Sch.2 para.3, SI 2013/1652 Art.3, Art.4, Sch.2 para.3, SI 2013/1655 Art.3, Art.4, Sch.2 para.3, SI 2013/1656 Art.3, Art.4, Sch.2 para.3, SI 2013/2013 Art.3, Art.4, Sch.2 para.3, SI 2013/2014 Art.3, Sch.2 para.3, SI 2013/2181 Art.4, SI 2013/2272 Art.3, Art.4, Sch.2 para.3, SI 2013/3074 Art.3, Sch.2 para.3, SI 2013/3075 Art.3, Sch.2 para.3, SI 2013/3076 Art.3, Art.4, Sch.2 para.3, SI 2013/3077 Art.3, SI 2013/3078 Art.3, Sch.2 para.3, SI 2013/3079 Art.3, Art.4, Sch.2 para.3, SI 2013/3080 Art.3, Sch.2 para.3, SI 2013/3081 Art.3, Art.4, Sch.2 para.3, SI 2013/3180 Art.5, Art.6, Sch.4 para.3, SI 2013/3184 Art.3, SI 2013/3185 Art.3, Art.4, Sch.2 para.3
Reg.2, amended: SI 2013/2815 Reg.3
Reg.2, applied: SI 2013/3074 Art.2, SI 2013/3075 Art.2, SI 2013/3077 Art.2, SI 2013/3078 Art.2, SI 2013/3079 Art.2, SI 2013/3080 Art.2, SI 2013/3081 Art.2, SI 2013/3180 Art.2, Art.3, Art.4, SI 2013/3184 Art.2, SI 2013/3185 Art.2
Reg.3, applied: SI 2013/516 Art.2, SI 2013/1652 Art.2, SI 2013/1655 Art.2, SI 2013/1656 Art.2, SI 2013/2013 Art.2, SI 2013/2014 Art.2, SI 2013/2181 Art.2, Art.3, SI 2013/2272 Art.2
Reg.3, substituted: SI 2013/2815 Reg.4
Reg.3A, added: SI 2013/2815 Reg.5
Reg.14, revoked: SI 2013/2815 Reg.6
Reg.15, amended: SI 2013/2815 Reg.7
Reg.18, amended: SI 2013/2815 Reg.8
Reg.38, revoked (in part): SI 2013/2815 Reg.9
Reg.39, added: SI 2013/2815 Reg.10
Sch.3 para.1, amended: SI 2013/2815 Reg.11
Sch.3 para.2, amended: SI 2013/2815 Reg.11

2108. Ecclesiastical Offices (Terms of Service) Regulations 2009
applied: SI 2013/1893 Sch.2

2131. Supreme Court Fees Order 2009
Sch.2 para.1, amended: SI 2013/388 Sch.1 para.45, SI 2013/534 Sch.1 para.21, SI 2013/591 Sch.1 para.43
Sch.2 para.1, substituted: SI 2013/2302 Sch.1
Sch.2 para.2, substituted: SI 2013/2302 Sch.1
Sch.2 para.3, substituted: SI 2013/2302 Sch.1
Sch.2 para.4, substituted: SI 2013/2302 Sch.1
Sch.2 para.5, substituted: SI 2013/2302 Sch.1
Sch.2 para.6, substituted: SI 2013/2302 Sch.1
Sch.2 para.7, substituted: SI 2013/2302 Sch.1
Sch.2 para.8, substituted: SI 2013/2302 Sch.1
Sch.2 para.9, substituted: SI 2013/2302 Sch.1
Sch.2 para.10, substituted: SI 2013/2302 Sch.1
Sch.2 para.11, substituted: SI 2013/2302 Sch.1
Sch.2 para.12, substituted: SI 2013/2302 Sch.1
Sch.2 para.13, substituted: SI 2013/2302 Sch.1
Sch.2 para.14, substituted: SI 2013/2302 Sch.1
Sch.2 para.15, substituted: SI 2013/2302 Sch.1
Sch.2 para.16, amended: SI 2013/2302 Art.7
Sch.2 para.16, substituted: SI 2013/2302 Sch.1
Sch.2 para.17, amended: SI 2013/2302 Art.7
Sch.2 para.17, substituted: SI 2013/2302 Sch.1
Sch.2 para.18, substituted: SI 2013/2302 Art.7, Sch.1
Sch.2 para.19, substituted: SI 2013/2302 Sch.1
Sch.2 para.20, substituted: SI 2013/2302 Sch.1
Sch.2 para.21, added: SI 2013/2302 Art.7
Sch.2 para.21, substituted: SI 2013/2302 Sch.1

2160. Limited Partnerships (Forms) Rules 2009
Sch.1 Part 2, amended: SI 2013/1388 Sch.1

2163. Eggs and Chicks (England) Regulations 2009
Reg.3, amended: SI 2013/3235 Reg.5
Reg.8, amended: SI 2013/3235 Reg.5
Reg.11, amended: SI 2013/3235 Reg.5
Sch.1 Part 1, amended: SI 2013/3235 Reg.5
Sch.2 Part 1, substituted: SI 2013/3235 Reg.5
Sch.2 Part 2, amended: SI 2013/3235 Reg.5
Sch.3, amended: SI 2013/3235 Reg.5

2205. National Health Service (Miscellaneous Amendments Relating to Community Pharmaceutical Services and Optometrist Prescribing) Regulations 2009
Reg.29, revoked: SI 2013/349 Sch.10 para.5

Reg.30, revoked: SI 2013/349 Sch.10 para.5
Reg.31, revoked: SI 2013/349 Sch.10 para.5
Reg.32, revoked: SI 2013/349 Sch.10 para.5
Reg.33, revoked: SI 2013/349 Sch.10 para.5
Reg.34, revoked: SI 2013/349 Sch.10 para.5

2263. Infrastructure Planning (Environmental Impact Assessment) Regulations 2009
Reg.2, referred to: SI 2013/522 Reg.7
Reg.6, applied: SI 2013/522 Reg.7
Reg.8, applied: SI 2013/522 Reg.7

2264. Infrastructure Planning (Applications Prescribed Forms and Procedure) Regulations 2009
applied: SI 2013/343, SI 2013/586, SI 2013/648, SI 2013/675, SI 2013/680, SI 2013/1203, SI 2013/1752, SI 2013/1873, SI 2013/3200
Reg.2, amended: SI 2013/522 Reg.3
Reg.3, applied: SI 2013/522 Reg.7
Reg.8, applied: SI 2013/522 Reg.7
Sch.1, amended: SI 2013/522 Reg.3, SI 2013/755 Sch.4 para.330
Sch.1, substituted: SI 2013/522 Reg.3

2268. Non-Domestic Rating (Alteration of Lists and Appeals) (England) Regulations 2009
Reg.4, see *West London Aero Club v Hazel (Valuation Officer)* [2013] R.A. 386 (VT), Graham Zellick Q.C. (President)

2269. Valuation Tribunal for England (Council Tax and Rating Appeals) (Procedure) Regulations 2009
Reg.10, amended: SI 2013/465 Reg.2
Reg.17, amended: SI 2013/465 Reg.2
Reg.20A, added: SI 2013/465 Reg.2
Reg.36, amended: SI 2013/465 Reg.2
Reg.37, amended: SI 2013/465 Reg.2
Reg.38, amended: SI 2013/465 Reg.2
Reg.43, see *Naz v Redbridge LBC* [2013] EWHC 1268 (Admin), [2013] R.V.R. 226 (QBD (Admin)), David Holgate QC
Reg.43, amended: SI 2013/465 Reg.2

2270. Council Tax (Alteration of Lists and Appeals) (England) Regulations 2009
Reg.3, amended: SI 2013/467 Reg.2

2401. European Public Limited-Liability Company (Employee Involvement) (Great Britain) Regulations 2009
applied: SI 2013/1893 Sch.2
Reg.39, amended: SI 2013/1956 Sch.1 para.15

2425. Companies (Authorised Minimum) Regulations 2009
Reg.4, amended: SI 2013/472 Art.4

2436. Unregistered Companies Regulations 2009
Reg.3, referred to: SI 2013/3008 Reg.3
Sch.1, referred to: SI 2013/3008 Reg.3
Sch.1 para.10, amended: SI 2013/1972 Reg.2
Sch.1 para.10, revoked (in part): SI 2013/1972 Reg.2

2437. Companies (Companies Authorised to Register) Regulations 2009
Reg.18, referred to: SI 2013/3008 Reg.3

2477. Water Industry (Special Administration) Rules 2009
referred to: SI 2013/1582 Sch.1 para.1
Part 1 r.3, varied: SI 2013/1582 Sch.1 para.7
Part 2 r.8, varied: SI 2013/1582 Sch.1 para.7
Part 2 r.11, amended: SI 2013/472 Art.4
Part 2 r.11, varied: SI 2013/1582 Sch.1 para.7
Part 2 r.17, varied: SI 2013/1582 Sch.1 para.7
Part 2 r.18, varied: SI 2013/1582 Sch.1 para.7
Part 3 r.23, varied: SI 2013/1582 Sch.1 para.7
Part 3 r.24, varied: SI 2013/1582 Sch.1 para.7
Part 3 r.25, varied: SI 2013/1582 Sch.1 para.7
Part 4 r.35, varied: SI 2013/1582 Sch.1 para.7
Part 6 r.65, varied: SI 2013/1582 Sch.1 para.7
Part 7 r.82, varied: SI 2013/1582 Sch.1 para.7

2562. Cosmetic Products (Safety) (Amendment No.3) Regulations 2009
revoked: SI 2013/1478 Sch.1

2615. Company, Limited Liability Partnership and Business Names (Sensitive Words and Expressions) Regulations 2009
Sch.2 Part 1, amended: SI 2013/642 Art.5

2657. Court Martial Appeal Court Rules 2009
Part 3 r.16, substituted: SI 2013/2524 r.3

2680. School Staffing (England) Regulations 2009
Reg.3, amended: SI 2013/1940 Reg.2
Reg.13, amended: SI 2013/1940 Reg.2
Reg.18, amended: SI 2013/1940 Reg.2
Reg.25, amended: SI 2013/1940 Reg.2
Sch.2 para.4A, added: SI 2013/1940 Reg.2
Sch.2 para.5A, added: SI 2013/1940 Reg.2

2726. Greater Manchester (Light Rapid Transit System) (Exemptions) Order 2009
revoked: SI 2013/339 Art.18

2767. RTM Companies (Model Articles) (England) Regulations 2009
Sch.1, revoked: 2013 c.8 s.3

2773. Criminal Justice Act 2003 (Conditional Cautions Financial Penalties) Order 2009
revoked: SI 2013/615 Art.3

2781. Crime and Disorder Act 1998 (Youth Conditional Cautions Financial Penalties) Order 2009
revoked: SI 2013/608 Art.3

2798. Statutory Auditors and Third Country Auditors (Amendment) Regulations 2009
revoked: SI 2013/1672 Sch.1

2957. Waste Electrical and Electronic Equipment (Amendment) Regulations 2009
revoked: SI 2013/3113 Reg.96

2971. Mutual Societies (Transfers of Business) (Tax) Regulations 2009
Reg.3, amended: SI 2013/496 Sch.11 para.17

2979. Audiovisual Media Services Regulations 2009
Reg.11, revoked (in part): SI 2013/2217 Reg.2
Reg.13, revoked (in part): SI 2013/2217 Reg.2

2981. Legislative and Regulatory Reform (Regulatory Functions) (Amendment) Order 2009
Sch.1, amended: SI 2013/1575 Sch.1 para.24

2982. Company, Limited Liability Partnership and Business Names (Public Authorities) Regulations 2009
Sch.1, amended: SI 2013/472 Sch.2 para.177, SI 2013/1466 Sch.1 para.8

2984. School Organisation (Establishment and Discontinuance of Schools)(England)(Amendment) Regulations 2009
revoked: SI 2013/3109 Reg.3

2999. Provision of Services Regulations 2009
Reg.2, amended: SI 2013/3115 Sch.2 para.73
Reg.18, see *R. (on the application of Hemming (t/a Simply Pleasure Ltd)) v Westminster City Council* [2013] EWCA Civ 591, [2013] P.T.S.R. 1377 (CA (Civ Div)), Lord Dyson (M.R.)

3001. Offshore Funds (Tax) Regulations 2009
Reg.2, amended: SI 2013/1770 Reg.2
Reg.12, applied: SI 2013/2819 Reg.22
Reg.17, amended: SI 2013/661 Reg.2
Reg.17, applied: SI 2013/2819 Reg.23
Reg.18, amended: SI 2013/2819 Reg.43
Reg.20, amended: SI 2013/605 Reg.7
Reg.21, amended: SI 2013/605 Reg.7
Reg.23, substituted: SI 2013/1810 Reg.4
Reg.24, amended: SI 2013/605 Reg.7
Reg.35, substituted: SI 2013/1400 Reg.15
Reg.36, substituted: SI 2013/1400 Reg.15
Reg.39, amended: SI 2013/1400 Reg.15
Reg.47, amended: SI 2013/1400 Reg.15
Reg.53, amended: SI 2013/1411 Reg.3
Reg.55, amended: SI 2013/1411 Reg.4
Reg.63, amended: SI 2013/1411 Reg.5
Reg.72A, added: SI 2013/1411 Reg.6
Reg.72B, added: SI 2013/1411 Reg.6
Reg.72C, added: SI 2013/1411 Reg.6
Reg.74, amended: SI 2013/472 Sch.2 para.178, SI 2013/1773 Sch.2 para.20
Reg.80, applied: SI 2013/2819 Reg.22
Reg.90, applied: SI 2013/1411 Reg.1
Reg.92, amended: SI 2013/1411 Reg.7
Reg.92A, revoked: SI 2013/1411 Reg.8
Reg.92B, revoked: SI 2013/1411 Reg.8
Reg.92C, revoked: SI 2013/1411 Reg.8
Reg.94A, amended: SI 2013/1411 Reg.9
Reg.99, amended: SI 2013/1411 Reg.10
Reg.104, amended: SI 2013/1411 Reg.14
Reg.106, amended: SI 2013/1411 Reg.11
Reg.124A, added: SI 2013/1770 Reg.2
Reg.124B, added: SI 2013/1770 Reg.2
Sch.3 Part 2, amended: SI 2013/1411 Reg.12

3008. Burma (Restrictive Measures) (Overseas Territories) Order 2009
revoked: SI 2013/1447 Art.15
Art.26, amended: SI 2013/472 Sch.2 para.179

3011. Double Taxation Relief and International Tax Enforcement (Guernsey) Order 2009
Sch.1, added: SI 2013/3154 Sch.1 Part 2

3012. Double Taxation Relief and International Tax Enforcement (Jersey) Order 2009
Sch.1, added: SI 2013/3151 Sch.1 Part 2

3015. Air Navigation Order 2009
applied: SI 2013/343 Sch.1 para.5, Sch.2 para.2, SI 2013/1203 Sch.1 para.16, SI 2013/1734 Sch.1 para.17
Art.52, amended: SI 2013/3169 Art.3
Art.52, revoked (in part): SI 2013/3169 Art.3
Art.79, amended: SI 2013/3169 Art.4
Art.161, enabled: SI 2013/52, SI 2013/54, SI 2013/76, SI 2013/86, SI 2013/87, SI 2013/88, SI 2013/89, SI 2013/90, SI 2013/94, SI 2013/95, SI 2013/156, SI 2013/254, SI 2013/255, SI 2013/256, SI 2013/392, SI 2013/406, SI 2013/424, SI 2013/831, SI 2013/832, SI 2013/834, SI 2013/835, SI 2013/836, SI 2013/837, SI 2013/839, SI 2013/878, SI 2013/918, SI 2013/919, SI 2013/921, SI 2013/922, SI 2013/930, SI 2013/931, SI 2013/932, SI 2013/1038, SI 2013/1040, SI 2013/1051, SI 2013/1052, SI 2013/1106, SI 2013/1107, SI 2013/1130, SI 2013/1131, SI 2013/1215, SI 2013/1216, SI 2013/1217, SI 2013/1218, SI 2013/1416, SI 2013/1417, SI 2013/1418, SI 2013/1459, SI 2013/1516, SI 2013/1757, SI 2013/1794, SI 2013/1833, SI 2013/1848, SI 2013/1885, SI 2013/2054, SI 2013/2262, SI 2013/2321, SI 2013/2322, SI 2013/2421, SI 2013/2585, SI 2013/2990
Art.246, amended: SI 2013/3169 Art.5
Art.255, amended: SI 2013/3169 Art.5
Sch.13 Part C, amended: SI 2013/3169 Art.6

3040. Administrative Justice and Tribunals Council (Listed Tribunals) (Amendment) Order 2009
revoked: SI 2013/2042 Sch.1 para.78

3042. Flood Risk Regulations 2009
Reg.8C, added: SI 2013/755 Sch.4 para.332
Reg.9, amended: SI 2013/755 Sch.4 para.333
Reg.10, amended: SI 2013/755 Sch.4 para.334
Reg.11, amended: SI 2013/755 Sch.4 para.335
Reg.12, amended: SI 2013/755 Sch.4 para.336
Reg.13, amended: SI 2013/755 Sch.4 para.337
Reg.14, amended: SI 2013/755 Sch.4 para.338

Reg.15, amended: SI 2013/755 Sch.4 para.339
Reg.16, amended: SI 2013/755 Sch.4 para.340
Reg.18, amended: SI 2013/755 Sch.4 para.340
Reg.19, amended: SI 2013/755 Sch.4 para.341
Reg.20, amended: SI 2013/755 Sch.4 para.342
Reg.21, amended: SI 2013/755 Sch.4 para.343
Reg.22, amended: SI 2013/755 Sch.4 para.344
Reg.23, amended: SI 2013/755 Sch.4 para.345
Reg.23, substituted: SI 2013/755 Sch.4 para.345
Reg.25, amended: SI 2013/755 Sch.4 para.346
Reg.26, amended: SI 2013/755 Sch.4 para.347
Reg.27, amended: SI 2013/755 Sch.4 para.348
Reg.28, amended: SI 2013/755 Sch.4 para.349
Reg.29, amended: SI 2013/755 Sch.4 para.350
Reg.29, substituted: SI 2013/755 Sch.4 para.350
Reg.32, amended: SI 2013/755 Sch.4 para.351
Reg.32, substituted: SI 2013/755 Sch.4 para.351
Reg.35, amended: SI 2013/755 Sch.4 para.352
Reg.36, amended: SI 2013/755 Sch.4 para.353
Reg.36, revoked (in part): SI 2013/755 Sch.4 para.353

3050. Crime and Disorder Strategies (Prescribed Descriptions) (Wales) Order 2009
Art.3, amended: SI 2013/755 Sch.5 para.55

3056. Scottish and Northern Ireland Banknote Regulations 2009
Reg.17, amended: SI 2013/472 Sch.2 para.180
Reg.31, amended: SI 2013/472 Art.4

3069. Ministry of Defence Police (Conduct) Regulations 2009
Reg.3, amended: SI 2013/602 Sch.2 para.95

3070. Ministry of Defence Police Appeals Tribunals Regulations 2009
Reg.3, amended: SI 2013/602 Sch.2 para.96
Reg.5, amended: SI 2013/602 Sch.2 para.96

3093. Local Government Pension Scheme (Management and Investment of Funds) Regulations 2009
Reg.3, amended: SI 2013/472 Art.4, Sch.2 para.181
Reg.4, applied: SI 2013/2356 Reg.69
Reg.6, amended: SI 2013/472 Art.4
Reg.7, amended: SI 2013/472 Art.4
Reg.12, applied: SI 2013/2356 Reg.57, Reg.58
Sch.1, amended: SI 2013/410 Reg.2
Sch.1, amended: SI 2013/472 Art.4

3097. Welsh Health Specialised Services Committee (Wales) Regulations 2009
Reg.2, amended: SI 2013/235 Sch.2 para.132

3101. Private Water Supplies Regulations 2009
Reg.17, amended: SI 2013/235 Sch.2 para.133
Sch.4 para.1, revoked (in part): SI 2013/235 Sch.2 para.133

3112. Care Quality Commission (Registration) Regulations 2009
Reg.2, amended: SI 2013/235 Sch.2 para.134
Reg.9, amended: SI 2013/235 Sch.2 para.134
Reg.9, revoked (in part): SI 2013/235 Sch.2 para.134
Reg.16, amended: SI 2013/235 Sch.2 para.134

3151. Child Support (Management of Payments and Arrears) Regulations 2009
Reg.12, revoked (in part): SI 2013/2380 Reg.7

3216. Waste Electrical and Electronic Equipment (Amendment) (No.2) Regulations 2009
revoked: SI 2013/3113 Reg.96

3219. Sheep and Goats (Records, Identification and Movement) (England) Order 2009
Art.21, applied: SI 2013/109 Sch.1 para.4
Art.22, applied: SI 2013/109 Sch.1 para.4
Art.24, applied: SI 2013/109 Sch.1 para.4

3222. Medicines (Products for Human Use) (Amendments to Fees for Variations) Regulations 2009
revoked: SI 2013/532 Sch.9

3226. Northern Rock plc Transfer Order 2009
Art.9, amended: SI 2013/472 Art.4
Art.20, amended: SI 2013/472 Sch.2 para.182
Art.21, amended: SI 2013/472 Sch.2 para.182

3235. Food Enzymes Regulations 2009
Reg.3, revoked: SI 2013/2210 Sch.5
Reg.4, revoked: SI 2013/2210 Sch.5
Reg.5, revoked: SI 2013/2210 Sch.5
Reg.6, revoked: SI 2013/2210 Sch.5
Reg.7, revoked (in part): SI 2013/2210 Sch.5
Reg.8, revoked: SI 2013/2210 Sch.5
Reg.9, revoked: SI 2013/2775 Reg.20

3238. Food Additives (England) Regulations 2009
Reg.3, revoked: SI 2013/2210 Sch.5
Reg.4, revoked: SI 2013/2210 Sch.5
Reg.5, revoked: SI 2013/2210 Sch.5
Reg.6, revoked: SI 2013/2210 Sch.5
Reg.7, revoked: SI 2013/2210 Sch.5
Reg.8, revoked: SI 2013/2210 Sch.5
Reg.9, revoked: SI 2013/2210 Sch.5
Reg.10, revoked: SI 2013/2210 Sch.5
Reg.11, revoked: SI 2013/2210 Sch.5
Reg.12, revoked: SI 2013/2210 Sch.5
Reg.13, revoked: SI 2013/2210 Sch.5
Reg.14, revoked: SI 2013/2210 Sch.5
Reg.15, revoked: SI 2013/2210 Sch.5
Reg.16, revoked: SI 2013/2210 Sch.5
Reg.17, revoked: SI 2013/2210 Sch.5
Reg.18, revoked (in part): SI 2013/2210 Sch.5
Reg.20, revoked: SI 2013/2210 Sch.5
Sch.1, revoked: SI 2013/2210 Sch.5

3245. Public Service Vehicles (Registration of Local Services) (Quality Contracts Schemes) (England and Wales) Regulations 2009

Reg.4, amended: SI 2013/1644 Sch.4
Reg.5, amended: SI 2013/1644 Sch.4
Reg.6, amended: SI 2013/1644 Sch.4
Reg.7, amended: SI 2013/1644 Sch.4
Reg.10, amended: SI 2013/1644 Sch.4

3246. Quality Contracts Schemes (Application of TUPE) Regulations 2009

Reg.2, amended: SI 2013/1644 Sch.4
Reg.9, amended: SI 2013/1644 Sch.4

3255. Official Feed and Food Controls (England) Regulations 2009

Reg.2, amended: SI 2013/2996 Reg.37
Reg.3, amended: SI 2013/2996 Reg.37
Reg.38, amended: SI 2013/264 Reg.11
Reg.41, amended: SI 2013/2996 Reg.37
Sch.2, amended: SI 2013/2996 Reg.37
Sch.3, amended: SI 2013/2996 Reg.37

3269. International Joint Investigation Teams (International Agreement) Order 2009

referred to: 2013 c.22 Sch.8 para.7
Art.2, varied: 2013 c.22 Sch.8 para.7

3276. Designation of Schools Having a Religious Character (Independent Schools) (England) (No.3) Order 2009

Sch.1, amended: SI 2013/2162 Sch.2

3293. Quality Partnership Schemes (Wales) Regulations 2009

Reg.2, amended: SI 2013/1644 Sch.6
Reg.5, amended: SI 2013/1644 Sch.6
Reg.7, amended: SI 2013/1644 Sch.6
Reg.8, amended: SI 2013/1644 Sch.6
Reg.10, amended: SI 2013/1644 Sch.6
Reg.11, amended: SI 2013/1644 Sch.6
Reg.12, amended: SI 2013/1644 Sch.6
Reg.13, amended: SI 2013/1644 Sch.6
Reg.14, amended: SI 2013/1644 Sch.6
Reg.15, amended: SI 2013/1644 Sch.6
Reg.16, amended: SI 2013/1644 Sch.6
Reg.18, amended: SI 2013/1644 Sch.6

3328. Criminal Defence Service (Contribution Orders) Regulations 2009

Reg.2, amended: SI 2013/591 Sch.1 para.41, SI 2013/626 Reg.5, SI 2013/630 Reg.67

3342. Town and Country Planning (Environmental Impact Assessment) (Undetermined Reviews of Old Mineral Permissions) (Wales) Regulations 2009

Reg.2, amended: SI 2013/755 Sch.5 para.56
Reg.2, revoked (in part): SI 2013/755 Sch.5 para.56

3344. Eels (England and Wales) Regulations 2009

Part 4, applied: SI 2013/1933 Art.4, Sch.16 para.12
Reg.2, amended: SI 2013/755 Sch.4 para.355
Reg.4, amended: SI 2013/755 Sch.4 para.356
Reg.6, amended: SI 2013/755 Sch.4 para.357
Reg.7, amended: SI 2013/755 Sch.4 para.358
Reg.8, amended: SI 2013/755 Sch.4 para.359
Reg.12, amended: SI 2013/755 Sch.4 para.359
Reg.13, amended: SI 2013/755 Sch.4 para.359
Reg.14, amended: SI 2013/755 Sch.4 para.359
Reg.17, amended: SI 2013/755 Sch.4 para.359
Reg.20, amended: SI 2013/755 Sch.4 para.359
Reg.21, amended: SI 2013/755 Sch.4 para.359
Reg.26, amended: SI 2013/755 Sch.4 para.360
Sch.1 para.3, amended: SI 2013/755 Sch.4 para.361
Sch.1 para.4, amended: SI 2013/755 Sch.4 para.361
Sch.1 para.5, amended: SI 2013/755 Sch.4 para.361

3365. Agriculture (Cross compliance) (No.2) Regulations 2009

Sch.1 para.1, amended: SI 2013/3231 Reg.2

3367. Cosmetic Products (Safety) (Amendment No.4) Regulations 2009

revoked: SI 2013/1478 Sch.1

3376. Official Feed and Food Controls (Wales) Regulations 2009

Reg.2, amended: SI 2013/3007 Reg.4, SI 2013/3049 Reg.3
Reg.38, amended: SI 2013/479 Reg.11
Reg.41, amended: SI 2013/3007 Reg.4
Sch.1, amended: SI 2013/3049 Reg.3

3377. Food Enzymes (Wales) Regulations 2009

Reg.3, revoked: SI 2013/2591 Sch.5
Reg.4, revoked: SI 2013/2591 Sch.5
Reg.5, revoked: SI 2013/2591 Sch.5
Reg.6, revoked: SI 2013/2591 Sch.5
Reg.7, revoked (in part): SI 2013/2591 Sch.5
Reg.8, revoked: SI 2013/2591 Sch.5
Reg.9, revoked: SI 2013/2750 Reg.20

3378. Food Additives (Wales) Regulations 2009

Reg.3, revoked: SI 2013/2591 Sch.5
Reg.4, revoked: SI 2013/2591 Sch.5
Reg.5, revoked: SI 2013/2591 Sch.5
Reg.6, revoked: SI 2013/2591 Sch.5
Reg.7, revoked: SI 2013/2591 Sch.5
Reg.8, revoked: SI 2013/2591 Sch.5
Reg.9, revoked: SI 2013/2591 Sch.5
Reg.10, revoked: SI 2013/2591 Sch.5
Reg.11, revoked: SI 2013/2591 Sch.5
Reg.12, revoked: SI 2013/2591 Sch.5
Reg.13, revoked: SI 2013/2591 Sch.5
Reg.14, revoked: SI 2013/2591 Sch.5
Reg.15, revoked: SI 2013/2591 Sch.5
Reg.16, revoked: SI 2013/2591 Sch.5

Reg.17, revoked: SI 2013/2591 Sch.5
Reg.18, revoked (in part): SI 2013/2591 Sch.5
Reg.20, revoked: SI 2013/2591 Sch.5
Sch.1, revoked: SI 2013/2591 Sch.5

2010

5. Employers Duties (Registration and Compliance) Regulations 2010
Reg.3, amended: SI 2013/2556 Reg.4
Reg.4, amended: SI 2013/2556 Reg.4

17. National Lottery (Annual Licence Fees) Regulations 2010
Reg.2, amended: SI 2013/2329 Sch.1 para.40

19. Social Security (Contributions Credits for Parents and Carers) Regulations 2010
Reg.2, amended: SI 2013/388 Sch.1 para.46, SI 2013/591 Sch.1 para.44

21. Transfer of Functions of the Asylum and Immigration Tribunal Order 2010
Sch.2 para.28, revoked: SI 2013/2042 Sch.1 para.80

22. Transfer of Tribunal Functions Order 2010
Sch.3 para.134, revoked: SI 2013/349 Sch.10 para.5
Sch.3 para.135, revoked: SI 2013/349 Sch.10 para.5
Sch.3 para.136, revoked: SI 2013/349 Sch.10 para.5
Sch.3 para.143, revoked: SI 2013/2042 Sch.1 para.81
Sch.3 para.146, revoked (in part): SI 2013/472 Sch.1

35. Banking Act 2009 (Exclusion of Insurers) Order 2010
Art.2, amended: SI 2013/472 Art.4

42. First-tier Tribunal (Gambling) Fees Order 2010
Art.2, amended: SI 2013/2302 Art.9
Art.3, substituted: SI 2013/2302 Art.9
Art.4, revoked: SI 2013/2302 Art.9
Art.5, revoked: SI 2013/2302 Art.9
Sch.1, substituted: SI 2013/2302 Art.9
Sch.2 para.1, added: SI 2013/2302 Sch.1
Sch.2 para.2, added: SI 2013/2302 Sch.1
Sch.2 para.3, added: SI 2013/2302 Sch.1
Sch.2 para.4, added: SI 2013/2302 Sch.1
Sch.2 para.5, added: SI 2013/2302 Sch.1
Sch.2 para.6, added: SI 2013/2302 Sch.1
Sch.2 para.7, added: SI 2013/2302 Sch.1
Sch.2 para.8, added: SI 2013/2302 Sch.1
Sch.2 para.9, added: SI 2013/2302 Sch.1
Sch.2 para.10, added: SI 2013/2302 Sch.1
Sch.2 para.11, added: SI 2013/2302 Sch.1
Sch.2 para.12, added: SI 2013/2302 Sch.1
Sch.2 para.13, added: SI 2013/2302 Sch.1
Sch.2 para.14, added: SI 2013/2302 Sch.1
Sch.2 para.15, added: SI 2013/2302 Sch.1
Sch.2 para.16, added: SI 2013/2302 Sch.1
Sch.2 para.17, added: SI 2013/2302 Sch.1
Sch.2 para.18, added: SI 2013/2302 Sch.1
Sch.2 para.19, added: SI 2013/2302 Sch.1
Sch.2 para.20, added: SI 2013/2302 Sch.1

60. Criminal Procedure Rules 2010
see *R. (on the application of Guardian News and Media Ltd) v City of Westminster Magistrates' Court* [2012] EWCA Civ 420, [2013] Q.B. 618 (CA (Civ Div)), Lord Neuberger (M.R.)

66. Private Water Supplies (Wales) Regulations 2010
Reg.17, amended: SI 2013/235 Sch.2 para.142
Sch.4 para.1, revoked (in part): SI 2013/235 Sch.2 para.142

76. National Health Service (Functions of the First-tier Tribunal relating to Primary Medical, Dental and Ophthalmic Services) Regulations 2010
Reg.2, amended: SI 2013/235 Sch.2 para.143
Reg.3, amended: SI 2013/235 Sch.2 para.143
Reg.4, amended: SI 2013/235 Sch.2 para.143
Reg.5, amended: SI 2013/235 Sch.2 para.143
Reg.6, amended: SI 2013/235 Sch.2 para.143
Reg.7, amended: SI 2013/235 Sch.2 para.143

93. Agency Workers Regulations 2010
Reg.18, amended: 2013 c.24 Sch.3 para.6

102. Infrastructure Planning (Interested Parties) Regulations 2010
Reg.2, amended: SI 2013/522 Reg.4
Sch.1, amended: SI 2013/522 Reg.4, SI 2013/755 Sch.4 para.362
Sch.1, substituted: SI 2013/522 Reg.4

103. Infrastructure Planning (Examination Procedure) Rules 2010
applied: SI 2013/586, SI 2013/648, SI 2013/675, SI 2013/1734, SI 2013/1752, SI 2013/1873, SI 2013/2809, SI 2013/3200

104. Infrastructure Planning (Compulsory Acquisition) Regulations 2010
Reg.2, amended: SI 2013/522 Reg.5
Sch.2, amended: SI 2013/522 Reg.5, SI 2013/755 Sch.4 para.363
Sch.2, substituted: SI 2013/522 Reg.5

105. Infrastructure Planning (Miscellaneous Prescribed Provisions) Regulations 2010
Sch.1 Part 1 para.11, revoked: SI 2013/520 Reg.2
Sch.1 Part 1 para.12, revoked: SI 2013/520 Reg.2
Sch.1 Part 1 para.13, revoked: SI 2013/520 Reg.2
Sch.1 Part 1 para.15, revoked: SI 2013/520 Reg.2
Sch.1 Part 1 para.18, revoked: SI 2013/520 Reg.2
Sch.1 Part 1 para.19, revoked: SI 2013/520 Reg.2

Sch.1 Part 1 para.22, revoked: SI 2013/520 Reg.2
Sch.1 Part 1 para.23, revoked: SI 2013/520 Reg.2
Sch.1 Part 1 para.24, revoked: SI 2013/520 Reg.2
Sch.1 Part 1 para.25, revoked: SI 2013/520 Reg.2
Sch.1 Part 1 para.33, revoked: SI 2013/520 Reg.2
Sch.1 Part 1 para.34, revoked: SI 2013/520 Reg.2
Sch.1 Part 1 para.35, revoked: SI 2013/520 Reg.2
Sch.1 Part 1 para.37, revoked: SI 2013/520 Reg.2
Sch.1 Part 1 para.40, revoked: SI 2013/520 Reg.2
Sch.1 Part 1 para.41, revoked: SI 2013/520 Reg.2
Sch.1 Part 2 para.37, added: SI 2013/520 Reg.2
Sch.1 Part 2 para.38, added: SI 2013/520 Reg.2
Sch.1 Part 2 para.39, added: SI 2013/520 Reg.2
Sch.1 Part 2 para.40, added: SI 2013/520 Reg.2
Sch.1 Part 2 para.41, added: SI 2013/520 Reg.2
Sch.1 Part 2 para.42, added: SI 2013/520 Reg.2
Sch.1 Part 2 para.43, added: SI 2013/520 Reg.2
Sch.1 Part 2 para.44, added: SI 2013/520 Reg.2
Sch.1 Part 2 para.45, added: SI 2013/520 Reg.2
Sch.1 Part 2 para.46, added: SI 2013/520 Reg.2
Sch.1 Part 2 para.47, added: SI 2013/520 Reg.2
Sch.1 Part 2 para.48, added: SI 2013/520 Reg.2
Sch.1 Part 2 para.49, added: SI 2013/520 Reg.2
Sch.1 Part 2 para.50, added: SI 2013/520 Reg.2
Sch.1 Part 2 para.51, added: SI 2013/520 Reg.2
Sch.1 Part 2 para.52, added: SI 2013/520 Reg.2

106. Infrastructure Planning (Fees) Regulations 2010
Reg.9, amended: SI 2013/498 Reg.2

123. Regulation of Investigatory Powers (Covert Human Intelligence Sources Matters Subject to Legal Privilege) Order 2010
Art.8, applied: SI 2013/2788 Art.3

127. Crime and Disorder Act 1998 (Youth Conditional Cautions Code of Practice) Order 2010
revoked: SI 2013/613 Art.3

132. Export Control (North Korea) (Amendment) Order 2010
revoked: SI 2013/3182 Sch.1

167. Hill Farm Allowance Regulations 2010
applied: SI 2013/109 Reg.4, Reg.5

231. Pharmacy Order 2010
Art.66, amended: SI 2013/235 Sch.2 para.144
Sch.1 para.1, revoked (in part): SI 2013/235 Sch.2 para.144
Sch.4 Part 2 para.37, revoked (in part): SSI 2013/50 Sch.5
Sch.4 Part 2 para.53, revoked: SI 2013/349 Sch.10 para.5
Sch.4 Part 2 para.65, revoked: SI 2013/1478 Sch.5 para.28

234. General and Specialist Medical Practice (Education, Training and Qualifications) Order 2010
Sch.3 Part 2 para.16, revoked (in part): SSI 2013/174 Sch.1

265. Mercury Export and Data (Enforcement) Regulations 2010
Reg.4, amended: SI 2013/755 Sch.4 para.364

288. Community Health Councils (Constitution, Membership and Procedures) (Wales) Regulations 2010
Reg.2, amended: SI 2013/235 Sch.2 para.145
Reg.12, amended: SI 2013/235 Sch.2 para.145
Reg.29, applied: SI 2013/898 Sch.4 para.2, Sch.5 para.1, Sch.6 para.2
Reg.29, revoked (in part): SI 2013/235 Sch.2 para.145

333. Notification of Conventional Tower Cranes Regulations 2010
revoked: SI 2013/448 Sch.1

405. National Health Service (Functions of Strategic Health Authorities and Primary Care Trusts and Administration Arrangements) (England) (Amendment) Regulations 2010
revoked: SI 2013/235 Sch.2 para.200

420. Fish Labelling (England) Regulations 2010
revoked: SI 2013/1768 Reg.16

424. Welfare Reform Act 2009 (Section 26) (Consequential Amendments) Regulations 2010
Reg.10, revoked: SI 2013/458 Sch.1
Reg.11, revoked: SI 2013/458 Sch.1

432. Rail Vehicle Accessibility (Non-Interoperable Rail System) Regulations 2010
Sch.1 Part 1, referred to: SI 2013/3031 Art.2

435. Rail Vehicle Accessibility (London Underground Metropolitan Line S8 Vehicles) Exemption Order 2010
Art.4, amended: SI 2013/1931 Art.4
Art.4, revoked (in part): SI 2013/1931 Art.4
Art.6, revoked (in part): SI 2013/1931 Art.4
Sch.1, revoked: SI 2013/1931 Art.4

447. Education (Student Support) (European University Institute) Regulations 2010
Reg.27, amended: SI 2013/630 Reg.53
Sch.2 Part 2 para.4, amended: SI 2013/1728 Reg.24

460. Animal Gatherings Order 2010
Art.8, amended: SI 2013/2952 Sch.2 para.8

473. Postgraduate Medical Education and Training Order of Council 2010
Art.6, applied: SI 2013/335 Reg.26
Art.10, amended: SI 2013/3036 Reg.3

480. Regulation of Investigatory Powers (Communications Data) Order 2010
referred to: SI 2013/1554 r.6_27
Sch.1, amended: SI 2013/602 Sch.2 para.97
Sch.2 Part 1, amended: SI 2013/472 Sch.2 para.184, SI 2013/602 Sch.2 para.97
Sch.2 Part 2, amended: SI 2013/602 Sch.2 para.97

490. Conservation of Habitats and Species Regulations 2010

see *Elliott v Secretary of State for Communities and Local Government* [2012] EWHC 1574 (Admin), [2013] Env. L.R. 5 (QBD (Admin)), Keith, J.; see *R. (on the application of Champion) v North Norfolk DC* [2013] EWHC 1065 (Admin), [2013] Env. L.R. 38 (QBD (Admin)), James Dingemans Q.C.; see *R. (on the application of Prideaux) v Buckinghamshire CC* [2013] EWHC 1054 (Admin), [2013] Env. L.R. 32 (QBD (Admin)), Lindblom, J.
Reg.5, amended: SI 2013/755 Sch.4 para.366
Reg.9, amended: SI 2013/755 Sch.4 para.367
Reg.9, see *Elliott v Secretary of State for Communities and Local Government* [2012] EWHC 1574 (Admin), [2013] Env. L.R. 5 (QBD (Admin)), Keith, J.; see *R. (on the application of Prideaux) v Buckinghamshire CC* [2013] EWHC 1054 (Admin), [2013] Env. L.R. 32 (QBD (Admin)), Lindblom, J.
Reg.9A, amended: SI 2013/755 Sch.4 para.368
Reg.17, amended: SI 2013/755 Sch.4 para.369
Reg.41, see *Eaton v Natural England* [2012] EWHC 2401 (Admin), [2013] 1 C.M.L.R. 10 (QBD (Admin)), Judge Waksman Q.C.
Reg.53, see *Elliott v Secretary of State for Communities and Local Government* [2012] EWHC 1574 (Admin), [2013] Env. L.R. 5 (QBD (Admin)), Keith, J.
Reg.56, amended: SI 2013/755 Sch.4 para.370
Reg.61, see *Feeney v Secretary of State for Transport* [2013] EWHC 1238 (Admin), [2013] Env. L.R. 34 (QBD (Admin)), Ouseley, J.
Reg.64, see *R. (on the application of Hughes) v Carmarthenshire CC* [2012] EWCA Civ 1509, [2013] Env. L.R. 17 (CA (Civ Div)), Sullivan, L.J.
Reg.99, amended: SI 2013/755 Sch.4 para.371
Reg.127, amended: SI 2013/755 Sch.4 para.372
Reg.129, amended: SI 2013/755 Sch.4 para.373

493. Employment Relations Act 1999 (Blacklists) Regulations 2010

Reg.5, see *Miller v Interserve Industrial Services Ltd* [2013] I.C.R. 445 (EAT), Underhill, J.

521. Regulation of Investigatory Powers (Directed Surveillance and Covert Human Intelligence Sources) Order 2010

Art.1, amended: SI 2013/2788 Art.8
Art.1A, added: SI 2013/2788 Art.9
Art.3, amended: SI 2013/2788 Art.10, Art.11
Art.4, amended: SI 2013/2788 Art.12
Art.5, amended: SI 2013/2788 Art.13, Art.14
Art.6A, added: SI 2013/2788 Art.15
Sch.1 Part 1, amended: SI 2013/472 Sch.2 para.185, SI 2013/602 Sch.2 para.98, SI 2013/2788 Art.16
Sch.1 Part 1A, added: SI 2013/2788 Art.16
Sch.1 Part 2, amended: SI 2013/755 Sch.4 para.374

534. Food Hygiene (England) (Amendment) Regulations 2010

revoked: SI 2013/2996 Sch.9

590. Children's Trust Board (Relevant Partners) (Exceptions) (England) Regulations 2010

Reg.2, amended: SI 2013/235 Sch.2 para.146

593. Excise Goods (Holding, Movement and Duty Point) Regulations 2010

Reg.3, amended: SI 2013/3210 Reg.3

634. National Health Service (Miscellaneous Amendments Relating to Ophthalmic Services) Regulations 2010

Reg.4, revoked: SI 2013/461 Sch.4

638. Federation of Maintained Schools and Miscellaneous Amendments (Wales) Regulations 2010

Reg.32, applied: SI 2013/2124 Reg.4, Reg.5
Reg.38, applied: SI 2013/2124 Reg.4, Reg.5
Reg.50, applied: SI 2013/2127 Reg.3, Reg.4
Reg.51, referred to: SI 2013/2127 Reg.3, Reg.4
Reg.64, applied: SI 2013/2127 Reg.4
Reg.65, applied: SI 2013/2127 Reg.4
Reg.66, applied: SI 2013/2127 Reg.4
Reg.67, applied: SI 2013/2127 Reg.4
Reg.67, referred to: SI 2013/2127 Reg.4
Sch.7, applied: SI 2013/2124 Reg.4, Reg.5
Sch.7 para.5, applied: SI 2013/2124 Reg.4, Reg.5
Sch.7 para.11A, added: SI 2013/2124 Reg.7
Sch.7 para.13, amended: SI 2013/2124 Reg.7

639. Water Resources (Control of Pollution) (Silage, Slurry and Agricultural Fuel Oil) (England) Regulations 2010

Reg.9, substituted: SI 2013/1001 Reg.26

649. Gangmasters Licensing (Exclusions) Regulations 2010

revoked: SI 2013/2216 Reg.3

650. Registered Pension Schemes etc (Information) (Prescribed Descriptions of Persons) Regulations 2010

Reg.2A, added: SI 2013/2259 Reg.25
Reg.3, amended: SI 2013/2259 Reg.26

658. Health Protection (Part 2A Orders) Regulations 2010

Reg.10, amended: SI 2013/235 Sch.2 para.147
Reg.11, amended: SI 2013/235 Sch.2 para.147

659. Health Protection (Notification) Regulations 2010

Reg.1, amended: SI 2013/235 Sch.2 para.148
Reg.4, amended: SI 2013/235 Sch.2 para.148
Reg.5, amended: SI 2013/235 Sch.2 para.148
Reg.6, amended: SI 2013/235 Sch.2 para.148

671. Housing and Regeneration Act 2008 (Consequential Provisions) (No.2) Order 2010
Sch.1 para.62, revoked: SI 2013/458 Sch.1
Sch.1 para.63, revoked: SI 2013/458 Sch.1

672. Authorisation of Frequency Use for the Provision of Mobile Satellite Services (European Union) Regulations 2010
Reg.1, amended: SI 2013/174 Reg.3
Reg.4, amended: SI 2013/174 Reg.4
Reg.5A, added: SI 2013/174 Reg.5
Reg.5B, added: SI 2013/174 Reg.5
Reg.5C, added: SI 2013/174 Reg.5
Reg.5D, added: SI 2013/174 Reg.5
Reg.5E, added: SI 2013/174 Reg.5
Reg.5F, added: SI 2013/174 Reg.5
Reg.6, revoked: SI 2013/174 Reg.6
Reg.7, revoked: SI 2013/174 Reg.6
Reg.8, revoked: SI 2013/174 Reg.6
Reg.9, revoked: SI 2013/174 Reg.6
Reg.10, amended: SI 2013/174 Reg.7
Reg.14, added: SI 2013/174 Reg.8

675. Environmental Permitting (England and Wales) Regulations 2010
applied: SI 2013/586 Art.12, SI 2013/3200 Art.14
Reg.2, amended: SI 2013/390 Reg.4, SI 2013/755 Sch.4 para.376, SI 2013/2952 Sch.2 para.9
Reg.2, revoked (in part): SI 2013/390 Reg.4
Reg.3, amended: SI 2013/390 Reg.5, SI 2013/766 Reg.2
Reg.5, amended: SI 2013/390 Reg.6
Reg.6, amended: SI 2013/390 Reg.7
Reg.7, amended: SI 2013/390 Reg.8
Reg.8, amended: SI 2013/390 Reg.9
Reg.12, amended: SI 2013/390 Reg.10
Reg.12, applied: SI 2013/198 Art.5, SI 2013/675 Art.16, SI 2013/1933 Art.13, SI 2013/1967 Art.13, SI 2013/2587 Art.20, SI 2013/2808 Art.16, SI 2013/2809 Art.13, SI 2013/3200 Art.14, SI 2013/3244 Art.17
Reg.17, amended: SI 2013/390 Reg.11
Reg.18, amended: SI 2013/390 Reg.12
Reg.32, amended: SI 2013/390 Reg.13, SI 2013/755 Sch.4 para.377
Reg.33, amended: SI 2013/755 Sch.4 para.378
Reg.35, amended: SI 2013/390 Reg.14
Reg.36, amended: SI 2013/390 Reg.15
Reg.37, see *R. (on the application of European Metal Recycling Ltd) v Environment Agency* [2012] EWHC 2361 (Admin), [2013] Env. L.R. 14 (QBD (Admin)), Judge Pelling Q.C.
Reg.38, applied: SI 2013/680 Art.15, SI 2013/1873 Art.11, SI 2013/2258 Sch.1 Part 2
Reg.40, amended: SI 2013/390 Reg.16
Reg.46, amended: SI 2013/755 Sch.4 para.379
Reg.58, amended: SI 2013/390 Reg.17, SI 2013/755 Sch.4 para.380
Reg.59, amended: SI 2013/755 Sch.4 para.380
Reg.61, amended: SI 2013/755 Sch.4 para.381
Reg.63, amended: SI 2013/390 Reg.18, SI 2013/755 Sch.4 para.381
Reg.65, amended: SI 2013/755 Sch.4 para.382
Reg.108, amended: SI 2013/755 Sch.4 para.383
Sch.1 Part 1 para.1, amended: SI 2013/390 Reg.19
Sch.1 Part 1 para.2, amended: SI 2013/390 Reg.19
Sch.1 Part 1 para.3, amended: SI 2013/390 Reg.19
Sch.1 Part 1 para.4, substituted: SI 2013/390 Reg.19
Sch.1 Part 1 para.6, revoked (in part): SI 2013/390 Reg.19
Sch.1 Part 2, revoked: SI 2013/390 Reg.21
Sch.1 Part 2, amended: SI 2013/390 Reg.21
Sch.1 Part 2, amended: SI 2013/390 Reg.22
Sch.1 Part 2, revoked (in part): SI 2013/390 Reg.22
Sch.1 Part 2, amended: SI 2013/390 Reg.22
Sch.1 Part 2, amended: SI 2013/390 Reg.24
Sch.1 Part 2, revoked (in part): SI 2013/390 Reg.24
Sch.1 Part 2, amended: SI 2013/390 Reg.26, Reg.27
Sch.1 Part 2, revoked (in part): SI 2013/390 Reg.26, Reg.27
Sch.1 Part 2, amended: SI 2013/390 Reg.33
Sch.1 Part 2, revoked (in part): SI 2013/390 Reg.30, Reg.31, Reg.32, Reg.33, Reg.34
Sch.1 Part 2, substituted: SI 2013/390 Reg.36
Sch.1 Part 2, substituted: SI 2013/390 Reg.37
Sch.1 Part 2, added: SI 2013/390 Reg.38, Reg.39
Sch.1 Part 2, revoked (in part): SI 2013/390 Reg.40
Sch.1 Part 2, revoked (in part): SI 2013/390 Reg.41
Sch.1 Part 2, amended: SI 2013/390 Reg.42
Sch.1 Part 2, revoked: SI 2013/390 Reg.44
Sch.1 Part 2 para.1, amended: SI 2013/390 Reg.22
Sch.1 Part 2 para.1, revoked (in part): SI 2013/390 Reg.22
Sch.1 Part 2 para.1, amended: SI 2013/390 Reg.22
Sch.1 Part 2 para.1, amended: SI 2013/390 Reg.23
Sch.1 Part 2 para.1, revoked: SI 2013/390 Reg.23
Sch.1 Part 2 para.1, revoked (in part): SI 2013/390 Reg.25
Sch.1 Part 2 para.1, amended: SI 2013/390 Reg.28
Sch.1 Part 2 para.1, amended: SI 2013/390 Reg.29
Sch.1 Part 2 para.1, revoked (in part): SI 2013/390 Reg.29
Sch.1 Part 2 para.1, amended: SI 2013/390 Reg.35

Sch.1 Part 2 para.1, substituted: SI 2013/390 Reg.35
Sch.1 Part 2 para.1, amended: SI 2013/390 Reg.40
Sch.1 Part 2 para.1, amended: SI 2013/390 Reg.43
Sch.1 Part 2 para.1, revoked (in part): SI 2013/390 Reg.43, SI 2013/2952 Sch.2 para.9
Sch.1 Part 2 para.2, amended: SI 2013/390 Reg.23
Sch.1 Part 2 para.2, revoked (in part): SI 2013/390 Reg.23
Sch.1 Part 2 para.3, amended: SI 2013/390 Reg.41
Sch.1 Part 2 para.5, revoked: SI 2013/390 Reg.21
Sch.2 para.2, amended: SI 2013/755 Sch.4 para.384
Sch.3 Part 1 para.3, amended: SI 2013/390 Reg.45
Sch.3 Part 1 para.6, amended: SI 2013/390 Reg.45
Sch.5 Part 1 para.5, amended: SI 2013/390 Reg.46
Sch.5 Part 1 para.10, amended: SI 2013/390 Reg.46
Sch.5 Part 1 para.16, amended: SI 2013/390 Reg.46
Sch.5 Part 1 para.20, added: SI 2013/390 Reg.46
Sch.7 para.1, amended: SI 2013/390 Reg.47
Sch.7 para.1, revoked: SI 2013/390 Reg.58
Sch.7 para.1, substituted: SI 2013/390 Reg.47
Sch.7 para.2, amended: SI 2013/390 Reg.47
Sch.7 para.2, revoked: SI 2013/390 Reg.58
Sch.7 para.3, amended: SI 2013/390 Reg.47
Sch.7 para.3, revoked: SI 2013/390 Reg.58
Sch.7 para.4, amended: SI 2013/390 Reg.47
Sch.7 para.4, revoked: SI 2013/390 Reg.47, Reg.58
Sch.7 para.5, amended: SI 2013/390 Reg.47
Sch.7 para.5, revoked (in part): SI 2013/390 Reg.47, Reg.58
Sch.7 para.6, amended: SI 2013/390 Reg.47
Sch.7 para.6, revoked: SI 2013/390 Reg.58
Sch.7 para.7, amended: SI 2013/390 Reg.47
Sch.7 para.7, revoked: SI 2013/390 Reg.58
Sch.7 para.8, amended: SI 2013/390 Reg.47
Sch.7 para.8, revoked: SI 2013/390 Reg.58
Sch.7A para.1, added: SI 2013/390 Reg.47
Sch.7A para.2, added: SI 2013/390 Reg.47
Sch.7A para.3, added: SI 2013/390 Reg.47
Sch.7A para.4, added: SI 2013/390 Reg.47
Sch.7A para.5, added: SI 2013/390 Reg.47
Sch.7A para.6, added: SI 2013/390 Reg.47
Sch.7A para.7, added: SI 2013/390 Reg.47
Sch.7A para.8, added: SI 2013/390 Reg.47
Sch.7A para.9, added: SI 2013/390 Reg.47
Sch.8 para.1, substituted: SI 2013/390 Reg.48
Sch.8 para.2, substituted: SI 2013/390 Reg.48
Sch.8 para.3, substituted: SI 2013/390 Reg.48
Sch.8 para.4, substituted: SI 2013/390 Reg.48
Sch.8 para.5, substituted: SI 2013/390 Reg.48
Sch.8 para.6, substituted: SI 2013/390 Reg.48
Sch.8 para.7, substituted: SI 2013/390 Reg.48
Sch.8 para.8, substituted: SI 2013/390 Reg.48
Sch.9 para.3, amended: SI 2013/390 Reg.49
Sch.10 para.5, amended: SI 2013/766 Reg.2
Sch.13 para.1, revoked: SI 2013/390 Reg.58
Sch.13 para.1, substituted: SI 2013/390 Reg.50
Sch.13 para.2, revoked (in part): SI 2013/390 Reg.50, Reg.58
Sch.13 para.3, revoked: SI 2013/390 Reg.58
Sch.13 para.4, revoked: SI 2013/390 Reg.58
Sch.13A para.1, added: SI 2013/390 Reg.50
Sch.13A para.2, added: SI 2013/390 Reg.50
Sch.13A para.3, added: SI 2013/390 Reg.50
Sch.13A para.4, added: SI 2013/390 Reg.50
Sch.14 para.1, substituted: SI 2013/390 Reg.51
Sch.14 para.2, substituted: SI 2013/390 Reg.51
Sch.14 para.3, substituted: SI 2013/390 Reg.51
Sch.15 para.1, revoked: SI 2013/390 Reg.58
Sch.15 para.1, substituted: SI 2013/390 Reg.52
Sch.15 para.2, revoked: SI 2013/390 Reg.58
Sch.15 para.3, revoked: SI 2013/390 Reg.58
Sch.15A para.1, added: SI 2013/390 Reg.52
Sch.15A para.2, added: SI 2013/390 Reg.52
Sch.15A para.3, added: SI 2013/390 Reg.52
Sch.15A para.4, added: SI 2013/390 Reg.52
Sch.17 para.1, revoked: SI 2013/390 Reg.58
Sch.17 para.1, substituted: SI 2013/390 Reg.53
Sch.17 para.2, revoked: SI 2013/390 Reg.58
Sch.17 para.3, revoked: SI 2013/390 Reg.58
Sch.17A para.1, added: SI 2013/390 Reg.53
Sch.17A para.2, added: SI 2013/390 Reg.53
Sch.17A para.3, added: SI 2013/390 Reg.53
Sch.20 para.12, amended: SI 2013/390 Reg.54
Sch.21 para.3, referred to: SI 2013/648 Art.21
Sch.23 Part 2 para.11A, added: SI 2013/755 Sch.4 para.385
Sch.26 Part 1 para.2, revoked: 2013 c.32 Sch.12 para.30

699. Environment Agency (Inland Waterways) Order 2010

Art.3, amended: SI 2013/1888 Art.2

713. Valuation Tribunal for Wales Regulations 2010

Reg.4, applied: SI 2013/2356 Sch.2 para.22
Reg.9, amended: SI 2013/547 Reg.2
Reg.27, amended: SI 2013/547 Reg.2
Reg.30, amended: SI 2013/547 Reg.2
Reg.32A, added: SI 2013/547 Reg.2
Reg.37, amended: SI 2013/547 Reg.2
Reg.38, amended: SI 2013/547 Reg.2
Sch.1, amended: SI 2013/547 Reg.2

724. Train Driving Licences and Certificates Regulations 2010

Reg.2, amended: SI 2013/950 Reg.4

Reg.3, amended: SI 2013/950 Reg.4
Reg.35, revoked (in part): SI 2013/2042 Sch.1 para.83
Reg.36, revoked (in part): SI 2013/2042 Sch.1 para.83
Reg.40, added: SI 2013/950 Reg.4
Sch.2 para.2, amended: SI 2013/950 Reg.4

727. Cambridgeshire Community Services National Health Service Trust (Establishment) Order 2010
Art.1, amended: SI 2013/593 Art.2

740. Detergents Regulations 2010
Reg.2, amended: SI 2013/1244 Reg.2
Reg.7, amended: SI 2013/1244 Reg.2
Reg.9, revoked: SI 2013/1244 Reg.2
Reg.11, amended: SI 2013/1244 Reg.2
Reg.12, amended: SI 2013/1244 Reg.2
Reg.13, amended: SI 2013/1244 Reg.2
Reg.26, amended: SI 2013/1244 Reg.2
Reg.31, added: SI 2013/1244 Reg.3
Sch.2, amended: SI 2013/1244 Reg.4

743. National Health Service Trusts (Consultation on Establishment and Dissolution) Regulations 2010
Reg.1, amended: SI 2013/235 Sch.2 para.149
Reg.2, amended: SI 2013/235 Sch.2 para.149
Reg.3, amended: SI 2013/235 Sch.2 para.149
Reg.4, amended: SI 2013/235 Sch.2 para.149

745. Biocidal Products (Amendment) Regulations 2010
revoked: SI 2013/1506 Reg.34
Reg.3, applied: SI 2013/1506 Sch.2 para.10
Reg.4, applied: SI 2013/1506 Sch.2 para.10

768. CRC Energy Efficiency Scheme Order 2010
applied: SI 2013/1119 Art.96, SI 2013/3103 Reg.13
revoked (in part): SI 2013/1119 Art.96
Art.3, amended: SI 2013/1119 Sch.9 para.2
Art.4, amended: SI 2013/1119 Sch.9 para.3
Art.5, amended: SI 2013/1119 Sch.9 para.4
Art.5, revoked (in part): SI 2013/1119 Sch.9 para.4
Art.6, amended: SI 2013/1119 Sch.9 para.5
Art.9, amended: SI 2013/755 Sch.4 para.387, SI 2013/1119 Sch.9 para.6
Art.12, substituted: SI 2013/1119 Sch.9 para.7
Art.29, amended: SI 2013/1119 Sch.9 para.8
Art.30, amended: SI 2013/1119 Sch.9 para.8
Art.31, substituted: SI 2013/1119 Sch.9 para.8
Art.34A, added: SI 2013/1119 Sch.9 para.8
Art.36, revoked: SI 2013/1119 Sch.9 para.8
Art.37, amended: SI 2013/1119 Sch.9 para.8
Art.38, amended: SI 2013/1119 Sch.9 para.8
Art.39, revoked: SI 2013/1119 Sch.9 para.9
Art.40, revoked: SI 2013/1119 Sch.9 para.9
Art.41, revoked: SI 2013/1119 Sch.9 para.9
Art.42, revoked: SI 2013/1119 Sch.9 para.9
Art.43, revoked: SI 2013/1119 Sch.9 para.9
Art.44, revoked: SI 2013/1119 Sch.9 para.9
Art.45, revoked: SI 2013/1119 Sch.9 para.9
Art.46, revoked: SI 2013/1119 Sch.9 para.9
Art.48, substituted: SI 2013/1119 Sch.9 para.10
Art.49, substituted: SI 2013/1119 Sch.9 para.10
Art.50, substituted: SI 2013/1119 Sch.9 para.10
Art.52, amended: SI 2013/1119 Sch.9 para.11
Art.53, amended: SI 2013/1119 Sch.9 para.11
Art.54, amended: SI 2013/1119 Sch.9 para.11
Art.55, amended: SI 2013/1119 Sch.9 para.11
Art.55, revoked (in part): SI 2013/1119 Sch.9 para.11
Art.56, revoked: SI 2013/1119 Sch.9 para.11
Art.58, amended: SI 2013/1119 Sch.9 para.12
Art.59, revoked (in part): SI 2013/1119 Sch.9 para.13
Art.59, substituted: SI 2013/1119 Sch.9 para.13
Art.61, substituted: SI 2013/1119 Sch.9 para.14
Art.75, substituted: SI 2013/1119 Sch.9 para.15
Art.76, substituted: SI 2013/1119 Sch.9 para.15
Art.77, substituted: SI 2013/1119 Sch.9 para.15
Art.78, substituted: SI 2013/1119 Sch.9 para.15
Art.79, substituted: SI 2013/1119 Sch.9 para.15
Art.80, substituted: SI 2013/1119 Sch.9 para.15
Art.96, revoked: SI 2013/1119 Sch.9 para.16
Art.98, amended: SI 2013/1119 Sch.9 para.16
Art.99, amended: SI 2013/1119 Sch.9 para.16
Art.99, revoked (in part): SI 2013/1119 Sch.9 para.16
Art.99, substituted: SI 2013/1119 Sch.9 para.16
Sch.1 Part 1 para.1, amended: SI 2013/1119 Sch.9 para.17
Sch.1 Part 1 para.2, amended: SI 2013/1119 Sch.9 para.17
Sch.1 Part 1 para.3, amended: SI 2013/1119 Sch.9 para.17
Sch.1 Part 1 para.3, revoked: SI 2013/1119 Sch.9 para.17
Sch.1 Part 1 para.4, amended: SI 2013/1119 Sch.9 para.17
Sch.1 Part 1 para.4, revoked: SI 2013/1119 Sch.9 para.17
Sch.1 Part 1 para.5, amended: SI 2013/1119 Sch.9 para.17
Sch.1 Part 1 para.5, substituted: SI 2013/1119 Sch.9 para.17
Sch.1 Part 3 para.8, amended: SI 2013/1119 Sch.9 para.17
Sch.1 Part 3 para.11, amended: SI 2013/1119 Sch.9 para.17
Sch.1 Part 4 para.12, amended: SI 2013/1119 Sch.9 para.17

Sch.1 Part 4 para.13, amended: SI 2013/1119 Sch.9 para.17
Sch.1 Part 4 para.15, amended: SI 2013/1119 Sch.9 para.17
Sch.1 Part 4 para.16, amended: SI 2013/1119 Sch.9 para.17
Sch.1 Part 4 para.17, amended: SI 2013/1119 Sch.9 para.17
Sch.1 Part 4 para.18, amended: SI 2013/1119 Sch.9 para.17
Sch.1 Part 4 para.19, amended: SI 2013/1119 Sch.9 para.17
Sch.1 Part 4 para.22, substituted: SI 2013/1119 Sch.9 para.17
Sch.1 Part 5 para.23, amended: SI 2013/1119 Sch.9 para.17
Sch.1 Part 5 para.24, amended: SI 2013/1119 Sch.9 para.17
Sch.1 Part 6 para.25, amended: SI 2013/1119 Sch.9 para.17
Sch.1 Part 6 para.27, revoked: SI 2013/1119 Sch.9 para.17
Sch.1 Part 7 para.28, amended: SI 2013/1119 Sch.9 para.17
Sch.1 Part 7 para.29, substituted: SI 2013/1119 Sch.9 para.17
Sch.1 Part 7 para.30, amended: SI 2013/1119 Sch.9 para.17
Sch.2 Part 1 para.1, revoked: SI 2013/1119 Sch.9 para.18
Sch.2 Part 1 para.2, revoked: SI 2013/1119 Sch.9 para.18
Sch.2 Part 1 para.3, revoked: SI 2013/1119 Sch.9 para.18
Sch.2 Part 1 para.4, revoked: SI 2013/1119 Sch.9 para.18
Sch.2 Part 1 para.5, revoked: SI 2013/1119 Sch.9 para.18
Sch.2 Part 2 para.6, revoked: SI 2013/1119 Sch.9 para.18
Sch.2 Part 2 para.7, revoked: SI 2013/1119 Sch.9 para.18
Sch.2 Part 2 para.8, revoked: SI 2013/1119 Sch.9 para.18
Sch.2 Part 2 para.9, revoked: SI 2013/1119 Sch.9 para.18
Sch.3 Part 1 para.4, amended: SI 2013/1119 Sch.9 para.19
Sch.3 Part 2 para.8, revoked (in part): SI 2013/1119 Sch.9 para.19
Sch.3 Part 3 para.10, substituted: SI 2013/1119 Sch.9 para.19
Sch.3 Part 3 para.15, amended: SI 2013/1119 Sch.9 para.19
Sch.3 Part 3 para.16, amended: SI 2013/1119 Sch.9 para.19
Sch.5 Part 1 para.1, revoked: SI 2013/1119 Sch.9 para.20
Sch.5 Part 1 para.1, substituted: SI 2013/1119 Sch.9 para.20
Sch.5 Part 1 para.2, revoked: SI 2013/1119 Sch.9 para.20
Sch.5 Part 1 para.2, substituted: SI 2013/1119 Sch.9 para.20
Sch.5 Part 1 para.3, revoked: SI 2013/1119 Sch.9 para.20
Sch.5 Part 1 para.3, substituted: SI 2013/1119 Sch.9 para.20
Sch.5 Part 1 para.4, revoked: SI 2013/1119 Sch.9 para.20
Sch.5 Part 1 para.4, substituted: SI 2013/1119 Sch.9 para.20
Sch.5 Part 1 para.5, revoked: SI 2013/1119 Sch.9 para.20
Sch.5 Part 1 para.5, substituted: SI 2013/1119 Sch.9 para.20
Sch.5 Part 1 para.6, revoked: SI 2013/1119 Sch.9 para.20
Sch.5 Part 1 para.6, substituted: SI 2013/1119 Sch.9 para.20
Sch.5 Part 1 para.7, revoked: SI 2013/1119 Sch.9 para.20
Sch.5 Part 1 para.7, substituted: SI 2013/1119 Sch.9 para.20
Sch.5 Part 2 para.8, revoked: SI 2013/1119 Sch.9 para.20
Sch.5 Part 2 para.8, substituted: SI 2013/1119 Sch.9 para.20
Sch.5 Part 2 para.9, revoked: SI 2013/1119 Sch.9 para.20
Sch.5 Part 2 para.9, substituted: SI 2013/1119 Sch.9 para.20
Sch.5 Part 2 para.10, revoked: SI 2013/1119 Sch.9 para.20
Sch.5 Part 2 para.10, substituted: SI 2013/1119 Sch.9 para.20
Sch.5 Part 2 para.11, revoked: SI 2013/1119 Sch.9 para.20
Sch.5 Part 2 para.11, substituted: SI 2013/1119 Sch.9 para.20
Sch.5 Part 2 para.12, revoked: SI 2013/1119 Sch.9 para.20
Sch.5 Part 2 para.12, substituted: SI 2013/1119 Sch.9 para.20
Sch.5 Part 2 para.13, revoked: SI 2013/1119 Sch.9 para.20
Sch.5 Part 2 para.13, substituted: SI 2013/1119 Sch.9 para.20

Sch.6 Part 1 para.6, revoked (in part): SI 2013/1119 Sch.9 para.21
Sch.6 Part 1 para.7, amended: SI 2013/1119 Sch.9 para.21
Sch.6 Part 1 para.10, revoked: SI 2013/1119 Sch.9 para.21
Sch.6 Part 1 para.11, amended: SI 2013/1119 Sch.9 para.21
Sch.6 Part 1 para.12, revoked (in part): SI 2013/1119 Sch.9 para.21
Sch.6 Part 2 para.3, revoked (in part): SI 2013/1119 Sch.9 para.21
Sch.6 Part 3 para.3, amended: SI 2013/1119 Sch.9 para.21
Sch.6 Part 3 para.6, amended: SI 2013/1119 Sch.9 para.21
Sch.6 Part 3 para.7, revoked (in part): SI 2013/1119 Sch.9 para.21
Sch.6 Part 3 para.9, amended: SI 2013/1119 Sch.9 para.21
Sch.6 Part 3 para.10, amended: SI 2013/1119 Sch.9 para.21
Sch.6 Part 3 para.10, revoked (in part): SI 2013/1119 Sch.9 para.21
Sch.6 Part 3 para.11, amended: SI 2013/1119 Sch.9 para.21
Sch.6 Part 3 para.11, revoked (in part): SI 2013/1119 Sch.9 para.21
Sch.6 Part 3 para.12, amended: SI 2013/1119 Sch.9 para.21
Sch.6 Part 3 para.12, revoked (in part): SI 2013/1119 Sch.9 para.21
Sch.8 para.1, revoked: SI 2013/1119 Sch.9 para.22
Sch.8 para.2, revoked: SI 2013/1119 Sch.9 para.22
Sch.8 para.3, revoked: SI 2013/1119 Sch.9 para.22
Sch.8 para.4, revoked: SI 2013/1119 Sch.9 para.22
Sch.8 para.5, revoked: SI 2013/1119 Sch.9 para.22
Sch.10 para.2, amended: SI 2013/755 Sch.4 para.388
Sch.10 para.6, amended: SI 2013/755 Sch.4 para.388

772. Occupational and Personal Pension Schemes (Automatic Enrolment) Regulations 2010

disapplied: SSI 2013/174 Reg.6
Reg.4, substituted: SI 2013/2556 Reg.5
Reg.5, substituted: SI 2013/2556 Reg.5
Reg.6, amended: SI 2013/2556 Reg.5
Reg.7, amended: SI 2013/2556 Reg.5
Reg.8, amended: SI 2013/2556 Reg.5
Reg.9, amended: SI 2013/2556 Reg.5
Reg.9, applied: SSI 2013/174 Reg.6
Reg.13, amended: SI 2013/2556 Reg.5
Reg.15, applied: SSI 2013/174 Reg.6
Reg.17, amended: SI 2013/2556 Reg.5
Reg.18, amended: SI 2013/2556 Reg.5
Reg.21, amended: SI 2013/2556 Reg.5
Reg.24, amended: SI 2013/2556 Reg.5
Reg.27, amended: SI 2013/2556 Reg.5
Reg.28, amended: SI 2013/2556 Reg.5
Reg.29, amended: SI 2013/2556 Reg.5
Reg.35, amended: SI 2013/2328 Reg.2, SI 2013/3115 Sch.2 para.74
Reg.37, amended: SI 2013/2556 Reg.5
Reg.38, substituted: SI 2013/2556 Reg.5
Reg.39A, substituted: SI 2013/2556 Reg.5
Reg.50, amended: SI 2013/2556 Reg.5
Sch.1, substituted: SI 2013/2556 Reg.5

778. Immigration and Nationality (Fees) Regulations 2010

Reg.6, see *R. (on the application of Omar) v Secretary of State for the Home Department* [2012] EWHC 3448 (Admin), [2013] Imm. A.R. 601 (QBD (Admin)), Beatson, J.
Reg.30, see *R. (on the application of Omar) v Secretary of State for the Home Department* [2012] EWHC 3448 (Admin), [2013] Imm. A.R. 601 (QBD (Admin)), Beatson, J.

781. Health and Social Care Act 2008 (Regulated Activities) Regulations 2010

Sch.2 para.3, amended: SI 2013/235 Sch.2 para.150
Sch.2 para.13, amended: SI 2013/235 Sch.2 para.150
Sch.2 para.17, amended: SI 2013/472 Sch.2 para.186

797. Fish Labelling (Wales) Regulations 2010

revoked: SI 2013/2139 Reg.13

801. Transmissible Spongiform Encephalopathies (England) Regulations 2010

Reg.2, amended: SI 2013/2952 Sch.2 para.10
Reg.4, amended: SI 2013/2952 Sch.2 para.10
Reg.15A, added: SI 2013/336 Reg.2
Sch.1, revoked (in part): SI 2013/2952 Sch.2 para.10
Sch.2 Part 1 para.1, revoked: SI 2013/336 Reg.2
Sch.2 Part 1 para.10, amended: SI 2013/336 Reg.2
Sch.2 Part 1 para.14, amended: SI 2013/2952 Sch.2 para.10
Sch.3 para.5, amended: SI 2013/336 Reg.2
Sch.3 para.9, substituted: SI 2013/336 Reg.2
Sch.4 para.4, amended: SI 2013/336 Reg.2
Sch.4 para.6, amended: SI 2013/336 Reg.2
Sch.4 para.7, amended: SI 2013/336 Reg.2
Sch.4 para.8, amended: SI 2013/336 Reg.2
Sch.4 para.11, amended: SI 2013/336 Reg.2
Sch.4 para.11, revoked (in part): SI 2013/336 Reg.2
Sch.4 para.18, amended: SI 2013/336 Reg.2

Sch.4 para.19, amended: SI 2013/336 Reg.2
Sch.4 para.20, amended: SI 2013/336 Reg.2
Sch.6 Part 1 para.1, revoked (in part): SI 2013/2952 Sch.2 para.10
Sch.6 Part 1 para.2, revoked (in part): SI 2013/2952 Sch.2 para.10
Sch.6 Part 1 para.3, revoked: SI 2013/2952 Sch.2 para.10
Sch.6 Part 2 para.18, amended: SI 2013/336 Reg.2, SI 2013/2952 Sch.2 para.10
Sch.6 Part 2 para.19, revoked: SI 2013/2952 Sch.2 para.10

811. Notification of Conventional Tower Cranes (Amendment) Regulations 2010

revoked: SI 2013/448 Sch.1

825. Right to Manage (Prescribed Particulars and Forms) (England) Regulations 2010

Reg.5, amended: SI 2013/1036 Sch.2 para.42
Sch.2, amended: SI 2013/1036 Sch.2 para.43
Sch.3, amended: SI 2013/1036 Sch.2 para.44

828. Banking Act 2009 (Inter-Bank Payment Systems) (Disclosure and Publication of Specified Information) Regulations 2010

Reg.7, amended: SI 2013/472 Art.4, Sch.2 para.187
Reg.7, revoked (in part): SI 2013/472 Sch.2 para.187
Sch.1, amended: SI 2013/472 Sch.2 para.187, SI 2013/1765 Art.9

868. National Health Service (Pharmaceutical Services) (Amendment) (Wales) Regulations 2010

revoked: SI 2013/898 Sch.8 para.22

906. Credit Rating Agencies Regulations 2010

Reg.2, amended: SI 2013/472 Sch.2 para.188
Reg.3, amended: SI 2013/472 Sch.2 para.188
Reg.4, amended: SI 2013/472 Sch.2 para.188
Reg.5, amended: SI 2013/472 Sch.2 para.188
Reg.6, amended: SI 2013/472 Sch.2 para.188
Reg.7, amended: SI 2013/472 Sch.2 para.188
Reg.31, revoked: SI 2013/3115 Sch.3
Reg.32, amended: SI 2013/472 Sch.2 para.188
Reg.33, amended: SI 2013/472 Sch.2 para.188

914. National Health Service (Pharmaceutical Services and Local Pharmaceutical Services) (Amendment) Regulations 2010

revoked: SI 2013/349 Sch.10 para.9

917. National Employment Savings Trust Order 2010

Art.1, amended: SI 2013/597 Art.2
Art.2, amended: SI 2013/597 Art.2
Art.13, amended: SI 2013/597 Art.2
Art.18, amended: SI 2013/597 Art.2
Art.19, amended: SI 2013/597 Art.2
Art.19, revoked (in part): SI 2013/597 Art.2
Art.20, revoked (in part): SI 2013/597 Art.2
Art.21, amended: SI 2013/597 Art.2
Art.21, revoked (in part): SI 2013/597 Art.2
Art.22, amended: SI 2013/597 Art.2
Art.23, amended: SI 2013/597 Art.2
Art.24, amended: SI 2013/597 Art.2
Art.26, amended: SI 2013/597 Art.2
Art.26, revoked (in part): SI 2013/597 Art.2
Art.32, amended: SI 2013/597 Art.2

937. Freedom of Information (Additional Public Authorities) Order 2010

Sch.1 Part 1, amended: SI 2013/64 Art.7

948. Community Infrastructure Levy Regulations 2010

applied: SI 2013/648 Art.11
see *Oxford Diocesan Board of Finance v Secretary of State for Communities and Local Government* [2013] EWHC 802 (Admin), [2013] J.P.L. 1285 (QBD (Admin)), Lang, J.
Reg.2, amended: SI 2013/982 Reg.3
Reg.5, amended: SI 2013/982 Reg.4
Reg.5, varied: SI 2013/648 Art.11
Reg.8, disapplied: SI 2013/982 Reg.12
Reg.10, amended: SI 2013/982 Reg.5
Reg.11A, added: SI 2013/982 Reg.6
Reg.14, amended: SI 2013/982 Reg.6
Reg.22, amended: SI 2013/982 Reg.6
Reg.55, amended: SI 2013/982 Reg.7
Reg.57, amended: SI 2013/982 Reg.7
Reg.58, amended: SI 2013/982 Reg.7
Reg.58A, added: SI 2013/982 Reg.8
Reg.59, amended: SI 2013/982 Reg.8
Reg.59A, added: SI 2013/982 Reg.8
Reg.59B, added: SI 2013/982 Reg.8
Reg.59C, added: SI 2013/982 Reg.8
Reg.59D, added: SI 2013/982 Reg.8
Reg.59E, added: SI 2013/982 Reg.8
Reg.59F, added: SI 2013/982 Reg.8
Reg.62, amended: SI 2013/982 Reg.8
Reg.62, revoked (in part): SI 2013/982 Reg.8
Reg.62A, added: SI 2013/982 Reg.8
Reg.63A, added: SI 2013/982 Reg.9
Reg.63B, added: SI 2013/982 Reg.9
Reg.70, amended: SI 2013/982 Reg.9
Reg.88, amended: SI 2013/982 Reg.10
Reg.122, see *R. (on the application of Mid Counties Co-operative Ltd) v Forest of Dean DC* [2013] EWHC 1908 (Admin), [2013] J.P.L. 1551 (QBD (Admin)), Stewart, J.
Reg.123, amended: SI 2013/982 Reg.11

959. Care Planning, Placement and Case Review (England) Regulations 2010

applied: SI 2013/706 Reg.14

see *S (A Child) (Interim Residence), Re* [2012] EWCA Civ 1915, [2013] 2 F.L.R. 446 (CA (Civ Div)), Ward, L.J.
Reg.2, amended: SI 2013/706 Reg.3
Reg.3, amended: SI 2013/706 Reg.4
Reg.9, applied: SI 2013/706 Reg.14
Reg.11, amended: SI 2013/3239 Reg.18
Reg.13, amended: SI 2013/235 Sch.2 para.151, SI 2013/3239 Reg.19
Reg.25A, added: SI 2013/984 Reg.3
Reg.33, amended: SI 2013/3239 Reg.20
Reg.39, substituted: SI 2013/706 Reg.5
Reg.39ZA, added: SI 2013/3239 Reg.21
Reg.47A, added: SI 2013/706 Reg.6
Reg.47B, added: SI 2013/706 Reg.6
Reg.47C, added: SI 2013/706 Reg.6
Reg.47D, added: SI 2013/706 Reg.6
Reg.47E, added: SI 2013/706 Reg.6
Reg.47F, added: SI 2013/706 Reg.6
Sch.1 para.2, amended: SI 2013/706 Reg.7
Sch.2 para.3, amended: SI 2013/984 Reg.4, SI 2013/3239 Reg.22
Sch.2 para.3, revoked (in part): SI 2013/984 Reg.4
Sch.2A para.1, added: SI 2013/706 Reg.8
Sch.2A para.2, added: SI 2013/706 Reg.8
Sch.2A para.3, added: SI 2013/706 Reg.8
Sch.2A para.4, added: SI 2013/706 Reg.8
Sch.2A para.5, added: SI 2013/706 Reg.8
Sch.2A para.6, added: SI 2013/706 Reg.8
Sch.2A para.7, added: SI 2013/706 Reg.8
Sch.2A para.8, added: SI 2013/706 Reg.8
Sch.2A para.9, added: SI 2013/706 Reg.8
Sch.2A para.10, added: SI 2013/706 Reg.8
Sch.7 para.5A, added: SI 2013/3239 Reg.23

976. Northern Ireland Act 1998 (Devolution of Policing and Justice Functions) Order 2010
Sch.18 Part 1 para.9, revoked: SI 2013/686 Sch.2

983. Beef and Veal Labelling Regulations 2010
Reg.2, amended: SI 2013/3235 Reg.3
Reg.4, amended: SI 2013/3235 Reg.3

990. Teachers Pensions Regulations 2010
Reg.18, amended: SI 2013/275 Reg.3
Reg.128, revoked: SI 2013/275 Reg.4
Sch.3 para.1, revoked: SI 2013/275 Reg.5
Sch.3 para.2, amended: SI 2013/275 Reg.5
Sch.3 para.2, revoked (in part): SI 2013/275 Reg.5
Sch.3 para.3, revoked: SI 2013/275 Reg.5
Sch.3 para.4, amended: SI 2013/275 Reg.5
Sch.3 para.4, revoked (in part): SI 2013/275 Reg.5
Sch.3 para.5, revoked: SI 2013/275 Reg.5
Sch.13 Part 3 para.11, amended: SI 2013/275 Reg.6
Sch.13 Part 5 para.24, revoked: SI 2013/275 Reg.6

994. Water Supply (Water Quality) Regulations 2010
Reg.2, amended: SI 2013/235 Sch.2 para.152
Reg.22, amended: SI 2013/235 Sch.2 para.152
Reg.26, amended: SI 2013/235 Sch.2 para.152
Reg.31, amended: SI 2013/1387 Sch.5 para.7
Reg.31, revoked (in part): SI 2013/1387 Sch.5 para.7
Reg.35, amended: SI 2013/235 Sch.2 para.152

995. Human Fertilisation and Embryology (Disclosure of Information for Research Purposes) Regulations 2010
Reg.2, amended: SI 2013/235 Sch.2 para.153
Reg.5, revoked: SI 2013/235 Sch.2 para.153

1000. National Health Service (Direct Payments) Regulations 2010
applied: SI 2013/1617 Reg.19
revoked: SI 2013/1617 Reg.20
Reg.1, amended: SI 2013/235 Sch.2 para.154
Reg.2, amended: SI 2013/235 Sch.2 para.154
Reg.2, revoked (in part): SI 2013/235 Sch.2 para.154
Reg.3, amended: SI 2013/235 Sch.2 para.154
Reg.3, revoked (in part): SI 2013/235 Sch.2 para.154
Reg.4, amended: SI 2013/235 Sch.2 para.154
Reg.5, amended: SI 2013/235 Sch.2 para.154
Reg.7, amended: SI 2013/235 Sch.2 para.154
Reg.8, amended: SI 2013/235 Sch.2 para.154
Reg.9, amended: SI 2013/235 Sch.2 para.154
Reg.10, amended: SI 2013/235 Sch.2 para.154
Reg.11, amended: SI 2013/235 Sch.2 para.154
Reg.12, amended: SI 2013/235 Sch.2 para.154
Reg.13, amended: SI 2013/235 Sch.2 para.154
Reg.14, amended: SI 2013/235 Sch.2 para.154
Reg.15, amended: SI 2013/235 Sch.2 para.154
Reg.16, amended: SI 2013/235 Sch.2 para.154
Reg.17, amended: SI 2013/235 Sch.2 para.154
Reg.18, amended: SI 2013/235 Sch.2 para.154
Reg.19, amended: SI 2013/235 Sch.2 para.154
Reg.20, amended: SI 2013/235 Sch.2 para.154

1004. Identification and Traceability of Explosives Regulations 2010
revoked: SI 2013/449 Reg.9

1011. Consumer Credit (Total Charge for Credit) Regulations 2010
revoked (in part): SI 2013/1881 Art.21

1013. Consumer Credit (Disclosure of Information) Regulations 2010
Reg.1, amended: SI 2013/1881 Art.26
Reg.1, revoked (in part): SI 2013/1881 Art.26
Reg.2, amended: SI 2013/1881 Art.26
Reg.3, amended: SI 2013/1881 Art.26
Reg.6, amended: SI 2013/1881 Art.26
Reg.7, amended: SI 2013/1881 Art.26
Sch.1 para.2, amended: SI 2013/1881 Art.26

Sch.1 para.3, amended: SI 2013/1881 Art.26
Sch.1 para.5, amended: SI 2013/1881 Art.26
Sch.2 para.1, amended: SI 2013/1881 Art.26
Sch.2 para.3, amended: SI 2013/1881 Art.26
Sch.2 para.4, amended: SI 2013/1881 Art.26
Sch.3 para.5, amended: SI 2013/1881 Art.26

1014. Consumer Credit (Agreements) Regulations 2010
Reg.1, amended: SI 2013/1881 Art.27
Reg.1, revoked (in part): SI 2013/1881 Art.27
Reg.2, amended: SI 2013/1881 Art.27
Sch.1, amended: SI 2013/1881 Art.27
Sch.4 para.1, amended: SI 2013/1881 Art.27
Sch.4 para.3, amended: SI 2013/1881 Art.27
Sch.4 para.4, amended: SI 2013/1881 Art.27

1051. Whole of Government Accounts (Designation of Bodies) Order 2010
Sch.1, amended: SI 2013/687 Sch.2

1060. Additional Statutory Paternity Pay (Weekly Rates) Regulations 2010
Reg.2, amended: SI 2013/574 Art.10

1090. Beef and Pig Carcase Classification (England) Regulations 2010
Reg.2, amended: SI 2013/3235 Reg.2
Reg.2, revoked (in part): SI 2013/3235 Reg.2
Sch.1 Part 1, amended: SI 2013/3235 Reg.2
Sch.2, amended: SI 2013/3235 Reg.2

1150. Cosmetic Products (Safety) (Amendment) Regulations 2010
revoked: SI 2013/1478 Sch.1

1155. Waste Electrical and Electronic Equipment (Amendment) Regulations 2010
revoked: SI 2013/3113 Reg.96

1172. Local Education Authorities and Children's Services Authorities (Integration of Functions) (Local and Subordinate Legislation) Order 2010
Sch.3 para.65, revoked: SI 2013/458 Sch.1

1188. Building Societies (Financial Assistance) Order 2010
Art.2, amended: SI 2013/496 Sch.11 para.18
Art.3, amended: SI 2013/496 Sch.11 para.18
Art.4, amended: SI 2013/496 Sch.11 para.18
Art.11, amended: SI 2013/496 Sch.11 para.18

1206. Damages-Based Agreements Regulations 2010
revoked: SI 2013/609 Reg.2

1228. Merchant Shipping (Ship-to-Ship Transfers) Regulations 2010
Reg.2, amended: SI 2013/755 Sch.4 para.389

1484. Wireless Telegraphy (Automotive Short Range Radar) (Exemption) (No.2) (Amendment) Regulations 2010
revoked: SI 2013/1437 Reg.3

1492. Drinking Milk (Wales) Regulations 2010
Reg.2, amended: SI 2013/3270 Reg.4
Reg.2, revoked (in part): SI 2013/3270 Reg.4
Reg.3, amended: SI 2013/3270 Reg.4
Reg.4, revoked: SI 2013/3270 Reg.4
Reg.5, amended: SI 2013/3270 Reg.4
Reg.6, amended: SI 2013/3270 Reg.4

1493. Water Resources (Control of Pollution) (Silage, Slurry and Agriculture Fuel Oil) (Wales) Regulations 2010
Reg.2, amended: SI 2013/755 Sch.5 para.58
Reg.3, amended: SI 2013/755 Sch.5 para.59
Reg.7, amended: SI 2013/755 Sch.5 para.59
Reg.8, amended: SI 2013/755 Sch.5 para.59
Reg.9, amended: SI 2013/755 Sch.5 para.59
Sch.2 para.5, amended: SI 2013/755 Sch.5 para.59
Sch.2 para.7, amended: SI 2013/755 Sch.5 para.59

1513. Energy Act 2008 (Consequential Modifications) (Offshore Environmental Protection) Order 2010
Art.5, revoked: SI 2013/971 Reg.38

1532. Electoral Law (Polling Station Scheme) (Northern Ireland) Regulations 2010
applied: SI 2013/3156 Art.6
Reg.5, varied: SI 2013/3156 Art.6
Reg.7, varied: SI 2013/3156 Art.6

1554. Pyrotechnic Articles (Safety) Regulations 2010
Reg.3, amended: SI 2013/602 Sch.2 para.99
Reg.3, revoked (in part): SI 2013/602 Sch.2 para.99
Sch.2 para.1, amended: SI 2013/1950 Reg.2
Sch.4 para.5, amended: SI 2013/1948 Reg.4

1620. Pharmacy Order 2010 (Approved European Pharmacy Qualifications) Order 2010
Sch.1, amended: SI 2013/3036 Reg.7

1627. Marine Strategy Regulations 2010
Sch.2, amended: SSI 2013/323 Reg.26

1635. Land Registration (Proper Office) Order 2010
revoked: SI 2013/1627 Art.4

1647. National Health Service (Miscellaneous Amendments Relating to Independent Prescribing) (Wales) Regulations 2010
Reg.2, revoked: SI 2013/898 Sch.8 para.23

1648. National Health Service (Pharmaceutical Services) (Amendment) (Wales) (No.2) Regulations 2010
revoked: SI 2013/898 Sch.8 para.24

1668. Zoonoses and Animal By-Products (Fees) (England) Regulations 2010
revoked: SI 2013/1240 Reg.11

1671. Eggs and Chicks (Wales) Regulations 2010
Reg.3, amended: SI 2013/3270 Reg.5
Reg.8, amended: SI 2013/3270 Reg.5
Reg.11, amended: SI 2013/3270 Reg.5
Sch.1 Part 1, amended: SI 2013/3270 Reg.5
Sch.2 Part 1, substituted: SI 2013/3270 Reg.5
Sch.2 Part 2, amended: SI 2013/3270 Reg.5

Sch.3, amended: SI 2013/3270 Reg.5

1675. Export Control (Burma) (Amendment) Order 2010

revoked: SI 2013/1964 Sch.1

1703. Child Minding and Day Care (Disqualification) (Wales) Regulations 2010

Sch.1 para.11, amended: SI 2013/1465 Sch.1 para.27
Sch.1 para.14A, added: SI 2013/1465 Sch.1 para.27
Sch.3 para.2, amended: SI 2013/1465 Sch.1 para.27
Sch.3 para.7, amended: SI 2013/1465 Sch.1 para.27

1704. Cancellation of Student Loans for Living Costs Liability (Wales) Regulations 2010

applied: SI 2013/1396 Reg.5

1771. Designation of Schools Having a Religious Character (Independent Schools) (England) (No.2) Order 2010

Sch.1, amended: SI 2013/2162 Sch.2

1821. Environmental Civil Sanctions (Wales) Order 2010

applied: SI 2013/755 Sch.7 para.12
Art.2, amended: SI 2013/755 Sch.5 para.60

1823. Wireless Telegraphy (Licensing Procedures) Regulations 2010

Reg.5, referred to: SI 2013/1787 Art.2

1837. Lord President of the Council Order 2010

Art.3, referred to: 2013 c.6 s.25

1881. Health and Social Care Act 2008 (Miscellaneous Consequential Amendments) Order 2010

Art.22, revoked: SI 2013/458 Sch.1
Art.23, revoked: SI 2013/458 Sch.1

1898. Parental Responsibility and Measures for the Protection of Children (International Obligations) (England and Wales and Northern Ireland) Regulations 2010

Sch.1 para.1, revoked: 2013 c.22 Sch.10 para.99

1903. Electricity (Competitive Tenders for Offshore Transmission Licences) Regulations 2010

applied: SI 2013/175 Reg.2
revoked: SI 2013/175 Reg.1
Reg.15, applied: SI 2013/175 Reg.2

1907. Employment and Support Allowance (Transitional Provisions, Housing Benefit and Council Tax Benefit) (Existing Awards) (No.2) Regulations 2010

applied: SI 2013/386 Reg.26, Reg.27, SI 2013/983 Art.9
referred to: SI 2013/3029 Sch.7 para.25, Sch.7 para.28
Reg.2, varied: SI 2013/983 Sch.4 para.2
Reg.4, varied: SI 2013/983 Sch.4 para.3
Reg.5, applied: SI 2013/381 Reg.16
Reg.5, referred to: SI 2013/3029 Sch.7 para.25, Sch.7 para.28, SI 2013/3035 Sch.1
Reg.5, varied: SI 2013/983 Sch.4 para.4
Reg.6, varied: SI 2013/983 Sch.4 para.5
Reg.7, applied: SI 2013/386 Reg.26
Reg.7, varied: SI 2013/983 Sch.4 para.6
Reg.8, varied: SI 2013/983 Sch.4 para.7
Reg.9, varied: SI 2013/983 Sch.4 para.8
Reg.10, varied: SI 2013/983 Sch.4 para.9
Reg.11, varied: SI 2013/983 Sch.4 para.10
Reg.12, varied: SI 2013/983 Sch.4 para.11
Reg.13, varied: SI 2013/983 Sch.4 para.12
Reg.14, varied: SI 2013/983 Sch.4 para.13
Reg.15, varied: SI 2013/983 Sch.4 para.14
Reg.16, varied: SI 2013/983 Sch.4 para.15
Reg.17, varied: SI 2013/983 Sch.4 para.16
Reg.18, varied: SI 2013/983 Sch.4 para.17
Reg.21, varied: SI 2013/983 Sch.4 para.18
Reg.22, varied: SI 2013/983 Sch.4 para.19
Sch.1 Part 1 para.2, varied: SI 2013/983 Sch.4 para.20
Sch.1 Part 1 para.6, varied: SI 2013/983 Sch.4 para.20
Sch.1 Part 2 para.7, varied: SI 2013/983 Sch.4 para.20
Sch.1 Part 2 para.8, varied: SI 2013/983 Sch.4 para.20
Sch.1 Part 2 para.9, varied: SI 2013/983 Sch.4 para.20
Sch.1 Part 2 para.10, varied: SI 2013/983 Sch.4 para.20
Sch.1 Part 2 para.10A, varied: SI 2013/983 Sch.4 para.20
Sch.1 Part 2 para.11, varied: SI 2013/983 Sch.4 para.20
Sch.1 Part 2 para.12, varied: SI 2013/983 Sch.4 para.20
Sch.1 Part 3 para.13, varied: SI 2013/983 Sch.4 para.20
Sch.2 Part 1 para.2, varied: SI 2013/983 Sch.4 para.21
Sch.2 Part 1 para.2A, varied: SI 2013/983 Sch.4 para.21
Sch.2 Part 1 para.3, varied: SI 2013/983 Sch.4 para.21
Sch.2 Part 1 para.4, varied: SI 2013/983 Sch.4 para.21
Sch.2 Part 1 para.4A, varied: SI 2013/983 Sch.4 para.21
Sch.2 Part 2 para.6A, varied: SI 2013/983 Sch.4 para.21
Sch.2 Part 3 para.7, varied: SI 2013/983 Sch.4 para.21

Sch.2 Part 3 para.8, varied: SI 2013/983 Sch.4 para.21
Sch.2 Part 3 para.9, varied: SI 2013/983 Sch.4 para.21
Sch.2 Part 3 para.10, varied: SI 2013/983 Sch.4 para.21
Sch.2 Part 3 para.11, varied: SI 2013/983 Sch.4 para.21
Sch.2 Part 3 para.12, varied: SI 2013/983 Sch.4 para.21
Sch.2 Part 3 para.13, varied: SI 2013/983 Sch.4 para.21
Sch.2 Part 3 para.14, varied: SI 2013/983 Sch.4 para.21
Sch.2 Part 3 para.15, varied: SI 2013/983 Sch.4 para.21
Sch.2 Part 3 para.16, varied: SI 2013/983 Sch.4 para.21
Sch.2 Part 4, varied: SI 2013/983 Sch.4 para.21
Sch.2 Part 4 para.17, varied: SI 2013/983 Sch.4 para.21
Sch.2 Part 4 para.18, varied: SI 2013/983 Sch.4 para.21
Sch.2 Part 4 para.19, varied: SI 2013/983 Sch.4 para.21
Sch.2 Part 4 para.20, varied: SI 2013/983 Sch.4 para.21
Sch.2 Part 4 para.21, varied: SI 2013/983 Sch.4 para.21
Sch.2 Part 4 para.22, varied: SI 2013/983 Sch.4 para.21
Sch.2 Part 4 para.22A, varied: SI 2013/983 Sch.4 para.21
Sch.2 Part 4 para.23, varied: SI 2013/983 Sch.4 para.21
Sch.2 Part 4 para.24, varied: SI 2013/983 Sch.4 para.21
Sch.2 Part 4 para.25, varied: SI 2013/983 Sch.4 para.21
Sch.2 Part 4 para.25A, varied: SI 2013/983 Sch.4 para.21
Sch.2 Part 4 para.27, varied: SI 2013/983 Sch.4 para.21
Sch.3, varied: SI 2013/983 Sch.4 para.22

1927. Cosmetic Products (Safety) (Amendment No 2) Regulations 2010
revoked: SI 2013/1478 Sch.1

1938. Academy Conversions (Transfer of School Surpluses) Regulations 2010
revoked: SI 2013/3037 Reg.3

1941. Apprenticeships, Skills, Children and Learning Act 2009 (Consequential Amendments to Subordinate Legislation) (England) Order 2010
Art.16, revoked: SI 2013/458 Sch.1
Art.17, revoked: SI 2013/458 Sch.1
Art.22, revoked: SI 2013/3109 Reg.3
Art.23, revoked: SI 2013/3110 Reg.8

1955. Serious Organised Crime and Police Act 2005 (Disclosure of Information by SOCA) Order 2010
referred to: 2013 c.22 Sch.8 para.7
Art.2, varied: 2013 c.22 Sch.8 para.7

1970. Consumer Credit (Advertisements) Regulations 2010
revoked (in part): SI 2013/1881 Art.21

2128. Equality Act 2010 (Disability) Regulations 2010
Reg.4, see *P v Governing Body of A Primary School* [2013] UKUT 154 (AAC), [2013] Eq. L.R. 666 (UT (AAC)), David Williams

2130. Care Standards Act 2000 (Registration)(England) Regulations 2010
disapplied: SI 2013/2668 Reg.2
Reg.2, amended: SI 2013/706 Reg.11, SI 2013/1394 Sch.9 para.1, Sch.9 para.2
Reg.3, amended: SI 2013/1394 Sch.9 para.1, Sch.9 para.3, Sch.9 para.6
Reg.4, amended: SI 2013/1394 Sch.9 para.1
Reg.6, amended: SI 2013/1394 Sch.9 para.1, Sch.9 para.7
Reg.7, amended: SI 2013/446 Reg.2, SI 2013/1394 Sch.9 para.1, Sch.9 para.8, SI 2013/3239 Reg.25
Reg.8, amended: SI 2013/1394 Sch.9 para.1, Sch.9 para.9
Reg.9, amended: SI 2013/1394 Sch.9 para.1
Reg.10, amended: SI 2013/1394 Sch.9 para.1, Sch.9 para.3, Sch.9 para.10
Reg.11, amended: SI 2013/1394 Sch.9 para.1
Reg.12, amended: SI 2013/1394 Sch.9 para.1
Reg.13, amended: SI 2013/1394 Sch.9 para.1, Sch.9 para.11
Reg.13, disapplied: SI 2013/1394 Sch.10 para.8
Sch.1 Part 1 para.1, amended: SI 2013/1394 Sch.9 para.1, Sch.9 para.5
Sch.1 Part 1 para.2, amended: SI 2013/1394 Sch.9 para.1
Sch.1 Part 1 para.3, amended: SI 2013/1394 Sch.9 para.1, Sch.9 para.5
Sch.1 Part 1 para.4, amended: SI 2013/1394 Sch.9 para.1
Sch.1 Part 2 para.5, amended: SI 2013/1394 Sch.9 para.1, Sch.9 para.12
Sch.1 Part 2 para.6, amended: SI 2013/1394 Sch.9 para.1, Sch.9 para.12
Sch.1 Part 2 para.7, amended: SI 2013/1394 Sch.9 para.1, Sch.9 para.12
Sch.1 Part 2 para.8, amended: SI 2013/1394 Sch.9 para.1
Sch.1 Part 2 para.9, amended: SI 2013/1394 Sch.9 para.1

Sch.1 Part 2 para.9A, added: SI 2013/1394 Sch.9 para.12
Sch.1 Part 2 para.9A, amended: SI 2013/1394 Sch.9 para.1
Sch.1 Part 2 para.10, amended: SI 2013/1394 Sch.9 para.1, Sch.9 para.12
Sch.1 Part 2 para.11, amended: SI 2013/1394 Sch.9 para.1
Sch.1 Part 2 para.12, amended: SI 2013/1394 Sch.9 para.1
Sch.1 Part 2 para.13, amended: SI 2013/1394 Sch.9 para.1, Sch.9 para.4, Sch.9 para.12, SI 2013/3239 Reg.26
Sch.1 Part 2 para.14, amended: SI 2013/1394 Sch.9 para.1, Sch.9 para.4, Sch.9 para.12
Sch.1 Part 2 para.15, amended: SI 2013/1394 Sch.9 para.1
Sch.1 Part 2 para.16, amended: SI 2013/1394 Sch.9 para.1, Sch.9 para.12
Sch.1 Part 2 para.17, amended: SI 2013/1394 Sch.9 para.1
Sch.1 Part 2 para.18, amended: SI 2013/1394 Sch.9 para.1, Sch.9 para.12
Sch.1 Part 3 para.19, amended: SI 2013/1394 Sch.9 para.1, Sch.9 para.7, Sch.9 para.12
Sch.1 Part 3 para.20, amended: SI 2013/1394 Sch.9 para.1, Sch.9 para.12
Sch.2 para.1, amended: SI 2013/1394 Sch.9 para.1
Sch.2 para.2, amended: SI 2013/1394 Sch.9 para.1, Sch.9 para.5
Sch.2 para.3, amended: SI 2013/1394 Sch.9 para.1
Sch.2 para.4, amended: SI 2013/1394 Sch.9 para.1
Sch.2 para.5, amended: SI 2013/1394 Sch.9 para.1
Sch.2 para.6, amended: SI 2013/1394 Sch.9 para.1
Sch.2 para.7, amended: SI 2013/1394 Sch.9 para.1
Sch.2 para.8, amended: SI 2013/1394 Sch.9 para.1
Sch.2 para.9, amended: SI 2013/1394 Sch.9 para.1
Sch.2 para.10, amended: SI 2013/1394 Sch.9 para.1
Sch.3 Part 1 para.1, amended: SI 2013/1394 Sch.9 para.1
Sch.3 Part 1 para.2, amended: SI 2013/1394 Sch.9 para.1
Sch.3 Part 1 para.3, amended: SI 2013/1394 Sch.9 para.1, Sch.9 para.5
Sch.3 Part 1 para.4, amended: SI 2013/1394 Sch.9 para.1
Sch.3 Part 1 para.5, amended: SI 2013/1394 Sch.9 para.1
Sch.3 Part 1 para.6, amended: SI 2013/1394 Sch.9 para.1
Sch.3 Part 1 para.7, amended: SI 2013/1394 Sch.9 para.1
Sch.3 Part 1 para.8, amended: SI 2013/1394 Sch.9 para.1, Sch.9 para.13
Sch.3 Part 2 para.9, amended: SI 2013/1394 Sch.9 para.1
Sch.3 Part 2 para.10, amended: SI 2013/1394 Sch.9 para.1, Sch.9 para.5
Sch.3 Part 2 para.11, amended: SI 2013/1394 Sch.9 para.1
Sch.3 Part 2 para.12, amended: SI 2013/1394 Sch.9 para.1
Sch.4 para.1, amended: SI 2013/1394 Sch.9 para.3, Sch.9 para.14
Sch.4 para.2, amended: SI 2013/1394 Sch.9 para.3
Sch.4 para.3, amended: SI 2013/1394 Sch.9 para.3, Sch.9 para.14
Sch.4 para.4, amended: SI 2013/1394 Sch.9 para.3
Sch.4 para.5, amended: SI 2013/1394 Sch.9 para.3
Sch.4 para.6, amended: SI 2013/1394 Sch.9 para.3, Sch.9 para.14
Sch.4 para.7, amended: SI 2013/1394 Sch.9 para.3
Sch.4 para.8, amended: SI 2013/1394 Sch.9 para.3, Sch.9 para.14
Sch.4 para.9, amended: SI 2013/1394 Sch.9 para.3, Sch.9 para.14
Sch.4 para.10, amended: SI 2013/1394 Sch.9 para.3, Sch.9 para.14
Sch.4 para.11, amended: SI 2013/1394 Sch.9 para.3, Sch.9 para.14
Sch.4 para.12, amended: SI 2013/1394 Sch.9 para.3
Sch.4 para.13, amended: SI 2013/1394 Sch.9 para.3, Sch.9 para.14
Sch.5 para.1, amended: SI 2013/1394 Sch.9 para.1
Sch.5 para.3, amended: SI 2013/1394 Sch.9 para.15
Sch.5 para.10, amended: SI 2013/1394 Sch.9 para.1

2136. Llangollen and Corwen Railway Order 2010
Art.9, amended: SI 2013/755 Sch.5 para.62
Art.21, amended: SI 2013/755 Sch.5 para.62
Sch.4 para.1, amended: SI 2013/755 Sch.5 para.63
Sch.4 para.2, amended: SI 2013/755 Sch.5 para.63
Sch.4 para.3, amended: SI 2013/755 Sch.5 para.63
Sch.4 para.4, amended: SI 2013/755 Sch.5 para.63
Sch.4 para.5, amended: SI 2013/755 Sch.5 para.63
Sch.4 para.6, amended: SI 2013/755 Sch.5 para.63
Sch.4 para.7, amended: SI 2013/755 Sch.5 para.63
Sch.4 para.8, amended: SI 2013/755 Sch.5 para.63
Sch.4 para.9, amended: SI 2013/755 Sch.5 para.63
Sch.4 para.10, amended: SI 2013/755 Sch.5 para.63
Sch.4 para.11, amended: SI 2013/755 Sch.5 para.63

Sch.4 para.12, amended: SI 2013/755 Sch.5 para.63
Sch.4 para.13, amended: SI 2013/755 Sch.5 para.63

2184. Town and Country Planning (Development Management Procedure) (England) Order 2010
Art.2, amended: SI 2013/1238 Art.3, Art.5, SI 2013/2136 Art.2
Art.3A, added: SI 2013/2932 Art.2
Art.3A, revoked: SI 2013/2932 Art.2
Art.3B, added: SI 2013/2932 Art.2
Art.3B, revoked: SI 2013/2932 Art.2
Art.6, amended: SI 2013/3194 Art.2
Art.8, substituted: SI 2013/1238 Art.4
Art.10, amended: SI 2013/1238 Art.5, SI 2013/2932 Art.2
Art.10, revoked (in part): SI 2013/2932 Art.2
Art.10A, added: SI 2013/1238 Art.5
Art.11, amended: SI 2013/3194 Art.2
Art.13, amended: SI 2013/2136 Art.2
Art.20, amended: SI 2013/1238 Art.6
Art.29, amended: SI 2013/1238 Art.5, SI 2013/2932 Art.2
Art.29, applied: SI 2013/2140 Art.8
Art.29, revoked (in part): SI 2013/2932 Art.2
Art.31, amended: SI 2013/1238 Art.7
Art.31, see *R. (on the application of Prideaux) v Buckinghamshire CC* [2013] EWHC 1054 (Admin), [2013] Env. L.R. 32 (QBD (Admin)), Lindblom, J.
Art.33, amended: SI 2013/2136 Art.2
Art.33, applied: SI 2013/2114 Reg.4, SI 2013/2137 r.6
Art.34, amended: SI 2013/235 Sch.2 para.155, SI 2013/2879 Art.2
Art.34, applied: SI 2013/1102 Reg.5, SI 2013/2879 Art.4
Art.34, revoked (in part): SI 2013/2879 Art.2
Art.36, amended: SI 2013/1238 Art.5
Art.36, applied: SI 2013/1102 Reg.5, Reg.6, SI 2013/2140 Art.2, Art.15, Art.26
Art.37, applied: SI 2013/1102 Reg.5
Art.37A, applied: SI 2013/1102 Reg.6
Sch.1A para.1, added: SI 2013/2136 Sch.1
Sch.1A para.2, added: SI 2013/2136 Sch.1
Sch.1A para.3, added: SI 2013/2136 Sch.1
Sch.1A para.4, added: SI 2013/2136 Sch.1
Sch.1A para.5, added: SI 2013/2136 Sch.1
Sch.2, amended: SI 2013/2136 Sch.2, Sch.3
Sch.3, amended: SI 2013/2136 Sch.4
Sch.5, applied: SI 2013/2140 Art.17
Sch.5, referred to: SI 2013/2140 Art.2, Art.17

2192. Equality Act 2010 (Qualifying Settlement Contract Specified Person) Order 2010
amended: SI 2013/1956 Sch.1 para.17
Art.1, amended: SI 2013/1956 Sch.1 para.17

2214. Building Regulations 2010
applied: SI 2013/2730 Reg.6, Reg.7
varied: SI 2013/2730 Reg.6, Reg.7
Part 7A, applied: SI 2013/2730 Reg.3
Reg.2, amended: SI 2013/10 Reg.4, SI 2013/747 Reg.3, SI 2013/1959 Reg.3
Reg.11, amended: SI 2013/747 Reg.4, SI 2013/1105 Reg.3
Reg.12, applied: SI 2013/747 Reg.35, Reg.36
Reg.14, revoked (in part): SI 2013/747 Reg.5
Reg.15, amended: SI 2013/747 Reg.6
Reg.16, amended: SI 2013/747 Reg.7
Reg.17, amended: SI 2013/747 Reg.8
Reg.17A, added: SI 2013/747 Reg.9
Reg.19, amended: SI 2013/747 Reg.10
Reg.20, amended: SI 2013/747 Reg.11
Reg.21, amended: SI 2013/747 Reg.12
Reg.23, substituted: SI 2013/747 Reg.13
Reg.25, amended: SI 2013/747 Reg.14
Reg.25, substituted: SI 2013/1959 Reg.4
Reg.25A, added: SI 2013/747 Reg.15
Reg.25B, added: SI 2013/747 Reg.15
Reg.26A, added: SI 2013/1959 Reg.5
Reg.27A, added: SI 2013/1959 Reg.6
Reg.29, amended: SI 2013/10 Reg.5, SI 2013/747 Reg.16
Reg.29, revoked (in part): SI 2013/747 Reg.16
Reg.29A, added: SI 2013/747 Reg.17
Reg.30, amended: SI 2013/747 Reg.18
Reg.33, amended: SI 2013/747 Reg.19
Reg.34, amended: SI 2013/1105 Reg.3, SI 2013/1959 Reg.7
Reg.34, substituted: SI 2013/181 Reg.7
Reg.35, amended: SI 2013/747 Reg.20, SI 2013/1959 Reg.8
Reg.37A, added: SI 2013/2730 Reg.4
Reg.37B, added: SI 2013/2730 Reg.4
Reg.43, amended: SI 2013/747 Reg.21
Reg.47, amended: SI 2013/747 Reg.22
Reg.48, amended: SI 2013/747 Reg.23
Sch.3, amended: SI 2013/747 Reg.24, Reg.25, Reg.26, Reg.27, SI 2013/1105 Reg.3
Sch.3, substituted: SI 2013/2621 Sch.1
Sch.4 para.3A, added: SI 2013/747 Reg.28
Sch.4A Part 1 para.1, added: SI 2013/10 Sch.1
Sch.4A Part 1 para.2, added: SI 2013/10 Sch.1
Sch.4A Part 1 para.3, added: SI 2013/10 Sch.1
Sch.4A Part 1 para.4, added: SI 2013/10 Sch.1
Sch.4A Part 1 para.5, added: SI 2013/10 Sch.1
Sch.4A Part 1 para.6, added: SI 2013/10 Sch.1
Sch.4A Part 1 para.7, added: SI 2013/10 Sch.1
Sch.4A Part 1 para.8, added: SI 2013/10 Sch.1

Sch.4A Part 1 para.9, added: SI 2013/10 Sch.1
Sch.4A Part 1 para.10, added: SI 2013/10 Sch.1
Sch.4A Part 1 para.11, added: SI 2013/10 Sch.1
Sch.4A Part 1 para.12, added: SI 2013/10 Sch.1
Sch.4A Part 1 para.13, added: SI 2013/10 Sch.1
Sch.4A Part 1 para.14, added: SI 2013/10 Sch.1
Sch.4A Part 1 para.15, added: SI 2013/10 Sch.1
Sch.4A Part 1 para.16, added: SI 2013/10 Sch.1
Sch.4A Part 1 para.17, added: SI 2013/10 Sch.1
Sch.4A Part 1 para.18, added: SI 2013/10 Sch.1
Sch.4A Part 1 para.19, added: SI 2013/10 Sch.1
Sch.4A Part 1 para.20, added: SI 2013/10 Sch.1
Sch.4A Part 1 para.21, added: SI 2013/10 Sch.1
Sch.4A Part 1 para.22, added: SI 2013/10 Sch.1
Sch.4A Part 1 para.23, added: SI 2013/10 Sch.1
Sch.4A Part 1 para.24, added: SI 2013/10 Sch.1
Sch.4A Part 1 para.25, added: SI 2013/10 Sch.1
Sch.4A Part 1 para.26, added: SI 2013/10 Sch.1
Sch.4A Part 2, added: SI 2013/10 Sch.1

2215. Building (Approved Inspectors etc.) Regulations 2010
applied: SI 2013/2730 Reg.6, Reg.7
varied: SI 2013/2730 Reg.6, Reg.7
Reg.8, amended: SI 2013/747 Reg.30, SI 2013/2730 Reg.5
Reg.16, amended: SI 2013/747 Reg.31
Reg.20, amended: SI 2013/747 Reg.32, SI 2013/1959 Reg.10
Reg.20, substituted: SI 2013/747 Reg.32
Sch.1, amended: SI 2013/747 Reg.33

2220. Financial Services and Markets Act 2000 (Contribution to Costs of Special Resolution Regime) Regulations 2010
Reg.17, amended: SI 2013/472 Sch.2 para.189

2228. Contaminants in Food (England) Regulations 2010
disapplied: SI 2013/264 Sch.1
revoked: SI 2013/2196 Reg.10

2232. Flood Risk Management Functions Order 2010
Art.2, amended: SI 2013/755 Sch.4 para.390

2317. Equality Act 2010 (Commencement No 4, Savings, Consequential, Transitional, Transitory and Incidental Provisions and Revocation) Order 2010
Art.10, disapplied: SI 2013/425 Reg.10

2394. Contaminants in Food (Wales) Regulations 2010
referred to: SI 2013/479 Sch.1
revoked: SI 2013/2493 Reg.10

2430. Employment and Support Allowance (Transitional Provisions, Housing Benefit and Council Tax Benefit) (Existing Awards) (No.2) (Amendment) Regulations 2010
referred to: SI 2013/3035 Sch.1
Reg.5, applied: SI 2013/3035 Sch.1

2460. Birmingham Community Healthcare National Health Service Trust (Establishment) Order 2010
Art.1; amended: SI 2013/593 Art.2

2462. Central London Community Healthcare National Health Service Trust (Establishment) Order 2010
Art.1, amended: SI 2013/593 Art.2

2463. Eastern and Coastal Kent Community Health National Health Service Trust (Establishment) Order 2010
Art.1, amended: SI 2013/593 Art.2

2464. Hertfordshire Community National Health Service Trust (Establishment) Order 2010
Art.1, amended: SI 2013/593 Art.2

2465. Liverpool Community Health National Health Service Trust (Establishment) Order 2010
Art.1, amended: SI 2013/593 Art.2

2466. Norfolk Community Health and Care National Health Service Trust (Establishment) Order 2010
Art.1, amended: SI 2013/593 Art.2

2476. Scottish Parliament (Disqualification) Order 2010
Sch.1 Part I, amended: SI 2013/1465 Sch.1 Part 3, SI 2013/2314 Art.8

2485. Ashton, Leigh and Wigan Community Healthcare National Health Service Trust (Establishment) Order 2010
Art.1, amended: SI 2013/593 Art.2

2503. Animal Feed (England) Regulations 2010
Reg.2, amended: SI 2013/3133 Reg.3
Reg.4, substituted: SI 2013/3133 Reg.3
Sch.1, substituted: SI 2013/3133 Sch.2

2512. Wireless Telegraphy (Exemption and Amendment) Regulations 2010
Reg.5, amended: SI 2013/1253 Reg.2

2537. Companies Act 2006 (Transfer of Audit Working Papers to Third Countries) Regulations 2010
Reg.1, amended: SI 2013/1672 Reg.13
Reg.4, substituted: SI 2013/1672 Reg.13

2571. Care Leavers (England) Regulations 2010
Reg.3, amended: SI 2013/706 Reg.12

2580. Building Society Special Administration (England and Wales) Rules 2010
Part 1 r.4, amended: SI 2013/496 Sch.11 para.19, SI 2013/1765 Art.7
Part 2 r.12, amended: SI 2013/472 Sch.2 para.190
Part 2 r.15, amended: SI 2013/496 Sch.11 para.19
Part 2 r.20, amended: SI 2013/472 Sch.2 para.190
Part 2 r.22, amended: SI 2013/496 Sch.11 para.19
Part 2 r.24, amended: SI 2013/472 Sch.2 para.190
Part 2 r.25, amended: SI 2013/472 Sch.2 para.190
Part 3 r.31, amended: SI 2013/472 Sch.2 para.190
Part 3 r.38, amended: SI 2013/472 Sch.2 para.190
Part 3 r.45, amended: SI 2013/472 Sch.2 para.190

Part 3 r.46, amended: SI 2013/472 Sch.2 para.190
Part 3 r.49, amended: SI 2013/472 Sch.2 para.190
Part 3 r.50, amended: SI 2013/472 Sch.2 para.190
Part 3 r.51, amended: SI 2013/472 Sch.2 para.190
Part 4 r.54, amended: SI 2013/472 Sch.2 para.190
Part 5 r.62, amended: SI 2013/472 Sch.2 para.190
Part 5 r.63, amended: SI 2013/472 Sch.2 para.190

2581. Building Society Insolvency (England and Wales) Rules 2010

Part 1 r.3, amended: SI 2013/472 Sch.2 para.191
Part 2 r.10, amended: SI 2013/472 Sch.2 para.191
Part 2 r.16, amended: SI 2013/472 Sch.2 para.191
Part 3 r.20, amended: SI 2013/472 Sch.2 para.191
Part 3 r.22, amended: SI 2013/472 Sch.2 para.191
Part 4 r.28, amended: SI 2013/472 Sch.2 para.191
Part 6 r.42, amended: SI 2013/472 Sch.2 para.191
Part 6 r.43, amended: SI 2013/472 Sch.2 para.191
Part 6 r.46, amended: SI 2013/472 Sch.2 para.191
Part 7 r.74, amended: SI 2013/472 Sch.2 para.191
Part 9 r.85, amended: SI 2013/472 Sch.2 para.191
Part 9 r.87, amended: SI 2013/472 Sch.2 para.191
Part 9 r.88, amended: SI 2013/472 Sch.2 para.191
Part 9 r.89, amended: SI 2013/472 Sch.2 para.191
Part 9 r.91, amended: SI 2013/472 Sch.2 para.191
Part 9 r.95, amended: SI 2013/472 Sch.2 para.191
Part 9 r.96, amended: SI 2013/472 Sch.2 para.191
Part 9 r.97, amended: SI 2013/472 Sch.2 para.191
Part 9 r.107, amended: SI 2013/472 Sch.2 para.191
Part 9 r.108, amended: SI 2013/472 Sch.2 para.191
Part 17 r.180, amended: SI 2013/472 Sch.2 para.191
Part 17 r.181, amended: SI 2013/472 Sch.2 para.191
Part 18 r.203, amended: SI 2013/472 Sch.2 para.191
Part 22 r.269, amended: SI 2013/472 Sch.2 para.191

2584. Building Society Insolvency (Scotland) Rules 2010

Part 1 r.3, amended: SI 2013/472 Sch.2 para.192
Part 2 r.8, amended: SI 2013/472 Sch.2 para.192
Part 3 r.11, amended: SI 2013/472 Sch.2 para.192
Part 3 r.12, amended: SI 2013/472 Sch.2 para.192
Part 4 r.17, amended: SI 2013/472 Sch.2 para.192
Part 6 r.25, amended: SI 2013/472 Sch.2 para.192
Part 7 r.31, amended: SI 2013/472 Sch.2 para.192
Part 8 r.32, amended: SI 2013/472 Sch.2 para.192
Part 8 r.33, amended: SI 2013/472 Sch.2 para.192
Part 8 r.37, amended: SI 2013/472 Sch.2 para.192
Part 8 r.38, amended: SI 2013/472 Sch.2 para.192
Part 8 r.39, amended: SI 2013/472 Sch.2 para.192
Part 8 r.40, amended: SI 2013/472 Sch.2 para.192
Part 8 r.42, amended: SI 2013/472 Sch.2 para.192
Part 8 r.43, amended: SI 2013/472 Sch.2 para.192
Part 8 r.45, amended: SI 2013/472 Sch.2 para.192
Part 8 r.51, amended: SI 2013/472 Sch.2 para.192
Part 12 r.87, amended: SI 2013/472 Sch.2 para.192
Part 12 r.88, amended: SI 2013/472 Sch.2 para.192
Part 12 r.90, amended: SI 2013/472 Sch.2 para.192
Part 13 r.95, amended: SI 2013/472 Sch.2 para.192

2600. Tribunal Procedure (Upper Tribunal) (Lands Chamber) Rules 2010

Part 2 r.10, substituted: SI 2013/1188 r.3
Part 2 r.20, amended: SI 2013/1188 r.4
Part 5 r.30, amended: SI 2013/1188 r.5
Part 5 r.30, revoked (in part): SI 2013/1188 r.5
Part 8 r.44A, added: SI 2013/1188 r.7
Part 8 r.44A, substituted: SI 2013/1188 r.6
Part 8 r.45, substituted: SI 2013/1188 r.6
Part 10 r.51A, added: SI 2013/1188 r.8
Part 11 r.55, amended: SI 2013/1188 r.9
r.8, see *Pitman v Nuneaton and Bedworth BC* [2013] UKUT 246 (LC), [2013] R.V.R. 334 (UT (Lands)), AJ Trott FRICS

2614. Education (Listed Bodies) (England) Order 2010

revoked: SI 2013/2993 Art.1
Sch.1 Part 1, amended: SI 2013/2318 Sch.1 para.118

2617. Ecodesign for Energy-Related Products Regulations 2010

Sch.1 para.4, amended: SI 2013/1232 Reg.2

2618. Education (Recognised Bodies) (England) Order 2010

revoked: SI 2013/2992 Art.1

2628. Capital Requirements (Amendment) Regulations 2010

revoked: SI 2013/3115 Sch.3

2649. National Health Service (Functions of Strategic Health Authorities and Primary Care Trusts and Administration Arrangements) (England) Amendment (No.2) Regulations 2010

revoked: SI 2013/235 Sch.2 para.201

2652. Animal Feed (Wales) Regulations 2010

Reg.2, amended: SI 2013/3207 Reg.3
Reg.4, amended: SI 2013/3207 Reg.3
Sch.1, substituted: SI 2013/3207 Sch.2

2655. First-tier Tribunal and Upper Tribunal (Chambers) Order 2010

Art.2, amended: SI 2013/1187 Art.3
Art.5A, added: SI 2013/1187 Art.4
Art.10, amended: SI 2013/1187 Art.5, SI 2013/2068 Art.3
Art.11, amended: SI 2013/2068 Art.4
Art.12, amended: SI 2013/1187 Art.6
Art.13, amended: SI 2013/1187 Art.7

2660. Protection of Vulnerable Groups (Scotland) Act 2007 (Consequential Provisions) Order 2010

Art.2, amended: SI 2013/2318 Sch.1 para.120

Art.2, revoked (in part): SI 2013/2318 Sch.1 para.120
Art.3, amended: SI 2013/2318 Sch.1 para.120

2797. Visits to Former Looked After Children in Detention (England) Regulations 2010
Reg.2, amended: SI 2013/706 Reg.13
Reg.3, substituted: SI 2013/706 Reg.13

2817. Flavourings in Food (England) Regulations 2010
Reg.3, revoked: SI 2013/2210 Sch.5
Reg.4, revoked: SI 2013/2210 Sch.5
Reg.5, revoked: SI 2013/2210 Sch.5
Reg.6, revoked: SI 2013/2210 Sch.5
Reg.8, revoked: SI 2013/2210 Sch.5

2818. Rate of Bereavement Benefits Regulations 2010
Reg.2, amended: SI 2013/574 Art.15
Reg.3, amended: SI 2013/574 Art.15

2839. Child Minding and Day Care Exceptions (Wales) Order 2010
Art.11, referred to: SI 2013/3029 Sch.1 para.19, Sch.6 para.21, SI 2013/3035 Sch.1
Art.12, referred to: SI 2013/3029 Sch.1 para.19, Sch.6 para.21, SI 2013/3035 Sch.1
Art.14, referred to: SI 2013/3029 Sch.1 para.19, Sch.6 para.21, SI 2013/3035 Sch.1

2841. Medical Profession (Responsible Officers) Regulations 2010
Reg.1, amended: SI 2013/391 Reg.2
Reg.5, substituted: SI 2013/391 Reg.3
Reg.9, amended: SI 2013/391 Reg.3
Reg.10, amended: SI 2013/391 Reg.3
Reg.11, amended: SI 2013/391 Reg.3
Reg.12, substituted: SI 2013/391 Reg.3
Reg.13, amended: SI 2013/391 Reg.3
Reg.14, amended: SI 2013/391 Reg.3
Reg.16, amended: SI 2013/391 Reg.4
Reg.18, amended: SI 2013/391 Reg.4
Reg.19, amended: SI 2013/391 Reg.4
Sch.1 Part 1 para.1, amended: SI 2013/391 Reg.5
Sch.1 Part 1 para.3, amended: SI 2013/391 Reg.5
Sch.1 Part 1 para.4, amended: SI 2013/391 Reg.5
Sch.1 Part 1 para.5, revoked: SI 2013/391 Reg.5
Sch.1 Part 1 para.14A, added: SI 2013/391 Reg.5
Sch.1 Part 1 para.14B, added: SI 2013/391 Reg.5
Sch.1 Part 2 para.20, amended: SI 2013/391 Reg.6
Sch.1 Part 2 para.25A, added: SI 2013/391 Reg.6
Sch.1 Part 2 para.25B, added: SI 2013/391 Reg.6
Sch.1 Part 2 para.25C, added: SI 2013/391 Reg.6
Sch.1 Part 2 para.25D, added: SI 2013/391 Reg.6
Sch.1 Part 2 para.25E, added: SI 2013/391 Reg.6

2880. Single Use Carrier Bags Charge (Wales) Regulations 2010
Sch.1 para.1, amended: SI 2013/898 Sch.7 para.6

2893. Official Statistics Order 2010
revoked: SI 2013/1163 Art.2
Sch.1, amended: SI 2013/472 Sch.2 para.193

2915. Sea Fish (Specified Area) (Prohibition of Fixed Engines) (Wales) Order 2010
Art.4, amended: SI 2013/755 Sch.5 para.64

2922. Flavourings in Food (Wales) Regulations 2010
Reg.3, revoked: SI 2013/2591 Sch.5
Reg.4, revoked: SI 2013/2591 Sch.5
Reg.5, revoked: SI 2013/2591 Sch.5
Reg.6, revoked: SI 2013/2591 Sch.5
Reg.8, revoked: SI 2013/2591 Sch.5

2955. Family Procedure Rules 2010
referred to: SI 2013/3204 r.137
see *A (Children) v Lancashire CC* [2013] EWHC 851 (Fam), [2013] 2 F.L.R. 1221 (Fam Div), Peter Jackson, J.; see *AI v MT (Alternate Dispute Resolution)* [2013] EWHC 100 (Fam), [2013] 2 F.L.R. 371 (Fam Div), Baker, J.; see *L (A Child) (Interim Care Order: Extended Family), Re* [2013] EWCA Civ 179, [2013] 2 F.L.R. 302 (CA (Civ Div)), Thorpe, L.J.; see *N (A Child) (Care Proceedings: Adoption), Re* [2012] EWCA Civ 1563, [2013] 1 F.L.R. 1244 (CA (Civ Div)), Hallett, L.J.
Part 2 r.2.1, substituted: SI 2013/3204 r.3
Part 2 r.2.3, amended: SI 2013/1472 r.3, SI 2013/3204 r.4
Part 2 r.2.5, amended: SI 2013/3204 r.5
Part 2 r.2.5, revoked (in part): SI 2013/3204 r.5
Part 4 r.4.3, amended: SI 2013/3204 r.6
Part 4 r.4.4, amended: SI 2013/3204 r.7
Part 4 r.4.8, amended: SI 2013/3204 r.8
Part 5 r.5.4, added: SI 2013/3204 r.9
Part 6 r.6.16, amended: SI 2013/3204 r.10
Part 6 r.6.18, amended: SI 2013/3204 r.11
Part 7 r.7.1, revoked (in part): SI 2013/3204 r.12
Part 7 r.7.2, revoked: SI 2013/3204 r.12
Part 7 r.7.3, revoked: SI 2013/3204 r.12
Part 7 r.7.5, revoked: SI 2013/3204 r.12
Part 7 r.7.7, applied: SI 2013/1407 Art.4
Part 7 r.7.17, revoked: SI 2013/3204 r.12
Part 7 r.7.20, amended: SI 2013/3204 r.13
Part 7 r.7.23, revoked: SI 2013/3204 r.14
Part 7 r.7.24, revoked: SI 2013/3204 r.14
Part 7 r.7.33, amended: SI 2013/3204 r.15
Part 8 r.8.7, revoked: SI 2013/3204 r.16
Part 8 r.8.14, substituted: SI 2013/3204 r.17
Part 8 r.8.19, revoked: SI 2013/3204 r.18
Part 8 r.8.24, substituted: SI 2013/3204 r.19
Part 8 r.8.28, amended: SI 2013/3204 r.20
Part 8 r.8.30, substituted: SI 2013/3204 r.21
Part 8 r.8.37, revoked: SI 2013/3204 r.22
Part 9, amended: SI 2013/3204 r.25
Part 9, substituted: SI 2013/3204 r.27
Part 9 r.9.3, revoked (in part): SI 2013/3204 r.22

Part 9 r.9.5, amended: SI 2013/3204 r.23
Part 9 r.9.5, revoked (in part): SI 2013/3204 r.23
Part 9 r.9.7, amended: SI 2013/1472 r.4
Part 9 r.9.10, amended: SI 2013/3204 r.24
Part 9 r.9.12, amended: SI 2013/3204 r.26
Part 9 r.9.18, amended: SI 2013/3204 r.28
Part 9 r.9.18A, added: SI 2013/3204 r.29
Part 9 r.9.21, amended: SI 2013/3204 r.30
Part 9 r.9.22, amended: SI 2013/3204 r.31
Part 9 r.9.22, revoked (in part): SI 2013/3204 r.31
Part 9 r.9.23, amended: SI 2013/3204 r.32
Part 9 r.9.23, revoked (in part): SI 2013/3204 r.32
Part 9 r.9.25, revoked (in part): SI 2013/3204 r.33
Part 9 r.9.27, revoked (in part): SI 2013/3204 r.34
Part 10 r.10.2, amended: SI 2013/3204 r.35
Part 10 r.10.2, revoked (in part): SI 2013/3204 r.35
Part 10 r.10.4, revoked: SI 2013/3204 r.36
Part 10 r.10.5, amended: SI 2013/3204 r.37
Part 10 r.10.11, amended: SI 2013/3204 r.38
Part 10 r.10.14, amended: SI 2013/3204 r.39
Part 10 r.10.15, amended: SI 2013/3204 r.40
Part 10 r.10.16, amended: SI 2013/3204 r.41
Part 10 r.10.17, amended: SI 2013/3204 r.42
Part 11 r.11.1, amended: SI 2013/3204 r.43
Part 11 r.11.5, revoked: SI 2013/3204 r.44
Part 11 r.11.14, amended: SI 2013/3204 r.45
Part 11 r.11.19, amended: SI 2013/3204 r.46
Part 12 r.12.3, amended: SI 2013/235 Sch.2 para.156
Part 12 r.12.9, revoked: SI 2013/3204 r.47
Part 12 r.12.10, revoked: SI 2013/3204 r.47
Part 12 r.12.11, revoked: SI 2013/3204 r.47
Part 12 r.12.16, amended: SI 2013/3204 r.48
Part 12 r.12.16, revoked (in part): SI 2013/3204 r.48
Part 12 r.12.33, amended: SI 2013/3204 r.49
Part 12 r.12.35, amended: SI 2013/3204 r.50
Part 12 r.12.36, amended: SI 2013/3204 r.51
Part 12 r.12.52, amended: SI 2013/1465 Sch.1 para.28, SI 2013/3204 r.52
Part 12 r.12.52, revoked (in part): SI 2013/3204 r.52
Part 12 r.12.73, amended: SI 2013/534 Sch.1 para.22
Part 13 r.13.2, amended: SI 2013/3204 r.53
Part 13 r.13.9, amended: SI 2013/3204 r.54
Part 13 r.13.15, amended: SI 2013/3204 r.55
Part 13 r.13.17, amended: SI 2013/3204 r.56
Part 13 r.13.18, amended: SI 2013/3204 r.57
Part 13 r.13.18, revoked (in part): SI 2013/3204 r.57
Part 13 r.13.22, amended: SI 2013/3204 r.58
Part 13 r.13.22, revoked (in part): SI 2013/3204 r.58
Part 14 r.14.8, amended: SI 2013/3204 r.59
Part 14 r.14.14, amended: SI 2013/534 Sch.1 para.22
Part 14 r.14.17, amended: SI 2013/3204 r.60
Part 14 r.14.20, amended: SI 2013/3204 r.61
Part 14 r.14.28, revoked: SI 2013/3204 r.62
Part 17 r.17.6, revoked (in part): SI 2013/3204 r.63
Part 18 r.18.2, amended: SI 2013/3204 r.64
Part 18 r.18.8, amended: SI 2013/1472 r.5
Part 18 r.18.9, revoked (in part): SI 2013/3204 r.65
Part 18 r.18.12, revoked (in part): SI 2013/3204 r.65
Part 18 r.18.13, amended: SI 2013/3204 r.66
Part 20 r.20.1, revoked: SI 2013/3204 r.67
Part 22 r.22.12, amended: SI 2013/3204 r.68
Part 22 r.22.12, revoked (in part): SI 2013/3204 r.68
Part 24 r.24.1, revoked (in part): SI 2013/3204 r.69
Part 24 r.24.12, amended: SI 2013/3204 r.70
Part 26 r.26.2, amended: SI 2013/534 Sch.1 para.22
Part 27 r.27.5, revoked (in part): SI 2013/3204 r.71
Part 27 r.27.6, amended: SI 2013/3204 r.71
Part 27 r.27.6, revoked (in part): SI 2013/3204 r.71
Part 28 r.28.2, amended: SI 2013/530 r.3, SI 2013/3204 r.72
Part 28 r.28.2, revoked (in part): SI 2013/3204 r.72
Part 28 r.28.3, amended: SI 2013/530 r.4, SI 2013/1472 r.6
Part 28 r.28.4, revoked: SI 2013/3204 r.73
Part 29 r.29.17, added: SI 2013/3204 r.74
Part 29 r.29.18, added: SI 2013/3204 r.74
Part 30 r.30.3, amended: SI 2013/530 r.5
Part 31 r.31.18, amended: SI 2013/3204 r.75
Part 32, amended: SI 2013/3204 r.78
Part 32, added: SI 2013/3204 r.104
Part 32 r.32.1, amended: SI 2013/3204 r.76
Part 32 r.32.2, amended: SI 2013/3204 r.77
Part 32 r.32.5, amended: SI 2013/3204 r.79
Part 32 r.32.5A, added: SI 2013/3204 r.80
Part 32 r.32.6, amended: SI 2013/3204 r.81
Part 32 r.32.6A, added: SI 2013/3204 r.82
Part 32 r.32.6B, added: SI 2013/3204 r.82
Part 32 r.32.7, amended: SI 2013/3204 r.83
Part 32 r.32.8, substituted: SI 2013/3204 r.84
Part 32 r.32.9, amended: SI 2013/3204 r.85
Part 32 r.32.9A, added: SI 2013/3204 r.86
Part 32 r.32.10, amended: SI 2013/3204 r.87
Part 32 r.32.10A, added: SI 2013/3204 r.88
Part 32 r.32.11, amended: SI 2013/3204 r.89
Part 32 r.32.12, amended: SI 2013/3204 r.90
Part 32 r.32.12A, added: SI 2013/3204 r.91
Part 32 r.32.15, amended: SI 2013/3204 r.92
Part 32 r.32.15A, added: SI 2013/3204 r.93

Part 32 r.32.16, amended: SI 2013/3204 r.94
Part 32 r.32.16A, added: SI 2013/3204 r.95
Part 32 r.32.17, revoked: SI 2013/3204 r.96
Part 32 r.32.18, revoked: SI 2013/3204 r.96
Part 32 r.32.19, amended: SI 2013/3204 r.97
Part 32 r.32.19A, added: SI 2013/3204 r.98
Part 32 r.32.20, revoked: SI 2013/3204 r.99
Part 32 r.32.21, revoked: SI 2013/3204 r.99
Part 32 r.32.22, amended: SI 2013/3204 r.100
Part 32 r.32.22A, added: SI 2013/3204 r.101
Part 32 r.32.22B, added: SI 2013/3204 r.101
Part 32 r.32.22C, added: SI 2013/3204 r.101
Part 32 r.32.22D, added: SI 2013/3204 r.101
Part 32 r.32.25, amended: SI 2013/3204 r.102
Part 32 r.32.27, amended: SI 2013/3204 r.103
Part 34, added: SI 2013/3204 r.124
Part 34 r.34.1, amended: SI 2013/3204 r.105
Part 34 r.34.2, amended: SI 2013/3204 r.106
Part 34 r.34.3, amended: SI 2013/3204 r.107
Part 34 r.34.6, amended: SI 2013/3204 r.108
Part 34 r.34.7, amended: SI 2013/3204 r.109
Part 34 r.34.8, amended: SI 2013/3204 r.110
Part 34 r.34.13, amended: SI 2013/3204 r.111
Part 34 r.34.15, amended: SI 2013/3204 r.112
Part 34 r.34.16, amended: SI 2013/3204 r.113
Part 34 r.34.16, revoked (in part): SI 2013/3204 r.113
Part 34 r.34.17, amended: SI 2013/3204 r.114
Part 34 r.34.18, amended: SI 2013/3204 r.115
Part 34 r.34.19, amended: SI 2013/3204 r.116
Part 34 r.34.19, revoked (in part): SI 2013/3204 r.116
Part 34 r.34.20, amended: SI 2013/3204 r.117
Part 34 r.34.21, amended: SI 2013/3204 r.118
Part 34 r.34.23, amended: SI 2013/3204 r.119
Part 34 r.34.24, amended: SI 2013/3204 r.120
Part 34 r.34.26, amended: SI 2013/3204 r.121
Part 34 r.34.27, amended: SI 2013/3204 r.122
Part 34 r.34.28, amended: SI 2013/3204 r.123
Part 34 r.34.28A, amended: SI 2013/3204 r.125
Part 34 r.34.29A, revoked: SI 2013/3204 r.126
Part 34 r.34.30, amended: SI 2013/3204 r.127
Part 34 r.34.30, revoked (in part): SI 2013/3204 r.127
Part 34 r.34.31, amended: SI 2013/3204 r.128
Part 34 r.34.32, amended: SI 2013/3204 r.129
Part 34 r.34.33, amended: SI 2013/3204 r.130
Part 34 r.34.35, substituted: SI 2013/3204 r.131
Part 34 r.34.36, amended: SI 2013/3204 r.132
Part 34 r.34.36C, added: SI 2013/3204 r.133
Part 34 r.34.38, amended: SI 2013/3204 r.134
Part 34 r.34.39, amended: SI 2013/3204 r.135
Part 34 r.34.40, amended: SI 2013/3204 r.136

Pt 18., see *DR v GR (Financial Remedy: Variation of Overseas Trust)* [2013] EWHC 1196 (Fam), [2013] 2 F.L.R. 1534 (Fam Div), Mostyn, J.
Pt 22., see *B (A Child) (Residence Order: Case Management), Re* [2012] EWCA Civ 1742, [2013] 1 F.L.R. 963 (CA (Civ Div)), Moore-Bick, L.J.; see *P-S (Children) (Family Proceedings: Evidence), Re* [2013] EWCA Civ 223, [2013] 1 W.L.R. 3831 (CA (Civ Div)), Elias, L.J.
Pt 25., see *A (A Child) (Wasted Costs Order), Re* [2013] EWCA Civ 43, [2013] 6 Costs L.R. 873 (CA (Civ Div)), McFarlane, L.J.
r.1.1, see *H-L (A Child) (Expert Evidence: Test for Permission), Re* [2013] EWCA Civ 655, [2013] 2 F.L.R. 1434 (CA (Civ Div)), Sir James Munby (President, Fam); see *JRG v EB (Abduction: Brussels II Revised)* [2012] EWHC 1863 (Fam), [2013] 1 F.L.R. 203 (Fam Div), Mostyn, J.
r.4.4, see *Vince v Wyatt* [2013] EWCA Civ 495, [2013] 1 W.L.R. 3525 (CA (Civ Div)), Thorpe, L.J.
r.9.26B, see *DR v GR (Financial Remedy: Variation of Overseas Trust)* [2013] EWHC 1196 (Fam), [2013] 2 F.L.R. 1534 (Fam Div), Mostyn, J.
r.12.66, see *M (A Child) (Foreign Care Proceedings: Transfer),Re* [2013] EWHC 646 (Fam), [2013] Fam. 308 (Fam Div), Cobb, J.
r.13.9, see *G v G* [2012] EWHC 1979 (Fam), [2013] 1 F.L.R. 286 (Fam Div), Hedley, J.
r.24.12, see *JG (A Child) v Legal Services Commission* [2013] EWHC 804 (Admin), [2013] 2 F.L.R. 1174 (QBD (Admin)), Ryder, J.
r.25.1, see *H-L (A Child) (Expert Evidence: Test for Permission), Re* [2013] EWCA Civ 655, [2013] 2 F.L.R. 1434 (CA (Civ Div)), Sir James Munby (President, Fam); see *R. (on the application of T) v Legal Aid Agency (formerly Legal Services Commission)* [2013] EWHC 960 (Admin), [2013] 2 F.L.R. 1315 (QBD (Admin)), Collins, J.; see *TG (A Child) (Care Proceedings: Biomechanical Engineering Evidence), Re* [2013] EWCA Civ 5, [2013] 1 F.L.R. 1250 (CA (Civ Div)), Sir James Munby (President, Fam)
r.28.1, see *A (Children) v Lancashire CC* [2013] EWHC 851 (Fam), [2013] 2 F.L.R. 1221 (Fam Div), Peter Jackson, J.; see *HB v PB* [2013] EWHC 1956 (Fam), [2013] P.T.S.R. 1579 (Fam Div), Cobb, J.
r.28.2, see *KS v ND (Schedule I: Appeal: Costs)* [2013] EWHC 464 (Fam), [2013] 2 F.L.R. 698 (Fam Div), Mostyn, J.
r.28.3, see *Ezair v Ezair* [2012] EWCA Civ 893, [2013] 1 F.L.R. 281 (CA (Civ Div)), Thorpe, L.J.;

see *KS v ND (Schedule I: Appeal: Costs)* [2013] EWHC 464 (Fam), [2013] 2 F.L.R. 698 (Fam Div), Mostyn, J.
r.29.10, see *J Council v GU* [2012] EWHC 3531 (COP), (2013) 16 C.C.L. Rep. 31 (CP), Mostyn, J.
r.30.3, see *HH v BLW (Appeal: Costs: Proportionality)* [2012] EWHC 2199 (Fam), [2013] 1 F.L.R. 420 (Fam Div), Holman, J.
r.31.8, see *JRG v EB (Abduction: Brussels II Revised)* [2012] EWHC 1863 (Fam), [2013] 1 F.L.R. 203 (Fam Div), Mostyn, J.
r.33.1, see *S v M (Maintenance Pending Suit)* [2012] EWHC 4109 (Fam), [2013] 1 F.L.R. 1173 (Fam Div), Coleridge, J.
r.33.14, see *Mohan v Mohan* [2013] EWCA Civ 586, [2013] C.P. Rep. 36 (CA (Civ Div)), Thorpe, L.J.; see *Zuk v Zuk* [2012] EWCA Civ 1871, [2013] 2 F.L.R. 1466 (CA (Civ Div)), Thorpe, L.J.
r.33.16, see *Zuk v Zuk* [2012] EWCA Civ 1871, [2013] 2 F.L.R. 1466 (CA (Civ Div)), Thorpe, L.J.

2956. Somalia (Asset-Freezing) Regulations 2010
Reg.2, amended: SI 2013/472 Art.4
Sch.1 para.5, amended: SI 2013/472 Sch.2 para.194, SI 2013/534 Sch.1 para.12

2969. National Assembly for Wales (Disqualification) Order 2010
Sch.1 Part 1, amended: SI 2013/2268 Art.2

2984. Merchant Shipping and Fishing Vessels (Health and Safety at Work) (Asbestos) Regulations 2010
Reg.2, amended: SI 2013/1473 Reg.2
Reg.4, amended: SI 2013/1473 Reg.2
Reg.30, added: SI 2013/1473 Reg.2

2999. Scottish Parliament (Elections etc.) Order 2010
Art.8, applied: 2013 asp 14 Sch.2 para.2
Art.11, applied: 2013 asp 14 Sch.2 para.6

3020. Higher Education (Higher Amount) (England) Regulations 2010
Reg.5, substituted: SI 2013/3106 Reg.11

3021. Higher Education (Basic Amount) (England) Regulations 2010
Reg.5, substituted: SI 2013/3106 Reg.10

3023. Financial Services and Markets Act 2000 (Administration Orders Relating to Insurers) Order 2010
Art.3, amended: SI 2013/472 Sch.2 para.195
Art.4, amended: SI 2013/472 Sch.2 para.195
Sch.1 para.2, amended: SI 2013/472 Sch.2 para.195
Sch.1 para.3, amended: SI 2013/472 Sch.2 para.195
Sch.1 para.4, amended: SI 2013/472 Sch.2 para.195
Sch.1 para.5, amended: SI 2013/472 Sch.2 para.195
Sch.1 para.8, amended: SI 2013/472 Sch.2 para.195
Sch.1 para.9, amended: SI 2013/472 Sch.2 para.195

2011

70. Rail Vehicle Accessibility (Non-Interoperable Rail System) (London Underground Metropolitan Line S8 Vehicles) Exemption Order 2011
revoked: SI 2013/1931 Art.5

99. Electronic Money Regulations 2011
applied: SI 2013/161 Art.6, SSI 2013/50 Sch.2 para.1
referred to: SI 2013/161 Art.6
Reg.2, amended: SI 2013/472 Sch.2 para.196, SI 2013/3115 Sch.2 para.75
Reg.7, applied: SSI 2013/50 Sch.2 para.1
Reg.21, amended: SI 2013/3115 Sch.2 para.75
Reg.31, revoked: SI 2013/1881 Sch.1 para.42
Reg.50, applied: SI 2013/418 Art.2
Reg.51, applied: SI 2013/418 Art.2
Reg.52, applied: SI 2013/418 Art.2
Reg.54, applied: SI 2013/418 Art.2
Reg.55, applied: SI 2013/418 Art.2
Reg.57, applied: SI 2013/418 Art.2
Reg.59, amended: SI 2013/429 Reg.2, SI 2013/472 Sch.2 para.196
Reg.61, amended: SI 2013/472 Sch.2 para.196
Sch.2 Part 2 para.6, amended: SI 2013/3115 Sch.2 para.75
Sch.3 Part 1 para.1, amended: SI 2013/472 Sch.2 para.196
Sch.3 Part 1 para.2, amended: SI 2013/472 Sch.2 para.196
Sch.3 Part 1 para.3, amended: SI 2013/472 Sch.2 para.196
Sch.3 Part 1 para.3, revoked (in part): SI 2013/472 Sch.2 para.196
Sch.3 Part 1 para.4, amended: SI 2013/472 Sch.2 para.196
Sch.3 Part 1 para.5, amended: SI 2013/472 Sch.2 para.196
Sch.3 Part 1 para.6, amended: SI 2013/472 Sch.2 para.196
Sch.3 Part 1 para.7, amended: SI 2013/472 Sch.2 para.196
Sch.3 Part 1 para.8, amended: SI 2013/472 Sch.2 para.196

122. Legal Services Act 2007 (Disclosure of Restricted Information) Order 2011
Sch.1, amended: SI 2013/472 Sch.2 para.197

134. Nuclear Decommissioning and Waste Handling (Finance and Fees) Regulations 2011

applied: SI 2013/126 Reg.3
revoked: SI 2013/126 Reg.2

209. Criminal Procedure and Investigations Act 1996 (Defence Disclosure Time Limits) Regulations 2011

applied: SI 2013/1554 r.22_9
referred to: SI 2013/1554 r.2_3

234. CRC Energy Efficiency Scheme (Amendment) Order 2011

revoked (in part): SI 2013/1119 Art.96

237. Air Navigation (Overseas Territories) (Amendment) Order 2011

revoked: SI 2013/2870 Sch.1

243. Promotion of the Use of Energy from Renewable Sources Regulations 2011

Reg.4, amended: SI 2013/829 Reg.2

245. Investment Bank Special Administration Regulations 2011

see *MF Global UK Ltd (In Administration), Re* [2012] EWHC 3068 (Ch), [2013] 1 W.L.R. 903 (Ch D (Companies Ct)), David Richards, J.; see *MF Global UK Ltd (In Special Administration), Re* [2013] EWHC 1655 (Ch), [2013] 1 W.L.R. 3874 (Ch D (Companies Ct)), David Richards, J.
Reg.2, amended: SI 2013/472 Sch.2 para.198, SI 2013/504 Reg.41
Reg.3, amended: SI 2013/472 Sch.2 para.198
Reg.5, amended: SI 2013/472 Sch.2 para.198
Reg.6, amended: SI 2013/472 Sch.2 para.198
Reg.7, amended: SI 2013/472 Sch.2 para.198
Reg.8, amended: SI 2013/472 Sch.2 para.198
Reg.8, varied: 2013 c.33 Sch.2 para.33
Reg.11, amended: SI 2013/472 Sch.2 para.198
Reg.12, amended: SI 2013/472 Sch.2 para.198
Reg.13, amended: SI 2013/504 Reg.41
Reg.15, amended: SI 2013/472 Sch.2 para.198
Reg.16, amended: SI 2013/472 Sch.2 para.198
Reg.17, amended: SI 2013/472 Sch.2 para.198
Reg.18, amended: SI 2013/472 Sch.2 para.198
Reg.19, amended: SI 2013/472 Sch.2 para.198
Reg.20, amended: SI 2013/472 Sch.2 para.198
Reg.22, amended: SI 2013/472 Sch.2 para.198
Sch.1 para.3, amended: SI 2013/472 Sch.2 para.198
Sch.1 para.4, amended: SI 2013/472 Sch.2 para.198
Sch.2, amended: SI 2013/472 Sch.2 para.198
Sch.2 para.1, amended: SI 2013/1765 Art.10
Sch.2 para.3, amended: SI 2013/472 Sch.2 para.198
Sch.2 para.6, amended: SI 2013/472 Sch.2 para.198, SI 2013/1765 Art.10
Sch.2 para.7, amended: SI 2013/1765 Art.10
Sch.2 para.8, amended: SI 2013/472 Sch.2 para.198
Sch.2 para.9, amended: SI 2013/472 Sch.2 para.198, SI 2013/1765 Art.10
Sch.2 para.10, amended: SI 2013/472 Sch.2 para.198
Sch.2 para.11, amended: SI 2013/472 Sch.2 para.198
Sch.2 para.12, amended: SI 2013/472 Sch.2 para.198
Sch.2 para.13, amended: SI 2013/472 Sch.2 para.198
Sch.2 para.15, amended: SI 2013/472 Sch.2 para.198
Sch.2 para.17, amended: SI 2013/1765 Art.10
Sch.4 para.4, amended: SI 2013/472 Sch.2 para.198
Sch.6 Part 2 para.3, amended: SI 2013/472 Sch.2 para.198

258. Food Additives (England) (Amendment) Regulations 2011

revoked: SI 2013/2210 Sch.5

409. Marine Licensing (Exempted Activities) Order 2011

Art.3, amended: SI 2013/526 Art.3
Art.13, amended: SI 2013/526 Art.4
Art.15, amended: SI 2013/526 Art.5
Art.15, revoked (in part): SI 2013/526 Art.5
Art.17, amended: SI 2013/526 Art.6
Art.17A, added: SI 2013/526 Art.7
Art.17B, added: SI 2013/526 Art.7
Art.18A, added: SI 2013/526 Art.8
Art.21, amended: SI 2013/526 Art.9
Art.22, amended: SI 2013/526 Art.10
Art.25, amended: SI 2013/526 Art.11
Art.25A, added: SI 2013/526 Art.12
Art.26A, added: SI 2013/526 Art.13

445. Immigration and Nationality (Fees) Order 2011

applied: SI 2013/617, SI 2013/617 Reg.10, SI 2013/749, SI 2013/749 Reg.9
Art.3, applied: SI 2013/617 Reg.3, Reg.4, Reg.5, Reg.6, Reg.9, SI 2013/749 Reg.3, Reg.4, Reg.5, Reg.6, Reg.8
Art.4, amended: SI 2013/249 Art.2
Art.4, applied: SI 2013/617 Reg.6, Reg.9, SI 2013/749 Reg.5, Reg.8
Art.5, amended: SI 2013/249 Art.2
Art.5, applied: SI 2013/617 Reg.4, Reg.5, SI 2013/749 Reg.5
Art.6, applied: SI 2013/617 Reg.7, Reg.8, SI 2013/749 Reg.7

452. Poultrymeat (England) Regulations 2011

disapplied: SI 2013/264 Sch.1
Reg.1, amended: SI 2013/3235 Reg.10

Reg.2, amended: SI 2013/3235 Reg.10
Reg.12, amended: SI 2013/3235 Reg.10
Sch.1 Part 1, amended: SI 2013/3235 Reg.10
Sch.1 Part 2, amended: SI 2013/3235 Reg.10

503. National Health Service (Functions of Strategic Health Authorities and Primary Care Trusts and Administration Arrangements) (England) (Amendment) Regulations 2011
revoked: SI 2013/235 Sch.2 para.202

517. Armed Forces and Reserve Forces (Compensation Scheme) Order 2011
applied: SI 2013/386 Reg.27, SI 2013/471 Reg.11, Reg.20, Reg.33, SI 2013/480 Reg.24, SI 2013/483 Reg.10, SI 2013/628 Sch.1 para.29
Art.2, amended: SI 2013/436 Art.2
Art.15, amended: SI 2013/436 Art.2
Art.15, applied: SI 2013/376 Reg.83, SI 2013/379 Reg.68
Art.24A, added: SI 2013/436 Art.2
Art.24B, added: SI 2013/436 Art.2
Art.24C, added: SI 2013/436 Art.2
Art.24D, added: SI 2013/436 Art.2
Art.24E, added: SI 2013/436 Art.2
Art.24F, added: SI 2013/436 Art.2
Art.29, applied: SI 2013/376 Reg.83, SI 2013/379 Reg.68
Art.39, applied: SI 2013/3029 Sch.4 para.1, Sch.9 para.20, SI 2013/3035 Sch.1
Art.40, amended: SI 2013/436 Art.2
Art.41, amended: SI 2013/436 Art.2
Art.42, amended: SI 2013/436 Art.2
Art.64, amended: SI 2013/436 Art.2
Art.65A, added: SI 2013/436 Art.2

548. Libya (Financial Sanctions) Order 2011
Art.2, amended: SI 2013/472 Art.4
Sch.1 para.5, amended: SI 2013/472 Sch.2 para.200, SI 2013/534 Sch.1 para.12

555. Marine Licensing (Application Fees) (Wales) Regulations 2011
applied: SI 2013/414 Art.3

557. Marine Licensing (Register of Licensing Information) (Wales) Regulations 2011
applied: SI 2013/414 Art.3

559. Marine Licensing (Exempted Activities) (Wales) Order 2011
applied: SI 2013/414 Art.3
Art.5, amended: SI 2013/414 Art.5
Art.6, applied: SI 2013/414 Art.3
Art.7, applied: SI 2013/414 Art.3
Art.8, applied: SI 2013/414 Art.3
Art.9, applied: SI 2013/414 Art.3
Art.10, applied: SI 2013/414 Art.3
Art.11, applied: SI 2013/414 Art.3
Art.12, applied: SI 2013/414 Art.3
Art.13, applied: SI 2013/414 Art.3
Art.14, applied: SI 2013/414 Art.3
Art.15, applied: SI 2013/414 Art.3
Art.16, applied: SI 2013/414 Art.3
Art.17, applied: SI 2013/414 Art.3
Art.18, amended: SI 2013/755 Sch.5 para.66
Art.18, applied: SI 2013/414 Art.3
Art.19, amended: SI 2013/755 Sch.5 para.66
Art.19, applied: SI 2013/414 Art.3
Art.20, applied: SI 2013/414 Art.3
Art.21, applied: SI 2013/414 Art.3
Art.22, applied: SI 2013/414 Art.3
Art.23, applied: SI 2013/414 Art.3
Art.24, applied: SI 2013/414 Art.3
Art.25, amended: SI 2013/755 Sch.5 para.67
Art.25, applied: SI 2013/414 Art.3
Art.26, applied: SI 2013/414 Art.3
Art.27, applied: SI 2013/414 Art.3
Art.28, applied: SI 2013/414 Art.3
Art.29, applied: SI 2013/414 Art.3
Art.30, applied: SI 2013/414 Art.3
Art.31, applied: SI 2013/414 Art.3
Art.32, applied: SI 2013/414 Art.3
Art.33, applied: SI 2013/414 Art.3
Art.34, applied: SI 2013/414 Art.3

581. Fostering Services (England) Regulations 2011
applied: SI 2013/3029 Sch.1 para.19, Sch.6 para.21, SI 2013/3035 Sch.1
Reg.2, amended: SI 2013/235 Sch.2 para.160, SI 2013/984 Reg.6
Reg.13, amended: SI 2013/3239 Reg.28
Reg.26, amended: SI 2013/984 Reg.7
Reg.28, amended: SI 2013/984 Reg.8
Reg.30, amended: SI 2013/984 Reg.9
Reg.31, amended: SI 2013/984 Reg.10
Reg.32, amended: SI 2013/984 Reg.11
Sch.3 para.1, substituted: SI 2013/984 Reg.12
Sch.3 Part 1 para.1, substituted: SI 2013/984 Reg.12
Sch.3 Part 1 para.2, substituted: SI 2013/984 Reg.12
Sch.3 Part 1 para.3, substituted: SI 2013/984 Reg.12
Sch.3 Part 1 para.4, substituted: SI 2013/984 Reg.12
Sch.3 Part 1 para.5, substituted: SI 2013/984 Reg.12
Sch.3 Part 1 para.6, substituted: SI 2013/984 Reg.12
Sch.3 Part 1 para.7, substituted: SI 2013/984 Reg.12
Sch.3 Part 1 para.8, substituted: SI 2013/984 Reg.12

Sch.3 Part 1 para.9, substituted: SI 2013/984 Reg.12
Sch.3 Part 1 para.10, substituted: SI 2013/984 Reg.12
Sch.3 para.2, substituted: SI 2013/984 Reg.12
Sch.3 Part 2 para.11, substituted: SI 2013/984 Reg.12
Sch.3 Part 2 para.12, substituted: SI 2013/984 Reg.12
Sch.3 Part 2 para.13, substituted: SI 2013/984 Reg.12
Sch.3 Part 2 para.14, substituted: SI 2013/984 Reg.12
Sch.3 Part 2 para.15, substituted: SI 2013/984 Reg.12
Sch.3 Part 2 para.16, substituted: SI 2013/984 Reg.12
Sch.3 para.3, substituted: SI 2013/984 Reg.12
Sch.3 para.4, substituted: SI 2013/984 Reg.12
Sch.3 para.5, substituted: SI 2013/984 Reg.12
Sch.3 para.6, substituted: SI 2013/984 Reg.12
Sch.3 para.7, substituted: SI 2013/984 Reg.12
Sch.3 para.8, substituted: SI 2013/984 Reg.12
Sch.3 para.9, substituted: SI 2013/984 Reg.12
Sch.3 para.10, substituted: SI 2013/984 Reg.12
Sch.3 para.11, substituted: SI 2013/984 Reg.12
Sch.3 para.12, substituted: SI 2013/984 Reg.12
Sch.3 para.13, substituted: SI 2013/984 Reg.12
Sch.7, amended: SI 2013/235 Sch.2 para.160, SI 2013/3239 Reg.29

582. Arrangements for Placement of Children by Voluntary Organisations and Others (England) Regulations 2011

Reg.2, amended: SI 2013/235 Sch.2 para.161
Reg.7, amended: SI 2013/235 Sch.2 para.161

605. Libya (Asset-Freezing) Regulations 2011

Reg.2, amended: SI 2013/472 Art.4
Reg.8, amended: SI 2013/2071 Reg.3, Reg.4
Sch.1 para.5, amended: SI 2013/472 Sch.2 para.201, SI 2013/534 Sch.1 para.12

655. Food Additives (Wales) (Amendment) Regulations 2011

revoked: SI 2013/2591 Sch.5

656. Home Energy Efficiency Schemes (Wales) Regulations 2011

Reg.2, amended: SI 2013/2843 Reg.3

666. Stamp Duty and Stamp Duty Reserve Tax (Eurex Clearing AG) Regulations 2011

Reg.2, amended: SI 2013/504 Reg.42
Reg.3, substituted: SI 2013/504 Reg.42
Reg.4, amended: SI 2013/504 Reg.42

667. Stamp Duty and Stamp Duty Reserve Tax (European Central Counterparty Limited) Regulations 2011

Reg.2, amended: SI 2013/504 Reg.43
Reg.3, substituted: SI 2013/504 Reg.43
Reg.4, amended: SI 2013/504 Reg.43

668. Stamp Duty and Stamp Duty Reserve Tax (European Multilateral Clearing Facility N.V.) Regulations 2011

Reg.2, amended: SI 2013/504 Reg.44
Reg.3, substituted: SI 2013/504 Reg.44
Reg.4, amended: SI 2013/504 Reg.44

669. Stamp Duty and Stamp Duty Reserve Tax (LCH.Clearnet Limited) Regulations 2011

Reg.2, amended: SI 2013/504 Reg.45
Reg.3, substituted: SI 2013/504 Reg.45
Reg.4, amended: SI 2013/504 Reg.45

670. Stamp Duty and Stamp Duty Reserve Tax (SIX X-CLEAR AG) Regulations 2011

Reg.2, amended: SI 2013/504 Reg.46
Reg.3, substituted: SI 2013/504 Reg.46
Reg.4, amended: SI 2013/504 Reg.46

673. Application of Pension Legislation to the National Employment Savings Trust Corporation Regulations 2011

Reg.2, revoked: SI 2013/2734 Sch.9 para.17
Reg.3, revoked: SI 2013/2734 Sch.9 para.17

688. Jobseeker's Allowance (Mandatory Work Activity Scheme) Regulations 2011

applied: 2013 c.17 s.1
Reg.4, applied: 2013 c.17 s.1
Reg.4, varied: 2013 c.17 s.1

690. Further Education Teachers Qualifications (England) (Amendment) Regulations 2011

revoked: SI 2013/1976 Sch.1

691. Student Fees (Qualifying Courses and Persons) (Wales) Regulations 2011

Sch.1 para.1, amended: SI 2013/1792 Reg.7
Sch.1 para.9, amended: SI 2013/1792 Reg.8

694. Flood and Water Management Act 2010 (Commencement No 3 and Transitional Provisions) Order 2011

Art.5, amended: SI 2013/755 Sch.4 para.391

695. Regional Flood and Coastal Committees (England and Wales) Regulations 2011

Reg.4, amended: SI 2013/755 Sch.4 para.393
Reg.5, amended: SI 2013/755 Sch.4 para.394
Reg.6, amended: SI 2013/755 Sch.4 para.394
Reg.7, amended: SI 2013/755 Sch.4 para.394
Reg.8, amended: SI 2013/755 Sch.4 para.394
Reg.9, amended: SI 2013/755 Sch.4 para.394
Reg.11, amended: SI 2013/755 Sch.4 para.395
Reg.14, amended: SI 2013/755 Sch.4 para.396
Reg.18, amended: SI 2013/755 Sch.4 para.396
Reg.19, amended: SI 2013/755 Sch.4 para.396
Reg.22, amended: SI 2013/755 Sch.4 para.396
Reg.27, amended: SI 2013/755 Sch.4 para.396

Reg.28, amended: SI 2013/755 Sch.4 para.396

696. Flood and Coastal Erosion Risk Management (Levies) (England and Wales) Regulations 2011

amended: SI 2013/755 Sch.4 para.398
Reg.1, amended: SI 2013/755 Sch.4 para.399
Reg.2, amended: SI 2013/755 Sch.4 para.400
Reg.3, amended: SI 2013/755 Sch.4 para.401
Reg.4, amended: SI 2013/755 Sch.4 para.401
Reg.5, amended: SI 2013/755 Sch.4 para.401
Reg.6, amended: SI 2013/755 Sch.4 para.401
Reg.8, amended: SI 2013/755 Sch.4 para.401
Reg.9, amended: SI 2013/755 Sch.4 para.401
Reg.10, amended: SI 2013/755 Sch.4 para.401
Reg.11, amended: SI 2013/755 Sch.4 para.401
Reg.12, amended: SI 2013/755 Sch.4 para.401

700. Fruit Juices and Fruit Nectars (Wales) (Amendment) Regulations 2011

revoked: SI 2013/2750 Reg.20

704. National Health Service (Concerns, Complaints and Redress Arrangements) (Wales) Regulations 2011

applied: SI 2013/898 Sch.4 para.33, Sch.5 para.21
Part 7, applied: SI 2013/235 Sch.3 para.23
Reg.34, amended: SI 2013/235 Sch.2 para.162
Reg.34, revoked (in part): SI 2013/235 Sch.2 para.162
Sch.2 para.2, revoked: SI 2013/898 Sch.8 para.25

723. Government Resources and Accounts Act 2000 (Estimates and Accounts) Order 2011

Sch.1, amended: SI 2013/687 Sch.2

731. Pension Protection Fund (Pension Compensation Sharing and Attachment on Divorce etc) Regulations 2011

Reg.31A, added: SI 2013/627 Reg.6
Reg.31B, added: SI 2013/627 Reg.6
Reg.31C, added: SI 2013/627 Reg.6
Reg.31D, added: SI 2013/627 Reg.6
Sch.1 para.2, amended: SI 2013/627 Reg.6

734. Independent Health Care (Wales) Regulations 2011

Reg.2, amended: SI 2013/472 Sch.2 para.202

736. Assembly Learning Grants (European Institutions) (Wales) Regulations 2011

revoked: SI 2013/765 Reg.4

745. Health and Safety at Work etc Act 1974 (Application outside Great Britain) (Variation) Order 2011

revoked: SI 2013/240 Art.1

748. Tunisia (Restrictive Measures) (Overseas Territories) Order 2011

Art.12, amended: SI 2013/472 Sch.2 para.203

750. Terrorist Asset-Freezing etc Act 2010 (Overseas Territories) Order 2011

Sch.2 para.10, amended: SI 2013/534 Sch.1 para.12

798. Derbyshire Community Health Services National Health Service Trust (Establishment) Order 2011

Art.1, amended: SI 2013/593 Art.2

799. Hounslow and Richmond Community Healthcare National Health Service Trust (Establishment) Order 2011

Art.1, amended: SI 2013/593 Art.2

800. Leeds Community Healthcare National Health Service Trust (Establishment) Order 2011

Art.1, amended: SI 2013/593 Art.2

802. Lincolnshire Community Health Services National Health Service Trust (Establishment) Order 2011

Art.1, amended: SI 2013/593 Art.2

804. Solent National Health Service Trust (Establishment) Order 2011

Art.1, amended: SI 2013/593 Art.2

805. Wirral Community National Health Service Trust (Establishment) Order 2011

Art.1, amended: SI 2013/593 Art.2
Art.4, amended: SI 2013/1698 Art.2

817. Accounts and Audit (England) Regulations 2011

Reg.2, amended: SI 2013/235 Sch.2 para.163

827. Pensions Increase (Review) Order 2011

applied: SI 2013/604 Sch.1

865. Flood and Coastal Erosion Risk Management Information Appeal (Wales) Regulations 2011

Reg.1, amended: SI 2013/755 Sch.5 para.68

881. Animal By-Products (Enforcement) (England) Regulations 2011

revoked: SI 2013/2952 Reg.28
Sch.2 para.16, revoked: SI 2013/1478 Sch.5 para.30

886. Assembly Learning Grants and Loans (Higher Education) (Wales) (No.2) Regulations 2011

applied: SI 2013/1965 Reg.2
Reg.2, amended: SI 2013/1965 Reg.3
Reg.29, amended: SI 2013/1965 Reg.4
Reg.32, amended: SI 2013/1965 Reg.5
Reg.42, amended: SI 2013/1965 Reg.6
Reg.77, amended: SI 2013/1965 Reg.7
Reg.93, amended: SI 2013/1965 Reg.8
Reg.98, amended: SI 2013/1965 Reg.9
Reg.101, amended: SI 2013/1965 Reg.10
Sch.5 para.5, amended: SI 2013/1965 Reg.11

887. Egypt (Asset-Freezing) Regulations 2011

Reg.2, amended: SI 2013/472 Art.4
Sch.1 para.5, amended: SI 2013/472 Sch.2 para.204, SI 2013/534 Sch.1 para.12

888. Tunisia (Asset-Freezing) Regulations 2011

Reg.2, amended: SI 2013/472 Art.4
Sch.1 para.5, amended: SI 2013/472 Sch.2 para.205, SI 2013/534 Sch.1 para.12

909. M1 Motorway (Junctions 25 to 28) (Variable Speed Limits) Regulations 2011
Sch.1 para.1, substituted: SI 2013/482 Reg.3
917. Jobseeker's Allowance (Employment, Skills and Enterprise Scheme) Regulations 2011
revoked: 2013 c.17 s.1
see *R. (on the application of Reilly) v Secretary of State for Work and Pensions* [2013] EWCA Civ 66, [2013] 1 W.L.R. 2239 (CA (Civ Div)), Pill, L.J.
Reg.2, see *R. (on the application of Reilly) v Secretary of State for Work and Pensions* [2013] EWCA Civ 66, [2013] 1 W.L.R. 2239 (CA (Civ Div)), Pill, L.J.
Reg.3, see *R. (on the application of Reilly) v Secretary of State for Work and Pensions* [2013] EWCA Civ 66, [2013] 1 W.L.R. 2239 (CA (Civ Div)), Pill, L.J.
Reg.4, see *R. (on the application of Reilly) v Secretary of State for Work and Pensions* [2013] EWCA Civ 66, [2013] 1 W.L.R. 2239 (CA (Civ Div)), Pill, L.J.
Reg.5, see *R. (on the application of Reilly) v Secretary of State for Work and Pensions* [2013] EWCA Civ 66, [2013] 1 W.L.R. 2239 (CA (Civ Div)), Pill, L.J.
925. Marine Licensing (Appeals Against Licensing Decisions) (Wales) Regulations 2011
applied: SI 2013/414 Art.3
Reg.6, substituted: SI 2013/414 Art.6
935. Road Traffic Exemptions (Special Forces) (Variation and Amendment) Regulations 2011
Reg.3, applied: SI 2013/19 Art.6, SI 2013/20 Art.7, SI 2013/21 Art.6, SI 2013/26 Art.7, SI 2013/27 Art.7, SI 2013/32 Art.6, SI 2013/33 Art.6, SI 2013/34 Art.6, SI 2013/35 Art.9, SI 2013/36 Art.7, SI 2013/42 Art.7, SI 2013/43 Art.6, SI 2013/44 Art.8, SI 2013/47 Art.7, SI 2013/48 Art.6, SI 2013/49 Art.5, SI 2013/56 Art.5, SI 2013/57 Art.4, SI 2013/58 Art.6, SI 2013/61 Art.5, SI 2013/71 Art.5, SI 2013/72 Art.6, SI 2013/101 Art.6, SI 2013/116 Art.5, SI 2013/118 Art.6, SI 2013/119 Art.7, SI 2013/131 Art.6, SI 2013/133 Art.6, SI 2013/134 Art.4, SI 2013/135 Art.4, SI 2013/136 Art.5, SI 2013/137 Art.6, SI 2013/142 Art.6, SI 2013/144 Art.6, SI 2013/150 Art.7, SI 2013/151 Art.6, SI 2013/153 Art.7, SI 2013/169 Art.6, SI 2013/171 Art.7, SI 2013/172 Art.4, SI 2013/183 Art.6, SI 2013/184 Art.7, SI 2013/187 Art.4, SI 2013/188 Art.4, SI 2013/196 Art.7, SI 2013/197 Art.6, SI 2013/200 Art.6, SI 2013/203 Art.6, SI 2013/204 Art.6, SI 2013/205 Art.6, SI 2013/206 Art.6, SI 2013/210 Art.8, SI 2013/212 Art.5, SI 2013/231 Art.7, SI 2013/286 Art.12, SI 2013/287 Art.7, SI 2013/288 Art.6, SI 2013/289 Art.9, SI 2013/291 Art.6, SI 2013/292 Art.7, SI 2013/293 Art.8, SI 2013/297 Art.6, SI 2013/299 Art.6, SI 2013/305 Art.6, SI 2013/306 Art.6, SI 2013/311 Art.7, SI 2013/312 Art.7, SI 2013/313 Art.8, SI 2013/314 Art.7, SI 2013/366 Art.6, SI 2013/370 Art.6, SI 2013/396 Art.6, SI 2013/397 Art.6, SI 2013/402 Art.6, SI 2013/403 Art.6, SI 2013/404 Art.6, SI 2013/681 Art.7, SI 2013/682 Art.9, SI 2013/696 Art.6, SI 2013/730 Art.8, SI 2013/742 Art.4, SI 2013/751 Art.5, SI 2013/752 Art.7, SI 2013/769 Art.6, SI 2013/774 Art.8, SI 2013/775 Art.7, SI 2013/776 Art.7, SI 2013/778 Art.7, SI 2013/779 Art.6, SI 2013/781 Art.6, SI 2013/782 Art.6, SI 2013/802 Art.4, SI 2013/845 Art.5, SI 2013/847 Art.5, SI 2013/848 Art.7, SI 2013/851 Art.8, SI 2013/853 Art.9, SI 2013/856 Art.6, SI 2013/857 Art.5, SI 2013/858 Art.7, SI 2013/859 Art.6, SI 2013/861 Art.6, SI 2013/864 Art.4, SI 2013/865 Art.4, SI 2013/866 Art.6, SI 2013/867 Art.9, SI 2013/868 Art.8, SI 2013/869 Art.7, SI 2013/872 Art.7, SI 2013/873 Art.6, SI 2013/897 Art.6, SI 2013/899 Art.6, SI 2013/900 Art.9, SI 2013/902 Art.7, SI 2013/905 Art.4, SI 2013/910 Art.7, SI 2013/912 Art.6, SI 2013/913 Art.5, SI 2013/915 Art.5, SI 2013/945 Art.9, SI 2013/947 Art.6, SI 2013/948 Art.6, SI 2013/960 Art.6, SI 2013/962 Art.10, SI 2013/963 Art.6, SI 2013/964 Art.4, SI 2013/970 Art.7, SI 2013/972 Art.6, SI 2013/974 Art.7, SI 2013/978 Art.6, SI 2013/990 Art.8, SI 2013/993 Art.7, SI 2013/994 Art.6, SI 2013/996 Art.7, SI 2013/997 Art.8, SI 2013/1003 Art.4, SI 2013/1004 Art.7, SI 2013/1005 Art.8, SI 2013/1006 Art.7, SI 2013/1007 Art.6, SI 2013/1009 Art.6, SI 2013/1016 Art.5, SI 2013/1017 Art.6, SI 2013/1023 Art.6, SI 2013/1025 Art.8, SI 2013/1027 Art.7, SI 2013/1056 Art.9, SI 2013/1062 Art.5, SI 2013/1063 Art.6, SI 2013/1067 Art.7, SI 2013/1068 Art.7, SI 2013/1069 Art.11, SI 2013/1071 Art.5, SI 2013/1073 Art.6, SI 2013/1075 Art.6, SI 2013/1078 Art.6, SI 2013/1079 Art.6, SI 2013/1093 Art.7, SI 2013/1094 Art.7, SI 2013/1137 Art.6, SI 2013/1149 Art.5, SI 2013/1150 Art.6, SI 2013/1183 Art.7, SI 2013/1186 Art.7, SI 2013/1220 Art.8, SI 2013/1224 Art.4, SI 2013/1225 Art.6, SI 2013/1231 Art.3, SI 2013/1234 Art.7, SI 2013/1235 Art.8, SI 2013/1247 Art.4, SI 2013/1249 Art.9, SI 2013/1251 Art.6, SI 2013/1258 Art.6, SI 2013/1259 Art.8, SI 2013/1261 Art.6, SI 2013/1262 Art.6, SI 2013/1263 Art.5, SI 2013/1265 Art.6, SI

2013/1266 Art.6, SI 2013/1267 Art.6, SI 2013/1268 Art.6, SI 2013/1269 Art.6, SI 2013/1270 Art.10, SI 2013/1272 Art.6, SI 2013/1273 Art.10, SI 2013/1275 Art.12, SI 2013/1276 Art.7, SI 2013/1283 Art.8, SI 2013/1284 Art.6, SI 2013/1286 Art.6, SI 2013/1292 Art.8, SI 2013/1293 Art.6, SI 2013/1298 Art.6, SI 2013/1307 Art.6, SI 2013/1312 Art.6, SI 2013/1314 Art.8, SI 2013/1320 Art.7, SI 2013/1326 Art.6, SI 2013/1327 Art.6, SI 2013/1332 Art.7, SI 2013/1333 Art.8, SI 2013/1338 Art.9, SI 2013/1344 Art.13, SI 2013/1345 Art.10, SI 2013/1347 Art.4, SI 2013/1350 Art.6, SI 2013/1351 Art.6, SI 2013/1362 Art.9, SI 2013/1371 Art.6, SI 2013/1377 Art.7, SI 2013/1383 Art.4, SI 2013/1386 Art.7, SI 2013/1398 Art.6, SI 2013/1404 Art.6, SI 2013/1428 Art.6, SI 2013/1439 Art.7, SI 2013/1449 Art.7, SI 2013/1450 Art.7, SI 2013/1451 Art.6, SI 2013/1454 Art.10, SI 2013/1457 Art.10, SI 2013/1464 Art.8, SI 2013/1484 Art.6, SI 2013/1490 Art.6, SI 2013/1492 Art.6, SI 2013/1494 Art.4, SI 2013/1502 Art.5, SI 2013/1522 Art.6, SI 2013/1524 Art.6, SI 2013/1534 Art.7, SI 2013/1545 Art.8, SI 2013/1548 Art.6, SI 2013/1549 Art.6, SI 2013/1551 Art.6, SI 2013/1556 Art.7, SI 2013/1602 Art.6, SI 2013/1606 Art.7, SI 2013/1607 Art.6, SI 2013/1610 Art.7, SI 2013/1611 Art.6, SI 2013/1612 Art.6, SI 2013/1613 Art.6, SI 2013/1622 Art.7, SI 2013/1630 Art.4, SI 2013/1639 Art.6, SI 2013/1641 Art.6, SI 2013/1645 Art.14, SI 2013/1646 Art.8, SI 2013/1647 Art.7, SI 2013/1650 Art.4, SI 2013/1685 Art.4, SI 2013/1688 Art.10, SI 2013/1691 Art.6, SI 2013/1696 Art.7, SI 2013/1699 Art.7, SI 2013/1702 Art.7, SI 2013/1732 Art.7, SI 2013/1737 Art.4, SI 2013/1835 Art.8, SI 2013/1836 Art.7, SI 2013/1839 Art.7, SI 2013/1845 Art.5, SI 2013/1847 Art.5, SI 2013/1850 Art.6, SI 2013/1886 Art.7, SI 2013/1890 Art.6, SI 2013/1891 Art.7, SI 2013/1898 Art.6, SI 2013/1901 Art.8, SI 2013/1904 Art.7, SI 2013/1909 Art.4, SI 2013/1912 Art.8, SI 2013/1914 Art.6, SI 2013/1915 Art.6, SI 2013/1927 Art.6, SI 2013/1951 Art.9, SI 2013/1953 Art.8, SI 2013/1954 Art.7, SI 2013/1955 Art.10, SI 2013/1989 Art.7, SI 2013/1990 Art.9, SI 2013/1991 Art.8, SI 2013/1992 Art.6, SI 2013/1993 Art.6, SI 2013/1994 Art.8, SI 2013/1999 Art.6, SI 2013/2000 Art.6, SI 2013/2001 Art.6, SI 2013/2003 Art.7, SI 2013/2004 Art.7, SI 2013/2008 Art.6, SI 2013/2010 Art.6, SI 2013/2011 Art.6, SI 2013/2016 Art.10, SI 2013/2026 Art.7, SI 2013/2028 Art.6, SI 2013/2031 Art.4, SI 2013/2035 Art.8, SI 2013/2037 Art.6, SI 2013/2040 Art.6, SI 2013/2041 Art.6, SI 2013/2049 Art.5, SI 2013/2073 Art.4, SI 2013/2088 Art.10, SI 2013/2096 Art.8, SI 2013/2101 Art.6, SI 2013/2113 Art.5, SI 2013/2126 Art.6, SI 2013/2131 Art.6, SI 2013/2134 Art.6, SI 2013/2138 Art.6, SI 2013/2144 Art.6, SI 2013/2150 Art.6, SI 2013/2151 Art.5, SI 2013/2163 Art.10, SI 2013/2165 Art.8, SI 2013/2166 Art.7, SI 2013/2167 Art.6, SI 2013/2168 Art.7, SI 2013/2169 Art.8, SI 2013/2170 Art.6, SI 2013/2171 Art.10, SI 2013/2176 Art.6, SI 2013/2177 Art.8, SI 2013/2178 Art.6, SI 2013/2179 Art.6, SI 2013/2182 Art.10, SI 2013/2186 Art.6, SI 2013/2187 Art.6, SI 2013/2189 Art.6, SI 2013/2205 Art.6, SI 2013/2207 Art.6, SI 2013/2208 Art.7, SI 2013/2211 Art.6, SI 2013/2218 Art.7, SI 2013/2222 Art.7, SI 2013/2225 Art.6, SI 2013/2229 Art.7, SI 2013/2239 Art.9, SI 2013/2240 Art.5, SI 2013/2250 Art.6, SI 2013/2253 Art.7, SI 2013/2260 Art.6, SI 2013/2261 Art.7, SI 2013/2263 Art.6, SI 2013/2267 Art.4, SI 2013/2282 Art.6, SI 2013/2283 Art.6, SI 2013/2284 Art.8, SI 2013/2285 Art.5, SI 2013/2288 Art.6, SI 2013/2291 Art.9, SI 2013/2293 Art.6, SI 2013/2303 Art.6, SI 2013/2304 Art.9, SI 2013/2305 Art.8, SI 2013/2307 Art.8, SI 2013/2308 Art.7, SI 2013/2309 Art.8, SI 2013/2310 Art.7, SI 2013/2361 Art.9, SI 2013/2362 Art.6, SI 2013/2363 Art.7, SI 2013/2364 Art.7, SI 2013/2365 Art.5, SI 2013/2368 Art.7, SI 2013/2382 Art.6, SI 2013/2383 Art.8, SI 2013/2387 Art.7, SI 2013/2391 Art.7, SI 2013/2393 Art.6, SI 2013/2394 Art.6, SI 2013/2395 Art.6, SI 2013/2400 Art.6, SI 2013/2401 Art.6, SI 2013/2402 Art.7, SI 2013/2407 Art.6, SI 2013/2413 Art.6, SI 2013/2414 Art.6, SI 2013/2442 Art.7, SI 2013/2446 Art.6, SI 2013/2447 Art.7, SI 2013/2448 Art.6, SI 2013/2450 Art.6, SI 2013/2453 Art.6, SI 2013/2455 Art.6, SI 2013/2456 Art.6, SI 2013/2458 Art.6, SI 2013/2463 Art.10, SI 2013/2469 Art.6, SI 2013/2478 Art.8, SI 2013/2483 Art.6, SI 2013/2484 Art.6, SI 2013/2486 Art.7, SI

2013/2487 Art.8, SI 2013/2492 Art.6, SI 2013/2499 Art.6, SI 2013/2504 Art.6, SI 2013/2511 Art.6, SI 2013/2512 Art.6, SI 2013/2515 Art.10, SI 2013/2516 Art.7, SI 2013/2518 Art.6, SI 2013/2520 Art.8, SI 2013/2521 Art.10, SI 2013/2523 Art.9, SI 2013/2528 Art.6, SI 2013/2529 Art.6, SI 2013/2530 Art.7, SI 2013/2531 Art.7, SI 2013/2543 Art.6, SI 2013/2546 Art.7, SI 2013/2566 Art.4, SI 2013/2567 Art.5, SI 2013/2573, SI 2013/2574 Art.6, SI 2013/2575 Art.6, SI 2013/2578 Art.6, SI 2013/2608 Art.7, SI 2013/2615 Art.6, SI 2013/2625 Art.7, SI 2013/2626 Art.6, SI 2013/2631 Art.4, SI 2013/2634 Art.4, SI 2013/2643 Art.6, SI 2013/2650 Art.7, SI 2013/2651 Art.6, SI 2013/2652 Art.7, SI 2013/2653 Art.8, SI 2013/2654 Art.5, SI 2013/2658 Art.6, SI 2013/2674 Art.5, SI 2013/2676 Art.7, SI 2013/2678 Art.6, SI 2013/2679 Art.7, SI 2013/2680 Art.6, SI 2013/2681 Art.6, SI 2013/2682 Art.7, SI 2013/2686 Art.7, SI 2013/2690 Art.8, SI 2013/2692 Art.6, SI 2013/2697 Art.6, SI 2013/2700 Art.6, SI 2013/2704 Art.14, SI 2013/2706 Art.5, SI 2013/2707 Art.9, SI 2013/2708 Art.6, SI 2013/2710 Art.6, SI 2013/2711 Art.7, SI 2013/2712 Art.6, SI 2013/2714 Art.7, SI 2013/2718 Art.6, SI 2013/2719 Art.9, SI 2013/2724 Art.6, SI 2013/2725 Art.4, SI 2013/2736 Art.6, SI 2013/2757 Art.6, SI 2013/2759 Art.10, SI 2013/2760 Art.9, SI 2013/2761 Art.10, SI 2013/2762 Art.7, SI 2013/2763 Art.6, SI 2013/2764 Art.8, SI 2013/2769 Art.7, SI 2013/2773 Art.6, SI 2013/2800 Art.6, SI 2013/2808 Art.12, SI 2013/2822 Art.6, SI 2013/2835 Art.5, SI 2013/2838 Art.7, SI 2013/2839 Art.5, SI 2013/2840 Art.4, SI 2013/2842 Art.4, SI 2013/2845 Art.4, SI 2013/2863 Art.7, SI 2013/2868 Art.7, SI 2013/2883 Art.6, SI 2013/2917 Art.6, SI 2013/2922 Art.6, SI 2013/2923 Art.5, SI 2013/2924 Art.7, SI 2013/2925 Art.6, SI 2013/2937 Art.7, SI 2013/2942 Art.6, SI 2013/2943 Art.7, SI 2013/2953 Art.6, SI 2013/2956 Art.8, SI 2013/2958 Art.6, SI 2013/2964 Art.7, SI 2013/2965 Art.6, SI 2013/2966 Art.5, SI 2013/2967 Art.6, SI 2013/2968 Art.13, SI 2013/2975 Art.6, SI 2013/3010 Art.5, SI 2013/3012 Art.7, SI 2013/3016 Art.6, SI 2013/3020 Art.6, SI 2013/3038 Art.6, SI 2013/3058 Art.6, SI 2013/3059 Art.9, SI 2013/3067 Art.6, SI 2013/3082 Art.6, SI 2013/3100 Art.6, SI 2013/3119 Art.5, SI 2013/3121 Art.6, SI 2013/3124 Art.7, SI 2013/3125 Art.6, SI 2013/3127 Art.8, SI 2013/3130 Art.4, SI 2013/3132 Art.6, SI 2013/3201 Art.7, SI 2013/3215 Art.8, SI 2013/3219 Art.6, SI 2013/3222 Art.6, SI 2013/3240 Art.6, SI 2013/3242 Art.6, SI 2013/3245 Art.6, SI 2013/3247 Art.6, SI 2013/3248 Art.7, SI 2013/3251 Art.6, SI 2013/3252 Art.6, SI 2013/3253 Art.6, SI 2013/3255 Art.6, SI 2013/3261 Art.6, SI 2013/3263 Art.5, SI 2013/3264 Art.7, SI 2013/3274 Art.7, SI 2013/3275 Art.6, SI 2013/3276 Art.7, SI 2013/3277 Art.7, SI 2013/3283 Art.6, SI 2013/3284 Art.6, SI 2013/3285 Art.7, SI 2013/3287 Art.8, SI 2013/3288 Art.9, SI 2013/3289 Art.6, SI 2013/3290 Art.6, SI 2013/3295 Art.6, SI 2013/3310 Art.9, SI 2013/3311 Art.5, SI 2013/3312 Art.6, SI 2013/3314 Art.7, SSI 2013/11 Art.4, SSI 2013/15 Art.7, SSI 2013/16 Art.7, SSI 2013/17 Art.7, SSI 2013/18 Art.7, SSI 2013/28 Art.6, SSI 2013/54 Art.7, SSI 2013/55 Art.7, SSI 2013/56 Art.7, SSI 2013/57 Art.7, SSI 2013/101 Art.7, SSI 2013/102 Art.6, SSI 2013/103 Art.7, SSI 2013/104 Art.7, SSI 2013/130 Art.7, SSI 2013/132 Art.7, SSI 2013/133 Art.7, SSI 2013/134 Art.7, SSI 2013/138 Art.7, SSI 2013/158 Art.7, SSI 2013/164 Art.7, SSI 2013/165 Art.7, SSI 2013/166 Art.7, SSI 2013/167 Art.5, SSI 2013/206 Art.7, SSI 2013/208 Art.7, SSI 2013/209 Art.7, SSI 2013/213 Art.7, SSI 2013/224 Art.4, SSI 2013/232 Art.7, SSI 2013/233 Art.7, SSI 2013/234 Art.7, SSI 2013/235 Art.7, SSI 2013/243 Art.7, SSI 2013/244 Art.7, SSI 2013/245 Art.7, SSI 2013/246 Art.7, SSI 2013/248 Art.6, SSI 2013/251 Art.3, SSI 2013/263 Art.3, SSI 2013/272 Art.7, SSI 2013/273 Art.7, SSI 2013/274 Art.7, SSI 2013/275 Art.7, SSI 2013/283 Art.4, SSI 2013/298 Art.7, SSI 2013/299 Art.7, SSI 2013/300 Art.7, SSI 2013/301 Art.7, SSI 2013/329 Art.7, SSI 2013/330 Art.7, SSI 2013/331 Art.7, SSI 2013/332 Art.7, SSI 2013/358 Art.7, SSI 2013/359 Art.7, SSI 2013/360 Art.7, SSI 2013/361 Art.7

962. Social Care Charges (Means Assessment and Determination of Charges) (Wales) Regulations 2011

Reg.14, amended: SI 2013/633 Reg.4

963. Social Care Charges (Direct Payments) (Means Assessment and Determination of Reimbursement or Contribution) (Wales) Regulations 2011

Reg.16, amended: SI 2013/633 Reg.5

976. Penalties, Offshore Income etc (Designation of Territories) Order 2011

Sch.1, amended: SI 2013/1618 Art.2

988. Waste (England and Wales) Regulations 2011
Reg.3, amended: SI 2013/755 Sch.4 para.403
Reg.9, substituted: SI 2013/755 Sch.4 para.404
Reg.10, amended: SI 2013/755 Sch.4 para.405
Reg.13, see *R. (on the application of UK Recyclate Ltd) v Secretary of State for the Environment, Food and Rural Affairs* [2013] EWHC 425 (Admin), [2013] 3 All E.R. 561 (QBD (Admin)), Hickinbottom, J.
Reg.25, amended: SI 2013/755 Sch.4 para.405
Reg.28, amended: SI 2013/755 Sch.4 para.405
Reg.29, substituted: SI 2013/755 Sch.4 para.406
Reg.30, amended: SI 2013/755 Sch.4 para.407
Reg.32, amended: SI 2013/755 Sch.4 para.408
Reg.34, amended: SI 2013/755 Sch.4 para.409
Reg.35, amended: SI 2013/755 Sch.4 para.409
Reg.37, amended: SI 2013/755 Sch.4 para.409
Reg.38, amended: SI 2013/755 Sch.4 para.409
Reg.39, amended: SI 2013/755 Sch.4 para.409
Reg.40, amended: SI 2013/755 Sch.4 para.409
Reg.42, applied: SI 2013/2258 Sch.1 Part 2
Reg.46, amended: SI 2013/755 Sch.4 para.409
Sch.1 Part 4 para.13, amended: SI 2013/755 Sch.4 para.410
Sch.4 Part 2 para.18, revoked: SI 2013/141 Reg.7

991. Beef and Veal Labelling (Wales) Regulations 2011
Reg.2, amended: SI 2013/3270 Reg.3
Reg.4, amended: SI 2013/3270 Reg.3

1005. Mobile Homes Act 1983 (Jurisdiction of Residential Property Tribunals) (England) Order 2011
Art.2, amended: SI 2013/1036 Sch.2 para.46
Art.4, revoked: SI 2013/1036 Sch.2 para.47

1006. Mobile Homes (Written Statement) (England) Regulations 2011
Sch.1, amended: SI 2013/1036 Sch.2 para.48

1007. Residential Property Tribunal Procedures and Fees (England) Regulations 2011
revoked: SI 2013/1036 Sch.2 para.49
Reg.24, revoked (in part): SI 2013/2042 Sch.1 para.89
Reg.32, revoked (in part): SI 2013/2042 Sch.1 para.90

1014. Recycling, Preparation for Re-use and Composting Targets (Monitoring and Penalties) (Wales) Regulations 2011
Reg.2, amended: SI 2013/755 Sch.5 para.70
Reg.3, amended: SI 2013/755 Sch.5 para.71

1015. M1 Motorway (Junctions 6A to 10) (Variable Speed Limits) Regulations 2011
Sch.1 para.1, substituted: SI 2013/2808 Sch.4 Part 1
Sch.1 para.2, substituted: SI 2013/2808 Sch.4 Part 1
Sch.1 para.3, substituted: SI 2013/2808 Sch.4 Part 1
Sch.1 para.4, substituted: SI 2013/2808 Sch.4 Part 1
Sch.1 para.5, substituted: SI 2013/2808 Sch.4 Part 1

1045. Family Procedure (Modification of Enactments) Order 2011
Art.3, revoked: 2013 c.22 Sch.10 para.99
Art.5, revoked: 2013 c.22 Sch.10 para.99
Art.6, revoked (in part): 2013 c.22 Sch.10 para.99
Art.7, revoked: 2013 c.22 Sch.10 para.99
Art.10, revoked (in part): 2013 c.22 Sch.10 para.99
Art.11, revoked: 2013 c.22 Sch.10 para.99
Art.12, revoked: 2013 c.22 Sch.10 para.99
Art.13, revoked: 2013 c.22 Sch.10 para.99
Art.14, revoked: 2013 c.22 Sch.10 para.99

1080. Libya (Restrictive Measures) (Overseas Territories) Order 2011
Art.9, amended: SI 2013/3160 Art.2
Art.12, amended: SI 2013/3160 Art.2
Art.15, amended: SI 2013/3160 Art.2, Art.3
Art.32, amended: SI 2013/3160 Art.3

1086. Ivory Coast (Asset-Freezing) Regulations 2011
Reg.2, amended: SI 2013/472 Art.4
Sch.1 para.5, amended: SI 2013/472 Sch.2 para.206, SI 2013/534 Sch.1 para.12

1094. Democratic People's Republic of Korea (Asset-Freezing) Regulations 2011
revoked: SI 2013/1877 Reg.22
Reg.2, amended: SI 2013/472 Art.4
Reg.9, applied: SI 2013/1877 Reg.23
Sch.1 para.5, amended: SI 2013/472 Sch.2 para.207, SI 2013/534 Sch.1 para.12

1128. Wireless Telegraphy (Licence Charges) Regulations 2011
Sch.2, amended: SI 2013/917 Reg.3
Sch.9, amended: SI 2013/917 Reg.4
Sch.13, amended: SI 2013/917 Reg.5

1129. Iran (Asset-Freezing) Regulations 2011
Reg.2, amended: SI 2013/472 Art.4
Sch.1 para.5, amended: SI 2013/472 Sch.2 para.208, SI 2013/534 Sch.1 para.12

1135. Fruit Juices and Fruit Nectars (England) (Amendment) Regulations 2011
revoked: SI 2013/2775 Reg.20

1194. Poultry Health Scheme (Fees) Regulations 2011
revoked: SI 2013/1240 Reg.11

1197. Trade in Animals and Related Products Regulations 2011
Reg.15, applied: SI 2013/1240 Reg.10, Sch.7
Reg.32, amended: SI 2013/2996 Reg.39
Sch.2 Part 1 para.4, applied: SI 2013/1240 Reg.4

1211. Offshore Funds (Tax) (Amendment) Regulations 2011
Reg.15, amended: SI 2013/1411 Reg.15

1215. Civil Jurisdiction and Judgments (Maintenance) (Rules of Court) Regulations 2011
Reg.2, revoked: 2013 c.22 Sch.10 para.99

1245. Pensions Act 2007 (Abolition of Contracting-out for Defined Contribution Pension Schemes) (Consequential Amendments) Regulations 2011
Reg.17, revoked: SI 2013/2734 Sch.9 para.18
Reg.19, revoked: SI 2013/2734 Sch.9 para.18
Reg.20, amended: SI 2013/2734 Sch.9 para.18

1265. Companies Act 2006 (Consequential Amendments and Transitional Provisions) Order 2011
Sch.3 para.2, amended: SI 2013/472 Sch.2 para.209

1296. Export Control (Eritrea and Miscellaneous Amendments) Order 2011
Art.7, revoked: SI 2013/3182 Sch.1

1301. Investment Bank Special Administration (England and Wales) Rules 2011
applied: SI 2013/472 Sch.2 para.211
Part 2 r.8, amended: SI 2013/472 Sch.2 para.210
Part 2 r.10, amended: SI 2013/472 Sch.2 para.210
Part 2 r.12, amended: SI 2013/472 Sch.2 para.210
Part 2 r.13, amended: SI 2013/472 Sch.2 para.210
Part 2 r.16, amended: SI 2013/472 Sch.2 para.210
Part 2 r.19, amended: SI 2013/472 Sch.2 para.210
Part 2 r.20, amended: SI 2013/472 Sch.2 para.210
Part 2 r.26, amended: SI 2013/472 Sch.2 para.210
Part 2 r.30, amended: SI 2013/472 Sch.2 para.210
Part 2 r.32, amended: SI 2013/472 Sch.2 para.210
Part 2 r.39, amended: SI 2013/472 Sch.2 para.210
Part 2 r.41, amended: SI 2013/472 Sch.2 para.210
Part 2 r.42, amended: SI 2013/472 Sch.2 para.210
Part 2 r.44, amended: SI 2013/472 Sch.2 para.210
Part 2 r.47, amended: SI 2013/472 Sch.2 para.210
Part 2 r.50, amended: SI 2013/472 Sch.2 para.210
Part 3 r.55, amended: SI 2013/472 Sch.2 para.210
Part 3 r.56, amended: SI 2013/472 Sch.2 para.210
Part 3 r.59, amended: SI 2013/472 Sch.2 para.210
Part 3 r.60, amended: SI 2013/472 Sch.2 para.210
Part 3 r.61, amended: SI 2013/472 Sch.2 para.210
Part 3 r.63, amended: SI 2013/472 Sch.2 para.210
Part 3 r.65, amended: SI 2013/472 Sch.2 para.210
Part 3 r.66, amended: SI 2013/472 Sch.2 para.210
Part 3 r.70, amended: SI 2013/472 Sch.2 para.210
Part 3 r.76, amended: SI 2013/472 Sch.2 para.210
Part 3 r.106, amended: SI 2013/472 Sch.2 para.210
Part 3 r.117, amended: SI 2013/472 Sch.2 para.210
Part 3 r.118, amended: SI 2013/472 Sch.2 para.210
Part 3 r.122, amended: SI 2013/472 Sch.2 para.210
Part 5 r.138, amended: SI 2013/472 Sch.2 para.210
Part 5 r.146, amended: SI 2013/472 Sch.2 para.210
Part 6 r.157, amended: SI 2013/472 Sch.2 para.210
Part 6 r.165, amended: SI 2013/472 Sch.2 para.210
Part 6 r.175, amended: SI 2013/472 Sch.2 para.210
Part 6 r.179, amended: SI 2013/472 Sch.2 para.210
Part 6 r.181, amended: SI 2013/472 Sch.2 para.210
Part 6 r.184, amended: SI 2013/472 Sch.2 para.210
Part 7 r.200, amended: SI 2013/472 Sch.2 para.210
Part 7 r.202, amended: SI 2013/472 Sch.2 para.210
Part 7 r.207, amended: SI 2013/472 Sch.2 para.210
Part 7 r.209, amended: SI 2013/472 Sch.2 para.210
Part 7 r.210, amended: SI 2013/472 Sch.2 para.210
Part 7 r.212, amended: SI 2013/472 Sch.2 para.210
Part 8 r.220, amended: SI 2013/472 Sch.2 para.210
Part 8 r.221, amended: SI 2013/472 Sch.2 para.210
Part 8 r.222, amended: SI 2013/472 Sch.2 para.210
Part 9 r.227, amended: SI 2013/472 Sch.2 para.210
Part 11 r.327, amended: SI 2013/472 Sch.2 para.210

1304. Export Control (Syria and Miscellaneous Amendments) Order 2011
Art.8, revoked: SI 2013/2012 Sch.1

1329. Magistrates Courts (Enforcement or Variation of Orders Made in Family Proceedings and Miscellaneous Provisions) Rules 2011
Sch.4 para.11, amended: SI 2013/534 Sch.1 para.25

1411. Land Registration (Proper Office) (Amendment) Order 2011
revoked: SI 2013/1627 Art.4

1414. Warm Home Discount (Reconciliation) Regulations 2011
Reg.9, amended: SI 2013/519 Reg.2
Reg.15, amended: SI 2013/519 Reg.3

1435. Credit Rating Agencies (Amendment) Regulations 2011
Reg.3, revoked: SI 2013/3115 Sch.3

1450. Food Additives (Wales) (Amendment) (No.2) Regulations 2011
revoked: SI 2013/2591 Sch.5

1456. Food Additives (England) (Amendment) (No.2) Regulations 2011
revoked: SI 2013/2210 Sch.5

1484. Civil Jurisdiction and Judgments (Maintenance) Regulations 2011
Sch.7 para.2, revoked (in part): 2013 c.22 Sch.10 para.99
Sch.7 para.8, revoked: 2013 c.22 Sch.11 para.210
Sch.7 para.9, revoked (in part): 2013 c.22 Sch.10 para.99

1505. Pollution Prevention and Control (Designation of Directives) (England and Wales) Order 2011
revoked: SI 2013/123 Art.3

1507. Wireless Telegraphy (Mobile Spectrum Trading) Regulations 2011

Reg.4, amended: SI 2013/646 Reg.2
Reg.5, amended: SI 2013/646 Reg.2
Sch.1, substituted: SI 2013/646 Reg.2

1519. Shropshire Community Health National Health Service Trust (Establishment) Order 2011
Art.1, amended: SI 2013/593 Art.2

1520. Worcestershire Health and Care National Health Service Trust (Establishment) and the Worcestershire Mental Health Partnership National Health Service Trust (Dissolution) Order 2011
Art.1, amended: SI 2013/593 Art.2

1524. Energy Information Regulations 2011
Sch.1 para.1, amended: SI 2013/1232 Reg.3

1543. Environmental Protection (Controls on Ozone-Depleting Substances) Regulations 2011
Reg.7, amended: SI 2013/755 Sch.4 para.411

1551. Care Quality Commission (Additional Functions) Regulations 2011
Reg.1, amended: SI 2013/1413 Reg.2
Reg.2, amended: SI 2013/1413 Reg.2
Reg.3, amended: SI 2013/1413 Reg.2
Reg.4, amended: SI 2013/1413 Reg.2

1556. National Health Service (Charges to Overseas Visitors) Regulations 2011
Reg.2, amended: SI 2013/235 Sch.2 para.164

1613. Undertakings for Collective Investment in Transferable Securities Regulations 2011
Reg.7, amended: SI 2013/472 Sch.2 para.212, SI 2013/1388 Reg.14
Reg.8, amended: SI 2013/1388 Reg.14
Reg.15, amended: SI 2013/472 Sch.2 para.212

1654. Cancellation of Student Loans for Living Costs Liability (Wales) Regulations 2011
applied: SI 2013/1396 Reg.5

1679. Egypt (Restrictive Measures) (Overseas Territories) Order 2011
Art.12, amended: SI 2013/472 Sch.2 para.213

1709. Criminal Procedure Rules 2011
Pt 76., see *R. v Smith (Ian) (Costs)* [2013] 3 Costs L.R. 516 (Sen Cts Costs Office), Costs Judge Campbell
r.5.8, see *R. (on the application of Guardian News and Media Ltd) v City of Westminster Magistrates' Court* [2012] EWCA Civ 420, [2013] Q.B. 618 (CA (Civ Div)), Lord Neuberger (M.R.)
r.63.10, see *R. (on the application of Chinaka) v Southwark Crown Court* [2013] EWHC 3221 (Admin), (2013) 177 J.P. 683 (DC), Fulford, L.J.
r.64.5, see *Adler v Crown Prosecution Service* [2013] EWHC 1968 (Admin), (2013) 177 J.P. 558 (QBD (Admin)), Sir John Thomas (President QBD)

1719. Poultrymeat (Wales) Regulations 2011
referred to: SI 2013/479 Sch.1
Reg.1, amended: SI 2013/3270 Reg.8
Reg.2, amended: SI 2013/3270 Reg.8
Reg.12, amended: SI 2013/3270 Reg.8
Sch.1 Part 1, amended: SI 2013/3270 Reg.8
Sch.1 Part 1, substituted: SI 2013/3270 Reg.8
Sch.1 Part 2, amended: SI 2013/3270 Reg.8

1734. Court Funds Rules 2011
Part 4 r.28, amended: SI 2013/534 Sch.1 para.9

1738. Extraction Solvents in Food (Amendment) (England) Regulations 2011
revoked: SI 2013/2210 Sch.5

1740. Adoption and Children (Scotland) Act 2007 (Consequential Modifications) Order 2011
Sch.1 Part 2 para.41, revoked: SI 2013/458 Sch.1
Sch.1 Part 2 para.42, revoked: SI 2013/458 Sch.1

1752. Registered Pension Schemes (Lifetime Allowance Transitional Protection) Regulations 2011
applied: SSI 2013/174 Reg.2
Reg.4, amended: SI 2013/1740 Reg.3
Reg.13, amended: SI 2013/1740 Reg.3

1788. Sexual Offences Act 2003 (Prescribed Police Stations) Regulations 2011
revoked: SI 2013/300 Reg.3

1794. Gaming Duty (Amendment) Regulations 2011
revoked: SI 2013/1819 Reg.3

1824. Town and Country Planning (Environmental Impact Assessment) Regulations 2011
see *R. (on the application of Catt) v Brighton and Hove City Council* [2013] EWHC 977 (Admin), [2013] B.L.G.R. 802 (QBD (Admin)), Lindblom, J.; see *San Vicente v Secretary of State for Communities and Local Government* [2012] EWHC 3585 (Admin), [2013] J.P.L. 642 (QBD (Admin)), Philip Mott Q.C.; see *Thomas v Carmarthenshire Council* [2013] EWHC 783 (Admin), [2013] J.P.L. 1266 (QBD (Admin)), Burton, J.
Reg.2, amended: SI 2013/2140 Art.27
Reg.2, see *R. (on the application of Lyon) v Cambridge City Council* [2012] EWHC 2684 (Admin), [2013] Env. L.R. 11 (QBD (Admin)), Judge Birtles
Reg.7, see *R. (on the application of Lyon) v Cambridge City Council* [2012] EWHC 2684 (Admin), [2013] Env. L.R. 11 (QBD (Admin)), Judge Birtles
Reg.10A, added: SI 2013/2140 Art.27
Reg.15, amended: SI 2013/2140 Art.27
Reg.17, amended: SI 2013/2140 Art.27
Reg.20, amended: SI 2013/2140 Art.27
Reg.23, amended: SI 2013/2140 Art.27
Reg.29, amended: SI 2013/2879 Art.3
Reg.29, revoked (in part): SI 2013/2879 Art.3

Sch.2, see *R. (on the application of Lyon) v Cambridge City Council* [2012] EWHC 2684 (Admin), [2013] Env. L.R. 11 (QBD (Admin)), Judge Birtles
Sch.2 para.2, see *R. (on the application of Lyon) v Cambridge City Council* [2012] EWHC 2684 (Admin), [2013] Env. L.R. 11 (QBD (Admin)), Judge Birtles

1826. Beef and Pig Carcase Classification (Wales) Regulations 2011
Reg.2, amended: SI 2013/3270 Reg.2
Reg.2, revoked (in part): SI 2013/3270 Reg.2
Sch.1 Part 1, amended: SI 2013/3270 Reg.2
Sch.2, amended: SI 2013/3270 Reg.2

1848. Defence and Security Public Contracts Regulations 2011
Sch.3 para.1, amended: SI 2013/1431 Reg.3
Sch.3 para.2, amended: SI 2013/1431 Reg.3
Sch.3 para.3, amended: SI 2013/1431 Reg.3

1849. Extraction Solvents in Food (Amendment) (Wales) Regulations 2011
revoked: SI 2013/2591 Sch.5

1856. Statutory Auditors and Third Country Auditors (Amendment) Regulations 2011
Reg.1, revoked (in part): SI 2013/1672 Sch.1
Reg.7, revoked: SI 2013/1672 Sch.1

1860. Railways and Other Guided Transport Systems (Safety) (Amendment) Regulations 2011
Reg.2, revoked (in part): SI 2013/2042 Sch.1 para.91

1893. Afghanistan (Asset-Freezing) Regulations 2011
Reg.2, amended: SI 2013/472 Art.4
Sch.1 para.5, amended: SI 2013/472 Sch.2 para.214, SI 2013/534 Sch.1 para.12

1939. School Governors Annual Reports (Wales) Regulations 2011
Reg.2, amended: SI 2013/437 Reg.2, SI 2013/1561 Reg.2
Reg.5, amended: SI 2013/1561 Reg.2
Reg.5, revoked (in part): SI 2013/1561 Reg.2
Reg.6, amended: SI 2013/1561 Reg.2
Sch.2 para.1, substituted: SI 2013/1561 Reg.2
Sch.2 para.1A, added: SI 2013/1561 Reg.2
Sch.2 para.1B, added: SI 2013/1561 Reg.2
Sch.2 para.5A, added: SI 2013/437 Reg.2

1943. Head Teacher's Report to Parents and Adult Pupils (Wales) Regulations 2011
Reg.3, revoked (in part): SI 2013/437 Reg.3
Reg.4, amended: SI 2013/437 Reg.3
Sch.1 Part 4A para.6A, added: SI 2013/437 Reg.3
Sch.1 Part 4B para.1, added: SI 2013/437 Reg.3

1944. School Information (Wales) Regulations 2011
Reg.2, amended: SI 2013/437 Reg.4
Reg.5, amended: SI 2013/437 Reg.4
Sch.3 para.31, added: SI 2013/437 Reg.4

1963. School Performance Information (Wales) Regulations 2011
Reg.2, amended: SI 2013/437 Reg.5

1986. Education (Student Support) Regulations 2011
see *Kebede v Secretary of State for Business, Innovation and Skills* [2013] EWHC 2396 (Admin), [2013] Eq. L.R. 961 (QBD (Admin)), Burnett, J.
Reg.2, amended: SI 2013/630 Reg.54, SI 2013/1728 Reg.4
Reg.5, amended: SI 2013/1728 Reg.5, SI 2013/3106 Reg.5
Reg.18, amended: SI 2013/1728 Reg.6
Reg.19, amended: SI 2013/1728 Reg.7
Reg.22, amended: SI 2013/1728 Reg.8, SI 2013/3106 Reg.6
Reg.23, amended: SI 2013/1728 Reg.9
Reg.23, revoked (in part): SI 2013/1728 Reg.9
Reg.38, amended: SI 2013/235 Sch.2 para.165, SI 2013/1728 Reg.10
Reg.38, applied: SI 2013/235 Sch.3
Reg.41, amended: SI 2013/1728 Sch.1
Reg.42, amended: SI 2013/630 Reg.54
Reg.44, amended: SI 2013/1728 Sch.1
Reg.45, amended: SI 2013/630 Reg.54, SI 2013/1728 Sch.1
Reg.46, amended: SI 2013/1728 Sch.1
Reg.56, amended: SI 2013/1728 Reg.11
Reg.57, amended: SI 2013/1728 Sch.1
Reg.58, amended: SI 2013/1728 Sch.1
Reg.59, amended: SI 2013/1728 Sch.1
Reg.60, amended: SI 2013/1728 Sch.1
Reg.61, amended: SI 2013/630 Reg.54, SI 2013/1728 Reg.12
Reg.62, amended: SI 2013/1728 Sch.1
Reg.63, amended: SI 2013/1728 Sch.1
Reg.64, amended: SI 2013/1728 Sch.1
Reg.65, amended: SI 2013/1728 Sch.1
Reg.67, amended: SI 2013/1728 Sch.1
Reg.68, amended: SI 2013/1728 Sch.1
Reg.69, amended: SI 2013/1728 Reg.13
Reg.72, amended: SI 2013/1728 Sch.1
Reg.73, amended: SI 2013/1728 Sch.1
Reg.74, amended: SI 2013/1728 Sch.1
Reg.75, amended: SI 2013/1728 Sch.1
Reg.76, amended: SI 2013/1728 Sch.1
Reg.77, amended: SI 2013/1728 Sch.1
Reg.78, amended: SI 2013/1728 Sch.1
Reg.79, amended: SI 2013/1728 Sch.1
Reg.80, amended: SI 2013/1728 Sch.1
Reg.81, amended: SI 2013/1728 Sch.1
Reg.86, amended: SI 2013/1728 Reg.14
Reg.87, amended: SI 2013/1728 Sch.1

Reg.105, amended: SI 2013/1728 Sch.1
Reg.116, amended: SI 2013/1728 Reg.15
Reg.119, amended: SI 2013/1728 Reg.16
Reg.122, amended: SI 2013/3106 Reg.7
Reg.124, amended: SI 2013/1728 Sch.1
Reg.125, amended: SI 2013/630 Reg.54, SI 2013/1728 Reg.17, Sch.1
Reg.127, amended: SI 2013/1728 Sch.1
Reg.139, amended: SI 2013/1728 Reg.18, SI 2013/3106 Reg.8
Reg.141, amended: SI 2013/1728 Sch.1
Reg.142, amended: SI 2013/630 Reg.54, SI 2013/1728 Reg.19, Sch.1
Reg.147, amended: SI 2013/1728 Sch.1
Reg.161, amended: SI 2013/1728 Reg.20, SI 2013/3106 Reg.9
Reg.166, amended: SI 2013/1728 Sch.1
Sch.2 para.6, revoked: SI 2013/1728 Reg.21
Sch.4 para.5, amended: SI 2013/1728 Reg.22

2007. Staffordshire and Stoke on Trent Partnership National Health Service Trust (Establishment) Order 2011

Art.1, amended: SI 2013/593 Art.2

2038. Legal Services Act 2007 (Designation as a Licensing Authority) Order 2011

Sch.1 para.2, amended: SI 2013/472 Art.4

2055. Infrastructure Planning (Changes to, and Revocation of, Development Consent Orders) Regulations 2011

Reg.2, amended: SI 2013/522 Reg.6
Sch.1, amended: SI 2013/522 Reg.6, SI 2013/755 Sch.4 para.412
Sch.1, substituted: SI 2013/522 Reg.6

2085. Postal Services Act 2011 (Consequential Modifications and Amendments) Order 2011

Sch.1 para.55, revoked (in part): SSI 2013/50 Sch.5

2123. Education (Information About Individual Pupils) (England) (Amendment) Regulations 2011

revoked: SI 2013/2094 Sch.2

2159. Veterinary Medicines Regulations 2011

revoked: SI 2013/2033 Reg.47

2185. Tonnage Tax (Training Requirement) (Amendment) Regulations 2011

revoked: SI 2013/5 Reg.4

2205. Stamp Duty and Stamp Duty Reserve Tax (Cassa Di Compensazione E Garanzia S.p.A.) Regulations 2011

Reg.2, amended: SI 2013/504 Reg.47
Reg.3, substituted: SI 2013/504 Reg.47
Reg.4, amended: SI 2013/504 Reg.47

2260. Equality Act 2010 (Specific Duties) Regulations 2011

Reg.2, varied: SI 2013/235 Sch.3 para.25
Reg.3, varied: SI 2013/235 Sch.3 para.26, Sch.3 para.27
Sch.1, amended: SI 2013/235 Sch.2 para.166, SI 2013/472 Sch.2 para.215, SI 2013/534 Sch.1 para.10, SI 2013/2318 Sch.1 para.125

2262. Investment Bank Special Administration (Scotland) Rules 2011

Part 2 r.9, amended: SI 2013/472 Sch.2 para.216
Part 2 r.11, amended: SI 2013/472 Sch.2 para.216
Part 2 r.14, amended: SI 2013/472 Sch.2 para.216
Part 2 r.17, amended: SI 2013/472 Sch.2 para.216
Part 2 r.18, amended: SI 2013/472 Sch.2 para.216
Part 2 r.22, amended: SI 2013/472 Sch.2 para.216
Part 2 r.26, amended: SI 2013/472 Sch.2 para.216
Part 2 r.28, amended: SI 2013/472 Sch.2 para.216
Part 2 r.31, amended: SI 2013/472 Sch.2 para.216
Part 3 r.36, amended: SI 2013/472 Sch.2 para.216
Part 3 r.37, amended: SI 2013/472 Sch.2 para.216
Part 3 r.39, amended: SI 2013/472 Sch.2 para.216
Part 3 r.40, amended: SI 2013/472 Sch.2 para.216
Part 3 r.42, amended: SI 2013/472 Sch.2 para.216
Part 3 r.44, amended: SI 2013/472 Sch.2 para.216
Part 3 r.45, amended: SI 2013/472 Sch.2 para.216
Part 3 r.49, amended: SI 2013/472 Sch.2 para.216
Part 3 r.55, amended: SI 2013/472 Sch.2 para.216
Part 3 r.83, amended: SI 2013/472 Sch.2 para.216
Part 3 r.94, amended: SI 2013/472 Sch.2 para.216
Part 3 r.95, amended: SI 2013/472 Sch.2 para.216
Part 3 r.99, amended: SI 2013/472 Sch.2 para.216
Part 5 r.114, amended: SI 2013/472 Sch.2 para.216
Part 5 r.122, amended: SI 2013/472 Sch.2 para.216
Part 6 r.127, amended: SI 2013/472 Sch.2 para.216
Part 6 r.132, amended: SI 2013/472 Sch.2 para.216
Part 6 r.134, amended: SI 2013/472 Sch.2 para.216
Part 7 r.136, amended: SI 2013/472 Sch.2 para.216
Part 7 r.138, amended: SI 2013/472 Sch.2 para.216
Part 7 r.140, amended: SI 2013/472 Sch.2 para.216
Part 7 r.141, amended: SI 2013/472 Sch.2 para.216
Part 7 r.142, amended: SI 2013/472 Sch.2 para.216
Part 8 r.149, amended: SI 2013/472 Sch.2 para.216
Part 8 r.150, amended: SI 2013/472 Sch.2 para.216
Part 8 r.151, amended: SI 2013/472 Sch.2 para.216
Part 11 r.187, amended: SI 2013/472 Sch.2 para.216
Part 11 r.194, amended: SI 2013/472 Sch.2 para.216

2330. A55 Trunk Road (Glan Conwy Conwy Morfa, Conwy County Borough) (Temporary 70 mph Speed Limit) Order 2011

varied: SI 2013/1 Art.11, SI 2013/195 Art.14, SI 2013/674 Art.11

2341. Health Research Authority Regulations 2011

Reg.1, amended: SI 2013/235 Sch.2 para.167

2344. Upper Tribunal (Immigration and Asylum Chamber) (Judicial Review) (England and Wales) Fees Order 2011

Art.1, amended: SI 2013/2069 Art.4
Art.2, amended: SI 2013/2069 Art.5
Sch.1, amended: SI 2013/2069 Art.6, SI 2013/2302 Art.10
Sch.2 para.1, amended: SI 2013/388 Sch.1 para.47, SI 2013/534 Sch.1 para.24, SI 2013/591 Sch.1 para.45
Sch.2 para.1, substituted: SI 2013/2302 Sch.1
Sch.2 para.2, substituted: SI 2013/2302 Sch.1
Sch.2 para.3, substituted: SI 2013/2302 Sch.1
Sch.2 para.4, substituted: SI 2013/2302 Sch.1
Sch.2 para.5, substituted: SI 2013/2302 Sch.1
Sch.2 para.6, substituted: SI 2013/2302 Sch.1
Sch.2 para.7, substituted: SI 2013/2302 Sch.1
Sch.2 para.8, substituted: SI 2013/2302 Sch.1
Sch.2 para.9, substituted: SI 2013/2302 Sch.1
Sch.2 para.10, substituted: SI 2013/2302 Sch.1
Sch.2 para.11, substituted: SI 2013/2302 Sch.1
Sch.2 para.12, substituted: SI 2013/2302 Sch.1
Sch.2 para.13, substituted: SI 2013/2302 Sch.1
Sch.2 para.14, substituted: SI 2013/2302 Sch.1
Sch.2 para.15, substituted: SI 2013/2302 Sch.1
Sch.2 para.16, substituted: SI 2013/2302 Sch.1
Sch.2 para.17, substituted: SI 2013/2302 Sch.1
Sch.2 para.18, substituted: SI 2013/2302 Sch.1
Sch.2 para.19, substituted: SI 2013/2302 Sch.1
Sch.2 para.20, substituted: SI 2013/2302 Sch.1

2377. Animal By-Products (Enforcement) (No.2) (Wales) Regulations 2011

Sch.2 para.15, revoked: SI 2013/1478 Sch.5 para.31

2378. Poultry Health Scheme (Fees) (Wales) Regulations 2011

revoked: SI 2013/1241 Reg.11

2379. Trade in Animals and Related Products (Wales) Regulations 2011

Reg.11, applied: SI 2013/1662 Reg.4
Reg.15, applied: SI 2013/1241 Reg.10
Sch.2 Part 1 para.4, applied: SI 2013/1241 Reg.6

2431. Civil Enforcement of Parking Contraventions Designation Order 2011

Art.3, revoked (in part): SI 2013/992 Art.4
Sch.1, revoked: SI 2013/992 Art.4
Sch.2, revoked: SI 2013/992 Art.4

2440. Belarus (Restrictive Measures) (Overseas Territories) Order 2011

Art.14, amended: SI 2013/472 Sch.2 para.218
Art.23, amended: SI 2013/472 Sch.2 para.218

2441. Double Taxation Relief and International Tax Enforcement (South Africa) Order 2011

see *Revenue and Customs Commissioners v Ben Nevis (Holdings) Ltd* [2013] EWCA Civ 578, [2013] S.T.C. 1579 (CA (Civ Div)), Jackson, L.J.

2491. Airport Charges Regulations 2011

Reg.23, revoked: SI 2013/610 Sch.2 para.5
Reg.24, revoked: SI 2013/610 Sch.2 para.5
Reg.25, revoked: SI 2013/610 Sch.1 para.7
Reg.26, revoked: SI 2013/610 Sch.1 para.7
Reg.32, revoked (in part): SI 2013/610 Sch.1 para.7

2499. Waste and Emissions Trading Act 2003 (Amendment) Regulations 2011

Reg.9, revoked: SI 2013/141 Reg.7
Reg.10, revoked: SI 2013/141 Reg.7
Reg.11, revoked: SI 2013/141 Reg.7
Reg.12, revoked: SI 2013/141 Reg.7
Reg.13, revoked: SI 2013/141 Reg.7

2581. Public Services Reform (Scotland) Act 2010 (Consequential Modifications of Enactments) Order 2011

Sch.2 Part 2 para.53, revoked: SI 2013/458 Sch.1
Sch.2 Part 2 para.54, revoked: SI 2013/458 Sch.1

2678. Immigration (Procedure for Marriage) Regulations 2011

Sch.1, amended: SI 2013/226 Reg.2

2679. Immigration (Procedure for Formation of Civil Partnerships) Regulations 2011

Sch.1, amended: SI 2013/227 Reg.2

2680. RTM Companies (Model Articles) (Wales) Regulations 2011

Sch.1 Part 2 para.23, revoked (in part): 2013 c.8 s.3
Sch.2 Part RHANa para.23, revoked (in part): 2013 c.8 s.3

2687. Legislative Reform (Industrial and Provident Societies and Credit Unions) Order 2011

Art.25, amended: SI 2013/472 Art.4

2699. Recognised Auction Platforms Regulations 2011

Reg.1, amended: SI 2013/642 Art.6
Reg.5A, applied: SI 2013/418 Art.2
Reg.5C, added: SI 2013/429 Reg.2
Reg.20, amended: SI 2013/3115 Sch.2 para.76
Sch.2 para.5, revoked: SI 2013/642 Art.6

2721. Fire and Rescue Services (Appointment of Inspector) (Wales) Order 2011

revoked: SI 2013/3155 Art.3

2724. Double Taxation Relief and International Tax Enforcement (China) Order 2011

Sch.1, substituted: SI 2013/3142 Sch.1

2742. Al-Qaida (Asset-Freezing) Regulations 2011

Reg.2, amended: SI 2013/472 Art.4
Sch.1 para.5, amended: SI 2013/472 Sch.2 para.219

2829. Incidental Flooding and Coastal Erosion (Wales) Order 2011
Art.3, amended: SI 2013/755 Sch.5 para.73, Sch.5 para.74
Art.4, amended: SI 2013/755 Sch.5 para.75
Art.6, amended: SI 2013/755 Sch.5 para.76
Art.8, amended: SI 2013/755 Sch.5 para.77

2832. Financial Services and Markets Act 2000 (Permissions, Transitional Provisions and Consequential Amendments) (Northern Ireland Credit Unions) Order 2011
Art.3, amended: SI 2013/472 Art.5
Art.5, amended: SI 2013/472 Sch.2 para.220
Art.6, amended: SI 2013/472 Sch.2 para.220
Art.7, amended: SI 2013/472 Sch.2 para.220

2841. First-tier Tribunal (Immigration and Asylum Chamber) Fees Order 2011
Art.5, amended: SI 2013/534 Sch.1 para.23

2855. Incidental Flooding and Coastal Erosion (England) Order 2011
Art.3, amended: SI 2013/755 Sch.4 para.414
Art.4, amended: SI 2013/755 Sch.4 para.415
Art.6, amended: SI 2013/755 Sch.4 para.416
Art.8, amended: SI 2013/755 Sch.4 para.417

2860. Renewable Heat Incentive Scheme Regulations 2011
Reg.2, amended: SI 2013/1033 Reg.3, SI 2013/2410 Reg.3
Reg.3, amended: SI 2013/2410 Reg.4
Reg.5, substituted: SI 2013/2410 Reg.5
Reg.5A, added: SI 2013/2410 Reg.6
Reg.8, amended: SI 2013/2410 Reg.7
Reg.9, amended: SI 2013/2410 Reg.8
Reg.12, amended: SI 2013/2410 Reg.9
Reg.13, amended: SI 2013/2410 Reg.10
Reg.16, amended: SI 2013/2410 Reg.11
Reg.17, amended: SI 2013/2410 Reg.12
Reg.17A, added: SI 2013/2410 Reg.13
Reg.20, amended: SI 2013/2410 Reg.14
Reg.22, amended: SI 2013/1033 Reg.8
Reg.23, revoked (in part): SI 2013/1033 Reg.8
Reg.24A, added: SI 2013/2410 Reg.15
Reg.25, amended: SI 2013/1033 Reg.8
Reg.25, revoked (in part): SI 2013/1033 Reg.8
Reg.26, amended: SI 2013/1033 Reg.8, SI 2013/2410 Reg.16
Reg.34, amended: SI 2013/2410 Reg.17
Reg.34A, added: SI 2013/2410 Reg.18
Reg.35, amended: SI 2013/2410 Reg.19
Reg.37, amended: SI 2013/1033 Reg.4
Reg.37A, added: SI 2013/1033 Reg.5
Reg.37B, added: SI 2013/1033 Reg.5
Reg.37C, added: SI 2013/1033 Reg.5
Reg.37C, amended: SI 2013/3179 Reg.3
Reg.37D, added: SI 2013/1033 Reg.5
Reg.37D, amended: SI 2013/3179 Reg.4
Reg.37E, added: SI 2013/1033 Reg.5
Reg.38, amended: SI 2013/1033 Reg.7, SI 2013/2410 Reg.20
Reg.39, amended: SI 2013/1033 Reg.7, SI 2013/2410 Reg.21
Reg.39A, added: SI 2013/2410 Reg.22
Reg.42, amended: SI 2013/1033 Reg.7
Reg.42A, added: SI 2013/2410 Reg.23
Reg.43, amended: SI 2013/1033 Reg.6, SI 2013/2410 Reg.24
Reg.47, amended: SI 2013/2410 Reg.25
Reg.48, amended: SI 2013/2410 Reg.26
Reg.51A, revoked: SI 2013/1033 Reg.8
Reg.51B, revoked: SI 2013/1033 Reg.8
Reg.53, amended: SI 2013/1033 Reg.7
Sch.A1 para.1, added: SI 2013/2410 Reg.27
Sch.A1 para.2, added: SI 2013/2410 Reg.27
Sch.A1 para.3, added: SI 2013/2410 Reg.27
Sch.A1 para.4, added: SI 2013/2410 Reg.27
Sch.A1 para.4, amended: SI 2013/3179 Reg.5
Sch.A1 para.5, added: SI 2013/2410 Reg.27
Sch.A1 para.6, added: SI 2013/2410 Reg.27
Sch.A1 para.7, added: SI 2013/2410 Reg.27
Sch.A1 para.7, substituted: SI 2013/3179 Reg.5
Sch.A1 para.8, added: SI 2013/2410 Reg.27
Sch.A1 para.8, substituted: SI 2013/3179 Reg.5
Sch.A1 para.9, added: SI 2013/2410 Reg.27
Sch.A1 para.9, substituted: SI 2013/3179 Reg.5
Sch.A1 para.10, added: SI 2013/2410 Reg.27
Sch.A1 para.11, added: SI 2013/2410 Reg.27
Sch.A1 para.12, added: SI 2013/2410 Reg.27
Sch.A1 para.13, added: SI 2013/2410 Reg.27
Sch.A1 para.14, added: SI 2013/2410 Reg.27
Sch.A1 para.15, added: SI 2013/2410 Reg.27
Sch.A1 para.16, added: SI 2013/2410 Reg.27
Sch.1 para.1, amended: SI 2013/2410 Reg.28
Sch.4, added: SI 2013/1033 Sch.1
Sch.5 Part 1, added: SI 2013/1033 Sch.1
Sch.5 Part 2, added: SI 2013/1033 Sch.1
Sch.5 Part 3, added: SI 2013/1033 Sch.1
Sch.5 Part 4, added: SI 2013/1033 Sch.1
Sch.5 Part 5, added: SI 2013/1033 Sch.1
Sch.5 Part 6, added: SI 2013/1033 Sch.1
Sch.5 Part 7, added: SI 2013/1033 Sch.1

2866. Legal Services Act 2007 (Designation as a Licensing Authority) (No.2) Order 2011
Art.4, amended: SI 2013/472 Art.4
Art.6, amended: SI 2013/534 Sch.1 para.11
Sch.2, amended: SI 2013/294 Sch.1

2907. National Health Service (Pharmaceutical Services) (Amendment) (Wales) Regulations 2011
revoked: SI 2013/898 Sch.8 para.26

2936. Wine Regulations 2011
Reg.2, amended: SI 2013/3235 Reg.13
Reg.4, amended: SI 2013/3235 Reg.13
Reg.14, amended: SI 2013/3235 Reg.13
Sch.1 para.1, amended: SI 2013/3235 Reg.13
Sch.2 para.1, amended: SI 2013/3235 Reg.13

2943. Social Security (Electronic Communications) (No.2) Order 2011
Art.4, revoked: SI 2013/458 Sch.1
Art.5, revoked: SI 2013/458 Sch.1

2989. Iran (Restrictive Measures) (Overseas Territories) Order 2011
Art.3A, amended: SI 2013/786 Art.3
Art.3B, amended: SI 2013/786 Art.4
Art.3C, amended: SI 2013/786 Art.5
Art.3I, substituted: SI 2013/786 Art.6
Art.12, amended: SI 2013/472 Sch.2 para.221

2999. Investment Trust (Approved Company) (Tax) Regulations 2011
Reg.19, amended: SI 2013/1406 Reg.2
Reg.20, amended: SI 2013/1406 Reg.2
Reg.22, amended: SI 2013/1406 Reg.2
Reg.22, revoked (in part): SI 2013/1406 Reg.2

3037. Cosmetic Products (Safety) (Amendment) Regulations 2011
revoked: SI 2013/1478 Sch.1

3038. Council Tax (Demand Notices) (England) Regulations 2011
Sch.1 Part 2 para.18, amended: SI 2013/2977 Reg.5
Sch.1 Part 2 para.19, amended: SI 2013/2977 Reg.5
Sch.1 Part 2 para.27, amended: SI 2013/2977 Reg.5

3045. Port Security (Port of Dover) Designation Order 2011
Art.4, amended: SI 2013/2728 Art.2

3049. Open-Ended Investment Companies (Amendment) Regulations 2011
Reg.2, amended: SI 2013/2984 Art.2
Reg.4, amended: SI 2013/2984 Art.2
Reg.4, applied: SI 2013/2984 Art.3
Reg.4, varied: SI 2013/2984 Art.3
Reg.10, applied: SI 2013/2984 Art.3
Reg.10, varied: SI 2013/2984 Art.3

3050. Elected Local Policing Bodies (Specified Information) Order 2011
Sch.1 Part 1 para.3, amended: SI 2013/1816 Art.3
Sch.1 Part 2 para.13, amended: SI 2013/1816 Art.4

3066. Railways (Interoperability) Regulations 2011
Reg.2, amended: SI 2013/3023 Reg.2
Reg.12, amended: SI 2013/3023 Reg.2
Reg.37, revoked (in part): SI 2013/2042 Sch.1 para.92

3076. Dartmouth-Kingswear Floating Bridge (Vehicle Classifications & Revision of Charges) (Amendment) Order 2011
revoked: SI 2013/2916 Art.4

2012

8. School Admissions (Admission Arrangements and Co-ordination of Admission Arrangements) (England) Regulations 2012
applied: SI 2013/3110 Sch.3 para.8

10. School Admissions (Infant Class Sizes) (England) Regulations 2012
applied: SI 2013/3104 Sch.2 para.11
Reg.4, see *R. (on the application of DD) v Islington LBC Independent Appeal Panel* [2013] EWHC 2262 (Admin), [2013] E.L.R. 483 (QBD (Admin)), Judge McKenna

80. A419 Trunk Road (Blunsdon to Calcutt, Wiltshire) (Prohibition of U Turns) (Experimental) Order 2012
revoked: SI 2013/1504 Art.4

129. Syria (European Union Financial Sanctions) Regulations 2012
Reg.2, amended: SI 2013/472 Art.4
Reg.3, amended: SI 2013/877 Reg.3
Reg.4, amended: SI 2013/877 Reg.4
Reg.5, amended: SI 2013/877 Reg.4
Reg.8B, added: SI 2013/877 Reg.5
Reg.9, amended: SI 2013/877 Reg.6, Reg.7
Reg.12, amended: SI 2013/1876 Reg.2
Sch.1 para.5, amended: SI 2013/472 Sch.2 para.222, SI 2013/534 Sch.1 para.12

148. Non-Domestic Rating (Small Business Rate Relief) (England) Order 2012
Art.4, amended: SI 2013/15 Art.2
Art.4, substituted: SI 2013/15 Art.2

199. Reporting of Injuries, Diseases and Dangerous Occurrences (Amendment) Regulations 2012
revoked: SI 2013/1471 Sch.4

212. Settlement Agreements (Automatic Enrolment) (Description of Person) Order 2012
amended: SI 2013/1956 Sch.1 para.16
Art.1, amended: SI 2013/1956 Sch.1 para.16

244. Smoke Control Areas (Exempted Fireplaces) (Wales) Order 2012
revoked: SI 2013/561 Art.3

245. Seed Marketing (Wales) Regulations 2012
Reg.3, amended: SI 2013/889 Reg.3
Reg.21A, added: SI 2013/889 Reg.4

249. Houses in Multiple Occupation (Specified Educational Establishments) (England) Regulations 2012

revoked: SI 2013/1601 Reg.3

335. School Finance (England) Regulations 2012

revoked: SI 2013/3104 Reg.2

417. National Health Service (Functions of Strategic Health Authorities and Primary Care Trusts and Administration Arrangements) (England) (Amendment) Regulations 2012

revoked: SI 2013/235 Sch.2 para.203

425. Street Works (Charges for Occupation of the Highway) (England) Regulations 2012

applied: SI 2013/1147 Art.2

444. Local Authorities (Conduct of Referendums) (Council Tax Increases) (England) Regulations 2012

Sch.1, substituted: SI 2013/409 Sch.1
Sch.3, amended: SI 2013/409 Sch.2
Sch.5, amended: SI 2013/409 Sch.2

502. National Health Service (Primary Dental Services) (Miscellaneous Amendments) Regulations 2012

Reg.5, revoked: SI 2013/469 Reg.5

504. Medicines (Products for Human Use) (Fees) Regulations 2012

revoked: SI 2013/532 Reg.59
Reg.57, applied: SI 2013/532 Reg.59
Reg.58, applied: SI 2013/532 Reg.59

516. Judicial Pensions (Contributions) Regulations 2012

Reg.3, amended: SI 2013/484 Reg.3

528. Pension Protection Fund and Occupational Pension Schemes (Levy Ceiling and Compensation Cap) Order 2012

revoked: SI 2013/105 Art.5

531. Residential Property Tribunal Procedures and Fees (Wales) Regulations 2012

Reg.2, amended: SI 2013/1723 Art.5
Reg.12, amended: SI 2013/1723 Art.5
Reg.21, amended: SI 2013/1723 Art.5
Reg.24, revoked (in part): SI 2013/2042 Sch.1 para.98
Reg.47, amended: SI 2013/1723 Art.5
Sch.1 Part 003, amended: SI 2013/1723 Art.5
Sch.1 Part 003 para.54, amended: SI 2013/1723 Art.5
Sch.1 Part 003 para.55, amended: SI 2013/1723 Art.5
Sch.1 Part 003 para.56, amended: SI 2013/1723 Art.5
Sch.1 Part 003 para.57, amended: SI 2013/1723 Art.5
Sch.1 Part 003 para.58, amended: SI 2013/1723 Art.5
Sch.1 Part 003 para.59, amended: SI 2013/1723 Art.5
Sch.1 Part 003 para.60, amended: SI 2013/1723 Art.5
Sch.1 Part 003 para.61, amended: SI 2013/1723 Art.5

632. Control of Asbestos Regulations 2012

Reg.3, amended: SSI 2013/119 Sch.2 para.27

637. Neighbourhood Planning (General) Regulations 2012

Reg.23, applied: SI 2013/1102 Reg.6
Sch.1 para.1, amended: SI 2013/235 Sch.2 para.168

638. Identification and Traceability of Explosives (Amendment) Regulations 2012

revoked: SI 2013/449 Reg.9

646. Rent Officers (Housing Benefit Functions) (Amendment) Order 2012

see *R. (on the application of Zacchaeus 2000 Trust) v Secretary of State for Work and Pensions* [2013] EWCA Civ 1202, [2013] P.T.S.R. 1427 (CA (Civ Div)), Sullivan, L.J.; see *R. (on the application of Zacchaeus 2000 Trust) v Secretary of State for Work and Pensions* [2013] EWHC 233 (Admin), [2013] P.T.S.R. 785 (QBD (Admin)), Underhill, J.

734. Housing (Right to Buy) (Limit on Discount) (England) Order 2012

applied: SI 2013/677 Art.3
revoked (in part): SI 2013/677 Art.4

745. Plant Health (Fees) (England) Regulations 2012

revoked: SI 2013/494 Reg.7

747. Further Education Teachers Qualifications, Continuing Professional Development and Registration (England) (Amendment) Regulations 2012

revoked: SI 2013/1976 Sch.1

749. Town and Country Planning (Compensation) (England) Regulations 2012

revoked: SI 2013/1102 Reg.8

767. Town and Country Planning (Local Planning) (England) Regulations 2012

Reg.2, amended: SI 2013/235 Sch.2 para.169
Reg.4, amended: SI 2013/235 Sch.2 para.169

780. Social Security Benefits Up-rating Order 2012

revoked: SI 2013/574 Art.26

782. Pensions Increase (Review) Order 2012

applied: SI 2013/604 Sch.1

786. Isle of Wight National Health Service Trust (Establishment) Order 2012

Art.1, amended: SI 2013/593 Art.2

788. Torbay and Southern Devon Health and Care National Health Service Trust (Establishment) Order 2012

Art.1, amended: SI 2013/593 Art.2

796. Barts Health NHS Trust (Establishment) and the Barts and The London NHS Trust the Newham University Hospital NHS Trust and the Whipps Cross University Hospital NHS Trust (Dissolution) Order 2012
Art.1, amended: SI 2013/593 Art.2
798. Consular Fees Order 2012
Sch.1 Part 1, amended: SI 2013/535 Art.2
Sch.1 Part 2, substituted: SI 2013/1720 Art.2
799. Copyright and Performances (Application to Other Countries) Order 2012
revoked: SI 2013/536 Art.1
801. Town and Country Planning (Development Management Procedure) (Wales) Order 2012
Art.27, amended: SI 2013/755 Sch.5 para.79
Art.27, revoked (in part): SI 2013/755 Sch.5 para.79
Sch.4, amended: SI 2013/755 Sch.5 para.80
808. Ministry of Defence Police (Performance) Regulations 2012
Reg.4, amended: SI 2013/602 Sch.2 para.100
810. Export Control (Syria Sanctions) and (Miscellaneous Amendments) Order 2012
revoked: SI 2013/2012 Sch.1
813. Immigration and Nationality (Cost Recovery Fees) Regulations 2012
revoked: SI 2013/617 Reg.11
819. Social Security Benefits Up-rating Regulations 2012
revoked: SI 2013/599 Reg.6
822. Income Tax (Pay As You Earn) (Amendment) Regulations 2012
Reg.53, amended: SI 2013/521 Reg.39
Reg.54, amended: SI 2013/521 Reg.40
842. National Assistance (Sums for Personal Requirements) (Assessment of Resources and Miscellaneous Amendments) (Wales) Regulations 2012
Reg.2, revoked: SI 2013/631 Reg.3
847. Data-gathering Powers (Relevant Data) Regulations 2012
Reg.6, amended: SI 2013/1811 Reg.4
Reg.6, revoked (in part): SI 2013/1811 Reg.3
Reg.11A, added: SI 2013/1811 Reg.5
852. Dunham Bridge (Revision of Tolls) Order 2012
revoked: SI 2013/653 Art.4
901. National Health Service Trust Development Authority (Establishment and Constitution) Order 2012
Art.1, amended: SI 2013/260 Art.2
Art.3, amended: SI 2013/235 Sch.2 para.170
Art.5A, added: SI 2013/260 Art.3
Art.6A, added: SI 2013/260 Art.4
Art.6B, added: SI 2013/260 Art.4
917. Capital Requirements (Amendment) Regulations 2012
revoked: SI 2013/3115 Sch.3
922. National Health Service Trust Development Authority Regulations 2012
Reg.1, amended: SI 2013/235 Sch.2 para.171
Reg.3, amended: SI 2013/235 Sch.2 para.171
Reg.3, revoked (in part): SI 2013/235 Sch.2 para.171
925. Iran (European Union Financial Sanctions) Regulations 2012
Reg.2, amended: SI 2013/472 Art.4
Reg.9A, added: SI 2013/163 Reg.3
Reg.10, amended: SI 2013/163 Reg.4
Reg.10, revoked (in part): SI 2013/163 Reg.4
Reg.10A, added: SI 2013/163 Reg.5
Reg.11, amended: SI 2013/163 Reg.6
Reg.14, amended: SI 2013/163 Reg.7
Reg.14, revoked (in part): SI 2013/163 Reg.7
Reg.15, amended: SI 2013/163 Reg.8
Reg.16, amended: SI 2013/163 Reg.9
Reg.19, amended: SI 2013/163 Reg.10
Sch.1 para.5, amended: SI 2013/472 Sch.2 para.223, SI 2013/534 Sch.1 para.12
936. Postal Services (Universal Postal Service) Order 2012
see *R. (on the application of TNT Post UK Ltd) v Revenue and Customs Commissioners* [2012] EWHC 3380 (Admin), [2013] S.T.C. 1306 (QBD (Admin)), Kenneth Parker, J.
Art.2, amended: SI 2013/3108 Art.3
Art.3, amended: SI 2013/3108 Art.4
Art.5, amended: SI 2013/3108 Art.5
Art.9, amended: SI 2013/3108 Art.6
Art.10, amended: SI 2013/3108 Art.7
Art.11, added: SI 2013/3108 Art.8
Sch.1 para.2, amended: SI 2013/3108 Art.9
Sch.1 para.2, revoked (in part): SI 2013/3108 Art.9
Sch.1 para.3, amended: SI 2013/3108 Art.10
Sch.1 para.3, revoked (in part): SI 2013/3108 Art.10
Sch.1 para.5, amended: SI 2013/3108 Art.11
Sch.1 para.6, amended: SI 2013/3108 Art.12
Sch.1 para.6A, added: SI 2013/3108 Art.13
Sch.1 para.7, amended: SI 2013/3108 Art.14
Sch.1 para.7, revoked (in part): SI 2013/3108 Art.14
Sch.1 para.7A, added: SI 2013/3108 Art.15
Sch.2 para.3, amended: SI 2013/3108 Art.16
Sch.2 para.4, amended: SI 2013/3108 Art.17
Sch.2 para.4, revoked (in part): SI 2013/3108 Art.17
Sch.2 para.5, revoked: SI 2013/3108 Art.18
Sch.3 para.1, amended: SI 2013/3108 Art.19

Sch.3 para.2, amended: SI 2013/3108 Art.20
Sch.3 para.3, amended: SI 2013/3108 Art.21

956. Young People's Learning Agency Abolition (Consequential Amendments to Subordinate Legislation) (England) Order 2012
Art.13, revoked: SI 2013/458 Sch.1
Art.14, revoked: SI 2013/458 Sch.1
Art.17, revoked: SI 2013/3109 Reg.3
Art.18, revoked: SI 2013/3110 Reg.8

971. Immigration and Nationality (Fees) Regulations 2012
revoked: SI 2013/749 Reg.10

985. M1 Motorway (Junctions 10 to 13) (Actively Managed Hard Shoulder and Variable Speed Limits) Regulations 2012
Sch.1 para.1, substituted: SI 2013/482 Reg.5
Sch.2 para.1, substituted: SI 2013/482 Reg.6

1020. Local Authorities (Committee System) (England) Regulations 2012
Reg.4, amended: SI 2013/235 Sch.2 para.172
Reg.4, revoked (in part): SI 2013/235 Sch.2 para.172
Reg.5, applied: SI 2013/643 Art.2
Reg.9, amended: SI 2013/218 Reg.33, SI 2013/235 Sch.2 para.172
Reg.9, revoked (in part): SI 2013/235 Sch.2 para.172

1034. School Governance (Constitution) (England) Regulations 2012
applied: SI 2013/1624 Reg.19, SI 2013/3110 Sch.4 para.2
Sch.4, applied: SI 2013/1624 Reg.17
Sch.4 para.9, applied: SI 2013/1624 Reg.17

1035. School Governance (Federations) (England) Regulations 2012
Reg.5, amended: SI 2013/1624 Sch.2 para.2
Reg.7, amended: SI 2013/1624 Sch.2 para.2
Reg.7, applied: SI 2013/1624 Reg.13
Reg.20A, added: SI 2013/1624 Sch.2 para.2
Reg.24, amended: SI 2013/1624 Sch.2 para.2
Sch.6 para.1, substituted: SI 2013/1624 Sch.2 para.2
Sch.6 para.2, substituted: SI 2013/1624 Sch.2 para.2
Sch.6 para.3, substituted: SI 2013/1624 Sch.2 para.2
Sch.6 para.4, substituted: SI 2013/1624 Sch.2 para.2
Sch.6 para.5, substituted: SI 2013/1624 Sch.2 para.2
Sch.6 para.6, substituted: SI 2013/1624 Sch.2 para.2
Sch.6 para.7, substituted: SI 2013/1624 Sch.2 para.2
Sch.6 para.8, substituted: SI 2013/1624 Sch.2 para.2
Sch.6 para.9, substituted: SI 2013/1624 Sch.2 para.2
Sch.6 para.10, substituted: SI 2013/1624 Sch.2 para.2
Sch.6 para.11, substituted: SI 2013/1624 Sch.2 para.2
Sch.6 para.12, substituted: SI 2013/1624 Sch.2 para.2
Sch.6 para.13, substituted: SI 2013/1624 Sch.2 para.2
Sch.6 para.14, substituted: SI 2013/1624 Sch.2 para.2

1128. Postal Services Act 2011 (Disclosure of Information) Order 2012
Art.3, amended: SI 2013/472 Sch.2 para.224
Art.4, amended: SI 2013/1575 Sch.1 para.25, SI 2013/3134 Sch.4 para.14

1155. Food Additives (England) (Amendment) and the Extraction Solvents in Food (Amendment) (England) Regulations 2012
revoked: SI 2013/2210 Sch.5

1197. Designation of Rural Primary Schools (England) Order 2012
revoked: SI 2013/2655 Art.3

1198. Food Additives (Wales) (Amendment) and the Extraction Solvents in Food (Amendment) (Wales) Regulations 2012
revoked: SI 2013/2591 Sch.5

1199. Apprenticeships (Alternative English Completion Conditions) Regulations 2012
Sch.1, amended: SI 2013/1968 Reg.2

1204. Police (Complaints and Misconduct) Regulations 2012
Reg.4, varied: SI 2013/1778 Reg.3
Reg.7, varied: SI 2013/1778 Reg.3
Reg.37, varied: SI 2013/1778 Reg.3

1243. Export Control (Iran Sanctions) Order 2012
Art.2, amended: SI 2013/340 Art.2
Art.6, substituted: SI 2013/340 Art.2
Art.6A, added: SI 2013/340 Art.2
Art.8A, added: SI 2013/340 Art.2
Art.9A, added: SI 2013/340 Art.2
Art.15, amended: SI 2013/340 Art.2
Art.18, amended: SI 2013/340 Art.2

1259. Education (Listed Bodies) (Wales) Order 2012
Sch.1 Part 1, amended: SI 2013/2318 Sch.1 para.126

1261. Velindre National Health Service Trust Shared Services Committee (Wales) Regulations 2012
Reg.2, amended: SI 2013/235 Sch.2 para.173
Sch.1 para.1, amended: SI 2013/235 Sch.2 para.173

1273. Health Education England (Establishment and Constitution) Order 2012
Art.4, amended: SI 2013/647 Art.2
Art.5A, added: SI 2013/647 Art.2
Art.5B, added: SI 2013/1197 Art.2
Art.5C, added: SI 2013/1197 Art.2
Art.5D, added: SI 2013/1197 Art.2

1290. Health Education England Regulations 2012
Reg.1, amended: SI 2013/235 Sch.2 para.174

1301. Guinea-Bissau (Asset-Freezing) Regulations 2012
Reg.2, amended: SI 2013/472 Art.4
Sch.1 para.5, amended: SI 2013/472 Sch.2 para.225, SI 2013/534 Sch.1 para.12

1302. Burma/Myanmar (Financial Restrictions) (Suspension) Regulations 2012
revoked: SI 2013/1096 Reg.2

1313. Community Right to Challenge (Expressions of Interest and Excluded Services) (England) Regulations 2012
Reg.4, amended: SI 2013/218 Reg.19
Sch.2 para.1, amended: SI 2013/218 Reg.19
Sch.2 para.5, added: SI 2013/218 Reg.19
Sch.2 para.6, added: SI 2013/218 Reg.19
Sch.2 para.7, added: SI 2013/218 Reg.19

1320. Criminal Justice Act 2003 (Commencement No 28 and Saving Provisions) Order 2012
Art.4, applied: SI 2013/1103 Art.2, Art.4
Art.5, applied: SI 2013/1103 Art.4

1386. CRC Energy Efficiency Scheme (Allocation of Allowances for Payment) Regulations 2012
applied: SI 2013/3103 Reg.13
revoked: SI 2013/3103 Reg.13
Reg.2, amended: SI 2013/1097 Reg.2
Reg.3, amended: SI 2013/1097 Reg.2
Reg.4, amended: SI 2013/1097 Reg.2
Reg.4A, added: SI 2013/1097 Reg.2
Reg.5, amended: SI 2013/1097 Reg.2
Reg.5, revoked (in part): SI 2013/1097 Reg.2
Reg.6, amended: SI 2013/1097 Reg.2
Reg.7, amended: SI 2013/1097 Reg.2
Reg.9, amended: SI 2013/472 Art.4
Reg.10, revoked (in part): SI 2013/1097 Reg.2
Reg.11, applied: SI 2013/3103 Reg.13

1425. National Patient Safety Agency (Amendment) Regulations 2012
revoked: SI 2013/235 Sch.2 para.204

1426. Medical Devices (Amendment) Regulations 2012
Reg.3, revoked: SI 2013/2327 Reg.22

1439. Supervision of Accounts and Reports (Prescribed Body) and Companies (Defective Accounts and Directors Reports) (Authorised Person) Order 2012
Art.2, amended: SI 2013/472 Sch.2 para.226

1467. National Health Service (Local Pharmaceutical Services) Amendment Regulations 2012
revoked: SI 2013/349 Sch.10 para.10

1472. A23 Trunk Road (Handcross Warninglid) (Temporary Restriction and Prohibition of Traffic) Order 2012
revoked: SI 2013/1377 Art.8

1483. Social Security (Information-sharing in relation to Welfare Services etc.) Regulations 2012
Reg.2, amended: SI 2013/41 Reg.2, SI 2013/454 Reg.3
Reg.4, amended: SI 2013/388 Sch.1 para.48
Reg.5, amended: SI 2013/41 Reg.2, SI 2013/454 Reg.3
Reg.6, amended: SI 2013/41 Reg.2, SI 2013/454 Reg.3
Reg.6, revoked (in part): SI 2013/458 Sch.1
Reg.7, amended: SI 2013/41 Reg.2, SI 2013/454 Reg.3
Reg.8, amended: SI 2013/41 Reg.2, SI 2013/454 Reg.3
Reg.9, amended: SI 2013/41 Reg.2, SI 2013/454 Reg.3
Reg.9A, added: SI 2013/454 Reg.3
Reg.9A, amended: SI 2013/41 Reg.2
Reg.9B, added: SI 2013/454 Reg.3
Reg.9B, amended: SI 2013/41 Reg.2
Reg.10, amended: SI 2013/41 Reg.2
Reg.10, substituted: SI 2013/454 Reg.3
Reg.11, amended: SI 2013/41 Reg.2, SI 2013/454 Reg.3
Reg.12, added: SI 2013/41 Reg.2
Reg.12, amended: SI 2013/454 Reg.3
Reg.13, added: SI 2013/41 Reg.2
Reg.13, amended: SI 2013/454 Reg.3
Reg.14, added: SI 2013/41 Reg.2
Reg.14, substituted: SI 2013/454 Reg.3
Reg.15, added: SI 2013/41 Reg.2
Reg.16, added: SI 2013/454 Reg.3
Reg.17, added: SI 2013/454 Reg.3

1489. Iraq (Asset-Freezing) Regulations 2012
Reg.2, amended: SI 2013/472 Art.4
Sch.1 para.5, amended: SI 2013/472 Sch.2 para.227, SI 2013/534 Sch.1 para.12

1493. Plant Health (Fees) (Wales) Regulations 2012
revoked: SI 2013/1700 Reg.7

1506. Automatic Enrolment (Earnings Trigger and Qualifying Earnings Band) Order 2012
Art.3, revoked: SI 2013/667 Art.4

1507. Sudan (Asset-Freezing) Regulations 2012
Reg.2, amended: SI 2013/472 Art.4
Sch.1 para.5, amended: SI 2013/472 Sch.2 para.228, SI 2013/534 Sch.1 para.12

1508. Republic of Guinea (Asset-Freezing) Regulations 2012
Reg.2, amended: SI 2013/472 Art.4
Sch.1 para.5, amended: SI 2013/472 Sch.2 para.229, SI 2013/534 Sch.1 para.12

1509. Belarus (Asset-Freezing) Regulations 2012
revoked: SI 2013/164 Reg.18
Reg.9, applied: SI 2013/164 Reg.19

1511. Democratic Republic of the Congo (Asset-Freezing) Regulations 2012
Reg.2, amended: SI 2013/472 Art.4
Sch.1 para.5, amended: SI 2013/472 Sch.2 para.230, SI 2013/534 Sch.1 para.12

1515. Eritrea (Asset-Freezing) Regulations 2012
Reg.2, amended: SI 2013/472 Art.4
Sch.1 para.5, amended: SI 2013/472 Sch.2 para.231, SI 2013/534 Sch.1 para.12

1516. Liberia (Asset-Freezing) Regulations 2012
Reg.2, amended: SI 2013/472 Art.4
Sch.1 para.5, amended: SI 2013/472 Sch.2 para.232, SI 2013/534 Sch.1 para.12

1517. Lebanon and Syria (Asset-Freezing) Regulations 2012
Reg.2, amended: SI 2013/472 Art.4
Sch.1 para.5, amended: SI 2013/472 Sch.2 para.233, SI 2013/534 Sch.1 para.12

1518. Cancellation of Student Loans for Living Costs Liability (Wales) Regulations 2012
applied: SI 2013/1396 Reg.5

1538. Prospectus Regulations 2012
Reg.10, amended: SI 2013/472 Sch.2 para.234

1579. M54 Motorway (Junction 1 to Junction 3) (Temporary Restriction and Prohibition of Traffic) Order 2012
revoked: SI 2013/1122 Art.8

1631. National Health Service (Clinical Commissioning Groups) Regulations 2012
Sch.4 para.3, amended: SI 2013/235 Sch.2 para.175
Sch.4 para.5, revoked: SI 2013/235 Sch.2 para.175
Sch.4 para.9A, added: SI 2013/235 Sch.2 para.175
Sch.4 para.9B, added: SI 2013/235 Sch.2 para.175
Sch.5 para.6, amended: SI 2013/235 Sch.2 para.175

1643. School Governance (Transition from an Interim Executive Board) (Wales) Regulations 2012
applied: SI 2013/2127 Reg.2
Reg.10, applied: SI 2013/2127 Reg.4

1652. Health and Safety (Fees) Regulations 2012
Reg.17, amended: SI 2013/1948 Reg.3
Reg.18, revoked: SI 2013/1512 Reg.2
Reg.21, revoked: SI 2013/448 Sch.1
Reg.24, amended: SI 2013/1506 Sch.5 para.10, SI 2013/1948 Reg.3
Sch.14, revoked: SI 2013/1512 Reg.2
Sch.16, revoked: SI 2013/448 Sch.1

1653. Education (Student Fees, Awards and Support) (Amendment) Regulations 2012
Reg.8, see *R. (on the application of Arogundade) v Secretary of State for Business, Innovation and Skills* [2013] EWCA Civ 823, [2013] E.L.R. 466 (CA (Civ Div)), Longmore, L.J.

1665. Public Record Office (Fees) Regulations 2012
revoked: SI 2013/3267 Reg.3

1715. Volatile Organic Compounds in Paints, Varnishes and Vehicle Refinishing Products Regulations 2012
Reg.3, amended: SI 2013/390 Reg.57

1726. Criminal Procedure Rules 2012
applied: SI 2013/1554 r.2_1
revoked: SI 2013/1554
Part 17, applied: SI 2013/1554 r.2_1
r.76.2, see *R. (on the application of Gray) v Aylesbury Crown Court* [2013] EWHC 500 (Admin), [2013] 3 All E.R. 346 (QBD (Admin)), Toulson, L.J.

1742. Food Hygiene (England) (Amendment) Regulations 2012
revoked: SI 2013/2996 Sch.9

1743. Merchant Shipping (Accident Reporting and Investigation) Regulations 2012
Reg.2, amended: SI 2013/2882 Reg.2
Reg.6, amended: SI 2013/2882 Reg.2
Reg.13, amended: SI 2013/2882 Reg.2

1745. Consumer Credit (Total Charge for Credit) (Amendment) Regulations 2012
revoked (in part): SI 2013/1881 Art.21

1754. Copyright and Performances (Application to Other Countries) (Amendment) Order 2012
revoked: SI 2013/536 Art.1

1755. Syria (Restrictive Measures) (Overseas Territories) Order 2012
Art.8, substituted: SI 2013/1719 Art.3
Art.9, substituted: SI 2013/1719 Art.4
Art.11, amended: SI 2013/2598 Art.2
Art.17, amended: SI 2013/2598 Art.2
Art.24, amended: SI 2013/472 Sch.2 para.235
Art.33, amended: SI 2013/1719 Art.5
Art.37, amended: SI 2013/2598 Art.2
Art.43, amended: SI 2013/1719 Art.6
Sch.2 para.1, amended: SI 2013/1719 Art.7
Sch.2 para.2, amended: SI 2013/1719 Art.7
Sch.4 para.1, amended: SI 2013/1719 Art.8
Sch.4 para.2, amended: SI 2013/1719 Art.8
Sch.5 para.5, amended: SI 2013/472 Sch.2 para.235
Sch.6 para.1, added: SI 2013/1719 Art.9
Sch.6 para.2, added: SI 2013/1719 Art.9

Sch.6 para.3, added: SI 2013/1719 Art.9
Sch.6 para.4, added: SI 2013/1719 Art.9
Sch.6 para.5, added: SI 2013/1719 Art.9
Sch.6 para.6, added: SI 2013/1719 Art.9
Sch.6 para.7, added: SI 2013/1719 Art.9
Sch.6 para.8, added: SI 2013/1719 Art.9
Sch.6 para.9, added: SI 2013/1719 Art.9
Sch.6 para.10, added: SI 2013/1719 Art.9
Sch.6 para.11, added: SI 2013/1719 Art.9

1756. Iran (Restrictive Measures) (Overseas Territories) Order 2012

Art.2, amended: SI 2013/1444 Art.2
Art.12, amended: SI 2013/1444 Art.2
Art.12, substituted: SI 2013/1444 Art.2
Art.12A, added: SI 2013/1444 Art.2
Art.13, amended: SI 2013/1444 Art.2
Art.14A, added: SI 2013/1444 Art.2
Art.14B, added: SI 2013/1444 Art.2
Art.15A, added: SI 2013/1444 Art.2
Art.19A, added: SI 2013/1444 Art.2
Art.19B, added: SI 2013/1444 Art.2
Art.20, amended: SI 2013/1444 Art.2
Art.26, amended: SI 2013/472 Sch.2 para.236
Art.31A, added: SI 2013/1444 Art.2
Art.32, amended: SI 2013/1444 Art.2
Art.32, substituted: SI 2013/1444 Art.2
Art.32A, added: SI 2013/1444 Art.2
Art.33, amended: SI 2013/1444 Art.2
Art.34, amended: SI 2013/1444 Art.2
Art.35, amended: SI 2013/1444 Art.2
Art.35, substituted: SI 2013/1444 Art.2
Art.43, amended: SI 2013/1444 Art.2
Art.48, amended: SI 2013/1444 Art.2
Art.54, amended: SI 2013/1444 Art.2
Sch.2 para.2, amended: SI 2013/1444 Art.2
Sch.4 para.2, amended: SI 2013/1444 Art.2
Sch.5 para.2, amended: SI 2013/1444 Art.2
Sch.5 para.6, amended: SI 2013/472 Sch.2 para.236

1757. Al-Qaida (United Nations Measures) (Overseas Territories) Order 2012

Art.23, amended: SI 2013/472 Sch.2 para.237

1758. Afghanistan (United Nations Measures) (Overseas Territories) Order 2012

Art.23, amended: SI 2013/472 Sch.2 para.238

1809. Treaty of Lisbon (Changes in Terminology or Numbering) Order 2012

Sch.1 Part 2, amended: SI 2013/458 Sch.1

1836. Tax Avoidance Schemes (Information) Regulations 2012

Reg.2, amended: SI 2013/2592 Reg.4, Reg.15
Reg.4, amended: SI 2013/2592 Reg.5, Reg.6, Reg.7, Reg.8
Reg.5, applied: SI 2013/2592 Reg.2
Reg.8A, added: SI 2013/2592 Reg.16
Reg.9, amended: SI 2013/2592 Reg.9
Reg.10, amended: SI 2013/2592 Reg.10
Reg.11, amended: SI 2013/2592 Reg.11, Reg.12
Reg.12, amended: SI 2013/2592 Reg.13, Reg.14
Reg.13, amended: SI 2013/2592 Reg.17, Reg.18, Reg.19
Reg.13A, added: SI 2013/2592 Reg.20

1846. Ecclesiastical Judges, Legal Officers and Others (Fees) Order 2012

revoked: SI 2013/1922 Art.3

1847. Legal Officers (Annual Fees) Order 2012

revoked: SI 2013/1918 Art.4

1848. Customs Disclosure of Information and Miscellaneous Amendments Regulations 2012

applied: SI 2013/1387 Reg.22

1865. M62 Motorway (Junctions 25 to 30) (Actively Managed Hard Shoulder and Variable Speed Limits) Regulations 2012

Sch.1 para.1, substituted: SI 2013/482 Reg.8
Sch.2 para.1, amended: SI 2013/482 Reg.9, Reg.10

1868. National Insurance Contributions (Application of Part 7 of the Finance Act 2004) Regulations 2012

Reg.5, amended: SI 2013/2600 Reg.3
Reg.8, applied: SI 2013/2600 Reg.1
Reg.14A, added: SI 2013/2600 Reg.4
Reg.16A, added: SI 2013/2600 Reg.5
Reg.22, amended: SI 2013/2600 Reg.6
Reg.25, amended: SI 2013/2600 Reg.7
Reg.26, amended: SI 2013/2600 Reg.8, Reg.9, Reg.10, Reg.11, Reg.12

1889. Waste (England and Wales) (Amendment) Regulations 2012

Reg.2, see *R. (on the application of UK Recyclate Ltd) v Secretary of State for the Environment, Food and Rural Affairs* [2013] EWHC 425 (Admin), [2013] 3 All E.R. 561 (QBD (Admin)), Hickinbottom, J.

1893. National Health Service (Dental Charges) (Wales) (Amendment) Regulations 2012

revoked: SI 2013/544 Reg.3

1903. Natural Resources Body for Wales (Establishment) Order 2012

applied: SI 2013/755 Sch.7 para.3
Art.2, substituted: SI 2013/755 Sch.1 para.2
Art.4, amended: SI 2013/755 Sch.1 para.3
Art.5A, added: SI 2013/755 Sch.1 para.4
Art.5B, added: SI 2013/755 Sch.1 para.4
Art.5C, added: SI 2013/755 Sch.1 para.4
Art.5D, added: SI 2013/755 Sch.1 para.4
Art.5E, added: SI 2013/755 Sch.1 para.4
Art.5F, added: SI 2013/755 Sch.1 para.4
Art.5G, added: SI 2013/755 Sch.1 para.4
Art.5H, added: SI 2013/755 Sch.1 para.4

Art.5I, added: SI 2013/755 Sch.1 para.4
Art.5J, added: SI 2013/755 Sch.1 para.4
Art.6, revoked: SI 2013/755 Sch.1 para.5
Art.7, revoked: SI 2013/755 Sch.1 para.5
Art.8, amended: SI 2013/755 Sch.1 para.6
Art.8A, added: SI 2013/755 Sch.1 para.7
Art.9, amended: SI 2013/755 Sch.1 para.8
Art.9A, added: SI 2013/755 Sch.1 para.9
Art.10, substituted: SI 2013/755 Sch.1 para.10
Art.10A, added: SI 2013/755 Sch.1 para.11
Art.10B, added: SI 2013/755 Sch.1 para.11
Art.10C, added: SI 2013/755 Sch.1 para.11
Art.10D, added: SI 2013/755 Sch.1 para.11
Art.10E, added: SI 2013/755 Sch.1 para.11
Art.11, amended: SI 2013/755 Sch.1 para.12, SI 2013/1821 Art.31
Art.11, applied: SI 2013/755 Sch.7 para.5, Sch.7 para.6, Sch.7 para.7
Art.11A, added: SI 2013/755 Sch.1 para.13
Art.11A, applied: SI 2013/755 Sch.7 para.7
Art.12, amended: SI 2013/755 Sch.1 para.14
Art.12A, added: SI 2013/755 Sch.1 para.15
Art.13, amended: SI 2013/755 Sch.1 para.16
Art.13A, added: SI 2013/755 Sch.1 para.17
Art.16, added: SI 2013/755 Sch.1 para.18
Art.17, added: SI 2013/755 Sch.1 para.18
Art.18, added: SI 2013/755 Sch.1 para.18
Sch.1 paraA.1, added: SI 2013/755 Sch.1 para.19
Sch.1 para.1, amended: SI 2013/755 Sch.1 para.19
Sch.1 para.1A, added: SI 2013/755 Sch.1 para.19
Sch.1 para.2, amended: SI 2013/755 Sch.1 para.19
Sch.1 para.3, revoked: SI 2013/755 Sch.1 para.19
Sch.1 para.4, revoked: SI 2013/755 Sch.1 para.19
Sch.1 para.5, amended: SI 2013/755 Sch.1 para.19

1909. National Health Service (Pharmaceutical Services) Regulations 2012

applied: SI 2013/349 Reg.2, Reg.7, Reg.36, Reg.40, Reg.42, Reg.48, Reg.50, Reg.66, Reg.115, Reg.117, Sch.4 para.25, Sch.4 para.26, Sch.5 para.15, Sch.5 para.16, Sch.9 para.1, Sch.9 para.3, Sch.9 para.5, Sch.9 para.7, Sch.9 para.8, Sch.9 para.9, Sch.9 para.10, Sch.9 para.11, Sch.9 para.13, Sch.9 para.14
referred to: SI 2013/349 Reg.24, Sch.9 para.1
revoked: SI 2013/349 Sch.10 para.11
Part 8, applied: SI 2013/349 Sch.9 para.5, Sch.9 para.14
Part 10, applied: SI 2013/349 Sch.9 para.13
Part 11, applied: SI 2013/349 Sch.9 para.13
Reg.24, applied: SI 2013/349 Reg.24
Reg.25, applied: SI 2013/349 Reg.64
Reg.35, applied: SI 2013/349 Reg.79, Reg.80
Reg.42, applied: SI 2013/349 Sch.9 para.8
Reg.44, applied: SI 2013/349 Reg.41
Reg.47, applied: SI 2013/349 Sch.9 para.14
Reg.47, referred to: SI 2013/349 Sch.9 para.14
Reg.48, applied: SI 2013/349 Sch.9 para.5
Reg.50, applied: SI 2013/349 Sch.9 para.9
Reg.51, applied: SI 2013/349 Reg.51
Reg.52, applied: SI 2013/349 Sch.9 para.5
Reg.55, applied: SI 2013/349 Reg.55
Reg.57, applied: SI 2013/349 Sch.9 para.10
Reg.58, applied: SI 2013/349 Sch.9 para.5
Reg.61, applied: SI 2013/349 Sch.9 para.5
Reg.63, applied: SI 2013/349 Sch.9 para.5
Reg.65, applied: SI 2013/349 Reg.65, Sch.4 para.24, Sch.5 para.14
Reg.66, applied: SI 2013/349 Reg.66
Reg.79, applied: SI 2013/349 Reg.79, Reg.80
Reg.88, applied: SI 2013/349 Reg.88
Reg.98, applied: SI 2013/349 Sch.9 para.13
Sch.2 Part 3, applied: SI 2013/349 Sch.9 para.3
Sch.4, applied: SI 2013/349 Sch.9 para.13
Sch.5, applied: SI 2013/349 Sch.9 para.13
Sch.7, applied: SI 2013/349 Sch.9 para.1, Sch.9 para.2, Sch.9 para.4
Sch.7 para.6, applied: SI 2013/349 Sch.9 para.8
Sch.7 para.10, applied: SI 2013/349 Sch.9 para.6, Sch.9 para.13

1916. Human Medicines Regulations 2012

applied: SI 2013/532 Reg.42
Part 3, added: SI 2013/1855 Reg.16
Part 3 regA.17, substituted: SI 2013/1855 Reg.4
Part 5, applied: SI 2013/532 Reg.50
Part 6, applied: SI 2013/532 Reg.43
Part 12, applied: SI 2013/235 Sch.3 para.28
Reg.5, applied: SI 2013/532 Reg.5, Sch.2 para.31, Sch.3 para.7
Reg.8, amended: SI 2013/1855 Reg.3, SI 2013/2593 Reg.2
Reg.8, applied: SI 2013/532 Reg.42
Reg.17, substituted: SI 2013/1855 Reg.4
Reg.18, substituted: SI 2013/1855 Reg.4, Reg.5
Reg.18, substituted: SI 2013/1855 Reg.4
Reg.19, revoked (in part): SI 2013/1855 Reg.6
Reg.19, substituted: SI 2013/1855 Reg.4
Reg.20, amended: SI 2013/1855 Reg.7
Reg.20, substituted: SI 2013/1855 Reg.4
Reg.21, substituted: SI 2013/1855 Reg.4
Reg.22, substituted: SI 2013/1855 Reg.4
Reg.23, substituted: SI 2013/1855 Reg.4
Reg.24, substituted: SI 2013/1855 Reg.4
Reg.25, substituted: SI 2013/1855 Reg.4
Reg.26, substituted: SI 2013/1855 Reg.4
Reg.27, amended: SI 2013/1855 Reg.8
Reg.27, substituted: SI 2013/1855 Reg.4
Reg.27, referred to: SI 2013/532 Reg.40
Reg.27, substituted: SI 2013/1855 Reg.4

Reg.28, substituted: SI 2013/1855 Reg.4
Reg.29, substituted: SI 2013/1855 Reg.4
Reg.29, applied: SI 2013/532 Reg.18, Sch.2 para.45
Reg.29, substituted: SI 2013/1855 Reg.4
Reg.30, substituted: SI 2013/1855 Reg.4
Reg.31, substituted: SI 2013/1855 Reg.4
Reg.31, applied: SI 2013/532 Reg.14
Reg.31, substituted: SI 2013/1855 Reg.4
Reg.32, revoked: SI 2013/1855 Reg.35
Reg.32, substituted: SI 2013/1855 Reg.4
Reg.33, substituted: SI 2013/1855 Reg.4
Reg.34, amended: SI 2013/1855 Reg.9
Reg.34, substituted: SI 2013/1855 Reg.4
Reg.35, substituted: SI 2013/1855 Reg.4
Reg.36, amended: SI 2013/1855 Reg.10
Reg.36, substituted: SI 2013/1855 Reg.4
Reg.37, substituted: SI 2013/1855 Reg.4, Reg.11
Reg.37, substituted: SI 2013/1855 Reg.4
Reg.38, substituted: SI 2013/1855 Reg.4
Reg.39, amended: SI 2013/1855 Reg.12
Reg.39, substituted: SI 2013/1855 Reg.4
Reg.40, substituted: SI 2013/1855 Reg.4
Reg.41, substituted: SI 2013/1855 Reg.4
Reg.42, amended: SI 2013/1855 Reg.13
Reg.42, substituted: SI 2013/1855 Reg.4
Reg.43, amended: SI 2013/1855 Reg.14
Reg.43, substituted: SI 2013/1855 Reg.4
Reg.44, substituted: SI 2013/1855 Reg.4, Reg.15
Reg.44, substituted: SI 2013/1855 Reg.4
Reg.45, substituted: SI 2013/1855 Reg.4
Reg.45A, substituted: SI 2013/1855 Reg.4
Reg.45B, substituted: SI 2013/1855 Reg.4
Reg.45C, substituted: SI 2013/1855 Reg.4
Reg.45D, substituted: SI 2013/1855 Reg.4
Reg.45E, substituted: SI 2013/1855 Reg.4
Reg.45F, substituted: SI 2013/1855 Reg.4
Reg.45G, substituted: SI 2013/1855 Reg.4
Reg.45H, substituted: SI 2013/1855 Reg.4
Reg.45I, substituted: SI 2013/1855 Reg.4
Reg.45J, substituted: SI 2013/1855 Reg.4
Reg.45K, substituted: SI 2013/1855 Reg.4
Reg.45L, substituted: SI 2013/1855 Reg.4
Reg.45M, substituted: SI 2013/1855 Reg.4
Reg.45N, substituted: SI 2013/1855 Reg.4
Reg.45O, substituted: SI 2013/1855 Reg.4
Reg.45P, substituted: SI 2013/1855 Reg.4
Reg.45Q, substituted: SI 2013/1855 Reg.4
Reg.45R, substituted: SI 2013/1855 Reg.4
Reg.45T, substituted: SI 2013/1855 Reg.4
Reg.45U, substituted: SI 2013/1855 Reg.4
Reg.45V, substituted: SI 2013/1855 Reg.4
Reg.68, amended: SI 2013/1855 Reg.17
Reg.68, applied: SI 2013/532 Reg.18
Reg.73, amended: SI 2013/2593 Reg.3
Reg.82, amended: SI 2013/2593 Reg.4
Reg.84, amended: SI 2013/1855 Reg.18
Reg.103, applied: SI 2013/532 Reg.44
Reg.110, amended: SI 2013/1855 Reg.19
Reg.113, amended: SI 2013/2593 Reg.5
Reg.127, applied: SI 2013/532 Reg.50
Reg.135, amended: SI 2013/1855 Reg.20
Reg.135, applied: SI 2013/532 Reg.18
Reg.142, amended: SI 2013/2593 Reg.6
Reg.149, applied: SI 2013/532 Sch.7 para.3
Reg.169, applied: SI 2013/532 Reg.26, Sch.2 para.30
Reg.177, amended: SI 2013/1855 Reg.21
Reg.182, amended: SI 2013/1855 Reg.22
Reg.196, amended: SI 2013/2593 Reg.7
Reg.206, amended: SI 2013/1855 Reg.23
Reg.210, amended: SI 2013/1855 Reg.24
Reg.210A, added: SI 2013/1855 Reg.25
Reg.213, amended: SI 2013/235 Sch.2 para.176
Reg.213, revoked (in part): SI 2013/235 Sch.2 para.176
Reg.214, amended: SI 2013/1855 Reg.26
Reg.223, amended: SI 2013/1855 Reg.27
Reg.229, amended: SI 2013/235 Sch.2 para.176
Reg.229, revoked (in part): SI 2013/235 Sch.2 para.176
Reg.230, amended: SI 2013/235 Sch.2 para.176
Reg.233, amended: SI 2013/235 Sch.2 para.176
Reg.233, revoked (in part): SI 2013/235 Sch.2 para.176
Reg.247, amended: SI 2013/235 Sch.2 para.176
Reg.256A, added: SI 2013/1855 Reg.28
Reg.256B, added: SI 2013/1855 Reg.28
Reg.256C, added: SI 2013/1855 Reg.28
Reg.256D, added: SI 2013/1855 Reg.28
Reg.256E, added: SI 2013/1855 Reg.28
Reg.256F, added: SI 2013/1855 Reg.28
Reg.256G, added: SI 2013/1855 Reg.28
Reg.256H, added: SI 2013/1855 Reg.28
Reg.256I, added: SI 2013/1855 Reg.28
Reg.256J, added: SI 2013/1855 Reg.28
Reg.256K, added: SI 2013/1855 Reg.28
Reg.256L, added: SI 2013/1855 Reg.28
Reg.256M, added: SI 2013/1855 Reg.28
Reg.256N, added: SI 2013/1855 Reg.28
Reg.327, amended: SI 2013/1855 Reg.29
Reg.330, amended: SI 2013/1855 Reg.30
Reg.346, amended: SI 2013/2593 Reg.8
Reg.346, substituted: SI 2013/1855 Reg.31
s.Art.3 Reg.45S, substituted: SI 2013/1855 Reg.4
Sch.5 para.1, substituted: SI 2013/1855 Reg.32
Sch.5 para.3, amended: SI 2013/1855 Reg.32
Sch.5 para.5, amended: SI 2013/1855 Reg.32

Sch.7A para.1, added: SI 2013/1855 Reg.33
Sch.7A para.2, added: SI 2013/1855 Reg.33
Sch.7A para.3, added: SI 2013/1855 Reg.33
Sch.7A para.4, added: SI 2013/1855 Reg.33
Sch.7A para.5, added: SI 2013/1855 Reg.33
Sch.7A para.6, added: SI 2013/1855 Reg.33
Sch.7A para.7, added: SI 2013/1855 Reg.33
Sch.7A para.8, added: SI 2013/1855 Reg.33
Sch.7A para.9, added: SI 2013/1855 Reg.33
Sch.7A para.10, added: SI 2013/1855 Reg.33
Sch.7A para.11, added: SI 2013/1855 Reg.33
Sch.7A para.12, added: SI 2013/1855 Reg.33
Sch.7A para.13, added: SI 2013/1855 Reg.33
Sch.7A para.14, added: SI 2013/1855 Reg.33
Sch.7A para.15, added: SI 2013/1855 Reg.33
Sch.7A para.16, added: SI 2013/1855 Reg.33
Sch.7A para.17, added: SI 2013/1855 Reg.33
Sch.7A para.18, added: SI 2013/1855 Reg.33
Sch.7A para.19, added: SI 2013/1855 Reg.33
Sch.7A para.20, added: SI 2013/1855 Reg.33
Sch.7A para.21, added: SI 2013/1855 Reg.33
Sch.7A para.22, added: SI 2013/1855 Reg.33
Sch.7A para.23, added: SI 2013/1855 Reg.33
Sch.7A para.24, added: SI 2013/1855 Reg.33
Sch.8 Part 1 para.9A, added: SI 2013/1855 Reg.34
Sch.11 Part 1 para.11, referred to: SI 2013/532 Reg.40
Sch.11 Part 1 para.13, referred to: SI 2013/532 Reg.40
Sch.11 Part 2 para.23, referred to: SI 2013/532 Reg.40
Sch.11 Part 3 para.30, referred to: SI 2013/532 Reg.40
Sch.16 Part 2, added: SI 2013/235 Sch.2 para.176
Sch.16 Part 2, amended: SI 2013/235 Sch.2 para.176
Sch.16 Part 2, revoked: SI 2013/235 Sch.2 para.176
Sch.17 Part 4, amended: SI 2013/2593 Reg.9
Sch.22, added: SI 2013/235 Sch.2 para.176
Sch.22, amended: SI 2013/235 Sch.2 para.176
Sch.22, revoked: SI 2013/235 Sch.2 para.176
Sch.32 para.3, applied: SI 2013/532 Sch.2 para.31
Sch.32 para.3, referred to: SI 2013/532 Reg.40

1917. Police and Crime Commissioner Elections Order 2012

Sch.2 Part 2 para.15, amended: SI 2013/388 Sch.1 para.49, SI 2013/591 Sch.1 para.46

1919. Education (Information About Individual Pupils) (England) (Amendment) Regulations 2012

revoked: SI 2013/2094 Sch.2

1926. National Curriculum (Exceptions for First, Second, Third and Fourth Key Stages) (England) Regulations 2012

revoked: SI 2013/1487 Reg.3

1943. School Premises (England) Regulations 2012

applied: SI 2013/3109 Reg.16
referred to: SI 2013/3109 Sch.1 para.25

1969. Land Registration Fee Order 2012

revoked: SI 2013/3174 Art.14

1976. Climate Change Agreements (Administration) Regulations 2012

Reg.2, amended: SI 2013/508 Reg.3
Reg.12, amended: SI 2013/508 Reg.4
Reg.15, amended: SI 2013/508 Reg.5

2029. Localism Act 2011 (Commencement No 7 and Transitional, Saving and Transitory Provisions) Order 2012

Art.5, revoked: SI 2013/797 Art.4

2031. Neighbourhood Planning (Referendums) Regulations 2012

Reg.2, amended: SI 2013/798 Reg.3
Reg.4, amended: SI 2013/798 Reg.4
Reg.6, amended: SI 2013/798 Reg.5
Reg.8, amended: SI 2013/798 Reg.6
Reg.11, amended: SI 2013/798 Reg.6
Reg.12, amended: SI 2013/798 Reg.6
Reg.17, added: SI 2013/798 Reg.7
Sch.3, amended: SI 2013/798 Reg.8
Sch.3, revoked: SI 2013/798 Reg.8
Sch.5, amended: SI 2013/798 Reg.8
Sch.5, revoked: SI 2013/798 Reg.8
Sch.6 Part 1 para.1, added: SI 2013/798 Sch.1
Sch.6 Part 1 para.2, added: SI 2013/798 Sch.1
Sch.6 Part 1 para.3, added: SI 2013/798 Sch.1
Sch.6 Part 1 para.4, added: SI 2013/798 Sch.1
Sch.6 Part 1 para.5, added: SI 2013/798 Sch.1
Sch.6 Part 1 para.6, added: SI 2013/798 Sch.1
Sch.6 Part 2 para.7, added: SI 2013/798 Sch.1
Sch.6 Part 2 para.8, added: SI 2013/798 Sch.1
Sch.6 Part 2 para.9, added: SI 2013/798 Sch.1
Sch.6 Part 2 para.10, added: SI 2013/798 Sch.1
Sch.6 Part 3 para.11, added: SI 2013/798 Sch.1
Sch.6 Part 3 para.12, added: SI 2013/798 Sch.1
Sch.6 Part 3 para.13, added: SI 2013/798 Sch.1
Sch.6 Part 3 para.14, added: SI 2013/798 Sch.1
Sch.6 Part 4 para.15, added: SI 2013/798 Sch.1
Sch.6 Part 4 para.16, added: SI 2013/798 Sch.1
Sch.6 Part 4 para.17, added: SI 2013/798 Sch.1
Sch.6 Part 4 para.18, added: SI 2013/798 Sch.1
Sch.6 Part 4 para.19, added: SI 2013/798 Sch.1
Sch.6 Part 4 para.20, added: SI 2013/798 Sch.1
Sch.6 Part 5 para.21, added: SI 2013/798 Sch.1
Sch.6 Part 5 para.22, added: SI 2013/798 Sch.1
Sch.6 Part 5 para.23, added: SI 2013/798 Sch.1
Sch.6 Part 5 para.24, added: SI 2013/798 Sch.1
Sch.6 Part 6 para.25, added: SI 2013/798 Sch.1
Sch.6 Part 7 para.26, added: SI 2013/798 Sch.1

Sch.6 Part 7 para.27, added: SI 2013/798 Sch.1
Sch.6 Part 7 para.28, added: SI 2013/798 Sch.1
Sch.6 Part 8 para.29, added: SI 2013/798 Sch.1
Sch.6 Part 8 para.30, added: SI 2013/798 Sch.1
Sch.6 Part 8 para.31, added: SI 2013/798 Sch.1
Sch.6 Part 8 para.32, added: SI 2013/798 Sch.1
Sch.6 Part 8 para.33, added: SI 2013/798 Sch.1
Sch.6 Part 8 para.34, added: SI 2013/798 Sch.1
Sch.6 Part 8 para.35, added: SI 2013/798 Sch.1
Sch.6 Part 8 para.36, added: SI 2013/798 Sch.1
Sch.6 Part 8 para.37, added: SI 2013/798 Sch.1
Sch.6 Part 8 para.38, added: SI 2013/798 Sch.1
Sch.6 Part 8 para.39, added: SI 2013/798 Sch.1
Sch.6 Part 8 para.40, added: SI 2013/798 Sch.1
Sch.6 Part 8 para.41, added: SI 2013/798 Sch.1
Sch.6 Part 8 para.42, added: SI 2013/798 Sch.1
Sch.6 Part 8 para.43, added: SI 2013/798 Sch.1
Sch.6 Part 9 para.44, added: SI 2013/798 Sch.1
Sch.6 Part 9 para.45, added: SI 2013/798 Sch.1
Sch.6 Part 10 para.46, added: SI 2013/798 Sch.1
Sch.6 Part 10 para.47, added: SI 2013/798 Sch.1
Sch.6 Part 10 para.48, added: SI 2013/798 Sch.1
Sch.6 Part 10 para.49, added: SI 2013/798 Sch.1
Sch.6 Part 10 para.50, added: SI 2013/798 Sch.1
Sch.6 Part 11, added: SI 2013/798 Sch.1
Sch.7, added: SI 2013/798 Sch.2
Sch.8, added: SI 2013/798 Sch.3

2051. School Teachers Pay and Conditions Order 2012
revoked: SI 2013/1932 Art.3

2079. Green Deal Framework (Disclosure, Acknowledgment, Redress etc.) Regulations 2012
referred to: SI 2013/1808 Art.2
Part 7, added: SI 2013/139 Reg.7
Reg.2, amended: SI 2013/139 Reg.3, SI 2013/1881 Sch.1 para.44
Reg.19, amended: SI 2013/139 Reg.4
Reg.24, amended: SI 2013/139 Reg.5
Reg.25, amended: SI 2013/1881 Sch.1 para.44
Reg.30, amended: SI 2013/139 Reg.6
Reg.52, amended: SI 2013/139 Reg.8, SI 2013/1881 Sch.1 para.44
Reg.57, substituted: SI 2013/139 Reg.9
Reg.57A, added: SI 2013/139 Reg.10
Reg.59, amended: SI 2013/139 Reg.11
Reg.60A, added: SI 2013/139 Reg.12
Reg.62, substituted: SI 2013/139 Reg.13
Reg.63, amended: SI 2013/139 Reg.14
Reg.65, amended: SI 2013/139 Reg.15
Reg.66, amended: SI 2013/139 Reg.16
Reg.67, amended: SI 2013/139 Reg.17
Reg.68, amended: SI 2013/139 Reg.18
Sch.1 Part 6 para.24, amended: SI 2013/1881 Sch.1 para.44
Sch.2 Part SECTION1 para.1, substituted: SI 2013/139 Reg.19
Sch.2 Part SECTION2 para.2, substituted: SI 2013/139 Reg.19
Sch.2 Part SECTION3 para.3, substituted: SI 2013/139 Reg.19
Sch.2 para.1, substituted: SI 2013/139 Reg.19
Sch.2 para.2, substituted: SI 2013/139 Reg.19

2125. Export Control (Syria and Burma Sanctions Amendment) and Miscellaneous Revocations Order 2012
revoked: SI 2013/2012 Sch.1
Art.4, revoked: SI 2013/1964 Sch.1

2166. Further Education Teachers Qualifications (England) (Amendment) Regulations 2012
revoked: SI 2013/1976 Sch.1

2186. Wireless Telegraphy (Register) Regulations 2012
Sch.2 Part 2, amended: SI 2013/640 Reg.2

2261. Schools Forums (England) Regulations 2012
Reg.1, amended: SI 2013/3104 Reg.3
Reg.4, amended: SI 2013/3104 Reg.3
Reg.7, amended: SI 2013/3104 Reg.3
Reg.8, amended: SI 2013/3104 Reg.3

2263. Cosmetic Products (Safety) (Amendment) Regulations 2012
revoked: SI 2013/1478 Sch.1

2281. Smoke Control Areas (Authorised Fuels) (England) (No.2) Regulations 2012
revoked: SI 2013/447 Reg.3

2282. Smoke Control Areas (Exempted Fireplaces) (England) (No.2) Order 2012
revoked: SI 2013/462 Art.3

2288. M4 Motorway (Junction 12) (Temporary Restriction and Prohibition of Traffic) Order 2012
revoked: SI 2013/978 Art.8

2371. National Health Service (Pharmaceutical Services) Regulations 2012 (Amendment) Regulations 2012
revoked: SI 2013/349 Sch.10 para.11

2387. A282 Trunk Road (Dartford-Thurrock Crossing Charging Scheme) Order 2012
revoked: SI 2013/2249 Art.17

2404. Tribunals, Courts and Enforcement Act 2007 (Consequential Amendments) Order 2012
Sch.3 para.2, revoked: SI 2013/687 Sch.2

2488. Local Authority (Duty to Secure Early Years Provision Free of Charge) Regulations 2012
revoked: SI 2013/3193 Reg.5
Reg.3, applied: SI 2013/3104 Reg.16

2546. Medicines (Products for Human Use) (Fees) (Amendment) Regulations 2012
revoked: SI 2013/532 Reg.60

2554. Financial Services and Markets Act 2000 (Short Selling) Regulations 2012

Reg.1, amended: SI 2013/472 Sch.2 para.239
Reg.2, revoked (in part): SI 2013/1773 Sch.2 para.21
Reg.5, amended: SI 2013/472 Sch.2 para.239

2568. Jobseeker Allowance (Sanctions) (Amendment) Regulations 2012
disapplied: 2013 c.17 s.1

2573. Agricultural Holdings (Units of Production) (England) Order 2012
revoked: SI 2013/2607 Art.3

2574. Criminal Justice Act 2003 (Commencement No 29 and Saving Provisions) Order 2012
Art.2, applied: SI 2013/1103 Art.4
Art.3, applied: SI 2013/1103 Art.4
Sch.1, applied: SI 2013/1103 Art.2

2596. Burma (Restrictive Measures) (Overseas Territories) (Suspension) Order 2012
revoked: SI 2013/1447 Art.15

2607. Port Security (Port of Aberdeen) Designation Order 2012
Art.4, amended: SI 2013/2728 Art.3

2608. Port Security (Port of Grangemouth) Designation Order 2012
Art.3, amended: SI 2013/2728 Art.4
Art.3, revoked (in part): SI 2013/2728 Art.4
Art.4, amended: SI 2013/2728 Art.4
Sch.2 para.1, revoked: SI 2013/2728 Art.4
Sch.2 para.2, revoked: SI 2013/2728 Art.4
Sch.2 para.3, revoked: SI 2013/2728 Art.4
Sch.2 para.4, revoked: SI 2013/2728 Art.4

2609. Port Security (Port of Portland) Designation Order 2012
Art.4, amended: SI 2013/2728 Art.5

2610. Port Security (Port of Tees and Hartlepool) Designation Order 2012
Art.4, amended: SI 2013/2728 Art.6

2611. Port Security (Port of Workington) Designation Order 2012
Art.4, amended: SI 2013/2728 Art.7

2619. Materials and Articles in Contact with Food (England) Regulations 2012
disapplied: SI 2013/264 Sch.1

2653. M25 Motorway and the M11 Motorway (M25 Junctions 23 27) (Temporary Restriction and Prohibition of Traffic) Order 2012
revoked: SI 2013/1259 Art.10

2675. Mobile Homes (Written Statement) (Wales) Regulations 2012
Sch.1, amended: SI 2013/1723 Art.6

2677. Child Support Maintenance Calculation Regulations 2012
Reg.2, amended: SI 2013/630 Reg.44
Reg.14A, added: SI 2013/2380 Reg.6
Reg.15, amended: SI 2013/2380 Reg.6
Reg.34, amended: SI 2013/1517 Reg.8
Reg.34, varied: SI 2013/1860 Art.7
Reg.42, amended: SI 2013/1517 Reg.8
Reg.42, varied: SI 2013/1860 Art.7
Reg.43, amended: SI 2013/1654 Reg.5
Reg.44, amended: SI 2013/630 Reg.44
Reg.44, referred to: SI 2013/380 Sch.7 para.5
Reg.45, amended: SI 2013/630 Reg.44
Reg.50, amended: SI 2013/1517 Reg.8
Reg.54, substituted: SI 2013/1517 Reg.8
Reg.64, amended: SI 2013/388 Sch.1 para.50, SI 2013/591 Sch.1 para.47
Reg.69, amended: SI 2013/1654 Reg.5
Reg.69, varied: SI 2013/1860 Art.7
Reg.70, amended: SI 2013/1654 Reg.5
Reg.74, amended: SI 2013/1654 Reg.5
Reg.75, amended: SI 2013/1517 Reg.8
Reg.77, substituted: SI 2013/1517 Reg.8
Sch.1 para.2, revoked: SI 2013/2380 Reg.6
Sch.1 para.3, revoked: SI 2013/2380 Reg.6
Sch.1 para.4, revoked: SI 2013/2380 Reg.6

2690. Community Radio (Guernsey) Order 2012
revoked: SI 2013/243 Art.2

2695. M5 Motorway (Junctions 11A-12) (Temporary Restriction and Prohibition of Traffic) Order 2012
revoked: SI 2013/20 Art.8

2705. Materials and Articles in Contact with Food (Wales) Regulations 2012
referred to: SI 2013/479 Sch.1

2711. Veterinary Medicines (Amendment) Regulations 2012
revoked: SI 2013/2033 Reg.47

2743. Industrial Injuries Benefit (Injuries arising before 5th July 1948) Regulations 2012
applied: SSI 2013/148 Reg.6

2748. Iraq (United Nations Sanctions) (Overseas Territories) (Amendment) Order 2012
Sch.5 para.7, amended: SI 2013/472 Sch.2 para.240

2751. Eritrea (Sanctions) (Overseas Territories) Order 2012
Sch.6 para.5, amended: SI 2013/472 Sch.2 para.241

2753. Zimbabwe (Sanctions) (Overseas Territories) Order 2012
Art.4, amended: SI 2013/1446 Art.2
Art.7, amended: SI 2013/1446 Art.2
Art.8, amended: SI 2013/1446 Art.2
Art.9, amended: SI 2013/1446 Art.2
Sch.2 para.3, amended: SI 2013/1446 Art.2
Sch.2 para.5, amended: SI 2013/1446 Art.2
Sch.5 para.1, amended: SI 2013/1446 Art.2
Sch.6 para.5, amended: SI 2013/472 Sch.2 para.242

2782. Feed-in Tariffs Order 2012
Art.2, amended: SI 2013/1099 Art.3
Art.11, amended: SI 2013/1099 Art.4
Art.24A, added: SI 2013/1099 Art.5
Art.24B, added: SI 2013/1099 Art.5
Art.27, amended: SI 2013/1099 Art.6
Art.27, revoked (in part): SI 2013/1099 Art.6
Art.29, amended: SI 2013/1099 Art.6
Art.30, amended: SI 2013/1099 Art.6
Art.30A, added: SI 2013/1099 Art.6
Art.30B, added: SI 2013/1099 Art.6
Art.30C, added: SI 2013/1099 Art.6
Art.30D, added: SI 2013/1099 Art.6
Art.38, amended: SI 2013/1099 Art.7
Art.38, revoked (in part): SI 2013/1099 Art.7
Art.38A, added: SI 2013/1099 Art.7

2785. Child Support (Meaning of Child and New Calculation Rules) (Consequential and Miscellaneous Amendment) Regulations 2012
Reg.1, amended: SI 2013/1517 Reg.9
Reg.9, revoked: SI 2013/1517 Reg.10

2791. Health Service Branded Medicines (Control of Prices and Supply of Information) Amendment Regulations 2012
revoked: SI 2013/2881 Reg.4

2822. Recovery of Costs (Remand to Youth Detention Accommodation) (England and Wales) Regulations 2012
revoked: SI 2013/507 Reg.2

2885. Council Tax Reduction Schemes (Prescribed Requirements) (England) Regulations 2012
Reg.2, amended: SI 2013/3181 Reg.2
Reg.3, amended: SI 2013/3181 Reg.2
Reg.8, amended: SI 2013/3181 Reg.2
Reg.12, amended: SI 2013/3181 Reg.2
Reg.13, amended: SI 2013/3181 Reg.2
Sch.1 Part 1 para.2, amended: SI 2013/3181 Reg.2
Sch.1 Part 2 para.6, amended: SI 2013/3181 Reg.2
Sch.1 Part 3 para.8, amended: SI 2013/3181 Reg.2
Sch.1 Part 6 para.25, amended: SI 2013/3181 Reg.2
Sch.2 Part 1 para.1, amended: SI 2013/3181 Reg.2
Sch.2 Part 1 para.2, amended: SI 2013/3181 Reg.2
Sch.2 Part 4, amended: SI 2013/3181 Reg.2
Sch.3 para.1, amended: SI 2013/3181 Reg.2
Sch.4 para.3, amended: SI 2013/3181 Reg.2
Sch.5 para.19, amended: SI 2013/3181 Reg.2
Sch.6 Part 1 para.21, amended: SI 2013/3181 Reg.2
Sch.6 Part 1 para.22, amended: SI 2013/3181 Reg.2
Sch.6 Part 1 para.29A, added: SI 2013/3181 Reg.2
Sch.8 Part 2 para.4, disapplied: SI 2013/215 Reg.4
Sch.8 Part 2 para.9, amended: SI 2013/3181 Reg.2
Sch.8 Part 2 para.9, applied: SI 2013/501 Reg.8, Reg.13

2886. Council Tax Reduction Schemes (Default Scheme) (England) Regulations 2012
Sch.1, amended: SI 2013/276 Reg.16
Sch.1, applied: SI 2013/501 Reg.8, Reg.13
Sch.1, disapplied: SI 2013/215 Reg.4

2904. Financial Restrictions (Iran) Order 2012
revoked: SI 2013/162 Art.2

2920. Town and Country Planning (Fees for Applications, Deemed Applications, Requests and Site Visits) (England) Regulations 2012
Reg.1, amended: SI 2013/2153 Reg.3
Reg.2A, added: SI 2013/2153 Reg.2
Reg.5A, added: SI 2013/2153 Reg.4
Reg.9A, added: SI 2013/2153 Reg.5
Reg.10, amended: SI 2013/2153 Reg.3
Reg.11A, added: SI 2013/2153 Reg.3
Reg.14, amended: SI 2013/2153 Reg.6
Sch.1 Part 1 para.7, amended: SI 2013/2153 Reg.7
Sch.1 Part 2, amended: SI 2013/2153 Reg.7

2991. School and Early Years Finance (England) Regulations 2012
Reg.10, applied: SI 2013/3104 Reg.9, Sch.4 para.1
Reg.11, applied: SI 2013/3104 Reg.8
Reg.16, applied: SI 2013/3104 Reg.19
Reg.20, applied: SI 2013/3104 Sch.4 para.1
Sch.2, applied: SI 2013/3104 Reg.8
Sch.2 Part 1, applied: SI 2013/3104 Sch.2 para.5
Sch.2 Part 2 para.8, applied: SI 2013/3104 Reg.8
Sch.2 Part 2 para.10, applied: SI 2013/3104 Reg.8
Sch.2 Part 4, applied: SI 2013/3104 Sch.4 para.1
Sch.2 Part 5, applied: SI 2013/3104 Reg.8
Sch.3, applied: SI 2013/3104 Sch.4 para.1
Sch.3 Part 1 para.1, applied: SI 2013/3104 Sch.4 para.1
Sch.3 Part 1 para.2, applied: SI 2013/3104 Sch.4 para.1
Sch.3 Part 1 para.11, applied: SI 2013/3104 Sch.4 para.1
Sch.3 Part 2 para.14, applied: SI 2013/3104 Sch.4 para.1
Sch.3 Part 2 para.15, applied: SI 2013/3104 Sch.4 para.1

2994. Benefit Cap (Housing Benefit) Regulations 2012
Reg.2, amended: SI 2013/388 Sch.1 para.51, SI 2013/546 Reg.2, SI 2013/591 Sch.1 para.48

2996. National Health Service Commissioning Board and Clinical Commissioning Groups (Responsibilities and Standing Rules) Regulations 2012
Part 7, applied: SI 2013/474 Reg.4
Part 8, applied: SI 2013/474 Reg.4
Part 9, applied: SI 2013/474 Reg.4
Reg.4, applied: SI 2013/350 Reg.2

Reg.5, amended: SI 2013/261 Reg.19
Reg.10, amended: SI 2013/261 Reg.20
Reg.17, applied: SI 2013/257 Reg.5, SI 2013/500 Reg.5
Reg.21, amended: SI 2013/2891 Reg.2
Reg.32A, added: SI 2013/2891 Reg.3
Reg.32B, added: SI 2013/2891 Reg.3
Reg.39, amended: SI 2013/2891 Reg.4
Reg.39, applied: SI 2013/257 Reg.13, Reg.15, SI 2013/500 Reg.13, Reg.15
Reg.39, revoked (in part): SI 2013/2891 Reg.4
Reg.40, amended: SI 2013/2891 Reg.4
Reg.40, revoked (in part): SI 2013/2891 Reg.4
Reg.41, amended: SI 2013/2891 Reg.4
Reg.42, amended: SI 2013/2891 Reg.4
Reg.42, applied: SI 2013/257 Reg.13, Reg.15, SI 2013/500 Reg.13, Reg.15
Reg.43, applied: SI 2013/257 Reg.13, Reg.15, SI 2013/500 Reg.13, Reg.15
Reg.48, applied: SI 2013/257 Reg.12, SI 2013/500 Reg.12
Reg.50, amended: SI 2013/2891 Reg.5
Sch.1 para.2, applied: SI 2013/350 Reg.2
Sch.1 para.3, amended: SI 2013/2891 Reg.6
Sch.1 para.5, amended: SI 2013/2891 Reg.6
Sch.5 para.2, revoked: SI 2013/2891 Reg.2

2999. Climate Change Agreements (Eligible Facilities) Regulations 2012

Reg.2, amended: SI 2013/505 Reg.2
Reg.3, amended: SI 2013/505 Reg.2

3018. Electricity and Gas (Energy Companies Obligation) Order 2012

Art.15, applied: SSI 2013/148 Reg.4

3025. Nursing and Midwifery Council (Midwives) Rules Order of Council 2012

applied: SI 2013/235 Sch.3 para.6
Sch.1, added: SI 2013/235 Sch.2 para.177
Sch.1, amended: SI 2013/235 Sch.2 para.177

3038. Greenhouse Gas Emissions Trading Scheme Regulations 2012

Reg.3, amended: SI 2013/755 Sch.4 para.419, SI 2013/1037 Reg.2, SI 2013/3135 Reg.4, Reg.5
Reg.8, amended: SI 2013/3135 Reg.5
Reg.8, revoked (in part): SI 2013/3135 Reg.5
Reg.20, amended: SI 2013/755 Sch.4 para.420
Reg.27, amended: SI 2013/755 Sch.4 para.421
Reg.44, amended: SI 2013/3135 Reg.5
Reg.45, amended: SI 2013/755 Sch.4 para.422, SI 2013/3135 Reg.5
Reg.52, amended: SI 2013/755 Sch.4 para.423, SI 2013/3135 Reg.3
Reg.69, amended: SI 2013/3135 Reg.6
Reg.73, amended: SI 2013/755 Sch.4 para.423
Reg.74, amended: SI 2013/3135 Reg.5
Reg.74, revoked (in part): SI 2013/3135 Reg.5
Reg.77, amended: SI 2013/3135 Reg.5
Reg.79, amended: SI 2013/3135 Reg.5
Reg.80, amended: SI 2013/3135 Reg.5
Reg.80, revoked (in part): SI 2013/3135 Reg.5
Reg.81, amended: SI 2013/3135 Reg.5
Reg.81, revoked (in part): SI 2013/3135 Reg.5
Reg.84, amended: SI 2013/3135 Reg.5
Reg.86, amended: SI 2013/755 Sch.4 para.424, SI 2013/3135 Reg.4
Reg.87, amended: SI 2013/755 Sch.4 para.425, SI 2013/1037 Reg.2, SI 2013/3135 Reg.4
Reg.87A, added: SI 2013/1037 Reg.2
Reg.87B, added: SI 2013/3135 Reg.4
Sch.3 para.1, amended: SI 2013/3135 Reg.6
Sch.4 para.3, amended: SI 2013/3135 Reg.5
Sch.5 para.3, amended: SI 2013/755 Sch.4 para.426, SI 2013/3135 Reg.6
Sch.5 para.6, amended: SI 2013/755 Sch.4 para.426
Sch.5 para.8, amended: SI 2013/3135 Reg.5
Sch.6 para.7, amended: SI 2013/3135 Reg.6
Sch.6 para.11, amended: SI 2013/3135 Reg.6
Sch.7 para.1, amended: SI 2013/3135 Reg.6
Sch.10 para.1, amended: SI 2013/755 Sch.4 para.427

3041. Controlled Foreign Companies (Excluded Banking Business Profits) Regulations 2012

Reg.2, amended: SI 2013/472 Sch.2 para.243

3042. Child Maintenance and Other Payments Act 2008 (Commencement No 10 and Transitional Provisions) Order 2012

Art.6, revoked: SI 2013/1860 Art.6

3050. Animals (Scientific Procedures) Act 1986 (Fees) Order 2012

revoked: SI 2013/509 Art.3

3053. River Tyne (Tunnels) (Revision of Tolls) Order 2012

revoked: SI 2013/3087 Art.3

3055. Excise Duties (Surcharges or Rebates) (Hydrocarbon Oils etc.) Order 2012

revoked: 2013 c.29 s.179

3056. Excise Duties (Road Fuel Gas) (Reliefs) Regulations 2012

revoked: 2013 c.29 s.179

3065. Somalia (Sanctions) (Overseas Territories) Order 2012

Art.3, amended: SI 2013/1443 Art.3
Art.4, amended: SI 2013/1443 Art.4
Art.7, amended: SI 2013/1443 Art.5
Art.8, amended: SI 2013/1443 Art.6
Art.9, amended: SI 2013/1443 Art.7
Art.10, amended: SI 2013/1443 Art.8

Sch.6 para.5, amended: SI 2013/472 Sch.2 para.244

3066. Democratic People's Republic of Korea (Sanctions) (Overseas Territories) Order 2012

Art.3, amended: SI 2013/1718 Art.3, SI 2013/2599 Art.3
Art.4, amended: SI 2013/1718 Art.4
Art.7, amended: SI 2013/1718 Art.5
Art.8, amended: SI 2013/1718 Art.6
Art.9, amended: SI 2013/1718 Art.7
Art.10A, added: SI 2013/1718 Art.8
Art.10B, added: SI 2013/1718 Art.8
Art.10C, added: SI 2013/1718 Art.8
Art.10D, added: SI 2013/1718 Art.8
Art.10E, added: SI 2013/1718 Art.8
Art.10F, added: SI 2013/1718 Art.8
Art.16, amended: SI 2013/1718 Art.9
Art.17, amended: SI 2013/1718 Art.10
Sch.3 para.1, amended: SI 2013/1718 Art.11
Sch.3 para.2, amended: SI 2013/1718 Art.11
Sch.5 para.1, amended: SI 2013/1718 Art.12
Sch.5 para.2, amended: SI 2013/1718 Art.12
Sch.6 para.5, amended: SI 2013/472 Sch.2 para.245

3067. Côte d'Ivoire (Sanctions) (Overseas Territories) Order 2012

Sch.6 para.5, amended: SI 2013/472 Sch.2 para.246

3068. Guinea-Bissau (Sanctions) (Overseas Territories) Order 2012

Sch.5 para.5, amended: SI 2013/472 Sch.2 para.247

3094. NHS Bodies and Local Authorities (Partnership Arrangements, Care Trusts, Public Health and Local Healthwatch) Regulations 2012

Part 5, applied: SI 2013/235 Sch.3 para.19, Sch.3 para.20
Reg.13, amended: SI 2013/349 Sch.10 para.12
Reg.14, amended: SI 2013/261 Reg.21
Reg.29, varied: SI 2013/235 Sch.3 para.21

3097. Education (Student Support) (Wales) Regulations 2012

applied: SI 2013/1733 Art.2, SI 2013/1965 Reg.12
Reg.2, amended: SI 2013/1965 Reg.13, SI 2013/3177 Reg.132
Reg.32, amended: SI 2013/1965 Reg.14
Reg.35, amended: SI 2013/1965 Reg.15
Reg.45, amended: SI 2013/1965 Reg.16
Reg.56, amended: SI 2013/1965 Reg.17
Reg.63, amended: SI 2013/1965 Reg.18
Reg.69, applied: SI 2013/1733 Art.2
Reg.74, applied: SI 2013/1733 Art.2
Reg.81, amended: SI 2013/1965 Reg.19
Reg.97, amended: SI 2013/1965 Reg.20
Reg.102, amended: SI 2013/1965 Reg.21
Reg.105, amended: SI 2013/1965 Reg.22
Sch.1 Part 2 para.5, amended: SI 2013/1965 Reg.23
Sch.3, applied: SI 2013/1733 Art.2
Sch.5 para.5, amended: SI 2013/1965 Reg.24
Sch.5 para.9, amended: SI 2013/765 Reg.34

3098. Civil Legal Aid (Procedure) Regulations 2012

applied: SI 2013/1179 Sch.2 para.2, SI 2013/1893 Sch.3 para.1
Reg.36, referred to: SI 2013/480 Reg.44
Reg.37, applied: SI 2013/2877 Reg.6

3110. Consumer Rights (Payment Surcharges) Regulations 2012

Reg.2, amended: SI 2013/3134 Sch.4 para.15
Reg.3, amended: SI 2013/3134 Sch.4 para.15
Reg.4, applied: SI 2013/761 Art.2, SI 2013/3168 Sch.1
Reg.7, amended: SI 2013/761 Art.3
Reg.7, applied: SI 2013/3168 Sch.1
Reg.8, applied: SI 2013/3168 Sch.1
Reg.9, applied: SI 2013/3168 Sch.1
Reg.10, applied: SI 2013/3168 Sch.1

3118. Energy Performance of Buildings (England and Wales) Regulations 2012

Reg.2, amended: SI 2013/10 Reg.8, SI 2013/181 Reg.9
Reg.4, amended: SI 2013/181 Reg.10
Reg.9, amended: SI 2013/10 Reg.9
Reg.27, amended: SI 2013/10 Reg.10
Reg.28, amended: SI 2013/603 Reg.2
Reg.30, amended: SI 2013/10 Reg.11
Reg.31, amended: SI 2013/10 Reg.12
Reg.32, amended: SI 2013/10 Reg.13
Sch.A1 Part 1 para.1, added: SI 2013/10 Sch.2
Sch.A1 Part 1 para.2, added: SI 2013/10 Sch.2
Sch.A1 Part 1 para.3, added: SI 2013/10 Sch.2
Sch.A1 Part 1 para.4, added: SI 2013/10 Sch.2
Sch.A1 Part 1 para.5, added: SI 2013/10 Sch.2
Sch.A1 Part 1 para.6, added: SI 2013/10 Sch.2
Sch.A1 Part 1 para.7, added: SI 2013/10 Sch.2
Sch.A1 Part 1 para.8, added: SI 2013/10 Sch.2
Sch.A1 Part 1 para.9, added: SI 2013/10 Sch.2
Sch.A1 Part 1 para.10, added: SI 2013/10 Sch.2
Sch.A1 Part 1 para.11, added: SI 2013/10 Sch.2
Sch.A1 Part 1 para.12, added: SI 2013/10 Sch.2
Sch.A1 Part 1 para.13, added: SI 2013/10 Sch.2
Sch.A1 Part 1 para.14, added: SI 2013/10 Sch.2
Sch.A1 Part 1 para.15, added: SI 2013/10 Sch.2
Sch.A1 Part 1 para.16, added: SI 2013/10 Sch.2
Sch.A1 Part 1 para.17, added: SI 2013/10 Sch.2
Sch.A1 Part 1 para.18, added: SI 2013/10 Sch.2
Sch.A1 Part 1 para.19, added: SI 2013/10 Sch.2
Sch.A1 Part 1 para.20, added: SI 2013/10 Sch.2

Sch.A1 Part 1 para.21, added: SI 2013/10 Sch.2
Sch.A1 Part 1 para.22, added: SI 2013/10 Sch.2
Sch.A1 Part 1 para.23, added: SI 2013/10 Sch.2
Sch.A1 Part 1 para.24, added: SI 2013/10 Sch.2
Sch.A1 Part 1 para.25, added: SI 2013/10 Sch.2
Sch.A1 Part 1 para.26, added: SI 2013/10 Sch.2
Sch.A1 Part 2, added: SI 2013/10 Sch.2

3119. Building Regulations &c (Amendment) Regulations 2012
Reg.41, amended: SI 2013/181 Reg.6
Reg.41, revoked (in part): SI 2013/181 Reg.6
Sch.1, amended: SI 2013/181 Sch.1

3122. Payments in Euro (Credit Transfers and Direct Debits) Regulations 2012
Reg.2, amended: SI 2013/472 Sch.2 para.248
Reg.5, applied: SI 2013/418 Art.2
Reg.6, applied: SI 2013/418 Art.2
Reg.8, applied: SI 2013/418 Art.2
Reg.9, applied: SI 2013/418 Art.2
Reg.14, amended: SI 2013/429 Reg.2, SI 2013/472 Sch.2 para.248
Reg.16, amended: SI 2013/472 Sch.2 para.248
Reg.17, amended: SI 2013/472 Sch.2 para.248
Sch.1 Part 1 para.1, amended: SI 2013/472 Sch.2 para.248
Sch.1 Part 1 para.2, amended: SI 2013/472 Sch.2 para.248
Sch.1 Part 1 para.3, substituted: SI 2013/472 Sch.2 para.248
Sch.1 Part 1 para.4, amended: SI 2013/472 Sch.2 para.248
Sch.1 Part 1 para.5, amended: SI 2013/472 Sch.2 para.248
Sch.1 Part 2 para.7, amended: SI 2013/472 Sch.2 para.248
Sch.1 Part 3 para.8, amended: SI 2013/472 Sch.2 para.248

3136. Severn Bridges Tolls Order 2012
revoked: SI 2013/3246 Art.3

3140. A11 Trunk Road (Fiveways to Thetford Improvement) (Temporary Restriction and Prohibition of Traffic) Order 2012
revoked: SI 2013/2521 Art.11

3144. Council Tax Reduction Schemes and Prescribed Requirements (Wales) Regulations 2012
applied: SI 2013/3029 Reg.36
revoked: SI 2013/3029 Reg.36
Reg.32, disapplied: SI 2013/111 Reg.6
Sch.1 Part 2 para.2, amended: SI 2013/112 Reg.3
Sch.1 Part 2 para.3, amended: SI 2013/112 Reg.4
Sch.2 Part 1 para.1, amended: SI 2013/112 Reg.5
Sch.2 Part 1 para.2, amended: SI 2013/112 Reg.5
Sch.2 Part 4, amended: SI 2013/112 Reg.5
Sch.6 Part 2 para.4, amended: SI 2013/112 Reg.6
Sch.6 Part 2 para.5, amended: SI 2013/112 Reg.7
Sch.6 Part 4 para.19, amended: SI 2013/112 Reg.8
Sch.6 Part 4 para.19, revoked (in part): SI 2013/112 Reg.8
Sch.6 Part 4 para.30, amended: SI 2013/112 Reg.9
Sch.6 Part 4 para.30, revoked (in part): SI 2013/112 Reg.9
Sch.7 Part 1 para.1, amended: SI 2013/112 Reg.10
Sch.7 Part 1 para.3, amended: SI 2013/112 Reg.10
Sch.7 Part 4, amended: SI 2013/112 Reg.10
Sch.7 Part 6 para.23, amended: SI 2013/112 Reg.10
Sch.7 Part 6 para.24, amended: SI 2013/112 Reg.10
Sch.8 para.18, amended: SI 2013/112 Reg.11
Sch.8 para.18, revoked (in part): SI 2013/112 Reg.11
Sch.13 Part 1 para.1, disapplied: SI 2013/111 Reg.6
Sch.13 Part 1 para.7, applied: SI 2013/588 Reg.8, Reg.10, Reg.17
Sch.13 Part 3 para.10, amended: SI 2013/112 Reg.12

3145. Council Tax Reduction Schemes (Default Scheme) (Wales) Regulations 2012
revoked: SI 2013/3035 Reg.1
Sch.1, amended: SI 2013/112 Reg.14, Reg.15, Reg.16, Reg.17, Reg.18, Reg.19, Reg.20, Reg.21
Sch.1, applied: SI 2013/588 Reg.8, Reg.10, Reg.17, SI 2013/3029 Reg.40
Sch.1, disapplied: SI 2013/111 Reg.6
Sch.1, revoked: SI 2013/112 Reg.16, Reg.17, Reg.21

3150. District of Craven (Electoral Changes) Order 2012
Sch.1, amended: SI 2013/221 Art.2

3214. M25 Motorway and the A13 and the A282 Trunk Roads (Junction 30) (Temporary 50 Miles Per Hour Speed Restriction) Order 2012
revoked: SI 2013/1307 Art.7

3249. A465 Trunk Road (Rhigos Roundabout, Rhondda Cynon Taf to Dowlais Top Roundabout, Merthyr Tydfil) (De-restriction) Order 2012
revoked: SI 2013/405 Art.3

3260. King's Lynn and West Norfolk (Electoral Changes) Order 2012
Art.1, revoked: SI 2013/220 Art.5
Art.2, revoked: SI 2013/220 Art.5
Art.3, revoked: SI 2013/220 Art.5
Art.4, revoked: SI 2013/220 Art.5

2013

5. Tonnage Tax (Training Requirement) (Amendment) Regulations 2013
revoked: SI 2013/2245 Reg.4

7. Scotland Act 2012 (Transitional and Consequential Provisions) Order 2013
applied: SSI 2013/72 r.5

9. Criminal Legal Aid (General) Regulations 2013
Part 5, applied: SI 2013/614 Reg.10
Reg.2, amended: SI 2013/2790 Reg.3
Reg.9, amended: SI 2013/472 Sch.2 para.249
Reg.9, applied: SI 2013/471 Reg.17
Reg.9, referred to: SI 2013/614 Reg.7, Reg.9
Reg.12, amended: SI 2013/2790 Reg.4
Reg.12, revoked (in part): SI 2013/2790 Reg.4
Reg.24, amended: SI 2013/2790 Reg.5
Reg.25, amended: SI 2013/2790 Reg.6
Reg.25, applied: SI 2013/471 Reg.17
Reg.26, applied: SI 2013/614 Reg.15

52. Air Navigation (Restriction of Flying) (Jet Formation Display Teams) (RAF Cranwell) Regulations 2013
Reg.3, amended: SI 2013/255 Reg.3

89. Air Navigation (Restriction of Flying) (Duxford Aerodrome) Regulations 2013
Reg.3, amended: SI 2013/835 Reg.2, SI 2013/1106 Reg.3

92. Recovery of Costs Insurance Premiums in Clinical Negligence Proceedings Regulations 2013
revoked: SI 2013/739 Reg.2

94. Air Navigation (Restriction of Flying) (Vauxhall Bridge) Regulations 2013
revoked: SI 2013/95 Reg.2

104. Civil Legal Aid (Merits Criteria) Regulations 2013
Part 2, referred to: SI 2013/422 Reg.2, SI 2013/480 Reg.2, SI 2013/503 Reg.2, SI 2013/512 Reg.8, SI 2013/611 Reg.2
Reg.2, amended: SI 2013/3195 Reg.2
Reg.53, amended: SI 2013/772 Reg.2
Reg.56A, added: SI 2013/3195 Reg.2

108. Non-Domestic Rating (Renewable Energy Projects) Regulations 2013
applied: SI 2013/452 Reg.7

126. Nuclear Decommissioning and Waste Handling (Finance and Fees) Regulations 2013
Reg.11, amended: SI 2013/1875 Reg.3

164. Belarus (Asset-Freezing) Regulations 2013
Reg.2, amended: SI 2013/472 Art.4
Sch.1 para.5, amended: SI 2013/472 Sch.2 para.251, SI 2013/534 Sch.1 para.12

165. Financial Services and Markets Act 2000 (Prescribed Financial Institutions) Order 2013
Art.1, amended: SI 2013/3115 Sch.2 para.77

184. M27 Motorway (Junctions 8 11) (Temporary Restriction and Prohibition of Traffic) Order 2013
Art.2, varied: SI 2013/826 Art.2

228. Rights of Passengers in Bus and Coach Transport (Exemptions) Regulations 2013
revoked: SI 2013/1865 Reg.3

240. Health and Safety at Work etc Act 1974 (Application outside Great Britain) Order 2013
applied: SI 2013/645 Reg.9, SI 2013/1471 Reg.19

242. Scotland Act 1998 (Modification of Schedule 5) Order 2013
Art.4, applied: 2013 asp 14 Sch.4 para.12, Sch.4 para.32

244. Guinea (Sanctions) (Overseas Territories) Order 2013
Sch.6 para.5, amended: SI 2013/472 Sch.2 para.252

253. Care Standards Act 2000 (Extension of the Application of Part 2 to Holiday Schemes for Disabled Children) (England) Regulations 2013
applied: SI 2013/1394 Reg.35

257. National Health Service (Procurement, Patient Choice and Competition) Regulations 2013
revoked: SI 2013/500 Reg.18

261. National Health Service and Public Health (Functions and Miscellaneous Provisions) Regulations 2013
Part 2, applied: SI 2013/2269 Reg.16
Reg.3, amended: SI 2013/2269 Reg.15
Reg.4, amended: SI 2013/2269 Reg.15
Reg.6, amended: SI 2013/2269 Reg.15
Reg.7, amended: SI 2013/2269 Reg.15

264. Food Safety (Sampling and Qualifications) (England) Regulations 2013
applied: SI 2013/2996 Reg.15
Sch.1, amended: SI 2013/2196 Reg.9
Sch.3, referred to: SI 2013/2996 Reg.15

276. Jobseeker's Allowance (Schemes for Assisting Persons to Obtain Employment) Regulations 2013
applied: 2013 c.17 s.1
referred to: 2013 c.17 s.1
Reg.3, amended: SI 2013/2584 Reg.2
Reg.3, applied: SI 2013/3029 Sch.10 para.2A, SI 2013/3035 Sch.1
Reg.3, referred to: 2013 c.17 s.1

335. National Health Service (Performers Lists) (England) Regulations 2013
Reg.4, amended: SI 2013/1869 Sch.1 para.5
Reg.9, amended: SI 2013/1869 Sch.1 para.5

358. Welfare Reform Act 2012 (Commencement No.8 and Savings and Transitional Provisions) Order 2013
Art.5, amended: SI 2013/983 Art.23

359. Civil Enforcement of Road Traffic Contraventions (Representations and Appeals) (Wales) Regulations 2013

applied: SI 2013/362 Reg.20
Reg.3, applied: SI 2013/362 Reg.8, Reg.18, Sch.1 para.1, Sch.1 para.2
Reg.3, referred to: SI 2013/362 Reg.8, Reg.18
Reg.4, applied: SI 2013/362 Reg.5, Reg.18, Reg.20, Reg.22, Sch.1 para.2
Reg.5, applied: SI 2013/362 Reg.10, Reg.19
Reg.6, applied: SI 2013/362 Reg.22
Reg.7, applied: SI 2013/361 Reg.6, SI 2013/362 Reg.20, Reg.22
Sch.1 Part 1 para.1, varied: SI 2013/361 Reg.6
Sch.1 Part 2 para.2, varied: SI 2013/361 Reg.6
Sch.1 Part 2 para.3, varied: SI 2013/361 Reg.6
Sch.1 Part 2 para.4, varied: SI 2013/361 Reg.6
Sch.1 Part 2 para.5, varied: SI 2013/361 Reg.6
Sch.1 Part 2 para.6, varied: SI 2013/361 Reg.6
Sch.1 Part 2 para.7, varied: SI 2013/361 Reg.6
Sch.1 Part 2 para.8, varied: SI 2013/361 Reg.6
Sch.1 Part 2 para.9, varied: SI 2013/361 Reg.6
Sch.1 Part 2 para.10, varied: SI 2013/361 Reg.6
Sch.1 Part 2 para.11, varied: SI 2013/361 Reg.6
Sch.1 Part 2 para.12, varied: SI 2013/361 Reg.6
Sch.1 Part 2 para.13, varied: SI 2013/361 Reg.6
Sch.1 Part 2 para.14, varied: SI 2013/361 Reg.6
Sch.1 Part 2 para.15, varied: SI 2013/361 Reg.6
Sch.1 Part 2 para.16, varied: SI 2013/361 Reg.6
Sch.1 Part 3 para.17, varied: SI 2013/361 Reg.6
Sch.1 Part 3 para.18, varied: SI 2013/361 Reg.6
Sch.1 Part 4 para.19, varied: SI 2013/361 Reg.6
Sch.1 Part 4 para.20, varied: SI 2013/361 Reg.6
Sch.1 Part 5 para.21, varied: SI 2013/361 Reg.6

362. Civil Enforcement of Road Traffic Contraventions (General Provisions) (Wales) Regulations 2013

applied: SI 2013/359 Reg.5
Reg.4, applied: SI 2013/359 Reg.8, SI 2013/361 Reg.3
Reg.9, applied: SI 2013/359 Reg.3, SI 2013/361 Reg.3
Reg.10, applied: SI 2013/359 Reg.3, Reg.6, SI 2013/1969 Sch.1 para.1
Reg.12, applied: SI 2013/359 Reg.8
Reg.13, applied: SI 2013/359 Reg.8
Reg.14, applied: SI 2013/359 Reg.8, Reg.9, SI 2013/1969 Sch.1 para.3
Reg.15, applied: SI 2013/359 Reg.4, Reg.8, SI 2013/361 Reg.3
Reg.18, applied: SI 2013/359 Reg.3
Sch.1 para.1, applied: SI 2013/359 Reg.3
Sch.1 para.1, referred to: SI 2013/359 Reg.4
Sch.1 para.2, applied: SI 2013/359 Reg.3

364. National Health Service (Primary Dental Services) (Miscellaneous Amendments and Transitional Provisions) Regulations 2013

Reg.46, revoked (in part): SI 2013/711 Reg.2
Reg.51, revoked: SI 2013/711 Reg.2

376. Universal Credit Regulations 2013

applied: SI 2013/378 Reg.18, SI 2013/379 Reg.51, SI 2013/386 Reg.30, Reg.32
Part 4, applied: SI 2013/386 Reg.23, Reg.24, Reg.25, Reg.26, Reg.27
Part 5, applied: SI 2013/379 Reg.16, Reg.27, Reg.31, SI 2013/381 Reg.26, SI 2013/386 Reg.24, Reg.25
Part 5, disapplied: SI 2013/386 Reg.24
Part 6, applied: SI 2013/383 Reg.16, SI 2013/386 Reg.9
Part 6, applied: SI 2013/381 Reg.41, SI 2013/383 Reg.13, SI 2013/384 Reg.6
Part 6, applied: SI 2013/384 Reg.6
Part 7, disapplied: SI 2013/386 Reg.20
Part 8, applied: SI 2013/386 Reg.30, Reg.32
Reg.2, amended: SI 2013/591 Sch.1 para.54, SI 2013/803 Reg.2
Reg.2, revoked (in part): SI 2013/1508 Reg.3
Reg.3, amended: SI 2013/630 Reg.38
Reg.3, applied: SI 2013/380 Reg.9, Reg.37
Reg.4, amended: SI 2013/1508 Reg.3
Reg.4, applied: SI 2013/386 Reg.11
Reg.4A, added: SI 2013/1508 Reg.3
Reg.9, amended: SI 2013/1508 Reg.3
Reg.11, applied: SI 2013/386 Reg.32
Reg.13, amended: SI 2013/630 Reg.38
Reg.17, referred to: SI 2013/380 Reg.6
Reg.19, amended: SI 2013/630 Reg.38
Reg.21, applied: SI 2013/381 Sch.3 para.3, SI 2013/383 Reg.13
Reg.22, applied: SI 2013/384 Reg.11
Reg.24, applied: SI 2013/765 Reg.28
Reg.27, applied: SI 2013/386 Reg.23, Reg.25, Reg.26, Reg.27, SI 2013/765 Reg.28
Reg.27, disapplied: SI 2013/386 Reg.23, Reg.26, Reg.27
Reg.28, applied: SI 2013/386 Reg.23, Reg.24
Reg.28, disapplied: SI 2013/386 Reg.23, Reg.24, Reg.25, Reg.26, Reg.27
Reg.29, applied: SI 2013/380 Reg.38, Reg.58, SI 2013/381 Sch.3 para.4
Reg.31, applied: SI 2013/380 Reg.37, Reg.38
Reg.35, amended: SI 2013/1508 Reg.3
Reg.35, referred to: SI 2013/380 Reg.37, Reg.38
Reg.36, applied: SI 2013/384 Reg.14
Reg.55, applied: SI 2013/381 Reg.41
Reg.57, applied: SI 2013/386 Reg.12
Reg.58, amended: SI 2013/1508 Reg.3

Reg.59, amended: SI 2013/1508 Reg.3
Reg.62, applied: SI 2013/383 Reg.13
Reg.64, applied: SI 2013/383 Reg.13
Reg.66, applied: SI 2013/386 Reg.21
Reg.66, varied: SI 2013/386 Reg.28
Reg.68, amended: SI 2013/630 Reg.38
Reg.73, applied: SI 2013/386 Reg.21
Reg.81, applied: SI 2013/381 Reg.19
Reg.83, amended: SI 2013/630 Reg.38
Reg.89, applied: SI 2013/386 Reg.11
Reg.98, amended: SI 2013/1508 Reg.3
Reg.101, varied: SI 2013/386 Reg.30, Reg.32
Reg.102, applied: SI 2013/378 Reg.19, Reg.30, SI 2013/379 Reg.61, SI 2013/386 Reg.33
Reg.103, applied: SI 2013/378 Reg.20, Reg.30, SI 2013/379 Reg.61, SI 2013/386 Reg.33
Reg.104, applied: SI 2013/378 Reg.21, Reg.30, SI 2013/379 Reg.52, Reg.61, SI 2013/386 Reg.31, Reg.33
Reg.105, applied: SI 2013/378 Reg.30, SI 2013/379 Reg.61
Reg.106, referred to: SI 2013/381 Reg.35
Reg.107, applied: SI 2013/386 Reg.34
Reg.107, disapplied: SI 2013/386 Reg.34
Reg.108, referred to: SI 2013/381 Reg.35
Reg.109, referred to: SI 2013/381 Reg.35
Reg.111, amended: SI 2013/630 Reg.38
Reg.111, varied: SI 2013/386 Reg.32
Reg.114, substituted: SI 2013/630 Reg.38
Reg.117, applied: SI 2013/381 Sch.1 para.27
Reg.117, substituted: SI 2013/630 Reg.38
Sch.1 para.2, applied: SI 2013/380 Reg.40
Sch.1 para.4, applied: SI 2013/380 Sch.6 para.6
Sch.4, applied: SI 2013/380 Sch.6 para.7
Sch.4 Part 1 para.2, amended: SI 2013/803 Reg.2
Sch.4 Part 3 para.9, amended: SI 2013/2828 Reg.4
Sch.4 Part 3 para.11, amended: SI 2013/803 Reg.2
Sch.4 Part 3 para.12, amended: SI 2013/803 Reg.2
Sch.4 Part 3 para.12, substituted: SI 2013/2828 Reg.4
Sch.4 Part 3 para.16, amended: SI 2013/803 Reg.2
Sch.4 Part 4 para.24, amended: SI 2013/1508 Reg.3
Sch.4 Part 5 para.35, amended: SI 2013/1508 Reg.3
Sch.5, applied: SI 2013/380 Sch.6 para.6
Sch.5 Part 3 para.5, applied: SI 2013/386 Reg.29
Sch.5 Part 3 para.5, disapplied: SI 2013/386 Reg.29
Sch.5 Part 3 para.6, disapplied: SI 2013/386 Reg.29
Sch.8 para.2, amended: SI 2013/630 Reg.38, SI 2013/1508 Reg.3
Sch.10 para.18, applied: SI 2013/3029 Sch.5 para.22, SI 2013/3035 Sch.1

377. Social Security (Personal Independence Payment) Regulations 2013

Part 3, applied: SI 2013/387 Reg.23
Reg.4, amended: SI 2013/455 Reg.2
Reg.8, applied: SI 2013/380 Reg.37, Reg.38, SI 2013/387 Reg.13
Reg.9, applied: SI 2013/387 Reg.13
Reg.9, disapplied: SI 2013/380 Reg.35
Reg.12, applied: SI 2013/387 Reg.23
Reg.13, applied: SI 2013/387 Reg.23
Reg.17, applied: SI 2013/387 Reg.26
Reg.17, referred to: SI 2013/387 Reg.26
Reg.18, applied: SI 2013/387 Reg.26
Reg.18, referred to: SI 2013/387 Reg.26
Reg.28, amended: SI 2013/2270 Reg.7
Reg.30, disapplied: SI 2013/387 Reg.25
Reg.30, referred to: SI 2013/387 Reg.25

378. Jobseeker's Allowance Regulations 2013

applied: SI 2013/379 Reg.51, SI 2013/983 Art.17, Art.18
Part 3, applied: SI 2013/983 Art.17, Art.18
Reg.15, amended: SI 2013/1508 Reg.4
Reg.18, varied: SI 2013/983 Art.17, Art.18
Reg.19, applied: SI 2013/376 Sch.11 para.2, SI 2013/983 Art.19
Reg.20, applied: SI 2013/376 Sch.11 para.2, SI 2013/983 Art.19
Reg.21, applied: SI 2013/376 Sch.11 para.2, SI 2013/379 Reg.52, SI 2013/983 Art.19
Reg.22, referred to: SI 2013/381 Reg.35
Reg.23, applied: SI 2013/983 Art.20
Reg.23, disapplied: SI 2013/983 Art.20
Reg.24, referred to: SI 2013/381 Reg.35
Reg.25, referred to: SI 2013/381 Reg.35
Reg.29, amended: SI 2013/630 Reg.39
Reg.31, applied: SI 2013/381 Reg.45
Reg.31, referred to: SI 2013/380 Reg.43
Reg.37, varied: SI 2013/983 Art.12
Reg.42, amended: SI 2013/591 Sch.1 para.52
Reg.44, amended: SI 2013/1508 Reg.4
Reg.45, applied: SI 2013/381 Reg.39
Reg.49, referred to: SI 2013/384 Reg.12
Reg.73, amended: SI 2013/1508 Reg.4
Sch.1 para.6, amended: SI 2013/1508 Reg.4

379. Employment and Support Allowance Regulations 2013

applied: SI 2013/378 Reg.18, SI 2013/983 Art.14, Art.15
Part 4, applied: SI 2013/376 Reg.39, Reg.41
Part 5, applied: SI 2013/376 Reg.40, Reg.41
Part 8, applied: SI 2013/983 Art.14, Art.15
Reg.2, varied: SI 2013/983 Art.10

Reg.3, varied: SI 2013/983 Art.10
Reg.6, applied: SI 2013/381 Reg.35
Reg.6, varied: SI 2013/983 Art.10
Reg.7, varied: SI 2013/983 Art.10
Reg.11, varied: SI 2013/983 Art.10
Reg.15, varied: SI 2013/983 Art.10
Reg.16, applied: SI 2013/381 Reg.26
Reg.21, amended: SI 2013/1508 Reg.5
Reg.21, applied: SI 2013/381 Reg.26
Reg.22, applied: SI 2013/381 Reg.26
Reg.26, applied: SI 2013/381 Reg.15
Reg.26, varied: SI 2013/983 Art.10
Reg.29, applied: SI 2013/381 Reg.26
Reg.30, varied: SI 2013/983 Art.10
Reg.49, amended: SI 2013/1508 Reg.5
Reg.51, varied: SI 2013/983 Art.14, Art.15
Reg.52, applied: SI 2013/376 Sch.11 para.1, SI 2013/378 Reg.21, SI 2013/983 Art.16
Reg.53, applied: SI 2013/376 Sch.11 para.1
Reg.54, referred to: SI 2013/381 Reg.35
Reg.55, applied: SI 2013/983 Art.20
Reg.55, disapplied: SI 2013/983 Art.20
Reg.56, referred to: SI 2013/381 Reg.35
Reg.57, referred to: SI 2013/381 Reg.35
Reg.62, referred to: SI 2013/384 Reg.13
Reg.86, applied: SI 2013/381 Reg.15
Reg.87, varied: SI 2013/983 Art.10
Reg.94, amended: SI 2013/591 Sch.1 para.51
Reg.94, revoked (in part): SI 2013/1508 Reg.5

380. Universal Credit, Personal Independence Payment, Jobseeker's Allowance and Employment and Support Allowance (Claims and Payments) Regulations 2013

applied: SI 2013/381 Reg.4, SI 2013/387 Reg.28, SI 2013/983 Art.3, Art.5, Art.6
Part 6, applied: SI 2013/381 Sch.3 para.1
Reg.6, applied: SI 2013/376 Reg.21, SI 2013/381 Sch.2 para.1, SI 2013/383 Reg.5, SI 2013/386 Reg.14
Reg.6, referred to: SI 2013/983 Art.3, Art.4
Reg.7, applied: SI 2013/381 Sch.2 para.1, SI 2013/383 Reg.5
Reg.8, applied: SI 2013/386 Reg.6
Reg.9, amended: SI 2013/1508 Reg.6
Reg.9, applied: SI 2013/376 Reg.21, Sch.5 para.7, SI 2013/381 Sch.2 para.1, SI 2013/386 Reg.3, Reg.14, Reg.19
Reg.9, referred to: SI 2013/983 Art.3, Art.4
Reg.11, applied: SI 2013/387 Reg.12
Reg.11, disapplied: SI 2013/387 Reg.8
Reg.11, referred to: SI 2013/387 Reg.8, Reg.12
Reg.12, disapplied: SI 2013/387 Reg.8
Reg.18, applied: SI 2013/381 Sch.3 para.1
Reg.25, applied: SI 2013/381 Sch.3 para.1
Reg.26, applied: SI 2013/376 Reg.21, SI 2013/983 Art.3, Art.5, Art.6
Reg.31, applied: SI 2013/387 Reg.15
Reg.32, applied: SI 2013/381 Reg.5, Reg.13, Reg.23
Reg.33, applied: SI 2013/381 Reg.5, Reg.13, Reg.18, Reg.23
Reg.34, applied: SI 2013/381 Reg.5, Reg.13, Reg.23
Reg.35, applied: SI 2013/387 Reg.13
Reg.37, applied: SI 2013/381 Sch.3 para.1, SI 2013/387 Reg.13
Reg.38, applied: SI 2013/387 Reg.20
Reg.40, applied: SI 2013/382 Art.7
Reg.46, applied: SI 2013/381 Sch.3 para.1
Reg.47, applied: SI 2013/381 Sch.3 para.1
Reg.48, applied: SI 2013/381 Sch.3 para.1
Reg.49, applied: SI 2013/381 Sch.3 para.1
Reg.50, applied: SI 2013/381 Sch.3 para.1
Reg.51, applied: SI 2013/381 Sch.3 para.1
Reg.52, applied: SI 2013/381 Sch.3 para.1
Reg.55, applied: SI 2013/379 Reg.97, SI 2013/381 Sch.3 para.1
Reg.56, applied: SI 2013/381 Reg.49, Sch.3 para.1
Reg.57, applied: SI 2013/381 Reg.49, Sch.3 para.1, SI 2013/384 Reg.4, SI 2013/387 Reg.29
Reg.58, applied: SI 2013/381 Sch.3 para.1, SI 2013/384 Reg.4
Reg.59, applied: SI 2013/381 Sch.3 para.1
Sch.2, applied: SI 2013/378 Reg.33, SI 2013/381 Reg.4
Sch.2 Part 2, referred to: SI 2013/387 Reg.8
Sch.6, applied: SI 2013/384 Reg.4, SI 2013/386 Reg.22
Sch.6 para.1, amended: SI 2013/1508 Reg.6
Sch.6 para.3, amended: SI 2013/1508 Reg.6
Sch.6 para.3, applied: SI 2013/386 Reg.22
Sch.6 para.4, amended: SI 2013/1508 Reg.6
Sch.6 para.4, applied: SI 2013/384 Reg.11, Reg.12, Reg.13
Sch.6 para.5, applied: SI 2013/384 Reg.11, Reg.12, Reg.13
Sch.6 para.8, amended: SI 2013/443 Reg.10, SI 2013/1881 Sch.1 para.45
Sch.6 para.11, amended: SI 2013/1881 Sch.1 para.45

381. Universal Credit, Personal Independence Payment, Jobseeker's Allowance and Employment and Support Allowance (Decisions and Appeals) Regulations 2013

applied: SI 2013/379 Reg.7, Reg.85
Reg.35, applied: SI 2013/983 Art.6
Reg.45, applied: SI 2013/380 Reg.38
Reg.46, referred to: SI 2013/384 Reg.11

Reg.55, disapplied: SI 2013/983 Art.21
Sch.1, applied: SI 2013/983 Art.6
Sch.1 Part 3 para.26, applied: SI 2013/380 Reg.47

382. Rent Officers (Universal Credit Functions) Order 2013

applied: SI 2013/380 Reg.40, SI 2013/381 Reg.19, Reg.30
Art.2, amended: SI 2013/1544 Art.4
Art.3, amended: SI 2013/2978 Art.4
Art.4, amended: SI 2013/1544 Art.4, SI 2013/2978 Art.4
Sch.1 para.2, substituted: SI 2013/2978 Art.4
Sch.1 para.3, amended: SI 2013/2978 Art.4
Sch.1 para.4, substituted: SI 2013/1544 Art.4, SI 2013/2978 Art.4
Sch.1 para.6, added: SI 2013/2978 Art.4
Sch.2, applied: SI 2013/380 Reg.40

383. Social Security (Payments on Account of Benefit) Regulations 2013

Reg.3, amended: SI 2013/1508 Reg.7
Reg.10, applied: SI 2013/381 Sch.3 para.14
Reg.13, amended: SI 2013/1508 Reg.7

384. Social Security (Overpayments and Recovery) Regulations 2013

applied: SI 2013/381 Sch.3 para.15
Reg.4, applied: SI 2013/381 Sch.3 para.15
Reg.7, applied: SI 2013/381 Sch.3 para.15
Reg.8, applied: SI 2013/381 Sch.3 para.15
Reg.9, applied: SI 2013/381 Sch.3 para.15
Reg.11, amended: SI 2013/1508 Reg.8

386. Universal Credit (Transitional Provisions) Regulations 2013

Reg.2, amended: SI 2013/2070 Reg.3
Reg.3, amended: SI 2013/2070 Reg.3
Reg.3, referred to: SI 2013/983 Art.3, Art.4
Reg.4, applied: SI 2013/983 Art.4
Reg.5, applied: SI 2013/1511 Art.2, SI 2013/2657 Art.2
Reg.5, varied: SI 2013/983 Art.5, Art.6
Reg.6, applied: SI 2013/1511 Art.2, SI 2013/2657 Art.2
Reg.6, varied: SI 2013/983 Art.5, Art.6
Reg.7, applied: SI 2013/1511 Art.2, SI 2013/2657 Art.2
Reg.7, varied: SI 2013/983 Art.5, Art.6
Reg.8, applied: SI 2013/1511 Art.2, SI 2013/2657 Art.2
Reg.8, varied: SI 2013/983 Art.5, Art.6
Reg.9, applied: SI 2013/1511 Art.2, SI 2013/2657 Art.2
Reg.9, varied: SI 2013/983 Art.5, Art.6
Reg.10, amended: SI 2013/803 Reg.3
Reg.10, applied: SI 2013/1511 Art.2, SI 2013/2657 Art.2
Reg.10, varied: SI 2013/983 Art.5, Art.6
Reg.11, applied: SI 2013/1511 Art.2, SI 2013/2657 Art.2
Reg.11, substituted: SI 2013/803 Reg.3
Reg.11, varied: SI 2013/983 Art.5, Art.6
Reg.12, amended: SI 2013/2070 Reg.4
Reg.12, applied: SI 2013/1511 Art.2, SI 2013/2657 Art.2
Reg.12, varied: SI 2013/983 Art.5, Art.6
Reg.14, amended: SI 2013/2070 Reg.3, Reg.5
Reg.14, revoked (in part): SI 2013/2070 Reg.5
Reg.15, amended: SI 2013/2070 Reg.3
Reg.16, amended: SI 2013/2070 Reg.3
Reg.18, amended: SI 2013/2070 Reg.3
Reg.20, revoked: SI 2013/2070 Reg.6
Reg.27, amended: SI 2013/591 Sch.1 para.53

387. Personal Independence Payment (Transitional Provisions) Regulations 2013

Reg.2, amended: SI 2013/2689 Reg.2
Reg.3, amended: SI 2013/2231 Reg.2, SI 2013/2689 Reg.2
Reg.4, amended: SI 2013/2231 Reg.2
Reg.4, substituted: SI 2013/2689 Reg.2
Reg.6, amended: SI 2013/2231 Reg.2
Reg.18, amended: SI 2013/2231 Reg.2
Reg.22, amended: SI 2013/2231 Reg.2, SI 2013/2689 Reg.2

405. A465 Trunk Road (Rhigos Roundabout, Rhondda Cynon Taf to Dowlais Top Roundabout, Merthyr Tydfil) (De-restriction) Order 2013

varied: SI 2013/673 Art.5, SI 2013/691 Art.5

418. Payment to Treasury of Penalties (Enforcement Costs) Order 2013

Art.2, amended: SI 2013/504 Reg.49

419. Financial Services and Markets Act 2000 (Qualifying EU Provisions) Order 2013

Art.1, amended: SI 2013/1773 Sch.2 para.22
Art.2, amended: SI 2013/1773 Sch.2 para.22
Art.3, amended: SI 2013/1773 Sch.2 para.22
Art.5, amended: SI 2013/1773 Sch.2 para.22
Art.6, amended: SI 2013/1773 Sch.2 para.22

422. Civil Legal Aid (Remuneration) Regulations 2013

Reg.7, amended: SI 2013/2877 Reg.2
Reg.9, amended: SI 2013/2877 Reg.2
Reg.9, revoked (in part): SI 2013/2877 Reg.2
Sch.1 Part 2, amended: SI 2013/2877 Reg.2
Sch.1 Part 2, substituted: SI 2013/2877 Reg.2
Sch.2, substituted: SI 2013/2877 Sch.1
Sch.5 para.1, amended: SI 2013/2877 Sch.2

424. Air Navigation (Restriction of Flying) (Trooping the Colour) Regulations 2013

Reg.3, amended: SI 2013/1459 Reg.2

435. Criminal Legal Aid (Remuneration) Regulations 2013
disapplied: SI 2013/534 Reg.12
Reg.2, amended: SI 2013/2803 Reg.3
Reg.3, amended: SI 2013/2803 Reg.3
Reg.12A, added: SI 2013/2803 Reg.3
Sch.1 Part 7, amended: SI 2013/862 Sch.1 para.3
Sch.1 Part 7, referred to: SI 2013/483 Reg.15
Sch.4 para.11, amended: SI 2013/2803 Reg.3
Sch.5, substituted: SI 2013/2803 Sch.1
Sch.6 Part 1 para.1, substituted: SI 2013/2803 Sch.2
Sch.6 Part 1 para.2, substituted: SI 2013/2803 Sch.2
Sch.6 Part 1 para.3, substituted: SI 2013/2803 Sch.2
Sch.6 Part 2, substituted: SI 2013/2803 Sch.2
Sch.6 Part 3, substituted: SI 2013/2803 Sch.2

440. Financial Services Act 2012 (Transitional Provisions) (Permission and Approval) Order 2013
Art.4, amended: SI 2013/1765 Art.11
Art.7, amended: SI 2013/1765 Art.11

447. Smoke Control Areas (Authorised Fuels) (England) Regulations 2013
revoked: SI 2013/2111 Reg.3

452. Non-Domestic Rating (Rates Retention) Regulations 2013
Reg.4, applied: SI 2013/737 Sch.1 para.1

453. Legal Aid, Sentencing and Punishment of Offenders Act 2012 (Commencement No 6) Order 2013
Art.3, referred to: SI 2013/534 Reg.6

461. National Health Service (Optical Charges and Payments) Regulations 2013
Reg.8, amended: SI 2013/2555 Reg.3
Reg.24, substituted: SI 2013/1856 Reg.2

462. Smoke Control Areas (Exempted Fireplaces) (England) Order 2013
revoked: SI 2013/2112 Art.3

471. Criminal Legal Aid (Financial Resources) Regulations 2013
Reg.2, amended: SI 2013/2791 Reg.4
Reg.2, revoked (in part): SI 2013/2791 Reg.4
Reg.7, amended: SI 2013/2791 Reg.5
Reg.11, amended: SI 2013/591 Sch.1 para.50
Reg.14, amended: SI 2013/2791 Reg.6
Reg.16, amended: SI 2013/2791 Reg.7
Reg.16, revoked: SI 2013/2791 Reg.8
Reg.17, amended: SI 2013/2791 Reg.7
Reg.17, substituted: SI 2013/2791 Reg.9
Reg.18, amended: SI 2013/2791 Reg.7
Reg.19, amended: SI 2013/2791 Reg.7
Reg.20, amended: SI 2013/591 Sch.1 para.50, SI 2013/2791 Reg.7, Reg.10
Reg.21, amended: SI 2013/2791 Reg.7, Reg.11, Reg.12
Reg.22, amended: SI 2013/2791 Reg.7
Reg.23, amended: SI 2013/2791 Reg.7
Reg.24, amended: SI 2013/2791 Reg.7
Reg.25, amended: SI 2013/2791 Reg.7
Reg.26, amended: SI 2013/2791 Reg.7
Reg.27, amended: SI 2013/2791 Reg.7
Reg.28, amended: SI 2013/2791 Reg.7
Reg.29, amended: SI 2013/2791 Reg.7
Reg.30, added: SI 2013/2791 Reg.13
Reg.31, added: SI 2013/2791 Reg.13
Reg.32, added: SI 2013/2791 Reg.13
Reg.33, added: SI 2013/2791 Reg.13
Reg.34, added: SI 2013/2791 Reg.13
Reg.35, added: SI 2013/2791 Reg.13
Reg.36, added: SI 2013/2791 Reg.13
Reg.37, added: SI 2013/2791 Reg.13
Reg.38, added: SI 2013/2791 Reg.13
Reg.39, added: SI 2013/2791 Reg.13
Sch.1 para.2A, added: SI 2013/2791 Reg.14
Sch.1 para.3A, added: SI 2013/2791 Reg.14
Sch.1 para.4, amended: SI 2013/2791 Reg.14

475. National Health Service (Charges for Drugs and Appliances), (Dental Charges) and (Travel Expenses and Remission of Charges) (Amendment) Regulations 2013
Reg.16, revoked (in part): SI 2013/711 Reg.3

477. Tribunal Procedure (Amendment) Rules 2013
r.55, referred to: SI 2013/534 Reg.14

479. Food Safety (Sampling and Qualifications) (Wales) Regulations 2013
Sch.1, amended: SI 2013/2493 Reg.9
Sch.2 Part 1 para.5, amended: SI 2013/3049 Reg.4

480. Civil Legal Aid (Financial Resources and Payment for Services) Regulations 2013
applied: SI 2013/512 Reg.16, SI 2013/534 Reg.9
Reg.5, amended: SI 2013/753 Reg.2
Reg.7, applied: SI 2013/534 Reg.9
Reg.8, applied: SI 2013/534 Reg.9
Reg.24, amended: SI 2013/591 Sch.1 para.49
Reg.25, applied: SI 2013/534 Reg.9
Reg.27, applied: SI 2013/534 Reg.9
Reg.28, applied: SI 2013/534 Reg.9
Reg.37, applied: SI 2013/534 Reg.9
Reg.38, applied: SI 2013/534 Reg.9
Reg.39, applied: SI 2013/534 Reg.9
Reg.41, applied: SI 2013/534 Reg.9
Reg.44, applied: SI 2013/534 Reg.9

483. Criminal Legal Aid (Contribution Orders) Regulations 2013
applied: SI 2013/480 Reg.29, SI 2013/1686 Reg.4, Reg.26
Reg.6, substituted: SI 2013/2792 Reg.4

Reg.7, amended: SI 2013/2792 Reg.5
Reg.8, amended: SI 2013/2792 Reg.6
Reg.17, amended: SI 2013/2792 Reg.7
Reg.18, applied: SI 2013/1686 Reg.16, Reg.17, Reg.23, Reg.24, Reg.26
Reg.25, amended: SI 2013/2792 Reg.7
Reg.34, amended: SI 2013/2792 Reg.7
Reg.35, applied: SI 2013/1686 Reg.16, Reg.17, Reg.23, Reg.24, Reg.26
Reg.39, applied: SI 2013/1686 Reg.16, Reg.17, Reg.23, Reg.24, Reg.26

488. Government Resources and Accounts Act 2000 (Estimates and Accounts) Order 2013
Sch.1, amended: SI 2013/3187 Art.2, Sch.1, Sch.2

494. Plant Health (Fees) (England) Regulations 2013
Sch.1, amended: SI 2013/3050 Reg.3
Sch.2, substituted: SI 2013/3050 Reg.4

503. Civil Legal Aid (Statutory Charge) Regulations 2013
Reg.4, varied: SI 2013/534 Reg.10

504. Financial Services and Markets Act 2000 (Over the Counter Derivatives, Central Counterparties and Trade Repositories) Regulations 2013
Reg.7, amended: SI 2013/1908 Reg.4
Reg.8, amended: SI 2013/1908 Reg.4
Reg.9, amended: SI 2013/1908 Reg.4
Reg.9, applied: SI 2013/418 Art.2
Reg.15A, added: SI 2013/1908 Reg.4

507. Recovery of Costs (Remand to Youth Detention Accommodation) Regulations 2013
Reg.3, amended: SI 2013/2243 Reg.2

512. Legal Aid (Financial Resources and Payment for Services) (Legal Persons) Regulations 2013
Reg.10, amended: SI 2013/754 Reg.2

534. Legal Aid, Sentencing and Punishment of Offenders Act 2012 (Consequential, Transitional and Saving Provisions) Regulations 2013
Reg.9A, added: SI 2013/621 Reg.3
Sch.1 Part 2 para.26, added: SI 2013/621 Reg.4

556. Financial Services and Markets Act 2000 (PRA-regulated Activities) Order 2013
Art.3, amended: SI 2013/3115 Sch.2 para.78

574. Social Security Benefits Up-rating Order 2013
applied: SI 2013/599 Reg.2, Reg.3

609. Damages-Based Agreements Regulations 2013
Reg.5, amended: SI 2013/534 Sch.1 para.26

611. Civil Legal Aid (Costs) Regulations 2013
Reg.7, varied: SI 2013/534 Reg.9A
Reg.8, varied: SI 2013/534 Reg.9A
Reg.10, varied: SI 2013/534 Reg.9A

614. Criminal Legal Aid (Determinations by a Court and Choice of Representative) Regulations 2013
Reg.11, applied: SI 2013/2814 Reg.1
Reg.12, amended: SI 2013/1765 Art.12
Reg.18, amended: SI 2013/2814 Reg.2
Reg.19, substituted: SI 2013/2814 Reg.2

628. Legal Aid (Information about Financial Resources) Regulations 2013
Reg.4A, added: SI 2013/2726 Reg.3
Sch.1 para.29, added: SI 2013/2726 Reg.4

637. Financial Services Act 2012 (Misleading Statements and Impressions) Order 2013
Art.2, amended: SI 2013/1773 Sch.2 para.23

644. Bank of England Act 1998 (Macro-prudential Measures) Order 2013
Art.1, amended: SI 2013/3115 Sch.2 para.79

648. Hinkley Point C (Nuclear Generating Station) Order 2013
Art.2, amended: SI 2013/2938 Sch.1
Art.8, amended: SI 2013/2938 Sch.1
Art.12, amended: SI 2013/2938 Sch.1
Art.16, amended: SI 2013/2938 Sch.1
Art.25, amended: SI 2013/2938 Sch.1
Art.27, amended: SI 2013/2938 Sch.1
Art.38, amended: SI 2013/2938 Sch.1
Art.44, amended: SI 2013/2938 Sch.1
Art.49, amended: SI 2013/2938 Sch.1
Art.52, amended: SI 2013/2938 Sch.1
Sch.1 Part 1, amended: SI 2013/2938 Sch.1
Sch.2 para.1, amended: SI 2013/2938 Sch.1
Sch.2 para.2, amended: SI 2013/2938 Sch.1
Sch.2 para.3, amended: SI 2013/2938 Sch.1
Sch.2 para.4, amended: SI 2013/2938 Sch.1
Sch.2 para.5, amended: SI 2013/2938 Sch.1
Sch.2 para.6, amended: SI 2013/2938 Sch.1
Sch.2 para.10, amended: SI 2013/2938 Sch.1
Sch.2 para.12, amended: SI 2013/2938 Sch.1
Sch.2 para.13, amended: SI 2013/2938 Sch.1
Sch.14 para.3, amended: SI 2013/2938 Sch.1
Sch.14 para.4, amended: SI 2013/2938 Sch.1
Sch.14 para.5, amended: SI 2013/2938 Sch.1

692. A55 Trunk Road (Pen-y-clip Tunnel, Conwy County Borough) (Temporary Traffic Prohibitions & Restrictions) Order 2013
Art.1, varied: SI 2013/820 Art.2

693. A55 Trunk Road (Glan Conwy Conwy Morfa, Conwy County Borough) (Temporary 70 mph Speed Limit) Order 2013
disapplied: SI 2013/729 Art.7
varied: SI 2013/729 Art.7, SI 2013/3238 Art.12, SI 2013/3257 Art.14

716. Guardian's Allowance Up-rating Order 2013
applied: SI 2013/746 Reg.2, Reg.3

717. Guardian's Allowance Up-rating (Northern Ireland) Order 2013
applied: SI 2013/746 Reg.2, Reg.3

755. Natural Resources Body for Wales (Functions) Order 2013

Sch.2 Part 1 para.41, revoked: 2013 c.32 Sch.12 para.30

761. Enterprise Act 2002 (Part 8 Domestic Infringements) Order 2013

revoked: SI 2013/3134 Sch.4 para.16

765. Education (European Institutions) and Student Support (Wales) Regulations 2013

applied: SI 2013/1965 Reg.25

Reg.28, amended: SI 2013/1965 Reg.26

Sch.2 Part 2 para.4, amended: SI 2013/1965 Reg.27

794. Electoral Registration (Postponement of 2013 Annual Canvass) Order 2013

referred to: SI 2013/3198 Reg.14, SI 2013/3206 Reg.14

802. A1 Trunk Road (Water Newton, Cambridgeshire) (Temporary 50 Miles Per Hour Speed Restriction) Order 2013

revoked: SI 2013/1451 Art.7

835. Air Navigation (Restriction of Flying) (Duxford Aerodrome) (Amendment) Regulations 2013

revoked: SI 2013/1106 Reg.2

836. Air Navigation (Restriction of Flying) (Jet Formation Display Teams) (No.2) Regulations 2013

Sch.1, amended: SI 2013/1417 Reg.2

837. Air Navigation (Restriction of Flying) (Folkestone) Regulations 2013

revoked: SI 2013/1216 Reg.2

878. Air Navigation (Restriction of Flying) (Funeral of Baroness Thatcher) Regulations 2013

Reg.3, amended: SI 2013/921 Reg.2

930. Air Navigation (Restriction of Flying) (Enniskillen, Northern Ireland) Regulations 2013

revoked: SI 2013/1416 Reg.2

932. Air Navigation (Restriction of Flying) (Royal International Air Tattoo RAF Fairford) Regulations 2013

Reg.3, amended: SI 2013/1215 Reg.2

981. Mobile Homes (Selling and Gifting) (England) Regulations 2013

Reg.7, applied: SI 2013/1179 Sch.1

983. Welfare Reform Act 2012 (Commencement No 9 and Transitional and Transitory Provisions and Commencement No 8 and Savings and Transitional Provisions (Amendment)) Order 2013

Art.2, applied: SI 2013/358 Art.5

Art.3, applied: SI 2013/1511 Art.3, SI 2013/2657 Art.3, SI 2013/2846 Art.3

Art.4, applied: SI 2013/1511 Art.4, Art.5, Art.8, Art.10, SI 2013/2657 Art.4, SI 2013/2846 Art.4, Art.5

Art.4, referred to: SI 2013/1511 Art.4, Art.8, Art.10, SI 2013/2657 Art.4, Art.6

Art.5, applied: SI 2013/1511 Art.4, SI 2013/2657 Art.4, SI 2013/2846 Art.4

Art.6, applied: SI 2013/1511 Art.5, Art.9, Art.11, SI 2013/2657 Art.6, SI 2013/2846 Art.5

Art.7, varied: SI 2013/1511 Art.6

Art.9, applied: SI 2013/1511 Art.5, SI 2013/2657 Art.6, SI 2013/2846 Art.5

Art.10, applied: SI 2013/1511 Art.5, SI 2013/2657 Art.6, SI 2013/2846 Art.5

Art.10, varied: SI 2013/1511 Art.8

Art.11, amended: SI 2013/2657 Art.5

Art.11, applied: SI 2013/1511 Art.5, SI 2013/2657 Art.6, SI 2013/2846 Art.5

Art.11, varied: SI 2013/1511 Art.9

Art.12, applied: SI 2013/1511 Art.5, SI 2013/2657 Art.6, SI 2013/2846 Art.5

Art.12, varied: SI 2013/1511 Art.10

Art.13, applied: SI 2013/1511 Art.5, SI 2013/2657 Art.6, SI 2013/2846 Art.5

Art.13, varied: SI 2013/1511 Art.11

Art.14, applied: SI 2013/1511 Art.5, SI 2013/2657 Art.6, SI 2013/2846 Art.5

Art.15, applied: SI 2013/1511 Art.5, SI 2013/2657 Art.6, SI 2013/2846 Art.5

Art.16, applied: SI 2013/1511 Art.5, SI 2013/2657 Art.6, SI 2013/2846 Art.5

Art.17, applied: SI 2013/1511 Art.5, SI 2013/2657 Art.6, SI 2013/2846 Art.5

Art.18, applied: SI 2013/1511 Art.5, SI 2013/2657 Art.6, SI 2013/2846 Art.5

Art.19, applied: SI 2013/1511 Art.5, SI 2013/2657 Art.6, SI 2013/2846 Art.5

Art.20, applied: SI 2013/1511 Art.5, SI 2013/2657 Art.6, SI 2013/2846 Art.5

Art.21, applied: SI 2013/1511 Art.5, SI 2013/2657 Art.6, SI 2013/2846 Art.5

Art.22, applied: SI 2013/1511 Art.5, SI 2013/2657 Art.6, SI 2013/2846 Art.5

Sch.4 para.21, amended: SI 2013/1511 Art.7

1045. Chemical Weapons (Licence Appeal Provisions) (Revocation) Order 2013

revoked: SI 2013/1129 Art.3

1046. Energy Supply Company Administration Rules 2013

Part 2 r.10, amended: SI 2013/2950 r.2

1054. A465 Trunk Road (Nant-ybwch Roundabout to Brynmawr Roundabout, Blaenau Gwent) (Temporary Traffic Restrictions and Prohibitions) Order 2013

revoked: SI 2013/2732 Art.11

1097. CRC Energy Efficiency Scheme (Allocation of Allowances for Payment) (Amendment) Regulations 2013

applied: SI 2013/3103 Reg.13

revoked: SI 2013/3103 Reg.13

1119. CRC Energy Efficiency Scheme Order 2013
Art.3, amended: SI 2013/1773 Sch.2 para.24
Sch.4 para.2, applied: SI 2013/3103 Reg.12
Sch.4 para.3, applied: SI 2013/3103 Reg.12
Sch.4 para.4, applied: SI 2013/3103 Reg.12

1130. Air Navigation (Restriction of Flying) (Shoreham-by-Sea) Regulations 2013
Reg.3, amended: SI 2013/1848 Reg.3

1163. Official Statistics Order 2013
Sch.1, amended: SI 2013/2329 Sch.1 para.41

1165. Penalties for Disorderly Behaviour (Amount of Penalty) (Amendment) Order 2013
revoked: SI 2013/1579 Art.2

1169. Tribunal Procedure (First-tier Tribunal) (Property Chamber) Rules 2013
Part 4 r.32, applied: SI 2013/1179 Art.4

1179. First-tier Tribunal (Property Chamber) Fees Order 2013
Sch.2 para.1, substituted: SI 2013/2302 Sch.1
Sch.2 para.2, substituted: SI 2013/2302 Sch.1
Sch.2 para.3, substituted: SI 2013/2302 Sch.1
Sch.2 para.4, substituted: SI 2013/2302 Sch.1
Sch.2 para.5, substituted: SI 2013/2302 Sch.1
Sch.2 para.6, substituted: SI 2013/2302 Sch.1
Sch.2 para.7, substituted: SI 2013/2302 Sch.1
Sch.2 para.8, substituted: SI 2013/2302 Sch.1
Sch.2 para.9, substituted: SI 2013/2302 Sch.1
Sch.2 para.10, substituted: SI 2013/2302 Sch.1
Sch.2 para.11, substituted: SI 2013/2302 Sch.1
Sch.2 para.12, substituted: SI 2013/2302 Sch.1
Sch.2 para.13, substituted: SI 2013/2302 Sch.1
Sch.2 para.14, substituted: SI 2013/2302 Sch.1
Sch.2 para.15, substituted: SI 2013/2302 Sch.1
Sch.2 para.16, substituted: SI 2013/2302 Sch.1
Sch.2 para.17, substituted: SI 2013/2302 Sch.1
Sch.2 para.18, substituted: SI 2013/2302 Sch.1
Sch.2 para.19, substituted: SI 2013/2302 Sch.1
Sch.2 para.20, substituted: SI 2013/2302 Sch.1
Sch.2 para.21, added: SI 2013/2302 Art.11
Sch.2 para.21, substituted: SI 2013/2302 Sch.1

1203. Galloper Wind Farm Order 2013
Art.30, amended: SI 2013/2086 Sch.1
Sch.1 Part 3 para.1, amended: SI 2013/2086 Sch.1
Sch.1 Part 3 para.4, amended: SI 2013/2086 Sch.1
Sch.1 Part 3 para.16, amended: SI 2013/2086 Sch.1
Sch.1 Part 3 para.21, amended: SI 2013/2086 Sch.1

1418. Air Navigation (Restriction of Flying) (Jet Formation Display Teams) (No.3) Regulations 2013
Sch.1, amended: SI 2013/1833 Reg.2, SI 2013/2054 Art.2

1455. Enterprise and Regulatory Reform Act 2013 (Commencement No 1, Transitional Provisions and Savings) Order 2013
Art.3, amended: SI 2013/2271 Art.2
Art.4, amended: SI 2013/2271 Art.2
Sch.3 para.10, revoked: SI 2013/2271 Art.2

1460. Accession of Croatia (Immigration and Worker Authorisation) Regulations 2013
Reg.5, applied: SI 2013/3029 Reg.28, SI 2013/3035 Sch.1

1506. Biocidal Products and Chemicals (Appointment of Authorities and Enforcement) Regulations 2013
Reg.13, applied: SI 2013/1507 Reg.4, Sch.1
Reg.27, amended: SI 2013/1948 Reg.2

1511. Welfare Reform Act 2012 (Commencement No 11 and Transitional and Transitory Provisions and Commencement No 9 and Transitional and Transitory Provisions (Amendment)) Order 2013
Art.5, varied: SI 2013/2657 Art.5

1542. Police and Criminal Evidence Act 1984 (Application to immigration officers and designated customs officials in England and Wales) Order 2013
Art.31, amended: SI 2013/2343 Art.2
Sch.2 Part 1, amended: SI 2013/2343 Art.2
Sch.2 Part 3, amended: SI 2013/2343 Art.2

1554. Criminal Procedure Rules 2013
Part 2 r.2.2, amended: SI 2013/3183 r.4
Part 3 r.3.8, amended: SI 2013/2525 r.3
Part 5 r.5.4, amended: SI 2013/2525 r.4
Part 5 r.5.8, amended: SI 2013/3183 r.5
Part 9 r.9.2, amended: SI 2013/3183 r.6
Part 9 r.9.7, amended: SI 2013/3183 r.6
Part 12 r.12.1, added: SI 2013/3183 Sch.1
Part 12 r.12.2, added: SI 2013/3183 Sch.1
Part 12 r.12.3, added: SI 2013/3183 Sch.1
Part 12 r.12.4, added: SI 2013/3183 Sch.1
Part 12 r.12.5, added: SI 2013/3183 Sch.1
Part 12 r.12.6, added: SI 2013/3183 Sch.1
Part 12 r.12.7, added: SI 2013/3183 Sch.1
Part 12 r.12.8, added: SI 2013/3183 Sch.1
Part 12 r.12.9, added: SI 2013/3183 Sch.1
Part 12 r.12.10, added: SI 2013/3183 Sch.1
Part 12 r.12.11, added: SI 2013/3183 Sch.1
Part 62 r.62.5, amended: SI 2013/3183 r.8
Part 62 r.62.9, amended: SI 2013/3183 r.8
Part 76 r.76.1, amended: SI 2013/3183 r.9
Part 76 r.76.4, amended: SI 2013/3183 r.9
Part 76 r.76.7, amended: SI 2013/3183 r.9

1569. Fixed Penalty (Amendment) Order 2013
Art.2, amended: SI 2013/1840 Art.2

1616. Coroners (Inquests) Rules 2013
Part 3, applied: SI 2013/1629 Reg.23

1617. National Health Service (Direct Payments) Regulations 2013

Reg.7, amended: SI 2013/2354 Reg.2
Reg.8, amended: SI 2013/2354 Reg.3
Reg.11, amended: SI 2013/2354 Reg.4
Reg.13, amended: SI 2013/2354 Reg.5

1624. School Governance (Roles, Procedures and Allowances) (England) Regulations 2013

Reg.13, amended: SI 2013/2688 Reg.2
Reg.26, amended: SI 2013/2688 Reg.2, Reg.3

1725. Crime and Courts Act 2013 (Commencement No 3) Order 2013

Art.3, revoked (in part): SI 2013/2200 Art.6

1747. Civil Enforcement of Parking Contraventions (County of Flintshire) Designation Order 2013

revoked: SI 2013/1982 Art.3

1773. Alternative Investment Fund Managers Regulations 2013

applied: SI 2013/1797 Sch.2 para.6
Reg.2, amended: SI 2013/1797 Sch.1 para.2, Sch.2 para.3
Reg.2, revoked (in part): SI 2013/1797 Sch.1 para.2
Reg.5, amended: SI 2013/1797 Sch.1 para.2
Reg.5A, added: SI 2013/1797 Sch.1 para.2
Reg.8, substituted: SI 2013/1797 Sch.1 para.2
Reg.10, amended: SI 2013/1797 Sch.1 para.2
Reg.29, amended: SI 2013/1797 Sch.1 para.2, Sch.2 para.3
Reg.33, amended: SI 2013/1797 Sch.1 para.2
Reg.34, substituted: SI 2013/1797 Sch.2 para.3
Reg.49, amended: SI 2013/1797 Sch.1 para.2, Sch.2 para.3
Reg.49, revoked (in part): SI 2013/1797 Sch.2 para.3
Reg.50, amended: SI 2013/1797 Sch.1 para.2
Reg.50, substituted: SI 2013/1797 Sch.2 para.3
Reg.54, amended: SI 2013/1797 Sch.1 para.2
Reg.56, substituted: SI 2013/1797 Sch.2 para.3
Reg.57, amended: SI 2013/1797 Sch.1 para.2
Reg.57, revoked: SI 2013/1797 Sch.2 para.3
Reg.58, amended: SI 2013/1797 Sch.1 para.2
Reg.58, applied: SI 2013/1797 Sch.2 para.4
Reg.58, revoked: SI 2013/1797 Sch.2 para.3
Reg.59, amended: SI 2013/1797 Sch.1 para.2
Reg.59, applied: SI 2013/1797 Sch.2 para.5
Reg.59, revoked: SI 2013/1797 Sch.2 para.3
Reg.60, revoked: SI 2013/1797 Sch.2 para.3
Reg.61, revoked: SI 2013/1797 Sch.2 para.3
Reg.62, revoked: SI 2013/1797 Sch.2 para.3
Reg.63, revoked: SI 2013/1797 Sch.2 para.3
Reg.64, revoked: SI 2013/1797 Sch.2 para.3
Reg.71, amended: SI 2013/1797 Sch.2 para.4
Reg.71, revoked (in part): SI 2013/1797 Sch.2 para.3
Reg.77, amended: SI 2013/3115 Sch.2 para.80
Sch.2 Part 2 para.13, revoked: SI 2013/3115 Sch.3

1783. Road User Charging Schemes (Penalty Charges, Adjudication and Enforcement) (England) Regulations 2013

Reg.4, enabled: SI 2013/2249
Reg.5, enabled: SI 2013/2249
Reg.17, applied: SI 2013/2249 Art.8
Reg.21, applied: SI 2013/2249 Art.10
Reg.22, enabled: SI 2013/2249
Reg.22, referred to: SI 2013/2249 Art.11
Reg.23, enabled: SI 2013/2249
Reg.23, referred to: SI 2013/2249 Art.12
Reg.24, applied: SI 2013/2249 Art.13
Reg.24, enabled: SI 2013/2249
Reg.25, applied: SI 2013/2249 Art.14, proviso.001
Reg.25, enabled: SI 2013/2249
Reg.27, applied: SI 2013/2249 Art.15
Reg.27, enabled: SI 2013/2249
Reg.28, applied: SI 2013/2249 Art.15

1813. Protection of Freedoms Act 2012 (Destruction, Retention and Use of Biometric Data) (Transitional, Transitory and Saving Provisions) Order 2013

Art.2A, added: SI 2013/2580 Art.3
Art.5A, added: SI 2013/2580 Art.4
Art.10, added: SI 2013/2770 Art.3

1893. Employment Tribunals and the Employment Appeal Tribunal Fees Order 2013

see *Fox Solicitors Ltd v Advocate General for Scotland* [2013] CSOH 133, 2013 S.L.T. 1169 (OH), Lord Bannatyne
Sch.3 para.1, substituted: SI 2013/2302 Sch.1
Sch.3 para.2, substituted: SI 2013/2302 Sch.1
Sch.3 para.3, substituted: SI 2013/2302 Sch.1
Sch.3 para.4, substituted: SI 2013/2302 Sch.1
Sch.3 para.5, substituted: SI 2013/2302 Sch.1
Sch.3 para.6, substituted: SI 2013/2302 Sch.1
Sch.3 para.7, substituted: SI 2013/2302 Sch.1
Sch.3 para.8, substituted: SI 2013/2302 Sch.1
Sch.3 para.9, substituted: SI 2013/2302 Sch.1
Sch.3 para.10, substituted: SI 2013/2302 Sch.1
Sch.3 para.11, substituted: SI 2013/2302 Sch.1
Sch.3 para.12, substituted: SI 2013/2302 Sch.1
Sch.3 para.13, substituted: SI 2013/2302 Sch.1
Sch.3 para.14, substituted: SI 2013/2302 Sch.1
Sch.3 para.15, amended: SI 2013/2302 Art.12
Sch.3 para.15, substituted: SI 2013/2302 Sch.1
Sch.3 para.16, substituted: SI 2013/2302 Sch.1
Sch.3 para.17, substituted: SI 2013/2302 Sch.1
Sch.3 para.18, substituted: SI 2013/2302 Sch.1
Sch.3 para.19, substituted: SI 2013/2302 Sch.1
Sch.3 para.20, substituted: SI 2013/2302 Sch.1

1961. Protection of Freedoms Act 2012 (Code of Practice for Surveillance Camera Systems and Specification of Relevant Authorities) Order 2013

Art.3, amended: SI 2013/2318 Sch.1 para.127

1971. Companies (Revision of Defective Accounts and Reports) (Amendment) Regulations 2013

revoked: SI 2013/2224 Reg.2

1984. Healthy Eating in Schools (Nutritional Standards and Requirements) (Wales) Regulations 2013

Reg.2, amended: SI 2013/2750 Sch.15 para.2

2012. Export Control (Syria Sanctions) Order 2013

Art.4, amended: SI 2013/3182 Art.15
Art.5, amended: SI 2013/3182 Art.15

2112. Smoke Control Areas (Exempted Fireplaces) (England) (No.2) Order 2013

Sch.1, amended: SI 2013/3026 Art.2

2140. Town and Country Planning (Section 62A Applications) (Procedure and Consequential Amendments) Order 2013

Art.3A, added: SI 2013/2932 Art.3
Art.3A, revoked: SI 2013/2932 Art.3
Art.3B, added: SI 2013/2932 Art.3
Art.3B, revoked: SI 2013/2932 Art.3
Art.8, amended: SI 2013/2932 Art.3
Art.8, revoked (in part): SI 2013/2932 Art.3
Art.9, amended: SI 2013/3194 Art.3
Art.9, applied: SI 2013/2141 r.9, r.10, SI 2013/2142 Reg.6, Reg.7
Art.13, applied: SI 2013/2141 r.9, r.10, SI 2013/2142 Reg.6, Reg.7
Art.14, applied: SI 2013/2141 r.9, r.10, SI 2013/2142 Reg.6, Reg.7
Art.16, applied: SI 2013/2141 r.9, r.10, SI 2013/2142 Reg.6, Reg.7
Art.17, applied: SI 2013/2141 r.6, r.9, r.10, SI 2013/2142 Reg.6, Reg.7
Art.18, applied: SI 2013/2141 r.6, r.9, r.10, SI 2013/2142 Reg.6, Reg.7

2162. Designation of Schools Having a Religious Character (Independent Schools) (England) Order 2013

Sch.1, amended: SI 2013/2867 Art.5

2321. Air Navigation (Restriction of Flying) (Dartford) Regulations 2013

revoked: SI 2013/2322 Reg.2

2400. A1 Trunk Road (A1(M) Junction 10 to Biggleswade, Bedfordshire) (Temporary Restriction and Prohibition of Traffic) Order 2013

revoked: SI 2013/2724 Art.7

2440. A45 and A46 Trunk Roads (South East of Coventry) (Temporary Restriction of Traffic) Order 2013

revoked: SI 2013/3117 Art.9

2493. Contaminants in Food (Wales) Regulations 2013

referred to: SI 2013/479 Sch.1

2568. M1 and M6 Motorways and the A14 Trunk Road (Catthorpe) (Temporary Restriction and Prohibition of Traffic) Order 2013

amended: SI 2013/2780 Art.2

2571. Annual Tax on Enveloped Dwellings Avoidance Schemes (Prescribed Descriptions of Arrangements) Regulations 2013

Reg.4, applied: SI 2013/2592 Reg.2

2804. Criminal Defence Service (Very High Cost Cases) (Funding) Order 2013

Sch.2 Part 2, applied: SI 2013/422 Reg.9

2847. A14 Trunk Road (Junctions 6 to 10, Kettering) (Temporary Restriction and Prohibition of Traffic) Order 2013

revoked: SI 2013/3097 Art.13

2952. Animal By-Products (Enforcement) (England) Regulations 2013

Reg.12, amended: SI 2013/2996 Reg.38
Reg.23, amended: SI 2013/2996 Reg.38

2964. A120 Trunk Road (Hare Green Interchange to Horsley Cross Roundabout, Essex) (Temporary Restriction and Prohibition of Traffic) (No.2) Order 2013

revoked: SI 2013/3265 Art.2

2980. Age-Related Payments Regulations 2013

applied: SI 2013/3029 Sch.5 para.33, Sch.10 para.63, SI 2013/3035 Sch.1

3109. School Organisation (Establishment and Discontinuance of Schools) Regulations 2013

Reg.20, referred to: SI 2013/3110 Sch.3 para.8

3134. Consumer Contracts (Information, Cancellation and Additional Charges) Regulations 2013

applied: SI 2013/3168 Sch.1

3198. Representation of the People (England and Wales) (Description of Electoral Registers and Amendment) Regulations 2013

Reg.45, applied: SI 2013/3197 Art.11
Sch.3, applied: SI 2013/3197 Art.11

3206. Representation of the People (Scotland) (Description of Electoral Registers and Amendment) Regulations 2013

Reg.47, applied: SI 2013/3197 Art.11
Sch.3, applied: SI 2013/3197 Art.11